Happy New Year 2014
4th Love and thanks
Sonny & Helen
xx

1001 GARDENS
YOU MUST SEE BEFORE YOU DIE

1001 GARDENS
YOU MUST SEE BEFORE YOU DIE

GENERAL EDITOR
RAE SPENCER-JONES

PREFACE BY
ALAN TITCHMARSH

A Quintessence Book

First published in Great Britain in 2007 by Cassell Illustrated
a division of Octopus Publishing Group Limited
Endeavour House, 189 Shaftesbury Avenue
London, WC2H 8JY
www.octopusbooks.co.uk

An Hachette UK Company
www.hachette.co.uk

A CIP catalogue record for this book is available from the British Library.

ISBN-13: 978-1-84403-737-7
QSS.KGAR

This book was designed and produced by
Quintessence
230 City Road
London EC1V 2TT

First edition published in 2007
This edition first published in 2012

Senior Editor	Ruth Patrick
Editors	Marianne Canty, Paul Docherty,
	Marcus Hardy, Carol King, Frank Ritter
Copy Editor	Richard Rosenfeld
Editorial Assistant	Jenny Evans
Picture Researcher	Joanne Forrest-Smith
Designers	Ian Hunt, James Lawrence, Rod Teasdale
Update Editor	Ruth Patrick
Update Designer	Tea Aganovic

Creative Director	Richard Dewing
Editorial Director	Jane Laing
Publisher	Mark Fletcher

Manufactured in Singapore by Pica Digital Pte Ltd.
Printed in China by Midas Printing International Ltd.

CASSELL
ILLUSTRATED

Contents

Preface

By Alan Titchmarsh

'Have you been to see the garden at so-and-so?' I get asked. Sometimes I can nod sagely and pass a remark about the topiary or the thyme walk, the formal canal or the parterre. But even more frequently I have to shake my head apologetically and admit that the place is on my wish list but that, as yet, I have not managed to walk through its gates.

This book only makes things worse. You see, I actually like visiting gardens. You might think that after a lifetime of digging and hoeing, weeding and pruning, that looking at other people's flowers would not be a high on my list of priorities. But it is. And for several reasons.

Firstly, I am always seeking inspiration. I pinch ideas frequently, on the grounds that most likely the perpetrators in question have already pinched them from somebody else. Of course, the trick is to give the ideas a twist—if I like the way lime trees are used in a pleached avenue, as at Chatsworth, I can copy the planting pattern in my own more modest patch using fewer of them and keeping them more restricted in their growth. Or I can construct a rill across my lawn which won't quite match that at Hestercombe in Somerset where Sir Edwin Lutyens and Gertrude Jekyll worked their magic, but it might create something vaguely reminiscent of their genius.

Folk with underdeveloped imagination will claim that there is little or nothing in large and stately gardens that can be of much use to those of us with smaller patches of ground, but I don't agree. Scale is not everything, but line and proportion are. I find that the longer I garden the more important shape and form become, and that colour seems to be of secondary importance.

Oh, there are gardens that are praised as being a 'riot' of colour, but nowhere else in society is rioting regarded as acceptable, so I don't see why it should be revered in gardens. Well, not always. I have to admit that banks of rhododendrons in full flower in the Savill Gardens in Windsor Great Park or Exbury take some beating. I'll concede that.

And I don't want to give the impression that it is only British gardens that turn me on. I love the tranquillity of the Alhambra and Generalife gardens in Spain, the splendour of the glorious fountains at Peterhof in St Petersburg and the spectacle of Versailles and Vaux-le-Vicomte in Paris.

I love formality more and more, but am equally captivated by the genius of 'Capability' Brown's parkland, particularly at Blenheim Palace, and Humphry Repton's and William Kent's Arcadian landscapes.

Then I go on holiday to the Mediterranean and wish I had a simple grove of olives or citrus trees. In the Flower Forest in Barbados I yearn to bring British gardening style to bear in a climate which has a phenomenal growth rate. What couldn't I do with that sort of plant material and a bit of English style?

But my imagination is running away with me. I do not always look at gardens as masterpieces to be copied. In many of them I can simply enjoy being there. When I am allowed to stroll around the Blandy Gardens on Madeira, Christopher Lloyd's creation at Great Dixter, or the Parc des Moutiers in Normandy I am a happy man, because as well as looking for ideas, I try to switch off and enjoy 'the genius of the place'.

Man has built some staggering architectural wonders, but when he works hand in hand with nature, then his creations take on a life and a power that architecture alone can never equal. The best gardens in the world are places that inspire, enrich and captivate, and this book contains a thousand and one of them.

So many riches, and so little time to enjoy them. I am already marking in red the gardens that must be at the top of my wish list. You can do the same. But do not be tempted to rush around them. Give yourself time to savour them. Find a quiet corner. Admire their spectacle by all means, but try, also, to get in touch with their souls. Let them reach inside you and touch your spirit. That way you will discover that there is more to gardening than brilliant flowers and a lifetime of weeding and watering. It is, as the poet remarked, 'the purest of human pleasures.' *

* Francis Bacon's Essays

Alan Titchmarsh

Introduction

By Rae Spencer-Jones

Humans have gardened for millennia and throughout history gardens have had myriad purposes. For the ancient Egyptians, gardens supplied shade and water—a necessary respite from the relentless North African sun (see Karnak, page 867). For the practical ancient Romans, the garden's principle objective was for growing food, and herbal cures for illness and injury (see Pompeii, page 695). Medieval gardens in Europe were built behind imposing boundary walls to protect the incumbents from what they perceived as the hostile wilderness beyond, while monastic gardens were as vital for spiritual sanctuary as the monastery itself.

In the seventeenth century, gardens such as the elaborate and majestic landscape of Versailles, France (see page 570), were created as expressions of political power. The English landscape movement of the eighteenth and nineteenth centuries was a backlash against the rigid formality of the seventeenth century, and gave garden owners the opportunity to exploit their landscape as a forum for expression through architecture, literature, and philosophy. Throughout the centuries, many wealthy property owners in Europe and the United States financed plant-hunting expeditions abroad, and numerous gardens and arboreta, such as Arnold Arboretum in Massachusetts (see page 64), still possess important plant collections from such expeditions.

In many cultures today, the garden is integral to people's lifestyles. Whether on an English rooftop or in a Spanish city park, gardens can be an outdoor gallery for art and sculpture, or a canvas for innovative hard landscaping or planting design. Several modern private gardens—unique expressions of the individuals who have created them—have become icons of their time for their design or plantsmanship. Examples include Helen Dillon's garden in Ireland (see page 448) and Dutch plantsman Piet Oudolf's garden (see page 534). More recently, gardens, parks, and landscapes have become vital substitutes for wildlife habitats, which are declining as a result of intensive farming practices and development. Botanical gardens, such as England's Royal Botanic Gardens, Kew (see page 386), now play a necessary role in preserving and conserving threatened or rare plants; others including the National Botanical Garden at Kirstenbosch in South Africa (see page 872) also celebrate the sheer diversity of their native flora.

1001 Gardens You Must See Before You Die celebrates this global diversity among gardens. It is a worldwide journey that pays homage to the influence of historic gardens and parks on those of today. It also challenges the conventional concept of the "garden" by including the disciplined landscape of the war graves in Kranji, Singapore (see page 837); the weird and wonderful such as Antoni Gaudí's own garden Els Jardins de Ca L'Artigas in Spain (see page 702), and the surrealist Las Pozas in Mexico (see page 842); the Dutch artist and philosopher Louis Guillaume Le Roy's eco-cathedral, which will take

1,000 years to complete (see page 520); and even the natural landscape of Namaqualand, South Africa (see page 869), with its breathtaking spring display of annuals.

How this book is organized

The chapters of this book have been organized geographically from west to east, and north to south beginning with North America and ending with Australia, New Zealand, and the islands. This method of breaking down the chapters is not purely continental, but groups them to reflect each area's separate gardening tradition and history. The countries, regions, and states are also organized in this way. The book traces the lines of latitude across the world map from left to right, and each country's position within the chapter was decided by measuring its most northerly point. Consequently, all the gardens in the same area are featured together, providing readers with a straightforward means of navigating their way around the book. All the geographical information has been drawn from *The Times Atlas* (11th edition, 2003) for consistency.

The Islands chapter is not a recognized geographical area, but gardening in the various islands tends to be influenced by the colonial styles that manifested themselves at various points in history. Grouping the islands together in this way has also eliminated any political or geographical issues, such as whether the Canary Islands should be grouped with Europe for political reasons or with Africa on the basis of climate.

The garden names are featured in their original language to preserve the romance of the gardens, for political reasons, and for aesthetic value. For the European gardens, a translation has been provided for languages where the meaning would not necessarily be easily derived by an English speaker. The gardens are indexed by their original language name as well as by their English translation. At the back of the book, a list of international gardening organizations, a climate zone chart, and a gardens directory— including addresses and web site links—provides practical details for the reader as well as further information regarding the gardens featured.

Fact boxes

Each garden entry is accompanied by a fact box that provides readers with information on the garden at a glance. It includes the designer, the owner, the garden style, size, and the garden's location and climate. Occasionally it has been impossible to source the designer of a garden and sometimes the size of a garden has been difficult to quantify. In the latter case we have simply aimed to give the reader a sense of scale. Climate information has been provided using the Köppen climate classification system; U.S. climate zones have been given for all U.S. entries.

Contributors

James Alexander-Sinclair (JA-S) is a garden designer of many years' experience whose commissions are mostly private country gardens all over the UK. He has presented television programs for both the BBC and Channel 4 and writes for a number of different publications.

Sharon Amos (SA) is a freelance writer and editor specializing in gardening. She lives in Kent and has a small garden crammed with campanulas, hollyhocks, foxgloves and hardy geraniums, plus a cruel plant (Araujia) that she grew from seed. She also has an allotment and irritates fellow plotholders with her refusal to use chemicals.

Lisa Amphlett (LA) recently left her job as a features editor on a busy London gardening magazine to become a full-time (but no less busy) mom in Perth, Western Australia. Somewhere between the diaper changing and baby feeding she still finds the time to visit and write about inspirational gardens across Australia.

Helena Attlee (HA) is the author of *Italian Gardens: A History*, Frances Lincoln, 2006. She is a visiting lecturer at Birkbeck College, London, and leads special-interest tours to Italy for a wide variety of groups.

Christopher Bailes (CBa) studied at Kew; from 1980–88 he grew orchids at Kew and the Eric Young Orchid Foundation, editing *The Orchid Review* from 1986–90. In 1988 he became Curator of Rosemoor Garden, and from 1996–2000 also ran Hyde Hall. He has written four books and more than 100 articles and papers.

Vanessa Berridge (VB) has worked in magazines for almost thirty years. She was editor of *Country Homes & Interiors* for five years, and more recently launched and edited *The English Garden*, to which she still contributes. Now freelance, she also writes regularly for *Homes & Gardens*, *The Garden*, *Saga Magazine* and *The Lady*.

Matthew Biggs (MB) is a gardening writer and broadcaster who travels the world in search of great gardens. He presented Channel 4 television's 'Garden Club', is a panel member on BBC Radio 4's 'Gardeners' Question Time' and has written several books, his latest *'Gardening at Eden—and how to do it at home'*.

Caroline Boisset (CB) After graduating in Horticulture from Bath University, Caroline Boisset joined the editorial team of a gardening part-work as Technical Editor. A year later she went to Wye College where she gained an M.Sc. in Landscape Ecology, Design and Maintenance and then became Assistant Editor at *The Garden*, the Journal of the Royal Horticultural Society. She is a founder member and Fellow of the Institute of Horticulture; she was the first editor of the IoH Newsletter. Now working as a freelance horticultural editor and author she has written several books and articles; she is currently the Editor of the IDS yearbook and Lilies and Related Plants, the Yearbook of the RHS Lily Group, and co-chairman of the European Garden Scholarships. In 1995 she was awarded an RHS Gold Medal for an exhibit of pumpkins and squashes.

Anneli Bojstad (AB) Swedish born Art historian, based in Madrid since 1989, where she has developed her professional activities, adjusting her knowledge of art, architecture and gardens. Curator of the acclaimed exhibition "Gardens From The Soul" at the Botanic Gardens of Madrid in 2002, she's the author of *La Gran Aventura de los Indianos* (Antonio Machado 2004). Her garden and interior features have been published extensively in magazines such as; *Elle, Vogue, Casa & Campo*. She is currently working on a book about Spanish gardens and designing roof top terraces.

Jan Borsky (JBo) Landscape Architect, education: horticultural college and university in the Czech Republic, further studies in Austria. Participated on various projects in the Czech Republic, Austria, Germany and South Africa. Currently works at the Silva Tarouca Research Institute for Landscape and Ornamental Gardening in Pruhonice, Czech Republic.

Melanie Brown (MBr) Since leaving university Melanie has worked for the International Development Charity Afghanaid. Here she has kindled her passion for Afghanistan and has visited the country. During these trips her keen interest in gardens and history have led her to visit some of Afghanistan's most impressive Mughal gardens (which inspired her to write about them).

Jim Buckland (JB) is Gardens Manager of West Dean Gardens, Sussex, UK. He is an

honours graduate of the Royal Botanic Gardens Kew, has managed historic, public and private gardens in both Australia and the UK and is a frequent lecturer and a regular contributor to gardening publications.

Rob Cassy (RCa) has written for *Arena, Garden Design, Garden Inspirations, Gardens Illustrated, Hortus, Living Etc* and *The Independent*. He is a regular contributor to *The Times*. Rob's books include *101 Ideas Gardens, Garden UK, A Shortcut to Perfect Planting*, and *Everything You Need to Know About Gardening but Were Afraid to Ask*.

Philip Cave (PCa) landscape architect and garden designer who creates commercial and private schemes worldwide. He wrote *Creating Japanese Gardens* (Aurum Press/CharlesTuttle) in 1993, after learning the art in Kyoto, and a section in *Garden UK* (Conran Octopus) in 2003. His London-based practice (www.philipcave.com) has won a number of awards.

Roy Cheek (RChe) has wide experience in gardens, nurseries and parks throughout Britain from gardener to director. He was senior lecturer and curator at Cannington College, Somerset, England for 20 years, where he founded several new courses and created a diverse collection of gardens, which included 10,000 different kinds of plants. He currently leads garden tours worldwide, lectures and reports for the RHS magazine *The Garden*. He is also RHS vice-chairman of Tender Plant and Floral Trials Committee and senior advisor for RHS Holidays. He is co-author of three best-selling books and many specialist plant and garden articles.

Ruth Chivers (RChi) is a UK garden writer and designer who lives in California. A book author, she is a consulting editor on *Garden Design* magazine, and writes for UK gardening titles. In addition, Ruth is a passionate garden visitor wherever she travels, and lectures on garden subjects, including design and garden history.

John Coke (JC) founded small specialist nursery Green Farm Plants in 1983, growing an eclectic mix of perennials, shrubs and tender plants. A move to nearby Bury Court in 1997 and the design of a show garden in the old farmyard there by Piet Oudolf precipitated greater specialisation in hardy, "naturalistic" perennials and grasses. A second, minimalistic garden was designed by Christopher Bradley-Hole in 2002.

Martyn Cox (MC) writes for many magazines and has been on the editorial teams at *Gardenlife, BBC Gardeners' World Magazine, Amateur Gardening* and *Horticulture Week*. He is trained in amenity and commercial horticulture, and is a Garden Writers' Guild committee member. His East London garden is full of unusual perennials, fruit and vegetables.

Pat Crocker (PC) (BAA, PHEc) Culinary Herbalist, is a garden writer, author of four cookbooks and the 'Herb Series' of handbooks, photographer, and lecturer. Passionate about gardens, herbs, and food, Pat loves her work and asks, "what other job requires that one wander alone in beautiful gardens, eat exquisite food, and share those pleasures with others?" www.riversongherbals.com

Will de Pury (WdP) is an art historian and antiques dealer with a particular interest in the grand estates of the former Soviet Union.

Caroline Donald (CD) is a writer and editor. This includes editing the gardening pages of the *Sunday Times* newspaper and writing a regular column in *Homes and Gardens* magazine. She has a cottage garden in Somerset that verges on the unkempt but keeps her, the neighbouring rabbits and the resident population of slugs in supply of vegetables.

Ambra Edwards (AE) is well known in Britain as a campaigning journalist, columnist and garden historian. She has written extensively on twentieth century garden design and more recently the iconic garden heritage of the National Trust. She confesses to a wildly eclectic taste in gardens, from the teasing wit of Little Sparta to the tranquillity of Forde Abbey to the sweet austerity of Barragan.

Susan Elderkin (SE) is the author of two novels, *Sunset over Chocolate Mountains* and *The Voices*. Based in London, she helped launch *Gardens Illustrated* magazine, and is now a freelance garden journalist, travel writer and critic. In 2003 she was listed by Granta as one of the best young British novelists of the decade.

Kristof Fatsar (KF) graduated as landscape architect (1994) and as Monument Conservator (1996). He completed his Ph.D. in 2001. He is currently Associate Professor of Garden History and Head of the Study Program for the Conservation of Historic Gardens at the Corvinus University of Budapest with his main research topic being the garden history of Hungary.

Clare Foster (CF) is the Garden Editor at *House & Garden* magazine and a freelance writer and author. Prior to *House & Garden* she spent ten years at *Gardens Illustrated* magazine, latterly as Editor. She has written several books including *Compost* (Cassell), and is currently working on a book about allotment gardening. She lives in a small cottage in Oxfordshire with her husband, two small children and a dog, and is slowly creating a garden there when time allows.

Antoinette Galbraith (AG) is a freelance writer who lives in Edinburgh and gardens in the Borders. She specialises in writing about Scottish gardens contributing regularly to *Scottish Field, Scotsman, Scotland on Sunday, The English Garden, Period Living* and numerous other publications.

Lei Gao (LG) is a Ph.D. candidate in the Department of Landscape, University of Sheffield. She has been studying architecture and garden history in China and the United Kingdom for more than 10 years and her current dissertation concerns the attitudes towards historic gardens in China in the twentieth century.

Sally Gregson (SG) is a trained horticulturist and owner of Mill Cottage Plants, the hydrangea specialists. She writes regular gardening columns in *The Country Gardener* magazine which is distributed in the south of England. Sally is also a well-known speaker on a variety of topics, including the gardens of Japan.

Jerry Harpur (JHa) has been photographing gardens from around the world since the eighties. This has earned him several awards on both sides of the Atlantic, including the Lifetime Achievement Award from the Garden Writers Guild in London, UK, and an Honorary Doctorate from Essex University. His book *Gardens in Perspective* was published in 2005.

Marcus Harpur (MH) began his career in book publishing before joining his father, Jerry, to form Harpur Garden Library in the early nineties. His photographs appear in numerous books and magazines such as *Homes and Gardens, Ideal Home, The English Garden* and *Country Life*. He lives in North Essex with his wife and three children.

Allyson Hayward (AH) is a landscape historian from Wellesley, Massachusetts. She has been awarded a Gold Medal from the Massachusetts Horticultural Society for promoting New England's garden history, served as chair of the New England Garden History Society, is a member of the landscape advisory committee for Historic New England, and president of the New England Farm and Garden Association, Inc. She lectures extensively, and her book on the life and gardens of British garden designer Norah Lindsay (1873–1948) will be published in 2007.

Jan Hendrych (JH) is a Landscape Architect with the Landscape Institute of Harvard University. He works on historic garden and park rehabilitation projects in the United States, Italy, and the Czech Republic. Currently, he lectures at the Czech Technical University, Faculty of Architecture in Prague and researches at the Silva Tarouca Research Institute for Landscape and Ornamental Gardening in Pruhonice, Czech Republic. Jan lives in Prague and is married with three children.

Jenny Hendy (JHe) trained in botany and afterwards worked on the staff of one of Britain's leading gardening publications. As a freelancer she now writes for magazines and periodicals and has had 17 books published internationally. She runs a thriving garden design practice, is BBC Radio Stoke's resident gardening expert and a busy lecturer.

Judith Hitching (JHi) lives in the Cotswolds, and spends most of her time in the garden. She writes for consumer magazines, and is the author of *A Guide to Garden Visits*, published by Michael Joseph. She has written about over 500 gardens, and is interested in garden history, old houses, books and music.

Caroline Holmes (CH) is a garden historian whose work encompasses the Romans to the present day. Author of 6 books, writer for a wide range of consumer magazines, lecturer in Europe, the States and Japan, TV and award winning Radio Presenter. A specialist designer from re-creations to poisons. www.Caroline-Holmes.com

Heidi Howcroft (HH) was born and educated in Britain, and she has worked as a landscape architect in all parts of Germany. She has written a number of a number of books on garden design, the most recent being an updated version of her best-selling book

Das Pflasterbuch für den Garten and *Geheime Gärten in Deutschland*. Heidi is a features writer for EDEN and commutes between her homes in Somerset, England and Munich, Germany.

John Hoyland (JHo) gardens in southwest France and in Hertfordshire, England, where he runs Pioneer Nurseries, a small nursery specialising in rare and unusual plants. He is a regular contributor to the gardening pages of national newspapers and to gardening magazines.

Erica Hunningher (EH) is a freelance writer, editor, lecturer and tour leader. Her articles have appeared in *The Times, Gardeners' World Magazine, The English Garden* and *Hortus*; she has edited a host of gardening classics by top gardening authors including David Austin, Beth Chatto, Penelope Hobhouse and the late Christopher Lloyd.

Leigh Hunt (LH) trained at the Royal Botanic Gardens, Kew in England. He now works for the Royal Horticultural Society as a horticultural advisor, providing information on all aspects of plant cultivation. However, when time allows, he likes nothing better than nosing around other people's gardens for inspiration and to see well-grown plants.

Anne Jennings (AJ) is a freelance garden designer, consultant and writer, and Head of Horticulture at the Museum of Garden History in London. She is author of *Knot Gardens and Parterres* (Barn Elms 1998) and wrote a series of six chronological garden history books published by English Heritage in 2004 / 5.

Alice Joyce (AJo) An award-winning gardener, lecturer, and author of a series of *Gardenwalks* guidebooks, she worked as a sculptor in Chicago before turning to garden writing. Now living in Northern California, she is the San Francisco *Chronicle*'s Garden Walks columnist; her articles and photographs appear widely in magazines and newspapers.

Noel Kingsbury (NK) has been writing about plants and gardens since running a nursery business in the 1990s. He is well-known for his advocacy of naturalistic planting schemes informed by ecological science, particularly for public space. Linking gardening and landscape with wider cultural and political issues is also a major interest.

Rosemary Legrand (RL) is an experienced horticultural speaker on the RHS speakers register who is regularly invited to lecture on cruise liners. Her enjoyment of photography is used to advantage in her range of illustrated talks. A former nursery owner, her late father George Hyde was a hybridist of award winning azaleas and rhododendrons, collections of

which can be seen at the RHS gardens Wisley, Exbury and Kingston Lacy. Rosemary lives in Dorset where she has created a garden of just under one acre.

Paula McWaters (PMcW) has written and edited gardening features for many years, for consumer and gardening magazines. Former Gardening Editor of *Good Housekeeping*, Assistant Editor of *Country Living* and Editor of *Gardenlife*. Her special interests are small gardens and garden visiting. She has project-managed two gold medal-winning gardens at the RHS Chelsea Flower Show.

Alasdair Moore (AM) is a horticulturalist, writer and international tour guide. For over half of his professional life he was Assistant-Head Gardener at the renowned Tresco Abbey Gardens, Isles of Scilly. His first book *La Mortola* was published in 2004. He regularly leads garden tours to South Africa, Japan and the Riviera.

Toby Musgrave (TM) is a horticulturist, garden historian and garden designer. As well as writing six books and contributing to numerous magazines and newspapers, he lectures widely and designs gardens around the world. www.TobyMusgrave.com

Carol Newman (CN) is a lifelong expatriate now retired to America, an alumni of the Architectural Association's Conservation of Landscape, Parks and Gardens course's first years, writes for *The World of Interiors* and cultivates her own garden (inspired by Russell Page) when not visiting her small grandson in St Petersburg, Russia.

Michèle Osborne (MO) French born, graduated from the Sorbonne as a linguist but her passion for architecture and design led her to start her own landscape design practice. She has collaborated with leading architects and developers to create award-winning outdoor spaces in Britain and abroad. Her work has been featured in many books and magazines. She is the author of *Gardens in the Sky* and *Lighting Gardens*.

Jane Owen (JO) writes *The Times'* garden blog and presents the Royal Horticultural Society's Chelsea Flower Show DVD. She is a journalist, editor, designer, speaker (British Library, V&A etc), and Women of the Year council member. Her books include *Gardens Through Time* (BBC) and *Eccentric Gardens* (Pavilion) and she co-presented BBC TV's landmark series, Gardens Through Time.

Jill Raggett (JR) is a Reader in Gardens and Designed Landscapes at Writtle College, England, and Adjunct Professor at the Nova Scotia College of Agriculture, Canada. She has

travelled extensively to study historic and contemporary gardens. One of her major areas of research concerns the origins and expression of the Japanese-style garden in Great Britain.

Christine Reid (CR) is an Australian writer whose wide interests include the social and cultural history of gardens and designed landscapes, both historic and contemporary. Based in Melbourne, she is the Garden Editor of *Australian Country Style* magazine and a regular contributor to many publications in Australia and the UK, including the recently published *Oxford Companion to the Garden, Gardens Illustrated* and *Hortus*.

Juliet Roberts (JRo) is Editor of *Gardens Illustrated*. Prior to garden journalism, she worked for the British Film Institute on variety of film magazines. But as her passion for gardening grew, she found she had somehow swapped cinema-going for nursery and garden visiting. A keen gardener, Juliet is particularly fond of vegetable growing and has had an allotment for many years. Her first book, *Organic Kitchen Gardening*, was published by Conran Octopus in 2005.

Richard Rosenfeld (RR) has written eleven gardening books, with articles for the *Times, Sunday Times, Independent* and *Guardian*, etc., and lives in New York and Sussex. He has designed gardens in Italy and Spain.

Vivian Russell (VR) is a photographer and writer. Her books include the award-winning *Monet's Garden*, together with *Monet's Landscapes, Monet's Water Lilies, Dream Gardens, Gardens of the Riviera, Edith Wharton's Italian Gardens, Dog Show* and *Gnomes*. She has photographed two recent books on the gardens at Levens Hall and Hampton Court Palace. A contributor to the *Daily Telegraph* gardening supplement, her forthcoming book is on Scottish gardens.

Barbara Segall (BS) is a horticulturist, freelance garden writer and garden traveller. For the touring guide to *The Gardens of Spain and Portugal* (March 1999, Mitchell Beazley) she made extensive visits to Spain and Portugal visiting some 140 garden and landscape sites. Her recent garden destinations include gardens and garden shows in South Africa and the United States, and is planning her own latest list of 'must-see' gardens. Her work appears in a number of specialist gardening and consumer publications such as *The Kitchen Garden, Country Life, Country Living, Gardens Illustrated, The English Garden, Herbs, Ideal Homes* and *Homes and Gardens*. Her latest book is *Pots and Plants* (Mitchell Beazley 2006).

Myfanwy Slade (MS) is a biologist and environmental scientist now working as a freelance writer and photographer. She lives with her husband and small son in Reading where she is currently restoring their tangled and long-neglected Victorian garden to its former glory.

Naomi Slade (NS) Freelance writer, editor, environmentalist and biologist; she is a regular contributor to magazines including *Gardeners' World*. Her interests include urban and community gardening, wildlife, plants—particularly native trees, garden visits, botanical artisans. Career highlights: three silver-gilt medals at Chelsea Flower Show; a teacher-training garden for the Department of Education; and linking *Wallace and Gromit* to gardening in schools.

Rae Spencer-Jones (RS-J) studied horticulture before joining the editorial team of *Gardens Illustrated* magazine. Now a freelance horticultural journalist and author, she has written on all areas of horticulture for a wide range of gardening pubilcations, including the gardening pages of the *Daily Telegraph* and *The Times, Gardener's World* magazine and *Gardens Illustrated*. Her own book, *Wild Flowers of Britain and Ireland*, was published by Kyle Cathie in 2005.

Edwinna von Baeyer (EvB) is a landscape historian living in Ottawa, Canada. She has written numerous articles and three books on Canadian landscape history. When not in front of the television watching English soccer, you can find her in her garden trying to beat the Canadian climate.

Isabelle van Groeningen (IvG) is an established garden historian, designer and consultant, lecturer and occasional writer. In 1983 she moved from Belgium to England to study horticulture at the Royal Botanic Gardens Kew, followed by a Ph.D. in conservations studies at York University. She has a particular interest in Herbaceous planting schemes, both traditional border planting and the more relaxed naturalistic style practiced on the continent. The practice Land Art Ltd, which she founded in 1992 with Gabriella Pape, covers a wide range of projects, from the historic to the new, both public and private, in Britain and on the Continent. Specialised in the creation of new schemes in historically sensitive settings, Isabelle was involved in the replanting of Jellicoe's Secret Garden at Cliveden and won English Heritage's Contemporary Gardens Competition in 1999 for the re-creation of the herbaceous borders at Eltham Palace.

Cleve West (CWe) From award-winning show gardens to private havens, Cleve West has built a reputation for innovative, contemporary landscapes in the UK. He is a member of the Society of Garden Designers (MSGD) and a judge for the Royal Horticultural Society. He contributes regularly to garden journals and writes a weekly column for *The Independent Magazine*.

Kim Wilkie (KW) is a landscape architect who searches to understand the special character of each place and let designs be inspired by both memory and imagination. Kim set up his practice, Kim Wilkie Associates, in London in 1989. He continues to teach sporadically at Berkeley; writes optimistically about land and place; and meddles in various national committees on landscape policy in the UK. Recent projects include the new V&A Garden and the Richmond Floodscape Project.

Angharad Williams (AW) With more than a decade's writing experience, Angharad is the founding partner of Proof in Translation, a brother/sister duo passionate about (copy)writing, proofreading and translation. Educated in Dutch, French and Italian at University College London in England and Leiden University in the Netherlands, Angharad's other passions are gardens, art history and alpine skiing.

Gwilym Williams (GW) Having worked in the heritage industry for nearly twenty years, Gwilym has excavated at Kew Gardens and Royal Hospital Chelsea. Inspired by an interest in gardens and garden archaeology, he has recently completed an excavation of a 17th-century manorial garden in Oxfordshire, England to be published in 2007. Together with his sister, he founded Proof in Translation.

Matthew Wilson (MW) is the Curator and Head of Site at RHS Harlow Carr, North Yorkshire, England. He contributes regularly to both local and national publications, including the *Daily Telegraph* and the magazines *BBC Gardeners' World, The Garden, Gardens Illustrated,* and *The English Garden*. Matthew has also appeared on local and national radio and television programs such as Gardeners' World, Gardening with the Experts, ITV's Britain's Best Back Gardens, BBC Countryfile, and Turf Wars.

Ted Wilson (TW) is a senior lecturer in history at Manchester Metropolitan University, specialising in economic and monetary history, and the history of the First World War. He has a keen interest in gardens and garden history and enjoys visiting and photographing them in his spare time.

Chris Woods (CW), a native of England but now a U.S. citizen, has worked in the horticultural world, as a garden manager and designer, for thirty years. He started his career at the Royal Botanical Gardens, Kew, where he worked as an apprentice horticulturist. He has worked in three other gardens in the UK, Portmeirion in Wales, Bateman's in Sussex, and Cliveden in Buckinghamshire.

He came to the U.S. in 1981 and was, until April 2003, Director and Chief Designer of Chanticleer, one of America's most vibrant public gardens. More recently, he was the Vice President for Horticulture and External Operations for the Santa Barbara Botanical Garden and then Executive Director of the Ojai Valley Land Conservancy in California. In 2006 he was appointed Director, the VanDusen Botanical Garden in Vancouver, Canada.

Among numerous other responsibilities, he was a member of the Board of the Fairmount Park Conservancy and a founding member of the Business Advisory Board for the Flora of North America Project.

He is the author of numerous articles and was a guest editor of the Brooklyn Botanic Garden's handbook *Perennials and Their Uses*. In April 1992, Facts on File published his book *The Encyclopedia of Perennials*.

In 2003, he was awarded the professional citation for achievements in public horticulture by the American Public Garden Association.

Jan Woudstra (JW) is a landscape architect and historian who has worked in private practice, but also pursued an academic career. He has taught at the Architectural Association in London, and currently at the Department of Landscape of the University of Sheffield. He is a former editor of *Garden History*.

Sam Youd (SY) has been gardening since the age of eight. He started as an apprentice with Liverpool Parks Department in 1962. There he trained as a propagator, became a training instructer, and finally technical adviser. He has been Head of Gardens at Tatton Park in Cheshire since 1983. Sam is a writer, broadcaster and photographer. He has lectured and travelled all over the world though his specialist subjects are the gardens of China and Japan. For this work he was awarded the Associate of Honour by the RHS in 2003.

Chris Young (CY) is a garden and landscape writer based in Lincolnshire, England. He trained as a landscape architect at the University of Gloucestershire, but always had an enthusiasm for writing and disseminating his love of gardens and landscapes to the wider world. His particular interest is in garden design, and especially the designers shaping our domestic and public space. He is currently deputy editor of *The Garden*, the journal of the Royal Horticultural Society, which is read by 365,000 readers internationally. He is married with one son.

Garden Names Index

From desert to mountain range, from a subtropical to a northern temperate climate, North American gardens exist in an enormous variety of conditions. Plants in North America vary from tough, hardy survivors to freewheeling, tolerant climbers. And the designs include everything from postmodern inner-city roof gardens to Beatrix Ferrand's rural, classical feel and the ultimate in retro gardening, Florida's Disney World.

NORTH AMERICA

Minter Gardens

British Columbia, Canada

DESIGNERS: Brian Minter, Faye Minter
OWNERS: Brian Minter, Faye Minter
GARDEN STYLE: 20th-century display and themed gardens
SIZE: 32 acres (12.9 ha)
CLIMATE: Temperate
LOCATION: Rosedale, British Columbia

British Columbia, Canada's most western province, is a vast wilderness of rivers, lakes, waterfalls, beaches, mineral hot springs, alpine meadows, and snow-capped mountains. Centuries ago, its eastern Fraser Valley witnessed a massive mountain rockslide that swept over fertile meadows, and created stunning and rugged land formations. With Mount Cheam as a spectacular natural backdrop, Brian and Faye Minter envisioned a world-class garden at the very site where the rockfall came to rest, a place where wild geraniums, aquilegias, roses, and bleeding hearts made their home. True to their dream, just a quarter century after their first encounter with the land and its features, the Minters' eleven themed gardens (with a maze, topiary, scented area, two aviaries, stream, and Chinese design) reflect the seasons in a magnificent Pacific Northwest coast fashion.

Hundreds of thousands of spring bulbs—tulips, daffodils, hyacinths, anemones, lilies, ranunculus, and alliums—combine in bold and stunning spring beds. As summer arrives, the Rhododendron Garden, planted in solid drifts on a north-facing bank above fern-laden rock wall terraces, offers awe inspiring vistas. Dogwoods and magnolias are grouped between the rhododendrons to heighten their effect Extra touches include brilliant annuals, cottage-garden-style perennial plants, a 12-foot-high (4 m) peacock topiary with a 50-foot-long (15 m) floral tail, Penjing rock bonsai, and the fall gold and russet hues of winter pansies and flowering kale—all making the gardens a thrilling, three-season experience. PC

Abkhazi Garden

British Columbia, Canada

DESIGNERS: Prince and Princess Abkhazi, John Wade
OWNER: The Land Conservancy of British Columbia
GARDEN STYLE: 20th-century Californian and Asian
SIZE: 1.4 acre (0.6 ha)
CLIMATE: Temperate
LOCATION: Victoria, British Columbia

Love affairs make great stories, and this one resulted in a great garden. Exiled Georgian Prince Nicholas Abkhazi married Marjorie (Peggy) Pemberton-Carter, in 1946, and so began the creation of a garden that they worked on for more than forty years and called their "child." Under the direction of John Wade, a protégé of Los Angeles modernist architect Richard Neutra, they built a dynamic house and garden overlooking the Strait of Juan de Fuca and the Olympic Mountains.

The garden is hidden from the street behind a hornbeam hedge, and has views to the water and mountains beyond. The garden wends its way around rocky outcrops, and mature Japanese maples. The Rhododendron Woodland Garden, originally planted with 50-year-old specimens, is now a jungle of tall, sculptural trunks and grand shrubs that flower. Rivers of bulbs, tiny alpine plants, and flowering woodland specimens, including wood anemones, trilliums, arisaemas, lilies, cyclamen, primulas, and ferns and hostas keep everything alive.

The South Lawn, bathed in sunlight, features a geometric plan with a central stone circle and sundial, bordered by standard lilacs. Mixed-herbaceous-bordered paths skirt the lawn, leading the visitor to the house, and to views at the edge of the property. One of the most remarkable is toward a path edged by soft tips of heather flowing gently along the edge of the property, ending at an immense rocky outcrop. Princess Abkhazi likened this sight to the River Yangtze, and it is easy to see what she means. AH

Dr. Sun Yat-Sen Classical Chinese Garden

British Columbia, Canada

DESIGNER: Wang Zu-Xin
OWNER: City of Vancouver
GARDEN STYLE: 20th-century classical Chinese
SIZE: 0.3 acre (0.1 ha)
CLIMATE: Temperate
LOCATION: Vancouver, British Columbia

Vancouver, with its bustling metropolitan core, vibrant Chinatown, Pacific Ocean views, and proximity to the Coast Mountain Range, has more than 190 parks. One exceptional garden in this multicultural green city is tucked behind protective walls—the Dr. Sun Yat-Sen Classical Chinese Garden—and it is a fitting tribute to the man known as Kuo Fu, "The Father of Modern China." Yat-Sen was the principal architect of the revolution that overturned the Manchu dynasty in China, and he devoted his life to Chinese economic development. In the sixteenth century, Wen Zhengming described the purpose of classical gardens of the Ming dynasty: "Most cherished in this mundane world is a place without traffic; truly in the midst of a city there can be mountain and forest." Designed by Taoist poets, these Chinese gardens were meant to calm the minds of busy scholars, and help them focus on harmony and balance—the yin and yang. Spare and highly structured, such gardens allow quiet contemplation of nature's elements within a perfect suspension of the opposing forces: light-dark, solid-empty, hard-soft, and straight-undulating.

The inscription above the entrance to the Dr. Sun Yat-Sen garden means the "garden of ease." Here the *qi*, or life force, found in the elements—rock, water, and plants—has a calming effect. Serpentine walkways, *yun wei ting* (rocks forming a mountain), typical Suzhou-type pavilions, and a winding double corridor set off a meticulously arranged landscape, where plants are used sparingly, with a mystical or symbolic purpose. PC

Butchart Gardens

British Columbia, Canada

DESIGNERS: Jennie Butchart, Ian Ross
OWNERS: The Butchart family
GARDEN STYLE: 20th-century themed gardens
SIZE: 55 acres (22.3 ha)
CLIMATE: Temperate
LOCATION: Vancouver Island, British Columbia

At the beginning of the twentieth century, cement manufacturing pioneer Robert Pim Butchart established his business and family near rich limestone deposits at Tod Inlet on Vancouver Island. Not long after, Butchart's wife, Jennie, conceived and executed a bold plan for a sunken garden in the exhausted quarry near their house.

As the garden took shape, Robert began collecting ornamental birds, and built elaborate birdhouses throughout the garden. By 1908 the Butcharts had created a Japanese Garden on the seaside of their home. Later an Italian Garden and Rose Garden were added to the grounds. Today his descendants still manage the four, all-season, main garden areas with their spectacular views and exquisite designs, which continue to draw more than a million visitors a year. The mild temperatures mean that there is nearly always something in flower, starting with spring tulips—100,000 bulbs in all—rhododendrons, azaleas, and Siberian wallflowers. Aquilegias, delphiniums, and Himalayan blue poppies (*Meconopsis betonicifolia*) share the spotlight with tuberous begonias and sweet William (*Dianthus barbatus*) in summer. PC

> "The mild temperatures mean that there is nearly always something in flower..."

Thomas Hobbs' Garden

British Columbia, Canada

DESIGNER: Thomas Hobbs
OWNER: Thomas Hobbs
GARDEN STYLE: 20th-century Mediterranean
SIZE: 0.5 acre (0.2 ha)
CLIMATE: Temperate
LOCATION: Vancouver, British Columbia

Marvelous, gorgeous, extraordinary: superlatives come to mind when you visit Thomas Hobbs' Garden high on a hill overlooking Vancouver's English Bay.

Hobbs says he was born "obsessed with plants" and began growing seeds when he was five years old. He bought this property in 1987 and transformed the Mediterranean-style house and garden into a statement of his horticultural design philosophy. A noted florist, plant collector, orchid breeder, and nursery owner, he has written books urging gardeners to be more creative and make personal, inspiring, intimate gardens. And he has applied this advice to his own garden. Hobbs loves creating "garden incidents" that make visitors catch their breath. The enclosed front garden is a carefully considered composition with all the plants complementing the peach color of the stuccoed house. His color palette includes rusts, peaches, salmons, and corals, with mauve flowers and silver and dark foliage plants being used as accents.

The slate-and-tile terrace has a Mediterranean flavor with a fountain, pond, and a profusion of varied pots. He grows angels' trumpets, canna lilies, and hardy palms, all set off by a small lawn and a chartreuse euphorbia hedge. The front garden leads to a shady side garden planted with ornamental cherry trees and large-leaved Japanese butterbur (*Petasites japonicus*) and yellow waxbells (*Kirengeshoma palmata*). At the back of the house, the garden opens up to the wider landscape with a view over the treetops to the sea, mountains, and city. EvB

Darts Hill

British Columbia, Canada

DESIGNERS: Edwin Darts, Francisca Darts
OWNER: City of Surrey
GARDEN STYLE: 20th-century native plant collection
SIZE: 7.5 acres (3 ha)
CLIMATE: Temperate
LOCATION: Surrey, British Columbia

Donated to the City of Surrey by the owner, Francisca Darts, on the death of her husband, Edwin, this horticultural paradise is without equal in the region for its variety of rare and native plants, shrubs and trees. The garden was created on a south-facing slope at the western end of the Hazelmere Valley in South Surrey, not far from the U.S. border, by the Darts.

The couple labored and tilled the land, which had been logged in the late 1880s, but never properly cleared. In 1947 they erected their house. Their first large garden project involved planting an orchard, including plum, peach, apple, pear, and nut trees, of which hardly anything remains.

The impressive rhododendron and magnolia collection includes *M. macrophylla*, *M. acuminata*, and *M. tripetala*. The rhododendron walk, leading to a small pond, follows a path lined with blue rhododendrons that flower in April, followed by a tall *Paulownia tomentosa* covered in lilac-blue flowers. Other ornamental trees include *Calocedrus decurrens*, *Corylus avellana* 'Contorta', and *Hamamelis mollis*. Nearer the house is a magnificent *Picea orientalis* with a *Wisteria floribunda* winding its tendrils to the highest reaches of the tree for a stunning display in spring. But the most famous tree in the collection is an eastern U.S./Canada and Japanese walnut cross (*Juglans cinerea* x *J. ailanthifolia* var. *cordiformis*) that has been deemed a City of Surrey heritage tree.

Today the Darts Hill Garden Conservancy Trust Society (a group of volunteers including Francisca Darts) assists the city in maintaining the garden. AH

Park and Tilford Gardens

British Columbia, Canada

DESIGNER: A community project
OWNERS: Various, including the City of
   North Vancouver
GARDEN STYLE: 20th-century themed gardens
SIZE: 3 acres (1.2 ha)
CLIMATE: Temperate
LOCATION: Vancouver, British Columbia

Eight spectacular themed gardens were created on this site in 1969 as a community service project for the enjoyment of the people of North Vancouver.

The Oriental Garden contains Japanese maples, pines, and bamboos gently placed next to a pond and manicured bonsai trees. A few steps away, the Native Garden features a natural footpath over a rustic, wooden bridge leading to a small, Pacific-style forest of cedar, hemlock, and rare, native azaleas. The floor of this quiet haven is planted with native plants. The Rock Pool, with its lush, rich vegetation, including a giant gunnera, skunk cabbages, ornamental grasses, and daylilies, has the rushing sound of a waterfall.

For the flower enthusiast, there are great choices. The White Garden has white, gray, and green leaves, and there's even a finch aviary packed with birds. For the lover of bright, contrasting colors, the Display Garden has colorful annuals. The Rose Garden has more than twenty-five varieties of rose: from delicate miniatures to showy floribundas. A short walk away is the Herb Garden, the smallest area on the site, filled with robust scents, and medicinal and culinary herbs. The Colonnade Garden has an aviary with parrots, cockatoos, mynas, and other tropical birds. The large rhododendron area is guarded by Douglas firs, big magnolias, and flowering dogwoods. This garden's variety means that there is almost always something eye-catching at any time of year. AH

UBC Botanical Garden

British Columbia, Canada

DESIGNERS: Justice and Webb Landscape Artists
OWNER: University of British Columbia
GARDEN STYLE: 20th-century display gardens,
   greenhouses, research plots
SIZE: 110 acres (44.5 ha)
CLIMATE: Temperate
LOCATION: Vancouver, British Columbia

Canada's longest continuously operating university botanical garden was founded in 1916 by John Davidson, British Columbia's first provincial botanist. A true botanical garden with teaching, research, and conservation as its mandate, the UBC Botanical Garden is known as one of the leading research institutions in North America. At the same time, its diverse collections, seasonal displays, and the sheer beauty of the gardens and plants draw visitors who simply want to experience its many pleasures.

In the Asian Garden, some of the most ancient-flowering specimens, the magnolias, are gathered from Tibet, Japan, China, Korea, Manchuria, and other eastern regions, in perhaps the greatest number on the North American continent. The Alpine Garden offers rare glimpses of mountainous rock and soil, as well as plants from the Andes to coastal Morocco, and the Canary Islands to Asia Minor. The Food Garden—a big hit with children—features established and experimental varieties of vegetables, berries, and fruit trees of the Pacific Northwest. The Native Garden unfolds in synchronization with nature, and the Physic Garden's formal design showcases plants used for medicinal purposes. Smaller gardens include the Arbor Garden, Winter Garden, Perennial Border Garden, and Contemporary Garden. The Nitobe Memorial Garden (see page 25) is an authentic Japanese tea and stroll garden. PC

Nitobe Memorial Garden

British Columbia, Canada

DESIGNER: Mori Kannosuke
OWNER: University of British Columbia
GARDEN STYLE: Japanese tea and stroll garden
SIZE: 2.5 acres (1 ha)
CLIMATE: Temperate
LOCATION: Vancouver, British Columbia

"I am in Japan," said Crown Prince Tsugo, now His Imperial Majesty Akihito, the 125th Emperor of Japan, as he toured the Nitobe Memorial Garden at the University of British Columbia in 1992. The traditional Japanese Garden is considered to be one of the most traditional, authentic Japanese tea and stroll gardens in North America, and is among the top five Japanese gardens outside Japan.

Sitting high on the cliffs overlooking the Strait of Georgia, the small, exquisite garden was created out of pristine forest by Japanese landscape architects and gardeners in honor of Inazo Nitobe, an international scholar who died a few years before World War II. Nitobe had devoted his life to peace and had worked tirelessly toward his goal of creating "a bridge across the Pacific."

On arriving here, the visitor encounters an idealized conception and symbolic representation of nature, which is richly layered with meaning and culture. The stone lanterns and bridges, the benches, the tea garden gate, the rocks, and the pagoda are built as, or are adorned with, symbols that represent Japanese life, religion, and beliefs.

The Memorial Garden is a tranquil space featuring waterfalls, rivers, forests, islands, and seas, striking the perfect balance between opposites, balancing yin and yang. Applying traditional Japanese pruning techniques to native Canadian trees and shrubs, while at the same time displaying native Japanese maple, cherry, azalea, and iris, the garden does indeed span the Pacific.

Visitors come to this subtle and serene place of contemplation and simple beauty to enjoy the spring cherry blossom, the irises in summer, and the brilliantly-colored maples in fall. They don't just encounter a different culture, but are exposed—intellectually and in their hearts—to a very different kind of garden art. PC

Van Dusen Botanical Garden

British Columbia, Canada

DESIGNERS: William Livingstone, Roy Forster
OWNER: City of Vancouver
GARDEN STYLE: 20th-century displays in landscape setting
SIZE: 55 acres (22.2 ha)
CLIMATE: Temperate
LOCATION: Vancouver, British Columbia

The mild Pacific Northwest climate, more than 7,500 species of plant assembled from six continents, beautifully designed lakes and rockwork, and the proximity to Vancouver's hip downtown combine to make the Van Dusen Botanical Garden a favorite haunt of photographers, garden enthusiasts, and tourists.

The garden evolves around majestic evergreen trees scattered throughout the former Shaughnessy golf course, and sports the largest Canadian collection of hollies, along with outstanding bamboos, magnolias, rhododendrons, and azaleas. Upon entering the central courtyard, you can walk straight ahead into the traditional Herb Garden, or stroll through the White Garden to the right. On the way to the Rock Garden, you will see dwarf conifers, a pool with water plants, miniature bulbs, and perennials. Stairs lead to the formal, renaissance-style Rose Garden planted with repeat-blooming roses, and outlined with box and santolina. The Perennial Garden has a late-nineteenth-century border and contemporary island plantings. Then it is on to the Heather Garden, via the little stone bridge, with Scots pine and birch, and heaths and heathers giving color for most of the year. Among others, there is also a Fragrance Garden and one of only three Elizabethan hedge mazes in North America.

With its rolling lawns, tranquil lakes, and dramatic rockwork, the Van Dusen Botanical Garden is one of the most picturesque landscape settings from which to glimpse the mountains and the vibrant Vancouver cityscape. PC

Edwards Gardens

Ontario, Canada

DESIGNER: Rupert E. Edwards
OWNER: City of Toronto
GARDEN STYLE: 20th-century naturalistic parkland
SIZE: 35 acres (14.1 ha)
CLIMATE: Continental cool summer
LOCATION: Toronto, Ontario

The largest city in the second-largest country in the world has an ecologically inspired vision for its public spaces. Toronto wants the world to know this multicultural Canadian financial and arts center as "the city within a park." As part of 593 parkland acres (240 ha) stretching along the valley floor of the River Don in central Toronto, Edwards Gardens, with its gardenesque planting, views of the rugged valley, large rock garden, teaching garden, and floral displays, contributes in no small way to that green dream. The dream began in 1944, when businessman Rupert E. Edwards purchased a home and created a picturesque, painterly, and irregularly planted landscape reminiscent of the previous century. He envisioned the land as a public garden, a wish granted when the encroaching city acquired the property in 1956.

Edwards Gardens is famous for rhododendrons, but also features seasonal perennials and roses on the uplands with wildflowers, an arboretum, and one of the largest rockeries in Canada in the eroded riverbed below. The wild, natural style of the gardens helps them merge seamlessly with the bordering parks, where paths follow the meandering Wilket Creek and bridges linking natural valley pockets filled with indigenous trees, shrubs, and wildlife.

At its northern entrance, Edwards Gardens is adjacent to the recently refurbished home of the Toronto Botanical Garden, a separate, volunteer-based gardening education and information center offering an excellent horticultural library. PC

Parkwood Estate Gardens

Ontario, Canada

DESIGNERS: Harries and Hall, H. B. and L. A. Dunington-Grubb Landscape Architects, John Lyle

OWNER: The Canadian State

GARDEN STYLE: 20th-century English Arts and Crafts

SIZE: 12 acres (4.8 ha)

CLIMATE: Continental cool summer

LOCATION: Oshawa, Ontario

One of Canada's foremost industrialists and philanthropists, Samuel McLaughlin, built Parkwood as a grand private estate featuring architectural, landscape, and interior designs of the early twentieth century. Now a National Historic Site, the large property still reflects the personal interests and style of the founder of General Motors of Canada.

During the early decades of the 1900s, the gardens at Parkwood evolved following the English Arts and Crafts gardening style that favored formal beds surrounding the house and a looser, less formal presentation, including a broad expanse of lawn, farther away. Visitors were drawn through gates to views contained and sheltered by cedar hedges. In fact Parkwood's first landscape designers linked each principal room of the house to an adjacent part of the garden, and established a wooded park beyond.

Spectacular outdoor garden "rooms," including the Italian Garden, the Sundial Garden, Summerhouse, and Sunken Garden, were created by the second team of designers. The last, and perhaps most outstanding, refinement was made by architect John Lyle, who created the Formal Garden in the mid-1930s. The three remaining greenhouses display palms, orchids, and tropical plants, and are home to the Japanese Garden and the Greenhouse Tea Room. The heritage gardens of Parkwood capture both the grandeur of life during the interwar years of the twentieth century, and the personal style of the man who envisioned this site. PC

Queen Victoria Park

Ontario, Canada

DESIGNER: Niagara Parks Commission
OWNER: Niagara Parks Commission
GARDEN STYLE: 19th-century formal and naturalistic public park
SIZE: 200 acres (81 ha)
CLIMATE: Continental cool summer
LOCATION: Niagara Falls, Ontario

With the roar of 600,000 gallons (2,727,600 l) of water per minute tumbling down 176 feet (54 m), visitors can stroll along the Canadian side of the Niagara Gorge and its river without having to leave Queen Victoria Park. A grand, royal garden, it provides the perfect vantage point for experiencing the nightly illumination of the falls and the summer fireworks displays held on Fridays.

Named after Queen Victoria, it is a fantastic setting for rich natural vegetation and exotic species. The park came into existence when the Queen Victoria Niagara Parks Act of 1887 brought 154 acres (62 ha) of land into public hands for the purpose of preservation. In the early days, rhododendrons and azaleas took center stage. Now native plants such as giant yellow hyssop (*Agastache nepetoides*) and purple giant hyssop (*A. scrophulariifolia*) or maidenhair fern can also be found among the spring daffodils (numbering half a million), magnolias, and tulips.

Besides the large Rock Garden, Hybrid Tea Rose Garden, and the sweeping lawns, summer visitors can enjoy carpetbedding displays with thousands of annuals. Then, in the crisp fall days when winter is just about to set in, fuchsia and lantana standards, lilies, and coleus give way to chrysanthemums and flowering kale. And as temperatures drop farther, the mist from the falls turns to ice, and the stark branches of deciduous trees and shrubs become ice-crusted, creating a glistening, magical winter sight. PC

Niagara Parks Botanical Gardens

Ontario, Canada

DESIGNER: Niagara Parks Commission
OWNER: Niagara Parks Commission
GARDEN STYLE: 20th-century themed gardens
SIZE: 100 acres (40.5 ha)
CLIMATE: Continental cool summer
LOCATION: Niagara Falls, Ontario

The Niagara Parks Botanical Gardens has its roots in plant education, focusing on the relationship of plants to the ecosystem that evolved around the erosion of the Niagara gorge. In 1936 it was founded as the School for Apprentice Gardeners. It remains a residential location for studying, gardening, and learning how to maintain such landscapes.

A passion for the art, science, and mystery of horticulture is evident in the design of the formal herb, rose, vegetable, and rock garden, and the magnificent arboretum. The garden also has one of Canada's finest collections of ornamental trees and shrubs, a greenhouse, and North America's largest butterfly conservatory.

In 1884, 915 naturalized plants were found and cataloged in the area, but there were no trees, so the Niagara Parks Commission reestablished 269 trees and has continued a steady planting program ever since.

The Niagara River corridor is part of Carolinian Canada, that part of the eastern deciduous forest that includes southern species such as tulip trees (*Liriodendrum tulipifera*), sassafras, sycamore, and black walnut (*Juglans nigra*). Thanks to the moderate temperatures and moderating effects of the Great Lakes, species diversity is very high. The sedimentary rock of limestone, sandstone, and shale that underlie the predominantly clay soils of the postglacial river corridor have given rise to astonishing scenes. PC

The Toronto Music Garden

Ontario, Canada

DESIGNER: Julie Moir Messervy
OWNER: City of Toronto
GARDEN STYLE: 20th-century interpretive
SIZE: 2 acres (0.8 ha)
CLIMATE: Continental cool summer
LOCATION: Toronto, Ontario

In the late 1990s, the celebrated cellist Yo-Yo Ma collaborated with several artists to make *Inspired by Bach*, a six-part film series. The first in the series was *The Music Garden*, in which he worked with landscape designer Julie Moir Messervy to interpret the theme of nature, the subject of Bach's first suite. As a result of the film a real-life Music Garden project began to take shape, with the City of Toronto pledging the site. A combination of impeccable vision, creative collaboration across many disciplines, and a bold design that envisioned each section of the garden as one of the six dance movements in Bach's *Suite No. 1 for Unaccompanied Cello* make the Toronto Music Garden internationally renowned.

In the Music Garden, visitors float from the Prelude, with its undulating riverlike walk of curves, to a forest grove of wandering trails, the Allemande (a movement in 4/4 time). They are then swept along a swirling path through a wildflower meadow to the Sarabande. Here the garden's centerpiece stone acts as a stage for poets and artists. A formal flower parterre symbolizes the Minuet, where architectural blacksmith Tom Tollefson's Music Pavilion shelters small musical ensembles or dance groups. The Gigue, a jaunty English dance, is artfully interpreted as a series of giant grass steps that propel visitors back to the outside world. This garden is clever, engaging, and fun—and it is a pity that more gardens are not based on works of art. PC

Royal Botanical Gardens

Ontario, Canada

DESIGNER: Carl Borgstrom
OWNERS: City of Hamilton, a charitable volunteer board
GARDEN STYLE: 20th-century display gardens
SIZE: 2,700 acres (1,093.5 ha)
CLIMATE: Continental cool summer
LOCATION: Hamilton/Burlington, Ontario

Like the country itself, Canada's Royal Botanical Gardens are wild, cultured, complex, serene, and, above all, vast. About one-tenth of the massive site is cultivated, and the remainder encompasses managed natural areas where the largest freshwater marsh restoration project of its kind in North America has been undertaken. The RBG is a living museum that helps people explore the relationship between the plant world, humanity, and the rest of nature.

The garden encompasses five separate areas. The Hendrie Park Rose Garden features roses, medicinal and scented plants, lilies, climbers, espaliers, and woodland species. In the Rock Garden can be found a spring bulb display, summer annuals, flowering cherries, azaleas, and many unusual trees and shrubs. The spectacular Arboretum includes indigenous trees, shrubs, conifers, hedges, dogwoods, hawthorns, and flowering crab apples.

The Katie Osborne Lilac Garden has the world's largest collection of lilacs, and the Laking Area includes irises, perennials, peonies, daylilies, ornamental grasses, and the Heritage Garden. In addition, there's an information center, and both indoor and outdoor floral displays, including a Mediterranean Garden.

For more robust types, there's also marshland, woodland, meadow, Niagara escarpment, and agricultural land in the four nature sanctuaries of Cootes Paradise, Hendrie Valley, Rock Chapel, and Berry Tract, all very varied natural habitats, linked by an 18 mile (30 km) trail system. PC

Parc Régional Bois de Belle-Rivière

Québec, Canada

DESIGNER: Ronald Leduc
OWNER: City of Montréal
GARDEN STYLE: 20th-century modern park landscaping
SIZE: 435 acres (176 ha)
CLIMATE: Continental cool summer
LOCATION: Montréal, Québec

The gardens at the Parc Régional Bois de Belle-Rivière were completed by the Québec horticulturist Ronald Leduc, who hosts a popular weekly radio gardening program. The main attractions are the collection of over 100 tree species and 132 different bird species. The forest also provides a shady haven for strollers, hikers, and cyclists during the summer, and a spectacular show of foliage colors in the fall.

A 27-mile-long (17 km) network of trails winds across the lawns and through the gardens and forest. There are five signposted routes that vary in length from 1 mile to 4 miles (1 km to 6 km), all of them easy walking. Trails in the arboretum-style forest feature hemlock, cedar bush, and sugar bush, with Japanese catalpas, European spindle trees, and buckeyes. Other trails pass through an ornamental garden, a labyrinth, and an aquatic garden.

The lawns are a popular choice for a summer picnic, while the nearby river offers a cool spot for swimming to beat the summer heat. In the winter, cross-country skiers use the trails and can even rent one of the park's huts for an overnight stay. In addition, the glistening snow beckons snowshoers, dogsledders, and tobogganers.

In the spring, the sap flows from the sugar maple trees. For a sweet treat, many Montrealers visit the park's sugar shacks to see how maple syrup is made. Educational activities such as nature interpretation programs are also offered by the park staff. EvB

Jardins de Métis

Québec, Canada

DESIGNER: Elsie Reford
OWNER: Les Amis des Jardins de Métis
GARDEN STYLE: 20th-century English natural
SIZE: 40 acres (16.1 ha)
CLIMATE: Continental cool summer
LOCATION: Grand-Métis, Québec

Four hours' drive from Québec City, on the beautiful Gaspe Peninsula, is a garden that has grown from its origins as a summer retreat into an internationally renowned center for garden art and design. Elsie Reford founded the Jardins de Métis, also known as the Reford Gardens, in the 1920s. The house is understated, but the view is amazing, down a straight path flanked by an avenue of shaped Pinus mujo, and through a "keyhole" across the wide waters of the River Mitis and St. Lawrence seaway beyond. The device of keeping outward vistas to a minimum has been used throughout the garden, so that there are just a few teasing glimpses—cut through a deep row of sheltering trees and shrubs—of the water.

The gardens demonstrate many of the fashions of the period while respecting the natural landscape, with natural streams linking a number of discrete garden spaces. Lovers of Sino-Himalayan plants are particularly pleased, not least by the sight of massed Himalayan blue poppies (Meconopsis betonicifolia).

The garden has also become home to an international festival of garden design, based on that at Chaumont-sur-Loire in France (see page 592). What distinguishes this festival is the total integration of the installations into the overall garden setting and surrounding woodland, adding to the allure of the original garden. The Jardins de Métis offer a blend of period style, intermingled with cutting-edge garden art that provokes and inspires. MW

Jardin Botanique de Montréal

Québec, Canada

DESIGNER: Henry Teuscher
OWNER: Museums Nature Montréal
GARDEN STYLE: 20th-century botanical
SIZE: 185 acres (75 ha)
CLIMATE: Continental cool summer
LOCATION: Montréal, Québec

As one of the largest French-speaking, metropolitan areas in the world, Montréal gets a high rating for its culture, architecture, and history, and its centrally located botanical garden certainly adds to the ambience. International in its scope, with an impressive collection of 22,000 plant species and cultivars, the garden is the grand legacy of Brother Marie-Victorin. Now ranking as one of the largest of its kind in the world, the garden celebrated its seventy-fifth anniversary in 2006.

Ponds, shrubs, tall grasses, and even the Flowery Book are situated at the very heart of the site, surrounded by the 7,000-specimen arboretum fanning out over half the grounds. The magical Tree House brings the forest ecosystem to life. There are also interactive displays, shows, and special events in the 6 acre (3 ha) First Nations Garden. Inspired by Amerindian and Inuit cultures, this contemporary garden features a variety of native traditions, ranging from gathering food and medicinal plants to making wooden boats and containers.

Other exceptional themed gardens on the site include an Insectarium, which houses around 160,000 live and mounted insect specimens, the Japanese Garden and Pavilion, the Marsh Garden, the Bog Garden, the Chinese Garden (with the largest bonsai collection in North America), the Alpine Garden, and the Rose Garden. Together with ten exhibition greenhouses, and year-round demonstrations, workshops, and activities, this is one of the best botanical gardens you will see. PC

> "...one of the largest of its kind... the garden celebrated its seventy–fifth anniversary..."

Parc du Bois-de-Coulonge

Québec, Canada

DESIGNER: Henry Atkinson
OWNER: City of Québec
GARDEN STYLE: 19th-century landscape
SIZE: 59.3 acres (24 ha)
CLIMATE: Continental cool summer
LOCATION: Québec City, Québec

Located just a few blocks from the historic center of Québec City, Parc du Bois-de-Coulonge shows just what can be achieved in a public green space when the appropriate resources are thrown at it. The park is approached through a wooded area that reveals little of what is to come. Closely planted trees have had meandering paths cut through them, leading visitors to the unforgettable sight of wide lawns sweeping down to the St. Lawrence River, broad and glittering between its high banks.

Given that this part of Canada is under snow for up to six months of the year, the diversity of planting is astonishing. The borders around the main administrative building, built in the style of a small French chateau, are filled with lush, subtropical plants, looking more like St. Tropez than northeastern America. Down near the river, an area of sweeping island beds has been filled with flowering perennials and ornamental grasses, augmented with half–hardy plants and annuals. The effect is lovely, especially with the backdrop of mature trees and an emerald-green lawn. Back near the chateau, a formal area of clipped box hedges is less satisfactory.

Visitors leave the park through a different woodland path, passing through a delightful planting of shade-tolerant perennials, ferns, and shrubs. You're left in no doubt that Parc du Bois-de-Coulonge is a fine public green space. If only more parks were as exciting as this. MW

Maison et Jardins Chénier-Sauvé

Québec, Canada

DESIGNER: Thérèse Romer
OWNER: Fondation Maison et Jardins Chénier-Sauvé
GARDEN STYLE: 20th-century eclectic
SIZE: 1.5 acres (0.6 ha)
CLIMATE: Continental cool summer
LOCATION: Saint Eustache, Québec

Thérèse Romer, a well-known Québec garden writer and heritage conservationist, has been experimenting with exuberant mixtures of plants surrounding her heritage house since 1972. The property, in a sheltered spot between two rivers, features a garden that unites rare and cultivated plants with wild, native plants. She has also preserved and propagated perennials and shrub roses found on the property that date from the mid-1800s. The result is spectacular, with deep perennial beds extending into the nearby forest.

The garden may be small, but it is packed with interest. Her great love of flowers is indicated by a mass of color including purple clematis, blue hydrangeas, red roses, and pink and yellow sedums. Lilies are everywhere, with the native Canada lily (*Lilium canadense*), cultivated daylilies, and martagon lilies. And there are extensive plantings of pink peonies for late spring, edging the broad lawn and upper terrace that is shaded by catalpa trees, with ligularia and coral bells beneath.

As the garden flows down toward the river, large plantings of wildflowers lead into a small forest of old trees carpeted with wild ginger, lily-of-the-valley, and evening primrose. Romer has also created a marsh garden, near the river, full of cardinal flowers, marsh marigolds, flowering rushes, and an interesting mix of ornamental grasses that she grew from seed, all collected together by the river's edge. EvB

Les Quatre Vents

Québec, Canada

DESIGNERS: The Cabot family
OWNERS: Francis Cabot, Anne Cabot
GARDEN STYLE: 20th-century mixed
SIZE: 8 acres (3.2 ha)
CLIMATE: Continental cool summer
LOCATION: La Malbaie, Québec

The Cabot family have owned the *seigneurie* at Cap à l'Aigle near La Malbaie on the northern shores of the St. Lawrence River for more than 100 years, but the story of the garden at Les Quatre Vents—French for "the four winds"—is more recent. Francis Cabot's parents built the original house at Les Quatre Vents in the late 1920s, and his mother and architect uncle laid out the original garden. The design consisted of a broad lawn, the Tapis Vert, flowing out from the house toward the distant Laurentian Mountains, and a number of garden "rooms," terraces, and raised alpine beds. When Francis and his wife, Anne, took over the house—rebuilt after a fire—in the 1960s, they began renovating the gardens.

Trees and shrubs were brought in from the surrounding fields to provide protection from the winds that give the garden its name, hedgerows of native species were installed to give a framework, and rock walls and terraces were rebuilt and replanted. Cabot's great skill was in identifying the strongest vistas and enhancing them with planting, a difficult task when faced with so much beautiful countryside.

Once the restoration had been completed, Cabot extended the garden, and it is these newer areas that raise the design to the level of greatness. Crossing a ravine, via an alarmingly wobbly rope bridge, reveals an entirely different garden space, dominated by the pigeonnier, a building based on traditional French dovecotes. The arch beneath the pigeonnier frames another view to the landscape beyond, and that, in turn, is heightened by the mirror of the canal water. From here radiate allées and pathways, leading on to farther garden spaces, including the superb Japanese Garden.

Les Quatre Vents is an object lesson in how to relate a garden to the landscape and create viable growing conditions within. It ranks among the finest gardens in North America. PC

Annapolis Royal Historic Gardens

Nova Scotia, Canada

DESIGNER: A community project
OWNER: Annapolis Royal Historic Gardens Society
GARDEN STYLE: 20th-century themed gardens
SIZE: 17 acres (6.8 ha)
CLIMATE: Continental cool summer
LOCATION: Annapolis Royal, Nova Scotia

The community of Port Royal, founded in the lush Annapolis Valley of Nova Scotia in 1605, was the first permanent European settlement in North America, after St. Augustine, Florida. Renamed Annapolis Royal when it fell to the British in 1710, the town is now a national historic district, and it is fitting that the extensive display gardens of the town reflect four centuries of history.

In the Annapolis Royal Historic Gardens, one begins the tour of Canadian garden history within the lavender-hedged knot garden, based on a 1638 English design. La Maison Acadienne et Potager demonstrates a seventeenth-century French settler's post-and-beam-structured house with typical four-square kitchen garden and orchard sporting early apples and pears. The eighteenth century is represented by the Governor's Garden, where four symmetrical beds are planted with herbs and flowers, enclosed by tall yew hedges. In the Victorian Garden, one senses the exuberance of the nineteenth century in the curved, cloverleaf–shaped beds filled with showy annuals, and rare and exotic plants. Modern techniques and experiments are a vibrant part of the Innovative Garden with its closely planted fruit and vegetable demonstration areas, which explore companion planting, espaliered and dwarf fruit tree varieties, and new and unusual introductions.

The Rose Garden, with 230 different cultivars, together with the Rose Maze, brings the number of rosebushes in this collection to more than 2,000. Also look out for the grass collection, the expanding collection of magnolias, the softwood plantation with dramatic specimens of eastern white pine (*Pinus strobes*), the 100 varieties and more of daylily, the Rock Garden, and the colorful perennial beds. Not only do the Annapolis Royal Historic Gardens pick up the threads of Canadian garden history, but they weave them into a rich botanical tapestry. PC

The Bloedel Reserve

Washington, U.S.

DESIGNERS: Prentice Bloedel, Thomas Church, Richard
Haag, Fujitaro Kubota
OWNER: The Arbor Fund
GARDEN STYLE: 20th-century modern
SIZE: 150 acres (60.7 ha)
CLIMATE: Zone 8b
LOCATION: Bainbridge Island, Washington

Prentice Bloedel, whose father ran a prosperous lumber enterprise, and his wife, Virginia, bought a house at the north end of Bainbridge Island in 1951, and in the decades that followed added dramatic areas of wilderness to their property overlooking Puget Sound. The setting came to be regarded as one of North America's foremost landscapes, and in 1988 the Bloedel Reserve was opened to the public.

The Bloedels wished to "capture the essence of the Japanese garden—the qualities of naturalness, subtlety, reverence, tranquillity—and construct a Western expression of it." Bloedel also wrote of feeling "the existence of a divine order…man is not set apart from the rest of nature." He wanted the artificial and natural to blend seamlessly. Paths weave through meadows, marsh, and woodland, and the garden blends natural forest growth with carefully managed areas that reflect a range of landscape designs. The house, formerly the family residence, boasts a patio designed by Thomas Church, and to the side are stunning vistas of Puget Sound.

Designer Fujitaro Kubota's graceful mastery of plants and design left its imprint on the Japanese Garden, while the Reflection Garden incorporates modernist elements in sublime proportions, with yew hedges surrounding a rectangular, spring-fed pool that mirrors the sky. Infinitely subtle, it all adds up to a rare, generous garden filled with clever touches. AJo

Elisabeth Carey Miller Botanical Garden,

Washington, U.S.

DESIGNER: Elisabeth Carey Miller
OWNERS: Pendleton and Elisabeth Carey Miller
Charitable Foundation
GARDEN STYLE: Woodland Garden
SIZE: 5 acres (2 ha)
CLIMATE: Zones 7a–8a
LOCATION: Seattle, Washington

The Elisabeth Carey Miller Botanical Garden is located on a steep slope on a bluff overlooking Puget Sound, with spectacular views of the Olympic Peninsula. The estate was the home of Elisabeth and Pendleton Miller, who moved to this area just north of Seattle in 1948. Elisabeth was a dedicated gardener and received many awards for her horticultural work.

The garden is best known for its excellent collections of trees and shrubs, and for its woodlands extensively planted with herbaceous perennials. The garden has a variety of microclimates due to its location above the sound, which has given scope for horticultural experimentation and the cultivation of plants not normally seen in the region. The relatively small landscaped area of 3 acres (1.2 ha) within the garden contains more than 4,000 different kinds of plants. In particular, Elisabeth was an avid fern collector and grower, and species native to the region grow abundantly in the garden. These include the giant chain fern (*Woodwardia fimbriata*) and the leatherleaf fern (*Polypodium scouleri*); unexpectedly, the Virginia chain fern (*Woodwardia virginiana*), a rarity so far to the west, also grows here.

Tours should be booked well in advance. Spring is the best and most popular time to visit, although the garden is beautiful all summer and is also noted for its outstanding fall color. Beware: traversing the steep slope may be difficult for some visitors. AH

Rhododendron Species Botanical Garden

Washington, U.S.

DESIGNER: American Rhododendron Society
OWNER: Rhododendron Species Foundation
GARDEN STYLE: 20th-century rhododendron collection
SIZE: 22 acres (8.9 ha)
CLIMATE: Zones 8a–8b
LOCATION: Federal Way, Washington

An extract from the mission statement for the Rhododendron Species Foundation (RSF) says it all: "The Rhododendron Species Foundation is a non-profit organization dedicated to the conservation, research, acquisition, evaluation, cultivation, public display, and distribution of Rhododendron species." Founded by the American Rhododendron Society in 1964, the RSF was set up to develop a collection of rhododendron species and pursue a conservation agenda, and to do this it started to develop the Rhododendron Species Botanical Garden. The garden had a mixed start in 1974, when the wood product and paper manufacturer Weyerhaeuser Company generously leased the land at no cost and developed the site, laying the service road and pathways, installing irrigation, and adding huge quantities of sawdust into the beds. However, as the sawdust decomposed, it led to waterlogging, and many plants died. In 1980 the garden opened to the public. By 1984 it had been replanted according to taxonomic groups rather than geographic origin.

The woodland garden now contains collections of ferns, primroses, irises, heathers, maples, magnolias, conifers, and other unusual plants. It has one of the world's largest collections of rhododendrons. For six months, peaking in March and May, the 10,000-plus rhododendrons put on a wonderful flowering display. To see such a show is fascinating because of the diversity. You can also see what the parents of the hybrids look like, gaining an insight into how rhododendron breeding has evolved. TM

The Chase Garden

Washington, U.S.

DESIGNERS: Ione Chase, Emmott Chase, Rex Zumwalt
OWNER: The Garden Conservancy
GARDEN STYLE: 20th-century natural
SIZE: 4.5 acres (1.8 ha)
CLIMATE: Zones 8a–8b
LOCATION: Orting, Washington

Childhood sweethearts Ione and Emmott Chase grew up in the hilly countryside at the foot of Washington's Cascade Mountains. In 1962, two decades after marrying, they began gardening nearby on sloping terrain crowned by a bluff overlooking the Puyallup River valley. The Chases envisioned a garden of picturesque beauty as they faced the daunting job of eradicating brambles, brush, and obstinate tree stumps. Some four decades later, an amazing sweep of alpine meadows coexists with island beds, and a bounty of shrubs and trees.

Emmott scaled the garden's lofty trees, which are mainly Douglas fir, pruning selectively to sustain spectacular vistas of the volcanic Mount Rainier, while Ione mapped out the garden's meandering paths in the snow. They also called in the landscape architect Rex Zumwalt to lay out the Japanese-style entry garden, giving it raked gravel, quiet pools, and a dry stream bed.

Springtime here is magical, with countless small flowering plants evoking the colors and textures of an impressionist painting. Beneath a canopy of evergreens in the woodland, the forest floor offers an equally irresistible panoply of wildflowers with native trilliums, erythroniums, vanilla leaf, and Solomon's seal. Adjacent to the house, Ione successfully cultivated an allée of lewisia (*Lewisia cotyledon*). The species—a native of the Siskiyou Mountains—usually rests under a winter covering of snow, but Ione found it flourished in a place beneath the eaves, away from heavy downpours. It makes a beautiful sight. AJo

Ohme Gardens

Washington, U.S.

DESIGNERS: Herman Ohme, Ruth Ohme
OWNER: The State of Washington
GARDEN STYLE: 20th-century alpine
SIZE: 9 acres (3.6 ha)
CLIMATE: Zones 7a–8a
LOCATION: Wenatchee, Washington

A uniquely expressive landscape, the Ohme Gardens embody the industriousness of Herman and Ruth Ohme. Married in 1929 during the Great Depression, the Ohmes acquired land for an orchard as their livelihood. At the end of each day, the hardworking couple took in breathtaking views of the Cascade Mountains and Wenatchee Valley, seen from a high bluff. It was the perfect site for a house, but bank loans were impossible to come by. Thus the couple began their alpine wonderland.

Ruth once said, "We just wanted to build a nice backyard," but that was no easy job, with endless driving up and down the mountain in a car loaded with plants, and hauling flagstones out of the riverbed. Taking a sledgehammer to rocky outcrops, Herman crafted stepping-stones, borders, benches, and tables. Mules and crowbars were indispensable, as tons of rock were carted away and paths were created to connect pools and picturesque waterfalls; lawns were presided over by noble conifers.

Hugely popular from the start, the garden captivated visitors when it opened to the public in 1939; a carload of people could enter for 25 cents. Tourists loved the atmosphere of rustic Americana with handcrafted log furniture and shelters made from cedar, not to mention sensational views. One of the Ohmes' sons, Gordon, took over in the early 1950s, and he doubled the size of the 2-acre (0.8 ha) garden. Today the venture is no longer a family affair, but it remains a place of naturalistic beauty, rooted in sweat, crowbars, and a very particular vision. AJo

Washington Park Arboretum and Japanese Garden

Washington, U.S.

DESIGNERS: Juki Iida, Olmsted Brothers
OWNER: City of Seattle
GARDEN STYLE: 20th-century arboretum, 16th-century Momoyama-style Japanese garden
SIZE: 230 acres (93.2 ha)
CLIMATE: Zones 7a–8a
LOCATION: Seattle, Washington

In the early twentieth century, Seattle was enjoying the gold rush, and tuning in to civic beautification and public parks. The Olmsted Brothers, landscape architects, made their case for preserving tracts of the city's splendid landscape, and the city's park authorities asked them to create a master plan in 1902. The Olmsteds worked in Seattle for decades, and were approached again in 1934 to design the Washington Park Arboretum. Twenty-three years later, an anonymous gift made it possible to involve Juki Iida in designing an authentic Japanese garden.

The maritime climate heightens the arboretum's year-round allure. Commanding collections of magnolia, rhododendron, and Japanese maple take center stage on a tracery of trails through forested areas and cultivated spaces, where the fiery foliage ignites in fall. Winter offers sculptural silhouettes, reptilian bark, and colorful berries, and a spectacle of trees, shrubs, and wildflowers abounds in spring, arguably the arboretum's best season. Juki Iida came from Japan to oversee the Japanese Garden's installation in 1960. Specifically she arranged massive boulders as symbolic elements in the 3.5-acre (1.4 ha) stroll garden. An arbor frames the tranquil scene, gradually revealing a sequence of stone lanterns, black pines, wisteria trellises, and camellias. AJo

Taliesin

Wisconsin, U.S.

DESIGNER: Frank Lloyd Wright
OWNER: Frank Lloyd Wright Foundation
GARDEN STYLE: 20th-century modern, Arts and Crafts
SIZE: Estate 600 acres (243 ha)
CLIMATE: Zone 4b
LOCATION: Spring Green, Wisconsin

Frank Lloyd Wright spent much of his childhood with relatives from Wales and considered the country his spiritual home. Hence he named his house Taliesin (pronounced Tally-ehssen)—Welsh for "shining brow." Today the house is owned by the Frank Lloyd Wright Foundation.

The buildings, gardens, roads, ponds, lights, and furniture were all designed by Wright. The buildings sit low in the landscape, and the transition from indoors to courtyards, gardens, farm buildings, and on to meadows, orchards, fields, and woodland is a natural one. Waterfalls cascade over steep, stone ledges, and wide, deep steps cut into the hillside link terraces and buildings. Everything is unassuming.

Wright began to build Taliesin in 1911, after he left his wife, six children, and studio in 1909. He set up a new life there with his former client Mamah Borthwick Cheney, and Taliesin became a work in progress until the end of his life in 1959. There are three distinct phases of its history, all linked to tragedy, mishap, and fulfillment. In 1914, during his absence, a servant set fire to the house, killing Cheney and her two children. A second fire, caused by faulty wiring, occurred in 1924. During a second rebuilding, Wright married his third wife, Olgivanna Hinzenberg, in 1928, and she remained his partner during the highly productive last third of his life. Taliesin continued to evolve as his home and studio, and later as an architecture school, when he took over buildings where his aunts ran an experimental boarding school. RChi

Wallace Gardens

Minnesota, U.S.

DESIGNER: Wally Marx
OWNER: Wally Marx
GARDEN STYLE: 20th-century formal and restored prairie
SIZE: 110 acres (44 ha)
CLIMATE: Zone 4a
LOCATION: Medina, Minnesota

Inspired by visiting such classics as Hidcote Manor in England (see page 305) and by reading up on English gardens, Wally Marx designed this centerpiece for his rolling acres west of Minneapolis. The site includes remnants of the Big Woods and restored prairie.

Dark woods by the house offer views of light-filled garden "rooms" set along a 275-foot-long (84 m) central axis running west–east, and linked by shallow steps and gravel paths. A subdued, black-and-white garden leads to the Victorian Rose Garden where geometric beds contain more than forty different rose varieties. The next room, beyond a hedge of Medora junipers (*Juniperus scopulorum*), is reached through a white arch smothered by vibrant pink roses. This is the Monet Garden, a floral crescendo complete with green steel arches that take color—red and white roses, red honeysuckles, and mauve wisteria—to heady heights, as in the Grande Allée at Giverny in France (see page 556). "The great Impressionist painter based his Clos Normand on the geometric principles of English gardens…," Marx explains.

A tranquil mood is restored in the Lattice Garden, an oasis of green. Then a transverse path takes you to a highly productive kitchen garden to the south. A 300-foot-long (91 m) ribbon of grass between shrub borders, and a knot chain of box and purple berberis run alongside the garden "rooms," inviting you to explore a golden temple. To the north is a broad lawn. All is quintessentially English, perhaps. On this vast scale and beneath wide skies, though, it looks and feels thoroughly American. EH

The Dow Gardens

Michigan, U.S.

DESIGNERS: Herbert H. Dow, Alden Dow
OWNER: Herbert Dow II
GARDEN STYLE: 19th-, 20th-century mixed
SIZE: 112 acres (45.3 ha)
CLIMATE: Zones 5a–5b
LOCATION: Midland, Michigan

On May 18, 1897, Herbert H. Dow's chemical company (now one of the world's largest) began manufacturing and selling bleach commercially. He made a fortune and put some of the money into his wonderful garden in Midland.

He began the garden in 1899 for his personal pleasure, expressing himself and his interest in garden design. Following his design philosophy to "never reveal the gardens' whole beauty at first glance" (now one of the basic tenets of garden design), he started on 8 acres (3.2 ha) of flat, sandy land. He raised hills and dug ponds, filling the whole with an exciting mix of plants, all carefully selected to withstand the cold winters.

When he died in 1930, the baton passed to his youngest son, Alden. An architect who had studied under Frank Lloyd Wright, Alden built an extraordinary house and studio on the grounds. He wrote, "I think this garden is a most interesting side of my father's character." He continued the garden's expansion and added new levels of interest, clearly influenced by the design ethics of the Chinese, Japanese, and art deco. Herbert Dow's grandson, Herbert Dow II, also continued to develop the garden. Today the extensive grounds are home to a delightful mix of more than 1,700 species of trees, shrubs, perennials, and annuals. The latest addition to the garden is the Whiting Forest, which is just to the north of the Grace A. Dow Library. It is dedicated to the study and conservation of native plants and the forest types indigenous to mid-Michigan. TM

Brooklyn Botanic Gardens

New York, U.S.

DESIGNERS: Various, including Takeo Shiota
OWNER: City of New York
GARDEN STYLE : 20th-century botanical
SIZE: 52 acres (21 ha)
CLIMATE: Zones 6b–7a
LOCATION: Brooklyn, New York

What a perfect way to reclaim a waste dump in one of the busiest cities in the world. Founded in 1910, this garden takes you on a journey of discovery the moment you step through the turnstile, with a plant collection of around 12,000 species, recreated native settings, and significant examples of garden design.

The formality of the Osborne Garden with its pergola and calm, green lawn welcomes the visitor, who can then wander through the Cranford Rose Garden. There are more than 1,000 different types of rose arranged in beds, around a pool, or climbing up a delicately trellised garden "room." Next go to the authentic recreation of a Japanese garden with its pool, pavilion, and swaths of bamboo. By following meandering paths, one can admire sheets of daffodils, be intoxicated by the scents of the Fragrance Garden, or be invigorated by the profusion of the Herb Garden. In summer the long formal pool in front of the Palm House disappears under multicolored water lilies. Through a beautifully designed gate, the Native Flora Garden reveals forgotten treasures.

A visit to the Steinhardt Conservatory, opened in 1988, offers a sense of wonder with its global display of plants from deserts, rain forests, and temperate climates. The most striking feature is the Cherry Esplanade. A broad lawn is bordered by a double avenue of cherry trees, creating a fantastic vista, but also an intimate space in spite of its size. This is the core of the garden where people sit and children play. The clouds of pink blossoms seen in spring from the terrace above stay in the memory forever. MO

Central Park

New York, U.S.

DESIGNERS: Frederick Law Olmsted, Calvert Vaux
OWNER: City of New York
GARDEN STYLE: 19th-century public park
SIZE: 843 acres (341 ha)
CLIMATE: Zones 6b–7a
LOCATION: New York, New York

Central Park is one of the world's most famous public parks. It covers 6 percent of the island of Manhattan and was the first landscaped public park in the United States. It also launched the career of the nation's most famous landscape architect. Although Frederick Law Olmsted's name is always remembered in connection with the park, the winning entry—the Greensward Plan—in a competition held in 1857 to determine the design of the park was also the work of the forgotten English-born architect Calvert Vaux.

From 1857 to 1869, some 20,000 workers transformed the damp, rocky site. Tons of soil were moved, rocky outcrops were obliterated using more gunpowder than was fired in the Civil War's greatest battle at Gettysburg (1863), and more than 270,000 trees and shrubs were planted. The result was an English-style, natural landscape with large expanses of open lawn, shrubberies, and tree-lined avenues providing a green haven for the city. With great insight, the plan also incorporated traffic via sunken roads and a network of bridges.

The park opened to the public in 1859, with the rich arriving by carriage and others on foot, and it has been extremely popular with New Yorkers ever since. Key additions have included a zoo, playgrounds, and a swimming pool. The 1980s saw the beginning of a major renovation program, which was privately funded by the Central Park Conservancy. Many of the projects focused on restoring features of the original Greensward Plan, including the Sheep Meadow, Bethesda Terrace, and Belvedere Castle. TM

Madoo Conservancy

New York, U.S.

DESIGNER: Robert Dash
OWNER: Robert Dash
GARDEN STYLE: 20th- and 21st-century contemporary
SIZE: 2 acres (0.8 ha)
CLIMATE: Zones 6b–7a
LOCATION: Sagaponack, Long Island, New York

Artist Robert Dash happily admits that the gardens at Madoo are all about seduction. Dash came to Sagaponack in 1962, fell in love with the area, and set about finding himself a permanent home there. Since 1967, Dash has strived to create gardens at Madoo for "calm, contemplation and rapture." It has been dubbed the artist's "ever-changing masterpiece," and is now on the National Register of Historic Places.

Shades of green provided by imaginatively pruned plants are the basis for this painter's garden, but accents of color make appearances in unexpected places. The simple, vibrant yellow arch is beloved of garden aficionados. The summer house, painted a delicate shade of mauve, is Dash's own comment on Manet's view that "the very color of the air is mauve." The shed, with its bright green doors, must be the most photographed shed of all time, not least of all because of the illusion created by its mirrored windows.

The planting takes into account the seasonal extremes on Long Island, from severe winters to very hot and dry summers. A wide range of plants flourish, from box balls and laburnum to rugosa roses, dicentra, peonies, and vegetables. Many of the plants are propagated by Dash himself, and the garden has always been cultivated without the use of chemicals.

Open to the public since 1993, this remains a very personal garden. Hats left hanging on gateposts and artistic touches such as a golden mask nestling amongst the foliage are further imprints of Dash's style and wit that leave you with an uncanny feeling that he has been there only minutes before you. RSJ

George Eastman House Gardens

New York, U.S.

DESIGNER: Alling Stephen DeForest
OWNER: George Eastman House Board of Trustees
GARDEN STYLE: 20th-century Arts and Crafts
SIZE: 12.5 acres (5 ha)
CLIMATE: Zones 6a–6b
LOCATION: Rochester, New York

George Eastman, the father of popular photography and founder of the Eastman Kodak Company, used his fortune to create this palatial estate. He built and lived in the magnificent classical revival house from 1905 until his death in 1932. The house had many modern conveniences behind its decorative façade. Outside Eastman enjoyed all the benefits of country living in the city. In what is a relatively compact plot for such an estate, DeForest's landscape plan combined working farmland, stables, barns, and pastures with elegant flower gardens, sweeping lawns, and several greenhouses.

In 1949 the estate became the George Eastman House Museum of Photography and was opened to the public. Its mission was to collect and present the history of photography and film. By the mid-1980s, finances were secured to restore the museum's grounds, using DeForest's plans, plant lists, historical photographs, correspondence, and invoices to reconstruct the majority of gardens and grounds as they were in Eastman's time.

Today the gardens make up a historic collection consisting of trees, ornamental shrubs, vines, and four gardens planted with perennials, bulbs, annuals, and groundcover. All of this is faithful to the original design. Architectural elements include the grape arbor, pergola, sunken oval lily pool, seventeenth-century Venetian wellheads, and a garden house. The gardens are a perfect example of how valuable photographic records are in researching and preserving garden history. RChi

Jacob Javits Plaza

New York, U.S.

DESIGNER: Martha Schwartz
OWNER: City of New York
GARDEN STYLE: 20th-century post-modernist
SIZE: 1.1 acres (0.4 ha)
CLIMATE: Zones 6b–7a
LOCATION: New York, New York

Swirling strands of bright green, elongated, New York City park benches make quite a startling sight as you approach this space—exactly the response that designer Martha Schwartz intended you to have. The garden occupies the rooftop of the underground garage beneath the plaza. The opportunity to revitalize the space arose when roof repairs were undertaken in 1992.

From the landscape architect's perspective, the aim was unequivocal—to transform an unwelcoming environment into a lively, open space in the heart of the city. Schwartz was partly influenced by Frederick Law Olmsted, creator of Central Park, and there is an underlying wit behind the tweak given to each element in the design. Visitors can either bask in the sun or relax in the shade, and the looping back-to-back benches weave through the area, providing plenty of seating options. Schwartz's design makes intimate circular niches for gregarious groupings, and outward-facing curves for lunching alone. It is quickly apparent that the seats make shapes and patterns that are an updated play on historic French parterres. Traditional topiary that punctuated such designs are also given a contemporary twist, with 6-foot-high (1.8 m) tousled grass hemispheres that exude mist on hot days, like upturned pots letting off steam. Also note the brightly colored garden features—actually street trash cans, drinking fountains, and seats—in the shadows cast by tall, gray buildings. Schwartz pushes the boundaries of landscape architecture in a way not commonly seen in New York. Or anywhere else. RChi

Boscobel

New York, U.S.

DESIGNER: States Morris Dyckman
OWNER: Boscobel Restoration, Inc.
GARDEN STYLE: 19th-century mixed
SIZE: 2.5 acres (1 ha)
CLIMATE: Zones 6a–6b
LOCATION: Garrison, New York

Take a train along the Hudson River valley, north from New York City, and it is remarkable how soon one leaves the city behind and enters the rugged, natural beauty of upstate New York. On the east bank, opposite the West Point Military Academy, and with spectacular views of the valley and the Hudson Highlands (part of the Appalachians), is Boscobel.

The early-nineteenth-century, neoclassical mansion was built by States Morris Dyckman, a descendant of one of the early Dutch families of New Amsterdam. Today it contains a fine collection of decorative arts from the federal period. However, the house was not always in its current location. Dyckman built it in nearby Montrose. In the 1950s it was sold for demolition. Only a rescue mission by Benjamin West Frazier saved what had survived. In 1956 a donation of $50,000 enabled the house (stored in pieces in various barns) to be rebuilt and restored at Garrison, and also funded restoration of the garden.

In front of the house is a great lawn and a belvedere with views. To one side is the Necessary House and the entrance to the woodland with its network of paths. On the other side is a rose garden with a fountain and more than 150 rose varieties. From here a brick walkway takes you through the apple orchard to the D-shaped herb garden. Enclosed by a rustic wooden pergola and trained fruit trees that shade the benches, the gravel paths run between a series of formal, board-edged, raised beds filled with herbs, vegetables, and fruit trees. At the back of the garden is the lovely brick and timber orangery. TM

John P. Humes Japanese Stroll Garden

New York, U.S.

DESIGNER: Douglas DeFaya
OWNER: John P. Humes Foundation
GARDEN STYLE: 20th-century Japanese
SIZE: 4 acres (1.6 ha)
CLIMATE : Zones 6b–7a
LOCATION: Mill Neck, New York

On this steeply sloping site, the Stroll Garden evokes a feeling of a remote mountain hamlet, or *yamazoto*. Japanese stroll gardens date back many centuries and are places of contemplation in which symbolism plays a major part.

Work started in 1960, when Humes returned from a visit to Japan, which had included a trip to the gardens of Kyoto. The garden was created over the next ten years with the aid of a Japanese garden designer. It went into decline when Humes became ambassador to Austria, but revived on his return. At his death, a foundation was set up to maintain the garden, and it opened to the public in 1985.

This stroll garden is a spiritual journey to enlightenment through meditation. Its pathway, or *roji*, always curves and is rarely a straight line. Your pace is controlled by the size of the stones in the path, small ones slowing the feet and larger ones encouraging you to stop and view a particular vista. At first the path zigzags up a hill, at the top of which symbolic items have been placed. The downward path is made from small pebbles that represent a stream flowing down over symbolic waterfalls to a pool (the "ocean") with koi and turtles. In fact water is evident in various forms, from delicate, trickling spouts to rocky waterfalls. It is also a garden of hundreds of different shades of green, from the large, dark, and glossy to the fine needles of trained and trimmed pines. The Humes Stroll Garden forces a change of pace—certainly no bad thing in the fast-paced world of today. RChi

"Japanese stroll gardens…are places of contemplation in which symbolism plays a major part"

Innisfree Garden

New York, U.S.

DESIGNERS: Walter Beck, Marion Beck, Lester Collins
OWNER: Innisfree Foundation
GARDEN STYLE: 20th-century Chinese landscape
SIZE: 150 acres (60.70 ha)
CLIMATE: Zones 5b–6a
LOCATION: Millbrook, New York

To visit Innisfree is to enter a different world. When they started work in 1929, owners Walter and Marion Beck had discovered scrolls of the works of eighth-century Chinese poet and painter Wang Wei during a visit to London. Inspired by the philosophy and aesthetic of Chinese gardens, the Becks began developing each area into what Walter termed "cup" (enclosed) gardens. The site at Innisfree is, in fact, one huge "cup" garden with Lake Tyrell at its center.

A path links individual garden spaces, making a progression of scenes that turn a series of Chinese-influenced, three-dimensional landscapes into an entity with a uniquely American atmosphere. Using the topography of the site to make enclosures, Walter worked in three dimensions, positioning rocks and grouping objects to form compositions that were balanced, no matter what angle they were viewed from. He also wrapped the stones before moving and repositioning them to preserve their covering of ancient lichen. Marion, a botanist, planted the carefully crafted spaces using predominantly native plants, chosen and placed with equal care to balance the *yin* and *yang*. Everywhere water in different guises was added to each scene.

The Becks hoped that Innisfree would stimulate an indigenous approach to garden and landscape design. Lester Collins, who became involved with the garden while a landscape architecture student, took over the management of the garden and continued to develop it after Walter's death in 1954. It opened to the public in 1960, as its creators wished. RChi

Longhouse Reserve

New York, U.S.

DESIGNERS: Jack Lenor Larsen, Charles Forberg
OWNER: Longhouse Reserve Ltd.
GARDEN STYLE: Late 20th-century contemporary
SIZE: 16 acres (6.5 ha)
CLIMATE: Zones 6b–7a
LOCATION: Long Island, New York

Along the southern peninsula, at the eastern tip of Long Island, a towering Japanese cedar (*Cryptomeria japonica* 'Yoshino') marks the entrance to Longhouse Reserve, also known as the Jack Lenor Larsen Garden. Textile designer Jack Lenor Larsen had his home—based on a seventh-century Shinto shrine—built here in the early 1990s. The aim was to link aesthetics and nature, to highlight art as an essential part of life, and to make the garden accessible to the public.

The area had been farming country before it became a fashionable place for the wealthy to make weekend and summer retreats. Larsen owned the land prior to building. He cleared the site of a tangle of vines and saplings. The only features were long, straight berms of soil, previously field boundaries, that almost divided the plot into equal quarters. He planted them with thousands of Canadian hemlock (*Tsuga canadensis*) to make fine-textured hedges.

Larsen believes gardening is like weaving: Both involve a balance of textures and colors. Visitors to Longhouse quickly discover an array of planting textures and colors offset by an inspiring collection of artwork. The artists include Dale Chihuly and Yoko Ono, whose *Play It by Trust* is a ghostly, all-white chess game in a simple green "room." Larsen's own *Red Garden* is an extraordinarily effective study in heightened perspective. The painted, flame-red cedar trunks are interspersed between azaleas covered in bright-red flowers along a grassy path, with a stoneware vessel, *Closed Form* by Toshiko Takaizu, as focal point. RChi

British Memorial Garden

New York, U.S.

DESIGNERS: Isobel Bannerman, Julian Bannerman
OWNER: City of New York
GARDEN STYLE: 21st-century traditional and contemporary
SIZE: 0.75 acre (0.3 ha)
CLIMATE: Zones 6b–7a
LOCATION: New York, New York

Just three blocks away from Ground Zero, the new British Memorial Garden at Hanover Square commemorates the sixty-seven British victims of the attacks on the World Trade Center in 2001, and celebrates historic ties between the United States and United Kindom. Planting started in spring 2006.

In 1714 Manhattan's Hanover Square was named in honor of the accession of the Elector of Hanover (George I) to the British throne. After the founding of the United States, Hanover Square disappeared from maps and became part of Pearl Street. But the name continued in popular usage and was officially restored to the map in 1830. It is a very appropriate location for this very British garden.

Julian and Isobel Bannerman have created a classic British flower garden in a contemporary style. The topiary and hedging use native British yew and box, and the curving contemporary walkways use a dark, reflective stone from Caithness in Scotland. Looping through this like a ribbon are paler stones carved with the names of the UK counties. Welsh slate is used for the water rill running through the garden, there are Portland stone benches, iron bollards from the City of London, and borders generously planted in an abundant English style.

Unity, a black granite monolithic work by Anish Kapoor, stands as a memorial sculpture. Its hollowed center is polished to a mirror finish to reflect light and symbolize an eternal flame. RChi

New York Botanical Garden

New York, U.S.

DESIGNERS: Beatrix Farrand, Penelope Hobhouse
OWNER: New York Botanical Garden
GARDEN STYLE: 19th-century botanical
SIZE: 250 acres (101.2 ha)
CLIMATE: Zones 6b–7a
LOCATION: The Bronx, New York

New York Botanical Garden is a leading research institution as well as the city's very own backyard. Across this site is something for everyone throughout the year. There are 40 acres (16.2 ha) of the only native forest left in New York, complete with a children's adventure garden and a Beatrix Farrand rose garden. Behind the scenes, the herbarium is one of the largest in the world. It includes plants from Lewis and Clark's expedition to the western United States in 1805.

The garden was the creation of two botanists, Dr. Nathaniel Lord Britton and his wife, Elizabeth. They returned from England inspired by the great Royal Botanic Gardens at Kew (see page 386). Their idea gained support and finance from New York's richest members of society, and the gardens opened in 1891.

Start your visit at the magnificent conservatory. Built in 1902, it is the largest conservatory in the country and has recently been extensively restored. It houses eleven computer-controlled, ecological habitats, ranging from rain forest to desert. Outside are "hot" and "cool" perennial borders, and then a quieter, more intimate, traditional herb garden designed by Penelope Hobhouse. Moving away from this area, the garden becomes more parklike where paths loop around the edges of the old native forest and nature is largely in charge. RChi

RIGHT The New York Botanical Gardens were inspired by the Royal Botanic Gardens at Kew, England.

The Abby Aldrich Rockefeller Sculpture Garden, Museum of Modern Art

New York, U.S.

DESIGNER: Philip Johnson

OWNER: Museum of Modern Art

GARDEN STYLE: 20th-century modernist

SIZE: 10 acres (4.5 ha)

CLIMATE: 6b–7a

LOCATION: New York, New York

From the moment it opened in 1953, this sculpture garden became a landmark in urban landscape design and was immediately loved by the public. The garden is set 4 feet (1.2 m) below the terraces that frame it at each end, and the minimal design includes two narrow water channels bridged by marble slabs that accentuate their length. The space is farther punctuated by several perfect squares of low planting, from which emerge groves of silver birch and beech. The sculptures are placed among these trees.

The current garden replaced another that was built in 1939, the first ever external space conceived to exhibit sculpture within a museum. The old garden had undergone several redesigns that had tended to separate the artworks with the use of various types of screens. The commission to design a completely new garden was finally awarded to Philip Johnson in the early 1950s, and was named after Abby Aldrich Rockefeller, who had secured the land.

Johnson described the garden as "really a sort of outdoor room," these days a familiar concept, but back in the 1950s very innovative. The sheer power of his design resides in the fact that it simply echoes the rectilinear look of the museum building and of the city beyond. The pristine space, which has been paved in a grid of pale gray marble slabs, is also a marvelous evocation of an Italian piazza. MO

> "From the moment it opened in 1953, this garden became a landmark in urban landscape design…"

Old Westbury Gardens

New York, U.S.

DESIGNERS: George A. Crawley, Jacques Greber
OWNER: Old Westbury Gardens
GARDEN STYLE: 20th-century Arts and Crafts
SIZE: 160 acres (64.8 ha)
CLIMATE: Zones 6b–7a
LOCATION: Long Island, New York

In the first years of the twentieth century, the wealthy flocked in droves out of New York City to Long Island and built hundreds of estates there. Today only a few of these estates remain. Of these, Old Westbury Gardens is undoubtedly a jewel. John S. Phipps had the house designed by London architect George A. Crawley for his English-born wife, Margarita.

Old Westbury is mock seventeenth-century English. With craftsmen hired from England, it took three years and cost $15–20 million to build, not bad for an "inexpensive little country home," as the client briefed his architect. Phipps' father was a partner in the Carnegie Steel Company and bequeathed Phipps his fortune. Out of new money, a truly elegant, old-world estate was made. Inside, European antiques are set off by paintings by Gainsborough, Reynolds, and Constable. Outside, landscape and gardens host an eclectic range of features—English, French, and Dutch—all of which have been beautifully laid out.

A particular highlight of Westbury is the walled garden. Handsome brick walls with limestone quoins have elaborate iron gates opening on to a spectacular 2-acre (0.8 ha) garden. Gravel paths lead past long, abundantly planted English borders with swags of roses trained on ropes. A wisteria-laden pergola frames great vistas across the lotus and lily pool with a classic fountain. Beyond is the intricately designed rose garden, and beyond that grand allées with common lime (*Tilia* x *europaea*), yew hedges, and precisely clipped topiary that give the impression that a slice of England has drifted across the Atlantic. Box plants, which were imported when they were 125 years old in 1928, have been closely trimmed and undulate around a rectangular lawn. Visitors to the gardens will also see sculptures arranged around the grounds and, overlooking the lake, the Temple of Love. Everything in this garden is meant to be glamorous and romantic. RChi

The High Line

New York, U.S.

DESIGNERS: James Corner Field Ops; Diler Scofidio & Renfro
OWNER: New York City
GARDEN STYLE: 21st-century contemporary
SIZE: 1.5 miles long (2.4 km)
CLIMATE: 6b-7a
LOCATION: New York City

The High Line has been hailed as New York's most visited park. Elevated approximately 33 feet (10 m) above the chaos of city life, this extraordinary landscape has risen out of the 1930s elevated freight rail. The trains stopped running in the 1980s and the line started to fall into disrepair. But in 2009, after nearly two decades of local campaigning and consultation, landscape architects James Corner Field Operations and architects Diller Scofidio & Renfro won a competition to reinvent the High Line as a public park.

The essence of the 1.5-mile-long (2.4 km) park lies in reflecting the biodiversity that crept in as the railway lay unused. A series of urban microclimates—sunny, shady, wet, dry, windy, and sheltered were created with units of paving and naturalistic planting by Piet Oudolf.

The transformation has taken place over three phases. The first section begins its journey in the industrial Meat Packing District at Gansevoort Street. The second phase travels via West 30th Street in the residential area of Chelsea. The third and final phase, which is yet to be built, is intended to wrap around the planned redevelopment of the Hudson Yards. Unlike the first and second phases, the original fabric of the railway will be left intact and indigenous flora encouraged to flourish. This phase will see a children's play area with rubberized beams and an area for performance—planned and spontaneous—accessed by a walkway. Despite these new initiatives, this phase is intended to be a reminder of the historical cityscape from which the park was borne. RSJ

Noguchi Museum

New York, U.S.

DESIGNER: Isamu Noguchi
OWNER: Isamu Noguchi Foundation and Garden Museum
GARDEN STYLE: 20th-century contemporary Japanese
SIZE: 16 acres (6.5 ha)
CLIMATE: Zones 6b–7a
LOCATION: Long Island City, New York

The most striking thing about the approach to the Noguchi Museum, also known as the Noguchi Sculpture Garden, is how unlike a museum or art gallery the building appears. That was the exact intention of twentieth-century sculptor Isamu Noguchi. He wanted the style of his sculpture to be reflected in the way in which it was displayed, in line with his underlying philosophy of how art relates to its surroundings. Together, the museum and walled sculpture garden, which the museum encircles, display hundreds of works.

Noguchi began designing gardens during a visit to Japan in 1951. His first major commission was for the new UNESCO Headquarters in Paris. He went on to build gardens for many corporations and large institutions. With an American mother and Japanese father, Noguchi acknowledged the influences of both cultures. For Noguchi, the art of garden creation was "the sculpture of spaces," which meant that he updated the conventions of the traditional Japanese garden, creating spaces for contemplation, with trickling fountains, abstract shapes, the play of light on solid forms, the pattern of shadows, and a broad palette of textures.

All of this is apparent at the museum garden. What really stands out is the selection, finish, and placement of the natural materials used. As Noguchi himself said, "The art of stone in a Japanese garden is that of placement. Its ideal does not deviate from that of nature. But I am also a sculptor of the West. I place my mark and do not hide." RChi

The Cloisters

New York, U.S.

DESIGNER: John D. Rockefeller Jr. (donated the structures)
OWNER: Metropolitan Museum of Art
GARDEN STYLE: 20th-century with medieval structures
SIZE: 4 acres (1.62 ha)
CLIMATE: Zones 6b–7a
LOCATION: New York, New York

The Cloisters (also called the Metropolitan Museum of Art Cloisters) occupy one of the most spectacular sites in New York, a rocky slice of Manhattan overlooking the Hudson River. The person who made this part of the Metropolitan Museum of Art possible, John D. Rockefeller Jr., also bought the bluffs on the opposite side so that the fantastic views would not be overlooked at least in one direction.

Rockefeller bought a collection of medieval architectural elements, some of which today make up The Cloisters. From the collection of mostly French architectural artifacts dating from the twelfth to the fifteenth century, a series of buildings was created using elements from five cloisters to house the museum's European medieval art and architecture. Where the buildings link together, three cloister gardens have been created with arcaded sides, as found in old monasteries. Each of these enclosed gardens is different. However, all show how medieval monastic gardens would have looked and been used.

The Cuxa Cloister is filled with a lawn divided by a crisscross of paths and beds filled with flowering plants. The aroma of herbs fills the air in the Bonnefont Cloister, reminding us that religious orders gardened for a purpose, using herbs for culinary, medicinal, and other purposes. Species shown in the tapestries inside the museum are planted in the Trie Cloister. A skylight covers a fourth courtyard with a simple stone fountain set on polished pebbles at its center. Throughout, fountains drip and wafts of ancient music add to the atmosphere. RChi

Donald M. Kendall Sculpture Gardens

New York, U.S.

DESIGNERS: Edward D. Stone Jr., Russell Page,
  François Goffinet
OWNER: PepsiCo, Inc.
GARDEN STYLE: 20th-century contemporary landscape
SIZE: 120 acres (48.6 ha)
CLIMATE: Zone 6b
LOCATION: PepsiCo Headquarters, Purchase, New York

Former PepsiCo CEO Donald M. Kendall conceived the idea for this landscape, which is also known as the Pepsico Sculpture Gardens. The gardens are located at the company's world headquarters, where Kendall commissioned the design and collected the sculptures. The list of artists reads like a *Who's Who* of twentieth-century sculptors, including Auguste Rodin, Henry Moore, and Joan Miró. As the collection grew, Kendall enlisted British landscape designer Russell Page in 1980 to reshape the landscape and place the artworks to best effect.

Page's preference for simplicity over the elaborate is evident. He worked for a year considering light and shade, masses and voids, and how plants and sculpture would work together throughout the seasons. Page also laid out the Golden Path and created vistas that unfold across sweeping lawns to woodland fringes. Three cool, contemporary courtyards with sunken pools make formal gardens between the seven linked, rectangular buildings. Braided trees combine with wide cobblestone paths to make a classically simple, formal entrance.

Close to the two rectangular lily pools with their central "floating islands" of lawn is a bronze plaque embedded in the concrete: "I am tired, it is raining, and I am not a water lily." This note was found on Page's desk after he had finished his work here at the end of 1985. He died shortly afterward. RChi

Wave Hill Gardens

New York, U.S.

DESIGNERS: Marco Polo Stufano, John Nally,
  George W. Perkins
OWNER: City of New York
GARDEN STYLE: 20th-century park
SIZE: 28 acres (11.3 ha)
CLIMATE: Zones 6b–7a
LOCATION: The Bronx, New York

The fabulous views of the 500-foot-high (150 m) Palisades across the Hudson River are just some of the attractions at Wave Hill. In 1903 George W. Perkins bought the estate and developed it to enhance its magnificent vistas. Land was graded, greenhouses were added, and a swimming pool and terraces built. The plantings included rare trees and shrubs to harmonize with the wider landscape. In 1960 Wave Hill was bequeathed to the City of New York and the gardens subsequently fell into disrepair. The 1967 arrival of Marco Polo Stufano, of the New York Botanical Garden, arrested the decline. He turned a tired estate into a vibrant horticultural experience.

Wave Hill's flower garden is its heart and includes a range of combinations with many unusual plants. A raised circular area showcases weekly displays of greenhouse specials amid the lushly planted borders. There is also an herb garden, an aquatic garden, dry and wild gardens, an alpine house, a conservatory, and a pergola, all of which make a refreshing change from nearby city streets. Theodore Roosevelt, Mark Twain, and Arturo Toscanini all lived here. Illustrious visitors included Charles Darwin and Thomas Huxley, who proclaimed the view across the river one of the world's greatest natural wonders. RChi

RIGHT Wave Hill Gardens, in the Bronx and begun in 1903, were bequeathed to the City of New York in 1960.

Manitoga Garden

New York, U.S.

DESIGNER: Russel Wright
OWNER: The Russel Wright Design Center
GARDEN STYLE: 20th-century modern American
SIZE: 75 acres (30.3 ha)
CLIMATE: Zones 5b–6a
LOCATION: Garrison, New York

Manitoga, hovering over the Hudson River, is recognized as the seminal mid-twentieth-century American garden. The small house sits imbedded in a granite cliff and overlooks a quarry pool with waterfall. No one could imagine a more picturesque natural site for a modern home, but it is all artifice.

The house and garden on a mountainside were the creation of Russel Wright, one of the greatest modern designers of the United States. Best known for his dinnerware and furniture, he was also a stage designer, sculptor, and great enthusiast for the natural East Coast landscape. In 1942 he bought an exhausted quarry, and over the next thirty years he hewed and hauled the land to create 4 miles (6.4 km) of paths from which the peaceful landscape could be viewed at particular times of day and season. Every granite boulder was artfully considered and moved into place, often with great effort, and every stream and pool was perfected. Native trees and shrubs, particularly the pink mountain laurel, were brought in, along with ferns, mosses, and wildflowers.

Believing that "good design is for everyone," Wright used the estate as an educational tool, hosting events, giving tours, and ultimately bequeathing it to the Russel Wright Design Center in 1976. The center now has a summer camp to introduce children to Wright's ideas. The innovative house and garden at Manitoga embody the idealism of Americans in the mid-twentieth century. CN

Vanderbilt Mansion Italian Garden

New York, U.S.

DESIGNERS: André Parmentier and others
OWNER: National Parks Service
GARDEN STYLE: 19th-, 20th-century formal Italian
SIZE: 3 acres (1.2 ha)
CLIMATE: Zones 5b–6a
LOCATION: Hyde Park, New York

Views of the Hudson River make a fine setting for the opulent Vanderbilt mansion. When Frederick William Vanderbilt, grandson of Cornelius "the Commodore" Vanderbilt, bought this estate in 1895, it already had beautiful grounds. The original house was replaced with a neoclassical building. Outside, Vanderbilt, who had graduated in horticulture from Yale, indulged his passion for gardening. He retained the naturalistic landscapes of Belgian designer André Parmentier, but made his own mark in the formal walled gardens.

Vanderbilt was active in developing the gardens until his death in 1938, after which Franklin D. Roosevelt, who knew the gardens from his youth, was instrumental in making the estate a National Historic Site in 1940. The gardens fell into disrepair through lack of funds. In the last twenty years, they have been restored, with planting added by volunteers.

A garden tour was a staple for house guests of the Vanderbilts. Imagine their surprise to see gardens walled by mellow brick in woodlands, and hillsides terraced into colored tiers. At the top, annuals pack into intricately shaped beds. A row of cherry trees and brick columns leads to a walled perennial garden. Space opens up at one end to a black reflecting pool with a sensuous statue known as Barefoot Kate framed in a classical gazebo. Beyond this, the path leads to the rose garden, with more than 1,000 plants. In the Vanderbilts' day, tours ended here, with Japanese tea served in the pale pinkish loggia. RChi

Harkness Memorial State Park

Connecticut, U.S.

DESIGNERS: Beatrix Farrand, Marian Coffin
OWNER: Connecticut State Parks and Forests
GARDEN STYLE: 20th-century Arts and Crafts
SIZE: 134 acres (54.2 ha)
CLIMATE: Zones 6a–6b
LOCATION: Waterford, Connecticut

This park, also known as Eolia, makes the perfect summer estate. It is perched on a promontory with panoramic views and refreshed by the sea breezes of Long Island Sound. Edward S. Harkness and his wife, Mary, aptly named this limestone mansion after Eolia, the Greek mythical god of the winds. After purchasing the property, they made changes to the house and had the surrounding gardens laid out by the Boston firm of Brett and Hall.

Between 1918 and 1929, landscaper Beatrix Farrand was hired to rethink parts of the formal grounds. Farrand replanted the Italianate west garden, softening the existing layout and limestone pergola with her signature planting style. She planted great drifts of herbaceous plants in graduated color schemes, very much in the style of Gertrude Jekyll, whom she much admired. Farrand also designed the rock garden and stone path, the entrance garden, and the Oriental-inspired East Garden. In recent years, the gardens at Eolia have been restored, and the planting has been restored in line with the work of landscape architect Marian Coffin, who was hired in 1949 to refurbish the East Garden plantings.

Eolia captures the spirit of the time and place when great estates were being created by a super-wealthy elite. Together with their designers and craftsmen, they left a stunning legacy. Bequeathed to the state of Connecticut in 1950, Harkness has been a state park, open to everyone, since 1952. RChi

Hollister House

Connecticut, U.S.

DESIGNERS: George Schoellkopf, Gerald Incandela
OWNER: The Garden Conservancy
GARDEN STYLE: 20th-century Arts and Crafts
SIZE: 2 acres (0.8 ha)
CLIMATE: 6a–6b
LOCATION: Washington, Connecticut

Hollister House unapologetically does not have a modern garden—no brushed steel or even native planting—but it is a brilliant American interpretation of the genius of Sissinghurst. George Schoellkopf has the talents of both Vita Sackville-West and Harold Nicolson—her fresh, creative, masterful planting and his architectural use of the landscape.

The house sits on a heavily wooded, quiet road, a dark pre-Revolutionary saltbox with additions, on a slope above a dammed stream. The garden "rooms" relate to the windows and size of the rooms within, as at the Alhambra in Spain (see page 720). It is intimate and, with the dropping levels, doesn't seem large until you keep finding yourself surprised by yet another room. Vistas are deliberately broken by asymmetry. High hedges, taller plantings, and glimpses of the farm buildings create the vertical lines with a backdrop of forest leaves. The low stretch of water, the big, wide stone steps, and the perfectly proportioned, large lawn create the horizontal.

George is a hands-on gardener, out there at 6 AM in spring and summer. Nothing escapes his notice. He has a brilliant eye for shape and color, and the bold, improvisational decoration of the 1840s is clearly evident, as are billowing curves, and the flashes of genius in his use of the otherwise unglamorous, red begonia throughout one area as a unifying filler. Keep an eye out for the rarities like *Lilium schellenbaum* and a variegated *Cercis canadensis*. CN

Blithewold Gardens

Rhode Island, U.S.

DESIGNERS: John De Wolf, Bessie Van Wickle
OWNER: Blithewold Mansion, Gardens and Arboretum
GARDEN STYLE: 20th-century naturalistic
SIZE: 33 acres (13.4 ha)
CLIMATE: Zones 6b–7a
LOCATION: Bristol, Rhode Island

Blithewold was built in 1896 as a retreat for Augustus and Bessie Van Wickle, whose wealth came from coal. The views down to the harbor and moorings for their yacht made the site perfect for them. Today visitors can enjoy the garden thanks to their daughter Marjorie's will, which specified that any funds be spent on the grounds first, and the house second.

It is a charming, informal estate, which is also called Blithewold Mansion, Gardens and Arboretum. The naturalistic grounds were laid out by landscape architect John De Wolf and carried on by Bessie, and finally by Marjorie. Many specimen trees were planted, and wide borders created with shrubs and flowering plants. Gravel paths make a pleasant meander around the property, from which you can also watch the boats in Narragansett Bay.

Since 1926 Blithewold has had a relationship with the Arnold Arboretum, whose staff came here to see the Chinese toon tree (*Cedrela sinensis*) bloom for perhaps the first time in the United States. In 1911 De Wolf satisfied the Van Wickles' request for exotic trees with more native plantings. He planted a giant redwood (*Sequoiadendron giganteum*) when it outgrew its previous home at Prospect Park, Brooklyn, where he was superintendent for a while. It is the oldest and largest of the sequoias on the grounds and marks the Enclosed Garden with its intriguing opening in the shrubbery. The thickets are another of Blithewold's charms, a magical forest whose trees make a canopy over an understory of rhododendrons, Solomon's seals, ferns, and daffodils in spring. PC

The Mount

Massachusetts, U.S.

DESIGNERS: Edith Wharton, Beatrix Farrand
OWNER: Edith Wharton Restoration, Inc.
GARDEN STYLE: 20th-century European formal
SIZE: Garden 3 acres (1.2 ha), estate 49 acres (19 ha)
CLIMATE: Zone 6a
LOCATION: Lennox, Massachusetts

Edith Wharton built The Mount (which is also known as Edith Wharton's Garden) in 1902. It is the only representation of Edith Wharton's design theories, both architectural and landscape, and is one of the few National Historic Landmarks created by a woman. A niece, Beatrix Farrand, was enlisted to help with aspects of the design. Wharton assimilated many influences from her European travels, and they are evident everywhere. Farrand designed the approach of the 0.5-mile-long (1 km) driveway, which sweeps through the landscape with the working buildings of the estate exposed to the view, a design that goes contrary to the English landscape tradition.

The gardens were planned as an extension to the house, and Wharton thought it was important that gardens should have "a charm independent of the seasons." But The Mount also has an elegance and charm reminiscent of the Italian renaissance. Descend from the back of the house, across a spacious terrace, and down wide steps to a pathway bisecting the lime walk, and you will come to the flower garden, where a delightful walled Italian garden is planted in shades of green and white. The rest of the flower garden is a riot of color with plenty of reds, crimsons, violets, and pinks, a real "mass of bloom" in four huge, 12-foot-wide (4 m) borders around a pool. In recent years, restoration has pulled the estate back from the brink of neglect. RChi

RIGHT Edith Wharton's unique garden, The Mount, incorporates elements of design brought back from Europe.

Arnold Arboretum

Massachusetts, U.S.

DESIGNERS: Charles Sprague Sargent, and others
OWNER: City of Boston
GARDEN STYLE: 19th-century arboretum
SIZE: 265 acres (107.3 ha)
CLIMATE: Zone 6a
LOCATION: Boston, Massachusetts

Founded in 1872, this is the oldest public arboretum in the United States. It is named for its benefactor, a whaling merchant from New Bedford, who bequeathed the land, from his estate, to the president and fellows of Harvard College. Today the arboretum boasts a large collection of woody plants, with an emphasis on eastern Asia and North America.

Designed by founding director Charles Sprague Sargent and Frederick Law Olmsted, the arboretum has woods, meadows, rock formations, brooks, hills, and valleys. Olmsted was a firm believer in the moral and spiritual sustenance derived from beautiful landscapes. Sargent, a scientist and Harvard professor, was interested in trees. The garden combines their twin visions, being a tranquil, beautiful space for the public, and also Harvard University's horticultural research and education institution, which handles the plant collection, herbarium, and library. The arboretum also occupies a central role in Olmsted's "Emerald Necklace," a chain of parks around Boston.

The arboretum, owned by the City of Boston, is on long-term lease to Harvard University. The collections include historic introductions from eastern Asia by Charles Sargent, Ernest Wilson, William Purdon, Joseph Hers, and Joseph Rock. The most recent collections are from Japan, Korea, China, and Taiwan. Today the garden houses more than 14,000 plants covering most genera, including *Fagus*, *Forsythia*, *Lonicera*, *Magnolia*, *Malus*, *Quercus*, *Rhododendron*, and *Syringa*. The fall foliage is particularly wonderful and comes from 130 different kinds of maple. JRo

Garden in the Woods

Massachusetts, U.S.

DESIGNER: Will C. Curtis
OWNER: New England Wild Flower Society
GARDEN STYLE: 20th-century naturalistic and botanical
SIZE: 44.9 acres (18.2 ha)
CLIMATE: Zone 6a
LOCATION: Framingham, Massachusetts

Also known as the New England Wild Flower Society's Garden in the Woods, this specialist botanical garden was founded by Will C. Curtis, a landscape designer with a great love of nature. He transferred the garden into the care of the New England Wild Flower Society in 1967. It is a unique amalgamation of wildflower sanctuary and garden, and was made possible by a highly focused mission to conserve wild plants and to showcase America's East Coast flora.

Curtis purchased the site in 1931 with the aim of achieving his dream of creating a garden for native North American plants. The site was ideal in its range of habitats with hillsides and shady valleys, a pond and boggy areas, and water from springs and a small brook. The opportunity for establishing a range of vegetation types has also been expertly realized here, with the woodland gardens being the most extensive. Even so, visitors should also note the meadow habitat, pines, and the New England Garden of Rare and Endangered Plants. An arid garden here is perhaps a less expected feature. However, the addition of extra drainage has allowed a number of western plateau desert species to grow.

The garden now contains a collection of more than 1,600 different plants, including more than 200 rare and endangered species. Although they are principally New England natives, there is a sprinkling of exotics and cultivars, including a number developed by the garden. As would be expected, spring is the best time for flowers, but there is floral interest throughout the summer before Massachusetts' fall foliage arrives. With the assistance of good cultivation and careful placement, it is remarkable how satisfying, naturalistic garden landscapes can be created almost entirely from native plants. Access is good throughout the garden, and plants are well labeled. A small specialist nursery on the site supplies a wide range of plants. CBa

Isabella Stewart Gardner Museum

Massachusetts, U.S.

DESIGNER: Isabella Stewart Gardner
OWNER: City of Boston
GARDEN STYLE: 15th-century Italianate courtyard
SIZE: Approximately 24 x 14 sq. yd. (20 x 12 sq. m)
CLIMATE: Zone 6a
LOCATION: Boston, Massachusetts

When Isabella Stewart Gardner opened her museum in 1903, it was considered one of the nation's finest art collections. As set out in her will, the collection has not changed since her death in 1924, apart from the theft of some important pieces in 1990.

A wealthy patron of the arts, Isabella designed her museum as a fifteenth-century, Venetian, renaissance-style palazzo, and incorporated architectural artifacts collected in Europe. However, Isabella also had a passion for flowers. The museum's four stories of stone columns and ornate galleries overlook a courtyard garden filled with a collection of horticultural treasures. This tranquil oasis, echoing a formal Italian garden, is capped by a glass roof, allowing for an ever changing array of Mediterranean-style planting. The displays are updated every four to six weeks with plants cultivated in a greenhouse behind the museum. In the early part of the year, there are white azaleas and cyclamen. In March this changes to cineraria, calla lilies, and orange trees. Every April 14, to celebrate Isabella's birthday, the garden's balconies are hung with nasturtiums.

The landscape architect Patrick Chassé was taken on as the museum's first curator of landscape in 2005. Having researched photographic archives, he is making subtle adjustments to ensure this iconic courtyard remains close to Gardner's original vision. There are two additional gardens at the museum: the Monk's Garden (named after Isabella's favorite niece, Olga Monks) and the South Garden (located between the museum and the neighboring building). JRo

Mount Auburn Cemetery

Massachusetts, U.S.

DESIGNERS: General Henry Dearborn, Dr. Jacob Bigelow
OWNER: Mount Auburn Cemetery
GARDEN STYLE: 19th-century landscaped cemetery
SIZE: 175 acres (70.8 ha)
CLIMATE: Zone 6a
LOCATION: Cambridge, Massachusetts

Mount Auburn Cemetery, founded in 1831, is one of Cambridge, Massachusetts' historic landscapes. It holds an impressive collection of more than 5,000 trees, including some 700 species and varieties. There are thousands of shrubs and herbaceous plants in clusters through the cemetery's undulating hills, dells, ponds, woodlands, and clearings. Despite the constant reminders of mortality, it is a place of beauty in every season, but probably more so in fall when it takes on the color of New England.

The landscape reflects a number of different styles, ranging from Victorian-style plantings to contemporary gardens, and from formal ornamental gardens to natural woodlands. The plant species come from all around the world, highlighting those that grow well when planted in a northern temperate climate. There are some individual specimens that are labeled as local champions. There is also a range of nineteenth-century architecture, including chapels, gateways, and towers.

The original design was inspired by Père-Lachaise Cemetery in Paris (see page 582), with ideas drawn from English picturesque gardens being incorporated into the natural landscape to create a "rural cemetery." It was the first large-scale, designed landscape in the United States to be opened to the public, and has been designated a National Historic Landmark.

Like Père-Lachaise, Mount Auburn Cemetery is the final resting place of thousands of ordinary and distinguished people, including the famous Boston-based author Oliver Wendell Holmes (1809–94). BS

> "The original design was inspired by Père-Lachaise Cemetery in Paris..."

Naumkeag Garden

Massachusetts, U.S.

DESIGNERS: Nathan Barrett, Fletcher Steele, Mabel Choate

OWNER: The Trustees of Reservations

GARDEN STYLE: 19th- and 20th-century themed

SIZE: Garden 8 acres (3.2 ha), woodland 40 acres (16.2 ha)

CLIMATE: Zone 5b

LOCATION: Stockbridge, Massachusetts

Legend has it that family picnics here beneath an old oak tree were so enjoyable that lawyer and diplomat Joseph Choate decided to buy the land. Designed by Stanford White in 1885, the house was called Naumkeag, the Native American name for Salem, Choate's birthplace.

Designer Nathan Barrett terraced the hilly site in 1889, creating a two-tier garden with a formal, topiary evergreen walk near the house and grassy terraces below, with views down to the Berkshires. The changes that were made by Joseph's daughter Mabel are what Naumkeag is now famous for. She began

work three years before she inherited the garden in 1929. After hearing landscape architect Fletcher Steel lecture at a local garden club, she hired him to help her. They worked together for the next thirty years and created a curving landform on the south lawn, the black, glass-lined pool in the Afternoon Garden, and a Chinese Garden with Mabel's collection of Asian ornaments. The wavelike series of beds in the Rose Garden was the last project they worked on.

Naumkeag is also known for the Blue Steps. Built in 1938, Fletcher Steele's acclaimed design turns a ribbon of water, running through a narrow brook at the top of the steps, into a cascade as it plunges down the hills through a series of pools on each of the four terraces. On each landing, white tubular railings echo the blue-painted, semicircular pool alcoves, and curving handrails accentuate the sweep of the terraces. Also note the clever mix of white-stemmed silver birch against dark green yew. RChi

The Fells

New Hampshire, U.S.

DESIGNER: Clarence Hay
OWNER: Department of Conservation and Recreation
GARDEN STYLE: 20th-century American colonial revival
SIZE: 164 acres (66.4 ha)
CLIMATE: Zones 4b–5a
LOCATION: Newbury, New Hampshire

You cannot see the house or gardens when you pull up to a sleepy, packed-dirt parking lot, but don't let that put you off. After a moderate walk along a sloping, wood-lined drive, you realize you're on a hill overlooking the eastern shore of Lake Sunapee, one of the most beautiful lakes in New Hampshire.

The Fells is a perfect example of an early-twentieth-century summer estate. It was built as a summer retreat and working farm for three generations of the Hay family—Secretary of State John M. Hay, who also served as private secretary to Abraham Lincoln; Clarence Hay, a noted archaeologist, who developed the gardens with his wife, Alice Appleton Hay; and nature writer John Hay, who chose the name The Fells, using the Scottish word for rocky, upland pastures.

The estate includes an understated, colonial revival main house and outstanding gardens. Local volunteers have done an admirable job bringing the once-decaying gardens back to the state of Clarence Hay's era with arbors and trellises, flowering trees and shrubs, and classic statuary. A 100-foot-long (31 m) perennial border, packed with butterflies and bees, runs next to the house. And from the formal Rose Terrace with its cascading fountain, designed by Alice Hay, are views to the lake beyond. At times, through the trees, you can see the old-fashioned tour boats that cruise the lake twice daily, always dipping into the cove so that the tourists can glimpse the house from the water's edge.

One of the loveliest period features is Clarence Hay's Rock Garden, which tumbles down the south-facing hill by a trickling brook that terminates in a water-lily pool surrounded by azaleas and Japanese iris. It includes more than 600 species of alpine and native plant. After that, meander through the garden along the many paths. And don't miss the masses of rhododendrons and Walled Garden. AH

Celia Thaxter's Garden

Maine, U.S.

DESIGNER: Celia Laighton Thaxter
OWNER: Shoals Marine Laboratory
GARDEN STYLE: 19th-century informal, cottage garden
SIZE: 0.02 acre (0.09 ha)
CLIMATE: Zone 5b
LOCATION: Appledore, Maine

Celia Laighton Thaxter was born in Portsmouth, New Hampshire, in 1835. When she was four, the family moved to White Island, Isles of Shoals, where her father became lighthouse keeper. Eight years later, Thaxter's father developed a hotel on Appledore, the largest of the islands, 9 miles (15 km) off Maine's rugged coast. One of the first on this coast, the resort became a gathering place for local literary and artistic figures in the late nineteenth century.

Celia gardened as a child, but moved away after marrying Levi Thaxter, her father's business partner. She returned ten years later to care for her mother and assist with the hotel. At the same time, she found fame as a writer of poetry and prose. Her most famous book, *An Island Garden*, was published in the last year of her life, 1896. It is a highly personal account of creating a garden, with observations on plants, pests, and the trials and tribulations of gardening illustrated in wonderful watercolors by Childe Hassam. The garden also inspired a generation of U.S. artists to try raised beds packed with old-fashioned flowers.

After her death, a fire burned down the hotel and her cottage in 1914, and the garden and resort were almost forgotten. An army barracks was built over her garden during World War II. It later became the Shoals Marine Laboratory, but, when the old cottages were being restored, the garden was recreated using her book as a guide. Tours are limited to fifty people at a time, and reservations are required. RChi

Garland Farm

Maine, U.S.

DESIGNER: Beatrix Farrand
OWNER: The Beatrix Farrand Society
GARDEN STYLE: 20th-century naturalistic
SIZE: 4.9 acres (2 ha)
CLIMATE: Zone 5b
LOCATION: Bar Harbor, Maine

The niece of the novelist Edith Wharton, and the only founding female member of the American Society of Landscape Architects, Beatrix Farrand was one of America's preeminent landscapers. She designed gardens at Dumbarton Oaks in Washington D.C., for affluent families, including John D. Rockefeller and Mrs. Henry Cabot Lodge, and landscaped the campuses of Princeton and Yale universities. A resident of Bar Harbor, Maine, she established her home at Reef Point, where she amassed an important horticultural library and outstanding collection of plants. Near the end of her life, she moved to Garland Farm, the coastal home of her Reef Point property manager, where he and his wife cared for her. Beatrix lived there until she died in 1959.

Beatrix brought some of her favorite plants and garden elements, including fencing and garden ornaments, to build her last garden. In the Japanese Garden are her favorite plants from the Far East, intermingled with native groundcover. The Terrace Garden is divided into rectangular parterres, containing heather and lavender. Perennials and annuals abound in the other beds, with clematis and roses climbing the fences. You'll also see plantings of rare cherry hybrids, and other trees and shrubs not normally grown in this part of Maine. A small greenhouse structure survives, originally built to grow annuals, and overwinter tubs of rosemary and lemon verbena. AH

Crystal Springs Rhododendron Garden

Oregon, U.S.

DESIGNERS: Ruth Hansen, Wallace K. Huntington
OWNERS: Portland Parks and Recreation, Portland Chapter of the American Rhododendron Society
GARDEN STYLE: 20th-century rhododendron collection
SIZE: 7 acres (2.8 ha)
CLIMATE: Zones 8a–8b
LOCATION: Portland, Oregon

The idea for a garden dedicated to rhododendrons was first broached by the Portland Chapter of the American Rhododendron Society in 1950. Sam Jackson, owner of the *Oregon Journal*, even donated land on Terwilliger Boulevard for the garden. Because of its precipitous terrain, though, it was not suitable, and instead, the current site was selected. Called Shakespeare Island by students of the nearby Reed College because of the plays that had once been performed there, it had become overgrown with scrub. With hard work, the site was cleared and planted. In 1964 the garden was officially named Crystal Springs Rhododendron Garden because of the spring-fed lake that is such a prominent feature.

The layout is the creation of two designers. The older part, The Island, is the work of Ruth Hansen. The more recent part, The Peninsula (from 1977), is by Wallace K. Huntington. One of the aims of the garden was to evaluate rhododendrons. Unfortunately this was unworkable, and the site evolved as a show garden. Today there are more than 2,500 rare and hybrid species of rhododendron and azalea. The spring/early-summer show of flowers is quite special. A number of other ericaceous plants and trees extend the season, with the fall show being particularly remarkable. The lake itself is another feature, as are the paths meandering gently through the gardens and by the lake, passing three waterfalls and crossing two formal bridges. This is a tranquil, beautiful place only minutes away from downtown Portland. TM

Japanese Garden

Oregon, U.S.

DESIGNER: Takuma Tono
OWNER: Japanese Garden Society of Oregon
GARDEN STYLE: 20th-century traditional Japanese
SIZE: 5.5 acres (2.2 ha)
CLIMATE: Zones 8a–8b
LOCATION: Portland, Oregon

"A Japanese garden is not just a place for the cultivation of trees and flowering shrubs, but one that provides secluded leisure, rest, repose, meditation, and sentimental pleasure... The garden that speaks to all the senses not just to the mind alone." These are the profound words of Professor Takuma Tono, designer of the Japanese Garden in Portland, which is praised as one of the most authentic Japanese gardens outside Japan.

Construction of the Japanese Garden began in 1963, and it was opened to the public in 1967. Despite being a mere babe when compared with the ancient gardens of Japan, it already has a sense of timeless maturity. In achieving this, Tono's design has been aided by the climate found in Portland and the ceaseless efforts of the many volunteers who became involved in the project.

The garden's design was strongly influenced by the three philosophies so closely associated with the Japanese garden style: Shinto, Buddhist, and Taoist. These are clearly evident throughout the garden with its five different areas seamlessly stitched together. The areas are the Strolling Garden and Pond Garden (*Chisen-kaiyu-shiki*), the Natural Garden (*Shukeiyen*), the Sand and Stone Garden (*Karesansui/Zen niwa*), the Flat Garden (*Hiraniwa*), and the Tea Garden (*Roji-niwa*). Each of these areas has its own distinctive feel, style, and look. What makes the overall design so clever is that there is no jarring or disharmony. The use of surprise and anticipation, of wondering what is coming next, is masterful as one keeps finding new vistas and new gardens, both intimate and with views out over the borrowed landscape. TM

"The garden that speaks to all the senses not just the mind alone"

Portland Classical Chinese Garden

Oregon, U.S.

DESIGNERS: A team of Chinese gardeners
OWNER: City of Portland
GARDEN STYLE: 20th-century traditional Chinese
SIZE: 0.9 acre (0.4 ha)
CLIMATE: Zones 8a–8b
LOCATION: Portland, Oregon

This is an extraordinary, classical Chinese garden in the heart of a modern U.S. city. Based on a Ming dynasty garden in Suzhou, China, it occupies a full city block and is a conscientiously arranged landscape of plants, water, and stone. The garden was designed by artisans and architects from China, who wanted to communicate the aesthetic and symbolic importance of the natural landscape and our place within it.

There are hundreds of native Chinese plants in the garden with specimen trees, rare and unusual shrubs and perennials, and collections of magnolia, osmanthus, rhododendron, and bamboo. There is also a beautiful collection of camellias, and an equally delightful collection of cymbidiums.

Water and stone are key ingredients throughout the garden. The magnificent limestone Taihu stones symbolize the mountain landscape, but also have a powerful abstract, sculptural look. Cut granite serves as the foundation stone for columns, bridges, and walkways, and softly rounded pebbles mixed with broken roof tiles and pottery make patterns in the walkways and courtyards. The solid nature of stone is softened throughout by the pools and streams.

As well as the garden, there is also the Courtyard of Tranquillity, the Celestial Hall of Permeating Fragrance, and the Tower of Cosmic Reflections. With these structures, the Portland Classical Chinese Garden brings a mystical sensibility to an otherwise bland, urban landscape. CW

Northwest Garden Nursery

Oregon, U.S.

DESIGNERS: Ernie O'Byrne, Marietta O'Byrne
OWNERS: Ernie O'Byrne, Marietta O'Byrne
GARDEN STYLE: 20th-century plantsman's garden
SIZE: 1 acre (0.4 ha)
CLIMATE: Zone 7a
LOCATION: Eugene, Oregon

Situated in a delightful area surrounded by meadows and woods, the Northwest Garden Nursery is not simply a source of rare and unusual plants, it is also a first-rate garden in its own right. Visitors to the nursery can see a connoisseur's collection of perennials displayed in a variety of different garden styles. Informality is the keynote, and this gives the impression that the garden has developed organically among and around the various buildings on the site. Because the beds and borders are often on a very small scale, the garden seems much larger than it really is. The wealth of plants here certainly keeps it alive and interesting.

The garden has many strengths. One is the Woodland Garden that comes alive from late winter to early summer with shade plants and has lush foliage throughout the season, including hellebores, podophyllums, cyclamens, epimediums, corydalis, primulas, arisaemas, and ferns. The Rock Garden's collection of alpines peaks in spring. The Sunny Border Garden is at its best in summer, being a fine example of a mixed border with disciplined color themes from both foliage and flowers. In late summer and fall, the grasses, cannas, and kniphofias in the Conifer Garden are in full cry, with hot colors contributing to the fall display. Finally the gravel Dryland Garden shows innumerable plants that thrive without regular watering. After that, head straight to the nursery. CBa

Ira Keller Fountain Park

Oregon, U.S.

DESIGNER: Angela Danadjieva
OWNER: City of Portland
GARDEN STYLE: 20th-century modern, terraced
   civic space
SIZE: 1 acre (0.4 ha)
CLIMATE: Zones 8a–8b
LOCATION: Portland, Oregon

The crags and commanding waterfalls of Oregon's Cascade Mountains inspired San Francisco landscape architect Lawrence Halprin when he tackled the Ira Keller Fountain, a centerpiece for a Portland public plaza. The setting was part of a 1960s urban renewal scheme, and completed a triad of interconnecting parks built to revive a downtown neighborhood.

In 1966 Halprin had brought a freshness and beauty to the city center in the creation of Lovejoy Fountain Park, followed by Pettygrove Park. The Brooklyn native with an egalitarian outlook chose associate Angela Danadjieva, a Bulgarian trained in Paris, to design the interactive water feature as the final link in the parkland spaces. She believed it was important that people had access to water to revel in its sensory pleasures. Opened in 1971, the fountain's abstract concrete profiles emerged as a meeting place. A sunken plaza muffles the clamor of traffic.

Ira's Fountain, as it is known locally, gives passersby a unique experience. The textural finishes and cobblestone surfaces of the fountain's bold geometry juxtapose angular, vertical walls and overlapping horizontal planes, forming sequestered nooks, inviting terraces, and wading areas. Visually stunning, the rush of 13,000 gallons (50,000 l) of water per minute from the fountain's upper level fills a series of pools that culminate in a breathtaking, beautiful cascade. This powerfully built, modern structure is a testament to the inventiveness and drive of contemporary U.S. landscape architecture. AJo

Chicago Botanic Garden

Illinois, U.S.

DESIGNERS: John O. Simonds, John Brookes, Wolfgang
Oehme, James van Sweden

OWNER: Forest Preserve District of Cook County

GARDEN STYLE: 20th-century botanical, display, naturalistic

SIZE: 385 acres (155.9 ha)

CLIMATE: Zones 5a–5b

LOCATION: Glencoe, Illinois

The *Urbs in Horto* (City in a Garden) motto was adopted in 1837, and the Chicago Horticultural Society has promoted gardens and gardening since 1890. However, it was not until 1972 that this garden, also known as Glencoe, actually opened. John O. Simonds' plan turned mosquito infested land into a naturalistic landscape. In a massive program of earthworks, gentle hillocks were shaped to create a water labyrinth of pools and basins. Following the Chinese aesthetic, the heart of the garden is a large island in the center of a lagoon, and a network of paths weaves around the site, linking woods, formal display gardens, and three native habitats.

Highlights include a Japanese stroll garden, *Sansho-en*, or the garden of three islands, designed in 1982 with layered, predominantly green, foliage, and a teahouse built out over the water. In contrast, the English Walled Garden illustrates six gardening traditions and highlights the country's influence on international horticulture. However, the guiding spirit is a focus on native plants, with vistas rooted in the midwestern landscapes of the Great Plains. In 2002 another major project, the Great Basin Gardens, added sweeps of perennial planting.

Chicago Botanic Garden offers a diverse garden experience, from intimate to panoramic, from formal to naturalistic, and from expansively open to mysteriously hidden. This is a horticultural marathon, and with twenty-six gardens spread out over a huge site, it takes at least a day to see it all. RChi

Lurie Garden, Chicago Millennium Park

Illinois, U.S.

DESIGNERS: Gustafson Guthrie Nichols Ltd., Piet Oudolf, Robert Israel

OWNER: City of Chicago

GARDEN STYLE: 21st-century contemporary

SIZE: Garden 2.5 acres (1 ha), park 24.5 acres (9.9 ha)

CLIMATE: Zones 5a–5b

LOCATION: Chicago, Illinois

Chicago's Millennium Park occupies a site previously considered untouchable, a desolate area of railroad tracks and parking lots. Despite its name, the park opened in 2004; it attracts millions of visitors.

The Lurie Garden, in the park's southeastern corner, is a collaboration between landscape architects Gustafson Guthrie Nichols Ltd., plantsman Piet Oudolf, and conceptual thinker and theater designer Robert Israel. Kathryn Gustafson derived inspiration from Chicago's natural and cultural history. The bold, powerful city with its array of tall buildings, many by leading architects, evolved out of flat, marshy origins. So, on two sides, high hedges fill rectangular steel structures to screen the garden from the park, making it a mysterious location and providing a protective barrier for delicate perennial planting. A shallow brook of water runs beside a wider hardwood pathway, both slashing diagonally through the space, dividing the garden into light and dark areas. Work started in 2001 to produce the thousands of herbaceous plants required for Oudolf's signature planting style. To create his vibrant prairie-in-the-city, he used native plants for his core palette. Additional cultivars, hybrids, and non-native plants were selected, if they were sufficiently hardy to withstand the climate. The result is a colorful, textured tapestry that changes with the seasons and shows visitors how beautiful native plants can be. The Lurie Garden perfectly embodies Chicago's *Urbs in Horto* (City in a Garden) motto. RChi

Lincoln Memorial Garden

Illinois, U.S.

DESIGNER: Jens Jensen
OWNER: Lincoln Memorial Garden
GARDEN STYLE: 20th-century woodland and prairie
SIZE: 110 acres (44.5 ha)
CLIMATE: Zone 5a
LOCATION: Springfield, Illinois

In the early 1930s, the city of Springfield, Illinois, at the urging of one of its wealthy community leaders, Harriet Knudson, donated land along the shores of Lake Springfield for a community garden project. She then selected and paid for the services of one of the country's foremost landscape architects, Jens Jensen, to design the garden.

Jensen's plan for the then 63-acre (26 ha) garden was to create a sense of the Midwest landscape with which Abraham Lincoln would have been familiar. The garden was designed as a series of interconnecting paths, bordered by various arrangements of native plants. This pattern of lanes was highlighted by eight "council rings," or circular stone benches, which were designed to foster friendly gatherings.

Today the garden comprises 110 acres (45 ha) of land encompassing the original garden, a Walnut Grove, and a 29-acre (12 ha) tract known as the Ostermeier Prairie Center. It is a combination of prairie, woodlands, wetland, babbling streams, a lake, and a mature cypress grove.

One of the greatest achievements of the garden's design is that every visit provides a different experience. Visitors can appreciate the changes of the seasons with the lush, green spring trees and wildflowers coming into early growth, the prairie flowers in the middle of summer, the stunning bright colors of the fall leaves, and the wintry snow with flecks of red berries dotting the landscape, with the lake in the background. The deer, shorebirds, and warblers provide the sound effects.

Jensen used many of his signature trademarks in the garden, including the sunny and shadowy areas along the curving trails that pull the visitor deep into the garden toward the light filled, exuberant, wild prairie area. The best time to visit is early in the day, when it is possible to see the dew covered grasses and spiders' webs, and hear the birds calling. AH

Stan Hywet Hall and Gardens

Ohio, U.S.

DESIGNERS: Warren Manning, Ellen Biddle Shipman
OWNER: Stan Hywet Halls & Gardens, Inc.
GARDEN STYLE: 20th-century Arts and Crafts
SIZE: 71 acres (28.7 ha)
CLIMATE: Zone 5a–5b
LOCATION: Akron, Ohio

Stan Hywet means "stone quarry" in Old English, and derives from the old sandstone workings found on this estate. The main hall, completed in 1915, has a strong English influence, which came about when the founder of the Goodyear Company, Franklin A. Seiberling, visited England with his architect, Charles S. Schneider. They were quite taken by the Tudor style they saw there, and copied it in a bid to return to "simpler" values.

Seiberling later hired the landscape architect Warren Manning, who positioned the hall to give five major views of the valley. The other feature that immediately stands out is the use of birch, which with its irregular trunk, makes an engaging, unusual choice for a 550-foot-long (167 m) allée. Overhanging branches turn this into a magical corridor with intriguing views to other parts of the grounds along the route. At the end of this, a fine pair of teahouses or pavilions provides a wonderful place to enjoy views of the landscape and the lagoon garden, which is situated in the old quarry.

In 1929 Manning recommended Ellen Biddle Shipman to design the walled garden. Known as the English Garden, it had a central pool and fountain surrounded by cottage-garden-style borders. Unfortunately, in time, trees shaded the space and, like many estates, Stan Hywet Hall suffered a period of neglect. However, from the late 1980s onward, the gardens and landscape have been restored using sketches and photographs from Manning's archives, which show how the garden looked originally. The Seiberling family also secured land in the lower valley, thus preserving the views in perpetuity. RChi

"Overhanging branches turn this into a magical corridor..."

The Topiary Garden

Ohio, U.S.

DESIGNERS: James Mason, Elaine Mason
OWNER: Columbus Recreation and Parks Department
GARDEN STYLE: 20th-century topiary park
SIZE: Garden 1 acre (0.4 ha), park 9 acres (3.6 ha),
CLIMATE: Zones 5a–5b
LOCATION: Old Deaf School Park, Columbus, Ohio

If you want to see the painting *A Sunday Afternoon on the Island of La Grande Jatte* by the French postimpressionist Georges Seurat rendered in topiary, this is the place to come.

It was created by James T. Mason after his wife, Elaine, asked him to install some topiary in their own garden. He had grander ideas, though, having envisioned the concept of "a landscape of a painting of a landscape." He took his project to the Columbus Recreation and Parks Department. James was given the go-ahead. He designed, created, and installed the metal armatures on which the evergreen yews are trained into the shapes that recreate the painting, which shows people relaxing on the banks of the River Seine. There are fifty-four people, eight boats with sails, three dogs, a monkey, and a cat, and the river is represented by a pond. The largest topiary is more than 12 feet (4 m) tall.

At first Elaine did all the tying in of stems and trimming, but for some years now, this has been handled by the Columbus Recreation and Parks Department. A topiary boat perpetually sails across the pond. In summer the long shadows made by the figures echo those in Seurat's famous orginal. In winter, though, when the topiary is covered in snow, the "painting" gets a natural remake. BS

"A topiary boat perpetually sails across the pond"

Bartram's Garden

Pennsylvania, U.S.

DESIGNER: John Bartram
OWNER: The Fairmount Park Commission
GARDEN STYLE: 18th-century botanical and parkland
SIZE: 45 acres (18.2 ha)
CLIMATE: Zones 6b–7a
LOCATION: Philadelphia, Pennsylvania

Born into an eighteenth-century Quaker family, John Bartram was the United States' first homegrown botanist and plant hunter. In 1728 he purchased a 102-acre (41 ha) farm and developed America's oldest botanical garden, growing many of the plants that he discovered and collected on his expeditions. Bartram traveled to Delaware, Maryland, and Virginia, and trekked through the Appalachians, North and South Carolina, New Jersey, and Florida, where he succumbed to malaria. After a period convalescing, he explored the St. Johns River for 400 miles (643 km).

Many of the more than 200 native American plants that John (and son William) introduced into cultivation were eagerly sought by gardeners in England. In 1765 he was appointed royal botanist by King George III on a salary of fifty British pounds per annum. His house survives and is open. It is next to his botanical garden, meadow, parkland, and wetland. The garden features three areas. The Upper Kitchen Garden contains herbs and edibles in raised beds. The Common Flower Garden is filled with herbaceous plants and bulbs. The New Flower Garden is dedicated to new plants that John collected on his trips and received from friends.

A highlight of the garden is the Franklinia tree (*Franklinia alatamaha*) that John discovered near the Altamaha river in Georgia in 1765. Named after John's great friend, Benjamin Franklin, the tree became extinct in the wild as early as 1803. Thanks to the Bartram family, who propagated and distributed the tree, it was saved from total extinction. TM

Hershey Gardens

Pennsylvania, U.S.

DESIGNERS: Various, including Jane Taylor
OWNER: The M. S. Hershey Foundation
GARDEN STYLE: 20th-century themed gardens
SIZE: 23 acres (9.3 ha)
CLIMATE: Zone 6b
LOCATION: Hershey, Pennsylvania

On a visit to Hershey Gardens, head to the Rose Garden planted by Milton Hershey's gardeners in 1937. The arbors, sunken garden, and flower beds are filled with 275 different roses around a half-moon pool, making a good place to start. After that, go either to the oak grove, the Children's Garden, and then the Japanese Garden, or straight to the gazebo.

From the gazebo, the path leads up to a simple memorial, topped by the five flags of the U.S. Armed Forces, dedicated to those who died preserving freedom. On either side are bed after bed of spectacular seasonal displays. In spring there are 30,000 tulips in 100 different varieties. The Perennial Garden in summer celebrates American natives such as coneflowers, echinacea, black-eyed Susan (*Rudbeckia fulgida*), and eupatorium. The Herb Garden is traditional and sensory, as is Mrs. Hershey's Rose Garden, planted with the old roses she grew in 1907. The Rock Garden lies at the farthest point with a display of shrubs, evergreens, and small trees, especially Japanese maples.

Then come the ornamental grasses, the shady, tranquil Japanese Garden, and the latest addition, the Children's Garden. Devised by Jane Taylor, a pioneer in this field, it has thirty themed areas, including a floral alphabet, a chocolate lane to the kisses fountain, the chocolate tropics, and the Spa-Tacular Garden featuring plants used in washing and cleaning with a bathtub and overhead shower. The butterfly house is small, but all species are clearly identified. There is also an education center on the site. CH

Fallingwater

Pennsylvania, U.S.

DESIGNER: Frank Lloyd Wright
OWNER: Western Pennsylvania Conservancy
GARDEN STYLE: 20th-century modern in natural wilderness
SIZE: 5, 000 acres (2,023 ha)
CLIMATE: Zones 6a–6b
LOCATION: Mill Run/Ohiopyle, Pennsylvania

Both the house and landscape at Fallingwater are of iconic status. The gushing waterfall is an integral part of the house that is also at one with the surrounding, mountainous woods. A typical western Pennsylvania Appalachian stream, Bear Run, dominates the site and cascades across the landscape. In 1935 architect Frank Lloyd Wright designed Fallingwater, arguably his most famous creation, for Edgar J. Kaufmann, the wealthy owner of the Kaufmann Department Store in Pittsburgh. Instead of building a house with a view, Lloyd Wright exploited the natural dynamism of the waterfall and gave the house a southerly aspect by having it straddle Bear Run itself. The house was constructed from sandstone quarried on site.

Visitors hear the rush of water and get tantalizing views of the house as they approach through the woodland garden. There is a refreshing lack of human intervention here, referring to a time when man had little desire or need to control nature.

The house itself also doubles as a garden because it has a series of terraces off the living rooms. Several rooms give the impression that the interior is at one with the exterior. Several sculptures—including one from Orissa in India, dated 750 CE—and containers contrast with the naturalized trees. The house has a guest annex that is approached by a covered walk and tree plantings leading to a courtyard pool. Most satisfying of all, the woodland path actually runs above Bear Run, which lets you savor the wildness of the site. It goes without saying that the bookshop at Fallingwater is to die for. CH

Chanticleer

Pennsylvania, U.S.

DESIGNER: Adolph Rosengarten
OWNERS: The Chanticleer Foundation
GARDEN STYLE: 20th-century botanical
SIZE: 35 acres (14.2 ha)
CLIMATE: Zones 6b–7a
LOCATION: Wayne, Pennsylvania

The house on this site, built by Adolph Rosengarten from 1912, is surrounded by the original 7 acres (3 ha) of gardens. An eclectic display of containers provides intimacy and individuality on the terraces around the house, and plantings are dropped into the paving and borders using decorative pots. Cannas and yuccas in the paving frame an ornate iron seat that looks like a stage set, and a brook terminates at the terrace flanked by pots of papyrus adjoining the swimming pool. The most secret of courtyard terraces is distinctly modern with pots of lavender.

These gardens are a joy to explore. The grass here is planted with bulbs and wildflowers, framed by and dotted with trees, and there's a backdrop of woodland with a middle ground of plants, water, and paving. The plantings in the woodland, under both deciduous and evergreen cover, are bold and include hostas, ferns, and hogweed. The perennials around the lake are in good health along with swaths of daylilies, and the slope up from the lake takes on a prairie-meets-pavement style with grasses, perovskia, and lavender. The steps are massed with asclepias, rudbeckias, and more. The "ruins" at the top provide a solid, architectural austerity with a reflecting pool and sculpture. Nearer the house, the original sunken garden with its central pool and arbor has a magnificent forest pansy (*Cercis canadensis*). Note the ingenious homemade vegetable frames. CH

RIGHT The Orchard Garden at Chanticleer is particularly beautiful in spring, when the fruit trees are in blossom.

Longwood Gardens

Pennsylvania, U.S.

DESIGNER: Pierre S. du Pont
OWNER: Longwood Gardens, Inc.
GARDEN STYLE: 20th-century display gardens
SIZE: 1,050 acres (425 ha)
CLIMATE: Zones 6b–7a
LOCATION: Kennett Square, Pennsylvania

Longwood Gardens (also known as Du Pont Gardens) is one of the world's largest display gardens. They were created from 1907 to the 1930s by Pierre S. du Pont, a dynamic force who was an industrialist, conservationist, philanthropist, farmer, designer, engineer, and impresario. The garden reflects his vitality, and is a tour de force in every sense of the word. Initially it consisted only of a showcase garden. However, it now has a seemingly never-ending series of gardens, woodlands, and meadows. There are twenty outdoor gardens, including a Rose Arbor, a Theater Garden, a tropical Cascade Garden, a Peony Garden, a Wisteria Garden, and various other flower gardens. There are lakes, meadows, and forest walks. An outdoor topiary garden dates back to the 1930s and includes rabbits, birds, furniture, and various decorative shapes. There are also twenty indoor gardens within 4 acres (2 ha) of heated greenhouses, and 11,000 different types of plant. Whenever you visit Longwood, there is always so much in bloom in special displays in the greenhouses, including dogwoods, witch hazels, bulbs, magnolias, and azaleas, as well as display vegetable plots, children's plots, and themed groups of plants.

There are also some stunning fountains. Pierre based his Italian Water Garden on the Villa Gamberaia near Florence, but he added six hundred jets of recirculating water. Over the years, several successive generations of Du Pont have contributed to the development of Longwood. Pierre undoubtedly made the most enduring contribution. BS

James Rose Center

New Jersey, U.S.

DESIGNER: James Rose
OWNER: James Rose Center
GARDEN STYLE: 20th-century contemporary
SIZE: 0.07 acre (0.02 ha)
CLIMATE: Zones 6a–6b
LOCATION: Ridgewood, New Jersey

James Rose was one of the leaders of the modern movement in landscape architecture in the United States. He was also one of the most colorful people in the field; his refusal to take the required courses resulted in his failure to graduate from high school. Although he was accepted for architecture courses at Cornell and Harvard, he was expelled from the latter institution for refusing to design landscapes in the Beaux-Arts manner.

Rose conceived the idea for his own home while stationed in Japan in the 1940s, and the Japanese influence is evident. He described it as a "tiny village" with three distinct buildings—the main house for his mother, a guesthouse for his sister, and a studio for himself. It is a complete fusion of indoor and outdoor space, with house and gardens entwined. There are terraces, balconies, and atrium-type spaces at tree-branch level, with timber skywalks linking sections together. On the second floor, it feels like you are in a large tree house. In the main courtyard, a water spout plays into a pool, but there are no traditional borders; it is a house in the woods and of the woods.

Although Rose shunned most academic institutions, he was influential as a visiting lecturer at numerous landscape architecture schools. Now his home and studio are a center for landscape design research and study. Rose described this unusual place as "neither landscape, nor architecture, but both; neither indoors, nor outdoors, but both." RChi

Van Vleck House and Gardens

New Jersey, U.S.

DESIGNER: Joseph Van Vleck Jr.
OWNER: The Montclair Foundation
GARDEN STYLE: 20th-century garden "room"
SIZE: 6 acres (2.5 ha)
CLIMATE: Zone 6b
LOCATION: Montclair, New Jersey

Van Vleck House and Gardens is the former private estate of the Van Vleck family, who began developing it in the late nineteenth century. The garden contains many ericaceous plants, including a fine showing of rhododendrons and azaleas.

The gardens surround a formal twentieth-century Italianate-style house built in 1916 by Joseph Van Vleck Jr. They are a succession of small "rooms" filled with hundreds of flowering shrubs and broad-leaved evergreens. The property is laced with sunny flagstone and dappled shady paths winding through the collections.

Howard Van Vleck, the last family member to reside here, was particularly interested in scientific aspects of horticulture. He experimented with hybridization of his vast rhododendron collection, working to create a clear yellow-flowering variety. His most notable successes were Rhododendron 'Howard Van Vleck', R. 'Elizabeth Van Vleck', and R. 'Goldsworth Yellow'.

The centerpiece of the garden is a Chinese wisteria (Wisteria sinensis) that comes into bloom in May, filling the garden with visitors eager to enjoy this beautiful spring sight. Planted in 1939 as two separate plants, the wisteria runs the length of the patio, wraps itself around two grand columns guarding the back portico, and clambers up over the balcony, clothing the entire back of the house in its tremendous, vigorous splendor. AH

Greenwood Gardens

New Jersey, U.S.

DESIGNER: William Whetten Renwick
OWNER: Self-owned, nonprofit conservation organization
GARDEN STYLE: 20th-century Arts and Crafts, Italianate
SIZE: 26 acres (10.5 ha)
CLIMATE: Zones 6a–6b
LOCATION: Short Hills, New Jersey

This innovative garden has wonderful water features and terraces inlaid with colorful, ornamental tiles. Originally built in 1906, the private estate was the home of Joseph P. Day and his wife, Pauline Martindale Pope. When their house was destroyed by fire in 1911, they hired architect William Whetten Renwick to design a new house and gardens. Called Pleasant Days, the estate featured an Italianate mansion, two stone summerhouses, water cascades, grottoes, arbors, pools, and a tile-inlaid terrace reflecting the Arts and Crafts movement. In 1949 new owners rebuilt the house in the colonial revival style and renamed the estate The Greenwoods.

The garden is inspired by Italian gardens of the past. Hundreds of pieces of sculpture decorate the "rooms," and the gentle sound of the water cascade adds a soothing dimension as you walk down one of the numerous allées. The space near the house is organized formally. Surrounding spaces initiate the transition to less formal plantings. Tall, majestic trees create a marvelous canopy over the gardens, which are surrounded by box and funky containers filled with plants. Amazingly, when you stand in the middle of the property, which is in the most densely populated county in the entire country, all your views are protected and preserved. There is no hint of any human activity. The garden is now undergoing an extensive restoration process, complete with a fascinating archaeological dig. Children love it. AH

Cornerstone Festival of Gardens

California, U.S.

DESIGNERS: Various
OWNER: Chris Hougie
GARDEN STYLE: 21st-century display/sculptural
SIZE: 13.9 acres (5.6 ha)
CLIMATE: Zones 9b–10a
LOCATION: Sonoma, California

The Cornerstone Festival of Gardens (or Cornerstone Gardens) opened in 2004. It was founded by Chris Hougie, who, while honeymooning in France, had visited the Chaumont Garden Festival (see page 592). Hougie realized that America did not have a similar venue, "where high-caliber landscape architects can demonstrate the fun and whimsical combination of art and gardens." So he bought some land and created one.

The aim of Cornerstone, according to Hougie, "is to create a place for the community where people can enjoy unique and creative visions of landscape as art. Designers have the freedom to create everything from traditional gardens to modern, conceptual installations." Cornerstone has twenty installations by some of the world's most well-respected garden designers and landscape architects. Some of the gardens are in place for only a season, others for longer. This combination provides Cornerstone with a sense of permanency while constantly providing opportunities for garden designers and gardeners.

The festival site offers its own design challenges because it is a windy location with high levels of strong sunlight, a limited budget, and a small space of approximately 1,800 square feet (167 sq. m). The results, though, speak for themselves. The gardens offer a wide range of novel solutions and an opportunity to see what truly innovative designers can achieve with skill, ingenuity, and enthusiasm. TM

Huntington Botanical Gardens

California, U.S.

DESIGNER: Henry E. Huntington
OWNER: The Huntington Library
GARDEN STYLE: 20th-century themed botanical
SIZE: 150 acres (60.7 ha)
CLIMATE: Zones 10a–10b
LOCATION: San Marino, California

Apart from a dazzling art collection and world-famous library of books, with works by Shakespeare and John Milton, Huntington has fabulous botanical gardens. In 1903 Henry E. Huntington bought the 600-acre (243 ha) San Marino Ranch and citrus plantation. Together with William Hertrich, he started to develop the gardens. When Huntington died in 1927, the gardens extended to well over 100 acres (450 ha) in twelve garden areas. The Rose Garden was planted in 1908 to provide a history of the evolution of the rose.

Today, there is a 10-acre (4 ha) Desert Garden with more than 4,000 species, an Australian Garden, and a Jungle Garden. Also note the rare, flowering trees, including the tabebuia's spring blooms.

The Japanese Garden here has an incredible, tranquil beauty, with ponds providing exquisite reflections of junipers and the moon bridge. The traditional Japanese House has rooms for sleeping, dining, and drinking tea, and is framed by acers, azaleas, camellias, and wisteria. Beyond is the gravel garden, and Zen and Bonsai courts. In addition a 12-acre (4.8 ha) classical Chinese garden is still under construction. When completed it will be one of the largest outside China. The central feature is a 1-acre (0.4 ha) lake surrounded by seasonal gardens of traditional plants, five pavilions, and a teahouse. RL

RIGHT Huntington Botanical Gardens, just one part of the San Marino Ranch, was bought by Henry E. Huntington in 1903.

Forestiere Underground Gardens

California, U.S.

DESIGNER: Baldasare Forestiere
OWNER: Underground Nature Conservancy
GARDEN STYLE: 20th-century underground
SIZE: 10 acres (4 ha)
CLIMATE: Zone 9a
LOCATION: Fresno, California

In hot climates, before air conditioning, a good way to stay cool in summer was to disappear underground. This works for humans, but is unconventional for a garden and plants. The Forestiere Underground Gardens are certainly unusual, if not dramatic.

After passing through the gate that leads from a very normal-looking American street, one enters the world created by Baldasare Forestiere, a Sicilian immigrant who learned his tunneling trade when he worked in New York City. Forestiere moved west and bought the plot of land, hoping to establish a citrus farm. However, his ambitions were thwarted because beneath the thin layer of topsoil, he hit bedrock. Then the California sun must have gone to his head because he changed tack, and digging became an obsession. For more than forty years, until he died in 1946, he dug a complex of more than fifty interconnected "rooms" up to 22 feet (7 m) below ground.

Yet this is no dark, dank labyrinth. Many of the 100 or so patios and courtyards are open to the sky, making for a strong visual contrast as the dark shade of the tunnels and "rooms" suddenly gives way to the bright blue sky and dazzling California sunlight. It also means that below the surface is a rambling garden, its sunlit spaces richly planted with an attractive mix of fruit trees (even citrus), climbing grape vines, and flowering plants. TM

The Pool Garden at El Novillero

California, U.S.

DESIGNER: Thomas Church
OWNER: Dewey Donnell
GARDEN STYLE: 20th-century contemporary
SIZE: 0.5 acres (0.2 ha)
CLIMATE: Zone 9b
LOCATION: Sonoma, California

The pool garden at El Novillero is one of the most iconic gardens of the 20th century. For its creator, Thomas Church, the opportunity to design and build a garden at a cattle ranch deep in the Sonama Valley in California was a welcome departure from the urban and suburban gardens that he had made his business since the end of the Second World War. His brief was to create a contemporary garden with plenty of room for entertaining. In so doing, Church drew his inspiration from surrounding salt marshes, the meandering river nearby, and the slopes of distant hills to create a garden of simple and seemingly free curves, yet the whole is bound within a carefully concealed and disciplined grid system.

Local flora has been incorporated in the design and is actively encouraged. Elderly gnarled and bent oak trees provide shelter and shadows. Out of the shade of the oaks, wooden decking is replaced by a concrete terrace, which frames the pool, the feature most recognized by garden lovers and disciples of landscape design. Its sinuous curves reflect those of the nearby river, although its original purpose was a reservoir in case of bush fires. At its center, a voluptuous sculpture by Adaline Kent appears to float languidly on the still surface of the pool. It too has dual practical purpose, being a diving board and sun lounger as well as an unforgettable work of art. RSJ

Forest Lawn

California, U.S.

DESIGNER: Dr. Hubert Eaton
OWNER: Forest Lawn Memorial-Parks and Mortuaries
GARDEN STYLE: 20th-century memorial park
SIZE: 300 acres (121 ha)
CLIMATE: Zones 10a–10b
LOCATION: Glendale, California

Forest Lawn is to the United States what the Parisian cemetery Père-Lachaise is to France, though on a far grander scale. It is a final resting place for the great and the good, and a hauntingly beautiful retreat for the living to visit. Whereas European cemeteries tend to focus on death, the memorial park at Glendale very much celebrates life. Strange as this might sound, Forest Lawn is a truly joyous place.

More than a million visitors pass through its monumental, wrought-iron gates each year, including thousands of children on school trips. More than 60,000 people have been married in the chapels,

Ronald Reagan and Jane Wyman being the most famous. Buildings in a wide range of architectural styles nestle into the wooded landscape, and original statuary and reproductions of hundreds of world-famous works add to the overall effect. There is even a museum with a large, permanent collection that also hosts ever changing exhibitions. Set up in 1906 as a nonprofit organization by a group of San Francisco businessmen, Forest Lawn came seriously into its stride when Dr. Hubert Eaton took over management in 1917. He envisaged "a great park devoid of misshapen monuments and other signs of earthly death, but filled with towering trees, sweeping lawns, splashing fountains." Then he made it reality.

Many famous people are buried here, including Hollywood stars, some of whom are at rest in enclosed gardens with no public access. This may disappoint celebrity hunters, but garden lovers will leave with a great sense of fulfillment. RCa

Sunset Garden

California, U.S.

DESIGNER: Thomas Church
OWNER: Sunset Publishing Corporation
GARDEN STYLE: 20th-century modern, abstract
SIZE: 1.5 acres (0.6 ha)
CLIMATE: Zones 9b–10a
LOCATION: Menlo Park, California

Sunset magazine was founded in 1898, in the early days of the Southern Pacific Railroad Company, to promote and encourage travel in the western region of the United States. Its editorial mission now includes food, gardening, and a range of other lifestyle issues. In 1951 the corporate offices moved to this huge, California ranch-style building, which is similar in appearance to a supersize suburban home.

Designed by local landscape architect Thomas Church, the garden is a large, calm space, like a suburban garden on steroids—it looks like a typical Californian backyard only ten times normal size, and its scale matches that of the oversized, ranch-style office building. The lawn is huge and is laid with bent grass, a type of grass that would not be used today, as it is not drought tolerant.

The garden today exerts a distinctly retro feel, taking the visitor back to Californian garden design in the 1950s. The concepts of indoor and outdoor living are almost seamlessly combined. From the glass-walled entrance hall, there is a panoramic view of the sinuous, curving path around a 1-acre (0.4 ha) velvet lawn. The Old Man, a magnificent oak, casts a lopsided presence near the start of the route, its heavy limbs supported by metal posts.

Various areas in the garden represent the West's major climate zones. There are plants from the deserts of Arizona and arid southern California, and from the cooler, wetter Pacific Northwest. A stroll around the curving path that surrounds the giant lawn is always a pleasant, relaxing experience. RChi

Filoli

California, U.S.

DESIGNERS: Bruce Porter, Isobella Worn, Lurline B. Roth
OWNER: National Trust for Historic Preservation
GARDEN STYLE: 20th-century formal
SIZE: 16 acres (6.5 ha)
CLIMATE: Zones 9b–10a
LOCATION: Woodside, California

The gardens at Filoli lie to the rear and south of the Georgian-style house, and were built between 1915 and 1920. Founded by William Bowers Bourn and designed by Bruce Porter, they take their inspiration from Europe. A formal layout encloses a series of set-piece gardens with lawns, terraces, pools, and parterres within discrete compartments. Among the major features are the Sunken Garden, imposing Pool Pavilion Garden, a large Walled Garden, the formal Rose Garden, and the Knot Garden. There are tightly manicured hedges and topiary, and many trees and shrubs have been skillfully trained, mostly in traditional ways. However, notes of humor have been injected by innovative or surreally shaped specimens. The Knot Garden is more conventional and features low, intersecting hedges of green, purple, and silver.

The Californian climate allows the garden to grow plants for color all year round. The formal layout includes a variety of floral displays, and the seasonal bedding is carefully color themed. Among permanent plantings are camellias, rhododendrons, magnolias, and a wide variety of roses and perennials. There is also a cutting garden, and displays of tropical plants and orchids.

Filoli is considered to be one of America's finest historical gardens. Now owned by the National Trust for Historic Preservation, the quality of maintenance and display is of the highest order. CBa

RIGHT Filoli is the site of a Georgian-style house and is considered to be one of America's finest historical gardens.

Hearst Castle

California, U.S.

DESIGNER: Julia Morgan
OWNER: State of California
STYLE: 20th-century Spanish, Mediterranean
SIZE: 127 acres (51.4 ha)
CLIMATE: Zone 10a
LOCATION: San Simeon, California

William Randolph Hearst inherited this site, also known as Hearst Mansion and San Simeon, in 1919. Until then it had been 40,000 acres (16,200 ha) of ranch with basic accommodation. Hearst camped out on family visits and called the property La Cuesta Encantada, meaning "the enchanted hill." He decided to use it to showcase his vast collection of European art, antiques, and sculptures, with gardens to match the fantastic buildings and opulent interiors.

With the family fortune from mining to fund his venture, he commissioned architect Julia Morgan to design the buildings and gardens. Their collaboration lasted until Hearst's failing health forced him to move out in 1947, by which time the estate had grown to 165 rooms with 127 acres (51.4 ha) of gardens. It was a huge feat of construction and engineering, with many tons of topsoil poured on the rocky site.

Coast live oaks (*Quercus agrifolia*) help to integrate the gardens with the surrounding landscape. The towering main house, La Casa Grande, resembles a Spanish cathedral, and Italian cypresses (*Cupressus sempervirens*) and Mexican fan palms (*Washingtonia robusta*) were planted to balance its scale with the smaller buildings. Courtyards of all sizes, terraces with gardens, staircases, pools, and fountains were also used to link the buildings. Scented jasmine and roses soften the retaining walls, and lantana and trailing geraniums are informally planted. The main European influences are Italian (hence the expanded terraces), Moorish, and Spanish (seen in the pools and paving). Fragments of ancient sculptures and whole classical statues add to the European style.

This garden has a real sense of place, and of the rich and famous who once walked along the terraces and lounged in the courtyards, from Winston Churchill (in 1929) to Cary Grant. Hearst loved to swim in the Neptune pool with his favorite dachshunds, by the enchanted hill. RChi

The Getty Villa

California, U.S.

DESIGNERS: Denis Kurutz, Matt Randolph, Amy Korn
OWNER: J. Paul Getty Trust
GARDEN STYLE: 20th-century Roman, classical
SIZE: 64 acres (26 ha)
CLIMATE: Zones 10a–10b
LOCATION: Pacific Palisades, California

At the Getty Villa, also known as the J. Paul Getty Museum, a Californian canyon is transformed into the ancient Mediterranean world, complete with cobblestone roads, all set against a scenic hillside backdrop that includes cypresses, cedars, and olive trees. John Paul Getty bought the site in 1945. The first museum bearing his name opened at his ranch house in 1954. The villa became the J. Paul Getty Museum in 1974, its architecture inspired by Villa dei Papiri, a first-century Roman villa destroyed by Vesuvius. It served in this role until the opening of the Getty Center in 1997. The villa remains an extraordinary educational center, housing Greek, Roman, and Etruscan antiquities, and demonstrates how gardens were integral to Roman life.

The Outer Peristyle is the grandest courtyard, with replicas of statues discovered at the Villa dei Papiri found in the same positions as the originals. Enjoy this space like Romans—recline in scented, shaded loggias, enjoy the cooling effects of the reflecting pool, stroll along its colonnade, and take in the 1,000-foot-long (304 m) trompe l'oeil mural. Then enjoy spectacular Pacific Ocean views.

The smaller Inner Peristyle is a calm, green space with a central pool and fountain. Outside the exterior walls of the villa, the Herb Garden is filled with plants grown for medicinal and culinary uses. The East Garden is a quiet space designed around a circular lily fountain. Together they help us understand exactly what the Romans—and the Greeks and Etruscans—contributed to our gardening heritage. RChi

Quarryhill Botanical Garden

California, U.S.

DESIGNER: Jane Davenport Jansen
OWNER: Quarryhill Botanical Garden
GARDEN STYLE: 20th-century botanical
SIZE: 20 acres (8.1 ha)
CLIMATE: Zones 9b–10a
LOCATION: Glen Ellen, California

If the temperate flora of Asia appeals, then Quarryhill is the place to go. Situated amid vineyards in the Sonoma Valley, against the background of the Mayacamus Mountains, clothed in knobcone pines and madrones, this botanical garden was created by the late Jane Davenport Jansen in 1987. China was then opening its doors to visitors, giving access to extraordinary flora that had been inaccessible to the West since before the Cultural Revolution. The aim was to house some of the most beautiful plants in the world, including rhododendrons, maples, magnolias, Oriental dogwoods, roses, and stewartias.

Annual plant hunting expeditions to China, Japan, Taiwan, Nepal, and India have secured the introduction of 1,600 different species from 300 genera, all of which are meticulously recorded in the Database of Asian Plants in Cultivation. Quarryhill claims to have one of the largest collections of scientifically documented, wild-source, temperate Asian plants in North America.

The garden was planted on the craggy outcrops and hollows left by the stone quarries once used for road building. Lakes and other water features were created where the heavy winter rains accumulated, and around the stream that flowed through the grounds in winter. Approximately 10,000 plants have been planted out in twenty years, all of them grown from seed sown in the garden nursery. The achievement is extraordinary. CB

The J. Paul Getty Museum

California, U.S.

DESIGNERS: Robert Irwin, Emet L. Wemple, Laurie Olin
OWNER: J. Paul Getty Trust
GARDEN STYLE: 20th-century modern
SIZE: 110 acres (45 ha)
CLIMATE: Zones 10a–10b
LOCATION: Los Angeles, California

The Getty Center, which houses collections of the J. Paul Getty Museum, cost a staggering $1 billion to build and opened to the public in 1997. It straddles the hillsides of the mountains near Santa Monica and has many views of the Los Angeles skyline, the distant San Gabriel Mountains, and the Pacific Ocean. The Central Garden, though, has become an icon. Commissioning the artist Robert Irwin to design this space was somewhat controversial. However, Irwin has made the visit a sensory experience

Irwin started designing this space in 1992. There are tree-lined paths and a natural ravine with a stream that cascades into a pool. Great, splay-topped tree shapes, formed out of rebar, provide structures for bougainvillea to scramble up and over, and elsewhere, steel arches make more familiar garden features. The central pool looks like an amphitheater stage, its terraces filled with a riot of more than 500 different plants, and right in the middle of the pool, an azalea maze resembles a floating labyrinth. It is a heady place. There are plenty of other areas for quieter contemplation, with huge, rough-hewn boulders for seats, cooling fountains, and a cactus garden on the Southern Promontory. Irwin's quote, "Always changing, never twice the same," is carved into the plaza floor of the Central Garden. RChi

RIGHT The gardens of the J. Paul Getty Museum were started in 1992 by the artist Robert Irwin.

Lotusland

California, U.S.

DESIGNERS: Madame Ganna Walska, and others
OWNER: Ganna Walska Lotusland Foundation
GARDEN STYLE: 20th-century plantswoman's garden
SIZE: 37 acres (14.9 ha)
CLIMATE: Zone 9b
LOCATION: Santa Barbara, California

Lotusland shares two things with not-so-far-away Hollywood. First it has the same warm climate. Second its creator and residing spirit, Madame Ganna Walska, was a larger-than-life character who would have been perfectly at home in Tinseltown.

Originally the home of a late-nineteenth-century nurseryman, the estate underwent a modest, but progressive, development during the first half of the twentieth century. Only with its purchase by Walska in 1941 did everything take off. A Polish opera singer who had been the toast of European and American society, she was drawn to California by its climate and freethinking residents. She originally purchased the Cuesta Linda Estate as a retreat for Tibetan monks, and christened it Tibet Land. Fortunately the monks never appeared, and Walska found gardening rather than God. Over the years, her energy, resources, and artistic talent, in collaboration with some of the top landscape architects and designers of the day, were poured into creating a fantasy world with stunning and dramatic plant combinations. When juxtaposed against the exotic hard landscaping and detailing, they produce a sense of surreal beauty. Trees drip with bromeliads. Palm trees tower over cacti. Paths are lined with huge diamonds of green glass. A Mediterranean blue, kidney-shaped pond is bordered by abalone shells.

Until the last years of her life, Walska was the creative dynamo at the center of this horticultural vortex. Her spirit still presides as the garden advances into the twenty-first century. JB

"Fortunately the monks never appeared, and Walska found gardening rather than God"

Oakland Museum and Garden

California, U.S.

DESIGNERS: Dan Kiley, Geraldine Knight Scott
OWNER: City of Oakland
GARDEN STYLE: 20th-century abstract, modern, architectural
SIZE: 7 acres (2.8 ha)
CLIMATE: Zone 9b–10a
LOCATION: Oakland, California

A green oasis tucked away in the heart of any city center is always an exciting discovery. At Oakland Museum, the architecture and landscape entwine magnificently. From the outset, the architects advised the city that what it really needed was a green, open space rather than yet another building—thankfully, that is what it got.

Designed in 1969, Oakland Museum is a multilevel roof garden. From the street, the tall, austere walls block the view inside. However, plenty of foliage spills over the ledges in some places, with branches and flowers peeking over walls in others, to give everyone

a clue about what is going on inside. The entry lawn has specimen trees, including cedar. It is very easy to forget that this is a roof garden, so successfully were the challenges met by the landscape architect Dan Kiley and his team.

Filling the structures and spaces created by the architects meant finding appropriate plants for the task. The plants have also been grouped according to their cultivation requirements. Certain key points around the garden, such as entrances and path intersections, are emphasized using particularly interesting plants. The clinging and climbing plants here include honeysuckle, wisteria, bougainvillea, and roses. Trees that grow well in the raised plant beds here include olive, lemon, pine, and Japanese pear (*Pyrus pyrifolia*). There is also a fish pool that can be viewed from above. As well as fish for visitors to look at, it has a particularly interesting selection of aquatic plants. RChi

Santa Barbara Botanic Garden

California, U.S.

DESIGNERS: Lockwood de Forest Jr., Beatrix Farrand,
Elizabeth Kellam de Forest
OWNER: Board of directors
GARDEN STYLE: Botanic garden
SIZE: 78 acres (31.8 ha)
CLIMATE: Zone 3
LOCATION: Mission Canyon Road, Santa Barbara, California

Blessed with a spectacular backdrop of the Santa Ynez Mountains and glorious views of the Pacific Ocean, Santa Barbara Botanic Garden is the oldest of its kind in California. Founded in 1926, the garden is dedicated to the study, conservation, and display of California's native flora, and contains around 5,800 species of trees, shrubs, wildflowers, cacti, and succulents. A third are threatened with extinction in the next 50 years.

When it was first established, the gardens were arranged into native plant groups to a design by Dr Frederic Clements, among others. In 1938, Beatrix Farrand and Lockwood de Forest Jr. developed the naturalistic design of the garden. There are 33 acres (13.3 ha) of cultivated garden and 5.5 miles (8.8 km) of nature trails through meadow, canyon, and forests of redwood and oak woodland.

Visiting between March and May is highly recommended when the California poppy, meadow foam, blue-eyed grass, tidy tips, lupine, gilia, and goldfields crescendo into a glorious symphony of color. The impressive collection of *Ceanothus*—some 30 taxa and over 50 cultivars—is also in full swing, having started in February and continuing until June.

For winter visitors, there is the Manzanita Section of over 60 taxa and 50 cultivars of *Arctostaphylos*, which range from flat ground cover plants to small trees. The delicate, urn-shaped white to pink blossoms are at their best in January and February, although their sculptural form and attractive red bark make them beautiful at any time of year. *RSJ*

Ruth Bancroft Garden

California, U.S.

DESIGNERS: Lester Hawkins, Ruth Bancroft
OWNER: Ruth Bancroft Garden, Inc.
GARDEN STYLE: 20th-century modern
SIZE: 2.5 acres (1 ha)
CLIMATE: Zones 9b–10a
LOCATION: Walnut Creek, California

The story goes that a single *Aeonium* 'Glenn Davidson' sparked Ruth Bancroft's interest in succulents. Visiting her garden today convinces even the most doubtful that a drought-tolerant garden can look fabulous, and not be just a tapestry of beiges and browns.

The garden gives no clues to casual passersby of the drama inside. Ruth and her husband, Philip, took over the house and garden of what was then a ranch with walnut and fruit orchards in the 1940s. Initially only the area close to the house was gardened in a more traditional manner. Then, from the 1950s onward, her growing succulent and cacti collection rapidly filled the shade houses and greenhouses. By the 1970s, space was running short, and the 2.5 acres (1 ha) of orchards had reached the end of their productive life. Local landscape designer Lester Hawkins laid out a meandering system of paths around mounded beds, or berms, their undulating organic shapes making ideal growing conditions, and an architectural shade structure provided more relief from the relentless summer sun in this sheltered, inland valley.

All in all, it is a dramatic, architectural garden with a diversity of plant shapes, habits, and forms. Vibrant flowers stand out against the textured foliage. African aloes, haworthias, and gasterias are well represented, their blooms sprinkling splashes of red, coral, orange, and yellow in late winter and early spring. Though many plants are dormant in summer, yuccas and agaves produce a later flush of blooms. Trees and shrubs from other dry regions, including Australia and Mexico, provide an upper canopy of structural planting. Pines, palo verde, and mesquite give form, as do native 300-year-old valley oaks (*Quercus lobata*). In 1992 the Ruth Bancroft Garden became the first sponsored by the Garden Conservancy, an organization devoted to preserving significant private gardens in the United States. RChi

The Leichtag Family Healing Garden

California, U.S.

DESIGNER: Topher Delaney
OWNER: Rady Children's Hospital and Health Center
GARDEN STYLE: 20th-century modern
SIZE: 0.5 acre (0.2 ha)
CLIMATE: Zone 10a
LOCATION: San Diego, California

At the heart of a complex of buildings in a suburb of San Diego, colorful giant globes dotted among willowy palm trees mark the entrance to the Leichtag Family Healing Garden, where Topher Delaney has designed a space that is full of joy.

The design concept was to make a garden that provides both distraction and relaxation. What you first see is the curving Constellation Wall that shields the garden from the road and is studded with glass circles that sparkle at night to reveal all twelve signs of the zodiac. Around the corner, a 20-foot-tall (6 m) metal-framed brontosaurus makes a remarkably friendly guardian. Windmills have been an important feature in the landscape of the United States— practical and graceful, interesting to observe—and the colorful blades on this version form a giant spectrum wheel that blurs to bright white in a strong breeze. And all around you are the colors of the sky, the earth, ocean, and plants on every surface, from curving walls to swirling patterns in the paving.

Animal shapes of all kinds are cut out of metal wall sections, casting interesting shadows and openings to peek through. Ceramic creatures of all types swim, fly, and slither. Taking center stage, though, is a magnificent, mosaic sea-horse fountain that spouts water into a raised, shallow pool. Visitors also love the wall seats around the raised plant beds, with larger mosaic-covered shapes making tables and benches. Everywhere you look, nature and art combine to make the garden a place of renewal and diversion from everyday concerns. RChi

> "Taking center stage, though, is a magnificent, mosaic sea-horse fountain that spouts water..."

Denver Botanic Gardens

Colorado, U.S.

DESIGNERS: Saco R. DeBoer, Garrett Eckbo
OWNER: Denver Botanic Gardens, Inc.
GARDEN STYLE: 20th-century modern botanical
SIZE: 23 acres (9.3 ha)
CLIMATE: Zones 4a–5b
LOCATION: Denver, Colorado

This is one of the top botanical gardens in the United States, and also one of the first to promote environmentally responsible practices such as water conservation and biological pest control. Established in 1959, its boundaries extend beyond the city, with three satellite sites at Chatfield, Mount Goliath Alpine Trail, and Centennial Gardens.

At the main site, the more than 32,000 plants from many different countries mean there is something for everyone throughout the year. The forty-five gardens fill 23 acres (9 ha). One of the highlights is the humid, tropical rain forest that fills the soaring arch of the 1960s conservatory, a Denver landmark. The most impressive outside sites are the Plains Garden; the Japanese Garden and teahouse; the Water Gardens; and the Rock Alpine Garden.

Tons of rocks were used to create slopes and berms spread over 1 acre (0.4 ha) of ground to make this alpine area one of the best in North America. Here Panayoti Kelaidis, curator of plant collections, has skillfully planted almost a quarter of the garden's entire collection. The alpines range from tiny, mat-like examples to bulbs, succulents, and shrubs from around the world. There is also a contrasting mix of native grasses with wildflowers turning a relatively small area into a plains garden. Planting in the Japanese garden has been adjusted to withstand regional temperatures and the high altitude. Note how the large, pink, red, and white water lilies are used in the Water Garden, giving a hint of Giverny in France (see page 556). What more could anyone want? RChi

Missouri Botanical Garden

Missouri, U.S.

DESIGNER: Dr. George Engelmann

OWNER: Missouri Botanical Garden

GARDEN STYLE: 19th-century botanical

SIZE: 51.5 acres (20.8 ha)

CLIMATE: Zones 5a–5b

LOCATION: St. Louis, Missouri

Missouri Botanical Garden, also known as Shaw's Garden, is one of America's finest and oldest botanical gardens. Its mission statement is "To discover and share knowledge about plants and their environment, in order to preserve and enrich life." It was created on what was prairie far outside the city, and was a philanthropic gift to St. Louis from Henry Shaw, the English entrepreneur. The gates opened to the public in 1859, since when the garden has continually strengthened. Today Missouri Botanical Garden is a National Historic Site and has one of the world's leading programs in botanical research.

The highlights include the oldest part of the garden—the Victorian Area—that surrounds Shaw's Tower Grove House. It has been restored to recreate a nineteenth-century garden feel. Also note the Linnean House. Built in 1882, it is the United States' oldest, continuously operating greenhouse and home to a wonderful collection of camellias. It is in complete contrast to the Climatron, a geodesic dome conservatory that covers more than 0.5 acre (0.2 ha) and is filled with 1,200 tropical species of plant in a natural-looking setting. One of the best highlights, though, is the 14-acre (5.6 ha) Japanese Garden that is promoted as the largest Japanese stroll garden in the West. Called Seiwa-en—meaning "the garden of pure, clear harmony and peace"—and designed by the late Professor Koichi Kawana, this is one of the finest and most authentic examples of its genre in the United States. Finish your visit with a walk by the 4-acre (1.6 ha) lake with its streams and waterfalls. TM

> "Missouri Botanical Garden...
> has one of the world's leading
> programs in botanical research"

Yew Dell Gardens

Kentucky, U.S.

DESIGNER: Theodore Klein
OWNER: Private community volunteer board
GARDEN STYLE: 20th-century arboretum, alpine garden, English walled garden, serpentine garden
SIZE: 33 acres (13.4 ha)
CLIMATE: Zone 6a
LOCATION: Crestwood, Kentucky

From 1941 the self-taught artisan and nurseryman Theodore Klein and his wife, Martha, developed Yew Dell Gardens. An exquisite private estate, it included a successful commercial nursery and an extensive collection of unusual plants. The gardens cover a wide range of styles, including formal topiary, a traditional English Walled Garden, and Yew Dell's signature Serpentine Garden with more than 1,000 rare specimen trees and shrubs, among them some that Klein introduced to the nursery trade. This plant lover's paradise is also graced by several thousand rare, unusual, and newly introduced plants among the architectural features, which include a small stone castle and the Kleins' Cotswolds-style home.

The arboretum contains an outstanding tree collection with cultivars of common beech (*Fagus sylvatica*) that were once described by famed plantsman J. C. Raulston as among some of the best in the United States. The Secret Garden has everything in abundance, from dwarf conifers to peonies with more than seventy Lenten roses, more than 100 hardy ferns, and numerous species and cultivars of hardy ginger. The stunning evergreen Serpentine Garden has an impressive collection of evergreens, including abies, piceas, and tsugas. And the Walled Garden is bounded on three sides by stone walls set off by a small round pool in the center.

The ever changing mood of the garden is determined by the likes of *Hakonechloa macra* 'All Gold', *Verbascum* 'Caribbean Crush', and the newly released, yellow-leaved, dwarf hydrangea, *H. quercifolia* 'Little Honey'. But if that implies everything here is fixed and unchanging, then the truth is a little more surprising. A process of ongoing research and experimentation in the gardens includes breeding and evaluation in various species, in particular tiarella, helleborus, baptisia, fothergilla, viburnum, cornus, and carex. AH

Monticello

Virginia, U.S.

DESIGNER: Thomas Jefferson
OWNER: The Thomas Jefferson Foundation
GARDEN STYLE: 19th-century English landscaped
SIZE: 40 acres (16.2 ha)
CLIMATE: Zone 7a
LOCATION: Charlottesville, Virginia

Besides his achievements as a politician, Thomas Jefferson, the third President of the United States and a renowned scholar, was also a highly talented gardener. He inherited this substantial country estate, where he expanded the house and developed the garden until his death in 1826. During the following hundred years, the garden at Monticello, unfortunately, all but vanished, and it was not until 1939 that the Garden Club of Virginia set in motion a two-year restoration program that brought it back to life. The researchers were greatly helped in this program of restoration by the meticulous records Jefferson had kept of all his gardening activities, including his garden book.

The main areas are the oval-shaped west lawn with its associated winding-walk flower border, laid out in 1808. Jefferson had also made twenty oval-shaped beds that were scattered around the house and planted with about 105 different herbaceous species. In 1979 a two-year archaeological dig heralded the start of the restoration of the vegetable garden, a 1,000-foot-long (305 m) terrace that was recreated with great accuracy. Today the beds are planted with appropriate vegetables, and many are grown for their seeds. Next to the vegetable garden, the south orchard, restored in 1981, is part of the larger fruit garden in which Jefferson grew 170 varieties. Beyond the immediate garden is the grove, an area that Jefferson planted with his "pet trees," which had had all their lower growth removed so that their beauty could be fully enjoyed. TM

Gunston Hall

Virginia, U.S.

DESIGNER: George Mason
OWNER: Commonwealth of Virginia
GARDEN STYLE: 18th-, 19th-, and 20th-century mixed
SIZE: 550 acres (223 ha)
CLIMATE: Zone 7a
LOCATION: Mason Neck, Virginia

"That all men are born equally free and independent, and have certain inherent natural Rights." For those who enjoy following in history's footsteps, Gunston Hall was the home of George Mason, one of the least known of America's Founding Fathers. Mason originally wrote these words in the Virginia Declaration of Rights, and inspired his good friend, Thomas Jefferson, to include the famous phrases in the Declaration of Independence. They remain a key part of the American Constitution to this day.

Gunston Hall is smaller than Washington's Mount Vernon, and much more accessible than Thomas Jefferson's home at Monticello. Built between 1755 and 1759, Gunston Hall was designed by the English craftsman William Buckland, one of the foremost architects of the colonial period. The surrounding formal gardens, designed by Mason, contain only plants from that era, including box now 12 feet (4 m) high. From the gardens, visitors can stroll along a pathway through a deeply shaded deer park that rambles along the Potomac River.

The garden was designed as an extension of the house, with porticos and pavilions linking to the garden spaces. It was created on top of a level, artificial platform that affords good views over the surrounding woods, the river, and the Maryland shore. The period touch here is reinforced additionally by the inclusion of rare breeds of domestic animal from Mason's day and by the reconstructed outbuildings, which are typical of those that were found on an eighteenth-century plantation. AH

Mount Vernon

Virginia, U.S.

DESIGNER: George Washington
OWNER: The Mount Vernon Ladies Association
GARDEN STYLE: 18th-century landscaped and botanical
SIZE: 50 acres (20.2 ha) garden, 500 acres (202 ha) estate
CLIMATE: Zone 7a
LOCATION: Mount Vernon, Virginia

The 2,126-acre (861 ha) Mount Vernon estate was inherited by George Washington, who spent the next forty-five years improving and expanding it, until it was nearly 8,000 acres (3,240 ha) by the time of his death in 1799. The gardens are bound by a ha-ha on three sides, with the Potomac River on the fourth. Trees, especially *Gleditsia triacanthos*, were used to frame the views, and the house was landscaped in front with a generous "bowling green" flanked by symmetrically designed flower and kitchen gardens. The outer edge of the entrance courtyard has the Gardener's House and the Clerk's Quarters, each sheltering original American hollies (*Ilex opaca*). More than a dozen of Washington's known tree plantings have survived, including two tulip trees (*Liriodendron tulipifera*).

The flower and kitchen gardens have boundaries about 125 feet (38 m) long, running parallel to the house facade. Peaches, cherries, apples, and pears were espaliered along the walls, and the Orangery in the Flower Garden was a source of pride to Washington—he collected plants from all over the world. Elsewhere you'll see crown imperials (*Fritillaria imperialis*), everlasting peas, larkspur, tulips, and phlox. The box hedging dates back to 1795.

Other areas of interest include the small botanical garden, and the slopes to the wharf with the family burial vaults and slave graves. Washington was fascinated by practicalities—gravel paths, construction, and crop rotation—and today's visitor gains a real sense of a pioneering, energetic, eighteenth-century man and his garden. CH

Colonial Williamsburg

Virginia, U.S.

DESIGNERS: Various
OWNER: The Colonial Williamsburg Foundation
GARDEN STYLE: 18th-century Italianate, kitchen, domestic
SIZE: 175 acres (70.8 ha)
CLIMATE: Zone 7a
LOCATION: Williamsburg, Virginia

The most imposing garden in Colonial Williamsburg is that of the Governor's Palace, which was completed in 1722. Its grand scale complemented the former capital of Virginia, founded here in 1698, and the garden's twenty-four "yards" give an insight into eighteenth-century domestic gardens. By 1926 Colonial Williamsburg was in ruins because of neglect, but thanks to the Reverend Dr. William Goodwin and John D. Rockefeller, it was restored and recreated.

An avenue of catalpa trees takes you to the palace gates. Excavations revealed foundations and gate openings that determined the lines of the garden walks during restoration, which was also helped by the discovery at Oxford University of the Bodleian Plate, showing the position of oval beds. Once inside, step into the Ballroom Garden, descend to a canalized pond, and explore the miniature Hampton Court Palace maze and the bowling green. The kitchen garden and orchard have also been restored. The elegant corner pavilions were once toilets, or "necessaries," whose "soil" was used for the gardens.

Allow time to visit the tiny herb garden by John Blair's Kitchen, red-flowering honeysuckle in Creasy's Garden, the slave gardens, and the modern courtyard and pool in the Lila Acheson Wallace Garden behind the DeWitt Wallace Decorative Arts Gallery. CH

> "...explore the miniature Hampton Court Palace maze..."

Enid A. Haupt Garden

Washington D.C., U.S.

DESIGNER: Jean Paul Carlihan
OWNER: Smithsonian Institution
GARDEN STYLE: 20th-century mixed
SIZE: 4.5 acres (1.8 ha)
CLIMATE: Zone 7a
LOCATION: Smithsonian Castle, Washington, D.C.

Enid A. Haupt was a major garden philanthropist. When new plans for the Quadrangle at the Smithsonian Institution were made in the 1980s, she was approached as a potential sponsor for a small part of the garden. After inspecting the plans, she decided to finance the entire project. The Enid A. Haupt Garden (also known as the Smithsonian Roof Garden) opened in 1987.

The garden contains three areas: the Moongate Garden, the Fountain Garden, and a parterre. The garden and architecture of the Temple of Heaven in Beijing, China, inspired the design of the Moongate Garden. Its strong geometrical layout, centered on the cardinal points of the compass, is realized in granite and water, and the shimmering reflections make the space appear larger than it actually is. The Fountain Garden reflects the design of the thirteenth-century Court of Lions at the Moorish Alhambra Palace in Granada, Spain. The parterre is a formal garden that incorporates complex patterns that alter seasonally.

Taking in the scope of the landscape—the brick paths, berms, pools, fountains, trees, shrubs, borders, and hanging plants—it is easy to forget that you are standing on the roofs of several museums and galleries. With the backdrop of the Castle and Independence Avenue, the garden makes a welcome refuge from the buzz of the museum and city. It is a living showcase and may be considered a living gallery of the Smithsonian. RChi

Dumbarton Oaks

Washington D.C., U.S.

DESIGNERS: Beatrix Farrand, Ruth Pavey, Alden Hopkins
OWNER: Harvard University
GARDEN STYLE: 20th-century Arts and Crafts, naturalistic
SIZE: 10 acres (4 ha)
CLIMATE: Zone 7a
LOCATION: Washington, D.C.

Beatrix Farrand, Edith Wharton's niece, accompanied her aunt around Europe, absorbing the finest classical education, and you can see the results here. Paths lead sinuously to different parts of the house and garden. Step from the conservatory, and you'll see terraces sculpted with grass, brick, mosaic pebbles, and planting. Descend through terraces, and you will see pools and massed plantings. Or take meandering brick walks into orchards and trees along Lovers' Lane to where a rocky stream glides into a naturalistic park.

Terraces include the Green and Zodiac Gardens, and then the Rose Garden that leads into the Fountain Terrace, each with vistas across and out of the garden. In spring the cherry blossom is magical, as is *Forsythia* 'Hill' and the white wisteria on the edges of the North Vista. The fall herbaceous borders are a triumph with drifts of yellow and red plants interspersed with clipped yew, culminating in a fine Norway Maple (*Acer platanoides*), which turns yellow before the leaves drop.

Farrand worked from 1922 for twenty-six years, her work continued by Ruth Pavey, who incorporated stone details and clipped ivy. In 1961 her Pebble Garden, a tour de force of pebbles from Mexico, replaced the tennis court. In 1941 Dumbarton Oaks was donated to Harvard University. CH

RIGHT Dumbarton Oaks was designed by, among others, Beatrix Farrand, Edith Wharton's niece.

Federal Reserve Garden

Washington D.C., U.S.

DESIGNERS: Wolfgang Oehme, James van Sweden
OWNER: The Federal Reserve System
GARDEN STYLE: 20th-century contemporary
SIZE: 2 acres (0.8 ha)
CLIMATE: Zone 7a
LOCATION: Washington, D.C.

Although the Federal Reserve Garden has been hailed as "The New American Garden," critics had to be won over. The planting was thought to look more like weeds than a bold, new kind of garden design. The style was deemed too domestic, the planting too naturalistic. It was thought not stately enough for a government site, five blocks from the White House.

Severe winter weather in 1977 had decimated the previous planting on this triangular site. David Lilly convinced the Board of Governors and the National Commission of Fine Arts that the redesign should break with tradition; the brief requested sitting areas on a human scale as a refuge from the pressures of the city, especially in summer. As a gardener himself, Lilly wanted a space where plants could be enjoyed and discovered. The garden was the first major commission for Washington landscape architects Wolfgang Oehme and James van Sweden.

The city's diagonal and right-angled streets influenced the design. Berms and planters sculpt the ground, channeling views to Washington landmarks and enclosing seating areas. Lawn provides a foil to the mass of planting in front of the main entry, and bold drifts of herbaceous plants (including many natives) combine with lush ornamental grasses and borrowed vistas.

A generous application of fertilizer boosted rapid, luxuriant growth of the young drifts of plants to silence the critics. It clearly worked. RChi

William Paca Gardens

Maryland, U.S.

DESIGNER: William Paca
OWNER: Historic Annapolis Foundation
GARDEN STYLE: 18th-century pleasure garden
SIZE: 2 acres (0.81 ha)
CLIMATE: Zones 7a–7b
LOCATION: Annapolis, Maryland

William Paca, later the governor of Maryland from 1782 to 1785, was a young lawyer when, in 1776, he became one of the four signatories from Maryland to the Declaration of Independence. His house and garden date from 1763–65. Paca's garden, an oasis in the center of the historic town, is unique. It is Paca's only garden from this period that has been restored.

Bringing the garden back to life in the 1970s was a challenge because any evidence of the original garden had gone. To make matters worse, when the restoration team began work, they discovered that no archival records had survived. They were dependent on the results of an archaeological dig. One of the aims of the restoration was to use plants known to have been cultivated in Paca's day.

The garden is characterized by series of terraces linked by a central path, and stone steps. The upper terrace, with its view over the garden, was used as an entertaining space. The middle terrace has topiary and two large, geometric parterres whose beds are filled with period roses and seasonal plants. The lower garden area is not a formal terrace, but an informal, grassy area with serpentine paths and beds of native plants. The main feature of this area is the fish-shaped pool crossed by a small, white, picturesque bridge, and a two-story, white summerhouse. TM

RIGHT William Paca's lower garden with its fish-shaped pool, picturesque bridge, and two-story summerhouse.

Ladew Topiary Gardens

Maryland, U.S.

DESIGNER: Harvey Ladew
OWNER: Ladew Topiary Gardens Foundation
GARDEN STYLE: 20th-century topiary and "rooms"
SIZE: 22 acres (8.9 ha)
CLIMATE: Zone 7a
LOCATION: Monkton, Maryland

Harvey Ladew described life as "perfectly delightful," and so he should. This wealthy, well-educated linguist had a great time traveling and hunting all over the world. In 1929 he bought the aptly named Pleasant Valley Farm, and from 1937 until his death in 1967, he developed a passion for imaginative gardens. The most striking feature here is his topiarized hunt with fox, hounds, horse, and rider charging across the lawn.

The chief components at Ladew are the garden "rooms" separated by sweeps of lawn and views, a small woodland, a berry garden, a terrace, and portico gardens. There is also a croquet lawn, a pink garden, a rose garden, and the Great Bowl with a central pool. There's wit in the Garden of Eden, which casts away the notion that Eve tempted Adam—just peer through the keyhole and all will be revealed. Other notable features include the water lily and yellow gardens (and they are gloriously yellow) that have just been restored, the Temple of Venus, and the former facade of the Tivoli Theater ticket booth that has been converted into a teahouse. The sculpture garden has a topiarized version of Winston Churchill's top hat and "V for victory" sign, a heart with an arrow, riding cup, menagerie, and aviary. The iris garden contains no fewer than sixty-five varieties. Also look out for the Japanese bridge, the Buddha, the pagoda topiary, and a bright-red, metal Chinese junk in the lowest pool. During his glamorous life, Ladew played piano with Cole Porter, ate snails in bed with Colette, and rode with Clark Gable. The Ladew Topiary Gardens have the same wow factor. CH

Mount Cuba

Delaware, U.S.

DESIGNERS: Pamela Cunningham Copeland, Marian Coffin, Seth Kelsey

OWNER: Mt. Cuba Center, Inc.

GARDEN STYLE: 20th-century woodland and naturalistic

SIZE: 630 acres (255 ha)

CLIMATE: Zone 6b

LOCATION: Greenville, Delaware

As a child walking through Connecticut's woodlands, Pamela Cunningham Copeland became enchanted by native wildflowers. These early influences were a major factor when, in 1935, she and her husband, Lammot du Pont Copeland, purchased the rolling landscape that became Mount Cuba. Whether by luck or judgment, she also purchased land that sits on the Appalachian Piedmont, part of the Piedmont zone that extends from the Hudson River 1,000 miles (1,600 km) south to central Alabama. It is bordered to the west by the Blue Ridge and Appalachian mountains, and to the east by the fall line and coastal plain, and it has a rich and unusual ecology.

The Piedmont boasts more than 3,000 species, many of which are excellent garden plants, enabling Pamela (assisted by landscape architect Seth Kelsey) to create a wildflower garden from 1950. The result is a naturalistic garden that takes full advantage of the natural, wooded topography and merges seamlessly with it. A series of paths winds through the glades and groves, all filled with native trees, shrubs, and wildflowers. Opening and closing vistas create a constantly changing scene, enhanced by occasional views of the pool garden.

The Copelands wanted their country estate to be seen by the public, and they left it to be administered by Mt. Cuba Center, Inc., a nonprofit organization that manages the garden and is dedicated to research, education, and the display of plants native to the Piedmont. Yet the highlight of Mount Cuba remains the Copelands' legacy, one of the most spectacular displays of wildflowers in a garden anywhere in the eastern states. The show is wonderful in spring. TM

"...one of the most spectacular displays of wildflowers..."

Winterthur Garden

Delaware, U.S.

DESIGNERS: Various
OWNER: Winterthur Museum & Country Estate
GARDEN STYLE: 20th-century woodland and naturalistic
SIZE: 60 acres (24 ha) garden, 982 acres (397.4 ha) estate
CLIMATE: Zone 6b
LOCATION: Wilmington, Delaware

Henry Francis du Pont's passion for gardening started at an early age, and he became a perfectionist plantsman with exacting standards. Apparently a team of twenty gardeners was on call when houseguests stayed, ready to move flowering azaleas into spaces where color was flagging in this "natural" garden. Some 25,000 daffodil bulbs were planted in one season. Du Pont laid tree branches on the ground as a guide for "random" results—with everything labeled and previous plantings left undisturbed. Du Pont inherited Winterthur in 1928, developed the gardens, and filled the house with U.S. decorative arts.

A horticulturist rather than landscape designer, he left Winterthur's hills and meadows largely intact. He created a flowering understory beneath a woodland canopy, and was meticulous with color grouping, planting different azalea cultivars together and waiting years for them to hybridize. The 8-acre (3 ha) Azalea Woods with its white, pink, lavender, salmon, and red azaleas appears to be a natural garden, but is, in fact, a mixture of native and exotic plants in freeflow colonies.

Close to the house, landscape architect and lifelong friend Marian Coffin collaborated with Du Pont to design the Sundial Garden, Reflecting Pool, and Peony Garden, linking the transition from the house to the wider landscape with Italianate steps and terraces. Here borders are filled with plants adapted to the hot Delaware summers. Du Pont planted for form and texture first. He also made sure that Winterthur is in flower year-round. RChi

Nemours Gardens

Delaware, U.S.

DESIGNER: Alfred I. du Pont
OWNER: The Alfred I. du Pont Testamentary Trust
GARDEN STYLE: 20th-century woodland and formal
SIZE: 300 acres (121.5 ha)
CLIMATE: Zone 6b
LOCATION: Wilmington, Delaware

It is not just the name "Nemours" that deceives visitors into thinking they are in Europe instead of the Brandywine Valley. Alfred I. du Pont had a 102-room chateau built in 1909–10. The house and gardens were designed as a unit, and the 2-mile-long (3 km) central axis brings drama to the garden and was created in stages over the next twenty-five years.

Nemours unfolds along this great central axis, a sense of progression echoed by allées of tall trees, including pink-flowering horse chestnuts (*Aesculus hippocastanum*). They form a backdrop to grassy areas, with terraces linked by broad, stone steps. A 1-acre (0.4 ha) reflecting pool mirrors the entire vista when its 157 water jets are not playing.

Halfway along the central axis, Du Pont created an impressive colonnade as a memorial to his ancestors, who were among the first immigrants to the United States. There are marble walls, pools, sculptures of cherubs, mythical beasts, classical busts, and water bubbling and spouting away. A pair of graciously curved, outdoor stairs leads down into a quieter sunken garden, with boxwood parterres, sculpted heads, and gentler waterspouts.

Traveling on past a small pool and up a grassy bank, the central axis ends in a classical Temple of Venus with an eighteenth-century, life-size statue of Diana the Huntress. Closer to the house at Nemours, intricate boxwood parterres are filled with colorful annuals to be enjoyed from crisp, white gravel paths. Of all the famous Du Pont gardens, Nemours stands out with its baroque sense of theater. RChi

Gibraltar

Delaware, U.S.

DESIGNER: Marian Coffin
OWNER: Preservation Delaware, Inc.
GARDEN STYLE: 20th-century formal
SIZE: 6 acres (2.4 ha)
CLIMATE: Zone 6b
LOCATION: Wilmington, Delaware

Gibraltar (also known as Marian Coffin Gardens) takes its name from the high rocky ledge on which it stands. In 1909 Hugh and Isabella Sharp bought the estate and began major renovations to the fifty-year-old house. Creating a formal garden on this tricky site was the most important of their changes.

Hugh was a preservationist and amateur horticulturist. As a member of the Du Pont family, Isabella also had a strong enthusiasm for horticulture. In 1919 they engaged Marian Coffin, one of the foremost landscape architects of the day, to design their garden. She designed a series of "rooms," each with its own atmosphere contributing something different to the overall plan. Handcrafted iron gates, railings, balustrades, and a collection of statuary, urns, and fountains were all integrated.

A marble garden staircase connects three main terraces in a grand, curving sweep down from the house. The paved Flagstone Terrace offers a breathtaking view of the garden, the exotic planting behind the iron railings, and of evergreen shrubs offsetting limestone urns and lead statues in the middle level, the Evergreen Terrace. The lower terrace has a reflecting pool, where lilac and white wisterias fill the air in spring, followed by African lilies in summer. Elsewhere there are lawns and a flower garden. Wrought-iron gates mark the entrance to another enclosure where an unusual bald cypress (*Taxodium distichum*) allée makes an impressive 200-foot-long (60 m) approach to the Italianate garden pavilion, which has an elegant fountain. RChi

Desert Botanical Garden

Arizona, U.S.

DESIGNERS: Various
OWNER: Desert Botanical Garden
GARDEN STYLE: 20th-century desert plant collection
SIZE: 145 acres (59 ha) desert, 50 acres (20 ha) garden
CLIMATE: Zones 9a–9b
LOCATION: Phoenix, Arizona

Set against rocky red buttes at Papago Park, in the northern part of the Sonoran Desert, the Desert Botanical Garden (also known as the Phoenix Botanical Garden) has one of the world's largest outdoor collections of succulent plants. Established in 1939, the garden's mission is to conserve, educate, and research the range of plants found in the world's arid regions. The garden shows five different habitats, and their communities of plants and wildlife.

Various demonstration gardens are designed to show how you can garden in such harsh conditions. If that sounds horribly worthy, the plants liven things up with their strange shapes and whimsical, wonderfully descriptive common names, from cow's tongue and bunny ears to the boojum tree. Tall and hairy, they shed their leaves in summer to conserve water. The delicate red flowers of the Baja fairy duster are a magnet to hummingbirds.

This site was originally a settlement of the native Papago people, who lived for thousands of years in and around the Sonoran Desert, and several trails document their life in the desert. Over the centuries, they developed extensive knowledge of their arid homeland's plant species. Several hundred are edible, many have medicinal uses, and others can be used in all kinds of ways, including construction.

The dramatic vistas of distant mountains make a perfect backdrop to the fantastic shapes of the cacti. It is a rich, colorful, and beautiful landscape. Enjoy it from the network of paths and meandering trails, and relax on the shaded patios under the arborlike ramadas. Then sit down, relax, and gulp down delicious, prickly pear cactus juice. RChi

> "It is a rich, colorful, and beautiful landscape. Enjoy..."

Taliesin West

Arizona, U.S.

DESIGNER: Frank Lloyd Wright
OWNER: The Frank Lloyd Wright Foundation
GARDEN STYLE: 20th-century desert landscape
SIZE: 600 acres (242.8 ha)
CLIMATE: Zones 9a–9b
LOCATION: Scottsdale, Arizona

Taliesin West (also known as The Frank Lloyd Wright Foundation) was started in 1937 when Frank Lloyd Wright, one of the leading architects of the twentieth century, was aged seventy. The latter part of his life was incredibly productive, and he worked with students from his school of architecture until his death in 1959. Like its counterpart in Wisconsin (see page 42), it served as his home, studio, and a campus.

Wright's theories of organic design are embodied in this bold, original approach to desert living. The house is hunkered into a broad, flat rock overlooking 600 acres (243 ha) of Sonoran Desert. Huge sloping walls, made of materials from the site, emerge from the rugged landscape. The house's lines are angular; a triangular terrace juts out into the desert. The roof supports acres of heat-reflecting, white canvas.

The entrance is by a courtyard with a backdrop of colorful sculptures. Gardens ebb and flow around complex, sculptural buildings, and the movement is from one pool of light to another, with spaces linked by terraces and steps. Wright's studio faces a sunken garden with an angular pool, and the main room of the house is known as the Garden Room—it's a real outdoor room beneath a sloping roof, and the planting echoes the architecture and boulders.

"Our new desert camp belonged to the Arizona desert as though it had stood there during creation," Wright said. Taliesin West is as elemental as its creator intended. As the headquarters of The Frank Lloyd Wright Foundation, it remains a working community of architects and students. RChi

Tucson Botanical Gardens

Arizona, U.S.

DESIGNERS: Rutger Porter, Bernice Porter
OWNER: Tucson Botanical Gardens Board
GARDEN STYLE: 20th-century botanical
SIZE: 5.5 acres (2.2 ha)
CLIMATE: Zones 9a–9b
LOCATION: Tucson, Arizona

Like other public gardens that started their lives as private refuges, Tucson Botanical Gardens retains a real charm and warmth. Once a family garden out in open country, it is now part of the city. It is a welcome, rich resource, full of plant and design ideas waiting to be discovered on a stroll through meandering pathways that loop through the site.

Rutger and Bernice Porter lived here throughout their marriage from the early 1930s until Rutger's death in 1968. He was a nurseryman, but neither was native to the area, so their garden began as an experiment. The entrance, patio, and historical gardens around the house, now the visitor center, give glimpses of how the Porters created this richly varied oasis out of acres once filled with creosote bushes and mesquite trees. Practicalities came first: Shade the living spaces from the scorching summer heat, and then add color and interest for each season. At the start, mixtures of native and Mediterranean plants were used, and over time, an extended palette of plants sturdy enough to cope with the challenging Tucson climate was added.

They created sixteen individual gardens in different styles. There are five sensory patios shaded by traditional arbors, an attractive xeriscape garden requiring very little water, and a vivid space full of the flair of Tucson's Mexican-American gardens. About 11,000 gallons (40,000 l) of water are stored on the site for irrigation when needed. Unusual plants include a crested variant of the giant saguaro (*Carnegiea gigantea*). It's a favorite nesting spot for birds, with nests walled off from each other inside the body of the cactus, which is stacked like a skyscraper.

The grounds became the Tucson Botanical Gardens in 1974, having been bequeathed by Bernice Porter. Her vision was that they should be a place of beauty, inspiration, and education, and this has certainly been achieved. RChi

Tohono Chul Park

Arizona, U.S.

DESIGNERS: Richard Wilson, Jean Wilson
OWNER: Tucson Botanical Gardens Board
GARDEN STYLE: 20th-century desert preserve
SIZE: 49 acres (19.8 ha)
CLIMATE: Zones 9a–9b
LOCATION: Tucson, Arizona

An oasis in the northern region of the rapidly expanding city of Tucson, Tohono Chul Park is a vibrant, living museum of Sonoran Desert flora and fauna, art, and culture. Although much of the site remains a natural landscape of saguaro and cholla cacti, Tohono offers the visitor an authentic and beautiful experience of the link between the plants and people of the region.

Started by Richard and Jean Wilson as a preserve to protect a small part of the desert from encroaching development, the park now includes a great diversity of gardens and landscapes. An incredibly colorful display is found in the Hummingbird Garden, where salvia, desert honeysuckle, and desert willow attract all kinds of hummingbird to their tubular flowers. The influence of the early European settlers is reflected in the Spanish colonial garden next to the original, Santa Fe-style house built in 1937. Here the visitor can sit under the shade of desert ironwood trees, whose flowers resemble sweet peas.

Plants used for food, basket making, medicinal purposes, and cultural ceremonies by the Tohono O'odham people can be seen in the ethno-botanical garden. However, the forest of jumping cholla cactus is what everyone comes to see. The joints of the cactus separate easily, enabling them to "jump" to attack passersby. Back-lit by the sun, the cacti glow with a strange, otherworldly presence. The site is also a nesting place for the curve-billed thrashers and cactus wrens that are perfectly at home in the harsh environment. CW

Peckerwood Garden

Texas, U.S.

DESIGNERS: John Fairey, Carl Schoenfeld
OWNER: John Fairey
GARDEN STYLE: 20th-century native and naturalistic
SIZE: 19 acres (7.7 ha)
CLIMATE: Zone 8b
LOCATION: Hempstead, Texas

"A garden is a journey that seems to have neither a beginning nor an ending…" So said John Gaston Fairey, owner and creator of Peckerwood, professor of architecture, and renowned painter, on the unfolding of a very remarkable garden created over the last thirty years. About an hour's drive from Houston, Peckerwood is an oasis of horticulture amid the undulating farmland of southeast Texas. It is a unique place with rare native plants from the southern states and Mexico, many unknown in cultivation.

A gentle stream divides the property where, on one side, an ever expanding arboretum includes a wide range of trees, including maples, hollies, liquidambars, styrax, yews, and oaks. The oaks include the loquat-leaf oak (*Quercus rysophylla*) with its beautiful veined leaves 7–10 inches (18–25 cm) in length, and the *Quercus sartorii* that Fairey introduced after a trip to the El Cielo Biosphere Reserve.

Near the modern, galvanized-metal house and museum lies an enclosed garden with mounds of drought loving plants, such as agave, yucca, and dasylirion, offset by the soft pinks and whites of zephyranthes. To the side of the dry garden, a refreshing, rectangular pool runs under a terra-cotta-colored wall augmented by multihued, ceramic bamboo sculpted by the garden artist Marcia Donahue. As if a tour of the garden were not enough, part of Fairey's house is a museum of traditional and contemporary Mexican folk art, a fantastic addition to a fantastic garden. The adjacent Yucca Do Nursery sells an extraordinary range of wonderful plants. CW

Lady Bird Johnson Wildflower Center

Texas, U.S.

DESIGNERS: Various
OWNER: Lady Bird Johnson Wildflower Center
GARDEN STYLE: 20th-century native and naturalistic
SIZE: 279 acres (113 ha)
CLIMATE: Zone 8b
LOCATION: Austin, Texas

The Lady Bird Johnson Wildflower Center was set up in 1982 by Lady Bird Johnson, former First Lady, and the late Helen Hayes, the actress, to preserve North America's native plants and natural landscapes. With a mission to respect the natural beauty and biological heritage of each region, and a commitment to conserve and restore natural landscapes, the center is one of the foremost conservation, research, and education gardens in the United States.

There are a number of trails and exhibit gardens throughout the property. The Savanna Meadow Trail is an effervescence of spring color, featuring the Texas bluebonnet (*Lupinus texensis*), the symbol for the center. The Woodland Trail is lined with many common Hill Country species, including oaks and elms, and the John Barr Inner Loop is the perfect place to see the flora of the Hill Country.

The architecture of the buildings and support facilities reflects the wild look of the garden—the structures are constructed by using a range of recycled, native, or natural materials. This means that the buildings are energy efficient and have a low impact on the environment. Look carefully, though, and you'll note three styles: Spanish mission with graceful elegance, the neat and tidy architecture of the German settlers, and the corrugated-tin buildings of twentieth-century ranchers.

The garden is best seen in spring when the bluebonnets are at their finest. Texas Hill Country does get furnace hot in summer, and as they say, "It's hotter than whoopee in woolens." CW

Biltmore Estate

North Carolina, U.S.

DESIGNER: Frederick Law Olmsted
OWNER: William Amherst Vanderbilt Cecil
GARDEN STYLE: 19th-century formal and woodland
SIZE: Approximately 8,000 acres (3,238 ha)
CLIMATE: Zone 7a
LOCATION: Asheville, North Carolina

Biltmore House was built by George Washington Vanderbilt II between 1896 and 1902, and is still owned by the family. Modeled in French renaissance style, the 250-room castle is the largest private residence in the United States. Vanderbilt hired the founding father of U.S. landscape architecture, Frederick Law Olmsted, to design the grounds, which contain perfectly manicured pleasure gardens, a large arboretum, a nursery, and the first managed forest in the United States. Working with architect Richard Morris Hunt, Olmsted created an Italian Garden, an English Walled Garden, a Rose Garden, and an Azalea Garden with more than 1,000 plants.

The formal gardens surrounding the house are spectacular. The Italian Garden, enclosed by hedges and stone walls, is a delightful symmetry of space and water. The Walled Garden, originally designed as a kitchen garden, is now a display garden of colorful annuals and perennials with tens of thousands of bulbs planted annually. The Azalea Garden has one of the United States' largest collections of native and hybrid azaleas, and is a blast of color in spring and early summer. If you like roses, head straight for the 1-acre (0.4 ha) Rose Garden with its 265 varieties and more than 1,700 plants. And don't miss the house, the farm, and winery. CW

> "...the grounds contain perfectly
> manicured pleasure gardens..."

Atlanta Botanical Garden

Georgia, U.S.

DESIGNERS: Various
OWNER: Atlanta Botanical Garden, Inc.
GARDEN STYLE: 20th-century botanical and woodland
SIZE: 30 acres (12.2 ha)
CLIMATE: Zone 7b
LOCATION: Atlanta, Georgia

Atlanta is known as the city of trees, and its streets are lined with dogwoods and azaleas. The awesome outlines of its skyscrapers make a dramatic backdrop to this buzzing botanical garden. Founded in 1976 and constantly being upgraded, the main site has 15 acres (6 ha) of formal gardens. They range from the gaudy Children's Garden, complete with oversized model animals, to the Fuqua Orchid Center with its tropical, desert, and endangered species, and they provide a welcome respite from the extremes of Atlanta's climate. A favorite is the Conservation Garden, which has drifts of bog and acid loving native plants around a 60-foot-wide (18 m) water lily pond with sundews and carnivorous plants.

Traditionalists can amble under the climber-clad pergola and see roses that thrive in this climate. The Herb Garden is tended by the Chattahoochee Unit of the Herb Society of America. The Japanese Garden is approached by narrow paths and enclosed by white walls, and exudes tranquillity. Don't miss walking through the 5-acre (2 ha) Woodland Shade garden, which is at its best in spring, and includes many native trees and plants. In addition, there are 15 acres (6 ha) of old-growth forest, known as the Storza Woods, just 3 miles (5 km) away.

As you would expect, all the plants are well labeled. The gardens run a wide variety of programs for all ages and interests, including moonlit tours, the Dogwood Festival, Asian gardening, and shows to celebrate herbs, rhododendrons, hemerocallis, roses, and ponds. This garden is busy and fun. CH

Callaway Gardens

Georgia, U.S.

DESIGNERS: Cason Callaway, Virginia Callaway
OWNER: Ida Cason Callaway Foundation
GARDEN STYLE: 20th-century formal and naturalistic resort
SIZE: 13,000 acres (5,265 ha)
CLIMATE: Zone 7b
LOCATION: Pine Mountain, Georgia

Cason Jewell Callaway and Virginia Hollis Hand Callaway, twentieth-century founders of Callaway Gardens, built their weekend retreat home in 1930 on 2,500 acres (1,013 ha) of land along the shore of a 14-acre (6 ha) artificial lake. It was made possible by the Callaway family fortune, amassed by Cason's father, Fuller Earle Callaway, in the late 1890s, on the back of cotton mills, banks, real estate, and insurance. Over time, with other Callaway family members making their homes on adjacent parcels of land, the property has grown into an almost 13,000-acre (5,265 ha) site known as Callaway Gardens.

The best way to view the site is to follow the trails that connect to each of the themed gardens. One of the most popular is the Callaway Brothers Azalea Bowl, a 40-acre (16 ha) garden with more than 3,400 hybrid azaleas erupting each spring. Additional plantings, including 2,000 trees and shrubs, provide a canopy over a large pavilion and gazebo. The garden is laced with paths, a stream, and a quaint bridge.

One of the last major projects initiated by Cason J. Callaway before his death was Mr. Cason's Vegetable Garden, set on 8 acres (3 ha). The design includes areas for fruit, herbs, and flowers. And don't miss the John A. Sibley Horticultural Center, named in honor of a local Georgia banker, a 5-acre (2 ha) site with greenhouses and gardens full of native and exotic plants, a rock garden, sculpture garden, fern grotto, and 22-foot-high (7 m) indoor waterfall. And there's also an opportunity to explore the foothills of the Appalachian mountains. AH

Middleton Place

South Carolina, U.S.

DESIGNERS: Henry Middleton, John Julius Pringle Smith
OWNER: The Middleton Place Foundation
GARDEN STYLE: 18th- and 19th-century French landscaped
SIZE: 65 acres (26.3 ha)
CLIMATE: Zone 8b
LOCATION: Charleston, South Carolina

Above the Ashley River, a live oak estimated to be more than 1,000 years old was used as a trail marker by native Americans. In 1741 Henry Middleton took over the rice plantation here as part of his wife's dowry and began building a Jacobean-style house with the aid of an English landscape designer. It took ten years to complete the grounds, which were designed on a triangular grid with a central axis running through the house. In 1865 Union troops burned down the house. Its smaller replacement is completely out of scale, although the axis is quite evident, and the views are still magnificent.

The green lawn, edged with flower beds, sweeps downhill and is terminated by terraces stepping down to two butterfly-shaped lakes by the river. Following the curve of the Ashley River to the west, a series of formal areas can be explored, including the Rose Garden, Azalea Pool, and Camellia Avenue. In 1786 French plant hunter and nurseryman André Michaux brought in the first four *Camellia japonica* plants to be introduced to the United States. One survives, and today Middleton showcases camellias.

The gardens suffered during the Civil War, but in about 1870 William Middleton planted some of the United States' first *Azalea indica* plants. John Julius Pringle Smith and his wife, Heningham Ellett Smith, inherited the property in 1925 and restored the grounds. Middleton Place is now acknowledged as the oldest extant garden in the United States. To the east, the working buildings of the former plantation can be visited, and there is a great café. CH

Cà d'Zan Mansion and Gardens

Florida, U.S.

DESIGNERS: John Ringling, Mable Ringling
OWNER: State of Florida
GARDEN STYLE: 20th-century U.S. version of formal Italian
SIZE: 66 acres (26.7 ha)
CLIMATE: Zone 9b
LOCATION: Sarasota, Florida

Cà d'Zan, which means "House of John" in Venetian dialect, is a fantastic Venetian Gothic mansion on Sarasota Bay. It was built in 1926 as a winter residence for John and Mable Ringling, famous for their circus. This magnificent, terra-cotta, thirty-room palazzo sits on the shore of the Sarasota Bay, rising majestically at the end of a long drive lined with palms and banyan (*Ficus benghalensis*) trees. Inside there are all kinds of artifacts that chronicle the history of the circus. The mansion is part of the luxurious Ringling Estate, which also includes the John and Mable Ringling Museum of Art.

The estate's grounds are vast with plenty of paths, benches, and beautiful gardens. The Circus Museum's courtyard is arcaded on three sides by loggias filled with potted palms and other containers brimming with tropical delights. And the statues of Greek and Roman gods and goddesses add to the twentieth-century U.S. version of a formal Italian garden.

The main view from the loggia into the garden looks down a broad, central axis path terminating at a grand statue, with majestic palm trees and an enchanting curving exedra that leads visitors down the pathway. The attention to detail captures the flamboyant lifestyle of the Ringlings. Best of all is the Rose Garden, completed in 1913 and recently restored to include hundreds of hybrid and old Roses. The Secret Garden is close by, where you are captivated by the soft hues of the flowering plants and shrubs. Bring the children and top off a lesson in Italian lore with a dash of the circus. AH

Walt Disney World Resort

Florida, U.S.

DESIGNERS: Various, including Walt Disney
OWNER: The Walt Disney Company
GARDEN STYLE: 20th- and 21st-century theme park
SIZE: 4,000 acres (1,620 ha)
CLIMATE: Zone 9b
LOCATION: Lake Buena Vista, Florida

One doesn't often equate Walt Disney World Resort, also known as Disney World, with gardening, but this attraction is not just for the children. These gardens were inspired by the formal gardens of Europe, and Walt Disney's intent for his original Disneyland in California, from its very inception, was to include landscaping as an integral part of the park. Walt traveled to Europe several times in the 1940s and 1950s, bringing home notebooks filled with techniques, and at each of the Disney theme parks built during the next fifty years, floriculture and horticulture have been big features.

Walt Disney World Resort is one of the largest gardens in the world. More than 350 horticultural professionals tend the three million bedding plants and care for the 175,000 trees, four million shrubs, 13,000 rosebushes, and 800 hanging baskets. There are more than 200 pieces of topiary, with figures ranging from traditionally sculpted hedges to fanciful three-dimensional shapes, including a menagerie of Disney characters. The plants come from about fifty countries and every continent except Antarctica.

One of the best features is the Behind-The-Scenes Tour, letting you explore the horticultural facilities and tree farm that service the park. You'll see the topiary in various stages of completion, and get to question the gardeners. There is also a short walking tour of the experimental gardens and greenhouses. After that, see how the plants are used in the main show features: the Desert of Big Thunder Mountain Railroad, Typhoon Lagoon's Tropical Atmosphere, the Carriage Path on the Sassagoula River between Dixie Landings and Port Orleans, the Rose Walk between Journey into Imagination and the World Showcase, the jungles and savanna of Disney's Animal Kingdom, the parterre garden in front of the train station as you enter the Magic Kingdom, and the Cottage Garden in the United Kingdom Pavilion. AH

Edison and Ford Winter Estates

Florida, U.S.

DESIGNERS: Thomas Edison, Mina Edison
OWNER: City of Fort Myers
GARDEN STYLE: 20th-century tropical botanical
SIZE: 14 acres (5.7 ha)
CLIMATE: Zone 10a
LOCATION: Fort Myers, Florida

Thomas Edison came across Fort Myers in 1885 while searching for the perfect material for a lightbulb filament. Not only did he find the perfect bamboo filament on the shores of the Caloosahatchee River, but he also purchased a winter home where he built a laboratory so he could enjoy working vacations. In 1916 Henry Ford purchased his own home, Mangoes, next door to his best friend's Seminole Lodge.

Today these two properties form one of the most outstanding tropical botanical gardens in the United States, containing more than 1,000 varieties of plant from all over the world. The centerpiece is an 84-foot-tall (26 m) banyan tree (*Ficus benghalensis*), whose circumference makes it one of the largest banyans in the country. Given to Edison by Harvey Firestone and planted in 1925 as a single-trunk, 4-foot-tall (1 m) specimen, this champion tree now covers more than 1 acre (0.4 ha) with its many trunks and rooted tentacles. The tree has inconspicuous flowers that no one can see and is heavily laden with small, dark, inedible orange figs each year. The parent tree from India apparently covered almost 14 acres (6 ha)

Edison began his garden as a means of obtaining plant products and by-products to use in his scientific investigations. His wife, Mina, later enhanced the gardens with roses, orchids, and bromeliads. The property now includes nine National Historic Register buildings, the Botanical and Research Gardens, 14 acres (6 ha) of tropical botanical gardens, 500 unique plants, flowers, and trees, nine champion trees, and orchid and propagation greenhouses. AH

Fairchild Tropical Botanic Garden

Florida, U.S.

DESIGNER: William Lyman Phillips
OWNER: Fairchild Tropical Botanic Garden
GARDEN STYLE: 20th-century tropical botanical
SIZE: 83 acres (33.6 ha)
CLIMATE: Zone 10a
LOCATION: Coral Gables, Miami, Florida

The Fairchild Tropical Botanic Garden is the ultimate example of a modern botanical garden. It combines displays, horticulture, and extensive plant collections with research, conservation, and education. The garden lies on the edge of Biscayne Bay and, as might be expected with South Florida's large lakes nearby, water is a key element here.

The garden was established in 1938 by the botanist and plant hunter David Fairchild and Col. Robert H. Montgomery. Palms (a particular passion of Montgomery's) and tropical plants immediately took pride of place. More than 400 palm species are now planted, with collections in the Montgomery Palmetum and the Bailey Palm Glade that overlook the Glade and Royal Palm lakes. An internationally important collection of more than 3,700 cycads has also been recently developed.

The Fairchild Garden provides a fascinating introduction into the world of tropical plants. Besides the extensive scientific and conservation collections, it hosts a number of exhibits and displays. These include a large tropical conservatory (Windows to the Tropics), where orchids, aroids, and bromeliads are featured. The Richard H. Simons Rainforest maintains a collection of tropical species outdoors with the aid of overhead irrigation, and the McLamore Arboretum contains a collection of more than 700 tropical, flowering trees. Besides the arboretum, a 568-foot-long (173 m) Vine Pergola supports a large collection of tropical, flowering vines.

Conservation is an important aspect of the modern botanic garden, and in the far southeastern section, the Keys Coastal Habitat has a collection of South Florida native plants in a naturalistic garden setting that attract birds and other wildlife. A collection of the endangered species of Florida and Puerto Rico is featured in a garden adjacent to the Gate House Museum. CBa

Marie Selby Botanical Gardens

Florida, U.S.

DESIGNER: Marie Selby
OWNER: William and Marie Selby Foundation
GARDEN STYLE: 20th-century tropical botanical
SIZE: 13 acres (5.3 ha)
CLIMATE: Zone 10a
LOCATION: Sarasota, Florida

The Marie Selby Botanical Gardens have come to be some of the most important botanical institutions in the world. Providing a showcase for more than 20,000 plants, taken from 214 plant families, and including 6,000 orchids, the gardens are not only a botanical powerhouse, but a genuine pleasure to visit. If there is a specific emphasis in the garden, it is on three major families of the tropical and subtropical world, the Orchidaceae, Bromeliaceae, and Gesneriaceae.

The gardens are in the grounds of the former home of Marie and William Selby of the Texaco Company. In the early 1920s the Selbys built a Spanish-style house among the laurel and banyan trees. Landscaping of the site was planned by Marie. The gardens contain twenty distinct types of habitat, including long avenues of oaks, sweeps of cycads, and huge bamboo groves. Visitors to the gardens will also find an increasingly endangered mangrove swamp bordering the Sarasota Bay with almost 2,300 plants that were collected from their native habitats, representing 165 plant families and 1,200 species.

For those with more of an interest in botanical study, rather than just looking at plants, the gardens' herbarium contains in the region of 90,000 specialized collections of tropical flora, particularly the flora of Ecuador and the Andes. The Spirit Collection contains nearly 26,000 flowers preserved in fluids, making it the second-largest collection in the world. If you also mention the Bromeliad and Orchid Identification Centers, it is clear that the Marie Selby Botanical Gardens is an incredible botanical tour de force. CW

> "...the gardens' herbarium contains in the region of 90,000 specialized collections..."

Vizcaya Museum and Gardens

Florida, U.S.

DESIGNER: Diégo Suarez
OWNER: Miami-Dade County
GARDEN STYLE: 20th-century Italianate botanical
SIZE: 180 acres (72.9 ha)
CLIMATE: Zone 10a
LOCATION: Miami, Florida

In 1912 industrialist James Deering purchased land on Biscayne Bay, near Miami, and built on the marshy ground near the sea, rather than on the limestone ridge, in order to preserve its native hardwood hammock growth. The pilings and solid foundations have protected the house, as has the great stone barge that is used as a breakwater. A terrace curves around with a yacht landing at one end and an elegant French tea pavilion at the other. With family wealth from farm machinery, he traveled to Europe and met landscape architect, Columbian Diégo Suarez, in Italy. And that's why these gardens exude renaissance inspiration. Deering hired Suarez in 1914. By 1921 the gardens were completed, and Deering died four years later. In 1952, they were restored and opened.

The magnificent gateways on either side of the forecourt were brought from the Palazzo Bevilacqua-Lamassa in Verona. They are made from pink marble and Istrian stone, and are surmounted by sea horses, one of Deering's symbols for Vizcaya. The gardens were planned along a central axis in a fan shape, to be balanced by architectural and water features highlighted by clipped hedges, trees, and sculpted grass. Look out on the south terrace for the playful lead frogs and lizards, by Charles Cary Rumsey, all over the fountain basin, which is shaped like a sarcophagus. A dramatic vista then extends from the south terrace across the island pool, and up the water staircase and grottoes, whose shellwork is superb, to the casino (a loggia, or roofed gallery, not a gambling den). Look down on the gardens leaning on Samuel Yellin's ornate railings backed by tall columns supporting eighteenth-century busts in Carrara marble and seventeenth-century urns from Messina. Other sights not to miss include The Theater, Secret, and Fountain gardens, the Peacock Bridge, and the sumptuous house. CH

Europe boasts a vast array of garden design styles. From the formal and impeccably geometric gardens of the grand châteaux to the informal cottage gardens filled with native perennials, and from the landscape gardens of Capability Brown to today's eco-friendly wildflower gardens, Europe enjoys a wealth of indigenous traditions. Add to those, influences from China, Brazil, and the Islamic world, and the result is a cornucopia of styles.

EUROPE

Khutor Ghorka

Arkhangel'skaya Oblast', Russian Federation

DESIGNERS: Monks in the 19th century
OWNER: Solovetskiye State Museum Reserve
GARDEN STYLE: 19th-century sheltered hill and dell garden
SIZE: 34.5 acres (14 ha)
CLIMATE: Subarctic
LOCATION: Solovetskiye, Arkhangel'skaya Oblast'

On the edge of the Arctic Circle, in the middle of the Solovetskiye Islands in the Russian White Sea, is one of the finest and most sacred monasteries in Russia, established by the Old Believers in the fifteenth century. The islands were the first in the Soviet gulag (labor camp) archipelago, described by Alexander Solzhenitsyn, and became associated with suffering. In 1990 the monastery was reconsecrated, and the monks returned. The archipelago, a remarkable cultural landscape, is now a World Heritage Site. It is a landscape that has been tended and molded by man, and in turn has tempered and molded its inhabitants. The sheer isolation of Solovetskiye gives it an aura of remote, arctic purity. The islands are inaccessible by sea for more than half the year.

In 1822 Arkhimandrite Makarii built a small hermitage with a 35-acre (14 ha) garden sheltered between three hills beside a pair of lakes. The garden became known as Khutor Ghorka, meaning "Farm Hill," and provided the monks with precious fruit, vegetables, and candles. A place for seclusion, prayer, and cultivation, the garden has an extraordinary peace and tranquillity. From the hermitage, there is a view to the white stone walls and golden domes of the monastery, which can be reached by a network of sixteenth-century canals. The garden is now being restored by the owner, with help from the Prince of Wales International Business Leaders Forum and the Moscow botanist Artyom Parshin. KW

Oranienbaum

Leningradskaya Oblast', Russian Federation

DESIGNERS: Giovanni Mario Fontana, Gottfried Shadel, Antonio Rinaldi
OWNER: The Russian State
GARDEN STYLE: 18th- and 19th-century landscaped
SIZE: 410 acres (165.9 ha)
CLIMATE: Continental cool summer
LOCATION: Lomonosov, Leningradskaya Oblast'

Oranienbaum was first the country estate of Peter I the Great's good friend Prince Alexander Menshikov, on the Gulf of Finland, 25 miles (40 km) from the summer heat of the city. The impressive palace—Menshikov's estate was grander than Peter I's own at Peterhof—with terrace, grand parterre, fountains, and statues, all connected by a canal to the naval bases on the gulf, was well cared for until 1727, when Menshikov was exiled, bankrupt, two years after Peter I's death. The estate declined until it was given to the heir of Empress Elizabeth, who became Peter III, Catherine the Great's husband. Peter III built a new palace and small fortress town in the park.

After her 1762 coup and Peter III's death, Catherine had Antonio Rinaldi modernize the existing palaces, and build the exquisite Chinese Palace and the amazing Coasting Hill Pavilion. This gilded building with humps was 1,746 feet (162 m) long, but was torn down in the 1850s, though the three-story rococo pavilion, with whimsical Italian interior plasterwork, has been beautifully restored. Rinaldi flanked the three tracks with colonnades of 100 pillars and landscaped the gardens to either side. There are many outbuildings in various states of repair, and lovely walks through glades of Russian landscape, with winding paths through birches and firs and wildflowers, punctuated by classical statues and thrilling vistas. The restoration of the park has been slow, and it is now a lovely, quiet place. CN

Pavlovsk

Leningradskaya Oblast', Russian Federation

DESIGNERS: Empress Maria Fyodorovna, Charles Cameron, Vincenzo Brenna
OWNER: The Russian State
GARDEN STYLE: Late 18th-century classic
SIZE: 1,500 acres (607 ha)
CLIMATE: Continental cool summer
LOCATION: Pavlovsk, Leningradskaya Oblast'

Pavlovsk is acknowledged as one of the greatest achievements of landscape gardening in Russia, a romantic, small, classical palace in thousands of acres of sublime forest and meadows. Catherine the Great gifted the land to her son, Paul, and his Danish wife, Maria Fyodorovna, on the birth in 1777 of her first grandchild, Alexander. Catherine insisted that they use her favorite architect, Charles Cameron. Lavish attention and astronomical sums were spent on the estate, inspired by the young couple's 1782 European tour, and Maria's own gardening family. Maria was the most beloved and caring of the Romanovs, helping many charities, including the first horticultural school. She loved flowers, particularly roses, and had ornamental plants imported from the Royal Botanic Gardens at Kew and all over the world. Large areas of virgin forest were made picturesque by her succession of great designers, and many follies and monuments were built. The Rose Pavilion by Andrei Voronikhin celebrated the return of her son Alexander after the defeat of Napoleon I in 1814.

Maria left the estate to her third son so that it would be kept as a family museum, but in the nineteenth century it became a huge concert hall and the terminus of Russia's first railroad. Loyal retainers saved the palace and park for the people during Soviet times, but both the local residents and the estate itself suffered greatly in the Nazi era. CN

Peterhof

Leningradskaya Oblast', Russian Federation

DESIGNER: Jean-Baptiste Alexandre Le Blond
OWNER: The Russian State
GARDEN STYLE: 18th-century formal French
SIZE: 296.5 acres (120 ha)
CLIMATE: Continental cool summer
LOCATION: St. Petersburg, Leningradskaya Oblast'

The Emperor Peter the Great wanted the gardens at his summer residence to surpass the gardens at Versailles, and more than ten sketches of his ideas still exist. He employed several architects, but primarily Jean-Baptiste Alexandre Le Blond, a pupil of André Le Nôtre, to create his elegant extravagance and the world's greatest water garden. A gravity-fed water system, 14 miles (22 km) long, designed by Vastly Tuvolkov, powers more than 176 fountains, including those of the great cascade, which were turned on for the first time in the summer of 1721. The system was extended in the first half of the nineteenth century and supplies enough water to keep the fountains working for up to ten hours a day.

Water from basins in the upper park flows under the palace, down the beautifully proportioned marble steps of a double cascade populated by gilded gods, mythical figures, and fountains, and into a canal flowing into the Gulf of Finland. At the base of the cascade, a fountain of Samson vanquishing a lion spouts a jet of water 66 feet (20 m) into the air, a celebration of the Russian victory over Sweden on St. Sampson's day, 1709, which won the Russian Empire new access to Europe. The formal Lower Park, with allées, trick fountains, bridges, and palaces, echoes many aspects of the style of Versailles.

The fastest way for the visitor to reach Peterhof is by hydrofoil; the journey takes thirty minutes from the jetty outside the Hermitage Museum. Note that the fountains do not operate in winter, and the gilded statuary is best viewed on a sunny day. MB

> "…a fountain of Samson vanquishing a lion spouts a jet of water…into the air…"

Tsarskoe Selo

Leningradskaya Oblast', Russian Federation

DESIGNERS: Charles Cameron, and others
OWNER: The Russian State
GARDEN STYLE: 18th-century baroque and classical
SIZE: 741.3 acres (300 ha)
CLIMATE: Continental cool summer
LOCATION: St. Petersburg, Leningradskaya Oblast'

Tsarskoe Selo, meaning "Emperor's Village," is the location of the Catherine and Alexander Parks, created around two palaces. The first, the Catherine Palace, was built in 1752 by Rastrelli for Empress Elisabeth and named after her mother, Catherine I, who built a love nest for her husband, Peter the Great, on the site in about 1720. The palace was then extensively expanded by Catherine the Great's architect, Charles Cameron, and can only be described as awesome—Russian bombast before classicism toned down the excess. It included the famous Amber Room, formal gardens, the Agate Pavilion, Cameron Gallery, and a glazed, covered walkway reaching above the gardens. A Chinese village once housed courtiers. The farther reaches of the park were in the English style; indeed Catherine's gardener was John Busch, a Scot. The many monumental pavilions and follies amid the lakes and streams were all open to a well-dressed public (including the young Alexander Pushkin).

The Alexander Palace, nearby, was built for Catherine's dear grandson Alexander I, on his marriage, and was also occupied rather modestly by the families of Nicholas I, Alexander III, and the last emperor, Nicholas II, just before they were killed in the Revolution. This Palladian building has pools on three sides and winding walks, laid out by another Scot, Adam Menelaws, with statues, pavilions, and outbuildings, including an elephant house and a chapel built as a ruin. The Catherine and Alexander Palaces and Parks were devastated by the Nazis, but have been restored with gilt and pomp. CN

> "…statues, pavilions, and outbuildings, including an elephant house…"

Gatchina

Leningradskaya Oblast', Russian Federation

DESIGNERS: Antonio Rinaldi, John Busch, Paul I
OWNER: The Russian State
GARDEN STYLE: 18th-century, 19th-century picturesque
SIZE: 1,729.7 acres (700 ha)
CLIMATE: Continental cool summer
LOCATION: St. Petersburg, Leningradskaya Oblast'

Gatchina is most often linked to Emperor Paul I, the militarily obsessed son of Catherine the Great. In his more carefree youth, Paul and his young wife, Maria Fyodorovna, made a grand tour of Europe, spending delightful months with the equally young Louis XVI and Marie Antoinette at Versailles in 1782.

Paul was given Gatchina by his mother after the death of its former owner, her lover, Grigory Orlov, who had it from 1765 to 1783. Orlov had improved the palace of Peter the Great's sister, Natalya, and developed the hunting park with the architect Antonio Rinaldi and two Scottish gardeners, the

brothers Sparrow. It became Paul's favorite residence, being fortresslike with parade grounds and cannon, whereas his wife preferred romantic Pavlosk.

Today you will see a wooded English landscape park and languid lakes with pavilions, all especially wonderful in the fall. It is a very large estate with pools and streams, though no fountains, with lovely bridges and architectural features. Paul built a replica of the French Priory Palace for his exiled friend, the Prince of Condé. The Temple of Venus, on a little islet, was inspired by the one at Chantilly.

The most extraordinary pavilion is the Little Birch House, which appears to be a large, square pile of birch logs in the woods. An inconspicuous door opens to a room of mirrors, garlanded with flowers under a painted ceiling, with breathtakingly exquisite luxury, a gift to Paul from his wife. The couple were quite competitive with their gardens, creating ever better effects. CN

Imperskijj Botanicheskiy Sad

Leningradskaya Oblast', Russian Federation

DESIGNER: Friedrich Ernst Ludwig von Fischer
OWNER: Komarov Botanical Institute
GARDEN STYLE: 19th-century botanical
SIZE: 22 acres (8.9 ha)
CLIMATE: Continental cool summer
LOCATION: St. Petersburg, Leningradskaya Oblast'
TRANSLATION: Imperial Botanical Garden

The Imperial Botanical Garden is now part of the Komarov Botanical Institute of the Russian Academy of Sciences, a world-class laboratory. Situated on Aptekarsky (Apothecary) Island on the west side of the River Neva delta, it was created by Peter the Great in 1714. Many exotic seeds and plants were brought in, and a greenhouse was soon constructed.

Friedrich Ernst Ludwig von Fischer was appointed director in 1826 at the bequest of Dowager Empress Maria Fyodorovna, and he oversaw the garden's greatest expansion until 1850. In the 1830s thousands of plants were imported from Rio de Janeiro, where there was a branch of the garden. The Palm House was erected in 1899, and an adjoining pavilion houses the giant water lily (*Victoria amazonica*). By 1917 there were 5,000 species in the open ground, another 26,000 under glass, and two million dried specimens in the herbarium.

The garden is now laid in the English landscape style with plants that can take the harsh climate. It is a wonderful place to wander amid the majestic trees, with greenhouse collections from the Caucasus, the Mediterranean, and Asia, including orchids, ferns, palms, and water lilies. The pride of the garden is the famous night-flowering Cereus cactus (*Selenicereus pteranthus*). Its large, fragrant, creamy white flowers bloom only once a year, in May. CN

Letniy Sad

Leningradskaya Oblast', Russian Federation

DESIGNER: Jean-Baptiste Alexandre Le Blond
OWNER: The Russian State
GARDEN STYLE: 18th-century Dutch baroque
SIZE: 27 acres (10.9 ha)
CLIMATE: Continental cool summer
LOCATION: St. Petersburg, Leningradskaya Oblast'
TRANSLATION: The Summer Garden

Peter the Great does not come to mind as a garden enthusiast, but he aspired to be another Sun King. His new city, St. Petersburg, was founded in 1703, and work began on the Summer Garden the next year, partly inspired by his visit to Het Loo on his first foreign trip. After visiting Versailles in 1715, he brought in André Le Nôtre's assistant, Jean-Baptiste Alexandre Le Blond, to help with the plans. His modern garden had hundreds of allegorical statues, arbors, grottoes, aviaries, menagerie cages, and fountains, all with the intention of introducing Russians to Western art. Explanations were posted, and sometimes given by Peter himself.

Shady, formal gravel walks between mature trees are still punctuated and lined with statues. Situated on the River Neva, east of where the Winter Palace and Hermitage buildings later went up, Peter's own small Summer Palace (by Domenico Trezzini) is in the far corner. The great iron railings by Georg Friedrich Veldten were erected between 1770 and 1784, the Coffee House and the Tea House were added in the 1820s, and the well-loved monument to Ivan Krylov was erected in 1855. After the garden was opened to well-dressed common folk by Nicholas I, the Whit Sunday Marriage Fair took place in the central allée, where the prospective partners and their families could make contact, view, and then haggle. CN

Elaginskii Dvorets

Leningradskaya Oblast', Russian Federation

DESIGNERS: Joseph Busch, Carlo Rossi
OWNER: The Russian State
GARDEN STYLE: 19th-century landscaped
SIZE: 237.2 acres (96 ha)
CLIMATE: Continental cool summer
LOCATION: Yelagin Island, Leningradskaya Oblast'
TRANSLATION: Yelagin Palace

Yelagin Island has long been St. Petersburg's most beautiful pleasure ground. A villa belonging to an imperial court official was here in the time of Peter the Great. In Catherine the Great's day, it was known for the splendid parties of General A. P. Melgunov, director of the Military School. The next owner was secretary and theatrical adviser to Catherine, Ivan Yelagin, who further embellished the island and even kept a Turkish dance band for his fireworks parties. In winter people were welcome to walk in the heated Winter Garden, 180 feet (33 m) long.

Alexander I bought the established house and extensive gardens for his elderly mother, Maria Fyodorovna, in 1817. Carlo Rossi rebuilt the small classical palace "of utmost refinement," and many handsome outbuildings and pavilions, while Joseph Busch, son of Catherine the Great's gardener, did extensive landscaping. The existing streams were made picturesque, thousands of trees were planted, and serpentine lakes and pleasant clearings were linked by long, winding walks. Alexander was so pleased with the work of Rossi that he gave him many more commissions, including the Mikhailovsky Palace (home of the Russian Museum) and the great General Staff Building opposite the Winter Palace.

In the 1930s the Soviets further popularized the island as a People's Park, with concrete and piped music, and slot machines in the Orangery. Now there is no through traffic, access is by a footbridge, and, at least on weekdays, it is wonderfully quiet again. CN

Gorkyi Park

Moskovskaya Oblast', Russian Federation

DESIGNER: Moisei Ginzburg
OWNER: City of Moscow
GARDEN STYLE: 20th-century amusement park with ice-skating network
SIZE: 300 acres (121.5 ha)
CLIMATE: Continental cool summer
LOCATION: Moscow, Moskovskaya Oblast'
TRANSLATION: Gorky Park

Opened in 1928 as the first Park of Culture and Rest in the Soviet Union, and named after the revolutionary writer Maxim Gorky, this sprawling curiosity began life as a comradely amalgamation of Moscow's Golitsyn Hospital gardens with those of the Nezkuchny Palace. It has since become better known thanks to Martin Cruz Smith's eponymous Cold War thriller, published in 1981, which begins with the discovery of three bodies here, their faces and fingerprints cut away to conceal their identities. Then the power ballad "Wind of Change" by the German rock band Scorpions became an international hit in the politically charged 1990s: "I follow the Moskva / Down to Gorky Park / Listening to the wind of change..."

The reality is very different. Gorky Park is a great place for families with children, young couples, and tourists. The park's less-than-perfect layout; inconsistent planting—one year being beautiful, the next puzzling; seedy, wooded areas; and fairground rides past their use-by date have terrific charm. There are also fine panoramic views from the dangling cages of the Ferris wheel, a genuine old spaceship for children to clamber over, and the monumental ice sculpture festival held each February. In the depths of winter, the lakes freeze over and pathways are deliberately flooded to create a wonderful icy network for skaters. At the height of summer, you can hire rowing boats by the hour. WdP

Aptekarsky Ogarod

Moskovskaya Oblast', Russian Federation

DESIGNERS: Peter the Great, Catherine the Great, Artyom Parshin, Kim Wilkie
OWNER: Moscow State University
GARDEN STYLE: 18th- and 19th-century botanical
SIZE: 24.7 acres (10 ha)
CLIMATE: Continental cool summer
LOCATION: Moscow, Moskovskaya Oblast'
TRANSLATION: The Old Apothecary's Garden

This garden, in the center of Moscow, has survived wars, fires, and revolutions. It was established by Peter the Great in 1706, when he returned from his tours around western Europe, enthusing about the cultivation of herbs and medicines and new scientific practices. In the 1850s the medicinal planting was replaced by romantic, curving walks and a lake, but the garden kept its scientific discipline and botanical role right through the Soviet period to its restoration at the end of the twentieth century.

Today the garden is still enclosed by great lime avenues, and an old larch is thought to date from Peter the Great's time. The restoration of the garden has been careful to retain the Chekhovian character of the lake and serpentine walks, but a fresh layer of design has been added to the adjacent areas. A new reflecting pool leads up to the restored nineteenth-century greenhouse, and there are plans to create fresh beds on the wasteland beside the original garden. The modern beds are going to be laid out on a three-dimensional, warped grid, designed by Kim Wilkie and supervised by the Moscow botanist and designer Artyom Parshin.

The garden is a popular urban park, even in the depths of winter. Long hot summer days at this latitude create brilliant herbaceous displays among the ancient trees, and the new greenhouses hold a rare botanical collection for winter interest. KW

Kuskovo

Moskovskaya Oblast', Russian Federation

DESIGNERS: Feodor Argunov, Aleksey Mironov, Grigory Dikushin
OWNER: The Russian State
GARDEN STYLE: 18th-century baroque garden, landscaped park
SIZE: 741 acres (300 ha)
CLIMATE: Continental cool summer
LOCATION: Moscow, Moskovskaya Oblast'

The estate of Kuskovo became the State Museum of Ceramics in 1938, and the substantial orangery complementing this wooden, pink-stuccoed palace now houses a world-class collection featuring Italian majolica, Venetian and English glassware, Meissen and Sèvres porcelain, Oriental antiquities, and some Imperial and Soviet masterpieces.

Kuskovo's rise to glory began in 1715 when Field Marshal Count Boris Sheremetev, hero of the Battle of Poltava, bought the estate from his younger brother. Four years later, his son, Peter Borisovich, inherited it. Marriage in 1743 to the Princess Cherkasskaya led to the initiation of a monumental program of works, guided by two serf architects, Fyodor Argunov and Alexei Mironov, who were part of the bride's dowry.

The garden's radiating ground plan is very elegant, but buildings were required as retreats from the climate, and this is where Kuskovo excels. Beneath its prominent dome with wrought-iron gates and windows, the elegant grotto features shellwork and plaster in yellow, white, and green. The Italian Cottage is a miniature palace in its own right, and the red-brick Dutch house with its blue-tiled interior conveys an idealized vision of life in the Netherlands. When visiting, be sure to note the curious mechanism that granted privacy from servants at intimate dinner parties. WdP

Moskva Botanicheskiy Sad

Moskovskaya Oblast', Russian Federation

DESIGNERS: Various

OWNER: Russian Academy of Sciences

GARDEN STYLE: 20th-century botanical garden, naturalistic, and arboretum

SIZE: 890 acres (360.4 ha)

CLIMATE: Continental cool summer

LOCATION: Moscow, Moskovskaya Oblast'

Founded in 1945, Moscow's Main Botanical Garden, among the world's largest and most impressive, is in the Ostankino Forest Park on the northern outskirts of the city. Coordinating more than 100 satellite gardens, ranging from the polar-alpine arboretum outside Kirovsk to the apple collection at Alma-Ata in Kazakhstan, this is a leading center for botanical, horticultural, and agricultural research. Plants of commercial interest are particularly well represented, and there are more than 2,000 species, forms, and cultivars of plants bearing fruit and berries. Trees are

of special interest: there is a 125-acre (50 ha) forest that is left more or less untouched to regenerate naturally. The more parklike Dendrarium is almost twice that size and is planted with some 4,000 trees, shrubs, and climbers, including beautiful Japanese maples, lilacs, and honeysuckles.

A huge area with landscaped terrain representing different regions of the former Soviet Union, the garden is a fascinating display of the diverse native flora of European Russia, the Caucasus, Asia, the Far East, and Siberia. Formal areas display a vast range of garden ornamentals as well as herbal, aromatic, and medicinal plants, while assorted greenhouses hold around 5,000 tropical and subtropical species.

The scale of the garden is so vast, and the collections so extensive, it cannot be appreciated in one day. Head straight for the rose gardens, the Japanese garden, and the hothouses before taking in the bigger picture at a more leisurely pace. WdP

Mon Repos

Leningradskaya Oblast', Russian Federation

DESIGNER: Baron Ludwig von Nicolay
OWNER: The Russian State
GARDEN STYLE: 18th- and 19th-century landscape
SIZE: 440 acres (180 ha)
CLIMATE: Continental cool summer
LOCATION: Linnassaari, nr Vyborg, Leningrad region

Mon Repos lies on the rocky and pretty 2.5-mile-long (4 km) island of Linnassaari near Vyborg, which is joined to the mainland by a bridge and characterized by Wiborgite granite and glacial formations, some up to 65.6 feet (20 m) high. Before Baron Ludwig Von Nicolay, Prince Friedrich of Wurttemberg had already set out paths, built an orangery and pavilions and planted trees. Von Nicolay already had experience of developing parks and gardens—he was involved in the creation of Gatchina and Pavlovsk parks—and Mon Repos became his life's work.

Dams were built to keep out the sea, more trees—limes, oaks, and birch—were planted, statues were erected, a viewing platform was constructed, and a hermit's hut installed among the many garden features. There were fruit and vegetable gardens, a formal flower garden, borders of shrubs, and arches for climbing plants.

While the park remained intact and in good condition into the 20th century, it began to decline toward the end of the Second World War, when it was used as a military rest home and suffered from vandalism and pillaging. Today, it is widely recognized and admired as an important historical landscape. There are over 50 species of indigenous plants, some of them rare, as well as numerous animals and birds. There has been restoration on features such as the Tea Arbour and Neptune's temple, while the 80,000 visitors a year are carefully managed to preserve the fabric of this precious place. RSJ

Marfino

Moskovskaya Oblast', Russian Federation

DESIGNERS: Pyotr Saltykov, Nikita Panin, Mikhail Bykovsky
OWNER: The Russian State
GARDEN STYLE: 19th-century formal garden and park
SIZE: Approximately 500 acres (202 ha)
CLIMATE: Continental cool summer
LOCATION: Marfino, Moskovskaya Oblast'

Marfino Palace, some 25 miles (40 km) north of Moscow, was built to resemble the kind of idealized medieval castle found only in picture books or immortalized in verse. The term "Gothic" is often taken to mean dark and sinister, but this sugary pink and white confection, completed in 1846, tells quite a different story. Terraces lead down toward a lake, where two gigantic griffins with upstretched wings flank the landing stage. The palace and its reflection, when viewed from the distant shore, are quite beautiful and magical.

Despite sitting so well in the watery and wooded landscape, the present Marfino Palace is a relatively new addition to this historic estate, its earlier baroque incarnation having been ransacked by French troops during the Napoleonic invasion of 1812. Luckily, most other structures within the landscaped grounds survived the onslaught more or less intact. Look out for two churches, the impressive kennels, and the coach house in the classical style, while the demi-lune music pavilion, with Tuscan columns supporting a semicupola, is a bravura exercise in simplicity. The more dramatic, but arguably less refined, Milovid, a two-tiered rotunda overlooking the lake, has a heavy-weight octagonal base surmounted by slender columns supporting a dome that shelters a statue of Apollo.

There is a touching poignancy here, a feeling not so much of neglect, but of times having moved on, leaving this extraordinary place behind. WdP

Vigelandsparken

Oslo, Norway

DESIGNER: Gustav Vigeland
OWNER: City of Oslo
GARDEN STYLE: 20th-century neoclassical
SIZE: 79 acres (31.9 ha)
CLIMATE: Temperate
LOCATION: Frogner, Oslo, Oslo Akershus
TRANSLATION: Vigeland Sculpture Park

Vigeland Sculpture Park is also known as Frogner Park. Its geometric layout, with its central axis, expansive lawns, and extensive avenues, is based on baroque garden design. Its style, though, belongs to the neoclassicism of the 1920s.

The park contains more than 600 sculptures by Gustav Vigeland, full-size nude figures portraying universal human emotions and relationships. The earliest sculpture is *The Fountain* with its six giants, which is encircled by twenty trees sculpted in bronze with human figures bound up in their sinuous branches. On the bridge across the ponds, figures of men, women, and children represent life's cycle of renewal and decay. At the park's highest point stands *The Monolith*, a 46-foot-high (14 m) column of tangled bodies surrounded by figures representing life from birth to death. The last sculpture on the park's main axis is *The Wheel of Life* (1933–34); bordered by beds of red and white annuals in summer, seven linked figures appear to rotate in a symbol of eternity.

The park is especially beautiful in winter, when the lawns and flower beds have a mantle of white and vistas are terminated by leafless trees. Come summer, colorful maples line the avenues, and yellow and scarlet shrub roses make blocks of strident color. EH

> "The earliest sculpture is
> *The Fountain* with...six giants..."

Villa Mairea

Länsi-Suomi, Finland

DESIGNER: Alvar Aalto
OWNERS: The Aalto family
GARDEN STYLE: 20th-century modern
SIZE: 1.5 acres (0.6 ha)
CLIMATE: Temperate
LOCATION: Noormarkku, Pori, Satakunta, Länsi-Suomi

One of the landmark houses of the twentieth century, Villa Mairea was designed during 1937–39 by the Finnish architect and designer Alvar Aalto. He loved native villages, which he described as having "grown directly out of natural conditions…forest architecture pure and simple." The house is set in a clearing in a pine forest, the trees making a fourth wall for the building and enclosing the garden. Aalto lived in Japan for a year prior to creating Villa Mairea. He admired the Japanese relationship with nature, their respect for the landscape in garden making, and their use of indigenous materials. The canopy has

a turf roof supported by treelike pillars, and a green roof is repeated on the sauna building. There is also a rough-stone fireplace spanning the link between the canopy and the smooth, concrete house walls. In addition, a naturalistic mound, rustic fence, and gate define the boundary between the garden and forest beyond. Note that the swimming pool is a soft, free-form shape surrounded by lawn and plants. Also note how a timber deck anchors the wood-walled sauna to the ground, part of it cantilevered over the pool as a diving board for swift, cold plunges.

Aalto was a highly successful and influential designer. Curvilinear lines were used in his furniture, buildings, and their surrounding gardens. Thomas Church, the American landscape architect, visited him in 1937 and was influenced by this fluidity. Aalto's garden legacy at Villa Mairea retains a timeless quality—simple, sleek, and modern, but warmed by traditional vernacular touches. RChi

Botaniska Trädgården

Uppsala, Sweden

DESIGNERS: Carl Hårlemann, Carl Peter Thunberg
OWNER: University of Uppsala
GARDEN STYLE: 18th-century botanic garden
SIZE: 34 acres (13.7 ha)
CLIMATE: Temperate
LOCATION: Uppsala, Uppsala
TRANSLATION: Botanic Garden

This garden's history is intertwined with that of Carl Linnaeus' Botanic Garden in Uppsala (see page 154). The original botanic garden was founded in 1655 and located in the middle of the town of Uppsala close to the River Fyrisån, on the site of what is now Linnaeus' garden. This garden, redeveloped by Linnaeus in the 1740s, has now been restored to his original design.

By the 1780s, the original garden, within the town, had become too small for the ever-expanding plant collection that Linnaeus' reputation continued to draw to Uppsala. Moreover, it was decided that the damp conditions, so close to the river, were not ideal for cultivation. So in 1787 (a year before Linnaeus' death), his former student and successor, Carl Peter Thunberg, persuaded King Gustaf III to give the garden at Uppsala Castle to the university, which he then proceeded to develop into a new botanic garden. The garden that Thunberg acquired had been laid out in the 1750s in the baroque style by the architect Carl Hårlemann and the new garden was officially opened on the centenary of Linnaeus' birth in 1807. Linnaeus' posthumous reputation ensured that the collection of plants at Uppsala continued to grow, while donations from the king financed the building of the new Linneanum to house the orangery.

At present there are over 11,000 taxa grown in a wide range of different habitats. There are collections of economic crops, shows of annuals, collections of troughs, xeriscapes, rockscapes, peat beds, and a tropical greenhouse with 4,000 tender taxa. TM

Linnéträdgården

Uppsala, Sweden

DESIGNERS: Carl Linnaeus, Olof Rudbeck, Carl Hårleman
OWNER: University of Uppsala
GARDEN STYLE: 17th-, 18th-, 19th-century botanic garden
SIZE: 2.5 acres (1 ha)
CLIMATE: Temperate
LOCATION: Uppsala, Uppsala
TRANSLATION: Carl Linnaeus' Botanic Garden

Located close to the River Fyrisån in Uppsala, the Linnaeus Garden is on the site of the original Uppsala University Botanical Garden. It shows how the original garden looked in the mid-eighteenth century.

Uppsala Botanic Garden—now in the grounds of Uppsala Castle (see page 152)—was originally founded here in 1655 by Professor of Medicine, Olof Rudbeck the Elder. It was primarily used to educate medical students in the art of pharmacology. By the end of the seventeenth century, it had a collection of over 1,000 species, many of which were cultivated here for the first time in Sweden. However, in 1702, a great fire destroyed much of the garden. The university was unwilling to fund its recreation, and it fell into decline for forty years. When, in 1741, Carl Linnaeus was appointed professor of medicine, he proceeded to restore it.

The garden became one of the finest in Europe primarily because of Linnaeus' zeal. His ever-rising reputation ensured a constant influx of new plants. The plants were crucial to his role both as an educator and a researcher. The latter particularly focused on his new classification system using Latin names and his interest in phenology. Following the move of the botanic garden to its new, and current, site in 1807, the old garden fell into a second period of neglect. This time it lasted for over a century until, in 1917, the Swedish Linnaeus Society began reconstructing Linnaeus´ garden. The society is still responsible for maintenance of the garden's museum. TM

Enköpings Parker

Uppsala, Sweden

DESIGNERS: Various
OWNER: The Enköping Park Office
GARDEN STYLE: Eclectic garden designs
SIZE: Various
CLIMATE: Temperate
LOCATION: Enköping, Uppsala
TRANSLATION: Enköping Parks

Enköping, a small town situated close to Lake Mälaren, is the most central in Sweden and also home to a remarkable series of seventeen public green spaces or small garden parks. Their ambience and style are as varied as their shapes, forms, and plantings. The seventeen attractions are: Afzelius Place, Blomberg's Park, Blue Garden, Dream Park, Fish Market Square, Fridegård's Park, Gustaf Adolf's Place, House of Westerlund, Kaplanen, Kölnback's Park, Monastery Park, Munksund Well, Pastor Spak's Park, Rosendal Pocket Park, Rådhusgården, School Park,

and the Travel Center. The gardens are varied in the features they offer to the visitor; unfortunately, there is not space here to go into detail about all of them.

Created at the end of the nineteenth century, Afzelius Place (named after a vicar called Arvid August Afzelius) is the oldest and most popular park. The focal point is the Johanna Fountain, which is characteristic of its time. It has a formal layout of parterres filled with bedding in the summer, lawns, and neat pathways. In the Monastery Park, the remains of the fourteenth-century Franciscan cloister building can still be seen. In contrast, the Dream Park (1966), designed by Piet Oudolf, features 220 different types of perennial plant. It is typical of Oudolf's style, being filled with subtle color compositions that contrast with the strong forms of the plants. Particularly effective are the "streams" of three types of blue *Salvia nemorosa* that contrast with the architectural beech hedges. TM

Drottningholms Slott

Island of Lovön, Stockholm, Sweden

DESIGNER: Nicodemus Tessin
OWNER: The Royal Court of Sweden
GARDEN STYLE: Baroque, English landscape
SIZE: 25 acres (10 ha)
CLIMATE: Temperate
LOCATION: Island of Lovön, Stockholm
TRANSLATION: Drottningholm Palace

Built on the island of Lovön, overlooking Lake Mälaren, the magnificent Drottningholm Palace is the residence of the Swedish royal family. Now a UNESCO World Heritage Site, it is Sweden's best-preserved, seventeenth-century royal castle. It was commissioned in the baroque style by Queen Hedvig Eleonora and designed by Nicodemus Tessin the Elder (possibly under the supervision of André Le Nôtre).

By the beginning of the nineteenth century, the parterres had been lost; they were restored 150 years later by King Gustaf VI Adolf in the 1950s and 1960s.

Today, the parterre de broderie is a simplified version of the original. Clipped box hedges and a large lawn have replaced the intricate embroidery pattern of box hedges and colored gravel. However, the bronze statues by Adriaen de Vries, including the centerpiece Hercules, are the original ones looted as trophies of war from Prague and Denmark.

Out in the park, the Chinese Pavilion was built in 1753 as a birthday present for Queen Louisa Ulrika. She had the building's architect, Carl Fredrik Adelkrantz, add tree groves and avenues to create a natural, romantic setting. Within the groves were aviaries (only one altered example of which remains), and beyond was a menagerie, though only the pool survives. A quarter of a century later, in 1780, Gustav III had Fredrik Magnus Piper create a new English landscape garden. To the north of the baroque garden, it features lawns, groves, tree avenues, and two ponds with canals, islets, and bridges. TM

Millesgården

Island of Lindingö, Stockholm, Sweden

DESIGNERS: Carl Milles, Evert Milles
OWNER: Carl and Olga Milles Lidingöhem Foundation
GARDEN STYLE: 20th-century sculpture garden
SIZE: 4.7 acres (2 ha)
CLIMATE: Temperate
LOCATION: Island of Lindingö, Stockholm

> "It features a mix of terraces, stairways, plants, vistas ... "

In 1906, the sculptor Carl Milles bought a plot of land on the cliff of Herserud high above Lake Värtan on the island of Lidingö. Two years later a house and studios were built. Carl and his artist wife, Olga, lived there until 1931. In 1936, the couple established their Lidingöhem Foundation, and toward the end of the decade the garden they created, called the Millesgården, was opened to the public.

The garden was a collaboration between Carl and his architect half-brother, Evert. It features a mix of terraces, stairways, plants, vistas, and Carl's sculptures, although most are duplicates. On the upper terrace is a marble portal that once belonged to the Hotel Rydberg in Stockholm, and a massive sandstone column from the eighteenth-century Stockholm Opera House capped with Milles' *The Wings* (1908).

Milles was deeply inspired by the gardens on Italy's Mediterranean coast. This is clear in the first phase of construction during 1911–13. The loggia was intended as an open-air studio to ease the symptoms of silicosis that Carl developed as a result of inhaling dust while carving stone. In the 1920s adjacent properties were purchased, and both the middle terrace and little studio (complete with Italian-inspired frescoes) were constructed. Little Austria was built in 1924. Here, within the naturally rugged hollow, Carl made a picturesque and sculptural landscape to remind his wife of her homeland. Below Little Austria is Olga's terrace with the Aganippe Fountain (1955). On the middle terrace is the *Sun Singer* on its high square base of granite.

From 1931 to 1950 Carl taught in the United States and garden developments stopped. However, Evert kept developing plans to implement upon their return. In 1950 the expansive lower terrace was created and became home to the three large fountain sculptures, *Poseidon*, *Europa*, and *Jonah and the Whale*. Carl died in 1955. TM

Hagaparken

Stockholm, Sweden

DESIGNER: Fredrik Magnus Piper
OWNER: Stockholm City Council
GARDEN STYLE: 18th- and 19th-century romantic, landscape
SIZE: 12.4 acres (5 ha)
CLIMATE: Temperate
LOCATION: Stockholm, Stockholm
TRANSLATION: Haga Park

Hagaparken is now part of the world's first National City Park, called Ekoparken, which extends around the Brunnsviken inlet. Given the wonderful natural setting near a bay beside the Baltic Sea, it is no wonder that the newlywed heir apparent, King Gustav III, having enjoyed his time here in 1776, bought Haga in 1781. A decade later, he united it with the neighboring Brahelund, creating the park as it is today.

As he was erecting himself a new palace-cum-museum, designed by the Frenchman Louis Jean Desprez, Gustav also had the architect Fredrik Magnus Piper repeat for him at Haga what he was creating for him at Drottningholm—an English landscape garden: a fashionable, tamed, romantic landscape of groves, winding paths, and picturesque vistas.

The landscape is also notable for its eclectic gathering of garden buildings, including the Turkish Pavilion, the Royal Pavilion (1782), and the Koppartälten (1790), a stable designed by Desperez to look like a Roman battle tent. All building work came to a halt in 1792 when Gustav was assassinated—what remains of the palace and cellars is what had so far been built. However, Gustaf IV continued to develop Haga. In 1802–04 he added the Queen's Pavilion, or Haga Slott as it is known today, which is now used to accommodate guests of the Swedish government. Also note the Ekotemplet, the summer dining room, and the Kinesiska Pagoden, or Chinese Pagoda. TM

Skogskyrkogården

Stockholm, Sweden

DESIGNERS: Erik Gunnar Asplund, Sigurd Lewerentz
OWNER: Stockholm City Council
GARDEN STYLE: 20th-century romantic naturalism
SIZE: 247 acres (100 ha)
CLIMATE: Temperate
LOCATION: Enskede, Stockholm, Stockholm
TRANSLATION: Woodland Cemetary

Built on the site of a disused gravel pit, now heavily wooded with pines interspersed with grassy slopes, Enskede Woodland Cemetary is beautifully peaceful. Approaching up a walled ramp, visitors are gently funneled through the gate toward the "ceremonial hills." Although looking natural, they are, in fact, carefully crafted. One ramp flanked by a giant, black granite cross, rises up one hill to the loggia of the crematorium, while a flight of steps ascends a second hill to a square of birch trees, which has been called the Grove of Remembrance.

Considered by many to be Sweden's most important twentieth-century architect, Erik Asplund had a deep and a profound interest in Nordic traditions and their symbolic impact on the Swedish landscape, and vice versa. He was the perfect man for the commission. It lasted twenty-five years, beginning in 1915 when he and Lewerentz—who designed the imposing Resurrection Chapel—won the design competition. Placed at the end of a woodland path, the small, enclosed Woodland Chapel (a mix of vernacular and classical) was Asplund's first building (1918–20). Right away it demonstrated the subtle naturalism and the careful, gentle mingling of woodland and topography, and of buildings and graves that is Asplund's hallmark. Indeed it is perhaps ironic that the first funeral to take place here was Asplund's own. In 1994 Skogskyrkogården became a UNESCO World Heritage Site, one of the very few twentieth-century designs to be so honored. TM

Gunnebo Slott

Gothenburg, Sweden

DESIGNER: Carl Wilhelm Carlberg
OWNER: City of Mölndal
GARDEN STYLE: Neoclassical, renaissance, formal
SIZE: 100 acres (40.4 ha)
CLIMATE: Temperate
LOCATION: Mölndal, Gothenburg
TRANSLATION: Gunnebo House and Gardens

In 1778, John Hall purchased the ailing Gunnebo estate as a summer home, and commissioned architect Carl Wilhelm Carlberg to design the house and gardens. Carlberg had just returned from a lengthy trip abroad, suffused with enthusiasm for the neoclassical influences he had witnessed, which is apparent in the gardens he created for the classical house.

The formal French Baroque Garden, with avenues of trees and hedges, is embellished with exotic plants and features furniture, urns, and statues among them. The English landscape park was laid out in the late 18th century. Geometry is at the core of its design, and reflects the changing relationship of the time between man and the landscape. A recently opened coffee house and restaurant is supplied with vegetables and herbs by the abundant harvest from the kitchen garden. This and the other garden areas were certified organic in 2006, and much effort goes into fostering historic gardening techniques, such as hand-pruning all the trees, shrubs, and hedges.

Gunnebo has had mixed fortunes. After John Hall's son inherited the property, it fell into disrepair and was auctioned off in 1832. After changing hands several times, the estate was bought by the City of Mölndal in 1948. A period of renovation took place until 1952, using archives of over 200 of Carlberg's original design drawings. Further restoration took place from 1996 to 2006, and now the estate is one of Gothenburg's premier visitor attractions. RSJ

Grönsöö Slottspark

Stockholm, Sweden

DESIGNERS: David von Schultzenheim, Willam Chambers
OWNERS: The von Ehrenheim family, The Grönsöö Cultural and Historic Foundation
GARDEN STYLE: 17th-century, 18th-century baroque, romantic
SIZE: 1,779 acres (720 ha)
CLIMATE: Temperate
LOCATION: Stockholm
TRANSLATION: Grönsöö Palace Gardens

High on a headland jutting out into the glittering Lake Mälaren, Grönsöö Palace creates a powerful impression. The magnificent original palace was built as a status symbol by Chancellor Johan Skytte between 1607 and 1611. Successive owners continued to develop it, and traces of each period have been preserved in a remarkable way.

One of the oldest features, dating from Skytte's time, is an early seventeenth-century orchard area containing Sweden's oldest commercial apple orchard, in front of which stands Queen Christina's lime tree, one of the oldest in Europe, planted in 1623. A century later, baroque influences resulted in disciplined greenery around the house and terraces, the addition of clipped lime and ash hedges, and a double chestnut avenue. Then came the romantic period of the late eighteenth century, with an artificial island, a maze, and English-style paths that wind around the palace, never losing sight of the lake, and one of the garden's main attractions, the Chinese pagoda. Exotic trees were added in the nineteenth century, and the grand maze was demolished to create a park, subsequently replaced by a 1920s flower garden, where an iron temple still remains.

Today, an ambitious project to restore the gardens at Grönsöö aims to highlight the history of Swedish garden architecture and design from the seventeenth century to the present day. NS

Japanska Trädgården

Blekinge, Sweden

DESIGNERS: Henry August Flindt, Sven-Ingvar
  Andersson, Akira Mochizuki
OWNER: Ronneby City Council
GARDEN STYLE: 20th-century public park
SIZE: 80 acres (32.4 ha)
CLIMATE: Temperate
LOCATION: Brunnsparken, Ronneby, Blekinge
TRANSLATION: Japanese Garden

Ronneby Japanese Garden, also known as Ronneby Brunnspark, came into being in 1705 because of the perceived health-giving qualities of its mineral water. The spa was a low-key operation until 1873, when the company Ronneby Hälsobrunns AB was established and the size of the grounds increased fortyfold.

The nineteenth-century park was laid out by the Danish landscape architect Henry Flindt in a German style with flower beds near the buildings, shrubberies concentrated around the paths, and grass in between. However, in 1929, the spa owners went bankrupt. In 1959 the hotel burned down. The replacement went up two years later. The garden buildings were restored and converted into office space.

To celebrate the town's six hundredth anniversary in 1987, the park was redesigned by Professor Sven-Ingvar Andersson. His new areas included the Garden of a Thousand Roses, the Rhododendron Mountain, the Scented Garden, ponds, water features, and the Japanese Garden (assisted by the Japanese landscape architect Akira Mochizuki and influenced by various different types of oriental gardens, including the tetra, roji, and Zen-Buddhist). Through a bamboo doorway, a path winds its way to the Meditation Pavilion enclosed by whistling mountain bamboos, Japanese maples, and Japanese irises. This garden focuses the mind and awakens the senses. TM

Uraniborgs Renässansträdgård

Island of Ven, Skåne, Sweden

DESIGNER: Tycho Brahe
OWNER: Swedish National
  Property Board (SFV)
GARDEN STYLE: 16th-century formal renaissance
SIZE: 0.6 acres (0.3 ha)
CLIMATE: Temperate
LOCATION: Island of Ven, Skåne
TRANSLATION: Uraniborg Renaissance Garden

The island of Ven lies in the sound between Denmark and Sweden. It was here that the sixteenth-century Danish astronomer Tycho Brahe—the first to observe and describe a supernova—had his observatory, house, and garden. His book *De Stella Nova* (1573) made him famous but caused controversy because the heavens were considered to be divinely created, perfect, and unchangeable. His fame brought job offers from all over Europe. However, King Frederik II persuaded him to stay by offering him Ven and a chance to build an observatory.

The garden's design is shown in Brahe's own books and copperplate engravings. It was square, enclosed within 16-foot-high (5 m) walls with an entrance at each corner and, within, the plot was divided into four quarters. Brahe grew 300 types of tree. He was probably inspired by his 1575 visit to the botanic garden in Padua, though his plantings were revamped following a visit to his sister at Eriksholm Castle (now Trolleholm) in 1592. There has been detailed recent archaeological research here, with seed and pollen found in the soil being used to identify what plants were grown in Brahe's time. The project is offering a unique opportunity to study the flora grown in Danish/Swedish gardens of the late sixteenth century. There is also a conservatory for the tender plants that Brahe probably also grew. TM

Slottsträdgården

Skåne, Sweden

DESIGNERS: Camilla Anderson, John Taylor
OWNER: City of Malmö Streets and Parks Department
GARDEN STYLE: 20th- and 21st-century English,
   new European
SIZE: 4.9 acres (1.9 ha)
CLIMATE: Temperate
LOCATION: Slottsparken, Malmö, Skåne
TRANSLATION: Castle Park Garden

Slottsträdgården is a vibrant, exciting, fluid garden masterminded by "Englishman abroad" John Taylor. He strolls about his domain chatting to volunteers and visitors alike in Swedish with a Yorkshire accent, and is informed, passionate, and amiable. His mission is to create a strong horticultural experience.

Slottsträdgården has something for everyone. The cutting, herb, and vegetable garden provides an attractive potager effect. Vast beds of towering sunflowers and eight demonstration gardens created by noted designers and schoolchildren make for endless variety and interest, but traditional Swedish it is not. John says, "Malmö is a dynamic and progressive place where a new wave of interest in both community and gardening is moving away from the traditional Scandinavian reserve."

Here nothing remains static for long. By the entrance, an island bed bears up to four displays a year. They include a dramatic mix of poppies following salvias, and a Salvia patens and Verbena bonariensis combination joined by delicate gaura and red-headed northern sugarcane (Sorghum vulgare). The garden responds well to the imaginative touch. The use of "garden rooms" enables discrete flights of fancy such as a "hanging garden" of climbers and ramblers suspended on a frame over a regimented group of clipped lonicera and buxus. The highlights of the year are the Trädgården festivals, held on the first Sunday in May and the first Sunday in September. NS

Sofiero Slott

Skåne, Sweden

DESIGNERS: King Gustav VI Adolf,
   Crown Princess Margareta
OWNER: Helsingborg City Council
GARDEN STYLE: 20th-century mixed, mainly rhododendrons
SIZE: 37 acres (14.9 ha)
CLIMATE: Temperate
LOCATION: Helsingborg, Skåne
TRANSLATION: Sofiero Castle

At the mouth of the Baltic Sea, a small stretch of water separates Denmark from Sweden. Just across the sound from Hamlet's Castle at Helsingor is the Swedish town of Helsingborg. A quick drive to the north is Sofiero Slott, which was given to King Gustav VI Adolf and his wife, Crown Princess Margareta, as a wedding present in 1905. It became the king's favorite summer retreat. When he died in 1973, he left the castle to the city. After two decades of neglect, it underwent a major restoration in 1993.

When the garden opens each year in April, the show of over ten million rhododendrons flowering their hearts out is absolutely breathtaking. The king was obsessed by these showy shrubs and became a renowned expert. He began his collection in the 1930s, planting many of the species rhododendrons and their hybrid descendants, discovered by such famous plant hunters as Ernest Wilson, George Forrest, Frank Kingdon Ward, and Joseph Rock. Following losses as a result of harsh winters in the 1940s, a second phase of planting was undertaken.

Rhododendrons are not the only attraction of Sofiero Slott. Crown Princess Margareta (who died at the age of 38 in 1920) also left her mark on the garden. The Flower Walk with its herbaceous borders was created in 1914 and is a striking sight in summer. Later additions include the King's Winery in the English Garden, Queen Ingrid's Fragrant Garden, the Lust Garden, and the Victorian Kitchen Garden. TM

Kadriorg

Harjumaa, Estonia

DESIGNER: Niccolo Michetti
OWNER: The Estonian State
GARDEN STYLE: 18th-century forest park and
   formal flower gardens
SIZE: 200 acres (80 ha)
CLIMATE: Temperate
LOCATION: Tallinn, Harjumaa

Known alternately as Katherinthal or Ekaterinthal, Kadriorg was created by a tsar for his tsarina and is by far the most notable garden of its kind in Estonia. Despite its imperial history, grand palace, and elaborate gardens, the park has a relaxed, informal atmosphere, combining wooded areas and meadows with shady, tree-lined paths and bridleways.

At the center of Kadriorg Park is the magnificent baroque Summer Palace designed for Peter the Great by the Italian architect, Niccolo Michetti, in 1718. The palace and surrounding park were named by Peter after his wife Catherine, known in Estonian as ëKadrií.

The palace lost much of its splendor during the communist period when Soviet-style renovations and neglect left the place a shadow of its former self. It has since undergone extensive restoration, and in 2000 opened its doors to the public as home to the Foreign Art Collection of the Estonian Art Museum. In front of the palace, the Swan Lake is popular with lovers and families with small children who feed the swans and ducks on summer days, or skate in winter.

The formal flower garden at the rear of the palace has also been restored to its eighteenth-century glory and further renovations are planned: botanical mazes and tunnels to replace the overgrown linden and maple trees that now encroach on the palace structure, and the opening up of views from the palace to reveal the old city and the sea beyond. Project directors hope restoration will be complete by 2018, Kadriorg's three hundredth anniversary. NS

Attadale

Highland, Scotland

DESIGNERS: Michael Innes, Nicolette Macpherson
OWNERS: Ewen Macpherson, Nicolette Macpherson
GARDEN STYLE: Traditional Highland garden, with
   contemporary plantings
SIZE: 20 acres (8.1 ha)
CLIMATE: Temperate
LOCATION: Strathcarron, Wester Ross, Highland

Attadale lies in a romantic Highland landscape overlooking Loch Carron with views of the Isle of Skye in the distance. The shelter of the hills combines with the warm North Atlantic drift to create a microclimate where artist Nicolette Macpherson has been able to indulge a passion for "painting with plants."

Twenty-five years ago, when her husband, Ewen, inherited Attadale, Nicolette found an old-fashioned garden with rhododendrons, azaleas, and conifers. As she was used to working with Sussex clay she was uncertain how to proceed. However, nature provided a helping hand in 1984 and 1989 when storms uprooted the conifers that lined the driveway, leaving a framework of peat-filled pools fed by a creek. At this point, the Macphersons called on landscape designer Michael Innes, who suggested damming each pool with a log to create a series of connecting ponds. As the water level rose, a nick was cut into each log, allowing the water to flow out to create a "waterfall." This system still works seventeen years later.

Growing in confidence at every stage, Nicolette has restored the sunken garden, added a red and green potager, and created a Japanese garden that fits into the sparse Highland landscape surprisingly well. Paths now lead through a woodland garden planted with meconopsis, and she has also housed a collection of ferns in a geodesic dome. AG

RIGHT The beautiful Highland landscape of Attadale, where an astonishing array of plants flourishes.

Castle of Mey

Highland Scotland

DESIGNER: Queen Elizabeth, the Queen Mother
OWNER: The Queen Elizabeth
   Castle of Mey Trust
GARDEN STYLE: Traditional cottage garden
SIZE: 9.5 acres (3.8 ha)
CLIMATE: Temperate
LOCATION: Thurso, Caithness, Highland

Mysterious pink sandstone turrets peep above a small forest of contorted sycamores through which a winding drive leads to the ancient Castle of Mey. It is set in the remote moorland landscape of Thurso in the most northerly region of the British Isles. It has views across the Pentland Firth to the Orkney Isles and was bought in 1952 and restored by the late Queen Mother. In fact, the castle was the only home Her Majesty ever bought. Her love of it is reflected in the comfortable, homely atmosphere of the reception rooms now open to the public.

The garden is quite remarkable, not least because winter winds can reach 90 miles per hour (144 km/h). Substantial stone walls surround the garden, which is divided into sections separated by hedging to create windbreaks. The overall appearance is of a cottage garden with colorful herbaceous plantings, astilbes, primulas, and old roses. The climber rose 'Albertine' frames a wooden seat, the favorite area of the Queen Mother. It is surrounded by small island beds and paths covered by shells from the nearby beach.

One of the best features is a yellow-flowering *Clematis orientalis* covering a hedge in front of the greenhouses, which are filled with a vivid selection of pot plants used for indoor display. In fact, everything in the gardens at Mey was timed to be perfect for the Queen Mother's annual vacations in August and October. This includes a superb selection of fruit such as strawberries, raspberries, rhubarb, and apples, and plums trained against the walls. RL

Cawdor Castle Gardens

Highland, Scotland

DESIGNERS: Sir Archibald Campbell, Arabella Lennox-Boyd
OWNER: Sixth Countess Cawdor
GARDEN STYLE: 18th-, 19th-, and 20th-century
    formal gardens
SIZE: 3.5 acres (1.4 ha)
CLIMATE: Temperate
LOCATION: Cawdor, Nairn, Highland

> *This castle hath a pleasant seat; the air*
> *Nimbly and sweetly recommends itself*
> *Unto our gentle senses*
> *Macbeth*, I, vi. William Shakespeare, 1606

In one sense, these lines describe Cawdor Castle. Surrounded by extensive woodlands in the eastern heart of the Scottish Highlands, the castle dates from the fourteenth century when it was built by the Thanes of Cawdor. Centuries of ownership have spun it into a confection of turrets and gables, though as far as the play goes, there is no connection between Shakespeare's Macbeth and the castle.

The walled garden dates from the seventeenth century. Originally a kitchen garden, it now has a maze based on Roman depictions of the Minotaur's labyrinth at Knossos in Crete. Laid out in the early eighteenth century, the flower garden is Edwardian in feel thanks to its cottage-garden favorites such as poppies, delphiniums, and double hollyhocks.

The steep, wild garden between the castle and the rocky, fast-flowing Cawdor creek is home to rhododendrons, daffodils, primulas, willows, and bamboos. The nearby Cawdor dower house of Auchindoune is a treasure trove of Himalayan plants brought from the Tsangpo Gorges of Tibet by the plant hunters Frank Kingdon Ward and Jack Cawdor, the young fifth earl. There is also a vegetable garden by Arabella Lennox-Boyd, an arboretum, salmon fishing, a golf course, and a hotel. RCa

Inverewe Garden

Highland, Scotland

DESIGNERS: Osgood Hanbury Mackenzie, Mairi T. Sawyer
OWNER: The National Trust for Scotland
GARDEN STYLE: 19th- and 20th century subtropical woodland
SIZE: 50 acres (20 ha)
CLIMATE: Temperate
LOCATION: Poolewe, Wester, Highland

How can this colorful, subtropical paradise possibly exist? Inverewe is on a remote coastal promontory in the northwest Highlands. It is susceptible to high winds and salt spray from the Atlantic, and lies farther north than Moscow. Yet it is one of Scotland's best-loved gardens and open all year. What is the secret?

The warming currents of the Gulf Stream keep the winters mild. However, Osgood Mackenzie, who bought the estates of Inverewe and Kemsary in 1862, planted shelter belts of trees, built high protective walls around the vegetable plot, and imported vast quantities of loam (reputedly by ship from Ireland) to transform shallow, rocky heathland into fertile garden soil. He also initiated an annual program of soil enrichment to keep it in shape and to replace nutrients leached away by the heavy rainfall. Around 220 tons (200 t) of peat, seaweed, and manure mulches are still applied each year.

What is the result? Himalayan blue poppies (*Meconopsis betonicifolia*), Chilean lantern trees (*Crinodendron hookerianum*), Californian dog's tooth violets (*Erythronium californicum*), Chatham Island forget-me-nots (*Myosotidium hortensia*), South African bulbs aplenty, eucalyptus from Tasmania and Australia, Mediterranean rock roses, and Chinese rhododendrons all grow. Mackenzie's redoubtable daughter, Mairi Sawyer, carried the flame until her death in 1953, when she bequeathed the estate to the National Trust for Scotland, which maintains it to this day. Inverewe is a mecca for midges, so a visit means insect repellent is a must. RCa

Dunbeath Castle Gardens

Highland, Scotland

DESIGNERS: David Bryce, Xa Tollemach
OWNERS: Stuart Threipland, Claire Threipland
GARDEN STYLE: 19th-century formal walled garden
SIZE: 20 acres (8.1 ha)
CLIMATE: Temperate
LOCATION: Dunbeath, Caithness, Highland

When Edinburgh architect David Bryce landscaped the driveway at Dunbeath Castle, perched on the top of a cliff overlooking the Moray Firth in Caithness, he designed a "keyhole" driveway that impresses as much today as it did in the mid-nineteenth century. As you enter the drive, you see the front door half a mile (1 km) away. As you continue down the hill, the castle slowly reveals itself, framed between banks of grass against the Firth of Forth in the background.

Known as Caithness' hidden gem, Dunbeath's gardens feature a walled garden laid out in 1860 to provide shelter. Claire Threipland, the current owner, explains, "In winter the strong winds blow at over 100 miles an hour [160 km/h], and we can hardly walk outside to our car." Despite the short summer, the long length of the days encouraged Claire to renovate the walled garden with the help of Xa Tollemach, a gold medal-winning designer at the Chelsea Flower Show. The collaboration has led to a brightly planted garden that contrasts with the castle's simple lines.

Hedges of red-flowering *Fuchsia magellanica* have been used to divide the space into "rooms" that open up into a series of surprises, including a neat vegetable patch with fruits, shrubs, and a metal arbor. The centerpiece of the garden is the double border that runs from east to west, the full length of the garden flanking a grass path. This generous border features perennials and roses that flower in July and August. A greenhouse is home to Scotland's most northerly fig and apricot trees, while a climb up the turret by the lower wall gives magnificent views. AG

Langwell

Highland, Scotland

DESIGNER: Unknown
OWNER: Lady Anne Bentinck
GARDEN STYLE: 19th-century traditional Scottish walled garden
SIZE: 2 acres (0.8 ha)
CLIMATE: Temperate
LOCATION: Berriedale, Caithness, Highland

Gardens often spread their interest over many months. Here, though, as at Balmoral, everything is timed to look its best for when the Royal Family arrives for the start of the grouse season on August 12. All the borders are in flower, and fruits and vegetables ready to harvest over the next six weeks. Unlike Balmoral, which remains firmly shut, Langwell is open to the public by appointment.

Sitting on the far northeast coast of Scotland, only 1 mile (1.6 km) from the sea, the nineteenth-century walled garden is laid out on a slope with an Italianate pond at the bottom. It bears the brunt of Arctic winds, and has little sunlight during winter and a short growing season. Head gardener Francis Higgins has twenty-two years' experience of gardening in a climate so cold that runner beans are grown in a polytunnel over summer.

Two sets of double herbaceous borders, each with sturdy, late-summer perennials, bisect the length and width of the garden to form a cross. Within each of the four quarters, protected by yew hedges, are vegetable plots and themed flower borders. The phlox border is superb. The dahlia border is vibrant with thirty varieties of cacti and decorative dahlias, grown to perfection by Higgins, who started his career in a dahlia nursery. Each year, he devises different schemes for his annual borders, with the burned orange, yellow, and copper hues of helichrysum, framed by a dark yew hedge, perhaps being the simplest and most effective of all. VR

Kerrachar Gardens

Highland, Scotland

DESIGNERS: Peter Kohn, Trish Kohn
OWNERS: Peter Kohn, Trish Kohn
GARDEN STYLE: 20th- and 21st-century English
    cottage garden
SIZE: 2.5 acres (1 ha)
CLIMATE: Temperate
LOCATION: Kylesku, Sutherland, Highland

When Peter and Trish Kohn bought Kerrachar, a small farm overlooking Loch Chairn Bhain on the northwest coast of Sutherland, the patch of cultivated ground near the house was enough to suggest that a garden might be possible. Eleven years on, the couple have a flower-filled paradise, with modern plant associations that sit happily in the remote surroundings.

As Kerrachar is accessible only by boat, bringing in machinery was impossible, so all work was done by hand. They also used available recycled materials. Although the garden benefits from the effects of the North Atlantic drift, the salt-laden winds are ferocious in winter. Peter, a lecturer who took early retirement, and Trish started by putting in windbreaks: lumber and netting barriers inside a framework of native alder, birch, sorbus, and Scotch pines (*Pinus sylvestris*), followed by plantings of shrubs. A polytunnel was erected to grow cuttings and plants from seed.

As they cleared the grounds, the Kohns found soils that allowed experiments with perennials and shrubs, including those from the Southern Hemisphere. Other surprises include a collection of lilies and roses. *Lilium canadense*, the yellow meadow lily, flourishes as does red *L. coccineum* and pink *L. mackliniae*.

Trish admits that in winter they listen closely to the weather forecast: "Occasionally we get a severe gale that drenches everything in salt and we've spent many January hours standing outside, hoses in hand, washing all the evergreens down to prevent the salt burning their leaves." AG

Kildrummy Castle

Aberdeenshire, Scotland

DESIGNER: Colonel James Ogsten
OWNER: Kildrummy Gardens Trust
GARDEN STYLE: 20th-century rock
    and water garden
SIZE: 20 acres (8.1 ha)
CLIMATE: Temperate
LOCATION: Alford, Aberdeenshire

Your first glimpse of the glen of Kildrummy is from the top of a bridge. On one side you look down into a lushly planted water garden, and on the other, the quarry garden that supplied stone for the now ruined castle on the hill nine centuries ago. When Colonel Ogsten, a soap manufacturer in Aberdeen, bought the estate in 1898, he built himself a home on the opposite bank to the castle. He connected the two with a replica of the fourteenth-century Auld Brig o' Balgownie, in Old Aberdeen. Apparently, when being shown the new home, a guest pointed out that he now had everything except a garden. Within five years, a team of Japanese landscape gardeners had turned the creek that flowed through the ravine into a large pond with a series of cascading pools. The disused quarry became an enormous rock garden.

The planting was made possible by the existing shelter of silver firs, larch, and hemlock. However, the site remains a serious frost pocket. The water garden is ringed with skunk cabbage, meconopsis, Asiatic primulas, and gunneras that thrive in the cool, moist, acidic soils of Scotland. The banks of the glen and rock garden are richly planted with hardy alpines, enkianthus, pieris, many rhododendrons, acers, and two rare purple oaks (*Quercus robur* 'Purpurascens').

Colonel Ogsten's home is now a luxury hotel. The garden operates independently, having been established as a private trust by the last owner in 1968. You will not find such a unique garden in a more natural setting anywhere else in Britain. VR

Crathes Castle

Aberdeenshire, Scotland

DESIGNER: The Burnett family
OWNERS: The Burnett family, the National Trust for Scotland
GARDEN STYLE: 18th-century formal
SIZE: 3.75 acres (1.5 ha)
CLIMATE: Temperate
LOCATION: Banchory, Aberdeenshire

Alexander Burnett started building Crathes in 1553 using funds provided by his marriage to wealthy Janet Hamilton, daughter of the prebendary of Kincardine (an unmarried grandee of the church). In the early eighteenth century, it was enlarged by what became known as the Queen Anne Wing. Space must have been urgently required, since the mistress of the castle at this time, Margaret, had twenty-one children in twenty-three years. The Burnett family continued to live here until 1951. The treasures on display include the Horn of Leys (pronounced to rhyme with "days") presented to Alexander Burnard by Robert the Bruce in 1323. Some of the interior decoration at Crathes Castle has close parallels with the decoration in the gardens of Edzell Castle.

The magnificent gardens enclosed by walls and yew hedges date back to 1702 and were the creation of Sir James and Lady Sybil Burnett from 1926. Sir James enjoyed a long friendship with Sir Harold Hillier of Winchester in England with, and through, whom he collected trees and shrubs. Lady Sybil was a disciple of Gertrude Jekyll, especially of her book *Colour Schemes for the Flower Garden*. Influenced by Jekyll, she created her own color schemes with drifts of herbaceous plants. Eight gardens are contained within the site. The White Borders, Red Garden, and Golden Garden were created in memory of Lady Sybil and all follow Jekyll's advice that "gold plants veer towards lighter yellows not oranges." The northerly site and long summer days ensure that the gardens look wonderful well into September. CH

Pitmedden Garden

Aberdeenshire, Scotland

DESIGNER: The National Trust for Scotland
OWNER: The National Trust for Scotland
GARDEN STYLE: 1950s recreation of 17th-century Scottish
 formal style
SIZE: 15 acres (6 ha)
CLIMATE: Temperate
LOCATION: Pitmeddon, Ellon, Aberdeenshire

Amid the beautiful, gently rolling, rich farmlands of Aberdeenshire, the green architectural crispness of Pitmedden always comes as a stunning surprise to the visitor. The spectacular formality of the Great Garden with its immaculately clipped topiary and box hedges, designed to be viewed from above, is a splendid recreation of seventeenth-century Scottish formal gardens. Brilliantly executed by the National Trust for Scotland in the 1950s, three of the garden's four giant-sized parterre patterns have associations with the Palace of Holyrood in Edinburgh. The fourth parterre pattern is based on the coat of arms of Sir Alexander Seton, who began to lay out a garden here in 1675. A stone in the garden even records this exact date. The central vista between the parterres is emphasized by a broad sweep of lawn punctuated by perfectly placed yews.

The ornamental patterns of the box hedging are divided by scrolls and arabesques following the French style of parterres de broderie. Every spring and summer, the beds between are filled with thousands of annual bedding plants, creating a striking effect. The jewel-like colors of the annuals, with yellow and orange marigolds, offer a brilliant contrast to the dark-green clipped box, granite chips, and mown lawn. Everything here is maintained to the very highest standard. As a visitor, it is absolutely essential to stroll along the terraces and to look down on such a brilliant design.

As well as annuals, flowers blossom in wonderful herbaceous borders that run along the south- and west-facing garden beds. There are also apple trees on the walls behind the beds. Espaliers, goblets, and fans are complemented by a tunnel of old Scottish apple varieties. Unfortunately the historical authenticity of the restoration at Pitmedden has been criticized by some garden historians. Nevertheless its spirit and charm are a great success. CR

Edzell Castle Gardens

Angus, Scotland

DESIGNERS: Lindsay family and others
OWNER: Historic Scotland
GARDEN STYLE: 17th-century formal; 1930s-formal;
   20th/21st-century planting
SIZE: 1 acre (0.4 ha)
CLIMATE: Temperate
LOCATION: Edzell, Angus, Scotland

Visitors do not make the trip to Edzell Castle Gardens for the planting, but rather to experience a garden steeped in history. This is the only garden in Scotland that still features a "pleasaunce"—a garden area devoted to giving pleasure to the senses but with no fruits or vegetables—that is in its entirety. The estate at Edzell belonged to the Lindsay family, who acquired it in 1358 when the residence consisted of a timber motte and bailey structure. The warm red sandstone castle, with its central tower house that exists now, was built in the 16th century.

The walled garden was built in 1604 by David, Lord Edzell; the walls of the garden carry a plaque of his coat of arms. Three of the garden's walls show carved stone panels, which are decorated with the Seven Planetary Deities: Mars, Venus, and Mercury on the east wall, while the Seven Liberal Arts and Seven Cardinal Virtues appear on other panels along the south and west walls respectively. A bath house and summer house were each constructed in two corners of the garden, well away from the castle. The bath house is now a ruin, but the summer house, with two stories and the castle's only surviving example of carved oak wall paneling, is still standing.

The current layout of the garden was created in the 1930s and consists of a parterre, which is picked out in low, clipped, box hedges. Here, the Lindsay family mottoes *Dum Spiro Spero* (As long as I breathe I hope) and *Endure Forte* (Hold firm), also in box, were designed to be viewed from the ruined keep. In the corners of the parterre are triangular-shaped borders, each with a Scottish thistle, English rose, or French fleur-de-lis made out of box. At the garden's center is an imposing block of yew surrounded by smaller clipped domes of yew, and there are roses planted in blocks. Visit Edzell to be impressed by the fact that it is a unique 17th-century example of garden design, drenched in atmosphere. RSJ

House of Pitmuies Gardens

Angus, Scotland

DESIGNER: Margaret Ogilvie
OWNER: Margaret Ogilvie
GARDEN STYLE: Scottish Edwardian
SIZE: 26 acres (10.5 ha)
CLIMATE: Temperate
LOCATION: Guthrie, Forfar, Angus

This eighteenth-century house has a long-established kitchen garden where decorative, ornamental, and edible plants are all grown together as though they were in a traditional French potager. Raised beds are filled with neat rows of vegetables, enhanced by tripods of exuberant sweet peas that fill the midsummer air with perfume. Follow the sweet scents farther, as the path from the kitchen garden leads straight to the chief axis of the garden, a long, narrow pair of herbaceous borders. Overflowing with well-grown perennials, they have a color scheme of mostly pastel shades, with many repetitions and an intermingling of white-flowering and silver-leaved plants. Singling out particular beauties is hard. However, the many roses, some of which are old-fashioned and some of which are modern, are exquisite, as are the old delphinium cultivars in spectacular blue. The soft pastel colors of these flowery borders in soft cream, white, and blue tones are aligned with a window in the drawing room and cleverly reflect the interior decor. They are all the more vivid and striking against the backdrop of lawns and mature trees in the woodland beyond.

Before leaving, take the gate through the wall into the woodland garden and walk along the banks of the Vinny, where you will find the tallest *Ilex aquifolium* 'Argentea Marginata' in the British Isles and a magnificent old paperbark maple (*Acer griseum*). The final surprise for the visitor is a decorative Gothic dovecot, an early building with later nineteenth-century additions. CR

Blair Castle

Perth and Kinross, Scotland

DESIGNER: Second Duke of Atholl
OWNER: Atholl Estates
GARDEN STYLE: 18th-century formal
SIZE: 2,500 acres (1,012 ha)
CLIMATE: Temperate
LOCATION: Blair Atholl, Pitlochry, Perth and Kinross

At the center of an estate that covers over 145,000 acres (58,725 ha), this striking white castle is home to both the Duke of Atholl and the Atholl Highlanders, Europe's last remaining private army. The second duke began to lay out the gardens in the 1730s, with geometric avenues radiating out from the castle in the French style. As you approach the castle, the first garden feature that comes into view is the eye-catching, Gothic-looking folly called The Whim. Dating from 1761, it is located on a rise in line with the Lime Avenue that forms the main drive to the castle. The main feature, however, is the Hercules Garden that dates from 1758. The restoration of the overgrown 9-acre (3.5 ha) walled garden began in 1984. The enclosure contains an interesting mix of edibles and ornamentals that is as attractive as it is diverse. Orchards are underplanted with vegetables, herbaceous borders rub shoulders with urns and statuary, and an unlikely mix of nineteenth-century folly, pavilion, and Chinese bridge actually works. Dominating the show is a series of pools and islands.

Other highlights include Diana's Grove, named after a statue of the Roman goddess of hunting. Begun in 1737, this 2-acre (0.8 ha) plantation is home to tall, mature trees. Adding to the scene, the Banvie Burn runs through the grove and is crossed by two eighteenth-century bridges. They lead to an area of high ground and the ruins of St. Bride's Kirk. The kirk is the resting place of Viscount Dundee, killed in the Battle of Killiecrankie (1689), although the site's origins date back to Celtic times. TM

Glendoick Gardens

Perth and Kinross, Scotland

DESIGNERS: Euan Cox, Peter Cox, Patricia Cox
OWNERS: Peter Cox, Patricia Cox
GARDEN STYLE: 20th-century rhododendron collection
SIZE: 10 acres (4 ha)
CLIMATE: Temperate
LOCATION: Glendoick, Perth and Kinross

Glendoick Gardens are home to one of the most comprehensive collections of rhododendrons in the world. In June the garden is filled with the voluptuous technicolor flowers of large rhododendrons as well as with the delicacy and fragrance of the dwarf species.

The collection began in 1919 when the garden's owner, Euan Cox, joined plant hunter Reginald Farrer on a trip to Burma. The pair discovered many new plants, but the voyage was to be Farrer's last. The task of recording and propagating the plants fell to Cox. Their finds formed the initial planting of the gardens, which have been extended with rare plants ever since.

Plant hunting did not end with wealthy Edwardian gentlemen venturing to the far corners of the British Empire. Euan Cox's son, Peter, and grandson, Kenneth, have continued traveling in Asia and China, and they are still discovering new plants.

The rhododendron beds here are underplanted with drifts of trilliums, meconopsis, lilies, and rare nomocharis, many of them collected by the Cox family. From the very first expedition is *Deutzia calycosa*, covered with white and pink flowers early in the season. Flowering nearby is a low-growing form of *Paeonia mareii* with large pink flowers, introduced by Peter Cox. The plants collected during nearly a century have been used by the Coxes to breed hundreds of new varieties of rhododendron. There are dwarf and scented varieties and, more recently, ones with red or purple foliage. They can be seen throughout the gardens, with the newest varieties in trial beds at the garden's entrance. JHo

Drummond Castle Gardens

Perth and Kinross, Scotland

DESIGNER: Lewis Kennedy
OWNER: Grimsthorpe and Drummond Castle Trust Ltd.
GARDEN STYLE: 19th-century formal parterre
SIZE: 18 acres (7.3 ha)
CLIMATE: Temperate
LOCATION: Muthill, Crieff, Perth and Kinross

In terms of wow factor, nothing in Britain matches the first impression of the great parterre of Drummond Castle. To pass through the arch of the fifteenth-century keep and to find oneself looking over a 60-foot (18 m) drop with a 5-acre (2 ha) tableau spread out below is absolutely stupendous.

Having evolved over five centuries, always in the Drummond family, the garden bears the imprint of many generations. It was supplying cherries to James IV of Scotland as early as 1508. Its famous obelisk sundial was added in 1630. Some 200 years later, the garden was laid out in the spirit of the formal revival by landscape gardener Lewis Kennedy. It was bisected from east to west with the diagonal lines of the cross of St. Andrew and from north to south with a long vista that cut a swathe into wooded hills. Sir Charles Barry, who was to build a grand castle (which was never executed) to match the new parterre, contributed Italianate terracing, baroque staircases, statues, and urns. Lewis Kennedy, having worked for Princess Josephine at Parc de Malmaison in France (see page 606), brought French features to the garden in the box broderie, ponds, and allées. Another layer was added to the garden, Victorian evergreens that gradually carpeted it. The real impact of the garden, though, comes from the 200 clipped hollies and yews of different heights, and the patriotic and heraldic color schemes. Blue lavender and silver anaphalis are used for the Scottish flag. The reds and yellows of hybrid tea roses, golden yews, *Prunus pissardii*, and thirty varieties of acer highlight the family crest. VR

Arduaine Garden

Argyll and Bute, Scotland

DESIGNER: James Arthur Campbell
OWNER: The National Trust for Scotland
GARDEN STYLE: 19th-century woodland garden
SIZE: 49 acres (20 ha)
CLIMATE: Temperate
LOCATION: Oban, Argyll and Bute

The wild and windy coast off the Sound of Jura in the western Highlands of Scotland hides a calm oasis. Protected by the warming air of the Gulf Stream, Arduaine (pronounced Ar–doo–a-nie) is a peaceful woodland garden set on a beautiful promontory.

James Arthur Campbell bought the land during the 1880s and realized that if the winds were tamed, this inhospitable site would make a superb garden. On his return from working on the family tea plantations in Sri Lanka, he began planting a shelter belt of exotic conifers and native, deciduous trees. With the winds and the salt-spray locked out, the garden was filled with his collection of rhododendrons, and rare trees and shrubs. By the time of his death in 1929, his garden contained one of the most important collections of species rhododendrons in Britain.

Ownership of the garden has passed to the National Trust for Scotland, and the mature trees and shrubs now protect a collection of plants from around the world. The warm air and high rainfall— usually 75 inches (190 cm) a year—favor lush growth and allow tender plants to flourish. Despite the exotic plants, the atmosphere at Arduaine is that of the relaxing calm of broadleaf woodland. Pools of native water lilies are bordered by collections of ferns that sit comfortably with the leathery leaves and intense blue flowers of the Chatham Island forget-me-not (*Myosotidium hortensia*). A collection of South American shrubs, particularly from Chile, contains plants rarely seen in Europe.

A walk past the enormous rhododendrons and up through the trees of the shelter belt leads to a viewing platform. Here you can feel the full force of the wind and appreciate the calming influence of the trees on the garden below. You also get a panoramic view of one of the most stunning seascapes in Scotland. The wind can be vicious, but the view is utterly worth it. JHo

Benmore Botanic Garden

Argyll and Bute, Scotland

DESIGNERS: Ross Wilson, Piers Patrick, James Duncan, the Younger family
OWNER: Royal Botanic Garden Edinburgh
GARDEN STYLE: 19th-century mountainside pinetum
SIZE: 130 acres (52.6 ha)
CLIMATE: Temperate
LOCATION: Dunoon, Argyll and Bute

An avenue of giant redwood trees (*Sequoiadendron giganteum*) makes an apt entrance to one of the finest collections of conifers in the world.

The mountainous site in the Eachaig Valley covers a huge area. It is the work of owners who clearly loved their trees and conifers. Ross Wilson was the first to plant here in 1820. Piers Patrick, in 1863, a year after he had bought the estate, planted the avenue of redwoods that now stands 128 feet (40 m) tall. The scale of planting grew with new owners in the late nineteenth century. From 1871 to 1883, James Duncan planted about six million trees. Henry Younger and his family carried on planting when he bought the estate in 1889. Today there are over 200 species and many varieties of conifer, from the Chilean monkey puzzle (*Araucaria araucana*) to the New Zealand podocarpus. The garden has over 650 different rhododendrons, many collected by plant hunter George Forrest in the early twentieth century. Although Benmore has some of the biggest conifers in Britain, they do not all reach huge proportions. The walled garden has 300 more modest varieties.

Since 1929, Benmore has been managed by the Royal Botanic Garden, Edinburgh. In recent years, a Chilean rainforest glade has been created using plants grown from seeds or materials gathered in the wild. Elsewhere a Bhutanese glade features plants from the Himalayas. For dramatic views, big plants, and gardening on a massive scale, Benmore cannot be beaten. Bring a sturdy pair of walking shoes. MC

Glenarn

Argyll and Bute, Scotland

DESIGNERS: Archie Gibson, Sandy Gibson,
   Sue Thornley, Mike Thornley
OWNERS: Mike Thornley, Sue Thornley
GARDEN STYLE: 20th-century rhododendron and magnolia
SIZE: 16 acres (6.5 ha)
CLIMATE: Temperate
LOCATION: Rhu, Glasgow, Argyll and Bute

Twenty-five years ago, when Michael and Sue Thornley first saw Glenarn, the hillside garden overlooking Gareloch, they were bowled over and immediately knew they wanted to spend the rest of their lives restoring the once-famous magnolia and rhododendron plantings. Three minutes later, their resolve was sorely tested when they saw the run-down house. With developers snapping at their heels there was no time to delay and they went ahead.

The garden came with an interesting history. It was planted by the brothers Archie and Sandy Gibson, two chartered accountants, who used the spaces left by trees uprooted in the storms that swept the west coast in 1928. They became friendly with well-known Scottish gardeners who gave them their excess stock, including rare and beautiful species of rhododendron grown from seeds introduced by plant collectors Frank Kingdon Ward, Frank Ludlow, and George Sherriff. Later, in the 1950s, they added magnolias, such as pink *Magnolia sprengeri* 'Diva' and white and crimson hybrids of *M. campbelli*, establishing a collection that is unique in Scotland.

The brothers died several years before Michael and Sue, both of whom are architects, arrived at Glenarn. The Thornley's budget was extremely tight, but they were undeterred. While their two small children, Hannah and Matthew, played happily in the greenhouse, the couple began the enormous task of restoring the garden. They were watched closely throughout the restoration process by rhododendron experts, who were worried they might destroy rare plants, but who also helped by finding a box of photographic negatives in the attic. Several surprises were uncovered, including a rockery and a damp area with candelabra primulas. Sue explains, "At the outset we couldn't identify anything, but apart from each other and our family, the garden is our greatest passion." AG

Crarae Garden

Argyll and Bute, Scotland

DESIGNER: The Campbell family
OWNER: The National Trust for Scotland
GARDEN STYLE: 20th-century woodland garden
SIZE: 50 acres (20.2 ha)
CLIMATE: Temperate
LOCATION: Minard, Inverary, Argyll and Bute

"The nearest you will get to a Himalayan Gorge in the UK", is how the eminent horticulturist and plant hunter Roy Lancaster described Crarae Garden.

The woodland garden lies on the shores of Loch Fyne on the western coast of Scotland, with some of the benefits of the Gulf Stream. It was created by Lady Campbell of Succoth at the beginning of the twentieth century. Her nephew was the great plant collector Reginald Farrer, who undoubtedly influenced and inspired her work in the gardens, which are planted with some of the rhododendron species that he introduced from his expeditions.

The gardens are owned now by the National Trust for Scotland, but Sir George Campbell and his son, Sir Ilay Campbell, originally recognized the potential for a unique garden ideally suited for all the rhododendron species. Sir George cleared thickets of native trees to open up a central ravine, where a natural creek tumbles down over rocky outcrops of stone to the lower slopes beneath. Father and son planted a wonderful selection of choice trees, including acers, cercidiphyllum, cornuses, and *Hamamelis* that give fabulous fall color and provide a canopy for the vast selection of shrubs and plants beneath. You will find an extensive collection of eucalyptus, embothrium, and crinodendron from Chile, and a collection of rare conifers. Candelabra primulas and the wonderful blue Himalayan poppy *Meconopsis* x *sheldonii* flourish in the bog garden. Before you leave, make a point not miss the fantastic panoramic view over Loch Fyne from the top of Flagstaff Hill. RL

Colonsay House and Woodland Gardens

Isle of Colonsay, Argyll and Bute, Scotland

DESIGNERS: Malcolm MacNeil, MacNeil family, Lord Strathcona
OWNERS: Alex Howard, Jane Howard
GARDEN STYLE: 19th-century woodland
SIZE: 20 acres (8.1 ha)
CLIMATE: Temperate
LOCATION: Isle of Colonsay, Argyll and Bute

If you are going to make the effort to visit a garden—and the effort involved in getting to the Isle of Colonsay is huge—then it helps if there are other things to do. Fortunately the gardens of Colonsay House are in the middle of one of the most beautiful islands in the world. It is 8 miles (13 km) long and surrounded by long, sandy beaches, sparkling seas, fantastic wildflowers, and sheep speckled hills.

True, this is Scotland and the winter weather can turn nasty with 60-mile-an-hour (97 km/h) winds. However, this garden had wise founders who, in the nineteenth century, planted broad-leaved woodland around the gardens. This was augmented in the 1930s, and as a result, the gardens are sheltered and capable of supporting many interesting and unusual shrubs. The bones of an older, grander garden layout are still visible among the woodland, though most recent plantings were masterminded by Lord Strathcona (the current owner's father). Closer to the house, the gardens are more domesticated: a beautifully planted and lively creek, immaculately mown grass terraces, and the Loggia Garden. This garden leads to the more recent Lighthouse Garden, the design for which is centered around the distorting glass of the abandoned lens from the Islay Lighthouse. In short, there is something for everyone. Is it worth the trip? You bet. JA-S

Ascog Hall Victorian Fernery and Gardens

Isle of Bute, Argyll and Bute, Scotland

DESIGNERS: Edward La Trobe Bateman, Wallace Fyfe, Katherine Fyfe
OWNERS: Wallace Fyfe, Katherine Fyfe
GARDEN STYLE: 19th-century fernery, modern plantings
SIZE: 3 acres (1.2 ha)
CLIMATE: Temperate
LOCATION: Isle of Bute, Argyll and Bute

Ascog Hall was built in the Scottish baronial style by Glasgow merchant Alexander Bannatyne Stewart. It has views of the Firth of Clyde and a recently rescued, glass-roofed Victorian fernery. After Stewart's death, the house and fernery lay neglected and consumed by undergrowth. The current owners stumbled upon it (literally) in 1990. After clearing years of rubbish, the mosaic paths and sandstone walls became visible. Later, a copy of the *Gardeners' Chronicle* (dated 1879), with a description of the place and an inventory of all the ferns, told them exactly what they had found.

The Fyfes were able to erect a new roof, identical in every way to the original, and the possibility of restoring the structure to its former glory became reality. Amazingly, one fern (a 1,000-year-old *Todea barbara*) had survived, and with help from the Royal Botanic Gardens in Edinburgh, the rest of the fernery has also been fully stocked. Around this extraordinary enterprise, the Fyfes are also renovating the rest of the gardens. These were designed by Edward La Trobe Bateman and, like the house and fernery, also lay under many years' worth of undergrowth. Now there are new plantings beside the original paths, a rose garden, and a brand-new gravel garden. JA-S

RIGHT The stunning Victorian fernery at Ascog Hall, restoration of which commenced in the 1990s.

Mount Stuart Gardens

Isle of Bute, Argyll and Bute, Scotland

DESIGNERS: Marquises of Bute, Thomas Mawson,
   Rosemary Verey, James Alexander-Sinclair
OWNER: Johnny Bute
GARDEN STYLE: 18th-century parkland, 19th-century
   rock garden, 20th- and 21st-century planting
SIZE: 300 acres (121.5 ha)
CLIMATE: Temperate
LOCATION: Rothesay, Isle of Bute, Argyll and Bute

Mount Stuart House sits in Gothic splendor on the Isle of Bute. Warmed by the Gulf Stream and nourished by good Scottish rain, the gardens and woodland have developed over three centuries. They were begun in 1717 and consolidated by the third Earl of Bute, a notable botanist and gardener (who helped found Kew Gardens, page 386) and, briefly, prime minister.

The gardens are divided into distinct areas. The oldest and largest is the Policies (the Scottish equivalent of English parkland). Areas of woodland are sliced by walks and rides. The Wee Garden—which belies its name by occupying a good 5 acres (2 ha)—was laid out in 1823. It concentrates on plants from the southern hemisphere. The Rock Garden occupies the most prominent position, by the house, and was designed by Thomas Mawson in the 1890s. It is set around two streams that were piped through stone conduits for over 1 mile (1.6 km), and houses plants from Asia. Farther out, the kitchen garden was laid out by Rosemary Verey around a glass pavilion and was enthusiastically replanted in 2000 by James Alexander-Sinclair. The newest garden is around the brand-new visitor center, where lines of plants are laid out in a pattern inspired by a paper clip.

For many generations, the Bute family has been unafraid of change. This is obvious in the architecture and decor of the house. It is also apparent in the gardens, which reflect many historical periods but which are not tied to any particular one. JA-S

Achamore Gardens

Isle of Gigha, Argyll and Bute, Scotland

DESIGNER: Sir James Horlick
OWNER: Isle of Gigha Heritage Trust
GARDEN STYLE: 19th- and 20th-century woodland garden
SIZE: 40 acres (16 ha)
CLIMATE: Temperate
LOCATION: Isle of Gigha, Argyll and Bute

Achamore Gardens is the highlight of any visit to Gigha, the most southerly of the Hebridean Islands. Getting there is quite a trip. It kicks off with a slow drive down the Kintyre Peninsula, before boarding a ferry that makes the 3-mile (5 km) journey across the Sound of Gigha. The trip is worthwhile in spring when the gardens fill with rhododendrons in every shape and size. You will see the *Rhododendron sinogrande*, with 31-inch-long (80 cm) leaves, and others with attractive foliage, such as *R. preptum,* whose leaves have brown, felted undersides. Many of the plants are imposing, though there are compact forms, like

R. 'Blue Tit'. Some have scented blooms, while others (*R. rubiginosum*) have aromatic foliage. There are also varieties from the Himalayas with attractive bark (*R. thomsonii*) and plum-colored stems.

The garden was started in 1884 when Captain William Scarlett bought the land and built Achamore House. He planted sycamore and spruce trees to provide shelter from the strong, salt-laden, westerly gales and to give cover for game birds. However, not until Sir James Horlick arrived in 1944 was the garden filled with rhododendrons and exotic plants. He cut a series of connecting clearings through thick stands of rampant *R. ponticum* and planted hundreds of trees and shrubs with nothofagus, cercidiphyllum, camellia, and eucryphia. After Horlick's death in 1972, the garden suffered for many years. However, the local community bought the island in 2002 and started a program of restoration. Few rhododendron gardens in Britain have such a beautiful location. MC

Dun Ard

Stirling, Scotland

DESIGNERS: Niall Manning, Alastair Morton
OWNERS: Niall Manning, Alastair Morton
GARDEN STYLE: 20th-century modern
SIZE: 3 acres (1.2 ha)
CLIMATE: Temperate
LOCATION: Fintry, Stirling

The idea underpinning this modern gem is that hidden gardens are more exciting because they demand exploration. Consequently all you see of it from the sliding glass doors at the back of the house is a long, green vista running up the hill. Dun Ard was made from scratch by Niall Manning and Alastair Morton in 1990 from a piece of hillside overlooking the Fintry Hills. The garden unfolds in a series of terraces and sloping banks, screened from each other by yew, holly, and hornbeam hedges. Strong architectural spaces, including a formal pond, terrace parterre, sandstone circle, and braided hornbeam

walk are counterpointed with a woodland garden, orchard, and meadow areas with naturalized bulbs and orchids. The early-summer border is a mass of tall, wavy veronica, airy fennel, and acid-green euphorbias. The late-summer garden is planted with grasses and hot colors. The owners are avid cooks, so the garden has a vegetable border, two greenhouses, an ornamental potager, and a herb garden, all organic, with emphasis on heritage varieties.

Niall is chairman of the Garden History Society in Scotland. The garden is woven with ideas that reach across centuries, gleaned from books, travel, and garden visiting. The long, green vista was inspired by Italy's Villa Cetinale, near Siena, and the terrace parterre by the hanging gardens of the Palazzo Piccolomina in Pienza. The pyramid is modeled on the ice house at the Désert de Retz in Paris, and the sandstone circle echoes the sky garden installations of artist James Turrell in west Cork in Ireland. VR

Stirling Castle

Stirling, Scotland

DESIGNER: Unknown
OWNER: Historic Scotland
GARDEN STYLE: 16th- and 19th-century formal
SIZE: 2.4 acres (1 ha)
CLIMATE: Temperate
LOCATION: Stirling Old Town, Stirling

The royal castle of Stirling gazes down over the sites of some of the most significant battles fought in Scotland. Below these walls, the armies of England were defeated at Stirling Bridge by William Wallace in 1297 and at Bannockburn by Robert the Bruce seventeen years later. Two-and-a-half centuries later, Mary Queen of Scots spent her childhood within the castle and was crowned here (1543). Her son, James VI of Scotland and I of England, was baptized here.

Given the castle's long history and elevated, defensive position, it may come as some surprise that its Queen Anne Garden was created as recently as the nineteenth century. With its series of manicured lawns, shady trees, and flower beds at the foot of ancient stone walls or flanking the stone paths where they are filled with roses, the design adds to the tranquil atmosphere. The most interesting garden is actually best viewed from the Queen Anne garden. Dating from the 1520s, the King's Knot was created outside the castle walls by James V (the father of Mary Queen of Scots) as a token to his French wife and queen, Mary of Guise. Today all that remains of the large formal garden (modified in the nineteenth century) are the clearly visible earthworks. There is also evidence to suggest that the sixteenth-century garden replaced an even earlier garden made by James I after his coronation in 1424. This is believed to have been an imitation of the King's Garden outside the walls of Windsor Castle. James had been imprisoned at Windsor. From his tower room, he first saw his future queen, Lady Jane, in the garden. TM

Cambo Estate

Fife, Scotland

DESIGNER: Catherine Erskine
OWNERS: Catherine Erskine, Peter Erskine
GARDEN STYLE: 20th-century formal and woodland
SIZE: 72.5 acres (29.3 ha)
CLIMATE: Temperate
LOCATION: Kingsbarns, St. Andrews, Fife

A long drive curves through deciduous woodlands on the Cambo Estate to the substantial Victorian house, built in 1881. Behind, a fast-running creek tumbles down the middle of the 2.5-acre (1 ha) walled garden, through the woodlands, and out to the North Sea. The garden blooms throughout the year, with snowdrops in late winter and daffodils in spring.

The estate has been the property of the Erskine family since 1688 and was inherited by Peter Erskine in 1976. His wife, Catherine, has developed the gardens over the past two decades, focusing on snowdrops, while planting up the walled garden to provide color from May until late fall. The main site for the snowdrops—beside the woodlands—is a small area, reclaimed from undergrowth, where cultivars such as the honey-scented Galanthus 'S. Arnott' flourish. They are followed by deep blue muscari, anemones, chionodoxa, and dog-toothed violets in the walled garden. Other features are a lilac walk, old apple trees covered with roses, roses scrambling over pergolas, and old and shrub roses beneath a plum tree in a bed edged with lady's mantle (Alchemilla mollis).

Down the center of the walled garden is a nepeta walk, backed by alliums, old roses, and hardy geraniums for early summer. In midsummer, the ornamental potager comes into its own with its loose, flowing design and low potentilla hedging. There are a number of herbaceous borders with late-flowering plants, such as Japanese anemones, Michaelmas daisies, eupatorium, and schizostylis interspersed in the modern style with tall grasses. VB

Earlshall Castle

Fife, Scotland

DESIGNER: Sir Robert Lorimer
OWNERS: Paul Veenhuijzen, Josine Veenhuijzen
GARDEN STYLE: Late 19th-century topiary garden
SIZE: 4 acres (1.6 ha)
CLIMATE: Temperate
LOCATION: Leuchars, Fife

With its enormous, freestanding, topiary peacocks and pepperpots rising from the lawn, Earlshall is the best topiary garden in Scotland. The late Christopher Lloyd's father, Nathaniel Lloyd, was so taken with it in the 1920s that he had his architect, Edwin Lutyens, copy the idea at Great Dixter in England (see page 424). Equally thrilling is the architecture that sets it off, a seamless blend spanning five centuries.

The restoration of the sixteenth-century castle, together with the design of the garden and pavilions in the late 1890s, is the work of the brilliant Arts and Crafts architect Sir Robert Lorimer. The example of his parents' restoration of nearby Kellie Castle and his own input into the design of the garden there won the twenty-six-year-old Lorimer this important first commission. Designed on a theme of surprise and contrast, Lorimer built the entrance lodge that opens onto a long double avenue of limes, with grass coming flush to the house, and open views to the park. The garden, however, remains hidden behind its walls. It is divided into an orchard, box parterre, sunken bowling green, topiary lawn, and kitchen garden, all divided by walls of clipped holly and yew.

Lorimer's love of craftsmanship can be seen in the wooden thistle gate, the curved arbor at the end of the yew walk, and the stone portal inscribed with a quote from *As You Like It*. Stone animals became Lorimer's signature motif. You will find a row of mischievous monkeys sitting on top of the Tool House, and both an owl and a basket of birds adorning the Dowry House. VR

Kellie Castle and Garden

Fife, Scotland

DESIGNER: Sir Robert Lorimer, Louise Lorimer
OWNER: The National Trust for Scotland
GARDEN STYLE: Traditional Scottish walled garden,
    17th-century with late 19th-century additions
SIZE: 1.5 acres (0.6 ha)
CLIMATE: Temperate
LOCATION: Pittenweem, Fife

As well as being the most atmospheric garden you can think of, Kellie Castle holds a special place in Scotland's affection. For over a century, it was the home of three of the country's best-loved, twentieth-century artists: the architect Sir Robert Lorimer, the painter John Henry Lorimer, and the sculptor Hew Lorimer. Fortunately there was also a gardener in the family, Louise Lorimer, to whom the garden owes its legacy of old roses.

It was rescued from dereliction in 1878 by Professor James Lorimer, his wife, and six nearly grown children, who used their formidable talents to create a garden in the spirit of the seventeenth-century castle. Paths edged with box lead you under rose arches into smaller, secret gardens and to a charming garden house designed by Robert Lorimer with a stone bird on top. You are met at every turn by flowers, fruits, and vegetables, all mingled together in the manner of an old Scottish garden.

Now owned by the National Trust for Scotland, the garden has been run organically since 1990. Signs in the garden explain how this is done. The head gardener follows a "gardening with friends" policy. Flowers are chosen to attract beneficial insects. Seed- and berry-bearing plants are grown to feed the birds. There are many examples of companion planting in the vegetable borders, with associations and methods designed to attract, deter, or confuse pests and also to improve the vigor of the plants. The garden participates in a seed saving program to safeguard heritage vegetables. It has a National Collection of rhubarb ranged along its north-facing wall together with many varieties of old and new disease-resistant potatoes.

Its sense of enclosure, cottage-garden planting, and old-world charm encourage a steady stream of painters to set up their easels here. Additionally, local children build a new scarecrow here every year. VR

Dirleton Castle and Gardens

East Lothian, Scotland

DESIGNER: Historic Scotland
OWNER: Historic Scotland
GARDEN STYLE: 19th-century Arts and Crafts
SIZE: 3.5 acres (1.4 ha)
CLIMATE: Temperate
LOCATION: Dirleton, East Lothian

Gardens have been at Dirleton Castle since the sixteenth century, and those seen here today are restorations of ones made in the mid-nineteenth and early twentieth centuries. The existing castle was built in the thirteenth century, but most of it was destroyed on the orders of Robert the Bruce 100 years later. About 300 years down the line, the castle belonged to the Ruthven family. They created formal gardens, a yew-hedged bowling green, and orchards.

The Victorian head gardener, David Thompson, brought the gardens at Direlton up to date, most noticeably by creating geometric parterres filled with colorful bedding. They continue to be planted each June for the summer displays. The Arts and Crafts herbaceous borders were introduced in the 1920s and are in the book of *Guinness World Records* because they are the longest in the world at 262 feet (80 m) long. They have been beautifully restored and flank the main axial paths through the site. The borders are edged in miniature box hedging. Within them, shrubs and more structural plants such as pampas grass (*Cortaderia selloana*), cardoon, and New Zealand flax (*Phormium tenax*) provide a backdrop to a wide range of softer herbaceous plants and herbs such as sedum, catmint, and bergamot as well as ornamental grasses. Best of all, the flame creeper (*Tropaeolum tuberosum*) weaves its way through a yew hedge, flashing scarlet flowers against dark green.

Although the planting at Dirleton is sumptuous, the setting makes it magical. Ruined castles are often evocative places, and Dirleton is one of the best. AJ

Shepherd House Garden

East Lothian, Scotland

DESIGNERS: Sir Charles Fraser, Lady Ann Fraser
OWNERS: Sir Charles Fraser, Lady Ann Fraser
GARDEN STYLE: Late 20th-century walled garden
SIZE: 1 acre (0.4 ha)
CLIMATE: Temperate
LOCATION: Inveresk, East Lothian

When Sir Charles and Lady Ann Fraser set about redesigning their unusual, triangular, walled garden at Shepherd House, they really had just two criteria. The first was to follow their passion for plants and design. The second was that Lady Ann, a botanical artist, would be allowed to concentrate on her work, which largely revolved around tulips.

The son of a Church of Scotland minister, who grew up in a garden full of "regimented rows of plants," Charles is the tidy one, while Ann prefers the more romantic touch. The result is a formal layout with informal plantings, the tulips taking center stage in spring. Directly in front of the house is the Millennium Terrace where a symmetrical design of redbrick paths divides lavender-edged beds planted with standard hollies underplanted with tulips. To the east, the wedge-shaped space that remains has been neatly filled with a parterre.

The upper garden is reached by a set of steps fixed into an alpine wall leading to a rectangular stone-edged pond dominated by a bronze statue of a nude girl. Note the formal brook running under a series of rose- and wisteria-covered arches linking the pond to a raised stone fountain at the top of the garden. The remaining space is dedicated to a wide variety of woodland plants, shrubs, roses, and a small bulb meadow. The couple cheerfully acknowledge that their ideas have resulted in some lively discussions at almost every stage of their twenty-year labor of love. "Ann is usually right about most things, but don't tell her I said so," Sir Charles says. AG

Royal Botanic Garden Edinburgh

Edinburgh, Scotland

DESIGNERS: McNab family, Balfour family, Robert Graham
OWNER: Royal Botanic Garden Edinburgh
GARDEN STYLE: Early 19th-century botanic garden
SIZE: 77 acres (32 ha)
CLIMATE: Temperate
LOCATION: Inverleith Row, Edinburgh

For botanists, Edinburgh's Royal Botanic Garden is an eminent institution at the forefront of describing and discovering plants, and also their uses, evolution, and biology. For gardeners, it is a beautifully landscaped garden and meticulous plant collection, providing inspiration and relaxation in the center of the capital.

The collection of rhododendrons is said to be the most comprehensive in the world, and its extent is a legacy of Scottish plant hunter George Forrest. While traveling in the Himalayas and China at the beginning of the twentieth century, he collected over 30,000 plant specimens that were sent directly to Edinburgh

Botanic Garden for classification and distribution. Beside 300 rhododendrons, he sent back magnolias, lilies, camellias, gentians, peonies, and primulas. The garden has continued to be planted with Chinese natives that, with Forrest's introductions, can be seen covering the Chinese hillside. Here there are winding paths, a waterfall, and Chinese pavilion, all of which evoke the plants' native habitat.

Many of Forrest's introductions can also be seen in the massive 2-acre (0.8 ha) rock garden that contains over 5,000 species. The mounds, gorges, screes, and streams replicate conditions in high alpine meadows, Arctic valleys, and Mediterranean scrub. More alpines are grown in the Alpine House, where you will see brightly colored draba, gentians, and primulas, and also fritillaria and Chilean crocuses.

The Botanics, as the garden is known, is situated on a hill north of Edinburgh, and many areas have stunning views of the city and Edinburgh Castle. JHo

Dawyck Botanic Garden

Scottish Borders, Scotland

DESIGNERS: Veitch family, Naesmyth family, Balfour family
OWNER: Royal Botanic Garden Edinburgh
GARDEN STYLE: 13th- to 20th-century woodland garden
SIZE: 60 acres (24.3 ha)
CLIMATE: Temperate
LOCATION: Stobo, Peebleshire, Scottish Borders

Dawyck has one of the best collections of trees in the world. The garden was created by many owners, all of whom have left their impression on the wooded site. From the thirteenth to the seventeenth centuries, the land was owned by the Veitch family, early ancestors of the famous dynasty of England-based nurserymen. In 1691 the estate was bought by James Naesmyth. His son and grandson planted widely and created terraces in front of the house. In 1897 the garden was bought by the Balfour family, who developed the garden until 1978, when management was taken over by the Royal Botanic Garden in Edinburgh.

The garden includes many important trees. In the nineteenth century, many plants found in North America were sent to Dawyck, including many specimens introduced by Scottish plant hunter David Douglas and some that he grew himself from seed. There is a very impressive Douglas fir (*Pseudotsuga menziesii*) that was planted in 1835. The garden also features a beech tree that has been named after the garden. *Fagus sylvatica* 'Dawyck' is an upright form that was found as a seedling in the 1850s and today is over 100 feet (33 m) high. Apart from this old-timer, Dawyck has another twenty-five champion trees. There is also something for those who like smaller plants. At the heart of the garden is a ravine where a stream rushes over rocks before flowing under a rustic, arched stone bridge. In spring the stream's steep banks are carpeted by massed ranks of snowdrops. You will also see the world's first reserve for fungi, mosses, and liverworts. MC

Mellerstain

Scottish Borders, Scotland

DESIGNER: Reginald Blomfield
OWNERS: Earl John Haddington, Countess Jane Haddington
GARDEN STYLE: 20th-century baroque
SIZE: 5 acres (2 ha)
CLIMATE: Temperate
LOCATION: Gordon, Scottish Borders

Located right in the heart of Sir Walter Scott country, this beautiful house is a unique example of both William and Robert Adam, this being the latter's first important commission in Scotland. It was built during 1770–78 for the Baillie family, the Earls of Haddington. However, initially the garden did not really take off. It wasn't until much later, in the early twentieth century, that Reginald Blomfield carried out a series of restorations for Lord Binning. He designed the garden in the style of André Le Nôtre, inserting a grandiose scheme that somehow managed to merge the architectural garden into the blue of the horizon.

As Blomfield said, "Indeed it would have required the resources of Louis XIV to carry out the whole of my design." He made further modifications to the scheme in 1911, when the lower terrace was removed to create the gardens.

The balustraded terraces have parterres that are planted with herbaceous perennials and sub-shrubs. With the borders along the house facade facing south, they include a good variety of Mediterranean climbers and herbs. The descent then takes you to a lower terrace and the croquet lawn. It is worth walking to the lake because the slope down here is so steep that you actually lose sight of the house. Incidentally, the north front is approached by a patte d'oie providing vistas out into the countryside. Tucked in among the trees is a charming cottage orné with a romantic cottage garden. Finally you should certainly not leave until you have visited the café and well-stocked nursery. CH

Stobo Castle

Scottish Borders, Scotland

DESIGNER: Hylton Philipson
OWNER: Stobo Castle Health Spa
GARDEN STYLE: 20th-century Japanese water garden
SIZE: 4 acres (1.6 ha)
CLIMATE: Temperate
LOCATION: Stobo, Peebles, Scottish Borders

When Georgina married Hugh Seymour, a farmer, in 1998, she found herself faced with a magnificent, but overgrown, Japanese water garden situated about 600 feet (182.8 m) from their farmhouse. Started in 1904 by the owner, Hylton Philipson, the gardens were a by-product of his attempt to generate electricity for Stobo Castle by building a dam across a creek at the foot of a valley. Shortly afterward he built another, lower dam at the head of a 30-foot (9 m) drop into a narrow gorge. The resulting waterfall, later framed by a Japanese-style trompe l'oeil bridge, was the foundation of the water garden.

By coincidence this project took place shortly after Japan had reopened itself to the West, and Philipson was persuaded to use some Eastern garden design ideas on his site. The narrow gorge and natural flow of water lent themselves to the naturalistic style of landscape, then popular in Japan. Exciting new arrivals such as Japanese maple (*Acer palmatum*), *Cornus kousa*, and the katsura tree (*Cercidiphyllum japonicum*) were planted on either side of the valley. A collection of Japanese artifacts was imported, and a network of narrow paths laid out.

Georgina admits she felt unqualified to tackle the garden at first. At that point nature stepped in. One storm uprooted 200 rhododendrons, while another took out a lot of the conifers. This encouraged a program of rejuvenation and the planting of as many original species as possible. New trees were combined with a collection of specialist rhododendrons, giving magical displays in the spring and autumn. AG

Brodick Castle

Isle of Arran, North Ayrshire, Scotland

DESIGNER: Duchess of Montrose
OWNER: The National Trust for Scotland
GARDEN STYLE: Edwardian garden, ornamental woodland
SIZE: 60 acres (24.3 ha)
CLIMATE: Temperate
LOCATION: Isle of Arran, North Ayrshire

The first thing to look out for when you take the ferry from Ardrossan is the peak of Goatfell, the highest mountain on Arran. Then, as you sail into Brodick Bay, you will see the sandstone castle 2,500 feet (762 m) below it, surrounded by terraces and a shelter belt of trees that make Brodick one of the mildest and most famous of Scotland's west-coast gardens.

Home of the Dukes of Hamilton for nearly 500 years, the woodland garden was transformed by the only child of the twelfth duke, Lady Mary Louise. She subscribed to the China and Himalayan expeditions of George Forrest and Frank Kingdon Ward, among others. Over the years, her garden was enriched by subtropical plants from Tresco Abbey in Cornwall (see page 442), thanks to the Duchess' son-in-law Major James Boscawen, whose uncle owned Tresco in the Scilly Isles. In 1957 Brodick passed to the National Trust for Scotland. For the next thirty years, head gardener John Basford planted twenty-two varieties of magnolia and many Australasian shrubs. Thanks to his friendship with the head gardener at Achamore (see page 189), Sir James Horlick's collection of rhododendrons and other plants there were propagated and brought to Brodick.

The 1710 walled garden, remodeled in Edwardian style, has a new scheme of half-hardy plants used for late summer interest, and a network of paths leads through woodland, densely planted with treasures, all the way down to the sea. The famous pond garden is planted with gunnera, candelabra primulas, and phormiums, while the Lower Rhododendron Walk has large-leaved rhododendrons. VR

Little Sparta

South Lanarkshire, Scotland

DESIGNER: Ian Hamilton Finlay
OWNER: The Little Sparta Trust
GARDEN STYLE: 20th-century philosophical garden
SIZE: 4 acres (1.6 ha)
CLIMATE: Temperate
LOCATION: Dunsyre, Lanark, South Lanarkshire

The poet and artist Ian Hamilton Finlay left school at fourteen, without a classical education, yet his garden in the Pentland Hills is the Stowe (see page 319) of our times. His design looks back to classical Greece and Rome and, through inscriptions, buildings, and artifacts in the landscape, invites us to examine our place in nature and how we live. It is a revolutionary garden, politically and aesthetically, and is widely considered to be the most significant of our time.

The garden gives the impression of being a series of natural groves and pools, extending gradually out to a sweep of loch and hillside. In fact it is all landscaped. When Finlay moved here in 1966, there was nothing but barren sheep pasture and a single, storm-blasted ash. It has grown piecemeal over the years, reflecting his preoccupations, namely social justice, freedom from tyranny, and personal and political virtue. He renamed the property Little Sparta, alluding to his long war with Scottish bureaucracy. The name conveys the austere dignity of the site and Finlay's fascination with martial imagery. The garden is peppered with images of grenades and tanks. A figure of Apollo in his shrine clutches a machine gun.

For all this, there is a lyrical quality to the garden. The groves are hung with poems celebrating the call of the curlew and the murmur of streams. The sudden juxtapositions between fury and gentleness, between busy enclosures and windy moorland, between the grand and the cozy, between the noble and the foolish (it is full of jokes) make this small garden seem as large as the restless mind of its poet-designer. AE

Culzean Castle and Country Park

South Ayrshire, Scotland

DESIGNERS: The Kennedy family

OWNER: The National Trust for Scotland

GARDEN STYLE: 19th-century woodland and
walled garden

SIZE: 30 acres (12.1 ha)

CLIMATE: Temperate

LOCATION: Maybole, South Ayrshire

On a cliff facing the Atlantic sits Culzean Castle, once home to the Kennedy family, the Earls of Cassillis, and the Marquises of Aisla. Remodeled into a Georgian masterpiece by Robert Adam in the 1790s, it went to the National Trust for Scotland in 1945, together with 560 acres (226.8 ha) of landscape. The transformation of Culzean in the past twenty years, under head gardener Susan Russell, has meant that it now offers a breadth of interest unsurpassed in Scotland: you can explore the sunken terraces of the Fountain Court, planted with tree ferns (*Dicksonia antarctica*)

and Chusan palms (*Trachycarpus fortunei*); the citrus-laden orangery; a camellia house filled with scented rhododendrons; and the 20-acre (8.1 ha) Happy Valley. There is also a 5.5-acre (2.2 ha) walled garden.

The south garden has a restored vinery and peach house set off by Victorian ribbon bedding. There is also a collection of peonies, hostas interplanted with shuttlecock ferns (*Matteuccia struthiopteris*), a rock garden grotto, and a jungle garden with perennials, ferns, *Angelica gigas*, cannas, and bananas.

The north garden is dominated by a long, double herbaceous border. It is bisected in the middle by annuals and forty varieties of kniphofia. There is an apple orchard, soft fruit in cages, rows of vegetables, sweet peas, and espaliered fruit grown against walls. At the foot of these are the cutting flower borders that start in May with fifty varieties of tulip. They unfold with a succession of Dutch irises, annuals, gladioli, dahlias, and chrysanthemums. VR

Cally Gardens

Dumfries and Galloway, Scotland

DESIGNER: Michael Wickenden
OWNER: Michael Wickenden
GARDEN STYLE: 20th-century walled nursery garden
SIZE: 3 acres (1.2 ha)
CLIMATE: Temperate
LOCATION: Gatehouse of Fleet, Castle Douglas,
  Dumfries and Galloway

Built as a kitchen garden to service Cally House, this walled garden went into decline after World War I but was turned around in 1987 by the nurseryman and plant hunter, Michael Wickenden. The resulting nursery, specializing in rare perennials, has become a popular landmark for visitors drawn to the subtle charms of the area. Taking full advantage of 15-foot-high (5 m) walls and a Gulf Stream climate, the fusion of garden-cum-nursery is choreographed with a sensitivity that is rare among plant hunters. Thankfully it is more like a garden than a museum of plants, but

pause at your peril. Lingering over labels will leave you jet-lagged and drooling over treasures from the Andes and the mountains of southern Ecuador to northwest Yunnan, China, and the central highlands of Irian Jaya, New Guinea. Seeds are also obtained from other nurseries and botanic gardens worldwide, so the collection is impressive. There are thousands of varieties in the borders and several hundred in the sales area. This is a gardener's paradise where plant associations are thoughtful and considered, while allowing room for experiment.

Sales from the garden's nursery and donations have helped fund the continuing restoration of the original eighteenth-century structures, including the gardener's cottage, potting sheds, fruit store, mushroom house, and 100-foot-long (31 m) lean-to vinery. An orchard has also been replanted, using original varieties. If you are in the area, do not miss it. It contains a stunning range of plants. CWe

Glenwhan Gardens

Dumfries and Galloway, Scotland

DESIGNER: Tessa Knott

OWNER: Tessa Knott

GARDEN STYLE: 20th- and 21st-century ornamental landscape garden with ponds

SIZE: 12 acres (5 ha)

CLIMATE: Temperate

LOCATION: Wigtownshire, Dumfries and Galloway

Twenty-five years ago, 12 acres (5 ha) of hilly rock, bracken, and gorse 300 feet (91 m) above the Bay of Luce were fenced off by Tessa Knot. Tessa had originally trained as a chef, but her latest ambition was to exclude the local deer and rabbits from this site and then to plant oak, larch, rowan, cherry, and pine around the perimeter to provide shelter.

The two ponds with native water lilies form the hub of the garden. They are ringed by moisture-loving plants such as the giant gunnera (*Gunnera manicata*), flag irises, and skunk cabbage—all are enclosed by banks with shrubs and trees. Meandering paths, which were initially mapped out with sawdust, follow the lie of the land that is so rocky that planting holes had to be hewn out of the ground with pickaxes. It was exposed to the wind in all directions, so the existing gorse was used as shelter for the large collection of hybrid rhododendrons and azaleas before being gradually replaced by hollies, pittosporums, and olearias. Glenwhan is certainly a place to come and lose yourself. You can wander ever higher and stop at numerous vantage points before leveling off at the top. There paths have been made through 17 acres (6.8 ha) of moorland with 120 species of fern, grasses, and wildflowers.

The garden manages to retain the character of a semiwild landscape. It has a mix of native plants, including willow and sorbus, and the much more exotic Australian eucalyptuses, Chilean embothriums, and Montezuma pines. This "mixing" technique is repeated in its understory of shrubs and perennials. As far as fauna goes, imported blue peacocks now mingle with local waterfowl, and brown trout swim alongside koi carp. Still relatively young, the canopy of trees has not grown so high as to obscure the fantastic views, the fate of many other west-coast gardens. Tessa Knott is keeping a watchful eye that her garden remains open and airy. VR

Castle Kennedy Gardens

Dumfries and Galloway, Scotland

DESIGNERS: The Earls of Stair
OWNER: Lochinch Heritage Estate
GARDEN STYLE: 19th-century landscaped garden
SIZE: 75 acres (30.3 ha)
CLIMATE: Temperate
LOCATION: Stranraer, Wigtownshire,
Dumfries and Galloway

A crumbling old castle on the banks of a loch makes a dramatic focus for the garden at Castle Kennedy. Surrounded by rolling hills, the gardens have been built on a peninsula between two bodies of water, simply called Loch White and Loch Black. At one end of the peninsula is the ruined castle, and about 1 mile (1.6 km) away, a nineteenth-century replacement.

The original castle was built for the Kennedy family. It was bought by Sir John Dalrymple, the first Earl of Stair, in 1677. However, fire destroyed the castle in 1716. The site remained unoccupied until the new Castle of Lochinch was built in the 1860s. Although the land could have been forgotten during those 150 years, it saw gardening on an industrial scale. The second earl decided to ape the great formal gardens he had seen while an ambassador in France. For many years, he had also been in the military, so he enlisted the help of the army to make his garden. Under his command, the Royal Scots Greys and the Royal Inniskilling Fusiliers set to work, landscaping the peninsula to form grass ridges, mounds, and terraces on the banks leading up from the lochs.

The warming effect of the Gulf Stream means that the garden has many tender plants, including rare rhododendrons that flower in spring, and, at 56 feet (17 m) high, the tallest New Zealand *Pittosporum tenuifolium* in the British Isles. Keep an eye out for the well-stocked walled garden with many exotic shrubs, including bottlebrushes, and masses of herbaceous plants that fill the garden with summer color. MC

The Garden of Cosmic Speculation

Dumfries and Galloway, Scotland

DESIGNERS: Maggie Keswick, Charles Jencks
OWNER: Charles Jencks
GARDEN STYLE: 20th-century mathematical, scientific, cosmological
SIZE: 40 acres (16.2 ha)
CLIMATE: Temperate
LOCATION: Portrack House, Portrack, Dumfries and Galloway

Before 1990, Portrack was just a conventional estate with vegetables and raspberries, and greenhouses full of begonias. Now it houses the Garden of Cosmic Speculation, with a Physics Garden and an astroturf and aluminium parterre depicting black holes.

The garden began when Maggie Keswick and her husband, Charles Jencks, started digging out a lake. The spoil would be built up into ramparts, echoing the shapes of the surrounding hills. For Maggie, an expert on Chinese gardens, it was natural that they should represent the "land dragons" on the horizon. It turned out that these sculptural forms could also express the scientific and cosmological concepts that Jencks, a pioneering architect, was exploring in his work. So the double helix and snail mount took shape, suggesting a complex of meanings from Marxist dialectic to chaos theory to the structure of DNA. There is a long tradition of gardens influenced by literature. This garden instead embraces mathematics and science, particularly fractal geometry, a concept coined in 1977 to describe natural phenomena. We are accustomed to gardens made in straight lines. Jencks instead uses waves and twists, right down to the sunk fence, the fences, and the gates. Maggie Keswick died in 1995. However, Jencks has continued to develop his garden ideas. For example, a water staircase now traces the thirteen billion years that have elapsed since the beginning of the universe. AE

Logan Botanic Garden

Dumfries and Galloway, Scotland

DESIGNERS: The McDouall family
OWNER: Royal Botanic Garden Edinburgh
GARDEN STYLE: 20th-century exotic
SIZE: 15.5 acres (6.5 ha)
CLIMATE: Temperate
LOCATION: Stranraer, Wigtownshire, Dumfries and Galloway

Logan Garden dispels the usual misconception of Scotland as a wild and windswept place where only the toughest plants survive. On the southwest tip of the country, it is caressed by the Gulf Stream that allows exotic and tender plants to thrive.

At the beginning of the twentieth century, the McDouall brothers, Kenneth and Douglas, inherited the garden from their parents and began to experiment with exotic plants. They built a peat garden to house the vast numbers of acid-loving plants that were appearing in Europe from plant expeditions to China and the Himalayas. In the walled garden, fuchsias, diascias, osteospermums, salvias, echiums, and other tender perennials grow in abundance, and there is a collection of Australian tree ferns (*Dicksonia antarctica*) and New Zealand cabbage palms (*Cordyline australis*). A grove of eucalyptus is underplanted with callistemon, olearia, and leptospermum to create Australian woodland.

Now the property of the Royal Botanic Garden Edinburgh, Logan is a garden for enthusiasts. The plants that grow here grow almost nowhere else in Scotland. The most popular area is the Gunnera Bog, where the enormous, rhubarb-like leaves of *Gunnera manicata* form a translucent canopy. JHo

RIGHT The Logan Botanic Garden, where the Gulf Stream provides a warm microclimate for exotic plants.

Botanisk Have Århus

Århus, Denmark

DESIGNER: Unknown
OWNER: University of Aarhus
GARDEN STYLE: 19th-century botanic
SIZE: 53 acres (21 ha)
CLIMATE: Temperate
LOCATION: Aarhus, Århus
TRANSLATION: Aarhus Botanical Garden

One of the most impressive gardens in Denmark, the botanic garden at Aarhus attracts over 70,000 visitors every year to its five greenhouses. They cover an area of over 0.5 acres (0.2 ha), providing an educational resource for biology and botany students, school groups, and the public. Århus exchanges plants and seeds with other international organizations and botanic gardens in a bid to save endangered species.

From desert to rainforest and from China to California, you will find the world's different climates. The frost-free Subtropical Winter Rain House contains oaks, including the cork oak (*Quercus suber*) and holm oak (*Q. ilex*). They are planted together with Mediterranean and Australasian species, including rosemary, cistus, and bay. In complete contrast, gingers are the dominant species in the Tropical Herbs, Lianas, and Vines House. They thrive beside cucurbits, cardamom, vanilla, chili peppers, cinnamon, and cycads.

The Subtropical Summer Rain House is ideal for growing citrus, pineapples, and tree ferns. The Succulent House is full of cacti and other plants that survive in arid places, such as Namibia and parts of the Sahara Desert. Many species in this house display unique adaptations designed for heat and drought. At the other end of the spectrum, the ultramoist Tropical Rain Forest House is kept at 80–100 percent humidity, reflecting life in Borneo and the Amazon Basin. Here foliage from the banana and arum families, cannas, strelitzias, figs, and guavas, rounds off a captivating, entirely global experience. NS

Fredensborg Slotshave

Frederiksborg, Denmark

DESIGNERS: Johan Cornelius Krieger, Nicolai Henri Jardin
OWNERS: Queen Margrethe II, the Danish State
GARDEN STYLE: 18th-century baroque
SIZE: 300 acres (121 ha)
CLIMATE: Temperate
LOCATION: Fredensborg, Frederiksborg
TRANSLATION: Fredensborg Palace Gardens

Fredensborg's royal association began in 1678 when King Christian V bought land for hunting here. The current baroque palace, overlooking Esrum Lake, was built by Frederik IV. He named the castle to celebrate the peace accord of 1720, marking the end of the Northern War. Fredensborg means "castle of peace."

The garden is French baroque inspired and is in perfect harmony with both the palace architecture and the natural woodland setting. From the semicircular lawn behind the palace radiate seven allées. They have been replanted over the past thirty years to give the garden a more modern feel. Between the allées are woodlands and winding paths.

The garden evolved under Frederik V who, in the 1760s, employed French architect Nicolai Henri Jardin. Jardin developed the French theme adding the Versailles style *tapis vert*, a long lawn flanked by a double allée, leading down the slope to the lake. The sculptures in the park date from the 1760s and were installed on the recommendation of Johannes Wiedewelt. Those in the Nordmandsdalen (Norwegian Valley) were carved by J. G. Grund, the subject matter somewhat odd for the time. Rather than classical gods and heroes, the valley, which reopened in 2002 after restoration, has sculptures of Norwegian and Faroese farmers and fishermen.

The gardens nearest the palace are private. They are open to the public in July when the royal family is not in residence. Kitchen gardens here supply fresh vegetables and there is an orangery. TM

Frederiksborg Slot

Frederiksborg, Denmark

DESIGNER: Johan Cornelius Krieger
OWNERS: The Danish State
GARDEN STYLE: 18th-century baroque, formal
SIZE: 22 acres (9 ha)
CLIMATE: Temperate
LOCATION: Hillerød, Frederiksborg
TRANSLATION: Frederiksborg Castle

In the center of Hillerød rises this huge castle. Set on three islets and surrounded by a large lake, it is now home to the National History Museum. What the visitor sees today is the castle rebuilt by the brewing magnate J. C. Jacobsen, following a devastating fire in 1859. The original, early-seventeenth-century castle, of which only the chapel survives, was commissioned in the Dutch renaissance style by King Christian IV.

Created for Frederik IV by the royal architect and landscape designer Johan Cornelius Krieger, the detached baroque garden dates from 1720. These ornate gardens lasted for forty years through the reigns of three kings. By the end of the eighteenth century, they had been removed, since, by then, they were old-fashioned and too expensive to maintain.

However, in 1993, a three-year restoration began with the aim of bringing the gardens back to life. With the help of 65,000 box plants, 7,000 hornbeams, 375 limes, and 166 pyramid-shaped clipped yews, the garden is now as Krieger intended. From an oval pool at the top of a terraced slope there is a main axis with a canal and a series of waterfalls that cascade into the lake. To both sides of the cascade axis are box hedge parterres with the royal monogram, thickets and avenues, and ornamental topiary. The wider romantic and informal park dates from the mid-nineteenth century, and was created by Frederik VII. TM

LEFT The castle at Hillerød, setting for the National History Museum and surrounded by ornate baroque gardens.

Gisselfeld Kloster

Vestsjælland, Denmark

DESIGNER: Edward Milner
OWNERS: The Danneskjold-Samsøe family
GARDEN STYLE: 19th-century landscape park
SIZE: 110 acre (44.5 ha)
CLIMATE: Temperate
LOCATION: Haslev, Vestsjælland
TRANSLATION: Gisselfeld Manor

Surrounded by a moat, Gisselfeld is an imposing Gothic renaissance castle of large, red brick. Built in 1547 by the statesman Peder Oxe, it was frequently visited by Hans Christian Andersen. The well-wooded park, filled with 400 species of tree and ornamental shrub, features a lake with fountains and a grotto with a waterfall. The "stew pools" date from the founding of the castle and were used to stock carp to serve at the dining table.

The garden is in the English style and was designed by the British landscape gardener Edward Milner in the late nineteenth century. He is one of the great, forgotten figures in British and European garden history. He began his career as an apprentice at Chatsworth, under the head gardener and designer of the Crystal Palace, Sir Joseph Paxton. He later established himself as a designer. His firm, Milner-White, survived until the retirement of Frank Marshall in 1995, making it the longest established garden design practice in Britain.

Another feature of the gardens is the magnificent range of greenhouses with the orangery, which were built in 1879. They underwent extensive restoration in the 1990s, and now feature art exhibitions and one of Denmark's trendiest nurseries. TM

"[Gisselfeld] was frequently visited by Hans Christian Andersen"

Tivoli

København, Denmark

DESIGNER: Georg Carstensen
OWNER: Tivoli Ltd.
GARDEN STYLE: 19th-century amusement park
SIZE: 15 acres (6.1 ha)
CLIMATE: Temperate
LOCATION: Copenhagen, København
TRANSLATION: Tivoli Gardens

A walk through the center of Copenhagen on a summer's day is accompanied by the screams and shouts of those on the rides of perhaps the world's most famous amusement park. Taking its name from two eighteenth-century pleasure gardens—Jardin de Tivoli in Paris, and the Vauxhall Gardens in London—the charter to establish Tivoli & Vauxhall was sought from King Christian VIII in 1841 by Georg Carstensen.

The layout of Tivoli has not changed much since it was established on the site of a part of the city's fortifications, the lake being part of the old moat.

The main entrance has not changed since 1843. The Chinese-style Pantomime Theater looks as it did on its opening night in 1874.

However, the number of attractions on offer has grown since Carstensen proposed billiards, a restaurant, swings, merry-go-rounds, slides, smoking salons, concert pavilion, and a bazaar for the trading of Danish and foreign products. Today over four million people pass annually through the gates to be thrilled by twenty-five rides, eat at the twenty-eight restaurants, enjoy shows, and marvel at the grounds. The beds are filled with seasonal bedding—each year the spring flower show requires 134,000 tulips and narcissi alone. The winding paths take the visitor through a fairyland mix of water features and lakes, rides and stalls, restaurants and bars. When darkness falls, the 110,718 outdoor lights transform Tivoli into a magical realm, even more special during the winter opening season in the runup to Christmas. TM

Botanisk Have København

København, Denmark

DESIGNER: H. Flindt
OWNER: University of Copenhagen
GARDEN STYLE: 18th- and 19th-century botanic
SIZE: 25 acres (10 ha)
CLIMATE: Temperate
LOCATION: Copenhagen, København
TRANSLATION: Copenhagen Botanic Garden

Copenhagen's botanic garden has Denmark's largest collection of plants. It includes 25,000 specimens from over 13,000 species, and, most importantly, houses the only gene bank for Danish wild species. The garden is actually the botanic garden's fourth incarnation. The first version, the Hortus Medicus, was founded in the city center in 1600, but no funds were forthcoming for its upkeep so it closed in 1778, the same year that the second garden also closed. Oeder's Garden, as it was known, had also been laid out in the city center by G. C. Oeder in 1752, but in 1778 the king repurchased it and donated a new piece of land near Charlottenborg for a third garden. The third garden became increasingly cramped and, in 1842, moved to larger premises. The present and fourth garden (also located in the center of the city) opened in 1874 on land that had been the city's former fortifications. Consequently the rock gardens and other higher areas are made up from parts of the old ramparts, while the lake is a remnant of a moat.

While there, take a look at the circular Palm House. It was planned by Tyge Rothe (the head gardener) and J. C. Jacobsen (the founder of the Carlsberg brewery), and was built during 1872–74. Today it is filled with a collection of tropical and subtropical plants, cacti and other succulents, a collection of species orchids from Thailand and the Far East, and a historical collection of cycads. Outdoor highlights in the garden include annuals and alpines from Greece and Greenland. TM

Egeskov Slot

Fyn, Denmark

DESIGNER: Niels Krag the Younger
OWNERS: The Ahlefeldt-Laurvig-Bille family
GARDEN STYLE: 18th- to 20th-century mixed
SIZE: 36 acres (14.6 ha)
CLIMATE: Temperate
LOCATION: Kværndrup, Fyn
TRANSLATION: Egeskov Castle

The castle you see today was completed in 1554, though it dates from the fourteenth century, and is one of Europe's best moated renaissance castles.

The beautiful gardens surrounding the castle are a collection of compartments that have evolved over the years. The layout dates from around 1730 when Niels Krag laid out the formal French garden that, in 1962, was replaced by the present renaissance garden designed by the Frenchman Ferdinand Duprat. It features fountains, red gravel paths, and topiary pyramids, spirals, squirrels, and peacocks.

More recently a 10-foot-tall (3 m) sundial was designed by mathematician and poet Piet Hein, and the Peasant's Garden added. There are four mazes: the oldest, which is several centuries old, is of beech hedges instead of traditional yew. The most recent, planted in bamboo, is an exact copy, but features a Chinese tower in its center—it is the world's largest bamboo maze. The Fuchsia Garden has 104 different species, Europe's largest collection. There are also an organic Kitchen Garden, an English Garden, and to the south, by the lake, a Cottage Garden. The more contemporary gardens include water and a semicircular herbaceous border that blooms from mid-summer to late fall. Bordering the lawns are the rose beds with the pink *Rosa* 'Egeskov', named in 1982. Other buildings contain a museum of agriculture and various vintage motor museums with vintage cars and motorcycles, emergency vehicles and, well, you name it. TM

Glorup Slot

Fyn, Denmark

DESIGNERS: Nicolai Henri Jardin, H. A. Flindt
OWNER: Private
GARDEN STYLE: 18th-century formal, informal
SIZE: Greater than 25 acres (10 ha)
CLIMATE: Temperate
LOCATION: Svindinge, Fyn
TRANSLATION: Glorup Castle

The earliest reference to the castle at Glorup—where Hans Christian Andersen was often a visitor—dates to 1390. However, the first description of this castle was in 1599 when the seneschal of Denmark, Christopher Valckendorf, built a four-winged house on two stories with four towers and a moat—of this, only the cellar remains. In 1762 Glorup and the neighboring manor of Rygaard were purchased by Count Adam Gottlob Moltke. Moltke had Nicolai Henri Jardin modernize the house, which today is almost as it was in 1765.

Originally there was a garden in front of the south wing. But with the revamped house, and English landscape gardens sweeping Europe, Moltke created a larger English garden to the southwest of the castle. Here he used French inspired lime avenues and an obelisk. In the 1860s the farm was moved, leaving space for a garden laid out during 1862–75 by H. A. Flindt. Between the house and formal lake with its island fountain is the formal French garden with its two rows of Greek and Roman deities, and its patterns of shrubs and flowers. In the nineteenth century, it was also filled with 100,000 bedding plants every year. The classical temple with an Italian sculpture of Andromeda was moved here from Moltke's house in Amalienborg, Copenhagen (now part of the royal residence). Not far from the temple, a 138-foot (42 m) bridge crossed a ravine, but today only the towers remain. The park is home to a number of fine trees, including a tulip tree (*Liriodendron tulipifera*), wellingtonias, and a *Ginkgo biloba*. TM

Liselund

Isle of Møn, Storstrøm, Denmark

DESIGNER: Anders Kirkerup
OWNERS: Krista Steffensen, Steffen Steffensen
GARDEN STYLE: 18th-century romantic picturesque
SIZE: 14.8 acres (6 ha)
CLIMATE: Temperate
LOCATION: Isle of Møn, Storstrøm
TRANSLATION: Liselund Park

Liselund was once part of the steep terrain—steep by Danish topographical standards—of Klinteskoven (the Cliff Forest). In 1783 the Prefect of Møn, Antoine de la Calmette, acquired the land, built the old castle, and with his wife, Catharina Elisabeth (or Lisa) Iselin, created the garden that bears her name.

Both husband and wife died young, as did their spendthrift son who left his wife, Martha, a pauper (this White Lady of Liselund apparently still haunts the grounds). The Baronecy of Rosenkrantz acquired Liselund in the 1820s, built the new castle in 1887, and sold it in the 1960s. There followed a period of decline until the sale in 1989 to the present owners, who have restored and converted it into a castle-hotel. Despite the changes in fortune, the romantic garden created in the 1790s by Antoine and Lise remains largely intact. Liselund is an excellent example of the Danish late-eighteenth-century Enlightenment garden. The park and garden buildings were the work of Anders Kirkerup and still contain many of its picturesque ingredients. With its paths winding through the woodland setting, augmented by streams and lakes, the visitor comes across the buildings as if by accident rather than as a result of ingenious design. Scattered throughout the park are memorial stones, a Norwegian log cabin, Chinese teahouse, and a small, thatched castle (which has a collection of sculptures), a grotto, Egyptian pyramid, Greek ruin, Danish burial mound, and Swiss cottage. Thankfully the garden has survived in a good condition to this day. TM

Palanga

Klaipeda, Lithuania

DESIGNER: Edouard Fransua André
OWNER: The City of Palanga
GARDEN STYLE: 19th-century formal botanic gardens set in the remnants of primitive pine forest
SIZE: 275 acres (110 ha)
CLIMATE: Temperate
LOCATION: Palanga, Klaipeda

The coastal botanic garden of Palanga, with its sand dunes and beaches, primitive pine forests, historic buildings, pagan shrine, and its own flock of trumpet swans, is a big draw for those tired of city life.

Created in 1897 for Count Feliks Tyszkiewicz by botanist and landscape architect Edouard Fransua André, some 500 species make up the planting scheme, with trees brought in from botanical gardens all over Europe. Pine trees dominate, and their aroma penetrates the paths and flower-filled squares laid out among remnants of the ancient forest.

Count Tyszkiewicz's neorenaissance palace, set in formal gardens, now houses the Amber Museum. Over 25,000 pieces of "Baltic gold" are on display, many complete with ancient insects that predate humans by a million years. Nearby is the popular statue of Eglë, Queen of the Serpents, created by the sculptor Robertas Antinis. Providing ample fodder for Freudian analysis, the legend of Eglë tells the tale of a young girl forced into marriage with a sea snake. Eglë reluctantly agrees, and discovers that the snake is really a handsome young man. Love blooms, but Eglë's brothers murder her husband. In despair, Eglë turns herself and her children into pine trees.

Behind the palace and its lovely rose garden is the highest point in Palanga, Birutė Hill. This ancient Lithuanian sacred place was once the site of a pagan shrine tended by vestal virgins, and is now the site of a nineteenth-century chapel with beautiful stained-glass windows and a glorious view of the sea. MS

Bide-a-Wee Cottage

Northumberland, England

DESIGNER: Mark Robson
OWNER: Mark Robson
GARDEN STYLE: 20th-century informal plantsman's garden
SIZE: 2 acres (0.8 ha)
CLIMATE: Temperate
LOCATION: Stanton, Netherwitton, Morpeth, Northumberland

A lifelong project by owner Mark Robson, who began developing the disused sandstone quarry around his parents' home while still in his teens, Bide-a-Wee Cottage's plot combines sophisticated plantsmanship with an innate feeling for design, rooting this small retreat firmly into the surrounding countryside. Visitors cannot fail to sense the warmth and hospitality that years of continuous occupation, hard work, and quiet observation have conferred upon this garden.

Imaginative use of the quarry face combined with dense interplanting at ground level takes optimum advantage of all the available space. Robson's well-honed sense of scale also creates an illusion. Though far from apparent at first sight, this is very much a landscape in miniature. Those conifers? That archway? How tall and imposing are they really? In terms of seriously clever perspective, the "David"-sized Bide-a-Wee has a close affinity to Capability Brown's "Goliath" Sheffield Park in East Sussex (see page 427). The plantings include rhododendrons, ferns, and drifts of grasses with astilbes and primulas beside the spring-fed pool. Giant Himalayan lilies (*Cardiocrinum giganteum*) grow up to 12 feet (4 m) high by the quarry's north face, while agapanthus and crocosmia thrive around the garden in sunny, sheltered pockets. Another feature is a wildflower meadow containing numerous beehives. There is a National Collection of *Centaurea*. Almost anything you admire in the garden can be purchased as seed or young plants from the nursery area. RCa

Belsay Hall

Northumberland, England

DESIGNERS: Sir Charles Monck, Sir Arthur Middleton
OWNER: Managed by English Heritage for the Belsay Trust
GARDEN STYLE: Italianate, Greek revival, wild, romantic
SIZE: 30 acres (12 ha)
CLIMATE: Temperate
LOCATION: Belsay, Northumberland

Belsay Hall offers an insight into how the other half lived and gardened in Northumberland between the fifteenth and nineteenth centuries. The castle dates from 1460 and the adjoining Jacobean house from 1614, though sadly both of these structures have been reduced to picturesque ruins.

The eighteenth century saw the estate extended by Sir William Middleton. In 1804 his son, Sir Charles Monck, took the Grand Tour on an eighteen-month honeymoon and, on their return, Sir Charles and Lady Monck built the new hall in Greek revival style, surrounding it with formal terraces and flower beds built out of local rock, including the dramatic Quarry Garden. The microclimate allows liverworts, hart's tongue ferns (*Asplenium scolopendrium*), and Chusan palms to flourish as well as a fine specimen of *Cornus kousa* and the autumnally resplendent *Acer circinatum*. Sir Charles' grandson, Sir Arthur Middleton added a croquet lawn and created a parallel garden, west of the Quarry Garden, in the "wild garden" style popularized by William Robinson.

A walk around the estate begins on the terraces surrounding the mansion, moving on to the ruined castle and house, the Magnolia Terrace and Winter Garden, then the Croquet Lawn, and into the Quarry Garden, returning through the Wild Garden. The hall itself is gradually being restored, although it is still a shadow of its former, glorious self. CH

RIGHT This tall arch in an imposing high wall lends an atmosphere of mystery to the walled garden at Belsay Hall.

The Concrete Menagerie

Northumberland, England

DESIGNERS: John Fairnington, James Beveridge
OWNER: Muriel Fairnington
GARDEN STYLE: 20th-century sculpture garden
SIZE: 0.2 acre (0.08 ha)
CLIMATE: Temperate
LOCATION: Branxton, Northumberland

The Concrete Menagerie is thirty minutes' drive from Northumberland's number one tourist attraction, Alnwick Castle (see The Alnwick Garden, opposite). Although children will enjoy both, it is debatable which will touch them more: the state-of-the-art waterworks at Alnwick or the animal sculptures and figures in this small village garden.

John Fairnington was a senior partner in his family's joinery business. When he retired in 1961, he started to make sculptures to entertain his only child, Edwin, who was born with cerebral palsy. The garden contains a wonderful mixture of the familiar and the exotic, with rabbits, horses, cattle, dogs, stags, and sheep mingling with pandas, zebras, hippos, giraffes, and elephants. The figures are based on people in the village and national figures such as Winston Churchill.

John made life-size drawings of the sculptures that were executed by another retired employee of the firm, James Beveridge. The larger pieces were erected in the garden, with iron stays for legs, the armature molded with galvanized wire netting 1 inch (2.5 cm) thick and stuffed with paper. This was cemented over and painted. Paths and low-growing plants were laid around the statues to set them off.

When Edwin died in 1971, John made the Memory Corner, a final piece dedicated to his son. Although John lived to the age of ninety-eight, he never made another statue. The garden now belongs to his great-niece, Muriel, and has weathered over time. Untouched by any restoration project, it is the genuine article. VR

The Alnwick Garden

Northumberland, England

DESIGNER: Wirtz International

OWNERS: Twelfth Duke and Duchess of Northumberland, Alnwick Garden Trust

GARDEN STYLE: 21st-century formal

SIZE: 42 acres (17 ha)

CLIMATE: Temperate

LOCATION: Alnwick, Northumberland

The first garden at Alnwick was laid down in 1750 by the first Duke of Northumberland, who employed locally born Capability Brown to landscape the parkland adjoining his castle grounds. A century of development followed during which coal-fired hothouses raised exotic fruits such as pineapples. Czar Alexander I then tempted Alnwick's skilled head gardener off to the even colder climes of Russia, so Decimus Burton helped to reconfigure the gardens to the highest standards of Victorian good taste. However, the two world wars saw a fall into obscurity.

By the 1950s, this once-great place was just a nursery for trees. The current garden was the brainchild of Jane, the twelfth Duchess. After much research, she commissioned her master plan from Belgian father-and-son team Jacques and Peter Wirtz.

The new garden at Alnwick opened in 2001. Old cynics might feign horror, but most people have great affection for this unparalleled and wildly enthusiastic work in progress that is far and away Britain's most exciting fresh start in large-scale contemporary gardening.

Alnwick is now a garden very much for everyone, especially young families. Aimed more at stimulating the mind and imagination than in pocketing a fast theme-park buck, this visionary charitable project has reinvigorated the surrounding area and made a major destination out of a charming historic town once merely passed through by tourists on the fast track north to Edinburgh. RCa

Herterton House

Northumberland, England

DESIGNERS: Frank Lawyley, Marjorie Lawyley
OWNERS: Frank Lawyley, Marjorie Lawyley
GARDEN STYLE: 20th-century "rooms"
SIZE: 1 acre (0.4 ha)
CLIMATE: Temperate
LOCATION: Hartington, Cambo, Morpeth,
Northumberland

When Frank and Marjorie Lawyley first saw Herterton House, there was little going for it. The Elizabethan building was all but derelict, and the surrounding land contained the remains of a 400-year-old farmyard. Inspired by the amazing views across the uplands of Northumberland, though, they bought Herterton in 1976 and immediately started work on the garden. As their starting point, they sought advice from *A Housewife's Garden* published in 1617. It inspired the five historic areas now crammed into the modest site.

At the front of the house is the Formal Garden. As its name suggests, it has a bold structure provided mainly by hedges and topiaries in contrasting shades of green and gold. Although these offer year-round interest, the Lawyleys also added plants, such as *Iris unguicularis*, crocuses, pulmonarias, snowdrops, and periwinkles, to ensure that Herterton is alive in winter. The Physic Garden, to one side of the house, contains plants cultivated for their medicinal properties, as well as dye plants and culinary herbs.

However, the Lawyleys' greatest achievement is to the rear of the property. The Flower Garden is bounded by crisply cut hedges and dotted with topiaries of all shapes and sizes with spirals, standards, balls, columns, and buttresses. Beyond lies the Fancy Garden. It contains some of Herterton's best herbaceous plantings, and is crowned by a gazebo raised on a terrace. Do not miss the nursery, where the plants are available at good prices. LH

"As their starting point, they sought advice from *A Housewife's Garden* published in 1617"

Cragside Gardens and Estate

Northumberland, England

DESIGNER: Lord William Armstrong
OWNER: The National Trust
GARDEN STYLE: High Victorian
SIZE: 1,000 acres (405 ha)
CLIMATE: Temperate
LOCATION: Rothbury, Morpeth, Northumberland

As its splendid name suggests, Cragside is a dramatic garden of rocks and waterfalls. It is also a monument to Victorian confidence and success, and was the creation of the industrialist William Armstrong. Born in Newcastle, this gentleman intended to become a lawyer. However, his interest in engineering led first to his invention of the hydraulic crane and then, some time later, to the breech-loading gun.

In the late 1880s, he employed more than 20,000 people on Tyneside, and used his huge wealth to buy and restore Bamburgh Castle and to build Cragside. The mansion, perched on a rocky crag high above the Debdon Burn, was the first house in the world to be lit by hydroelectricity. The variety and scale of the grounds match it in their towering ambition. Surrounding the house on all sides is one of the largest artificial rock gardens in Europe. In the pinetum below, England's tallest Douglas fir (*Pseudotsuga menziesii*) soars above the other lofty woodland trees, many of them already large, established specimens when they were planted. Other features include the magnificent Dahlia Walk, in full bloom by late summer. Seven hundred dahlias are planted annually, with thirty different varieties. Bold and brash, the bed is edged with 2-foot-tall (60 cm) dahlias with taller blocks of semicactus, cactus, decoratives, and water lily types behind. Only double dahlias are used, developed in the 1860s. Everything here is designed to impress, including the labor-intensive carpet bedding that demonstrated how many gardeners Armstrong could afford. VB

Dalemain

Cumbria, England

DESIGNERS: The Hasell family

OWNER: Robert Hasell-McCosh

GARDEN STYLE: 20th-century formal and informal with 17th-, 18th-, and 19th-century features

SIZE: 5 acres (2 ha)

CLIMATE: Temperate

LOCATION: Penrith, Cumbria

Dalemain, which means "manor in the valley," has belonged to the Hasell family for over 300 years, and although open to the public, it is still a family home. The house at Dalemain started life as a defensive pele tower; in the 14th century a hall was built onto the tower, turning it into a manor house. Two wings were added in Elizabethan times, then a Georgian facade to the front of the house was built in 1744, followed by a matching facade facing the gardens in 1748.

A spectacular silver fir (*Abies cephalonica*), thought to be the largest in the UK, announces the beginnings of the landscape gardens. The Tudor knot garden is filled with 20th-century-style plantings of, among other things, santolina and rue. Beyond is the Rose Garden, which is infused by the delicious, heady perfume of over 150 old-fashioned varieties in June and July. Here too is an orchard where "apricock trees" were first planted in 1684. At the other end of the garden, there are abundant color-themed herbaceous borders and mixed borders of shrub roses, geraniums, pulmonaria, and rodgersias. An 18th-century alcove seat is shrouded in *Clematis tangutica*, while the roof of the 17th-century summer house is a pyramid with a sphere at its pinnacle.

Pass through a gate to beyond the ornamental gardens and enter Lob's Wood, where cherries, birch, and beech create dappled shade. A woodland walk travels by the edge of Dacre Beck, and in this place of simplicity, the peace and tranquillity allows one to absorb the spirit of this beautiful place. RSJ

Sizergh Castle

Cumbria, England

DESIGNER: Rock garden by T. R. Hayes & Son
OWNER: The National Trust
GARDEN STYLE: 20th-century informal
SIZE: 16 acres (6.5 ha)
CLIMATE: Temperate
LOCATION: Sizergh, Kendal, Cumbria

When Sizergh Castle's tower was first built in the fourteenth century, its purpose was to defend the surrounding countryside from marauders. The castle slowly became a home rather than a fortress, and the next logical step was to cultivate the grounds. This process was started in the eighteenth century and continued through to the 1920s, resulting in amazingly varied gardens. There are ponds, borders, lawns, and a kitchen garden.

Yet the most impressive addition is the 1926 rock garden. Flanked by harsh castle walls that have been carefully softened with climbers, the large rock garden almost looks like the remains of a quarry. It dips toward the center to form a watery dell, and the surrounding craggy terraces are densely planted with shrubs and perennials. Tucked out of sight behind the rock garden is the walled kitchen garden, which produces cut flowers as well as fruit and vegetables. Also, sheltered by the castle's north-facing walls, is part of the National Collection of ferns, of which Sizergh holds four representative genera.

The imposing castle crowns the gardens to the south. They are mainly terraced. One provides space for a deep herbaceous border with the giant yellow scabious rising majestically from the back in midsummer. Even the walls and steps contain plants, especially *Erigeron karvinskianus*, with its cheerful, daisylike flowers. There is also a formal Dutch garden, on a smaller, more intimate scale, and home to an avenue of "Shirotae" flowering cherries that are packed with blossoms in spring. A superb sight. LH

Hill Top

Cumbria, England

DESIGNER: Beatrix Potter
OWNER: The National Trust
GARDEN STYLE: 20th-century cottage garden
SIZE: 0.5 acre (0.2 ha)
CLIMATE: Temperate
LOCATION: Sawrey, Hawkshead,
Ambleside, Cumbria

The most evocative gardens are not necessarily the grandest. The garden that belonged to Beatrix Potter, writer and illustrator of some of the best-loved stories for children, is a modest plot typical of Lake District cottages. It is long and thin, surrounded by stone walls that enclose a charming jumble of fruit, vegetables, flowers, and herbs.

The garden is virtually as Beatrix Potter left it. By her own admission, her interest in gardening waned as her passion for farming grew. Her diary entries describe the garden as being untidy and full of weeds. Consequently, the current custodian, the National Trust, is not too worried if the odd tuft of grass sprouts between the paving slabs or the occasional weed peeps out between the flowers.

The stories written here include *The Tale of Tom Kitten* and *The Tale of Jemima Puddleduck*. Parents of small children, and aficionados, will recognize the rhubarb patch from the illustration in the latter. It forms part of the vegetable garden opposite the house, along with a hodgepodge of raspberry canes, strawberries, salads, globe artichokes (*Cynara scolymus*), and neat rows of potatoes. From here a stone-flagged path leads between long flower borders crammed with peonies, verbascum, tansy, and poppies, and favorite cottage-garden annuals such as sweet peas, pot marigolds, and love-in-a-mist. All this is thanks to Beatrix Potter's diaries and the books' illustrations, which have been invaluable in ensuring the planting stays much as it was. SA

Muncaster Castle

Cumbria, England

DESIGNERS: First Lord Muncaster, Sir John Ramsden
OWNERS: Peter Frost-Pennington, Iona Frost-Pennington
GARDEN STYLE: 18th-, 19th-, and 20th-century
woodland garden
SIZE: 77 acres (31.2 ha)
CLIMATE: Temperate
LOCATION: Ravenglass, Cumbria

The gardens at Muncaster Castle are set beneath the natural splendor of Scafell Pike, England's tallest peak, and were started in the 1780s by the first Lord Muncaster. He planted thousands of beech, chestnut, elm, and oak. Some survive to this day although many have been lost to disease and storms. What everyone comes to see are the rhododendrons. The acid soil and warming influence of the Gulf Stream are ideal for the tender varieties planted in the 1840s when a flood of new forms entered the country following plant-hunting expeditions to China.

In 1917 Sir John Ramsden inherited the estate and continued the tradition of planting rhododendrons. He helped fund plant collecting expeditions by George Forrest and Frank Kingdon-Ward. Many of the plants at Muncaster were grown from seeds brought back from their trips to China and the Far East. Ramsden was also an avid plant breeder, and he raised many new hybrids before his death in 1958. During his lifetime, the garden had the largest collection of rhododendron species in Europe. Also look out for the magnolias, cherries, hydrangeas, pieris, camellias, maples, and a 99-foot-high (30 m) *Nothofagus obliqua* that usually reaches monumental heights only in its native Chile and Argentina—it is the tallest of its type in the UK.

Finish off a visit by taking in the amazing views across the Lakeland Hills and Esk Valley from the curved grass terrace. From here you can see why Lord Muncaster chose this spot to build his garden. MC

Levens Hall

Cumbria, England

DESIGNER: Guillaume Beaumont
OWNER: Hal Bagot, Susan Bagot
GARDEN STYLE: Late 17th-century formal garden of hedges and topiary
SIZE: 10 acres (4 ha)
CLIMATE: Temperate
LOCATION: Kendal, Cumbria

The most famous topiary garden in Britain was laid out by a Frenchman. Guillaume Beaumont trained under André Le Nôtre at Versailles, and had worked at Hampton Court before he started laying out the garden at Levens Hall in 1694. Levens is a rare survivor of the period, saved from redevelopment by the inertia, poverty, or indifference of previous owners.

Over three centuries, Beaumont's yews have grown into mighty trees, clipped into a great variety of gloriously eccentric shapes. There are chess pieces, crowns, giant mushrooms, and fat-chested peacocks. You can also make out a lion, a British judge's wig, and even a jug of Moroccan ale. Two giant trees, styled the King and Queen, dominate the proceedings. These shapes may well be the work of Alexander Forbes, head gardener from 1810 to 1862, who restored much of the garden and introduced a number of golden yews.

Topiary is only part of Levens Hall's appeal. It has an orchard to make the saddest heart sing, with old mossy trees underplanted with bright red tulips. A long walk leads to a smoking house, set, appropriately, in the wilderness. Behind the ancient beech hedges lie a rose garden, fountain garden, and some superb mixed borders. The original bowling green, dug up for vegetables during World War II, is being returned to pristine flatness. Beyond the sunk fence (one of the earliest in the land) lies an enormous park, but most visitors will be drawn irresistibly back to the topiaries in the yew garden. AE

Holker Hall

Cumbria, England

DESIGNERS: Lord George Cavendish, Thomas Mawson
OWNERS: Lord Hugh Cavendish, Lady Grania Cavendish
GARDEN STYLE: Late 18th and early 19th-century formal, Italianate, wild gardens and woodland, 20th- and 21st-century additions
SIZE: 25 acres (4 ha), with 125 acres (50.6 ha) of parkland
CLIMATE: Temperate
LOCATION: Cark-in-Cartmel, Grange-over-Sands, Cumbria

The 200-year-old landscaped parkland at Holker Hall, created by Lord George Cavendish, left the present family members with a wonderful legacy. Like all good gardens, Holker (pronounced Hooker) has not remained static. Contemporary plantings and developments always ensure something fresh and exciting to see. Benefiting from the warm, Gulf Stream climate, Holker contains many choice shrubs and trees, and even some record breakers. For instance a 400-year-old lime tree with a girth measuring over 72 feet (22 m) that, in 2002, was listed by the Tree Council as one of Britain's fifty great trees.

Though the Hall dates back to the late sixteenth century, most of the garden's main architectural features appeared in the early 1900s. They include the balustraded terrace surrounding the hall, and the impressive limestone cascade and fountain reminiscent of those found in Italian renaissance gardens. Below the house the gardens have a vibrant, modern feel, containing a mix of herbaceous, bulbs, tender perennials, roses, and climbers. Hedges of clipped box and yew add formality.

The annual Holker Garden Festival attracts thousands of visitors, but you can always escape the crowds. A new turf labyrinth lies in the midst of a wildflower meadow. With its stark Cumbrian slate monoliths, it forms a link between the gardens proper and the park and natural landscape beyond. Through the trees you will glimpse the sea. JH

Brantwood

Cumbria, England

DESIGNERS: John Ruskin, Joan Severn
OWNER: The Brantwood Trust
GARDEN STYLE: 19th-century woodland garden, romantic
SIZE: 30 acres (12 ha)
CLIMATE: Temperate
LOCATION: Brantwood, Coniston, Cumbria

Located on the steeply rising shores of Coniston, in the heart of England's beautiful Lake District, Brantwood was the retirement home of the art critic John Ruskin. Ruskin championed the painter J. M. W. Turner, who was languishing in obscurity at the time, and, as Slade Professor of Fine Art at Oxford University, he lectured to many eminent students, including Oscar Wilde.

In 1889, Ruskin retired to his adopted home of Brantwood and largely remained there until his death in 1900, rarely speaking in public and publishing no further books or essays. Instead, he concentrated his efforts on improving the house and garden, although a number of his plans for the garden never came to be enacted during his lifetime. On his death, the property passed to his niece. She developed new features in the garden, such as the High Walk, a trail laid on land above the house that afforded extensive views to the beautiful Lakeland scenery all around.

What makes Brantwood especially interesting is that many of the features that can be seen today originated in ideas that Ruskin either considered for the garden or was generally interested in, without ever turning them into a practical reality. The Zig Zaggy is based on sketches that Ruskin made in the 1870s, and represents an allegorical journey to paradise, influenced by Dante's purgatorial mount. The Hortus Inclusus contains more than 200 native herbs laid out in the form of a medieval manuscript, and these are organized according to their medicinal, cosmetic, or culinary uses. MW

Newby Hall Gardens

North Yorkshire, England

DESIGNER: Major Edward Compton
OWNER: Richard Compton
GARDEN STYLE: 20th-century formal
SIZE: 40 acres (16.2 ha)
CLIMATE: Temperate
LOCATION: Ripon, North Yorkshire

The Weddell family has lived at Newby Hall in Yorkshire since they bought it in 1748, and William Weddell transformed the late seventeenth-century mansion into a neoclassical showcase for the treasures he brought back from his Grand Tour.

The gardens, however, had to wait until the twentieth century. Then, Major Edward Compton—a descendent of William Weddell—laid out most of the formal areas near the house and planted a shelterbelt of trees to protect the garden from the fierce Yorkshire winds. He created a series of enclosed gardens, including Sylvia's Garden. This was subsequently replanted by his son, Robin, with flowers in soft, subtle colors, and silver and purple foliage plants to maintain interest throughout the year. This garden is approached by a walkway known as the Wars of the Roses, after the fifteenth-century civil war in England, and is planted with the red rose of Lancaster (*Rosa gallica* var. *officinalis*), and the white rose of York (*R. rugosa*), with the beautiful, striped *R. gallica* 'Versicolor' dividing them. Newby Hall also holds a National Collection of *Cornus*, featured throughout the garden.

Finally, look out for Major Compton's majestic double herbaceous borders, sweeping down from the south side of the house to the River Ure, and divided by a broad swathe of lawn. They are backed by bold hedges of yew and are planted with a range of herbaceous perennials to ensure color from late spring to early fall. Visitors wishing to explore beyond the garden will find an ornamental woodland walk, with rustic bridges and cascades. VB

Castle Howard

North Yorkshire, England

DESIGNERS: Sir John Vanbrugh, Nicholas Hawksmoor, William Andrews Nesfield

OWNER: Castle Howard Estates Ltd.

GARDEN STYLE: 18th-century formal gardens, 20th-century arboretum

SIZE: 1,000 acres (405 ha)

CLIMATE: Temperate

LOCATION: York, North Yorkshire

Ostentatiously positioned to take advantage of the view across the surrounding landscape, Castle Howard—famous as the Brideshead estate in the television adaptation of Evelyn Waugh's *Brideshead Revisited*—was designed for the third Earl of Carlisle by Sir John Vanbrugh. It was built between 1699 and 1712. Vanbrugh, assisted by Nicholas Hawksmoor, also laid out the grounds, which remain more or less intact. Vanbrugh was responsible for the South Lake and the Temple of the Four Winds (1724–26), inspired by Andrea Palladio's Villa Rotunda in Vicenza, and Hawksmoor for the Mausoleum (1728–29).

There have been many changes and additions over the years. By 1750, the Walled Garden had doubled in size to its present 11 acres (4.5 ha), while the 70-acre (28 ha) Great Lake on the north front was filled with water in 1798. One notable nineteenth-century addition to the south of the house is the informal garden with its impressive parterres and fountains. In 1975, Lord Howard (1920–84) and plantsman Jim Russell began to create one of the most comprehensive collections of hardy, woody plants in Europe. In 1997, the 127-acre (51 ha) site became the Castle Howard Arboretum Trust (CHAT), a cooperation between Castle Howard and the Royal Botanic Gardens, Kew. It opened to the public in 1999. The garden at Castle Howard continues to evolve. Recent additions include the planting of 5 tons (4.5 t) of daffodil bulbs. TM

Duncombe Park

North Yorkshire, England

DESIGNERS: Charles Bridgeman, Stephen Switzer
OWNER: Sixth Lord Feversham
GARDEN STYLE: 18th-century English landscape
SIZE: 35 acres (14 ha), in 400 acres (160 ha)
   of parkland
CLIMATE: Temperate
LOCATION: Duncombe Park, Helmsely,
   North Yorkshire

The gardens at Duncombe Park are among a handful of remaining baroque landscapes in England. Exactly who was responsible for the creation of the garden is somewhat shrouded in mystery, but it is believed to have been Thomas Browne, brother-in-law of Sir Charles Duncombe, who inherited the estate and took the name Duncombe in the early 1700s. The design is attributed to Charles Bridgeman, while the architect Sir John Vanbrugh is believed to have advised Thomas Duncombe on the choice of site for the house. What is beyond doubt is that Duncombe Park has two features of great significance: the unique grass terraces and a prototype sunk fence.

The grass terraces are unique in design and execution, following the contours of the land rather than cutting across them. They are so effective that the writer Christopher Hussey described them as being "among the most spectacularly beautiful of English landscape conceptions of the 18th century." The sunk fence—a ditch and wall designed to keep livestock from the garden without cluttering the view—is believed to be one of the earliest in Britain. Among the architectural features in the garden is an Ionic temple, attributed to Vanbrugh.

The current owner, Lord Feversham, has kept the garden much as its founders envisaged. Today the park is a National Nature Reserve, and the management of trees and grassland is undertaken with wildlife in mind. MW

Scampston Hall

North Yorkshire, England

DESIGNER: Piet Oudolf
OWNERS: Lord Charles Legard, Lady Caroline Legard
GARDEN STYLE: 21st-century walled
   plantsman's garden
SIZE: 4.5 acres (1.82 ha)
CLIMATE: Temperate
LOCATION: Malton, Ryedale,
   North Yorkshire

In the past, the walled kitchen gardens of British stately homes were the powerhouses of the estates, where food would be produced in great quantities through the year. They were places where horticulture reached its apogee during the Victorian and Edwardian eras, but World War I and social change meant that many gardens became neglected.

When Sir Charles and Lady Caroline Legard took on Scampston Walled Garden, it still had its original walls, the remains of the greenhouses, the gardeners' outbuildings, and a central, oval pool, but was very different from how it once must have been. A full-scale restoration to a productive kitchen garden was unthinkable because of the excess produce. Instead, they appointed renowned Dutch designer Piet Oudolf to create a new oramental garden within the old walls.

With the site cleared of everything but the pool and the solid old walls, Oudolf created a series of garden "rooms" each with its own character. The result includes a number of bold ideas. The square reflective pool with its dyed black water is, arguably, the least successful element when compared with the broad, curving ribbons of molinia grasses, or Oudolf's trademark naturalistic, perennial plantings—both showstoppers in late summer. Around the perimeter of the garden is a plantsman's walk, full of interesting and often surprising plants, offering the more cautious gardener an idea of just what can be grown in North Yorkshire. MW

Studley Royal Water Garden

North Yorkshire, England

DESIGNER: John Aislabie
OWNER: The National Trust
STYLE: 18th-century landscape
SIZE: 150 acres (60.7 ha)
CLIMATE: Temperate
LOCATION: Ripon, Harrogate, North Yorkshire

Studley Royal Water Garden was always going to be special. One of very few eighteenth-century "green gardens" to survive in its original form, it was created by John Aislabie and his son, William, in the wild wooded valley of the River Skell. It uses the dramatic ruins of Fountains Abbey to maximum effect.

When the 1720 South Sea Bubble disaster ruined his political career, John Aislabie made the garden his life's work. He leveled the valley floor, confining the river to a central canal and creating geometric ponds at either side. From the romantic ruins of the great Cistercian abbey, a series of lawns and cascades leads,

via fine views and picturesque details, to the other end of the garden where they merge into a great lake and deer park. The acquisition of the abbey in 1768 was the crowning glory.

The final design of still water, lawns, and temples against a dark background of trees became the perfect fusion between the wild landscape and the polished planning of the eighteenth century. Over a period of ten years, two temples, a banqueting house, and the Octagon Tower were constructed as well as the Rustic Bridge, Grotto, and Serpentine Tunnel. Thanks to extensive restoration, clipped yew hedges border walks and frame views as the original design intended and native trees, such as beech and Scots pine (*Pinus sylvestris*), punctuate the landscape.

Artfully contrived to mimic and reflect nature, and with features arranged to infer antiquity from the start, Studley Royal and its romantic vistas, surprise views, and statuary are the epitome of elegance. NS

RHS Garden Harlow Carr

North Yorkshire, England

DESIGNERS: Geoffrey Smith, RHS
OWNER: Royal Horticultural Society
GARDEN STYLE: 20th-century informal
SIZE: 58 acres (23.5 ha)
CLIMATE: Temperate
LOCATION: Beckwithshaw, Harrogate, North Yorkshire

The Northern Horticultural Society (NHS) founded Harlow Carr in the late 1940s when a group of Manchester-based gardeners decided to demonstrate the plants and gardening techniques pertinent to horticulturalists in northern Britain. In Harlow Carr, on the edge of Harrogate, they found a site to challenge most gardeners. The virgin site was difficult, little more than grazing pasture with a spring-fed ditch in the cleft of a valley, exposed to strong winds and prone to long periods of frost.

Work on the garden began with the appointment of Geoffrey Smith as superintendent in 1954. Youthful and energetic, Smith and his team used basic equipment to shift tons of rock. This turned the meandering stream into one of the finest waterside gardens in Europe and gave Harlow Carr a reputation as one of the UK's best. By the late 1960s, the garden boasted fine collections of Sino-Himalayan plants including primula, rhododendron, and Himalayan blue poppy. Smith left the garden in 1975, and his departure signaled the beginning of the garden's decline. By 2001, the NHS and Harlow Carr were close to collapse. The RHS then agreed to take it over.

Since then, a lot of hard work has gone into the garden. While respecting the traditions and existing plant collections of Harlow Carr, the RHS is altering the garden to a more naturalistic arrangement, with the woodland gardens and streamside likely to reemerge as among the finest anywhere. MW

The Himalayan Garden at The Hutts

North Yorkshire, England

DESIGNERS: Peter Roberts, Caro Roberts
OWNERS: Peter Roberts, Caro Roberts
GARDEN STYLE: 20th- and 21st-century woodland garden
SIZE: 8 acres (3.24 ha)
CLIMATE: Temperate
LOCATION: Grewelthorpe, Ripon, North Yorkshire

When Peter and Caro Roberts bought The Hutts in 1996, they took on a garden with immense potential but tremendous challenges. Among the mature plantation conifers on the vertiginous slopes were the remains of hundred-year-old rhododendrons that had been engulfed by later woodland planting. The temptation to peel back the layers proved irresistible and the woodland clearance began in 1997, with the first new plantings following in 1998.

The Himalayan Garden is now one of those rare entities, being a garden dominated by plants from another continent. The topography of the site, with steep, often almost vertical, banks, streams, and a lake, has been a major factor in its success. The Roberts have had to be careful with their plant selection though, given the extremely acidic soil, often so thin that rocks are exposed. The garden now has about 1,000 rhododendrons and excellent collections of magnolias and cornus. Many shrubs and trees, including the rare and unusual, have been grown from seed collected by contemporary plant hunters in China, Burma, and Tibet. In recent years, the Roberts' have added extensive ground cover and understory planting with more unusual woody plants, this time emphasizing Far Eastern specimens.

The Himalayan Garden is both evocative and unusual, and affords a glimpse of the Himalayas in a beautiful corner of North Yorkshire. Many of the plants here are on sale in the nursery. MW

The Old Zoo

Lancashire, England

DESIGNERS: Gerald Hitman, David Smith
OWNER: Gerald Hitman
GARDEN STYLE: Eclectic landscape
SIZE: 15 acres (6 ha)
CLIMATE: Temperate
LOCATION: Old Langho, Blackburn, Lancashire

The Old Zoo, Gerald Hitman's wonderful, reed-faced contemporary house used to be a vast asylum for the mentally challenged. The garden's name comes from the former petting zoo for the 3,500 hospital residents. Hitman bought the hospital site in 1992 and kept back 15 acres (6 ha) for himself. The rest became a village development and the training ground for the Blackburn Rovers football club.

The Old Zoo looks out over the Ribble Valley and is screened from the village by high banks of clay planted with native trees. Hitman has had fun doing what he fancied rather than following traditional lines, so what you see is a sloping landscape garden, flavored with a big man's whimsy—he is 6 feet 5 inches (2 m) tall—rather than an overall plan. The life-sized nude sculpture of Hitman at the center of the beech maze certainly grabs the eye.

Elsewhere, green oak constructions by Derek Goffin dot the landscape, including a vast hot tub in the densely planted woodland stream area. There is a pavilion by the croquet lawn bordered by a bank of 12,000 white roses and cloud-pruned trees in pots, and a hedge-walled, open-air chapel. There are several figurative sculptures, many by Sophie Dickens and the Czech artist Obram Zoubek, the latter's in bright colors. At the bottom of the garden is a lake, beside which are 400 native trees underplanted with cotoneaster and outcrops of topiary yew. On the opposite clay bank are sixteen varieties of Lancashire apple, with more trees to come. This is an exciting, original garden and it is not finished yet. CD

Gresgarth Hall

Lancashire, England

DESIGNER: Lady Arabella Lennox-Boyd
OWNER: Lady Arabella Lennox-Boyd
GARDEN STYLE: 20th-century, contemporary
SIZE: 15 acres (6 ha)
CLIMATE: Temperate
LOCATION: Caton, Lancaster, Lancashire

Lady Arabella Lennox-Boyd has made them all: private gardens, roof gardens, public spaces, and gold-medal-winning gardens at the RHS Chelsea Flower Show. However, her own garden at Gresgarth Hall is her most ambitious achievement.

Born in Italy, Lennox-Boyd moved to Gresgarth Hall in 1978. The garden serves as her laboratory and contains elements of most styles of garden design with classical and modern sculpture, terraces, bog garden, lake, wild garden, kitchen garden, herbaceous borders, orchard, bluebell wood, and nuttery.

From her castellated home, which largely dates from the nineteenth century, a series of terraces leads down to a stream called the Artle Beck. It is crossed by a red-painted Chinese bridge en route to a woodland garden and a spring show of azaleas and bluebells under the canopy of mature trees. Elsewhere there is a Zodiac Garden with a mosaic by British artist Maggie Howarth and an attractive kitchen garden.

The fact that there is a garden here at all is testament to Lennox-Boyd's gardening prowess. There were complications with drainage, and the bad soil and weather conditions would have put off most gardeners. What of the future? When Lennox-Boyd finds time off from designing gardens around the world, she plans to add more fountains, build a new bridge over the stream, and plant a hundred white magnolias in her Millennium Wood. MC

RIGHT Viewed from one of its terraces, castellated Gresgarth Hall catches the last rays of the afternoon sun.

Bramham Park

West Yorkshire, England

DESIGNER: Robert Benson
OWNER: George Lane Fox
GARDEN STYLE: 18th-century formal garden with
    French influences
SIZE: 68 acres (27 ha)
CLIMATE: Temperate
LOCATION: Wetherby, West Yorkshire

Bramham Park holds the distinction of being the best-preserved, early seventeenth-century, French-style formal garden in the UK. Subsequent movements in landscape design saw formal gardens swept away, yet Bramham survived.

When he acquired the 611 acres (248 ha) of Bramham Moor in 1698, Robert Benson—the first Lord Bingley—employed the architect Thomas Archer to design and build the house, no doubt influenced by the great classical architecture that he would have seen on the Grand Tour. Around the house, the garden was developed on the lines of many of the great contemporary French formal gardens, with tree-lined walks and allées radiating from the house, though Benson was also clearly a man with his own ideas.

Key features include the octagonal Gothic temple, a replica of a design featured in Batty Langley's 1742 book *Gothic Architecture*. Many of the garden's allées are lined with beech hedges, now towering up to 25 feet (7.5 m) high, but perhaps the grandest period features are the obelisk ponds, a series of connected formal pools and cascades. It is these features that make Bramham an exceptional and important garden because it provides a chance to experience the height of good taste and fashion in English landscaping in the early 1700s, when so many other contemporary gardens flowered only briefly before succumbing to the next fashion. The Lane Fox family, direct descendents of Robert Benson, continue to care for and develop Bramham Park. MW

Harewood

West Yorkshire, England

DESIGNERS: Capability Brown, Charles Barry
OWNER: Seventh Earl of Harewood
GARDEN STYLE: 18th-century landscape, Italianate, kitchen garden
SIZE: 36 acres (14.6 ha)
CLIMATE: Temperate
LOCATION: Leeds, West Yorkshire

Home to the Lascelles, the Earls of Harewood, the eighteenth-century building (designed by John Carr of York) sits perfectly in Capability Brown's landscape. The other great set piece is the parterre—added during the 1840s by Charles Barry and Harewood to give an Italian palazzo look—that overlooks the lake. It was restored by former head gardener Michael Walker, whose specialty is the restoration of High Victorian parterres. The arabesques in the parterre at Harewood are seasonally planted, outlined in dwarf hedging box, white chippings, mown grass, and stone edgings. Orpheus has always been the centerpiece, but the current statue by Astrid Zydower of Orpheus and the Leopard replaces Barry's original, which was damaged by frost in 1982.

The south-facing borders on the upper and lower levels sport plants that you would not expect to be hardy even hundreds of miles to the south. The small Dolphin Terrace was suggested by an idea from the designer David Hicks. The Lakeside Walk includes an extensive collection of rhododendrons and other Himalayan plants. However, it is the lake that grabs the eye. The cascade leads to an extensive and well-planted rockery that is boggy and profuse in spring with primulas, astilbes, hostas, and gunnera. In complete contrast, the kitchen gardens were designed on a grand scale and are now being restored. Another recent addition is the substantial Bird Garden, home to over one hundred threatened and exotic birds. CH

York Gate Garden

West Yorkshire, England

DESIGNER: Robin Spencer
OWNER: Perennial
GARDEN STYLE: 20th-century garden
   of compartments
SIZE: 1 acre (0.4 ha)
CLIMATE: Temperate
LOCATION: Adel, Leeds, West Yorkshire

From the age of seventeen until his death in the early 1980s, Robin Spencer designed and maintained this exceptional garden. For thirty years, he was able to indulge his three main passions: gardening, design, and plant collecting. He said that he had reworked every area of the garden at least once if not two or three times, all in the pursuit of perfection.

No fewer than fifteen distinct features can be identified in which the attention to detail is critical. Every plant, path, ornament, and composition nears perfection. In the last ten years of his life, he became particularly interested in the paving. He used stones, setts, flagstones, cobblestones, millstones, and gravel in different sizes and shades to play an important role in defining the atmosphere of each area, be it the iris borders, white and silver garden, herb garden, alley, vegetable garden, miniature pinetum, or fern borders. The choice of strictly utilitarian ornaments was made to help maintain the atmosphere of a cottage garden. That is why stone troughs and sinks, old boilers and kitchen pans, grinding wheels, pump heads, and millstones double up as planters.

For nearly twenty years after Spencer's death, his mother continued to look after the garden in his memory. She left it in her will to Perennial, the Gardeners' Royal Benevolent Society. In his lifetime Spencer had hoped that visitors could identify with the small scale of the garden, and be constantly surprised and charmed by its intimacy. Today Spencer would probably have been delighted with how well the garden has been maintained. CB

> "Every plant, path, ornament, and composition nears perfection"

Brodsworth Hall

South Yorkshire, England

DESIGNERS: Philip Wilkinson; English Heritage, David Avery
OWNER: English Heritage
GARDEN STYLE: 19th-century Victorian eclectic
SIZE: 15 acres (6 ha)
CLIMATE: Temperate
LOCATION: Doncaster, South Yorkshire

The gardens at Brodsworth Hall are a catalog of High Victorian taste. Created around an Italianate house that mirrors Queen Victoria's Osborne on the Isle of Wight (see page 431), they contain geometric bedding displays, formal terraces, and a scented rose garden, with more relaxed plantings farther away. From the 1860s, they formed the private playground of Charles Thellusson, whose wealthy family was best known for horse racing and yachting.

Much of what visitors can see today is due to recent restoration work. The house had suffered subsidence and slipped into decay, and the gardens had become overgrown in the twentieth century. Thankfully, much of this has been reversed since English Heritage took over the property in 1990. The underlying nineteenth-century structure has survived and, now that the plants have been pruned, can be seen and enjoyed again. As well as the vistas, fountains, and statues, there is a fine legacy of mature plants, including two 30-foot-high (10 m) strawberry trees. The rock garden has been planted with more than 350 types of fern, recalling the Victorian pteridomania, or passion for ferns. The latest feature to be recovered is the rose dell in the pleasure grounds, which boasts 80 different species of rose.

Elsewhere there is a noticeable number of garden buildings. The Target House was once the den where the family practiced archery. The Eye Catcher is more whimsical, featuring the facade of a building halfway up a cliff. And do not miss the game larder and ornamental lavatory. LH

Easton Walled Gardens

Lincolnshire, England

DESIGNERS: Ursula Cholmeley, Fred Cholmeley
OWNERS: Ursula Cholmeley, Fred Cholmeley
GARDEN STYLE: 20th-century informal
SIZE: 11 acres (4.5 ha)
CLIMATE: Temperate
LOCATION: Easton, Grantham, Lincolnshire

The gardens at Easton, home of the Cholmeley family for fourteen generations, reached their zenith in the late Victorian to early Edwardian era; they featured walled gardens, terraces, elaborate bedding displays, and tightly clipped lawns. Famous visitors to the gardens at Easton included Franklin D. Roosevelt, who proclaimed them to be "a dream of Nirvana… almost too good to be true."

Easton's decline came during World War II when it was requisitioned by the War Ministry—locals reported grenades exploding in the glasshouses. By 1951 damage to the house was irreversible and, by 1999, the gardens were entirely lost. At this point the Cholmeleys took back the estate. Over the next four years, the gardens rang to the sound of chainsaws and heavy machinery as their hidden treasures were slowly revealed. The owners did not attempt a full restoration but made the most of the remaining features—including the venerable yew tunnel and imposing bridge that spans the River Whitham—while developing new plantings and exploring contemporary design ideas.

The resulting garden is like a ghost brought back to life. Features such as the Pickery, a cutting garden with over one hundred different plants, and the sumptuous Velvet Border have injected a mass of color. In late winter, the wooded glades are awash with snowdrops, and Easton's fine old trees can now be seen in all their glory. The garden is a good example of how the great can fall and how they can be colorfully brought back to life. MW

Cholmondeley Castle Gardens

Cheshire, England

DESIGNER: Lady Lavinia Cholmondeley
OWNER: Lady Lavinia Cholmondeley
GARDEN STYLE: Late 20th-century formal and informal
SIZE: 18 acres (7.3 ha)
CLIMATE: Temperate
LOCATION: Malpas, Cheshire

The gardens located at Cholmondeley (pronounced chum-lee) have a romantic, fairytale quality about them. Right at their heart lies a mock Gothic castle built in the nineteenth century, and surrounding it are formal and flowingly informal gardens. They were laid out in 1690 by royal gardener George London, but his walled garden and canals are long gone. Instead, the current romantic garden owes much to the present Lady Cholmondeley who, since the 1960s, has developed the planting by a process of constant experimentation.

Of all the areas in the grounds, the Temple Garden draws most visitors. It features a pillared temple with an ironwork cupola that is reflected in the lake below, as are the specimen trees and shrubs. In spring there are azaleas and rhododendrons that are followed in summer by bold clumps of large-leaved gunnera and the stately royal fern (*Osmunda regalis*). At the lake's edge, Koi carp can be seen gliding through the water, and visitors can take the path across rustic bridges to the grassed islands in the middle. This is a good vantage point over the surrounding gardens, allowing visitors a great view of the contrasting shapes, textures, and colors of the complex planting.

Beneath the castle and on the terrace, the plants are predominately silver. They were planted in 1977 for Queen Elizabeth II's Silver Jubilee (the twenty-fifth anniversary of her reign, which was celebrated with considerable enthusiasm across the UK). To the west of the castle are some of the most impressive plants: camellias with luscious blooms, a liquidamber that turns gold and red in fall, and a large handkerchief tree (*Davidia involucrata*) planted in a glade, which blooms in late May. Cholmondeley's latest addition is a rose garden. Other highlights include the wild orchids in the lawns and primroses on the lower levels beneath the castle. LH

Arley Hall

Cheshire, England

DESIGNERS: Rowland Egerton-Warburton, Lady Ashbrook
OWNER: Eleventh Viscount Ashbrook
GARDEN STYLE: 19th-century informal
SIZE: 12 acres (4.8 ha)
CLIMATE: Temperate
LOCATION: Northwich, Cheshire

It is rumored that the superb, double herbaceous borders at Arley Hall are the oldest in England. Although this is difficult to prove, they are certainly among the earliest, dating from before 1846. Remarkably, they look today much as they do in watercolor paintings executed in 1889.

The borders are designed to provide a fine display from early summer to early fall. The display kicks off with tall blue delphiniums and quickly progresses to richer colors. Red crocosmia and yellow helianthus appear in late summer, with early fall marked by fleshy sedums and the seedheads of blood-red orache. The borders are backed by strategically placed yew trees—clipped into buttresslike shapes—creating marked divisions. A second element is a long lawn that runs up the middle. At one end is a shady shelter with a classically inspired frontage; the other gives views of the countryside beyond.

Step away from the borders and there is still much to see. An avenue of 33-foot-high (10 m) holm oaks (*Quercus ilex*) have been trimmed into symmetrical cylinders. There are two walled gardens. One is planted with vegetables and old-fashioned fruit. The other has mixed borders of shrubs and perennials, carefully married by color. Hidden corners include the herb and richly scented rose gardens. In recent years, Viscount Ashbrook has developed The Grove and Woodland Walk with around 300 species of spring-flowering rhododendrons and azaleas. Additionally, exotic trees and flowering shrubs make sure that the show never flags. LH

Tatton Park

Cheshire, England

DESIGNERS: Humphry Repton, Joseph Paxton, and others
OWNER: The National Trust; managed by
Cheshire County Council
GARDEN STYLE: 18th-century landscape, 19th-century
formal and kitchen gardens, 20th-century
Japanese garden
SIZE: 49 acres (19.8 ha)
CLIMATE: Temperate
LOCATION: Knutsford, Cheshire

When designer Humphry Repton produced his plans for the parkland at Tatton Park in 1791, he was particularly clear about one point. The driveway that went in a straight line up to the front of the mansion had to go. He replaced it with a winding road that provides a tour of the picturesque parkland. Repton's obstinacy may seem whimsical, but it gave Tatton two important legacies. The first was the glorious eighteenth-century parkland and the second a cleared area around the house that later became the gardens. Tatton is, basically, a collection of gardens.

The earliest formal areas include a beech maze from 1795 and Charlotte's Garden, named after Charlotte Edgerton who was part of the wealthy Edgerton family who owned Tatton for more than 400 years. Joseph Paxton (the designer of the Crystal Palace) created many new features here, including, in 1847, the Italian Garden— its terracotta balustrading was added in 1887. The fernery, once known as the Tatton Palm House, was designed by George Stokes in 1859, and is now planted with large tree ferns (*Dicksonia antarctica*).

Tatton is best known, though, for its recently restored Japanese Garden. Constructed between 1910 and 1913 for Alan de Tatton Edgerton, it is rated as one of the finest in Europe. It is in the style of a tea garden, complete with teahouse, flowing streams, islands, and rocks. However, it may soon be eclipsed by the walled kitchen garden. At approximately 4 acres (1.6 ha), the kitchen garden is one of the largest to be restored in England to date. LH

> "Tatton is best known…
> for its recently restored
> Japanese Garden"

Lyme Park

Cheshire, England

DESIGNERS: Lewis Wyatt, Graham Stuart Thomas
OWNER: The National Trust
GARDEN STYLE: 19th- and 20th-century formal, woodland
SIZE: 17 acres (6.8 ha)
CLIMATE: Temperate
LOCATION: Disley, Stockport, Cheshire

The eighteenth-century Palladian mansion of Lyme Park is famous as the exterior of Pemberley in the BBC's 1995 adaptation of Jane Austen's novel *Pride and Prejudice*. The gardens near the house are predominantly formal and have a number of features and focuses from different periods of the nineteenth century. The elegant conservatory designed by Lewis Wyatt was built in 1814 and is justly famous for two camellias, said to be over 150 years old, and the beds on the terrace outside that often boast a show of *Penstemon* 'Rubicundus', first raised at Lyme in 1906.

To the east of the conservatory are the Rose Garden and the Herbaceous Border. The former was created in 1913 and replanted in 1995, the latter in the 1920s and redesigned in 1966 for the National Trust in the style of Gertrude Jekyll by the plantsman Graham Stuart Thomas, who knew the great lady. The Dutch Garden, which underwent restoration in the 1980s, was originally laid out in the 1860s when it was called the Italian Garden. Each spring and summer the geometric beds are filled with brightly colored displays of bedding plants. The English Garden is now being restored based on Wyatt's 1814 plan.

If you want the calm of green plants after the exuberance of the formal gardens, then take a stroll through Killtime. This ravine-cum-woodland garden is filled with shade- and moisture-loving plants, including, in spring, a fine show of rhododendrons. The 1,400-acre (567 ha) medieval deer park has a number of marked trails and "The Cage"—an early eighteenth-century hunting tower. TM

Ness Botanic Garden

Cheshire, England

DESIGNERS: Arthur Kilpin Bulley, Ken Hulme
OWNER: University of Liverpool
GARDEN STYLE: Botanical gardens
SIZE: 64 acres (25.9 ha)
CLIMATE: Temperate
LOCATION: Ness, Neston, Cheshire

Arthur Kilpin Bulley changed the face of British gardening. Born with an insatiable appetite for plants and a burning desire to communicate it, his major interest was introducing Chinese and Himalayan mountain plants to Britain. Many of his now-familiar introductions can be seen at Ness. A cotton merchant by trade, he started to create a garden in 1898 —presented to the University of Liverpool by his daughter in 1948. He also sponsored expeditions to the Far East, launching the careers of renowned plant hunters George Forrest and Frank Kingdon-Ward.

Bulley introduced hundreds of new plants. Hybrids of *Rhododendron griersonianum* and *Camellia saluenensis* have resulted in many new forms, and the glorious *Pieris formosa* var. *Forrestii*, which can be seen on the Specimen Lawn in spring, was actually grown from seed collected by Forrest in China.

Set on the banks of the River Dee, the garden includes landscaped terraces, a rock garden, and a water garden full of candelabra primulas and the beautiful, blue, fall-flowering *Gentiana sino-ornata*. By the time Ken Hulme became director in 1957, the gardens were in sore need of attention. He spent the next three decades remodeling the garden from Bulley's regimented collections to its current, more naturalistic style. The gardens increased in size, and collections of rhododendrons, azaleas, camellias, cherries, and heathers were established. Today the commitment to maintain and develop the beauty of the gardens still remains, though with an emphasis on research, conservation, and education. NS

Haddon Hall

Derbyshire, England

DESIGNER: Ninth Duchess of Rutland
OWNER: Lord Edward Manners
GARDEN STYLE: 20th-century informal
SIZE: 2 acres (0.8 ha)
CLIMATE: Temperate
LOCATION: Bakewell, Derbyshire

Perched on an outcrop, the castlelike Haddon Hall would be an unforgiving and imperious building if it were not for the softening effect of its romantic landscape and gardens. Mature trees thrust their branches across the sight of the uncompromising, mainly sixteenth-century building, while its lovely meadows burgeon with wildflowers in summer. The gardens were established on the terraces to the side and rear of the hall. They were created in earnest over the last hundred years, with most of the work carried out in the first two decades of the twentieth century by the ninth Duchess of Rutland.

Although the duchess imposed some additional architectural plantings on the existing terraces, such as the collection of yew trees, the richly scented roses are her greatest legacy. Over the years, they have been replanted. You will now find hybrid teas providing summerlong blooms in occasional bright shades and long-flowering modern English roses with their old-fashioned looks. Other kinds of rose also grow in profusion. One of the most fascinating aspects of the rose collection is the way individual flowers are partnered with other plants to extend and increase the display. Clematis trained on obelisks are especially successful, as are delphiniums in early summer and tender perennials later in the season. Horticultural detail is plentiful throughout the garden, though one of the best reasons to visit is the magnificent setting. The garden has been seamlessly merged into the glorious Derbyshire countryside that surrounds it. LH

Renishaw Hall Gardens

Derbyshire, England

DESIGNERS: Sir George Sitwell, Sir Reresby Sitwell
OWNERS: Sir Reresby Sitwell, Lady Penelope Sitwell
GARDEN STYLE: 19th- and 20th-century English Italianate
SIZE: 5 acres (2 ha)
CLIMATE: Temperate
LOCATION: Renishaw, Sheffield, Derbyshire

An early seventeenth-century manor house that was substantially enlarged and remodeled in the Georgian period, Renishaw Hall is steeped in history. However, its formal gardens are a deceptively recent addition. Stylistically inspired by the Italian renaissance, with manicured lawns partitioned by magnificent yew hedges and full of antique statuary, the grounds you see today are largely as laid out by Sir George Sitwell in 1895 and effectively belong to the twentieth century. *On the Making of Gardens*, an essay outlining his design theories, was published in 1909. Though Sir George's literary output was eclipsed by the modernist poetry and art criticism of his children—Dame Edith, Sir Osbert, and Sir Sacheverell—his reputation as a gardener and his gardening legacy show more endurance.

Precisely the width of the house, the south-facing garden descends in a series of gentle terraces, the lowest of which commands striking views of the surrounding countryside and distant, industrial town. The present resident, the seventh Baronet, has improved Sir George's various garden "rooms" by widening existing flower borders and creating many new planting opportunities. A profusion of tender climbers cloaks the facade of the house, hundreds of romantic shrub roses bring summer scent and color, and fountains add sparkle. There is also a National Collection of yuccas and a working vineyard. It is this dynamic tension between formality and exuberance, between old and new, that gives Renishaw its edge over other gardens. RCa

Chatsworth

Derbyshire, England

DESIGNERS: Thomas Archer, Capability Brown,
George London, Henry Wise, Joseph Paxton,
Jeffry Wyattville
OWNERS: Chatsworth House Trust, twelfth Duke
of Devonshire
GARDEN STYLE: Baroque and landscape
SIZE: 100 acres (40 ha)
CLIMATE: Temperate
LOCATION: Bakewell, Derbyshire

Despite the seemingly natural landscape, the grounds and gardens at Chatsworth have been sculpted by generations of the Cavendish family and their designers. From 1686, the first Duke of Devonshire employed George London and Henry Wise to create an English Versailles. The intricate parterres, walks, and wildernesses are now long gone, but the sense of geometry remains in the sinuous Serpentine Walk and the 1960s injection of box and golden yew, additions to Jeffry Wyattville's nineteenth-century stone-edged beds. You can also see Thomas Archer's Cascade House, which still carries water down steps designed by a Frenchman, Grillet, a pupil of André Le Nôtre. The 1698 greenhouse is now a camellia house.

In the eighteenth century, Capability Brown designed this stunning landscape with both beauty and utility in mind. The skyline is still largely unaltered, and so too are the legacies of Joseph Paxton, the great Victorian head gardener. There is the great, 45-foot-high (14 m) Wellington Rock that was hauled into position to dominate the placid pond, the Strid, while other boulders form the Rockeries, the 331-foot-long (100 m) Conservative Wall—a stone wall with a series of glass cases set up against it—and the site of the Great Stove. When you have seen all of them, take the walk above Stand Wood to see the four reservoir lakes that were dug to supply the Cascade and the stunning 280-foot-high (85 m) jet of the Emperor Fountain.

The historic roots of Chatsworth are rich and alive. They continue to yield new ideas and designs, ranging from new plantings and topiary cottages to Angela Conner's water sculpture (*Revelation*), a mill, and an upstream bridge on the reformed River Derwent. The Great Slope, which now forms the Salisbury Lawns, is a site of special scientific interest for its rare wildflowers and grasses. CH

Melbourne Hall

Derbyshire, England

DESIGNERS: George London, Henry Wise, and others
OWNERS: Lord Ralph Kerr, Lady Marie-Claire Kerr
GARDEN STYLE: 17th-century formal French,
   20th- and 21st-century additions
SIZE: 20 acres (8.1 ha)
CLIMATE: Temperate
LOCATION: Melbourne, Derbyshire

Melbourne Hall has the magical atmosphere of a garden that has stood still for several centuries. However, there is a hint of gentle evolution and a maturity still to be reached.

It was Queen Anne's vice-chamberlain, Thomas Coke, who commissioned London and Wise to design a garden in the style of the French garden designer André Le Nôtre. The 1704 plan—the original drawings are still kept in the family archive—included a yew tunnel, grassed terraces to the east of the house leading to the Great Basin planted with four swamp cypresses (*Taxodium distichum*), and Robert Bakewell's unique arbor, known as the Birdcage. It is an exquisite piece of partly gilded, lacy ironwork. Avenues of braided limes, underplanted with beech and yew, lead away from the central composition into atmospheric thickets. At the intersection of the paths are dark, still pools and statues. A beautiful lead urn provides the focal point for the main avenue at the top of the garden.

Early in the twentieth century, a water garden was planted in the woodland area near the house. In the last twenty years, Lady Kerr, the current owner, has been making a significant contribution to the beauty of this part of the garden. She has cultivated the woodland by removing some of the overgrown tree seedlings to let in light and make room, and this has allowed the introduction of a huge collection of exceptional species. These days, London and Wise must be smiling in their eternal garden. CB

Clumber Park

Nottinghamshire, England

DESIGNERS: Capability Brown, Humphry Repton
OWNER: The National Trust
GARDEN STYLE: 18th-century English landscape
SIZE: 3,800 acres (1,539 ha)
CLIMATE: Temperate
LOCATION: Worksop, Nottinghamshire

Clumber Park, designed with help from Capability Brown and Humphry Repton, provided the magnificent setting for the home of the Dukes of Newcastle. Everything at Clumber was built on a grand scale to reflect the importance of its owners. The house is no more (demolished in 1938 to avoid inheritance tax), but what remains is a nostalgic reminder of the estate's former glory. A 2-mile-long (3 km) avenue of lime trees, the longest in Europe, leads through rolling parkland, densely planted woodlands, and rhododendron dells to the serpentine lake at the heart of the park.

Near the ruins of the house stands the restored walled kitchen garden. Built during the 1770s, the 4-acre (1.5 ha) garden was at the forefront of eighteenth-century horticultural techniques. The garden supplied newly introduced peaches, nectarines, and figs, and even produced that most prized of fruits, the pineapple. The greenhouses and flued walls needed for growing these fruits have been renovated, and many of the tools and techniques used are on display. Within the garden, among delphiniums and dahlias, are varieties of vegetables and fruits that were popular before 1910.

The park stands in what was Sherwood Forest. During the eighteenth and nineteenth centuries, as trees were felled to build the ships for Britain's navy, parks and mansions were constructed in the clearings. They provided homes for many newly created dukes and earls, giving the area the name by which it is still known—The Dukeries. JHo

Felley Priory Garden

Nottinghamshire, England

DESIGNER: The Hon. Mrs. Maria Chaworth-Musters
OWNER: The Hon. Mrs. Maria Chaworth-Musters
GARDEN STYLE: 20th-century romantic English
SIZE: 5 acres (2 ha)
CLIMATE: Temperate
LOCATION: Underwood, Nottinghamshire

Three minutes' drive from the highway, Felley Priory is a haven of quiet. Founded in 1156, the priory was dissolved by Henry VIII in 1536, but traces of it still remain. A high wall, a perfect backdrop for tall shrubs, is thought to be part of the medieval boundary.

There are terraced lawns, a rose- and clematis-covered pergola, a knot garden, yew hedging with nineteenth-century-style topiary birds and roundels, a rose garden, and a lavish mixture of shrubs, perennials, and herbaceous plantings. Harking back to the priory's origins is a square, medieval garden planted with irises, lilies, basil, and box.

The garden's open setting amid fields and hills adds to its charm. Since it is 600 feet (183 m) above sea level and very exposed, the high yew hedges are necessary to protect the more delicate herbaceous perennials in the double borders that line the terraced lawns. The range of planting is enormous. Near the house are beds of wallflowers and fritillaries for spring, followed by tree peonies, parahebes, viburnums, and euphorbias. For late summer, there are different varieties of hydrangea. Outside the walls is the meadow and shrubbery, where paths are cut through the grass when the fritillaries have died down. The rose garden is approached through a beech hedge and has beds edged with lavender. The old roses are intertwined with clematis, and include gallicas, bourbons, moss roses, damasks, and albas.

Several periods in the long history of English gardening style are represented in this garden. The overall effect is wonderfully romantic and relaxed. VB

Biddulph Grange Garden

Staffordshire, England

DESIGNERS: James Bateman, Maria Bateman
OWNER: The National Trust
GARDEN STYLE: High Victorian
SIZE: 15 acres (6 ha)
CLIMATE: Temperate
LOCATION: Biddulph, Stoke-on-Trent, Staffordshire

To visit Biddulph Grange is to take a round-the-world trip in a single day. It is a brilliant example of how dividing a garden into "rooms" can have maximum impact. Cleverly planned frameworks of hedges, rocks, banks, and plantings conceal each area from the next, leading you from one surprise to another. The garden is the work of James Bateman and his wife Maria, both passionate plant lovers who came to Biddulph in 1840; they were aided in their grand design by the painter Edward Cooke. Between them they concocted a series of global tableaux, all interconnected by tunnels and passageways.

In China, you enter through the temple and the garden is laid out before you like the design on a willow-pattern plate. In Egypt, stone sphinxes guard a hidden court and flank a pyramid cleverly constructed out of yew topiary. The world tour continues with Italian terraces and a Scottish glen, complemented by a pinetum, rock garden, and that most curious Victorian creation, the stumpery, where a narrow path winds through a forest of uprooted oaks turned on their heads so that the roots provide an unusual backdrop for a collection of ferns.

The garden at Biddulph Grange was created when Victorian plant hunters were returning with new species from around the world. There are rhododendrons collected from the Himalayas and exotic conifers in the pinetum. It is an ambitious vision, which survives with help from the National Trust to astonish visitors today no less than it did more than 160 years ago. SA

The National Memorial Arboretum

Staffordshire, England

DESIGNERS: Various
OWNER: Royal British Legion
GARDEN STYLE: Wooded parkland
SIZE: 150 acres (60.70 ha)
CLIMATE: Temperate
LOCATION: Croxall Road, Alrewas, Staffordshire

In this time of global unrest, there is no more appropriate landscape to visit than the National Memorial Arboretum. There are over 50 memorials dedicated mainly to the military but also to the police, fire brigade, and ambulance services as well as charities and local and overseas organizations. The poignant memorials range from the powerful stone architecture of the Armed Forces Memorial set at the top of a 19.5-foot-high (6 m) earth mound, with a spiraling walkway that takes visitors up grassy tree-planted slopes, to the Children's Woodland, planted with trees in memory of children who have passed away. There are memorials from conflicts long ago; others are dedicated to more recent events. At the Arboretum's center is the Millennium Chapel of Peace and Forgiveness, where every day visitors can observe a minute's silence at 11 o'clock for those who have lost their lives in conflict.

Over 50,000 trees have been planted in the Arboretum since 1997 as a living tribute to those people and events that they commemorate, and they have already grown together to create a series of thriving wildlife habitats. In many cases, specific trees have been chosen for their relevance to the various memorials. Among them, The Beat is an avenue of chestnuts, which was funded by every police force in the UK, with trees grown from conkers taken from the grounds of Sir Robert Peel's home Drayton Manor.

The memorials, trees, and wildlife here remind us that this very special place is, and always will be, as much about life as it is about death. RSJ

The Dorothy Clive Garden

Staffordshire, England

DESIGNERS: Frank Knight, John Codrington, George Lovatt
OWNER: Willoughbridge Garden Trust
GARDEN STYLE: Picturesque, informal
SIZE: 8 acres (3.2 ha)
CLIMATE: Temperate
LOCATION: Willoughbridge, Staffordshire

The Dorothy Clive Garden began in a small way in 1939 when Colonel Harry Clive began clearing pathways in the disused gravel quarry above his house so that his invalid wife, Dorothy, could take walks there. The quarry had been worked out over one hundred years earlier and was colonized mainly with oak. The sheltered microclimate, deep accumulations of leaf mold, and well-drained acidic gravel were also perfect for rhododendrons—an early wartime association with Frank Knight, manager of the old Knap Hill Nursery, had made Clive an avid collector of the genus.

Clive used a number of landscape architects, including John Codrington. However, most of the new developments have occurred in the last thirty years under head gardener George Lovatt. He has linked areas of differing character to create surprises at every turn. The south-facing slope is a giant scree garden with a pool at its base, and there are herbaceous borders, Mediterranean-style plantings, and a bog garden. Viewing points take in the Staffordshire countryside, with sometimes a glimpse of distant Mount Snowdon in neighboring North Wales.

Much of the original plantings remain, including some important Knap Hill hybrid azaleas. Mature tree magnolias, giant cardiocrinums, and lush architectural foliage add to the spectacle. The garden's fiftieth anniversary was marked by the construction of a dramatic waterfall plunging to the base of the quarry. This should be a parched, windswept heath, but artful gardening has created a veritable oasis. JHe

Hawkstone Historic Park and Follies

Shropshire, England

DESIGNERS: Richard Hill, Rowland Hill, Sir Richard Hill
OWNER: Mark Boler
GARDEN STYLE: 18th-century picturesque
SIZE: 300 acres (121.5 ha)
CLIMATE: Temperate
LOCATION: Weston-under-Redcastle, Shrewsbury, Shropshire

Hawkstone was designed to thrill. It is still an awesome experience, as Dr. Johnson noted on July 25, 1774, "[I was] conducted by Miss Hill over a large tract of rocks and woods, a region abounding with striking scenes and terrific grandeur . . . its prospects, the awfulness of its shades, the horrors of its precipices, the verdure of its hollows and the loftiness of its rocks. The ideas which it forces upon the mind, are the sublime, the dreadful, and the vast . . ."

Richard Hill became rich in London and so, looking for a way to invest his money, he and his nephew, Rowland, started to improve Hawkstone Hall. A great deal of the landscaping survives—the Summerhouse and Cold Bath, the Grotto, the Ravens' Shelf, the Hermit's Summer Residence, the Fox's Knob, St. Francis' Cave, the Terrace Walk, and the White Tower. Red Castle Hill, glimpsed from the Grotto, was believed to have belonged to King Arthur, while the Temple of Patience, where visitors were served gingerbread, has been renamed the Gingerbread Hall. Paoli's Point was named after the Corsican general Paschal Paoli, who commented that nowhere had afforded him such delight.

In 1783, the second (Sir) Richard Hill introduced a guidebook. He put his philanthropic ideals into large-scale local employment and continued landscaping for a further twenty-six years. Look out for the 100-foot-high (30 m) monument that you can climb, Hawk River, and the Gothic Arch. CH

Hodnet Hall Gardens

Shropshire, England

DESIGNER: Brigadier A. G. W. Heber-Percy
OWNER: Algernon Heber-Percy
GARDEN STYLE: 20th-century informal
SIZE: 60 acres (24.3 ha)
CLIMATE: Temperate
LOCATION: Hodnet, Market Drayton, Shropshire

The gardens at Hodnet Hall focus on a series of pools that were built in 1922. They were the creation of Brigadier Heber-Percy who, as a young man, took over the estate and started his gardening career with the grudging approval of his father. What Heber-Percy created is now recognized as one of the most important twentieth-century gardens in England.

The gardens surrounding the pools are still the main attraction. Fine swamp cypress (*Taxodium distichum*), a collection of flowering cherries, and a handkerchief tree (*Davidia involucrata*) help form a canopy and backdrop. They also provide shelter for the rich understory and the mass plantings of candelabra primulas, *Iris kaempferi*, giant-leaved gunnera, and astilbes in shades of pink.

Hodnet's topography slopes steeply away from the house and levels by the pools. These flat areas made it possible to create a series of interconnecting gardens around what has now become the tearoom and store. In spring the Camellia Garden is a major attraction, planted with cultivars of early-flowering *Clematis sasanqua* as well as the large-flowered hybrids such as 'Donation' and 'Cornish Snow'. There is also a Magnolia Walk that is full of blossom in the spring season. Midsummer sees roses in the Circular Garden at their peak together with the borders along the Broadwalk. The latter is just beneath the house and provides an opportunity to admire views over the Shropshire countryside. LH

Wollerton Old Hall

Shropshire, England

DESIGNER: Lesley Jenkins
OWNER: Lesley Jenkins
GARDEN STYLE: Arts and Crafts
SIZE: 4 acres (1.6 ha)
CLIMATE: Temperate
LOCATION: Wollerton, Market Drayton, Shropshire

A garden has been on this site for over 500 years. It is the childhood home of Lesley Jenkins, who moved back to the property in 1984 and set about designing a new garden. Made in a classical English Arts and Crafts style, it consists of a series of linked garden "rooms" filled with modern plantings that lend the whole a vibrant and imaginative liveliness.

The old black-and-white hall demands strong linear formality from its garden. The Lime Allée is central to the main vista, with many smaller gardens leading off it. In front of the house was an Elizabethan knot garden. After box disease took hold, it was replaced by a simple design of standard Portugal laurel (*Prunus lusitanica*) that leads down the York stone path. The Rill Garden consists, as its name suggests, of gentle trickling water, being in direct contrast to the Lanhydrock Garden, a cacophony of loud, jubilant color and form from the brilliant reds, russets, and yellows of rudbeckias, heleniums, oriental poppies, and the fine collection of salvias. The main perennial border follows the traditional Gertrude Jekyll style with plantings in large, painterly drifts. From here one enters the reflective Font Garden where a quiet, cloistered oak loggia faces a stone font. In spring, there is a sea of crown imperials (*Fritillaria meleagris*). The attention to detail in every post, seat, gate, and obelisk points straight to the Arts and Crafts movement. It is no surprise then that Wollerton Old Hall has become a honeypot for garden photographers and TV producers. People cannot get enough of it. JHi

"The attention to detail... points straight to the Arts and Crafts movement"

The David Austin Rose Gardens

Shropshire, England

DESIGNER: David Austin
OWNER: David Austin
GARDEN STYLE: 20th-century formal
SIZE: 2 acres (0.8 ha)
CLIMATE: Temperate
LOCATION: Albrighton, Wolverhampton, Shropshire

David Austin has been breeding and hybridizing roses for more than sixty years. The gardens at Albrighton display not only his fragrant English roses, but also the best old roses and modern shrub roses. With more than 800 rose varieties growing here, from the purest white and palest yellow to the brightest copper and darkest burgundy, these gardens offer a gorgeous feast for the eyes and nose.

The gardens are enclosed and divided by neat, evergreen hedges with sculptures by Pat Austin as focal points. All but the Species Garden, which contains the true wild roses and their near hybrids, are of formal design. The largest and most established area is the pergola-lined Long Garden—about 290 feet (85 m) long—with a collection of old roses and modern shrub roses plus some English roses to extend the flowering season.

Adjacent areas include the Victorian Garden with concentric borders that are planted with English roses and other repeat-flowering shrub roses. A 9-foot-high (3 m) circular wall shows how climbing roses perform facing north, south, east, and west. The Renaissance Garden, so-called because of the loggia overlooking a long canal, is just for English roses. They are grown low in snakelike borders edged with box and massed in swaths at shoulder height. The Lion Garden has formal beds planted with hybrid teas, floribundas, and English roses plus miniatures and patios around a lion sculpture. A welcome feature is the strategically placed seats where visitors can stop and marvel at the beauty of so many different roses. EH

Clipsham Yew Tree Avenue

Rutland, England

DESIGNER: Amos Alexander
OWNER: The Forestry Commission
GARDEN STYLE: Topiary garden
SIZE: 0.3 mile (0.5 km)
CLIMATE: Temperate
LOCATION: Clipsham, Oakham, Rutland

If you find yourself in this part of Lincolnshire, be sure to break your journey to see Clipsham Yew Tree Avenue. There is no house or garden, just a double avenue of clipped yews rising majestically next to the road, all leading, in a delightfully surreal way, to nowhere. It once formed part of the carriage drive to Clipsham Hall, but has been under the care of the Forestry Commission since 1955.

That this totally unique feature has survived from the time Amos Alexander, head forester of the Clipsham Estate, started clipping the trees in 1870 is almost miraculous. Only enthusiasts know how long it takes to grow and shape such a feature, and how quickly and easily it can be overwhelmed by surrounding vegetation or lost to disease.

Some 150 pieces of yew line the two sides of the avenue. They are all different, some short and squat, but most shaped like elongated domes, crowned with birds or tiered heads. What makes this avenue so engaging is the way the trees have been decorated over the years with bas relief. Events, such as Queen Elizabeth II's coronation in 1953 and the fortieth anniversary of her accession in 1992, have been commemorated in letters and numbers. Neil Armstrong's landing on the moon in 1969 and a Spitfire (representing the Battle of Britain) have also been etched out. There are also depictions of deer, a baby elephant, and three bears.

Children love weaving in and out of the topiary while solving the eight riddles on the Treasure Trail. Their reward is hidden in one of the box bushes. VR

East Ruston
Old Vicarage Garden

Norfolk, England

DESIGNERS: Alan Gray, Graham Robeson
OWNERS: Alan Gray, Graham Robeson
GARDEN STYLE: 20th-century informal
SIZE: 20 acres (8.1 ha)
CLIMATE: Temperate
LOCATION: East Ruston, Norwich, Norfolk

Located less than 1.5 miles (2.5 km) from the North Sea coast, this is one of the UK's most eclectic gardens. Despite much of the garden being twenty years old or less, it displays remarkable maturity thanks to the rich Norfolk soil and the benign influence of the maritime climate that keeps frosts away, and ensures an almost nonstop growing season.

The owners took on the near-derelict Arts and Crafts vicarage and surrounding, empty land in the 1980s. They soon appreciated that although the climate and soil were on their side, the dry summer and cold winter winds were not, and set about planting a network of sheltering hedges surrounded by thick belts of trees. Within these hedges the site has gradually developed into a garden of "rooms," with cleverly framed internal vistas.

What sets this garden apart is the attention to detail and the experiments with composition and color. The Kings' Walk is a broad, tapering lawn dotted with topiaries leading to a superbly constructed walk-through summerhouse, designed to have exactly the same roof pitch as the vicarage. Simple green spaces of mown grass and topiary, boxed into "rooms" by hedges, give way to riotously colorful arrangements of tender perennials, annuals, and subtropical plants. One area has been set out with massive *Cyathea* tree ferns, planted on a grid like the columns in a cathedral, with the lofty fronds casting dappled shade below. The Desert Wash is an arid scheme that includes a dry stream bed crossed by a bridge resembling the backbone of a dinosaur, the suggestion being that you just missed the downpour and flashflood. Gray and Robeson do not appear to be showing any signs that their inventiveness and horticultural joie de vivre may be waning. The garden continues to develop and change. MW

The Plantation Garden

Norfolk, England

DESIGNER: Henry Trevor
OWNER: Plantation Garden Preservation Trust
GARDEN STYLE: High Victorian quarry garden
SIZE: 3.2 acres (1.3 ha)
CLIMATE: Temperate
LOCATION: Norwich, Norfolk

Tucked away between the Catholic cathedral and Norwich's busy Earlham Road, the Plantation Garden was hidden until 1980, when a local midwife prowled through deep undergrowth and rediscovered it.

Built in an abandoned chalk quarry, the Plantation Garden is an ostentatious Victorian garden in miniature. All the crucial elements of a country estate are contained within it—tumbling rocks, formal gardens and woodland walks, Gothic ruins, a grotto, Italian terraces, and rustic buildings, together with the latest in conifers, carpet bedding, and a palm house. But whereas the owners of most estates were fantastically wealthy, Henry Trevor was merely a prosperous Norwich businessman, and the garden he laid out between 1856 and 1897 reflects this.

The main side wall of the garden is composed of brick, flint, pieces of kiln lining, and terracotta brickwork that came from a local brickworks and were probably seconds and spoils. The wall is like a collage with bits of heraldry and even little faces like gargoyles. More pieces from the brickworks feature in the Gothic fountain, while the Italianate terraces are a collection of building materials, drainpipes, flint, and even old bottles.

Period planting in the garden's rocky scree includes cordylines, cannas, and acanthus with such Victorian staples as hypericum, antirrhinums, stocks, and dianthus in the formal beds. The result is a garden of rare quirkiness and charm. VB

Sheringham Park

Norfolk, England

DESIGNER: Humphry Repton
OWNER: The National Trust
GARDEN STYLE: English landscape
SIZE: 1,000 acres (405 ha)
CLIMATE: Temperate
LOCATION: Sheringham, Norfolk

Described by Humphry Repton, the last of the great English landscape designers, as "my most favourite work" and "darling child," the landscape at Sheringham, dating from 1812, is his best-preserved work. It was designed for Abbot Upcher, who never lived to see it, but Repton did not stop at the landscape, he also designed (with his son) Sheringham Hall.

Repton wrote in his Red Book, "I hope I may be here allowed to indulge my favourite propensity for humanising as well as animating beautiful scenery." Located in a secluded valley at the edge of the Cromer/Holt ridge, not more than half a mile (1 km) from the sea, it more than met Repton's aim.

The mature, ornamental woodland imbues a sense of enclosure and intimacy. Creating the canopy and enlivening the understory is a great diversity of broad-leaved trees with conifers, ornamental trees, and shrubs. There is a collection of Ernest Wilson's Chinese introductions from the early 1900s that includes maples, magnolias, camellias, pieris, and the handkerchief tree (*Davidia involucrata*). The highlight though is the spectacular show of rhododendrons and azaleas in late spring and early summer.

In contrast there are open meadows rife with wildflowers in summer and stunning views to the sea. There is also a classical temple—based on an original Repton design—erected in 1975 for the seventieth birthday of Thomas Upcher, the last descendant of the original owner to live at Sheringham. TM

Felbrigg Hall

Norfolk, England

DESIGNER: The Windham family
OWNER: The National Trust
GARDEN STYLE: 18th-century kitchen garden,
  parkland
SIZE: 6 acres (2.4 ha)
CLIMATE: Temperate
LOCATION: Felbrigg, Norwich, Norfolk

Felbrigg Hall, which lies 2 miles (3 km) from the North Sea coast, belonged to the Windham family and their descendents from the seventeenth century until 1969, when it was bestowed to the National Trust. It is well worth visiting because it boasts one of the best eighteenth-century kitchen gardens in England.

With 12-foot-high (3.5 m) walls and a nearly 2-acre (1 ha) site, the kitchen garden is bursting at the seams with fruits, vegetables, and flowers. Even though it is no longer fully productive, it is still an awesome sight. Vegetables are grown in neat rows, and the figs, pears, and plums are trained against the walls. The lean-to vine house is dominated by a large Black Hamburgh grapevine (*Vitis vinifera* 'Schiava Grossa'), and a wide range of local fruit varieties is grown in the orchard.

Also look out for one of the garden's most eccentric features, the octagonal brick dovecote crowned by a distinctive lantern. The remainder of Felbrigg's landscape is classic parkland with a large lake and woods full of mature trees. Nearby, the American Garden contains fine tulip trees, robinia, and liquidamber, planted in the nineteenth century.

Felbrigg was once described by Humphry Repton as "one of the most beautiful situations in Norfolk." Some believe that Repton, who lived on the edge of the estate from the 1770s, helped to create it, but there is no evidence of this. Repton himself used to complain that his friend William Windham III often asked for advice, but then gave the work to a rival. MC

The Exotic Garden

Norfolk, England

DESIGNER: Will Giles
OWNER: Will Giles
GARDEN STYLE: 21st-century interpretation
  of Victorian exotic
SIZE: 1 acre (0.4 ha)
CLIMATE: Temperate
LOCATION: Norwich, Norfolk

Prepare to expect the unexpected at The Exotic Garden—behind the uninspiring entrance in the center of Norwich is one of Britain's most exhilarating gardens. Will Giles has capitalized on the microclimate and transformed a horticultural desert into a lush, tropical garden. Plants that are not supposed to survive outdoors over winter in Britain actually thrive.

The garden is broken up by narrow paths, forming carefully crafted vistas and giving the illusion of extra size. Above and below it is packed with plants, creating an urban jungle that energizes and cheers. Under canopies of climbers and arching bananas are large-leaved gingers, palms, and colocasias and flashes of orange, pink, and purple. Houseplants are planted annually, and chlorophytum, monstera, and tradescantia are crammed into borders, with bromeliads tied to trees, in a twenty-first-century take on a Victorian passion for the exotic.

The bland house frontage has an added colonial balcony, while a tree house—topped by a giant gold leaf obelisk—sits among the boughs of a giant oak. Below, surrounded by lush foliage, a Caribbean-style shack is the garden store and, in a shady corner, is an Edwardian summer house. Also look out for the cascade, planted with ferns, tumbling into a pool below. The garden reaches a colorful crescendo from midsummer on. It is the perfect place to visit on a hot summer day when the air is filled with the intoxicating fragrance of jasmine and angels' trumpets. The tropics hit the UK. MB

Blickling Hall

Norfolk, England

DESIGNERS: John Adey Repton, Eighth Marquis of Lothian, Sir Digby Wyatt, Markham Nesfield, Norah Lindsay
OWNER: The National Trust
GARDEN STYLE: 19th- and 20th-century formal parkland
SIZE: 43 acres (17 ha)
CLIMATE: Temperate
LOCATION: Blickling, Norwich, Norfolk

The superb parkland gardens at Blickling Hall are the result of over three centuries of work by some of the greatest garden designers. The house, a spectacular redbrick mansion, was built in 1618 for Sir Henry Hobart and is set among sweeping lawns, fine ornamental gardens, and mature woodland. During the eighteenth century, John Hobart, the Second Earl of Buckinghamshire, commissioned the enlargement of the lake and improvements to the gardens. After his death, a striking pyramid-shaped mausoleum was built in the grounds. In the early 1800s, John Adey Repton created decorative schemes, which, along with much of the earlier eighteenth-century designs, have long been lost. Then, in 1856, the house passed to the Eighth Marquis of Lothian. He cut large, formal paths through mature woodland and, in 1870, employed Sir Digby Wyatt and Markham Nesfield to work on the east garden. They built terraces and steps, and they dug out a parterre, planted by Lady Lothian.

In the 1930s, Norah Lindsay, the doyenne of society gardens, was asked to update the parterre. She divided the area into four squares, each with a corner yew cone, filled with bright perennials. From the parterre, a path with lawns to either side leads the eye uphill to a temple, and bordering the lawns are mature stands of oak and beech. Close by is the Secret Garden, heavily planted with scented flowers in the nineteenth century. In short, the gardens are a marriage of the grand formal schemes of the past and artful, twentieth-century plantsmanship. MC

Sandringham

Norfolk, England

DESIGNERS: William Broderick Thomas, Geoffrey Jellicoe, Sir Eric Savill

OWNER: Queen Elizabeth II

GARDEN STYLE: 19th- and 20th-century formal and informal

SIZE: 60 acres (24.3 ha)

CLIMATE: Temperate

LOCATION: King's Lynn, Norfolk

Now the East Anglian country retreat of Queen Elizabeth II and the Royal Family, the Sandringham Estate was purchased in 1862 by Queen Victoria in an attempt to keep the Prince of Wales (later Edward VII) away from the temptations of the capital.

The nineteenth-century garden was laid out by William Broderick Thomas in the natural style, with the lawns, pair of lakes, and woodland gardens all making a tranquil setting for the house that was built in 1902. The edges of the lakes and the stream walk are flanked by plantings of moisture-loving species,

and to the eastern side of the upper lake is the large rockery now covered with dwarf conifers. Below is a grotto and above is a summerhouse built for Queen Alexandra, the Danish wife of Edward VII.

The large lawn is studded with memorial oaks planted by Queen Victoria and members of the Royal Family. The belt of woodland, enclosing the lawn and bordered by the two lakes, contains several notable specimens, including a lovely handkerchief tree (*Davidia involucrata*). The woodland is pierced by a path running between ornamental plantings of rhododendrons, magnolias, camellias, hydrangeas, and dogwoods. The last big change made to this area was in the 1960s when Sir Eric Savill designed the perimeter shrubberies and Woodland Walk.

To the north of the house is Jellicoe's garden, designed in 1947 for King George VI. Positioned to be viewed from his bedroom, it was enclosed by thick box hedges and surrounded by interlaced limes. TM

Pensthorpe
Millennium Garden

Norfolk, England

DESIGNER: Piet Oudolf
OWNERS: Bill Jordon, Deborah Jordan
GARDEN STYLE: 21st-century naturalistic
SIZE: 1 acre (0.4 ha)
CLIMATE: Temperate
LOCATION: Fakenham, Norfolk

A wildlife and waterfowl park in East Anglia may not seem the obvious location for a garden by one of Europe's leading designers. However, amid the lakes and waterways at Pensthorpe lies the Millennium Garden with plantings by the Dutch designer Piet Oudolf. Created to mark the new century, the garden shows the virtue of simplicity in planting composition. Oudolf's style is usually referred to as naturalistic because the plants tend to be chosen as much for their texture and foliage as for their blooms.

They also require less maintenance than other more highly bred plants, remaining stronger and more compact and less likely to need staking and tying in.

The design is based on blocks and drifts of one particular plant, with ornamental grasses used to create highlights. What comes out most is the value of repetition in the planting, sometimes with blocks of the same plant repeated three or four times. The background to the garden is largely neutral although the presence of an old farmhouse, now reduced to a shell, does provide ambience.

The garden is, arguably, Oudolf's most successful in Britain to date. The big horizons and high light levels of Norfolk are akin to the prairies of North America, from where the wild cousins of many of the plants in the garden come. Lovers of naturalistic planting, and waterfowl, will adore it. MW

Birmingham Botanical Gardens and Glasshouses

West Midlands, England

DESIGNER: John Claudius Loudon
OWNER: Birmingham Botanical and Horticultural Society
GARDEN STYLE: 19th-century collection, modern gardens
SIZE: 15 acres (6 ha)
CLIMATE: Temperate
LOCATION: Edgbaston, Birmingham, West Midlands

When botanical gardens began to pop up in cities around nineteenth-century England, it became a matter of civic pride for the Birmingham Botanical and Horticultural Society to create one. The society employed the leading garden designer of the day, John Claudius Loudon, who submitted a plan in 1830. It was impressive but too grand—initial financial constraints prevented building of the huge circular greenhouse that he proposed. However, the rest of the gardens were laid out to his specification.

The oldest greenhouse is the Tropical House, built in 1852 to house the giant water lily (*Victoria amazonica*) that had flowered in Britain for the first time three years earlier. The Tropical House was joined by the Subtropical House in 1871, with the range of Terrace Glasshouses being erected in 1873. They house orchids, citrus, succulents, and tall palms. In the Subtropical House there are chattering mynah birds to entertain visitors.

The greenhouses form the gateway to the rest of the gardens, beginning with the Loudon Terrace, from which you will see the main sloping lawn enclosed by trees. At one end of the terrace is a domed lawn aviary with exotic birds and, to the right, the bandstand dating from 1873. There is also a cottage garden, fernery, National Collection of bonsai, and rhododendron walk. LH

Castle Bromwich Hall Gardens

West Midlands, England

DESIGNERS: William Winde, the Bridgeman family
OWNER: Castle Bromwich Hall Gardens Trust
GARDEN STYLE: 17th-century formal English
SIZE: 10 acres (4 ha)
CLIMATE: Temperate
LOCATION: Castle Bromwich, Birmingham, West Midlands

The urban sprawl of Birmingham is the unlikely home of one of Britain's most important historic gardens. Developed by generations of the Bridgeman family, Castle Bromwich Hall and Gardens are a rare example of a Jacobean country house and garden. Captain William Winde, who had developed the parks and gardens at Combe Abbey in Warwickshire, Cliveden in Buckinghamshire (see page 324), and Powis Castle in Wales (see page 547), laid out the design of these gardens in the early seventeenth century.

Winde conceived the gardens, laid out in the formal Dutch style, as an arrangement of self-contained areas, some ornamental and some utilitarian, separated by walls, hedges, and changes in level. The next 400 years saw continual development. The gardens survived changes in fashion, in particular the landscape movement, which saw the destruction of many formal gardens. They even survived being engulfed by the growth of a huge city. However, they could not survive the economics of maintaining a large garden in the twentieth century. By the 1980s, the gardens were overgrown and derelict.

Local garden enthusiasts came to the rescue and are restoring the site. Remember, as you walk through the gate of the walled garden to see the recreated parterre, that this is a garden created by volunteers. The flower gardens filled with culinary and medicinal herbs, the elegance of the orangery, and the fun of the holly maze are all a tribute to them. JHo

Upton House

Warwickshire, England

DESIGNERS: Percy Morley Horder, Kitty Lloyd-Jones
OWNER: The National Trust
GARDEN STYLE: 20th-century informal
SIZE: 37 acres (14.9 ha)
CLIMATE: Temperate
LOCATION: Banbury, Warwickshire

Upton House garden has many features of the classic English country house landscape, but it possesses one real surprise to make it stand out. The house—late seventeenth century with 1920s additions made by the second Viscount Bearsted, who was also responsible for the current form of the garden—features a pretty blue, silver, and yellow color scheme to the back with roses and perennials. Beyond this, a lawn sweeps away to a distant view of hills with sheep and clumps of trees, framed by magnificent cedars and yews at either side. Nothing is odd so far. However, a walk to the end of the lawn reveals a whole valley at one's feet, completely concealed until the very edge. The view below is over terraces of shrubs and perennials. There is a lake at the bottom and another to one side.

Fruit and vegetables grow well on the warm slopes of the valley and have apparently done so for centuries. Now the microclimate also provides a home for ornamentals. Particularly notable is a National Collection of asters, at their best in fall. Down in the valley bottom is a rose garden and, beyond, another surprise—a bog garden with sinuous paths between lush and expansive hostas, rodgersias, and ferns. Upton also has a rock garden, secret herb garden, an orchard, and a wilderness. It is not a major garden, but it has a quiet, English sophistication. NK

RIGHT A steep, grass pathway at Upton House garden creates an unusual reflection in one of the park's lakes.

Hall's Croft

Warwickshire, England

DESIGNER: Shakespeare Birthplace Trust
OWNER: Shakespeare Birthplace Trust
GARDEN STYLE: English country garden
SIZE: 1 acre (0.4 ha)
CLIMATE: Temperate
LOCATION: Old Town, Stratford-upon-Avon, Warwickshire

Some think that Hall's Croft is the most haunted of the five properties owned by the Shakespeare Birthplace Trust in and around Stratford-upon-Avon and, over the years, there have been a number of unexplained happenings and sightings. Standing opposite Holy Trinity Church, where England's most famous playwright is buried, the timbered house was built in 1613. It is covered at the front with a *Magnolia grandiflora* and wisteria. Its relative grandeur reflects the wealth and status of its original owner, Dr. Hall, husband of Shakespeare's daughter Susanna.

At the back of the house there is a wide stone terrace with steps leading up to a double border, planted with a mixture of herbaceous and meadow flowers. They include the tall yellow meadow rue (*Thalictrum flavum* ssp. *glaucum*), nigella, cornflowers, goat's rue, and leucanthemums, all threaded through with drifts of goldenrod. Standard roses, such as Ballerina and Winchester Cathedral, edge the path that leads to a sundial and arbor.

To the left of the house is an expanse of lawn and, at its center, a mulberry tree dating from 1609 when King James I decreed that mulberries should be planted to provide food for silkworms—unfortunately the wrong mulberry variety was used. Another important ingredient is the box-edged herb bed—with a central bay tree (*Laurus nobilis*)—based on Dr. Hall's casebook. The bed contains some 40 of the 150 herbs he listed, including lemon balm, garlic, dandelion, soapwort, hyssop, French tarragon (*Artemisia dracunculus*), and white mallow. VB

> "The bed contains some 40 of the 150 herbs [Dr. Hall] listed, including lemon balm, garlic..."

Garden Organic Ryton

Warwickshire, England

DESIGNER: Garden Organic
OWNER: Garden Organic (formerly Henry Doubleday Research Association)
GARDEN STYLE: 20th-century demonstration garden
SIZE: 10 acres (4 ha)
CLIMATE: Temperate
LOCATION: Ryton-on-Dunsmore, Coventry, Warwickshire

"This garden is all about demonstrating organics in action," says Sally Smith, Head of Information and Training at Garden Organic. At Ryton they practice what they preach. There are thirty demonstration gardens, with exhibitions, walks, and a well-stocked store to provide all the information you could need.

The gardens buzz with wildlife because there are no fertilizers or chemical pest controls. "The ethos is one of working in harmony with nature," says Sally. "Seeing is believing. We have been gardening this way here for twenty years and the gardens are far from overrun with weeds or pests!" A wildflower meadow, native woodland, and lake provide food, shelter, and breeding areas for birds, insects, and small mammals. There is also a highly productive garden, heritage vegetable patch, and outstanding cook's garden. A children's garden has a willow tunnel, raised pond, and turf bench and table.

The health of the planet is acknowledged because all the buildings are as energy efficient as possible. Meanwhile, the Heritage Seed Collection stands as staunch guardian of native biodiversity. "Soil management is the key to the success of organic growing, and garden compost, leafmold, and green manures are all used to produce a healthy soil and healthy plants," is the main advice given, backed up by numerous practical examples of organic pest- and disease-control and compost-making displays. If all this palls, seek out the amazing vegetables and perennials in the Vegetable Inspirations Garden. NS

Packwood House

Warwickshire, England

DESIGNERS: John Fetherston, Baron Ash
OWNER: The National Trust
GARDEN STYLE: 17th-century formal,
   20th-century informal
SIZE: 7 acres (2.8 ha)
CLIMATE: Temperate
LOCATION: Lapworth, Solihull, Warwickshire

Few gardens can claim to depict a Bible story in topiary, but Packwood House is one. The huge collection of yew shapes are traditionally known as the Sermon on the Mount and were originally set out by John Fetherston between 1650 and 1670. The mount itself is clothed with yew and box and is crowned with a large, single yew said to represent Christ. On the terraces below are twelve impressive, if slightly irregularly shaped, yew-tree apostles.

It is thought that this biblical allusion may have been propagated by Baron Ash, who carried out the historical-style restoration in the 1930s. Although the layout had changed little since the early eighteenth century, it was hidden by a great deal of Victorian planting. Baron Ash decided to remove this and reinstated two castellated gazebos and the west wall of the garden. However, he did add his own touch, namely a sunken garden with pool and colorful borders in the Carolean Garden. Thankfully, this does not detract from the Carolean Garden's seventeenth-century structure with cream-red brick walls, the restored gazebos at each corner, and a raised terrace.

With their countless steps, the terrace and gazebos demand to be explored. This makes them popular with children, and many are surprised by the holes that were once used for woven beehives, known as skeps. For adults, there are herbaceous borders along the terrace and around the edges of the Carolean Garden, where red-hot pokers and yellow achillea harmonize with the brickwork. LH

Boughton House

Northamptonshire, England

DESIGNERS: Van der Meulen, second Duke of Montagu
OWNERS: Ninth Duke and Duchess of Buccleuch,
the Living Landscape Trust
GARDEN STYLE: 17th-century Dutch formal, 18th-century
English garden
SIZE: 350 acres (141.7 ha)
CLIMATE: Temperate
LOCATION: Kettering, Northamptonshire

The second Duke of Montagu had grounds that, in his day, were among the finest in England— hardly surprising because he was also known as John the Planter. However, the work at Boughton actually began with the previous generation and Ralph Montagu, the first duke. Between 1684 and 1709, he developed the gardens in the Dutch style that had become popular following the crowning of King William III of Holland. With the help of Dutch gardener Van der Meulen, the garden's network of avenues, ponds, and now long-gone parterres was created.

The gardens were expanded during 1720–49 by John the Planter. He added a large lake, avenues that extend for 23 miles (37 km), and rides that total about 20 miles (32 km). These vast additions were conceived by Charles Bridgeman, the royal gardener who spearheaded the transition from formal parterres to the naturalistic English landscape style. Unfortunately some of Bridgeman's plans were too grand even for John the Planter, and he was dismissed.

After 1750, little happened to the gardens and they fell into decline. Since 1900, though, the family has regularly lived at Boughton House and restored the avenues. The work continues, most recently on the square-shaped Star Pond with arcs cut into each side to create the points. Nearer the house are other additions: herbaceous borders, planted urns, a small circular rose garden, and a lily pond. All of these bring interest to a garden dominated by structure. LH

Kelmarsh Hall

Northamptonshire, England

DESIGNERS: Norah Lindsay,
Geoffrey Jellicoe
OWNER: The Kelmarsh Trust
GARDEN STYLE: Italian, Colonial American
SIZE: 25 acres (10 ha)
CLIMATE: Temperate
LOCATION: Kelmarsh, Northampton,
Northamptonshire

The Palladian Kelmarsh Hall is discreetly set in an eighteenth-century landscape. A sunk fence makes the nearby road invisible from the entrance, while the rear of the property has stunning views toward a lake.

Between 1928 and 1933, Ronald Tree and his Virginian wife, Nancy, rented and transformed the house and gardens. The socialite garden designer Norah Lindsay helped out. Later she married the property's owner, Colonel Jubie Lancaster, and, together, they commissioned Geoffrey Jellicoe.

Today the house is empty but open, and the gardens are well tended and being restored. The deep back terrace retains Jellicoe's framing of interlaced limes and magnificent vistas. In 1933 a 540-foot (165 m) gap was cut through Shipley Wood on the far side of the lake, opening up the distant landscape. The flower gardens are restored with Lindsay's massed perennials and richly scented old roses, their ebullience framed by low box hedges.

The Sunken Garden, surrounded by box hedges filled with scented plants, leads through the former laundry drying area into double borders that open out into a final garden. The adjacent Walled Garden is being reinstated, and the orangery and Edwardian vinery have already been restored. Also note the rose garden laid out in Colonial American style with board-edged beds. As you bask in this sun trap, ponder the fact that Nancy Lancaster demolished a farmhouse because it blocked the glorious view. CH

Coton Manor Garden

Northamptonshire, England

DESIGNERS: Ian Pasley-Tyler, Susie Pasley-Tyler
OWNERS: Ian Pasley-Tyler, Susie Pasley-Tyler
GARDEN STYLE: Arts and Crafts
SIZE: 10 acres (4 ha)
CLIMATE: Temperate
LOCATION: Guilsborough, Northamptonshire

Nestling in the hills of Northamptonshire, Coton Manor's mellow stone provides the perfect backdrop for this exquisitely planted garden. It was originally laid out in the 1920s by the grandparents of the current owner and gradually developed by subsequent generations. The current generation of Pasley-Tylers certainly fully appreciate and maximize the setting and architectural core of the house, outbuildings, and water.

Terraces laid out immediately around the house provide a microclimate for sun-loving Mediterranean climbing plants, gray-leaved and scented species, and imaginative containers. A mixed rose garden flourishes by the conservatory. There is also a stone-edged reflecting pool at the foot of the terraces. Just below that, you will marvel at what can be grown under a holly hedge (the list of plants includes *Astrantia* 'Sunningdale Variegated', *Delphinium* 'Pandora', and *Rosa* 'Fred Loads'). Well-placed seats allow visitors to the garden plenty of time to soak up the scents and sights. Also note the shady winding path beside a naturalistic brook leading to the water garden, the water staircase, rose walk, and gravel garden.

The boundary between the upper and lower gardens features mixed borders that have been carefully planted to extend the seasons. They are Susie Pasley-Tyler's specialty and are constantly updated and maintained. Farther away, the lawns merge into grassy landscape as the gardens fall away to the stream—complete with flamingos—that supports the water and bog plants. Another big highlight for visitors is the walk into the 5-acre (2 ha) woods that are at their most exciting in the bluebell season. When returning up the garden, pause for a while in the peace and small enclosure of the herb garden. Then, wallet in hand, go straight to the nursery—guarded by a noisy parrot—which is definitely worth exploring. CH

Holdenby House Gardens

Northamptonshire, England

DESIGNERS: Rosemary Verey, Rupert Golby
OWNERS: James Lowther, Karen Lowther
GARDEN STYLE: Late 20th-century informal
SIZE: 15 acres (6 ha)
CLIMATE: Temperate
LOCATION: Holdenby, Northampton, Northamptonshire

For all the obvious beauties of Holdenby's gardens, it is their history that makes them unique. Descend the steps to the farthest lawn and there is an incongruously large and highly ornamented archway, part of a vast house built for Queen Elizabeth I's chancellor, Sir Christopher Hatton. Only one-eighth now survives because much of it was demolished in the seventeenth century. However, even this portion is magnificent and hints at how imposing the original structure and garden must have been.

Some elements of the sixteenth-century garden do survive, including several of the 1580 terraces that were built to impress Elizabeth when she stayed there. Much of what is now visible is modern recreation. The period garden was actually made in 1980 by Rosemary Verey. It is a smaller version of Hatton's original centerpiece to the gardens, including plants that were introduced to England before 1580. These pretty plantings reach their peak in early summer, but continue to provide structure and some interest for the rest of the season.

From the Elizabethan Garden, paths lead to distinctly different areas. There is a kitchen garden planted to create an attractive potager with fruit and vegetables. A wide terrace runs along the back of the house and features large yew hedges. There is a network of fragrant borders—mainly shrubs and perennials—that have been replanted by Chelsea Flower Show medal-winner Rupert Golby. Near the Falconry Centre are long borders with the current owners' collection of silver-leaved plants. LH

Cottesbrooke Hall

Northamptonshire, England

DESIGNERS: Sylvia Crowe, Geoffrey Jellicoe,
Robert Weir Schultz, Catherine Macdonald-Buchanan
OWNERS: Capt. John Macdonald-Buchanan,
Elizabeth Macdonald-Buchanan
GARDEN STYLE: Italianate, Arts and Crafts, wild
SIZE: 30 acres (12.1 ha)
CLIMATE: Temperate
LOCATION: Cottesbrooke, Northampton,
Northamptonshire

As if from the pages of a Jane Austen novel, the Queen Anne brick facade at Cottesbrooke Hall, dressed with Duston and Ketton stone, exudes understated elegance. Although the north side of the house blends into eighteenth-century English parkland, to the south the latter stops at the forecourt terraces designed by Geoffrey Jellicoe. Balustraded and paved, the clipped boxwood and four boxwood-edged beds of *Rosa* 'Pascali' add classical elegance, as do the carefully placed statues of Diana, Mercury, Cupid, and Venus.

The house is flanked by a series of gardens. Along the Statue Walk are statues from the Temple of Ancient Virtue in Buckinghamshire's Stowe Landscape Garden: Socrates, Lycurgus, Epaminondas, and Homer—all opposite the excellent herbaceous borders—and framed by clipped yew hedging. A gap in the hedge takes you into a section called Dilemma where tulips, the golden Indian bean tree (*Catalpa bignonioides* 'Aurea'), the handkerchief tree (*Davidia involucrata*), mulberry, and medlar trees thrive. The classical theme is perpetuated elsewhere by the statue of a gladiator by the interlaced limes known as Gladiator Avenue. Two brick gateways then lead into the Pool Court, now covered with grass, designed by Robert Weir Schultz and embellished with an elegant arbor by Dame Sylvia Crowe. A plant-swathed Edwardian brick pergola guides visitors on to the Pine Court and Dutch Garden.

Visitors to Cottesbrooke should also look out for the newer East and West Wild Gardens, separated by Hunter's Bridge, with a fusion of artificial and natural landscaping. The East Garden has a series of trails opening into a glade with a bronze horse's head sculpted by Nic Fiddian-Green. The West Garden, on the other hand, has a distinctly Chinese theme, and was created with the purpose of celebrating the new millennium. CH

The Menagerie

Northamptonshire, England

DESIGNERS: Gervase Jackson Stops, Ian Kirby

OWNER: Alexander Myers

GARDEN STYLE: 20th-century modern,
    18th-century themes

SIZE: 3.5 acres (1.4 ha)

CLIMATE: Temperate

LOCATION: Horton, Northamptonshire

The Menagerie is one of the most enchanting gardens in England. It stems from a love affair with a Palladian folly, built by the architect, astronomer, and grottomaker Thomas Wright for the Earl of Halifax in 1749. Originally a banquet house, it was discovered decaying in a field by Gervase Jackson Stops, formerly buildings advisor to the National Trust. He bought it in the 1970s and spent the rest of his life restoring it.

Only a dedicated specialist with such a thorough understanding of garden history could have had such fun restoring it. The starting point for the garden,

created largely by Jackson Stops's friend, Ian Kirby, is the *patte d'oie* layout from the early eighteenth century: three straight walks, marked out by limes and hornbeam hedges, radiate out from the house. Each vista is terminated by a garden feature in the correct manner. However, a classical obelisk sits atop a Tudor spiral mount, and the Thomas Wright-inspired summerhouses that terminate the outer vistas are not what they seem. A classical frontage conceals a chapel, dedicated to St. Francis of Assisi. From here, a second door entices visitors into a formal garden that turns out to be a wilderness of ponds and reeds.

Following the death of Jackson Stops, the garden saw a brief decline, but it was rescued by its current owner. He has restored the fabulous shell grotto Stops made and created a magnificent walled kitchen garden. Work is now focused on developing the wilder areas so that the garden melts seamlessly back into nature, a secret jewel among the bean fields. AE

Cambridge University Botanic Garden

Cambridgeshire, England

DESIGNER: Professor John Stevens Henslow
OWNER: Cambridge University
GARDEN STYLE: Botanical garden
SIZE: 40 acres (16.2 ha)
CLIMATE: Temperate
LOCATION: Cambridge, Cambridgeshire

In 1831 the Reverend Professor John Stevens Henslow, clergyman and inspirational teacher of the naturalist (and author of the theory of natural selection) Charles Darwin, established a botanical garden as a teaching and research resource for the University of Cambridge. Henslow believed that trees were the most important plants in the world and should be studied in their own right. You can still see the avenue of *Pinus nigra* planted by Henslow to demonstrate the variation within a single species.

The collection of trees is magnificent, with giant and dawn redwoods, cedars, and a large collection of *Sorbus*, all providing a beautifully landscaped garden framework. Around the lake, on a smaller scale, are two rock gardens—one of limestone, one sandstone—with alpine and rock plants from around the world. In fact you will quickly notice that plants from the same geographic area are grown together and are, like all 10,000 plants in the garden, clearly labeled. Scented gardens, greenhouses (alpine, temperate, and tropical), herbaceous beds, a winter garden, and an intricate layout of 144 island beds, grouping together plants of the same botanical family, are all found here.

Despite being owned by the university, the gardens are much more than a center for study—they are a valued asset that benefits the whole of Cambridge. They are a place for children to romp, for undergraduates to unwind, for professors to walk in thoughtful reflection, and for garden visitors to relax in a tranquil oasis in the heart of the city. JHo

Crossing House Garden

Cambridgeshire, England

DESIGNER: Margaret Fuller
OWNERS: Douglas Fuller, Margaret Fuller
GARDEN STYLE: 20th-century plantsman's
English cottage garden
SIZE: 0.3 acres (0.1 ha)
CLIMATE: Temperate
LOCATION: Shepreth, Royston, Cambridgeshire

"Plant-lovers are welcome to walk round this garden," reads the handwritten sign as you enter through the gate of the Crossing House Garden. The garden's owners, Douglas and Margaret Fuller, were once the railroad-crossing keepers. Ever since the late 1950s when a few curious pedestrians, waiting for the crossing to open, asked to see the garden, the sign has been there and the garden has been open to visitors every single day of the year.

The Fullers have packed the tiny garden with plants from the rare to the popular. The year-round flowering is achieved by densely planting bulbs, perennials, and shrubs and overplanting with annuals when the plants are past their peak. In spring there are carpets of hellebores and snowdrops defying the hard frosts. Species tulips follow the primroses. Magnolias lead the way in to summer with alliums and *Nectaroscordum siculum* that self-seed around the beds. Peer into the tiny greenhouses and you will see orchids, a collection of auriculas, and new plants biding their time for an outside place.

There is also a fun seedbed that definitely lives up to the name—it is actually an old iron bedstead sown with rows of annuals in spring. In winter it is covered by a candlewick counterpane of pink *Cyclamen coum* and *C. hederifolium*. Topiary sheep graze dangerously close to rare saxifrages, and an old railway sign warns you to proceed slowly. Going around slowly, is the best way to enjoy this little jewel of garden. JH

Clare College Fellows' Garden

Cambridgeshire, England

DESIGNER: Nevill Willmer
OWNERS: The Masters and Fellows, Clare College, University of Cambridge
GARDEN STYLE: Mid-20th-century informal
SIZE: 2 acres (0.8 ha)
CLIMATE: Temperate
LOCATION: Cambridge, Cambridgeshire

The long herbaceous borders of the Fellows' Garden at Clare College flow down to the River Cam, while the college's mellow stone walls sit behind with the grander pinnacles of King's College Chapel. This picture-perfect view is the work of Nevill Willmer. He redesigned the garden in 1947 after years of neglect, the gardening staff having been reduced to one aged gardener during World War II. Willmer conceived the garden as a series of real-life landscape paintings. The best views are from the west front of the college, the Master's Lodge, the bridge over the Cam, and the causeway that runs to Queens' Road.

At the center of the garden, enclosed by a clipped yew hedge, lies a formal sunken pond. From here a path leads to the riverbank along a double-sided herbaceous border planted in gold and blue. Behind the old wall is the White Walk, which leads to an informal lawn, backed by borders devoted to summer and fall colors. Willmer used visual trickery to give this essentially traditional English garden a twist. The alleys gradually narrow to make them appear longer, and bright orange-red flowers are placed in the foreground with paler colors behind to make the borders appear longer than they really are.

The garden is now tended by five gardeners. It has billowing borders and immaculate lawns, with a restoration program underway—ten years will see the garden returned to Willmer's original master plan. LH

Anglesey Abbey Gardens

Cambridgeshire, England

DESIGNERS: Huttleston Broughton, first Lord Fairhaven
OWNER: The National Trust
STYLE: 20th-century English
SIZE: 98 acres (39.6 ha)
CLIMATE: Temperate
LOCATION: Lode, Cambridgeshire

With a family fortune made in American mining and railroads, Huttleston Broughton, the first Lord Fairhaven, spent the 1930s transforming the grounds of 900-year-old Anglesey Abbey into one of the most sumptuous, twentieth-century British gardens. Every year Fairhaven had his gardeners plant more than 5,000 hyacinths in rows. He created tree-lined avenues and wide, open areas of sculpture lawns that feature Britain's finest collection of seventeenth- and nineteenth-century garden statuary. The lawns lead to enclosed gardens, an arboretum, and a pinetum.

In total there are twenty-three garden areas at Anglesey Abbey. A stroll along the Fairhaven Centenary Walk demonstrates that even in bleak midwinter, gardens can still be colorful, scented, and beautiful. Created after Fairhaven's death, the impressive scale of the 1-mile-long (1.6 km) walk echoes his own extravagance. It is not unusual in winter to come across visitors crawling along on all fours. Snowdrop enthusiasts, in particular, flock to the gardens to admire, close up, Anglesey Abbey's famous snowdrop collection.

The house and gardens became the property of the National Trust in 1966. The trust's then garden advisor, Graham Stuart Thomas, was shocked to see so many dahlias being used, and he ordered their removal. Fortunately, the gardeners ignored the great man and, in high summer, dahlias still roar out. JH

Peckover House and Garden

Cambridgeshire, England

DESIGNERS: Main designer unknown, Graham Stuart Thomas
OWNER: The National Trust
GARDEN STYLE: 19th-century, eclectic Victorian
SIZE: 2 acres (0.8 ha)
CLIMATE: Temperate
LOCATION: Wisbech, Cambridgeshire

Peckover House grounds are like a grand country house in miniature, with a kitchen garden, croquet lawn, orangery, and two pools. The fine redbrick house was built in 1722 and overlooks the Georgian boomtown of Wisbech, but the gardens date from the Victorian era. The town is a pretty backwater now, but Peckover has survived and has been restored.

Peckover is one of the finest examples of a walled town garden in the country. Most visitors enter the gardens from the side, emerging into the ornamental kitchen garden. Surrounding the main lawn are old espalier pear trees encrusted by lichen, and mixed borders. Against the adjacent wall are rows of cut flowers and stock plants for the main borders. The central area of the garden is a series of interconnected "rooms." The first has a modest orangery with orange plants more than 300 years old. Other sections of the central area include herbaceous borders and a circular pool with a fountain overlooked by trellised gazebos.

The area most typical of the Victorian period is near the rear of the house. It includes dense shrubberies and nineteenth-century favorites such as a monkey puzzle tree (*Araucaria araucana*) and a Chusan palm (*Trachycarpus fortunei*). Croquet hoops are set in the lawn below the main steps. Balls and mallets are usually provided, so have a game. LH

The Manor

Cambridgeshire, England

DESIGNER: Lucy Boston
OWNER: Diana Boston
STYLE: 20th-century country garden with topiary
SIZE: 4 acres (1.6 ha)
CLIMATE: Temperate
LOCATION: Hemingford Grey, Huntingdon, Cambridgeshire

This garden has two bonuses. First, the manor house, dating from 1130, is said to be the oldest inhabited house in England. Second, Lucy Boston used it as the setting for her children's books in the 1930s.

Many features here are described in the books, including the topiary deer under the huge copper beech tree (*Fagus sylvatica* Purpurea Group). An avenue of yews are in the shape of a crown and orb and topiary horses guard the Norman-fronted house. A bridge over a stream leads through pink roses into a maze of borders and rose-covered archways.

Lucy Boston spent many years restoring the house and creating a garden that is every bit as imaginative and mysterious as her stories. That is why you will see a chess set among the topiary figures, while the 300 varieties of old roses here were apparently planted by Graham Stuart Thomas. Two hundred or so still thrive, some in double 100-foot-long (30 m) herbaceous borders stretching down to the river. A gentle walk though a grove of trees on the lawn is meant to resemble a mystical ballet. You should come early when the mist is rising—with the trees emerging out of the haze, the magic is still strong. MH

> "You should come early when the mist is rising… the magic is still strong"

Wimpole Hall

Cambridgeshire, England

DESIGNERS: Charles Bridgeman, Capability Brown,
William Emes

OWNER: The National Trust

GARDEN STYLE: 18th- and 19th-century English landscape

SIZE: 74 acres (29.9 ha)

CLIMATE: Temperate

LOCATION: Arrington, Royston, Cambridgeshire

The first garden at Wimpole Hall was laid out in the formal, French style in the 1690s by royal gardeners George London and Henry Wise. It was an ambitious project, and creating the garden was enough to bankrupt the second Earl of Radnor.

Throughout the eighteenth century, successive owners employed nearly all the great landscape designers of their day, including Charles Bridgeman, Robert Greening, Capability Brown, William Emes, and Humphry Repton. Later, in the early twentieth century, Wimpole Hall languished and decayed, but was saved by Rudyard Kipling's daughter, Elsie Bambridge, funded by royalties from her father's books. More recently, the gardens have seen remarkable restoration. Of the seventeenth-century garden nothing remains. A Victorian parterre on the north front, though, was restored in 1996. Some of Bridgeman's long avenues leading to the cardinal compass points have also been replanted, while Brown's serpentine lake, which replaced Bridgeman's canalized ponds, has been dredged. The Gothic Tower, by Sanderson Miller, has also been restored.

A nineteenth-century pleasure ground to the northeast of the house is enclosed by a sunk fence, and contains a fine collection of trees, including the National Collection of walnuts. Beyond is the 2-acre (1 ha) mid-eighteenth-century Walled Garden, back in production again. A new project is under way to rebuild the greenhouses designed by Sir John Soane (1790–94) and destroyed by a bomb in 1941. TM

East Bergholt Place

Suffolk, England

DESIGNER: Charles Eley
OWNERS: Rupert Eley, Sarah Eley
GARDEN STYLE: 20th-century collection of unusual trees and shrubs
SIZE: 15 acres (6 ha)
CLIMATE: Temperate
LOCATION: East Bergholt, Suffolk

East Bergholt Place is a historic garden very much of its time, but brought right up to date. Set right in the heart of Constable country, the Edwardian house is surrounded by topiary yew hedges and lawns. It is all very traditional. Beyond the hedges are a brook and a rectangular pool leading to the main part of the garden, a largely unstructured and free-flowing space containing a first-rate collection of flowering shrubs and trees.

The present owner's great-grandfather subscribed to the plant hunting expeditions of George Forrest in the 1920s and built up an impressive collection of magnolias, rhododendrons, and camellias. Mown paths meander around a sloping valley through hidden dells and glades with something of interest at every step. Oddities such as oemleria, *Nyssa sinensis*, and *Acer triflorum* are in abundance. Fall is especially spectacular when the sun glows through *Viburnum opulus* 'Roseum' or shines on swagged red berries of cotoneaster. In the spring there is the new foliage of acers and towering columns of flowers from massive rhododendrons. An open meadow turns yellow with primroses, and glades of daffodils set off a white-flowering *Magnolia soulangeana*. Benefiting from a warm microclimate and proximity to the sea, there are many plants that are not easy to grow elsewhere in East Anglia. A Chusan palm (*Trachycarpus fortunei*) has reached 100 feet (30 m) high, and *Eucryphia* x *nymansensis* provides a profusion of waxy yellow flowers in late summer.

A nursery for plantaholics, connoisseurs, and beginners, the Place for Plants, has been created within the walls of the old kitchen garden. Whereas the turn-of-the-century planting here was done by a collector, keen to build up an impressive array of plants from around the world, today's plants are chosen either to replace old plants or because they are the right plant for the right place. MH

Ickworth House

Suffolk, England

DESIGNERS: Capability Brown, Lord Howard de Walden
OWNER: The National Trust
GARDEN STYLE: English landscape, 19th-century
   formal gardens
SIZE: 1,800 acres (729 ha)
CLIMATE: Temperate
LOCATION: Horringer, Bury St. Edmunds, Suffolk

The cedar and oak trees that screen the approach to Ickworth were planted in the nineteenth century by the first Marquis of Bristol. They were meant to hide the construction of the east wing, but were left to grow to maturity. To the south of the wing is the early nineteenth-century, formal Italianate-style garden laid out by the marquis' great-nephew, Charles Ellis. Here are box hedges, bedding plants, the Temple Rose Garden, the Silver and Gold Gardens, with many Mediterranean species, and an example of a Victorian stumpery—tree stumps pulled from the ground and inserted upside down into the ground. There is also an orangery and adjoining terrace.

From the Italianate garden, a path from the rotunda leads up to a terraced walk, with views over the park and the site of the earlier Ickworth Hall. Here, the walled kitchen garden (now a vineyard producing Ickworth wines) is part of remnants of an eighteenth-century garden created by the first earl, including a canal and summerhouse (c.1703).

The sculpting of the ornamental landscape was also started by the first earl who, between 1700 and 1731, removed tenants from over 1,200 acres (486 ha). They were rehoused in Horringer village, while the earl flattened buildings and removed hedges. Improvements were made on behalf of the second earl by Capability Brown between 1769 and 1776. Exactly what these consisted of is not recorded, but it is likely that Brown laid out the woodland in which the first marquis created the Albana Walk, named for his wife, Elizabeth Albana Upton. TM

> "From the Italianate garden,
> a path from the rotunda leads
> up to a terraced walk..."

Shrubland Park Gardens

Suffolk, England

DESIGNERS: Sir Charles Barry, William Robinson
OWNER: Seventh Lord de Saumarez
GARDEN STYLE: Formal Italianate
SIZE: 5 acres (2 ha)
CLIMATE: Temperate
LOCATION: Coddenham, Ipswich, Suffolk

Sir Charles Barry, the architect of the Houses of Parliament, was also the leading light of the mid-nineteenth-century Italianate style of formal garden design, which was in essence a mix of French, Dutch, English, and Italian renaissance influences. His most famous garden, Trentham in Staffordshire, was his first. However, the flat site at Trentham did not offer the same opportunity as the steep slope at Shrubland Park, where the most striking feature, built in the 1850s, is the Grand Descent.

Taking full advantage of the fact that the house was deliberately positioned on the brink of the steep chalk escarpment to make the most of the fine views across the landscape, Barry installed the stairway that descends from the pavilion, via a series of terraces, to the Fountain Garden and the lower loggia. From this lower level, the Green Terrace runs north into the parkland and south to the Swiss Chalet with its alpine rockery. A series of individual gardens was made along its length. Of these, the French Garden—the walls heated by hot water—the Witches Circle, a set of stone basins and a raised flower bed, the box maze, and the Swiss Garden survive. West of the terrace, the Wild Garden also survives. From there the garden melds into woodland and park, where some of the trees are believed to be over 800 years old. The gardens were subsequently modified in 1888 by William Robinson. A strong advocate of the natural style and to whom the Italianate style was an abomination, he simplified the seasonal planting schemes and introduced a flower garden feel.

Garden historians should note that Shrubland was the site of one of the master landscaper Humphry Repton's earliest commissions in the late eighteenth century. Later maps show that many of his suggested improvements were implemented, including the Brownslow Terrace that extends west from the hall to the statue of Diana. TM

Somerleyton Hall

Suffolk, England

DESIGNERS: William Nesfield, Joseph Paxton, and others
OWNERS: Third Baron and Baroness Somerleyton
GARDEN STYLE: Victorian Italianate
SIZE: 12 acres (4.8 ha)
CLIMATE: Temperate
LOCATION: Somerleyton, Lowestoft, Suffolk

The yew maze at the heart of this Suffolk garden—part of William Nesfield's original design—dates back to 1846. In Victorian times, the maze hedge took eight gardeners three months to cut. Today it takes four gardeners only three or four days with gas-powered hedge trimmers.

Greenhouses in the kitchen garden deserve special attention thanks to the ridge-and-furrow roof design that was invented, or at least popularized, by Joseph Paxton, the designer of London's immense Crystal Palace. The greenhouses have recently been renovated, as have Paxton's peach cases. All are now planted with tender ornamentals. Renovation has also seen the Victorian aviary brought back to life. For plant lovers there are lashings of wisteria, old-fashioned roses, and ornamental vines on the long iron pergola (part of the original garden). The vast double herbaceous border is another lively attraction. A new flower garden around a pond at one edge of the garden has become a haven for a wide variety of wildlife, including some lovely green woodpeckers. Those with a penchant for raucous flower color should head for the bedding-filled sunken garden near the house or to the azalea and rhododendron areas in early summer. Somerleyton also has a collection of specimen trees, including a multistemmed giant redwood (*Sequoiadendron giganteum*), a large *Eucalyptus gunnii*, a Monterey pine (*Pinus radiata*), a splendid ginkgo, and an Atlas cedar (*Cedrus atlantica*).

What ultimately separates Somerleyton from other better-known Victorian gardens is that it is still a family home, and it is this detail that gives it a more intimate and exciting atmosphere. Added interest also comes from the fact that the house at Somerleyton was built for Sir Morton Peto, the father of Harold Peto, the great twentieth-century garden maker. JO

Wyken Hall

Suffolk, England

DESIGNERS: Sir Kenneth Carlisle, Lady Carla Carlisle
OWNERS: Sir Kenneth Carlisle, Lady Carla Carlisle
GARDEN STYLE: 20th-century formal
  country-house garden
SIZE: 5 acres (2 ha)
CLIMATE: Temperate
LOCATION: Stanton, Bury St. Edmunds, Suffolk

Wyken Hall is a medieval, half-timbered manor house in the wide, open plains of Suffolk, which, with its garden, was transformed in the 1980s. The hall is the heart of the garden, large and rambling with many gables and rooflines. Once painted the standard white, it is now a deep, lustrous Suffolk pink, making its presence felt all around the garden, its color chiming in with the plantings.

Perhaps to act as a barrier against rattling winds, the formal area of the garden, largely sheltered in "rooms" of yew hedges, is arranged on one side of the house. A croquet lawn sits alongside, bounded at the far end by a brilliantly colored border. One of the features here is a cast-iron gate, which has been decorated with golden ears of corn. Gothic ornaments and seating are found all around the garden, especially in the formal herb parterre where a striking pattern has been created by planting chives, box, and oregano.

Farther away from the house is a magnificent, partly-walled rose garden, arranged around an old church font, where the color and scent have been turned up high. Every part of the planting performs. If you want some peace after all this visual noise, you should proceed to a deck that peers out over a natural pond that is surrounded by flowering meadows and woods. At the front of the house is a twist on the normal carriage drive with an unusual arrangement of circular box hedges laid out in the shape of a quincunx. MH

Heveningham Hall

Suffolk, England

DESIGNERS: Capability Brown, Kim Wilkie
OWNERS: Mr. and Mrs. Jon Hunt
GARDEN STYLE: Capability Brown with modern
  landform gardens
SIZE: 2,500 acres (1,012.5 ha)
CLIMATE: Temperate
LOCATION: Heveningham, Suffolk

Heveningham Hall is the classic ideal of a country seat. Built for successful city bankers in the 1790s, the house was designed by Sir Robert Taylor and the landscape by Capability Brown. However, Brown died the year after he drew up the designs for the park, and they were not implemented until 200 years later when a 1.2-mile-long (2 km) lake was dug through the center of the valley and over 740 acres (300 ha) of arable land were returned to parkland. The woodland was also revived, and a further 334 acres (135 ha) of woods are now being planted.

Behind the house, the garden front has always posed a problem. A typical Victorian parterre had been built on the site in 1877, but the scale and ornamentation jarred beside the 80-yard-long (73 m) Georgian façade, and the retaining walls blocked the views from the main reception rooms. The listed garden beside the Grade I listed house was certainly clumsy for its setting, and the design was not exactly smart. In a groundbreaking decision, English Heritage consented to its demolition and replacement with a completely new garden of sweeping grass terraces.

The terraces now flow with, and fit comfortably in, the rising land, arcing in a fan shape, giving the house plenty of space to breathe. The grass steps are contained within a colonnade of pleached evergreen oaks, though you can still actually see the roots of the old cedars bulging through the geometric pattern. And to set it all off, a 55-yard-long (50 m) reflecting canal separates the stone terrace from the grass. KW

Helmingham Hall Gardens

Suffolk, England

DESIGNER: Lady Xa Tollemache
OWNERS: Fifth Baron Tollemache, Lady Xa Tollemache
GARDEN STYLE: 18th-century country garden,
   20th- and 21st-century additions
SIZE: 10 acres (4 ha) within a 400-acre (162 ha) park
CLIMATE: Temperate
LOCATION: Helmingham, Stowmarket, Suffolk

Helmingham Hall has been the home of the present Lord and Lady Tollemache (whose family has owned it for over 500 years) since 1975. The Tudor house—where plotters planned to restore Charles II to the throne in 1660—was finished in 1510 and is surrounded by a 60-foot-wide (18 m) moat, the sloping sides being covered in narcissi and primroses.

Xa Tollemache has become a well-known garden designer, not only for Helmingham, but for gardens at many great houses. In her own walled garden, she has maintained long, double herbaceous borders, where she is always experimenting with new combinations. Either side of the borders, and between the vegetable beds, are tunnels of arches trained with colorful gourds, sweet peas, runner beans, and roses. The existing parterre garden now includes box hedging with pyramid topiary. The wall borders are edged with 'Hidcote' lavender, overflowing in midsummer with scented hybrid musk roses.

On the east side of the house, Lady Tollemache had the idea of asking the Marchioness of Salisbury to design the herb and knot garden so that it could be seen from the upper windows of the house. It is divided into four beds, one of which has the interwoven Tollemache family pattern delineated in boxwood. The plants here were chosen by Lady Tollemache from those introduced before 1750. Recent additions include gray-painted garden seats designed by George Carter, and a weatherboard summerhouse by the swimming pool. JH

Hergest Croft

Herefordshire, England

DESIGNERS: William Banks, Dorothy Banks,
   Lawrence Banks, Elizabeth Banks
OWNERS: Lawrence Banks, Elizabeth Banks
GARDEN STYLE: Late 19th-century informal
SIZE: 56 acres (22.6 ha)
CLIMATE: Temperate
LOCATION: Kington, Herefordshire

In fall at Hergest Croft, the delicious scent of toffee that is given off by the Katsura tree (*Cercidiphyllum japonicum)* hangs enticingly in the air. It may not be a rare garden experience, but it comes from the tallest Katsura in Britain. The gardens contain fifty other trees of record proportions and a collection of more than 4,000 plants that have been planted by three generations of the Banks family since 1895.

The first generation of Banks', William and Dorothy, laid out the four main areas. Greatly influenced by William Robinson's *The English Flower Garden* (1883), the gardens reflect his relaxed, naturalist ideals. A fine example is Park Wood, with its secluded valley encircled by ancient oak woodland and containing huge rhododendrons. In fact Hergest Croft is best known for its rhododendrons and the Azalea Garden, home to some magnificent displays, as well as less conspicuous treasures such as National Collections of birch and maple. The Maple Grove was started in 1985 by Lawrence and Elizabeth Banks, and contains many new trees from China.

In contrast, the gardens around the Edwardian house are more formal. Herbaceous borders backed by exotic trees provide color throughout the summer and, slightly hidden away, is a croquet lawn with urns planted with lilies. The last of the four main areas is the kitchen garden with its ancient apple trees. These are underplanted with spring flowers, the daffodils and auriculas giving way to tulips and grape hyacinths as the season progresses. LH

The Laskett

Herefordshire, England

DESIGNERS: Sir Roy Strong, Dr. Julia Trevelyan Oman
OWNER: Sir Roy Strong
GARDEN STYLE: 20th-century formal,
   theatrical
SIZE: 4 acres (1.6 ha)
CLIMATE: Temperate
LOCATION: Much Birch, Hereford, Herefordshire

It has been said that gardens often look like their owners. Take Sir Roy Strong's garden, tucked into the Herefordshire countryside on the English–Welsh border. It is stylized, fascinating, and personable. What makes it so extraordinarily different from everything else, though, is its heavy reliance on vistas, allées, focal points, rooms, sculpture, and planting— the hallmarks of formal French and English gardens.

Sir Roy and his late wife, Dr. Julia Trevelyan Oman, moved into The Laskett in May 1973. Over time, they made a remarkable garden around a somewhat unremarkable house. Julia was a movie and theater designer, and Sir Roy a historian, writer, and director of London's National Portrait Gallery (1967–73) and the Victoria and Albert Museum (1974–87). He was more interested in garden structure and grand gestures, she in the detail and more delicate planting. The garden was developed piecemeal. Specific areas such as Covent Garden, Elizabeth Tudor Avenue, and Torte's Garden, were named after a place, pet, friend, event, and so on. The statuary is largely replica, being large, romantic, and bold.

The Laskett is a success because it was built by two people living in harmony. It is deeply personal and representative of the owners' outlook over three decades. Eccentric, formal, purposeful, (sometimes) contrived, above all it is magnificently theatrical. CY

RIGHT The Laskett expresses Sir Roy Strong's taste for theater and also his late wife's subtle eye for planting.

Bryan's Ground

Herefordshire, England

DESIGNERS: David Wheeler, Simon Dorrell
OWNERS: David Wheeler, Simon Dorrell
GARDEN STYLE: 20th-century with
   Arts and Crafts influences
SIZE: 7 acres (2.8 ha), plus 22 acres (8.9 ha) of meadows
CLIMATE: Temperate
LOCATION: Stapleton, Presteigne, Herefordshire

The extensive garden at Bryan's Ground, on the border with Wales, is little over a decade old and is already famous. The comfortable, rambling 1912 Arts and Crafts house has been home to David Wheeler and Simon Dorrell since 1993, and doubles as the office where *Hortus*, the upmarket gardening journal, is published. Readers of *Hortus* who are interested in how the garden is developing are kept up to date by way of David's pen and Simon's drawings.

When David and Simon arrived here, the Sunk Garden, at the front of the house, was already established, as were mature yew hedges and fine trees. They have expanded the garden, creating a series of interlocking "rooms" featuring flowers and foliage. There is a Sulking House (a perfect hideout for grumpy old men), a Dutch garden with canal, and an old rose garden. Fragrant flowers and follies, towers and topiaries, pools, and a potager have all been planned with a witty personal style. The entrance garden is wonderfully dramatic with around thirty square beds laid in a grid, planted with a heritage apple variety and underplanted with *Iris sibirica*.

Away from the cultivated areas, the development of Cricket Wood, the arboretum David began planting in 2000, continues. Bisected by a stream and with mown walks, its informality is in contrast to the more formal gardens around the house. The trees and shrubs, many uncommon and chosen for their fall color, blend harmoniously into the countryside with its delightful pastures and rolling hills. CR

Croome Park

Worcestershire, England

DESIGNER: Capability Brown
OWNER: The National Trust
GARDEN STYLE: 18th-century English landscape
SIZE: 670 acres (271.3 ha)
CLIMATE: Temperate
LOCATION: High Green, Severn Stoke, Worcestershire

In 1996, the National Trust acquired this historically important yet neglected landscape. After a decade of dedicated restoration work, the landscape has been returned to its eighteenth-century glory. Croome was the first large-scale design project undertaken by Capability Brown after he had resigned his position as head gardener at Stowe to become a freelance designer. The man who was so quick off the mark to recognize the thirty-five-year-old's budding brilliance when Brown hired him in 1751 was George William.

The earl inherited Croome in 1744, and the estate became his passion. In the following fifty-eight years until his death, he spent a staggering £400,000 (about £30 million today) creating the garden and landscape. By the turn of the nineteenth century, the ornamental gardens were said to have a collection of exotic plants second only to London's Royal Botanic Gardens at Kew (see page 386).

Brown built the church, the mansion, and the stable blocks, and from the surrounding swampy ground he created a spectacular landscape. An integral part of it was the lake and artificial river that were, and still are, fed by Brown's cunning land-drainage system. The lake is a perfect foil for the lovely garden buildings by Robert Adam and James Wyatt and for the landscape walks.

Over 1,400 trees have now been replanted, and the shrubberies are once again in great shape. This much-overlooked garden is a wonderful place for wandering through the so-called natural English countryside and to marvel at Brown's skill. TB

Stone House Cottage

Worcestershire, England

DESIGNERS: James Arbuthnot, Louisa Arbuthnot
OWNERS: James Arbuthnot, Louisa Arbuthnot
GARDEN STYLE: 20th-century informal
SIZE: 0.7 acre (0.3 ha)
CLIMATE: Temperate
LOCATION: Stone, Kidderminster, Worcestershire

A young garden, Stone House encapsulates so much of what is good about the British gardening tradition. It also illustrates an eccentricity and creative individuality that is quintessentially British. Though quite small, it actually feels much larger because it is divided into a series of small intimate spaces. There is a long, hedged axis that runs the length of the garden—the kind of feature normally found in larger gardens, but effective if used carefully in smaller plots. From this axis, entrances lead to different areas, giving a pervasive feeling of the unexpected.

Very much the effort of a husband-and-wife team, Stone House demonstrates how effectively two people working together, with very different skills, can collaborate. James Arbuthnot is a self-taught bricklayer—having previously been in the army—who delights in making towers and walls out of recycled bricks (hence the garden's nickname of the San Gimignano of the Midlands). Louisa is a dedicated gardener and plantswoman. The walls and hedges create a sheltered microclimate and habitat for a variety of tender shrubs and a great many climbers. The site of an old greenhouse has been made into a well-drained bed for alpines, and there are borders of roses and perennials. On the other side of the long axis is a more informal area of mown grass with large shrubs.

Stone House is a delightful garden with many features that one would expect to find only in a much larger garden. A visit at almost any time of year is rewarding, and there is a well-stocked nursery. NK

Spetchley Park

Worcestershire, England

DESIGNERS: Ellen Wilmott, Rose Berkeley
OWNER: John Berkeley
GARDEN STYLE: Victorian
SIZE: 30 acres (12.1 ha)
CLIMATE: Temperate
LOCATION: Spetchley, Worcester, Worcestershire

Set within a deer park and providing the setting for the Georgian mansion, the gardens at Spetchley Park are primarily Victorian. One of the garden's architects, the famous plantswoman Miss Ellen Wilmott, was known for carrying pockets full of seed of her favorite plant, *Eryngium giganteum*, that she would scatter liberally when visiting friends. This earned the plant the nickname Miss Wilmott's Ghost because it would appear long after she had departed. As is typical of so many late nineteenth- and early twentieth-century country-house gardens, those at Spetchley are composed of a series of "rooms." The gardens are aptly described as a plantsman's paradise because each area possesses its own flavor and atmosphere—informal, formal, natural, exotic, and woodland.

One of the garden's most spectacular features is the spring show of bulbs with swaths of daffodils, primroses, and crocuses. They are followed by tender and semitender exotics in the warmth of the Melon Yard walls. Also note the South Border with clematis, wisteria, and climbing roses forming a backdrop to peonies, irises, mulleins, and the Chinese gooseberry (*Actinidia deliciosa*). In the West Border, the containing wall is cloaked with hydrangea, clematis, and Virginia creeper (*Parthenocissus quinquefolia*), while the border itself has roses, tree peonies, and camellias. In contrast, the Fountain Gardens have a formal air with four areas enclosed by a clipped yew hedge. In the Kitchen Garden is the new Millennium Garden that is semitropical and part Italianate. TM

Burford House

Worcestershire, England

DESIGNERS: John Treasure, Charles Chesshire
OWNER: The Burford Garden Company
GARDEN STYLE: Mainly 20th-century informal
SIZE: 7 acres (2.8 ha)
CLIMATE: Temperate
LOCATION: Tenbury Wells, Worcestershire

The gardens at Burford House are mainly associated with the cultivation of clematis. Not surprisingly, they also contain the National Collection of clematis, and it is estimated that there are currently over 500 varieties growing on the site that runs down to the River Teme, with up to eighty of them possibly in flower at any one time during the summer.

The collection of plants at Burford is the legacy of the late John Treasure, who started designing the gardens around the elegant Georgian house in 1952. In essence, they contain a fluid series of borders planted with a backdrop of interesting shrubs that double as supports for the clematis. The other main garden ingredient found in abundance here is water, and the streamside gardens provide ideal conditions for moisture-loving plants. Across the Teme, visitors can enjoy the wildflowers and naturalistic Meadow Garden that provide a relaxed contrast to the rest of the manicured schemes.

Since 1993, garden designer Charles Chesshire has breathed new life into Burford. Besides improving the existing gardens, he has been responsible for the addition of the new Clematis Maze, the Mediterranean and Herb Garden, and the Clematis and Rose Garden. They are still in keeping with the ideas of John Treasure, but ensure that the gardens develop over time rather than being set in stone. One spectacular element of the gardens that never seems to change is the giant *Wisteria* 'Burford' that cascades down the back of the house. Planted in 1960, it still drips with scented, mauve flowers in late spring. LH

Eastgrove Cottage Garden

Worcestershire, England

DESIGNERS: Malcolm Skinner, Carol Skinner
OWNERS: Malcolm Skinner, Carol Skinner
GARDEN STYLE: 20th-century cottage garden, arboretum
SIZE: 1.5-acre (0.6 ha) garden, 2-acre (0.9 ha) arboretum
CLIMATE: Temperate
LOCATION: Shrawley, Little Witley, Worcestershire

The Skinners were bowled over with excitement when they first laid eyes on the seventeenth-century, black-and-white, timber-framed Eastgrove Cottage. They immediately recognized the potential of the outdoor space and, more than thirty years later, the resulting garden, arboretum, and nursery are full of horticultural riches. Although much of the garden is laid out in traditional cottage style, the couple's expert eye for design and immaculate maintenance ensures it is a modern interpretation.

The different areas are carefully color coordinated to reinforce a series of distinctive atmospheres. The Secret Garden, a haven of mauves, pinks, and blues, is the perfect place to relax. There are livelier, eye-catching borders packed with rust-red irises, orange poppies, and yellow achilleas. The Great Wall of China is a series of raised beds that bring diminutive plants closer to eye level for easier inspection.

In 2005, the Skinners created the Meadow, an arboretum with spectacular views across the Worcestershire countryside. Other features include a grass labyrinth, which visitors can follow in the manner of medieval monks, and a "seat of hope" that was constructed on the day after the Indian Ocean tsunami of December 2004.

All the garden plants are carefully selected by the Skinners, and the best are sold in the nursery. It stocks over 1,000 plants and concentrates on those that are reliably hardy in temperate climates, with specialties including aquilegias, heleniums, hardy chrysanthemums, peonies, and salvias. LH

Painswick Rococo Garden

Gloucestershire, England

DESIGNER: Benjamin Hyett
OWNER: Painswick Rococo Garden Charitable Trust
GARDEN STYLE: 18th-century rococo
SIZE: 6 acres (2.4 ha)
CLIMATE: Temperate
LOCATION: Painswick, Gloucestershire

This is a unique garden where the buildings dotted around are as important as the plants, and where ornate hideaways are tucked into the landscape as vantage points from which to admire the view, or to sit and gossip as they might have done in the eighteenth century. The extraordinary colonnaded Exedra was specifically designed for people to socialize and talk, the Eagle House is a gorgeous pale pink hexagon with elaborate tracery and oversize finials, while the Red House is a gingerbread Gothic building with no particular purpose other than to perfectly suit the setting in which it sits.

All the structures in the garden date from the 1740s, when Benjamin Hyett embraced the rococo era with enthusiasm and used its flamboyant style to turn the valley behind his father's house into a secret pleasure garden with winding serpentine paths and formal elements. The rococo style is extremely rare, especially for gardens, because the fashion was so short-lived, and Painswick is thought to be the only example in Britain.

Besides the architecture, visitors to the garden should also note the wonderful kitchen garden—a marvel of straight edges and geometric shapes filled with heritage varieties of brassicas and potatoes, such as pink fir apple. It is bordered by espaliered apple trees, greengages, and mulberries. The thick carpets of snowdrops in the woodland garden are a big spring attraction, enticing snowdrop enthusiasts from all over.

The garden was derelict until very recently, with its restoration beginning in 1988. In order to bring it back to its former glory, the restorers have had to rely heavily on a 1748 watercolor by Thomas Rubins, which shows the garden when it was at its peak. A maze has been planted in golden and green privet to celebrate Painswick's 250th anniversary and its subsequent survival into the twenty-first century. SA

Rodmarton Manor

Gloucestershire, England

DESIGNER: Ernest Barnsley, William Scrubey
OWNER: Simon Biddulph
GARDEN STYLE: Arts and Crafts
SIZE: 8 acres (3.2 ha)
CLIMATE: Temperate
LOCATION: Rodmarton, Cirencester, Gloucestershire

Rodmarton Manor was built for the Biddulph family slowly, and in stages, by the architect Ernest Barnsley from 1909. In fact, the house grew almost organically out of its own land. The timbers were felled on the estate and seasoned there; the stone was quarried nearby and worked by local stonemasons; and the village blacksmith made the door and catches in the Arts and Crafts style.

The garden (also planned by Barnsley) is arranged into separate "rooms," each divided by hedges of yew, box, holly, and beech. The perfect symmetry of the topiary and hedges echoes the lines of the house,

and most of the original garden features are still here. They include the Leisure Garden and Trough Garden, with many old stone farmyard troughs planted with alpines and creeping plants, a sunken garden, and a cherry orchard. The vast herbaceous borders are still planted up in the Jekyll style with perennials— Ernest Barnsley knew Jekyll and had read her books. Credit, though, should also be given to the first head gardener to have worked at the manor, William Scrubey, who was responsible for most of the original planting.

In late winter, the garden opens for three days when the extensive collection of snowdrops is in full bloom. Do not miss them or the kitchen garden in summer, with its arches of old apples and scented old roses. Other must-see attractions are the Lime Avenue and the Wild Garden, both of which link this romantic and inspiring garden to the beautiful Cotswold countryside that surrounds it. JHi

Highgrove

Gloucestershire, England

DESIGNERS: Sir Roy Strong, Rosemary Verey,
Isabel Bannerman, Julian Bannerman,
Miriam Rothschild, Sixth Marchioness of Salisbury
OWNER: The Duchy of Cornwall
GARDEN STYLE: 20th- and 21st-century formal and informal
SIZE: 15 acres (6 ha)
CLIMATE: Temperate
LOCATION: Tetbury, Gloucestershire

The Prince of Wales' garden was started in 1981 and allowed him to realize some of his long-held beliefs about organic gardening. He called on the great and the good—including Sir Roy Strong and the late Rosemary Verey—and together they got to work.

When Prince Charles moved to Highgrove, the garden was virtually nonexistent. Therefore, anchoring the house to the garden and the garden to the landscape were two priorities. Now it has a number of intimate areas, each with its own special atmosphere and identity. Close to the house, the Sundial Garden is planted entirely in black and white with dogwood, violas, poppies, roses, scabious, aquilegia, and primulas. The Terrace Garden on the west side is a mass of lady's mantle (*Alchemilla mollis*), honesty, wild strawberries, lavender, forget-me-nots, and pinks. The walled kitchen garden is a dream, with tunnels of espaliered fruit trees and box-edged beds brimming with vegetables. Elsewhere, the Stumpery is an unusual feature, housing some of the prince's amazing collection of ferns and hostas. A fairly recent addition is the Carpet Garden, Moorish in style and based on an oriental carpet owned by the prince.

Eye-catchers are one of the keys to the garden's success. They include a statue, dovecote, fountain, gate, and archway, all playing a prominent part. The prince also loves terracotta pots, and they are placed around the garden, all artfully planted. This is gardening on a grand scale and a joy to see. PM

Bourton House

Gloucestershire, England

DESIGNERS: Richard Paice, Monique Paice
OWNERS: Richard Paice, Monique Paice
GARDEN STYLE: 20th-century English with modern plantings
SIZE: 3 acres (1.2 ha)
CLIMATE: Temperate
LOCATION: Bourton on the Hill, Moreton-in-Marsh, Gloucestershire

The garden surrounds a charming eighteenth-century village house. It was started in 1983 by the Paices, who arrived at Bourton House to find it smothered with bindweed. Like any great scheme, it is still evolving largely thanks to the talented gardener Paul Williams and his successor, Paul Nicholls.

Attention to detail is evident in the rigorously clipped box parterre at the front of the house that mirrors the formality of the architecture. The Topiary Garden, with an oval pool at its center, is hidden behind tall yew hedges and never has a leaf out of place. Precise pruning and tying in give the garden a high degree of formality that gives way to bold and exuberant planting in the wide borders. Clipped box is widespread throughout the garden. Other prominent features include the large lawn sweeping behind the house to a raised border, two Persian ironwoods (*Parrotia persica*) near the house, which lend fiery colors in the fall, the wide stone steps leading to the raised walk, and a seat with a screen of modern stained glass where you can sit and enjoy the beauty of the Cotswold Hills.

This is a classical English garden, worked very intensively, but its bold use of modern planting gives it an exciting edge. Note the wide borders containing perennials, bulked up in summer with tender plants in their pots, and the tropical border. If you are looking for inspiring ideas for your own pot plantings, do not miss the beautiful pot displays in the courtyard. JHi

Westonbirt Arboretum

Gloucestershire, England

DESIGNERS: Robert Holford,
The Forestry Commission
OWNER: The Forestry Commission
GARDEN STYLE: Early 19th-century arboretum
SIZE: 600 acres (243 ha)
CLIMATE: Temperate
LOCATION: Westonbirt, Tetbury,
Gloucestershire

The history of the British Empire is the history of the trees of Westonbirt. The park's creator—the wealthy Victorian landowner Robert Holford—helped finance plant expeditions to the far corners of the Empire. Holford used the plant hunters' finds to create this picturesque landscape, acquired by the state fifty years ago as the home of the National Arboretum.

Whatever time of year you visit, Westonbirt is magnificent. There are over 18,000 trees and shrubs, accessible via 17 miles (27 km) of paths. Around Holford's original planting, the cerulean haze of hundreds of thousands of bluebells, with celandines, wood anemones (*Anemone nemorosa*), and primroses, evokes the ancient woodlands of England. Later in the year, there are large collections of camellias, magnolias, and rhododendrons. However, the pyrotechnics of the fall colors, when the whole garden is ablaze, are the big attraction. Also look out for the color circle of maples, katsuras, spindles, and Persian ironwoods (*Parrotia persica*), planted by Holford in the 1850s, that was used as a picnic site where friends were invited to "color parties."

As a recent attraction, if you come at Christmas time, trees are floodlit or hung with lights to create magical winter walks. Westonbirt is also a scientific resource. There are more than 100 trees that are either rare, endangered, or extinct in the wild. The oldest trees—a group of coppiced limes—are said to be over 2,000 years old. JHo

Barnsley House

Gloucestershire, England

DESIGNERS: Rosemary Verey, David Verey
OWNERS: Rupert Pendered, Tim Haigh
GARDEN STYLE: Late 20th-century informal
SIZE: 5.5 acres (2.2 ha)
CLIMATE: Temperate
LOCATION: Barnsley, Cirencester, Gloucestershire

Barnsley House had a huge influence up until the death of its creator, Rosemary Verey, in 2001. Prince Charles and Elton John approached Rosemary for advice on designing their own gardens, while visitors poured into her garden from all around the world to see a series of richly planted areas that sum up mid-twentieth-century English gardening. With the plot around the house divided into individual sections, each with its own character and linked by vistas, the sheer variety makes sure that visitors keep exploring.

David Verey, Rosemary's husband, inherited the seventeenth-century house in 1951, and he was the one who initially tackled the garden's structure. However, it was Rosemary's talent for planting that turned Barnsley into a mecca. A garden tour kicks off next to the house with two distinct areas. First is the knot garden with entwining dwarf hedging making a neat, snaking pattern. Next is an informal area that spills out from the back of the house. The main path is planted with a tapestry of rock roses and is bordered by stout Irish yews (*Taxus baccata* 'Fastigiata'), and a path to the side has a box-edged herb garden. Both lead to the sweeping mixed borders that are well stocked with shrubs, perennials, and masses of bulbs.

A little deeper into the garden is a braided lime walk that stands opposite the Temple Garden with its reflective lily pond. Through the gates in the adjacent garden wall is the potager, planted for ornamental effect. The house is now a country inn, so extra vegetables are grown in an extended area to ensure there is enough produce for the kitchens. LH

Kiftsgate Court Gardens

Gloucestershire, England

DESIGNERS: Heather Muir, Diany Binny
OWNERS: Anne Chambers, Johnny Chambers
GARDEN STYLE: 20th-century semiformal
SIZE: 3.5 acres (1.4 ha)
CLIMATE: Temperate
LOCATION: Chipping Camden, Gloucestershire

Perched at the edge of the Cotswold escarpment, Kiftsgate Court has views of the Bredon and Malvern Hills. To the left of the entrance, the ground sweeps away below a stone balustrade. In early summer, the mixed woodland along the slopes is decked out in myriad greens, and silver limes line the drive.

The garden was laid out in the 1920s and 1930s by Heather Muir, in part inspired by her neighbor, Lawrence Johnson at Hidcote. Heather planted the hedges, laid the paths, and terraced the steep banks. Her daughter, Diany Binny, took over in the 1940s, building a swimming pool in the lower garden and paving the White Garden. Since the 1980s, Kiftsgate has been home to Heather Muir's granddaughter, Anne Chambers, and her husband, Johnny.

Wide, very English borders bulge with plants that are encouraged to sprawl abundantly across lawns or paths. Signature plants, such as philadelphus, pop up again and again. There are tapestry hedges of copper and green beech, and a rose garden half filled with the vigorous rambler *Rosa filipes* 'Kiftsgate', bought as a small, unrecognized rose by Heather in the 1940s.

By contrast, there are soaring pines on the sheltered terraced banks, planted with cistus, ceanothus, Chusan palms (*Trachycarpus fortunei*), and Mediterranean herbs, all similar to plants you might find on the Côte d'Azur. On the site of a former tennis court there is a rectangular pool filled with ink-black water. It is surrounded by slim, white paving stones, with stepping stones leading to a grassy island in the middle. It is all, quite simply, breathtaking. VB

Snowshill Manor

Gloucestershire, England

DESIGNERS: Charles Paget Wade, H. M. Baillie-Scott
OWNER: The National Trust
GARDEN STYLE: Arts and Crafts
SIZE: 2 acres (0.8 ha)
CLIMATE: Temperate
LOCATION: Snowshill, Broadway, Gloucestershire

How would you define an overriding obsession? One answer to this question might be Charles Paget Wade's Tudor house with its seventeenth- and eighteenth-century additions—the gardens enclosed by Cotswold stone walls—that enabled him to pursue the Arts and Crafts movement with no concessions to the twentieth century. Wade also deserves recognition because he was the first to use turquoise-blue paint on garden woodwork and house windows to complement foliage greens and flowers. He was quite modern in that he viewed the garden as an extension of the house.

What you will see today are mellow walls, expanses of grass, sculpted hedges contrasting with the profusion of flowers, structures, and the play of shade and light. There is also a green court with a central flagged path leading to the house, with the rest of the gardens being terraced to the south. As a testament to Wade's conversion to Catholicism, there is a distinctly shrinelike, devotional spirit in the garden—the Virgin Mary quietly gazes into a pool from the immaculately restored cow barn that encloses the Well Court. Also note St. George in blue and gold looking down from the cottage and house across the green terraces, and the Bacchus fountainhead in the Armillary Court where there is a gilded sundial on a stone column in the center.

The garden is managed organically, and the kitchen garden still thrives. In keeping with Wade's principles, the parking lot is some distance from the house so that you can arrive and leave on foot. CH

Sezincote

Gloucestershire, England

DESIGNERS: Thomas Daniell, Graham Stuart Thomas
OWNERS: David Peake, Susanna Peake
GARDEN STYLE: 18th- and 19th-century Anglo-Indian
SIZE: 5 acres (2 ha)
CLIMATE: Temperate
LOCATION: Moreton-in-Marsh, Gloucestershire

The garden at Sezincote is one of those delightful expressions of mild English eccentricity. The approach to the house and garden is along a drive that could not be more English. At the last bend, though, you see a mansion built in the Hindu-Mughal style.

The house was designed in 1805 by Samuel Pepys Cockerell for his brother, Sir Charles, who wanted a reminder of India. Humphry Repton assisted Samuel in selecting sketches from Thomas and William Daniell's *Select Views of India* (1788), but it is not known if he helped lay out the grounds. The parkland has a definite Reptonian feel about it though.

As the driveway approaches the house, it passes over the ornamental Indian Bridge, complete with statues of Brahman bulls. Beneath, and attributed to Thomas Daniell, is the Thornery, a small valley, again with a strong hint of India, and a water garden. At the top is the Temple to Surya (the sun god) with a formal pool in front. A stream passes from here under the bridge to the Snake Pool, featuring a bronze serpent coiled around a trunk. There are two more pools, a fine collection of trees, and additional planting by Graham Stuart Thomas from the 1960s.

Graham Stuart Thomas was also involved in planting the Paradise Garden, which is adjacent to the house. Positioned in front of the orangery, complete with minarets, is an Islamic cruciform *chahar bagh* added by Lady Kleinwort in 1968 on her return from India. Another eccentric feature is the Tent Room, a sort of detached orangery, that Sir Charles used as his bedroom. TM

Hidcote Manor Garden

Gloucestershire, England

DESIGNER: Lawrence Johnston
OWNER: The National Trust
GARDEN STYLE: 20th-century garden "rooms"
SIZE: 4 acres (10 ha)
CLIMATE: Temperate
LOCATION: Hidcote Bartrim, Gloucestershire

Hidcote is one of the most influential British gardens of the twentieth century. Most significantly, it was responsible for establishing the fashion for garden "rooms," here embellished by borders packed with unusual plants. Although none of these ideas was revolutionary when the garden's creator, Lawrence Johnston, moved to Hidcote in 1907, it was he who succeeded in turning them into something exciting.

Johnston was born in Paris to a wealthy family of stockbrokers from Baltimore. He moved to England to study at Cambridge University and, after graduating, soon became a naturalized English citizen. His mother, Gertrude Winthrop, acquired Hidcote Manor, and the property suited them both perfectly. By 1910, Lawrence had begun to lay out the garden's key features. No more than ten years later, the garden was requiring the labor of twelve gardeners and was already looking much as it does today.

There are about a dozen garden "rooms" or areas clustered around the manor; perhaps the best-known feature is the red borders (dating from 1913). They are said to be the first single-colored borders in England, and contain a firework display of red- and orange-flowering plants. At the far end, two redbrick pavilions with elegantly incurved roofs offer spectacular views of the garden. Be sure to visit the Cottage Garden, full of old roses and phlox, the White Garden with the peacock topiary, and Mrs. Winthrop's Garden with its purple cordylines and acid-green lady's mantle (*Alchemilla mollis*). The long grass avenue has views across the Cotswold countryside, aerial hedges on stiltlike trunks, and a thatched gazebo.

Hidcote is currently undergoing a £1.6-million restoration by the National Trust. The Shelter House has already been reconstructed. Among other features, the dilapidated Rock Bank is due to be resurrected. The work is not due for completion until 2012, but is definitely worth waiting for. LH

Stancombe Park

Gloucestershire, England

DESIGNERS: The Reverend David Edwards, Lanning Roper, Gerda Barlow, Nada Jennett
OWNER: Gerda Barlow
GARDEN STYLE: 19th-century eccentric, Arts and Crafts style
SIZE: 15 acres (6 ha)
CLIMATE: Temperate
LOCATION: Dursley, Gloucestershire

The secret, Regency section of Stancombe Park is an essay in romantic eccentricity, while the upper part is a late twentieth-century interpretation of the Arts and Crafts style by current owner Gerda Barlow and designer Nada Jennett. A circle of gold acers around an Italian urn and a lime avenue complete this area. It is linked to the lower, secret garden by a menagerie walk of topiary leading down past a stone niche bubbling with spring water into brick tunnels, one guarded by Cerberus (Hades' canine sentry). The Egyptian-style entrances to two of the tunnels also celebrate Nelson's victory on the Nile. The tunnels open on to a lake with a temple at one end that, in the nineteenth century, was the love nest of the owner, the Reverend David Edwards. Legend maintains that this naughty clergyman designed the tunnels to make sure that his unfortunate wife would never interrupt him and his gypsy lover.

The path glides around the lake where, on one side, azaleas bloom in this otherwise alkaline garden. Farther on, two lead-windowed summerhouses stand beside the remains of stone- and cast-iron-edged triangular beds. There is a circular tufa trough that was once a fountain, but is now planted with box. The final feature was designed for the Millennium—doves and olive branches resting on either side of a brick facade with eighteenth-century plaques.

When the Barlows arrived in the 1960s, the garden was derelict. They have breathed in new life without disturbing its intimacy and mystery. JO

Westbury Court Garden

Gloucestershire, England

DESIGNER: Maynard Colchester
OWNER: The National Trust
GARDEN STYLE: Dutch 17th-century water garden
SIZE: 5 acres (2 ha)
CLIMATE: Temperate
LOCATION: Westbury-on-Severn, Forest of Dean, Gloucestershire

On the banks of the River Severn in Gloucestershire, Westbury Court is a rare British example of a Dutch seventeenth-century water garden. This style of gardening came to Britain during the reign of William and Mary (1689–1702), but was soon superseded by the landscape movement of the eighteenth century.

The garden was begun in 1696 by a courtier, Maynard Colchester, who was influenced by a nearby garden. He was responsible for the long canal and for the tall pavilion besides which stands a vast holm oak (*Quercus ilex*), probably the largest in the country.

His nephew, who succeeded Colchester in 1715, probably created both the T-canal, which lies parallel to the long canal, and a small walled garden.

The long canal is flanked by yew hedging, punctuated by lollipop yew pyramids and box balls, their regular shapes reflected in the water. At either end of a formal box parterre is a quincunx, consisting of five trees with domed standard Portugal laurels (*Laurus nobilis*) and a *Phillyrea angustifolia*. There are only occasional splashes of color: from period plantings of antirrhinums, nigella, lupins, and aquilegias that soften the geometry of the parterre; from the espaliered fruit on the old redbrick walls; and from the blossom in the cherry orchard.

Westbury is a delightful oddity because it is a garden without a house—Colchester's Palladian-style house was demolished in 1805. One big advantage to this is that there is no distraction from its canals when they are smudged by mist in the morning light. VB

Batsford Arboretum

Gloucestershire, England

DESIGNERS: First Lord Redesdale,
  second Lord Dulverton
OWNER: The Batsford Foundation
GARDEN STYLE: Arboretum
SIZE: 55 acres (22.2 ha)
CLIMATE: Temperate
LOCATION: Moreton-in-Marsh, Gloucestershire

In 1886, Algernon Bertram Freeman-Mitford (later the first Lord Redesdale) inherited the Batsford Estate. After building a new house, he turned his attention to the grounds in the 1890s. Inspired by the landscapes and plants (especially bamboos) of China and Japan that he had enjoyed on his travels in the 1860s, he designed a garden in a natural style. Within it, he replicated many of the planting associations he had seen in the wild. This collection of unusual plants, including the country's finest gathering of bamboos, was supplemented by a 0.4-mile-long (0.6 km) watercourse with waterfalls, lake, rocks, bronze statues, a thatched cottage, and a hermit's cave.

In 1919, the estate was sold to the first Lord Dulverton, who continued to add plants. Following a period of neglect after World War II, the second Lord Dulverton reversed the decline in the 1960s and added to the collection. Dulverton's dedication and work raised the garden's status to one of international repute, and to secure its long-term future he handed over the arboretum to a charitable trust in 1984. The arboretum now boasts collections of plants from around the world, with an emphasis on the Far East. There are over 3,050 labeled specimens, including approximately 1,600 different trees, shrubs, and bamboos. Stars of the show are the magnolias and the National Collection of Japanese flowering cherries that are spectacular in spring. In the fall, the hillside has a breathtaking display of color thanks to the Japanese maples, oaks, and mountain ash. TM

Kelmscott Manor

Gloucestershire, England

DESIGNER: William Morris, restored by Colvin
  and Moggridge
OWNER: The Society of Antiquaries of London
GARDEN STYLE: English Arts and Crafts
SIZE: 3.5 acres (1.5 ha)
CLIMATE: Temperate
LOCATION: Kelmscott, Lechlade, Gloucestershire

William Morris, the noted poet, craftsman, and socialist, described Kelmscott Manor as "heaven on earth… and what a garden! Close down on the river [Thames], a boat house and all things handy."

Morris was delighted with the gabled house and its rural setting, with grounds running down to water meadows. It was his country retreat from 1871 until his death in 1896. The simple Arts and Crafts garden was inspired by the enclosed trellised gardens of illuminated manuscripts, "Four little square gardens making a big square together, each of the smaller squares having a wattle fence round it, with roses growing thickly," as described by Georgiana Burne-Jones. With its old stone walls, wattle fences, straight paths, fruit trees, yew topiary, and yew hedges around separate "rooms," Morris considered it ideal.

From a door in the wall, a stone pathway, lined with standard pink roses set in close-mown grass, leads to a front porch covered with roses and honeysuckle. To the north and west of the house are walls of yew, low hedges of box, fruit orchards, and borders planted with simple, old-fashioned, cottage-garden flowers. Plants and birds in the garden, and in the countryside around, inspired the textiles and wallpaper designs on display in Kelmscott Manor. The wild strawberry that appears in Morris's classic textile *Strawberry Thief*, still grows in the kitchen courtyard, while down by the river are the trees that he drew for *Willow Boughs*, the fabric and wallpaper design that still adorns many English living rooms. EH

Le Manoir aux Quat' Saisons

Oxfordshire, England

DESIGNER: Raymond Blanc
OWNER: Raymond Blanc
GARDEN STYLE: 20th-century formal,
 kitchen garden
SIZE: 2 acres (0.8 ha)
CLIMATE: Temperate
LOCATION: Great Milton, Oxfordshire

The gourmet restaurant Le Manoir aux Quat' Saisons also has an excellent garden designed by its celebrity proprietor, the chef Raymond Blanc. When he took over the ancient stone manor house in 1984, Blanc set out to make a garden that would complement the house and could be used by the guests. He also wanted a kitchen garden, from which he would be able to supply his team of chefs with the fresh, organic produce they needed.

The manor house is surrounded by manicured lawns, abundant herbaceous borders, and a double row of fragrant lavender that leads the visitor to the entrance of the restaurant. Separated from the formal part of the garden by honeyed stone walls, the vegetable and herb gardens are absolutely immaculate. The vegetable plot, a large rectangular area, is divided into quadrangles. Each contains long rows of vegetables that have been planted with military precision. In 2005, Blanc created a new Malaysian garden with a range of exotic and unusual plants, including lemon grass, different gingers, and tamarind. The herb garden is as attractive as it is productive of first-rate plants for Blanc's kitchens. Diamond-shaped beds containing the herbs are bordered by clipped box and lavender, and they point to a central water feature and sculpture.

Beyond the kitchen gardens is a series of water gardens. One of the ponds dates all the way back to the seventeenth century, and there is also a Japanese garden with a rather more contemporary tea house that was created in 1995.

Raymond Blanc is almost as passionate about gardening as he is about food, which is saying something. His dedication is evident in every part of this garden. One thing is certain: this is a garden that will not stay still. With its owner's energy and propensity for new ideas, it will continue to evolve and grow from year to year. CF

Blenheim Palace

Oxfordshire, England

DESIGNERS: Capability Brown, Achille Duchêne
OWNER: Eleventh Duke of Marlborough
GARDEN STYLE: 18th-century Brownian landscape,
   20th-century formal additions
SIZE: 2,100 acres (850 ha)
CLIMATE: Temperate
LOCATION: Woodstock, Oxfordshire

When Lady Randolph Churchill caught sight of her new home at Blenheim, she was bowled over not so much by the palace as by "the finest view in England." This view is Capability Brown's masterwork.

Brown's achievement was to sweep away the rigid formality that had gone before to establish an English garden style that deliberately blurred the boundaries between art and nature. Geometric plantations now gave way to gently curving belts of trees, and wide lawns swept serenely down to a splendid river or lake. Brown did not flatten but followed the land's contours, subtly remodeling them—it was his genius for discovering the natural "capabilities" of his clients' estates that earned him his nickname.

Above all, he was a master of water, damming streams to create lakes. Nowhere did he do this more triumphantly than at Blenheim, where Sir John Vanbrugh had erected a majestic bridge to the palace. However, the River Glyme, which it spanned, was just a trickle, and visitors ridiculed the contrast. Brown dammed the River Glyme to create "the most superb piece of water, in which art has any share, in this kingdom." Features were now united by the lake, and the exit point of the river became a dramatic cascade.

Inevitably, the simplicity of Brown's design was overlaid by later generations. Formality returned with the Italian Garden and Water Terraces, designed by Achille Duchêne in the early twentieth century. In 1991 a maze was opened in the former kitchen garden, symbolizing the history of Blenheim. AE

University of Oxford Botanic Garden

Oxfordshire, England

DESIGNER: University of Oxford
OWNER: University of Oxford
GARDEN STYLE: 17th-century walled botanic garden
SIZE: 4 acres (1.8 ha)
CLIMATE: Temperate
LOCATION: Oxford, Oxfordshire

Founded in 1632 by the Earl of Danby, Britain's oldest botanic garden is situated opposite Magdalen College in the heart of Oxford. Entry is through a magnificent archway by Nicholas Stone. Exceptionally high walls shelter many tender climbers, including powder-blue ceanothus and pineapple-scented broom (*Cytisus battandieri*). The grounds hold a national reference collection of over 7,000 different types of plant. So great is the collection, and so compact the space, that this is a hotspot of biodiversity. It is also exceptionally beautiful: great effort is made to arrange the plants in exciting, sympathetic, and attractive ways.

The family beds are a fascinating way to discover which plants are related to each other. Plants used for food, fiber, dyes, and medicines are laid out in "economic" beds, and geographically themed borders display collections from South Africa, South America, the Mediterranean, and Australasia. Heated greenhouses extend the range of growing conditions. There is an arid house full of cacti and succulents, an insectivorous house, tropical palm house, lily house with giant water lilies, alpine house, and fernery. There is also a rock garden, bog garden, and a National Collection of euphorbia.

The university's collection of trees and shrubs is 6 miles (10 km) south of Oxford in the Harcourt Arboretum at Nuneham Courtenay. The 80-acre (32 ha) site has a fern gully, a wildflower meadow, and a collection, Plants from High Places, with species from the Pyrenees, Pinhos Mountains, Himalayas, Andes, and the South Island of New Zealand. *RC*

Westwell Manor

Oxfordshire, England

DESIGNER: Anthea Gibson

OWNERS: Thomas Gibson, Anthea Gibson

GARDEN STYLE: Late 20th-century traditional, land art

SIZE: 6 acres (2.4 ha)

CLIMATE: Temperate

LOCATION: Burford, Oxfordshire

The thoughtful amalgamation of ideas orchestrated by the owner/designer Anthea Gibson, and executed to a high standard, make Westwell Manor a near perfect series of twenty "rooms" in a late twentieth-century garden design. Westwell's position, on the edge of the Cotswolds in some of England's prettiest countryside, adds to the sense of perfection.

At first glance, the garden, screened from the country road by high stone walls, seems highly traditional. It also appears quite traditional inside, but every feature has a twist. There are two brooks not one, and they run beside braided limes. The Moonlight Garden, planted to capture moonbeams, contrasts with the inky black reflecting pool. The herbaceous borders near the house are huge and heavily planted. There is a kitchen garden with lavishly painted watering cans, nuttery, sundial garden, circular sitting area within a meadow, orchard, topiary, rose garden, lily pond, lavender terrace, wall of clematis, and—the biggest surprise of all—a miniature paddy field that has been planted with Camargue rice.

The boundaries between the areas are very attractive, ranging from woven willow and hazel, to flying hedges, to more traditional hedges and walls. Beyond the planted areas are mown paths through longer grass, a mount, and even a turf amphitheater.

Westwell Manor showcases some of the best of Britain's traditional twentieth-century garden ideas. It is particularly interesting when compared with some of the more tired examples of a dominant British theme, the Arts and Crafts garden revived. JO

Rousham House

Oxfordshire, England

DESIGNER: William Kent
OWNER: Charles Cottrell-Dormer
GARDEN STYLE: 18th-century landscape
SIZE: 30 acres (12.1 ha)
CLIMATE: Temperate
LOCATION: Steeple Aston, Bicester, Oxfordshire

This arcadia remains very much the work of the designer William Kent, who undertook to create the gardens between 1737 and 1741 as the place for his patron, General James Dormer, to settle down to his "philosophic retirement." Rousham is still in the same family, which is why even now it retains the feel of a private pleasure garden.

William Kent was the first landscape designer to "leap the fence" and "borrow" the adjoining countryside, making it part of the garden. You can clearly see how that works as you wander through the glades and around the beautifully proportioned classical buildings that he situated to punctuate the promenade. The surrounding landscape is not just an accidental backdrop, but is used in several ways. One of its roles is as an aid to contemplation, prompted by the statues—for example, the dying gladiator, the exquisite Praeneste—and the lovely arcaded building (again by Kent) with arched openings framing views across the River Cherwell. Again, a gloomy path overhung by evergreens is lit up by reflections from the rippling river water, stimulating the beholder to fresh meditations. In fact Rousham is an object lesson in understatement and restraint. Foliage takes the dominant role and flowers hardly register at all, except in the enclosed world of the adjoining seventeenth-century walled garden.

Horace Walpole, wandering around the house and gardens, thought that Rousham was "the most engaging of all Kent's works. It is Kentissimo." Who could disagree with that sentiment? JB

> "…a gloomy path overhung by evergreens is lit up by reflections from the rippling river water…"

Waterperry Gardens

Oxfordshire, England

DESIGNERS: Beatrix Havergal, Waterperry students
OWNER: Waterperry Gardens
GARDEN STYLE: 20th-century informal
SIZE: 8 acres (3.2 ha)
CLIMATE: Temperate
LOCATION: Wheatley, Oxfordshire

In 1932, the stern-sounding Horticultural School for Ladies at Waterperry opened its doors for the first time. The indomitable Beatrix Havergal was in charge, often cutting a dash with a smock tied around her ample waist. She is said to have left an indelible impression on author Roald Dahl, who immortalized her as Miss Trunchbull in his children's book *Matilda*. Nonetheless, many graduates became instrumental in shaping Britain's mid-twentieth-century gardens.

The gardens surround an eighteenth-century house, but their origins can be traced back to the *Domesday Book* of 1086. Although some of the ancient features survive, they are far less significant than the gardens created in the twentieth century. One of the hallmarks of a typical twentieth-century garden is the herbaceous border, and Waterperry's is in full bloom from late spring to mid-fall. It is backed by mellow brick walls covered with climbers. The nearby island beds were originally planted by Alan Bloom, who is credited with starting the island bed revival in the second half of the twentieth century.

In the Mary Rose Garden, formal beds of bright, scented roses are blended by color, and include hybrid teas and floribundas. There are also informal beds containing old-fashioned and species roses. Elsewhere, the Formal Garden has a traditional knot garden surrounded by herbs, and walls in the Alpine Garden contain a comprehensive collection of alpines.

Do not miss the museum of horticultural and agricultural tools, and note that Waterperry still runs educational gardening courses. LH

Buscot Park

Oxfordshire, England

DESIGNERS: Peter Coats, Sir Harold Peto, Tim Rees

OWNER: Administered by Lord Faringdon on behalf of the National Trust

GARDEN STYLE: Early 20th-century Italianate water garden, 18th-century park

SIZE: 5 acres (2 ha), within a 120-acre (48.6 ha) park

CLIMATE: Temperate

LOCATION: Faringdon, Oxfordshire

The original mansion at Buscot was built around 1880. The remains of the eighteenth-century park, substantially redeveloped during the twentieth century, provide a pleasing landscape of woodland walks and vistas over the lake. Modern additions include a colorful octagonal garden in the former kitchen garden, some finely planted new borders and walkways, and a playful, circular "swinging garden" hidden in a glade. The great glory of Buscot, though, is the water garden, created by Sir Harold Peto for the first Lord Faringdon between 1904 and 1913.

Peto spent many years on the Italian Riviera and was greatly influenced by the Italian renaissance. His genius was to integrate the architecture of the formal renaissance garden into softer British landscapes. At Buscot he forged a link between the house and lake, by means of a long, narrow water garden enclosed by box hedges and tall trees, running down to the sheet of water below. The view is powerfully controlled, up to the house and down to the lake where a mysterious pavilion draws the eye to the far shore.

The elements in the overall composition are few—grass, hedge, water, and stone. Within these constraints, Peto created a garden of extraordinary richness and theatricality. A stone-edged canal descends the hill, opening into a succession of brooks and pools edged by quiet green lawns austerely adorned with stone columns or figures. In the highest pool, a fountain with a boy and dolphin (feet and tail in the air) sends water tumbling down the slope in a narrow cascade, slipping on through another pool to dive under a hump-backed bridge with balustraded sides. The water ends its journey by entering a final pool, where swaths of water lilies attract the eye finally, and calmly, to the lake beyond. Powerful, tranquil, and chaste, Buscot Park is one of the great gardens designed in the early twentieth century. AE

Brook Cottage Garden

Oxfordshire, England

DESIGNERS: David Hodges, Kathleen Hodges
OWNERS: David Hodges, Kathleen Hodges
GARDEN STYLE: 20th-century cottage garden
SIZE: 4 acres (1.6 ha)
CLIMATE: Temperate
LOCATION: Alkerton, Banbury, Oxfordshire

Kathleen Hodges, a plantswoman of distinction, and David Hodges, an architect very much in tune with nature, began the gardens at Brook Cottage in 1964. David has since died, but their partnership created a garden that is still a masterpiece in variety.

The Hodges began by planting around the seventeenth-century stone house and barn, blending the building into the surrounding countryside. The old farmyard was turned into a lawn, and formal hedges of yew and copper beech (*Fagus sylvatica* Atropurpurea Group) were installed. Up the steep hillside they added a hanging garden of over 200 shrub roses, making a visit in early summer a must. Over fifty varieties of clematis provide extra color at this time, and elsewhere are many fine trees, including hollies, conifers, birch, ash, crab apples, and flowering cherries (*Sorbus aucuparia*), all of which have now reached splendid maturity. Also look out for the brook that allows bog plants to thrive around a pond, where the cattle used to drink. After going underground, the water spills into a serpentine lake with its own tiny island. The calm sheet of water reflects the trees, the swallows, and the sky.

The garden year at Brook Cottage kicks off with snowdrops, crocuses, and daffodils, followed by cherry blossoms. Summer flower borders are color schemed in pink and blue, and purple and red, with silver and white against a dark green yew hedge for maximum effect. The yellow border is perfectly positioned against the copper beech hedge for high drama. All in all, a thoughtful, exciting design. JHi

> "...their partnership created a garden that is still a masterpiece in variety"

Stowe Landscape Gardens

Buckinghamshire, England

DESIGNERS: Charles Bridgeman, Sir John Vanbrugh, William Kent, Capability Brown
OWNER: The National Trust
GARDEN STYLE: 18th-century landscape
SIZE: 250 acres (101.2 ha)
CLIMATE: Temperate
LOCATION: Stowe, Buckingham, Buckinghamshire

Representing the apotheosis of the landscape style, Stowe Landscape Gardens were laid out by several of the greatest names of eighteenth-century design. They are full of symbolism and illusion, embodied by the temples and obelisks. These buildings appear and disappear, tantalizing visitors and leading them down the serpentine byways of the garden.

Royal gardener Charles Bridgeman enclosed the garden with a 3.5-mile (5.5 km) sunk fence. Sir John Vanbrugh—also architect of Castle Howard in North Yorkshire (see page 234) and of Blenheim Palace in Oxfordshire (see page 310)—worked on the early phase of the garden for General Sir Richard Temple, later Viscount Cobham. In the garden's second phase, William Kent created the intimate Elysian Fields and the Temple of British Worthies, a curved stone screen of busts in niches, including King Alfred and Queen Elizabeth I. The original layout, however, was altered after 1746 by Capability Brown, who was Lord Cobham's head gardener. Brown preferred a more natural and open style of landscaping, and the great vistas are his work. The buildings dating from his period include the Temple of Concord and Victory, which marked British military achievements.

The wide views contrast with groves of oak, ash, and beech, underplanted with cherry laurel (*Prunus laurocerasus*) and thickets of viburnum, sweetbriar, and lilac. Many of the buildings are encircled by trees, with box, yew, holly, and laurel around the monument to make it stand out in the landscape. VB

Ascott House

Buckinghamshire, England

DESIGNER: Sir Harry Veitch

OWNER: The National Trust

GARDEN STYLE: High Victorian formal, naturalistic,
20th- and 21st-century additions

SIZE: 30 acres (12.1 ha)

CLIMATE: Temperate

LOCATION: Wing, Leighton Buzzard, Buckinghamshire

The garden at Ascott was laid out for Lionel de Rothschild in 1874 by Sir Harry Veitch. Sir Harry was the driving force behind the Veitch Nurseries, the most famous nursery of the nineteenth century.

Ascott was primarily a winter residence, and Veitch employed evergreen plants to provide color in the garden during the leafless months. Today the view over the terraced lawns toward the Chiltern Hills is enlivened by a noteworthy collection of mature and ornamental trees. The garden's natural feel has been further enhanced by twentieth-century plantings.

However, in the gardens near the house, Victorian formality still reigns supreme. By 1890, the golden yew topiary—animals and birds of almost every kind, with tables, chairs, churches, and other objects—was receiving widespread acclaim, especially the large sundial in clipped box with the inscription, "Light and shade by turn but love always" in golden yew.

The formal gardens have been altered in the past century. The fern garden has been replanted as a formal parterre in box and is now the Sunken Garden. In the southeastern part of the garden the Coronation Grove has become a wild garden. Other highlights are the Madeira Walk with its juxtapositions of formal and informal planting schemes along its length. The Dutch Garden boasts spring and summer bedding displays. There is also a Cupid fountain by Thomas Waldo Story, whose extravagant bronze Venus in her shell stands in the Circular or Venus Garden. Also look out for the Tea House and Skating Hut. TM

Bekonscot Model Village

Buckinghamshire, England

DESIGNER: Rolland Callingham

OWNER: Bekonscot Board of Trustees

GARDEN STYLE: Miniature landscaped, 1930s model railway village

SIZE: 1.5 acres (0.6 ha)

CLIMATE: Temperate

LOCATION: Beaconsfield, Buckinghamshire

Bekonscot is the oldest model village in the world. With its wonderful period detail, it has been a much-loved landmark for just over seventy-five years. If you are curious to see what rural England looked like in the 1930s, do not miss it.

The brainchild of Roland Callingham, a London accountant, and Tom Berry, his head gardener, the project started with a few model houses for an alpine garden. It gradually expanded to six model villages connected by a gauge1 railway, installed by the well-known model railway company Bassett-Lowke.

It opened to the public for charity in 1929 and, since then, has raised £5 million for the Church Army.

The most striking feature of this utopian vision of rural life is how the whole ensemble has been landscaped in proportion to the 1:12 scale of the houses. Some 3,000 shrubs and trees, including acers, elms, and oaks, are planted in the grounds. However, they are rigorously clipped and shaped using bonsai techniques so that they continue to remain in scale with the surrounding models. The green mantle of conifers, hedges, and grass is perked up by dwarf spring bulbs and, later, by summer bedding. Miniature gardens behind the model houses include model people clipping, mowing, or relaxing in deck chairs. There is even a little maze, an exact miniature of the one at Hampton Court Palace. This could make your visit even more fruitful, since if you drew a map or took a photo of the model, you could probably use it to avoid getting lost in the real maze. VR

Gipsy House

Buckinghamshire, England

DESIGNERS: Roald Dahl, Felicity Dahl, Keith Pounder
OWNER: Felicity Dahl
GARDEN STYLE: 20th- and 21st-century informal
SIZE: 1.5 acres (0.6 ha)
CLIMATE: Temperate
LOCATION: Great Missenden, Buckinghamshire

The author and poet Roald Dahl lived and worked at Gipsy House from 1954 until his death in 1991. Yet it was only when Felicity (Liccy), Roald's second wife, arrived at the modest Buckinghamshire farmhouse in 1983 that Roald, Liccy, and gardener Keith Pounder turned the garden from a neglected and exposed blank canvas into a series of "rooms" burgeoning with color and enclosed by dense yew hedges.

Parts of the garden were established when Roald was still alive, including his much-loved walled kitchen garden, where he cultivated his champion onions and old-fashioned varieties of fruit and vegetables, and a pleached lime avenue that lines the path toward his famous yellow writing hut. Much of the garden, however, has been developed since Roald's death. There is now the White Garden with its octagonal, glass birdhouse, and the Sunken Garden with sunken lawn, soporific water feature, and yellow plants (yellow being Roald's favorite color).

In fact, the garden remains a work in progress, with Liccy ensuring that it evolves in Roald's spirit. Just one area is dedicated to the author's memory. Behind a yew hedge, and sheltering beneath a canopy of nineteen whitebeams (*Sorbus aria*), a 1-foot-high (30 cm) box maze is paved with Yorkstone slabs, each engraved with a quotation chosen by close family and friends from Roald's books and poems. The spirit of the place is deeply moving and, with the wind rustling in the whitebeams, it exudes the kind of magic that Roald Dahl so magnificently conjured with words. RS-J

Turn End

Buckinghamshire, England

DESIGNERS: Peter Aldington, Margaret Aldington
OWNER: Peter Aldington
GARDEN STYLE: 20th-century informal
SIZE: 0.6 acre (0.2 ha)
CLIMATE: Temperate
LOCATION: Townside, Haddenham, Buckinghamshire

In many ways, Turn End is a lesson in effective garden design on a domestic scale. Architect Peter Aldington set out in the mid-1960s to show how modern houses could be incorporated into a traditional English village setting. He intended to build three houses here, sell two, live in one for a while, and then move on. As it turned out, Peter and his family never did get around to moving.

The garden is informally planted. However, its success relies on a bold framework of sightlines. From the garden door your eye is led on a series of journeys to various focal points, each tempting you to explore. A large stoneware pot draws you to a huge chestnut tree, and a sawn elm bench sends you down another path. Your eyes are constantly on the move.

Close to the house is a woodland area with specimen birches and limestone paths. Snowdrops, bluebells, primroses, and dwarf narcissi all flourish, followed by bluebells mixed with white and green tulips. Beyond is a grass "glade" with curved beds where agapanthus, salvias, and ornamental grasses are bulked out with summer annuals.

What strikes one most is how this garden packs so much into a small size. A pergola clad with roses and vines leads to an octagonal daisy garden, enlivened with pelargoniums and salvias in summer and then by late summer flowers such as Michaelmas daisies. Through an archway is a self-contained courtyard garden, bounded by traditionally made "wychert" or clay walls topped with tiles, giving it a distinctly Moorish flavor. It is all very simple, but it works. PM

West Wycombe Park

Buckinghamshire, England

DESIGNERS: Sir Francis Dashwood, and others

OWNER: The National Trust

GARDEN STYLE: Rococo, 18th-century English landscape

SIZE: 46 acres (18.6 ha)

CLIMATE: Temperate

LOCATION: West Wycombe, Buckinghamshire

Created by Sir Francis Dashwood, founder of the notorious Hellfire Club, this eighteenth-century park can be read in several ways. The classical temples and statuary dotted around the lake are a monument to Sir Francis' extended Grand Tour, taking in Russia, Asia Minor, and Europe. It can also be interpreted as a satire on the political and moral landscape of Stowe at the other end of Buckinghamshire.

The park was well ahead of its time with one of the earliest versions of the Temple of the Winds in Britain. The Venus Garden captures the sporty nature of the Dashwood family home that was, and still is, the venue for some lavish parties. The goddess' temple sits on top of a mount with paths descending on either side—a splendidly obvious suggestion of "legs akimbo." At their apex is an oval aperture opening into a small, oval cave. No subtlety here. This part of the garden was restored in the late twentieth century with the help of a small, contemporary painting. A flint pillar is thought to have stood directly in front of the oval cave with Mercury posing on top (at the time mercury was used to cure syphilis).

Sir Francis probably designed most of West Wycombe Park, including some of the buildings. They range from the Music Temple on one of the islands to the Temples of Apollo and Daphne. The park began life in 1735 and, in the 1770s, was softened in the English landscape style probably by Thomas Cook, a pupil of Capability Brown. The park makes a great walk through woodland, and around the lake with its three islands and cascade guarded by nymphs. JO

Cliveden

Buckinghamshire, England

DESIGNERS: Charles Bridgeman, Sir Charles Barry, Sir Geoffrey Jellicoe, and others
OWNER: The National Trust
GARDEN STYLE: Formal Italianate with woodland
SIZE: 376 acres (152.2 ha)
CLIMATE: Temperate
LOCATION: Taplow, Maidenhead, Buckinghamshire

Ever since the first house was built at Cliveden, it has been a focus for political intrigue and social notoriety. It is probably most famous for twentieth-century scandals, including the anti-Churchillian activities of the Cliveden Set during World War II and the Profumo Affair of the 1960s. The house, designed by Charles Barry in 1850, became the country home of Waldorf and Nancy Astor in the 1930s. Today it is an exclusive hotel, although the grade-one listed garden and woodland are open to the public.

Seventeenth-century earth-moving activity created a dramatic raised area on which the original and replacement houses were built. Barry's Italianate terrace, later elaborated with a balustrade bought by the Astors from the Villa Borghese in Rome (see page 727), forms an elevated platform from which to view the formal gardens and the beautiful Thames Valley landscape beyond. Although some of the box hedging, yew topiary, and internal herb plantings of the Italian-style parterre are a little unkempt, the drama of the setting and the scale of this part of the garden are absolutely breathtaking. To the front of the hotel, flanking the lawns, color-themed herbaceous borders are maintained in pristine condition thanks to plastic bean netting used to provide almost invisible yet effective support for lax stems and foliage. Elsewhere in the garden, enormous, slightly frivolous yew topiary competes with formal Italianate statuary, creating an almost *Alice in Wonderland* confusion of scale and proportion.

Though there are some lovely garden features and planting at Cliveden, perhaps one of the most delightful aspects of a visit here is the almost voyeuristic appeal of walking through gardens that once formed the backdrop to historical events and society scandals. Gardens are as much about people as plants and landscapes, and nowhere is that better demonstrated than at Cliveden. AJ

Chenies Manor

Buckinghamshire, England

DESIGNERS: Elizabeth MacLeod Matthews,
  Alistair MacLeod Matthews
OWNER: Elizabeth MacLeod Matthews
GARDEN STYLE: 20th-century garden with Tudor influences
SIZE: 8 acres (3.2 ha)
CLIMATE: Temperate
LOCATION: Chenies, Rickmansworth, Buckinghamshire

The warm, rosy tones of Tudor brickwork of the fifteenth- and sixteenth-century manor house at Chenies form the perfect backdrop to what is essentially a domestic garden. Lucy, the Duchess of Bedford, lived here in 1594 and was reputed to be a fine gardener. The present owner of Chenies, Elizabeth MacLeod Matthews, has, in turn, been heavily influenced by the ancient spirit of the place and has, rather brilliantly, conceived and planted a series of linked gardens around the house. Plump topiary birds perch on top of hedges. There is a gentle white garden, a sunken Dutch garden that erupts in May when the thousands of tulips open, and beyond, a series of lawns and deep herbaceous borders.

There are four other key features that are well worth looking out for. Among them is the physic garden—a vital ingredient in Tudor gardens. This example, with an octagonal well at its center, is a first-rate replica of the original and is home to at least 200 herbs that have been carefully chosen for their medicinal and culinary uses. The turf maze is in the old orchard, but Chenies also has a larger yew maze. Both serve to remind us of how the Elizabethans made their garden spaces for play and entertainment. In the immaculate kitchen garden, which has been delineated by gravel paths defined by blowsy catmint at their edges, fruit such as pears, gooseberries, and currants are grown as cordons. Apparently Queen Elizabeth I loved playing at Chenies when she was a child. You can certainly see why. JHi

Waddesdon Manor

Buckinghamshire, England

DESIGNER: Elie Laine

OWNER: The National Trust

GARDEN STYLE: 19th-century French formal, English landscape, 20th-century additions

SIZE: 160 acres (64.8 ha)

CLIMATE: Temperate

LOCATION: Aylesbury, Buckinghamshire

The huge French-style château at Waddesdon Manor is filled with priceless collections and, in terms of grandeur, has a garden to match. In 1874, Ferdinand Rothschild bought a 700-acre (283.5 ha) plot of countryside at Waddesdon. He commissioned the French designer Elie Laine to lay out terraces, the principal roads, and plantations, adding plenty of ideas of his own. The top of the hill was removed, a railway built to import all the materials, and the site was protected by shelterbelts. The statuary, basins, and fountains around the grounds were probably purchased from impoverished Italian aristocrats.

The drive winds through well-planted parkland culminating in a long, straight axis to the house front, lined with statuary, two Mentmore vases, and bedding schemes close to the house. The elaborate parterre de broderie was restored by Michael Walker and the current Lord Rothchild's daughter, Beth Tomassini. Its annual resplendence requires 230,000 plants, including geraniums and other brightly colored plants. An adjacent "carpet" is designed annually by a celebrity from the world of couture or the arts. The centerpiece of the park is a spectacular statue of Andromeda, which shows her chained to rocks, being saved by Perseus as the hippocampi rear up out of the water.

Away from the terraces, Waddesdon includes an aviary, rose garden, wood sculpture, tropical bedding, and a rock garden. The latter stretches from one side of the drive deep into the gardens, is partly artificial and partly real, and disguises a vast underground lake that ensures water is supplied for the house and gardens. A wire bird, brightly plumed in elaborate bedding plants, graces the center of the ornate, nineteenth-century aviary.

Spend a day walking and strolling in the grounds here, and then enjoy a delicious lunch accompanied by a glass of Mouton Rothschild. CH

Woburn Abbey

Bedfordshire, England

DESIGNERS: Isaac de Caus, George London, Charles
   Bridgeman, Humphry Repton, George Sinclair
OWNER: Fifteenth Duke of Bedford
GARDEN STYLE: 18th- and 19th-century landscape
SIZE: 3,000 acres (1,215 ha)
CLIMATE: Temperate
LOCATION: Woburn, Bedfordshire

The twelfth-century Woburn Abbey was established
as a Cistercian monastery. It remained so until Henry
VIII's dissolution in 1543 when the abbot was hanged
from the oak tree that still stands at the abbey's gate.

The garden took off when Humphry Repton
arrived at Woburn in 1802. He created a series of
linked compartments, such as a Chinese Garden to
the Chinese dairy that had been designed in 1780 by
the architect Henry Holland—who also remodeled
the abbey, an American garden, rose garden,
menagerie, and aviary. Repton also changed the
southern road and remodeled the lakes to the west
of the abbey. The deer park is home to ten species,
including the rare Père David deer from China, saved
from extinction by the eleventh Duke.

Woburn is a garden with layers of different styles.
Repton overlayed Charles Bridgeman who, by 1738,
had deformalized the French formal parterres of
George London. Even in the twentieth century, Percy
Cane was making changes. However, one feature
from the 1620s survives intact in the basement of the
abbey. The beautiful grotto room is a rare example of
Isaac de Caus' Italian, renaissance-influenced style.

Recently two biologists identified head gardener
George Sinclair's early nineteenth-century garden
at the Abbey as "arguably the world's first ecological
experiment." Sinclair's experimental garden contained
242 square plots with combinations of herbs, grasses,
and soils, and was detailed in Darwin's work *Hortus
Gramineus Woburnensis* (1816). TM

Wrest Park Gardens

Bedfordshire, England

DESIGNERS: George London, Henry Wise, Thomas Archer,
   Capability Brown
OWNER: English Heritage
GARDEN STYLE: Baroque, 18th-century English landscape
SIZE: 90 acres (36.5 ha)
CLIMATE: Temperate
LOCATION: Silsoe, Bedfordshire

This engaging landscape, home to the De Grey
family from the fourteenth to the twentieth century,
is steeped in history and has rare garden buildings,
statues, and fountains. It is an original.

Instead of focusing on the scenery of surrounding
Bedfordshire, Wrest is inward looking, which is
unusual for an eighteenth-century park. So, too, is
the grand, formal style around the house that owes
more to Versailles than to England, although the
original eighteenth-century Great Garden scheme
was probably by George London and Henry Wise.
Later that century, Capability Brown wrapped a
river around the perimeter. The current house is
nineteenth century, and replaced one from the early
eighteenth century. The terrace and parterres outside
give a flavor of the once dominant, formal style at
Wrest, and feature many stone and lead statues.

From the parterres, the canal leads down to an
impressive brick-domed pavilion created by Thomas
Archer (1710) to look like a small cathedral. Though
mazes, parterres, and fountains have vanished over
the years, there is still a mass of interesting features,
including the recently restored Chinese temple, a
Swiss cottage, the magnificent orangery, a grottolike
rustic bathhouse, a white stuccoed bowling green
house by Batty Langley, and woodland. Take a picnic
with you and explore. JO

RIGHT The early eighteenth-century pavilion at Wrest Park,
like a small cathedral, overlooks the ornamental canal.

The Swiss Garden

Bedfordshire, England

DESIGNER: Third Lord Ongley
OWNER: Bedfordshire County Council
GARDEN STYLE: 19th-century Swiss landscape
SIZE: 10 acres (4 ha)
CLIMATE: Temperate
LOCATION: Old Warden, Biggleswade, Bedfordshire

Laid out in the 1820s, this is an unusual twist on the idea, popular at the time, of gardens with natural landscapes and picturesque architecture. The Swiss motif was a romantic gesture by the third Lord Ongley for his mistress, who came from Switzerland.

There are many miniature buildings throughout the garden, but the principal one is a thatched Swiss cottage, which stands on its own little dome of grass, swathed in a spectacular sheet of daffodils in spring. The building may have been designed by John Buonarotti Papworth, and its interior is ornately decorated with pine cones and bark. Elsewhere a

thatched shelter encircles the trunk of a tall conifer, and a small Indian pavilion has intricate patterns in stained glass. Running throughout the garden is a network of canals spanned by wrought iron bridges that were made by the blacksmith uncle of Lady Emma Hamilton. Old Warden Park was later bought by the Shuttleworth family, whose collection of vintage planes is housed next door. One of their additions to the garden was a fernery grotto, with pulhamite—a very realistic rock substitute—forming the entrance tunnel, complete with stalactites.

The gardens fell into disrepair until leased and restored by Bedfordshire County Council in 1939. Visit in spring when the massed narcissus and hellebores emerge beneath azaleas and rhododendrons. Visit at other times for the trees, especially the wonderful cedars of Lebanon (*Cedrus libani*), arolla pines (*Pinus cembra*), and variegated sweet chestnut (*Castanea sativa* 'Aureomarginata'). MH

Benington Lordship Gardens

Hertfordshire, England

DESIGNER: Lilian Bott
OWNERS: Harry Bott, Sarah Bott
GARDEN STYLE: Edwardian
SIZE: 7 acres (2.8 ha)
CLIMATE: Temperate
LOCATION: Benington, Stevenage, Bedfordshire

The parkland at Benington Lordship is the brilliant antithesis of a designer's garden. There are no obvious signs that anyone has ever been at work here, scheming, meddling, and planting. Instead, it is as if the garden has just grown up organically around the eighteenth-century house, the ancient ruined Norman keep, and the nineteenth-century folly. The overall effect is of a garden that appears artless and uncontrived, which merges effortlessly into the surrounding landscape.

An adroit and confident designer's hand is needed to achieve an effect like this. Lilian Bott and her brother masterminded the garden in the early 1900s, and it is still in the same family, essentially, as when first planted with a strong Edwardian feel. However, there is now an overlay of twenty-first-century simplifications. For example, the kitchen garden has raised beds that make it far easier to grow vegetables, and the high-maintenance rockery has been grassed over.

Where the keep, folly, and old walls come together, they create a sheltered courtyard, which is ideal for tender azaras, *Carpenteria californica,* and a magnolia underplanted with hellebores. Benington Lordship's snowdrops are an absolute must-see and are followed by the scillas that turn the ground brilliant blue for two weeks, usually in perfect combination with drifts of spring daffodils. In summer the herbaceous borders are at their very peak. The planting here is big, blowsy, and bold—there are no modern grasses or tame color-coordinated schemes here. The borders flow in a great swath downhill so that you can look down from the top and appreciate every glorious detail. This is a beautiful spot where, unlike most other more densely inhabited corners of England, it is the plants and the stunning landscape that are all there is to see. SA

Hatfield House

Hertfordshire, England

DESIGNERS: John Tradescant the Elder,
Sixth Marchioness of Salisbury
OWNERS: Seventh Marquis and Marchioness
of Salisbury
GARDEN STYLE: English Jacobean
SIZE: 56 acres (22.6 ha)
CLIMATE: Temperate
LOCATION: Hatfield, Hertfordshire

Since the sixteenth century, the Cecil family has been woven into the fabric of British political life, and their seat at Hatfield is one of the most important homes in the country. In the late twentieth century—and into the twenty-first—the wife of the sixth Marquis of Salisbury, Marjorie "Mollie" Gascoyne-Cecil, recreated the gardens to equal the stature of the house.

A knot garden, with plants that would have been available in Britain before 1620, stands in front of the Old Palace. At its center the gilded statue of a boy "sounds" a trumpet when the wind blows. The adjacent Privy Garden is richly planted and leads to an enclosed scented garden, filled with secret corners where you can sit, relax, and inhale the aromas. Box hedges have been formed into bowers to stop the scents from wafting away.

One day a week the private gardens to the east of the house are open. Here, two avenues of tightly clipped holm oaks (*Quercus ilex*) surround a box parterre and topiary garden. However, the beauty of Hatfield lies in the tiny details as much as in the grand design. Look out for the stone fountains, wrought iron gates, rattan cloches in the vegetable gardens, and Lady Salisbury's elegant planting schemes.

Queen Elizabeth I spent a great deal of her childhood at the Old Palace at Hatfield. Tradition has it that she was sitting under an oak tree when the news of her accession to the throne of England arrived. The oak tree, now known as the Queen Elizabeth Oak, is still alive in the splendid park that surrounds the gardens. JH

> "…the beauty of Hatfield lies
> in the tiny details as much as
> in the grand design."

St. Paul's Walden Bury

Hertfordshire, England

DESIGNERS: Fergus Bowes-Lyon, Simon Bowes-Lyon
OWNER: Simon Bowes-Lyon
GARDEN STYLE: French 18th-century, formal landscape
SIZE: 60 acres (24.3 ha)
CLIMATE: Temperate
LOCATION: Whitwell, Hitchin, Hertfordshire

At the childhood home of the late Queen Elizabeth the Queen Mother is a garden that is sometimes thought to have always been outmoded, even from the very outset. Its layout and influences are debated, some saying that it was inspired by André Le Nôtre, and some that it is one of the earliest remaining gardens in the formal English landscape style. Despite all this "controversy," we can say for certain that it was laid out between 1720 and 1730 and features long, mown vistas, clipped beech hedges, and classical statuary.

The centerpiece of the garden is the house, a stately eighteenth-century building, built from red brick in a classical style, with stone facings. Three long rides, or allées, radiate from the house in the form of a patte d'oie. Striking out through deciduous woodland, the allées are terminated by classical statues, with further views of the stunning landscape beyond. There are various garden buildings, the principal one being a little octagonal structure known as the Organ House, which sits at the end of an allée. Additional garden buildings were shipped in from other gardens and carefully placed to enhance the spirit of the place. Extra features include a wonderful lake with a temple, a green theater amid the trees, and a medieval church, while in more recent times much color has been added by the planting of rhododendrons, magnolias, and camellias. Overall, though, this is still an original garden with wonderful green spaces, made for the purpose of quiet contemplation. MH

"The childhood home of
the late Queen Elizabeth
the Queen Mother..."

Saling Hall

Essex, England

DESIGNERS: Hugh Johnson, Judy Johnson
OWNERS: Hugh Johnson, Judy Johnson
GARDEN STYLE: 20th-century formal and woodland
SIZE: 12 acres (4.8 ha)
CLIMATE: Temperate
LOCATION: Great Saling, Braintree, Essex

Saling Hall is a glorious, late seventeenth-century redbrick house on the outskirts of an Essex village. Its owner, Hugh Johnson, has had two careers, one as a wine writer and one as a horticultural expert specializing in trees. The latter is amply illustrated by the remarkable garden he has created over more than thirty years.

Located near the vine-covered house, the garden is quite formal, with a front courtyard enclosed by yew hedges and braided limes. There is a walled area made in 1698 by the builder of the house. Irish junipers and clipped box give structure to beds that overflow in high summer with herbaceous perennials. The walls are covered by roses in different colors.

Several enclosed woodland areas and hidden gardens include one with a swirl of box cloud hedging beside a beautiful white mulberry. There are also a number of different landscapes, including the miniature French oak forest, a Norway maple glade, a pinetum of Californian pines, and Japanese cascade.

The suggested route around the site echoes that of an eighteenth-century landscape garden because it allows the visitor to catch sight of statues and garden buildings that keep disappearing and then reappearing. A small Greek temple marks the limit of the garden. There is a walk across its front planted with blocks of shrubs, including willows, dogwoods, berberis, and honeysuckle. The arboretum here, with its young pines, oaks, beeches, maples, ashes, sorbus, and limes, offers lovely contrasts of leaf texture, form, and color. VB

The Beth Chatto Gardens

Essex, England

DESIGNER: Beth Chatto
OWNER: Beth Chatto
GARDEN STYLE: 20th-century informal
SIZE: 12 acres (4.8 ha)
CLIMATE: Temperate
LOCATION: Elmstead Market, Colchester, Essex

The Beth Chatto Gardens are always beautiful. Even in early spring, the grasses, seed heads, and foliage set off the earliest flowers. There are buds of early snowdrops pushing up through stones in the gravel garden, aconites, the little *Narcissus* 'Cedric Morris', and hellebores among carpets of lamium in the wood. As the seasons roll on, every area becomes a richer and more varied tapestry of shapes and colors.

When Beth Chatto set out to make a garden in 1960, the site in the driest county of England was a windswept wasteland between two farms. Faced with widely differing soils—starved, arid gravel; dense, water-retaining silt; and sticky clay—and dry and damp areas in both sun and shade, she gradually created several distinctly different types of garden. All display a range of plants for problem places.

In the gravel garden, pathways wind between beds of rich color woven into foliage, all of which grow in drought-stricken conditions and are never watered. On the other side of the house, on a hot summer's day, you can descend the steps to the cool grass surrounding the ponds and enter another world. Here color is used sparingly among a hundred shades and tones of green. In the woodland garden, shade-loving plants carpet the floor in the light soil beneath trees. Shrubs, such as mahonias, viburnums, sorbus, and eucryphias, provide shelter for perennials and bulbs. The colchicums, cyclamens, and Japanese anemones among the berrying shrubs take the display into fall and are followed by a blaze of glorious foliage. EH

The Gibberd Garden

Essex, England

DESIGNER: Sir Frederick Gibberd
OWNER: The Gibberd Garden Trust
GARDEN STYLE: 20th-century garden of "rooms"
SIZE: 7 acres (2.8 ha)
CLIMATE: Temperate
LOCATION: Harlow, Essex

In 1946 the architect Sir Frederick Gibberd was appointed master planner for Harlow New Town. As an expression of commitment, he moved to Harlow in 1956. Here, on fields that slope down to Pincey Brook, he and Lady Gibberd created their secluded "private pleasure," a project that evolved until he died in 1984.

The garden is a highly individual creation and is the only one Sir Frederick ever made. Of it he wrote, "Garden design is an art of space, like architecture and town design. The space, to be a recognizable design, must be contained and the plants and walls enclosing it then become part of the adjacent spaces. The garden has thus become a series of rooms each with its own character, from small intimate spaces to large enclosed prospects."

The compartmentalized garden has a mix of semiformal and natural areas. There are woodlands and glades, pools and streams, lawns, a gazebo approached by a lime tree avenue, and even a castle with a moat and drawbridge that Sir Frederick created for his grandchildren. To call the compartments "rooms," though, is too formal. Rather, the garden is crammed with drama and consists of a series of interlocking experiences and surprises.

The garden's evolution was an organic process because Sir Frederick never drew a master plan or wrote down anything, which makes the current restoration tricky. Besides creating different areas, he also added carefully positioned objects within each, building up a collection of eighty sculptures, pots, and pieces of architectural salvage. TM

Glen Chantry

Essex, England

DESIGNERS: Wol Staines, Sue Staines
OWNERS: Wol Staines, Sue Staines
GARDEN STYLE: 20th-century informal plantsman's garden
SIZE: 2.5 acres (1 ha)
CLIMATE: Temperate
LOCATION: Wickham Bishops, Witham, Essex

In some gardens, a love of plants and the determination of owners to collect and grow as wide a range as possible are clearly apparent. That is how you would label Glen Chantry. It is crammed with interesting and unusual plants deftly displayed and grown to perfection. Wol and Sue Staines began creating the garden on difficult, fast-draining, gravelly soil in 1977. Today the garden is well established, and the Staines's hobby is their business—a well-stocked nursery offering many of the plants that are grown in the garden.

The slightly elevated position of the house has enabled the owners to create sweeping island beds that work with the gentle folds of the land. A large rock garden dominates the area to the front of the house with alpines and other choice plants. From the heart of it, a stream falls away to a series of pools, each planted with bold foliage perennials. Farthest from the house are two new beds with plants grown for their colorful winter stems. One of the signature beds of the garden features a planting of white, pink, and gold in mirrored segments. Elsewhere borders are devoted to Piet Oudolf-style naturalistic plants. There is little in the way of formality here, more an attempt to create a naturalistic environment where the plants can shine. The only formal area is to the rear of the house where the White Garden is also known as "the nunnery," in deference to the two wire-framed nuns who preside there. It is worth pointing out that the Staines have one of the most extensive snowdrop collections in the UK—they're not for sale though! MW

Audley End House

Essex, England

DESIGNERS: Capability Brown, Placido Columbani,
William Sawrey Gilpin, Richard Woods
OWNERS: English Heritage, Garden Organic
GARDEN STYLE: 18th-century landscape,
Victorian kitchen garden
SIZE: 50 acres (20.2 ha)
CLIMATE: Temperate
LOCATION: Saffron Walden, Essex

The history of the gardens at Audley End began in earnest in the mid-eighteenth century when the canalized River Cam was transformed into a sinuous lake, where you will now find white and black swans. Capability Brown took three years to transform the rigid, formal, sixteenth-century gardens into the beautiful landscape we see today. Robert Adam designed the classic bridge, the Temple of Victory, and the Tea House as well as the interiors of the Jacobean mansion.

Other features include the Elysian Gardens, designed by Placido Columbani and Richard Woods, now undergoing further restoration. You can step from the gloom into a pool of light where a waterfall falls into silence and slides away under the Tea Bridge. Behind the house, the early nineteenth-century flower parterre, attributed to William Sawrey Gilpin, has been fully restored and, incidentally, was one of the first gardens to be restored using advanced archaeological techniques. These days, planted with roses, peonies, herbaceous plants, and up to 14,000 bedding plants, it colorfully sets off the rear of the Jacobean house. Away from the back of the house, separated by a sunk fence, the Temple of Concorde dominates the pastures in the distance.

The Pond Garden is in High Victorian style, complete with seasonal and exotic bedding, a rockery, and in days gone by, an Irish otter called Paddy. A step away, on the other side of the retaining wall, is the extensive walled kitchen garden, restored to its former glory by Garden Organic. You will find clearly labeled historic fruits and heritage vegetables, a Thomas Rivers orchard house, a mushroom house, and vineries. The aspect of each wall and bed has been put to good use, with the center of the garden flanked by flowers. Produce grown by traditional methods is on sale. Additionally, this is a garden that delightfully exercises the mind and body with regular seasonally-themed walks. CH

RHS Garden Hyde Hall

Essex, England

DESIGNERS: Dick Robinson, Helen Robinson, the RHS
OWNER: Royal Horticultural Society
GARDEN STYLE: 20th- and 21st-century informal
and formal garden
SIZE: 28 acres (11.3 ha)
CLIMATE: Temperate
LOCATION: Rettendon, Chelmsford, Essex

Ignorance can be a wonderful thing. When Dick and Helen Robinson took on Hyde Hall Farm in the early 1950s, they had not intended to make a garden, and when they began to do so, they were complete novices. Conditions at Hyde Hall were tough, with rainfall lower than Jerusalem; sticky, orange clay soil; and a hilltop site exposed to the winds. Through trial and error, and with the help of a number of the UK's leading horticulturalists of the 1960s and 1970s, they managed to create a diverse 12-acre (4.8 ha) garden with collections of roses, viburnums, and crab apples.

In 1992 the Robinsons handed over the garden and surrounding farmland to the Royal Horticultural Society. A new garden was integrated into the landscape with the Robinsons' old garden at its heart. Perhaps the key development to date is the Dry Garden, a boulder-strewn slope designed to look like the kind of arid hillside found in the Mediterranean or Near East. About 6,000 drought-tolerant plants were added in early 2001. None has received any artificial irrigation since, no matter how hot or dry the weather. Despite difficult conditions, the Dry Garden has proved to be a highly successful, immensely popular, and much imitated feature.

Other developments include the ongoing Wild Wood planting of over 70,000 native trees and 5 miles (8 km) of hedgerows, the recreation of traditional wildflower meadows, and cornfield annual sowings. As an environmentally-conscious garden, Hyde Hall is relevant for gardeners of today and the future. MW

Forde Abbey and Gardens

Somerset, England

DESIGNERS: The Roper family

OWNER: Mark Roper

GARDEN STYLE: 18th-century landscape, 20th-century English romantic

SIZE: 30 acres (12.1 ha)

CLIMATE: Temperate

LOCATION: Chard, Somerset

Guillaume Beaumont, a pupil of André Le Nôtre, is said to have influenced the landscaping at Forde Abbey when, in the early eighteenth century, the Great Pond at the top of the garden was augmented by three lower ponds linked by cascades. Also at this time, walls were built and lawns were laid out like a giant's shawl spread around the building, an Italianate mansion of golden stone grafted onto the abbey built in the previous century.

Subsequent owners of Forde Abbey have gone on to contribute the extensive walled kitchen garden and the bog and rock gardens, and have planted trees such as Douglas firs (*Pseudotsuga menziesii*), cedars, and redwoods that lend the place an atmosphere of timelessness. Most of the garden, however, has been created since the mid-twentieth century by two generations of the Roper family. Geoffrey, father of Mark, the present owner, added the arboretum in 1947 and planted many of the woods.

There is plenty of horticultural interest for every season as well as fine statues, an Ionic temple, and an interlaced beech pavilion. Snowdrops in late winter are followed in early spring by carpets of Dutch crocuses (*Crocus vernus*) covering approximately 10 acres (4 ha) of lawns. "The crocus appear like mustard and cress," says Mark Roper, "so long as we leave them to die down in the long grass and resist cutting until the end of June." The regimen here also suits the daffodils that take over through spring, when magnolias, camellias, witch hazels, and *Cyclamen coum*, followed by azaleas and rhododendrons, bring on a riotous abundance of color. The herbaceous borders reflected in the long canal are at their best from midsummer onward, with rich displays of dahlias, asters, and delphiniums. The magnificent views of the abbey from the mount, and lush plantings that are spread out beside the streams and in the bog garden, are not to be missed. EH

Cothay Manor

Somerset, England

DESIGNER: Reginald Cooper
OWNERS: Alastair Robb, Mary-Anne Robb
GARDEN STYLE: Formal herbaceous
SIZE: 12 acres (4.9 ha)
CLIMATE: Temperate
LOCATION: Greenham, Wellington, Somerset

Hidden away in the rolling landscape of rural Somerset, Cothay Manor is a wonderfully romantic garden attached to a fifteenth-century manor house. It was designed in the 1920s by a previous owner, Reginald Cooper, who created a splendid 5-acre (2 ha) formal garden around the house. Cooper was a friend of both Harold Nicolson at Sissinghurst in Kent (see page 370) and Lawrence Johnston at Hidcote Manor in Gloucestershire (see page 305). Certain elements in Cothay are reminiscent of both these famous gardens (although, interestingly, Sissinghurst was created in 1932, *after* Cothay was conceived).

The structure of the formal garden, very much as it was when laid out in the 1920s, is simple and strong, anchored to a long yew walk. Leading off it are different garden "rooms." In front of the house, a stone pool complements the medieval facade, looking as though it has been there for centuries—it was actually added by Cooper. The gatehouse leads to a lavender-filled entrance courtyard.

The current owners, Alastair and Mary-Anne Robb, have lived here since 1993, and new areas have been added in keeping with the original design. These include an avenue of mop-headed *Robinia pseudoacacia* 'Umbraculifera' underplanted with nepeta and *Tulipa* 'White Triumphator'. Beyond the formal garden, 7 acres (2.8 ha) of informal gardens include a wildflower meadow, a bog garden next to the River Tone, and a woodland area with specimen trees and shrubs. There is so much detail here that visitors should pace themselves to take it all in. CF

Greencombe Gardens

Somerset, England

DESIGNER: Joan Lorraine
OWNER: Joan Lorraine
GARDEN STYLE: 20th-century formal, woodland
SIZE: 3.5 acres (1.4 ha)
CLIMATE: Temperate
LOCATION: Porlock, Somerset

Greencombe is a remarkable achievement. It is a north-facing garden—without any sun for two months a year—perched on the edge of the hillside overlooking the Bristol Channel and would be an impossibility for most gardeners. Not so for Joan Lorraine who, over a period of thirty years, has created a magical setting.

Around the house, carved into the slope, is an immaculately kept formal garden with an abundance of unusual roses, hydrangeas, lilies, and herbaceous plants surrounding an emerald lawn. Behind the house is a substantial walled vegetable plot bisected by stone paths. In contrast, a ribbon of woodland with a winding path leads off from the far side of the garden, offering dappled shade and spectacular bird's-eye views across the water. Here, in spring, the ground is carpeted with pretty erythroniums of many different species and varieties. A good range of rhododendrons and azaleas provides splashes of intense color under the tree canopy. At the far end of the woodland walk is a surprise: a delightful circular wooden chapel, made by a local craftsman, that blends into the woodland scene. The garden features bulbs and rhododendrons in spring, and maples and woodland color in fall. Everything is grown organically and mulched with leaf mold and compost.

Joan has traveled widely in search of interesting plants, and she holds four National Collections in her garden: *Erythronium*, *Polystichum*, *Gaultheria*, and *Vaccinium*. The garden is worth visiting for these alone. Most of all, a visit to Greencombe shows just what can be achieved with limited resources. CF

Lady Farm

Somerset, England

DESIGNERS: Judy Pearce, Mary Payne
OWNERS: Malcolm Pearce, Judy Pearce
GARDEN STYLE: Prairie and steppe, cottage garden
SIZE: 8 acres (3.2 ha)
CLIMATE: Temperate
LOCATION: Chelwood, Somerset

Located between Bristol and Bath, the garden at Lady Farm was begun by Malcolm and Judy Pearce in 1992. The catalyst was the removal of working buildings at the hilltop farm. It enabled 3 acres (1.2 ha) to be enclosed with windbreaks to improve the microclimate in readiness for planting. After the poor ground had been improved with additions of topsoil from a nearby paddock, the vegetable patch, lawns, and mixed planting got underway.

Soon after, a natural spring was discovered. This enabled a watercourse and two lakes to be created in the valley that falls rapidly from the house. A shaded alley of silver birch underplanted with hostas and alliums also proved an early success, and was later moved so that it could be given an even grander design. Perhaps the most important development at Lady Farm came with the involvement of garden designer Mary Payne. Her influence came to bear on the most challenging part of the garden, the south-facing valley side that drops steeply from the house lawn to the bottom lake. With thin soil and full sun, it was a potentially hostile environment for most garden plants, yet this is now arguably the most successful part of the garden and one for which Lady Farm has become well known. Mary Payne suggested prairie- and steppe-style plantings, and employed the matrix technique where plants are scattered randomly across the hillside. The plantings have great longevity, and remain as impressive in the winter months as in midsummer with grasses and perennials left standing until late winter. MW

Hadspen Garden

Somerset, England

DESIGNERS: Sandra Pope, Nori Pope
OWNER: Niall Hobhouse
GARDEN STYLE: Contemporary, color-themed
SIZE: 5 acres (2 ha)
CLIMATE: Temperate
LOCATION: Castle Cary, Somerset

Created largely within the kitchen garden of the eighteenth-century house, Hadspen has enjoyed two recent periods of distinction. The first was under Penelope Hobhouse during the 1970s, the second from 1987, under Nori and Sandra Pope. The Popes have become famous for their innovative use of color in over 1.6 miles (1 km) of color-themed borders.

In the D-shaped walled garden, a brilliant arc of color follows the curve of the walls. Taking as its starting point the rich plum of the old brickwork, a deep border swashbuckles through crimson and red to blazing orange and yellow in one direction, and blends subtly through half-tone shades in the other. Also within the D, a kitchen garden is set out in a patchwork of red, blue, and green. The double-yellow border is spectacular, with groupings of yellow foliage and flowers intensified by injections of blue. There are dramatic foliage displays in the pond garden and in the National Collection of rodgersias.

All these bold effects are skillfully managed so they never become overbearing, and there are many delicious quiet places to be savored, like the silvers and lavenders of the potting shed garden and a simple tunnel of beech underplanted with hostas, many of them bred at Hadspen. Besides being pioneering gardeners, the Popes are successful plant breeders. A nursery at the gate stocks the many choice "Hadspen" varieties now available. AE

RIGHT A recent addition to 18th-century Hadspen House, the garden is famous for its innovative use of color.

Hestercombe Gardens

Somerset, England

DESIGNERS: Coplestone Warre Bampfylde, Edwin Lutyens, Gertrude Jekyll
OWNERS: HGP Ltd., Somerset County Council
GARDEN STYLE: 18th-century landscape, 20th-century formal
SIZE: 50 acres (20.2 ha)
CLIMATE: Temperate
LOCATION: Cheddon Fitzpaine, Taunton, Somerset

Here are two must-see gardens in different styles on the same site. There is the formal Edwardian garden, designed in 1906 by Edwin Lutyens and planted by Gertrude Jekyll, and the idyllic 40-acre (16.2 ha) Georgian pleasure grounds created between 1759 and 1786. Known as the Secret Landscape Garden, it was opened in 1997 for the first time in 125 years.

Lutyens' design takes advantage of the south-facing sloping site and its views over the Vale of Taunton. A series of terraces joined by formal stone steps overlooks a sunken garden, known as the Great Plat, with long, narrow water brooks to east and west. A massive pergola with chestnut crossbeams on alternating square- and round-shaped pillars frames the countryside beyond. The architecture, down to the smallest detail, is superb, a perfect foil to Jekyll's planting plans, most of which survive and underpin the restoration. On the east terrace, a pale blue and yellow color scheme gives way to oranges and reds, with yellow irises and white arum lilies planted in the brook. Leathery-leaved bergenias edge the triangular beds in the Great Plat, surrounding peonies, white lilies, pink roses, and delphiniums.

From the Dutch Garden, a parterre of lavender, yuccas, roses, and lamb's ears, is a glimpse through the gate of the lake and wooded hills of the eighteenth-century landscape garden to the north. This has been restored and provides fascinating walks beside the pear-shaped lake to the woodland where classical temples, a mausoleum, and witch's hut offer resting points with lakeside views. Perhaps the most impressive sight is the Great Cascade, fed by water that runs in stone conduits from higher up the valley.

The two gardens at Hestercombe are superb examples of English garden style separated by 150 years or so—Bampfylde's romantic landscape park and Lutyens' architectural ingenuity overlaid by Jekyll's art of planting. EH

Montacute House

Somerset, England

DESIGNER: Sir Edward Phelips
OWNER: The National Trust
GARDEN STYLE: Formal Elizabethan
SIZE: 25 acres (10.1 ha),
     plus 300 acres (121.5 ha) parkland
CLIMATE: Temperate
LOCATION: Montacute, Yeovil, Somerset

The stunning Elizabethan manor house that stands at Montacute was built in 1600 by Sir Edward Phelips. The hard landscaping—the raised terraces, balustrades, sweeping steps, and exquisite garden pavilions—all date from that time. Sir Edward was an MP, Master of the Rolls, and chancellor to the Prince of Wales. The house and garden were built to impress. In 1915 Lord George Curzon rented the house and lived here with his mistress, the saucy novelist Elinor Glyn. She penned her potboilers in one of the gazebos. Constructed from the golden Ham stone typical of this region, the house is often said to be the most beautiful in England. The original garden had all the features expected from such a property, with knot gardens, parterres, peaches, vine houses, melon and cucumber frames, vegetables, herbs, and beehives. There are clipped yews and ancient yew hedges, and a Cedar Lawn that was once a bowling green. Wide borders viewed from the terraces contain old shrub roses underplanted with hostas, peonies, and spring bulbs. The surrounding parkland has a Lime Avenue and an Oak Avenue, while walks to nearby St. Michael's Hill end with the folly tower on its crest.

Many famous gardeners have influenced and worked on this awe-inspiring setting: Vita Sackville-West, William Robinson, Graham Stuart Thomas, and Phyllis Reiss from nearby Tintinhull House (see page 347), who would regularly bicycle over on Monday afternoons, with her own gardener in tow, to put in some work on the borders. JHi

East Lambrook Manor Gardens

Somerset, England

DESIGNER: Margery Fish
OWNERS: Robert Williams, Marianne Williams
GARDEN STYLE: 20th-century cottage garden
SIZE: 2 acres (0.5 ha)
CLIMATE: Temperate
LOCATION: South Petherton, Somerset

In 1956, Margery Fish published a book entitled *We Made a Garden*. It told the story of the garden that she and her husband were creating at East Lambrook. The garden was inspired by a cottage rather than a great house, and became a haven for plants so long neglected that they were in danger of being lost. This unassuming book changed the way we look at gardens, setting a precedent for the natural, informal style of planting so widely enjoyed today.

Seven more books followed, and Margery Fish became a celebrity. Her romantic, reassuringly messy garden showed the way for a new approach that did not need staff. Her garden featured ground cover plants to smother weeds, and sturdy, adaptable, hardy perennials—often improved forms of native plants that we now think of as cottage-garden favorites—including snowdrops, spurges, hardy geraniums, and columbines. A loose, informal design divided the garden into areas with ideal conditions for different plants. You will still see a moist ditch, shady wooded area, and free-draining slope for silver foliage plants, all quite novel in the 1940s. Lonicera hedges and an avenue of topiarized cypress "puddings," or large blobs, gave structure to the design.

After her death, the garden was looked after by her family before being sold in 1985 to Andrew and Dodo Norton, who were dedicated custodians of the garden until 1999. The new owners, who have been guided by Margery Fish's books and over 2,000 of her photos, have embarked on a major restoration. There is an excellent adjoining nursery. AE

Tintinhull House

Somerset, England

DESIGNERS: Dr. S. J. M. Price, Phyllis Reiss, Penelope Hobhouse
OWNER: The National Trust
GARDEN STYLE: 20th-century formal
SIZE: 2 acres (0.8 ha)
CLIMATE: Temperate
LOCATION: Yeovil, Somerset

An exquisite manor garden created between the world wars by Phyllis Reiss, Tintinhull has been described as the most perfect garden in England. Reiss used mellow stonework and crisp yew hedges to create elegant garden "rooms" linked by beguiling vistas. Her lyrical planting style was entirely her own, a style later elaborated on by Penelope Hobhouse when she became the tenant at Tintinhull.

The garden is entered through the house, which opens on to a wide stone terrace. From here a pathway lined with bulging box leads through Eagle Forecourt, down through a collection of azaleas to a small, sunken garden where white roses, lilies, and anemones bloom in turn around a central fountain. From here one path leads to a delightful rustic kitchen area, another to the pool garden.

The latter is the most significant part of the garden and was created by the childless Phyllis Reiss in memory of her favorite nephew, a pilot shot down during World War II. An open-fronted loggia stands at one end of the glassy pool dotted with lilies. To one side rises a magnificent hot border, to the other a silvery pastel one, and huge terracotta pots overflow with flowers. It is a powerfully still, quiet place. Phyllis was well aware of its special qualities, so the garden was opened to airmen from the nearby American base and anyone who had suffered a similar loss.

Tintinhull is beautiful throughout the year: on mid-summer afternoons, when the shadows are long and the air heavy with the scent of lilies, and in early fall, with windflowers around the fountain pool. AE

Broadleas Gardens

Wiltshire, England

DESIGNER: Lady Anne Cowdray
OWNER: Broadleas Gardens Charitable Trust
GARDEN STYLE: 20th-century woodland garden
SIZE: 10 acres (4 ha)
CLIMATE: Temperate
LOCATION: Broadleas, Devizes, Wiltshire

Plunging dramatically into the valley below, the dell garden at Broadleas is breathtaking. Although it is only 300 feet (29 m) long, this woodland garden covers 4 acres (1.6 ha) because of its wide, steep sides. Flanking the slopes is a lifetime's worth of rare plants that have been lovingly collected by the owner.

When Lady Cowdray bought the pretty Regency house in 1946, the garden was in a poor state. She says it was a "jungle that you couldn't walk through" and needed to be completely overhauled. With considerable effort she soon tamed the rampant *Rhododendron ponticum* and the massive clumps of old bamboo choking the dell. It has now been extensively planted with choice specimens that thrive in the special microclimate, with several of the plants more usually found in milder parts of southwest Cornwall. Among the highlights are magnolias, camellias, Persian ironwood (*Parrotia persica)*, and a rare *Paulownia fargesii*—a foxglove tree with mauve flowers. All of this is underplanted with perennials such as hostas, ferns, and *Primula whitei*. In spring the ground is packed with bulbs, and there are thousands of dog-toothed violets, trilliums, and sanguinaria. Although the dell is the highlight, there is also a winter garden, sunken rose garden, and secret garden veiled by a sprawling Japanese maple. In summer a silver border shimmers with the combined foliage of cistus, elaeagnus, olearia, and rosemary.

This is a garden for all seasons, and it keeps on improving. Despite being in her later years, Lady Anne is still working on it as energetically as ever. MC

Stourhead

Wiltshire, England

DESIGNER: Henry Hoare II
OWNER: The National Trust
GARDEN STYLE: 18th-century landscape
SIZE: 100 acres (40 ha)
CLIMATE: Temperate
LOCATION: Stourton, Warminster, Wiltshire

Banker Henry Hoare returned to England, inspired by his European Grand Tour, to create an eighteenth-century classical masterpiece in the grounds below his Palladian home. His imagination stimulated by the paintings of Claude and Poussin, Hoare turned the painters' nymph-haunted lakes, classical ruins, and grottoes into a magical reality. A walk through this landscape reveals Hoares' visions in a sequence of wonderful Arcadian scenes from Virgil's *Aeneid*.

The Turf Bridge (1762) marks the beginning of the route around the lake. At each vantage point, another beautiful composition appears: the Temple of Flora, Temple of Apollo, Pantheon or Bristol Cross, each set superbly in the parkland. Only the grotto is hidden from view. Here, in a high-domed chamber, a white lead statue of the nymph Ariadne lies on a plinth with the water bubbling below. In another chamber, a river god commands the source of the Stour. The dramatic notion of passing from broad daylight into a dark grotto was key in the eighteenth-century landscape, and Stourhead's is one of the finest examples.

The reflections in the lake of the trees here add further beauty, with each season having its own special highlights. For many, winter's quiet is when the Stourhead composition of splendid architectural interludes between grass, trees, and water is at its romantic best. Today Stourhead ranks as one of the world's most beautiful landscape gardens. CR

RIGHT Palladian Stourhead was inspired by the eighteenth-century Grand Tour and the works of Claude and Poussin.

Iford Manor

Wiltshire, England

DESIGNER: Harold Peto
OWNER: Elizabeth Cartwright-Hignett
GARDEN STYLE: Early 20th-century Anglo-Italianate
SIZE: 2.5 acres (1 ha)
CLIMATE: Temperate
LOCATION: Bradford-on-Avon, Wiltshire

In 1899 the disenchanted architect Harold Peto discovered Iford Manor, and the remainder of his life was set. Born in 1854, Peto was a direct contemporary of Gertrude Jekyll, the great plantswoman who, with her architect partner Sir Edwin Lutyens, defined late nineteenth- and early twentieth-century gardening. At Iford, Peto took their blueprint and gave it his own inimitable Italianate twist to produce a masterpiece.

The house, Elizabethan with an eighteenth-century classical facade, is set in the valley of the River Frome. Built of honey-colored stone, it sits close by the riverbank with the garden rising in a series of terraces to one side and behind. Planted with a selection of cypresses and junipers to provide a counterpoint to the surrounding sophisticated plantings, they form galleries where a treasure trove of artifacts, accumulated during a lifetime of travel and discerning collecting, is displayed.

After entering through a deceptively modest gate, one passes through a small court toward the Italian loggia and the sound of water in the form of a semicircular pool fed by one of a number of rivulets—fed in turn from high in the woods above. A succession of stairways takes you up the hillside. Terraces lead off, culminating in the Great Terrace, terminated by a handsome, semicircular stone seat. On either side, small enclosures act as side chapels.

The climax is found at the eastern end of the garden where Peto's Cloisters, built of local Westwood stone but incorporating many antique treasures, close the garden off from the outside world. JB

Longleat House

Wiltshire, England

DESIGNERS: Capability Brown, Humphry Repton, Russell Page
OWNER: Seventh Marquis of Bath
GARDEN STYLE: 18th-century English landscape with later additions
SIZE: 900 acres (364.5 ha)
CLIMATE: Temperate
LOCATION: Warminster, Wiltshire

Longleat is a paradox. On one hand it has stunning English landscape-style parkland. On the other it is home to lions and giraffes from the savannahs of Africa, definitely the star attractions in the safari park that opened here in 1966, overshadowing the eighteenth-century parkland. Ironically this is one of the best examples of Capability Brown's work.

Brown was employed by the third Viscount of Weymouth in 1757 to sweep away the formal gardens designed by Henry Wise and George London. He created Elysian drifts of trees and grass and a chain of lakes, though the scheme was modified in 1804 by Humphry Repton, who reshaped the Half Mile Pond. Repton made it more irregular and added the island where two gorillas, Nico and Samba, now live.

In the nineteenth century, exotic trees were planted in the parkland. The current formal gardens were also added to the north side of the house. However, the greatest changes came in the next century. Besides starting the safari park, the sixth Marquis of Bath employed the designer Russell Page to improve the gardens and create displays of rhododendrons along Longcombe Drive. The seventh marquis, who has a passion for mazes, is now in charge. The world's longest hedge maze, installed in 1975, covers an area of 1.5 acres (0.6 ha) and has a total pathway length of 1.7 miles (2.7 km). Other Longleat attractions include the Butterfly Garden, a railway, and safari boat rides. LH

Heale Garden

Wiltshire, England

DESIGNERS: Harold Peto, Louis Greville
OWNER: Greville family
GARDEN STYLE: 20th-century formal and informal
SIZE: 8 acres (3.2 ha)
CLIMATE: Temperate
LOCATION: Middle Woodford, Salisbury, Wiltshire

As the garden stands today, it was mainly designed by Harold Peto, who was employed by Greville in both 1906 and 1911. To the west of the house are two terraces. The beds on the upper terrace are backed by clipped yew, and planted with tall perennials and two stately wisterias. The stone path to the lower terrace, flanked by clipped trees, is smothered with lady's mantle (*Alchemilla mollis*). On the lower terrace are two stone lily ponds and two small borders. To the south, a lawn leads to the bank of a clear brook, a tributary of the River Avon that is well stocked with trout. This, the garden's most delightful and

natural feature, is the setting for its most famous and manmade feature, the Japanese Garden. Here the stream is divided and spanned by a red Nikko bridge straddled by a thatched teahouse. The latter, complete with authentic traditional straw mats, was brought from Japan and assembled in 1910 with the help of four Japanese gardeners. Next to the bridge, and under the shade of tall trees, is the bog garden, planted with a selection of moisture-loving plants.

The Long Border contains many dark-leaved plants, while a brick-and-flint wall encloses the delightful kitchen garden on three sides, leaving it open to the south. This compartment is filled with edible crops and ornamental displays. The beds are planted with vegetables and divided by espaliered fruit trees. A nice touch here are the tunnels of apples and pears over the paths. There are also ancient fig and mulberry trees, and the second tallest Katsura tree (*Cercidiphyllum japonicum*) in Europe. TM

Home Covert Garden and Arboretum

Wiltshire, England

DESIGNERS: John Phillips, Sarah Phillips
OWNERS: John Phillips, Sarah Phillips
GARDEN STYLE: Late 20th-century plantsman's garden
SIZE: 6 acres (2.4 ha)
CLIMATE: Temperate
LOCATION: Roundway, Devizes, Wiltshire

John and Sarah Phillips began work in 1960 on this informal plantsman's garden, perched on a plateau above rolling countryside. At the time it was a patch of ancient mixed woodland. Over the years, they have planted thousands of shrubs, bulbs, perennials, and approximately 25,000 choice trees. Like many a plantsman's garden, it was created gradually, without a plan. Many of the plants have been provided by the Phillips' famous gardening friends, including the late Christopher Lloyd, plant collector Roy Lancaster, and botanist Martyn Rix.

Close to the house are shaded borders, a rock garden, and raised beds that lead to the woodland garden with hydrangeas, magnolias, and eucryphias. Dropping 90 feet (27.4 m) from the plateau is a series of three water gardens that are reached by a precarious path. Here you will find moisture-loving plants, such as giant-leaved gunnera, rodgersias, and huge clumps of candelabra primulas. Though the garden performs right through the year, it is most rewarding for visitors in spring when camellias, rhododendrons, and thousands of dog's-tooth violets are in flower, and in midsummer for the cup-shaped flowers of the stewartias.

The sheer number of rare plants and informal, slightly eccentric atmosphere makes Home Covert unique. It is held in high esteem by the gardening elite and first-time visitors, not that John will admit this, describing it as "mad and rather weird." MC

Abbey House Gardens

Wiltshire, England

DESIGNERS: Ian Pollard, Barbara Pollard
OWNERS: Ian Pollard, Barbara Pollard
GARDEN STYLE: Mixed formal and woodland, knot garden
SIZE: 5 acres (2 ha)
CLIMATE: Temperate
LOCATION: Market Cross, Malmesbury, Wiltshire

To give you an idea of the energy that has gone into this magnificent garden—dominated by the tower of the great ruined abbey at Malmesbury—the owners have planted 2,000 roses and 50,000 tulips. Plants are everywhere. The walls of the sixteenth-century house are covered by wisteria, clematis, yellow *Rosa banksiae*, ivy, and jasmine. To the front lies the Celtic Cross knot garden.

The design, laid out in box, with clipped yew and spirals of holly, was taken from St. Martin's Cross on the Island of Iona. Plantings within the knot include santolina, teucrium, and dwarf red berberis, with added color from dianthus, muscari, and lady's mantle (*Alchemilla mollis*). The Celtic Cross is just the start, though. There are more box-edged beds packed with tulips and roses, planted in exuberant colors. An arch formed by four crab apples leads to Paradise with a stainless-steel sculpture in the center, down which water cascades over disks that appear to spin. There are also triple herbaceous borders, with apple trees set among the plants, a reminder that this was once a monastery orchard. Beyond the herbaceous borders is a vast pergola surrounding a herb garden.

The levels constantly change. The most notable is behind the house where the ground drops steeply away to what were the monastery's fishponds. The banks are covered with snowdrops, hellebores, crocuses, narcissuses, and primulas in spring, with geraniums and ferns providing summer interest. VB

Bowood House and Gardens

Wiltshire, England

DESIGNERS: Capability Brown, Charles Hamilton,
    Josiah Lane
OWNER: Ninth Marquis of Lansdowne
GARDEN STYLE: English landscape, woodland
SIZE: 100 acres (40 ha)
CLIMATE: Temperate
LOCATION: Calne, Wiltshire

Bowood is a fine example of a great estate and landscape, whose history has seen an accumulation of features. It has also been brought into the modern world and made into a thriving concern. The landscape around the house (just an annex, since the main house was demolished in the 1950s) is Capability Brown at his best, with a long stretch of lake dominating wide vistas, all so well done that it is difficult to know what is natural and what is not.

At the northern end of the lake is an extensive and convincing naturalistic cascade, designed in 1785 by Charles Hamilton (of Painshill Park in Surrey, see page 384), with a number of grottoes to one side. It adds another dimension to the landscape without impinging on Brown's more sober work and is as good an example of eighteenth-century landscape fantasy as one could wish to see. Josiah Lane, who designed the grottoes, also made a hermit cave decorated with tufa, fossils, and stalactites.

Bowood's owners have placed rhododendrons at a safe distance from the house, in a belt of woodland designed by Brown. For much of the year, their somber foliage creates a setting for the mausoleum. For a short spell in late spring and early summer, though, the woods—with bluebells—are splashed with color. The terraces by the house are an extra feature, with Irish yews (*Taxus baccata* 'Fastigiata') and roses. Together with the adventure playground, they create a well-handled mix of historical planting and modern tourism that is highly enjoyable. NK

Folly Farm

Berkshire, England

DESIGNERS: Edwin Lutyens, Gertrude Jekyll
OWNER: Anonymous private owner
GARDEN STYLE: Arts and Crafts
SIZE: 4 acres (1.6 ha)
CLIMATE: Temperate
LOCATION: Sulhamstead Abbots, Reading, Berkshire

Folly Farm is the best house and garden to have come out of the Edwin Lutyens-Gertrude Jekyll hard landscaping-planting partnership. Designed in 1906 for H. H. Cochrane, it was extended by Lutyens six years later for Zachary Merton, a wealthy benefactor of Great Ormond Street Hospital for Children. It was then that the Tank Court, the formal Dutch canal, and a sunken rose garden were added. With its yew hedges, curved brick and stone paths, an ornamental pool, and beds of roses and lavender, the rose garden is a triumph of the architecture-planting combination for which Lutyens and Jekyll became so well known.

All the key Lutyens features are here: herringbone brick pathways, shallow semicircular steps, clipped yew hedges, and lime walks. Gateways, pergolas, and garden doors are all made from the finest oak, with Arts and Crafts hinges and handles. The garden benches were also designed by Lutyens. His hard landscaping is softened by Jekyll's lush planting, with deep borders of perennials in carefully graded colors. Also note the range of different moods. The entrance court and Barn Court have a domesticated intimacy and beauty, with their carefully arranged pot plants, statues, and seats. All this is in contrast to the sweep of mown lawn and magnificent trees, the kitchen garden with its organic vegetables, and greenhouses full of tropical plants.

Money and ease of maintenance mean that not all of Jekyll's planting plans have been strictly adhered to. However, the spirit of these two Edwardian giants still resonates, one very good reason for visiting. JHi

Reading International Solidarity Centre Roof Garden

Berkshire, England

DESIGNERS: Team of volunteers

OWNER: Reading International Solidarity Centre

GARDEN STYLE: 21st-century permaculture roof garden

SIZE: 3,000 square feet (278 sq m)

CLIMATE: Temperate

LOCATION: Reading, Berkshire

The town center of Reading is devoted more to the corporate needs of people than to flora and fauna, and it is not, generally, a lovely place. Yet, on a rooftop three stories up is a haven for humans and wildlife alike. The garden belongs to an education charity concerned with sustainable development and social justice, so it is only right that it should be planted using permaculture. Here is a forest garden, consisting of tiers of plants to maximize the space, and it is almost self-maintaining.

The site has 120 different species from all over the world and they are planted for any of several purposes: medicinal, fruit, shade, ground cover, and/or nitrogen for the soil. There is a large cherry tree as well as vines, peaches, medlars, and mulberry bushes; vegetables in raised beds; shrubs and perennials; and plenty of food and shelter for the wildlife.

The garden's location, between tall buildings and above offices, provides a warm microclimate. Even banana plants survive. Rainwater is collected for irrigation, and kitchen waste from the café downstairs used for composting. The soil is potato peels, mulched with newspaper and bark chippings, and a wind turbine and solar panels power the irrigation pump. The garden is used by schools and other groups as an educational tool. It is a lovely place to visit: a little natural woodland in the urban jungle. CD

Chelsea Physic Garden

London, England

DESIGNER: The Society of Apothecaries
OWNER: Chelsea Physic Garden
GARDEN STYLE: 17th-century walled botanic garden
SIZE: 4 acres (1.6 ha)
CLIMATE: Temperate
LOCATION: Chelsea, London

Founded by the Society of Apothecaries in 1673 as a center for medicinal learning, the Chelsea Physic is one of the world's most botanically significant yet most secret and special gardens. Just a five-minute walk from the bustle of Sloane Square and the Kings Road, time palpably runs slow in this shabby-chic enclave of calm tranquility, where hard science still runs on apace behind the scenes despite a shoestring budget. A roll call of curators down the years includes such leading botanical figures as Philip Miller, Robert Fortune, William Hudson, William Forsyth, William Curtis, and Thomas Moore.

If you take a visit to the garden today, you can see Britain's largest outdoor fruiting olive tree, thanks to the garden's mild microclimate close to the River Thames; admire the eccentric rockery made from "forty tons of old stone from the Tower of London, flints and chalk and lava brought from Iceland"; take a walk through plant introductions of great medicinal and commercial importance; learn the value of ethnobotany; and experience firsthand beautifully scented plants used in perfumery and aromatherapy. You can also purchase cuttings and seeds from the age-old plants or join the admirable Friends of the Garden scheme, not only buying into history but helping to ensure the survival of a world-class institution that may yet discover more cures through research into over 5,000 species. But whatever you do, enjoy! RCa

John Madejski Garden

London, England

DESIGNER: Kim Wilkie
OWNER: Victoria and Albert Museum
GARDEN STYLE: Modern
SIZE: 0.75 acres (0.3 ha)
CLIMATE: Temperate
LOCATION: South Kensington, London

In 2004, landscape architect Kim Wilkie won an international competition to transform the gloomy central courtyard of London's Victoria and Albert Museum into an attractive, usable space. He responded to the bombastic, operatic architecture of the place by turning the courtyard into an urban stage set.

By day, the garden is filled with tourists and nannies lounging on the sunny lawns while their charges stampede through a shallow, elliptical pool. By night, everything changes thanks to the fiber-optic lighting that illuminates the building and planters—twenty-two huge cubes of glass—that edge the lawn. The water drains away to reveal a red sandstone floor, and the ellipse, outlined by interlocking bands of light, makes an amazing setting for parties.

The bold simplicity of Wilkie's design is upheld thanks to the discreet and effective planting. Two long rows of blue hydrangeas flower all summer and soften the terracotta, while the planters provide seasonal variety. The Italianate lemon trees feature in summer, the crisp, clipped hollies in winter, and the pair of liquidambars stand out in autumn when they inject brash reds and orange. With so much space and coolness, there's even room for a few flashy flowers—including eremurus, echiums, salvias and dahlias—all of which thrive in the sheltered microclimate.

Bright and buzzy on a summer's day, the garden is equally satisfying in winter when there's a sense of stylish, cloistered calm. AE

Kyoto Garden

London, England

DESIGNER: The Kyoto Garden Association
OWNER: Royal Borough of Kensington and Chelsea
GARDEN STYLE: 20th-century Japanese
SIZE: 1 acre (0.4 ha)
CLIMATE: Temperate
LOCATION: Holland Park, London

One of the most popular and distinctive areas of Holland Park, in west London, is the Kyoto Garden, created by Japanese gardeners for the 1991 London Festival of Japan. In traditional style, it is beautiful and calming, sculptured, restrained, and elegant. If you sit here in peace, you will quickly forget that you are in one of the world's busiest cities.

Japanese gardens, with their minimalism and restraint, their muted colors, and restricted planting, are the absolute antithesis of exuberant Western gardens. The underlying principle is a regard for the beauty and simplicity of nature, incorporating philosophy, symbolism, and even religion with the placing of every stone and tree. Natural materials, especially stone and water, are the essential elements, with the sparse planting being used to emphasize texture. All of these elements are set out here.

In accordance with Japanese tradition, there is an old lake (essential in the garden), the reflective surface of the pool drawing down the trees and the sky. Exquisitely laid paths wind between carefully placed rocks and ornaments. Acers, with finely divided leaves, erupt into fall color, and natural granite stepping stones cross a waterfall. To appreciate it all fully, it is worth reading this anonymous piece of advice, "The skill of enjoying life presented, rejoicing at sun, delighting in taste of water and breath of wind, birds' song, admiring the grasses and flowers instead of burning in fire of empty wishes—this is a wisdom of simplicity penetrating the philosophy of the Japanese garden." Read, reflect, and visit. NS

The Roof Gardens

London, England

DESIGNER: Ralph Hancock
OWNER: Virgin Limited Edition
GARDEN STYLE: 20th-century themed roof garden
SIZE: 1.5 acres (0.6 ha)
CLIMATE: Temperate
LOCATION: Kensington, London

Some 98 feet (29.8 m) above Kensington High Street, in the heart of London, this 1930s, Grade II-listed roof garden is perhaps one of the world's most effective horticultural fantasies. It is impossible to believe that the garden, with its Moorish architecture, exotic birds, and tender plants, is on the sixth floor of a former department store.

The garden still retains many of the plantings and features of the original, with three main themes dominating the layout: the Spanish Garden, Tudor Garden, and the English Woodland Garden. The first is an exotic oasis where olives, a Chusan palm

(*Trachycarpus fortunei*), mimosa *(Mimosa pudica)*, and bay trees (*Laurus nobilis*) provide a backdrop to colorful bedding displays. Water fountains, brooks, ceramic tiles, and a quartered courtyard provide a Moorish feel to the area. In contrast, the lush greenery of the Woodland Garden is provided by 100 different species of tree—protected by a preservation order— that thrive in less than 3 feet (90 cm) of soil. In the Tudor Garden, enclosed by walls and a timber pergola walkway, some early plants such as old roses and myrtle (*Myrtus communis)* contribute to the period feel. Unfortunately, later plant introductions, such as wisteria, can seem out of character.

The gardens, still in immaculate condition, play a crucial part in the commercial activities of the owner, and retain the intimate character of the original design and vision. The general public are allowed to visit the Roof Gardens throughout the week if no private function is taking place. AJ

Myddelton House Gardens

London, England

DESIGNER: Edward Augustus Bowles
OWNER: Lea Valley Regional Park Authority
GARDEN STYLE: Edwardian plantsman's garden
SIZE: 4 acres (1.6 ha)
CLIMATE: Temperate
LOCATION: Bulls Cross, Enfield, London

Edward Augustus Bowles developed the fascinating plant collection at Myddelton House at the end of the nineteenth century by gradually transforming an overgrown Victorian shrubbery into a plantsman's paradise. Bowles was an Edwardian gentleman who could afford to devote his time almost entirely to his great passion, and he became a highly respected plant collector and garden writer. Many of his favorite plants still grow at Myddelton today, including a National Collection of bearded iris. One of Bowles' most famous plant groupings was his "lunatic asylum" where plants with distorted growth habits are still grown, such as a contorted hazel (*Corylus avellana* 'Contorta') and a laburnum with oaklike leaves.

There is also a collection of plants named after Bowles, including the grass *Carex elata* 'Bowles' Golden' and the wallflower *Erysimum* 'Bowles' Mauve'. The Tulip Terrace is decorated with box-edged beds planted with different varieties of tulip each spring, and Tom Tiddler's Ground is filled with plants bearing gold or silver variegation on their leaves. Beyond the more formal gardens is a spring-flowering meadow.

This delightful garden is a magical place, which exudes the charm of its creator, a gentle, shy plant collector. It has no fancy tearoom or shop, no glossy guide or audio tour, but instead demands a dignified scrutiny that perhaps only the most passionate gardeners will fully appreciate. Edward Bowles was a plant custodian and his garden is a treasure. AJ

Museum of Garden History

London, England

DESIGNER: Sixth Marchioness of Salisbury
OWNER: Museum of Garden History
GARDEN STYLE: 17th-century reproduction knot garden
SIZE: 0.5 acre (0.2 ha)
CLIMATE: Temperate
LOCATION: Lambeth, London

This garden and museum are one of London's best-kept secrets. Set against the walls of Lambeth Palace Gardens, the small reproduction seventeenth-century knot garden and themed borders were designed in the 1980s by Lady Salisbury, the museum's president, and are a smaller version of gardens she created at Hatfield House in Hertfordshire (see page 332).

In honor of the plant-hunting activities of the two John Tradescants, father and son, whose tomb can be found nearby, the knot garden was designed in early seventeenth-century style. The hedge is planted with box, which at that time in history was gaining popularity over the woody herbs that had been used in Elizabethan and Tudor knot gardens. A large square, a circle, and a smaller square dominate the design. Multicolored parrot tulips pay homage to the "Tulipomania" that swept British horticulture in the seventeenth century, and roses, perennials, biennials, and annuals transform the formality of the knot to an almost cottage-gardenlike, early-summer spectacle. A topiarized spiral of the holly *Ilex* x *altaclerensis* 'Golden King' dominates the center of the knot with myrtle, viburnum, bay, and box. Plants in the knot garden and borders were, on the whole, available in Britain during the lifetimes of the two Tradescants (1570–1662).

This lovely garden is an important information center as well as a beautiful and peaceful haven close to the center of England's capital. AJ

Chiswick House Grounds

London, England

DESIGNERS: Charles Bridgeman, William Kent, Lord Burlington
OWNER: London Borough of Hounslow
GARDEN STYLE: 18th-century English landscape
SIZE: 65 acres (26.3 ha)
CLIMATE: Temperate
LOCATION: Chiswick, London

Chiswick, now a public park, was once the meeting place of an aesthetic and intellectual elite, pivotal not only to the history of gardening, but also to the formation of eighteenth-century taste.

Chiswick's owner, the third Lord Burlington, traveled extensively in Italy and admired the works of the ancients and the architects they inspired. His villa at Chiswick, begun in 1725, was modeled on the work of Palladio. His vision for the surrounding garden, probably realized by Charles Bridgeman during the 1720s, was of a Roman garden of straight avenues, classical pavilions, and an amphitheater. However, he had returned from a visit to Italy in 1719 with the painter William Kent, who remained his friend and employee for the rest of his life. Kent believed that "all gardening is landscape painting." By 1731, he had reinvented the garden in the manner of paintings of the Roman *campagna*, reworking straight lines into curves and contours, and adding statuary and buildings rich in classical allusion.

William Kent is credited with founding the English landscape tradition when he famously "leaped the fence and saw all nature was a garden." So pervasive is his influence that it is difficult now to appreciate just how radical he was, converting Chiswick's straight canal into the first natural-looking lake, or building a cascade that appeared centuries old. AE

Goodnestone Park Gardens

Kent, England

DESIGNERS: Emmy FitzWalter, Lady Margaret FitzWalter
OWNER: Lady Margaret FitzWalter
GARDEN STYLE: 20th- and 21st-century formal, woodland,
  walled flower gardens
SIZE: 14 acres (5.6 ha)
CLIMATE: Temperate
LOCATION: Wingham, Canterbury, Kent

Statuesque and imposing holm oaks (*Quercus ilex*) guard the gate to Goodnestone Park, an elegant, early eighteenth-century house resplendent with a Doric portico that was added in the nineteenth century. Much of the property's garden was created in the early twentieth century by an aunt of the present owner, who, after discovering a pocket of acid soil in the Kent chalk, built a huge rock garden and planted rare shrubs and trees through the woodland.

Since the current chatelaine, Lady FitzWalter, arrived at Goodnestone as a young wife in 1955, the garden has been her life's work. Money for the near-derelict site was limited, so many of the trees and shrubs in the woodland, including the dominant *Magnolia* x *soulangeana*, were propagated at Goodnestone from existing plants. An avenue of large-leaved limes was planted to draw the eye from the front door up a gentle incline. To one side of this avenue is a small arboretum, where daffodils appear in spring beneath branches of birch, malus, acer, and prunus. There is an extensive collection of cornus.

In the summer, the walled garden comes into its own, the borders brimming with roses, bulbs, and herbaceous plants. The main grass path centers on the Norman church beyond the garden that provides a dramatic focal point. Sixteenth-century walls are hung with ceanothus, clematis, fremontodendron, and *Wisteria sinensis*. Nearer the house, a fine wall-backed herbaceous border is best in late summer. Goodnestone is truly a garden for all seasons. VB

Penshurst Place and Gardens

Kent, England

DESIGNERS: Henry Sidney, Lanning Roper, John Codrington
OWNER: Second Viscount De L'Isle
GARDEN STYLE: Tudor, renaissance, 19th- and 20th-century formal additions
SIZE: 11 acres (4.5 ha)
CLIMATE: Temperate
LOCATION: Penshurst, Tonbridge, Kent

Penshurst Place is one of the few gardens in Britain that retains significant elements of its original late medieval and Tudor layout. In the mid-sixteenth century, fashionable renaissance ideas inspired the owner, Sir Henry Sidney, to take on the challenge of creating formal Italian-style terraced gardens close to the building. Overall, they have survived periods of neglect and changes in horticultural fashion.

Within the larger landscape, thick yew hedges, dating back to the mid-nineteenth century, form "rooms" within which a series of individual gardens has been created. Some retain features from earlier times. Others, such as the peony border and the red, white, and blue Union Jack garden, are twentieth-century additions. The style and character of these gardens vary enormously. They include an orchard, formal pool, Italianate parterre, herb gardens, and topiary. Apart from the hedges and trees, much of the planting is modern and has been designed to provide year-round interest: bulbs, hellebores, and fruit blossom in spring; the full color of the herbaceous borders and bedding in high summer; the nuts and fruit, including crab apples, in the fall.

Finances dictate the need to attract large numbers to Penshurst, and the associated events sometimes impact on the garden. Go just after opening time, though, to savor the magic of the garden—not just in the obvious features, but in details such as the simple beauty of gnarled, arthritic, espalier limbs and lichen-encrusted pools. AJ

Great Comp Garden

Kent, England

DESIGNERS: Roderick Cameron, Joyce Cameron
OWNER: Great Comp Charitable Trust
GARDEN STYLE: 20th-century
   plantsman's garden
SIZE: 7 acres (2.8 ha)
CLIMATE: Temperate
LOCATION: Platt, Borough Green, Kent

The Gothic ruins around this garden look ancient, but were built by the owner Roderick Cameron who moved, with his late wife, Joyce, to Great Comp in 1957. The ruins are actually a bit of cunning thrift. Roderick fashioned them from lumps of ironstone dug out of the garden, which were cemented together to make eccentric features among the planting.

The gardens contain at least seventy magnolia trees, with about thirty varieties, including a stately *Magnolia veitchii*. Over 50-feet (15 m) tall, it has been known to produce as many as 2,000 blooms in a season. Elsewhere, rhododendrons, conifers, heathers, and herbaceous perennials bring the tally of plants in the garden to over 3,000, all crammed into just 7 acres (2.8 ha). Large swaths are planted with ground cover plants to minimize maintenance, yet there is nothing dull about this thanks to the ingenious and creative plant combinations.

Paths crisscrossing the gardens offer ever-changing views, tempting visitors to wander off course, especially where glimpses of the ruins, a statue, or a wide expanse of lawn are purposefully provided. Near the house is the Italian Garden. Plants that would need protection from the winter cold in southern England thrive here, including a wide range of salvias, which are the great love of the garden's curator, William Dyson. As well as breeding new varieties such as 'Silas Dyson', named after his son, William runs the nursery that offers many of the first-rate plants on view in the garden. LH

Brogdale

Kent, England

DESIGNERS: Horticultural Association, The National Fruit
   Trials, Brogdale Horticultural Trust
OWNER: Brogdale Horticultural Trust
GARDEN STYLE: Orchards
SIZE: 150 acres (60.7 ha)
CLIMATE: Temperate
LOCATION: Faversham, Kent

In the Garden of England, in the heart of fruit growing country, lies Brogdale Horticultural Trust, a living museum of fruit trees spanning centuries of cultivation. It is not strictly a garden but a series of traditional, working orchards that boast every variety of apple, pear, and plum you have ever heard of—and plenty that you will not have.

This is the largest collection of fruit tree varieties in the world. There are well over 2,000 varieties of apple, including 'Decio', brought to England by the conquering Romans; 'Tower of Glamis', an eighteenth-century culinary apple from the orchards of Scotland that cooks to a sweet, pale lemon puree; and 'Red Sauce' with flesh stained delicate pink that was raised in the United States in 1910. There are also 337 varieties of plum and 502 of pear (including perry pears for producing a sparkling alcoholic brew), cherries, quinces, and medlars. The latter are often referred to in a robust Chaucerian style as "hairy arse," and they have to be nearly rotten before the flesh can be scooped out with a spoon and enjoyed. Also look out for the red, white, black, and even pink currants; nuts; grapevines; and raspberries.

Besides being preserved for posterity, the fruit trees and shrubs at Brogdale are a valuable genetic resource for growers planning to reintroduce old varieties or create new hybrids. The best times to visit are spring (for blossoms), and late summer and fall (for fruit). If you ask your tour guide nicely, you may even get to taste some. SA

Port Lympne Mansion

Kent, England

DESIGNERS: Sir Philip Sassoon, Russell Page
OWNER: Damian Aspinall
GARDEN STYLE: Arts and Crafts
SIZE: 15.5 acres (6.3 ha)
CLIMATE: Temperate
LOCATION: Lympne, Hythe, Kent

Country Life magazine described Port Lympne as the last great historic house to be built in the twentieth century, and this lovely Arts and Crafts mansion has gardens to match. The house was built for Sir Philip Sassoon, who also designed the gardens. They are set on a cliff above the English Channel, looking across Romney Marsh and out to sea (to France on a clear day), giving some superb views.

The sloping site means that the garden was laid out as terraces linked by sets of steps. The Trojan Stairs—a great sweep of 125 stone steps—lead to a terrace in front of the house. Walk east and you will find the Striped Garden, called that because of its rows of annual bedding. To the west lies the Chess Board Garden where grass and bedding plants are laid in squares. More steps lead to a vineyard on the right and a figyard on the left, again both terraced to cope with the slope. There is even a spectacular dahlia terrace where visitors will find plants that survive outside all year in the frost-free coastal climate, albeit under a protective blanket of straw during winter.

When the late animal conservationist John Aspinall bought the house in 1973, both mansion and gardens were in need of restoration. He enlisted designer Russell Page to help with the latter. You can now see a mix of historic plantings and new additions, including a collection of mock orange and penstemon. As if all this were not enough, there are 300 acres (121.5 ha) of adjoining wildlife park with elephants ambling across the Kent countryside and wolves skulking in the shrubbery. SA

Hever Castle and Gardens

Kent, England

DESIGNER: Joseph Cheal & Son
OWNER: Broadland Properties Ltd.
GARDEN STYLE: Tudor, Italianate
SIZE: 30 acres (12.1 ha)
CLIMATE: Temperate
LOCATION: Hever, Edenbridge, Kent

Dating from the thirteenth century, Hever Castle was where Anne Boleyn was raised and later courted by Henry VIII, and this Tudor link is celebrated inside and out. The castle's more recent topiary and bulb packed lawns are thanks to the wealth and enthusiasm of William Waldorf Astor, who bought Hever in 1903. The houses around the castle were demolished, the River Eden diverted, and a new Tudor village built.

Astor, who had been American minister to Italy, sought a monumental garden in which to display his Italian statuary and sculptures. He commissioned Joseph Cheal & Son to create 30 acres (12.1 ha) of gardens and 35 acres (14 ha) of lake that are impressive by any standards. Look at the 600-foot-long (183 m) buttressed Pompeian Wall that shelters Astor's collection of Roman and renaissance antiques, wonderfully canopied by extensive wisteria and underplanted by colorful bedding and small shrubs. The terraces, framed by archways, overlook the 35-acre (14 ha) lake that took 748 men two years to complete and that is decorated by W. S. Frith's 1908 fountain in Pentilic marble. The pergola here is embellished by shady grottoes inspired by the Gallery of a Hundred Fountains at the Villa d'Este in Italy.

Whatever happens, do not forget the long Rhododendron Walk leading to the Golden Stairs, and the Spring Garden and Half Moon Pool leading to the walled 4-acre (1.6 ha) Italian Garden. Historical or not, Hever is an impressive sight gardened to the highest standards, with a good sense of fun in the Water Maze—where a soaking is almost obligatory. CH

Garden Organic Yalding

Kent, England

DESIGNER: Garden Organic
OWNER: Garden Organic
GARDEN STYLE: Themed 13th- to 21st-century gardens
SIZE: 5 acres (2 ha)
CLIMATE: Temperate
LOCATION: Yalding, Maidstone, Kent

Yalding is the Kent outpost of the UK's leading organic gardening organization, Garden Organic. Sixteen gardens here bring garden history to life and encourage visitors to take up the organic way.

The history lesson starts with the Woodland Walk, which illustrates the cycles of the seasons and how early Britons cultivated the land. Farther on, the path leads to the thirteenth-century Apothecary's Garden, with plants that were cultivated for their medicinal properties. By the time visitors reach the Medieval Garden, gardening has become the preserve of lords and ladies. This remains the case in the sixteenth- and seventeenth-century formal Knot Garden, which has clipped, formal hedges symbolizing the power of the owners. In the early nineteenth-century Cottager's Garden, you can see the garden of more ordinary people, with a thatched house and intensively cultivated vegetable plot. This is in stark contrast to the Victorian Artisan's Garden, with its greenhouse and pergolas for pleasure rather than food.

In the twentieth century, visitors can see borders inspired by Gertrude Jekyll and a vegetable plot reflecting the World War II "Dig for Victory" campaign. The 1950s Allotment Garden explains the introduction of synthetic pesticides and why so many had to be banned. The Modern World's five gardens cover attracting wildlife and how to encourage children to garden. The Low Water Garden shows how to conserve water in the light of global warming. LH

Sissinghurst Castle Garden

Kent, England

DESIGNERS: Harold Nicolson, Vita Sackville-West
OWNER: The National Trust
GARDEN STYLE: Arts and Crafts
SIZE: 10 acres (4 ha)
CLIMATE: Temperate
LOCATION: Sissinghurst, Cranbrook, Kent

Thanks to its owners and creators, Sissinghurst graduated from ruinous dump in 1930 to modern icon. Harold Nicolson transformed the few remaining structures using carefully placed hedging to create an architectural backbone, while Vita Sackville-West filled the formality with a voluptuous outpouring of herbs, perennials, roses, shrubs, and climbers.

A living museum, its design and plants are readily accessible, the former clearly visible from the central tower while the latter are all clearly labeled. First time around it can be slightly confusing as garden "room" leads to yet another "room," and you are never quite sure where you are. The Rose Garden has a large D-shaped, clematis-clad wall. The roses—trained up an array of supports set inside the low box-edged beds—ensure texture and color as the season progresses. Then comes the rondelle, the Lime Walk that is stunning in spring, and the nuttery. Close by, the reds and yellows of the Cottage Garden mingle and fall across the crazy paving. There is more—the Azalea Walk, the Herb Garden with a Persian carpet created out of thyme, and the orchard. Leave the best for last. The famous White Garden, which spawned a thousand imitations, peaks in early summer with its centerpiece, a mock-Gothic arbor designed by the Nicolsons' son, Nigel, covered in *Rosa mulliganii*. CH

RIGHT In this cottage-style planting at Sissinghurst, Sackville-West specifically chose plants for their vivid "sunset" palette.

Stoneacre

Kent, England

DESIGNERS: Graham Fraser, Richard Nott
OWNER: The National Trust
GARDEN STYLE: 21st-century reworking of an Arts
and Crafts garden
SIZE: 1.5 acres (0.6 ha)
CLIMATE: Temperate
LOCATION: Otham, Maidstone, Kent

In 1928 the antiquarian Aymer Vallance left his house, a temple to the Arts and Crafts movement, to the National Trust. Today, two contemporary designers—the tenants—have breathed new life into Stoneacre. They have given this dramatic house an exhilarating setting—modern, bold, and full of joie de vivre.

Although the house remains a treasury of Arts and Crafts artifacts, Richard Nott and Graham Fraser felt strongly that the garden must not be a museum piece. With little previous gardening experience, they called on their fashion skills to make a garden that would complement the graphic architecture of the house. They stripped away huge climbers to reveal black-and-white timbering, and surrounded it with flamboyant new plantings. Cannas and hardy bananas tap on the library windows, and pots of the castor oil plant (Ricinus communis) and kangaroo paw jostle around the doors. The color palette is sumptuous—reds and purples, burgundies and golds, all set off by crisp balls and pyramids of box.

The garden progresses through a series of "rooms"—an entrance court, a hedged enclosure with formal borders, and a Mediterranean bank garden. To the rear is a courtyard. It is jam packed with tulips in spring, while in summer massed containers of eucomis, ligularia, pelargonium, and the chocolate plant (Cosmos atrosanguineus) mirror the colors of the house. A low wall divides it from the orchard, where a summerhouse looks out over the meadows.

Although gardening is generally a shared enterprise, Fraser and Nott have each used a "room" of their own to indulge their planting passions. Fraser has chosen the inner garden, replanting the long-standing red and purple borders with astrantias and cannas, and with broody, purple eupatorium. Nott has replanted the entrance court with grasses, golden flowers, and phormium—a lively, richly textured welcome to a joyous, life enhancing garden. AE

Scotney Castle Garden

Kent, England

DESIGNERS: Edward Hussey III, William Sawrey Gilpin
OWNER: The National Trust
GARDEN STYLE: Picturesque
SIZE: 24 acres (9.7 ha)
CLIMATE: Temperate
LOCATION: Lamberhurst, Tunbridge Wells, Kent

If you would like to surprise someone, try leading them blindfolded to the balustraded bastion (a lookout point) in Scotney Castle Garden and then whipping the blindfold off with a flourish. You will be guaranteed to hear a gasp of delight. You could even quote some eighteenth-century poetry by Richard Payne Knight to complete the effect: "Blessed too is he, who, 'midst his tufted trees, Some ruin'd castle's lofty towers sees." This view of a fourteenth-century moated castle in ruins, nestling in the valley, has to be one of the most romantic in England. In spring, when the azaleas are in full bloom, it is breathtaking.

Edward Hussey III saw its potential when he inherited the Scotney Castle estate in the mid-1830s. He set about building an Elizabethan-style country house on a terrace overlooking the castle ruins, using stone quarried from the slope below. Steps run down through the shady quarry that is planted with ferns, heavily scented azaleas, hardy fuchsias, and willow gentians. The lawns that slope toward the moat are carpeted with snowdrops, then primroses and narcissi, and there are beds of the pink- and white-flowered mountain laurel (*Kalmia latifolia*).

The walls of the ruined castle drip with white wisteria, climbing roses, lilacs and vines, and the borders around it are filled with a profusion of roses and herbaceous perennials. The colors here are soft and mellow so that the overall effect, with the stone of the castle acting as a backdrop, is magical. Herbs, planted in a series of semicircular beds, surround a carved stone Venetian wellhead. PM

Walmer Castle and Gardens

Kent, England

DESIGNERS: Successive Lord Wardens (including William Pitt and Earl Granville), Penelope Hobhouse

OWNER: English Heritage

GARDEN STYLE: 17th-century formal Italianate, 19th-century formal and informal, 20th-century additions

SIZE: 10 acres (4 ha)

CLIMATE: Temperate

LOCATION: Walmer, Deal, Kent

Walmer Castle is the sort of castle you could imagine living in—small, manageable, and cozy, with gardens on a similar scale. As you approach the low cluster of buildings, evergreen oaks can be seen outside the walls. Within are an immaculate croquet lawn, free-form topiary, and herbaceous borders flanked by mature yew hedges. The moat has been grassed over since the nineteenth century and is planted with fuchsias, hydrangeas, and lilacs, while fruit trees are trained along encircling walls. A kitchen garden has pear and apple trees, beans, and sweet peas, all fenced off with a latticework of living willow.

Once part of Henry VIII's coastal defenses, the castle became the official residence of the Lord Warden of the Cinque Ports in 1708. Incumbents over the years have included the Duke of Wellington and, more recently, the Queen Mother. Penelope Hobhouse designed a commemorative garden in her honor. It opened in 1997 and features a formal lily pool, colonnaded summerhouse, evergreen plantings in the shape of an "E," and exuberant mixed borders.

Each generation has added its own elements to the castle gardens, including the yew-lined Broad Walk, the woodland plantation, and the grass terraces. The most recent restoration project has been the greenhouses, now housing succulents, scented indoor plants, ferns, and seasonal displays. These gardens have flourished for three centuries and look set to carry on for many more years. SA

Hampton Court Palace

Surrey, England

DESIGNERS: Various, including Henry VIII,
William III, Mary II
OWNERS: Queen Elizabeth II, Historic Royal Palaces
GARDEN STYLE: Tudor, Stuart, classical French,
baroque
SIZE: 60 acres (24.3 ha)
CLIMATE: Temperate
LOCATION: East Molesey, Surrey

The earliest, relatively modest gardens at Hampton Court Palace were created for Cardinal Wolsey, probably on the site of the present Fountain Court. However, it was under the auspices of Henry VIII that today's ground plan largely took shape, although the king was more interested in the sport and spectacle of the tiltyard and deer park. The gardens were formalized in a *patte d'oie* design after Mollet by Charles II, and vastly improved in the baroque manner under William and Mary, although Queen Anne subsequently tried to obliterate all memory of her Dutch brother-in-law. Five hundred checkered years of royal gardening make Hampton Court fascinating to historians and a source of controversy for would-be restorers. What period to evoke? And how to show the many footprints of time? As far as visitors are concerned, though, it is best to enter into the spirit of the place, treating your trip as one glorious pageant.

The stateliest approach to Hampton Court is by Thames riverboat from Westminster. In July the Royal Horticultural Society's flower show is held here, and if you visit at the end of August, be sure to buy a bunch of Black Hamburgh (*Vitis vinifera* 'Schiava Grossa') grapes. The Great Vine, planted by Capability Brown in 1768, is the oldest in the world and produces around 700 pounds (320 kg) of fruit in a good year. Also make a point of seeing the Privy Garden, Knot Garden, Pond Gardens, and Maze. RC

Jellicoe Roof Garden

Surrey, England

DESIGNER: Geoffrey Jellicoe
OWNER: House of Fraser
GARDEN STYLE: 20th-century modernist roof garden
SIZE: 0.2 acre (0.08 ha)
CLIMATE: Temperate
LOCATION: Guildford, Surrey

In 1956, the first modern British roof garden of any size was designed by Geoffrey Jellicoe for Harvey's Department Store (now a House of Fraser store) in Guildford. It was a garden that was resolutely modern, expressing the same spirit of optimism and innovation epitomized by the 1951 Festival of Britain. It shared the same joy in bold, abstract shapes; the same delight in modern materials; and the same democratic desire to create worthy spaces for ordinary people.

Jellicoe once described it as his "sky-garden," and it is, indeed, a water garden in the sky. Rows of white concrete stepping stones, planters, and viewing platforms (once gaily topped by sun umbrellas) are scattered across a still expanse of water, arranged around a rooftop restaurant. In its simplicity, it recalls Japanese water gardens, a theme developed in a refurbishment carried out by House of Fraser in 2000 that has far more evocative planting than the original.

Jellicoe might not have been a plantsman, but he was a great conceptual thinker. This garden, designed in the year of the first Russian space mission, is meant to be a hymn to the sky. The reflecting water, poised in midair, makes the sky appear below as well as above. The circular stepping stones and planters wheeling around the pool suggest the orbit of Sputnik. Unfortunately, modern health and safety fears preclude entry to the garden, but it can still be enjoyed from any window table in the store's restaurant. AE

The Isabella Plantation

Surrey, England

DESIGNER: Unknown
OWNER: The Royal Parks Agency
GARDEN STYLE: 20th-century woodland garden
SIZE: 42 acres (17 ha)
CLIMATE: Temperate
LOCATION: Richmond Park, Richmond, Surrey

On the southwest edge of London, Richmond Park is Europe's largest walled park. In the center of the park, hidden like a secret garden, is the magnificent woodland garden known as the Isabella Plantation.

Streams and ponds line the paths that meander through the garden under a shady canopy of native oak, birch, and beech, exotic magnolias, and the occasional handkerchief tree (*Davidia involucrata*). In early spring there is a mass of bluebells, and primroses emerge in the clearings. In late spring and early summer, however, the garden really comes alive thanks to the collection of rhododendrons, azaleas, and camellias. Since they are packed together, they form a breathtaking tapestry of vibrant red, yellow, purple, orange, pink, and white, all reflected in the still waters of the garden's ponds. In fact the combination of fertile soil under the canopy of mature trees and the cooling effect of the streams provides the perfect conditions for rhododendrons and azaleas. Many were first brought to Europe by the plant explorer Ernest Wilson, and the plantation has fifty cultivars of azalea introduced by him.

Both Richmond Park and the Isabella Plantation are full of native British wildlife. However, interlopers, in the form of flocks of squawking, bright-green parakeets, occasionally interrupt the tranquility. Aptly enough, like many of the rhododendrons and azaleas in the garden, the birds are natives of the Himalayan foothills. If you stroll through the garden when the rhododendrons are flowering and the parakeets are swooping around, you could be in the Himalayas. JHo

Claremont Landscape Garden

Surrey, England

DESIGNERS: Charles Bridgeman, William Kent, and others
OWNER: The National Trust
GARDEN STYLE: 18th-century English landscape
SIZE: 50 acres (20.2 ha)
CLIMATE: Temperate
LOCATION: Esher, Surrey

Claremont's turf amphitheater is an icon of eighteenth-century landscaping. In 1726 it inspired the poet Alexander Pope to build his Bridgmannick Theatre at Twickenham. As Pope's name for his theater suggests, the amphitheater at Claremont is by Charles Bridgeman—the list of landscapers who worked here reads like a roll call of some of the greatest British garden designers, ranging from Sir John Vanbrugh (who once owned the place) to William Kent and Capability Brown.

Kent deformalized and enlarged the lake at the base of the amphitheater and added a cascade. The latter is now a stalactite and feldspar crystal-encrusted grotto and seems similar, although smaller, to the grotto at nearby Painshill Park (see page 384), created by the great grotto makers of the day, Joseph and Josiah Lane of Tisbury. Kent also removed Bridgeman's obelisk from the original lake and added the island and pavilion in its center. Contemporary accounts mention fishing parties and picnics in the cozy pavilion interior, which had a kitchen to one side. There was also a thatched house—the one you can see today is a smaller replacement—and a temple called Nine Pin Alley. Typically, this landscape was a playground as much as a visual feast. The specimen trees, bar the magnificent cedars of Lebanon (*Cedrus libani*), were added in the nineteenth century when Queen Victoria (who bought the estate for her youngest son) was a regular visitor.

Today the entrance is at the bottom of the hill, although this landscape was designed to be seen from the castellated belvedere. Views from this garden are as important as the garden itself. Here Kent, who famously "leaped the fence and saw that all nature was a garden," introduced a series of sunken fences so that the surrounding landscape could be viewed without impediment and so be incorporated into the overall design. JO

Munstead Wood

Surrey, England

DESIGNER: Gertrude Jekyll
OWNERS: Sir Robert Clark, Lady Clark
GARDEN STYLE: Edwardian
SIZE: 10 acres (4 ha)
CLIMATE: Temperate
LOCATION: Busbridge, Godalming, Surrey

There are few more illustrious English gardeners than Gertrude Jekyll. It is fitting, then, that one should make a pilgrimage to her garden in Surrey, where she lived and gardened for more than thirty years, and devised some of the theories that feature in her books, such as *Wood and Garden* (1899) and *Colour in the Flower Garden* (1908). It is also thrilling for garden lovers to walk the paths she walked and to see for themselves the planting schemes she devised.

Munstead Wood has now been split into several plots. The house that her working partner Edwin Lutyens designed in 1896 covers the largest area. As far as the garden goes, the current owners, Sir Robert and Lady Clark, with help from various head gardeners, have done a commendable job in restoring its best-known features. The Spring Garden is now very similar to how it appeared in Jekyll's day, with drifts of narcissi, primroses, and irises mixed with aubretia, white arabis, and purple and scarlet tulips. Jekyll's famous Munstead bunch primroses still feature, as do the azaleas and rhododendrons she planted, and the river of daffodils running through the woodland garden. The nut walk was replanted in 1989 and is now maturing well.

The herbaceous border remains a splendid illustration of Jekyll's planting skill. Colors move from fiery reds, oranges, and yellows at one end to blues, grays, and lilacs at the other. It is 200 feet (60.9 m) long and 14 feet (4.3 m) wide, broken only in the middle by a wooden door in the high sandstone wall that backs the border. PM

Bury Court

Surrey, England

DESIGNERS: Piet Oudolf, Christopher
  Bradley-Hole
OWNER: John Coke
GARDEN STYLE: Contemporary, naturalistic
SIZE: 3 acres (1.2 ha)
CLIMATE: Temperate
LOCATION: Bentley, Surrey

When Green Farm Plants, the nursery owned by John Coke, moved to Bury Court in 1996 the place was a working farm. The enclosed courtyard, then covered in concrete, was an obvious site for a display garden, and a fortuitous visit by the Dutch designer Piet Oudolf resulted in his very first garden in England.

The design is strongly asymmetrical, with clipped shapes in box and yew acting as focal points, and they contrast with the seven borders planted with the classic range of Oudolf perennials. They were carefully selected for their variety of color and form, and for their ability to evoke a natural meadow or prairie landscape. Grasses play a major role, and every border includes some, while many naturally occurring species of flowering plants—for example some lesser-known umbellifers—enhance the wild look. He also uses cultivars of more typical border plants like monardas, phlox, asters, achilleas, and veronicas, all included for their unparalleled richness of color and contrasting flower shapes, while others have been selected for their striking winter silhouettes.

The newer, quite separate front garden by Christopher Bradley-Hole attempts to show the value of minimalism. A grid of twenty-two 13-foot square (4 m) beds, rigidly contained within raised sides of used steel, are planted with a range of grasses and are intersected by paths of compacted gravel. The garden reaches a height of 6.5–10 feet (2–3 m) in summer, giving the impression that you're walking through a dreamlike meadow. JC

RHS Garden Wisley

Surrey, England

DESIGNERS: Various
OWNER: Royal Horticultural Society
GARDEN STYLE: 20th-century themed demonstration
  gardens, plantsman's garden
SIZE: 240 acres (97.2 ha)
CLIMATE: Temperate
LOCATION: Woking, Surrey

The Royal Horticultural Society (RHS) took over the garden at Wisley in 1903. It was a gift from Sir Thomas Hanbury enabling the RHS to move its garden out of Chiswick and the cramped, polluted environs of London. At the time some viewed it as a risky strategy. Wisley, though, is now one of Britain's most popular gardens, with around 750,000 visitors annually.

The RHS mission is to encourage and develop horticulture in all its forms and that sets the tone for the garden. You can walk up one of the finest and largest double mixed borders in the world and then find yourself in a country garden designed by Penelope Hobhouse. Other highlights include a series of award-winning model gardens transplanted from the Chelsea Flower Show; terrific displays in the Orchid House; classic, formal gardens designed by Geoffrey Jellicoe and Lanning Roper; vast collections of heathers; swaths of delphiniums undergoing trials; blazing displays of azaleas; perfect rows of cabbages; bold Piet Oudolf borders; and glorious rose gardens.

The missionary zeal of the RHS in promoting horticulture has made any overall unity of style and design impossible at Wisley. There is simply too much going on. It would be wrong, however, to think that this busyness impairs the beauty of Wisley. A day spent here is not just a walk around a garden. It is an immersion in all things horticultural. AM

RIGHT Wisley is beautiful and practical—the gardens are used to demonstrate innovative design and cultivation techniques.

The Savill Garden

Surrey, England

DESIGNER: Eric Savill
OWNER: Crown Estate
GARDEN STYLE: 20th-century woodland garden
SIZE: 35 acres (14.1 ha)
CLIMATE: Temperate
LOCATION: The Great Park, Windsor, Surrey

In the early 1930s, King George V and Queen Mary asked one of their park rangers to create a garden for them in an unpromising corner of Windsor Great Park. On a rolling, boggy site, dominated by massive oaks and horse chestnuts (*Aesculus hippocastanum*), Eric Savill managed to create the finest woodland garden in England. It's no wonder, then, that this beautiful garden was named after him.

The garden is a collection of several gardens that seamlessly merge together. The woodland garden, though, is the high point. In spring, rivers of *Narcissus bulbocodium* and other dwarf bulbs flow around collections of magnolias, camellias, and rhododendrons. Woodland paths meander among ferns, herbaceous perennials, and massed plantings of primulas. There is nothing half-done here. Thousands of hostas flourish among breathtaking carpets of blue Himalayan poppies (*Meconopsis betonicifolia*). By midsummer, the focus of the garden shifts from the coolness of the woodland to the fiery herbaceous borders and scent-filled rose garden. Away from this excitement are the formal beds of the Golden Jubilee Garden, made to celebrate the accession of Queen Elizabeth II to the throne and planted in a froth of pastel colors. What is certainly very surprising for a nation of garden lovers is that Eric Savill is one of the very few professional gardeners to have received a knighthood. He deserved it. JHo

LEFT The majestic, ever-changing beauty of Eric Savill's woodland garden is a delight throughout the year.

Vale End

Surrey, England

DESIGNERS: John Foulsham, Daphne Foulsham
OWNERS: John Foulsham, Daphne Foulsham
GARDEN STYLE: 20th-century cottage garden
SIZE: 1 acre (0.4 ha)
CLIMATE: Temperate
LOCATION: Albury, Guildford, Surrey

This cottage-style garden at the foot of the North Downs is on sandy soil on a steep, west-facing slope. The richly planted borders around sweeping lawns at different levels make the most of the charming view—of wooded hills encircling a millpond—beyond the old garden walls.

Plants rising high above the wall in the lowest border are chosen for their see-through qualities so as not to obscure the landscape. There are wafting miscanthus and frothy thalictrums, plume poppies, and the palm-leaf marshmallow (*Althaea cannabina*), all found towering above cottage-garden favorites such as blue delphiniums, border phlox, achilleas, and sedums. The owners—the Foulshams—welcome linarias in the shaded sitting area and encourage lady's mantle (*Alchemilla mollis*) to blur path edges, but they "edit" vigorously so nothing is obscured.

Pink roses—'Pompon de Paris', 'Blairii Number Two', and 'New Dawn'—festoon the catenary on the garden's upper level, along with vines, clematis, and wisteria. Daphne Foulsham grows striped *Rosa mundi* (*Rosa gallica* 'Versicolor') beneath the old apple trees on the tea lawn. She loves old rose blooms, particularly 'Charity' and 'Generous Gardener', bred by David Austin and named on behalf of the National Gardens Scheme when she was chairperson from 1994 to 2002. The Foulshams adore their garden, but admit that it takes hard work They love visitors and "work like lunatics" to prepare for open days, but they add, "The garden is not too manicured, because its main purpose is simply for being in." EH

Vann

Surrey, England

DESIGNERS: William Douglas Caroe, Gertrude Jekyll
OWNER: Mary Caroe
GARDEN STYLE: Arts and Crafts
SIZE: 5 acres (2 ha)
CLIMATE: Temperate
LOCATION: Hambledon, Godalming, Surrey

The gardens at Vann are at their best in spring and early summer. The house is an amalgam of historic styles completed belatedly in 1907 by the Arts and Crafts architect William Douglas Caroe. He incorporated the existing barn, put a suitable wellhead in the center of the drive, and built an attached stone pergola that leads to the lakes.

The front of Vann fulfills the green court look so beloved of the Arts and Crafts movement—a straight path in local brick leading to the front door through a yew hedge. Primroses and forget-me-nots, lavender, and alchemilla gently congregate in the flowerbeds. The pergola around the south side of the house is an architectural highlight, swathed in clematis and wisteria, and offset by displays of seasonal containers.

Caroe split the garden into yew-hedged "rooms" that still exist, but his former large kitchen garden has been transformed into double mixed borders. Above the lake, he diverted the stream through a rockery-cum-brook, almost invisible under the spring flowers. The narrow beds that flank it are packed with native and naturalized flowers, contrasting with the dark green of the enclosing yew hedge. Below the lake, Caroe wanted to create a water garden that evolved into woodland, but he was dissatisfied with his attempts. In 1911 he approached Gertrude Jekyll, who was living just a few miles away at Munstead Wood (see page 378). With consummate skill, she designed the lower water garden with her hallmark plantings of hostas, rodgersias, ferns, and irises leading into the natural woodland. CH

Painshill Park

Surrey, England

DESIGNER: The Hon. Charles Hamilton
OWNER: The Painshill Park Trust
GARDEN STYLE: 18th-century landscape park
SIZE: 168 acres (68 ha)
CLIMATE: Temperate
LOCATION: Cobham, Surrey

In 1738, the young Charles Hamilton took out a lease on some unpromising land by the River Mole and began to create a new kind of garden—a garden as a journey through the emotions. The centerpiece was a natural-looking lake. Around it Hamilton created "living pictures" inspired by the art and architecture he had admired on the Grand Tour. While walking around a carefully designed circuit, viewers would come across buildings, vistas, or garden features calculated to provoke dramatic changes of mood. A hillside was crowned by a classical temple of Bacchus, while a rustic hermitage was hidden away in a gloomy wood. Coming to a bleak mausoleum, visitors were astonished to pass through "the arch of death" onto a sunny riverbank with views across the Mole.

Hamilton was clever at manipulating landscape for dramatic effect, nowhere more so than in his Gothic temple where the land falls unexpectedly away to reveal the lake below. Most wonderful of all was a grotto, a mermaid cave hung with stalactites and glittering with crystal, with water running naturalistically down the walls. It is no surprise to learn that Charles Hamilton was always short of money. Parts of his garden buildings were made of papier-mâché or wood painted like stone. In the end, he had to sell Painshill. It remained in loving hands until the 1940s when it fell into decline. It was rescued in 1980 by Elmbridge Borough Council, which set up a restoration trust. The original plantings have been reinstated and, after painstaking research, many garden buildings faithfully reconstructed. AE

Hannah Peschar Sculpture Garden

Surrey, England

DESIGNERS: Anthony Paul, Hannah Peschar
OWNERS: Anthony Paul, Hannah Peschar
GARDEN STYLE: 20th- and 21st century naturalistic, exotic
SIZE: 10 acres (4 ha)
CLIMATE: Temperate
LOCATION: Ockley, Surrey

If there was ever a garden to make you jealous, it is the Hannah Peschar Sculpture Garden. Just 32 miles (51 km) from London, secreted in the gentle folds of the North Downs, the potent mix of woodland, running water, and art will leave you drooling. The garden has been designed by the landscape designer Anthony Paul. His deft, almost invisible touch creates an air of intimacy that is usually achieved only in private gardens. His bold, but subtle, handling of plants in a natural setting with a restrained use of color and lashings of chiaroscuro make this one of the most dramatic and yet serene landscapes in the UK. Paul, together with his wife, Hannah, has turned a secret glade into one of Britain's best-loved sculpture gardens. Working with over 100 sculptors, Peschar has selected many exciting artworks, most of which are by British artists. They are carefully sited in, and framed by, the landscape. And because they are on sale, the show is never the same.

Water also plays a prominent part. It is carefully channeled into ponds and rivulets to isolate and enhance the cottage where the owners live, accentuating the peace and beauty of its position. Bridges and waterfalls add mystery and excitement to the visitor's journey through the garden, while meandering paths reveal subtly juxtaposed natural woodland and subdued, ornamental revelry. Note how much of the garden's success lies in the careful handling of space between bold groupings of plants and the existing trees that form the backbone of the garden. A great success. CWe

Winkworth Arboretum

Surrey, England

DESIGNER: Dr. Wilfred Fox
OWNER: The National Trust
GARDEN STYLE: 20th-century arboretum
SIZE: 123 acres (49.8 ha)
CLIMATE: Temperate
LOCATION: Godalming, Surrey

Thousands of rare specimens have been planted at Winkworth, making it one of the most important tree collections in the UK. The arboretum was started in 1937 by Dr. Wilfred Fox, a renowned dermatologist, who bought woodland from the neighboring estate. Over the next thirty years, he planted masses of trees and shrubs, often calling on the professional help of W. J. Bean, the famous curator of London's Royal Botanic Gardens at Kew (see right).

Oaks, liquidambars, tupelos, stewartias, maples, and birches dominate, among them six record-breaking trees. The garden also has a National Collection of whitebeam, and includes the large-leaved *Sorbus* 'Wilfred Fox'. With so many trees the arboretum has a big show of fall color, but spring is equally impressive. Magnolias, scented witch hazel, and camellias come into flower, while carpets of bluebells spread far into the distance. There are also hundreds of azaleas, at their most impressive flanking the Azalea Steps, a 100-step outdoor staircase. The view across the massed ranks of carmine, pink, and white flowers is breathtaking.

In 1952 Fox handed over part of his arboretum to the National Trust and the remaining part five years later. However, he remained an influence over its management until he died in 1962. Work continues on its development. Recent projects include turning a leaking reservoir into a wetland area, and adding an ecofriendly, recycled plastic boardwalk. MC

Royal Botanic Gardens, Kew

Surrey, England

DESIGNERS: Various
OWNER: Trustees of the Royal Botanic Gardens
GARDEN STYLE: Formal
SIZE: 300 acres (121.5 ha)
CLIMATE: Temperate
LOCATION: Kew, Richmond, Surrey

This garden, also known as Kew Gardens, is arguably the world's number one botanical garden. Its unrivaled plant collection is the largest and most comprehensive anywhere. The constantly evolving garden is a who's who of great British landscape designers: William Nesfield, Charles Bridgeman, Capability Brown, and William Kent, who designed the famous pagoda. The architecture could not be better—there is a combination of Victorian elegance in Decimus Burton's Temperate and Palm House and contemporary excitement in both the Princess of Wales Conservatory and the new Alpine House. Also look out for the Museum of Economic Botany, the Marianne North art gallery, Kew Palace, Queen Charlotte's Cottage, several temples, and a bridge known as the Sackler Crossing.

The glorious plant collections, maintained to the highest standards, range from arboretum, woodland, and rock garden to the stunning beds, Berberis Dell, Holly Walk, and Winter Garden. In the greenhouses are plants from alpine zones, desert, and tropical rain forests. There is also a display of marine habitats in the basement of the Palm House. Impressive stuff from a garden that began as a physic garden of 9 acres (3.6 ha) in 1759, set in royal pleasure grounds. In 2003 Kew became a UNESCO World Heritage Site. MB

RIGHT The Sackler Crossing, spanning the main lake, references Capability Brown's love of undulating curves in its design.

Loseley Park

Surrey, England

DESIGNERS: Michael More-Molyneux, Sarah More Molyneux
OWNERS: Michael More-Molyneux, Sarah More-Molyneux
GARDEN STYLE: 20th-century informal, Gertrude Jekyll
SIZE: 6.5 acres (2.6 ha)
CLIMATE: Temperate
LOCATION: Compton, Guildford, Surrey

Sir William More's Elizabethan manor house at Loseley Park is one of the finest in Surrey and has the distinction of having remained in the More family to this day. The current generation has turned its hand to producing delicious Jersey ice cream, but since 1993 the restoration and creation of 2.5 acres (1 ha) of walled gardens with planted periphery walks have been high on the agenda.

The lawns and majestic trees that frame the facade of the house belie the horticultural activities within the walled garden. Its design is inspired by Gertrude Jekyll, who was a neighbor. The layout consists of a series of quadripartite gardens where you can lose yourself as you wander along the vine walk and into a rose garden with over 1,000 old-fashioned roses elegantly laid out in box-edged beds, with a gazebo in the center. The White Garden is a microcosm of the White Garden at Sissinghurst in Kent (see page 370). It has large-scale plantings of white flowers, and silver and gray foliage that contrast with the fiery red borders elsewhere in the ornamental garden. There are organically grown vegetables, including striking specimens of super-sized chard and an excellent range of over 200 herbs that illustrate there is so much more to herbs than green leaves. It is also home to a collection of rare and heritage plants grown for their seeds. Following that, visit the grand fountain gardens and then take a walk along the raised bed by the ornamental canal looking away across the countryside. This is English gardening at its best—traditional, but distinct. CH

Bicton Park Botanical Gardens

Devon, England

DESIGNER: Unknown

OWNER: Bicton Park Botanical Gardens

GARDEN STYLE: 18th- and 19th-century formal, parkland

SIZE: 63 acres (25.5 ha)

CLIMATE: Temperate

LOCATION: East Budleigh, Budleigh Salterton, Devon

Starting life in about 1735, the collection of gardens at Bicton Park is as diverse as it is large, and reflects nearly two centuries of changing horticultural styles and fashions. The earliest is the Italian Garden that took its inspiration from Versailles and was reputedly laid out to a design by André Le Nôtre. Sweeping down from the conservatory, the borders and flower beds, with brightly colored displays of bedding plants in the summer months, were nineteenth-century additions. So, too, was the Rose Garden, although its neighbor, the Mediterranean Garden with its show of drought-tolerant plants, is a more recent addition.

The American and Stream Gardens were created in the 1830s when, to have a collection of plants from "across the pond," was all the rage. The Hermitage Garden, the centerpiece of which is a rustic garden house, was built to overlook the waterfalls, ponds, and a notable gathering of dwarf conifers.

Full-sized conifers are a feature of the Pinetum with over 1,000 specimens and 300 species, among which are twenty-five champion trees. At 135 feet (41 m) high, the Grecian fir (*Abies cephalonica*) is the tallest ever recorded in the UK. The area increased in size in 1910 to accommodate new plants introduced from China by the plant hunter Ernest Wilson. A new-old feature is the restored Victorian Fernery, and ferns have been replanted in the rocks surrounding the flint Shell House, home to a wonderful collection of seashells. However, perhaps the garden's greatest treasure is the striking curvilinear palm house, built between 1825 and 1830. TM

Castle Drogo

Devon, England

DESIGNERS: Edwin Lutyens, George Dillistone
OWNER: The National Trust
GARDEN STYLE: 1920s formal, woodland
SIZE: 12 acres (4.8 ha)
CLIMATE: Temperate
LOCATION: Drewsteignton, Devon

Castle Drogo was one of the last true country houses to be built in Britain. Designed by Edwin Lutyens between 1910 and 1930, it looks like a cross between a medieval fortress and a power plant. Then again, it is located in Dartmoor with its singular, uncompromisingly open, dramatic landscape.

The drive winds its way past blocks of yew—echoing the bluff character of the house—and a naturalistic planting scheme of native shrubs and wild roses in which Gertrude Jekyll, with whom Lutyens regularly collaborated, had a hand. The garden sits to the north of the house, behind yew hedges, and is divided into two distinct areas with a woodland backdrop of oak and beech. The substantial sunken garden is dominated by a Persian ironwood (*Parrotia persica*) in each corner, trained over a metal frame to form an arbor. A pair of central lawns are edged with abundantly planted borders on each side, while the influence of Lutyens' architectural hand is evident in the Mughal-style, scalloped shape of the paths, which run through the planting. To one side, steps lead to a scented herb garden, and then to a grove of magnolias, Japanese maples, and azaleas. This grove leads to a lawn originally designed for tennis, enclosed by a vast circular yew hedge. The emptiness of the space acts as the classic palette cleanser for the mind after the richness of the planting elsewhere.

Castle Drogo is an unusual garden, one that balances a strong sense of architecture with good planting—befittingly, the garden avoids self-conscious prettiness. It is at its best in early summer. NK

Hotel Endsleigh

Devon, England

DESIGNER: Humphry Repton
OWNER: Alex Polizzi
GARDEN STYLE: Regency picturesque
SIZE: 108 acres (43.7 ha)
CLIMATE: Temperate
LOCATION: Milton Abbot, Tavistock, Devon

In the early part of the nineteenth century, Georgiana, the Duchess of Bedford, came upon a small thatched cottage on the duke's west-country estate. She was captivated by its rural isolation and its "picturesque beauties"; it was a world away from the hubbub of the family seat at Woburn Abbey. She instructed Humphry Repton, who had designed the classic landscape at Woburn (see page 328), to create a garden that would meld into the landscape and subsume the cottage orné in vines, creepers, and lush vegetation. She wanted to live a simple, rustic life, but with all the comforts of home, namely hunting lodges,

stables, a dairy, salmon larder, and a Swiss cottage set in its own alpine garden, with dozens of servants, grooms, and chambermaids. Repton designed canals to carry water throughout the garden down to the River Tamar below, with ponds, cascades, fountains, a swimming pool, and a basin of water set in the floor of the Shell House, engineered to startle unwary visitors with sudden, mellifluously flatulent belches.

As for the planting here, the Duke of Bedford was a latter-day plantaholic, bankrolling the early nineteenth-century plant hunters to bring him seeds. Now, 200 years later, the garden can boast the widest Caucasian fir (*Abies nordmanniana*), the largest stand of golden bamboo (*Phyllostachys aurea*), and the British national champion weeping beech (*Fagus sylvatica* 'Pendula'). Meanwhile, the old buildings have been converted into a country house hotel, the canals repaired, and the weeds and the thorns cleared. Georgiana would have been delighted. SG

Coleton Fishacre House and Garden

Devon, England

DESIGNERS: Oswald Milne, Edward White,
  Lady Dorothy D'Oyly Carte
OWNER: The National Trust
GARDEN STYLE: Edwardian with Arts and Crafts elements
SIZE: 20 acres (8.1 ha)
CLIMATE: Temperate
LOCATION: Coleton, Kingswear, Dartmouth, Devon

Created in 1925 for Lady Dorothy D'Oyly Carte, this garden is one that should really be kept a secret for fear of it becoming too popular on the garden visiting circuit. It is a garden to stumble across while driving along Devon's country roads and is one of those few places that manages to retain the character and intimacy of a private garden while benefiting from the care and security of a national organization.

Located in a county with a mild climate and positioned within a protected river estuary, it is a plant lovers' delight. Familiar garden plants rub shoulders with tender and exotic specimens without the latter appearing like uncomfortable antipodean relatives. Combine this mouthwatering planting with the structural bones provided by Lutyens-inspired hard landscaping, and the beautiful location and views, and what more could you want? Away from the house and the Seemly Terrace, the formal gardens, bowling-green lawn, herbaceous border, and the iris-planted brook, a path leads to a breathtaking view of the valley below. It meanders steeply through a wooded area, down to the sea.

The garden forces the visitor's pace to slow to an amble so that every plant, view, and moment is savored. It reflects a golden age of gardening, long past, when the wealthy owned country retreats where they made exquisite gardens, immaculately cared for by teams of gardeners. Financial restraints aside, Coleton Fishacre still maintains the gentility and dignity of a bygone era. AJ

Killerton

Devon, England

DESIGNERS: Sir Thomas Acland, John Veitch, John Coutts, William Robinson
OWNER: The National Trust
GARDEN STYLE: 18th- to 20th-century informal, woodland
SIZE: 21 acres (8.5 ha)
CLIMATE: Temperate
LOCATION: Broadclyst, Exeter, Devon

The garden at Killerton was started in the 1770s by Sir Thomas Acland and James Veitch. Veitch was founder of one of the most important British nurseries ever, and one of the first to invest in plant hunting abroad. Not surprisingly, there are many first introductions here, all of great historical and genetic importance.

Near the house is a large terrace with mixed borders, part of what was once a much larger scheme designed by William Robinson in around 1900. Mediterranean and warm-climate plants are now a particular feature here. Another early twentieth-century period piece is the rock garden planted with Japanese maples, ferns, and primulas. Nearby stands a splendid rustic-style, fussily decorated summerhouse called the Bear's Hut that was, alarmingly, originally built to house an American black bear.

The property's private chapel stands in its own tree-dominated garden, where you will find some of the oldest wellingtonia (*Sequoiadendron giganteum*) in Britain. Other conifers include Japanese cedar (*Cryptomeria japonica*) and *Taiwania cryptomerioides*. Notable deciduous trees include cork oak (*Quercus suber*), Japanese walnut (*Juglans ailanthifolia*), and a Japanese zelkova (*Zelkova serrata*).

Large numbers of rhododendrons, azaleas, and cherries make for a very colorful scene in spring and early summer. There are also extensive drifts of daffodils—many old or rare varieties. Anyone who loves plants, particularly trees, should enjoy this garden at any time of the year. NK

The Garden House

Devon, England

DESIGNER: Lionel Fortescue, Katherine Fortescue, Keith Wiley

OWNER: The Fortescue Garden Trust

GARDEN STYLE: 20th-century naturalistic garden

SIZE: 8 acres (3.2 ha)

CLIMATE: Temperate

LOCATION: Buckland Monachorum, Yelverton, Devon

"The church provides a focus for one of many superb views..."

The Garden House has been greatly admired in recent years for its outstanding naturalistic planting carried out by former head gardener Keith Wiley. The core of the garden stems from 1945 when Lionel Fortescue, a notoriously exacting Eton schoolmaster, started a walled garden around the ruins of the sixteenth-century vicarage of Buckland Monachorum. When Henry VIII dissolved England's monasteries, the last abbot of Buckland Abbey, less than 1 mile (1.6 km) away, became vicar of Buckland Monachorum. The church provides a focus for one of many superb views from the garden and remains connected to it by an ancient avenue of limes.

Fortescue was a passionate plant collector and stocked his garden with choice wisterias and rare camellias, rhododendrons, and azaleas. Today the Garden House boasts over 6,000 varieties, arranged in a sequence of informal gardens, where plants are encouraged to spread and self-seed as if they had sprung unaided from the rocky Dartmoor soil. Billowing South African perennials, showy subtropical bulbs (the current head gardener, Matt Bishop, is a noted bulb enthusiast), and Himalayan acers all manage to blend seamlessly with long views over Dartmoor. The strong sense of place is reinforced by the extensive use of local stone in urns, temples, walls, and terracing, and even, in a particularly haunting part of the garden, an apparently ancient stone circle. The still, quiet heart of this exuberant garden remains Fortescue's 2-acre (0.8 ha) walled garden, a romantic spot with terraces and secret stairways, a Rapunzel tower, and swags of wisteria. Another prime feature is the series of terraces undulating down from a circular, thatched summerhouse. A quarry garden rich in alpines, a flowery meadow, a native cottage garden, and the newly refurbished display of late-summer South African perennials grab center stage at different times of the year. AE

The Gnome Reserve

Devon, England

DESIGNER: Ann Atkin
OWNER: Ann Atkin
GARDEN STYLE: 20th-century woodland and wildflower garden
SIZE: 4 acres (1.6 ha)
CLIMATE: Temperate
LOCATION: West Putford, Bradworthy, Devon

There are infinite variations on every style of garden, from parterres to prairies, but you will never find anything like the Gnome Reserve anywhere in the world. Over the last few years, gnomes have become something of a cultural icon, featuring in such movies as *Amelie*, high-profile commercials, and fashionable store windows. It may be some time before their banishment from the RHS Chelsea Flower Show is lifted, but gnomes are spirits of the forest anyway, and at their happiest in nature. That is exactly where Ann Atkin has put them.

Founded by Ann just over twenty-five years ago, the Gnome Reserve has become the spiritual home of gnome lovers from all over the world. From the moment you enter the stillness of the woodland and see them spread out under a canopy of beeches, it really is a magical experience. There are over 1,000 gnomes dotted around the reserve, fishing in streams, waiting for buses, playing chess, pushing wheelbarrows, and reading quietly in mossy nooks. Some were made by Ann, a landscape artist. Most of the gnomes, though, have sprung directly from the imagination of Ann's son, Richard, who lives in the house with his family and makes the gnomes in his workshop. A recent project has been the addition of a wildflower garden in the meadow next to the gnome wood, with some 250 labeled species of flower, herb, grass, and fern included here. There is also a small gnome museum on the reserve and a shop selling gnomes. Be a sport, buy one, and give the lovely little creature a good home. VR

> "There are over 1,000 gnomes dotted around the reserve, fishing in streams, waiting for buses…"

Dartington Hall

Devon, England

DESIGNERS: Henry Avray Tipping, Beatrix Farrand, Percy Cane, Preben Jacobsen

OWNER: Dartington Hall Trust

GARDEN STYLE: Modernist

SIZE: 30 acres (12.1 ha)

CLIMATE: Temperate

LOCATION: Dartington, Totnes, Devon

Dartington is famous for innovative social and artistic projects, all thanks to Dorothy and Leonard Elmhurst, who bought the estate in 1925. In line with their progressive thinking, the garden of the fourteenth-century hall avoids looking backward and is modern in feel. It includes the only work in Britain of American designer Beatrix Farrand. Other designers have had a more recent hand in the garden, notably Preben Jacobsen, who created a herbaceous border.

The centerpiece of the garden is a wide, open, level lawn surrounded by gently sweeping, grassy terraces. Popularly believed to have been a medieval tiltyard for jousting, it is known as the Tournament Ground, though it is more likely an eighteenth-century feature. This area has two very striking stone staircases with accompanying balustrades designed by Percy Cane. There are spring flowering shrubs, herbaceous plants, and eleven Irish yews (*Taxus baccata* 'Fastigiata') representing the twelve apostles.

Above the grassy terraces of the Tournament Ground are paths through almost wild, woodland plantings, with extensive drifts of primroses, anemone species, and small bulbs in spring. Fine mature trees and shrubs abound: the Chinese dogwood (*Cornus kousa*), the handkerchief tree (*Davidia involucrata*), as well as cherries and crab apples. A Henry Moore statue of a reclining woman can be found at the end of an avenue of ancient sweet chestnuts. Dartington's garden is theatrical, but restful, and illustrates how a modern approach can work in a heritage setting. NK

Knightshayes Court

Devon, England

DESIGNER: Edward Kemp, the Heathcoat-Amory family
OWNER: The National Trust
GARDEN STYLE: Victorian, formal, woodland
SIZE: 50 acres (20.2 ha)
CLIMATE: Temperate
LOCATION: Tiverton, Devon

There is something for everyone at Knightshayes with its formal terraces and borders, its woodland walk, and its wonderful walled kitchen garden. Complementing an imposing Victorian gothic mansion, the large garden was laid out in the late nineteenth century by the landscaper Edward Kemp, who trained under Joseph Paxton at Chatsworth in Derbyshire (see page 250).

The house overlooks the Vale of Tiverton and was built in 1869 for Sir John Heathcoat-Amory, who had made his fortune in textiles and wanted a home from which he could survey his life's work—a large, lacemaking factory in Tiverton itself. The Victorian gardens remained largely unchanged until the 1950s when they were developed by a new generation of Heathcoat-Amorys. They undertook an ambitious replanting scheme both in the formal garden and woodland area. Today the house and garden are managed by the National Trust.

The formal garden in front of the house is delightful in spring and summer when the 120-foot-long (36 m) herbaceous borders are at their best. At the top of the terrace are several small garden compartments, including a paved garden with standard wisterias and a tranquil pool garden enclosed by battlemented yew. A grand sweep of lawn studded with spring bulbs takes the eye down to the woody edges of the garden. The woodland walk is stuffed full of interesting trees and shrubs, including magnolias, rhododendrons, and hydrangeas.

Set apart from the formal and woodland gardens on a south-facing incline, the 4-acre (1.6 ha) kitchen garden has been restored to its Victorian glory. It is now a triumph, bursting with organic produce and laid out in original design with a central stone pool, herbaceous borders, greenhouses, and outbuildings. The kitchen garden is one good reason for visiting Knightshayes, but there are plenty of others. CF

RHS Garden Rosemoor

Devon, England

DESIGNERS: Lady Anne Berry, Elizabeth Banks Associates
OWNER: Royal Horticultural Society
GARDEN STYLE: 20th- and 21st-century varied
SIZE: 65.5 acres (26.5 ha)
CLIMATE: Temperate
LOCATION: Rosemoor, Great Torrington, Devon

Tucked into the valley of the River Torridge, Rosemoor features a wide range of gardens built and planted over the past eighteen years, with the distinctive plantsman's garden created by Lady Anne Berry, who donated Rosemoor to the RHS in 1988.

Rosemoor has a strong sense of place, and makes use of traditional techniques and local materials. It lies within a mixed woodland estate, with new garden areas subtly fitted into the pre-existing field pattern with restored hedge banks and native plants. The major features include informal landscape parkland and arboretum plantings. The largest is the formal garden with a number of display gardens, while hedged "rooms" contain modern and shrub roses, and hot and cool color themes. There are also mixed herbaceous borders, herb and cottage gardens, a potager, foliage garden, demonstration gardens, a winter garden, raised beds, and glasshouse alpines.

To the north of the formal garden, marginal plantings line the stream leading to an ornamental lake. The fruit and vegetable garden, tucked behind an orchard of local fruit tree varieties, features a wide range of produce and growing techniques. A rock gully rich in bamboos and woodland plants then leads east to Lady Anne's original garden around Rosemoor House. Still maintained in her distinctive style, there is a series of small gardens, which feature rare, unusual, and tender plants. Extensive woodland gardens have also been developed here, and there is a new arboretum of trees and shrubs from the northern hemisphere. CBa

Abbotsbury Sub Tropical Gardens

Dorset, England

DESIGNER: First Countess of Ilchester
OWNER: Ilchester Estates
GARDEN STYLE: 19th-century subtropical
SIZE: 20 acres (8.1 ha)
CLIMATE: Temperate
ADDRESS: Abbotsbury, Weymouth, Dorset

Abbotsbury nestles in a hidden valley, like a secret Shangri-la. To one side lies the wild, stony sweep of Chesil beach, and to the other an Arthurian tor, surmounted by a mysterious chapel. In this deep, sheltered combe, with its mild, moist microclimate, successive generations of the Ilchester family created a private Himalayan kingdom, importing countless rare and tender plants new to Britain, many considered too delicate to grow outside. Here they thrived, creating a garden of exotic, junglelike luxuriance.

The beginnings of the garden at Abbotsbury were prosaic enough. In 1765 the central walled garden, now home to towering Chusan palms (*Trachycarpus fortunei*), was the first Countess of Ilchester's kitchen garden. Gradually the garden grew to its present size, becoming famous for its camellia groves, magnolias, and vast collection of rhododendrons and azaleas. Today it nurtures an ever-wider range of exotics from all parts of the globe.

From the original kitchen garden, which is now a Victorian garden planted with gaudy, summer subtropicals, winding paths lead to the West Lawn, through gentle woodland and thickets of bamboo to the Sino-Himalayan glade, a breathtaking sight in spring and fall. A sunny, open New Zealand garden injects a change of mood, leading in turn to formal lily ponds and a Mediterranean bank garden. Below is a romantic sunken garden filled with pots and the shriek of kookaburras. One exciting new feature at Abbotsbury is a new viewing point looking out over Dorset's "Jurassic Coast." AE

> "Today it nurtures an ever-wider range of exotics from all parts of the globe"

Athelhampton House and Gardens

Dorset, England

DESIGNERS: Alfred Cart de Lafontaine, Francis Inigo Thomas
OWNER: Patrick Cooke
GARDEN STYLE: Formal Italianate
SIZE: 15 acres (6 ha)
CLIMATE: Temperate
ADDRESS: Athelhampton, Dorchester, Dorset

Sir William Martyn began construction of the house at Athelhampton in 1485. He was then followed by four generations of Martyn and later a succession of owners until the Cooke family acquired the house and gardens in 1957. Between 1891 and 1899, Alfred Cart de Lafontaine constructed the formal gardens. However, the Great Court, Terrace and Pavilions, the Corona, Private Garden, and Lion's Mouth were all the brilliant creation of Francis Inigo Thomas.

Athelhampton is a magical place encompassing intimate and exquisite formal gardens that have a strong Italianate feel. The Terrace has a summerhouse at either end—the House of Joy and Summer, and the House of Sorrow and Winter—and leads down to the Great Court with a sunken lawn, its elegant fishpond surrounded by awe-inspiring yew topiary pyramids. The centrally situated, circular Corona is a pivotal point in the garden. It is Elizabethan in style with tall, stone obelisks on top of undulating walls that are positioned in front of clipped yew hedges around an ornamental fountain. In contrast, the Private Garden, with its views of the canal, is a study in simplicity. One side is bordered by the old kitchen garden wall where mature specimens of evergreen *Magnolia delavayi* and *M. grandiflora* thrive in its warmth. The Lime Walk leads to the octagonal Cloister Garden with interlaced lime trees that frame an octagonal pool. The garden ends on a high note with a walk along the banks of the River Piddle toward the large, open lawn where there is an ancient dovecote that can accommodate up to 1,500 birds. RL

Boveridge House

Dorset, England

DESIGNERS: Gertrude Jekyll, Thomas Mawson
OWNER: Philip Green Memorial School
GARDEN STYLE: Edwardian
SIZE: 15 acres (6 ha)
CLIMATE: Temperate
LOCATION: Cranborne, Wimborne, Dorset

The garden here is a fine example of a collaboration between Gertrude Jekyll, author of such works as *Colour in the Flower Garden* (1908), and landscape architect Thomas Mawson, who wrote *The Art and Craft of Garden Making* (1900). They made a formidable team, although they disliked each other intensely and neither knew of the other's involvement. Apparently Mawson's name was erased on plans sent to Jekyll.

Tucked away deep in the Dorset countryside, the gardens fell into disrepair after World War II. However, Mawson's hand was still evident in the long avenues, terraces, controlled views extending far into the park, architectural features, and structural planting. Jekyll's plants, however, had all but disappeared as beds and borders slipped into neglect. However, with aerial photographs taken by the German Air Force in 1938 and the Royal Air Force in 1942, a team, including English garden designer Chris Beardshaw, was able to bring the garden back to its Edwardian-era glory.

In the restored sundial garden, encircled by a yew hedge, trapezoid beds were planted radiating from the octagonal sundial base, as specified by Jekyll, with two varieties of phlox framed by *Bergenia cordifolia* and *Aster divaricatus*. The water lilies she loved, such as *Nymphaea* 'Marliacea Carnea', which originally came from the celebrated Latour-Marliac nursery, grace the formal lily pool. Most exciting of all, especially in late summer, is the long walk between drifts of verbascums, sedums, achilleas, and echinops—some of the Jekyll stalwarts that are known to have flowered here in the 1920s. EH

Cranborne Manor

Dorset, England

DESIGNER: John Tradescant the Elder
OWNER: Seventh Marquess of Salisbury
GARDEN STYLE: 17th-century, 20th-century Arts and Crafts
SIZE: 8 acres (3.2 ha)
CLIMATE: Temperate
LOCATION: Cranborne, Wimborne, Dorset

Cranborne Manor Garden successfully combines a Jacobean layout with twentieth-century Arts and Crafts-style planting and contemporary sculpture.

The house, thought to have been one of King John of England's favorite hunting lodges, was gifted by King James the First to Robert Cecil, the first Lord Salisbury, in the early seventeenth century. Cecil's gardener was John Tradescant the Elder, who is said to have laid out the structure of the gardens and the small mount for viewing the parterres. Today the box-edged beds around the mount are filled with lavender and the area enclosed by yew. Further beds are filled with clematis, roses, salvias, lilies, and, in early spring, flowering bulbs.

Close by the mount is a sculpture of a head, *In Memoriam* by Elizabeth Frink. A similar juxtaposition of the ancient and modern can be seen in front of the seventeenth-century gatehouse, where a modern water sculpture by Angela Connor stands in the center of a grass circle. A further series of garden "rooms" includes a herb garden whose beds are edged in santolina and contain *Rosa gallica* and honeysuckles. In high summer, pergolas drip with roses and exuberant herbaceous borders complete the picture of a quintessential romantic English garden. In the orchard, fruit trees are expertly trained against walls, and vegetables are grown inside cages to protect them from the bantams and chickens. JH

RIGHT Cranborne Manor, where styles from different eras combine to create a garden of timeless beauty.

Springhead

Dorset, England

DESIGNERS: Harold Squire, Rolf Gardiner, Marabel Gardiner, Rosalind Richards
OWNER: The Springhead Trust
GARDEN STYLE: 20th-century wild, semiformal, formal
SIZE: 7 acres (2.8 ha)
CLIMATE: Temperate
LOCATION: Fontmell Magna, Shaftesbury, Dorset

Pure water bubbling up through soft sand gives Springhead its name. Flowing in a silver stream to fill a lake, it gathers force before disappearing beneath the eighteenth-century mill house. The courtyard at the entrance has roses on the thatched house and shrub borders frame the mill, while the garden is a glorious secret waiting to be discovered. Emerging from shade into light at the top of a path, you find an expanse of water, rising in terraces like an amphitheater.

In the 1930s Rolf Gardiner made Springhead a center for rural regeneration, while Marabel Gardiner created extensive herbaceous borders and set a Venetian rotunda by the lakeside as a setting for music and festivals. When their daughter, Rosalind Richards, returned to Springhead in 1997, she had to rescue the then derelict garden. She has succeeded in making it beautiful in every season, yet far less labor intensive. On the terraces, shrubs and mixed plantings are in colors that range from pale creams, silver-grays, and lilacs to moody blues and rich reds, plums, and purples. Arbors between the lower flower beds provide places to enjoy views of the rotunda that seems to float on water. The rotunda disappears from sight as the ground rises and wilder plantings prevail, with wildflowers, bog gardens, a copper beech, and a katsura tree (*Cercidiphyllum japonicum*). A bridge across the stream gives views over the water and of the springs at the head of the valley. Beyond are huge evergreen holm oaks (*Quercus ilex*) that stand over Springhead like guardian spirits. EH

The Coach House

Dorset, England

DESIGNER: Penelope Hobhouse
OWNER: Penelope Hobhouse
GARDEN STYLE: Informal, 20th-century modern country garden
SIZE: 1 acre (0.4 ha)
CLIMATE: Temperate
LOCATION: Bettiscombe, Dorset

There are two gardens at the Coach House: an enclosed, richly planted, essentially Mediterranean garden to the rear of the house and an open, green garden to the front, joined by a single strong axis that sweeps right through the house. The perennial problem for the country gardener is making sure the garden blends into the landscape. Penelope Hobhouse's solution was to create a green front garden of grass and hedges to merge into the adjacent hills of the beautiful Marshwood Vale. The center of the design is a rectangular reflecting pool edged by stainless steel and a line of pear trees marking the boundary. To either side of the central yew avenue, tight hornbeam enclosures conceal fruit, vegetables, and cutting flowers—here a fruit cage or fat zucchini scrambling over the compost heap, there a froth of white blossom or a line of sweet peas.

Penelope Hobhouse has recently claimed to have tired of color, but the small garden behind the house remains a testament to her skills as a colorist. Every summer, when she opens the garden in aid of the local church, it is packed with acolytes taking notes. A luxuriant tangle of fragrant shrubs and sun lovers mulched in gravel, its simple geometry, deliciously complicated with many changes of level, groaning pergolas, secret, shady corners, and rampant growth, is all in heady contrast to the clean lines at the front.

Mrs. Hobhouse, in her seventies, says that the garden is now too much work and threatens to dig it all up. Hurry to see it, before she keeps her word! AE

Mapperton Gardens

Dorset, England

DESIGNERS: Ethel Labouchere, Victor Montagu
OWNER: Eleventh Earl of Sandwich
GARDEN STYLE: 17th century, 20th-century Italianate
SIZE: 14 acres (5.6 ha)
CLIMATE: Temperate
LOCATION: Beaminster, Dorset

Few surprises in gardens are greater than that offered on a first visit to Mapperton in Dorset. In front of the sixteenth- and seventeenth-century manor house is a courtyard of roses and clematis. To one side is a wide lawn, with only a narrow strip of flower beds along the wall that is pretty, but unassuming. Then, as you walk across the lawn, you suddenly realize that below a steep bank ahead the garden drops dramatically away to the right in a series of Italianate terraces.

Flight after flight of stone steps lead down elegantly through the valley, between clipped yew hedges and sculptured topiary acorns. At the top end is a neoclassical orangery and below, on a central, topiary-framed terrace, an octagonal pool with a central fountain. Beyond is a pergola covered with vines, wisteria, roses, and honeysuckle. Below that, the garden gradually becomes less formal, eventually merging into a small arboretum of trees and shrubs.

The planting around the orangery is suitably Mediterranean with a number of gray-leaved plants, including *Artemisia* 'Powis Castle' as well as *Phlomis italica* and salvia species. The great sweep of stone stairs is punctuated by terracotta pots of clipped box pyramids and other containers of sun-loving plants, such as *Helichrysum petiolare* and pelargoniums, that continue to flower into fall. Statues are positioned for dramatic effect in yew niches on pedestals at the top of each flight. Most appealing of all, though, is the way this formal, Italianate garden appears dropped, as if by magic, into English fields of grazing cattle. VB

Minterne

Dorset, England

DESIGNER: Admiral Robert Digby, the Digby family
OWNER: Twelfth Lord Digby
GARDEN STYLE: 18th- and 19th-century woodland garden
SIZE: 25 acres (10.1 ha)
CLIMATE: Temperate
LOCATION: Minterne Magna, Dorchester, Dorset

Minterne was rented to the Churchill family until 1768, when Admiral Robert Digby bought the estate and started landscaping. He planted shelterbelts of beech trees, built bridges, and made lakes and cascades. A diverse collection of trees was planted with aucuba, box, holly, laurel, and *Rhododendron ponticum*. For shelter, bamboo was added in the 1890s. With protection established and with the advantage of the green sand in the Minterne Valleys, huge-leaved *Rhododendron falconeri* were planted with ericaceous shrubs and trees. Conditions were now perfect for the introduction of a succession of different rhododendrons, discovered by the great plant hunters—E. H. Wilson, Reginald Farrah, George Forrest, Joseph Rock, and Frank Kingdon-Ward. In total, four generations of the Digby family have now maintained and expanded this horticultural legacy.

The wild woodland here is laid out in a horseshoe below Minterne House itself with over 1 mile (0.6 km) of rhododendron and azalea walks. The walks lead down the valley to a lovely, natural pond planted with colorful and attractive marginals and bog plants, and are framed with magnificent specimens of the handkerchief tree (*Davidia involucrata*).

Minterne House is one of the finest examples of Edwardian architecture. It was built in 1906 of honey-colored Ham Hill stone and replaced the original house that had to be demolished in 1903 because of dry rot. Quintessentially English in its setting, Minterne looks across fields and valleys that resemble the background of a Gainsborough painting. RL

Sticky Wicket

Dorset, England

DESIGNER: Pam Lewis, Peter Lewis
OWNER: Pam Lewis
GARDEN STYLE: 20th-century wildlife-friendly rural garden
SIZE: 3.5 acres (1.4 ha)
CLIMATE: Temperate
LOCATION: Buckland Newton, Dorchester, Dorset

At Sticky Wicket, conservationist Pam Lewis and her late husband Peter created a complex garden intended to protect and nurture birds and other wildlife. Lewis is passionate about the need to develop gardens as green oases for Britain's wildlife—that her creature-friendly garden also delights people is a great bonus. The garden has habitats of wetland and meadow, hedgerow and woodland coppice, with plants selected to provide food or cover. Grasses echo fluttering wings, native plants attract insects for food, and hedgerows provide food and nesting sites.

Color, though, is one of the chief joys of Sticky Wicket. The Bird Garden is pink and plum, while the Frog Garden—an area of pond and bog—is blue and yellow. However, the high point is the Round Garden, a series of exquisitely planted concentric circles, blending softly from pastel pinks and lavender to vivid violet, magenta, and crimson. Sunny and open, with warm gravel paths and plentiful herbs and nectar plants, this is sheer paradise for bees, butterflies, and garden photographers. Beyond lies a white-flowering wilderness rich in autumn fruit and berries, and two magnificent wildflower meadows. Finally, there is an organic vegetable garden and a relatively recent coppice of birch and Scots pine (*Pinus sylvestris*).

Although first and foremost a haven for wildlife, Sticky Wicket is simultaneously the most painterly of gardens. It is one of the best in Britain. AE

RIGHT Effusive planting at Sticky Wicket, a conservationist's dream set in the heart of the Dorset countryside.

Bramdean House

Hampshire, England

DESIGNER: Victoria Wakefield
OWNERS: Hady Wakefield, Victoria Wakefield
GARDEN STYLE: 20th-century formal, naturalistic
SIZE: 6 acres (2.4 ha)
CLIMATE: Temperate
LOCATION: Bramdean, Alresford, Hampshire

A mown pathway cuts a swath of green through the three main garden compartments at Bramdean House. A glimpse of a blue door might entice you straight to the Apple House at the end of the vista, but there is much of interest along the way. The journey begins with a masterpiece of planting—the mirror-image borders for which the garden is famous.

These double borders contain more than 100 different species that create endless waves of color and texture, all in perfect symmetry. Strong foliage plants give the structure, while sweet peas growing over hazel birdcages add color at eye level. Finally, repeated catmint (*Nepeta grandiflora* 'Bramdean' and *N.* 'Six Hills Giant') establish a satisfying rhythm. After that the ribbon of grass continues along the gently rising slope to fine, wrought iron gates in mellow brick walls. It runs through the square kitchen garden, where espalier and cordon fruit trees screen beds packed with rows of vegetables, fruits, and flowers for cutting. On both sides of the high walls is a vast array of unusual shrubs and climbers as well as rambling roses, among them 'Rambling Rector', named after a reverend who once lived here. A gate in the far wall of the kitchen garden marks a change of mood, from produce in ordered abundance to wilder planting that flanks the wide grass path through the orchard.

To either side of the main compartments are the working areas, with propagation to the west and compost to the east. They keep the beds and borders brimming with fine, healthy plants, injecting a long season of color, shape, and form. EH

Exbury Gardens

Hampshire, England

DESIGNER: Lionel de Rothschild
OWNER: Edmund de Rothschild
GARDEN STYLE: 20th-century, woodland
SIZE: 250 acres (101.2 ha)
CLIMATE: Temperate
LOCATION: Exbury, Southampton, Hampshire

Lionel de Rothschild was described as "a banker by hobby and a gardener by profession," so it is little wonder that he created one of the most celebrated rhododendron gardens in the world between 1919 and his death in 1942. His enthusiasm for discoveries made by plant hunters Frank Kingdon-Ward, George Forrest, Joseph Rock, and Ernest Wilson resulted in many of their finds being introduced to Exbury. Lionel's passion for rhododendrons fired his interest in the creation of an unsurpassed collection of some of the finest named hybrids, and they can be viewed in Exbury's huge woodland gardens.

The grounds include some large ponds that, in spring, reflect the rich hues of brightly colored azaleas and acers. In the fall there are breathtaking displays of multicolored foliage. The rock garden took more than two years to complete and is probably the largest in Europe, covering over 2 acres (0.8 ha)—a miniature railway was installed to move the huge stone used in its construction.

Lionel's son, Edmund de Rothschild, the present owner of Exbury, opened the gardens to the public in 1955. He has continued to expand the diversity of the gardens, and also added a steam railroad, while over the years a fine collection of trees has been planted in the grounds by a succession of royal visitors. RL

> "In the fall there are breathtaking displays of multicolored foliage"

Brandy Mount House Gardens

Hampshire, England

DESIGNERS: Michael Baron, Caryl Baron
OWNERS: Michael Baron, Caryl Baron
GARDEN STYLE: 20th-century plantsman's garden
SIZE: 1.5 acres (0.6 ha)
CLIMATE: Temperate
LOCATION: Alresford, Hampshire

Hundreds of pilgrims flock to a small town in rural Hampshire every February. They are snowdrop fanatics, and Brandy Mount House is their Mecca. It is unusual to find such an important collection of plants in a town-center garden. However, behind the ordinary-looking house in Alresford, on the northern edge of the South Downs, is a collection of bulbs that gets the pulses racing of the visiting galanthophiles.

The neat and tidy garden was created by Michael and Caryl Baron, who moved into the property in the early 1980s. At the time they had only a handful of snowdrop varieties. Twenty-three years later there are around 250 different types, and the collection now has National Collection status. From late winter to early spring, the snowdrops bloom in beds, troughs, and huge clumps piercing the lawn. Michael is very hands-on and gives guided tours, reeling off the long and complicated names with ease. Among the gems are *Galanthus elwesii* 'Moya's Green' with a light green tip to the edge of the petals, and *G. koenenianus* with corrugated leaves. These peculiarities explain Michael's love of snowdrops: "It's the tiny differences, which drive some people bonkers, that I like."

A spring visit here is filled with the perfume of a hundred varieties of daphne in full bloom, many of which are on a terrace beside the house. Part of Michael's collection of alpines, including dwarf narcissi and saxifrages, can be seen here, though his rarer bulbs are kept in the alpine house. MC

Longstock Water Garden

Hampshire, England

DESIGNERS: John Spedan Lewis, and others
OWNER: John Lewis Partnership
GARDEN STYLE: 20th-century water garden
SIZE: 75 acres (30.3 ha)
CLIMATE: Temperate
LOCATION: Stockbridge, Hampshire

The contemporary gardens that were laid out at Longstock were principally the vision of John Spedan Lewis, who acquired the estate in 1946. With the help of his butler, Jim Saunders, who exchanged the butler's pantry for the gardener's punt, the gardens tripled in size to become the Venice of water gardens where borders have been replaced by lagoons and paths by channels of crystal-clear water.

In many gardens the water is the subtext. At Longstock, though, it is the main narrative, with a bewildering array of brooks and rivulets, all fed by the nearby River Test. Although the place has something of the spirit of a William Robinson wild garden, the overwhelming impression is one of carefully groomed excellence. The islands, linked by simple board bridges, are meticulously mown, and their edges are softened by bold, naturalistic plantings of herbaceous plants such as geraniums, hostas, irises, ligularias, lysichitons, and primulas, with great sweeps of astilbes. Fine trees and substantial shrubs create a sense of enclosure and a canopy, and in spring, brilliant rhododendrons light up the surrounding woodlands, while the cut-leaf common alder (*Alnus glutinosa* 'Laciniata') and swamp cypress (*Taxodium distichum*) provide vertical accents as they soar skyward. Well worth a detour. JB

RIGHT Lush plantings in one of the many beautiful swampy lagoons at Longstock Water Garden.

Mottisfont Abbey Garden

Hampshire, England

DESIGNERS: Graham Stuart Thomas, and others
OWNER: The National Trust
GARDEN STYLE: 20th-century walled rose garden, landscape
SIZE: 35 acres (14.1 ha)
CLIMATE: Temperate
LOCATION: Mottisfont, Romsey, Hampshire

The walled former kitchen garden of the thirteenth-century priory has been home to the National Collection of Old Roses since the 1970s, when rosarian Graham Stuart Thomas designed the rose garden for the National Trust. Using climbers and shrubs grown from his own collection of old-fashioned, pre-1900 roses, he adapted the site. He kept the old paths, box hedges, and fruit trees, introduced roses everywhere, and pioneered the use of hardy perennials, such as lavender and catmint, to complement them. Consequently, Mottisfont has become synonymous with historic roses with the most romantic names.

Rosa 'Great Maiden's Blush', the crimson-and-white striped *R. mundi,* and *R.* 'Ispahan' from ancient Persia are just a handful of the 520 varieties to flourish here.

For a short, but spectacular, season in early summer, Mottisfont takes off when the roses are in full bloom. In the evenings, a magical alchemy takes place. The cooling night air traps the warm scents, heavy inside the walls. It is like stepping into a cloud of fragrance with the lightest lemony scents intermingling with rich, spicy aromas. The garden gates remain open into the evening throughout June so visitors can experience this delight for themselves.

Elsewhere in the garden are an intricate box- and lavender-edged parterre in front of the house and an avenue of limes leading to an octagonal yew enclosure by Geoffrey Jellicoe. A great plane (*Platanus x hispanica*) here, reputed to be the largest in Britain with a spread of 1,794 square yards (1,500 sq m), is part of a National Collection of *Platanus.* SA

Sir Harold Hillier Gardens

Hampshire, England

DESIGNERS: Sir Harold Hillier, Hampshire County Council
OWNER: Hampshire County Council
GARDEN STYLE: 20th-century arboretum, plantsman's garden
SIZE: 180 acres (72.9 ha)
CLIMATE: Temperate
LOCATION: Ampfield, Romsey, Hampshire

Sir Harold Hillier was one of the greatest plantsmen of the twentieth century. "While others are talking about conservation I'm doing it," he said. "I'm putting roots in the ground. I'm planting, planting, planting." You can see the results in the gardens of his former home in Hampshire, now open to the public. This is Sir Harold's personal "stamp collection" of rare and unusual plants and trees, started in 1953. He traveled widely, amassing material from all over the world, even sending back cuttings on his honeymoon. The result is a site stuffed with goodies—42,000 plants at the last count, including 12,500 different types.

First is the Winter Garden, the largest in Europe, containing hundreds of plants that provide color and inspiration for the dull winter months. Other highlights here include the peaceful pond and bog garden, which is shaded by swamp cypress trees (*Taxodium distichum*) and numerous bamboos; the Gurkha Memorial garden, featuring plants from Nepal; the camellia-clad Spring Walk; and Acer Valley that erupts in the fall, as does the tree-filled Three-acre Paddock. There is an extensive pinetum, and you will also find a populetum—a collection of over forty different poplar trees, featuring a massive gray *Populus* x *canescens* over 101 feet (30.7 m) high.

This is an all-year-round garden. As you pass through the impressive Visitor and Education Pavilion, it is worth picking up a "Plants of Current Interest" leaflet, updated weekly, to help you pick out seasonal highlights. For families there are plenty of child-focused activities and seasonal trails. PM

Spinners Garden

Hampshire, England

DESIGNERS: Peter Chappell, Diana Chappell
OWNER: Peter Chappell
GARDEN STYLE: Natural woodland garden
SIZE: 2 acres (0.8 ha), with additional arboretum and nursery
CLIMATE: Temperate
LOCATION: Boldre, Lymington, Hampshire

This superb, natural woodland garden was created by the renowned plantsman Peter Chappell and his late wife, Diana. Started in 1960, it is packed to the brim with choice and rare plants.

A visit in early spring means a walk through the woodland glades to enjoy the species bulbs emerging before the densely planted herbaceous perennials. Erythroniums and a fine collection of trilliums light up the woodland floor, magnolias sparkle with blossoms, and camellias and rhododendrons abound. There is also a comprehensive selection of first-rate trees, among them a choice range of cornus, including the magnificent 'Satomi', the first of its kind to be grown in a private garden in Britain, and the superb *Cercis canadensis* 'Forest Pansy' with wonderful purple foliage all season. Garden interest continues with an extensive collection of rodgersias, bog plants and hostas, as well as species and lace cap hydrangeas. For fall beauty, you cannot beat the acers and stewartias that abound here.

The plantings here are inspiring, and the different aspects of the garden show where they are best grown. After you have noted down some gems, head straight for the nursery, where there is a good chance they will be on sale. RL

> "…it is packed to the brim with choice and rare plants"

West Green House Gardens

Hampshire, England

DESIGNER: Marylyn Abbott
OWNER: The National Trust
GARDEN STYLE: 20th-century interpretation of 18th-century formal gardens
SIZE: 10 acres (4.5 ha)
CLIMATE: Temperate
LOCATION: Hartley Wintney, Hook, Hampshire

A series of delightful walled gardens surrounds the eighteenth-century West Green House. In one garden, characters from *Alice in Wonderland* are surrounded by topiary and roses in white and red, and another area has fabulous informal herbaceous borders. In the outstanding potager, designer Marylyn Abbott mixes edibles and ornamentals using neat globes of standard weigela and spring-flowering viburnum to create a formal structure, with chard or leeks beside the tulips and fritillaries. Each spring the area is changed from a color garden to a storybook garden. In the past, she has included medieval, Roman, and Native American ingredients. The last was complete with a tepee and boat packed with Native American medicinal plants surrounded by potatoes, chilies, amaranthus, sunflowers, and rudbeckias. Marylyn worked at the Sydney Opera House for many years as the marketing and tourism manager, so it is no surprise that she instils a sense of theatrical exuberance into her gardens.

The gardens are enveloped by an elegant neoclassical park dotted with birdcages, follies, monuments, and a lake fringed with fritillaries and snowdrops in spring. A trompe-l'oeil nymphaeum with restored steps and Italianate planting, the new formal Water Garden, and a spectacular Paradise Garden add extra elegance. A picturesque orangery, green theater, and formal allées add formality around the house. It is no wonder that West Green is regarded by many as one of Britain's top gardens. MB

Bayleaf Farmstead at the Weald and Downland Museum

West Sussex, England

DESIGNER: Weald and Downland Museum
OWNER: Weald and Downland Museum
GARDEN STYLE: Medieval recreation
SIZE: 0.1 acre (0.04 ha)
CLIMATE: Temperate
LOCATION: Singleton, Chichester, West Sussex

The Weald and Downland Museum is an extraordinary place, a sort of rescue center for old buildings that have been stuck in the path of highways, reservoirs, and general redevelopment. This collection of fifty or so dwellings has been immaculately reassembled, repaired, furnished and, in the case of Bayleaf Farmstead, been given an authentic period garden.

The farmhouse is a timber-framed building from the fifteenth century. The garden looks much as it would have done to the original inhabitants, who relied on their plot for fruits, vegetables, and herbs. The herb beds are marked out in traditional wattle edging, and are crammed with rosemary, lavender, winter savory, tansy, artemisia, thyme, and borage. Herbs were all-important and not just for cooking— strewing herbs helped repel fleas and bedbugs, and gruit herbs were used for flavoring homebrewed ale. The garden is fenced with hazel wattle. The margins have been left to run wild with rare corn cockles, oxeye daisies, foxgloves, and meadow grasses.

In the orchard are medlar trees, bullace (wild plums), and warden pears "so hard you could fire them from a canon and kill a man at a 1,000 yards," says head gardener Bob Holman. There are also three medieval "shaws"—little wooded areas planted with ash, oak, blackthorn, and hazel that were coppiced for thatching spars, fencing, and sticks for the fire. SA

Leonardslee Lakes and Gardens

West Sussex, England

DESIGNERS: Sir Edmund Loder, the Loder family
OWNERS: Robin Loder
GARDEN STYLE: 19th- and 20th-century woodland landscape
SIZE: 240 acres (97.2 ha)
CLIMATE: Temperate
LOCATION: Lower Beeding, Horsham, West Sussex

Synonymous with the *Rhododendron* Loderi Group, Sir Edmund Loder raised these hybrids, acclaimed for their noble appearance and gorgeous fragrance, in the grounds of Leonardslee. Sir Edmund acquired the estate in 1889 and created an exceptional woodland garden that opened to the public in 1907. Incredibly enthusiastic about rhododendrons and exotic conifers, he hybridized numerous rhododendrons and planted rare specimen trees including the clump-forming variety of the Chusan palm (*Trachycarpus fortunei* 'Surculosa'), which is unique to the garden. He also introduced antelopes, beavers, wallabies, and kookaburras. Today only the wallabies remain—they "mow" the grass and attract plenty of visitors.

Generations of the Loder family have been guardians of Leonardslee. The present owner, Robin Loder, found the devastation caused by the great storm of 1987 an enormous challenge. He has redesigned and replanted areas to include a "querkery" with over 100 species of oaks and 140 species of maples. All this merges seamlessly into the steep wooded valley sides, crisscrossed by innumerable paths giving views of the lakes below.

Spring and fall are the best times to visit Leonardslee for the rich colors, the magnolias and camellias, and the delicious fragrance of the azalea *Rhododendron luteum*. Also worth seeing is the collection of the Loders' Victorian automobiles and the Doll's House Exhibition. RL

High Beeches Gardens

West Sussex, England

DESIGNER: Colonel Giles Loder
OWNER: High Beeches Gardens Conservation Trust
GARDEN STYLE: 20th-century landscaped woodland garden
SIZE: 25 acres (10.1 ha)
CLIMATE: Temperate
LOCATION: Handcross, West Sussex

Capturing the drama and tranquility of a classic English country idyll, High Beeches Gardens inspire. It was begun in 1906 by Colonel Giles Loder, who spent the next sixty years exchanging plants and ideas with his botanical friends and cousins at Wakehurst Place, refining and developing his woodland garden with trees and shrubs from around the world.

His passion for plants is evident throughout. At the top of the hill, the best acid hay meadow in Sussex presents a vision worthy of John Constable. Small heath butterflies and bumblebees rise and dip over native flowers and grasses. Deep, damp gullies, filled with gunnera, plunge through open woodland to a lake and a spectacular aerial display from dragonflies.

The woods consist mainly of carefully chosen native oaks, towering like cathedral pillars over more exotic species. The rhododendron collection and gorgeously scented azaleas are spectacular. Beneath the trees, naturalized willow gentians (*Gentiana asclepiadea*) thrive alongside Asiatic primulas, ferns, and irises. *Magnolia macrophylla* with its enormous umbrella leaves is juxtaposed with the white flowers of *Cornus* 'Norman Hadden'. Vast rhododendrons sport young leaves covered in chocolate-colored felt, and *Primula helodoxa* follows the bank and ditch of an old boundary in a river of delicate yellow.

High Beeches is graceful in maturity. Elegantly designed and well managed to maximum effect, this garden wears its heritage well. NS

Denmans Garden

West Sussex, England

DESIGNER: John Brookes
OWNER: John Brookes
GARDEN STYLE: 20th-century naturalistic planting
with structural form
SIZE: 4 acres (1.6 ha)
CLIMATE: Temperate
LOCATION: Fontwell, Arundel, West Sussex

John Brookes, one of the most influential and significant designers in Britain for many years, brought the concept of the "outside room"—the garden as a place to eat, sit, and relax—to a British society that was already ripe for change in the 1960s. Taking his cue from American peers, such as Thomas Church, John set about making the creation of beautiful gardens accessible to all, spreading the word via books, television appearances, and articles.

Located in the comfortable Sussex landscape in southeast England, Denmans is a garden that excites designers and enthuses plant lovers. There are areas of gravel garden, open expanses of lawn, different uses of water, pockets of naturalistic and prairie planting, shrub borders, perennials, clumps of trees, hedging, focal points, and always a choice of routes. Denmans also includes most principles of garden design, without them being in any way contrived or unsuitable for the site. Considering how large it is, the garden has a very relaxed, domestic feel. Ultimately, though, it is a reassuring garden because no matter what combination or structure you look at, there is a real sense that you can achieve this at home. CY

"Considering how large it is, the garden has a very relaxed, domestic feel"

Borde Hill Garden

West Sussex, England

DESIGNER: Colonel Stephenson Clarke, the Clarke family
OWNERS: Andrewjohn Clarke, Eleni Stephenson Clarke
GARDEN STYLE: Early 20th-century formal, woodland garden
SIZE: 17-acre (6.8 ha) formal garden, 160-acre (64.8 ha)
  park and woodland
CLIMATE: Temperate
LOCATION: Haywards Heath, West Sussex

Borde Hill stands on a ridge in the High Weald of mid-Sussex, with leafy panoramas on either side. The gardens here represent the work of four generations of the same family, having been bought in 1892 by Andrewjohn Clarke's great-grandfather, Colonel Stephenson Clarke, a talented naturalist. He created a garden that has become internationally famous for its collection of rare trees and shrubs.

Stephenson Clarke's work developing the garden coincided with a fevered period of plant hunting. He sponsored expeditions to China, the Himalayas, the Andes, and Tasmania. Throughout the garden and woodland there is a rich variety of trees, magnolias, and rhododendrons raised from seeds and seedlings brought back by these plant collectors.

A series of linked gardens surrounds the stunning sixteenth-century house, while the Rose Garden, with lavender- and box-edged beds, is full of scent and color in midsummer and early fall. The herbaceous borders, designed to give maximum impact from midsummer to fall, are hot colored with rudbeckias, kniphofias, heleniums, and euphorbias. Peaches and nerines grow in the restored Victorian greenhouses, and there are aromatic gray-leaved plants in the gravel of the small, walled Mediterranean Garden. Beyond are wide lawns, wooded dells, and views over the Sussex countryside. The Old Rhododendron Garden features some of the first Chinese rhododendrons to be introduced to Britain. In late spring it is an impressive sea of pinks, oranges, and yellows. VB

Fishbourne Palace

West Sussex, England

DESIGNER: Unknown
OWNER: Sussex Archaeological Trust
GARDEN STYLE: Roman
SIZE: 1 acre (0.4 ha)
CLIMATE: Temperate
LOCATION: Fishbourne, Chichester, West Sussex

The Roman Palace at Fishbourne went up between C.E. 75 and 80. It is not known exactly who built it, though it was probably Tiberius Claudius Togidubnus, a client king to the Romans.

Archaeologists have now excavated half of the original central courtyard garden, which would have had colonnaded walks on all sides rising at the west wing into the porch of the Audience Chamber. The surviving drainage system is impressive, with tile-lined culverts feeding water from the north wing into possible water features, thereby irrigating the plantings. Clearly visible after 1,900 years, the bedding trenches for the clipped box hedging, shaped to enhance the statuary and benches, are replanted and line the central 40-foot-wide (12 m) walk from the entrance to the Audience Chamber.

The bedding trenches along the east side of the garden have been replanted. Flowering trees have been trained along a timber framework, putting into practice the advice of Pliny the Younger, who reportedly said that "a row of fruit trees alternating with posts [should be planted] to give an air of rural simplicity in surroundings of otherwise studied formality." A collection of Roman utilitarian plants has also been arranged systematically in a new display area. A new triclinium (from *tri clinos*, meaning "three couches"), or outdoor dining room, has been constructed to give visitors an idea of how the incumbents would have eaten alfresco. A model of a gardener potting in the shed demonstrates practical gardening techniques, Roman style. CH

Parham House

West Sussex, England

DESIGNER: The Pearson family
OWNER: Parham House Charitable Trust
GARDEN STYLE: Parkland, 20th- and 21st-century ornamental
SIZE: 875 acres (354.4 ha)
CLIMATE: Temperate
LOCATION: Pulborough, West Sussex

Built in the 1570s, Parham is a beautiful, gray stone house, matched by a perfect setting. Beyond the formal gardens, visitors will find the Deer Park and the northern slope of the South Downs, a landscape untouched by the modern world.

The gardens today are mainly the work of the last twenty or so years, but they build substantially on Parham's history. The boundary between Pleasure Grounds and the ancient park, for example, is concealed by a sunk fence. Although modern, it is in keeping with the period features, such as walls that date from the eighteenth century or earlier and ancient clipped yews. The design of the maze, laid out in 1991, is derived from needlework on the four-poster bed in the house's Great Chamber.

Other features include the broad, graveled path that leads down a gentle slope through the Pleasure Grounds, with lawns and huge trees, to a wrought iron gate guarded by a pair of stone lions. Within lies the 4-acre (1.6 ha) Walled Garden, which is divided into four by broad walks and includes an orchard and vegetable garden. This garden, now planted for year-round interest, supplies cut flowers for the house to match its decor and furnishings. The redbrick wall is covered with vines, clematis, and roses. In one corner, valerian threads its way out of a pineapple broom (*Cytisus battandieri*), while the paths froth with lady's mantle (*Alchemilla mollis)* and nepeta. A purple solanum grows over the fences near the greenhouse. This romantic, informal garden is particularly magical early on a summer morning. VB

Gravetye Manor Hotel

West Sussex, England

DESIGNER: William Robinson
OWNER: Relais & Chateaux
GARDEN STYLE: Late 19th-century naturalistic
SIZE: 30 acres (12.1 ha)
CLIMATE: Temperate
LOCATION: East Grinstead, West Sussex

William Robinson, the designer of Gravetye Manor, was partly responsible for changing garden history. Appalled by the gaudy displays of Victorian bedding, he championed a return to informal planting. While much of his influence was spread via articles and books, such as *The Wild Garden* (1870) and *The English Flower Garden* (1883), he also created a garden where he could practice what he preached.

Unlike many of his peers, Robinson was a practical gardener. He had worked for the Botanical Gardens of Regent's Park in London and for one of Veitch's leading nurseries. When he bought Gravetye Manor in 1885, he had plenty of experience. The whole site slopes steeply and had to be amended around the house with a series of rustic stone terraces. They are edged with mixed borders, although one terrace does have a rectangular water lily pond. To the south of the house are the original Robinsonian wildflower meadows. This type of meadow became fashionable in the late nineteenth century, and this one contains naturalized bulbs as well as native flowers. Walking past the lake and back up the slopes again, visitors reach a magnolia walk that blooms in midspring, and shrubberies with pines, parrotias, and rhododendrons. There is also an important legacy of trees here, including maples, pines, oaks, and many North American species.

After Robinson's death in 1935, the gardens suffered from neglect. Since 1958, they have been restored, and the main house is now a hotel. The food here is as good as the garden. LH

West Dean Gardens

West Sussex, England

DESIGNERS: Edward James, Harold Peto, Ivan Hicks, and others
OWNER: The Edward James Foundation
GARDEN STYLE: 19th century
SIZE: 100 acres (40.5 ha)
CLIMATE: Temperate
LOCATION: West Dean, Chichester, West Sussex

Like so many historic houses and gardens, West Dean seems to grow organically from its beautiful setting in the rolling folds of the South Downs. The house, once the venue for grand Edwardian house parties, is now a thriving arts foundation named after its founder, the eccentric patron of the surrealists, Edward James.

Having evolved over centuries and never having undergone a systematic makeover, the gardens lack a strong sense of coherence and order compared with other large historic gardens. However, they make up for that in variety and presentation. There are 35 acres (14.1 ha) of ornamental gardens, a 49-acre (20 ha) arboretum, a walled Victorian kitchen garden, and a 300-foot-long (91.4 m) pergola. The latter was the masterwork of Harold Peto, garden designer to the late nineteenth-century great and good, who created the massive stone and timber covered walkway for people to wander and enjoy the heady scents of honeysuckle and roses. Even better is the magnificently restored walled garden, where an extensive range of gleaming Victorian greenhouses is packed with everything from orchids to eggplants. Outside there are herbaceous borders, row upon row of perfect vegetables, and shaped fruit trees. JB

> "…West Dean seems to grow organically from its beautiful setting…"

Nymans Garden

West Sussex, England

DESIGNERS: Ludwig Messel, Leonard Messel, Maud Messel
OWNER: The National Trust
GARDEN STYLE: 19th- and 20th-century English country
SIZE: 30 acres (12.1 ha)
CLIMATE: Temperate
LOCATION: Handcross, Haywards Heath, West Sussex

The path of gardening is never smooth, and some gardens seem to have more than their fair share of setbacks. Nymans is no exception, with a fire that gutted the grand house in 1947 and the devastating loss of 486 trees in one night during the hurricane of 1987. Thanks to the dedication of its owners and gardeners, Nymans still stands as one of the great gardens of the Sussex Weald.

Developed by three generations of the Messel family from the 1890s until 1953, when it was passed to the National Trust, Nymans is very much a plantsman's garden. It has magnificent spring and summer mixed borders, and an exquisite circular rose garden with a central fountain that has graced many a calendar. The ruins of the old house still stand, wreathed with clematis, wisteria, and roses, a romantic backdrop and a key part of the garden's charm.

At the garden's heart is the Wall Garden that houses many rare plants. There are some lovely period features such as a croquet lawn and wisteria-clad pergola, a sunken garden, heather garden, lime avenue, and a laurel walk where the Messel children learned to ride their bicycles. Time is never allowed to stand still here, and the National Trust has done an admirable job in breathing new life into Nymans. Many areas were rethought and replanted after the hurricane, including the Rose Garden and the Pinetum. The Forecourt and Knot Garden have been recently renewed. It is a gardening commonplace that one year's setback is the next year's opportunity, and you will not see better proof than at Nymans. PM

Highdown Gardens

West Sussex, England

DESIGNERS: Sir Frederick Stern, Lady Stern
OWNER: Worthing Borough Council
GARDEN STYLE: 20th-century informal
   plantsman's garden
SIZE: 10 acres (4 ha)
CLIMATE: Temperate
LOCATION: Goring-by-Sea, Worthing,
   West Sussex

A huge Himalayan musk rose cascades down the vertical face of a gleaming white chalk cliff at the heart of this plantsman's garden. At its feet are masses of shrubs, perennials, and countless spring bulbs, including dwarf narcissi and snowdrops.

The former big-game hunter, amateur jockey, and civil servant Sir Frederick Stern started work on Highdown in 1909. He was keen to prove that it was possible to create a garden on this high, sloping site of almost pure chalk. At first he experimented to see what would survive, and later used plants brought back from plant collecting trips abroad by the likes of Reginald Farrer and Ernest Wilson. The chalk makes a stunning feature on the hellebore bank, where the purple, chocolate, and green shades of the *orientalis* varieties contrast brilliantly with the white stone. Elsewhere a network of island beds has been cut into the sloping side of the garden. The beds are filled with rare shrubs and trees, including a *Carpinus turczaninowii*, planted in 1937 by Queen Mary.

The garden is open all year and has many seasonal highlights. In summer there is a long rose pergola walk with mature specimens and beds, also packed with daylilies, agapanthus, and bearded irises. The leaves of the trees perk things up in the fall. In winter the tree bark stands out. Since Stern's death in 1967 the garden has been sympathetically managed by the local council and has won awards for using sustainable methods of gardening. MC

Marchants Hardy Plants

East Sussex, England

DESIGNERS: Graham Gough, Lucy Goffin
OWNERS: Graham Gough, Lucy Goffin
GARDEN STYLE: 21st-century plantsman's garden
SIZE: 2 acres (0.8 ha)
CLIMATE: Temperate
LOCATION: Laughton, East Sussex

The best inspiration often comes when least expected. For Graham Gough, the owner of Marchants Hardy Plants, it came when he was slumped in a deckchair overlooking his garden-to-be. Spurred on, he started up the lawnmower sitting next to him and carved the shape of beds, borders, and paths in the grass. Just a few years later, the garden was alive with swaying grasses and vibrant perennials that harmonize with the spectacular views of the hilly South Downs.

Graham and his partner, Lucy Goffin, set up Marchants in 1998. First and foremost, the site next to their Victorian cottage is a nursery. It sells an array of unusual and stalwart plants, and the plants sold also grow in the garden, creating a living catalog and providing innovative ideas for plant combinations. The garden faces broadly south but is exposed to the wind. To provide shelter without detracting from the garden's appearance, lashed wooden fences mirror the undulating hills beyond. Apart from two straight gravel paths, there is little hard structure. Instead, the space focuses on a raised grassy mound and a spiraling hornbeam hedge. Surrounding them are beds that begin to bloom in early spring with slate-blue hellebores and the vivid stems of willow. Then summer brings daylilies and more than forty grasses, including *Miscanthus sinensis* 'Silberspinne'.

The Marchants garden is always changing, partly with the seasons, partly by design. There is always something fresh for visitors to see and buy. LH

Merriments Gardens

East Sussex, England

DESIGNERS: David Weeks, Peggy Weeks
OWNERS: David Weeks, Peggy Weeks
GARDEN STYLE: 20th-century plantsman's garden
SIZE: 4 acres (1.8 ha)
CLIMATE: Temperate
LOCATION: Hurst Green, East Sussex

The garden at Merriments belongs to the neighboring nursery of the same name that sells an eclectic and interesting range of plants. The owners, David and Peggy Weeks, are talented designers and plant lovers, and the level of maintenance is exceptionally high. Not one plant among the thousands growing here seems to be out of place in character, color, or form.

The garden takes the visitor on a meandering journey past island beds planted with an artful combination of herbaceous perennials, ornamental grasses, shrubs, and roses that create dense but transient screens, separating one area from the next. Despite the scale of the garden, which was developed from an open field in the mid-1990s, there is an intimate atmosphere and great variety. The gently sloping garden has matured rapidly, and today is a vision of bold colors and imaginative planting. Warm colors dominate the Golden Border that comes into its own in late summer. A sophisticated Blue Gravel Garden is full of earlier flowering specimens, such as *Verbena bonariensis* and agapanthus. The tropical planting style around the ponds presents a cool, lush alternative to the vitality and exuberance of the borders, and, in 2004, a striking bridge was built over the ponds. Most recently a new entrance garden has been created in the style of Monet's Grande Allée at Giverny. The garden at Merriments is not just a superb store window for the plants on sale; it also offers plenty of lessons in clever combinations. AJ

Charleston

East Sussex, England

DESIGNERS: Roger Fry, Vanessa Bell, Duncan Grant;
restored by Sir Peter Shepheard
OWNER: The Charleston Trust
GARDEN STYLE: 20th-century informal, idiosyncratic
SIZE: 1 acre (0.4 ha)
CLIMATE: Temperate
LOCATION: Firle, Lewes, East Sussex

On a hot summer day, when the artist Vanessa Bell's favorite roses and hollyhocks are in full bloom and the scent of tobacco plants fills the air, you can almost hear the sound of laughter bouncing off Charleston's high walls. Few gardens have such strong associations with a cast of characters so creative and idiosyncratic as the artists, writers, and intellectuals known as the Bloomsbury Group. Therein lies its charm.

The walled garden behind the north facade of the farmhouse is based on a simple grid of gravel paths and lawns, with Italian-style box hedges and generous borders of intense color devised by the art critic Roger Fry in the 1920s. Inspired by their love of the Mediterranean, Vanessa Bell and her lover, Duncan Grant, added a small rectangular pool, created places for sitting, set statuary to terminate vistas, and placed casts of antique heads along the tops of the brick and flint walls.

English cottage-style plants, such as roses, zinnias, flowering shrubs, sunflowers, and hollyhocks, fill the beds beneath the old apple trees. Chrysanthemums, gladiolus, and globe artichokes are still grown as if to furnish vases with material for still-life paintings. The lawn, sloping down to a rectangular pool, which was a setting for family theatricals, is edged with silvery cotton lavender, creating a touch of formality. Around the mosaic piazza in the sheltered northeast corner of the garden, damson, fig and peach trees, and creamy-white *Rosa* 'Félicité Perpétue' thrive against the sun-baked walls. EH

Great Dixter

East Sussex, England

DESIGNERS: Edwin Lutyens, Nathaniel Lloyd, Christopher Lloyd
OWNER: The Great Dixter Charitable Trust
GARDEN STYLE: Semiformal Edwardian layout,
with late 20th- and 21st-century planting
SIZE: 5 acres (2 ha)
CLIMATE: Temperate
LOCATION: Northiam, Rye, East Sussex

There is a feeling that both plants and people are enjoying themselves while working their socks off in the dynamic garden created by the late Christopher Lloyd. The team, headed by Fergus Garrett, keeps up the spirit of adventure, experimenting with new plants in new combinations for a succession of interest that is best summed up as "never a dull moment."

In the 1910s, at the same time as restoring and adding to the house, Edwin Lutyens designed the framework of the surrounding gardens. The design is largely formal, but, as Lloyd wrote, "never stodgily so." The yew topiary pieces planted by his father, Nathaniel, contribute humor as well as gravitas. There is also plenty of informality with the areas of rough grass to either side of the entrance path, where blue camassias have naturalized. On the other side of the house, the margin of the upper orchard lawns, filled with daffodils and wild orchids, runs parallel with the highly organized and justifiably famous Long Border, making a "juxtaposition of near-wild and tame" that appealed to Lloyd. Here trees, shrubs, climbers, hardy and tender perennials, annuals, biennials, and bulbs contribute to the overall tapestry of daring colors.

In the sheltered exotic garden, which replaced Lutyens's formal rose garden in 1993, bold palms and bananas tower above vibrant cannas and dahlias. Be sure to see it all. EH

RIGHT The exuberant and uncontrived mixed borders at Great Dixter masterfully combine every sort of color.

Wakehurst Place

East Sussex, England

DESIGNERS: Gerald Loder, Kew Royal Botanic Gardens
OWNER: The National Trust
GARDEN STYLE: 20th-century botanic collection
SIZE: 561 acres (227.2 ha)
CLIMATE: Temperate
LOCATION: Ardingly, Haywards Heath, West Sussex

Wakehurst Place is the sister garden to the Royal Botanic Gardens, Kew, in London (see page 386). Often called "Kew in the country," it has been leased by the Botanic Gardens since 1965 to ensure that those plants that fail to thrive in city conditions can still be grown as part of Kew's collection. Where Kew often suffers from pollution and has poor alluvial soil, Wakehurst enjoys a comparatively clean atmosphere and deep earth. This has allowed the gardeners to create a complementary botanical collection specializing in Himalayan plants, birches, hypericum, *Nothofagus,* and skimmias.

The more formal gardens hug the imposing Tudor mansion, which was built in 1590 for Sir Edward Culpeper. They include features that provide year-round interest. In summer, the Sir Henry Price Walled Garden overflows with tender perennials in muted shades. Late in the season, the Winter Garden provides unexpected color from plantings of heathers, snowdrops, and vivid willows.

Away from these formal areas, the gardens descend into the Loder Valley, named in honor of former owner Gerald Loder, who bought the estate in 1903 and really began to shape the garden as it is now. The slopes are relaxed and tranquil. They contain groves of *Daphne bholua* that scent the wooded glades in spring. Midsummer brings the 7.8-foot-tall (2.4 m) Himalayan lilies (*Cardiocrinum giganteum*), which make a spectacular show near the Iris Dell. At the base of the valley is a nature reserve burgeoning with the native flora of Sussex. LH

Pashley Manor Gardens

East Sussex, England

DESIGNER: Anthony du Gard Pasley
OWNERS: James Sellick, Angela Sellick
GARDEN STYLE: 20th-century formal
SIZE: 10 acres (4 ha)
CLIMATE: Temperate
LOCATION: Ticehurst, Wadhurst, East Sussex

There are two sides to Pashley Manor. The front of the house is timber-framed and dates from the 1550s. The south-facing Georgian facade was added in 1720. The garden reflects the house and is full of contrasts between formality and relaxed woodland. At its heart is a lake—the remnant of a medieval moat—on which stands a small temple commemorating family events.

The garden was rundown when the Sellicks moved in. It has been gradually redesigned and extended over the past half century, with the help of Anthony du Gard Pasley. The main lawn rolls down from the Georgian facade toward the lake, dominated by what is believed to be one of the oldest Scots pines (*Pinus sylvestris*) in England. Formal, walled gardens slope away to the southeast of the house, each offering a different view of the Sussex countryside. The first terrace, planted with spring tulips in shades of white through to cream and yellow, leads through a doorway to the swimming-pool garden, edged with cistus, cornus, lavender, and white roses. Enclosed within redbrick walls are a rose garden, full of old shrub roses, and a vegetable garden large enough to supply all the needs of the house. Beyond the walls is a hot garden of deep reds, bronze, and orange with sedums, kniphofias, bronze fennel (*Foeniculum vulgare* 'Purpureum'), penstemons, heleniums, and coral schizostylis with phormiums as spiky accents.

In the lower reaches of the garden, the path winds through mauve *Rhododendron ponticum*, a laurel tunnel, and layered planting of eucryphia. It eventually leads to the lowest of a series of ponds. VB

Sheffield Park Garden

East Sussex, England

DESIGNERS: Capability Brown, Humphry Repton, Pulham and Sons, Arthur Gilstrap Soames
OWNER: The National Trust
GARDEN STYLE: Late 18th-century landscape garden, with 20th-century planting
SIZE: 200 acres (81 ha)
CLIMATE: Temperate
LOCATION: Uckfield, East Sussex

Landscape gardens by their very nature are always changing and evolving. The challenge for their owners is to manage the change well, and this is what makes visiting Sheffield Park Garden so satisfying.

The first lakes in the extensive grounds at Sheffield Park were designed in 1776 by Capability Brown for John Holroyd, the first Earl of Sheffield. Humphry Repton excavated further large pools in 1789 to bring the water closer to the mansion. Then, in 1883, the third earl employed Pulham and Sons to build cascades and waterfalls from reconstituted stone to link all these different elements. This has created a park that is a seamless, naturalistic whole.

From 1885, multiple conifers, rhododendrons, azaleas, and Japanese maples were planted. Arthur Gilstrap Soames, who purchased the estate in 1910, instigated a massive program of tree planting; mostly North American species, all notable for their fall color. The combined effect of shapely trees and flowering shrubs reflected in vast, still waters with countless lily pads can be described only as breathtaking.

Now safely in the hands of the National Trust after a period of postwar deterioration, Sheffield Park has been radically enhanced. Bluebells and the National Collection of rare Ghent azaleas are delights in early summer. Fall crocuses and long beds of blue gentians complement the deep reds, bright scarlets, and soft yellows of turning foliage. Whatever time you visit, you cannot escape the wow factor. RC

Osborne House

Isle of Wight, England

DESIGNERS: Thomas Cubbitt, Rupert Golby, Ludwig Gruner
OWNER: English Heritage
GARDEN STYLE: Italianate
SIZE: 50 acres (20.2 ha)
CLIMATE: Temperate
LOCATION: East Cowes, Isle of Wight

On her marriage to Prince Albert of Saxe-Coburg-Gotha, Queen Victoria was looking for "a place of one's own, quiet and retired." Osborne House on the Isle of Wight, set in 342 acres (138.5 ha) with a private beach for boating and bathing, was ideal. Even better, on a sunny day the view from the terraces (now magnificently planted) across the waters of the Solent reminded Albert of the Bay of Naples. In 1846 he planted a *Magnolia grandiflora,* and the family stayed there for the first time.

The house and gardens were designed in the Italianate style, but, as an economic measure, the balustrades and vases were molded in cement by Thomas Cubitt's workshops. The garden statuary was mostly factory-made cement or bronze-coated zinc casts of antique models. The Andromeda Fountain on the upper terrace was manufactured by the Coalbrookdale Foundry in 1851.

The vegetable plots and monogrammed garden tools given to the nine royal children, and a furnished Swiss cottage are all still there. The Victoria Fort and Albert Barracks, a miniature earthen fort completed in 1856 for battles between the young royals, is also present. Make sure you see the 1-acre (0.4 ha) Walled Garden built for producing cut flowers and fruit, restored and redesigned by Rupert Golby in the 1990s. The parterre gardens and terraces have also been restored, with seasonally changing bedding. Keep an eye out for the individual and entwining V and A monograms that dominate the pergola, seats, and pots. CH

Ventnor Botanic Garden

Isle of Wight, England

DESIGNERS: Sir Harold Hillier, Simon Goodenough
OWNER: Isle of Wight Council
GARDEN STYLE: 20th-century formal botanic garden
SIZE: 22 acres (8.9 ha)
CLIMATE: Temperate
LOCATION: Ventnor, Isle of Wight

One of Britain's youngest botanic gardens, Ventnor was started in 1970 on the site of a former hospital in the heart of the Undercliff. Protected to the north and east by chalk downs, the garden has a microclimate more akin to the Mediterranean, enabling plants that would otherwise be too tender in mainland Britain to flourish. In the early days of its development, the garden was enthusiastically supported by the late Sir Harold Hillier, the internationally renowned Hampshire plantsman, who supplied it with many shrubs and trees from his nurseries. Other rare and exotic plants have been introduced from around the world.

There are some very good plantings here, with dozens of salvias still in flower in early winter. The shallow, well-drained alkaline soil is ideal for the evening primroses, rock roses, verbascum, rosemary, curry plants, palms, and echiums planted on the Mediterranean Terrace among bare stone, mimicking the harsh landscape of the region. All the plants have to cope well with the salt-laden winds that blow in from the south and west.

Approached through a courtyard planted with cannas, agapanthus, and pampas grass, the gardens represent several different countries. The Australian Terraces, for instance, are planted with phormiums, cordylines, verbascums, and euphorbia. The New Zealand Garden is in a shaded glade with holm oaks (*Quercus ilex*), senecios, palms, and phormiums. The clifftop grassland path is dotted with British native wildflowers, and gives a view of both garden and sea crashing onto the beach far below. VB

Antony House

Cornwall, England

DESIGNERS: Humphry Repton, Mr. Pole-Carew, Sir John
  Carew Pole, Sir Richard Carew Pole
OWNER: The National Trust, Sir Richard Carew Pole
GARDEN STYLE: Formal, woodland
SIZE: 25 acres (10.1 ha), plus 50 acres (20.2 ha) woodland
CLIMATE: Temperate
LOCATION: Torpoint, Cornwall

Many Cornish gardens received new plants brought to Britain from North America and Asia during the nineteenth century, and the woodland planting at Antony House is a fine example of such a collection. The mild, moist climate and acidic soils provide ideal conditions for camellias, rhododendrons, azaleas, and other ericaceous plants that thrive in this beautiful valley by the banks of the River Lynher.

The huge woodland is still under the ownership and care of the Carew family, who have lived at Antony House for over 600 years. The current custodian, Sir Richard Carew Pole, president of the Royal Horticultural Society, is a keen plantsman with a special interest in trees and shrubs. He introduces many new specimens to the garden each year. The National Trust manages the formal gardens immediately surrounding the eighteenth-century mansion. They include a knot garden, roses, and herbaceous plants, a Japanese pond, and a National Collection of daylilies. Richard Carew Pole is a keen collector of modern sculpture, and examples can be found throughout the gardens. The dramatic conical water sculpture by William Pye was added in 1996.

The garden is open to the public for eight months of the year. With over 100 varieties of magnolia and many other early flowering shrubs and bulbs, a spring visit is essential, with the summer borders and fall color extending interest through the following seasons. The immediate and wider landscape provides one of the most beautiful settings imaginable. AJ

Trebah

Cornwall, England

DESIGNER: Charles Fox
OWNER: Trebah Garden Trust
GARDEN STYLE: 19th-century exotic woodland garden,
  Cornish valley garden
SIZE: 26 acres (10.5 ha)
CLIMATE: Temperate
LOCATION: Mawnan Smith, Falmouth, Cornwall

Trebah is one of a Cornish trio of exotic woodland gardens—alongside Glendurgan (see page 439) and Penjerrick (see page 438)—created by the Fox family of Falmouth during the nineteenth century. Wealthy Quaker shipping merchants, the Fox brothers wished to honor their Creator by creating their own vision of "Heaven on Earth." In a series of steep valleys running down to the sea, they nurtured exotics brought from all over the world and transformed the rugged ravines into lush, richly flowered woodlands with spectacular views over the treetops down to the River Helford.

At Trebah, Charles Fox placed every tree with meticulous care, and the collection of rare trees and shrubs continued to grow until World War II when, like many large gardens, it fell into decline. It was rescued in 1981 by Tony and Eira Hibbert who, having planned a peaceful and carefree retirement, discovered too late that the jungle surrounding their new home concealed the remains of a once outstanding garden. By 1987 the garden was open to the public, and restoration continues year by year.

Today Trebah is a garden to be enjoyed for its beautifully composed views and richly atmospheric planting. Summer blazes with showy subtropicals and a sea of blue and white hydrangeas. But Trebah does not need sunshine to enchant. While sheltering from a shower under the giant leaves of gunnera or wandering through a grove of tree ferns (*Dicksonia antarctica*) on a misty Cornish morning, Fox's vision of paradise seems supremely realized. AE

Barbara Hepworth Museum and Sculpture Garden

Cornwall, England

DESIGNER: Barbara Hepworth
OWNERS: Tate Gallery, Hepworth Estate
GARDEN STYLE: 20th-century informal sculpture garden
SIZE: 0.2 acre (0.1 ha)
CLIMATE: Temperate
LOCATION: St. Ives, Cornwall

Dame Barbara Hepworth settled in St. Ives with her family in 1939. By then she was already recognized as one of the most exciting of a new generation of British artists, which included her husband, Ben Nicholson, and Henry Moore. In 1949 Dame Barbara bought Trewyn Studios and continued to develop her skills, becoming established as one of Britain's leading abstract sculptors. She was famous for creating pieces from a wide range of different materials, including various types of stone, bronze, and wood.

Following her death in 1975, her studios and garden were opened to the public at her bequest. Set on a sloping hillside in the middle of the bustling fishing port, the high-walled garden has a delightfully calm atmosphere. Dame Barbara developed the garden over the years, installing paths, creating beds, and adding new plants as well as carefully placing a number of her favorite sculptures. In fact the planting is not just a backdrop to the sculptures, it is a key part of the experience. The mixed forms of the architectural specimens and soft planting, together with the varied shades of green, harmonize with and emphasize the sculptures. The play of shadows cast by the trees adds dynamism to the immobile works. The garden was vital to Dame Barbara, and offers a unique insight into her view of the correlation between the natural world and her abstract style. TM

Caerhays Castle Gardens

Cornwall, England

DESIGNER: John Charles Williams
OWNER: Julian Williams CBE
GARDEN STYLE: 19th- and 20th-century woodland garden
SIZE: 60 acres (24.3 ha)
CLIMATE: Temperate
LOCATION: Gorran, St. Austell, Cornwall

On a steeply wooded hillside, rising up behind a romantic gray-stone castle, is one of the greatest springtime gardens in Cornwall. It has been the home of the Williams family since 1853, but it was the third generation of the family who finally decided to do something about the garden. Julian Williams was eighteen and studying at university when he inherited the rambling estate after his father died. Eventually he gave up his job as an MP, and retreated to Cornwall to start gardening. The site now consists of a series of winding paths through a superb collection of camellias, magnolias, and rhododendrons.

John Charles Williams financially backed the intrepid plant hunters in the 1890s, including Ernest Wilson and George Forrest. They traveled to the remote mountainous regions of the Far East and returned to Britain with many rare and unknown plant specimens. Those planted in this sheltered spot with its rich acid soil have now grown to magnificent proportions. Also look out for the National Collection of magnolias, their cream and pink waxy petals standing out perfectly against the deep blue Cornish sky. Other magnificent specimens in the woodland include azaleas, nothofagus, oaks, acers, and ferns, all with an underplanting of bulbs. Caerhays Castle also bears the distinction of being the place of origin for Camellia x williamsii, one of the most popular and widely grown camellias. Visitors should note that the garden is steep, and the paths can be slippery. JH

The Lost Gardens of Heligan

Cornwall, England

DESIGNERS: The Tremayne family, Heligan Gardens Ltd.
OWNERS: The Tremayne family, Heligan Gardens Ltd.
GARDEN STYLE: Victorian, Edwardian
SIZE: 80 acres (32.4 ha)
CLIMATE: Temperate
LOCATION: Pentewan, St. Austell, Cornwall

Hidden for seventy-five years beneath a blanket of decayed leaves and encroaching trees, and neglected because many of the gardeners perished in World War I, the Lost Gardens of Heligan were the subject of a dramatic rediscovery by machete-wielding enthusiasts that has passed into gardening legend. In 1991, Tim Smit, John Nelson, and a team of volunteers gradually revealed the history of one of the most mysterious estates in England—the ancestral seat of the Tremayne family for over 400 years.

The once-spectacular gardens have now been restored. Delightful pleasure grounds with Italian and New Zealand gardens, summerhouses, a crystal grotto, pools, and a rocky ravine are linked by a network of walks. There are also extensive working gardens that originally met the needs of the Tremayne family. The walled vegetable and flower gardens are once again full to bursting. A cornucopia of traditional varieties is being grown alongside catacomblike beehives. There are also areas dedicated to the Victorian passion for exotic fruits, with a manure-warmed pit for growing pineapples, and greenhouses brimming with vines, peaches, and melons. Also make sure you see the "Jungle," packed with luxuriant, subtropical foliage, and the boardwalk that snakes downward, through palm-lined avenues, past groves of banana palms, magnificent giant rhubarb, and the richly textured trunks of exotic trees. Even without the history, this garden is stunning. NS

St Michael's Mount

Cornwall, England

DESIGNERS: St. Aubyn family
OWNERS: Lord St. Levan, The National Trust
GARDEN STYLE: 17th- to 21st-century informal exotic
SIZE: 5 acres (2 ha)
CLIMATE: Temperate
LOCATION: Marazion, Cornwall

An island capped by a castle is a dramatic setting for a garden, even by Cornwall's extravagant standards. Like its geographical sister, Mont St. Michel in France, St. Michael's Mount is a tidal island reached by foot at low tide via a causeway. The present house is a fascinating ensemble of medieval monastic buildings and later additions, including some delightful eighteenth-century "Gothick." Within this landscape and architecture is the loosely structured and rather wild garden, created by the St. Aubyn family.

The wind can be relentless, and yet whatever survives its buffeting benefits from an exceptionally mild climate and the excellent drainage offered by the rocky slopes. Monterey pines (*Pinus radiata*) and evergreen holm oaks (*Quercus ilex*) are the first line of defense, backed by an understory of salt-tolerant shrubs such as *Griselinia littoralis* and species euonymus and escallonia. Red-hot pokers (*Kniphofia* species) love it here, and succulents such as aloes, agaves, aeoniums, and varous Aizoaceae flourish in soil-filled nooks and crannies around massive granite boulders. Clumps of the terrestrial bromeliad *Fascicularia bicolor*, with its spiny rosettes and exotic red bracts, grow to several feet wide.

Sprawling over several terraces, the garden's architectural and exotic palms and yuccas are reminiscent of a Mediterranean garden. At times precipitous, with stout footwear being a visitor's prerequisite, this is a garden that exploits its exceptional location to the full. As a result, the garden is in season from spring to late summer. NK

The Eden Project

Cornwall, England

DESIGNERS: Tim Smit, Nicholas Grimshaw
OWNER: The Eden Trust
GARDEN STYLE: 21st-century giant greenhouses
SIZE: 37 acres (14.9 ha)
CLIMATE: Temperate; tropical, warm temperate in biomes
LOCATION: Bodelva, St. Austell, Cornwall

Drive along the winding Cornish road that leads to the Eden Project and the sight of the huge soap bubble-shaped domes at the bottom of the old quarry will take your breath away. You may have seen the photographs, but nothing prepares you for this.

Established in 2000, the Eden Project aims to foster an understanding of the importance of plants in the delicate relationships among all living things. In other words, it is hoped that by seeing how the natural world works, we will be able to create a sustainable future. If this sounds very lofty and high-minded, the experience is anything but. There are two giant domes or biomes: a tropical environment is recreated in one, a warm temperate climate in the other. The Humid Tropics Biome is, in effect, the largest conservatory in the world with over 1,000 plant species, streams, and crashing waterfalls. The walkways through this jungle are punctuated with easily digestible information about paper, coffee, rubber, and the other plants essential to our lives. The Warm Temperate Biome captures the natural and cultivated landscapes of the Mediterranean, California, and South America, where plants have adapted to their challenging environments through their waxy leaves, spines, or gray, hairy foliage.

Outside the massive domes, a long walk meanders through recreations of prairies, steppes, and other environments. Work by local artists is woven through the plants, and there are frequent performances by musicians and dancers from around the world. Prepare to be amazed. JH

Penjerrick Garden

Cornwall, England

DESIGNERS: Robert Were Fox, Barclay Fox
OWNER: Rachel Morin
GARDEN STYLE: 19th- and 20th-century naturalistic
SIZE: 10 acres (4 ha)
CLIMATE: Temperate
LOCATION: Budock Water, Falmouth, Cornwall

Penjerrick is one of a number of famous Cornish gardens that lie nestled away in valleys along the south coast of this mildest corner of England. They enjoy particularly gentle microclimates and, throughout the nineteenth and early twentieth centuries, were "proving grounds" for many of the exotic and tender species brought back from all over the world by the plant hunters.

One family who created several such plant paradises was the Fox family, and Penjerrick was the jewel in the crown. The garden was made by Robert Were Fox, a mining engineer, natural philosopher, and plantaholic, and his son Barclay. At its peak, the garden contained over 300 different species. Many were new introductions, but many other plants were raised in the garden, including some notable *Rhododendron* hybrids, in particular 'Penjerrick', 'Barclayi', and 'Penjerrick Cream'.

As with other valley gardens, World War I rang the death knell for Penjerrick's vast collections of expensive perennials, bulbs, and climbers that required an army of gardeners. Yet the garden remains a lush paradise filled with many mature and unusual subtropical specimens. As with most Cornish gardens, it is at its very best in spring. Lawns sweep down the slope, offering wonderful views toward the sea. Winding paths weave their way through forests of rhododendrons, tree ferns (*Dicksonia antarctica*), bamboos, magnolias, camellias, and many rare and magnificent trees and shrubs. Farther down the slope, reached via the wooden bridge, the valley garden contains a series of four ponds shaded in summer by the enormous leaves of *Gunnera manicata*. A network of paths also offers a range of different perspectives and vistas. One is lined with an avenue of towering tree ferns reaching over 16.4-feet (5 m) tall. They date back to the early phase of the garden and are some of the first tree ferns planted in England. TM

Glendurgan Garden

Cornwall, England

DESIGNER: Alfred Fox
OWNER: The National Trust
GARDEN STYLE: Subtropical woodland
SIZE: 25 acres (8.1 ha)
CLIMATE: Temperate
LOCATION: Mawnan Smith, Falmouth, Cornwall

Created by devout Quaker shipping merchant Alfred Fox in the 1820s, this lush garden of woods, wildflower meadows, and giant subtropical plants runs down a wide ravine from the private family home to the picturesque fishing hamlet of Durgan. As you glimpse bracing views of the River Helford through myriad rhododendrons, rare camellias, and magnolias in full bloom, there is no denying that Fox, with help from successive generations, achieved his aim of creating "a small piece of heaven on earth."

Although Glendurgan is at its most colorful in late spring, midsummer is when the garden becomes truly magical. Bamboos, bananas, unfurling tree ferns (*Dicksonia antarctica*), palms, massive poolside gunnera, and jagged clumps of aloes with 20-foot-high (6 m) flower spikes send all visitors, children in particular, into transports of delight, making Glendurgan one of the best English gardens for young families to explore. This is surely by design: Fox and his wife Sarah had twelve children.

Dating from 1833, the curious, asymmetrical maze with plump hedges of laurel has a straw-thatched clay schoolroom at its heart. It is overlooked by the contemplative Holy Bank where plants with biblical associations include the tree of heaven (*Ailanthus altissima*) and Christ's thorn (*Paliurus spina-christi*). Elsewhere the extraordinary flowers of venerable tulip trees (*Liriodendron tulipifera*) and handkerchief trees (*Davidia involucrata*) are well worth looking out for, as is a recent gift of rare tender conifers from the Royal Botanic Garden Edinburgh. RC

Trelissick Gardens

Cornwall, England

DESIGNER: The Copeland family
OWNER: The National Trust
GARDEN STYLE: 19th- and 20th-century informal, woodland
SIZE: 20 acres (8.1 ha), plus 375 acres (151.8 ha) parkland
CLIMATE: Temperate
LOCATION: Feock, Truro, Cornwall

Trelissick combines the characteristic, and perpetually exciting, planting style of Cornish gardens with wonderful views across some of the most beautiful coastal scenery in England. The garden rises up above the banks of the Fal, more of a creek than a river, with densely wooded slopes and protected coves, framing a view to the open sea beyond. A splendid "rustic" pavilion, ornamented with pinecones and a pebble floor, is a good place to admire the view when it rains.

Essentially a large estate, with a rather checkered history, Trelissick's garden is a relatively recent one. The serious planting started with the Copeland family in 1928, although the parkland framework of tree planting was carried out in the nineteenth century. Mature trees shelter a rich array of shrubby planting, dominated by magnolias, hybrid rhododendrons, camellias, and many other, often tender, species. A dell, sheltered from the prevailing winds, is home to tree ferns (*Dicksonia antarctica*) and exotically scented *Rhododendron maddenii*. A high water table in the lower parts of the garden provides an excellent home for the giant leaves of *Gunnera manicata*, skunk lilies, rodgersias, and Himalayan primulas.

The garden at Trelissick is split by a road leading down to the local ferry. A rustic bridge spans the canyon below to a newer part of the garden—Carcadden—noted for its fine, open lawns. These create a sense of space in contrast to the almost dominant woodland feel of the rest of Trelissick. Also note, near the entrance to the garden, two walled enclosures of interest to fruit and vegetable growers. One holds a collection of fig varieties. The other, known as the Parsley Garden, was designed to create a warm microclimate for early vegetables.

Trelissick is a particular joy for those interested in rare and unusual plants, but all will enjoy its location and setting. Spring and early summer are the best times to visit. NK

Trewithen Gardens

Cornwall, England

DESIGNER: George Johnstone
OWNER: Michael Galsworthy CBE
GARDEN STYLE: 20th-century informal, woodland
SIZE: 25 acres (10.1 ha)
CLIMATE: Temperate
LOCATION: Truro, Cornwall

If one had to visit only one garden to appreciate what is so special about Cornish gardens, this would probably be the best. It has all the classic features—informal woodland planting, tender shrubs, and fine trees—all of the highest quality.

The estate was inherited by George Johnstone in 1904. He began planting the extensive areas of woodland around the house. As one of a close-knit circle of gardening aristocrats, he obtained a wide range of newly introduced plants, mostly of Asian origin. What makes Trewithen so exciting is not just the choice plants—*Ceanothus arboreus* 'Trewithen

Blue' comes from here—but the way the lawn stretches out from the house. It can only be described as a double border on a spectacular scale, dominated by vast magnolias that graduate down to smaller shrubs. Its scale and proportions are perfect, and introduces that sense of architecture and planning that Cornish gardens so frequently lack. Ironically, this magnificent area partly owes its existence to the compulsory requisition of trees for timber during World War II.

Elsewhere, narrow snaking paths enable visitors to explore a rich plant collection, best appreciated in spring or early summer, although there is plenty of fine foliage later. There is also a lovely walled garden, laid out in a more formal vein, with a lily pond, summerhouse, well-planted borders, and a pergola draped in wisteria. Orderly and restful, Trewithen is one of the finest examples of a garden style that is highly distinctive and almost uniquely Cornish. NK

Tresco Abbey

Isles of Scilly, Cornwall, England

DESIGNERS: Augustus Smith, the Dorrien-Smith family
OWNER: Robert Dorrien-Smith
GARDEN STYLE: 19th- and 20th-century ornamental botanic
SIZE: 20 acres (8.1 ha)
CLIMATE: Temperate
LOCATION: Tresco, Isles of Scilly, Cornwall

The Abbey Garden on the tiny island of Tresco is unlike any other British garden. Its gorgeous setting on the Isles of Scilly is special enough, but nowhere else will you find proteas from South Africa, succulents from Mexico, New Zealand flame trees (*Metrosideros excelsus*), aloes, banksias, and a host of exotic plants all flourishing outdoors in Britain. The garden has often been described as Kew's Temperate House with the lid off, but this goes only a small way to explain the delights of Tresco.

The garden was started in the late 1830s by Augustus Smith, a dictatorial philanthropist who came to the islands full of charitable fervor to better conditions for their inhabitants. He made his home on Tresco and began his garden. He soon understood that the benign maritime climate would allow him to experiment with plants far too tender for mainland Britain. His descendents have always shared his passion for the garden, making it the extraordinary and beautiful place it now is. Today, Tresco contains a unique collection of subtropical plants with over 20,000 plants from over eighty countries.

The garden is laid out on a series of terraces that progress up a low hillside. The lower terraces are cooler and damper, home to lush tree ferns (*Dicksonia antarctica*). The drier upper terraces are decked with succulents and proteas, and the spectacular plants are framed by handsome stonework made from local granite. Tall windbreaks composed of cypresses and pines provide additional shelter for the exotic varieties, channeling the Atlantic winds up and over the terraces. At the heart of the garden are the ruins of the twelfth-century Benedictine priory where Augustus Smith began his horticultural vision. Since its conception, each generation of the family has added to the gardens, from specimen trees and a Mediterranean garden to fountains and sculpture. Few gardens are worth a major detour; this one is. AM

Rowallane Garden

Co. Down, Northern Ireland

DESIGNERS: John Armytage Moore, Hugh Armytage Moore
OWNER: The National Trust
GARDEN STYLE: 19th- and 20th-century informal
plantsman's garden
SIZE: 52 acres (21 ha)
CLIMATE: Temperate
LOCATION: Saintfield, Ballynahinch, Co. Down

Rowallane was started in the 1860s by the Reverend John Moore, who built the walled garden and planted the Pleasure Grounds. Following his death in 1888, Rowallane passed to Moore's nephew, Hugh Armytage Moore. Hugh filled the garden with plants that enjoyed the varied conditions here, and the garden has many rare and exotic specimens sent back from China and the Far East by plant hunters Ernest Wilson, George Forrest, and Frank Kingdon-Ward.

One of the delights of the design is how it incorporates the natural landscape, blurring the boundary between garden and nature. Within the garden is a fine mix of garden styles, and the plant collection is so diverse that there is something to enjoy at any time of year. By the entrance to the walled garden is *Hypericum* 'Rowallane', a cultivar raised here. Within are herbaceous plants with shrub roses, fuchsias, the gorgeous Himalayan blue poppy (*Meconopsis betonicifoila*), the National Collection of large-flowered penstemons, and two more plants that were bred in the garden: *Viburnum plicatum* f. *tomentosum* 'Rowallane', and the original *Chaenomeles* x *superba* 'Rowallane'.

The Rock Garden has a large outcrop of local rocks, and is home to primulas, heathers, and dwarf shrubs. In summer the wildflower meadow is studded with rare orchids. There is also a fine collection of conifers giving good color all year. Further highlights are the rhododendrons and azaleas, which give a show of flowers from mid-fall to late summer. TM

Mount Stewart

Co. Down, Northern Ireland

DESIGNER: Seventh Marchioness of Londonderry
OWNER: The National Trust
GARDEN STYLE: 20th-century formal
and informal
SIZE: 97 acres (39.2 ha)
CLIMATE: Temperate
LOCATION: Greyabbey, Newtownards, Co. Down

This is gardening on a gigantic, witty, outrageous scale, all thanks to Edith, Marchioness of Londonderry. Her husband inherited the stately house and grounds (now managed by The National Trust) in 1915. In 1921 she got stuck in. The garden is a bit like those completely over-the-top classical Chinese gardens, with everything thrown in and with a twist.

There are 98-foot-high (30 m) Tasmanian gum trees (*Eucalyptus globulus*), giant rhododendrons, and cardiocrinums—eucalyptuses like space rockets and roses that cannot stop climbing. Everything, especially the rare and tender (and their numbers are astonishing), is pampered by the Gulf Stream and the woods that block out the wind. The design includes Spanish and Italian parterres, and also a pergola with vines, terraces, and a sunken garden based on a Gertrude Jekyll plan. There is a 5-acre (2 ha) lake, 15 acres (6 ha) of rhododendrons, the family cemetery or Tir Nan Og (Land of the Ever Young), a red, white, and blue avenue, and a hillside with multiple views.

Everything is so incredibly immaculate. Add to that the imagery, with fun statues of fabulous creatures on the Dodo Terrace based on friends and public figures, Japanese ornaments, and the garden of Irish symbolism, and it is clear why this isn't just one of Northern Ireland's, but Europe's best. Allow a day to get around the garden. RR

RIGHT The immaculate grounds of Northern Ireland's Mount Stewart, where everything grows in abundance.

Glenveagh Castle Garden

Donegal, Republic of Ireland

DESIGNERS: Lanning Roper, James Russell
OWNER: The Irish State
GARDEN STYLE: 19th- and 20th-century Italianate, landscape
SIZE: 22,000 acres (8,910 ha)
CLIMATE: Temperate
LOCATION: Letterkenny, Donegal

J. G. Adair created this vast 22,000-acre (8,910 ha) estate in the 1850s. Originally boggy hillside sloping down to Loch Veagh, it was planted with pines and oaks as background for the castle that Adair built beside the loch. His wife, Cornelia, created the original garden, but it really took off when it was bought in 1937 by American Henry McIlhenny. He called in Lanning Roper and James Russell to advise on design and planting: they increased the range of rhododendrons and, for texture and structure, added palms, tree ferns, pseudopanax and *Trochodendron aralioides*, also including camellias, magnolias, and acers for color.

They added walks through woods, inserting themed openings—a pool in one, and blue poppies in others.

In 1966 a formal slate terrace was built, with Italian statues, Sicilian oil jars, and Italian cypresses (*Cupressus sempervirens*). Along the loch shore, sphinxes signal the entrance to the Italian garden, which features Italian busts set in griselinia hedges, eucryphias, and rhododendrons. As well as these formal features, there are boulder-strewn streams, open heath, oak groves, and a climb up sixty-seven granite steps to the top of the castle tower where there are views to the castle, loch, and mountains. Don't miss the kitchen garden and its grand entrance. Outside are terraces, lawns, spiral topiary, and box-edged beds with a mix of vegetables and flowers. In 1983 Henry gave the garden to the Irish State. Since then, the head gardener has been Sean O'Gaoithin. He added old Donegal roses, and new rhododendron and sorbus species—the place is still changing! RChe

Altamont Garden

County Carlow, Republic of Ireland

DESIGNER: Feilding Lecky Watson
OWNER: Heritage Ireland
GARDEN STYLE: 20th-century formal and informal
SIZE: 100 acres (40.5 ha)
CLIMATE: Temperate
LOCATION: Tullow, County Carlow

Had it not been for the indomitable Carona North, the estate of Altamont would have been sold off upon the death of her mother Isabel Lecky Watson in 1983, depriving Ireland of what would become one of the country's most romantic and best-loved gardens. She dedicated the rest of her life to restoring the mostly derelict grounds to their former glory.

Mrs. North inherited her father's passion for collecting plants. Feilding Lecky Watson came from a family that sponsored several plant-collecting trips during the 19th and early 20th centuries. It was he who created the gardens at Altamont around a house that, although dating from the 18th century, has its original foundations in the 16th century, and is thought to be on the site of an ancient convent.

Supremely romantic and mostly informal in style, there is still a hint of formality to the gardens behind the house with three parallel walks of lawns, clipped yews, and borders full of roses. After this, however, the gardens become distinctly naturalistic. The walks travel down toward a lake that was dug out after the Irish Famine in the 1850s to provide employment for locals. On its banks is a vast collection of rare trees and shrubs, including a collection of rhododendrons. Many of those rhododendrons came from the plant-collecting trips and one in particular, 'Corona', was the inspiration for Mrs. North's name.

Beyond the lake, the spirit of wilderness takes over the garden. Here lies the Ice Age Glen where there is a glorious river walk, a bog garden, an arboretum, and sublime views of the rural landscape. RSJ

The Dillon Garden

Dublin, Republic of Ireland

DESIGNER: Helen Dillon
OWNERS: Val Dillon, Helen Dillon
GARDEN STYLE: 20th- and 21st-century semiformal town garden
SIZE: 0.5 acre (0.2 ha)
CLIMATE: Temperate
LOCATION: Ranelagh, Dublin, Dublin

The garden writer, broadcaster, and plantswoman Helen Dillon moved to her elegant Regency house in the suburbs of south Dublin over thirty years ago. Here she created what was to become a mecca for plant lovers, a garden packed with rarities from around the globe and with a very clever design.

Stepping up from the sunken terrace, which has been decorated with an artfully staged collection of terracotta-potted specimens, the main event comes into view. What was once a lawn is now a limestone pavement bisected by a narrow canal or brook incorporating pools and cascades. Guarding the entrance is a pair of stone sphinxes, each backed by a clipped box pyramid. The long borders on either side of the canal are triumphs of color coordination. Hot reds, orange, purple, bronze, and black highlights are on the left. Opposite, cool blues and soft purples are sprinkled with white and silver. Unusual species and cultivars mingle with familiar varieties and are constantly being rearranged for more effective color combinations. There are also raised beds for alpines, including silvery-leaved celmisias from New Zealand.

Despite the owner's frenetic activity—weeding, deadheading, and tweaking—the garden has a relaxed air. Many plants are encouraged to self-seed, including angel's fishing rods, whose purple and pink wands arc over pathways. Despite the garden's poor soil, and with only 30 inches (76 cm) of rainfall a year, the lush displays are extraordinary and largely owing to Helen's husband's homemade compost. JHe

National Botanic Gardens

Dublin, Republic of Ireland

DESIGNERS: Various
OWNER: Irish Office of Public Works
GARDEN STYLE: 18th-century botanic garden
SIZE: 48 acres (19.5 ha)
CLIMATE: Temperate
LOCATION: Glasnevin, Dublin, Co. Dublin

These gardens, which are also known as Glasnevin, were established in 1795 by the Irish Parliament. They occupy a beautiful site on the banks of the River Tolka, and now contain in excess of 20,000 plant taxa and some striking nineteenth-century greenhouses.

The greenhouses were made famous by William Robinson who, as a trainee at Glasnevin, left in a fit of resentment, having first extinguished the fires in the boilers. In recent years the greenhouses and plant collection have experienced a period of restoration, with the Great Palm House of 1884 having reopened in 2004. The striking Curvilinear Range (1843–69), which was designed and built by Dublin ironmaster Richard Turner, is over 400 feet (122 m) in length. It has been planted with cycads and related plants, tender rhododendrons taken from southeast Asia, and collections from South Africa, and dry, temperate parts of Australia and South America. Further treats in the Fern House are the Irish native Killarney fern (*Trichomanes speciosum*) and the Australian king fern (*Todea barbara*) that came to Glasnevin in 1969 from Trinity College Botanic Gardens and is 400 years old.

Outdoors there are collections of alpines in the rock garden, moisture lovers in the bog, poisonous and economic plants, and roses. New developments include the Sensory Garden and an expansion of the Chinese plants collection. Native plants include those from the Burren in the west of Ireland. Two further highlights are the last rose of summer (*Rosa chinensis* 'Old Blush') and the early Victorian chain tent, with a monumental wisteria planted in 1836. TM

> "The striking Curvilinear Range . . . is over 400 feet (122 m) in length"

The Irish National Stud

Kildare, Republic of Ireland

DESIGNERS: Tassa Eida, Martin Hallin
OWNER: The Irish National Stud
GARDEN STYLE: 20th-century Japanese style, informal
SIZE: 5.5 acres (2.2 ha)
CLIMATE: Temperate
LOCATION: Tully, Kildare, Co. Kildare

County Kildare has been synonymous with horses since the fourteenth century—warhorses were likely bred here for the Knights of Malta. However, it was not until 1900 that the first stud farm was established by Colonel William Hall-Walker. He also had a passion for gardens. With Japanese gardens all the rage, he hired the famous Japanese landscape gardener Tassa Eida who, assisted by his son Minoru, laid out the garden between 1906 and 1910. Consequently, the garden is also known as the Japanese Garden.

Decorated by stone lanterns and a Geisha House, the gardens symbolize the "Life of Man," tracing the soul's journey "from Oblivion to Eternity and the human experience of its embodiment as it journeys by paths of its own choice through life." The path takes the visitor on a winding route through artificial caves to a stream and on to the reflective ponds and the weeping trees of the grave. The planting is highly ornamental, with highlights of old Japanese maples and mature Scotch pines (*Pinus sylvestris*).

Created in 1999 is St. Fiachra's Garden, "a garden to commemorate the Patron Saint of Gardeners in his home country of Ireland." Designed by Professor Martin Hallin and set in woodlands and wetlands, it emulates the natural Irish landscape of rock and water that inspired the monastic spirituality of the sixth and seventh centuries. It features monastic cells of fissured limestone surrounded by water. The inner subterranean garden lies in the main monastic cell and, entered through a tunnel, is filled with shaped rocks, ferns, and orchids, and is lit by fiber optics. TM

Larchill Arcadian Garden

Kildare, Republic of Ireland

DESIGNER: Unknown
OWNERS: Michael de las Casas, Louisa de las Casas
GARDEN STYLE: 18th-century ornamental farm
SIZE: 63 acres (25.5 ha)
CLIMATE: Temperate
LOCATION: Kilcock, Kildare

Both an ornamental farm and landscaped garden, constructed by diverse hands from the 1750s onward, Larchill fell long ago into ruin. Neglect, though, was ultimately to prove its savior. Unlike many gardens "improved" down the centuries, its bones were left intact. When this country estate 19 miles (30 km) west of Dublin was purchased by the de las Casas family in 1994, its significance both to Ireland and to Europe, as an unaltered ferme ornée (ornamental farm), immediately became apparent. Extensive work was undertaken to restore the place to its former glory and to make it a serious tourist destination.

Vaguely modeled on Marie Antoinette's hamlet in the grounds of le Petit Trianon at Versailles, and on Stowe in England, the park is home to ten classical and gothic follies, an artificial lake, and a farmyard. Ireland's largest collection of rare breed livestock grazes the land. An assortment of visitors from the most diehard historians to carloads of tourists walk the beech and ash avenues, enjoy the wildflower meadow, and admire the formal walled gardens with their flower borders, box hedging, water features, and ornamental herb and vegetable plots.

Gibraltar is the highlight of an hour-long stroll—a miniature fortress in the middle of the lake, it was modeled on a castle in Gibraltar. In its heyday, it was the scene of mock naval battles. The Foxes Earth feature comes a close second. On the fun side there is pets' corner, an adventure playground, a science room, and a program of outdoor events: alfresco Shakespeare, falconry, and Punch and Judy. RCa

Killruddery House and Gardens

Wicklow, Republic of Ireland

DESIGNER: Monsieur Bonet
OWNER: Fifteenth Earl of Meath
GARDEN STYLE: 17th-century formal
SIZE: 90 acres (36.4 ha)
CLIMATE: Temperate
LOCATION: Bray, Wicklow

When Tom Cruise and Nicole Kidman came galloping across the lawns of Killruddery in *Far And Away* (filmed in 1992), the theatricality of the location struck gardeners. This is the best surviving example of seventeenth-century gardening in the UK, having been laid out on a grand scale in the 1680s expressly for entertaining. It still has a magical atmosphere.

The Brabazon family, the Earls of Meath, who still own it, commissioned Bonet, a French Huguenot, to fashion them a trendsetting garden. His trademark French flourishes, reminiscent of Versailles, remain. Twin ponds (known as *miroirs d'eau*), some 540 feet

(165 m) long, reflect the facade of the mock-Elizabethan mansion. There are long, converging walks known as angles, laid out in a patte d'oie or goose-foot design, flanked by hornbeam, beech, and lime hedges. In fact hedges play a big part at Killruddery. Framed by a soaring double beech hedge with a hidden path between, there is an enchanting circular pond complete with elaborate fountain and cast-iron statues of the four seasons guarding the entrances. Farther on is a classical, eighteenth-century Sylvan theater with tiered grassy banks enclosed by tall bay hedges, the only one of its kind in Ireland.

Statuary is well used at Killruddery. It provides both a focal point in the shady wooded walks of the wilderness and a feature in the nineteenth-century orangery. The balustrade here is noteworthy, having been modeled on the tiara Lady Meath sold to finance the orangery's construction. Such attention to detail makes Killruddery very special. PMcW

Powerscourt House and Gardens

Wicklow, Republic of Ireland

DESIGNER: Daniel Robertson
OWNER: Tenth Viscount Powerscourt
GARDEN STYLE: 19th-century formal and informal
    landscape
SIZE: 45 acres (18.2 ha)
CLIMATE: Temperate
LOCATION: Enniskerry, Wicklow

Powerscourt is one of Ireland's greatest showpiece gardens. Bizarrely, though, the striking eighteenth-century Palladian mansion house, built in 1731 and gutted by fire in 1974, now contains shops, a terrace café, and exhibitions. However, given the garden's history, perhaps this is not so odd.

With verdant lawns that incontrovertibly prove why Ireland is the Emerald Isle, the garden as seen today dates from 1841. It is largely the design of inimitable London architect Daniel Robertson. The story goes that he worked only when drunk, and he had to be moved around the site in a wheelbarrow. This is not bad when you see what he achieved. A central stairway descends through the amphitheater of six terraces with statuary and formal beds to the Triton Pool, which has a fountain that jets to a height of 70 feet (21 m). There is a striking view from the top terrace over the pool to the natural beauty of the River Dargle and beyond, to Sugar Loaf Mountain.

Later additions at Powerscourt include a richly planted woodland garden filled with North American tree specimens. This, and Killing Hollow, are sights that are best viewed from the top of the Pepperpot, a fortified folly that stands to one side of the terraces. There is also a fine avenue of monkey puzzle trees (*Araucaria araucana*), the famous perspective gate, and a Japanese garden created in 1906. A little more distant, at 3 miles (5 km), is another must-see for the visitor, the Powerscourt Waterfall. At 398 feet (121 m) high, it is the tallest in Ireland and a wonderful spot to sit and have a picnic. TM

> " . . . verdant lawns that incontrovertibly prove why Ireland is the Emerald Isle . . . "

Mount Usher Gardens

Wicklow, Republic of Ireland

DESIGNER: Edward Walpole
OWNER: Madelaine Jay
GARDEN STYLE: 19th- and 20th-century wild garden
SIZE: 20 acres (8.1 ha)
CLIMATE: Temperate
LOCATION: Ashford, Wicklow

If you are seeking an antidote to modernism and the controlling hand of humans, then this wild garden is for you. Ranged along the River Vartry in a glorious, sheltered valley, the garden was inspired by Irish gardening maverick William Robinson. He eschewed formal Victorian bedding schemes in favor of a more naturalistic style. The garden was started in the 1860s by Edward Walpole, a Dublin businessman, and developed by four generations of the Walpole family, all ardent gardeners. It is now owned by Madeleine Jay, who bought it from the Walpoles in 1980 and is every bit as passionate about the place as they were.

Although she insists that "it is *not* a manicured showpiece or a botanical warehouse," she might agree that it is a botanical jewel because it does have many rare and champion trees, the tallest of their kind in Ireland and the UK. There are more than 5,000 species and cultivars in all. These include some exceptional species from the southern hemisphere that thrive in the mild, Irish climate, such as a wonderfully scented Japanese *Magnolia obovata*, and collections of eucryphia and eucalyptus species.

The river provides the focal point for the garden. Meandering paths take you on either side of it and over a series of bridges with views that will have your camera twitching. In fall, the Maple Walk bursts with color as do the riverside plantings of amelanchiers, liquidambars, and tupelo trees. Mount Usher is equally lovely in spring when the Azalea Walk and thousands of bulbs bloom, and in summer when the herbaceous and subtropical plants flower. PMcW

Kilfane Glen and Waterfall

Kilkenny, Republic of Ireland

DESIGNERS: Sir John Power, Lady Power

OWNERS: Nicholas Mosse, Susan Mosse

GARDEN STYLE: 18th-century picturesque

SIZE: 60 acres (24.4 ha)

CLIMATE: Temperate

LOCATION: Thomastown, Kilkenny

The two very different gardens at Kilfane are united by their shared woodland setting, but that really is about all. In the 15-acre (6 ha) upper garden that surrounds the house (closed to the public), the visitor wanders on gravel paths, admiring the plantings and collection of contemporary sculptures and artworks commissioned and positioned by the Kilfane Trust. If the visitor takes the woodland path to the lower garden, the scene is very different.

Dating from the 1790s, the carefully manipulated landscape here is as romantic as it is beautiful. The designer's aim was to create a picturesque scene—in effect a garden that looks like a picture. Thanks to some very sensitive restoration (the cottage orné was no more than foundations when work began in 1992) the effect is exactly that. In fact the scene greeting the visitor is so perfect that it is like walking on to a film set. You descend into the glen accompanied by the sound of the waterfall, an effect achieved by diverting a stream for 1 mile (1.6 km) and sending it tumbling over the edge of a 30-foot-high (10 m) cliff, to crash into the pool below. At the foot is a hermit's cave or grotto, where the pool becomes the source of the stream that crosses a meadow. A stepping-stone crossing takes visitors to the door of the ornamental cottage, from where paths lead through the woodland with bridges, seats, and fountains. The whole is so carefully designed, and the ambience of the woodland so wonderfully calming, that one cannot immediately tell what has been manipulated and what is real. TM

Ballymaloe Cookery School Gardens

Cork, Republic of Ireland

DESIGNERS: The Allen family, and others
OWNER: Darina Allen
GARDEN STYLE: 20th-century productive garden
SIZE: 10 acres (4 ha)
CLIMATE: Temperate
LOCATION: Shanagarry, Midleton, Cork

Although some parts of the garden at Ballymaloe date back to the early nineteenth century, and some of the layout and planting are original, the existing gardens are the passion and creation of the Irish celebrity chef Darina Allen. She has created a garden that is highly productive—generating a supply of ingredients for the cooking school—and simultaneously one of the most beautiful in Ireland.

The herb garden, fruit garden, and potager are also ornamental gardens, with box hedging and geometric beds providing the structure. The produce from the garden is harvested daily. Because many of the plants are "cut and come again" types, bare gaps do not keep popping up. Peach, apricot, and olive trees thrive in the fruit garden thanks to the mild climate found here. Flowers, such as calendula, edible chrysanthemum, lavender, and cornflower, are grown for recipes, with violets being crystallized to decorate cakes. The mix of high rainfall and liberal quantities of farmyard manure applied to all the beds in spring means that there is an abundance of lush growth. Beyond the productive gardens are exuberant herbaceous borders, a yew maze, a water garden, and an arboretum, and several interesting structures, including a tree house and shell grotto. The Allens built the latter, and it is said that every shell on the ceiling was salvaged from the kitchens.

The overriding impression is of the blending of the productive and ornamental, the recent and historic, the formal and informal. All of these make Ballymaloe such a delightful place to explore. AJ

Annes Grove

Cork, Republic of Ireland

DESIGNER: Richard Grove Annesley
OWNERS: The Annesley family
GARDEN STYLE: 20th-century Robinsonian-style wild garden
SIZE: 35 acres (14.1 ha)
CLIMATE: Temperate
LOCATION: Castle Town Roche, Cork

Set in a wooded limestone gorge of the River Awbeg, Annes Grove has belonged to the Annesley family since 1628. The first things you see are large parkland trees and the drive with conifers from the Victorian period, and the fine Georgian house.

Richard Grove Annesley inherited the property in 1907 and passionately planned and planted for almost sixty years in the Robinsonian style. He also sponsored plant collecting expeditions, especially those of Frank Kingdon Ward, and filled the garden with new and rare plants. A wrought-iron gate leads between herbaceous borders, backed by yew hedges, to steps edged with lavender, and then on to a mount with a rustic, Gothic-windowed summerhouse of Victorian twigwork. Don't miss the water and rock garden with its serpentine pool, or the woodland garden. The entrance is signaled by the statue of a girl set in grass scattered with blue forget-me-nots, silvery alchemillas, and lemon-yellow globe flowers, all backed by Japanese cherry blossom.

Hundreds of rhododendrons—many the first introductions from abroad—billow by the tracks through this Himalayan-like valley. Great conifers provide background and shelter from the sun and wind, and there are *Magnolia wilsonii* and *M. sieboldii* with hanging white flowers and dark crimson stamens. Descending to the valley floor, you'll find the water garden where the River Awbeg was diverted and weirs made to create white rapids and calm, dark reflective surfaces that mirror the lush foliage. It all creates a jungly, watery wonderland. RChe

Ilnacullin Gardens

Cork, Republic of Ireland

DESIGNER: Harold Peto
OWNERS: Irish Government Heritage
GARDEN STYLE: Italianate Arts and Crafts garden
SIZE: 37 acres (14.9 ha)
CLIMATE: Temperate
LOCATION: Glengarriff, Cork

There is something quite magical about taking a boat trip to an island garden, and often a feeling of expectation as you approach the unknown and exotic. That is just what you experience when you visit Ilnacullin, a short sea journey across Bantry Bay off the southern coast of Ireland. It is a jewel of an Italianate Arts and Crafts garden that thrives because of the gentle climate here.

The architect Harold Peto designed much of the garden and its structures for the owner, Annan Bryce, in the early twentieth century. Peto combined his love of the Arts and Crafts style with a passion for Italianate architecture. The elegant *casita*, or Italian tearoom, is a fine demonstration of this marriage. The building overlooks the Italian garden, a classic of its type, which features terraces, shallow steps, a rectangular pool, and a temple forming the focal point. From the temple there is a view toward the Caha Mountains on the mainland beyond. There is another equally fine view across the bay at the Grecian temple, which visitors can reach by walking along an avenue of beautiful Italian cypress trees (*Cupressus sempervirens*). Also note the walled garden with its microclimate within a microclimate. Not only does southwest Ireland benefit from the Gulf Stream, but Ilnacullin also nestles between protective mainland peninsulas. The garden's boundary walls provide ample shelter and warmth too. Tender and exotic plants thrive here, including agapanthus, nerine, and other Mediterranean, South African, and antipodean plants. AJ

Grosser Garten

Niedersachsen, Germany

DESIGNERS: Duchess Sophia of Hanover, Martin Charbonnier
OWNER: State Capital Hanover
GARDEN STYLE: 16th- and 17th-century baroque
SIZE: 138.4 acres (56 ha)
CLIMATE: Temperate
LOCATION: Hanover, Niedersachsen

The Grosser Garten (Great Garden) is a breathtaking testament to the baroque garden. It is part of the Herrenhause gardens, which include the Berggarten, Georgengarten, and Welfengarten, and was developed from the mid-seventeenth century until 1866.

Herrenhausen was the summer residence of the dukes, later the electors, of Hanover, who played a major role in British politics. Sophia, wife of Elector Ernst August, was the creative force of the garden. From 1689 to 1714, she set about transforming the gardens of Herrenhausen. When Sophia's son, Georg-Ludwig, succeeded to the throne of England in 1714, the whole court moved to London, and Herrenhausen's garden lay forgotten, sidelined from trends and fashions. That accounts for its period look.

The layout is pure baroque—formal, regular, and stately, with a hierarchy of spaces for different occasions. The main parterres, originally intended as decor to be seen from the staterooms of the palace, are like intricate embroidery, interwoven with shapes and colors. The bell fountain in the center is a 1937 addition, dating back to the time when the town took over the responsibility of the garden. To the side of the parterres is the hedge theater, adorned with gilt lead figures, which is still used for productions, and the parterre d'orangerie where citrus plants are displayed. Beyond the parterres is a 230-foot-high (70 m) jet fountain as a focal point. The garden is exhausting, exhilarating, and hugely impressive even without the backdrop of the palace, which was destroyed by wartime bombing. HH

Botanischen Gartens in Göttingen

Niedersachsen, Germany

DESIGNERS: Albrecht von Haller,
   Heinz Ellenberg
OWNER: University of Göttingen
GARDEN STYLE: 18th-century botanical
SIZE: 98 acres (36 ha)
CLIMATE: Temperate
LOCATION: Göttingen, Niedersachsen

A green oasis in the center of Göttingen, the original botanical garden was founded by Albrecht von Haller in 1736, and is as old as the university. Now called the Old Botanical Garden to distinguish it from the New Botanical Garden founded in 1967, it contains more than 10,000 species of hardy and tropical plant. The two gardens are components of the Botanical Garden of the Georg-August University.

The eight greenhouses of the Old Garden feature collections of tropical rain forest and water plants: carnivorous plants, bromeliads, ferns, orchids, cycads, cacti, aroids, and succulents. There is also a large coldhouse and a collection of European wild plants. Beyond the greenhouses, the arboretum gets top billing with its rockery, pond, wonderful show of spring bulbs, and collection of 1,200 species.

The New Botanical Garden, to the northeast of the city, was created by the geobotanist Professor Heinz Ellenberg when he needed more space for his ecological experiments. The 24 acres (9.7 ha) of the experimental Biotope Mackenrodt area have naturalized plant associations, including woodland and meadow communities. Elsewhere are temperate forest communities from Europe, Asia, and America, a 1.2-acre (0.5 ha) rockery, and an area dedicated to mid-European agriculture. A large collection of woody plants and forest perennials, the Forstbotanischer Garten, is next to the New Botanical Garden. TM

Berggarten und Regenwaldhaus

Niedersachsen, Germany

DESIGNERS: Duchess Sophia of Hanover, Martin
   Charbonnier
OWNER: State Capital Hanover
GARDEN STYLE: 17th-century botanical garden
SIZE: 51.9 acres (21 ha)
CLIMATE: Temperate
LOCATION: Hanover, Niedersachsen

The Berggarten, or Mountain Garden—the name refers to the sandy hill dating from the ice age that dominates an otherwise flat landscape—lies to the north of Hanover's Grosser Garten (see opposite) and forms part of the complex of royal gardens. What is now an impressive botanical garden had humble beginnings. It was begun in the seventeenth century as a kitchen garden, but as more new and exotic plants were gradually introduced, it changed shape. Duchess Sophia was instrumental in the development of the garden, encouraging her daughter to collect unusual species. By 1706 there were so many mulberry trees here that they could feed the royal silkworm farm in Hameln. The number of exotic plants steadily grew, and with it the reputation of the garden; by 1850 the Palm House held the largest collection of palms in Europe, and the first African violet in Europe was grown here.

Many of the greenhouses were destroyed in World War II and later rebuilt. These now house cacti, succulents, and one of the largest collections of orchids in the world. The latest addition is the Regenwaldhaus, the tropical Rain Forest House, containing more than 6,000 plants with birds, bats, frogs, and other exotic animals. Close ties with Hanover University's landscape department have led to the development of various themed gardens, the latest of which is the prairie garden. HH

Sanssouci

Brandenburg, Germany

DESIGNERS: Friedrich II, King of Prussia; Peter Joseph Lenné
OWNER: Prussian Palaces and Gardens Foundation
GARDEN STYLE: 19th-century romantic park
SIZE: Set within a park of 700 acres (283.5 ha)
CLIMATE: Temperate
LOCATION: Potsdam, Brandenburg

Little remains of the original, groundbreaking garden at Sanssouci commissioned by Friedrich II, King of Prussia, because it was later reworked into a great romantic landscape by Peter Joseph Lenné in 1822. Fortunately, though, the most distinctive features of the original garden have survived.

Sans souci means "carefree." Friedrich desired a summer palace where he could live the simple life, reading and philosophizing, free of the cares of state. He began by ordering a vineyard to be laid out. This, of course, was no ordinary vineyard. The slope was sculpted into six huge, concave terraces shaped to catch the sun. The walls were built of heat retaining brick studded with 168 niches. Vines were trained along the walls, and the niches were filled with figs. Glazed screens protected them from the weather.

A grand, central staircase bisected the terraces, with a monumental fountain at its foot. From the topmost terrace, a pair of tree-lined avenues extended to either side, terminating in fanciful trelliswork pavilions decorated with golden stars.

All this can still be seen today. So can Friedrich's other great treasure, an extraordinary Chinese teahouse topped with a golden parasol and adorned with life-size, gilded statues of Chinese people. You can also see Friedrich's last resting place, next to his faithful dogs. In 1990 Sanssouci was declared a World Heritage Site under the protection of UNESCO. With nearly 44 miles (70 km) of footpaths, and its collection of palaces and follies, Sanssouci is far removed from Friedrich's dream of rural simplicity. AE

Gartenanlage–Gedenkstätte Karl Foerster

Brandenburg, Germany

DESIGNER: Karl Foerster
OWNER: German Foundation for Monument Protection
GARDEN STYLE: 20th-century modern
SIZE: 1.2 acres (0.5 ha)
CLIMATE: Temperate
LOCATION: Potsdam-Bornim, Brandenburg

Tucked away southwest of Berlin, within easy reach of Sanssouci, is the birthplace of the garden style that epitomizes the modern German garden. Karl Foerster created this garden in 1912 as a showcase for his new cultivars and revolutionary plant combinations. Driven by a desire to create flower borders that would be long flowering, have year-round interest, and stand up to the harsh German winters, he developed an original approach to planting that influenced generations of garden designers worldwide.

Foerster broke with tradition by combining ornamental grasses with herbaceous plants, emphasizing not only color, but also form. The strict structure of the formal English beds was changed and new dynamic drifts were created. A prolific author, Foerster passed on many of his ideas through his books. Nothing can beat this garden, though. Thanks to the watchful eye and enthusiasm of Marianne Foerster, visitors can share her grandfather's vision and experience the garden much as it was in his day.

The Sunken Garden is laid out with terraced beds around a central oval water basin. It may not be spectacular in size, but it certainly is in detail. Many of Foerster's numerous signature plants populate the beds, including ornamental grasses such as *Calamagrostis* x *acutifolia* 'Karl Foerster', *Helenium* 'Königstiger', a multitude of phlox, and the delphiniums with which he made his name. Late summer and early autumn see a spectacular rush of colors, hues, and form. All the plants are labeled, and many are on sale in the adjoining nursery. HH

Schlosspark Rheinsberg

Brandenburg, Germany

DESIGNERS: Various, including Kurt Tucholsky
OWNER: Prussian Palaces and Gardens Foundation
GARDEN STYLE: 18th-century rococo park
SIZE: 64 acres (26 ha)
CLIMATE: Temperate
LOCATION: Rheinsberg, Brandenburg

Built close to the water's edge, this eighteenth-century castle appears to float on Grienericksee. The palace was given to Friedrich II by his father in 1734 and, ten years later, Friedrich gave it to his brother Prince Heinrich. Both made alterations.

Opposite the castle, a grass checkerboard parterre leads to a flight of stairs, overlooked by a pair of sphinxes, that takes you up into the park. Straight avenues then lead through the park to the main features. Along the park's southern edge, columns—dating back to 1741—frame the entrance, where the goddesses Flora and Pomona greet visitors.

One of the best features is the Salon, a small circular temple that was originally conceived as an orangery but became a bathhouse in the eighteenth century. The open-air theater, created in 1752, uses trees and hedges as a natural backdrop to the stage. Also note several features in the park, erected in memory of Prince Heinrich's deceased friends, relatives, and favorite servants. The Tempel für teure Verstorbene (1790) is a small, squat building, and the Malesherbes Säule is a ruined column erected in honor of Malesherbes, a French politician decapitated during the French Revolution.

There are two grottoes in the park, the Egeria Grotte—named after the water nymph Egeria—which is located at one end of the main axis, and the Feldsteingrotte, which overlooks the water. The latter consists of three grotto rooms that were originally decorated with shells and glass, but sadly these have disappeared. IvG

Branitzer Park

Brandenburg, Germany

DESIGNER: Prince Hermann von Pückler-Muskau
OWNER: Prince Pückler Museum Foundation
GARDEN STYLE: 19th-century landscape
SIZE: 247 acres (100 ha)
CLIMATE: Temperate
LOCATION: Cottbus, Brandenburg

After the sale of Muskau in 1845, Hermann, Prince of Pückler-Muskau, moved to the old family estate of Branitz. Heavily in debt, but with his passion for gardens undampened, he set about transforming the uninspiring landscape around the castle of Branitz, encouraged by his wife, Lucie, who wanted "this desert transformed into an artificial oasis." Like Muskau, the Branitzer Park became a lengthy, costly enterprise that, as time went on, increased in size.

The park was a culmination of all Pückler had seen and experienced in his travels. Its layout is an expression of his journey through life. He reshaped the landscape, building artificial watercourses, digging out lakes, heaping up the earth to create landforms, and creating interest where there was none. He also divided the site into zones, starting in the east, then moving to the pleasure ground around the castle, and ending in the west at the Tumulus, or Water Pyramid, which now contains Pückler's tomb. The pleasure ground, with its flower beds, ornaments, sculptures, ornamental trees, and shrubs, was in contrast to the gentle landscape, punctuated by the monumental earth pyramids that acted as focal points and viewing platforms.

Only indigenous or naturalized trees were used in the parkland, sensitively distributed to create interest and frame vistas. The Branitzer Park remains a highly impressive achievement, an interpretation of a landscape garden, interweaving influences from all over the world and setting new standards for centuries to come. HH

Pfaueninsel

Berlin, Germany

DESIGNER: Peter Joseph Lenné
OWNER: Prussian Palaces and Gardens Foundation
GARDEN STYLE: 19th-century landscape
SIZE: 370.7 acres (150 ha)
CLIMATE: Temperate
LOCATION: Berlin-Zehlendorf, Berlin

The Pfaueninsel—the Peacock Island, so called because of the peacocks introduced to the island in 1795—lies in Lake Havel to the west of Berlin. Accessible only by boat, it was a favorite retreat for the Prussian kings. Following the fashion at the time for rustic buildings, King Friedrich Wilhelm II had a ruined castle built on the island. His son, Friedrich Wilhelm III, continued the development by commissioning Peter Joseph Lenné to redesign the island as a landscape park, using the Jardin des Plantes in Paris (see page 575) as a model.

In addition to redefining the contours of the woodlands, creating glades and pastures, and making an extensive, sweeping network of paths, Lenné introduced many rare plants. He wanted to create an idyllic landscape as a refuge for the royal family. Several buildings, such as a dairy, built as a neo-Gothic ruin with cows and play areas for the royal children, completed the image. They were progressively added to, with a Palm House built by Schinkel in 1830–31, which later burned down, and menageries for the exotic animals, later moved by Friedrich Wilhelm IV to form the basis of Berlin's now-famous Tiergarten.

Pfaueninsel's garden and parkland, and many of the buildings, have now been comprehensively restored, painstakingly reestablishing the atmosphere of a nineteenth-century island retreat. A regular ferry links the island to the mainland. In 1990 the entire island was designated a World Heritage Site under the protection of UNESCO. HH

> "He wanted to create an idyllic landscape as a refuge for the royal family"

Klein-Glienicke

Berlin, Germany

DESIGNER: Peter Joseph Lenné, Karl Friedrich Schinkel, Prince Karl of Prussia
OWNER: Prussian Palaces and Gardens Foundation
GARDEN STYLE: 19th-century landscape
SIZE: 222.9 acres (90.2 ha)
CLIMATE: Temperate
LOCATION: Berlin-Zehlendorf, Berlin

Klein-Glienicke is part of the landscape, stretching far beyond its boundaries and drawing in the views and vistas of its surroundings. It is a testimony to the power of nineteenth-century landscape design, and the talents of a landscape designer, architect, and patron working together on a grand plan.

Peter Joseph Lenné, who was to become one of the most influential landscape gardeners in Germany, worked from 1816 on the comprehensive redesign of the estate, progressively extending and refining it as the owners' wealth and status increased. After the death in 1824 of the first owner, the then Prussian State Chancellor, Prince Hardenberg, Prince Karl of Prussia took the estate as his summer residence, and used it to house his collection of antiquities. Obviously impressed by the work that Lenné had already done in creating a pleasure ground between the house, the casino, and the banks of the Havel, Prince Karl commissioned him to design all the remaining areas. It was, however, the appointment of the great classical architect Karl Friedrich Schinkel that set the seal on Klein-Glienicke. The Italian influence is apparent throughout, from the sculptures to the water features. The cleverly placed network of paths makes sure that visitors do not miss a thing, from the immaculately restored features right down to the design of the flower beds. Klein-Glienicke is under UNESCO World Heritage protection. HH

Schlosspark Oranienbaum

Sachsen-Anhalt, Germany

DESIGNERS: Cornelis Ryckwaert, Prince Leopold Friedrich Franz of Anhalt-Dessau
OWNER: DessauWörlitz Cultural Foundation
GARDEN STYLE: 17th- and 18th-century landscape
SIZE: 93.90 acres (38 ha)
CLIMATE: Temperate
LOCATION: Oranienbaum, Sachsen-Anhalt

The area between Dessau and Wörlitz is rich in garden history. Its network of gardens includes the Wörlitzer Anlagen and Luisium, which have been named a UNESCO World Heritage Site. The town, castle, and garden at Oranienbaum were built between 1683 and 1698 to a grand baroque master plan drawn up by a Dutchman, Cornelius Ryckwaert, for the Dutch-born Princess Henriette Catharina of Anhalt-Dessau. The garden's layout is formal and precise. In front of the castle are parterres facing the town's marketplace. To the rear is an extensive, almost rectangular, garden with parterres grouped around a fountain. Extending from here are walkways, thickets, and a deer park.

After Henriette's death, the garden was initially used as a hunting lodge. Then Prince Leopold Friedrich Franz of Anhalt-Dessau, having redesigned the castle and grounds at Wörlitz, focused on Oranienbaum. Here he incorporated classic elements and the English landscape style into the existing garden in a masterly way. In 1795 the island garden was redesigned as an English-Chinese garden, the first of its type. Complete with pagoda, teahouse, and bridges, it reflected Prince Franz's interest in chinoiserie. Another addition was an orangery, built in the classical style.

For many years, Schlosspark Oranienbaum was familiar only to a few garden enthusiasts. With the reunification of Germany, it is thankfully now accessible to a far wider audience. HH

Wörlitzer Anlagen

Sachsen-Anhalt, Germany

DESIGNERS: Prince Leopold Friedrich Franz of Anhalt-Dessau, Friedrich Wilhelm von Erdmannsdorff
OWNER: DessauWörlitz Cultural Foundation
GARDEN STYLE: 18th-century landscape
SIZE: 276.8 acres (112 ha)
CLIMATE: Temperate
LOCATION: Wörlitz, Sachsen-Anhalt

Prince Leopold Friedrich Franz of Anhalt-Dessau was educated, wealthy, and aged only eighteen when he took over the family estates in 1758. Together with his great friend, the young architect Friedrich Wilhelm von Erdmannsdorff, he set off on a grand tour of France and England. They were among the first Germans to experience the new English landscape style. It impressed them so much that they set about recreating it at Wörlitz. A later trip to Italy instilled in them yet more ideas, and the Wörlitzer garden was born. The result was groundbreaking, marking a new era of architecture and landscape design in Germany. All the accepted rules of design were dismissed and natural parks with classical buildings were "in."

The castle was rebuilt by Erdmannsdorff between 1769 and 1773 in the classical style of an English country house. It was followed by many other small buildings peppered throughout the park, including a pantheon, a Gothic house, and various temples and grottoes. At the center of the garden are the lake and five garden areas that were created more or less simultaneously from 1765 onward, including the Schloss Garten, Kleines Walloch, Grosses Walloch, and the Neumarks Garten. The actual parkland covers about 98.8 acres (40 ha), and is cleverly linked by avenues and vistas to form a whole. One fact of particular interest is that the grounds were open to the public from the beginning. Indeed, not only the park but also the surrounding countryside were included in the makeover, creating a garden kingdom that spread to neighboring estates and is unique in the history of garden design. HH

"All the accepted rules of
design were dismissed…"

Wilhelmsbad Hanau

Hessen, Germany

DESIGNER: Unknown
OWNER: Administration of National Castles and Gardens
GARDEN STYLE: 18th-century English landscape
SIZE: 93 acres (37.6 ha)
CLIMATE: Temperate
LOCATION: Wilhelmsbad, Hessen

Wilhelmsbad was one of the earliest landscape parks in Germany and *the* spa frequented by society between 1777 and 1785. It then fell out of favor, and it is largely thanks to its dwindling popularity that it has survived, in immaculate condition, in its original late-eighteenth-century layout.

The architect Franz-Ludwig Cancrin erected the late-baroque thermal buildings along the promenade. More in keeping with the baroque architecture of these buildings than the other rustic or picturesque eye-catchers in the park is the building where the healing water was drawn, a small, brightly painted, hexagonal pavilion. The park also features a stream, the Braubach, that was dammed and altered to form a lake and small islands. It is liberally sprinkled with small, decorative buildings and ornaments, including a stone-arched bridge, stone pyramid, hermitage, grotto, and a wooden devil's bridge draped across a rocky abyss. And mirrored in the stream is one of the earliest, mock-ruined, medieval castles in Europe. Within its tower is a highly ornate apartment that was built for Prince Wilhelm von Hessen-Kassel, after whom the resort was named.

The most notable feature of this park, though, is probably its horsedrawn carousel that would have provided great entertainment for its many visitors, and is a fine example of early engineering. Built on a small hill that contains its extensive mechanics, this delightful, round pavilion, with its domed roof, still houses the collection of enchanting horses and carriages, and is currently being restored. IvG

Palmengarten

Hessen, Germany

DESIGNER: Heinrich Siesmayer
OWNER: City of Frankfurt
GARDEN STYLE: 19th-century botanical
SIZE: 50 acres (20.2 ha)
CLIMATE: Temperate
LOCATION: Frankfurt am Main, Hessen

Although the Palmengarten has outside gardens, it is best known for its Tropicarium, a complex of greenhouses with 1.2 acres (0.4 ha) of glass-covered climatic zones, ranging from rain forest, mangrove, mountain rain forest, monsoon, and trade-wind forest to savanna, thorn forest, and desert. The oldest greenhouse is the Palmenhaus, constructed in 1869.

Nineteenth-century garden designer Heinrich Siesmayer bought the collection of exotic plants from Duke Adolph von Nassau and, on a plot of land provided by the city, created a garden and built an assembly room, onto which the Palmenhaus was built. The garden and greenhouses were redeveloped and replanted in the early 1990s when the rose, rock, and rhododendron gardens and herbaceous beds were upgraded, and the new Tropicarium was built.

The Herbaceous Garden, dedicated to Germany's famous twentieth-century plantsman Karl Foerster, has several different habitats with marginal and waterside plants by the stream, behind which ornamental herbaceous perennials flower into late autumn. The Steppe Meadow is mown twice a year and features plants from Eurasian and North American steppes, and provides planting in dry, sunny conditions. The Cactus Garden by the entrance to the Tropicarium is planted with hardy succulents, accompanied by exotics and annuals from America, Africa, and the Canary Islands. If a serious collection sounds rather off-putting, the Palmengarten proves it can be great fun, being packed with ideas for every kind of garden, from the grand to the minuscule. IvG

Sichtungsgarten Hermannshof

Hessen, Germany

DESIGNERS: Urs Walser, Cassian Schmidt
OWNER: Freudenberg
GARDEN STYLE: 20th-century informal
SIZE: 5.5 acres (2.2 ha)
CLIMATE: Temperate
LOCATION: Weinheim, Hessen

Hermannshof is perhaps the most exciting garden in Europe for those interested in plants and design. It beautifully showcases the contemporary, naturalistic style for which Germany has become so renowned, and it does this using perennials on a relatively small and intimate scale compared with other large-scale plantings.

The area has one of the best climates in Germany. The garden has a framework of majestic trees, and since 1980 Hermannshof has been the scene of much new planting. A series of different garden habitats has been created. Each was planted with combinations designed to suit the site and to simplify maintenance. The garden is both inspirational and educational, and belongs to a network of sites that evaluates perennials and planting combinations.

In spring there are vast numbers of tulips. These are followed by early-summer drifts of woodland flowers along the garden's periphery, succeeded by the spectacular achillea-salvia bed, possibly the most striking border in Europe, a perfect balance of color and form. For the rest of the summer, there are extensive beds of prairie plants and annual borders. Unusual plants abound. The prairie beds in particular contain many introductions new to Europe and unorthodox plant combinations. NK

> "...followed by early-summer drifts of woodland flowers..."

Schlosspark Wilhelmshöhe

Hessen, Germany

DESIGNER: Giovanni Guerniero
OWNER: Administration of National Palaces and Gardens
GARDEN STYLE: 18th-century baroque, landscape park
SIZE: 593 acres (240 ha)
CLIMATE: Temperate
LOCATION: Kassel, Hessen

Towering high above the valley, the house and the main axis of the Wilhelmshöhe Palace gardens dominate the wooded slopes outside Kassel. They are an impressive sight not to be missed, visible even from the high-speed train as it rushes past. The house and the park are the work of three generations, each building on what the predecessor had created and adapting it to the style of the day.

Landgrave Karl of Hessen-Kassel (1670–1730) replaced the old hunting lodge with a baroque house that crowned the top of the hill. In 1701 he had a garden laid out in the Italian baroque style by Giovanni Guerniero. A dramatic series of cascades was meant to be the central feature, exploiting the topography of the site and extending from the garden into the valley. Despite the fact that only the upper section was built, Schlosspark Wilhelmshöhe is now the biggest hill park in Europe.

Work on the park continued under Karl's son Landgrave Friedrich I, in the then popular English style. The central dramatic axis remained the dominant feature, but it was softened by landscaping. Other buildings were added to the park, including a Chinese village. The cascade remained untouched, though. Make sure you time your visit to coincide with when the cascade is running. HH

LEFT The water features at Wilhelmshöhe Palace were designed to exploit the hilly topography.

Schloss Belvedere

Thüringen, Germany

DESIGNER: Unknown
OWNER: Stiftung Weimarer Klassik
GARDEN STYLE: 19th-century landscape park, botanical garden
SIZE: 106 acres (43 ha)
CLIMATE: Temperate
LOCATION: Weimar, Thüringen

From the city center of Weimar, you can reach Belvedere Castle by a gentle stroll through the 1-mile-long (1.6 km) Park an der Ilm (see page 474), carrying on up through the Belvederer Allée, which was designed in the late nineteenth century as a link between the two parks. Both castle and park are part of the wider Weimar landscape, which was recognized by UNESCO as a World Heritage Site in 1998.

The Duke Ernst August von Sachsen-Weimar laid out the castle, now a music school, and its baroque garden between 1724 and 1732. Under instruction from the Grand Duchess Maria Pawlowna, daughter of the Russian Czar Paul I, the park was transformed into a landscape park in the early nineteenth century with an open-air theater, fountains, and follies. She also laid out the Russian garden to the west of the park, inspired by the czar's garden in Pawlowsk.

In 1820 the Hortus Belvedereanus was created, a botanical collection that promoted the study of natural sciences. The beautiful orangery buildings, laid out in a horseshoe shape with the gardener's house at the center, housed an important collection of tender palms, citrus trees, and other exotics, including pomegranates and myrtles, that are still displayed in the courtyard in summer. Inside there are raised beds and a tufa rockery that has recently been restored. Next to the orangery is a formal garden with a small pavilion and pool, with seasonal displays of lovingly tended bedding plants. IvG

Park an der Ilm

Thüringen, Germany

DESIGNER: Johann Wolfgang von Goethe
OWNER: Society for the Classical Weimar Period
GARDEN STYLE: 18th- and 19th-century landscape park
SIZE: 118 acres (47.8 ha)
CLIMATE: Temperate
LOCATION: Weimar, Thüringen

The poet Goethe was given the Gartenhaus in the Ilmtal in 1776. A major influence on the Romantic Movement in Germany, he was instrumental in the early design stages of the landscape park that was planned between 1778 and 1833, creating a number of garden buildings and carrying out a lot of planting. The park is 1 mile long (1.6 km), starting by the Stadtschloss in the town center of Weimar. It runs south, parallel to the River Ilm, and provides a green corridor between the Schloss, Park Tiefurt, and the Schlosspark Belvedere. It spreads across both riverbanks, providing visitors with a perfect walk from the town center to the Belvedere.

The Römische Haus, which was built as a hermitage, lies on the opposite bank from Goethe's Gartenhaus, and together they form the key features in the park, backed up by sculptures, bridges, rocky outcrops, temples, and memorials to the "greats," such as William Shakespeare and Franz Liszt. The gardener's cottage nestles in the greenery, and the architecture of the hermitage is unmistakably Roman. The numerous bridges, all of differing design, range from simple wooden constructions to the stone-arched and suspension kinds. They provide variety and link the two parts of the park. Some also offer views out across the landscape to local landmarks.

Though many of the trees here—limes, oaks, and beeches—are native to Germany, a few exotic species, including copper beeches, the maidenhair tree (*Ginkgo biloba*), and the tulip tree (*Liriodendron tulipifera*), have been added to spice things up. IvG

"The poet Goethe…was instrumental in the early design stages of the landscape park…"

Schloss Pillnitz

Sachsen, Germany

DESIGNERS: Matthäus Pöppelmann, Peter Joseph Lenné
OWNER: Saxonian Palace Administration
GARDEN STYLE: 18th-century French parterre, 19th-century
English park
SIZE: 70 acres (28.3 ha)
CLIMATE: Temperate
LOCATION: Pillnitz, Sachsen

To visit Schloss Pillnitz, make the one-hour journey on the old-fashioned paddle wheeler from Dresden's city center along one of the most beautiful stretches of the River Elbe with the early-eighteenth-century River Palace and Mountain Palace.

The French Garden, with its formal bedding parterres, is situated between the two palace buildings and gives way to formal vistas, between which lie hedge-enclosed garden "rooms" with different themed plantings. On the opposite side, framed on three sides by a later extension to the palace, is the famous Fliederhof, a courtyard lined with lilacs, which are grown just as if they are standard trees. The complex of palace buildings is embraced by an English landscape park, which was remodeled between 1838 and 1867 following Peter Joseph Lenne's design principles. It contains the orangery (a former games room), the palm house, and a small lake, at the end of which lies the English pavilion, inspired by the Tempietto in the cloister of San Pietro in Montario, Italy. It is well worth going inside because the walls have been hand painted beautifully with a design of insects and butterflies.

The park is planted with many beautiful, mature trees of botanical note, making this part of the grounds feel like a marvelous arboretum. Do not miss the camellia, the largest in the country and one of the most impressive in Europe. It is the only one to survive of four Japanese plants introduced by the Swedish botanist Carl Peter Thunberg in 1778. IvG

Zwinger

Sachsen, Germany

DESIGNER: Matthäus Daniel Pöppelmann
OWNER: Saxonian Palace Administration
GARDEN STYLE: 18th-century baroque
SIZE: 13.3 acres (5.4 ha)
CLIMATE: Temperate
LOCATION: Dresden, Sachsen

The Zwinger is better known for its museum, old masters, and porcelain collection than for the garden, which is often treated as only an ornamental addition. However, although the garden is comparatively small, it is a good example of a baroque town garden.

Prince Friedrich August I, who is also known as "August The Strong," commissioned Matthäus Daniel Pöppelmann to build an orangery in the area between the inner walls and the town walls, known as the Zwinger. The construction took place between 1711 and 1728, and includes the Curved Gallery, a number of pavilions, the Nymphenbad, and the Crown Gates, which were later adopted as the symbol of Dresden. During the eighteenth century, the central area was used to display the plants grown in the orangery. In the 1820s, the gardens and lake were redesigned by the court gardener, C. A. Terscheck. They were altered again in 1924, when the Zwinger palace and its gardens were restored to Pöppelmann's original designs.

The garden, with its fountains, water features, and statues, makes a complete contrast to the rest of the city. Because very few of Dresden's historical gardens survived the combined forces of bombing and the Communist era, the Zwinger is all the more poignant and special. HH

"The garden…makes a complete contrast to the rest of the city"

Barockgarten, Grossedlitz

Sachsen, Germany

DESIGNERS: Various
OWNER: Free State of Saxony
GARDEN STYLE: 18th-century baroque
SIZE: 44.5 acres (18 ha)
CLIMATE: Temperate
LOCATION: Heidenau, Sachsen

This garden was created by Count August Christoph von Wackerbarth in 1719. He sold the property to "August the Strong" in 1723, who employed the leading gardeners of the time—Knoeffel, Longuelune, and Pöppelmann—to create a grand garden for parties and events. Although the garden was never completed, it has largely remained unchanged, and is one of Germany's finest baroque designs.

The attached Friedrichsschloss is quite small and dominated by the upper orangery, which is actually smaller than the main orangery on the lower terrace. The main orangery is a grand building, similar in size to one at Versailles, and impressive in its simple geometry. Orange trees and agapanthus tubs come out during the summer onto a horseshoe terrace.

The terrace in front of the castle is framed by a box-enclosed, narrow parterre with mingled bedding plants, providing the only touch of color in the garden. The water features are restricted to the terraces nearest to the castle, and consist mostly of narrow brooks. Huge water cascades and basins had been planned, but a shortage of water put a stop to that. Instead a great turf cascade, flanked by a pair of stone steps, sweeps down the hillside. Grand stone staircases also sweep down to the lower terraces, and formal vistas, often framed by lines of pleached limes or hedges, cross the garden and take the eye into the surrounding landscape. Everything here is formal and grand, but it is not ostentatious. IvG

Fürst-Pückler Park Bad Muskau

Sachsen, Germany

DESIGNER: Prince Hermann von Pückler-Muskau
OWNER: Prince Pückler Park Foundation
GARDEN STYLE: 19th-century landscape
SIZE: 1,853 acres (750 ha)
CLIMATE: Temperate
LOCATION: Bad Muskau, Sachsen; Leknika Town, Poland

Prince Ludwig Heinrich Hermann of Pückler-Muskau was an ambitious man, an outspoken liberal who loved riding, shooting, and travel and was passionate about landscape gardens. After visiting England and seeing Humphry Repton's work, he set about creating his own idyllic landscape in Muskau in 1815. It was a massive undertaking. The setting was ideal: a conical-shaped valley with the River Neisse gently flowing through it, with land stretching over a plateau to both sides. Views of the nearby town were carefully orchestrated, blocks of plantings were expertly positioned to create depth, and water and buildings added interest.

Muskau was a huge financial commitment, swallowing all the money of Pückler and his wife. Heavily in debt, they were forced to sell the property in 1845 to one of the wealthiest aristocrats of the time, Prince Friedrich of the Netherlands. With fresh funds and Pückler advising from a distance, work on the landscape park was finished. Later owners adapted the park. However, the greatest threat was the division of Germany in 1945, which split the park into two. The smaller section to the west of the river with the castle stayed in Germany, and the larger portion to the east became part of Poland.

Muskau is a colossal achievement. Even though exploring the whole of it is not possible, Pückler's spirit is very much alive among the trees, the glades, and the delightful views. HH

Schloss Fantasie

Bayern, Germany

DESIGNER: Duchess Elisabeth Friederike Sophie of Württemberg
OWNER: Administration of Palaces, Gardens, and Lakes
GARDEN STYLE: 18th-century rococo, landscape
SIZE: 42 acres (17 ha)
CLIMATE: Temperate
LOCATION: Bayreuth-Eckersdorf, Bayern

Duchess Elisabeth Friederike Sophie of Württemberg greatly wished to transform the estate that she had been given by her parents in 1763. Recently divorced, she poured her energy into creating a summer residence and garden. Renaming the estate Fantasie, she worked extensively on the Schloss and garden over the next seventeen years, until her death in 1780. Parterres, terraces, water features, and a hermitage were all added, with meadows grazed by cows in homage to the new, English, landscape style. The English landscape theme was continued by the next owner, Duchess Friederike Dorothee Sophie, who left the central section virtually intact and incorporated the surrounding landscape into the garden, adding monuments and statues to create staged scenes.

The third stage of the garden was undertaken from 1839 to 1881 by her grandson, Duke Alexander of Wittenberg. No doubt influenced by the work of Peter Joseph Lenné, the great Prussian gardener and landscape designer of the time, Duke Alexander brought new elements into the garden, although he did little to alter the rococo garden.

Despite changes in ownership, the garden has survived and is a good example of how various styles can be successfully combined. Schloss Fantasie was chosen as the venue for the recently opened Museum of Garden Art, which explores the development of gardens in Germany. Although small, the museum provides valuable insights into the world of gardens and garden design. HH

Park Schönbusch

Bayern, Germany

DESIGNER: Friedrich Ludwig von Sckell
OWNER: Administration of Palaces, Gardens, and Lakes
GARDEN STYLE: 18th-century neoclassical landscaped park
SIZE: 395 acres (160 ha)
CLIMATE: Temperate
LOCATION: Aschaffenburg, Bayern

At the heart of the vast Schönbusch estate, overlooking an artificial lake, stands the country house built by the Portugese architect Emanuel Joseph von Hérigoyen in 1778 for the Elector and Archbishop of Mainz, Friedrich Karl von Erthal. After the Congress of Vienna, the estate became the property of the royal family of Bavaria.

"Alles scheint Natur, so glücklich ist die Kunst versteckt." This famous quotation, from the influential German garden theorist C. C. L. Hirschfeld, means "Everything appears natural, so well concealed is the design." The title of an enlightening exhibition at Schönbusch tracing the history of the grounds, it perfectly describes this classically landscaped garden, one of the first and finest in Germany. Laid out in the English manner by Friedrich Ludwig von Sckell from 1785 onward, Schönbusch is complete artifice and completely convincing. Apparently an enclave of perfectly preserved, wooded countryside with meadows and waterways, all traversed by serpentine walks, it is actually a picturesque remodeling of a game park and the surrounding agricultural land.

Just as people today build rockeries after digging a pond, so the earth dredged from the two lakes (only one of which remains) was used to build steep hillsides, joined by the soaring Devil's Bridge. Individual buildings scattered around the grounds include the Observation Tower, the Temple to Friendship, the Philosopher's House, and the glorious Banqueting Hall. Shepherds' huts and a village of Dutch-style cottages add plenty of charm. RCa

Botanischer Garten München–Nymphenburg

Bayern, Germany

DESIGNER: Karl Ritter von Goebel
OWNER: Free State of Bayern
GARDEN STYLE: 20th-century botanical garden
SIZE: 54.4 acres (22 ha)
CLIMATE: Temperate
LOCATION: Munich-Nymphenburg, Bayern

Plant enthusiasts should not miss an opportunity to visit Munich's botanical garden, a tram ride away from the city, next to Schloss Nymphenburg. This garden opened in 1914 and replaced the old botanical garden, which had run out of space for its expanding collection of plants. The botanical garden now contains more than 9,000 outdoor plants and an additional 6,200 in the greenhouses. What sets this botanical garden apart, though, are its displays.

The only formal areas are the Schmuckhof, a sunken garden in front of the main building, expertly planted with seasonal bedding plants, and the Rose Garden, which has old and hybrid roses. From here the garden radiates out into systematically divided habitats, and includes the Spring Garden, the peony and iris beds, the Rhododendron Grove and Fern Gully, the Bavarian Plant Communities, the magnificent Rock Garden, the Moor and Heather Gardens, and the Arboretum. Of particular interest are the Ecological and Genetic Section and the small Protected Plants Areas.

Throughout the garden, visitors learn to appreciate the relationships among plants and their place in the ecosystem. It is this approach that makes the garden such a valuable learning site for everyone, from designers to beginners. HH

> "…visitors learn to appreciate the relationships among plants…"

Hofgarten Eremitage

Bayern, Germany

DESIGNER: Wilhelmine von Bayreuth
OWNER: Administration of Palaces, Gardens, and Lakes
GARDEN STYLE: 18th-century rococo
SIZE: 116.1 acres (47 ha)
CLIMATE: Temperate
LOCATION: Bayreuth, Bayern

Today Bayreuth is known more for its music festivals than its gardens, but that was not always so. More than 200 years ago, the gardens attracted all the attention. Tucked away in the northeastern tip of Bavaria is a collection of gardens created between 1735 and 1780 by two artistic, well-educated women.

Wilhelmine, Margravine of Brandenburg-Bayreuth, was given the Eremitage in 1735 as a present from her husband, Friedrich. She set about redesigning the castle and grounds, which had previously been used as a retreat by Margrave Georg Wilhelm and his court. While dressed as monks, the court would enjoy the simple life of hermits in the seven hermitages that were built in the woodlands. Wilhelmine had grander plans and transformed the grounds into an elaborate baroque garden with grottoes, water features, a variety of buildings, avenues, and thickets. The placing of these features seems random, which adds to the rustic theme of the original garden. Many of the buildings were constructed as ruins, including a theater and spectacular grotto.

The garden was landscaped at the end of the eighteenth century. The thickets were replaced by meadows and groups of trees, but much of the architecture remained intact. In the early nineteenth century, parts were sold off by the Bavarian State, and the garden fell into decline. A restoration program began after 1945, which included the repurchase of many parts of the original estate. This succeeded in bringing the gardens back to their former glory, once again putting Bayreuth on the gardening map. HH

Sichtungsgarten Weihenstephan

Bayern, Germany

DESIGNERS: Karl Foerster, Richard Hansen
OWNER: Weihenstephan Technical College
GARDEN STYLE: 20th-century demonstration garden
SIZE: 12.4 acres (5 ha)
CLIMATE: Temperate
LOCATION: Freising, Bayern

Far more than just a collection of plants, this university plant research center and demonstration garden has been at the forefront of plant design for a number of years. The garden was initiated by the great gardener and grower Karl Foerster, and was developed by another German plantsman, Professor Richard Hansen. Since 1948 garden plants have been examined and evaluated on this site, and valuable research has been undertaken. Whereas botanical gardens often feature only a few plants of a particular species, demonstration gardens focus on groupings as well as on individual plants. The main aim is to demonstrate to students and gardeners how trees, shrubs, herbaceous plants, and grasses can be combined to form aesthetically pleasing, long-flowering displays suited to the environment.

At the Sichtungsgarten, the woodland planting is impressive, and the spring planting is magical. However, the summer and early-autumn herbaceous beds steal the show with dynamic compositions of color and form, subtle yet bold, punctuated by fountains of ornamental grasses. In direct contrast are the wild, indigenous flowers that are spread throughout the garden, at the woodland edge, under the shrubs, and on the slopes at the water's edge, creating a beautiful, natural scene. The garden is constantly evolving and responding to new demands. Every season sees changes, but the framework remains the same. At Weihenstephan, they have built on the work of Karl Foerster and established an inspirational style. HH

"...the woodland planting
is impressive, and the spring
planting is magical"

Veitshöchheim Hofgarten

Bayern, Germany

DESIGNER: Prince Bishop Adam Friedrich von Seinsheim
OWNER: Administration of Palaces, Gardens, and Lakes
GARDEN STYLE: 18th-century rococo
SIZE: 29.7 acres (12 ha)
CLIMATE: Temperate
LOCATION: Veitshöchheim, Bayern

This compact, almost rectangular, hedge garden is one of the best surviving examples of German rococo. The gardens at Veitshöchheim, the summer residence of the prince bishops of Würzburg, were first designed as a pleasure ground at the beginning of the 1700s. The rococo garden, built on the site of a kitchen garden, is surrounded by a high wall and linked to the palace by a sweeping staircase. Adam Friedrich von Seinsheim, probably assisted by the head gardener of the time, J. Prokop Mayer, began work on the garden in 1763. Lines of hedges, straight walks, and triangular planting beds were laid out, dividing the garden into geometric shapes and forming small, intimate, hedged "rooms." The overall effect was mazelike. The proportions of the garden were distorted, making it appear far larger than it is.

The garden's statues of gods, noblemen, the four seasons, and allegories are copies of originals made by Ferdinand Tietz and Johann Wolfgang van der Auvera. They are carefully positioned for maximum effect in niches and hedged "rooms." The original sandstone sculptures are now in the Mainfränkischen Museum in Würzburg. The central feature of the garden, though, is the Grosser See, an impressive, large, irregular, baroque water basin dating from 1702–03 that was embellished by Tietz with statuary and a hidden glockenspiel.

Veitshöchheim is essentially a green and white refuge populated by mystical and classical figures, and softened by water features. It is not to everyone's taste, but is definitely worth a look. HH

Schlosspark Linderhof

Bayern, Germany

DESIGNER: Carl von Effner
OWNER: Administration of Palaces, Gardens, and Lakes
GARDEN STYLE: 19th-century mock baroque, Italianate
SIZE: 142.3 acres (57.6 ha)
CLIMATE: Temperate
LOCATION: Ettal, Bayern

King Ludwig II left a legacy of fantasy castles, palaces, and gardens. Although the castle of Neuschwannstein is firmly on the tourist map, his smaller alpine residence of Linderhof, just over the mountain to the south, is not as well known. Nestling on the side of the valley, both house and gardens are a delight.

Linderhof marks the beginning of Ludwig's fascination with the Sun King, Louis XIV of France. Carl von Effner was initially commissioned in 1870 to create a Versailles-like palace and garden, a project he soon abandoned and transferred to Herrenchiemsee (see page 490) when it became apparent that more space and a different terrain were required. What was finally built at Linderhof was a very successful mixture of baroque, Italian, and landscape ingredients. A strong, dominant axis runs north–south down the slope. It incorporates a water cascade with thirty marble steps behind the house, and a water basin with an 82-foot-high (25 m) fountain leading to a temple of Venus in front of the building. Terraces are carved into the hillside, with paths leading into the parkland and away into the woodland.

As is to be expected of such an eccentric as Ludwig, the buildings scattered around the grounds are special. They reflect his interest in the Orient and in Germanic mythology. Both the Moorish Kiosk and the Moroccan House were shown at the World Exhibition in Paris. No expense was spared, and the grotto is thought to be the first place in Bavaria to use electricity, the power for its lighting being produced by one of the first dynamos made by Siemens-Schuchers. Ludwig relived his Wagnerian fantasies by staging full-scale operas here. HH

"…both house and gardens
are a delight"

Schlossgarten Nymphenburg

Bayern, Germany

DESIGNERS: Dominique Girard, Joseph Effner, Friedrich
Ludwig von Sckell
OWNER: Administration of Palaces, Gardens, and Lakes
GARDEN STYLE: 18th-century baroque parterre, landscape
SIZE: 444.8 acres (180 ha)
CLIMATE: Temperate
LOCATION: Munich-Nymphenburg, Bayern

The Nymphenburg Palace features water, vistas, delightful buildings, and seemingly endless parkland. Built in 1664 by Elector Ferdinand Maria and his consort, Henriette Adelaide, the garden and the palace were extended from 1701 by their son, Elector Maximilian II Emanuel. The designers were the Bavarian court architect Joseph Effner and Dominique Girard, a pupil of André Le Nôtre and an expert in the construction of fountains. The garden was a massive undertaking involving the construction of a series of canals and an intricate water-pumping station.

The overall design used the canal as the main axis to divide the garden in two. As was the fashion, the garden was remodeled in the early nineteenth century by the landscape gardener Friedrich Ludwig von Sckell. He retained many features, such as the main canal, cascade, parterres, fountains, thickets, and side canals. Everything else was reworked in the landscape style, and Sckell succeeded in incorporating the pavilions scattered through the park into his design, positioning a lake in front of both the Badenburg and Pagodenburg. Both buildings are gems: Badenburg (built 1719–21) is a splendid bathhouse; Pagodenburg (1716–19) is a delightful teahouse with fine examples of chinoiserie. The Magdalenenklause (1725–28) is a small chapel built on a favorite spot of Ludwig II. The exquisite Amalienburg (1739) is a small rococo hunting lodge. What makes Nymphenburg so special is that it is a reflection of German garden history. HH

Rockgarden Sanspareil

Bayern, Germany

DESIGNER: Wilhelmine von Bayreuth
OWNER: Administration of Palaces, Gardens, and Lakes
GARDEN STYLE: 18th-century rococo
SIZE: 32.1 acres (13 ha)
CLIMATE: Temperate
LOCATION: Bayreuth-Wonsees, Bayern

The garden of Sanspareil, so-called because of the general cry of wonder, *"C'est sans pareil!"*—"There is no comparison!"—from first-time visitors, was inspired by rock formations in the beech woodland. It was another creation by Wilhelmine, Margravine of Brandenburg-Bayreuth. She used the existing features and the natural backdrop to create an extraordinary garden. Work began in 1744, when picturesque and rustic buildings were distributed through the woodlands with all manner of accessories. Many of these buildings were built out of timber and have disappeared over the years. However, the old theater ruin and the Oriental Building are still there, and these give a good impression of what the garden must have been like at its height.

The garden was meant not only to express beauty, but also to carry a deeper philosophical message. A novel, *The Adventures of Télémaque*, by the French writer François Fénelon, inspired the picturesque and often wild beauty of Sanspareil. Visitors were encouraged to reenact scenes from the book in the hope that they would soak up the novel's vision. Sanspareil is a strange, but wonderful, garden that is not quite fully in the rococo style, yet is too stylized to be a landscape garden. That is probably why there is nothing with which one can compare it. HH.

> "Sanspareil is a strange, but wonderful, garden…"

Westpark Munich

Bayern, Germany

DESIGNERS: P. Kluska, R. Weisse, G. Teutsch
OWNER: State Capital Munich
GARDEN STYLE: 20th-century modern
SIZE: 148.3 acres (60 ha)
CLIMATE: Temperate
LOCATION: Munich, Bayern

Postwar Germany has enjoyed a marvelous tradition of national and international garden shows. These not only create opportunities to establish new parks, but also provide a chance for designers to showcase new styles of gardening. Westpark, to the south of Munich city center, was home to the International Garden Festival of 1983 and is a lasting legacy to the power of garden design.

Westpark was created from wasteland that was tucked away behind housing and straddling a major freeway. The park, with its lakes, valleys, and slopes, is more than just a great, open space because they contain many gems left over from the garden festival. Several such delights are grouped like a string of pearls in the western section, where one theme garden flows into the next. This makes for a lively experience for visitors.

The main attractions here are the Rose Garden, the Chinese Garden, the Shady Garden, and the much-admired herbaceous, daylily, and iris beds. These beds in particular have become a mecca for plant enthusiasts and designers. Located on the fringes of a large, grassy area, the herbaceous borders are designed like an amphitheater around a central, exuberant flower bed. Narrow, ramped paths weave between the plantings on the slopes. Although naturalistic plantings dominate, nothing is wild about this carefully managed display. Also note how the warmth radiates off the rocks, the stepping-stones, and the thin soil, creating the feeling of an open, almost Mediterranean landscape. HH

Englischer Garten

Bayern, Germany

DESIGNER: Friedrich Ludwig von Sckell
OWNER: Administration of Palaces, Gardens, and Lakes
GARDEN STYLE: 19th-century landscape
SIZE: 921 acres (373 ha)
CLIMATE: Temperate
LOCATION: Munich, Bayern

What Hyde Park is to London, and Central Park is to New York, so the Englischer Garten is to Munich. This open space, stretching from the heart of the city out to the north, is *the* city escape. It was conceived at the end of the eighteenth century by Bavarian Elector Carl Theodor and British-American scientist Sir Benjamin Thompson as a garden for the people. Not until 1804, when the new court gardener, Friedrich Ludwig von Sckell, took office did the garden really take shape.

Sckell was influenced by the work of the great English landscape gardeners Capability Brown and Humphry Repton, a style in complete contrast to the strict forms of the baroque garden. He did not so much copy as amend the style to the site, adding slopes, mounds, glades, and grass. Paths and roads flow through the park, linking and crisscrossing to create a relaxed atmosphere. The lake, with its small island, slots into the landscape in a completely natural way. Buildings occur throughout the site to form a focal point or to frame a view. They include the Chinese Tower with its world-famous beer garden, the Monopteros—a temple crowning a small hill designed by the famous German classical architect Leo von Klenze, with views to Munich's historic center—and the Japanese Garden, added in 1972.

In summer you will see families out for a stroll, expatriates playing cricket and baseball, couples rowing on the lake, tourists taking a ride in a horsedrawn carriage, and students chilling out. Do not be surprised to see sunbathers in their own area, baring all for a complete tan. HH

Schlossgarten Schleissheim

Bayern, Germany

DESIGNERS: Enrico Zuccalli, Dominique Girard,
  Joseph Effnerl
OWNER: Administration of Palaces, Gardens, and Lakes
GARDEN STYLE: 17th- and 18th-century baroque
SIZE: 192.8 acres (78.8 ha)
CLIMATE: Temperate
LOCATION: Oberschleissheim, Bayern

Schleissheim is one of the best-preserved baroque gardens in Germany. It was created by Maximilian Emanuel, Elector of Bavaria, and with interruptions took more than thirty years to build, from 1684 until his death in 1726. Emanuel had stayed in the Netherlands, reflected in the Dutch inspired garden plan drawn up by Enrico Zuccalli that included a network of canals and bosquets. In France Emanuel was so impressed by Versailles that, in 1715, he recruited Dominique Girard, who had trained with André Le Nôtre. Girard gave the design a fashionably elegant, French overlay with parterres, additional water features, and fine statuary.

After Max Emanuel's death, the garden fell into gradual decline. In 1781 the long central lawn was turned into a canal. Although the woodlands and glades were neglected, they escaped the landscape makeover that befell most baroque gardens. In the reign of Ludwig I, the gardens were rediscovered and reconstruction was commissioned from Carl von Effner. In the late twentieth century, the forecourt and the water cascade were renovated.

The beauty of Schleissheim lies in its compact and logical layout. The garden is sandwiched between the main palace and the smaller garden house, the Lustheim, which appears to be on an island. Clever use of the central vista makes the garden appear longer, and extra depth is achieved by having the woodland dissected by paths and punctuated by bosquets on either side of the main canal. HH

Schlosspark Herrenchiemsee

Bayern, Germany

DESIGNER: Carl von Effner
OWNER: Administration of Palaces, Gardens, and Lakes
GARDEN STYLE: 19th-century mock baroque
SIZE: 103.8 acres (42 ha)
CLIMATE: Temperate
LOCATION: Chiemsee, Bayern

King Ludwig II created his idea of paradise on one of the larger islands in the Chiemsee, a lake in the foothills of the Alps. Between 1878 and 1885, he transformed the island into his version of Versailles with the help of the German landscape architect Carl von Effner. He trimmed his ambitions to fit the site, concentrating on what could be seen and used as a backdrop for the main reception rooms, particularly the spectacular Mirrored Gallery.

The palace is higher than the lake, and the garden sweeps down to its shore. With the clever use of perspective, the distance seems greater than it is.

A 600-foot-long (200 m) canal links the lake and the upper levels. The formal parterres, elaborate water sculptures (all recently restored), and wide gravel paths create a grand gesture, and disguise the fact that the garden is not very big. Although Ludwig II died before he could complete this project, it is quite possible that the huge cost would have prevented its completion. Even unfinished, though, this is a superb creation. The element of surprise, and contrast with the surrounding landscape and mountain backdrop, are unique. You can explore the parkland by foot, horse, or cart. Ideally combine the trip with a visit to the neighboring island of Fraueninsel, using the ferry that departs from the island's own jetty. HH

> "Even unfinished…this is a superb creation"

Insel Mainau

Baden-Württemberg, Germany

DESIGNER: Grand Duke Friedrich I of Baden
OWNER: Mainau GmbH
GARDEN STYLE: 19th-century botanical
SIZE: 111.2 acres (45 ha)
CLIMATE: Temperate
LOCATION: Lake Constance, Baden-Württemberg

Known as the Garden Island, Insel Mainau is one of the most popular gardens in Germany. It is a garden of superlatives, a plant collectors' paradise, and the work of a family of enthusiasts. Although there had been earlier gardens on the islands, the present version was created under the Grand Duke Friedrich I of Baden, who bought the island in 1853. He was an avid plant collector and traveled extensively. He laid out the extensive gardens to reflect his interests. The arboretum, Italian gardens, orangery, and landscape park were all laid out in his time, though his work has been continued into the twenty-first century by his great-grandson, Count Lennart Bernadotte, who took over the administration of the island in 1932. When Lennart Bernadotte married a commoner, he renounced his title and concentrated on the garden.

Insel Mainau is a garden for all seasons. This region's mild climate means that plants that are usually found in more southerly regions can be grown. The show of spring bulbs attracts visitors from north and south of the Alps. During the summer, the roses in the Italian Garden, the Promenade (with 800 planted), and the demonstration garden are a superb sight. Further attractions include the Herb, Scented, and Butterfly gardens, and the collections of rhododendrons and dahlias. The approach to the island is via a long bridge that seems to float above the lake, a clear sign that you are about to encounter something special. The garden and the park may not win any design awards, but without doubt they are a horticultural showpiece. HH

Rosengarten Gönneranlage

Baden-Württemberg, Germany

DESIGNER: Max Läuger
OWNER: City of Baden-Baden, Park Maintenance
GARDEN STYLE: 20th-century art deco rose garden
SIZE: 4 acres (1.6 ha)
CLIMATE: Temperate
LOCATION: Baden-Baden, Baden-Württemberg

It is almost possible to say that the whole of Baden-Baden is one big garden. Trees line the streets, tubs of bedding plants and flowering shrubs decorate the pedestrian zones, and even the main road is lined with roses. The centerpiece is the town park, the Lichtentaler Allee and, close by, the wonderful Gönneranlage. The latter was designed by Max Laüger, the German ceramicist and landscape architect, and was sponsored by the American-German coffee magnate Hermann Sielcken. It was named after the then mayor, Albert Gönner. This is one of the best rose gardens in Germany.

The rose garden was laid out between 1909 and 1912, and has since been excellently restored. It contains an impressive water feature and a green, leafy tunnel built to offer shade. Hedges divide the garden into "rooms" where color-coordinated arrangements can be displayed. The composition of the rose beds is well thought out. Standards are underplanted with a variety of old roses, miniatures, and hybrid teas. Pillars of ramblers and climbers are systematically dotted throughout the site. More than 11,000 roses flower here for an impressively long period from May to October. HH

"Standards are underplanted with a variety of old roses, miniatures, and hybrid teas"

Schlossgarten Schwetzingen

Baden-Württemberg, Germany

DESIGNERS: J. L. Petri, Nicolas de Pigage, Friedrich Ludwig
von Sckell

OWNER: Land Baden-Württemberg

GARDEN STYLE: 18th-century classical, English landscape

SIZE: 178 acres (72 ha)

CLIMATE: Temperate

LOCATION: Schwetzingen, Baden-Württemberg

This castle is a gem of baroque architecture built by Prince Karl Theodor in the eighteenth century as a summer residence, and the formal gardens are an absolute masterpiece. Set in a huge, circular box parterre with two long, parallel beds in the center, the formal gardens are planted with an array of brightly colored annuals in summer and bulbs in spring, with yew clipped to pinnacles in the corners. These gardens are perfect examples of large-scale parterres de broderie. Beyond them are smaller parterres with white and purple marble chips, with box shapes framing the view of the fountain and the magnificent, white marble stags. Behind the parterres are long, elegant allées formed by braided limes, the avenues seeming to go on and on forever. The influence of Versailles is obvious.

Look for the Garden of Pan beneath a canopy of trees, which is secret and shady, and has a sinuous brook covered by tiny pebbles to look like a serpent. The canal surrounds the orangery. Look out for a series of intriguing green gardens, one a famous theater garden visited by Voltaire. The classical architectural features of temples, bridges, and even a mosque were created by Nicolas de Pigage. The circular Temple of Botany has an exterior texture like an oak tree's bark. Beyond the formal section lies the English landscape garden, created by Friedrich Ludwig von Sckell, which has a stream meandering through the tranquil setting of lawns and specimen trees, and bridges crossing the water. RL

WALA Garten

Baden-Württemberg, Germany

DESIGNER: Rolf Bucher
OWNER: WALA
GARDEN STYLE: 20th-century biodynamic
SIZE: 11 acres (4.5 ha)
CLIMATE: Temperate
LOCATION: Eckwälden, Baden-Württemberg

There are only a few gardens in the world that, when you step into them, make you feel instantly at peace. The WALA garden in the village of Eckwälden in southern Germany is one of them. How extraordinary, then, that it is also the hub of a multi-million-euro industry. For the beautifully tended rows of calendula, nasturtium, echinacea, roses, sunflowers, tobacco, and camomile, plus all manner of roots, barks, and berries, are the ingredients of the Dr. Haushka organic skin-care products and WALA remedies that are manufactured here. What makes it a garden and not just a commercial growing space is the fact that it is run on biodynamic principles. If you are lucky enough to chat with the head gardener, Rolf Bucher, you will learn that "biodynamism"—a term coined by Rudolf Steiner—means taking account of the whole ecosystem. You must not care only about the well-being of the plants, but consider the soil, the surrounding trees, and the wildlife in the garden.

You will find a pond to keep the dragonflies and frogs happy, wild areas with trees, and dead wood and nettles for the birds, beetles, and hedgehogs that will keep the slugs and snails at bay, and hives for the bees. To keep the gardeners happy, there are borders billowing with yellow rudbeckia, verbascum, fennel, and giant thistles, alpines sprouting from the roofs of the outbuildings, and delicious honey for tea. This is a garden where nature and man live together in absolute harmony—and make a profit to boot. SE

Schlossgarten Weikersheim

Baden-Württemberg, Germany

DESIGNER: Daniel Matthieu
OWNER: City of Weikersheim
GARDEN STYLE: 18th-century baroque
SIZE: 22 acres (9 ha)
CLIMATE: Temperate
LOCATION: Weikersheim, Baden-Württemberg

The baroque garden of Schloss Weikersheim, a renaissance hunting palace now serving as a music academy, is within easy reach of the historic town of Rothenburg ob der Tauber. To understand how the garden was used, it is important first to explore the house. The visitor then steps into the nearby rectangular formal garden, which is approximately 755 x 395 feet (230 x 120 m) in size and was originally laid out in the renaissance style. In 1708 Count Karl Ludwig of Hohenlohe replaced that design with a French baroque garden, modeled on the one at Versailles, with a large parterre.

After the death of Ludwig, in 1756, the garden fell into gradual decline. Only the statues, more than fifty in number, gave an indication of how marvelous the garden must have been. These included Greek and Roman gods and goddesses, figures symbolizing the elements, and the garden's best-known feature, a row of dwarves ornamenting the wall of the moat.

Since 1945 the garden has been progressively restored, culminating in 1997 with the reconstruction of the Orangery to the original designs of Johann Christian Lüttich. This building, placed at the end of the garden, extends over the whole width of the parterre and has semicircular recesses that offer spectacular views over the Tauber valley. HH

RIGHT Since its restoration, Schlossgarten Weikersheim is again a fitting setting for its historic collection of statues.

Karlsruhe Schlossgarten

Baden-Württemberg, Germany

DESIGNERS: Christian Thran, Friedrich Dyckerhoff, Heinrich Hübsch
OWNER: Land Baden-Württemberg
GARDEN STYLE: 18th-century landscape park
SIZE: 94.8 acres (38.4 ha)
CLIMATE: Temperate
LOCATION: Karlsruhe, Baden-Württemberg

Karlsruhe's castle and town make up a homogenous whole because they were planned together in 1715, as instructed by the margrave, Karl Wilhelm von Baden-Durlach. From a tower built just behind the castle, thirty-two avenues radiate out into the wider landscape. Although the town has expanded since the eighteenth century, the development has fanned out following the pattern of the radiating roads.

The original garden design was inspired by formal French baroque gardens. In 1787 the gardens were largely remodeled and turned into an informal landscape park. Alterations to the park were made in 1967, when trees were thinned and pruned.

To the front of the castle, along the axis that links the building with the town, the formal garden layout survives on the Schlossplatz. To the west is the greenhouse and the orangery with its copper-domed roof, and the Botanischer Garten, a botanical collection started in the eighteenth century by botanist Karl Christian Gmelin. On the eastern edge of the garden is the Fasanenschloss. Of many other buildings here, the Little Castle is the oldest building in the town. It was the hunting lodge of Margrave Karl Wilhelm Hardtwald, and was built in 1709. Also of note are the two small Chinese tea pavilions. IvG

LEFT Karlsruhe Schlossgarten's tall tower is the focal point of the neighboring town's thirty-two radiating avenues.

Stadtgarten Karlsruhe

Baden-Württemberg, Germany

DESIGNERS: Hartweg, Karl Meyer, Friedrich Ries, Friedrich Scherer
OWNER: City of Karlsruhe
GARDEN STYLE: 19th-, 20th-century landscape park
SIZE: 54.61 acres (22.1 ha)
CLIMATE: Temperate
LOCATION: Karlsruhe, Baden-Württemberg

In the center of town, located right opposite the main train station, Karlsruhe's town park has an interesting history and a tradition for combining its conventional parkland with exotic attractions.

The public park was initially laid out in the landscape style in 1823 and, bit by bit, more new features were added. A rose garden was created in 1894 and, in 1913, a Japanese garden, one of the oldest in Germany. The park was extensively revamped as part of the Federal Garden Show of 1967, with the rose garden becoming a fan-shaped kaleidoscope of color, new extensive planting, and water features. An open-air, lakeside theater was added to the garden's facilities.

The Japanese garden is particularly worth a mention. Redesigned in 1967 by a Japanese landscape architect and a Shinto priest, it consists of two parts: the Zen Garden on the shores of the lake, and the larger garden—complete with Shinto temple, teahouse, and stream—on the other side of a main path. It is a garden within a garden, a beautiful, idyllic place, with its very own hermitlike poet.

Different eras of garden history are still visible in the Stadtgarten, each enhancing and blending with the next, creating a marvelous mix. And do not worry about the very popular zoo located in a corner of this large park—in fact the occasional sight of an elephant or a giraffe is a great plus. HH

Ogród w Nieborowie

Łódzkie, Poland

DESIGNERS: Szymon Bogumił Zug, Tylman van Gameren
OWNER: National Museum of Warsaw
GARDEN STYLE: 18th-century formal baroque in English park
SIZE: 49 acres (20 ha)
CLIMATE: Temperate
LOCATION: Nieborów, Łódzkie
TRANSLATION: Nieborów Palace Garden

Nieborów Palace, home of the National Museum of Warsaw, is an enormously popular tourist attraction. In various forms, the site has been the residence of powerful families since the thirteenth century, and in the late seventeenth century it was the site of the Nieborowski family's marvelous Gothic residence. It was remodeled by Tylman van Gameren into an opulent palace for Primate Michał Radziejowski.

After changing hands in the eighteenth century, the palace became property of the Radziwiłł family, one of the most powerful aristocratic families in all of Poland. They lived here until the end of World War II. The well-maintained building of sand-colored exteriors, a mansard roof, and sculpted tympanum, is now considered one of the most beautiful palaces in the country. Its rococo and neoclassical interiors house a collection of paintings, sculptures, furniture, and a library with over 10,000 books.

The palace is surrounded by an extensive and elegant park. A geometric French baroque garden, also designed by Van Gameren, includes alleés of trees, neat hedges, symmetrical flower beds, and box mazes. Both the formal garden and wider park are enhanced by a collection of European sculptures.

In the 1890s, the Radziwiłł family commissioned the rest of the park to reflect the growing popularity of English landscape parks. It boasts a huge pond and many carefully planted trees and shrubs, including rare specimens. An avenue of lime trees stretches 4 miles (7 km) from Nieborów Palace to Arkadia. NS

Ogród w Arkadii

Łódzkie, Poland

DESIGNER: Princess Helena Radziwiłł
OWNER: Nieborów Museum
GARDEN STYLE: 18th-century romantic
SIZE: Approximately 700 acres (280 ha)
CLIMATE: Temperate
LOCATION: Łowicz , Łódzkie
TRANSLATION: Arkadia Garden

Created in 1778 for Princess Helena Radziwiłł, Arkadia is believed to be the most beautiful garden in Poland. In Helena's hands, this rural idyll of Greek mythology became a huge romantic park, "a land of happiness and peace," and mock antique and Gothic buildings evoke the pastoral paradise fashionable at the time.

The park's pavilions were designed by the best architects and painters of the day. The pavilion names —Sybil's Grotto, the Melancholy Spot—were typically romantic, while the level of detail was astonishing: the Philemon and Baucis House was set within magnificent flower gardens; the Swiss Cottage yard was full of chickens; the Waterfall House had a library of philosophical works; while the Isle of Emotions featured a ring of altars where flowers were placed.

To add classical allure and make Arkadia more attractive, Princess Helena brought back fragments of sculpture from her travels. Thanks to her energy, avid collecting, and vision, Arkadia enjoyed the status of one of Poland's greatest cultural centers at the turn of the eighteenth century, and was exalted by poets.

The surviving buildings include the High Priest's House and the Temple of Diana, a classical structure that stands at a meeting of paths and has a painting of the morning star by Jean-Pierre Norblin on its ceiling. The delightful Gothic Cottage is also well worth a visit, as is the Margraves House with an adjoining tower and Greek arch. NS

Ogród Botaniczny Warszawa

Mazowieckie, Poland

DESIGNERS: Various, including Micha Szubert
OWNER: Polish Academy of Sciences
GARDEN STYLE: 20th-century botanical
SIZE: 100 acres (40 ha)
CLIMATE: Temperate
LOCATION: Warsaw, Mazowieckie
TRANSLATION: Warsaw Botanical Garden

Conceived as a seat of scientific learning, the focus of the largest botanical garden in Poland was built between 1977 and 1980 beside the laboratory complex. It now has approximately 10,000 species.

Since the garden was opened to the public in 1990, collections have been organized increasingly for public education and recreation. An extensive arboretum features collections of trees and shrubs, including many slow growing and acid-loving species like heathers, pieris, rhododendrons, and azaleas. It includes dwarf pines and rarer species such as the Franklin tree (*Franklinia alatamaha*), extinct in its native habitat of Georgia, U.S., for over 200 years. The Education Center for Nature and Ecology takes a look at the native species of Poland with a selection of foreign oddities. The Flora of Poland collection has species that are rare or endangered in the wild, particularly plants from the Carpathian Mountains.

In late spring and summer, the ornamental garden sees an explosion of daylilies, hostas, old roses, alliums, tulips, gladioli, and dahlias. A huge greenhouse has tropical and subtropical plants, including citrus, tree ferns, and fuchsias. The newest greenhouse hosts ferns and succulents. According to legend, visitors have suffocated from the scent of the spring flowers—perhaps not a bad way to go, but it may be worth hanging on a little longer, if only to see the sixty-two varieties of magnolia in bloom. NS

Park Łazienkowski

Mazowieckie, Poland

DESIGNER: Tylman van Gameren
OWNER: The Polish State
GARDEN STYLE: 18th-century baroque
SIZE: 198 acres (80 ha)
CLIMATE: Temperate
LOCATION: Warsaw, Mazowieckie
TRANSLATION: Łazienki Park

This large, beautiful, romantic landscaped park was designed as the summer retreat of King Stanisław August Poniatowski. Surprisingly close to the city center, and with a grand statue of Frédéric Chopin, Poland's great composer, standing outside the gates, this is Warsaw's most famous recreation spot.

Wide avenues are lined with tall, mature trees, and sculptures pop up in the most unexpected of places. Adorned with busts of Roman emperors and elegant fountains, the main promenade leads to the old orangery that houses an exhibition of Polish sculpture. Peacocks roam freely across broad lawns. The many interesting buildings include a second orangery, and a selection of palaces and pavilions, largely built in the eighteenth century.

Two good water features are the amphitheater with its stage actually built over the water, and the Palace On The Water. The work of architect Domenico Merlini, the palace casts a grand reflection in a formal pool, dappled by overhanging trees and foliage. One of the finest examples of neoclassical architecture in Poland, it was earmarked for destruction during World War II, narrowly avoiding a sticky end when the Nazis ran out of time for blowing up things and settled merely for setting it on fire. It has since been fully restored. The park is at its best in spring and summer, and the open-air Chopin concerts in the rose garden every summer Sunday at noon—when music lovers can often be seen scrambling genteelly for prime seats—are extremely popular. NS

Pałac Wilanòw

Mazowieckie, Poland

DESIGNER: Stanisław Kostka Potocki
OWNER: The Polish State
GARDEN STYLE: 18th-century English, French-Italian baroque
SIZE: 110 acres (45 ha)
CLIMATE: Temperate
LOCATION: Wilanòw, Mazowieckie
TRANSLATION: Wilanòw Palace

Often referred to as the "small Versailles," Wilanòw Castle and garden were commissioned by King Jan III Sobieski as a summer residence. The palace is remarkable for its authenticity and is one of the few significant buildings to have survived the destruction of World War II intact. The exterior is extensively and artistically decorated. Its delightful grounds—now three gardens in one—were enlarged and refined by Stanisław Kostka Potocki in the eighteenth century. One of his additions was a tranquil English park, where a pathway runs between a lake and perfectly ranked trees, and neatly laid out flower beds, sculptures, monuments, and pavilions add to the idyll. To the south of the palace is an English-Chinese romantic garden where pagodas, summerhouses, and artful bridges overlooking the lake are offset by promenades and mature planting. Potocki's neo-Gothic tomb can be seen as you approach the palace.

The most splendid of the three gardens is the baroque design in formal French-Italian style. It has a patte d'oie, or goosefoot, layout like Versailles. Long avenues are flanked by perfectly trimmed flower beds and trees, interspersed with statues. Smaller paths meander between trimmed shrubs and hedgerows. The palace—now an art gallery—just manages to steer clear of grandiosity by the humor of its frescoes and decoration. The artistic theme continues in the grounds with temporary exhibitions held in the orangery. The old stables contain a permanent display of poster art, a Polish specialty. NS

Pałac Czartoryskich

Lubelskie, Poland

DESIGNER: Unknown
OWNER: Institute of Soil Science and Plant Cultivation
GARDEN STYLE: 19th-century English romantic
SIZE: 60 acres (24.3 ha)
CLIMATE: Temperate
LOCATION: Puławy, Lubelskie
TRANSLATION: Czartoryski Palace

The most striking landmark in the quiet Polish fishing village of Puławy is the dramatic, baroque-classical Czartoryski Palace, surrounded by its elegant park. Dating from 1676, the palace was remodeled several times to attain its current perfect symmetry. A formal, rectangular pool in front of the palace reflects the central section of the building, and a semicircular walkway, originally punctuated by ornamental trees, curves around the pool in front of the palace. Well-groomed lawns invite you to stroll among tulips, narcissi, and other bulbs blooming beside the pool.

The park, an English-style romantic garden, was started in the early nineteenth century. Its rolling landscape has grassy, open spaces and mature trees, including a huge *Ginkgo biloba*, tulip trees, and English and native Polish species.

There are a number of buildings, including the Chinese House and the Marynki Palace, built by Czartoryski for his daughter, Marynka, on whom he doted. Pavilions from the early nineteenth century include the Temple of Sybil and Gothic House, said to be the first museum buildings in Poland. The 1980s saw reconstruction of historic caves in the garden.

After Poland was partitioned in 1795, the palace became the center of Polish political and cultural life. In 1862 the Institute of Agriculture and Forestry, one of the first in central Europe, was set up here. Courses continued until the start of World War I. NS

Ogród Botaniczny Krakowa

Małopolskie, Poland

DESIGNER: Unknown
OWNER: Jagiellonian University
GARDEN STYLE: 18th- to 21st-century botanical
SIZE: Approximately 15 acres (6 ha)
CLIMATE: Temperate
LOCATION: Kraków, Małopolskie
TRANSLATION: Kraków Botanical Garden

There is no doubt that Kraków is an exciting place. It was inhabited in neolithic times, and subsequently by Celts and Romans; legend has it that King Krak slew a fiery dragon awakened from slumber by the human noise above and that the city was named in his honor. It is also the site of the oldest botanical garden in Poland. It is relatively well preserved, with the patterns of an earlier baroque-style layout and an English-Chinese garden still evident. It adjoins a renaissance palace, built in 1792 as an observatory. A meteorological station and a greenhouse complex are relatively recent additions to the site that is a monument to culture and the art of gardening.

The 5,000 plant species include collections from the end of the eighteenth and beginning of the nineteenth centuries, a garden of healing plants, exotic and native species, and a great palm house dating back to 1882. The Jagiellonian Oak, the oldest tree in the garden, is approximately 500 years old. It is the sole remnant of the vast forests that once covered the whole region.

As a university garden, it offers an extensive range of scientific activities, including plant geography, ecology of vascular plants, and the monitoring of Poland's rare and endangered species. There are also a number of educational activities open to the public, lectures popularizing botany, and exhibitions of photography and paintings. NS

Zamek w Łancucie

Podkarpackie, Poland

DESIGNERS: Various, including Szymon Bogumił Zug
OWNER: The Polish State
GARDEN STYLE: 19th-century eclectic, parkland
SIZE: 35 acres (20 ha)
CLIMATE: Temperate
LOCATION: Łancut, Podkarpakie
TRANSLATION: Łancut Castle

Gardeners often have a fair amount to worry about. Pests and diseases can ravage treasured plants and rogue weather systems can cause drought or deluge without warning. The head gardener and guests at Łancut Castle have another reason for concern, however: it is said that on wild and stormy nights, the ghost of Stanisław Stadniki can be seen galloping through the castle grounds on a black horse, his cloak billowing in the wind. A local hoodlum, he came to the obligatory bad end and was doomed to remain on earth as penance for his disreputable life.

The castle, now a museum of period interiors, has five-pointed, star-shaped fortifications, and, in May, when the magnolia blooms, neither elaborate defences nor spectral horsemen can deter music lovers who flock to the international festival of chamber music here.

The castle was reconstructed and modernized in the nineteenth century to become one of the most luxurious residences in Europe, and the park is equally impressive and beautiful. The grounds include a park with *Ginkgo biloba*, plane trees, tulip trees, and Chinese junipers, all of which are rarely seen in Poland. Other features include an orangery, rosarium, and orchid house. An Italian garden was created on the eastern side of the castle, while a rose garden was arranged on the southern side of the orangery. Though the marvelously floriferous ornamental borders aren't scarred by the hoofs of Stanisław Stadniki's horse, these days the gardener still lies awake during stormy weather. NS

Plas Brondanw

Gwynedd, Wales

DESIGNER: Sir Clough Williams-Ellis
OWNER: Susan Clough Williams-Ellis
GARDEN STYLE: Arts and Crafts
SIZE: 2 acres (0.8 ha)
CLIMATE: Temperate
LOCATION: Llanfrothen, Penrhyndeudraeth, Gwynedd

Plas Brondanw was the home of the architect Bertram Clough Williams-Ellis, creator of the Italianate village Portmeirion on the North Wales coast. From 1908, when he inherited the estate from his father, to his death at the age of 95, Williams-Ellis was passionate about Plas Brondanw. Over the years, he developed a characterful garden that is still largely unaltered. Dominated by the brooding peaks of Snowdonia, it is very much at one with the surrounding landscape, despite its formal layout and design. Ingenious vistas give breathtaking views of the mountains so

that visitors can never quite escape their dramatic presence. Inspired by the Arts and Crafts movement as well as the classical gardens of Italy, the garden is constructed on a sloping site with terraces, hedged walks, and yew-enclosed "rooms." Tall yews clipped into weird and wonderful shapes are a dominating theme. Statuary and sculpture form focal points throughout, very much in the Portmeirion style.

This was never designed to be a flower garden. However, rhododendrons and azaleas add color, and interesting shrubs thrive in the Gulf Stream climate. A long border on the edge of the garden contains hydrangeas and ferns, while the dark-gray walls of the house are brightened by Japanese anemones (*Anemone* x *hybrida*). A visit to the watchtower is a must. Built at the end of a woodland walk behind the house, it has spectacular views over the mountains as well as down toward the Porthmadog Estuary and Clough Williams-Ellis' beloved Portmeirion. CF

Plas Newydd

Gwynedd, Wales

DESIGNERS: Humphry Repton, seventh Marquis of Anglesey
OWNER: The National Trust
GARDEN STYLE: 18th-century English landscape, late-20th-century formal and informal
SIZE: 49 acres (19.8 ha)
CLIMATE: Temperate
LOCATION: Llanfairpwll, Anglesey, Gwynedd

In many ways, the glory of this garden is its setting. The lawns sweep down to the waters of the Menai Straits that split the Isle of Anglesey from Wales. Behind, the craggy mountains of Snowdonia provide a breathtaking backdrop. It is hard to compete with this natural beauty. That is why generations of owners and garden designers have framed the view with plants or concentrated on enclosed areas.

Humphry Repton made original plans for the grounds in 1798–99 in one of his famous Red Books. It shows watercolors of areas that needed improving, and ideas on how they would look once work was completed. His major contributions were an informal, open-plan layout and trees that provided shelter from vicious winds that whip along the straits. The present Marquis of Anglesey and the National Trust have made more recent developments. There is an Australasian arboretum with eucalyptus and nothofagus. Elsewhere in the grounds are frost-sensitive Chilean fire bushes (*Embothrium coccineum*) and snowy white eucryphias.

The Terrace Garden is the best maintained area. Running the entire length of the lowest level is a narrow border of agapanthus. When in full flower in summer, it forms a river of blue that mirrors the Menai Straits beyond. In sharp color contrast, the adjacent borders are planted with a fiery mixture of hardy and tender perennials in shades of red, orange, and yellow. On the top terrace is a ferny grotto enclosed by trellis and cooled by a bubbling fountain. LH

Crûg Farm Plants

Gwynedd, Wales

DESIGNERS: Bleddyn Wynn-Jones, Sue Wynn-Jones
OWNERS: Bleddyn Wynn-Jones, Sue Wynn-Jones
GARDEN STYLE: Informal plantsman's garden
SIZE: 0.75 acre (0.3 ha)
CLIMATE: Temperate
LOCATION: Caernarfon, Gwynedd

The views from Crûg Farm are unforgettable. Mount Snowdon feels as if it is in the back garden. At the front, views of the Menai Straits have the Isle of Anglesey as their focal point. Those who can tear themselves away from the landscape will find a superlative collection of temperate-zone plants from the late twentieth and early twenty-first centuries.

For most of the year, Bleddyn and Sue Wynn-Jones run the nursery. Every fall, they leave the nursery and head off on annual seed collecting expeditions. Concentrating on woodland herbaceous flora and climbers, the Wynn-Jones family has traveled to the Far East, Himalayas, and South America. They are also very good at seeking out and exploring high-altitude zones throughout the tropics where many plants are hardy enough to survive in maritime temperate climates. Since woodland flora is very much their focus, many of the Wynn-Jones' introductions display exceptionally good foliage, and some of the asarums and arisaemas could almost be tropical. A particular interest of theirs is the Convallariaceae family, including lily-of-the-valley and Solomon's seal, and nearly all woodland floor species. They have also introduced good climbers.

During spring and early summer, rhododendrons and bulbs provide plenty of color. Later in the year, the decorative focus is on herbaceous plants, including a huge collection of hardy geraniums. This is a delightful "stroll garden" with little paths leading off through woodlands, a walled garden, and around old farm buildings. Do not miss it. NK

Portmeirion

Gwynedd, Wales

DESIGNER: Clough Williams-Ellis
OWNER: The Second Portmeirion Foundation
GARDEN STYLE: Fantasy Italianate
SIZE: 70 acres (28.3 ha)
CLIMATE: Temperate
LOCATION: Penrhyndeudraeth, Gwynedd, Wales

Countless British gardens have acted as backdrops to television programs. None, though, has achieved the cult status that Portmeirion enjoys thanks to the surreal 1960s series *The Prisoner*.

Sir Williams-Ellis, mastermind of the village, was born with two great advantages—enormous private wealth and architectural talent. The former enabled him to buy the site in 1925. The latter meant he could put his theories about town planning to the test by creating an entire, surreal, Italianate-style village in almost one fell swoop. The majority of the buildings were erected by 1939, the rest from 1954 to 1976.

The village benefits from dramatic bedding, tall Irish yews (*Taxus baccata* 'Fastigiata'), mature cabbage palms, yuccas, and an abundance of topiary. The surrounding woods also have a fairytale quality. In the early Victorian period, landowner Henry Seymour Westmacott planted firs—Douglas (*Pseudotsuga menziesii*), noble (*Abies procera*), and Himalayan (*A. spectabilis*)—coast redwoods (*Sequoia sempervirens*) and wellingtonia (*Sequoiadendron giganteum*) as well as pines—Monterey (*Pinus radiata*) and Scotch (*P. sylvestris*). In the Edwardian era, Caton Haigh introduced rhododendrons, camellias, and other shrubs. Williams-Ellis planted avenues and excavated lakes. All this is in addition to spring cherry blossoms, azaleas, and a weeping silver lime that scents the village in late summer. RCa

RIGHT The surreal setting of Portmeirion, where the plantings are as much of a surprise as the buildings.

Bodnant Garden

Conwy, Wales

DESIGNER: Edward Milner
OWNER: The National Trust
GARDEN STYLE: Picturesque, Arts and Crafts, woodland
SIZE: 80 acres (32.4 ha)
CLIMATE: Temperate
LOCATION: Tal-y-Cafn, Conwy

On top of high ground above the River Conwy, Bodnant enjoys spectacular views of Snowdonia. This distant brooding landscape, which changes dramatically with the weather, adds enormously to the romance of what is Wales' finest garden. Henry Pochin, whose fortune was based on a process for whitening soap, bought the estate in 1874. The 1792 house was significantly enlarged and remodeled, and its existing garden and surrounding plantations developed. Succeeding generations of Pochin's family and three generations of head gardeners are responsible for bringing Bodnant to its present-day perfection.

The first grand designs were by the landscape architect Edward Milner. He laid sweeping lawns to the west of the house and conceived the much-copied, 180-foot-long (55 m) laburnum tunnel that is breathtaking in early June, when noonday sunshine strikes thousands upon thousands of dangling, yellow flower chains. Pochin's grandson, Henry Duncan, terraced the lawns at the beginning of the twentieth century. Henry began collecting, planting, and hybridizing the Chinese rhododendrons for which the gardens have become so renowned. He and his son were such great plantsmen that they became presidents of the Royal Horticultural Society. Also look out for the waterfall—a fairytale masterpiece—and the eighteenth-century garden pavilion, transported from Gloucestershire in 1938 and rebuilt stone by stone. Above all else, do not miss the view down to the Lily Terrace and over to the mountains, a souvenir that every visitor will take home in their hearts. RCa

Chirk Castle

Wrexham, Wales

DESIGNER: Richard Myddelton Biddulph
OWNER: The National Trust
GARDEN STYLE: Topiary, hedges, shrub borders, parkland
SIZE: 5 acres (2 ha)
CLIMATE: Temperate
LOCATION: Chirk, Wrexham

Old topiary gardens are as rare as they are precious, taking decades to grow and shape, and hours to maintain. Chirk Castle is one of them, though it is not as well-known as it should be, perhaps because the pieces are not massed in a concentrated area, as with other topiary gardens. Chirk is different, with the topiary and hedges thrown open to the landscape.

An avenue of twenty yews, six of which are cut into enormous Welsh hats, the rest into elongated drums reflecting the rounded bastions of the castle, crown the top terrace. From here, crenellated yew hedges echo the castle's battlements, embellished with topiary buttressing or cut into alcoves. Hedges also mark the east and west boundaries of the garden, with freestanding topiary along the way.

Chirk is not just about topiary. Originally built as part of a chain of defensive hilltop border castles, it has been the home of the Myddelton family since 1595. With every succeeding century, the garden has undergone a different layer of development. The mid-seventeenth-century formal garden was swept away in the eighteenth century by a disciple of Capability Brown and then partly reinstated in the nineteenth when the topiary and yew hedges were planted. The final flourish came in the twentieth century, bringing a mantle of ornamental trees and shrubs, notably flowering cherries, magnolias, cornus, eucryphias, hydrangeas, and rhododendrons. It is said that seventeen counties can be seen from the castle. The view of the lime avenue into the wilderness with its statue of Hercules as a focal point, is a marvel. VR

Powis Castle and Garden

Powys, Wales

DESIGNERS: William Winde, William Emes, various others
OWNER: The National Trust
GARDEN STYLE: 17th-century garden with later additions
SIZE: 24 acres (9.7 ha)
CLIMATE: Temperate
LOCATION: Welshpool, Powys

Powis is blessed with both natural and artificial attributes. The first is its location, since the stunning Welsh scenery here provides a peerless backdrop. The second is the castle, which was built at a time when the area was a stronghold for the Welsh Princes of Powys, and which theatrically straddles an outcrop of pink, limy rock. The garden was originally laid out in an Italian- and French-influenced style, and the southeast face of the castle rock provides a series of stately terraces, possibly the closest thing to an Italianate Renaissance-style garden in Britain. Laid out in the late seventeenth century, they are the defining feature of Powis. Massive in scale at around 600 feet (182 m) long, and highlighted by innovative planting and architectural ornaments, such as the orangery and an aviary, they are a total delight. Edging one side are venerable yew hedges that rise over 50 feet (15 m) high in places. These giants provide a sense of gravitas to the hanging gardens of Wales.

From the top terraces, overlooking the Severn Valley, you get an overview of the rest of the garden beneath. To the left is a series of formal gardens crafted from the skeleton of an old kitchen garden created in 1911 by Lady Violet, wife of the fourth earl. Here unusual, tender plants prosper in the shelter of the walls and hedges. Immediately opposite, on an adjoining crag, is the Wilderness, a miniature woodland garden first laid out in the 1770s by William Emes. It contains beautiful trees, underplanted with ornamental shrubs, and in spring, the air here is heavy with the sweet scent of *Rhododendron luteum*. JB

National Botanic Garden of Wales

Camarthenshire, Wales

DESIGNERS: Various

OWNER: The National Botanic Garden of Wales

GARDEN STYLE: 21st-century botanic garden set in 18th-century landscaped park and gardens

SIZE: 500 acres (204 ha)

CLIMATE: Temperate

LOCATION: Llanarthne, Carmarthenshire

Varied, interesting, dramatic, and idiosyncratic, the first botanic garden to be created in Britain for over 200 years compensates for a modest lack of maturity with boundless enthusiasm. Conceived as a world-class resource for the twenty-first century, it delivers an engaging and ultimately contemporary message on the value of plants, perfectly pitched for our time.

Set in parkland belonging to a Regency estate, the gardens, lakes, woodlands, hills, and wildflower meadows provide varied habitats for flora and fauna to thrive. The entire site is dedicated to the care of threatened plants across the globe and to conserving the plant heritage of Wales. The world's largest single span greenhouse shelters some of the world's most endangered plants. Emphasis is on education, and the Physicians of Myddfai exhibition highlights the relationship between plants and medicine.

Wales is notoriously damp. The beautiful necklace of lakes and streams across the site is sprinkled with memorable water features. These include a brook, meandering down the entire length of the hill from conservatory to entrance, and the Scaladaqua Tonda (curving water steps), a water sculpture of five steps by William Pye. The garden bubbles with life. Modern sculpture abounds, children are well catered for, and some of the pieces of art are pure comedy.

The rich and intelligent blend of wildlife and sculpture, horticulture, design, history, and geology, combined with an unfettered ambition to save the world, make it a zesty and unmissable experience. NS

Aberglasney House and Gardens

Camarthenshire, Wales

DESIGNERS: Bishop Rudd, and others

OWNER: Aberglasney Restoration Trust

GARDEN STYLE: 17th-century historic garden with 20th-
and 21st-century additions and modern plantings

SIZE: 10 acres (4 ha)

CLIMATE: Temperate

LOCATION: Llangathen, Camarthenshire

Although its exact origins are shrouded in obscurity, Aberglasney has an ancient pedigree. The remarkable survival of the garden structure created by Bishop Rudd in the mid-1600s makes the site unique. However, there are records of a garden on the site long before that, and coins dating back to 1288 were discovered during work on the cloister garden.

Over the centuries, the fortunes of the inhabitants rose and fell. Great wealth was interspersed with periods of debt and decay. By 1995 the house was derelict and the gardens were drowning in a sea of weeds. Saved by the Aberglasney Restoration Trust in the nick of time, it is now considered one of the finest gardens in Wales. The cloister garden beside the house is surrounded on three sides by a long, arcaded walkway supporting a broad parapet. This is a rare piece of garden history, the sole survivor of a style of garden architecture popular around the time of Queen Elizabeth I. Two walled gardens that once supplied the house with fruits and vegetables have, however, been given a new incarnation. Clipped box patterns give a historical slant and a modern twist thanks to the adjoining ornamentals from around the world. The many unusual species make this garden a planter's paradise. Extra attractions include the pool area, sunken garden, lawns, vistas, and a tunnel of gnarled yew. The transformation from sleeping beauty to superstar is not over quite yet. After the better part of a millennium, the newly maturing garden is entitled to bide its time. NS

Ridler's Garden

Swansea, Wales

DESIGNER: Tony Ridler
OWNER: Tony Ridler
GARDEN STYLE: 20th- and 21st-century formal
SIZE: 0.5 acre (0.2 ha)
CLIMATE: Temperate
LOCATION: Swansea, Swansea

Tony Ridler is a graphic designer, which is evident in his Swansea town garden. It is an ordered, magical garden where nature is brought firmly to heel. Like so many before him, Ridler found inspiration in Lawrence Johnston's garden at Hidcote Manor in Gloucestershire (see page 305). Consequently design is paramount, with an *Alice in Wonderland* feel as endless "rooms" lead into each other, vistas open where least expected, and a surprise appears around every corner. There is no "borrowed landscape" because the garden is inward-looking, a microcosm of neatly clipped hedges, spirals, balls, and sight lines.

The garden is in its second incarnation and once had chickens, a pond, and meandering paths. Then Ridler created a formal courtyard, liked the effect, and the rest of the garden grew from there. It was never planned as a whole, and that explains why the original courtyard is off-center, a fact that still irritates.

Box, yew, Portugal laurel (*Prunus lusitanica*), and ophiopogon grass, along with sett and gravel paths, make up the backbone of the garden. Walls are painted black or as trompe l'oeil as a backdrop. Sculptures form the focus for a vista, the punctuation points on paths. However, the garden is not entirely at the mercy of Ridler and his clipping shears. Tulips supply bright patches of startling color in spring, followed by annuals and perennials, such as pink penstemon and orange marigolds, in summer. In winter, when they have died back and the mess of fallen leaves is over, Ridler is happiest: "I prefer quiet, somber spaces," he says. CD

Clyne Gardens

Swansea, Wales

DESIGNERS: The Vivian family
OWNER: Swansea City Council
GARDEN STYLE: 20th-century woodland
SIZE: 50 acres (20.4 ha)
CLIMATE: Temperate
LOCATION: Blackpill, Swansea

Clyne is a great example of what once belonged to a wealthy family, but later passed to the community. The house, built in 1791 with nineteenth-century Gothic additions, was home to the Vivian family. The last, Admiral A. Walker-Heneage Vivian, was responsible for the high quality of the planting and for selling the estate to Swansea City Council in 1952.

Sweeping lawns with clumps of trees and shrubs dominate the upper parts of the garden. The lower part—Brook Hole Valley—is essentially woodland. Beech, oaks—English (*Quercus robur*) and Turkey (*Q. cerris*)—and Scotch pine (*Pinus sylvestris*) form a backdrop to bluebells and exotic shrubs dominated by rhododendrons. The last form two National Collections: the large-leaved *falconeri* subsection that revels in the mild climate, and the subsection *triflorum*. There are also some *R. niveum* hybrids that Vivian raised. Best described as being in the colors of fruit yogurts, they make an idiosyncratic, early-summer touch and can be viewed from the tower that Vivian built for surveying his plants from above.

A particularly interesting touch at Clyne is that a variety of herbaceous plants have naturalized over the years, including Himalayan candelabra primulas. They create a stunning, multicolored effect in summer and are later followed by giant far-eastern meadowsweet (*Filipendula camtschatica*), gunnera, irises, and in early fall, crocosmias. A scarlet, Japanese-style bridge at the upper end of the garden is popular with wedding parties, a sign that the garden now functions as a much-loved park for the people. NK

Tredegar House

Newport, Wales

DESIGNERS: The Morgan family
OWNER: Newport City Council
GARDEN STYLE: 19th-century, 17th-century (recreated),
   and 20th-century formal gardens
SIZE: 90 acres (36.42 ha)
CLIMATE: Temperate
LOCATION: Newport, Newport

Since Tredegar House was built in the late seventeenth century, the industrial city of Newport has gradually encroached on its grounds. They remain an oasis of green, however, with sandy walks through a park of deciduous and coniferous trees, nineteenth-century shrubs, sequoias, and rhododendrons. Eighteenth-century landscaping swept away all but one of the oak and chestnut avenues radiating from the house.

The red brick mansion that belonged to the Morgan family from the seventeenth century until 1951 is one of the finest Restoration houses in the country. It still has the original entrance and well-preserved interiors with pictures from the Dulwich Picture Gallery, and furniture from the Victoria and Albert Museum—both in London. The late-seventeenth-century stable block was not demolished as planned, so can still be visited.

The medieval plan of the garden survives on two sides of the house in a series of formal walled gardens that have been rescued from the brink of decay and recently replanted. The Sunken Garden has also been restored with an early-twentieth-century planting scheme. The highlight of a visit, however, must be the discovery made some years ago by researchers in the Orangery Garden. While working with documentary and archaeological evidence, they pieced together a late-seventeenth-century mineral parterre. Its recreation is the first of its kind in Britain. The parterre is made of coal and brick dust, colored sands, and seashells, and would have been particularly fashionable when created. VB

De Eco-Kathedraal

Friesland, Netherlands

DESIGNER: Louis Guillaume Le Roy
OWNER: Louis Guillaume Le Roy
GARDEN STYLE: 20th-century eco-tectural
SIZE: 5 acres (2 ha)
CLIMATE: Temperate
LOCATION: Mildam, Friesland

In the somewhat unlikely context of a private, twentieth-century garden, the Dutch artist and philosopher Louis Guillaume Le Roy has created an eco-cathedral that embodies his theories about ecologically sustainable societies. Influenced by the mood of the late 1960s, particularly the counter-culture against contemporary urban architecture and industrialized agricultural monoculture, Le Roy promoted sustainable practices. These included the creation of separate communities located on the edges of cities where waste would be recycled, with the emphasis on small-scale, organic agriculture.

Le Roy had three bases. He worked at his home in Oranjewoud and his experimental garden at Mildam, but he tested his ideas more fully at a strip of public open space in nearby Heerenveen, where he involved the local community, aiming to promote local creativity and form a link with nature outside the city. Local politics proved quite a stumbling block at Heerenveen, so when he retired, he returned to work at Mildam, where he began to lay the foundations for an eco-cathedral that will take 1,000 years to complete, helped by volunteers. In the process, he has converted thousands of tons of building rubble and paving waste into a network of walls, creating spaces for the benefit of animals, plants, and people.

His *laissez-faire* approach toward planting has created an extraordinary lush place that challenges the notion that ecology equates with nativeness. JW

In de Tuinen van Ruinen

Drenthe, Netherlands

DESIGNERS: Ton ter Linden, Hanneke Clabbers
OWNERS: Frans Neuteboom, Janneke Neuteboom
GARDEN STYLE: 20th-century naturalistic
SIZE: 3.7 acres (1.5 ha)
CLIMATE: Temperate
LOCATION: Ruinen, Drenthe

These gardens were made famous by the artist Ton ter Linden, who developed a new manner of planting perennials. Plants, instead of being set in groups, were arranged incidentally, and often singularly, so as to achieve a meadowlike appearance. Acquiring 4 acres (2 ha) of meadowland, Ter Linden aimed to develop gardens around his newly built, farmhouse-style home and studio. The house was conventional, but the gardens—intended to be the subject and inspiration for his watercolors—were not.

Starting to experiment as a novice gardener, he despised conventional ways of growing irises and roses, finding ways to achieve an impressionistic appearance. To create a harmonious look, with everything in proportion, he restricted the choice of his plantings by height—nothing taller than 16–20 inches (40–50 cm). Detail was the key, creating blends and contrasts. The gardens were laid out in a regular manner, but the lush planting allows little of the asymmetric layout to remain visible. The only preexisting element was an ancient apple tree that provided a pivotal function within the layout.

In 2000 Ter Linden sold the gardens to dedicate more time to his art. New owners Frans and Janneke Neuteboom have organized a trust to maintain the spirit of the garden and reopen it to the public. JW

RIGHT In Ton ter Linden's garden, colorful, cultivated varieties appear in a seemingly natural, meadowlike setting.

Jac P. Thijsse Park

Noord-Holland, Netherlands

DESIGNER: Jac P. Thijsse

OWNER: Amstelveen City Council

GARDEN STYLE: 20th-century heem park (mixed woodland, wildflower meadows, native planting)

SIZE: 59 acres (24 ha)

CLIMATE: Temperate

LOCATION: Amstelveen, Noord-Holland

The Netherlands is one of the most densely populated places on Earth, and the home park movement is a response to intense population pressures. The need to create green lungs in ever expanding suburbia, and to reconnect the urban population with their ecological roots, inspired one of the first attempts anywhere to produce holistic, municipal open spaces using native flora to create beautiful natural habitats.

If all of this sounds terribly dull, it is not. This is one of the most exquisite and subtly unusual gardens you could hope to visit. The garden is made even more surprising by the location. Tucked away behind nondescript suburban housing, the long, narrow site, with its intricate network of canals, ponds, lakes, woods, and plant communities, seems infinitely larger than it actually is, with a bewildering number of paths. You can wander through thickets of birch brightened by sheets of greater celandine (*Chelidonium majus*), glades awash with drifts of harebell (*Campanula rotundifolia*) and heartsease (*Viola tricolor*), and by mysterious, still ponds fringed by luxuriant ferns.

The experience here is of an enchanted landscape where each community of native plants seems so right for its site that it becomes almost impossible to believe that everything was planned and designed. Developed since the late 1930s, its seeming serendipity is the result of an intense understanding of ecological conditions and plants. The result is a miracle of subtle beauty. JB

Museum Beeckestijn

Noord-Holland, Netherlands

DESIGNERS: Johann Georg Michael, Leonard Springer,
  Buro Albers, Copijn Utrecht
OWNER: Velsen Municipality (Friends of Beeckestijn)
GARDEN STYLE: 18th-century baroque, rococo landscaped
SIZE: 116 acres (47 ha)
CLIMATE: Temperate
LOCATION: Velsen, Noord-Holland

Beeckestijn is famous thanks to a surviving survey of 1772 by the architect and garden designer Johann Georg Michael. At the time of the survey, the estate was owned by a lawyer, Jacob Boreel, who had acquired it in 1742. Previously, the house and garden had been poorly documented. First recorded in 1380, it was bought in 1686 by Jan Trip, the mayor of Amsterdam, who sold it to his son in 1716. The son modified the house and gardens, and it has been suggested that he created the baroque layout.

The Michael survey appears to show the surviving baroque framework with a number of features reminiscent of what was being proposed in Batty Langley's *New Principles of Gardening* (1728) and the Dutch version of Philip Miller's *The Gardener's Dictionary* (1745). This included wildernesses with winding walks, planted with flowering shrubs; in other areas, walks wound through open groves. Dotted around the grounds there were follies, a Corinthian arch, and a hermitage, as well as a gardener's cottage in the shape of a Gothic chapel.

After some neglect, the estate was sold by the Boreel family to Velsen Council in 1953. There have been some attempts to restore the gardens, using the Michael plan as the basis for the work. In the first restoration of 1963, the original kitchen garden became a rose and herb garden. In 1994 a master plan by Buro Albers Adviezen proposed more accurate reconstruction work based on archaeology. Further work followed in 1996. LL

ING Bank

Noord-Holland, Netherlands

DESIGNERS: Alberts and Van Huut
OWNER: International Netherlands Group (ING)
GARDEN STYLE: Late 20th-century organic, commercial
  office space
SIZE: 133 acres (5 ha)
CLIMATE: Temperate
LOCATION: Amsterdam, Noord-Holland

The ING Bank in Amsterdam (completed in 1986) is one of the world's most remarkable "green buildings." It is also termed an autonomous building, because of its independence from normal infrastructure building requirements such as an external electricity supply, storm drains, and sewage processing. The complex is a prime example of the organic style for which the architectural practice of Alberts and Van Huut—founded by Anton Alberts and Max van Huut—has become so well known.

The gardens and plants form an integral part of the organic concept, which features a series of interconnected, irregular towers surrounding courtyards. The latter have been designed as intricate, richly planted, themed areas and include gardens in a Japanese style, a Scandinavian style, and an English style. The building contains extensive water features, and the waterfalls and swampy areas with seminaturalistic plantings were designed to provide the employees of the banking giant with a refreshing alternative to their working environment. Inside the building there is an abundance of indoor plants, with the result that the lush planting outside seems to flow indoors and promote the feeling of a totally green environment.

When the ING building was first occupied, its radically different design resulted in a significant drop in employee absenteeism. Sadly, in today's highly competitive banking environment, workers stay at their desks, and the gardens seem underused. JW

Hortus Bulborum

Noord-Holland, Netherlands

DESIGNERS: Pieter Boschman, Dr. Willem de Mol
OWNER: Hortus Bulborum Foundation
GARDEN STYLE: 20th-century botanical, functional
SIZE: 2.5 acres (1 ha)
CLIMATE: Temperate
LOCATION: Limmen, Noord-Holland

As the most important collection of historic bulb cultivars in the world, this garden holds a special position for garden historians and botanists. The collection is wholly funded by the Dutch bulb industry as a gene pool for the cultivation of new varieties. Started in the 1920s as a private collection of old tulip cultivars by schoolteacher Pieter Boschman, it extended to about 400 varieties. In 1928 Dr. Willelm de Mol from Amsterdam added a collection of hyacinths. When, in 1935, the newly founded Neversie, the Netherlands Society for the Promotion of Scientific Breeding of Ornamental Plants, took over responsibility for the collection, it was extended to include daffodils, fritillaries, and various other bulbous species. The collection has recently been expanded to make daffodils as important as tulips. Large donations for the expansion were received from hobby collectors of heirloom plants.

In order to maintain a good genetic pool, minimum numbers of each plant are required. However, they are not generally exceeded because maintenance would then become an increasing issue. As a result, plants are grown in small blocks of individual cultivars, ensuring a checkered carpet of spring color.

The collection has also been useful in being able to provide plant material for garden restorations abroad, for example in Italy, Germany, and the UK, as well as in the Netherlands. Although the garden is small, it is a popular plant lovers' destination during April and May. JW

Hortus Botanicus Amsterdam

Noord-Holland, Netherlands

DESIGNERS: Various
OWNER: Amsterdam City Council
GARDEN STYLE: 17th-century botanical, functional
SIZE: 2.5 acres (1 ha)
CLIMATE: Temperate
LOCATION: Amsterdam, Noord-Holland

Herbs, spices, exotic ornamentals, more than fifty historic trees, including a cinnamon, a Turkish hazel planted in 1795, and a 300-year-old giant cycad all vie for attention in this tranquil enclave just beyond the center of the city. The Amsterdam Botanic Garden was founded in 1638 as a medicinal herb garden by the elders of a city ravaged by plague. The collection of what was known as the Hortus Medicus expanded rapidly thanks to plants brought home by ships of the Dutch East India Company.

These days the greenhouses and outdoor beds provide six climate zones for 6,000 specimens of more than 4,000 species. The outdoor garden was designed in 1863 and includes plants from unusual environments. There is a dune bed with plants from the north Holland coast, a pond of swamp plants, and an area for carnivorous species. Another series of beds has plants that evolved during specific prehistoric periods. In the more formal area, concentric semicircles of box hedging show genetic relationships among plants.

A small greenhouse built in 1896 is alive with insects and tropical plants of economic significance such as cacao trees, tea, rice, peppers, and sugarcane. The tall palm house is home to palms and cycads, and is a winter retreat for tender plants like citrus that spend summers outdoors. The three-climate greenhouse, built in 1993 by architects Zwarts and Jansma, holds tropical, subtropical, and desert plants. A sophisticated computer system automatically controls the temperature and humidity. RCa

Mien Ruys Tuinen

Overijssel, Netherlands

DESIGNER: Mien Ruys
OWNER: Mien Ruys Garden Foundation
GARDEN STYLE: 20th-century personal, mixed
SIZE: 2 acres (0.8 ha)
CLIMATE: Temperate
LOCATION: Dedemsvaart, Overijssel

This garden, created in what was the orchard and vegetable garden of her parents' plant nursery, is the life's work of garden designer and landscape architect Mien Ruys. As she experimented, the garden that began life in 1925 continued to expand until 2000. Today there are about twenty-five compartments, each reflecting different phases in the creator's life.

The two earliest areas are the Wild Garden (1925) and the Old Experimental Garden (1927). The former, arranged around a rectangular pool, exemplifies Ruys' style. There is a geometric outline softened by luxuriant planting in a traditional, English, Gertrude

Jekyll-style, herbaceous border, measuring 98 x 13 feet (30 x 4 m). Then followed an intermission of twenty-five years while Ruys studied architecture and taught landscape architecture.

In 1954 she returned, adding the Water Garden and Herb Garden. As her garden design career took off, so too did development of her garden. The year 1960 was a particularly busy one with the creation of five new areas: the Standard Perennial Borders, the Sun Border, the Reed Pond, the City Garden, and the Sunken Garden—the latter being one of the first gardens to feature railroad ties.

The 1970s saw four more additions, the 1980s yet another four, and the 1990s six new areas: the Marsh Garden, Grasses, the New Perennial Collection, the Roof Garden, Corner Garden, and Clipped Garden. The final garden to be added was the New Border. If you want to learn how to link garden compartments together, this is the place to come. TM

Twickel

Overijssel, Netherlands

DESIGNERS: Various
OWNER: The Twickel Foundation
GARDEN STYLE: 17th-century to contemporary, mixed
SIZE: 9,900 acres (4,000 ha)
CLIMATE: Temperate
LOCATION: Delden, Overijssel

Although Twickel dates back to the Middle Ages, little was known about the gardens until the end of the seventeenth century, when it consisted of a rectangular moat with a house and moated gardens. The last consisted largely of orchards, with two kitchen gardens, a lawn, and parterre. A late-eighteenth-century survey reveals a remarkable layout with an English thicket to one side of the house. This was a cross between a Batty Langley-type wilderness and an English landscape garden that was primarily planted with trees and shrubs. This layout remained until the landscape architect

Jan David Zocher Jr. opened up the gardens to create a more traditional landscape park in 1835, and gave the central section of the park its present form. The character of the layout, as it survived into the twentieth century, was largely determined by alterations proposed in 1885. The rock garden was created by its last private owner, Baroness of Heeckeren van Wassenaer who remained an avid gardener until her death in 1975.

Currently the park is being altered following designs by Michiel van Gessel. The historic elements within the formal gardens surrounding the castle have been restored in recent years, and they are maintained to an adequate standard. The largest designed landscape park in the Netherlands, which surrounds the formal gardens, dominates the estate, and provides an idyllic character of mature trees and tree clumps, interspersed by meadows and informal lakes, and interconnected by a network of vistas. JW

Weldam

Overijssel, Netherlands

DESIGNERS: Edouard André, Hugo Poortman
OWNER: Alfred Otto Friedrich Graf zu
  Solms-Sonnenwalde
GARDEN STYLE: 19th-century formal, neoclassicist
SIZE: 9.8 acres (4 ha)
CLIMATE: Temperate
LOCATION: Markelo, Overijssel

The fourteenth-century castle at Weldam (rebuilt in 1645) has one of the grandest, nineteenth-century neobaroque gardens in the Netherlands. It was designed by Edouard André in 1879 and executed by his protégé, Hugo Poortman, for the Van Aldenburg Bentinck-Van Heeckeren van Wassenaar family. It is likely that the Dutch classical layout of the grounds, based on a double-moated site, was also carried out at around this time.

This layout was initially retained in the neobaroque garden, but then André emphasized the symmetry by filling in one of the moats. Two parterres de broderie, a large maze, and a spectacular beech bower then became the main features of the garden. The garden also included two sunken lawns and interesting topiary box, including the name "Mary" spelled out to commemorate Mary Cornelia Bentinck, the Countess Bentinck. Since André did not include a framework of avenues around the layout, it was more open than traditional seventeenth-century Dutch gardens where such an enclosure was customary. The relationship of the house with the wider landscape was strengthened by the views.

Look out for the beautifully sculpted vases, some dating back to the seventeenth century, and a collection of orangery plants that decorate the gardens. Over winter, these exotic plants are kept in a nineteenth-century orangery in the kitchen gardens, which also contain a number of other cast-iron greenhouses. JW

De Wiersse

Gelderland, Netherlands

DESIGNERS: The De Stuers family, the Gatacre family
OWNER: E. V. Gatacre
GARDEN STYLE: 20th-century formal, landscape,
  Arts and Crafts
SIZE: 40 acres (16 ha)
CLIMATE: Temperate
LOCATION: Vorden, Gelderland

As probably the best-maintained private estate in the Netherlands, De Wiersse holds a special position in Dutch gardening. The medieval castle is set within an arm of the local stream, which had been regularized by the end of the seventeenth century. The present garden's layout was largely determined during the early twentieth century when Victor de Stuers, who had been instrumental in setting up heritage protection in the Netherlands, restored and enlarged the moated house in 1912. His daughter, Alice, took charge of the gardens and produced designs for the Rose Garden in 1912, and the Sunken Garden in 1913. Alice married W. E. Gatacre in 1918; they converted the old pleasure grounds into a wild garden, and renovated and replanted following English models. By this stage, the gardens had doubled in size.

The garden got a new lease on life when Peter and Laura Gatacre took over in the late 1970s. While carefully retaining the historic structure of the estate, they have invigorated the gardens with perennial plantings in the Sunken Garden and wilderness areas, the latter containing both native and exotic plants. Although rhododendrons form a major feature, a carefully contrived framework of trees and shrubs creates smaller and larger spaces. One of the main issues over the years has been the maintenance of stable water levels, vital for healthy tree growth. After extensive research, as well as negotiations with the relevant authorities, higher levels were reestablished through a system of weirs and sluices. JW

Park Sonsbeek

Gelderland, Netherlands

DESIGNERS: Jan David Zocher Jr., Hugo Poortman,
  Leonard Springer, Wim van Krieken
OWNER: Arnhem Council
GARDEN STYLE: 19th-century landscape
SIZE: 165 acres (67 ha)
CLIMATE: Temperate
LOCATION: Arnhem, Gelderland

Sonsbeek public park is well known for holding postwar sculpture exhibitions. The present house at Sonsbeek is located on the site of a fifteenth-century castle, and was designed by Anthony Viervant and built after 1742. The estate was given its current name only after it was acquired by Mayor M. G. Pronck in 1778. He was also responsible for a landscape-style garden, planted with exotic trees and shrubs. The old moat around the former castle was extended into a large, informal lake in 1806 for Baron de Smeth, leaving the foundations of the castle as an island.

It was acquired by Baron van Heeckeren in 1821, and by the local council in 1899, whereupon landscape architects Hugo Poortman and Leonard Springer adapted it as a public park. They altered the location of the entrances while maintaining the historic path system, restored the deer enclosure and tea pavilion, and put the children's playground in the old kitchen garden. Since then it has regularly been a location for exhibitions, the first, in 1915, being on the history and science of the rose.

Today the park has a predominantly open character with large clumps of mature trees. It retains the impression of a private estate owing to the lawns with grazing animals, the river, and the dominant position of the historic house on the naturally sloping site. In 1998 the former kitchen garden was transformed—now with water features and extensive perennial plantings, this area has been named the Sloping Garden. JW

Zypendaal

Gelderland, Netherlands

DESIGNERS: J. P. Posth, C. E. A. Petzold, Hugo Poortman,
M. E. Canneman-Philipse
OWNER: Arnhem Council
GARDEN STYLE: 19th-century landscape, Arts and Crafts
SIZE: 225 acres (91 ha)
CLIMATE: Temperate
LOCATION: Arnhem, Gelderland

Zypendaal is uniquely situated in an undulating part of the Netherlands that enables it to make spectacular use of the natural springs. A series of rectangular fishponds had been created with a moated house, built in 1650. This was acquired by Hendrik Willem Brantsen in 1743, but he demolished the seventeenth-century house, replacing it with a larger one. The house was then inhabited by four generations of Brantsen, and the garden saw successive changes. In 1883 the house was extended and given a tower, following designs by Pierre Cuypers, designer of the Rijksmuseum in Amsterdam. In 1890 the landscape architect Hugo Poortman redesigned the parterre area in front of the house and enlarged the lake. And in 1930 the estate was acquired by the city of Arnhem, with the house becoming a museum in 1983.

Sections of the gardens were consequently reconstructed, and a modern border and rose beds were added according to designs by M. E. Canneman-Philipse, a popular garden designer during the 1980s, who occupied the Walenburg estate in Langbroek, and was much inspired by Vita Sackville-West. The setting for the house and surrounding formal gardens is still determined by its running water and the sinuous lines of the late-nineteenth-century landscape park, although the vegetation has now become slightly overgrown. This gives Zypendaal a wooded character that contrasts markedly with the adjoining Sonsbeek public park (see page 529), which is more open. JW

Huis Bingerden

Gelderland, Netherlands

DESIGNER: Eugenie van Weede
OWNERS: The Van Weede family
GARDEN STYLE: 17th-century formal,
20th-century country
SIZE: 22 acres (9 ha)
CLIMATE: Temperate
LOCATION: Angerlo, Gelderland

Bingerden House has five areas of parkland, woods, and gardens, surrounded by a 1-mile-long (2 km) moat from 1791. Owned by the Van Weede family since 1660, it had a formal garden even then. A hundred years ago, yew hedges were planted and cut into topiary figures, known as the Monks. Beyond these lie water and Dutch countryside.

The house was destroyed in the last days of World War II and rebuilt on a smaller scale. Jonkheer Dirk van Weede and his wife, Eugenie, inherited it in 1974, moving in permanently in 1994. Eugenie was daunted by the neglected garden, but she visited Sissinghurst in England (see page 370) and was inspired by its similar scale, overall design, and the plants.

Her three key aims were that her garden should complement the buildings, the planting should encourage wildlife and wherever possible be scented, and the whole scheme should be low maintenance.

The result is that six gardens have been restored or created: the Children's Garden, the Mount, the Rose Garden, the 1660s-style Formal Garden, and the Park with wildflowers and herbs among ancient trees. The most recent feature is the potager, where Eugenie has brightened up the great stretch of green with plenty of color. Here flowers grow, climb, and twist among the edible plants in geometric borders.

On the third weekend of June each year, the Van Weede family hold their International Specialist Nursery Days. If you love garden shows, then this is the place to be. JHa

Kröller–Müller Museum

Gelderland, Netherlands

DESIGNER: Jan Tijs Pieter Bijhouwer
OWNERS: The Dutch State, Stichting Nationale Park De Hoge Veluwe
GARDEN STYLE: 20th-century modernist, landscaped
SIZE: 61 acres (25 ha)
CLIMATE: Temperate
LOCATION: Otterlo, Gelderland

Kröller-Müller houses one of the earliest modernist sculpture gardens in Europe. The site excels in its setting, design, and content. Conceived as a centerpiece for a hunting estate acquired by Anton George Kröller between 1909 and 1917, the museum was seen by his wife, Helene Kröller-Müller, as a symbol of unity for the arts, architecture, and nature.

The aim was to locate the museum on what had been poor agricultural land, but economic recession stopped that. The estate was then given to the Dutch government on the condition that it would complete the plan and create a national park in order to protect the area. Henri van de Velde was commissioned to provide the designs for the museum that was completed in 1938.

The sculpture garden was realized only after World War II. The director of the museum, Abraham Marie Hammacher, asked the landscape architect Jan Tijs Pieter Bijhouwer to design an initial phase in 1955, and an extension to it in 1965. These designs maintained the natural landscape of the area, with its wooded sand dunes providing a backdrop to modernist, abstract sculptures. A number of open-air "rooms" were created within the woodland structure that were sown with grass and connected by winding paths. These "rooms" created spaces for the display of sculptures. The site was further extended in 1988, with a complete reassessment taking place in 1995. This saw a change in the location of the entrance, with proposed new ornamental plants. JW

Paleis Het Loo

Gelderland, Netherlands

DESIGNERS: Jacob Roman, Daniel Marot
OWNER: The Dutch State
GARDEN STYLE: 17th-century renaissance,
  20th-century baroque
SIZE: Set within Royal Forest of 24,710 acres (10,000 ha)
CLIMATE: Temperate
LOCATION: Apeldoorn, Gelderland

If you sense something is wrong when you walk the grounds of Paleis Het Loo, then you would be right. Too bright? Too brash? Too new? Call it a restoration, a pastiche, or a fake, but what you see of the garden today dates mostly from the 1970s and early 1980s.

Originally laid out for William and Mary of Orange between 1686 and 1695 by the Dutch architect Jacob Roman, and ornamented by the French Huguenot Daniel Marot, the outer parts of these formal baroque gardens slowly gave way to a naturalistic, English style of landscaping more favored by subsequent Princes of Orange. By 1807 Louis Napoleon had given it an English makeover by replacing the statuary, walls, and stairways close to the palace with an assortment of fine trees. Given that Het Loo had many parallels with Versailles, these changes might be regarded as vandalism. However, they were appropriate for the creative direction of the times.

When it was decided to return to the seventeenth-century ground plan, most of the eighteenth- and nineteenth-century modifications were swept aside, only some of the parterres being reinstated, and raw-looking, cast stonework was substituted for the genuine article. So, on one level, the restoration of the gardens at Het Loo is incomplete, unsatisfactory, and inaccurate. However, as an exercise in late-twentieth-century showmanship, it dazzles. In this sense, it carries on the long tradition of all great gardens in expressing the spirit of its age—which is exactly what the long-lost garden of William and Mary did. RCa

Kwekerij Piet Oudolf

Gelderland, Netherlands

DESIGNER: Piet Oudolf
OWNERS: Piet Oudolf, Anja Oudolf
GARDEN STYLE: 20th- and 21st-century modernist
SIZE: 1 acre (0.4 ha)
CLIMATE: Temperate
LOCATION: Hummelo, Gelderland

Garden designer Piet Oudolf has achieved a reputation as a leading figure in the so-called New European Wave of gardening. Unusually, Oudolf is someone who combines skill in both the architectural and the planted elements of the garden landscape. Assisted by his wife, Anja, he has been developing Kwekerij Piet Oudolf, "The Piet Oudolf Plantation," actually the family garden, since 1981. It is a splendid example of his style, and has been a testing ground for new ideas and new plants.

The layout, with its prominent, sculpted hedges and architectural elements, is clearly in the Mien Ruys tradition. (Ruys was the Bauhaus influenced designer who dominated Dutch garden art for most of the twentieth century.) Like so much of Oudolf's work, this is pure pleasure, with good examples of perennials and modern, clipped hedges. Oudolf demonstrates that herbaceous plants can look well when arranged in drifts, just as bulbous plants are more commonly planted. Influenced by the German plantsman Karl Fürster and English gardening, Oudolf's scheme is at its best in late summer and fall. Note the use of grasses and umbellifers grown for their structure, texture, and skeletal shapes toward the end of the year. Another feature is generous use of plants suited to swampy conditions, such as *Echinacea purpurea*.

This is an iconic garden. It is in a style relevant to anyone wishing to grow plants native to the northern temperate zone. It is a lesson in plantsmanship for the architect, and in architecture for the gardener. NK

Rosendael

Gelderland, Netherlands

DESIGNERS: Various
OWNER: Gelderland Trust
GARDEN STYLE: 18th-century landscaped
SIZE: 158 acres (64 ha)
CLIMATE: Temperate
LOCATION: Rozendaal, Gelderland

Rosendael is best known for its surviving features from an early-eighteenth-century, rococo phase designed by the eminent French architect and designer Daniel Marot, but there certainly is more to it than that.

The estate has a rich history. During the late seventeenth century, the medieval castle was owned by one of William III's confidants. Jan van Arnhem embellished the gardens within an irregular framework while making the most of an undulating site that was famed for its waterworks. When the estate was inherited by Lubbert Adolf Torck in 1721, he altered the castle to its present form. He developed the estate and gardens, calling on Marot to assist him. In went a shell gallery, garden pavilion, and water cascade with fountain jokes.

Later the gardens were given a landscape look, first by Philip Willem Schonck in 1781 and then by Jan David Zocher Jr., who, in a two-year period from 1836, completely reorganized the park. This created an open valley with flowing lines more consistent with the natural topography.

A large orangery was built on a prominent position near the castle. The area in front of it was redesigned by Dirk Wattez in 1874, providing a more open character. In 1904 a formal rose garden was added. Because of war damage, the orangery was lost, but it was rebuilt after the Gelderland Trust acquired the estate in 1977. It has also been responsible for a gradual restoration of the grounds as well as the castle, which opened to the public in 1990. JW

Bulb Fields

Zuid-Holland, Netherlands

DESIGNER: Commercial enterprise
OWNER: The Dutch bulb industry
GARDEN STYLE: Commercial horticulture
SIZE: 40,000 acres (16,200 ha)
CLIMATE: Temperate
LOCATION: From Leiden, Zuid-Holland northward to
Haarlem, Noord-Holland

Of all the horticultural treats in this book, the bulb fields of Holland must represent the greatest bargain. Entry to the 40,000 acres (16,200 ha) is free.

Brought from Turkey in the sixteenth century, the tulip proved to be completely at home in the dry, sandy soils bordering the North Sea between Haarlem and Leiden. Tulips became very popular with the Dutch people during their Golden Age. Later joined by narcissi, crocuses, hyacinths, lilies, and gladioli, the tulip became the subject of an intense, speculative frenzy in the mid-seventeenth century known as the Tulip Craze, when a particularly rare specimen sold for as much as 6,000 florins, then a great fortune. Desirable bulbs could be exchanged for a brace of fine horses or even a house, until an edict of 1636 forbade the trade that by then was threatening the Dutch economy.

Although the gladiolius flowers through to August, the most exciting time to visit is in late April. To drive around the bulb fields at this time is a pure delight, with new and ever changing vistas of color at every turn. The bulb fields are centered on the town of Lisse. You will get particularly striking views near Noordwijkerhout and Kasteel Tellingen. However, striking combinations of primary colors, often in long, continuous strips or huge squares, are almost everywhere. Although the bulbs are planted according to strictly commercial, rather than aesthetic, criteria, this seems only to add to the appeal of the great blocks of color. TW

Museumpark

Zuid-Holland, Netherlands

DESIGNERS: Office of Metropolitan Architecture
OWNER: City of Rotterdam
GARDEN STYLE: 20th-century new urbanist
SIZE: 9.8 acres (4 ha)
CLIMATE: Temperate
LOCATION: Rotterdam, Zuid-Holland

The Museumpark is of interest as a representation of much of the latest design philosophy that has dominated new Dutch urbanism. Conceived in the Office of Metropolitan Architecture, the practice of the architect Rem Koolhaas, in 1988–89, it was intended as a public park to link a number of proposed museums (now completed), alongside the 1932 Museum Boymans van Beuningen.

Koolhaas first challenged the concept of the public park as an escape from the city and a relief from urban stresses when he participated in the 1982 competition for the Parc de la Villette in Paris. In Rotterdam, as in Paris, he and the landscape architect Yves Brunier chose to emphasize an urban character by introducing the theme of the highway. The detailing of the park is robust with highwaylike materials: Tarmac abounds in the events area, the main path that leads from north to south is aligned with heavy concrete benches, and an overpass reminiscent of a viaduct crosses a dry river. This winds through an area where existing trees have largely been retained; this is referred to as the "romantic garden" and is planted with large, bold groupings. The river has been shaped provocatively as a spermatozoid, perhaps challenging the "romantic" notion. The interest of the park lies in the way it challenges the traditional concept of the public garden and what it ought to provide. It was the starting point of a new urban vision in the Netherlands that has become predominant and has influenced park design ever since. JW

Park Zorgvliet

Zuid-Holland, Netherlands

DESIGNERS: Jacob Cats, Hans Willem Bentinck
OWNER: The Dutch State
GARDEN STYLE: 18th-century landscaped park
SIZE: 55.6 acres (22.5 ha)
CLIMATE: Temperate
LOCATION: The Hague, Zuid-Holland

This park is best known as the Catshuis, the official residence of the Dutch prime minister, and is named after the original owner, the poet Jacob Cats, who bought the estate in 1643. At that time, it consisted of a series of sand dunes, but he began reclaiming them in 1652. He created the garden around a single-story house designed by Lodewijk Huygens. Cats celebrated his achievements in a poem published in 1656 that idealized country life, in the manner of ancient Roman authors.

Hans Willem Bentinck became the owner of the estate in 1675. Greatly interested in garden making, he later became the superintendent of gardens to William III and was granted the title of Duke of Portland. He altered the gardens to include a Mount Parnassus and circular maze as central features of the extensive plantations that lay to one side of the house and parterres. The estate remained in the hands of the Bentinck family, who made it into a landscape park in the late eighteenth century, until it was sold to Crown Prince William in 1837. The prince extended it by acquiring neighboring estates. Following his death, parts of the estate were sold off for housing, but the original estate was left.

Today the historic gardens are rather overgrown with woody vegetation, and the structure of the historic layout can no longer be discerned, although some features from the various periods in its development can still be identified. The park is well known for its rich, naturalized vegetation of bulbs and spring flowering plants. JW

Hortus Botanicus Leiden

Zuid-Holland, Netherlands

DESIGNERS: Carolus Clusius, Daniel Marot
OWNER: Leiden University
GARDEN STYLE: 16th-, 17th-, and 20th-century botanical
SIZE: 6.4 acres (2.6 ha)
CLIMATE: Temperate
LOCATION: Leiden, Zuid-Holland

Hidden away in the middle of the city center, the Hortus Botanicus Leiden, also known as the Leiden Botanic Garden, is the oldest botanic garden in the Netherlands and one of the oldest in the world (Pisa and Padua were the first, laid out in 1545.)

Originally founded in 1587 as a medical garden—a place where trainee doctors came to learn their cures—it became a botanic garden in 1594 with the arrival of Carolus Clusius (Charles de l'Ecluse) as the first prefect. He was responsible for introducing new plants to Europe. One of his most significant moves was bringing tulips with him to Leiden. These bulbs were the ancestors of those that started tulipomania in the 1630s. Clusius' garden was originally only about 115 x 131 feet (35 x 40 m), but it contained more than 1,000 different taxa.

The garden has been painstakingly restored to Clusius' original plan with its brick-edged beds and white, crushed-shell walks; the laburnum he planted in 1601 is also still there. It is an active center for academic study, and a lovely, tranquil place to walk. There is a beautiful, seventeenth-century orangery designed by Daniel Marot, and a collection of tender exotics and citrus trees. There is also a large herbaceous border, rock garden, and rose garden from the 1930s that perfumes the air in summer.

Throughout the grounds you will find many prize specimen trees and collections of shrubs, with paths winding through them. There are also fine collections of Asian Araceae (including *Amorphophallus titanum*), hoya, dischidia, Asian orchids, and ferns. TM

Keukenhof

Zuid-Holland, Netherlands

DESIGNERS: The Zocher family
OWNER: Keukenhof Gardens
GARDEN STYLE: 19th-century English informal
SIZE: 79 acres (32 ha)
CLIMATE: Temperate
LOCATION: Lisse, Zuid-Holland

Despite its name meaning "kitchen garden", there is nothing domestic or small-scale about Keukenhof. With around seven million bulbs being planted every year, including 1,000 tulip varieties, it is a flagship of the Dutch bulb growing industry.

The garden at Keukenhof was originally created in the fifteenth century by the Countess of Holland, Jacoba van Beieren, who wanted to use part of her estate to grow fresh fruit and vegetables for her household. By the 1840s, it was in the hands of a landscaping family, the Zochers (designers of Amsterdam's Vondelpark), who replanted the park in the then fashionable English pattern, eschewing straight lines and any regularity. Keukenhof's lake and many of its trees may be traced to their work.

Today besides the parkland, you will see 1 acre (0.5 ha) of greenhouses and covered garden, not to mention regular exhibitions and demonstrations for gardeners held throughout the year. Only the neighboring bulb fields, glimpses of which can be caught from the top of the windmill at the northern end of the park, can rival the spectacle of Keukenhof. Great swaths of tulips, crocuses, and daffodils burst out of the gently rolling landscape, displaying huge blocks of pure color beneath great avenues of trees. Depending on the weather conditions, the best time to view the tulips is in late April and early May. Be warned of potential crowding; the site attracts 700,000 visitors a year, and many come at this time. However, the color is sensational. Keukenhof also hosts a National Flower Bulb Market in October. TW

Arboretum Trompenburg

Zuid-Holland, Netherlands

DESIGNERS: Hendrik Wachter, Jan David Zocher Jr.,
Louis Paul Zocher, James van Hoey Smith
OWNER: Arboretum Trompenburg Foundation
GARDEN STYLE: 20th-century arboretum
SIZE: 15 acres (6 ha)
CLIMATE: Temperate
LOCATION: Rotterdam, Zuid-Holland

The van Hoey Smith family have gardened at Arboretum Trompenburg over a period of 100 years. Created through the acquisition of a number of adjoining properties between 1857 and 1867, the estate included the seventeenth-century gardens of Trompenburg, the suburban Vredenoord and Zomerlust estates, some meadows, and a nursery.

The new Trompenburg was built on the site of Zomerlust, which had a mature garden in the landscape style, designed by Hendrik Wachter. This was largely retained while the renowned landscape gardener Jan David Zocher Jr. and his son Louis Paul were commissioned to convert the meadows and nursery into a landscape park, with screen plantings. The canal that split the site in two was retained, providing a formal feature within an otherwise informal layout. From about 1900, a further section was gradually changed to incorporate a rhododendron collection. The final section was developed into typical Arts and Crafts-inspired gardens consisting of several square gardens, one with roses and another with heathers. These were gradually converted into an arboretum.

Thanks to the efforts of James van Hoey Smith, a keen dendrologist, the gardens achieved worldwide acclaim. They were extended twice to the east side, in 1965 and 1993, with important collections of conifers, beech, oaks, hollies, and rhododendrons. There are also interesting collections of perennials and bulbs, including hostas and rodgersias. JW

Sophievka

Cherkas'ka Oblast', Ukraine

DESIGNER: Ludovic Metzel
OWNER: National Science Academy of Ukraine
GARDEN STYLE: 18th- and 19th-century landscape park
  inspired by Greek mythology
SIZE: 383 acres (155 ha)
CLIMATE: Steppe
LOCATION: Cherkasy, Cherkas'ka Oblast'

Work began here in 1796 against enormous odds to reshape a wilderness of granite. Explosives were used to blow out basins for large, artificial lakes and to reshape the hillsides. The excavated stone was used to build walls, form waterfalls, and create romantic and naturalistic rockfalls. Sculptures were commissioned in Italy, and saplings ordered from all around Europe. Despite crippling inherited debts, no expense was spared to make this even better than Arkadia, the fabulous park at Nieborow created by Helena and Michal Radziwill.

The landowner and prime mover was a well-connected Polish business magnate, Stanislav Schensny Pototsky, who was inspired by his adventuress Greek wife, Sophia, daughter of a courtesan, to create a lavish garden that would pay homage through symbolism and statuary to the ancient gods of her homeland. On Sophia's birthday, in May 1802, he finished the project, but he died soon afterward and never saw the garden in its full glory.

Visitors should look for the water-washed grotto of Venus, the naturalistic waterfalls, and the impressive fountain representing the snakes that killed the Trojan priest Laocoön and his sons. If nothing else, take the boat through the tunnel connecting both lakes. Representing the River Styx, through which sinister Chiron rowed the dead into Hades, this subterranean canal has a strong emotional effect on visitors, with its journey from light into dark and then back again. WdP

Alupka

Respublika Krym, Ukraine

DESIGNERS: Karl Kebach, William Hunt
OWNER: The Ukranian State
GARDEN STYLE: 19th-century Italianate formal garden,
  romantic landscape
SIZE: 120 acres (49 ha)
CLIMATE: Continental cool summer
LOCATION: Alupka, Respublika Krym

An extraordinary building with gardens and fountains to match, Alupka Palace offers expansive views north to the mountains and south to the Black Sea. Amazingly the English architect Edward Blore, who designed this luxurious residence for Count Mikhail Semyonovich Vorontsov, never once set foot here. Completed in the late 1840s under the supervision of William Hunt, Alupka remains Blore's masterpiece.

The landward facade of Alupka is Gothic revival that, on first sight, is cool, well measured, and Scottish, but in fact is cleverly mannered. The seaward front is extravagantly Moorish, resembling the fourteenth-century Alhambra Palace in Granada, Spain, but is even grander. Although the southern central portico earns most plaudits today, Alupka is astonishing on all fronts. It is geographically out of place and out of time, but it remains at one with its surroundings.

The romantic, landscaped grounds to the north are the work of German gardener Karl Kebach; the Italianate terracing and formal gardens to the south are generally attributed to Hunt; and the exotic planting throughout owes much to the Nikitsky Botanical Gardens, located along the coast (see page 544). The gardens' second director, Nikolai Hartvis, supplied specimens and commissioned deliveries from the famous London nursery firm of Loddiges.

Should you experience déjà vu on seeing Alupka's lion terrace featuring animals in Carrara marble by Bonanni, they are based on those by Antonio Canova at the tomb of Pope Clement XII in Rome. WdP

Nikitskyi Botanichnyi Sad

Respublika Krym, Ukraine

DESIGNER: Christian Steven
OWNER: Ukraine Academy of Agrarian Sciences
GARDEN STYLE: 19th-century landscaped botanical garden
SIZE: 2,718 acres (1,100 ha)
CLIMATE: Continental cool summer
LOCATION: Yalta, Respublika Krym
TRANSLATION: Nikitsky Botanical Gardens

Established in 1812 by order of Tsar Alexander I, the gardens at Nikitsky were laid out in landscape style by the founder and first director, the Swedish-born Russian botanist Christian Steven. Although the initial work was arduous because so much rock had to be removed and so much topsoil imported, Steven took great care to leave exceptional examples of the native flora intact; today visitors can admire a 1,000-year-old juniper and a 500-year-old oak, among other exquisite trees. There are also expansive views of the mountains, Black Sea, and woodland promontories.

Easily ranking among the finest botanical gardens in the world, Nikitsky has picturesque terraces facing the sea where flowers are in bloom year round thanks to the warm, dry climate. At the height of summer, the gardens stay open until late evening, and a stroll in the grounds, with their Italianate pergolas and pavilions, is a fine way to round off the day.

Nikitsky is also a living museum with 50,000 different plants from the Mediterranean, Southeast Asia, and South America, and is a major research institution with behind-the-scenes experimental grounds. The fruit department alone is a valuable gene pool with around 100 species and 5,000 varieties, cultivars, and hybrids. Half the peaches and apricots now growing in the Ukraine are from varieties raised and trialed at Nikitsky. And, unusually for the Crimea, you can see olive trees—olives were thought nonproletarian after the 1917 revolution and only botanical specimens were tolerated. WdP

Kalmthout Arboretum

Antwerpen, Belgium

DESIGNERS: Charles Van Geert, Antoine Kort, Robert de Belder, Jelena de Belder
OWNER: Province of Antwerp
GARDEN STYLE: 18th-century botanical garden
SIZE: 29 acres (11.7 ha)
CLIMATE: Temperate
LOCATION: Kalmthout, Antwerpen

If you are looking for a way to escape the dreary winter months, then visit Kalmthout Arboretum and you will be uplifted by the sight of an extraordinary winter garden in full bloom. This garden is Belgium's best example of the gardenesque style, characterized by unrestrained wildness and irregularity.

The arboretum boasts a world-famous collection of witch hazels, and the annual Hamamelis Festival celebrates these wonderful winter flowers, though the gardens also contain hundreds of other winter-flowering plants. In fact the gardens are delightful all year round. They contain more than 6,000 varieties from right around the world. The oldest specimens are trees planted more than 150 years ago by the arboretum's founder, Charles Van Geert, and include some magnificent Japanese cherries and maples, as well as an endangered species of Chinese conifer and one of only three American snowdrop trees (*Halesia diptera*) to be found in Europe.

As the last hamamelis flowers of winter fade, spring is heralded by the delicate blossom on the branches of the cherry and apple trees throughout the arboretum. Then the Japanese maples start to flower, followed a few weeks later by hundreds of riotous rhododendrons. In summer, the arboretum's butterfly garden reaches its peak, exploding into life, teeming with butterflies and other insects. The Wild Rose Garden is always a big attraction, as is the show of fruit in fall. The arboretum calls itself a "garden for all seasons," and that is absolutely right. MS

Tuinen van Hex

Limburg, Belgium

DESIGNERS: Franz-Karl von Velbrück, Louis Fuchs, Jules Janlet, Countess Michel d'Ursel, Jacques Wirtz

OWNERS: Count and Countess Ghislain d'Ursel

GARDEN STYLE: 18th-century gardens, landscape park

SIZE: 12.5 acres (5 ha)

CLIMATE: Temperate

LOCATION: Heers-Heks, Limburg

The gardens at Kasteel Hex, built on a hill in 1780 by Prince-Bishop Franz-Karl von Velbrück, are well known in Belgium. They are laid out in the formal French manner, and successive owners have made their mark while respecting the past. The atmosphere today is one of quiet, aristocratic comfort. Everything seems effortless and uncontrived. The surrounding landscape, remodeled as parkland in the manner of Capability Brown, is an example of his influence on design in continental Europe. Legend has it that Masonic symbolism plays some part in the composition.

Distinct areas include the Prince's Garden, composed of box parterres filled with flowers and aromatic herbs; a rose garden with an interesting collection of wild and old roses, including three original China roses imported through the Dutch East India Company; a Chinese garden with a painted wooden Buddha; three minimalist terraces remodeled in 1990 by Jacques Wirtz; and an extensive kitchen garden with a cellar used for winter storage and blanching. Features in the park include a driveway of plane trees, a column commemorating a family wedding, a stone folly, and a thatched hermitage.

The gates open to the public for just two weekends a year: the second weekend of June (rose festival) and the second weekend of September (rare and unusual vegetables), with lectures and demonstrations from famous gardeners, writers, and academics. There are also stalls selling plants, bulbs, and seed from specialist nurseries. RCa

Serres Royales de Laeken

Bruxelles, Belgium

DESIGNERS: Alphonse Balat, Victor Horta
OWNER: The Belgian royal family
GARDEN STYLE: 19th-century early art nouveau
SIZE: 6 acres (2.4 ha)
CLIMATE: Temperate
LOCATION: Brussels, Bruxelles
TRANSLATION: The Royal Greenhouses of Laeken

A fairy-tale labyrinth of eleven interconnecting glasshouses packed with fuchsias the size of trees, a world-class collection of camellias, serried ranks of clivias in antique Chinese pots, with soaring palms and giant tree ferns (*Dicksonia antarctica*), this treasure trove of historic plants and architecture opens to the public for barely three weeks toward the end of spring. For the rest of the year, it is the preserve of the Belgian royal family, the jewel in the crown of their 70-acre (28 ha) private estate. Time your visit with care and book tickets in advance.

The first greenhouse at Château de Laeken was the classical orangery built for William I in 1818; by 1859 it had been joined by a circular hothouse enclosing a pool for the giant water lily (*Victoria amazonica*). It was not until the reign of Leopold II that Laeken's mint-green glasshouses became the envy of all Europe. Leopold, known as *le Roi Bâtisseur*, the Builder King, commissioned Alphonse Balat and the young Victor Horta in 1873 to design a vast complex of pavilions and cupolas linked by wide arcades like covered streets. Funded by enormous wealth from the Belgian Congo, the Serres de Laeken were an early blooming of art nouveau architecture.

Built between 1874 and 1876, the dome-shaped Winter Garden was the first completed project in what was to become a thirty-year schedule of works. Some 111 feet (34 m) high and 223 feet (68 m) in diameter, with a style of planting that is formal rather than naturalistic, it was often used for state receptions. The later Pier Greenhouse (1886–87) was conceived as a suitably imposing entrance chamber. The smaller glasshouses, equally splendid in ornamental terms, reflect the same hierarchy of use as rooms at court, reminding us that, though full of rare and beautiful plants, this is not a botanical garden as such but a statement of empire, a crystal palace. And it still inspires awe, as intended. RCa

Château de Beloeil

Hainaut, Belgium

DESIGNERS: Prince Claude-Lamoral II de Ligne, Jean-Baptiste Bergé, François-Joseph Belanger
OWNER: Prince Michel de Ligne
GARDEN STYLE: 18th-century high renaissance
SIZE: 62 acres (25.1 ha)
CLIMATE: Temperate
LOCATION: Beloeil, Hainaut

The Château de Beloeil has been in continuous ownership by a single family for almost seven centuries. This vast, stately home of the Princes de Ligne began as a medieval fortress. However, progressive alterations and enlargements by successive generations, especially from the sixteenth to eighteenth centuries, transformed both it and the surrounding landscape. Essentially French, and often described as the Belgian Versailles (see page 570), Beloeil is in fact more akin to Chantilly in France (see page 552) because of its vast, reflective waters. Ravaged by fire in 1900, the château was rebuilt to its former glory in 1920. Apart from a brief decline at the time of the French Revolution, the gardens have always flourished. There is a great sense of continuity.

The grounds were mostly laid out in the mid-eighteenth century according to the vision of Prince Claude-Lamoral II de Ligne, as interpreted by the French architect Jean-Baptiste Bergé. They are on a grand scale, the centerpiece being a rectangular lake almost 550 yards (500 m) long that runs from the moat around the château to a monumental fountain group, featuring Neptune at the rounded, farthest end. This main vista, framed by trees on either side, leads the eye out into the countryside. In contrast, the canals and pools in the many formal enclosures and flower gardens to the east and west take an introspective turn. In the late eighteenth century, François-Joseph Belanger was employed to turn part of the traditional garden into an English garden. RCa

Enghien

Hainaut, Belgium

DESIGNER: Father Charles de Bruxelles
OWNER: The Town of Enghien
GARDEN STYLE: 17th-century Italian renaissance, baroque
SIZE: 450 acres (182 ha)
CLIMATE: Temperate
LOCATION: Enghien, Hainaut

In French-speaking Wallonia, the gardens at Enghien (to German speakers, Edingen) were unique until quite recently because they were the only gardens in Belgium to offer visitors a genuine audiovisual experience. Using interactive kits, the listeners are directed along a choice of three tracks: the Park for lovers of history, the Garden for lovers of flowers, and Nature for a botanical-ecological adventure.

Created between 1630 and 1665, the parkland was the playground of the dynastic House of Arenberg. It is now open all year following extensive restoration of the historic gardens and buildings such as the castle, the Church of St. Nicholas, and the Capuchin Museum. In 1998, one of the most celebrated gardens of the architect Father Charles de Bruxelles was relaid, following the design of the original—an enclosed, four-sided flower garden with a dominant shell leitmotif. Careful attention has been paid to the Italianate renaissance-style planting.

The Seven Stars Baroque Park has a heptagonal pavilion and mysterious statues of the planets and the stars. From July until September, the European Dahlia Conservatorium has an impressive display of long-forgotten and rarely seen shapes and colors from their collection of 750 plants. The Rose Garden, created in 1997, has hundreds of roses planted on two levels; one is devoted to new and recently forgotten roses, the other to roses with a Belgian connection and to historic varieties, such as 'Parmentier', named after the great American landscape gardener. AW

Les Jardins d'Annevoie

Namur, Belgium

DESIGNERS: Charles-Alexis de Montpellier, Nicolas Charles de Montpellier
OWNER: The Wallone Region
GARDEN STYLE: 18th-century water gardens
SIZE: 69 acres (27.9 ha)
CLIMATE: Temperate
LOCATION: Annevoie-Rouillon, Namur

At Les Jardins d'Annevoie, some twenty ornamental lakes, ponds, and canals with more than fifty fountains and cascades are fed by natural springs and the River Rouillon, which crosses the gardens before flowing into the River Meuse. The 1,312-foot-long (400 m) Grand Canal at the top of the site acts as a reservoir. There are no machines or pumps, just naturally flowing water, the force of gravity, and the dynamics of communicating vessels (water levels in vertical tubes equalize if water is poured into one tube and the tubes are all connected at the bottom).

Designed and laid out from 1758 to 1776 by Charles-Alexis de Montpellier, the gardens combine three distinct European styles: French, English, and Italian. The French element, art correcting nature, is best illustrated by the small, formal canal, which is perfectly rectilinear, and by the tiered cascade. The English Cascade is the finest example of the English landscape style, art imitating nature, where white water tumbles and sprays down a moss-covered rockfall. The Italianate approach, art accommodating nature, can be seen throughout the grounds.

The highlights include a fountain that spits water 23 feet (7 m) into the air, and a fan-shaped fountain that is unusual for the eighteenth century. A series of scallop-edged weirs produces a soft murmuring sound. A grotto contains a trompe l'oeil image of the god of water and the seas that looks uncannily three-dimensional when viewed from the correct angle. And do not miss the steps of the "water buffet." RCa

Les Hortillonages

Picardie, France

DESIGNERS: A collective of market gardeners
OWNERS: Mostly privately owned
GARDEN STYLE: 20th-century potager, domestic
SIZE: 742 acres (300 ha)
CLIMATE: Temperate
LOCATION: Amiens, Picardie

This is probably one of the most unexpected and enchanting garden excursions you could undertake anywhere in western Europe. To see the gardens, you spend over one hour aboard a 30-foot-long (10 m) flat boat that carries up to twelve passengers. The boat's front is raised to protect the banks and it has a silent electric engine instead of traditional wooden paddles. This is the only way you can explore this extraordinary network of wide irrigation canals that have been reclaimed from the marshes. The whole network extends over 30 miles (48 km) but only 1.5 miles (2.5 km) are open to visitors.

Early in the twentieth century, the canals were created to feed working gardens run by over 1,000 small farmers who lived off their produce. Few of the gardens remain, and these are mainly privately owned and used as allotments. On the slow-paced trip, you enter a watery world where you only meet ducks and coots as you glide through green arches of weeping willows, observing the landscape from below, passing a mysteriously abandoned house. Some of the smaller lateral canals are overrun by grasses and reeds, and they are often covered with water lilies, adding to the romance.

Every summer, most of the gardeners compete for the best canalside garden with exuberant displays of multicolored annuals. The succession of vegetable gardens offer more delights with their immaculate rows and vertical supports for beans or peas in the dark, rich-looking soil. They are a reminder of the original purpose of this extraordinary site. MO

Château et Parc de Chantilly

Picardie, France

DESIGNERS: André Le Nôtre, and others
OWNER: Institut de France
GARDEN STYLE: 17th- and 18th-century high baroque
SIZE: 284 acres (115 ha)
CLIMATE: Temperate
LOCATION: Chantilly, Picardie

Chantilly is world famous for its historic château, its extensive collection of Old Masters that is second only to the Louvre, horse racing, the living equestrian museum Musée Vivant du Cheval, and the international fireworks competition, Les Nuits de Feu, held biennially in June. Above all else, it is famous for the landscaped grounds of its château, which rival Versailles in size and splendor. Chantilly is the cream of the crop of French gardens.

The estate has been owned by many wealthy families that have left their mark in an assortment of architectural styles. At the end of the seventeenth century, the great André Le Nôtre remodeled the gardens, pulling the buildings together visually, using vast reflecting pools and canals to strike a single chord. Water is the great unifier here. In scarce supply around Versailles, but abundant in this region, it is used to optimum effect.

Besides Le Nôtre, many other respected architects and designers had a hand in the creation of Chantilly, and the grounds as a whole are a unique testament to the French imagination.

The only problem is that Chantilly offers far too much to absorb on a single visit. The fun way to get around is by miniature train or horse-drawn carriage. If you become tired and need a temporary change of pace, then visit Le Hameau, where peasant cottages conceal surprising interiors, or take a relaxing half-hour boat trip down the Grand Canal. RCa

Le Parc Jean-Jacques Rousseau

Picardie, France

DESIGNERS: René-Louis de Girardin, Jean-Marie Morel
OWNER: Council General of Oise
GARDEN STYLE: 18th-century Arcadian landscape
SIZE: 61 acres (24.7 ha)
CLIMATE: Temperate
LOCATION: Ermenonville, Picardie

René-Louis de Girardin sought to create Rousseau's dream garden of *La Nouvelle Heloise* (1761), which was effectively an English landscape garden. The park and farm were decorated with classic and rustic buildings designed by Jean-Marie Morel, though most were destroyed during the French Revolution.

This park's style was Arcadian and the adjoining wilderness (now belonging to the Abbaye de Chaalis) was more Anglo-Chinese in style and was left uncultivated. The target ground for archery has survived, as has a rough bowling green. You can climb to the deliberately unfinished Temple of Philosophers dedicated to Montaigne. Each column represents a philosopher—Descartes, Newton, Penn, Montesquieu, Voltaire, Rousseau, and the remainder, to quote Girardin, "that lie here will stay for several centuries; for it is far easier to achieve a place at the Academy than merit a column at Ermenonville." Below the temple is the small, self-explanatory Altar to Dreams. Jean-Jacques Rousseau arrived on May 20, 1778, but unexpectedly died on July 2. His island tomb, framed by poplars, recalls the ancient, endless meadows and waters of eternal oblivion.

Two sculptures, *La Table* (*The Table*) and *Le Banc des Mères* (*The Mothers' Bench*), were created after Rousseau's death because Rousseau exalted maternal love. The painter Georges-Frederic Mayer's sepulchre lies on the edge of the Arcadian Meadow. Marie Antoinette once came to visit and pay homage. CH

Château de Brécy

Basse-Normandie, France

DESIGNER: Attributed to François Mansart
OWNER: Jacques le Bas
GARDEN STYLE: 17th-century formal baroque
SIZE: 4.4 acres (1.7 ha)
CLIMATE: Temperate
LOCATION: Brécy, Basse-Normandie

The gardens of this charming château are on a much smaller scale than those more usually seen as examples of the French formal style and are much more accessible to visitors.

The residence was built in the early seventeenth century and has been attributed to François Mansart, who may also have designed the gardens. The entrance forecourt has a superb arched gateway and walls ornamented with urns. However, the major ornamental gardens are found behind the château. These gardens are enclosed by beautiful stone walls, and some have wonderful carvings acting as accents.

There is a central axis, with the garden rising away from the building on a series of four terraces.

The first terrace, inspired by the works of seventeenth-century designer Claude Mollet, is planted as a pair of parterres de broderie in scrolled patterns of clipped box. The initial terrace is the width of the château, but each subsequent one becomes wider and features a different style of planting. The farther terraces are planted with clipped geometric forms of topiary set in lawns, and one has matching water basins. Throughout the garden are some fine stone ornaments with carved lions, urns, and garlands of flowers ideally suited to the formal design.

Elsewhere you will find herbaceous plants, roses, climbing plants, and clipped evergreens, which are not allowed to outgrow their place in this elegant design. The gardens are a gem of formal planting with carefully crafted and controlled views, both out to the surrounding landscape and back to the château. JR

Vauville Botanical Gardens

Basse-Normandie, France

DESIGNERS: Guillaume Pellerin, Eric Pellerin, Nicole Pellerin
OWNER: Eric Pellerin, Nicole Pellerin
GARDEN STYLE: 20th-century personal
SIZE: 10 acres (4 ha)
CLIMATE: Oceanic
LOCATION: Vauville, Basse-Normandie

With more than 900 species, including exotic plants from Tasmania, the Canary Islands, and South Africa, the botanical garden of Vauville is the work of a family of enthusiasts. It was in 1947 that a couple, Eric and Nicole Pellerin, introduced the first plants to the site, which is bathed by the mild temperatures of the Gulf Stream and lies on the northwest point of the Cherbourg peninsula.

Tirelessly extending their collection, they have acclimatized echiums from the Canaries, aloes, and Australian cordylines, as well as numerous examples of New Zealand flora, in particular evergreen species.

Their son, Guillaume Pellerin, has enthusiastically continued the creative work of his parents, creating a tropical oasis in which the imagination can run free. Exposed to the west winds, the garden is protected from spray from the sea by windbreaks of Monterey cypress, phormium (*P. tenax*), and eucalyptus. The tree echium (*E. pininana*) flourishes in the courtyard of the château, displaying its gigantic blue spikes in the month of June.

Divided into several areas of varied character, the garden is watered by streams and basins, where the shade is favorable for growing crinums and royal ferns (*Osmunda regalis*). The botanical variety and richness of the foliage make Vauville an exceptional collection. The site has been listed in the France's supplementary inventory of historic monuments since 1992. Vauville is also a very individual garden, where Guillaume Pellerin is planning to establish one of the largest groves of palm trees in northern Europe. ML

Château de Miromesnil

Haute-Normandie, France

DESIGNER: Unknown
OWNERS: M. and Mme Romatet
GARDEN STYLE: 19th- and 20th-century potager
SIZE: 35 acres (14 ha)
CLIMATE: Temperate
LOCATION: Tourville-sur-Arque, Haute-Normandie

This château and its gardens are a delight of French symmetry, being small and perfectly formed, rather like the short stories of Guy de Maupassant, who was born here in 1850. Set in woodland, the château is approached by an arrow-straight avenue of beech trees. Lawns sweep up to the entrance court that is punctuated by clipped yew and urns.

The potager is a working garden in which picked produce leaves gaps. The gnarled bark of the fruit trees adds a sculptural feel. The flowers used to inject life and color here include peonies and nasturtiums. You will also see them as floral displays inside the château because excellent tours can be taken with members of the resident de Voguë family. As you leave this living pantry, the garden and its borders open out. The outer walls have deep borders with roses, delphiniums, and, later, dahlias backed by a comprehensive collection of clematis offering color and interest over many months. The gardens then merge into an orchard underplanted with an impressionistic meadow, punctuated by wildflowers. Do not miss the sixteenth-century chapel hidden in the beech trees. Its plain exterior belies the beauty of the stained glass and paneling within. CH

> "The gnarled bark of the fruit trees adds a sculptural feel"

Le Clos du Coudray

Haute-Normandie, France

DESIGNER: Jean Le Bret
OWNER: Jean Le Bret, Marie-Christine Le Bret
GARDEN STYLE: 20th-century plantsman's garden
SIZE: 7.4 acres (2.9 ha)
CLIMATE: Temperate
LOCATION: Etaimpuis, Haute-Normandie

The French have always designed gardens brilliantly, but, until recently, have been less interested in plants. An outstanding exception to this rule is Jean Le Bret.

He opened Le Clos du Coudray in 1993 and it now houses the most comprehensive private collection of plants in France. Just under half of the 8,000 varieties found here are propagated and sold at the nursery, including alpines, perennials, grasses, ferns, dahlias, and roses. The garden also contains many trees, rare shrubs, and bamboos. Remarkably, no pesticides, fungicides, weed killers, or chemical fertilizers are used. "My garden," says Le Bret, "is about a philosophy based on a respect for nature and my belief that biodiversity is fundamental to the health of a garden. I give the plants the conditions they require, and then leave them to find their own equilibrium."

Laid out around the family home, the garden unfolds in a series of color-themed borders, "rooms," and water features, where you will find a huge range of plants. Divided by hedges and pergolas, and also crossed by two streams, the garden reveals something unexpected around every corner. The habitats range from a rockery, gravel gardens, and an exotic glen with bananas, cannas, and tree ferns, to a light woodland of rhododendrons, meconopsis, and cardiocrinums. You will find the National Collection of epimediums. Primulas, hostas, gunneras, and dahlias have a garden each. It all reflects Le Bret's love of the diversity found in the plant kingdom. VR

Giverny

Haute-Normandie, France

DESIGNER: Claude Monet
OWNER: The Claude Monet Foundation
GARDEN STYLE: 19th-century impressionistic
SIZE: 2.5 acres (1 ha)
CLIMATE: Temperate
LOCATION: Giverny, Haute-Normandie

The artist Claude Monet used his wealth to create this horticultural paradise of design and plantsmanship. After a long search for a suitable home, he wrote, "I am filled with delight, Giverny is a splendid spot for me."

The garden has two distinct halves. The Flower Garden was created around the Grande Allée and side paths. Monet took "the pictorial composition into the sky" by training climbers over an extensive network of iron frames that turn, over summer, into an amazing flowery, leafy tunnel as the climbing and rambling roses fill out. Climbing, spreading nasturtiums inch their way across the path beneath. The flower beds running parallel to the Grande Allée have a mix of climbers, perennials, and annuals, giving an impressionistic effect, focused by spikes of color and standard roses.

In 1893, inspired by landscapes on Japanese prints, Monet bought the meadowland that lay across the railroad line below the Flower Garden. The River Ru was then diverted into the meadow to form The Water Garden, a naturalistic pool that mirrors the water lilies, willows, sky, sun, and the celebrated Japanese Bridge. Five other bridges each provide a platform from which to view the sparkle of light on the water. The prettiest one is undoubtedly where Monet launched his boat and frequently painted. CH

> "...a naturalistic pool that mirrors the lilies, willows, sky..."

Manoir d'Ango

Haute-Normandie, France

DESIGNERS: Robert Mallet, Corinne Mallet
OWNERS: Robert Mallet, Corinne Mallet
GARDEN STYLE: 20th- and 21st-century nursery, informal
SIZE: 5 acres (2 ha)
CLIMATE: Temperate
LOCATION: Varengeville-sur-Mer, Haute-Normandie

Hydrangeas bloom with great profusion all summer long in Normandy, in every possible shade from pale pink to deep lilac. They are in public spaces, in cottage gardens, and at the foot of many châteaux. So when visitors come to the lovely village of Varengeville near Dieppe, hydrangeas are what they get.

Most visitors come to see the world-famous Parc du Bois des Moutiers, a collaboration between Edwin Lutyens, Gertrude Jekyll, and the owner, Guillaume Mallet. However, Mallet's grandson, Robert, a plantsman, developed a garden on the family estate dedicated solely to hydrangeas (with the tireless input of his wife, Corinne, who hunted for them all over the world). The couple recently acquired a larger plot on the edge of the village and created what is now the largest collection of hydrangeas in the world. It is named the Shamrock Collection in homage to the Irish soil where the plant is happiest. Because the land was riddled with blackberry bushes and rough grass, they cleared it and created mounds in which they planted paulownias. This was an excellent choice because their roots ensured good drainage and conserved moisture, while their large leaves formed an instant canopy for the hydrangeas.

Over 200 species and 1,000 cultivars are now beautifully arranged in separate beds, each with a theme (such as the plants' country of origin) and a star exhibit. The owners are on hand to answer questions about pruning and the mysterious color change that occurs in hydrangeas, which is due to the aluminum levels in the soil, not the iron levels. MO

Les Jardins Agapanthe

Haute-Normandie, France

DESIGNER: Alexandre Thomas

OWNER: Alexandre Thomas

GARDEN STYLE: 20th-century informal

SIZE: 1.4 acres (0.6 ha)

CLIMATE: Temperate

LOCATION: Grigneuseville, Haute-Normandie

This private Normandy garden, created by landscape architect Alexandre Thomas, would seem at home in the UK. Possibly as a reaction against the formal rigidity of French garden design, Thomas has created a welcoming space to make visitors feel as if they were walking around their own garden, allowing a profusion of plants to take center stage so that the design is not the dominating factor. You would never guess that fifteen years ago this was a flat, barren site. Now it is a succession of intimate spaces divided by mounds, hedges, and dry stone walls, with ponds indicating the end of a vista. Many changes of levels add an element of surprise and make the garden appear much bigger than it is.

The extraordinary number of different areas takes you on a journey from the Mediterranean Garden to the Exotic Garden via the English Path, down the Exuberant Descent to the Sunken Garden with its grid of lavender, and finally to the eponymous Agapanthus Walk, with plenty of sitting areas along the way. The sheer variety of plants is breathtaking. They are always used to set a scene. For example, a sweep of grasses and verbenas leads to a little wooden bridge, rows of hydrangeas in terracotta pots lie around a patio, and topiary yews frame a garden of roses and lavender. The hard landscaping provides a strong structure, using wide granite slabs, stone steps, gravel, and pebbles, with cobblestones and stone walls to rope everything together. Thomas has not created a show garden, but one packed with beautiful plants underpinned by a clever design. MO

Le Vasterival

Haute-Normandie, France

DESIGNER: Princess Greta Sturdza
OWNER: Princess Greta Sturdza
GARDEN STYLE: 20th-century woodland garden
SIZE: 29.7 acres (12 ha)
CLIMATE: Temperate
LOCATION: Sainte-Marguerite-sur-Mer, Haute-Normandie

Le Vasterival is the finest French private garden. This plantsman's paradise is the creation of Princess Greta Sturdza, who started its development in 1958. It holds an unrivaled collection of the rarest and choicest trees, shrubs, and plants, surpassing the collections of many botanical gardens. The princess is Vice-president of the Royal Horticultural Society, President of Honour of the International Dendrological Society, and holder of the RHS Veitch Gold Medal, to name only a few of her honors in the horticultural world.

The gardens are set in woodland that slopes down to a valley fed by natural springs. Even in the depths of winter, the favorite time of the princess, the garden is radiant with an ever-changing palette of colors that complement the plantings, textures, and shapes. A burst of "sunshine" from the fine collection of golden hamamelis and the subtle copper of *Hamamelis* 'Le Vasterival', raised by the princess, herald an exceptional array of plants. These include hellebores, an unequaled magnolia collection, camellias, cornus, rhododendrons (even a standard *Rhododendron yakushimanum*), and azaleas, which are waiting to give a glittering display.

In spring, blossoms on trees and shrubs give the garden a delicate beauty. The vivid summer colors of roses, perennials, astilbes, hostas, primulas, and ferns are enthralling. There is an extensive hydrangea collection of note, followed by a feast of vibrant fall hues. Your lasting memory of this garden may be a spellbinding glimpse of *Cornus controversa* 'Variegata' across the valley. RL

Le Bois des Moutiers

Haute-Normandie, France

DESIGNERS: Gertrude Jekyll, Edwin Lutyens
OWNERS: The Mallet family
GARDEN STYLE: English Arts and Crafts, woodland
SIZE: 30 acres (12.1 ha)
CLIMATE: Temperate
LOCATION: Varengeville-sur-Mer, Haute-Normandie

Where house and garden have been designed as one, there is a special kind of magic. Such is the case at Le Bois des Moutiers, an Arts and Crafts house designed by Edwin Lutyens for Guillaume Mallet in 1898. It sits at the head of a gently rolling valley that runs right down to the sea, and the location could not be better. At the front is a garden of "rooms," laid out by Lutyens and planted by Gertrude Jekyll. Behind the house, on the north side, is an extensive woodland garden with paths weaving down the hill to the sea.

Guillaume, a passionate gardener, enjoyed a fruitful collaboration with Lutyens and Jekyll. He admired their English styling and was delighted by their design here. Lutyens took great care with his use of materials; stucco, stone, and tiling are used in both the garden and house. A white garden, enclosed by yew hedges and filled with 'Iceberg' roses, white hydrangeas, lupins, and tulips, offers a calm, tranquil place to linger on a hot summer day. There are also shady retreats with built-in seating.

Behind the house is a wide lawn with paths leading into the woodland. Guillaume oversaw this area, filling it with ornamental trees, shrubs, and perennials. Rhododendrons, azaleas, and camellias thrive on the sandy soil, providing great splashes of color in spring. Take a tour of the house and view the garden from its windows. The Mallet family are still in residence and may even guide you around. PMcW

RIGHT Trees cast a light, protective shade over the vibrant coral pink rhododendrons of the woodland garden.

Château de Courances

Ile-de-France, France

DESIGNERS: Cosme Clausse and son, Claude Gallard, André
Le Nôtre, Achille Duchêne

OWNER: Marquis Jean-Louis de Ganay

GARDEN STYLE: 17th-century renaissance, later additions

SIZE: 190 acres (76.9 ha)

CLIMATE: Temperate

LOCATION: Courances, Ile-de-France

The tranquil park that surrounds the Louis XIII château dates back to the Clausse family taking over the medieval castle and land during the renaissance period. Richly endowed with natural springs and pools, and with access to the nearby river, the setting was ideal for a grand water garden. A network of formal pools and watercourses was built, including a 2,000-foot-long (600 m) Grand Canal and the Salle d'Eau, a huge trapezoid-shaped pool fed by spouts from the sculpted heads of monsters. By 1622, though, the son and heir was a ruined man, being forced to sell to Claude Gallard, advisor and secretary to the king. It was Gallard who hired landscape architect André Le Nôtre to develop the park further and rebuild the château.

The French Revolution brought turmoil to Courances, and, from 1830, the château was abandoned for forty years. During this time, a tree grew up through the dining room ceiling, and the property was said to be "falling apart like a piece of sugar forgotten in a wet place." It was rescued by Baron de Haber, a wealthy banker, and the park and building were restored using original plans. Through marriage, the château then passed to the Ganay family, who still live here. They commissioned landscape architect Achille Duchêne to complete the restoration. He did this by incorporating symmetrical box embroideries to link the château with the park and a giant reflecting pool.

Contemporary adaptations to enable ease of maintenance include replacing the original pathways with lawns, allowing the trees to overhang the watercourses, and cutting miles of formal box and yew hedging using laser-guided machines. With the exception of the little Anglo-Japanese garden, this is a highly stylized and formal landscape with magical vistas and exquisite symmetry, breathtakingly enhanced by water. JHe

Saint-Jean de Beauregard

Ile-de-France, France

DESIGNER: Mme de Curel
OWNERS: M. and Mme. de Curel
GARDEN STYLE: 17th-century formal
SIZE: Potager 5 acres (2 ha), parkland 37 acres (15 ha)
CLIMATE: Temperate
LOCATION: Saint-Jean de Beauregard, Ile-de-France

Saint-Jean de Beauregard is set up high, with views over hills and woodlands. When standing on the parterre in front of the elegant seventeenth-century château, it is difficult to imagine that you are less than 20 miles (32 km) from the center of Paris.

The château's parkland is extensive, with groves of oaks and chestnuts, and with avenues of centuries-old limes. In one corner, near the house, is a rare seventeenth-century dovecote. Behind the house, however, lies the real gem, a magnificent potager that the de Curels have restored to the original seventeenth-century design. It is perfectly proportioned with walls built at precisely the right height to provide a warm microclimate for the fruits and vegetables. Gaps in the walls allow the circulation of air, while a pool prevents wild animals from jumping in through the openings.

Wide grass paths lead around the outside of the potager, which is divided into four squares, each with four square beds to allow for crop rotation. The beds are edged with flowers, and espaliers of apples and pears. Vegetables grow within this decorative framework, with cardoons at each corner as focal points. There are red fruit on the east-facing wall, peaches and apricots on the west, kiwis and figs on the south, and buttresses of box on the south and north walls. Beyond the formal potager is an orchard with long grass around the trees in the English fashion. Old roses scramble up the end wall. VB

Parc de Courson

Ile-de-France, France

DESIGNERS: Louis-Martin Berthault, Timothy Vaughan
OWNER: M. and Mme. de Nervaux-Loÿs, M. and Mme. Fustier
GARDEN STYLE: 19th-century botanic and romantic
AREA: 86 acres (35 ha)
CLIMATE: Temperate
LOCATION: Courson-Monteloup, Ile-de-France

The park in this estate, well known for its plant shows and situated 22 miles (35 km) south of Paris, is a living example of the art of landscape gardening in the nineteenth century. The successive owners of this château, which was built in the seventeenth century by Nicolas de Lamoignon, have always maintained a perfect balance between architecture and landscape.

In about 1820 the Duc de Padoue entrusted the landscape gardener Louis-Martin Berthault with the challenging task of transforming his French-styled garden into a romantic, landscaped one. Berthault was a pupil of Bellanger, who had designed the gardens of the Empress Joséphine at Malmaison. A little later, in about 1860, further additions were made in the form of two glass houses, typical of the industrial architecture of the Second Empire.

The landscape of Courson came back to life in 1980 as a result of a meeting between the owners and the landscape gardener Timothy Vaughan, who created new beds and plantations. Courson has seen the introduction of new plants and trees, such as yews, prunus, and rare oak species. A new drive, created on the advice of the landscape gardener Louis Benech, has recently been added to emphasize the axes of the kitchen garden, which has been brought back into use. Within its walls, covered with ancient rose bushes, many new fruit trees have been planted: apples, plums, berries, and peaches including the famous 'Madeleine de Courson'. ML

Parc de Malmaison

Ile-de-France, France

DESIGNERS: Jean-Marie Morel, Louis Martin Berthault
OWNER: The French State
GARDEN STYLE: Early 19th-century informal English garden
SIZE: 15 acres (6 ha)
CLIMATE: Temperate
LOCATION: Rueil-Malmaison, Ile-de-France

The name of this beautifully proportioned pink manor house and its park is instantly evocative of Napoleon and of his first wife, the Empress Joséphine, who remained there all her life. Joséphine opted for an English garden designed by Louis Martin Berthault, the contemporary expert, with sweeps of lawns, open views, groups of trees, and even a river for boating. Berthault completed the largest heated greenhouse of the time. Here the specimens and seeds passionately collected by the Empress were exhibited and cultivated. Joséphine was the first to import to Europe some of our most familiar plants, such as the tree peony, the purple-flowering magnolia, camellias, and phloxes. Most famously, she promoted the rose with 400 varieties displayed in pots and beds. It was here that the repeat-flowering modern rose was developed and exported to England, where it became the hybrid tea.

Although the greenhouse no longer exists, there are walks among beautiful trees, including a stunning group of purple beeches (*Fagus sylvatica Atropurpurea*) and a magnificent cedar from Marengo in northern Italy, planted by Joséphine. The English-style river scene, with its bridge and pools reflecting trees and statues, has immense charm. You can also see the Emperor's Pavilion, where the young Bonaparte used to work in summer. The forest and pond of Saint-Cucufa, formerly part of the domain, offer a wonderful woodland walk. MO

Les Jardins du Musée Albert Kahn

Ile-de-France, France

DESIGNER: Achille Duchêne
OWNER: Département des Hauts-de-Seine
GARDEN STYLE: 20th-century eclectic
SIZE: 10 acres (4 ha)
CLIMATE: Temperate
LOCATION: Boulogne-Billancourt, Ile-de-France

This little-known garden, just outside Paris, is worth seeking out not only because it is enchanting, but because of its guiding principles. Albert Kahn, a businessman and philanthropist, acquired the land in 1895. He promoted education at the highest level through scholarships and commissioned a vast collection of photographs to be taken in fifty countries, which formed the Planetary Archives. He also created a garden using different types of landscaping from around the world, with the aim of broadening vision and understanding.

Visitors enter the garden though a forest of Blue Atlas cedars (*Cedrus atlantica* Glauca Group), whose low branches screen a small lily pond surrounded by a wild meadow. After crossing the meadow and passing through a group of slender birches, paths lead to a vast forest of conifers planted on steep, rocky soil, a reproduction of the Vosges Mountains. A bamboo gate marks the entrance to a Japanese garden filled with temples, lanterns, stone paths edged with azaleas, and streams crossed by stone or timber bridges. Formal French gardens are included, with a greenhouse, orchard, and rose garden.

Before 1936, when it opened to the public, this utopian space was visited only by visiting dignitaries, including Einstein, various poets and philosophers, and kings and queens. Today the concept of recording and preserving the world seems more relevant than ever. MO

Château d'Ambleville

Ile-de-France, France

DESIGNER: Marquise de Villefranche, Mme de Villefranche
OWNER: M. Coutau Begarie
GARDEN STYLE: 20th-century Italianate
SIZE: 10 acres (4 ha)
CLIMATE: Temperate
LOCATION: Ambleville, Ile-de-France

If you parachuted down into the middle of these gardens, their terraced layout and planting might make you think that you were in Italy. Then you would see the impressive renaissance château and its medieval tower, both unmistakably French.

The design of these gardens is unusual in France. They were recreated in 1928 by the Marquise de Villefranche when she bought the château. After her death, they were expanded and maintained by her granddaughter, and their new owners are now restoring them. The grander part of the design is the Moon Garden. There are wide lawns, a pool in the shape of a half moon, and, most strikingly, a vast yew hedge pierced with arches. The Secret Garden has four squares filled with black and white tulips around an Italian marble urn. It overlooks a stone reservoir built in the seventeenth century. The Sun Garden represents a chessboard with pieces made out of box topiary, though the squares are visible only in spring when they are marked by thousands of narcissi.

Also note the romantic cascade with mossy stone shells that flows through the garden, the wide avenues of ancient lime trees, and a handsome fence that frames a vista toward twelve sun rays. The Glasshouse Garden has tree peonies, hellebores, and black tulips in twenty-four squares with topiarized yew. Finally, the Garden of the Eye uses 200 yews to create four green Italianate "rooms." It is now officially named the Extraordinary Garden. MO

Les Jardins de Villarceaux

Ile-de-France, France

DESIGNERS: Nicolas de Mornay, Jean-Baptiste Courtonne
OWNER: Conseil régional d'Ile-de-France
GARDEN STYLE: 16th- and 18th-century French
SIZE: 156 acres (63 ha)
CLIMATE: Temperate
LOCATION: Chaussy, Ile-de-France

With its wooded slopes on the Vexin plateau, its pools and lakes, and its Renaissance garden, Villarceaux is a magnificent fortified estate. The lower château, the Manoir de Ninon, and the first terrace, called the François I garden, were designed in the sixteenth century by Nicolas de Mornay, the owner at the time.

At the foot of the St. Nicolas tower and the manor there is a charming, unpretentious herb garden of medieval inspiration. A stream still runs at the end of the terrace where it is said that the beautiful Ninon de Lenclos, friend of Nicolas, used to bathe. Later, in 1755, the upper château and its formal grounds in the French style were built by the Marquis de la Bussière and his architect, Jean Baptiste Courtonne. Few significant changes have been made to the gardens since that time, apart from the installation of eight Italian statues of groups of children, and an orangery built in the mid-nineteenth century. The upper château is ornamented with terraces, carpet bedding, and vertugadins (rigid banks). Open wolf-leaps surround the basins of the lower château.

From the upper château, the view includes the gardens with their beds in French embroidery style, the broad expanse of the sloping lawns, the cascade, and the "mirror basin." Near the manor, the Renaissance water gardens have been recreated with their canals and patterns of clipped box. Five centuries after reflecting the beauty of Ninon de Lenclos, their attraction is undiminished. ML

La Roseraie du Val-de-Marne

Ile-de-France, France

DESIGNERS: Jules Gravereaux, Edouard André
OWNER: General Council of Val-de-Marne
GARDEN STYLE: Late 19th-century botanical rose garden
SIZE: 4.2 acres (1.7 ha)
CLIMATE: Temperate
LOCATION: L'Haÿ-les-Roses, Ile-de-France

The Rose Garden of Val-de-Marne is seriously exciting to botanists, but something of a sleeping beauty for visitors because it comes into its own for just one month a year. For the rest of the year, this garden is by turns a bewilderment of well-pruned winter stems, glossy green spring leaves, and countless scarlet clusters of plump fall hips.

Come June, however, the garden is breathtaking. The layout is exquisite, the air positively drips with perfume, the colors are overwhelming, and the entire history and development of arguably the world's finest flower is laid bare in one fell swoop. All of this is a mere 5 miles (8 km) south of Paris. The founding genius was Jules Gravereaux, whose fortune came from the Bon Marché department store. He retired to L'Haÿ in 1892, and began sourcing and cultivating roses in 1894. He established links with botanical gardens, nurseries, and rosarians on all continents with the express intention of forming the most complete collection ever of the genus *Rosa*. In 1899 he commissioned landscape architect Edouard André to orchestrate the shrubs, standards, climbers, and ramblers into a coherent whole. The result is a virtuoso composition of beds, archways, pergolas, trelliswork, and a magical reflecting pool. Today there are some 16,000 plants on display, representing about 3,500 varieties. The gardens are of enormous significance to breeders as a gene bank.

There's an enclave devoted to the history of the rose, and the Allée de la Malmaison contains all the surviving roses grown by the Empress Joséphine. There are burnet roses, hedgerow roses, gallicas, orientals, species roses, new French roses, foreign roses, and countless areas devoted simply to the rose as an ornamental. All of this is utterly enchanting. In 1968 the county council took the bold and imaginative step of purchasing the garden outright to assure its long-term survival. RCa

Parc de Saint-Cloud

Ile-de-France, France

DESIGNER: André Le Nôtre
OWNER: The French State
GARDEN STYLE: 19th-century French formal
SIZE: 1,140 acres (461.7 ha)
CLIMATE: Temperate
LOCATION: Saint-Cloud, Ile-de-France

Perhaps because this historic site lost its château, it is not as well known as Versailles. However, its position, size, and wonderful waterworks demand a visit.

Louis XIV bought the domain from a rich Italian financier as a gift to his brother. The airy site on a steep slope above the River Seine was a favorite with French monarchs from Marie Antoinette to Napoleon I and Napoleon III, the last inhabitant before its destruction during the Franco-Prussian War of 1870–71. In the spirit of brotherly rivalry, André Le Nôtre was commissioned to expand the already beautiful gardens and remodel an existing cascade. The hilly situation and abundance of natural ponds and springs led to the construction of a vast network of channels and pools with complicated fountain patterns. These are fed by gravity and end in the spectacular Grand Cascade with terraces near the river.

The perspectives created by Le Nôtre are breathtaking. Originally on the axis of the château, they have retained their grandeur with rows of tall pyramid yews, curtains of clipped horse chestnut, large formal lawns, and sunken "rooms." They always lead the eye to the reflection of a pool or to wide inviting paths on one side, and the view of Paris and the Eiffel Tower on the other. In spite of this grand formality, the park has a very romantic atmosphere, so well captured by the photographs of Eugène Atget in the early twentieth century. An English garden, Le Jardin du Trocadéro, was added by Napoleon III to educate his children in botany. Beautifully cared for, the park certainly lingers in the memory. MO

Parc de Sceaux

Ile-de-France, France

DESIGNER: André Le Nôtre
OWNER: Département des Hauts-de-Seine
GARDEN STYLE: 17th- and 20th-century French formal
SIZE: 445 acre (180 ha)
CLIMATE: Temperate
LOCATION: Sceaux, Ile-de-France

This is a vast park in the grand French tradition. From the highest point, an immaculately ordered landscape can be seen at a glance.

This public space, in the middle of the urban bustle, was originally bought in 1670 by Colbert, the great financier to Louis XIV. However, it did not open its gates until the beginning of the twentieth century. André Le Nôtre, who designed all the important gardens of the period, was called in. He created a spectacular double perspective with a huge lawn and parterres in front of the raised château, leading to a series of cascades crossed by a very long canal bordered by clipped trees. Following the devastating storm of 1999, many trees were lost, and it will take a few years for the young trees along the canal to recreate the original effect. Still there is much to admire in this fantastic example of a site being reclaimed from violent destruction during the French Revolution of 1789 and consequent years of neglect.

The original château was rebuilt in the nineteenth century in the Louis XIII style, and the cascades were restored in the 1930s with decorative elements by Rodin. The jets and cascades add fun grandeur to the pools but are not always turned on, so check their running times. The garden around the orangery by Mansart has been rethought with beds of scented plants edged with box. The enclosed garden around the Dawn Pavilion is planted with sweeps of iris to echo the colors of the frescoes inside. This careful restoration, mixing original plans and contemporary concepts, is a big success. MO

Château de Rambouillet

Ile-de-France, France

DESIGNER: Joseph Fleuriau, Louis Jean-Marie de Bourbon
OWNER: Ministry of Culture
GARDEN STYLE: 18th-century French; English garden
AREA: 371 acres (150 ha)
CLIMATE: Temperate
LOCATION: Rambouillet, Ile-de-France

The park and gardens around the château of Rambouillet are enhanced by the green setting of 77 square miles (200 sq km) of surrounding forest. The estate, which became the presidential residence in 1895 and continues to be used as such in the summer, has been restored with the greatest care. The gardens were developed in two stages by successive owners.

The creation of the first gardens was inspired by Joseph Jean-Baptiste Fleuriau, who acquired the estate in 1700. It is said that he spent three times the estate's purchase price embellishing the gardens with manmade lakes, radiating canals, terraces, and parterres, a kitchen garden, and a fruit orchard—in the process creating a magnificent garden in the French style. In front of the château lies a wide lake; a landing stage enabled the château's occupants and guests to take a boat and row on the water, a popular pastime among the eighteenth-century aristocracy. Only a few staggered lines of the original planting remain. The contemporary French-styled garden, created by the landscape gardener Jacques Sgard in the 1990s, follows the layout of the original parterres.

The second part of the garden at Rambouillet was designed by Louis Jean-Marie de Bourbon, Duke of Penthièvre, who inherited the estate in 1737. English landscape gardens had become very fashionable, and the Duke of Penthièvre decided to landscape 62 acres (25 ha) in the picturesque style. He built waterways and transformed the resulting six islands into meadows or groves. Also in the fashion of the day, he also built follies: the shell cottage, decorated with splendid patterns of shells and mother-of-pearl; the Chinese pavilion, of which only the rockwork base has survived, known as "the lovers' cave"; and the hermitage. In 1783 the estate was bought by Louis XVI, who added a beautifully appointed dairy for the amusement of his queen, complete with Sèvres porcelain buckets and an adjacent tasting salon. ML

Vaux-le-Vicomte

Ile-de-France, France

DESIGNERS: André Le Nôtre, Louis Le Vau, Charles Le Brun
OWNER: Comte de Vogüé
GARDEN STYLE: 17th-century formal French baroque
SIZE: 100 acres (40 ha)
CLIMATE: Temperate
LOCATION: Maincy, Ile-de-France

The garden at Vaux-le-Vicomte is one of the greatest achievements in the history of French garden design. Nicolas Fouquet conceived the creation of a grand landscape soon after he had been appointed superintendent of finances under Louis XIV in 1653. He entrusted the design of his project to the famous landscape architect André Le Nôtre. By the latter part of the nineteenth century, the garden had fallen into ruin and was restored to its former glory by Alfred Sommier, with advice from Achille Duchêne. The garden was first opened to the public in 1949 and is still under private ownership.

The design makes full and subtle use of the gentle slope to the south side of the house and includes all the classical elements of a formal garden. The central axis from the house extends into the valley and ends at a monumental statue of Hercules. On either side of this axis are parterres de broderie, immaculately clipped topiary yew, statues and urns, cross axes accentuated by walks leading to the iron gates of the potager, water features, reflective pools, fountains, and a portico terrace known as the Confessional. There is even a great canal with grottoes to one side and a cascade on the other.

It took five years to complete the work at Vaux, and in 1661, Fouquet invited the Sun King to a celebratory party. Three weeks later, Louis XIV had Fouquet arrested and tried for misappropriation of state funds. However, the king was so impressed with the garden that he ordered Le Nôtre to create a bigger version at Versailles. CB

Château de Versailles

Ile-de-France, France

DESIGNERS: André Le Nôtre, Louis Le Vau, Charles Le Brun
OWNER: The French State
GARDEN STYLE: 17th-century French baroque
SIZE: 7,400 acres (3,019.2 ha)
CLIMATE: Temperate
LOCATION: Versailles, Ile-de-France

In creating the famous park of Versailles in the seventeenth century, the Sun King Louis XIV and landscape architect André Le Nôtre developed a long and faithful friendship. Together they were able to change a marshy plain into the greatest of baroque French formal gardens.

Shocked to discover that Nicolas Fouquet, the king's superintendent of finances, possessed an estate at Vaux-le-Vicomte (see page 569) that was grander and more imposing than any of his own, Louis commanded the three great creators of Vaux (Le Brun, Le Vau, and Le Nôtre) to start work immediately on his own scheme to the west of Paris. In 1661 the three great men set out to transform what was then a modest château and grounds into the magnificent estate it is now. A classical Italianate palace emerged, and Versailles became the capital of France. After the French Revolution in 1789, Louis XVI was forced to evacuate Versailles. In the nineteenth century, Louis-Philippe rescued it and made it into a museum of "all the glories of France." In 1919, President Woodrow Wilson made the first-ever journey by an American president to Europe in order to oversee the making of the treaty with which Versailles has become synonymous.

On days when the fountains are operating, the park comes to life again. No fewer than 607 jets play against the backdrop of a view that all gardening enthusiasts must surely see before they die. Mythical beasts and classical gods spout water, rivaling the palace in magnificence. TW

Château de Fontainebleau

Ile-de-France, France

DESIGNER: André Le Nôtre
OWNER: The French State
GARDEN STYLE: Renaissance, 17th-century baroque, romantic
SIZE: 13.2 acres (5.3 ha)
CLIMATE: Temperate
LOCATION: Fontainebleau, Ile-de-France

Surrounded by massive hunting forests, Château de Fontainebleau was built out of marshy ground, and a series of moats and the Grand Canal had to be built to prevent the possibility of flooding. The estate was very popular with the French royal family until Louis XIV developed Versailles. A series of renaissance gardens was created here on axes radiating from the château, and you can still see the outlines of these and the later baroque magnificence.

Courts are aligned around the palace, paved and decorated with elegant containers. The Court of the White Horse is patterned with grass, yew, and bay trees. There are fountains in the restored Court of Henri IV. The Queen's Garden to the north has been resurfaced and the fountain restored. To the south, the shadow of Le Nôtre's intricate Grand Parterre provides an enormous sense of space and grandeur. The 4,000-foot-long (1,200 m) Grand Canal, like that at Versailles, reaches out and draws in the farthest countryside, simultaneously displaying its power over its surroundings. You hardly notice the road that cuts across the garden. The park rolls away to the east to the town and château. To the west, the renaissance Garden of Pines was changed by Napoleon into the then-fashionable romantic landscape.

The statue of Tiber created in 1540 that once stood in these grounds was lost in the French Revolution of 1789. The statue was copied in the late twentieth century and reinstated, along with statues representing the twelve months of the year, and the formal pools in the Great Meadow. CH

Château de Breteuil

Ile-de-France, France

DESIGNER: Achille Duchêne
OWNERS: M. and Mme. Henri-François de Breteuil
GARDEN STYLE: Early 17th-century French
SIZE: 185 acres (75 ha)
CLIMATE: Temperate
LOCATION: Choisel, Ile-de-France

These remarkable gardens in an immense park of 185 acres (75 ha) have seen four centuries of history pass by. The parterres of yew and box and the mirrors of water designed by the landscape gardener Achille Duchêne are harmoniously set in the slopes of the Chevreuse valley. Having a somewhat informal appearance, the park landscaped in the English style comes to life with a carpet of rhododendrons in the spring and cyclamen in the autumn. In the hollow of a valley there is a group of chestnut trees dating from the time of Louis XIV. The park also has one of the earliest cedars of Lebanon in France, which may have been planted by Geneviève de Breteuil, lady-in-waiting to Queen Marie Antoinette.

A marked-out route passes by many ancient trees: oaks, American tulip trees, swamp cypresses, planes, and many others. Recently the park has been enhanced by new plantings on the Italian terraces, which were constructed in the seventeenth century. One of the terraces contains the Jardin des Princes and its collection of 300 plant varieties: hardy perennials, peonies, shrubs planted around a basin, and a pergola of roses. Since the year 2000 another terrace has been planted with a maze, made of thousands of box plants, reminiscent of the "visionary grove" that disappeared in the nineteenth century. The Château of Breteuil's remarkable trees, water features, glades, and Classical gardens make it a place of timeless charm. ML

Le Jardin du Palais Royal

Paris, France

DESIGNER: Claude Desgots
OWNER: Ministry of Culture
GARDEN STYLE: 17th- and 18th-century classical French
SIZE: 7 acres (3 ha)
CLIMATE: Temperate
LOCATION: Paris

The Palais Royal and its gardens could not be a more perfect representation of French classicism. To get the full impact, enter from the side street rather than from the main square next to the Comédie Française Theater. After passing through a dark arcade, you suddenly find yourself in a very grand space enclosed on three sides by identical buildings, about eight stories high above arcaded walkways. A colonnade leading on to a smaller inner courtyard closes the fourth side. This sense of order is reinforced by rows of immaculately clipped hornbeams, their dark trunks creating a parallel colonnade.

A circular pool at the center of the garden is flanked by two cultivated areas of colorful flowers within clipped hedges and fences. In summer this part of the garden is full of people sitting by the edge of the pool and its tall fountain. It has certainly had a very rich history from the seventeenth century, when the palace was built for Cardinal Richelieu, through to the eighteenth century, when it was redesigned by a nephew of André Le Nôtre. The garden became a meeting place for the great thinkers of the time and harbored the first stirrings of the French Revolution. Today the buildings around the inner courtyard house the Ministry of Culture and the Constitutional Council, while the courtyard is home to a permanent installation of black-and-white truncated columns by Daniel Buren. All these ingredients contribute to the continuous appeal of this stunning space. MO

Parc de Montsouris

Paris, France

DESIGNERS: Baron Haussmann, Adolphe Alphand
OWNER: City of Paris
GARDEN STYLE: 19th-century romantic
SIZE: 38 acres (15.4 ha)
CLIMATE: Temperate
LOCATION: Paris

Conceived as a place where Parisians could wander in the city, this green space was created during the reign of Napoleon III. Baron Haussmann was entrusted with the task of improving this insalubrious district, which was also infested with mice (*souris* in French), hence the name of the area. After the underground quarries and catacombs had been reinforced, the gardens finally opened to the public in 1878.

The garden's irregular layout, its large groups of trees and shrubs, and its broad avenues are typical of urban parks in the nineteenth century. Montsouris also has several large lawns, punctuated by groves of trees and shrubs. The railway lines that cross the park are concealed in a ravine hidden by luxuriant vegetation. The park has about 1,400 trees, several of them over 100 years old: oriental plane trees, ginkgo biloba, sequoias, and many others. In the middle of the park a manmade lake with an area of more than 2.5 acres (1 ha) provides a home for swans, coots, and ducks. The lake is fed by a cascade and an artificial stream, which provide welcome coolness in summer.

Montsouris has numerous sculptures scattered on the lawns and among the shrubs, including works by Henri Bouchard, Jules Coutan, and other artists. The park also houses the meteorological observatory, built in 1947; its obelisk marks the Paris meridian. A place of relaxation, ideal for strolling and nature-watching, the park has become one of the green treasures of the French capital. ML

Parc des Buttes Chaumont

Paris, France

DESIGNERS: Baron Haussmann, Adolphe Alphand
OWNER: City of Paris
GARDEN STYLE: 19th-century romantic baroque
SIZE: 61 acres (24.7 ha)
CLIMATE: Temperate
LOCATION: Paris

Often described as the most romantic park in Europe, this large urban space is remarkable in many ways. During the Universal Exhibition in Paris in 1867, the park opened on land bought by the city when Napoleon III had the very modern idea of bringing green spaces to the workers of the recently annexed area of Belleville. The task of designing a park was given to the famous Baron Haussmann, who was then reshaping Paris, with the engineer Adolphe Alphand. They took four years to create this new landscape.

Every element is artificial. The most spectacular is certainly the vast rocky cliff sculpted by dynamite, from which a dramatic 100-foot-high (30 m) waterfall plunges into a circular lake below. On top of the cliff is a replica of the Temple of the Sybil, located in Tivoli, Italy. All the steps, edgings, and walls are made of cement, another innovation, so that they resemble timber and rocks and give consistency to the whole design. As this park is meant for people to enjoy and admire nature, its 3 miles (5 km) of sinuous paths cross lawns and many wooded areas with unusual trees, from ginkgo and zelcova to a stately cedar of Lebanon (*Cedrus libani*). Boating to the island in the middle of the lake is a popular pastime, where 200 steps lead to the breathtaking viewing terrace at the top of the giant rock needle. A long suspension bridge and foot bridge (called the suicide bridge) soar 100 feet (30 m) above ground. For a city park, this is superb. MO

Le Jardin des Plantes

Paris, France

DESIGNER: Guy de la Brosse
OWNER: Muséum Nationale d'Histoire Naturelle
GARDEN STYLE: 17th- to 21st-century formal botanic
SIZE: 64 acres (25.9 ha)
CLIMATE: Temperate
LOCATION: Paris

The Jardin des Plantes, founded in 1635 by Guy de la Brosse, physician to Louis XIII, began life as a physic garden for the cultivation and study of medicinal herbs. Today, it is a huge botanical garden that houses the Muséum Nationale d'Histoire Naturelle (National Museum of Natural History) and contains a small zoo and an aquarium.

Le Jardin d'Iris et Vivaces (Iris and Perennials Garden), at its best in May, boasts 150 varieties of iris and more than 450 other species of hardy perennial. The botanical order beds are referred to as L'Ecole Botanique (Botanical School) and hold around 4,000 plant species of medicinal, culinary, commercial, and scientific interest. Le Roserie (Rose Garden) speaks for itself and is drenched with perfume throughout summer. Le Jardin Alpine (Alpine Garden) is a collection of more than 2,000 species from mountainous regions across the globe. Many remarkable trees are spread throughout the grounds. The most famous, a false acacia (*Robinia pseudoacacia*) from the U.S., survives from 1636.

La Serre Mexicaine (Mexican Greenhouse) maintains a hot and arid atmosphere perfect for sun-loving succulents. It was such a breakthrough in technology, when designed by Rohault de Fleury in 1836, that copies were built all around the world. Another, larger, greenhouse, the exquisite art deco Jardin d'Hiver (Winter Garden), recreates tropical rain forest conditions. Both greenhouses were closed for extensive restoration during 2004–06, but will carry the flag for a long while to come. RCa

Le Jardin du Luxembourg

Paris, France

DESIGNERS: Jacques Boyceau, Nicolas Deschamps,
Thomas Francini
OWNER: The French State
GARDEN STYLE: 17th- to 19th century French formal
SIZE: 55 acres (22 ha)
CLIMATE: Temperate
LOCATION: Paris

Extensive and elegant, lying in Paris' sixth arrondissement, the Jardin du Luxembourg is the perfect antidote to city life. This explains the large numbers of Parisians strolling or jogging beneath the shady walks and around the sculptures.

In 1612 Marie de Medici, wife of King Henry IV of France, built the palace. The garden had plantations, parterres, and waterworks installed, so that she could get away from court life and imagine she was back in Tuscany. From the mid-nineteenth century, as the Parisian boulevards grew, Luxembourg became one of the finest parks in Paris from the point of view of its layout, and the plants and sculptures it contained. The orangery, which was built in 1839 and extended fifty years later, is set off by no fewer than 180 exotically planted Versailles boxes containing oleander, pomegranates, oranges, and palms.

Grander parterres provide the setting for superb statuary, which was created between 1846 and 1850, and includes the queens and great ladies of France. The Fountains of the Medici feature a stone-edged mirror of water centered on an Italian-style grotto containing statues of Polypheme, Acis, and Galatee, the Young Faun, and *Diane the Huntress* by Auguste Ottin. Nearer to the Rue Medici is a copy of the *Dancing Faun from Pompeii* by Eugène Louis Lequesne. Also look out for Jules Dalou's bronze of Eugène Delacroix or his working of *The Triumph of Silène*, and magical views of other Parisian buildings, including the Pantheon. CH

Parc de la Villette

Paris, France

DESIGNERS: Alexandre Chemetoff, Daniel Buren,
Bernhard Leitner

OWNER: Éstablissement Public du Parc de la Villette

GARDEN STYLE: Late-20th century modern, abstract

SIZE: 0.7 acre (0.3 ha)

CLIMATE: Temperate

LOCATION: Paris

A competition to create a park on the grounds of Paris' ancient slaughterhouses was won in 1983 by the architect Bernard Tschumi, whose design approach followed the philosophical theory of deconstructivism. The result is a lively and popular space. Its layout is based on points, lines, and curves, with each of their twenty-six intersections marked by bright-red steel pavilions.

The striking Cinematic Promenade curves through a series of themed areas, from the Wind and Dune Garden to the Fog Garden, the Mirror Garden, and the Garden of Childhood Fears, each by a different designer. The Bamboo Garden by Alexandre Chemetoff sets industrial archaeology against a lush display of hundreds of bamboo varieties. A space has been excavated 16 feet (5 m) below ground to uncover a network of drains and pipes, which is incorporated into the design. A footbridge, saddling an enormous pipe, overlooks this mysterious enclave.

Steps down are edged by tiny cascades, with water channels and fountains everywhere. Simple black-and-white stone bands, by Daniel Buren, follow the length of the site, contrasting with the exuberance of the plants while keeping to the geometric theme. Their abstract order guides you through more multicolored, towering bamboos, until you discover a concrete cylinder designed by Bernhard Leitner. Inside is an acoustic chamber filled with the sounds of leaves, wind, and water. All in all, this garden is quite an extraordinary feat. MO

Parc de Bercy

Paris, France

DESIGNERS: Philippe Lecaisne, Ian Raguin
OWNER: City of Paris
GARDEN STYLE: 20th-century contemporary
SIZE: 34.5 acres (14 ha)
CLIMATE: Temperate
LOCATION: Paris

Created in 1995 on the site of the former Bercy wine depot to the east of Paris, the park has a resolutely contemporary appearance. However, a few traces of the past have been deliberately retained, such as the railway tracks that formerly linked the wine depot's cellars and warehouses.

The park consists of three gardens: the large meadow, the parterres or plant beds, and the romantic garden, situated on the other side of the footbridge from the depot, across Rue Joseph Kessel. To the west, the large meadow opens up onto a vast terrace punctuated by lime trees, overlooking the River Seine, and a large fountain-sculpture by the artist Gérard Singer. In the middle of the park are the parterres, consisting of nine themed gardens: the kitchen garden, vine arbors, rose garden, maze, perfumed garden, bulbs, orchard, observatory, and Maison de Jardinage ("House of Gardening"), a former tax office. This space displays the symbol of a season or an element: air, fire, earth, water, expressed by flowers with emblematic colours, such as white for winter and green for spring.

Situated to the east of the park is the romantic garden, which combines several elements: trees with interesting bark (birches and willows), and a valley with a variety of grasses, trees, and shrubs, with foliage providing welcome shade. A small manmade lake surrounds the Maison du lac (the lake house), which has been restored for the purpose of holding exhibitions. The Parc de Bercy has established itself as a garden full of life and character. ML

Parc André Citroën

Paris, France

DESIGNERS: Alain Provost, Gilles Clément, and others
OWNER: City of Paris
GARDEN STYLE: Late 20th-century postmodern eclectic
SIZE: 57 acres (23 ha)
CLIMATE: Temperate
LOCATION: Paris

This park in contemporary urban surroundings on the site of the old Citroën factory by the River Seine is the result of a landscape design competition and a fine example of postmodernist geometry. Even the rectangular lawn is bisected by a long, diagonal path.

Two impressive greenhouse pavilions, containing a Mediterranean garden and orange grove, are surrounded by a gently sloping plaza featuring blocks of magnolias, which have been pruned into columns that are spotlit at night. In front of the pavilions, the use of water and clipped plants echoes the French baroque style. One side of the lawn is edged by a canal—the Garden of Metamorphosis—with an elevated reflecting pool. Opposite, alongside a raised walkway with smaller cuboid pavilions, are six Sense Gardens, as well as areas themed around color. These include the White Garden and the Black Garden, which is full of dark foliage. In the Garden In Movement, grasses that respond to differing wind speeds have been planted, so that there is always something blowing about. In the Wild Garden, the overall geometric design relaxes into an informal mass of roses, poppies, bamboos, and foxgloves.

The park is packed with imaginative slants on familiar ideas, with rectangular lawns being laid at acute angles, low clipped hedges popping out of borders, and irises growing through grids of steel. One of the most spectacular sites is the entrance arch formed from two specimens of rarely planted *Sequoiadendron giganteum* 'Pendulum'. As parks go, few are as fun and as inventive as this one. MB

Parc de Bagatelle

Paris, France

DESIGNERS: Thomas Blaikie, Jean-Claude Nicolas Forestier
OWNER: City of Paris
GARDEN STYLE: 18th- to 21st-century English rose garden
SIZE: 59 acres (23.8 ha)
CLIMATE: Temperate
LOCATION: Paris

This was one of the first *jardins anglais* (English gardens). Its grounds were laid out in the late eighteenth century by the Scottish gardener Thomas Blaikie in association with François-Joseph Belanger, the architect who famously demolished the original hunting lodge and rebuilt it as an elaborate folly in less than three months for the Comte d'Artois. Ornamental construction in many styles punctuated the landscape, including a Gothic grotto, a Chinese bridge, a classical mausoleum, and a Temple of Love.

More or less spared during the French Revolution, Bagatelle became a restaurant in 1797 and then reverted to a hunting lodge under Napoleon. By 1905 it had fallen into neglect and was saved by Jean-Claude Nicolas Forestier, the commissioner of gardens for Paris. He redeveloped the site, saving what he could of the original and planting the formal rose beds for which Bagatelle is now chiefly renowned. Forestier largely created the garden as it is today. About 10,000 rose bushes representing more than 1,000 varieties are surrounded by low box hedging and grass. There are also significant displays of spring bulbs, peonies, irises, water lilies, and dahlias in early fall, followed by trees with colored foliage, then winter-flowering trees, shrubs, and snowdrops. A National Collection of clematis was established in 1992. Other delights include peacocks strutting across the lawns, massive koi carp in the lakes, and the annual international rose competition in June. There is no more delightful place in Paris to while away the hours on a sunny summer's day. RCa

Le Cimetière du Père-Lachaise

Paris, France

DESIGNER: Alexandre-Théodore Brongniart
OWNER: City of Paris
GARDEN STYLE: 19th-century formal
SIZE: 17 acres (6.8 ha)
CLIMATE: Temperate
LOCATION: Paris

Père-Lachaise Cemetery is no ordinary burial ground; it is more of an open-air museum. As the most prestigious of the city's twenty cemeteries, it receives two million visitors a year. With more than 5,000 trees spread across the site, Père-Lachaise is the largest "park" in Paris.

It takes its name from the onetime owner of the site, Père François de la Chaise d'Aix, Louis XIV's confessor. Alexandre Brongniart's plan combined formal straight avenues, a circular area planted with poplars, and a system of winding paths to cope with the sloping site. Its status was secured when Nicolas Frochot persuaded the city authorities to rebury well-known French citizens, among them Molière and La Fontaine, along with the original inhabitants, those formerly buried in churchyards of the fifth, seventh, and eighth arrondissements (administrative districts).

Père Lachaise became so popular that it had been enlarged five times by 1850, with a crematorium and wall memorial added at the end of the century. The oldest inhabitants are Abelard (1079–1141) and Héloise (1101–64). They were united here in 1817, the same year that Louis XVIII's remains were moved out to Saint-Denis, in a kind of celebrity plot swap. Other famous residents at Père-Lachaise include Sara Bernhardt, Frédéric Chopin, Edith Piaf, and Oscar Wilde. Since his mysterious death in Paris in 1971, the tomb of Jim Morrison, lead singer of The Doors, has particularly drawn large numbers of visitors.

Among the graves of the famous, there are plenty more of those whose fame has faded. However, the high-quality sculptures and outstanding memorials that mark their final resting places remain. RChi

> "…Père-Lachaise is the largest 'park' in Paris"

Parc Monceau

Paris, France

DESIGNERS: Thomas Blaikie, Louis Carrogis Carmontelle,
Gabriel Davioud, George Haussmann
OWNER: City of Paris
GARDEN STYLE: 18th- and 19th-century picturesque
SIZE: 12 acres (4.8 ha)
CLIMATE: Temperate
LOCATION: Paris

The Duke of Chartres, later Duke of Orleans, bought this land in 1769 with the intention of creating a grand, picturesque garden suitable for holding parties. Louis Carrogis Carmontelle drew up the first plans for a fantasy landscape with Gothic ruins, a ruined Temple of Mars, a minaret, Dutch mill, the extant Naumachie, a semicircular colonnade of Corinthian columns, and an Egyptian pyramid. After acquiring more land, he called in the fashionable Scottish landscaper Thomas Blaikie to design an English garden with a winter area and greenhouse.

In 1860 the park was taken over by the City of Paris. Baron Haussmann, assisted by the horticulturist Barillet-Deschamps and the architect Gabriel Davioud, tackled the site. Their work and the vestiges of the early landscaping are still intact. The main entrance is under a grand rotunda. Note the handkerchief tree (*Davidia involucrata*) straight ahead to your right and the four monumental gilded entrance gates. The park is peopled by monuments to writers, musicians, and composers, including Guy de Maupassant, Gounoud, Frédéric Chopin, and Alfred de Musset.

Apart from the main paths, there are sinuous smaller routes over rustic bridges, around the lake and streams, and under some fine trees. Spring bulbs enliven the park, as does excellent fall color. Exit by the Avenue Ruysdael, noting the mature paulownias, silver-leaved limes, and gleditsia. Visit the nearby Musée Nissim de Camondo to get an idea of affluent Parisian life in the mid-twentieth century. CH

Les Jardins des Tuileries

Paris, France

DESIGNERS: André Le Nôtre, Jacques Wirtz, Louis Benech, Pascal Cribier, François Roubaud

OWNER: City of Paris

GARDEN STYLE: 18th-century formal French, contemporary

SIZE: 74 acres (29.9 ha)

CLIMATE: Temperate

LOCATION: Paris

Sitting in the Tuilerie Gardens on one of the 3,000 green metal chairs or on a double wooden bench is a quintessentially Parisian experience. It is not difficult to realize why this very open garden in the middle of the city, bordered by a busy road, is such a magnet.

It is an immaculately ordered garden, structured by wide, gravel-covered avenues, some bordered by tall trees, with statues everywhere. Along the length of the gardens, steps lead to raised terraces. The one overlooking the River Seine has views of the orangery, built in 1851, which was adapted to house eight large panels of Claude Monet's *Water Lilies* series. On the other side, along the Rue de Rivoli, stands the famous Jeu de Paume Gallery, where the first democratic assembly took place in 1789, marking the beginning of the French Revolution. The Tuileries Palace, now destroyed, where Louis XVI and Marie Antoinette had taken refuge, was stormed by the Parisians in 1792, heralding the end of the monarchy.

In spite of these dark memories, the park is peaceful and works extremely well as a public space where beautifully restored, seventeenth-century sculptures can be admired along with works by Rodin, Henry Moore, and Giacometti. New features include majestic yew edges radiating from the Arc de Triomphe du Carrousel, generous borders, raised lawns, trees, and a water basin. The immense axis running from the Louvre to the Arc de Triomphe goes through the gardens, creating one of the most breathtaking urban perspectives in the world. MO

Les Jardins de Kerdalo

Bretagne, France

DESIGNER: Prince Peter Wolkonsky
OWNER: Isabelle Vaughan
GARDEN STYLE: 20th-century Arts and Crafts
SIZE: 44 acres (18 ha)
CLIMATE: Temperate
LOCATION: Trédarzec, Bretagne

The Russian aristocrat Prince Peter Wolkonsky spent over thirty years working and reworking his Breton masterpiece, which is now looked after by his daughter, Isabelle. It is little wonder that this is often called a fairy-tale garden. Nestled into a hillside overlooking the River Jaudy, it is famed for its interplay of light and shade, of water and stone, and for the quite extraordinary quality and variety of the plantsmanship.

When he took over the property, Wolkonsky rerouted water from a nearby spring and it now flows under the Chinese pavilion into the formal canal. The oriental theme is echoed by flanking rhododendrons and magnolias. Next the pergola curves around the lower sunken garden and looks out toward a spectacular, massive bank of hydrangeas. The two pavilions at the outer corners of the lower garden can barely be seen under cascades of *Wisteria floribunda* 'Macrobotrys' and clematis.

After stepping back up from the lower garden, you will find a small arboretum with over 50 varieties of magnolia, witch hazels, and azaleas. Appropriately, the Fountain of Saint-Fiacre, the patron saint of gardeners, is found along the path to the large pond. That is followed by the cascade into a substantial bog garden with giant gunnera, bamboos, shade-loving lysichytum, and ferns. As with all the thousands of plants at Kerdalo, these are superb specimens collected from all corners of the globe.

This is one of the best gardens in France and is definitely worth a visit. CH

Le Jardin du Bâtiment

Pays de la Loire, France

DESIGNER: William Christie
OWNER: William Christie
GARDEN STYLE: Formal 17th-century French
SIZE: 20 acres (8.1 ha)
CLIMATE: Temperate
LOCATION: Thiré, Pays de la Loire

There is little about the flat landscape around the village of Thiré to hint at the treasure it conceals in the garden of Le Bâtiment, home of the well-known Franco-American conductor and harpsichordist William Christie. When entering from the modest side entrance of the building, one is greeted by a breathtaking parterre de broderie in box, outlined by crushed brick. The lush green of the box and the dark red of the brick harmonize with the white facade of the elegant house. In spring, large urns of tulips, followed by summer pots of succulents, punctuate the formal rhythms of the parterre.

Christie rescued the house, built in the early 1600s, from centuries of neglect and created the garden from surrounding barren fields. The garden is a sensitive evocation, rather than a slavish recreation, of a garden of the period. It is a garden of contrasts in which the sober formality is lightened, for example, by a green area extravagantly sculpted in yew.

At the rear of the house, one can appreciate the scope and grandeur of Christie's creation. A formal enclosure of hornbeam and braided lime contains yew topiary. Beyond this, on a central axis stretching far into the distance, a small river has been diverted into a formal basin—a mirror to reflect the ever-changing sky. The tranquillity is broken only by the murmur of a small fountain in the nearby cloister garden. Christie discovered his garden's seventeenth-century dovecote in the path of a new road, had it dismantled stone by stone and reassembled in the garden. It is just one of the many clever touches. JHo

Le Potager Extraordinaire

Pays de la Loire, France

DESIGNER: Michel Rialland
OWNER: Le Potager Extraordinaire
GARDEN STYLE: 20th-century potager
SIZE: 2.5 acres (1 ha)
CLIMATE: Temperate
LOCATION: La Mothe-Achard, Pays de la Loire

If vegetables are your passion, then this is the place for you. You will never find so many assembled in one place, and none so curious.

What began ten years ago with Michel Rialland's passion for cucurbits (the melon, cucumber, marrow, pumpkin, and gourd family) has grown into an astonishing collection of edible and useful plants sourced from specialists and botanical gardens all over the world. The garden contains plants you have never heard of, in unimaginable combinations of shape, texture, and color. In its sixteen themed areas, you can see everything from a model organic vegetable garden and edible wildflowers to African peanuts and forty varieties of tomato. There's even a corner for the truly bizarre—the square pea, the exploding gherkin, and the oyster plant.

The best time to visit is from August onward, when even the most blasé teenager will be excited by the 200-foot-long (60 m) gourd tunnel, in which some twenty-five varieties from the Americas, Africa, and Asia hang suspended in the air. From the smallest child to the tallest adult, everyone will come eye to eye with curiously beautiful shapes and textures that you are actually encouraged to touch.

Children love the 3-foot-long (90 cm) snake gourd, complete with coils and stripes. Harry Potter fans will head for the Wizard's Garden, which has a real mandrake, belladonna, and henbane. Grown-ups can come away with a list of weird vegetables to be grown at home to entertain their dinner guests. There are also seeds for sale here. VR

Le Château du Pin

Pays de la Loire, France

DESIGNER: Gerard Gignoux
OWNER: SCI Château du Pin
GARDEN STYLE: Early 20th-century formal, parkland
SIZE: 300 acres (121.5 ha)
CLIMATE: Temperate
LOCATION: Champtocé-sur-Loire, Pays de la Loire

Away from the main tourist trail, the gardens of the Château du Pin have an undiscovered quality. A square stone tower is all that remains of the twelfth-century castle that has experienced a cycle of destruction and rebuilding over the centuries. The present eighteenth- and nineteenth-century Gothic architecture provides a wonderfully romantic backdrop to a descending series of formal terraced gardens that seamlessly merge with the surrounding countryside. Designed by Gerard Gignoux, who purchased the property in 1921, the gardens have a surprisingly sheltered and intimate feel.

Immaculately clipped yews are a signature of the château. In one of the pool gardens, topiary figures, including chess pieces crowding at the water's edge, create an *Alice in Wonderland* touch. The topiary's quirky styling contrasts with the rigid, geometric forms found in French renaissance gardens.

Next to the orangery is a dining terrace with terracotta pots filled with citrus, banana, avocado, and date trees. The Mediterranean influence is present in the billowing aromatic herbs and fragrant flowers that spill over the garden's stone paving. The plantings are often themed and include a yellow rose garden with lavender and acanthus, a delphinium garden, and a sage collection. The Persian garden is built around a long pool with two stepped cascades. Linking the wild woods with the formal gardens is a yew walk, an impressive avenue of topiary that lines up with the château's main entrance. The château is not open to the public, but the gardens are. JHe

Parc Oriental de Maulévrier

Pays de la Loire, France

DESIGNER: Alexandre Marcel
OWNER: Commune de Maulévrier
GARDEN STYLE: 19th-century oriental
SIZE: 30 acres (12 ha)
CLIMATE: Oceanic
LOCATION: Maulévrier, Pays de la Loire

Situated in Cholet in Maine-et-Loire, the oriental garden of Maulévrier was inspired by the Japanese Edo gardens of the seventeenth to nineteenth centuries. The gardens occupy part of the old estate of Château Colbert, owned by Louis XIV's famous minister. Acquired in 1895 by the industrialist Eugène Bergère, the estate was restored by the architect Alexandre Marcel, builder of the "Pagoda" in Paris.

Marcel laid out the gardens and set out to design a Japanese landscape centered round a lake with a deliberately exaggerated shoreline and islands. The water beautifully reflects the shades of the flowers and foliage of the many exotic trees, among them Japanese maple, Chinese larch, and catalpas. Subtle in spring and green in summer, the colors become vibrant in the fall. The water is like a silver ribbon leading the visitor through the gardens, starting from a small spring that symbolizes birth. Streams and cascades evoke the ups and downs of youth, eventually leading to the serenity of the lake, punctuated by landing stages, rocks, bridges, and a Khmer temple. This building was constructed for the Universal International Exhibition of 1900, as were the many sculptures representing figures of the temple of Angkor Wat in Cambodia.

Abandoned for forty years, the gardens were bought by the commune of Maulévrier in 1980, restored in their original style, and named the Parc oriental. A combination of exoticism and serenity, the landscape of Maulévrier's oriental gardens constantly changes with the passing of the seasons. ML

Château de Beauregard

Centre, France

DESIGNER: Gilles Clement
OWNER: Comtesse du Pavillon
GARDEN STYLE: 16th- to 18th-century French, postmodern
SIZE: 173 acres (70 ha)
CLIMATE: Temperate
LOCATION: Cellettes, Centre

Centuries of changing fashions can be traced in the evolution of this park, its buildings, and its gardens. In 1543 the château was acquired by Jean du Thiers, controller of finances to Henri II and a great plant collector. In 1551 about 1,500 rare plants and trees such as oaks, elms, beeches, hollies, and walnuts were recorded growing at Beauregard. In the seventeenth century, Paul Ardier planted a grand allée of fruit trees and created a paneled gallery of 327 portraits in the château. In the nineteenth century, the park surrounding Beauregard was restyled as an English garden. It survives today as informal parkland with grassy swards interspersed with clumps of trees in the style of an eighteenth-century English landscape as opposed to the intricacies of the French style.

In 1992 Beauregard was listed as a Historic Monument, marking the start of extensive renovation by the Comte and Comtesse du Pavillon. The Garden of Colors was created in the former kitchen garden by Gilles Clement. Inspired by Ardier's gallery, Clement has created living portraits in white-, black-, green-, pink-, blue-, red-, yellow-, orange-, and violet-flowering drifts. The twelve sections of paintings in the Great Gallery are mirrored in the dozen garden "rooms" filled with over 400 species of perennial. The rooms are divided by clipped hornbeam. The walls are smothered in clematis, honeysuckle, hops, ivies, jasmine, vines, passionflowers, and wisterias. Tucked under the trees is a romantic ruined chapel dedicated to the owner's husband, Comte Alain du Pavillon. Take a moment for peace and contemplation. CH

Château de Chenonceau

Centre, France

DESIGNERS: Philibert de l'Orme, Jacques Androuet du Cerceau, Henri Duchêne, Achille Duchêne
OWNER: Gaston Menier
GARDEN STYLE: 16th-century French renaissance
SIZE: 4 acres (1.6 ha)
CLIMATE: Temperate
LOCATION: Chenonceaux, Centre

Appropriately surrounded by ancient hunting woods, the domain of Chenonceau was given by Henri II to his mistress, Diane de Poitiers, in 1547. In early French renaissance style, her rectangular garden is a massive, separate, self-contained unit visible from, but not in symmetry with, the château. Today the quadripartite layout is decorated with gentle scrolls of santolina hedges punctuated by hibiscus and bedding plants. The broad perimeter levée offers views both across the river and into the simply patterned parterre. Philibert de l'Orme, who designed the Château d'Anet

for Diane, built a bridge to link the château to the far bank of the Cher.

After Henri's death in 1559, his wife, Catherine of Medici, demanded Chenonceau, where she hosted "magnificences" with elaborate fireworks, masques, and water spectacles. In 1563 the royal party came up the tree-lined avenue to be met by singing sirens who were answered by wood nymphs. Satyrs entered and tried to carry off the nymphs, who were rescued by knights. The Catherine de Medici garden today is a modest version of the original. A two-story gallery above the bridge provides a cool sanctuary.

Chenonceau later lapsed into obscurity, although the avenue that leads to the bridge inspired Jean-Jacques Rousseau to write *The Avenue de Sylvie*. In the nineteenth century, the Menier family commissioned Henri Duchêne and his son, Achille, to restore the gardens. The kitchen garden improves every year, and the orangery operates as a restaurant. CH

Festival des Jardins de Chaumont–sur–Loire

Centre, France

DESIGNERS: Jacques Wirtz (site); various show designers
OWNER: Conservatoire International des Parcs
· et Jardins
GARDEN STYLE: 20th- and 21st-century experimental
SIZE: 7.4-acre (2.9-ha) showground
CLIMATE: Temperate
LOCATION: Chaumont-sur-Loire, Centre

Every year from May to October, 150,000 visitors flock to a nineteenth-century château in the Loire Valley to be amused, inspired, provoked, sometimes appalled, and often baffled. The International Garden Festival of Chaumont-sur-Loire was established in 1992 by Jean-Paul Pigeat with the aims of restoring gardening to the realms of art, and introducing the public to imaginative and innovative new design.

Jacques Wirtz, a contemporary designer, created a site for the show, using a design inspired by the tulip tree (*Liriodendron tulipifera*). Undulating avenues correspond to the branches of the tree. The thirty show gardens are in leaf-shaped enclosures, hedged in by beech or hornbeam.

There is a woodland walk; a ravine garden that mimics a misty, jungle valley; a magnificently restored greenhouse; and the curious Experimental Garden, where eye-popping plant combinations are presided over by a giant yew rabbit. Each year's show gardens share a theme, such as vegetables, water, weeds, eroticism, or memory. Unlike the confections at London's Chelsea Flower Show, these gardens change and grow throughout the summer, and some are retained for several years. As well as wild flights of fancy, scientific exploration, humor, and social commentary, visitors see garden ideas that actually work. So whether it is a flying duck in carpet bedding that inspires you, water-squirting benches, or a vegetable garden in a suitcase, you will leave with an invigorating sense of what is possible. AE

Arboretum National des Barres

Centre, France

DESIGNERS: Philippe André de Vilmorin,
   Maurice de Vilmorin
OWNER: The Ministry of Agriculture
GARDEN STYLE: 19th-century botanical
SIZE: 86. 5 acres (35 ha)
CLIMATE: Temperate
LOCATION: Nogent-sur-Vernisson, Centre

Whether you are a landscape professional, a novice, or just someone interested in the conservation of the environment, this arboretum is a must. Established nearly 200 years ago on the property of the famous family of plantsmen, De Vilmorin, it opened to the public in 1985. This invaluable site, also called "A Forest from Five Continents," is divided into three areas. In the Geographic Collection, started in 1873, you will see some remarkable trees from 164-foot-tall (50 m) sequoias, a giant purple beech (*Fagus sylvatica* Atropurpurea Group), and a *Ginkgo biloba*, to the startling snake-bark acer (*Acer capillipes*) and monkey puzzle tree (*Araucaria araucana*).

In spring the Systematic Collection, started in 1894, seduces the senses with the scents of wisterias, magnolias, and honeysuckles; the colors of rhododendrons; and the spectacular drooping white bracts of the handkerchief tree (*Davidia involucrata*). The scents of lime blossom and viburnums make the summer visit magical, while the fiery colors of fall and the carpets of tiny cyclamens offer extra delights.

In the Ornamental Collection, marvel at oddities like a thuja with eighty trunks, a corkscrew hazel (*Corylus avellana* 'Contorta'), weeping cedars, and creeping conifers. Also look out for the flourishing numbers of flora and fauna. There are twenty different types of wild orchid in the forest; two are extremely rare and worth searching for in early spring. MO

Château de la Bourdaisière

Centre, France

DESIGNER: Prince Louis-Albert de Broglie
OWNERS: Prince Louis-Albert de Broglie,
   Prince Maurice-Philippe de Broglie
GARDEN STYLE: 16th-century Italianate, 19th-century walled
SIZE: 100 acres (40.50 ha)
CLIMATE: Temperate
LOCATION: Montlouis-sur-Loire, Centre

This renaissance château was built on the site of Maréchal Boucicault's fourteenth-century fortress by the Babou family, one of whom, Marie Gaudin, became mistress of King François I. Her great-granddaughter, Gabrielle d'Estrées, was born here and lived in the château. Gabrielle, in turn, became the mistress of Henri IV. Further architectural changes were made to the château by the Duc de Luynes and the Duc de Choiseul, who destroyed part of the building to obtain materials to use in his own estate. In 1795 La Bourdaisière was rebuilt. Finally, in 1840, Baron Angelier commissioned the construction of a facade in the renaissance style.

Today it is set in a huge park with a sixteenth-century, Tuscan-style pavilion and a nineteenth-century walled garden. The terraces around the house provide a good viewing platform, and there is an ornate arch on the Italian terrace designed by Leonardo da Vinci. The restored kitchen and herb gardens include 400 varieties of tomato (described as tiny marbles, great golden hearts, and little pears), 100 of lettuce, and twenty of basil. The greenhouse is bulging with different plants. Note that the kitchen gardens are at their most interesting from August to October, when tasting sessions can be organized. You must also visit the shop because it stocks an excellent range of seeds. The owner has high-end gardening shops in Paris and London. CH

Parc Botanique du Prieuré d'Orchaise

Centre, France

DESIGNER: Hubert Treuille
OWNER: Hubert Treuille
GARDEN STYLE: 20th-century botanical, informal
SIZE: 7.5 acres (3 ha)
CLIMATE: Temperate
LOCATION: Orchaise, Centre

This award-winning garden is situated on the side of a hill overlooking the river in the Cisse Valley. It belongs to Hubert Treuille, a widely traveled amateur botanist, who has gathered a collection of more than 2,000 plants from around the world.

A visit begins with the Grand Esplanade, which has straight paths edged by wide beds full of flowering shrubs. These are punctuated by rows of clipped, cylindrical yew, leading to a semicircular terrace edged with more yew. This whole area competes with a gigantic cedar at one end, which acts as an entrance to the less formal part of the garden. The path then leads to a lily pool and a terrace with views to the rock garden, a birch wood, and a modern sculpture. Farther on are trees and shrubs, including magnolias, flowering cherries, an area dedicated to rhododendrons and Japanese acers, then crab apples, heathers, and shrubs, with crinodendrons and American cornus. A second pool offers visitors a chance to rest before taking in the collection of roses and the potager. Alternatively, take a walk through fields of sheep with uninterrupted rural views to the forest. The Romanesque tower of an ancient monastery adds a historic touch. MO

> "This award-winning garden is...
> a collection of more than 2,000
> plants from around the world"

La Chatonnière

Centre, France

DESIGNER: Béatrice de Andia

OWNER: Béatrice de Andia

GARDEN STYLE: 20th- and 21st-century renaissance

SIZE: 17 acres (7 ha)

CLIMATE: Temperate

LOCATION: Azay-le-Rideau, Centre

Paris historian Béatrice de Andia inherited from her father this small renaissance château overlooking the Indre River and the forest of Chinon. In the hundred years before 1950, when he bought the château, it had been bought and sold twenty times. Then, in 1980, with failing agriculture, the apple orchards were razed and the house was left, in effect, in a farmyard.

In 1992 Madame de Andia's dream to create a series of gardens was given momentum when Robert Carvallo of Villandry (see page 605) recommended the services of his gardener of twenty years, Ahmed Azéroual. Béatrice described the result of this partnership as, "Secret and colorful, the nine gardens of La Chatonnière give impressions, provoke awakenings of the soul. As you walk the circuit, they symbolize, one by one, Elegance, the Senses, Silence, Intelligence, the Sciences, Improbability, Abundance, Exuberance, and Romance." The concepts and execution are fresh and exciting.

The best gardens include the Senses (created in 1996), with its 150 varieties of perfumed perennial in a box-edged parterre. Abundance (created in 2000) is laid out in the shape of a leaf whose veins act as paths. They are all edged by low box hedging and filled with massed herbs or vegetables. Snaking over the slope above Abundance is Improbability (1999), shaded by a lengthy pergola that leads away to the meadows. Silence (1997) is an inner court viewed from above with simple box hedging. All in all, it is a novel garden with a rich range of designs, based on an extremely clever idea. CH

"…the nine gardens of La Chatonnière give impressions, provoke awakenings of the soul"

Château de Chamerolles

Centre, France

DESIGNERS: Brigitte Barbier, Thierry Gilson, Jacques Moulin
OWNER: The Council General of Loiret
GARDEN STYLE: 20th-century French renaissance
SIZE: 368 acres (149 ha)
CLIMATE: Temperate
LOCATION: Chilleurs-aux-Bois, Centre

Chamerolles, on the northern perimeter of the Loire region, was built by Lancelot I of the Lake in the fifteenth century. In the seventeenth century, it became a bastion of new Protestant thought. Since 1988, the château and gardens have been magnificently recreated in a renaissance style inspired by the drawings of Jacques Androuet du Cerceau.

The two large, architecturally imposing trellised and galleried arbors that border the garden give a true sense of the scale—and the seclusion and intimacy—of early renaissance gardens. The arbors are gradually being turned green by hornbeam, and there are vines, sweetly scented honeysuckle, and hops on the trellises. The garden is divided by a low trellis into squares with an obelisk in the middle. The yew maze aims to take the eye or body on a spiritual journey to the beech tree at its center. A flowery square with turf seats has medieval echoes. There is also an open knot with arabesques of herbs, a rare plants square echoing an early renaissance physic garden, and two pot herb or vegetable squares. Farther away, a series of sinuous paths cross streams, giving a long, clear view to the fairy-tale pointed towers that top the moated château.

The Loiret region is famous for its perfume industry. In recognition of this, a "Walk through the history of perfumes" has been created within the château. This, in turn, refers back to the scented plants in the gardens. CH

Parc de la Pagode de Chanteloup

Centre, France

DESIGNER: Louis-Denis Le Camus
OWNER: Thierre André
GARDEN STYLE: Picturesque
SIZE: 35 acres (14 ha)
CLIMATE: Temperate
LOCATION: Amboise, Centre

Chanteloup's pagoda and its lake are the sole survivors of a great domain belonging to the Duke of Choiseul, minister to Louis XV. Following Choiseul's fall from power between 1775 and 1778, and the French Revolution of 1789, the Count of Chaptal took possession. However, he was forced to sell it in 1823 to a merchant who gradually destroyed the château and gardens, which were once compared to Versailles (see page 570). All that remained were the pagoda, lakes, forest avenues, and, of course, the views to Amboise across the Loire Valley. The park is also known as the Jardin de Chanteloup.

In 1907, the land was bequeathed by Princess Clementine d'Orléans to the landscape architect René Edouard-André, who ensured its survival. Today, Thierre André has made a visit to the pagoda an enjoyable experience and in many respects put the humor back into the garden. The garden has thirty different traditional eighteenth-century games to test your skills, played either individually or in groups. You can also climb the seven floors of the pagoda or take a boat trip around the half-moon pool. CH

"The garden has thirty different traditional eighteenth–century games to test your skills…"

Château du Rivau

Centre, France

DESIGNERS: Eric Laigneau, Patricia Laigneau
OWNERS: Eric Laigneau, Patricia Laigneau
GARDEN STYLE: Contemporary, with medieval references
SIZE: 15 acres (6 ha)
CLIMATE: Temperate
LOCATION: Lémeré, Centre

The first sight of the gleaming white château, with its pointed, slate roofs emerging from rows of vines in the gentle countryside of the Loire Valley, is straight out of a fairy tale. Built in the fifteenth and sixteenth centuries, this is a unique example of medieval architecture restored with passion by the owners, Eric and Patricia Laigneau. They are greatly interested in the art of the garden, and have created a contemporary space divided into twelve areas full of references to medieval legends and literature.

You can visit the gargantuan potager with its giant vegetables, admire ancient roses in the Secret Garden, learn how to make love potions in Lovers' Wood, wonder whom you might meet in the Enchanted Forest, be amazed by the Carpet of 1,000 Flowers and the stunning Lavender Knot Garden, while making sure not to get lost along Tom Thumb's trail. Elves and ogres spring up everywhere, some made out of flowerpots and old garden tools. Shrubs and trees have been trained in extraordinary shapes, and woven chestnut fences evoke forgotten skills. Another unique feature is the collection of ancient vines using old methods of cultivation. Every year, the owners invite an artist to create a work relating to the gardens. "The Running Forest," "The Nest," and "The Sphere" have all raised questions about the environment, provided new places to sit, or created new angles from which to view the garden. Most of all, they add a contemporary idiom to this extraordinary place that takes so much of its inspiration from a mythical past. *MO*

Le Jardin d'André Eve

Centre, France

DESIGNER: André Eve
OWNERS: Société des Roses Anciennes, André Eve
GARDEN STYLE: 21st-century historic rose garden
SIZE: 0.75 acre (3,000 sq m)
CLIMATE: Temperate
LOCATION: Morailles, Centre

Driven by his passion for old roses, André Eve has revived and re-established many cultivars that have been falling into oblivion, roses that he says made "our grandmothers and great-grandmothers dream" with their fragrance and delicate beauty. 'Blanc double de Coubert', 'Belle Poitevine', 'Louise Odier', 'Westerland', 'Fée des Neiges', 'Penelope', and many others appear in his list of favorite shrub roses. Among the climbing roses, Eve has selected some favorites such as 'Ghislaine de Féligonde', 'Sourire d'Orchidée', 'Blush noisette', 'Phyllis Bide', and 'Maréchal Niel'. The roses clamber over pergolas and fences everywhere in the garden. Eve has himself bred several attractive cultivars; one of these he has named 'Red Parfum'.

André Eve created this enchanted garden and its magnificent floral display some twenty years ago, close to his nursery. It is completely different from traditional rose gardens in that Eve has used circles and soft curves to express what he sees as the femininity of the rose. He has planted more than 500 varieties of old roses, plus other unusual varieties of more recent origin. Eve believes that roses appear more beautiful growing alongside other plants than on their own, so his rose bushes rub shoulders with shrubs, and bulbs and perennials thrive in the gaps between them. As for climbing roses, he often grows them intertwined with clematis so that on their pedestals each can highlight the other. ML

Château d'Ainay-le-Vieil

Centre, France

DESIGNER: Marie-Sol de la Tour d'Auvergne
OWNERS: d'Aligny family
GARDEN STYLE: 17th-century enclosed gardens
SIZE: 17 acres (7 ha)
CLIMATE: Temperate
LOCATION: Ainay-le-Vieil, Centre

Pleasingly composed of contrasting areas, the park of Ainay-le-Vieil has a delightful atmosphere. The several enclosed, walled gardens date from the seventeenth century and give the grounds a special personality. The feudal château, which is still inhabited, faces two seventeenth-century pavilions, from where the visitor passes over a stone bridge spanning the canal. The peaceful water soon inspires a mood of contemplation, as does the nineteenth-century park, which contains some remarkable trees including catalpas, cedars of Lebanon, and cypresses.

The successive walled gardens, restored twenty years ago, are devoted in turn to English herbaceous borders, a sculpted orchard, a meditation garden, a cloister of medicinal plants, and embroidery patterns formed with box. The entrance to the orchard consists of an alley crowned by hoops of pear trees and carpeted with roses. Within the meditation garden and its wall of living willow, a fresco shows St. Francis of Assisi talking to the birds; the woven hedge encloses a parterre of box and germanders as well as some yew topiary. Surrounded by a path, the medieval garden consists of a series of arcades linked by lime trees trained in vaults. The next walled garden pays tribute to Pomona, goddess of fruit trees, gardens, and orchards, with a statue of the goddess crowned with flowers. Finally, there is a collection of old roses, not to be missed at the end of spring when their form and scent are at their finest. ML

Parc Floral d'Apremont

Centre, France

DESIGNER: Gilles de Brissac
OWNER: Mme de Brissac
GARDEN STYLE: 20th-century informal
SIZE: 12 acres (4.8 ha)
CLIMATE: Temperate
LOCATION: Apremont-sur-Allier, Centre

Part of the experience of visiting this lovely park is going through the medieval village of Apremont, built around a towering château and classified as one of the "most beautiful villages in France." Restored with great care in the early twentieth century, it is an enchanting stage set with wonderful buildings.

The gardens were designed by the well-known landscaper Gilles de Brissac. The ancient houses, covered with clematis and climbing roses, now emerge from exuberant flower beds. Huge bunches of white wisteria cover a 300-foot-long (90 m) tunnel, echoing the white flowers of an imposing albizia.

Several follies are dotted around. The belvedere, of Russian inspiration, is decorated with glazed panels. The pagoda bridge crosses an artificial lake created by damming a local river. The Turkish Pavilion evokes the splendors of the Ottoman Empire.

A spectacular cascade was built in one of the quarries that originally occupied the site. It looks completely natural thanks to judicious planting of groundcover plants, ferns, and blue irises. Many interesting trees and shrubs are found in the garden, notably a metasequoia, some extraordinary crab apples, deutzias, a *Cornus alternifolia*, amelanchiers, and a group of stunning *Nyssa sylvatica*. The crowning glory is the white garden, inspired by Vita Sackville-West's garden at Sissinghurst in Kent (see page 370). With evergreen hedges, sharply clipped pyramids of box, and a profuse collection of white-flowering herbaceous and silver-leaved plants, it adds an elegant formality to this part of the garden. MO

Jardins du Prieuré d'Orsan

Centre, France

DESIGNERS: Patrice Taravella, Sonia Lesot
OWNERS: Patrice Taravella, Sonia Lesot
GARDEN STYLE: 20th-century enclosed medieval gardens
SIZE: 5 acres (2 ha)
CLIMATE: Temperate
LOCATION: Maisonnais, Centre

When an architect and a stage designer fell in love with this ancient priory, they brought the buildings back to life and teamed up with a gardener to create gardens of great beauty. Taking their inspiration from the study of medieval miniatures and avoiding slavish reconstruction, they gave the new garden a strong spiritual and symbolic character. The space reserved for meditation and prayer, traditionally enclosed within the U-shape of the buildings, lent itself perfectly to this purpose. Grass paths divide this central core into four squares of grape vines, symbolizing the four rivers of paradise, with a central fountain. Fields of broad beans and wheat create a spectacular, unexpected parterre. Eight arbors mark entrances to more enclosed gardens that glorify earthly abundance or symbolize virtues.

You can wander through the garden of medicinal herbs, the orchard, the olive grove, the vegetable garden laid out as a labyrinth, the green cloister with its beech arches covered in clematis and wisteria, or the rose garden. The most memorable features, though, are the structures used to separate spaces, train fruit trees, create fragrant seats covered in thyme, or edge raised beds overflowing with cucumbers and pumpkins. The garden is punctuated by an array of chestnut branches, either beautifully woven or used for support in various geometric patterns, creating vertical accents, diagonal lines, heart shapes against walls, or circles within arbors. The design is immensely satisfying and succeeds in reinterpreting a centuries-old tradition. MO

Jardins du Prieuré de Saint-Cosme

Centre, France

DESIGNER: Service des Jardins d'Indre et Loire
OWNER: General Council of Indre and Loire
GARDEN STYLE: 20th-century medieval, renaissance
SIZE: 5 acres (2 ha)
CLIMATE: Temperate
LOCATION: La Riche, Centre

This monastery, built on an island in the Loire River, owes its fame to Pierre de Ronsard, one of its priors in the sixteenth century and an illustrious poet.

These modern gardens, built around the ruins of the monastery, are a homage to Ronsard, whose tomb is ornamented by roses on a lawn. Inspired by the walled "rooms" of medieval gardens and the tapestry parterres of renaissance gardens, it is divided into eight spaces and is stepped over three terraces.

The Pink Garden has three parterres edged with box and filled with iris, followed by roses in front of an ancient box tree. The Cut Flower Garden spills over with tulips and dahlias next to the more formal Francis Poulenc Garden, where annuals enhance standard roses inside the shelter of a hornbeam hedge. Farther along, the Androuet du Cerceau Garden evokes motifs drawn by the fifteenth-century architect, with more roses and herbaceous plants in pastel tones. The Velvet Garden presents rows of fruit trees trained in cordons and espaliers around a pergola covered with climbing roses and grape vines. On the lower terrace, borders of lavender delineate the Cloister Garden, which is enclosed by banks covered in creeping juniper and backed by cypresses. There is an immaculately maintained potager and a grassy orchard planted with fruit trees trained into cones. This garden successfully mixes historic and contemporary references. Once a year it hosts a festival dedicated to roses. MO

Parc Floral de la Source

Centre, France

DESIGNERS: Various private owners, town planners, designers
OWNER: Public Authority of Gestion
GARDEN STYLE: Mid to late-20th-century eclectic, botanic
SIZE: 86.5 acres (35 ha)
CLIMATE: Temperate
LOCATION: Orléans, Centre

When this huge park was acquired by the city of Orléans, it was divided to accommodate a new town and a park that would showcase regional horticulture. The original château and parterres are now surrounded by beautiful gardens.

Visit at the end of spring and you will never forget the extraordinary Iris Garden, the National Collection with 1,000 varieties blooming in vast sweeps or in contained arrangements and exuding the most delicate scent. The Rose Garden, in the axis of the château and its pool, has symbols of love and passion in colors from pink to red, and white for innocence. Climbing varieties are displayed on pergolas and trellises. The Extraordinary Potager sheltered behind a 100-foot-long (30 m) "wave" of multicolored woven willow is truly remarkable, while the dazzling Dalhia Garden has beds edged in woven willow.

The mysterious Jardin de la Source contains the source of the River Loiret, and spray from the bubbling spring bathes the surrounding area in a fine mist. The Butterfly House recreates a tropical forest, and a delicate metallic mesh hung between trees creates an aviary. All in all, this park has a very impressive, very grand vision. MO

"...you will never forget the extraordinary Iris Garden..."

Villandry

Centre, France

DESIGNER: Joachim Carvallo
OWNERS: The Carvallo family
GARDEN STYLE: 20th-century formal renaissance garden
SIZE: Formal gardens 12 acres (5 ha)
CLIMATE: Temperate
LOCATION: Villandry, Centre

In the nineteenth century, many formal French gardens were destroyed to make way for the informality of the English landscape garden. As the twentieth century dawned, the pendulum of garden fashion swung back in favor of geometric exactitude. In 1906 Dr. Joachim Carvallo purchased Villandry and began his masterwork, a task that took him eighteen years to complete. An eighteenth-century network of canals, waterworks, and terraces clustered around the renaissance château provided the framework into which Carvallo poured his vision of a recreated renaissance garden.

The garden has three levels. Each has its own character, though they are all intricately patterned. The uppermost is simple and serene, with grass plots, a mirrorlike pond, and shady walks of braided limes with splendid views of the more extravagant areas below. The middle level is more complex, with ornamental parterres bordered by box hedges filled with spring and summer bedding. In typical Gallic style, they share the themes of music and love.

Shelter from the sun can be found beneath the shade of a vine-covered arbor overlooking the parterre below. Here you will find Villandry's fabulous potager. Surrounded by espaliered apple and pear trees, it is made up of nine squares of different geometric designs in box that are filled with color-coordinated, perfectly grown vegetables that are changed twice a year. This is vegetable gardening raised to the level of art, and it is the equal of any château in the nearby Loire valley. JB

Château de Cormartin

Bourgogne, France

DESIGNERS: Marc Simonet-Lenglart, Pierre Almendros
OWNERS: Anne-Maria Joly, Marc Simonet-Lenglart, Pierre Almendros
GARDEN STYLE: 17th-century renaissance
SIZE: 29.6 acres (11.9 ha)
CLIMATE: Temperate
LOCATION: Cormartin, Bourgogne

During the past twenty years, this château has been restored to its original splendor. Built in 1605 for the Marquise of Huxelles in the style of a water castle, the building and its gardens had fallen into a state of neglect by the time an extensive restoration program started in 1981.

Positioned between the small town of Cormartin and the Grosne River, the château's grounds offer extensive views over the river meadows to the other side of the valley. The garden plan is based on a grid of two rows, each of which contains three large squares. The castle, surrounded by water, occupies the central square and has a potager positioned to one side. There is also a grand parterre that is geometrically divided into smaller grass parterres, flower beds, and a parklike landscape with a small lake. The other two squares are quite different. Best of all is the quincunx, which has trees planted at regular intervals and, in complete contrast, a maze surrounded by a canal. At its center stands a belvedere that gives a superb view from the top. Beyond lies the hedge theater and, running parallel to the river, planted on top of the protective dike, is a long avenue of lime trees that provides much-needed summer shade. HH

> "...this château has been restored to its original splendor"

Le Jardin des Rosiers

Poitou-Charentes, France

DESIGNER: Patsy Boughton
OWNER: Patsy Boughton
GARDEN STYLE: Late 20th-century informal English
SIZE: 3.7 acres (1.5 ha)
CLIMATE: Temperate
LOCATION: La Puye, Poitou-Charentes

Patsy Boughton's garden near the village of La Puye is an oasis of Englishness among fields of flat French farmland. This is seriously rural countryside, and the garden is approached via a dusty track. Patsy sits under an awning at the gate, warning visitors that it is not a real rose garden, but a natural garden with some 350 roses and other garden plants. About 60 percent of the roses are old-fashioned varieties, including gallicas, damasks, and albas, with a good showing of unusual botanical species. The rest are David Austin, repeat-flowering English roses.

Boughton moved from England to Les Rosiers in 1992. There was little garden to speak of then, lost under a wilderness of brambles and weeds. Now it is a romantic series of "rooms," each separated by hedges and rose-covered arches. French visitors, more used to clipped order and having heeded Boughton's warning, are delighted by the informality of her approach, in which roses are but one element in the billowing, cottage-style borders. If it were not for the heat of the sun, you could be in Oxfordshire or Sussex. Dotted around the garden are chairs and benches where you are encouraged to linger, and little slate notices bearing lines of poetry or quotes that have caught Patsy's eye. The farther away from the house, the more wild the garden gets, with an orchard and an avenue of field trees leading to a bench beside the fields. On the way back, mindful of the limited season of some of her roses, she has planted a gravel garden with shrubs and herbaceous plants for year-round interest. CD

Le Labyrinthe

Rhône-Alpes, France

DESIGNER: Alain Richer
OWNERS: Yves Bouvier, Anne-Monique Bouvier
GARDEN STYLE: 20th-century medieval garden
SIZE: 4.5 acres (1.8 ha)
CLIMATE: Temperate
LOCATION: Yvoire, Rhône-Alpes

Built on a promontory overlooking Lake Geneva, the beautiful village of Yvoire acquired its castle in the fourteenth century. Today only the castle keep remains. However, the old, walled kitchen garden in the center of the village has been lovingly restored by Alain Richer to reflect the essence of its medieval origins. It is also called the Jardin des Cinq Sens.

Built on two levels as a series of interconnecting gardens, the alpine meadow at the top recalls the glacial Geneva valley, while the "weaving" area symbolizes the meeting of humans and nature. The medieval cloister has a lovely pergola of hornbeams enclosing a symmetrical garden that contains herbs and medicinal plants, with a birdbath at its center. Below, the maze uses the five senses as a unifying concept, and four gardens surround a central aviary. The Garden of Taste is seasonally planted with vegetable varieties that were common in the Middle Ages, with soft fruits and edible flowers. The Garden of Scent is filled with delicately scented flowers and aromatic foliage. A wonderfully tactile experience awaits visitors to the Garden of Touch, where textures vary from the downy soft to fearsomely thorny, sticky, or even rubbery. Rainbow hues from light blue to crimson characterize the Garden of Sight, while hearing is represented by birdsong and the murmur of water in fountains.

Verdant, abundant, and atmospheric, it is no wonder that Le Labyrinthe is winner of several awards. It is one of the finest gardens of its type in France and certainly the most poetic. NS

Le Jardin d'Erik Borja

Rhône-Alpes, France

DESIGNER: Erik Borja
OWNER: Erik Borja
GARDEN STYLE: 20th-century Japanese and Mediterranean
SIZE: 7 acres (3 ha)
CLIMATE: Temperate
LOCATION: Domaine des Clairmonts, Beaumont Monteaux

Two words encapsulate Erik Borja's garden—unity and harmony. These two concepts are also at the heart of the Japanese gardens created by Zen Buddhists that provided so much of Borja's inspiration. Japanese gardens and Le Jardin d'Erik Borja also share a puzzling symbolism. In the case of Zen gardens, this is a deliberate policy to help stimulate the meditating monks. In Borja's garden, it is more a case of East meets West and the melding of Japanese and Mediterranean ideas and styles. The question is, is this a successful marriage?

At an aesthetic level, the union certainly does work. Borja is a sculptor, and he takes his art into his garden. The natural materials seen here, the living and the lifeless, are treated as sculptural elements of a larger composition. So, in the Zen Garden, minimalist rock and raked gravel are juxtaposed with bold, exuberant plant forms and foliage. Throughout the garden, clipped greens are also extensively used as sculpture, maintained with Japanese-style cloud pruning. Three forms of pyracantha are grown together to create a massive, living backdrop to the Mediterranean garden. The gently undulating and curvaceous masses of box or honeysuckle (*Lonicera nitida*) gently massage the eye.

Yet for all the many bold statements in the garden, Borja pays much attention to the details. Countless delightful vignettes and subtle touches reduce the big scale down to the small. All of these add a great deal of charm to the composition and underscore the designer's skill. It is a triumph. TM

> "Countless delightful vignettes and subtle touches reduce the big scale down to the small"

Terre Vivante

Rhône-Alpes, France

DESIGNERS: Gilles Clément, Sue Stickland, and others
OWNER: Centre Terre Vivante
GARDEN STYLE: 21st-century informal, rural
SIZE: 50 acres (20.2 ha)
CLIMATE: Temperate
LOCATION: Mens, Rhône-Alpes

This extraordinary creation, protected by untouched woodlands in a remote, mountainous region near the Alps, was devised by the founders of France's first magazine dedicated to organic gardening and ecological living, *Les Quatre Saisons du Jardinage* (The Four Seasons of Gardening). They decided to put their theory into practice to demonstrate how to live in the twenty-first century by using solar power, saving water, fertilizing with green manure, installing a composting toilet, and building a wood house insulated with hemp. Visitors, a publishing house, and courses held here provide the financial support.

Beside the five ornamental gardens representing the elements, designed by Gilles Clément, one of the designers of Parc André Citroën, there is a family garden with a lawn edged with flowers, and space for growing vegetables, fruits, and herbs. The unusual vegetables include swedes, parsnips, and Jerusalem artichokes, which in France are considered fit only for animal fodder or times of famine. There are demonstration areas with plants that attract birds and bees, a potager, and a meadow full of wild roses. The stunning lily pond doubles as a reservoir. This is a refreshing garden packed with good ideas. MO

> "…ornamental gardens… vegetables…demonstration areas…a meadow of wild roses"

Château de Hautefort

Aquitaine, France

DESIGNERS: The Count of Choulot, Baroness de Bastard
OWNER: General Durosoy
GARDEN STYLE: 19th- and 20th-century classical French
SIZE: 6-acre (2.5 ha) garden, 74-acre (30 ha) park
CLIMATE: Temperate
LOCATION: Montignac-Grottes de Lascaux, Aquitaine

This magnificent château holds a commanding position surrounded by the woodland landscape of the Perigord region. It was originally a medieval fortress known as the Castrum de Autfort and belonged to the viscounts of Limoges. It has a colorful history, having been besieged by Richard the Lionheart in 1183, before Bertran de Born, a famous warrior-troubadour, restored it. The Count of Choulot completely redesigned the park and gardens in 1853. The castle's recent history dates from 1929 when the Baron and Baroness de Bastard bought the castle, and the formal gardens were restored.

A unique thuja conifer tunnel, with windows cut out to give framed views across the surrounding countryside, leads to a series of formal box parterres on the three sides of the château. The most prominent has wonderful sculptured shapes in box and yew. A filigree of semicircles, squares, cones, globes, scrolls, and mushrooms creates a green broderie (an embroiderylike design), with glorious plantings of jewel-colored flowers in summer and bulbs in springtime. When you gaze down on these beds from viewpoints high up in the building, they look just like pieces of tapestry.

There is also superb, classical topiary to the south and west. On the south-facing side of the château, the walls are furnished with mature specimens of *Magnolia grandiflora*, with large, glossy, evergreen leaves and strongly scented flowers. Beyond the parterres to the west is a natural woodland park packed with wildflowers. RL

Château Marqueyssac

Aquitaine, France

DESIGNERS: Bernard Vernet, Julien de Cerval
OWNER: Kleber Rossillon
GARDEN STYLE: 19th-century Italian, French
SIZE: 49 acres (20 ha)
CLIMATE: Temperate
LOCATION: Vézac, Aquitaine

The park at Château Marqueyssac has a series of terraced gardens that give a superb panoramic view of the Dordogne Valley from this natural bastion on a high ridge. If you like box, Marqueyssac has 150,000 box plants in borders and flower beds that create a captivating scene. There is even a short tunnel of mature box trees.

In 1861 Julien de Cerval inherited the property. His passion for gardens was much influenced by his time in Italy. He redesigned the pleasure gardens of the terraces with box, clipped in cloudlike shapes that reflect the surrounding countryside. Then he built the tower and belvederes 425 feet (130 m) above the Dordogne River, with winding paths, small staircases, three enchanting, dry stone gazebos, rock gardens, and benches carved into the rock. He also gave the chapel a neo-Gothic look and dedicated it to St. Julien, the patron saint of ferrymen. It had been built earlier by Julien Bessiere, who constructed the Great Path, which is 487 feet (148 m) long. Modern additions include the sinuous, serpentine path of santolinas and rosemary in subtle shades of green and silver-gray foliage, and the cascading waterfall. De Cerval introduced the limes, Judas trees (*Cercis siliquastrum*), laburnums, and umbrella pine trees (*Pinus pinea*) with the carpets of *Cyclamen hederifolium*.

Marqueyssac becomes magical every Thursday night in July and August, when the gardens are lit by 1,000 candle lights, an unforgettable sight. Everything about these romantic gardens and their unique setting is totally captivating. RL

Les Jardins du Manoir d'Eyrignac

Aquitaine, France

DESIGNERS: Gilles Sermadiras, Patrick Sermadiras
OWNER: Patrick Sermadiras
GARDEN STYLE: 20th-century French and Italian
SIZE: 10 acres (4 ha)
CLIMATE: Temperate
LOCATION: Salignac, Aquitaine

The unusual gardens of Eyrignac in Perigord were created over forty years ago in the spirit of the Italian Renaissance. Gilles Sermadiras, father of the present owner, set out to recreate a garden with topiary such as might have existed four centuries ago. Following the layout and paths of the pre-existing park with its low walls, steps, ornamental lakes, and fountains, he created an architecture of greenery with yews, box trees, hornbeams, and cypresses. The topiary sculptures have a variety of forms, including embroidery and French-style parterres, as well as forming garden "rooms." Impeccably clipped, the topiary has now reached full maturity, punctuating the park with a variety of sophisticated shapes and opening up beautiful perspectives—the hornbeam avenue with its double enfilade of columns of yews and hornbeam spirals; the avenue of vases with its green alcoves; the French garden punctuated by box trees pruned into spheres and arabesques; and the remarkably elegant garden of white roses.

Seven inexhaustible springs supply water to the garden's fountains and ponds, which welcome visitors with their cheerful babbling and coolness. Within the magnificent setting of the gardens is the seventeenth-century manor, whose particular attraction is that it remains beautiful whatever the season—the owner, Patrick Sermadiras, has made sure of that. The garden of the Manoir d'Eyrignac is recognized as having one of the most beautiful ensembles of plant sculpture in France, and has been listed as a *jardin remarquable* since 2004. ML

Les Jardins de L'Imaginaire

Aquitaine, France

DESIGNER: Kathryn Gustafson
OWNER: Terrasson-La-Villedieu Council
GARDEN STYLE: Late 20th-century contemporary
SIZE: 14 acres (5.6 ha)
CLIMATE: Temperate
LOCATION: Terrasson-La-Villedieu, Aquitaine

This new park, completed in 1999 in southwestern France, is the brainchild of an enterprising mayor. In order to attract tourists away from the medieval towns of Dordogne, he launched a competition to design a park on a large site above the town. Kathryn Gustafson won, and the result is hugely popular.

The publicity leaflet promises "a quest for paradise" through a sensual walk across centuries and civilizations, up and down a very steep slope. First there is the Sacred Wood with a clearing of wildflowers, and then the Plant Tunnel leads to a garden evocative of medieval monasteries. While walking through the trees, you notice golden ribbons symbolic of the rocky journey of life. Farther on, a straight row of pylons, topped by metal weather vanes and adorned by hanging bells, makes the direction and sound of the wind visible and audible.

The pleasing shape of an amphitheater nestles perfectly in the contours of the site, each step marked by elegant, metal benches. Visitors can rest and admire the view of the town beyond the roof of the greenhouse on one side, designed by British architect Ian Ritchie, and the metal structure of the rose pergola on the other. The water garden is spectacular, with a grid of fountains emerging from textured cobblestones beside a narrow canal. It cascades down a tall flight of concrete steps edged with blue perovskia and silver salix. Elsewhere a powerful, single jet emerges from a metal grille set in a lawn while, on the terrace below, a concrete brook creates another axis. This is a superb success. MO

Les Jardins des Paradis

Midi-Pyrénées, France

DESIGNERS: Eric Ossart, Arnaud Maurieres
OWNER: Conseil de Cordes-sur-Ciel
GARDEN STYLE: Late 20th-century contemporary
SIZE: 1 acre (0.4 ha)
CLIMATE: Mediterranean
LOCATION: Cordes-sur-Ciel, Midi-Pyrénées

Everything about these magical gardens, where traditional design is given a contemporary spin, seems slightly larger than life and more colorful. They were laid out in 1997 by two leading French garden designers, Eric Ossart and Arnaud Maurieres, who decided to create their own public garden in the former Cathar stronghold of Cordes-sur-Ciel in southwestern France. The setting, which is part of the gardens' charm, is a terraced hillside with views through trees over the surrounding countryside.

The design consists of a series of enclosed gardens, each with a distinct atmosphere. Influences range from the Mediterranean and the great abbeys of northern France to North Africa. There is even a hint of the Brazilian landscape architect Robert Burle Marx. As you enter the garden, a path of cannas leads to a medieval-style cloister, shaded by bamboo, with a floor of broken slates surrounded by box. In the background, you can hear the continuous sound of water coming from the various pools and the stepped fountain of metal buckets that runs down the main stairs leading to the other garden "rooms." These include a banana grove with a series of blue tile fountains, a terrace of broken terracotta with pots of agapanthus, and a series of colorful, late-summer gardens enclosed by willow screens.

On the bottom terrace is the modern, experimental potager with alternating rows of beans, cardoons, onions, colored chards, and salvias. Throughout, accents of color are provided by terracotta pots containing lantanas and marigolds. VB

Abbaye Saint-Michel de Cuxà

Languedoc-Roussillon, France

DESIGNERS: Dr. Jean Segui, Elisabeth Segui
OWNER: Abbaye Saint-Michel de Cuxà
GARDEN STYLE: 20th-century display garden
SIZE: 0.25 acre (0.1 ha)
CLIMATE: Mediterranean
LOCATION: Codalet, Languedoc-Roussillon

Most people discover this charming little garden by chance when visiting the Abbaye of Saint-Michel de Cuxà. It is a Romanesque abbey whose twelfth-century medieval cloister now forms part of the Metropolitan Museum of Art's "The Cloisters" complex. Settings do not come much lovelier than this. The snowcapped peak of Canigou rises in the distance, presiding over a garden that resounds, three times a day, to the tolling of the bell that calls the monks to prayer. The garden is now a place of pilgrimage, visited each May, when the irises are in flower. Some 500 varieties, mostly bearded, but with some species, have been planted in rows in a field below the abbey enclave, producing the horticultural equivalent of a painting by Monet.

The collection was started by Dr. Jean Segui over forty years ago. He went on to breed some of France's most renowned irises, including a handful of hybrids in red and gold, which are much valued by regional gardeners for the way their hues reflect the light and landscape of the Catalan. His daughter-in-law, Elisabeth Segui, built up the stock and opened a nursery, Iris de Thau, in nearby Meze. It champions old and rare varieties among the more popular hybrids. Marie Pal, Elisabeth's aunt, looks after the irises and can be found, every afternoon, sitting on a bench under the walnut tree, dispensing advice and catalogs. Although no irises are for sale, you can order them on the spot. Visitors find it hard to tear themselves away from this alluring garden. By the time they remember it is the abbey that they have come to see, the doors have long since shut. VR

La Bambouseraie de Prafrance

Languedoc-Roussillon, France

DESIGNERS: Eugène Mazel, Muriel Nègre
OWNER: Muriel Nègre
GARDEN STYLE: 19th-century natural
SIZE: 84 acres (34 ha)
CLIMATE: Mediterranean
LOCATION: Générargues Anduze,
   Languedoc-Roussillon

As soon as you enter the deep valley where this extraordinary garden is situated in the Cévennes region of southeastern France, it is easy to imagine that you are on another continent. Tall bamboos arch over the wide avenue leading to the entrance of the park and could not be in sharper contrast to the nearby dry, Mediterranean landscape. This sense of disorientation persists right through the garden as you make your way from seemingly impenetrable bamboo forests, with their eerie green light, to a bamboo maze and a Laotian village built on stilts. There is even a Japanese garden with its still pool overhung by acers. Because of their vast size and their location at the bottom of an extremely fertile valley, the gardens have their own microclimate, helped by a large network of irrigation canals.

This utopian creation was drummed up by Eugène Mazel, a successful spice merchant in the mid-nineteenth century. Thanks to his commercial activities, he was able to import from Asia a large collection of plants totally unknown in France at the time. However, the upkeep of this fabulous creation unfortunately ruined him, and he had to hand it over to a bank before the Nègre family eventually bought it. There is so much to see. Make sure to look for the gigantic, 100-foot-tall (30 m) *Ginkgo biloba* by the stream in the Valley of the Dragon. It symbolizes the resilience and success of a place that might have succumbed to the demands of visitors by installing interactive information points, but instead has defiantly retained its original look. MO

> "…make your way from…
> impenetrable bamboo forests,
> with their eerie green light…"

Domaine du Rayol

Provence-Alpes-Côte d'Azur, France

DESIGNER: Gilles Clément
OWNER: Conservatoire du Littoral
GARDEN STYLE: 20th-century contemporary
SIZE: 17 acres (7 ha)
CLIMATE: Mediterranean
LOCATION: Le Rayol-Canadel, Provence-Alpes-Côte d'Azur

A combination of botanical and landscape gardens, the Domaine du Rayol evokes the flora of nine regions of the world that share climatic conditions similar to those of the Mediterranean. The gardens are situated on the corniche (coast road) of the Maures in the Var and now belong to the Conservatoire du Littoral (Coast Conservancy).

The garden has its origins in the estate of a rich banker, Alfred-Theodore Courmes, who built a villa in the Art Nouveau style on the site in 1910, along with a grand Classical pergola and a summer house. He surrounded the structures with a variety of exotic gardens. The next owner, an aeronautics engineer, constructed a cypress-lined staircase to the sea and added a bamboo plantation. After a long period of neglect, the domaine been restored with its promontories, coves, and natural vegetation of mastic trees, pines, cistus, arbutus, and other species.

In the small wooded valley leading to the sea and the Pointe du Figuier, the nine Mediterranean gardens were created by landscape gardener Gilles Clément, the creator of "gardens of movement." Each garden brings together plants that are typical of a particular region of the world and others associated with it: the South African garden with its aloes enhanced by strelitzia species (birds of paradise); the Australian garden with bottlebrush trees such as callistemon and melaleuca; the arid Central American garden with agaves, yuccas, and other succulent plants; the oriental garden with bamboos and cycads; the Chilean garden with the giant araucaria or monkey puzzle tree of the Andes and the honey palm; the New Zealand garden with its cordylines and phormiums (New Zealand flax); the Californian garden; the American subtropical garden, and finally the maritime garden. All these remarkable, amazing plants can be admired in the gardens, either by walking unaccompanied or in guided tours ML

Fontana Rosa

Provence-Alpes-Côte d'Azur, France

DESIGNER: Vicente Blasco Ibanez
OWNER: City of Menton
GARDEN STYLE: 20th-century riviera
SIZE: 1.5 acres (0.6 ha)
CLIMATE: Mediterranean
LOCATION: Menton, Provence-Alpes-Côte d'Azur

Film buffs will remember the silent classic *The Four Horsemen of the Apocalypse*, which made a star of Rudolph Valentino. It was based on a novel by the Spanish writer, Vicente Blasco Ibanez, a political dissenter, who fled Spain to settle in Menton. He bought Fontana Rosa, a Belle Epoque villa that stood on a steep, narrowly terraced hillside overlooking the Mediterranean. It was here, from 1922 until his death six years later, that he created the lavish Novelist's Garden. Among the palm trees, plane trees, and magnolias, he built a cinema, library, and aquarium, and honored his literary heroes, Dickens, Victor Hugo, and Dostoevsky by mounting their busts on pedestals. The greatest homage of all was paid to Cervantes, in an elaborate rotunda depicting 100 scenes from Don Quixote.

The garden was inspired by the public garden of Valencia with its columns, benches, and pergolas, where he had played as a child. Everything he built was decorated with Moorish ceramics imported from the small town of Manises, near Valencia. Roses and carnations were grown in pots then planted in soil brought from Valencia in sacks. The garden was scented with jasmine, lilies, pomegranates, and orange and lemon trees.

Vicente Blasco Ibanez wanted Fontana Rosa to be turned into a sanctuary for aging writers after his death, but his son, Sigfrido, sold the upper half of the property to developers in 1970 and gave the lower half to the city of Menton. By the time it was classed as a historical monument twenty years later, the villa had been demolished and the buildings and features ravaged by World War II and neglect. The garden features have been restored little by little over the past few years and the city has plans for a complete restoration. Until then, you will have to use your imagination to picture it in its heyday. However, the ceramicwork alone makes this garden worth a visit. VR

Le Jardin Exotique d'Eze

Provence-Alpes-Côte d'Azur, France

DESIGNER: Jean Gastaud
OWNER: Ville d'Eze
GARDEN STYLE: 20th-century cactus and succulent garden
SIZE: 3.7 acres (1.4 ha)
CLIMATE: Mediterranean
LOCATION: Eze, Provence-Alpes-Côte d'Azur

Clinging to the mountainside 1,400 feet (430 m) above sea level and overlooking the Mediterranean is the Exotic Garden of Eze. The term "exotic" refers here not to banana and palm trees, but to a full range of cacti and succulents that are not normally grown in Mediterranean gardens. Although pear cactus and agave do grow wild on the lower slopes of the mountains in this region, here in the garden they have been joined by all manner of exotic South American cacti and succulents.

The collection was started in 1949 by Jean Gastaud on the site of the ruins of the old castle of Eze. It is not a place for anyone with vertigo—the winding, often narrow, paths weave and climb through the towering spires and the squat, marrow-shaped cacti to the top of the garden. There you will find a spectacular panorama of the Mediterranean, including the peninsula of Cap Ferrat, and, on a good day, a hint of far away Corsica.

They say that cactus collectors live the longest—just the expectation of a flower keeps them going. You can understand that when, among all the grayish-greens and dull blue-greens, you see a splash of color, bright intense sparks of yellow and pink bursting from the inert forms.

The garden was renovated during 2003–04. Although Eze is very much on the tourist route, the garden, which lies at the end of a long, narrow street, tends to be overlooked. This is a great shame because visitors are guaranteed a superb garden and some of the best views on the Riviera. HH

Villa Ephrussi de Rothschild

Provence-Alpes-Côte d'Azur, France

DESIGNER: Achille Duchêne
OWNER: Institut de France
GARDEN STYLE: Early 20th-century eclectic
SIZE: 19 acres (7.7 ha)
CLIMATE: Mediterranean
LOCATION: Cap Ferrat, Provence-Alpes-Côte d'Azur

In 1905, Maurice Ephrussi de Rothschild acquired 17.2 acres (7 ha) at Cap Ferrat. Seven years and eleven architects later, the house and garden, which was landscaped like the decks of a ship, were completed. The site has been run by the Institut de France since 1934. It is also known as the Jardins de Musée Ephrussi de Rothschild.

Breathtaking views make this garden a joy to visit at any time of year. The palazzo-style pink villa is approached via the Grand Court with a grotto. Behind the villa lies a formal French creole-style garden with palm trees and agaves lined up with the Temple of Love. To the west, approached by a horseshoe staircase, lies the Spanish-Moorish-style garden. Sunset is the best time to visit the Florentine Terrace, a series of gentle steps lined with cypresses and stone balustrades with spectacular views over the Mediterranean. There is also a Japanese Garden with a ceramic pagoda, and an Exotic Garden with steep winding paths around impressive cacti.

The formal beds in the rosary fan out from a hexagonal pavilion, climbers scramble over columns, and pots of santolina give a Persian air. The garden then disappears into a wilderness of windswept, gnarled olives and aloes that evoke a wild landscape. The Provençal Garden falls away to the easterly seaboard. Sinuous paths wind through the pine-wooded area of the English Garden with a small, shady temple. CH

Le Clos du Peyronnet

Provence-Alpes-Côte d'Azur, France

DESIGNER: Humphry Waterfield
OWNER: William Waterfield
GARDEN STYLE: 20th-century English Arts and Crafts
SIZE: 1.5 acres (0.6 ha)
CLIMATE: Mediterranean
LOCATION: Menton-Garavan, Provence-Alpes-Côte d'Azur

Le Clos du Peyronnet was originally laid out and planted by the artist and gardener Humphry Waterfield. Today his nephew, William, cares single-handedly for the garden.

Le Clos du Peyronnet was built when the Arts and Crafts influence on garden making was at its strongest. Structures such as the pergola, terrace, and pool reflected the quality of craftsmanship lavished on the garden. It is the planting, however, that makes this place so precious. The garden was made by a plantsman, and it is still cared for by an amateur botanist and plant collector.

The garden was created on a steeply sloping site that was terraced by Humphry Waterfield. The elegant Italianate house nestles into the hillside, surrounded by plants. Clipped Italian cypresses, citrus trees, echiums, and wisterias flourish in this climate. A vast number of potted South African bulbs are laid out in orderly fashion on identical stone tables where they are cared for as part of William Waterfield's personal collection. The heat is taken out of the garden by the dramatic series of pools on different levels, with water cascading from one to the next, eventually falling into the lily pond and fishponds at the bottom of the garden. Visitors may need to make a reservation on an organized tour. AJ

RIGHT Ancient wisteria snakes around the columns on the stunning pergola at Le Clos du Peyronnet.

Les Cèdres

Provence-Alpes-Côte d'Azur, France

DESIGNER: Julien Marnier-Lapostolle
OWNERS: The Marnier-Lapostolle family
GARDEN STYLE: 19th- to 21st-century botanic
SIZE: 34.5 acres (14.3 ha)
CLIMATE: Mediterranean
LOCATION: Saint-Jean-Cap-Ferrat, Provence-Alpes-
   Côte d'Azur

Les Cèdres has the finest private collection of plants in the world. It contains 16,000 different species ranging from succulent Madagascan rarities to vast stands of giant bamboo. Previous owners have included King Leopold II of Belgium and Sir Ernest Cassel. In 1924 the house and garden were purchased by the Marnier-Lapostolle family, in whose hands the garden has remained. Julien Marnier-Lapostolle was twenty-two years old when his family acquired Les Cèdres, and the garden became his great passion. His gifts as a botanist and horticulturalist made Les Cèdres the extraordinary garden it is today, though its unifying style is not in the same league. The sheer abundance of wonderful plants, however, is overwhelming.

In 1908 the basic structure of the garden around the house was laid out by the architects Harold Peto and Jules Vacherot, employed by King Leopold II. Pools, cascades, Italianate terraces, and staircases form the bones of the site that has a series of twenty-six gardens. Each has its own theme, such as tropical, wild, palms, and Mexico. There are also twenty-five greenhouses accommodating 600 species of orchid, carnivorous plants, and aquatics.

Five gardens, including the Mexican, the Philodendron Arbor, and Large Tropical, are covered over for the winter each year using scaffolding: a process that demands the attention of ten people for ten weeks. This illustrates the profound personal dedication to plants that makes Les Cèdres such a unique horticultural and botanical jewel. AM

Les Colombières

Provence-Alpes-Côte d'Azur, France

DESIGNER: Ferdinand Bac
OWNERS: Michael Likierman, Margaret Likierman
GARDEN STYLE: Early 20th-century classical
SIZE: 7.4 acres (2.9 ha)
CLIMATE: Mediterranean
LOCATION: Menton, Provence-Alpes-
   Côte d'Azur

In 1912 the caricaturist Ferdinand Bac began to design the house and garden at Les Colombières for Monsieur and Madame Ladan-Bockairy. The work was finally completed in the 1920s, by which time Bac had created a garden full of wit, brilliance, and beauty. The garden sits on a steep hillside above Menton's little harbor, overlooking the Mediterranean.

The garden is laid out on the site of an ancient olive grove and is studded with elegant Mediterranean cypresses (*Cupressus sempervirens*), which provide its thematic core. Within this framework, Bac laid out a series of walks, allées, follies, ornamental constructions, and trompe l'oeil with plenty of references to the classics, in particular Homer's *Odyssey*. The combination of the highly designed detail and the natural world is wonderfully executed. A six-hundred-year-old carob tree (*Ceratonia siliqua*) is the centerpiece of an avenue of huge olive jars. A flight of stone steps is interrupted by an olive tree, around which the steps were built. Les Colombières is a garden rooted in the Mediterranean that inspires both the intellect and the imagination. It has been superbly restored by Michael and Margaret Likierman. Though it is possible to visit only on certain days of the year, it is well worth waiting for. AM

"…a garden full of wit, brilliance, and beauty"

Serre de la Madone

Provence-Alpes-Côte d'Azur, France

DESIGNER: Lawrence Johnston
OWNER: Conservatoire du Littoral
GARDEN STYLE: Early to mid-20th-century formal
SIZE: 17 acres (6.8 ha)
CLIMATE: Mediterranean
LOCATION: Menton, Provence-Alpes-Côte d'Azur

What makes this garden fascinating is the spirit and time in which it was created. Its owner, the American-born Lawrence Johnston, carved a garden out of a hot, dry Mediterranean slope at a time when plant hunting, grand gestures, and, for many, social one-upmanship were rife.

Johnston was not just the fortunate owner of this site in southern France, overlooking the coast between Monaco and Italy. He was also the creator, with his mother, of Hidcote Manor in Gloucestershire (see page 305). By the time he bought Serre de la Madone in 1924, some of the exciting developments at Hidcote were bearing fruit, and he had certainly gained plenty of experience. However, the two gardens are very different. Serre was used for plants collected from far away, giving it a luxuriant feel. In many ways, it is a more successful garden than Hidcote ever was. The garden is nicely related to the house with paths, lines, and areas emanating from it. In addition, there is Johnston's ability to make intimate and personal spaces using water, walls, and trees. At times, in fact, the scale of Serre is more domestic than many similar-sized gardens, though its planting in its heyday was far from that. Johnston died in 1958, and the garden declined from then on.

In 1999, the Conservatoire du Littoral (the Coastal Protection Agency) purchased the property and handed over the restoration to a dedicated group. The restored garden is not a historical replica, but an example of a fascinating and beautiful garden, reawakened for a long-term future. CY

Villa Noailles

Provence-Alpes-Côte d'Azur, France

DESIGNER: Vicomte Charles de Noailles
OWNER: Charles de la Haye Jousselin
GARDEN STYLE: 20th-century formal
SIZE: 4.5 acres (1.8 ha)
CLIMATE: Mediterranean
LOCATION: Grasse, Provence-Alpes-Côte d'Azur

This garden is a superb highlight of any Mediterranean tour, partly thanks to its amazing setting.

When the Vicomte de Noailles began the project in 1947, he kept the olive grove intact to preserve the link with the surrounding countryside. A natural spring enabled the creation of wonderful fountains and the cultivation of plants not usually found in this dry landscape. The moment you enter the garden you are taken into a watery world of grottoes and seemingly endless fountains and pools, leading to the stream on the edge of the property. More fountains flow from decorative spouts set in a series of terraced walls, evoking the Hundred Fountains of the Villa d'Este in Italy (see page 688).

The viscount liked visual references to favorite places, which accounts for the obelisk reminiscent of the Villa Aldobrandini in Frascati (see page 686) and the grassy path lined with colorful borders of perennials that echoes Hidcote Manor in England (see page 305). The garden has a very strong structure with vistas framed by box hedges, a magnificent covered walk under Judas trees (*Cercis siliquastrum*), and green "rooms." Paved steps follow the slope of the olive grove, worth seeing in spring when thousands of naturalized bulbs are in full bloom, and lead to a field with eighteen different varieties of deciduous magnolia, an unforgettable visual delight when they disappear under great swelling clouds of flowers. Viburnums and camellias usually grown in very different climates are also found here, looking perfectly happy under the relentless blue sky. MO

Le Parc Saint Bernard

Provence-Alpes-Côte d'Azur, France

DESIGNERS: Gabriel Guévrékian, Charles de Noailles
OWNER: Hyères Municipality
GARDEN STYLE: Early 20th-century cubist, Mediterranean
SIZE: 0.5 acre (0.2 ha)
CLIMATE: Mediterranean
LOCATION: Hyères, Provence-Alpes-Côte d'Azur

Charles and Marie-Laure de Noailles were great patrons of the arts. Their close friends included F. Scott Fitzgerald and Edith Wharton, though quite what she thought of the garden no one knows.

In 1924, the de Noailles commissioned architect Robert Mallet-Stevens to design a modern, cubist villa on a hilly site above Hyères. Charles also asked the Armenian-born architect and garden designer Gabriel Guévrékian to add an appropriate garden in 1926. Guévrékian's creation was one of the earliest expressions of cubism in a garden setting. It also contained something of the Japanese gardens that so inspired the modernists, making it not a garden to stroll through but a "viewing" garden to be admired from without and above. It is in the shape of an isosceles triangle, with the apex farthest from the house. He also divided the interior of the triangle into a series of painted (now tiled) square and rectangular beds in yellow, blue, violet, gray, and black. They were planted with a mix of carpeting species and seasonal plants, tulips being a spring favorite. The house and garden fell into disrepair, but have now been restored.

For those less enthused by all things modern, below the house is a more conventional cascade of terraces created by Charles. These gardens capture both the exquisite views out to the aquamarine sea, and the wildernesslike beauty found in the best Mediterranean gardens. TM

RIGHT Gabriel Guévrékian's cubist creation Le Parc Saint Bernard has been restored, but with some loss of subtlety.

Zámek Veltrusy

Středočeský Kraj, Czech Republic

DESIGNERS: Rudolf Chotek, Jan Rudolf Chotek,
   Christian Hirschfeld, Richard van der Schott,
OWNER: The Czech State
GARDEN STYLE: 18th-century baroque, landscape
SIZE: 665 acres (269.3 ha)
CLIMATE: Temperate
LOCATION: Veltrusy, Středočeský Kraj
TRANSLATION: Veltrusy Castle

This summer château with its original French baroque gardens, created from 1720 by Count Václav Antonín Chotek, has been added to and changed many times. The most important additions were executed by Chotek´s son Rudolf, in the style of an ornamental farm in the second half of the eighteenth century, and by his grandson Jan Rudolf. Rudolf began with an ornamental farm that had been destroyed by floods, and worked on a romantic landscape park, helped by Christian Hirschfeld and Richard van der Schott,

director of Schönbrunn gardens (see page 640). The architect M. Hummel designed some of the romantic follies and neoclassical pavilions in the park.

The château was built on an island formed by two arms of a river, one of which became a stylized canal. The main outlook of the park is aligned with the Czech mythical mountain of Říp in the distance. Also contributing to the unique scenic mix are the island itself, a small lake, and ornamental bridges, including a Palladian bridge and an Egyptian bridge with a sphinx and a nearby grotto. An old central avenue of trees was saved to connect the château with the rest of the park and the neo-Gothic building of the Red Mill. Some buildings have disappeared; only recently, a flood in 2002 badly damaged some of the structures.

In his time, Rudolf Chotek established very early landscape parks, including one in Veltrusy and another in Kaèina near Kutná Hora. Both of them are first class and deserve to be restored. JH

Zámek Průhonice

Stredočeský Kraj, Czech Republic

DESIGNERS: Count Ernest Emanuel Silva-Tarouca,
František Thomayer
OWNER: Institute of Botany of the Czech Academy of
Sciences
GARDEN STYLE: 19th-century landscape park
SIZE: 617 acres (250 ha)
CLIMATE: Temperate
LOCATION: Průhonice, Stredočeský Kraj
TRANSLATION: Průhonice Castle

This classical, continental landscape park was designed at the end of the nineteenth century by its last noble owner, Count Ernest Emanuel Silva-Tarouca. He was also the cofounder and an important supporter of the third-oldest European dendrological society, the Dendrological Gardens Society of the former Austro-Hungarian Empire.

The central part of this park lies in a picturesque site of deep valleys, the edges being on an upper plain. Count Silva-Tarouca planted approximately 1,000 species to create a central Bohemian landscape in which indigenous plants were complemented by exotics. "I am creating a green oasis in the middle of this agricultural desert of sugar beet," he said.

At the same time, the count and the architect Jirí Stibral rebuilt the medieval fortress as a château in the Bohemian, neo-renaissance style, and this fairy-tale-like building dominates part of the park. The château overlooks the main park entrance and houses the Institute of Botany of the Czech Academy of Sciences. The grounds contain the new Dendrological Garden, designed in a late-twentieth-century post-modern style. The garden showground covers some 99 acres (40 ha) and has a mass of flowering plants, approximately 5,000 garden species. The local nursery offers plants for sale, including some very rare specimens that owe their existence to the Silva-Tarouca Institute's heritage tree collection. JBo

Zámek Trója

Praha, Czech Republic

DESIGNERS: Jean Baptista Mathey, Jiří Seeman,
Jan Prokop Mayer
OWNER: City of Prague
GARDEN STYLE: 17th-century dynamic baroque
SIZE: 8.7 acres (3.5 ha)
CLIMATE: Temperate
LOCATION: Prague, Praha
TRANSLATION: Trója Castle

The artist Jean Baptista Mathey designed this summer château for the Czech nobleman Václav Vojtěch of Šternberk in the last quarter of the seventeenth century. Mathey's academic education in classical painting is evident in the garden's emphasis on perspective and the exceptional baroque statues on the massive garden stairway. On the lower part of the stairs there is a grotto with a statue of fighting gods and giants, and the presence of many large terra-cotta vases brings the upper parterre terrace walls to life.

Classical clipped box and later parterres de broderie were built on two levels, one being a very high terrace that is level with the château, the lower part extending toward the ornamental grillework gates. At each side are symmetrical orangeries with terra-cotta busts of Roman emperors. At this point, the central view continues out across the River Vltava into the Old Royal Hunting Preserve and toward Prague Castle on the horizon. To the east side are former baroque fruit gardens, complete with bas-relief, an open-air theater, and numerous terra-cotta vases.

The last renovation of the garden was in 1980 by the architect Otakar Kuča. A new labyrinth of tall, clipped hornbeam circles was added to the center of the fruit orchard. Reconstruction of the château and the garden took place under Communist supervision, during the Cold War, so it is no great surprise that the water tricks on the garden stairs and other jokes were not restored, and are now long gone. JH

Zahrady Prazský Hradu

Praha, Czech Republic

DESIGNERS: Giovanni Spatio, Paolo della Stella, Reinhardt Bros., J. Dinebier, František Zinner, Josip Plečnik, Jan Ondřej, František Ritschl
OWNER: City of Prague
GARDEN STYLE: 18th-century French baroque, modern
SIZE: 15 acres (6 ha)
CLIMATE: Temperate
LOCATION: Prague, Praha
TRANSLATION: Prague Castle Gardens

Of Prague Castle's gardens, the most important is the Royal Garden, which originated with Emperor Ferdinand I in the mid-sixteenth century. The simple, Italian-style renaissance fruit and flower garden gradually gives way to an elaborate and compartmented mannerist garden, based on Vredeman de Vries' ideas, where the first tulips in Europe were cultivated and Andreae Matthioli worked on his world-famous herbarium. In the eighteenth century, the garden was given a French baroque design by František Zinner, and was later turned into a landscape park by František Ritschl.

On the south slope, above the Malá Strana, is the Paradise Garden. The later-nineteenth-century landscape design of this space by František Ritschl turned the old gardens into one grand, long space, adding new entrances and stairs from the ramparts and from the third court of the castle, and erecting a number of new pavilions. Similarly, Josip Plečnik's design of the new Bašta Garden connected it to the old Deer Moat, and to the Plečnik Vineyard Garden on the opposite slope of the Deer Moat—the favorite site of former President Tomáš Garique Masaryk. In this way, Plečnik united all the castle garden spaces, which former president Václav Havel had begun to open to the public in 1989. JH

Správa Pražského Hradu

Praha, Czech Republic

DESIGNERS: Jan Santini Aichl, Giovanni Alliprandi, Jan Ignác Palliardi, František Kaška, Matyáš Bernard Braun
OWNER: City of Prague
GARDEN STYLE: 17th-, 18th-century high baroque, classical
SIZES: 0.3–3. 8 acres (0.1–1.5 ha)
CLIMATE: Temperate
LOCATION: Prague, Praha
TRANSLATION: Prague Palace Gardens

The former vineyards and fruit gardens of the old houses in the Malá Strana (Lesser Town) district of Prague were, in the late baroque period, redesigned and converted into picturesque palace gardens for numerous noble families. The ground behind the remodeled baroque palaces rose sharply up the hill, and there was never enough room to design a connection between the outdoors and indoors, traditionally achieved by a linking loggia, ornamental stairway, balustrade, or terrace.

On the top terrace, a breathtaking vista over Prague was designed to surprise noble visitors. This view takes in six gardens—the Gardens of Ledebour, Small and Large Pálffy, Kolowrat, and Small and Large Fürstenberg—and on the slope opposite the castle hill are three major Palace Gardens—Schönborn, Lobkowitz, and Vrtba. Only the high-baroque Vrtba Garden, created on a gentle ridge in the form of concave and convex terraces, is open to the public. The garden was literally sculpted to represent the Garden of Hesperides, guarded by Atlas at the gate.

By the 1970s the palace gardens were in a thoroughly neglected state and closed to the public, but since then they have all been reconstructed. With the original plants lost forever, the designers have had no hesitation in using new cultivars. JH

Valdtšejnský Palác

Praha, Czech Republic

DESIGNERS: Giovanni Pieroni, Andrea Spezza, Nicolo Sebregondi
OWNER: The Czech State
GARDEN STYLE: 17th-century mannerist to early baroque
SIZE: 4.9 acres (2 ha)
CLIMATE: Temperate
LOCATION: Prague, Praha
TRANSLATION: Valdstein Palace, Wallenstein Palace

Space for the new mannerist garden of Duke Albrecht of Wallenstein had to be made by clearing a large number of older buildings in Prague's Malá Strana (Lesser Town). The city's biggest palace of the time was intended to command a spectacular panorama, rivaling that of the emperor's Prague Castle (see page 629)—a symbolic assertion of the duke's power. The garden, especially the loggia and parterre, was given a classical Roman scale and appearance, and bronze statues were sculpted especially for the garden by Adrian de Vries from 1624 to 1627.

The garden was further developed with an aviary for birds of prey and a grotto, and much later a square basin of reflecting water in front of the horse-riding school (now the National Gallery). This new area, designed by Nicolo Sebregondi with a baroque touch, is a grand, open, elegant space. Later an island with a statue of Hercules was added. At the beginning of the nineteenth century, some parts of the garden were redesigned in the landscape style; these were reconstructed in the middle of the twentieth century.

A second Wallenstein garden was built at the same time as the one in Prague at Valdice near Jicín, the seat of the Wallenstein domain. This garden has undergone many changes since that time and is now being restored by the local community. JH

LEFT The statues of the Wallenstein garden are copies of originals stolen by the Swedish army in the Thirty Years' War.

Villa Müller

Praha, Czech Republic

DESIGNERS: Camillo Schneider, Karl Fürster, Hermann Matern
OWNER: City of Prague
GARDEN STYLE: 20th-century functionalist with baroque influences
SIZE: 0.2 acre (0.08 ha)
CLIMATE: Temperate
LOCATION: Prague, Praha

When, in 1928, the young architect Adolf Loos and builder Karel Lhota decided on a steeply sloping plot for this functionalist villa, they were mindful of the open vista toward Prague Castle, Château Troja, and the meandering River Vltava by the Royal Hunting Preserve. The house was completed in 1930, and work began on the garden in the following year. Creating a garden on this site was difficult, and connecting it to the house involved some smart thinking.

The complexity of the garden—its design clearly imitates the corner of a baroque fortification—is evident from the terraces of the villa. The best view is afforded by the roof terrace, from where Prague Castle is framed by an elegant window. A dominant element of the garden design is the snakelike stairway that leads down from the garage platform to a low part of the garden. In the garden, visitors notice ingredients of Japanese and English gardens that were typical of many of the private gardens in the Ořechovka Garden Quarter in the 1930s, including the perennial border to the upper open lawn.

The owners lost control of the villa when they used part of it as a tax payment in 1945, and for years much of it was leased. Following the villa's naming as a national cultural monument in 1995, careful restoration of the garden began in 1998 under the landscape architects Vítězslava and Jan Ondřej. The original trees were saved, including a pyramidal oak (*Quercus robur* 'Fastigiata') at the entrance. JH

Zámek Jaroměřice

Vysočina, Czech Republic

DESIGNERS: Jean Trehet, Břetislav Storm, Dušan Riedl
OWNER: The Czech State
GARDEN STYLE: 18th-century baroque garden, English park
SIZE: 19 acres (7.7 ha)
CLIMATE: Temperate
LOCATION: Jaroměřice nad Rokytnou, Vysočina
TRANSLATION: Jaroměřice Castle

Originally a medieval castle, Jaroměřice was reworked as a renaissance château at the end of the sixteenth century by the Austrian baroque architect Jakob Ptandtauer. The château was to emerge in its baroque appearance, and the park its French layout, under the ownership of Count Jan Adam Questenberg, between 1700 and 1737. The château, one of the greatest baroque edifices in Europe, dominates the town of Jaroměřice nad Rokytnou.

The garden was designed by the French architect Jean Trehet in 1716, and combines French and Italian styles. It is now accessible from the château through the garden forecourt. Visitors pass through highly ornamental parterres and clipped box hedges down to where the River Rokytná is channeled into a formal canal. A second part of the garden lies on an artificial island, reached by a footbridge. This part has an open-air theater with adjacent sculptures of ancient gods within highly ornamental parterres. There is also an English park of about 15 acres (6 ha) on the west side of the château, behind the canalized river, with what used to be a fruit garden. The English park was established in the nineteenth century and has a network of radial paths that reflects the plan of the original baroque garden.

Since 1945 the garden has been owned by the Czech State, and it underwent extensive restoration from 1959 to 1962. Count Jan Adam Questenberg began an association between the château and music that continues today; many of the salons within the château—principally the China Lounge and the sala terrena—were created for concerts. The château hosts the Peter Dvorský International Classical Music Festival in June. For lovers of Antonio Salieri, court composer of Hapsburg Emperor Joseph II (and rumored without foundation to be the murderer of Mozart), there are regular festivals of his music because he spent many summers here. JBo

Lednicko–Valtick Areal

Jihomoravský Kraj, Czech Republic

DESIGNER: Bernhard Petri
OWNER: The Czech State
GARDEN STYLE: 17th-century English park, 19th-century additions, 20th-century tree plantings
SIZE: Lednice Park: 49.2 acres (19.9 ha)
CLIMATE: Temperate
LOCATION: Břeclav District, Jihomoravský Kraj
TRANSLATION: Lednice-Valtice Cultural Landscape

The grandiose Lednice–Valtice Cultural Landscape covers 77 square miles (200 sq km) that were given an English landscape makeover in the seventeenth century by Duke Karel I of Liechtenstein. The duke made the château in Valtice his residence and nearby Lednice his summer seat. Tree-lined avenues were added to connect Valtice with other parts of the estate. In the early nineteenth century, Duke Jan Josef I continued the project with the help of his estate manager-cum-landscape artist, Bernhard Petri.

The ground level of the Lednice Park was raised to prevent flooding, a new channel for the River Dyje was dug, and large numbers of romantic buildings and follies were built. They included castles, the Colonnade, the Rendezvous Chalet, the Fishpond Manor, the Pohansko Chalet, the Obelisk, a Temple of Apollo, and, on the historical boundary between Moravia and Lower Austria, the Boundary Manor.

English landscape parks were created at the château and around the three fishponds. The mannerist château of Valtice dominates the landscape, and the romantic neo-Gothic Lednice château sits on a low plain. The dominant feature in the Lednice Park itself is the tall minaret tower, from whose balcony Vienna may be seen on a clear day.

In the twentieth century, a wide selection of native and rare exotic tree species was planted. The Lednice–Valtice Cultural Landscape was added to the UNESCO World Heritage List in 1996. JBo

Zámek Milotice

Jihomoravský Kraj, Czech Republic

DESIGNERS: Anton Zinner, Dušan Riedl
OWNER: The Czech State
GARDEN STYLE: 18th-century French baroque
SIZE: 11 acres (4.5 ha)
CLIMATE: Temperate
LOCATION: Milotice nad Bečvou, Jihomoravský Kraj
TRANSLATION: Milotice Castle

This formal garden was completed in 1722 by the garden architect Anton Zinner, replacing older mannerist gardens. In 1740 two orangeries were added. An attempt was made by Maximillian Erras to transform the garden into an English park, but he did not really succeed in changing the garden's character. The garden suffered gradual deterioration until the late 1960s, when the garden architect Dušan Riedl proposed a program of restoration. This did not reproduce the original historic plans, because no evidence of them was found, and was emphatically baroque. Today's visitors can see the gracious mannerist château area with its court d´honneur, riding hall, stable, and the two surviving orangeries.

What is immediately clear to visitors is how the French baroque-style garden gradually changes into an English landscape-style park in its more remote areas. The main axis starts at the sala terrena (the area that connects the château to the garden) and leads over a small terrace parterre garden with two formal rose beds, clipped hedges, and an ornamental basin. A quick detour leads to the two orangeries, one of which contains Moravian baroque sculptures. The axis continues on, taking the visitor down a monumental, centrally built staircase to the main part of the garden—revealing a fountain surrounded by lawns and a wall of high, clipped hedges—and eventually leading to the tall trees of the park behind. To the left side of the garden boundary is a wooded area where pheasants were hunted. JBo

Zámek Lysice

Jihomoravský Kraj, Czech Republic

DESIGNER: Unknown
OWNER: The Czech State
GARDEN STYLE: 17th-century English landscape park
SIZE: 8.6 acres (3.5 ha)
CLIMATE: Temperate
LOCATION: Lysice, Jihomoravský Kraj
TRANSLATION: Lysice Castle

The château and garden were established during the renaissance alteration of an older fortress in the early seventeenth century. Terraces were added, and a Dutch garden created with rich, sculptural decorations and a fountain. Other significant changes included a court for ball games, and a compartment with a round, ornamental basin encircled by lawn. In the eighteenth century, the garden was enlarged southward to include the area of a former castle pond, and eastward where there had once been a fruit garden. The renaissance separation of each part of the garden was replaced by baroque links.

In the nineteenth century, the boundary wall of the middle terrace was replaced by a high gallery on a Doric colonnade above the garden, which replaced the area of the former ball court, and a new stucco and brick raised pathway was constructed. The whole garden was enlarged by a formal vegetable garden, and was gradually transformed into an English landscape park featuring some sophisticated planting. Look out for the bridge and staircase linking the gallery and garden, and note how the connecting sala terrena was embellished with a garden pavilion and grotto built into the retaining wall.

Elsewhere there are a number of period-piece sculptures, as well as a collection of indigenous and exotic woody plant species. Behind the garden walls, a large game reserve for hunting was designed as a forest landscape park. Other attractions at Lysice include the orangery and fig house. JBo

Botanická Zahrada a Arboretum, Mendelova Zemedelska a Lesnicka Universita

Jihomoravský Kraj, Czech Republic

DESIGNER: Ivar Otruba

OWNER: Mendel University of Agriculture and Forestry

GARDEN STYLE: 20th-century modernist

SIZE: 25 acres (10.1 ha)

CLIMATE: Temperate

LOCATION: Brno, Jihomoravský Kraj

TRANSLATION: Botanical Gardens and Arboretum, Mendel University of Agriculture and Forestry

The first botanical garden at Mendel University was founded in 1926 as an inspiration for students of systematic botany. An arboretum followed in 1938, this time for forestry students. Expansion of the university necessitated a brand-new garden in 1970. It consists of separate, integrated units featuring stone and metal sculptures, and was built as a resource for scientific research at the university.

One of the most exciting areas is the gorge, 16.5 feet (5 m) deep, with a cliff made of concrete and stone, and dry stone packing filled with alpines. At the bottom of the gorge, there is what might best be described as a mini sea, where water collects in spring, and another part of the gorge is shaped as an amphitheater. Around the garden, you will see 5,000 species of woody plant, 2,000 perennial species, alpine plants, and a large selection of cotoneasters, irises, willows, and porophyllums. Among the 2,000 orchids in the greenhouses are specialized collections of the genera *Paphiopedilum* and *Dendrobium*.

Every year there is a huge exhibition of irises, and another called The Colors of the Fall. Also note the greenhouse with about thirty species of tropical butterfly, and the clever use throughout the garden of all kinds of unusual industrial elements. JBo

Zámek Kroměříž

Zlínský Kraj, Czech Republic

DESIGNERS: Filiberto Lucchese, Giovanni Pietro Tencalla
OWNER: The Czech State
GARDEN STYLE: 17th-century Italian baroque, landscape park
SIZE: 32 acres (12.9 ha)
CLIMATE: Temperate
LOCATION: Kroměříž, Zlínský Kraj
TRANSLATION: Kroměříž Castle

Near the historic center of Kroměříž, the château garden—completed in 1675—is based on a rectangular ground plan, one side being enclosed by an 800-foot-long (243.8 m) ornamental gallery. Formerly an entrance to the garden, the gallery now serves as a viewing point for part of the garden. The spacious and high-quality stucco-ornamented first-floor rooms of the Italian mannerist sala terrena form the main entrance to the park itself. Today the entrance is through a court, built between two greenhouses in the first half of the nineteenth century. The garden's main features include two mazes, an octagonal rotunda, and the four fountain grottoes in the center. There are also flower beds, bordered by clipped, low hedges, two hills, and two rectangular fishponds. To one side is an adjoining old Dutch garden and a swan pond with an island and aviary. A small, hidden, neobaroque terrace garden communicates with the château via an arcaded, secret corridor with a double staircase.

A short distance from the town center lies a separate Flower Garden. Consisting of more than 116 acres (47 ha), it offers panoramic views of the town. In the late eighteenth century, it was restyled as a romantic landscape park. The work was completed in 1845, inspired by the ideas of Prince Pückler of Bad Muskau and under the supervision of the architect Antonín Arche. The Flower Garden, the Bishop's Mint, and the château and its garden were placed on the UNESCO World Heritage List in 1998. JBo

Zámek Buchlovice

Zlínský Kraj, Czech Republic

DESIGNER: Josef Lacowsky
OWNER: The Czech State
GARDEN STYLE: 18th-century baroque with English park
SIZE: 46.5 acres (18.8 ha)
CLIMATE: Temperate
LOCATION: Buchlovice, Zlínský Kraj
TRANSLATION: Buchlovice Castle

This baroque château, consisting of two three-winged buildings facing each other, was built in the style of an Italian villa. The château is enclosed by Italian baroque, terraced parterre gardens. The garden went through two transformations in the eighteenth century. In the first half of the century, the Italianate garden was partially transformed into the new classical French style. Later the château acquired more land that was shaped in the style of an English park. The landscaped park contains an excellent tree collection and some superb rhododendrons.

From the second half of the nineteenth century, Buchlovice's landscape park was developed according to the design of Josef Lacowsky. The terrain slopes down from west to east, and various terraces were formed, the upper and smallest terrace occupied by the château courtyard with its central fountain and obelisk. A stream was incorporated into the layout, separating the first and second terraces. A stretch of water accentuates the lower terrace as it adjoins the main parterre of the baroque garden.

In the twentieth century, a new gatehouse and entrance were built, and the park gained its collection of rhododendrons and decorative potted plants. Fuchsias are important at Buchlovice, and there is an annual summer exhibition of more than 800 species and varieties grown in the garden. Visitors are also attracted to the château by the rococo furniture that has remained in many of the rooms since the owners fled to Austria at the end of World War II. JBo

Schlossgarten Laxenburg

Niederösterreich, Austria

DESIGNERS: Isidore Canevale, Le Februe-d'Achambault, Christoph Lübeck, Peter Joseph Lenné
OWNER: City of Vienna
GARDEN STYLE: 18th-century baroque and landscape
SIZE: 593 acres (240 ha)
CLIMATE: Temperate
LOCATION: Laxenburg, Niederösterreich

When the Hapsburgs needed to escape the pomp and grandeur of their summer residence at Schönbrunn (see page 640), they retreated to the gentle pace of life at Laxenburg, 17 miles (27.2 km) to the south of Vienna. It was as if the imperial family were looking for a lost romantic time that would distract them from the upheavals of nineteenth-century Europe.

The gardens began as a hunting ground, then became a baroque garden and, finally, a more natural landscape garden. In 1782, following the orders of Emperor Joseph II, the architect Isidore Canevale produced a plan that was realized by Le Februe-d'Achambault and Christoph Lübeck, a gardener from Dessau. Throughout the next few years, during the reign of Franz II, various features were added to the park, and even the famous German landscape gardener Peter Joseph Lenné was commissioned to reduce the impact of the baroque elements. Very few of the buildings remain, and of these the most impressive are the Franzensburg, a baronial castle of 1799–1801 on the shores of the lake, the Gothic bridge, and the Rittersäule in the woodland. The exquisite Diana temple, with a painting by Vinzenz Fischer, is quite exceptional and has, like many other parts of the park, been restored.

Laxenburg is closely associated with the Empress Sissy, a beautiful, romantic, and tragic figure who sought solitude and refuge in the grounds. HH

Schlossgarten Belvedere

Wien, Austria

DESIGNERS: Lukas von Hildebrandt, Dominique Girard, Anton Zinner
OWNER: City of Vienna
GARDEN STYLE: 18th-century Austrian baroque
SIZE: 42.7 acres (17.3 ha)
CLIMATE: Temperate
LOCATION: Vienna, Wien

The Belvedere is better known today for its art collection and museums than for its gardens, which are a unique blend of French baroque and Italian mannerism. What appears to be one garden is, in fact, a series of gardens backing on to one another. At the top end of the sloping site is the Upper Belvedere; at the lower end is the Lower Belvedere. Separating and linking the two gardens is a high wall, broken at both ends by an unusual flight of steps and ramps (for horsedrawn carriages), situated in the center as a backdrop to the magnificent cascade and fountain.

The gardens are compact and complex, the confined space manipulated to make the grounds appear much larger than they are. Built for Prince Eugen of Savoy in 1700–23, the formal garden follows the principles laid out in the best-selling garden design book of the day, *La Théorie et la Pratique du Jardinage* by Dezallier d'Àrgenvilles. The theme, very much a favorite of Prince Eugen, is a celebration of victories, battles, and war heroes. Hercules, Apollo, Neptune, et al make their appearance as statues and in elaborate water features around the garden.

The name Belvedere—meaning "a beautiful view"—is entirely appropriate because from the Upper Garden, the city of Vienna unfolds before you, a magnificent panorama. But the garden is above all a private garden, the personal refuge of a prince who, as well as fighting battles, enjoyed gardening. HH

Schlossgarten Schönbrunn

Wien, Austria

DESIGNERS: Jean Trehet, Louis Gervais, Jean Nicolas
Jardot, Johann Ferdinand Hetzendorf
OWNER: City of Vienna
GARDEN STYLE: 17th- and 18th-century baroque
SIZE: 457 acres (185 ha)
CLIMATE: Temperate
LOCATION: Vienna, Wien

Built to rival Versailles, the Schönbrunn garden is a living reminder of the power of the Hapsburg monarchy. Viewed from the raised terrace in the center of the palace, the garden unfolds in a spectacular, 180-degree panorama. A star-shaped system of avenues radiates out, with the grand, central parterre in its center, all flanked by acres of woodland that seem to be held back by massive hedges. This leads to the Neptune Fountain, behind which, towering in the background and crowning the horizon, is the artificial ruin, the Glorietta.

The design of the garden cannot be attributed to a single person. Schönbrunn is the result of a progressive development from 1693 to 1780, and it reflects the interests and tastes of two monarchs, Leopold I and Empress Maria Theresia. The initial plans, dating from 1695, are attributed to Jean Trehet, who set out the parterre and the woodland with 20,000 beeches, and imported French yews for the hedges. Interest in the garden stagnated between 1700 and 1740, but was rekindled when Maria Theresia came to the throne. Her husband, Franz Stephan, added a menagerie, redesigned the Kammergärten (intimate gardens close to the palace), and cut a system of strong, diagonal avenues through the wooded areas. Seven years after his death, Maria Theresia commissioned Johann Ferdinand Hetzendorf to build the Glorietta in the *bosquets*, a block of closely planted trees with paths, and the obelisk at the end of the east diagonal. HH

Salzburger Freilichtmuseum

Salzburg, Austria

DESIGNERS: Various farmers
OWNER: Province of Salzburg
GARDEN STYLE: 17th- and 18th-century farmhouses
SIZE: 123 acres (49.8 ha)
CLIMATE: Temperate
LOCATION: Grossgmain, Salzburg

While grand historic and modern gardens attract a lot of attention, private gardens often go unnoticed. The traditional farmers' gardens of the alpine region are hard to track down, and that is why the open-air museum at Grossgmain, at the foot of Untersberg, is so special. Not only have traditional farmhouses and rural buildings from the region around Salzburg been saved, carefully dismantled, and meticulously rebuilt in regional "hamlets," but many of the gardens have been recreated. They provide a valuable insight into rural life and attitudes to gardening in the seventeenth and eighteenth centuries.

These gardens provided flowers for medicinal purposes, not decoration, as well as fruit, vegetables, and herbs, and relied on the farmers' wives to produce as much as possible in a compact area within a limited season. The gardens have a wonderful old-world charm, especially the three gardens in the Flachgau section of the museum. The Lohnergütl, Zischkhäusl, and Knotzinger Hof gardens are all excellent recreations of traditional country gardens. Of interest are minute details such as, in the Zischkhäusl garden, the ornamental glass "rose" balls placed on the ends of pea sticks to prevent eye injury to stooping gardeners. The gardens themselves are rarely open, but are so compact that they can be seen over the picket fence. Americans may see similarities between these small, enclosed gardens and the historic gardens of Williamsburg. The whole layout of the museum, with its clusters of traditional buildings, flower meadows, and woodland, is exemplary. HH

Hellbrunn

Salzburg, Austria

DESIGNER: Santino Solari
OWNER: City of Salzburg
GARDEN STYLE: 18th-century rococo mannerist, landscape
SIZE: 111 acres (44.9 ha)
CLIMATE: Temperate
LOCATION: Hellbrunn, Salzburg

A guided tour and waterproof clothing are obligatory when visiting this extraordinary garden. For just under 200 years, from 1613 to 1803, Hellbrunn was the summer residence of the archbishops of Salzburg, where they would hold court, entertain, and surprise guests. The gardens are divided into three sections— the large "natural garden," the French baroque water parterre, and the famous rococo mannerist garden to the side of the house. The palace and the grounds are based on the model of the Italian *villa suburbana*, and were built during 1613–15 by Santino Solari for Markus Sittikus, Prince Archbishop of Salzburg.

Stone for the building work was quarried from within the estate, from the slopes of the Untersberg. The quarry was transformed into an amphitheater, setting a trend that later inspired the theaters at Eremitage and Sanspareil in Bavaria. But Hellbrunn is best known for the "water toys" in the alcoves, temples, grottos, and paths of the enclosed garden immediately next to the palace. Sittikus took delight in surprising and playing jokes on his guests, a tradition that the guides are only too happy to continue. Watch out for the water jets concealed in the stone seats around the banqueting table in the Roman Theater, the stag's head that sprays water from its antlers, and the singing birds in the Orpheus Grotto. During 1748–52 a water-powered marionette-theater, designed and built by Lorenz Rosenegger, depicting life in a baroque town, was added as a grand finale. The mixture of formality, hydraulics, and playfulness makes Hellbrunn a hot attraction. HH

Mirabellgarten

Salzburg, Austria

DESIGNERS: Johann Bernhard Fischer von Erlach,
Matthias Diesel, Lukas von Hildebrandt,
Franz Anton Danreiter, Friedrich Ludwig von Sckell
OWNER: City of Salzburg
GARDEN STYLE: 17th-century baroque
SIZE: 9 acres (3.6 ha)
CLIMATE: Temperate
LOCATION: Salzburg, Salzburg

The Mirabellgarten is compact, but ingeniously planned to make the most of its space and the views. But while guided tours of Salzburg go through the parterre and past the rose garden to the Voiliere, they often miss other interesting sections of the garden.

Prince Bishop Wolf Dietrich von Raithenau built the first palace in 1601 for his mistress and her children. In the first half of the seventeenth century, a protective battlement was laid around the garden, and parts of this are still visible. The basic layout of the parterres originates from this period, but it was improved in a plan drawn up in 1687 by Johann Bernhard Fischer von Erlach and Matthias Diesel for Archbishop Johann Ernst von Thun-Hohenstein. The hedge theater, the dwarf's garden with macabre figures, a shooting range, and other small gardens all date from this period. Further improvements were made to the palace and the garden by Fischer von Erlach's successor, Lukas von Hildebrandt, who worked closely with the new court gardener for Prince Bishop Franz Anton Graf von Harrach. By 1810 the palace was the residence of the Crown Prince of Bavaria, who wanted a more contemporary garden. From a radical plan drawn up by the landscaper Friedrich Ludwig von Sckell, only the landscape garden to the north of the palace was realized. HH

RIGHT The parterres of the Mirabellgarten channel the gaze irresistibly toward the grandeur of Salzburg Castle.

Eszterháza

Győr-Moson-Sopron, Hungary

DESIGNERS: Anton Zinner, Nicolas Jacoby, Anton Umlauft
OWNER: The Hungarian State
GARDEN STYLE: 18th-century baroque, 20th-century neobaroque
SIZE: 575 acres (232 ha)
CLIMATE: Temperate
LOCATION: Fertőd, Győr-Moson-Sopron
TRANSLATION: Eszterházy Palace

Eszterháza is universally known as the Hungarian Versailles. The core of the current castle was built in the town of Süttör for the second son of Prince Eszterházy, later to become Count Miklós, in the late 1720s. His older brother died in 1762 without an heir, so Miklós inherited the title, enabling him to create his dream garden. Miklós later changed the name of the town to Eszterháza, later to become famous because Joseph Haydn was the *kapellmeister* of its opera house. Today the town's name is Fertőd.

The first garden, which was constructed during the 1720s, was designed by Anton Zinner. He already had experience creating gardens for members of the aristocracy, notably for Eugene of Savoy in and around Vienna, including Vienna's world-famous Belvedere. From the 1760s onward, construction of the entire Eszterháza site was overseen by Nicolas Jacoby. The gardens were given a French formal look, with a patte d'oie leading to the castle. Behind the parterre, small woods hid numerous pavilions, and the garden was surrounded by a game park.

Eszterháza was abandoned after Miklós died in 1790, but a later heir rediscovered it in the late nineteenth century, and a few additions followed. A neobaroque parterre was also added by Viennese imperial head gardener Anton Umlauft in the early years of the twentieth century. The site lost vast areas of the game park under the Communists, but is now starting to regain its splendor. KF

Tata

Komárom-Esztergom, Hungary

DESIGNER: Charles Moreau
OWNER: The Hungarian State
GARDEN STYLE: Early-19th-century landscape garden
SIZE: 175 acres (70.8 ha)
CLIMATE: Temperate
LOCATION: Tata, Komárom-Esztergom
TRANSLATION: Tata Fortress

Tata has been a royal residence since the first half of the fifteenth century, when Sigismund of Luxemburg, King of Hungary and later Emperor of the Holy Roman Empire, built a fortified castle here. The marshy area was brought under control for the Counts Eszterházy in the middle of the eighteenth century by the creation of two large lakes. A short while later, a new residence was started that was inherited by Count Ferenc Eszterházy in 1765. It was much easier to create a landscape garden in Tata than at other sites because of the vast local water supplies. However, one drawback was the lack of space for a large garden on the site because the town of Tata surrounded the royal residence. This meant that the garden had to be small. The medieval royal palace was transformed into a mock castle by Charles Moreau.

The new garden at Tata was initially designed by Isidore Ganneval as a moderate-sized square garden, divided by a star-shaped system of alleys with a small castle in its center. This idea was soon abandoned, though, when the garden was extended to surround the entire lake. The designer of the new garden was probably Charles Moreau. Ferenc Karsa, a visiting Hungarian army officer, wrote in in his diary in 1849: "The Count's garden is an abundant source of nature's beauty with its tarns, lake of swans, winding streams, and a Turkish mosque towering in the middle." Today many of the numerous buildings originally placed in different parts of the garden are still there, and strollers find them as eye-catching as ever. KF

Martonvásár

Fejér, Hungary

DESIGNER: Heinrich Nebbien
OWNER: The Hungarian State
GARDEN STYLE: Early-19th-century landscape garden
SIZE: 175 acres (70.8 ha)
CLIMATE: Temperate
LOCATION: Martonvásár, Fejér
TRANSLATION: Martonvásár Castle

Three generations of the Counts Brunszvik are responsible for the great garden here. After numerous decades of economic growth, which had affected the entire surrounding landscape, the first ornamental garden was created at Martonvásár in the last years of the eighteenth century. The garden was famously visited by Ludwig van Beethoven, who came here several times in the early nineteenth century

The garden had a sentimental character, with monuments dedicated to great emotions. Friendship, for instance, was symbolized by the Republic of the Lime Tree Ring, actually a group of lime trees planted in a circle, with each tree representing a member of a close group of friends, including Beethoven. He often came here to give piano lessons to the Brunszvik girls because he was in love with one of them.

When this style of garden fell out of fashion in the early nineteenth century, Ferenc Brunszvik decided to reshape it in a classic landscape style in 1809. He commissioned Heinrich Nebbien, who created a large lake—by damming the St. Ladislaus Creek that flows through the site—with an island in the middle of it. Numerous exotic trees were planted here, including cedars, white cypresses, plane trees, and ginkgos. An English traveler, Richard Bright, visited Martonvásár in 1815 and said that it felt like England. The park has not changed much since Nebbien's time, although the castle itelf was enlarged and altered according to the neo-Gothic style in 1875, giving the garden an unusual romantic twist. KF

Alcsút

Fejér, Hungary

DESIGNERS: Archduke Joseph of Hapsburg, Karl Tost
OWNER: The Hungarian State
GARDEN STYLE: Early-19th-century landscape garden
SIZE: 100 acres (40.5 ha)
CLIMATE: Temperate
LOCATION: Alcsút, Fejér
TRANSLATION: Alcsút Castle

The barren land of Alcsút came into the possession of the Palatine, Viceroy of Hungary, in 1818. The Palatine was then Archduke Joseph, a younger son of Emperor Leopold II, whose ambition was to create a thriving agricultural business. He hoped his model farm would help others implement the latest farming technology and revive his undeveloped country.

Joseph's changes also applied to the surrounding landscape, and he planted his favorite plane trees along the roads, and cedars of Lebanon (*Cedrus libani*) in the woods. The center of the estate was marked by an excellent neoclassical castle on a hill, but only a few buildings were erected in the garden. The Palatine and his wife preferred planting trees to commemorate events or as dedications to their family. They planted a pine grove for the birth of their son, Stephan, and birch trees for their daughter Maria Henrietta, later Queen of Belgium. An island was dedicated to their other daughter, Hermina, while the Doll House was built as a playroom for the children.

After the Palatine's death, his descendants made more improvements. A greenhouse was erected next to the castle, and the lake was enlarged. An extensive alpine garden was created, and bears were kept in a special enclosure. During World War II, the castle was badly damaged, and the Communists' revenge on the former ruling class culminated in the dismantling of the castle and the greenhouse. The garden, other edifices, and the remnants of the castle, however, can still be seen. And they are exceptionally beautiful. KF

Csákvár

Fejér, Hungary

DESIGNER: Ferdinand Zart
OWNER: The Hungarian State
GARDEN STYLE: Early-19th-century landscape garden
SIZE: 210 acres (85 ha)
CLIMATE: Temperate
LOCATION: Csákvár, Fejér
TRANSLATION: Csákvár Castle

Creating an English-style landscape garden at the Eszterházy Castle of Csákvár was a great challenge because the area lacks sufficient water resources. On the other hand, when the first residence was built in the middle of the eighteenth century, there was no intention of creating an ornamental garden. The nearby game park, called Alley Wood because of its grid of vistas, served the owner's needs for hunting, and that was all that he really ever needed.

Ferenc and János Eszterházy shared the family inheritance after their father's death in 1765. Csákvár was the secondary, less prestigious residence that came into the possession of the younger brother, János. He started putting money into Csákvár in the late 1770s and created a new, ornamental, English-style garden. Surprisingly his input initially meant that four separate gardens were created, each detached from the other by fences or walls. The design also became more and more irregular. The numerous garden pavilions in each area were partly designed by the Italian-born painter Pietro Rivetti, who was later convicted of forgery and died in prison.

The inner parts of the park were brought together and redesigned by Ferdinand Zart in 1801, in the classic landscape style, but the previous design wasn't completely eradicated. And, although more changes have meant that many of the pavilions have disappeared in the course of time, the garden still has an arcadian character with large clearings and groves, and long, clear vistas. KF

Városliget

Budapest, Hungary

DESIGNER: Heinrich Nebbien
OWNER: City of Budapest
GARDEN STYLE: 19th-century landscape garden
SIZE: 250 acres (101.2 ha)
CLIMATE: Temperate
LOCATION: Pest, Budapest
TRANSLATION: Városliget Park

The Városliget city park was one of the earliest urban public parks in Europe—not a princely garden open to the public, but a piece of land owned by the city and specially designed for the recreation of the citizens. The Embellishment Committee of the City of Pest had initiated a design competition in 1813 for the Városliget—Heinrich Nebbien completed his entry in 1816 and won the commission.

The western outskirts of Pest—part marshy, part sandy desert, with westerlies blowing the sand into town—gave the city council a headache for a long time. The first attempt, in 1799, to convert this land to a fruitful area and block the wind was ordered by the Primate of the Hungarian Clergy, the Archbishop of Esztergom, with the help of the garden designer Rudolph Witsch. Unfortunately the primate died too soon to see the project completed.

Although Nebbien considered himself mainly a business adviser, he designed the buildings in the garden himself. They were not implemented because of a shortage of funds, but the new plantations and the creation of the large lake with two islands gave the place plenty of character, and Városliget soon became popular and fashionable. In 1896 the World Exhibition was held here, and the layout had to be changed, with trees being felled to provide space for the exhibition pavilions. Visitors today find a huge, open space that retains parts of its early nineteenth-century layout, with botanical gardens, a castle, a zoo, and a spa noted for its giant floating chess boards. KF

Margitsziget

Budapest, Hungary

DESIGNERS: Archduke Joseph of Hapsburg, Karl Tost
OWNER: City of Budapest
GARDEN STYLE: 19th-century landscape garden
SIZE: 237 acres (95.9 ha)
CLIMATE: Temperate
LOCATION: Margaret Island, River Danube, Budapest
TRANSLATION: Margaret Island

The Margitsziget was originally used by lepers who needed to be quarantined, but part of it was handed over to a Dominican convent in the middle of the thirteenth century. St. Margaret, the daughter of a king, became a nun and spent almost her entire life on the island. After her death, the island became a pilgrimage site and subsequently took her name.

The island lies between the two parts of the Hungarian capital, Buda and Pest (once two cities), on the River Danube, and was presented to the Palatine, the Viceroy of Hungary, at the end of the eighteenth century. From 1795 until 1847, the Palatine was Archduke Joseph, a younger son of Emperor Leopold II, who enjoyed immense popularity because he was so actively involved in reviving the country. When the Enlightenment reached the Hapsburgs, it meant that the archdukes had to learn a profession during their childhood. Joseph chose gardening, and apparently was capable of recognizing 6,000 different plants. He loved working in his gardens and planted many exotic trees. When transforming Margaret Island from farmland to a landscape garden, he built a garden villa in the rather plain, rural environment, well aware of the historic importance of the medieval ruins.

The garden has always been open to the public as the palatines wished. At the end of the nineteenth century, the island underwent further developments, including the construction of a thermal spa and hotel. Today it has managed to preserve some of the character of its previous incarnations. KF

Regal Grădina in Săvârsin

Arad, Romania

DESIGNER: Andrei Forray
OWNER: The Romanian royal family
GARDEN STYLE: 20th-century wooded parkland
SIZE: 50 acres (20.2 ha)
CLIMATE: Temperate
LOCATION: Săvârsin, Arad
TRANSLATION: Royal Garden of Săvârsin

The connection between Săvârsin and the Romanian royal family began when King Michael and Queen Elena, charmed by this region of Transylvania and the beauty of the castle at Săvârsin, bought the estate and began to restore the parklands and buildings. They added several features to the original design by Andrei Forray, including a beautiful, ornamental lake. However, in 1947 the estate was confiscated and passed into state ownership. The castle became a hospital, then the private residence of dictator Nicolae Ceaucescu, and the abandoned parkland drifted into a wilderness. After Ceaucescu's death, and a prolonged court case, the estate was returned to its royal owners in 2000. Crown Princess Margarita, daughter of King Michael, is the estate manager and says she is "nursing the estate back to life."

The park has been well and truly reclaimed. In the center of the estate is the much restored and renovated castle, its appearance much enhanced by the informality of the surrounding parkland. Rare species of trees abound, many of them wonderfully ancient and gnarled. Particularly impressive are the centuries-old oaks and nut trees lining the main avenues of the park. The signs of neglect and turmoil have virtually been erased in the last five years, and Săvârsin is now well on its way to being the lovely, tranquil place with which the Romanian king and queen fell in love nearly a century ago. KF

Cluj Grădina Botănica

Cluj, Romania

DESIGNER: Unknown
OWNER: University Babes-Bolyai
GARDEN STYLE: 20th-century botanical garden
SIZE: 35 acres (14.1 ha)
CLIMATE: Temperate
LOCATION: Cluj-Napoca, Cluj
TRANSLATION: Botanic Gardens of Cluj

This is one of the most beautiful and complex botanical gardens in southeastern Europe. Founded in 1920 by Professor Alexandru Borza, and affiliated to the University Babes-Bolyai, the garden is rigorously scientific. The 10,000 plant species are systematically divided according to their taxonomy and phytogeography, but the overall effect is far from dry and academic because the gardens are thoughtfully and artistically designed. Formal education is combined with aesthetic values to create a site packed with variety and color.

The garden is spread over hilly land, and is split by the River Piriul Tiganilor and its tributaries into three islands creating microclimates that enable plants from all over the world to be grown. There is an excellent collection of Romanian flora, from the Transylvanian Plain to the Carpathian Mountains, Banat, Oltenia, and beyond. A major attraction is the Roman Garden, with its statue of the goddess Ceres and locally found ancient archaeological artifacts.

The hothouse complex is an impressive achievement. While outside winter temperatures regularly reach −148°F (−100°C) or lower, inside there are six greenhouses and a jungle of tropical plants. Palms, ferns, and orchids jostle for space around an Amazonian water lily (*Victoria amazonica*) with leaves the size of rowing boats and huge white flowers that fade to deep pink and die within a day. KF

Târgu Jiu Sculpture Park

Gorj, Romania

DESIGNER: Constantin Brancusi
OWNER: The Romanian State
GARDEN STYLE: 20th-century sculpture park
SIZE: 22 acres (8.9 ha)
CLIMATE: Temperate
LOCATION: Târgu Jiu, Gorj

The gardens at Târgu Jiu are a leafy setting for some of the most spectacular outdoor artworks of the twentieth century. Created by the sculptor Constantin Brancusi, not far from his birthplace in Hobita, the park marks the spot where the Romanian people fought off the advancing German armies of 1916.

Perhaps the most impressive piece in the park is *The Endless Column*, 100 feet (31 m) tall. The work is a stylized version of the traditional funeral pillars of southern Romania. Its soaring elegance belies the scale of the engineering effort required to assemble its seventeen cast-iron modules. Less imposing but more atmospheric is *The Table of Silence*, nestling in a clearing by the banks of the River Jiu. The circular limestone table is surrounded by twelve empty, hourglass-shaped chairs, leading one to contemplate both the passing of time and the empty places belonging to those who died in the war. Walking on, visitors pass the huge stone *The Gate of the Kiss* and the *Alley of Chairs*, and eventually reach the Avenue of Heroes, which rises up to give a stunning view of the great open space of the Carpathian landscape.

Monumental, subtle, and intimate, Brancusi's sculptures combine with the sweeping spaces of gentle woodland at Târgu Jiu to create a beautiful place to consider the best, and worst, of man. KF

LEFT *The Endless Column* in Târga Jiu Sculpture Park rises like a string of gargantuan beads pulled taut toward the sky.

Parco Botanico del Canton Ticino

Ticino, Switzerland

DESIGNER: Baroness Antoinette de Saint-Léger
OWNER: Canton of Ticino
GARDEN STYLE: Late-19th-century private botanical garden
SIZE: 6 acres (2.4 ha)
CLIMATE: Mediterranean
LOCATION: Isole di Brissago, Lake Maggiore, Ticino

Lake Maggiore is Switzerland's southernmost lake and, with more than 2,300 hours of sunshine a year, its sunniest area. Mountains to the north shelter it from wind, and Mediterranean warmth sweeps up from Venice and Genoa. On the lake are two islands, the Isole di Brissago. The smaller island, Isola di Sant'Apollinaire is closed to the public. The larger island, Isola di San Pancrazio, is home to a botanical garden with 1,600 plant species. Close to Italy, these gardens house plants that normally do not grow in Switzerland's alpine landcape.

Both islands were acquired in 1885 by Russian adventuress Baroness Antoinette de St-Léger for a mere 21,000 francs. Over the next four decades, she turned San Pancrazio into a personal paradise, cultivating rare and exotic plants, and patronizing sculptors, artists, composers, and writers, who flocked to her villa. By 1927 her looks, her last husband, the artists, and her wealth were gone. The islands were sold to the German industrialist Max Emden, who remodeled the villa and built a marina.

The islands were purchased for the public in 1949, and today, San Pancrazio has mature rhododendrons, azaleas, camellias, magnolias, palms, cistus, proteas, bamboos, tree ferns, eucalyptus, and citrus trees. The beneficent spirit of the baroness haunts it still: Buried in the village cemetery of Intragna, where she died in penury in 1948, her remains were moved to a quiet corner of the woods here in 1972. RCa

Vico Morcote

Ticino, Switzerland

DESIGNER: Sir Peter Smithers
OWNERS: The Smithers family
GARDEN STYLE: 20th-century informal
SIZE: 1 acre (0.4 ha)
CLIMATE: Mediterranean
LOCATION: Vico Morcote, Ticino

In his book, *Adventures of a Gardener*, Sir Peter Smithers described his gardening apprenticeship—through childhood and then his career, first as an MI6 agent, and then in national and international politics. The book set out twelve principles for the garden at Vico Morcote, where in 1970 he settled on the shores of Lake Lugano at the southern end of the Alps.

The first two principles were that the garden should be a source of pleasure and increasingly easy to maintain as the owner grew older. In practice this meant that the bare slopes of the hill became a self-sustaining ecosystem of exotics that blended into the landscape. The plants do all the work by supporting each other, and by shouldering out any unwanted ones. Sixteen different plant communities have been established in the garden according to the lay of the land, and each, in turn, surprises and delights the visitor. A stream runs through the central patio, around which the house was built, and cascades down the hill, filling the air with the sound of water.

Sir Peter, who died in 2006, chose his plants with care. Only the best forms of any species were included, and to this end Sir Peter sourced them from all over the world. Among his collections are magnolias, daphnes, camellias, nerines, peonies, and wisterias. He also bred some very good strains that bear the name "Vico." Two other guiding principles were that scent was all important—virtually all the species grown are scented, fragrant, or aromatic—and that plants that flower early or late in the season should be included to keep the garden alive. CB

Isola Bella

Isola Bella, Piemonte, Italy

DESIGNER: Antonio Crivelli
OWNERS: The Borromeo family
GARDEN STYLE: 17th- and 18th-century baroque
SIZE: 15 acres (6 ha)
CLIMATE: Mediterranean
LOCATION: Isola Bella, Lake Maggiore, Piemonte

At one end of Lake Maggiore lie three islands. Each is beautiful, but one is unique: nowhere is quite like the baroque extravaganza of Isola Bella. The palace and its gardens were constructed on what was originally barren rock in 1650–71 for the noble and wealthy Borromeo family, and named by Count Carlo III for his wife, Isabella. The island forms the shape of a barge. Landing at the stern, the visitor is guided through the magnificent, but unfinished, summer palace and out, blinking, into sunshine. Ahead stands a vast wedding-cake structure with shell-lined grottoes, stone pillars, and statues. Flights of steps lead up either side to the topmost terrace, where marble figures gaze toward the shore and the snowcapped Alps beyond. Splendid banquets were held there, with fireworks and mock naval battles on the lake below. Theatrical and musical performances were attended by princes and statesmen, the rich and famous.

At the prow of the island, ten levels below the top terrace, there is an ornate parterre. Low box hedges delineate green curlicues around brilliantly colored flowers, each pattern enclosed within an outer hedge. Pure white peacocks patrol the narrow paths between. Exotic blue and pink water lilies adorn the central pond. A giant camphor tree (*Cinnamomum camphora*), more than two centuries old, dominates the lush planting of oranges and grapefruit, orchids and papyrus. It is not hard to imagine the impression this magnificent palace must have made on everyone who visited Isola Bella—from Alexandre Dumas to Stendhal and Dickens. SG

Isola Madre

Isola Madre, Piemonte, Italy

DESIGNERS: The Borromeo family, the Arese family
OWNERS: The Borromeo family
GARDEN STYLE: 18th-century botanical
SIZE: 20 acres (8 ha)
CLIMATE: Mediterranean
LOCATION: Isola Madre, Lake Maggiore, Piemonte

Like a jewel emerging from the lake, Isola Madre, the largest of the Borromeo Islands, has none of the theatrical spectacle of its sister island, Isola Bella. However, it does not need it, because of its wonderful collection of choice plants and trees.

The mild climate in this part of northern Italy allows tender varieties to grow successfully outdoors. A magnificent Kashmir cypress (*Cupressus cashmeriana*) that dominates the garden around the villa is over two hundred years old and is the largest example in Europe. There are banks of evergreen azaleas and rhododendrons, with camellias planted in a woodland setting, and in another area banana trees and palms. At one end of the sixteenth-century villa there is a beautiful garden that complements the Moorish architecture. The garden also has definite North African influences. An ornamental pond is planted with papyrus plumes, while an Arabian carpet of colors surrounds the garden, complementing the grotto where there are classical figures, orchids in hanging baskets, and a striking climber, *Aristolochia gigantea*. Elsewhere you'll see purple bougainvillea, blue plumbago, black bamboo (*Phyllostachys nigra*), *Ginkgo biloba*, espaliered citrus trees, and hibiscus.

If possible, tour the villa to see the treasures, including a room devoted to an exquisite puppet theater made for the Borromeo family. The scenery and costumes rival those of La Scala in Milan. The antique puppets are works of art, and the handwritten accounts of their purchase are on display, together with a remarkable collection of dolls. RL

Villa Taranto

Piemonte, Italy

DESIGNER: Neil McEacharn
OWNER: Ente Giardini Botanici Villa Taranto
GARDEN STYLE: 20th-century botanical
SIZE: 50 acres (20 ha)
CLIMATE: Mediterranean
LOCATION: Verbania Pallanza, Piemonte

This exceptional garden, located by Lake Maggiore in northern Italy, was created by Scotsman Captain Neil McEacharn. It was named after his ancestor, Marshal MacDonald, who was given the title Duke of Taranto by Napoleon. Having established a lovely garden at his Galloway Castle in Scotland, McEacharn bought the estate in Italy in 1931. Work began by clearing 2,000 trees and installing irrigation to pump water from the lake to a reservoir, and then through the garden via a 5-mile-long (8 km) system of pipes.

In 1935, the terraced gardens were created with stepped brooks and beds of brilliantly colored annuals in summer and bulbs in spring. From the terraces, visitors can look out over a pergola covered with varied climbers. There is a fern glade with *Dicksonia antarctica*, and one of the finest mature collections anywhere of rare and choice trees, including *Emmenopterys henryi* from China. In spring, magnolia and rhododendron woods glisten with blossom, and there are outstanding azaleas and camellias.

The best time to visit Villa Taranto is in the fall, when it is possible to see the spectrum of gorgeous tints produced by the acers, particularly the fabulous *Acer* f. *atropurpureum* 'Villa Taranto'. With the beautiful foliage and the sensational dahlia garden, they give a kaleidoscope of color as you walk along a winding path. Visitors should also make sure that they take a look inside the Victoria Amazonica glasshouse with its huge and fabulous water lilies. Fittingly, after Neil McEacharn's death in 1964, he was buried in the chapel in the grounds of his beloved garden. RL

Villa San Remigio

Piemonte, Italy

DESIGNERS: Sophie and Silvio della Valle di Casanova
OWNERS: Piedmont Region
GARDEN STYLE: 20th-century baroque, English landscape
SIZE: 19.7 acres (8 ha)
CLIMATE: Mediterranean
LOCATION: Verbania Pallanza, Piemonte

"We are Sophie and Silvio della Valle di Casanova, and this garden was born of the dreams that we shared in our youth. We planned it as children, and as man and wife we have created it." These words introduce the garden of Villa San Remigio, set high above Lake Maggiore. First cousins Sophie and Silvio married in 1896, and the garden is a celebration of their love.

The formal element of the garden consists of two sets of terraces. The most dramatic are the six baroque terraces set against the ravishing backdrop of lake and mountain south of the villa. Sophie created them by working on models made from wood and cloth, adjusting them until she was happy with the effect at all times of day, even on moonlit nights. The balustrade of the first terrace is decorated with statues of the *Four Seasons* by Francesco Rizzi. The second is a little *salon*, or room, furnished with a topiary armchair and shell seats supported by dolphin pedestals. Under the third terrace Sophie designed a vaulted grotto for subtropical plants, ferns, and orchids. The circular sundial on the terrace outside is a fine excuse for another inscription: "Put here by Silvio and Sophie so that the new light of day may dispel the shadows of fled hours." The climax of the terrace garden is a fountain on the penultimate level, where the goddess Diana rides through the pool in a shell chariot pulled by two web-footed horses. Between the terraces and the lake, Sophie and Silvio created a romantic English landscape of winding woodland paths, and informal plantings of rhododendrons and azaleas, with exotic and native trees. HA

Villa Carlotta

Lombardia, Italy

DESIGNERS: Marquis Giorgio Clerici, and others
OWNER: The Italian State
GARDEN STYLE: 18th-century neoclassical
SIZE: 14 acres (5.7 ha)
CLIMATE: Mediterranean
LOCATION: Tremezzo, Lombardia

This villa was built in 1690 by Marquis Giorgio Clerici, and was given a baroque look in 1747, with the present neoclassical facade being added in 1880. Notable owners have included the wealthy Milanese banker Sommariva, who was responsible for the present facade, and Princess Marianna of Prussia, who gave the villa to her daughter Carlotta as a wedding gift. It is now owned by the Italian State.

To get the full effect of the dramatic terraces rising up to the villa, you must arrive by boat. Five stone staircases, with ornamental balustrades and statues, take visitors up through the terraces lined with pergolas swathed in citrus fruit. The garden's extremely fertile, acid soil means that a magnificent collection of over 150 camellias, rhododendrons, and azaleas can flourish here, along with tropical plants and collections of tree ferns, cacti, bamboos, roses, pittosporums, and giant gunneras.

Behind the villa itself is a romantic English-style park, containing many magnificent trees. There are also some remarkable marble statues by Canova inside the villa. But no matter where you stand, your eyes will always be drawn back to the stupendous view across Lake Como. JHi

> "To get the full effect of the dramatic terraces rising up to the villa, you must arrive by boat"

Isola del Garda

Isola del Garda, Lombardia, Italy

DESIGNERS: Duke Gateano de Ferrari, and others
OWNERS: The Borghese Cavazza family
GARDEN STYLE: 19th-century formal, woodland
SIZE: 15 acres (6 ha)
CLIMATE: Mediterranean
LOCATION: Isola del Garda, Lake Garda, Lombardia

The Isola del Garda is a small island on Lake Garda. Privately owned, it has only recently opened to the public. It has been inhabited since Roman times—with a respite as a game reserve during the decline of the empire—by an ever-changing stream of monks (including St. Francis of Assisi, who built a hermitage here in the thirteenth century), scholars, soldiers, and some of the oldest families in Italy (including the Dukes of Ferrari and Prince Scipione Borghese). The house (an extravagant neo-Gothic villa) and gardens were laid out between 1880 and 1900.

The island is only 1,000 yards (1 km) long, but it manages to pack a great deal into a small space. It divides into multilayered formal gardens that skitter around the outskirts of the villa, and the woodland beyond. The formal area consists of clipped parterres marking out geometric patterns and the coats of arms of the Ferrari family (who initially developed the gardens), and some artificial stucco caves planted with Canary Island date palms (*Phoenix canariensis*). Planted around, and among, the formal areas are roses and tall, columnar cypresses. The lower terraces have fruit trees, including pomegranates, capers, jujube, and citrus.

The rest of the island consists of a captivating mix of mature trees, grassy clearings, and, in particular, a fantastic grove of swamp cypresses (*Taxodium*) dabbling their long horny toes in the waters of the lake. Unusual architecture, interesting plants, a unique site, and the majesty of Lake Garda are four very good reasons to visit. JA-S

Villa Cicogna Mozzoni

Lombardia, Italy

DESIGNER: Unknown

OWNERS: The Cicogna family

GARDEN STYLE: 15th-century renaissance

SIZE: 44.4 acres (18 ha)

CLIMATE: Mediterranean

LOCATION: Bisuschio, Lombardia

Villa Cicogna Mozzoni has been home to the Cicogna family for over 400 years. It is an enchanting rural palace with a fine renaissance garden, beautiful views, and a dramatic water staircase.

The entrance to the garden is framed by an arcade, exquisitely frescoed with a trellis of leaves, flowers, cherubs, and peacocks. Beyond the arcade, the Sunken Garden is bathed in sunlight. It is enclosed on one side by the villa, and on the other three by high walls. To the right, the retaining wall of the upper terrace is decorated with niches containing busts and statues, and the far wall contains a fine grotto. Below the retaining wall, there are two large fishponds surrounded by balustrades. Fountains at the center of the ponds fill the enclosed space with the delightful sound of running water.

A flight of steps through a short tunnel—entered through a pair of wrought-iron gates decorated with the stork (*cicogna*) from the family coat of arms—links the Sunken Garden to the upper terrace that spans the width of the garden. It passes between the villa and the base of the water staircase that is marked by two supine maidens. The staircase was designed to be seen from the windows of the drawing room, and it is only from here that the intended perspective can be properly appreciated.

The terrace was an essential element of the renaissance garden. It provided a sheltered, private space where the family could take their exercise. At Villa Cicogna Mozzoni, the upper terrace offers fine views over the Sunken Garden and the landscape beyond its walls. On a fine day, Lake Lugano, on the border of Italy and Switzerland, is clearly visible. HA

Villa Monastero

Lombardia, Italy

DESIGNERS: Various
OWNER: Consiglio Nazionale delle Ricerche
GARDEN STYLE: 18th- to 20th-century classical Italian
SIZE: 12 acres (4.9 ha)
CLIMATE: Mediterranean
LOCATION: Varenna, Lombardia

Just outside the ancient town of Varenna is the magnificent terraced garden of a former convent. It was founded by the Cistercians in 1208, but was later dissolved in 1567 because of the nuns' reputation for promiscuity. It is now owned by the Consiglio Nazionale delle Ricerche, part of the Italian State, and is used as a research center.

The garden runs along the lake for over a mile (1.6 km), and climbs up the hill in a series of terraces and walks. Italian cypresses (*Cupressus sempervirens*) line the avenues, while the gentle climate and rich soil in the garden enable many exotic and rare trees to grow to an enormous height. Keep your eyes open, and you will see that African and American palms, yuccas, oleanders, and agaves are bigger here than usual. Also eight different species of citrus thrive here, besides the cordylines, erythreas, and myrtles under the lofty Montezuma pines (*Pinus montezumae*). Botanical rarities abound everywhere in this fabulous garden, as do architectural features. The best of these include statues, temples, urns, and wellheads, and there's a marvellous stone balustrade by the side of the lake covered with a magnificent, clambering wisteria. JHi

"...a former convent...dissolved in 1567 because of the nuns' reputation for promiscuity"

Villa del Balbianello

Lombardia, Italy

DESIGNERS: Count Monzino, and others
OWNER: Fondo per l'Ambiente Italiano
GARDEN STYLE: 18th-century, 20th-century Italianate
SIZE: 30 acres (12.1 ha)
CLIMATE: Mediterranean
LOCATION: Lenno, Lake Como, Lombardia

What could be more romantic than arriving at an Italian villa garden by boat? The setting of Villa del Balbianello is glorious. Perched on a promontory on the western shore of Lake Como, it has views across the water in all directions. Catching the boat from nearby Lenno, you can take in Balbianello's magical situation, punctuated by slender Italian cypress trees (*Cupressus sempervirens*) as you cruise toward the iron-gated steps of the landing stage. Once through the gates, gravel paths lead up through a steeply terraced garden to a magnificent loggia, adorned with a living trellis of creeping fig (*Ficus pumila*).

The original structure of the villa and gardens dates to the late eighteenth century, when a cardinal needed a meeting place for his friends. Many owners followed and made adaptations. The gardens today stem from major reworking by the last owner, Count Monzino, who left the villa to the Fondo per l'Ambiente Italiano in 1988.

Green, in its many shades, is the dominant color, and every tree, shrub, and climber is immaculately clipped, which, given the steep terrain, is a marvel in itself. Guided house tours take in the small museum Count Monzino set up in the attic, dedicated to his exploits as an explorer and mountaineer. At the turn of the nineteenth century, Villa del Balbianello was a highly popular tourist destination, and that still holds true. The motto carved in stone by the small harbor reads, "*Fait ce que voudras*" ("Do as you please"); indicating the spirit in which the gardens were conceived. PMcW

Villa Pisani

Veneto, Italy

DESIGNER: Girolamo Frigimelica
OWNER: Countess Maria-Pia Ferrari de Lazara
GARDEN STYLE: 18th-century French, 20th-century classical
SIZE: 24.7 acres (10 ha)
CLIMATE: Mediterranean
LOCATION: Stra, Veneto

Alvise Pisani originally commissioned Count Girolamo Frigimelica to transform his modest family home into a grand villa. However, in 1735 Alvise was elected Doge of Venice, and a more elaborate plan by Francesco Maria Prete was chosen. Fortunately Frigimelica's design for the garden was retained.

Until 1911 the area behind the villa was filled by French parterres de broderie. They were replaced by a long pool of water that was used to test naval models. At one end, the pool reflects the palace, and at the other, an ornate pavilion by Frigimelica, converted by Francesco Maria Prete into luxurious stables.

On each side of the original parterres, Frigimelica planted avenues that create views along the length of the garden. Additional avenues once radiated from the vertical axis, and led the eye across the parterres and through the trees beyond. At one end of the vertical avenue, on the east side of the garden, there was an elaborate, eighteenth-century maze from the original garden. Frigimelica designed a circular tower to stand in the middle of it. At the center of six radiating avenues, he built a hexagonal belvedere with stone steps that lead up through the building to a terrace overlooking the avenues in all directions. Beyond the belvedere, the coffee house stands on a mound containing an ice house. High walls enclose Villa Pisani's impressive array of greenhouses, where prize-winning camellias were grown right up until the mid-nineteenth century and, under the Pisani family, 22,000 lemons were produced and sold from the lemon house each year. HA

Villa Barbaro

Veneto, Italy

DESIGNERS: Andrea Palladio, Daniele Barbaro
OWNERS: Heirs to the Volpi family
GARDEN STYLE: 16th-century Palladian villa garden
SIZE: 0.5 acre (0.2 ha)
CLIMATE: Mediterranean
LOCATION: Maser, Veneto

Villa Barbaro was built for Daniele and Marcantonio Barbaro during 1560–68 as a farmhouse at the center of an agricultural estate. It is a beautiful place with the unique attraction of being the only Palladian villa in the Veneto to retain some of its original garden. The garden was laid out in front of the villa, but all that remains is a single axis that stretches from the ocher-colored facade over the road and into fields beyond.

Daniele Barbaro was a distinguished botanist. He was closely involved in the foundation and design of the Botanic Garden in Padua, and it is likely that the spaces to either side of the main axis were filled by parterre beds stocked with exotic plants. The garden was a public space, bound on one side by the road and on the other by the villa, and with *barchesse*, or barns, to each side of it. These barns, which Andrea Palladio designed as elegant garden arcades, were for housing tools and animals, and would have been used throughout the day by farm workers. The garden was also overlooked by the surrounding fields where the peasants worked, perhaps the reason that Palladio designed the *giardino segreto*, or secret garden, behind the villa. This small, enclosed courtyard is dominated by Palladio's magnificent nymphaeum, where stucco statues of classical gods, some by Marcantonio Barbaro, decorate the facade.

Palladio's great achievement at Villa Barbaro was to link the villa, garden, and the wider landscape together, seemingly to create a single, architectural structure. In so doing, he created a blueprint for the Venetian villa that lasted over two hundred years. HA

Villa Barbarigo

Veneto, Italy

DESIGNER: Unknown
OWNER: Count Fabio Pizzone Ardemani
GARDEN STYLE: 17th-century baroque
SIZE: 24.7 acres (10 ha)
CLIMATE: Mediterranean
LOCATION: Valsanzibio, Veneto

Here the sun's rays shine more brightly
Venus rises more lovely from the sea
The phases of the moon are clearer
Jupiter plays with carefree smile
And Mercury sets aside all clever deceits.

This inscription encapsulates the carefree atmosphere of Barbarigo, one of the most entertaining gardens in Italy, created for Antonio Barbarigo during 1665–69. A north–south axis runs down the slope opposite the villa, across the level ground and up Monte degli Staffoli, the hill behind the building. Hedges flanking this axis serve a dual function: they focus the view, drawing the eye toward the villa, and they also conceal a series of garden "rooms" that the architect furnished with surprises. On one side of the axis, the hedge hides a large and effective maze, and on the other, a charming rabbit island. *Giochi d'acqua*, or water tricks, add more unexpected amusement.

The garden's second axis consists of ascending pools decorated with statues. A graceful watergate has Diana, goddess of hunting, astride the pediment with her dogs close at hand. The facade below is decorated with bas-reliefs of neatly hung game.

In the eighteenth century, Villa Barbarigo was home to one of the finest and most extensive plant collections in Italy, and featured in Paolo Bartolomeo Clarici's book, *Istoria e cultura delle piante* (1726). HA

RIGHT One of a series of pools at Villa Barbarigo, considered to have one of the most entertaining gardens in Italy.

Giardino Giusti

Veneto, Italy

DESIGNER: Count Agostino Giusti
OWNERS: The Giusti family
GARDEN STYLE: 16th-century Italian renaissance
SIZE: 4.4 acres (1.8 ha)
CLIMATE: Mediterranean
LOCATION: Verona, Veneto

For at least three-and-a-half centuries, this fantastic garden in Verona has been one of the show gardens of Italy. In the early seventeenth century, Thomas Conyat wrote that it was "a second paradise" and "a delectable place of solace," and this still holds true in the twenty-first century. Others moved to write about the garden in its heyday include John Evelyn, Joseph Addison, and Johann Wolfgang von Goethe.

Tucked away under the steep hill of San Zeno, away from the lively bustle of the city with its Roman arena and early renaissance house that is now synonymous with Shakespeare's *Romeo and Juliet*, the garden is approached through the palazzo built by the Giusti family. Elegant obelisks adorn the gateposts that form the entrance to the garden, leading to an avenue of tall, pencil-thin cypresses and the ancient grotto carved out of tufa. Above is the striking image of a giant stone mask, from whose mouth it is not difficult to imagine great flames, actually stoked in a chamber behind it. Also note the steps leading up the hillside to the terraces. From both the restored pavilion halfway up and the top level, there are amazing views of the garden and out over the city. There are no original plans for the garden's layout, but recent work has reinstated planting features at ground level—including a maze that is said to be one of the oldest in Europe, and parterres believed to be the oldest in Italy—using an early eighteenth-century plan. Giardino Giusti was a "must see" on most eighteenth-century Grand Tours. You can certainly see why. CB

> "Giardino Giusti was a 'must see' on most eighteenth-century Grand Tours"

Orto Botanico di Padova

Veneto, Italy

DESIGNER: Daniele Barbaro
OWNER: University of Padua
GARDEN STYLE: 16th-century botanical
SIZE: 5.4 acres (2.2 ha)
CLIMATE: Mediterranean
LOCATION: Padua, Veneto

The Orto Botanico di Padova was established in 1545, making it the oldest university botanical garden in the world. It is still a library, classroom, and laboratory used by university students. During the nineteenth century, a series of greenhouses was built, and one of them contains the garden's most famous possession, a dwarf fan palm (*Chamaerops humilis*) from 1781.

The site allocated to the garden in the sixteenth century was irregular. By imposing a square or rectangular layout, half the ground would have been lost, but the problem was resolved by surrounding the area with a circular wall and arranging the site into quadrants, divided by four axes that corresponded to the four points of the compass. In each quadrant the beds were originally composed of every imaginable geometric shape, although the layout was revised in the nineteenth century. A circular moat was dug around the garden to provide water for irrigation and to protect the garden from intruders. Despite this precaution, the beds were stripped almost immediately in a series of nocturnal raids. A higher, and much more substantial, wall was erected and, shortly after, a list of rules affixed to it forbidding any kind of damage to the garden or the plants. Anyone found disobeying these rules was likely to face fines, imprisonment, and, in some cases, even exile.

Despite nineteenth-century alterations to the site, Padua's botanical garden is the finest example of a sixteenth-century botanical garden in Italy. It is a shady and tranquil space in the city center, with a fine collection of plants from all over the world. HA

> ". . . the Botanical Garden of Padua [. . .] represents the birth of science"

Giardini Botanici Hanbury

Liguria, Italy

DESIGNER: Sir Thomas Hanbury
OWNER: The Italian State
GARDEN STYLE: 19th-century botanical
SIZE: 44 acres (18 ha)
CLIMATE: Mediterranean
LOCATION: La Mortola, Ventimiglia, Liguria

Thomas Hanbury, second son of well-to-do Quakers, was so successful that he retired at the age of thirty-five. In 1864 his brother, Daniel, a pharmaceutical chemist interested in botanical origins of drugs and spices, came across a small Riviera promontory close to Menton containing a large ruined villa surrounded by olive terraces. Sheltered from alpine winds by surrounding hills and open to the sea on the south-east, Punta della Mortella was ripe for horticultural experimentation, and the Palazzo Orengo cried out for restoration. By 1867 this was Thomas' home.

Showered with honors by the Italian and British governments, and awarded a Victoria Medal of Honor by the Royal Horticultural Society—he donated its HQ at Wisley in Surrey—Hanbury is a "gardening great." After he died in 1907, the garden declined, but its condition today is thanks to the Italian State, the University of Genoa, and to the friends of the garden.

Instead of laying out formal beds in botanical order, Hanbury arranged his plants thematically or by country of origin. As you wander down flights of steps, past pools, fountains, and pergolas, you will encounter an Australian forest, citrus groves stocked with ancient varieties, an orchard with exotic fruit, extensive collections of passionflowers and sages, living fossils like cycads, the Garden of Perfumes, the Giardinetti full of roses and peonies, and many beds of rare succulents. The plant list is magnificently extensive with over 6,000 species on site. RCa

Giardino di Boboli

Toscana, Italy

DESIGNER: Niccolò Tribolo
OWNER: The Italian State
GARDEN STYLE: 16th-century formal with additions
SIZE: 79 acres (32 ha)
CLIMATE: Mediterranean
LOCATION: Florence, Toscana

During the sixteenth century, Boboli was one of the greatest gardens in Europe, a showcase for Florence's architects and sculptors. Designed in 1549 by Niccolò Tribolo for Duke Cosimo I de' Medici and his wife, Eleanora di Toledo, each successive generation of the Medici family added to the original layout and Boboli evolved into a rich renaissance, mannerist, and baroque history of the Italian garden in miniature.

Tribolo designed Boboli on rough hillside located between the Pitti Palace and the Porta Romana. He transformed the area behind the palace into a level, grassy field that he enclosed on all sides with trees. A colossal fountain marked the axis from the palace to the top of the hill; today, this space is occupied by a magnificent amphitheater, designed by Giulio Parigi in 1618. Tribolo's fountain was moved to the center of the Isolotto, a flamboyant feature of Cosimo I de' Medici's baroque additions to the garden. The Isolotto is a delightful island with pots of lemons, surrounded by a balustrade and a narrow, oval moat. It is linked to the shore by two gated bridges topped by figures of Capricorns, Cosimo I's personal motif. In 1589 Francesco de' Medici commissioned Buontalenti to build the grand grotto. This extraordinary mannerist structure consists of three, richly frescoed, furnished "rooms" and is the climax of a visit to Boboli. HA

RIGHT Within the Boboli Gardens is this small villa, the Casino del Cavaliere, now occupied by a porcelain museum.

Villa Chigi Cetinale

Toscana, Italy

DESIGNERS: Carlo Fontana, Lord Anthony Lambton
OWNER: Lord Anthony Lambton
GARDEN STYLE: 17th- and 18th-century baroque
SIZE: 58 acres (23.4 ha)
CLIMATE: Mediterranean
LOCATION: Ancaiano, Toscana

A visit to Villa Chigi Cetinale will take you deep into the truly ravishing countryside that unravels as you head west out of Siena. Traveling though narrow lanes, past bountiful olive groves and vineyards, you will eventually see Carlo Fontana's baroque villa and bold garden landscape set against the backdrop of the stunning, wooded Montagnola hills.

Fontana was commissioned to build the villa and garden in 1676 by Cardinal Flavio Chigi. He remodeled the villa from a simply constructed, Tuscan farmhouse, making it the midpoint of a north–south axis. From the windows of the drawing room on the first floor, the view stretches to the far end of the axis in both directions. To the south, the axis plunges down into a valley, where it eventually meets a colossal statue of Hercules. The northern axis opens onto the main garden and the original entrance from the road. It is flanked by cypress trees, creating an avenue pointing to the densely wooded hillside beyond. At the end of the avenue, Fontana built a semicircular theater, and 200 stone steps link the lower garden to the *romitorio*, or hermitage, at the top of the hill. Chigi had the garden extended to the east when he commissioned a *tebaide*, or holy wood, where frescoed chapels, and statues of saints and hermits line the grassy paths through the trees. The *tebaide* was completed by Chigi's nephew and heir, Buonaventura Chigi Zondadari. From 1690 to 1717, the Palio, Siena's world-famous horse race, was run several times through the wood.

Cetinale continues to grow and develop, even to this day. The house now belongs to the English Lord Lambton. He has set about restoring the garden landscape and, together with his partner, Claire Ward, has created two new gardens below the main axis. The first of these is a wonderfully romantic cottage garden, while the second is a charming green garden of clipped hedges and espaliered fruit trees. HA

Orto Botanico di Pisa

Toscana, Italy

DESIGNER: Joseph Goedenhuitze
OWNER: University of Pisa
GARDEN STYLE: 16th- to 20th-century botanical garden
SIZE: 7.4 acres (3 ha)
CLIMATE: Mediterranean
LOCATION: Pisa, Toscana

This is the world's first botanical garden, set up in 1543—shortly before those in Padua (1545) and Florence (1550)—by Luca Ghini, who went on to help found the latter two. All three gardens were created to teach students about the medicinal properties of plants, and one of his teaching tools was a series of mounted dried plants that formed the beginnings of an early herbarium. Pisa's living plant collection was expanded by plant-hunting trips to northern Italy.

The garden's original site, on the River Arno, was commandeered as a naval dockyard. Its next site, southeast of the city, brought a storm of complaints from students and others that it was too far from the center. Then, in 1591, the garden moved to its present site, where it was set up by the Flemish botanist Joseph Goedenhuitze (known as Giuseppe Casabona). Here, during the renaissance, painters were invited to record special collections; in keeping with the philosophy of the time, links were forged between art, medicine, botany, and horticulture.

The garden expanded during the eighteenth and nineteenth centuries when glasshouses were added. An arboretum was planted in about 1900. Look for the rare nineteenth-century Coquito palms (*Jubaea chilensis*) and the impressive Oriental planes (*Platanus orientalis*). The garden originally had a formal design, and, although it was altered over the centuries, some elements, such as the central pools and the stone edges on some beds, probably date back to the renaissance. This is a peaceful, historic oasis, close to the tourist-heavy center of Pisa. JO

Villa di Castello

Toscana, Italy

DESIGNER: Niccolò Tribolo
OWNER: Accademia della Crusca
GARDEN STYLE: 16th-century Italian renaissance
SIZE: 2.5 acres (1 ha)
CLIMATE: Mediterranean
LOCATION: Castello, Toscana

Built in 1477, Villa di Castello became the favorite residence of Cosimo I, who began the garden in 1538. The front of the villa commands a magnificent view to the city of Florence, and behind it the garden rises up on the hillside. The walled garden next to the villa is rather unusual because it's not aligned around a central axis emanating from the villa. It has remained largely unchanged since the sixteenth century.

The formal design is softened by 500 citrus trees of varying ages in ornamental terracotta pots. Other Italian features include the bases for fountains, though the actual fountains—a bronze of Hercules and Anteus by Bartolomeo Ammannati, and Venus-Florence wringing out her hair by Giambologna—are in the nearby Villa Petraia. The most unusual feature is the grotto of beasts, designed by Niccolò Tribolo in 1550 and set in the retaining wall. It is now dry, but you can imagine the marble basins, carved with fish and shell motifs, filled with water, jets emerging from the beasts. The tableau of statues is said to represent animals from the biblical flood.

The upper terrace walk is reached by ascending the twin flights of steps set in the retaining wall. There are lovely views over the villa to Florence in the distance, and from this high point the garden becomes more informal. Winding paths lead through the woodland and, in the middle of a grove of holm oaks (*Quercus ilex*) is a large pool. On the island in the center is the bronze statue of *Appennino o Inverno* (*Appenines or Winter*) by Bartolomeo Ammanati (dated 1564) that was originally a fountain. TM

La Foce

Toscana, Italy

DESIGNER: Cecil Pinsent
OWNER: Benedetta Origo
GARDEN STYLE: 20th-century Anglo-Italian
SIZE: 6 acres (2.4 ha)
CLIMATE: Mediterranean
LOCATION: Chianciano Terme, Siena, Toscana

La Foce is one of the most important twentieth-century gardens in Italy, and is set in a spectacular position above the vast spaces of the Orcia valley.

The garden was designed by the English architect Cecil Pinsent for the villa of author and historian Iris Origo. Pinsent began work on the garden in 1926, creating a series of garden spaces and walks behind the villa. The Lemon Garden lies at the heart of his design, a serene, geometric layout of broad terraces lined by box hedges, decorated with pots of lemons on stone plinths. Iris designed brilliant herbaceous borders at the base of the walls enclosing the garden and, in 1938, Pinsent added a raised pergola, rose garden, and a *limonaia* (lemon house). The wisteria-covered pergola strikes out to the west from the house before curving around the shoulder of the hill. At its far end, it opens into woods, where Pinsent had already built a small chapel and a cemetery.

In 1939, just before Italy entered World War II, Pinsent embarked on the final addition, the Lower Garden, which projects out over the Orcia valley. The space is entirely enclosed by tall cypresses and filled with wedge-shaped, double box hedges that taper toward a pool at the far end of the garden. Pinsent has created a mathematically controlled, enclosed landscape built on a human scale, and created the perfect foreground to the view over the wide, wild spaces of the valley below. HA

RIGHT La Foce, begun between the World Wars, in 1926, by English architect Cecil Pinsent.

Villa La Pietra

Toscana, Italy

DESIGNERS: Arthur Acton, Sir Harold Acton, Kim Wilkie
OWNERS: The Acton family, New York University
GARDEN STYLE: 20th-century Anglo-Italian
SIZE: 8.5 acres (3.5 ha)
CLIMATE: Mediterranean
LOCATION: Florence, Toscana

Villa La Pietra's influence is rarely acknowledged. But take a look at the layout and it becomes clear how its twentieth-century take on the Italianate—a temple, open-air theater, cypress and citrus trees, and box-hedged compartments filled with statues or sculptures—inspired a generation of garden makers. Hidcote's creator, Lawrence Johnston, and Sissinghurst's creators, Vita Sackville West and Harold Nicholson, were guests here; Edith Wharton, American novelist and garden maker, wrote about Villa La Pietra in *Italian Villas and Their Gardens*.

La Pietra dates from 1462, but, by the twentieth century, when it was bought by Arthur and Hortense Acton, little was left of the original park. He British, she American, they shared a love of fine art. Arthur, who had studied under Henri Duchêne at the École des Beaux Arts, set about making an Italianate garden around the villa, despite the fashion for informal English gardens. His interpretation created a new Italianate garden style, which became the vogue in Tuscany, England, and the United States. The Actons' son, Sir Harold, art connoisseur and model for Evelyn Waugh's Anthony Blanche in *Brideshead Revisited*, maintained the garden as his parents had left it.

La Pietra has attracted European and American artists, royals, and politicians for over a century. D. H. Lawrence, Pablo Picasso, Winston Churchill, Queen Elizabeth II, the Prince and Princess of Wales, Bill Clinton, Serge Diaghilev, Brigitte Bardot, and Jean Cocteau have all stayed here. The garden has now been restored by British designer Kim Wilkie. JO

Villa Gamberaia

Toscana, Italy

DESIGNER: Unknown
OWNER: Luigi Zalum
GARDEN STYLE: 18th-century Tuscan
SIZE: 3 acres (1.2 ha)
CLIMATE: Mediterranean
LOCATION: Settignano, Toscana

The intimate scale of Villa Gamberaia is part of an irresistible charm that makes it one of Italy's most popular gardens. It had numerous owners before the Capponi family bought it in 1717 and created the garden that exists today. Few archival records survive, and even the garden architect's name has been lost. The villa stands at the midpoint of the finest "bowling alley" in Italy, a smooth lawn stretching the length of the garden. It is flanked almost continuously on one side by buildings; on the other, by the high retaining wall of the upper terrace. In the eighteenth century, the alley would have been used to play bowls or Pall Mall, a form of croquet. To the north, the vista is stopped by a mossy nymphaeum, and to the south a statue of the Roman goddess Diana stands against the view. Opposite the villa, wrought-iron gates lead to the *giardino segreto*, the secret garden that was an essential element of the Italian baroque garden. The small space is enclosed by the retaining walls of the upper terraces and overlooked by smiling statues.

Gamberaia's most famous feature is the water parterre to the south of the villa. Instead of flowerbeds, the box parterres contain pools of water. The narrow paths that run between the clipped hedges are embellished with lemon trees in ancient, terracotta pots. The pools were an early twentieth-century invention, but they are the crowning glory of Gamberaia's perfect baroque garden. HA

RIGHT The understated Villa Gamberaia, site of one of Italy's most intimate and popular gardens.

Villa Garzoni

Toscana, Italy

DESIGNERS: Ottavio Diodati, and others
OWNER: Federico Bertola
GARDEN STYLE: 17th- and 18th-century baroque
SIZE: 10 acres (4 ha)
CLIMATE: Mediterranean
LOCATION: Collodi, Toscana

Villa Garzoni is certainly many things: flamboyant, humorous, theatrical, and extravagantly ornate. Italian baroque gardens often took a villa as the focus of their design, but at Garzoni, this was not at all possible. The villa is perched on a cliff, and the level ground behind it is occupied by a medieval village. Consequently, the original architect, whose name is unrecorded, made the garden at some distance from the villa. In order to reach the garden, the family had to descend from the clifftop and cross a bridge suspended above a deep gorge.

The garden at Garzoni was originally designed in the middle of the seventeenth century. It consists of a circular space on level ground, enclosed by an impressive series of yew hedges, with a grand, balustraded staircase, a spectacular cascade on the hillside immediately above the site, and a series of terraces. In the lower garden, the swirling arabesques of parterres de broderie are set against simple rectangular parterres planted with an array of vibrant annuals. A strange assembly of topiary figures creates a green menagerie that includes trees in the shapes of a peacock, dinosaur, and elephant, while sculpted swans swim in the two circular pools of the fountains.

In 1786 Ottavio Diodati was commissioned to embellish the original layout. He designed the cascade, managing to cunningly widen it toward the summit to create the sensational illusion of water descending a particularly steep and dramatic fall. He also added terracotta statues to every part of the garden, among them the collection of strange little monkeys that perch on the balustrades of the staircase. Water tricks were installed in the grotto above the second flight of steps, and a green theater was built on one of the terraces, its stage lit by griffins holding flaming torches. As a result of Diodati's additions, Villa Garzoni is considered one of the most amusing baroque gardens in Italy. HA

Villa I Tatti

Toscana, Italy

DESIGNER: Cecil Pinsent
OWNER: Harvard University
GARDEN STYLE: 20th-century Anglo-Italian
SIZE: 11 acres (4.5 ha)
CLIMATE: Mediterranean
LOCATION: Settignano, Toscana

Villa I Tatti was designed in 1908 by the English architect Cecil Pinsent for Bernard Berenson, the U.S. art historian and critic. It is a beautiful haven, an enclosed and tranquil space where the great man might retire to think or entertain a large, international circle of friends.

Villa I Tatti was the first major commission of Pinsent's career, but the layout clearly displays his firm belief in the order and symmetry that were at the heart of Italian baroque garden design. He used the old *limonaia* (lemon house) to the south of the villa as a screen to shield the main garden from the house. Today Pinsent's formal terraces are revealed beyond the *limonaia* as a delightful surprise to the first-time visitor. Four narrow terraces descend the hill, intersected by a central staircase; on the terraces to either side of the steps, are neat squares of box. That is the overview of the garden, but as one descends the steps, the details of Pinsent's design unfold. The steps are decorated with an elaborate pebble mosaic, and inside the box hedges there are low, geometric parterres that are invisible from above. On the lowest terrace, he made an oval pool flanked by tiers of box. Beyond it was a wood of holm oaks (*Quercus ilex*) that were already 40 feet (12 m) high when they were planted—so that Berenson could enjoy them fully during his lifetime. Aubrey Waterfield was commissioned to plant a woodland garden among the trees. To the west of the house, Pinsent designed an entirely separate space. It is a charming *giardino pensile*, or hanging garden, enclosed by a decorative, neobaroque wall that is swathed in wisteria. HA

"...a beautiful haven, an enclosed and tranquil space..."

Villa Reale di Marlia

Toscana, Italy

DESIGNERS: Jean-Marie Morel, Jacques Gréber
OWNERS: The Pecci-Blunt family
GARDEN STYLE: 17th-century formal baroque
SIZE: 50 acres (20.2 ha)
CLIMATE: Mediterranean
LOCATION: Marlia, Lucca, Toscana

In the hills around Lucca, in northwest Italy, there is an unusual proliferation of formal *palazzi*, created by seventeenth-century noblemen who had made fortunes in the textile trade. One of the grandest is the Villa Reale di Marlia, with a splendid baroque garden, in the hills overlooking Lucca.

The wealthy Orsetti family commissioned an unknown architect to design the grounds, and the formal garden was very much in the tradition of the day, with a vast sweep of lawn in front of the building and a series of smaller "rooms" hidden in the *boschi* (woodland) on one side of the lawn, an idea designed to create a sense of theater and surprise. The enclosures are different in character, ranging from the ornate lemon garden, with its large, balustraded pool, to the witty *teatro verde* (green theater), complete with grassy stage and wonderful terracotta statues standing in the yew and box wings. The theater was used for concerts by Napoleon I's sister, Elisa Bonaparte, who came to live here in the early nineteenth century. She adored the garden and commissioned the French landscape designer Jean-Marie Morel to redesign the parkland surrounding the house. They added a large lake at the bottom of the sweep of lawn, in the English landscape tradition, and modeled the parkland in the naturalistic style then fashionable. More changes to the garden took place in the early twentieth century when the property was acquired by the Pecci-Blunt family. They designed a Spanish garden with brooks, fishponds, and a splendid swimming pool. The garden has inevitably evolved over the centuries, but its original baroque heart is still very much in evidence. CF

> "...a splendid baroque garden, in the hills overlooking Lucca"

Villa Medici

Toscana, Italy

DESIGNERS: Michelozzi Michelozzo, Cecil Pinsent
OWNER: Anna Mazzini
GARDEN STYLE: 15th-century renaissance
SIZE: 5 acres (1 ha)
CLIMATE: Mediterranean
LOCATION: Fiesole, Toscana

The garden of Villa Medici is both beautiful and immensely important. One of the earliest renaissance gardens in Italy, its situation on a rocky hillside above Florence affords stunning views of the city. The villa and garden were designed and built by Michelozzi Michelozzo between approximately 1455 and 1461 for Giovanni de' Medici. Michelozzo designed two terraces. The first extends from the frescoed loggia on the east-facing facade, and is accessible from the first floor of the villa. Originally the terrace was planted with small parterre beds of herbs and flowers, but today the layout is a simple design of square lawns with lemon trees in pots. There is nothing but a low brick wall to divide the terrace from the view of Florence across the Arno Valley.

Michelozzo designed a second terrace at ground floor level on the west side of the villa. The area was originally used as a vegetable garden, a convenient arrangement because it is on the same level as the kitchen. In 1915 it was renovated by the English architect Cecil Pinsent. Four lawns are set around a central pool, and in the center of each lawn, Pinsent planted magnolia. He was also commissioned to restore the lower of the two south-facing terraces. He removed a series of modern flower beds, demolished the greenhouse that had been built against the retaining wall, and created a simple geometric layout of parterre beds and lawns around a circular pool. The greenhouse was replaced by a raised pergola that linked the two garden terraces to the third terrace on the west side of the villa. HA

Villa Vico Bello

Toscana, Italy

DESIGNER: Baldassare Peruzzi
OWNER: RVA Group
GARDEN STYLE: 16th-, 17th-, and 18th-century formal
SIZE: 5 acres (2 ha)
CLIMATE: Mediterranean
LOCATION: Siena, Toscana

The distinctive silhouette of Siena forms the skyline from this charming garden laid out on a sunny, south-facing slope above the city. Baldassare Peruzzi, Siena's most distinguished architect during the renaissance, designed Vico Bello for the Chigi family in 1576. He laid out the garden later in 1580.

Much of Peruzzi's layout was destroyed in the eighteenth century, when a terrace was added below the villa. However, a sixteenth-century lemon garden has survived intact. A path runs down the center, and lemon trees of an extraordinary size, some over 300 years old, highlight the parterre beds to either side. Peruzzi's beautiful apse stands at the far end of the path, and its curving inner wall has niches and two Roman busts standing at either side of the roof.

The terrace below the lemon garden is planted with fruit trees in parterre beds. There are two oval fish pools with wide stone rims at each end of the terrace; the narrow terrace below the fruit garden is shaded by a massive cedar planted in 1620. Azaleas fill the garden with a blaze of color in spring, and twenty different kinds of orchid hang in baskets suspended from the trees. A passage leads from the terrace into the eighteenth-century flower garden. The greenhouse just inside the entrance was once a family museum containing geological specimens from all over Tuscany. Beds of brightly colored annuals surround a ginkgo tree at the center of the garden, and a small balcony, set in the retaining wall on the far side of the terrace, gives another breathtaking view of Siena. HA

Villa Le Balze

Toscana, Italy

DESIGNER: Cecil Pinsent
OWNER: Georgetown University, United States
GARDEN STYLE: 20th-century Anglo-Italian
SIZE: 3 acres (1.2 ha)
CLIMATE: Mediterranean
LOCATION: Fiesole, Toscana

Villa Le Balze is an ingenious garden built on an awkward site in Fiesole. It was designed by the English architect Cecil Pinsent, an expert in the Anglo-Italian style so popular among expatriates in Florence. Pinsent was commissioned in 1911 by Charles Strong, a U.S. philosopher. Wrestling with a difficult and restricted space, Pinsent made one of the finest gardens of his career. He was unable to impose strict symmetry on the site because it was too narrow and irregular. Instead he made a series of interlocking, but enclosed, spaces linked by long views. At the end of each perspective, he placed an urn or a statue to catch the eye. In this way, he emphasized the length of the garden rather than its width.

Strong's bedroom window overlooked the *giardino segreto*, or secret garden, enclosed to the south by a high wall that concealed the view over Florence. The simple layout of box-edged grass parterres around a central pool is densely furnished with pots of lemons, and the air is full of the scent of the jasmine that Pinsent grew up the walls. In the narrow space to the north of the villa, Pinsent built an elaborate grotto, cladding it in shells and pebble mosaics and decorating it with busts of philosophers. Beside the grotto, a handsome, baroque staircase leads up to a raised pergola that Pinsent used to create a new north–south view over the garden and the valley beyond. Strong's library overlooked the garden to the west, where Pinsent made the Philosopher's Walk, lining the path with irises and lavender backed by holm oaks (*Quercus ilex*). HA

La Scarzuola

Umbria, Italy

DESIGNER: Tommaso Buzzi
OWNER: Marco Solari
GARDEN STYLE: 20th-century folly and landscape
SIZE: 10 acres (4 ha)
CLIMATE: Mediterranean
LOCATION: Montegabbione, Umbria

La Scarzuola, or the Cittá Buzziana, is a fascinating folly and landscape garden designed by Tommaso Buzzi between 1958 and his death in 1981. Buzzi trained as an architect. But in a brilliant career, he was also the artistic director of the Verini glassworks in Venice, cofounded the architecture magazine *Domus*, taught architecture at the Politecnico in Milan, designed ceramics, embroidery, and furniture, and wrote cook books.

In 1956, Buzzi bought the ancient, but derelict, Franciscan monastery of La Scarzuola. In the vicinity of the monastery, he created a garden modeled on one in Francesco Colonna's fifteenth-century book, *Hypnerotomachia Poliphili*. At the heart of this shady, atmospheric space, he made a pool and built a concrete copy of the boat that Colonna used to carry Polyphilus to the island of Cytherea. He created his folly—a city of miniature buildings— below the monastery. Some of the buildings, such as the Colosseum and the Parthenon, formed part of a visual index of architectural history. Others, including the transparent pyramid of iron and glass and the butterfly-shaped theater built in a pool, were Buzzi's own invention. Interestingly, he also used poor materials to encourage nature to invade the site, breaking down his structures and infesting them with moss and weeds. Since Buzzi's death, La Scarzuola has belonged to his nephew, Marco Solari, who continues to develop it. In a series of fine garden "rooms" created above the folly, you can enjoy that rare thing in Italy, a thriving herbaceous border. HA

Castello Ruspoli

Lazio, Italy

DESIGNER: Ottavia Orsini Marescotti
OWNER: Princess Claudia Giada Ruspoli
GARDEN STYLE: 17th-century topiary garden
SIZE: 1.2 acres (0.5 ha)
CLIMATE: Mediterranean
LOCATION: Vignanello, Lazio

Castello Ruspoli has one of the most well-preserved, and delicate topiary gardens in Italy. The garden was planted at the beginning of the seventeenth century for Ottavia Orsini Marescotti. The assassination of her husband had left Ottavia in charge of seven children, so, acting as regent for her sons, she ruled Vignanello and transformed the inside of the magnificent, but brutal, Marescotti fortress into a renaissance palace. She also opened a new door in the east wall, put a drawbridge across the moat, prepared the ground for planting, and obtained a supply of water that could be used to feed the fish pools and the fountains.

Ottavia's garden had three elements: a *giardino segreto*, or secret garden, for bulbs and rare plants; a hunting enclosure for small game; and the topiary garden. Beyond the garden, there was a larger hunting wood. The topiary garden is thought to have been planted in 1612 and consists of twelve parterres set out on level ground beneath the east facade of the castle. The perfectly clipped enclosures are planted in laurel, cherry bay, myrtle, and box, arranged around a fish pool with a balustrade of Peperino stone. Inside the parterres are twelve unique designs of dwarf box.

The garden was designed to be viewed from the windows of the *salotto*, or drawing room, on the first floor of the castle. The parterre below these windows spells out the initials of Ottavia Orsini's two sons, Sforza and Galeazzo. Her initials encircle theirs protectively. Rigorously formal, and perfectly maintained, the garden was a metaphor for Ottavia's dual role as governor and protective mother. HA

I Giardini della Landriana

Lazio, Italy

DESIGNERS: Marquise Lavinia Taverna, Russell Page
OWNERS: Marquis Gallarati-Scotti, Marquise Lavinia Taverna
GARDEN STYLE: 20th-century themed rooms
SIZE: 62 acres (25.1 ha)
CLIMATE: Mediterranean
LOCATION: Rome, Lazio

In 1956 the Marquis Gallarati-Scotti and his wife, Lavinia Taverna, acquired a property near Ardea, 3 miles (4 km) from the sea. It was a bare, windswept wasteland scattered with bombs and land mines from World War II, the site of the Anzio landing.

Originally only pines and eucalyptus were going to be planted as a windbreak around the manor, but Lavinia became interested in gardening. From then on, her collection of fine plants increased and, during the mid-1960s, she realized that her garden needed the guiding hand of a landscape artist. In 1967, Russell Page, the famous English expert, was hired. The first area to be designed was around the manor, followed by the larger garden, which was divided into intimate garden "rooms." An English rose garden was created with a comprehensive selection of old roses and white cottage-garden perennials that became the dazzling White Walk. This was in complete contrast to informal Mediterranean orange and olive gardens with citrus fruits, olives, and herbs, and the formality of the Italian gardens, the Little Garden, and the Spanish Pool. There is also a valley planted with gorgeous *Rosa* x *odorata* 'Mutabilis', and underplanted with *Ophiopogon japonicus* to give interesting ground cover.

In total there are twenty-three different gardens at Landriana, two of the best being the Gray Garden with a fine selection of lavender, cistus, santolinas, echiums, and *Convolvulus cneorum*, and the striking Blue Meadow. Visitors should also note the splendid collection of Australasian plants. RL

Villa Adriana

Lazio, Italy

DESIGNERS: Emperor Hadrian, and others
OWNER: The Italian State
GARDEN STYLE: Roman
SIZE: 296.5 acres (120 ha)
CLIMATE: Temperate
LOCATION: Tivoli, Lazio

Compared to the coherent design of Villa d'Este just up the road (see page 688), Villa Adriana is less obviously a garden. In fact, it is a series of courtyard gardens, all of which were a source of ideas and artifacts for later renaissance gardens. For example, the Marine Theater, almost certainly designed by Hadrian, with an island in the center of a pool, inspired parts of the Boboli gardens in Florence.

Hadrian, nicknamed the "Greekling" after his enthusiasm for Hellenic culture, was an intellectual and a poet. He became emperor in 117 CE. The estate he created at Tivoli is sometimes seen as a monument to his conquests, sometimes as a celebration of the places he had seen on his travels. The Canopus, a huge ornamental canal complete with stone crocodile, representing part of the Nile, is 390-feet (119 m) long. Hadrian dug out an existing valley to make the canal, with its curved northern point punctuated by a colonnade, and further colonnades along the sides. Six caryatids form the columns along the west side.

What remains today is impressive in its way, but gives little idea of the site's former opulence. You must use your imagination to see the sparkling water falling over the Canopus' curving apse and splashing into the brooks around the couches where Hadrian's guests lay feasting. Imagine the scent of the climbers that clothed the pergola to one side of the canal, and the peace and luxury of the place, particularly if you had just returned after a few years of campaigning around the outer reaches of the Roman Empire. JO

Villa Farnese

Lazio, Italy

DESIGNER: Giacomo Barozzi da Vignola
OWNER: The Italian State
GARDEN STYLE: 16th-century Italian renaissance, mannerist
SIZE: 50 acres (20 ha)
CLIMATE: Mediterranean
LOCATION: Caprarola, Lazio

Commissioned in 1559 by a nephew to Pope Paul III, Cardinal Alessandro Odorado Farnese, Villa Farnese and its mannerist garden sit above the surrounding village, a dominant statement of power and money. The architect for the house and garden was Giacomo Barozzi da Vignola. Today the pentagonal villa-cum-fortress constructed around a circular, colonnaded courtyard is unique and contains one of the best-preserved sixteenth-century villa interiors.

As befits a fort, the summer and winter gardens are reached by a bridge over the moat. Both gardens are squares, divided into four beds, each of which is quartered. Both squares are disappointingly planted, but the dripping, tufa-encrusted grotto is fun, and there's a woodland walk through a grove of sweet chestnuts (*Castanea sativa*) to the Casino del Piacere (House of Pleasure). Although it's odd to have a formal garden so far from the main residence, the Casino and its garden are a masterpiece. They are approached by a walled ramp, down the center of which runs a raised watercourse. The ornamentation here depicts dolphins, and at the top of the ramp is the imposing Fountain of Rivers.

Two curved flights of steps descend to the terrace below. The terrace is embellished with parterres of clipped box, and twenty-eight statues by Girolamo Rainaldi were added in 1620. More stairs on either side of the Casino, with carved dolphins jetting out water, lead to the Casino entrance and pebbled mosaic forecourt. Originally a colorful flower garden, it now includes fountains and stone spheres. TM

Il Giardino di Ninfa

Lazio, Italy

DESIGNERS: The Caetani family
OWNER: Fondazione Roffredo Caetani
GARDEN STYLE: 20th-century English romantic
SIZE: 20 acres (8.1 ha)
CLIMATE: Mediterranean
LOCATION: Sermoneta, Lazio

Ninfa is a beautiful garden set among the remains of a medieval town. Roses, jasmine, and wisteria scramble over the ruins, and tender plants shelter within the walls of houses and churches, some of which are still decorated with Byzantine frescoes. Plants thrive in the microclimate created by the river that cuts the site in two. Transforming the ruined town was the work of three women over ninety years. The first was Ada Wilbrahaim, English wife of Duke Onorato Caetani, who worked with her son, Gelasio. They gave the site structure by planting strategic groups of holm oak (*Quercus ilex*), cedar, and plane trees, and marking the main street with an avenue of cypresses. Ada also planted roses, and Gelasio brought in water, using underground channels and miniature aqueducts.

In 1934 Ninfa was inherited by Gelasio's nephew, Camillo. He died during World War II, so it went to Camillo's American mother, Marguerite Chapin, and his father, Roffredo Caetani. Marguerite planted ornamental cherries that flower in spring, when Ninfa floats on a raft of blossom, magnolias, and roses. She also added silver birch (*Betula pendula*) groves and arum lilies along the banks of the streams.

Marguerite gardened with her daughter, Lelia, who later took Ninfa's Anglo-American connections into a third generation by marrying Hubert Howard, another of Rome's Anglo-Italian nobility. After Marguerite's death, Lelia and Hubert worked with the legacy of three generations of Caetani gardeners, adding to the planting and safeguarding Ninfa's future by setting up the Caetani foundation. HA

Villa Aldobrandini

Lazio, Italy

DESIGNERS: Giacomo della Porta, Carlo Maderno
OWNER: The Italian State
GARDEN STYLE: 16th- and 17th-century baroque
SIZE: 1.2 acres (0.5 ha)
CLIMATE: Mediterranean
LOCATION: Frascati, Lazio

Villa Aldobrandini possesses the earliest example of baroque garden design and one of the most lavish water features in Italy. The villa and garden were designed in 1598 for Cardinal Pietro Aldobrandini by Giacomo della Porta, and later by Carlo Maderno.

The narrow space behind the villa is occupied by Della Porta's magnificent water theater, and above it a water staircase climbs the steep hillside. The theater was the final destination of a powerful torrent that tumbled down the staircase, gathering momentum as it fell. It entered the theater with a deafening roar and a force that generated a storm of intensely theatrical and constantly changing effects, including music, thunder, snow, and rain. The facade of the theater is decorated with statues by Jacques Sarrazin, brought to life by the water. Enceladus, the defeated Titan, groaned and spat, Pan played his pipes, centaurs sounded horns, and a lion and tigress roared.

A room at the right-hand end of the theater was known as the Temple to Apollo and the Muses. A model of Mount Parnassus was constructed at one end, complete with Pegasus and wooden automata of Apollo and the nine Muses. All the wooden figures played musical instruments, although the music was generated by a waterpowered organ installed under Parnassus. The other wonder in the room was a spinning copper ball suspended just above the floor on a current of air. Elsewhere the garden was peppered with *giochi d'acqua*, water tricks that made victims of Aldobrandini's visitors. Della Porta's design made Villa Aldobrandini famous all over Europe. HA

Villa Borghese

Lazio, Italy

DESIGNERS: Girolamo Rainaldi, and others
OWNER: The Italian State
GARDEN STYLE: 17th-century baroque, English landscape
SIZE: 198 acres (80 ha)
CLIMATE: Mediterranean
LOCATION: Rome, Lazio

The great park of the Villa Borghese can be found at the top of the Spanish Steps, a short stroll from the hectic shopping streets of Rome. It began life in 1605 with a formal layout around the villa, and further formal areas dotted about within parkland, though what is there today owes more to an eighteenth- and nineteenth-century English landscape makeover.

The original park, centered on the great villa, was divided into sections. The first was used for hunting, with two loggias for guests. The second included woods, hills, and a *ragnaia* for catching birds. The third, immediately around the Casino Nobile (now the Galleria Borghese), was built by the Flemish architect Ivan van Santen to exhibit the Borghese collection of antique sculpture. It had a formal layout of avenues and twenty-three compartments filled with statuary, columns, grottoes, fountains, and stone seats. However, many of the artifacts were sold or stolen and the park's structure altered in line with changing fashions. In fact, a sizable chunk was bulldozed during the wars to make way for food production.

Today the Villa Borghese has five museums, thirty-five fountains, twenty or so minor buildings, ten monuments, and a mass of sculpture, even if much of it is copied, some from Cliveden, Buckinghamshire, England (see page 324). It also includes some charming planting. The Secret Gardens around the Casino Nobile have been restored and planted with citrus (including oddities like 'Buddha's Hand'), roses, yuccas, iris, tulips, carnations, sunflowers, anemones, narcissi, and hyacinths. JO

Villa d'Este

Lazio, Italy

DESIGNER: Pirro Ligorio
OWNER: The Italian State
GARDEN STYLE: 16th-century high renaissance
SIZE: 10 acres (4 ha)
CLIMATE: Mediterranean
LOCATION: Tivoli, Lazio

Imagine a landscape caught between fantasy and reality, a place where statues might easily move, fountains spell out complex, allegorical messages, and the air is full of strange noises and distant music. This is the garden of Villa d'Este, the finest and most flamboyant of Italy's high renaissance gardens. It was built for Cardinal Ippolito II d'Este, the richest cardinal in Rome, who commissioned archaeologist, architect, and painter, Pirro Ligorio, as his garden architect. Building work began in 1560, and Ligorio's complex invention was almost complete by the time of Ippolito's death in 1572.

The garden consists of a central axis that runs from the level area at the bottom of the site and up the steep, terraced slope toward Ippolito's villa. This simple layout is complicated by several cross axes and eight other vertical axes, creating a structure that compels the visitor to engage with the garden. The visitor's role changes from that of passive spectator to active protagonist who is repeatedly faced with a choice between different paths or different kinds of entertainment. Originally these entertainments included a labyrinth, pools of exotic fish, complex fountains, grottoes, statues, hydraulic instruments, automata, and cascades. There was nothing casual about these features, for they all belonged in Ligorio's iconographic program. Ligorio's visual language drew from architecture, statues, and fountains; such references were an enormously important element of the high renaissance garden. Ligorio arranged all the different elements of Villa d'Este to create a narrative that would unfold as the visitor progressed through the garden.

It is delightful to visit Villa d'Este today, as many of the fountains have been restored to their original glory. Several times a day the garden is filled with the curious hydraulic music of the Organ Fountain and the singing of birds in the Fountain of the Owl. HA

Villa Lante

Lazio, Italy

DESIGNER: Giacomo Barozzi da Vignola
OWNER: The Italian State
GARDEN STYLE: 16th- and 17th-century mannerist
SIZE: 3.7 acres (1.5 ha)
CLIMATE: Mediterranean
LOCATION: Bagnaia, Lazio

Villa Lante was designed for Cardinal Gianfrancesco Gambara from 1568 by the architect Giacomo Barozzi da Vignola, with help from the engineer Tommaso Ghinucci. A study in geometry and symmetry, the site revolves around a main axis, to which even the villa—divided into twin *palazzine*—is subordinate.

The dominant theme is water, and in front of the *palazzine* is a central water parterre with stone boats. The Fountain of the Moors by Taddeo Landini—with four men holding aloft Cardinal Alessandro Peretti di Montalto's coat-of-arms—is a later addition (the cardinal owned the villa during 1590–1623), as is the ornate French-style parterre de broderie. With intricate shapes in clipped box set against a ground cover of reddish gravel, it was planted during the ownership of Duke Ippolito Lante in the second half of the seventeenth century.

Behind the *palazzine*, and shaded by mature plane trees, the garden ascends in a series of four terraces. The Fountain of the Dolphins, on the top terrace, sends water down a slope into the Catena d'Aqua (literally Chain of Water) that dominates the second terrace. Falling onto the third terrace, the water enters the Fountain of the River Gods with its shell-shaped water bowl. From here it moves into the Fountain of the Table that is both beautiful and practical because it kept food and wine cool. The lower terrace, that leads to the sloping ground between the *palazzine*, is dominated by the tiered, circular Candle Fountain, the 160 jets of which rise from cups and look like candles. TM

Villa Orsini

Lazio, Italy

DESIGNER: Vicino Orsini
OWNERS: The Bettini family
GARDEN STYLE: 16th-century sculpture-filled wood
SIZE: 123.6 acres (50 ha)
CLIMATE: Mediterranean
LOCATION: Bomarzo, Lazio

There are no herbaceous borders or gentle parterres at the Villa Orsini. Instead visitors find a garden filled with terror, sex, and violence: a 400-year-old theme park whose meaning is now a mystery. Created by Vicino Orsini, Duke of Bomarzo, in the late sixteenth century, this *sacro bosco*, or sacred wood, is filled with macabre sculptures hewn from a stony outcrop. Giants sleep in the undergrowth, dragons fight with lions, women bare their breasts, an elephant carries the body of a soldier, and a colossus tears open a rival's body. Best of all, the giant face of an ogre invites you to step into its mouth and enter Hades.

Its creator was a philosopher and patron of the arts whose life as a soldier was punctuated with imprisonment and stormy personal relationships. His private demons and turbulent life are clearly reflected in his creations. The exact meanings of the carvings and inscriptions have puzzled academics and garden historians since the garden was rediscovered in the 1950s. For some, the garden mocks the symmetry and order of contemporary renaissance gardens. Others see it as a traditional allegory of the journey of life. It may be that there is no great significance, that it is a piece of fun, "just to set the heart free," as an inscription on one of the obelisks says. Whatever the garden's meaning, it makes as great an impression today as it must have done 400 years ago. The "Park of Monsters," as it is known locally, also inspired the work of Jean Cocteau and Salvador Dalí. JHo

> "...visitors find a garden filled with terror, sex, and violence: a 400-year-old theme park whose meaning is now a mystery"

Palazzo Reale di Caserta

Campania, Italy

DESIGNERS: Luigi Vanvitelli, Carlo Vanvitelli
OWNER: The Italian State
GARDEN STYLE: 18th-century baroque
SIZE: Canal, 3 miles (4.8 km); English garden, 50 acres (20 ha)
CLIMATE: Mediterranean
LOCATION: Caserta, Campania

In 1751, King Carlo VII of the Two Sicilies commissioned Luigi Vanvitelli to transform the village of Caserta into a capital city, with a royal palace and a park in its center. The garden—designed by Vanvitelli and largely built by his son, Carlo—is the largest eighteenth-century landscape design in Italy. After a painstaking restoration, it was added to the UNESCO list of World Heritage Sites in 1997.

Caserta has the grandeur and simplicity of a French landscape. Its main feature is the straight 3-mile-long (5 km) canal, excavated in 1777, that runs across the plain between the palace and the foot of Monte Briano. An aqueduct brought water to the brow of the hill and released it in a rugged, naturalistic cascade to fill the canal. The water descends toward the palace through a series of deep basins filled with fish, down a number of cascades, and past groups of life-size statues carved from pure white marble. Carlo Vanvitelli flanked this startling view with clipped hornbeam hedges, rows of trees, and ribbons of turf seeded in the royal cowsheds. This cleverly articulated combination of water, light, foliage, and statuary was both the axis of the garden and an extraordinarily successful expression of the power of the Bourbon dynasty.

Caserta is a virtually perfect example of the internationalism of Italian garden design during the eighteenth century. In 1785, only eleven years after Vanvitelli's original Italian-French project reached its conclusion, plans were afoot for a new English addition to the garden. This was the brainchild of Sir William Hamilton, British ambassador to Naples, who appointed Giovanni Antonio Graefer as head gardener. The result of this English addition is an extraordinary undulating park of 50 acres (20 ha) planted with exotic trees and plants and furnished with intriguing false ruins, genuine archaeological remains, and classical sculptures. HA

Giardini La Mortella

Isola d'Ischia, Campania, Italy

DESIGNERS: Russell Page, Lady Susana Walton
OWNER: The William Walton Trust (Fondazione William Walton)
GARDEN STYLE: 20th-century tropical retreat
SIZE: 5 acres (2 ha)
CLIMATE: Mediterranean
LOCATION: Forio, Isola d'Ischia, Campania

Reached by boat from nearby Naples, there is no more enchanting place on the ancient volcanic island of Ischia than La Mortella—The Place of Myrtles. In 1949 the English composer William Walton and his young Argentinean bride, Susana, purchased a vast, quarrylike ravine in which to build their lifelong home. Work on the garden began in 1956 to a ground plan by English garden designer Russell Page and, over the following decades, Lady Walton's energy and vision have made it a masterpiece.

This enchanting garden has been laid out on a number of levels, and thanks to the site's valley and hillside terrain, La Mortella is also artistically multilayered, giving dramatic themes, quiet variations, sudden surprises, and subtle depths. The garden contains a variety of fountains, brooks, and waterfalls with lily and lotus pools, and there are also some interesting buildings for the visitor to look at: a subterranean temple, nymphaeum, Thai pavilion, tropical glasshouse teeming with hummingbirds, and even a purpose-built house for the giant-leaved water lily (*Victoria amazonica*).

Years of careful planting throughout the garden have created areas that are now heavily canopied with trees, resulting in a rain forest microclimate. This pushes back the boundaries of what's possible to grow here, and the collection holds in excess of 1,000 different species. Besides the obvious Mediterranean subjects, you'll also find ginger lilies, bromeliads, tree ferns, cycads, papyrus, and orchids galore.

On Sir William's death in 1983, Lady Walton established a benevolent trust to provide training and performance opportunities for young musicians and singers. This, in turn, led to the building of a recital hall in the grounds for international master classes and evening concerts at weekends. What could be a more sublime way to round off your visit than to attend a performance? RCa

Villa Cimbrone

Campania, Italy

DESIGNERS: Lord Ernest Grimthorpe, Nicola Mansi
OWNERS: Giorgio Vuilleumier, Paola Vuilleumier
GARDEN STYLE: 20th-century eclectic and Gertrude Jekyll
SIZE: 14.8 acres (6 ha)
CLIMATE: Mediterranean
LOCATION: Ravello, Campania

In 1904, Lord Ernest Grimthorpe spent 100 lira on a ruined farmhouse with woods, vineyard, walnut grove, and a view of the Gulf of Salerno. He recruited Nicola Mansi, a local man, to help him renovate the house and design a garden. Together they transformed the farmhouse into Villa Cimbrone, with towers, battlements, and Arabic, Venetian, and Gothic details. They made a garden between the house and the cliff edge, and down the rocky slope to the sea.

The garden has a mixture of features: formal flower gardens, temples, eighteenth-century statues, a grotto, and a Moorish loggia. A clear view of the sea and the Cilento mountains adds drama to every part of the site. A scattering of inscriptions in English and Latin adorn the house and the garden buildings.

The site is divided into an upper and lower garden, and an area of woodland is intersected by narrow paths. The main axis is known as the Viale dell'Immenso—a reference to boundless sea views. It is spanned by bridges and covered by a magnificent wisteria pergola. A Doric temple—one of many classical structures—shelters a statue of Ceres that is silhouetted against the sea. The terrace beside it is the most dramatic feature in the garden. Suspended 1,000 feet (300 m) above the Gulf of Salerno, it is bounded only by a balustrade decorated with eighteenth-century busts. Below the terrace, a grassy slope leads down to a wood and a winding path to the Temple of Bacchus. Lord Grimthorpe died in London in 1917, but his ashes are buried beneath the statue of Bacchus at the center of the temple. HA

Scavi Pompei

Campania, Italy

DESIGNERS: Unknown
OWNER: Soprintendenza Archeologica di Pompei
GARDEN STYLE: Roman
SIZE: 163 acres (66 ha)
CLIMATE: Mediterranean
LOCATION: Pompeii, Campania

The eruption of Vesuvius on August 29, 79 CE left the volcanic dust sealing the site for nearly 1,700 years, giving a good idea of what contemporary Pompeian gardens looked like. The wall paintings, tree root molds, outlines of flower beds, and extensive written references build up quite a detailed picture.

The houses face straight on to the street with the owner's offices near the entrance, an atrium providing a pool of light and natural air conditioning in summer. Frequently aligned with the entrance was a peristyle, a colonnaded square with a centerpiece water feature and clipped evergreen shrubs, including myrtle and scented flowers. If space was at a premium, one or more walls were painted with columns to create an illusory country scene. Up to seven layers, consisting of sand, lime, and marble with ceramic fragments, were used on the wall, leveling the surface and insulating against damp. Another key feature was the *larium*, or small altar, a tiny niche where offerings to the *lares*, or household gods, were placed. Also note the banked beds that flank the House of the Mysteries, once a luxury villa, and the cherry tree in the House of the Ship Europa, which takes its name from a grafito here, alluding to the Greek myth of Europa kidnapped by Jupiter.

Many gardens were restored and then neglected, but recently six teams from four European countries have studied and restored the *insulae* (appartment blocks) within the ancient town. Before leaving, make sure you see the House of the Vettii, House of Loreius Tiburtinus, and the House of the Dancing Faun. CH

Villa Gucetic

Dubrovacko-Neretvanska, Croatia

DESIGNERS: The Gucetic family
OWNER: Croatian Academy of Sciences and Arts
GARDEN STYLE: 17th-century renaissance Ragusian
SIZE: 63 acres (25.5 ha)
CLIMATE: Mediterranean
LOCATION: Trsteno, Dubrovnik, Dubrovacko-Neretvanska

These gardens are not visible from the coastal road, but the tiny village of Trsteno cannot be missed because of the towering pair of plane trees that, at over 200 feet (61 m) high, are the tallest in Europe. Beside them, a small road leads downhill to the simple gate of the garden and arboretum. Inside the grounds, the broad, straight path passes through woodland, with well-labeled mature trees, to the ancient aqueduct bringing water from the mountains. A tunnel of palms and bay trees then leads past The Green Loggia, a shady, rectangular clearing with the little chapel of St. Jerome, emerging at the villa.

The building, the country home of the Gucetic family, was rebuilt in 1667 and given to the state in 1948. It is a simple, stone building covered with climbers and several bougainvilleas. The area fronting the building has many strong, structural plants, including palms, cycads, agaves, and yuccas, and the softer shapes of lavender, cistus, irises, aubrieta, and scented stock. Plants from similar climates include jasmine, China roses, oleander, honeysuckle, and wisteria. From South Africa are osteospermums, euryops, pelargoniums, and freesias. There is also a rectangular herb garden with Italian cypresses and palms, and a citrus garden with oranges and lemons.

Other features include stone-pillared, vine-covered pergolas, one with views to the sea and islands, the other with a snapshot of the pretty little harbor. The path to the garden gate has billowing lantanas that attract hummingbird hawk moths and rare fritillary butterflies. RChe

Villa Skocibuha

Dubrovacko-Neretvanska, Croatia

DESIGNER: Unknown
OWNER: Gordana Marusic
GARDEN STYLE: 16th-century renaissance Ragusian
SIZE: 1 acre (0.4 ha)
CLIMATE: Mediterranean
LOCATION: Sudurad, Dubrovacko-Neretvanska

An old, three-decked ferry links a group of islands, where everything is hand loaded onto little carts. Sudurad is the last of the islands, and in the center of the village green is Villa Skocibuha, built in 1530 by Tomo and Vice Stjepovic-Skocibuha as their country retreat. Alhough it has been closed and somewhat forgotten in recent years, it is now open again after a major restoration in 2001.

The slim stone pillars support numerous pergolas covered with vines, occasionally interspersed with climbing roses, white jasmine, and bougainvilleas. Low stone walls join the pillars and double as

shaded seats, though in places they become stone troughs planted with irises, rosemary, muscari, stock, osteospermums, and pelargoniums. One long side border has fruit trees, with olives and a range of citrus fruit, almonds, and *Diospyros kaki* with apricot-colored fruit and good fall foliage. The lawns are actually four large square shapes, but where the grass grows poorly *Dichondra microphylla* is used instead. The edges are planted mostly with gray-leaved Mediterranean subjects, including several kinds of lavender, rosemary, fine-leaved helichrysum, and silver-leaved *Senecio bicolor*.

The Ladies Terrace has a good view of the vegetable garden at the rear of the villa, and a charming chapel. Orange trees are planted here, with fruit and good scent, and more rich perfume comes from the *Magnolia grandiflora*. The end is signaled by a large pavilion with fantastic views of the main garden, harbor, and the other islands. RChe

Ayazmo Park

Stara Zagora, Bulgaria

DESIGNER: Bishop Metody Kusev
OWNER: Municipality of Stara Zagora
GARDEN STYLE: 19th-century forest park
SIZE: 790.7 acres (320 ha)
CLIMATE: Temperate
LOCATION: Stara Zagora, Stara Zagora

Deep in the woods of Ayazmo Park is a small chapel next to the *ayazmo*, or healing spring, after which the park is named. Breathing in the rich scents of pine, cypress, and almond in this tranquil spot, it is hard to believe that just over 100 years ago this hillside was so blasted and barren that it was referred to derisively by the locals as Ahmak, or the Stupid Hill.

Today, the formal center of the park is planted with horse chestnut (*Aesculus hippocastanum*), linden, and pine trees, interspersed with clusters of the black locust tree (*Robinia pseudoacacia*). The Cypress and Cedar Walk, lined with *Cedrus atlantica* and *Cupressus sempervirens*, forms a restful green tunnel through the heart of the park and is a very popular place for summer visitors seeking to escape the heat of the sun. At the end is a monumental aleppo pine (*Pinus halepensis*) that marks the beginning of the less formal reaches of the park. Here, mixed stands of broadleaved trees, dominated by oaks, merge with pine, cedar, and cypress. Higher up the park you'll find hornbeam (*Carpinus orientalis*), turkey oak (*Quercus cerris*), and downy oak (*Q. pubescens*).

The transformation of the park from scrubby hillside to nearly 1,000 acres (405 ha) of magnificent woodland is a testament to the efforts of its founder, Bishop Metody Kusev. He began the tree-planting program in 1895 believing, "The beauty of the living tree, of the living forest, ennobles and elevates a man's moral stature." While the park may not quite live up to this ideal, it is a wonderfully calm and peaceful place to relax. MS

Le Jardin Exotique

Monaco

DESIGNERS: Prince Albert I of Monaco, Louis Notari
OWNER: Principality of Monaco
GARDEN STYLE: 20th-century succulent collection
SIZE: 2.8 acres (1.1 ha)
CLIMATE: Mediterranean
LOCATION: Monaco

Monaco's Le Jardin Exotique was begun in 1912 when the principality's collection of succulent plants, including cacti and aloes, was relocated. Land use has long been a problematic issue in this tiny state, and the site chosen by Prince Albert I was both improbable and brilliant. Using all the skills of Louis Notari, Monaco's chief engineer, Albert constructed a garden that clings to a rocky promontory 492 feet (150 m) above the bustling streets, looking out over the Mediterranean. The garden was finally opened in 1933. As a feat of engineering, Le Jardin Exotique is impressive, but as a garden it is remarkable.

The ornamental planting of succulents in bold and tightly grouped designs was pioneered in this area of the Cote d'Azur in the nineteenth century, but Le Jardin Exotique is unquestionably the pinnacle of this style. Ranks of huge cacti and chunky succulent euphorbias jostle for room beside clumps of bristling aloes and agaves, and flashes of brilliant color are provided by swaths of mesembryanthemums among prickly pears and yuccas. But Le Jardin Exotique is not just concerned with the big and the flashy; there are also tiny floral gems here, including pebble plants, lithops, and conophytum.

Le Jardin Exotique is pinned to a rock face and threaded with paths and footbridges. The views out across Monaco, the Mediterranean, and along the coast to Italy are spectacular. AM

RIGHT Le Jardin Exotique, perched spectacularly on the rock faces above Monaco's tall buildings and bustling streets.

Pazo de Oca

Galicia, Spain

DESIGNER: Unknown
OWNER: Unknown
GARDEN STYLE: 18th-century formal, informal
SIZE: 3.7 acres (1.5 ha)
CLIMATE: Temperate
LOCATION: Pontevedra, Galicia

Every year, thousands of pilgrims make the journey by foot along the *camino francés* route to Santiago de Compostela and the tomb of St. James. Along the route there are many hostels and guest houses, but one of the greatest and most surprising treats is the eighteenth-century garden at Pazo de Oca. What immediately strikes the visitor is the sense of unity between the delightful manor house and garden, since both are hewn from the same local gray granite.

The garden was built on a sloping site and, prior to its inception, there was a mill near the reservoir at the top of the garden. It is no surprise that the key element is water, and the various ways in which it is retained and moves. The water travels from the reservoir to the central pool, and throughout the garden, the sound of moving water is present as it tumbles down channels, squirts from fountains, and falls into pools. Then all becomes calm as it enters the hidden rectangular pool, enclosed in the middle of the garden. Here the still water introduces a note of tranquillity. Also here is the garden's most amusing feature. Making its stately progress across the middle of the stone-edged, crenellated pool is a stone boat with its two crew (or fishermen) at the prow and stern, taking good care of their cargo of plants.

Now covered with a patina of lichen, the gray granite has a softer look, giving the garden a romantic feel overall. This is in large part due to the lush planting with large specimen trees, such as *Camellia reticulata* 'Captain Rawes'—a remarkable 43 feet (13 m) high. TM

El Jardín de la Finca, Puente San Miguel

Cantabria, Spain

DESIGNERS: Javier de Winthuysen, Carmen Anon
OWNERS: Puente San Miguel, the Botin family
GARDEN STYLE: 19th-century renaissance revival, modernist
SIZE: 24.7 acres (10 ha)
CLIMATE: Temperate
LOCATION: Puente San Miguel, Cantabria

El Jardín de la Finca de la Sociedad Anónima Puente San Miguel has the great honor of being one of the historical gardens on the Spanish General Register of Assets of Cultural Interest.

Don Marcelino Sanz de Sautuola, who discovered the caves of Altamira, now classified as a World Heritage Site, owned the estate in the nineteenth century and was the original developer of the garden. He is believed to have been the first person to introduce *Eucalyptus globulus* to the province, in 1863, and the tree is in the garden. Other exceptional specimens include the largest magnolia in Europe—more than 200 years old and covering 0.2 acre (0.08 ha); a sequoia with a circumference of 18 feet (5 m); and a 98-foot-high (30 m) atlas cedar (*Cedrus atlantica*).

Wandering through his landscaped park, Don Marcelino was surrounded by fine examples of trees, from red maples to cork oaks (*Quercus suber*). He decided to embellish the park with two monuments—one, by the sculptor Jesus Otero, commemorated the discovery of the Altamira caves; the other, by Victorio Macho, recalled to memory the writer and journalist Victor de la Serna.

The twentieth century brought radical changes to the gardens. In the 1930s, garden designer Javier de Winthuysen introduced a renaissance revival style. Almost a half century later, landscape architect Carmen Anon introduced steel and mirrors. AW

Monasterio de Piedra

Aragón, Spain

DESIGNER: Juan Federico Muntadas
OWNER: The Spanish State
GARDEN STYLE: 19th-century romantic
SIZE: Unknown
CLIMATE: Mediterranean
LOCATION: Nuévalos, Aragón

Juan Federico Muntadas discovered the Iris Cave on property owned by his father, located on the site of the former twelfth-century Cistercian monastery of Piedra. He set about landscaping the grounds in the romantic style, of which he was a noted exponent, and opened them to the public. He created a wild and natural-looking park using the River Piedra, which runs through the property, and its limestone canyon as the main focus for his watery creation. Waterfalls, cascades, lakes, caves, and grottoes are all part of his romantic design. The remaining buildings of the former Monastery of Stone have been extended and are now part of a three-star hotel.

There is a marked trail through the park, which takes about three hours to complete. The trail moves up and down from viewpoint to valley, with one of the most dramatic sights overlooking a waterfall called the Horse's Tail. At its base is the Rainbow Grotto, which leads to the fish farm (Muntadas created Spain's first fish farm, intending to breed trout to restock Spain's rivers). The route goes up to the Devil's Cliff and down again to the Mirror Lake.

Before Muntadas worked his transformation, the site was covered by thick forest. In the wooded areas that remain, bordering the river, there are good stands of ash, elder, and plane trees, as well as *Celtis australis*. Care is needed because parts of the route are precipitous, and some moss- and lichen-covered paths make the steps very slippery. BS

Els Jardins de Ca l'Artigas

Cataluña, Spain

DESIGNER: Antoni Gaudí
OWNER: Municipality of La Pobla de Lillet
GARDEN STYLE: Early 20th-century New European
SIZE: 9.9 acres (4 ha)
CLIMATE: Mediterranean
LOCATION: La Pobla de Lillet, Cataluña

This garden gem, hidden from view for nearly fifty years, is a rare example of the horticultural work carried out by one of Cataluña's best-loved sons and one of the world's greatest architects, Antoni Gaudí.

While working on Park Güell in Barcelona (see page 710), Gaudí found time in 1904 to create his one-and-only humid garden for Joan Artigas i Alart. For inspiration, Gaudí needed to look no further than his Catalan homeland. But at the start of the Spanish Civil War, in 1939, the wealthy industrial family was forced to leave the Catllaràs Castle and to abandon their beloved Artigas Garden. In 1989, it was rediscovered and restored to its former glory.

The River Llobregat flows through the middle of the garden, and is undoubtedly the highlight, with other water features including waterfalls, fountains, and springs, all nicely blending with the static architecture of the cylindrical summerhouse, the artificial grotto, and the bridges. You will also find statues, such as the eagle on top of the bridge. An angel statue is believed to have stood in the grotto by the waterfall prior to 1939. If true, that suggests that Gaudí used his leitmotif of the four evangelists here. It is possible that he dotted them strategically around the garden in the shape of a cross. The most important feature of the garden is the Arches Bridge. The carved figures adorning it were reworked during the restoration under the sculptor Ramon Millet. AW

Jardí Botànic de Barcelona

Cataluña, Spain

DESIGNERS: Carlos Ferrater, Josep Lluís Canosa, Bet Figueras, Artur Bossy, Joan Pedrola
OWNER: Barcelona City Council
GARDEN STYLE: 20th-century botanical
SIZE: 34 acres (13.7 ha)
CLIMATE: Mediterranean
LOCATION: Barcelona, Cataluña

Cascading down the hillside of Montjuic, Barcelona's botanical garden combines hard-edged design, plants from around the world, and a mission to conserve the flora of the Mediterranean and Cataluña in particular. Opened in 1999 with plant collections from the five Mediterranean-climate regions of the world—California, central Chile, southern South Africa, south and southwest Australia, and the European Mediterranean—the garden is a dynamic and distinctly modern balance of geometrical architecture, the soft curves of nature, and the formality of regional plantings.

Eucalyptus and banksia mark the beginning of the Australian collection. California is signaled by bottle trees (*Brachychiton populneus*), Monterey pine (*Pinus radiata*), Californian live oak (*Quercus agrifolia*), and ceanothus species, while the giant baobab (*Adansonia digitata*) leads the visitor to the South African garden with its bright yellow and orange gazanias. The less widely known Chilean flora is marked by the monkey puzzle tree (*Araucaria araucana*); the European Mediterranean is represented by the cork oak (*Quercus suber*), sweet chestnut (*Castanea sativa*), and a woody, herbaceous understory of sasparilla (*Smilax aspera*) and butcher's broom (*Ruscus aculeatus*). The tour ends with an angled boardwalk among linear pools of water lilies, rushes, and other aquatic plants. CW

Jardí de Santa Clotilde

Cataluña, Spain

DESIGNER: Nicolau Rubió i Tudurí
OWNER: Lloret de Mar City Council
GARDEN STYLE: 20th-century Italianate
SIZE: 6.6 acres (2.7 ha)
CLIMATE: Mediterranean
LOCATION: Lloret de Mar, Cataluña

Built on the site of an old vineyard, this garden has a romantic, dreamlike quality. Begun in the 1920s by the Marquis of Roviralta, with the services of the young landscape architect Nicolau Rubió i Tudurí, it has now reached maturity.

One of the hallmarks of Tudurí's style is a naturalistic look. This is in evidence here, with cypresses towering above the neatly clipped hedges of scented *Pittosporum tobira* that follow the lay of the land. There is also an Italianate garden in the renaissance style, where the symmetry of paths, planting, and focal points, including statuary and fountains, is the key characteristic. The trees and shrubs include stately Italian cypresses (*Cupressus sempervirens*), Monterey cypresses (*C. macrocarpa*), and stone pines (*Pinus pinea*) that, with the help of the hedges, keep the sea hidden from full view, giving just occasional glimpses.

You can wander in any direction, but the hillside directs you either downward on magnificent stairways lined with statuary, or along the wide, impeccably raked gravel terraces. The main staircase leads to the Plaza de las Sirenas, with green-bronze statues made for the marquis.

One of the most attractive features of the stairs is the risers. Glossy ivy has been trained over them, from side to side, softening the stairs so that they blend in with the overall greenery of the garden. In every season, the greens of pines, pittosporum, oleander, and viburnum make the strongest impact; in summer, the agapanthus, oleander, hydrangeas, roses, and clivia certainly compete, as do the scented pittosporum and pine needles. BS

> "...this garden has a romantic, dreamlike quality"

El Parc de L'Estació del Nord

Cataluña, Spain

DESIGNERS: Andreu Arriola, Carme Fiol, Enric Pericas
OWNER: Barcelona City Council
GARDEN STYLE: 20th-century public park
SIZE: 11.9 acres (4.8 ha)
CLIMATE: Mediterranean
LOCATION: Barcelona, Cataluña

El Parc is not a massive space—covering two blocks of the grid pattern of the Eixample area of the city—but it manages to be both modern and green. Acting as a link to surrounding areas, and to the train station next to it, the park merges land art with open space. The design is meant to depict a dragon rising from the sea, with the beast leaving one world and entering another. As a result, the sculptor Beverly Pepper has created an interpretation of a dragon at one end and a decreasing circular amphitheater at the other, with a ceramic-tiled entrance in the middle.

Between these bursts of imagination is flat, open land, covered either in hard landscaping or grass. Areas of shade, openness, and intimacy exist, as do stunning, vertical columns with light emanating from the center, mimicking lightning reaching the earth. This may not be to everyone's taste, and many people may not appreciate this fable's reinterpretation as land-art, but, as is so often the case with Barcelona's public areas, successful urban planning has created a lively, imaginative space. If only other cities could also achieve results like these. CY

> "El Parc is not a massive space… but it manages to be both modern and green"

Jardí Botànic Marimurtra

Cataluña, Spain

DESIGNERS: Karl Faust and team of botanists
OWNER: Karl Faust Foundation
GARDEN STYLE: 20th-century botanical
SIZE: 37 acres (15 ha); 12.3 acres (5 ha) open to public
CLIMATE: Mediterranean
LOCATION: Blanes, Cataluña

Begun in 1921 by the German businessman Karl Faust, the Jardí Botànic Marimurtra was intended to be a scientific site, preserving the indigenous plants and character of the coastal flora of the Mediterranean. Today the garden is maintained by the Karl Faust Foundation, and about one-third of the property is open to the public.

Faust was an inveterate plant collector, bringing plants here from all over the world. He created several different areas in which to grow them and, although this is essentially a plant collectors' garden, it has interesting focal points and a wonderful position overlooking the Mediterranean coast. The main sections here are the Tropical, Temperate, and Mediterranean gardens, which house between them 3,500 species, including cacti, succulents, conifers, palms, and bamboos. Clearly marked routes lead the visitor through a variety of plantings, from African and American arid zones, past huge clumps of well-established bamboos in the temperate area, and then down the slope toward the sea, where the indigenous Mediterranean plants thrive with those from Australia, South Africa, and Chile. All the routes down the hill lead to a classical temple named in honor of Linnaeus, the eighteenth-century Swedish botanist, with wonderful views out to sea. BS

RIGHT Stunning views out to sea are just one of the attractions of the Jardí Botànic Marimurtra.

Jardí Botànic Cap Roig

Cataluña, Spain

DESIGNERS: Nicolai Woevodsky, Dorothy Woevodsky
OWNER: Caixa de Girona
GARDEN STYLE: 20th-century Anglo-
   Catalan romantic
SIZE: 100 acres (40 ha)
CLIMATE: Mediterranean
LOCATION: Calella de Palafrugell, Cataluña

Cap Roig was bought by the Russian colonel Nicolai Woevodsky and his British wife, Dorothy, in 1927 when it was just a precipitous headland with a ruined castle. The castle was restored to resemble the famous Castillo de Poblet, and the couple spent fifty years developing the gardens.

The drive and its long wide borders pass through an arch and curve away into the distance. One border has old olive trees before merging into conifers, some rare with contrasting shapes and colors. In spring the shrubs are backed by yellow clouds of mimosa and rosemary trailing over the wall. Rounding the curve, one sees the castle with its crenellated towers and a great Gothic door framed in the trees.

The Woevodskys first created terraced gardens, each with a different theme, on the steep slopes below the castle. One area has arum lilies, jasmine, and blue *Echium candicans*, another gnarled olive trees; a further area has a pool of water lilies and cyperus; the cloisterlike, stone-arched wall of the Nun's Terrace has *Pittosporum tobira* and bright seasonal bedding at the base. Below the terraces is the Spring Garden with its seasonal flowers set in light shade. On the steepest slopes there are plantings of cacti and succulents, with spiky agaves and aloes set in carpets of flowering gazanias, all within a light framework of *Pinus halepensis*. In more open areas, with very little shade, there are cacti. The Geranium Promenade is edged with scented-leaf pelargoniums as well as other colorful, seasonal flowers. RChe

Parc del Laberint d'Horta

Cataluña, Spain

DESIGNERS: Marquis of Alfarràs, Joan Anton Desvalls i d'Ardena, Domenico Bagutti
OWNER: Barcelona City Council
GARDEN STYLE: 18th-century romantic, neoclassical
SIZE: 22 acres (9.9 ha)
CLIMATE: Mediterranean
LOCATION: Barcelona, Cataluña

One of the loveliest parks in Barcelona because of its trees, the Parc del Laberint d'Horta has the largest maze in Spain. Fashioned from 2,460 feet (750 m) of Italian cypress (*Cupressus sempervirens*), the maze was designed by Joan Anton Desvalls i d'Ardena, in collaboration with the Italian architect Domenico Bagutti. At the center of the labyrinth is a statue of Eros, one of many classical figures scattered throughout the park.

The whole site is a good example of a restored, eighteenth-century, romantic-classical garden, with work beginning on its construction in 1791, and continued by descendants of the Marquis of Alfarràs through several generations. Financial difficulties in the late nineteenth century saw a change of ownership, and it passed into the hands of the municipality. The garden has benefited from comprehensive restoration, and you can now choose from one of the five paths that lead out from the Square of the Lions, where two marble lions commemorate the visit in 1827 of Fernando VII and his mother, Maria Luisa. All paths seem to head up to the main pavilion, a pink, classical-style building with friezes and blue shutters. The pavilion's back is reflected in the, dark, still waters of a square pool. In spring flowering trees, including the Judas tree (*Cercis siliquastrum*), ornamental orange (*Citrus aurantium* var. *amara*), the tree of heaven (*Ailanthus altissima*), cherry plum (*Prunus cerasifera atropurpurea*), and *Pittosporum tobira*, provide lots of scent and color. BS

Parc de Joan Miró

Cataluña, Spain

DESIGNERS: Antoni Solanas, Marius Quintana, Beth Gali, Andreu Arriola
OWNER: Barcelona City Council
GARDEN STYLE: 20th-century public park
SIZE: 14 acres (5.7 ha)
CLIMATE: Mediterranean
LOCATION: Barcelona, Cataluña

Covering the site of a former slaughterhouse, the Parc de Joan Miró (originally known as El Parc de L'Escorxador) takes up four city blocks, making it a sizable part of Barcelona. It is named after one of Cataluña's most famous sons, surrealist and abstract painter, sculptor, and ceramist Joan Miró. You will find works by Miró throughout the city, mostly in the Fundació Joan Miró at Parc de Montjuïc. But murals, sculpture, and ceramics also adorn the Casa de la Ciutat (City Hall); the pavement of the Ramblas, near the Liceu Opera House and La Boqueria market; and even the outside of Terminal B at Barcelona Airport.

Parc de Joan Miró is the home of one of Miró's last works, a mosaic-covered sculpture called *Dona i Ocell* or "Woman and Bird". Created in 1982 in collaboration with artist Gardy Artigas, the 70-foot-tall (22 m) sculpture stands in one corner of the park near a shallow pool. The phallic form of the abstract sculpture is said to have caused controversy when it was first installed. Yet it stands a colorful and playful icon that dominates this corner of the park, while the hard landscaping is a civic space for public use.

When you step down into the larger expanse of the park, the atmosphere is more intimate and attractive. Featuring pines, palms, and plane trees, it gives a respite from the hard landscaping, the surrounding roads, and buildings. Pockets of open space provide children's play areas, games of boule, dog walking, and outdoor table tennis. Note the gridlike pattern of the tree planting—common in Barcelona—and the unique lighting. CY

> "...it stands a colorful and playful icon that dominates this corner of the park"

Monestir de Pedralbes

Cataluña, Spain

DESIGNER: Unknown
OWNER: Barcelona City Council
GARDEN STYLE: 14th-century cloister
SIZE: 0.37 acre (0.15 ha)
CLIMATE: Mediterranean
LOCATION: Barcelona, Cataluña

The cloister gardens at the Monastery of Pedralbes, which takes its name from the white stone used in its construction, was, until quite recently, a traditional, monastic herb garden. Founded in 1326 by Queen Elisenda, the monastery was the home for the Poor Clares, a Franciscan order of nuns. On the death of her husband, Elisenda moved into the convent, and lived and worked among the community for the remaining thirty-three years of her life. In 1983 the Poor Clares moved out of the monastery to a nearby building, and the monastery—including its well-preserved, three-story cloister—was opened to the public.

Sitting on the stone, tile-faced benches of the fourteenth-century cistern that was used for drinking, washing, and also watering the cloister garden, it is easy to imagine the tranquil and meditative life of the monastic community. Each side of the magnificent Gothic cloister boasts twenty-six columns, making it the largest in the world. Originally orange blossom, roses, and jasmine were grown, but today tall cypresses, palms, oranges, and loquats offer shade, scent, and fruit, while the small herb garden—arranged in traditional rectangles—is filled with herbs, including lavender and rosemary. BS

> "…it is easy to imagine the tranquil and meditative life of the monastic community"

Parc Samà

Cataluña, Spain

DESIGNERS: Josep Fontserè i Mestres, Antoni Gaudí
OWNERS: The Samà family
GARDEN STYLE: 19th-century romantic park
SIZE: 34 acres (13.7 ha)
CLIMATE: Mediterranean
LOCATION: Cambrils, Cataluña

Parc Samà has all the ingredients of a romantic garden, and the elegance of a plantation-style mansion. It was founded by Salvador Samà Torrens, Marquis of Mariano, who began the garden in 1881. His family had lived in Cuba, and he brought to the property much that is reminiscent of the colonial style. He commissioned Josep Fontserè i Mestres, whose pupil was Antoni Gaudí—the exotic tower, the park's hallmark, is thought to be the work of Gaudí.

Although some of the plantings are relaxed and informal, much of it has an agricultural touch, with mandarin trees (*Citrus reticulata*), for example, arranged in rows for ease of harvest.

The most stunning and surreal of all Samà's features is the lake, with a canal and waterfall, fed by water from an underground source. There are three islands, the largest being a mountain made of large stones, complete with a grotto. Bridges to the island are balustraded with rustic-looking sides, though they are made of cement, while the star feature is the swamp cypress (*Taxodium distichum*), a great beauty with terrific fall color. In front of the house are several hundred-year-old specimens of lime, chestnut, and common oak (*Quercus robur*), and a fountain formed by shells of giant clams, decorated with huge snail shells. The park is also known for its collection of palms, including *Phoenix canariensis*, *Chamaerops excelsa* and *C. humilis*, and *Washingtonia filifera*. At the back of the house, a path leads to a wooded area with very fine specimens of *Pinus pinea*, *P. halepensis*, and the deodar cedar (*Cedrus deodara*). BS

Parc Güell

Cataluña, Spain

DESIGNER: Antoni Gaudí
OWNER: Barcelona City Council
GARDEN STYLE: 20th-century modernist park
SIZE: 42 acres (17 ha)
CLIMATE: Mediterranean
LOCATION: Barcelona, Cataluña

The skyscape of Barcelona is dominated by the fantastical designs of Antoni Gaudí, whose great patron was Eusebi Güell.

Altruistic and idealistic, Gaudí conceived the idea of a garden city in Gracia, on the northern outskirts of Barcelona, with sixty houses and private gardens linked by landscaped roads and walks. The market place is scooped out from the rocky hillside with a curvaceous perimeter seat, brightly decorated with broken tiles, and beyond are waving palms whose trunks echo the natural rock. Pathways take you to Gaudí's own house and beyond, under pergolas swathed in colorful bougainvillea and wisteria. From this vantage point, you can choose whether to climb higher, shaded by the grays and greens of pines, olives, eucalyptus, holm oak (*Quercus ilex*), and privet, to the stark crest of the hill. Throughout the park, there are agaves and palms; the 150 round stones represent rosary beads, suggesting that visitors enter into prayer as they ascend.

The entrance pavilion and iron balustrading lead to a double staircase with a central, water spouting dragon. Look up to the eighty-six columns of the Hypostile that supports the flat-roofed market place; the columns cleverly disguise pipes for winter rain that is then recycled. As Juan Bassegoda Nonell wrote in 1988, "Gaudí understood that Nature used magnificent structural forms…" CH

RIGHT Parc Güell, built by Antoni Gaudí and named for Gaudí's patron, Eusebi Güell.

Parc de la Ciutadella

Cataluña, Spain

DESIGNER: Jean-Claude Nicolas Forestier
OWNER: Barcelona City Council
GARDEN STYLE: 19th- and 20th-century mixed public park
SIZE: 76.5 acres (30.9 ha)
CLIMATE: Mediterranean
LOCATION: Barcelona, Cataluña

Located on the site of a former military citadel, from which it takes its name, this park was founded in 1888 as the setting for the International Exhibition. Today it is the largest expanse of green space in Barcelona, and it also contains 32 acres (13 ha) of zoo, the Parlament de Cataluña, the Museu d'Art Modern, and the Museu de Zoologia.

The imposing Arc de Triomphe, built as an entrance to the exhibition, now does the same job for the park, and once inside the green area it is clear how popular it is with the locals. Although given a formal cruciform layout by the two large avenues—one lined with white poplars, the other with limes and horse chestnut (*Aesculus hippocastanum*)—the park is predominantly informal, with lawns, and tall specimen trees and palms casting welcome shade. An interesting collection of mainly Mediterranean plants can be found at the Plaça d'Armes, in the center of the park, a modernization of the early twentieth-century design by the French landscape architect, Jean-Claude Nicolas Forestier.

Look for the circular lake with island, and an impressive cascade by Antoni Gaudí and Josep Fontserè i Mestres. Surrounded by a curving and balustraded stairway, and surmounted by a statue of Venus in her shell, the water cascades down greenery-encrusted steps to a large pool containing smaller fountains. Other structures of note are the brick and wood shade house that is filled with tropical plants, and the wrought-iron-framed greenhouse that has been converted into a café and cultural center. TM

Pinya de Rosa

Cataluña, Spain

DESIGNER: Dr. Fernando Riviere de Caralt
OWNER: Municipality of Blanes
GARDEN STYLE: 20th-century botanical with cacti
SIZE: 121.8 acres (49.3 ha)
CLIMATE: Mediterranean
LOCATION: Blanes, Cataluña

A coastal setting, with stunning views out to the Mediterranean sea, may not be the most obvious location for a botanical garden with a rich range of plants, but Pinya de Rosa is an exception to the rule. Growing the right plants in the right place has meant that the garden has developed slowly and surely over a period of fifty years.

Developed by Dr. Fernando Riviere de Caralt, a civil engineer, soon after he purchased the property in 1945, the garden is packed with cacti and other succulents. Intense acquisition from all over the world resulted in 7,000 species by the early 1990s, ranging from the now standard Mediterranean fare of yuccas and agaves, to the spikier opuntias and echinocactus. Some plants are laid out in botanical groups, others to an attractive design. In addition to the planterly benefits of a visit, there is the atmosphere: in the day, the light gives intense brilliance, adding to the spectacle of the shapes of plants, while in the cooler evening light, the garden can breathe and relax. The different areas combine to make it an incredibly private place that cannot be seen from the beach below. The result is a garden that makes people feel immediately relaxed and at home. CY

> "...an incredibly private place that cannot be seen from the beach below"

La Granja de San Ildefonso

Castilla Y León, Spain

DESIGNER: René Carlier
OWNER: The Spanish State
GARDEN STYLE: 18th-century baroque
SIZE: 360 acres (145.8 ha)
CLIMATE: Mediterranean
LOCATION: Segovia, Castilla Y León

The name derives from a monastic grange, or farm, that once stood on the site. In 1724 King Philip V, who was French by birth and spent his childhood at Versailles, retired to La Granja, also known as Jardines de la Granja de San Ildefonso. Here, with the help of 5,000 workers, he passed the next two decades making the gardens. Despite constant royal use until the reign of King Alfonso XIII in the late nineteenth and early twentieth centuries, the gardens were almost unaltered; they are Spain's premier example of this style and period. Philip clearly remembered his childhood, for there is a flavor of Versailles at La Granja. However, because of the setting—on a hillside with views of the Guadarrama Mountains—the garden has a definite Spanish ambience, and the baroque is self-evident in the ornate parterres, the radiating avenues of lime and horse-chestnut trees with their gravel paths, the groves bound by clipped hornbeam hedges, and the spectacular show of statuary and water features.

This is a place to wander along the paths and to come unexpectedly upon the many water features with their mythological sculptural scenes. All the fountains are stunning; of particular note, in the main cascade, are the fountains of Neptune, Apollo, and Andromeda that together form part of the long perspective known as The Horse Race. The tallest, the Fountain of Fame, shoots water to a height of 131 feet (40 m). The garden is lovely in summer, but a winter visit when it's empty, with snow on the ground and icicles hanging from the fountains, is magical. TM

La Mirada

Castilla-La Mancha, Spain

DESIGNER: Eduardo Mencos
OWNER: Eduardo Mencos
GARDEN STYLE: 20th-century experimental
SIZE: 2.5 acres (1 ha)
CLIMATE: Mediterranean
LOCATION: Guadalajara, Castilla-La Mancha

This garden, created during the 1990s on the Castile plateau, some 31 miles (50 km) from Madrid, by the versatile Spanish landscaper Eduardo Mencos, offers a large experimental backdrop where plant and sculptural elements form a challenging, dreamlike world. The surprising compositions of *objets trouvés*, organic constructions, and native plants provide a strong visual sense of narration that reflects Mencos' previous role as a movie director.

Facing a valley formed by a prehistoric river and situated among a wild landscape composed of a natural Mediterranean forest, the garden interacts with its surroundings in a very special way. Its outline, based on three circles, is inspired by the setting, and the numerous tree sculptures—a key part of its design—have been created using dead specimens of holm oak (*Quercus ilex*), whose naked branches have been turned into sculptures.

It certainly was a challenge to create a garden in such a harsh land with poor soil and the fierce Castilian climate. The Spanish proverb "nine months of winter and three of burning hell" gives an idea of the challenge. A total of 800 truckloads of good topsoil had to be used before the trees, starting with catalpas, cedars, chestnuts, and cypresses, were planted here, offering shade and structure. Mencos also imported oaks and junipers to the site from the countryside, with a large number of plants that grow in the wild, but best of all he introduced the glass ponds and the enormous, showy, steel pergola with its egg-shaped openings. AB

Palacio de Galiana

Castilla-La Mancha, Spain

DESIGNER: Carmen Marañón
OWNERS: Alejandro Fernández-Araoz, Carmen Marañón
GARDEN STYLE: 20th-century formal
SIZE: 2.5 acres (1 ha)
CLIMATE: Mediterranean
LOCATION: Toledo, Castilla-La Mancha

This simple, yet elegant, garden, designed around carved monumental cypresses, trimmed hedges, and large areas of ivy, was created during the 1960s to complement a 1,000-year-old building located in Toledo, on the banks of the River Tajo.

Most of the building was built in the hybrid *mudéjar* style by Alfonso X El Sabio during the thirteenth century, on the site of an old Moorish palace known as the Pabellón de la Noria. Chronicles from that time describe the palace as one of the most beautiful in the world. It was also considered to be Europe's first botanical garden.

After years of neglect, the palace was in ruins when, in 1959, Carmen Marañón bought it with her husband, Alejandro Fernández-Araoz. After exhaustive research, and on the advice of architects Manuel Gómez Moreno and Fernando Chueca Goitia, they started to restore the building. To avoid having to change any aspect of the original structure, they decided not to live in the palace, but instead to build a new house close by, taking their inspiration from traditional Toledo buildings.

The most interesting feature of the garden is without doubt a sunken patio at the center of the building, with a pond in the middle, reflecting the topiary in its many precise and compact forms that merge with the architectural elements. But the dominating features are the sculptured conifers. As its creator put it, "With their trunks wrapped in ivy, the cypresses seem to float, suspended in space, taking on a metaphysical nature." AB

Jardín del Palacio de Aranjuez

Madrid, Spain

DESIGNERS: Felipe II, Felipe V, Carlos IV, Juan de Villaneuva
OWNER: Patrimonio Nacional (National Heritage)
GARDEN STYLE: Various
SIZE: 741 acres (300 ha)
CLIMATE: Mediterranean
LOCATION: Aranjuez, Madrid

Over several centuries, Felipe II, Felipe V, and Carlos IV all took turns to build their palaces and pleasure gardens on this site, a former royal hunting ground. Felipe II's plans were executed by Dutch gardeners, while Felipe V was assisted by a duo of French gardeners, the Boutelous, father and son. Carlos IV and his architect, Juan de Villanueva, were responsible for the Prince's Garden. In all, four distinct areas can be found here: the Old and New Parterre Gardens, the Island Garden, and the Prince's Garden, with their mature trees and shady walks ranging along the banks of the River Tagus. The garden that is closest to the Royal Palace is the small parterre dating from the reign of Felipe II (1556). This lovely old relic was recently excavated and carefully restored. Each of its box-edged beds has a fruit tree in the center. The main French-style Parterre Garden, which dates from the eighteenth century, has its own river that flows along the northern side.

The trio of gardens at Aranjuez can be found spread over a large area, and it would need days to explore them fully, though it is possible to take in the Parterre Garden and some areas of the palace gardens before or after a tour of the palace. There is also the Chiquitren, a tourist train that offers visitors a bone-shaking ride over the cobbled streets, disconcertingly accompanied by a continuous recording of Rodrigo's *Concierto de Aranjuez*—said to have been inspired by a visit to these gardens. BS

Jardín del Monasterio de El Escorial

Madrid, Spain

DESIGNERS: Juan de Bautista, Juan de Herrara
OWNER: The Spanish State
GARDEN STYLE: 16th-century formal
SIZE: Approximately 6 acres (2.5 ha)
CLIMATE: Mediterranean
LOCATION: El Escorial, Madrid

A UNESCO World Heritage Site, El Escorial was built between 1562 and 1584 by Felipe II, and is the largest renaissance building in Spain. It houses a monastery, basilica, palace, library, mausoleum, and gardens.

The main garden is in the cloister, the Patio of the Apostles, named after the white marble statues of the apostles within, and which can only be visited with prior permission. At the center of this area is a large, octagonal, domed building. Around it, and edging the start of the four paths that run at right angles to one another, are four square pools. Beds contains a formal parterre of clipped box hedges and a fountain.

Outside the monastery, on a terrace that extends along the whole of the southern facade, with views over the surrounding countryside and to the distant Sierra de Guadarrama, is the Jardín de los Frailes (Garden of the Friars). Today the geometric parterres look a touch severe but Felipe loved flowers and had the gardens filled with color: "like fine Turkish carpets brought from Cairo or Damascus." Two more formal geometric gardens in the complex are open, and are attached to small eighteenth-century palaces where they are shaded by tall conifers. For something a little more bizarre, visit the monastery to see a panel of a version (not the one in the Prado) of Hieronymus Bosch's *Garden of Earthly Delights* (1500). TM

RIGHT Madrid province's most amazing site—both the palace and gardens at El Escorial were designed to impress.

Parque del Buen Retiro

Madrid, Spain

DESIGNERS: Felipe IV, Cosimo Lotti
OWNER: City of Madrid
GARDEN STYLE: 17th-century renaissance
SIZE: 296 acres (119.8 ha)
CLIMATE: Mediterranean
LOCATION: Madrid

This park offers air, light, and, because of its size, a sense of infinite space. Its origins date back to its incarnation as the garden around the Monasterio de los Jerónimos. Later it became part of the estate and gardens of Felipe IV's seventeenth-century palace. Cosimo Lotti was responsible for the layout of the garden areas and plantings of this period, when the large boating lake, El Estanque, was also created.

Carlos III opened the park to the public, but only if people followed a strict dress code, and enclosed its entire perimeter with iron railings. During the War of Independence, del Buen Retiro was devastated, but was subsequently restored, with many new features and buildings added by Ferdinand IV.

To see all the buildings and statuary in one visit would require several hours. The most interesting statue is in the Plaza del Angel Caído (The Square of the Fallen Angel) and may be the only public statue of the devil in the world. Within the park there are many fountains, including Fuente de la Alcachofa, which is shaped like an artichoke. While large areas of the park are densely wooded, there are several separate and distinct gardens, such as the rose garden—La Rosaleda. It is a beautiful and tranquil area in spring and summer, when the roses are at their best.

The iron and glass Palacio de Cristal and the Palacio de Velázquez, which are used for modern art exhibitions, are worth seeking out. In front of the Palacio de Cristal is a lake with a fountain and damp grotto tunnel. Swamp cypresses (*Taxodium distichum*) thrive here and make a beautiful fall display. BS

Real Jardín Botánico

Madrid, Spain

DESIGNERS: Francesco Sabatini, Leandro Silva Delgado
OWNER: Superior Council of Scientific Research
GARDEN STYLE: 18th-century botanical
SIZE: 20 acres (8.1 ha)
CLIMATE: Mediterranean
LOCATION: Madrid

Despite its scientific role, Madrid's botanical garden offers in its terraced and sheltered layout a sense of calm and peace in the middle of a modern city. It has been on this site for over two centuries and its predecessor, the first Royal Botanic Garden in Madrid, was created for King Ferdinand VI in the mid-eighteenth century on the banks of the River Manzanares. It held a collection of over 2,000 plants, many of them obtained by the botanist-surgeon José Quer during his travels. In 1774 King Carlos III moved the garden to its present location, and it was opened in 1781. Francesco Sabatini, the king's architect, and Juan de Villanueva, the architect responsible for the Prado Museum, were hired for the task.

The garden survived various pressures from nature and man until a major restoration was carried out in the twentieth century, under the direction of the renowned Spanish landscape architect Leandro Silva Delgado. Much of the original layout was retained, and many of the important surviving plants remain. The garden is divided into several distinct areas or terraces. Although the character of each terrace is different, there is a unity provided by the well-proportioned staircases, the wide paths, and the bowl-like granite pools (with fountains) at regular intervals along the paths. Shade is provided by a collection of mature and important trees such as cork oaks (*Quercus suber*), camphor trees, olives, walnut, and eucalyptus. The latest addition is the Rose Garden, made possible by the donation of some 300 varieties from a collector, Don Angel Esteban. BS

Jardín de Montforte

Valencia, Spain

DESIGNER: Sebastián Monleón Estellés
OWNER: City of Valencia
GARDEN STYLE: 19th-century neoclassical
SIZE: 3 acres (1.2 ha)
CLIMATE: Mediterranean
LOCATION: Valencia, Valencia

This romantic, nineteenth-century garden, heavily influenced by the neoclassical, with an injection of the relaxed and sinuous, is the only vestige of countless gardens and orchards that occupied this part of Valencia. Given the aggressive level of construction that has led to a plethora of large, dull buildings where there were once groves of orange trees, cypresses, and myrtles, the existence today of the Montforte garden is something of a miracle.

Originally an orchard, the garden and the mansion were created after 1849 by the Valencian architect Sebastián Monleón Estellés for the future Marquis of San Juan. The garden is still enchantingly beautiful, evoking the past with intimate and secluded spaces where time seems to have stopped.

The series of hedged garden "rooms" includes some near the house that are formal and walled by cypress, with the informal being farther away. Extra touches include the large pond, the forest, the artificial mountain, the pergola covered with bougainvillea, and the rose garden with a fountain in the center surrounded by orange trees. There are also a great number of striking classical sculptures made from Carrar marble, representing philosophers and mythological characters, especially Ceres, the goddess of agriculture, and Mother Earth. AB

"The garden is still enchantingly beautiful…"

Casa de los Bates

Andalucía, Spain

DESIGNER: Unknown
OWNERS: The Marlin-Feriche family
GARDEN STYLE: 17th-century Cuban-Spanish
SIZE: 7 acres (2.8 ha)
CLIMATE: Mediterranean
LOCATION: Motril, Andalucía

The forgotten, private garden of Casa de los Bates opened in 2002. It is set on a hill surrounded by avocado and cherimoya orchards. In the fifteenth century the estate was owned by the Moors but, after the Christian conquest, it was given by the Spanish monarchy to an English botanist in their service, Mr. Bates. Though the palace has gone, the splendid guest house, built in 1800 in the Cuban colonial style, remains. The present owners spent five years upgrading the property. Ancient palm and cypress trees hide the isolated house, while giving fine views between their trunks and foliage.

The drive enters through ornamental iron gates and skirts the hill, leading to a circular turning point. In its center is a pool with an ornate triple fountain set with statues, all surrounded by pots of red petunias. Twin balustraded steps lead down from the house to the winter garden with its blue and white tiled fountain. The formal beds are edged with clipped box or myrtle, and the clipped cypresses give a green background that is an excellent foil for the red and pink roses, white and pink watsonias, white lilies, strelitzias, and *Hibiscus mutabilis*, whose flowers open white, turn pink, and then darken.

The descent takes in palm trees and two tufa grottoes, the yellow spring *Jasminum mesnyi*, and white summer jasmine. At each side, there are cypress trees clipped to form "rooms" with a Gothic arched entry. The lowest section, the Generalife, has a narrow canal with side jets enclosed by clipped cypresses. It is atmospheric, beautiful, and exotic. RChe

La Alhambra

Andalucía, Spain

DESIGNERS: Various during the Nasrid dynasty
OWNER: Andalucía Regional Government
GARDEN STYLE: 13th-century Moorish
SIZE: 32 acres (12.9 ha)
CLIMATE: Mediterranean
LOCATION: Granada, Andalucía

In the thirteenth century, the Alhambra was a citadel of power, towering over Granada. Today it provides an insight into the importance and integration of courtyards and patios in the day-to-day life of this palace complex; there are also gardens beyond the buildings and on the adjacent hillside.

Within the royal palace, there are several major courtyards. The Patio of the Myrtles, otherwise known as the Patio of the Pool, was created for the Moorish ruler Yusuf I, and dates from the fourteenth century. The absence of elaborate ornament, and the simplicity of the pool and its courtyard, make a strong impact, while the planting of straight hedges of fragrant myrtle reinforce the design. The Patio of the Lions was built by Yusuf's son, Muhammad V, during the fourteenth century. It perfectly embodies Persian pleasure gardens, with an enclosed space divided by channels or watercourses symbolizing the rivers of Persia, and also the paradise gardens of the Koran. The central feature here is a stone basin surrounded by twelve carved lions. Water flows along the channels, and thin jets of water spill from the lions' mouths; the planting consists of aromatic herbs. Beyond are the remnants of another palace, the Portal, with terraces and pools, shrubs and hedges. Dating from 1924, they are by the architects responsible for restoration at the Alhambra, Modesto Cendoya and Leopoldo Torres Balbás. BS

RIGHT The Alhambra, perhaps Spain's most memorable monument, offers a wealth of restrained Moorish details.

Carmen de la Victoria

Andalucía, Spain

DESIGNER: Unknown
OWNER: University of Granada
GARDEN STYLE: 16th-century Moorish-Spanish
SIZE: 0.5 acre (0.2 ha)
CLIMATE: Mediterranean
LOCATION: El Albaicín, Granada, Andalucía

Unique to Granada, a *carmen* is a house with a garden and a kitchen garden attached, with fruit trees, vegetables, herbs, ornamental plants, and a predominant show of scented plants. El Albaicín has many of these secret little gardens enclosed by high walls, and they are very difficult to find, let alone enter.

It is not known how old the Victoria garden is, but the adjacent one is sixteenth century, which gives a good indication. Huge cedar cypresses and palm trees hide the house and garden, high up on a terrace. Entering through the wrought-iron gates, steps lead up past the porter's lodge to a small garden with a wonderful domed "pavilion" with slim pillars and arches of clipped cypress. On the same terrace, half-shaded by cedars, the white flowers of *Viburnum opulus* merge with the branches of diervilla wreathed in rose pink flowers, and there are also oleanders, argyranthemums, white banksian roses, and red climbing roses on the edge of the terrace.

After that, the Pergola Terrace with Italian cypresses forms an arcade with framed views of the palace on the wooded hill. Terraces with pergolas and wisterias follow; the main terrace has palms, cedars, cypress trees, water jets, bougainvillea, jasmine, philadelphus, agapanthus, red and pink roses, blue and white irises, red hibiscus, blue larkspur, and pomegranates and vines. All in all, this beautiful, extravagantly planted garden is one that visitors will find difficult to forget. RChe

Casa de Don Juan de Bosco

Andalucía, Spain

DESIGNER: Jean-Claude Nicolas Forestier
OWNER: Congregation of Salesians
GARDEN STYLE: 19th-century Andalucían
SIZE: 0.5 acre (0.2 ha)
CLIMATE: Mediterranean
LOCATION: Ronda, Andalucía

Curving steps lead down each side of the balcony of the Casa de Don Juan de Bosco and almost embrace the central pool of the main garden, which is full of goldfish with glazed, ceramic frogs spouting water into the center of the pool. The borders around the garden are planted with clipped gray santolina to balance the bright marigolds and roses, and the whole design is surrounded by a swirling pattern of cobbles inset with blue tiles that draw the eye down to ground level. Then visitors come across a sudden contrast. Beyond the stone balustrade is a stunning panoramic view of fields, river, woods, mountains, and a bridge built in 1793, all clearly seen from this high shelf 328 feet (100 m) up in the sky.

Located behind the pool, and tucked underneath the steps, is a beautifully tiled, stone-columned loggia decorated with ceramic pictures. Potted evergreens help frame the scene, and seasonal highlights include crimson Virginia creeper (*Parthenocissus quinquefolia*), mauve wisteria, pink roses, and blue plumbago. From the right of the pool, on a raised patio that is edged with pink and crimson climbing roses, and giant fig leaves, you can look down to another raised garden. Visitors will enter this garden between Arabic pillars, and see a large cedar and a mop-headed palm tree, which makes a superb contrast with the tight columns of cypress trees found elsewhere. It makes an excellent background to what is, overall, a fabulous garden. RChe

Carmen de los Mártires

Andalucía, Spain

DESIGNER: Various
OWNER: Granada Town Council
GARDEN STYLE: 19th-century eclectic
SIZE: 17.5 acres (7 ha)
CLIMATE: Mediterranean
LOCATION: Granada, Andalucía

This gem of a garden on the Alhambra hill, once known as "the best and most beautiful country house in the province of Granada," is an eclectic nineteenth-century garden, with a romantic spirit. Its size and amalgamation of different styles set it apart from traditional gardens of Granada, known as *carmens*, though it does share many of their characteristics. It belongs to the Islamic tradition, and offers amazing views of Granada, the plain, and the Sierra Nevada.

The place was named in honor of the Christians who were martyred there during the days of the Moors. On reconquering Granada, Isabel La Católica ordered a chapel to be built in their memory and, during the sixteenth century, it became a convent. The cypress planted by San Juan de la Cruz (who wrote *La Noche Oscura del Alma* beneath it) and the aqueduct in the ancient monastic garden still remain.

After the area was disentailed in the first half of the nineteenth century, together with other church lands, the property was acquired in 1846 by General Carlos Calderón, who built the mansion and the gardens, giving them the same appearance they maintain today, with different garden "rooms" on the terraced site. After passing through various private hands, today the estate is a public park. Visitors love the formal areas next to the house, with their geometric box hedges, fountains, ponds, and sculptures, and farther away, the romantic garden and the great lake with its little island. AB

Palacio de las Dueñas

Andalucía, Spain

DESIGNER: Unknown
OWNER: Duque de Alba
GARDEN STYLE: 15th-century Moorish
SIZE: 2 acres (0.8 ha)
CLIMATE: Mediterranean
LOCATION: Seville, Andalucía

This fifteenth-century *mudéjar* palace and gardens are a great surprise. Unusual for an Andalucían garden, the entrance courtyard and its plantings can be seen through the wide iron gates from the street.

A graveled drive leads up to the palace between two large, stone-edged beds, both featuring a tall Canary Island palm (*Phoenix canariensis*) emerging from densely planted citrus trees. Beneath the trees, red- and yellow-flowering cannas grow, their large, purplish, vertical leaves contrasting with the neat dwarf box hedging. A branch of the drive curves off to the left where purple-magenta bougainvilleas, sky-blue plumbago and other climbers cover the walls, with ivy-leaved pelargoniums and yellow euryops.

The central patio is reached through the palace. Surrounded by columns and Moorish arches, the diagonal paths center on an octagonal, ceramic-covered fountain with a raised marble bowl. Palms give height, dwarf box and myrtle give structure, and the beds are filled with richly scented, old shrub roses.

Other gardens surround the palace, one being rectangular with cross paths and a central fountain, and bordered by box hedges from which emerge tall, square obelisks of Italian cypress (*Cupressus sempervirens*). Orange-red clivias are used as infill, with marble statues acting as focal points. Additional features include a thicket of trees, a patio with a small, glazed, circular pool and fountain with a stone coat of arms, and a marvelous water tank. RChe

Casa del Rey Moro

Andalucía, Spain

DESIGNER: Jean-Claude Nicolas Forestier
OWNER: Unknown
GARDEN STYLE: 20th-century Spanish-Islamic
SIZE: 0.5 acre (0.2 ha)
CLIMATE: Mediterranean
LOCATION: Ronda, Andalucía

The dramatic, 328-foot-deep (100 m) gorge of the River Tajo divides the old town of Ronda from the new. In 1042 the house of a Moorish king was built right on the edge of the gorge; the present house is eighteenth century, but the ancient 250 steps going through tunnels right down to the river are still there; this is where a constant stream of slaves would carry up buckets of water to supply the town. In 1912 the owner, the Duchess of Parcent, commissioned Jean-Claude Nicolas Forestier to design a garden in this setting. He was the main instigator of the Andalucían Spanish-Moslem garden style that he implemented in Seville, Malaga, Casablanca, and Cuba.

His exquisite terracotta and blue-tiled top terrace has an octagonal pool with a little fountain, where tiled seats backed by clipped evergreen hedges and pots of geraniums guide the eye to the main vista. Here, on each side, are stone-columned pergolas topped with climbers that join in the middle, where a concave pool is set under the terrace, with a narrow brook taking water out into the garden. All the paths and the brook are lined with small, delicate, square blue tiles, the steps are all edged with scarlet perlagoniums, and the brook with myrtle, box, and almond trees. The brook then disappears, but the water emerges from the mouth of a lion's head and spouts into a pool, where white water lilies and green cyperus feature heavily, the surrounding terrace adding extra color with terracotta pots of blue flowers. Best of all are the large conifer trees that frame the view across the open countryside. RChe

Casa de Pilatos

Andalucía, Spain

DESIGNER: Unknown
OWNER: Duke of Medinaceli
GARDEN STYLE: 15th-, 16th-century Italian renaissance
SIZE: 2.5 acres (1 ha)
CLIMATE: Mediterranean
LOCATION: Seville, Andalucía

This palace dates from the fifteenth and sixteenth centuries, when the gardens were laid out. Today they have many original Andalucían features, but they still have more in common with the Italian renaissance. The main entrance is through the well-restored, breathtakingly decorated rooms and salons on the lower floor of the house.

Trails of climbers, including bougainvillea and plumbago, hang sumptuously over the typical Andalucían covered walkway, or *apeadero*. In the courtyard, orange trees grow against the walls, where they were once trained into fan shapes, though many have grown away from the wall. The first garden is the delightful, enclosed Chico Garden with the original water tank that served the palace, a pond with a fountain, and a bronze statue of Bacchus. Mature palms, figs, and a *Magnolia grandiflora* are the grandest specimens among the small, box-edged beds for roses, with the pathways between covered in yellow sand. The Grand Garden is more intimate and varied than the Chico. Its eleven rectangular beds are the direct descendants of the original kitchen garden of the fifteenth century. Two loggias for sculpture were later added at either end of the garden. Palms, citrus, and banana plants hold the high ground in the garden today, with climbers such as crimson-mauve bougainvillea, jasmine, and wisteria draping themselves over walls and arches. BS

RIGHT The Casa de Pilatos in Seville was constructed using a mixture of Italian renaissance and Andalucían styles.

Casas del Chapiz

Andalucía, Spain

DESIGNER: Unknown
OWNER: Council of Scientific Research
GARDEN STYLE: 16th-century Moorish
SIZE: 0.3 acre (0.1 ha)
CLIMATE: Mediterranean
LOCATION: Granada, Andalucía

This sixteenth-century building, which was once the home of two Moriscos (converts to Christianity) Hernan Lopez el Feri and Lorenzo el Chapiz, is one of the best examples of the Moorish style. Once two houses, it is built around two patios; the first is enclosed on all sides and has a raised wooden balcony, being paved below with pebbles, and there is a central, brick-edged, rectangular pool. Matching containers of slim Italian cypresses (*Cupressus sempervirens*) and aspidistras provide the greenery.

The second patio has elegant Moorish arches and balconies on two sides, while the third side is extended with closely planted cypress trees that form a green wall; their trunks are similar in shape and size to the pillars of the arches opposite. Within this balanced U-shape area is a long, rectangular pool, full of white water lilies. A narrow brick path separates the pool from the short-clipped box hedge, and there are orange trees at each corner.

A narrow path leads through a cypress screen to reveal a secret garden on a long terrace, with circular "pavilions" of cypress giving shade and privacy. A series of short box and myrtle hedges contain a range of trees, shrubs, and other plants. Typical of a *carmen* (a house with a garden and kitchen garden), there is a wide range of fruit trees, including orange, lemon, grapefruit, pomegranate, almond, pear, and diosporus, with roses, oleanders, philadelphus, abelias, and myrtle as the fragrant fillers. This long terrace gives magnificent views of the entire length of the Alhambra. RChe

El Festival de los Patios Cordobeses

Andalucía, Spain

DESIGNERS: Various
OWNERS: Various
GARDEN STYLE: Moorish and others
SIZE: Various
CLIMATE: Mediterranean
LOCATION: Córdoba, Andalucía

Córdoba has hundreds of beautifully planted patios that are usually hidden from public view. However, for two weeks in May, the heavy street doors are thrown open and householders compete in the annual Festival of the Patios. Every conceivable surface is festooned with flowers in brightly painted pots on whitewashed walls and wellheads. In one garden, head-high ironwork cakestands are hung with containers frothing with pink and crimson blooms, and in another, lines of succulents stand to spiky attention on the white steps. Under an arch painted red and yellow, a crowd of scarlet pelargoniums jostles around a doorway, packed in oil drums and paint buckets, saucepans, and tureens, and there are fat lemons on potted trees.

Córdoba's patios are the legacy of 700 years of Moorish rule—the enduring emblem of a desert culture that valued the garden as a domestic paradise—a hidden oasis of abundance, ease, and protection from the sun. Some of the loveliest are in the oldest parts of the city, particularly the Jewish quarter, but even among modern apartment blocks, the patio remains the place to eat, chat, and party.

The city's tourist office provides visitors with maps with numbered routes to help find the patios, but it's more fun to lose yourself in the labyrinth of narrow streets, stumbling unexpectedly on hidden gems. Patios are classified as aristocratic, middling, or *populares* (people's patios). And for those without one, there is an equally competitive contest for the most beautiful balcony. AE

> "…for two weeks in May… householders compete in the annual Festival of the Patios"

El Generalife

Andalucía, Spain

DESIGNER: Francisco Prieto-Moreno
OWNER: Andalucía Regional Government
GARDEN STYLE: 14th-century Moorish
SIZE: 0.07 acre (0.03 ha)
CLIMATE: Mediterranean
LOCATION: Granada, Andalucía

The Gardens of the Architect are the oldest in Granada, dating from the early fourteenth century. The palace and its gardens were intended as a summer retreat or country house for the sultans, and the hillside was duly terraced and water channels created. Vegetables and herbs were grown here, as they still are, though not to the same extent. The gardens nearer the palace are the work of Francisco Prieto-Moreno and date from the 1950s, when he was the palace architect and curator. His designs include many elements of what might previously have been on the site, including parterres and hedged garden "rooms," some with pools and fountains.

The famous water garden is inside the palace. The Court of the Long Pond is essentially an enclosed terrace, having buildings on three of its sides and a covered walkway on the fourth side. At the center of the space is a long, narrow channel of water with thin jets seemingly hopping across from one side to the other. Originally there were no jumping water jets; these were added in the eighteenth century, and for some visitors seem an intrusion into the peaceful nature of the patio. Brightly-colored flowers tumble from pots, and climbers cling to the surrounding walls. The former royal inhabitants, strolling in the shady arcaded walkway, would have seen it adorned with festoons of climbing roses, but over the years these have been changed or replaced.

Above this part of the palace, a doorway leads to the Patio of the Cypresses, also called the Patio of the Sultana; the water jets playing here were added in the nineteenth century. Square islands of oleander float in water channels with the water jets dancing from island to island. Higher up the hillside is a Moorish water staircase with water flowing down what is, in effect, a stone bannister. The staircase once had an additional water channel in its center, but sadly this was removed for safety reasons. BS

Hospital de los Venerables Sacerdotes

Andalucía, Spain

DESIGNER: Leonardo de Figueroa
OWNER: Seville City Council
GARDEN STYLE: Late 17th-century courtyard
SIZE: Unknown
CLIMATE: Mediterranean
LOCATION: Seville, Andalucía

Founded in 1697 by the Hermandad del Silencio (Brotherhood of Silence) as an asylum where old, poor, and homeless priests could live out their final years in peace, this hospital has one of the loveliest courtyard gardens in Seville. The buildings have recently been restored and are now administered by a cultural organization, Fundación FOCUS; daily tours of the buildings offer a perspective on life in one of Seville's typical seventeenth-century houses.

In style the hospital building combines the characteristics of restrained Spanish convent architecture with the opulence of a Sevillian noble's baroque mansion. Whitewashed walls and detailing create a strong contrast with rich, red brick, most strikingly in the central courtyard with its sunken center. The garden courtyard itself is a beautiful, open space, part cloister and part square patio, with arcaded columns supporting the upper galleries of the building, containing large French windows.

In the middle of the courtyard stands a simple fountain. Concentric steps in brick and tile lead down to the fountain, the circles contrasting with the patio's square floor plan. Greenery is provided by groups of terracotta pots holding leathery aspidistras, arum lilies, and myrtle, and standard citrus trees ranged around the upper level of the patio.

The Hospital de los Venerables Sacerdotes, which had fallen into disuse in the 1960s after serving as a storehouse, a textile factory, and a match factory, was renovated with the purpose of returning it to the people of Seville. Visitors come to see the murals in its church, painted by Valdés Leal and his son, Lucas. The building is now a popular setting for cultural events, and also offers a specialized library, a collection of engravings, and a musical auditorium equipped with a newly constructed organ, as well as conference rooms and various exhibition rooms equipped with the latest museum technology. BS

Jardín Botánico La Concepción

Andalucía, Spain

DESIGNER: Amalia Livermore
OWNER: Municipality of Malaga
GARDEN STYLE: 19th-century botanical
SIZE: 61 acres (24.7 ha)
CLIMATE: Mediterranean
LOCATION: Malaga, Andalucía

The gardens at La Concepción were begun in the 1850s as private pleasure grounds for Amalia Livermore and her husband, Jorge Loring Oyarzábal, Marquis of Casa Loring. The grounds were attached to the house of her grandfather, Thomas Livermore, who had been the British consul in Malaga. Amalia and Jorge traveled around the world, bringing back plants from wherever they visited. The result was a tropical garden of great distinction with over 3,000 separate species.

Bamboo groves, stands of the ginger lily (*Alpinia zerumbet*), and huge specimens of *Ficus microcarpa* are among the many plants that now thrive here. There are over 500 individual palms of twenty-five species holding court in this tree-lover's paradise. The garden boasts the tallest aruacaria in Malaga.

Two species of strelitzia—the small, brightly colored bird of paradise (*Strelitzia regina*) and the giant *Strelitzia nicolai*—make strong statements, whether they are in flower or not, with clivias, hibiscus, and dombeyas backing up the show. Much of the garden is perfumed by the fragrance of *Pittosporum tobira*, and wisteria and jasmine have leapt from their stately iron pergolas to sweep through the mature trees.

The house and garden were sold to the municipality of Malaga, and the gardens opened to the public in 1994. Visitors are taken around the garden in groups by well-informed guides. The route followed is along sandy paths lined with stone irrigation channels, past many water features, including a waterfall, and an avenue lined with palms from the Canary Islands and shade-giving *Platanus* x *acerifolia*. In the fall the plane trees provide a coppery glow to this lush hillside, and the avenue leads to a viewpoint where, from a classical gazebo, you gaze across the humming highway to the urban sprawl of Malaga. BS

Medina Azahara

Andalucía, Spain

DESIGNER: Caliph Abd-ar-Rahman III
OWNER: Andalucía Regional Government
GARDEN STYLE: 10th-century historic landscape
SIZE: 276.7 acres (112 ha)
CLIMATE: Mediterranean
LOCATION: Sierra Morena, Córdoba, Andalucía

The Medina Azahara, built as the new capital of al-Andalus in 929, commands an imposing view across a valley toward the modern city of Córdoba. The city flourished on three tiers, descending to the River Guadalquivir, but its vibrant existence was short-lived, and it was destroyed by warfare some seventy-five years later. Its ruins lay undisturbed until the early twentieth century.

It is not difficult to imagine, as you walk among the excavated footings, walls, and columns, and lightly planted gardens, the beauty of the palace with its courtyards and patio gardens, built here by the Caliph Abd-ar-Rahman III. The statistics reveal the fantastic amount of manpower and materials required; while the lavishness and beauty of the site, with its elaborate system of canals, aqueducts, and tunnels bringing water for the city from 10 miles (16 km) away, overwhelmed visitors in its heyday. The palace that dominates the upper terrace was built for the Caliph's favorite, al-Zahra, and for her entertainment an aviary, zoo, four large fishponds, and an estimated 300 pools or baths were created.

Descriptions of the site's original garden speak of pools, canals, and fountains, and a dazzling basin filled with quicksilver that, if touched, sent sunbeams around the great hall. Today, within the partially excavated foundations, the relatively recent plantings have matured into romantic, free-flowing shapes. Pencil-thin cypresses rise skyward, their dark outlines accentuated against the open landscape. In summer oleanders, a strawberry tree (*Arbutus unedo*), and pomegranates provide stylish focal points, while clouds of mauve bougainvillea hang in swaths across ruined archways, walls, and columns. Rosemary, myrtle, and roses would have scented the air of the original gardens; today palms create a more desertlike landscape, and in spring, the site is full of wildflowers and butterflies. BS

Palacio de Mondragón

Andalucía, Spain

DESIGNER: Unknown
OWNER: Municipal Museum of Ronda
GARDEN STYLE: 14th-century Moorish
SIZE: 0.1 acre (0.04 ha)
CLIMATE: Mediterranean
LOCATION: Ronda, Andalucía

The original courtyard patio of this former Moorish palace has triple arcades on three sides. The brick arches have marble capitals and ornamental molding, and the paving of terracotta squares has little blue tile inserts, while palms and potted plants enhance the scene. Passing beneath the columns and through a Moorish filigree door, visitors enter the jewel of a garden. A hexagonal raised pool in terracotta and blue tiles contains a pedestal and bowl with a gently bubbling trickle of water. Beyond is a small rectangular pool. A series of water jets on each side add movement and flashing light as they eject and splash. The water then continues into a lotuslike dish and narrow brook that enters a circular pool. The planting is a perfect balance, with a cedar tree overhanging the garden, and other shrubs arching up to create a light, semitransparent foil, like beaded curtains. The cyperus (papyrus) arch out over the water jets, backed by tiny, red-flowering plants.

The white walls are hung with pots of scarlet pelargoniums, and two narrow brooks lead you to a rectangular pool with cyperus in the center, ending in a round stone bowl set at the end. Both sides of the path are edged with dark clipped myrtle and box, and within them cerise bougainvillea, lemon trees, scarlet bottle brushes, and myrtles with their peeling bark give color and contrast. At the end there is a superb view over the countryside to the fields, woodlands, and mountains. It really is quite spectacular. RChe

Jardines de las Reales Alcázares

Andalucía, Spain

DESIGNERS: Pedro I, Carlos V
OWNER: Seville City Council
GARDEN STYLE: Various: Moorish, renaissance, landscape
SIZE: 40 acres (16.2 ha)
CLIMATE: Mediterranean
LOCATION: Seville, Andalucía

Construction of the Royal Fortress began in the tenth century, and successive rulers and monarchs added to it over the centuries, but little now remains of the original, save for a dividing wall between the orchards and domestic gardens. Palm trees, bitter oranges, *Magnolia grandiflora*, peaches, almonds, and roses, as well as scented *Pittosporum tobira*, are the key components in this "paradise" garden in the midst of one of Spain's busiest and most crowded cities.

Pedro I was the first of the Christian kings involved in the construction of the gardens. His workers provided many Islamic, or *mudéjar*, elements such as water, fountains, tiles, and enclosures. (*Mudéjar* comes from the Arabic, meaning "allowed to remain," which refers to the elements of Moorish style practiced by Moorish craftsmen who stayed in Spain after the Christian reconquest.)

Paths lead from the palace to several patios and courtyards. Enclosed patios near the palace are filled with the scent of orange blossom and jasmine. There are also eighteen garden areas to explore; the farther from the palace, the more expansive and relaxed they appear. The farthest away from the palace is the English Garden, laid out like a landscape park. Best of all are the places to sit and enjoy the shade, especially the poolside seats in the Poet's Garden. BS

RIGHT Las Reales Alcázares, built by Moors who ruled Seville, and later by *mudéjar* craftsmen for the Christian King Pedro I.

Palacio de los Marqueses de Viana

Andalucía, Spain

DESIGNER: Unknown
OWNER: Caja Provincial de Ahorros de Córdoba
GARDEN STYLE: 14th-century formal
SIZE: 1.6 acres (0.65 ha)
CLIMATE: Mediterranean
LOCATION: Córdoba, Andalucía

Set around a rather formal and austere palace, dating from the fourteenth century, is a collection of twelve patios/courtyards and an enclosed garden. Each patio is well marked and has its own character, informed by the planting and architecture. Climbers such as plumbago and bougainvillea clothe the walls, while clipped box hedging adds formality.

The first patio, the Reception Patio, is framed by a covered, arcaded walkway of pillars and arches, hung with dainty fairy roses and bougainvillea. It has a floor of delicately colored pebble mosaic tiles. At the center is a towering palm tree, circled by a incongruously low box hedge. The orange-flowered Cape lily, *Clivia miniata*, is grown in ancient terracotta pots. Next is the Archive Patio, so called because of its proximity to the Palace's archive library, which overlooks the courtyard. With a tiled fountain at its center, the patio is renowned for its 100-year old tangerine trees (*Citrus deliciosa*). The fifth patio, The Gardeners' Courtyard, is a long, narrow area that takes its name from the nearby gardeners' shed where all the tools are kept. One of the walls is smothered with Cape leadwort (*Plumbago capensis*). The final patio, the Courtyard of the Cats, has walls almost completely covered by foliage and flowers in wall-mounted pots.

At the heart of the outdoor areas is the Palace Garden, a large rectangle divided into numerous smaller, formal areas. Roses, oleander, citrus, and lilies scent the air, and in the center is an ancient holm oak (*Quercus ilex*) that is even taller than the native palms.

In 1980, the Palacio de los Marqueses de Viana became the property of the provincial bank, which opened the patios and garden to the public. Depending on the timing of your visit, some patios will be in deep, cool shade and others in bright, near blinding sunlight. The water in the pools and fountains calms the heat, while seasonal herbs and flowering plants add to the remarkable beauty. BS

Parque de María Luisa

Andalucía, Spain

DESIGNERS: Various
OWNER: Seville City Council
GARDEN STYLE: 20th-century art deco, mock Moorish
SIZE: 93 acres (37.6 ha)
CLIMATE: Mediterranean
LOCATION: Seville, Andalucía

Once part of the San Telmo Palace grounds, the María Luisa Park was given to the people of Seville in 1893 by María Luisa, the Duchess of Montpensier. It was laid out as a park and intended as the site for the ill-fated Latin-American Exposition of 1914 that eventually took place in 1929. The French landscape architect Jean-Claude Nicolas Forestier was responsible for much of the park's design before 1929.

Many of the pavilions and sites for the Expo are still in use, and one in particular, the Plaza de España, is a major attraction. It has a semicircular canal between the large plaza and the brick pavilion behind it. All around the walls of the pavilion are tiled benches and murals, each representing individual Spanish provinces, where Spaniards love to pose for photographs. There are numerous buildings and at least twenty *glorietas* (distinct, enclosed arbors) named in honor of sculptors, poets, writers, and artists. Each *glorieta* has statuary, benches, and mature plantings of trees and shrubs.

Throughout the María Luisa Park there are many long shady avenues of plane trees, and huge specimens of *Magnolia grandiflora*. Water features are abundant with a well-landscaped lake at the center of the park, complete with a domed, island gazebo. BS

> "…there are many long shady avenues of plane trees…"

Topkapi Sarayi

Istanbul, Turkey

DESIGNER: Unknown
OWNER: The Turkish State
GARDEN STYLE: 15th-century imperial courtyard
SIZE: 150 acres (60.7 ha)
CLIMATE: Mediterranean
LOCATION: Istanbul

Ottoman Sultan Mehmed II built the remarkable Topkapi Palace in 1459. He made full and clever use of the location, and one of the site's best features is its Byzantine olive grove, located on the Seraglio hill overlooking the Sea of Marmara, with spectacular views toward the Bosphorus.

According to surviving records, original designs for the gardens appear to have drawn more on the style of Persian paradise gardens than on the Greek-Roman courtyard gardens of Constantinople. The remains of the olive groves were kept as woodland, and the garden pavilions, with flowers and water throughout, were also retained. Now the largest of four interlinked courtyards spans the entire Seraglio Point. The Gate of Felicity leads from the second to the third courtyard, situated right at the heart of the palace, and the final courtyard, which was the sultan's private garden with pavilions, features some terraces and a variety of lush plantings.

The Ottomans loved to enjoy views over their luxuriant gardens, and the inner courtyards have ornate cloisters, decorative Byzantine fountains, and geometrically designed flower and vegetable beds. Pools provide coolness, and areas of lawn are punctuated by elegant, mature cypresses and plane trees that cast welcome, dappled shade.

The architecture of the palace is attractive, with many panels decorated in a floral style. But while time may have taken its toll, the gardens' formality has mellowed and they appear to have adapted well to a new life without the presence of royalty. NS

Casa do Campo

Braga, Portugal

DESIGNER: Unknown
OWNER: Maria Armanda Meireles
GARDEN STYLE: 18th-century formal Portuguese
SIZE: 2 acres (0.8 ha)
CLIMATE: Mediterranean
LOCATION: Celorico de Basto, Braga

This mansion dates from at least the eighteenth century. The estate is unusual in that the rectangular gardens are at an oblique angle to the mansion, and also higher, so that the view, in places, is actually over the mansion to the hills beyond.

Grand, ornamented gateways open on to the triangular courtyard, from where a flight of steps leads up to the garden. Erigeron daisies grow between the joints in the stones of the retaining walls, and raised pedestals with pots of colorful plants sit on top of the wall. In places, plants cascade down the wall, and these clever touches balance the pair of 30-foot-high (9 m) trimmed cylinders of camellia that are directly inside the wrought-iron garden gate. Topiary is a monumental feature, and the camellias have been confirmed as the oldest in Europe. Despite their age and trimming, they still produce some flowers.

The center of the garden has a circular pool with a simple fountain, enclosed by walls of camellia topped by rounded finials. Four arches in this green wall connect cross paths, and four more arches act as windows to the surrounding flower beds with cerise- and white-flowering Japanese azaleas and *Camellia reticulata* with its huge, wavy petals.

Along the main vista are two "houses" of clipped camellias, giving shade in summer and wind protection in winter. There are other examples of camellia topiary with spherical, acorn, and pyramid shapes, with stepped sides. In a far corner of the garden there is another camellia house with stone benches providing views of the hills beyond RChe

Casa de Mateus

Vila Real, Portugal

DESIGNER: Nicolau Nasoni
OWNER: Casa de Mateus Foundation
GARDEN STYLE: 18th-century romantic, baroque
SIZE: Unknown
CLIMATE: Mediterranean
LOCATION: Vila Real, Vila Real

The first glimpse of the elaborately ornamented baroque facade of Casa de Mateus—which is thought to be the work of the eighteenth-century Italian architect Nicolau Nasoni—prepares the visitor to appreciate the striking effects found in the gardens beyond. These include reflecting pools, tunnels of cypress, and terrace upon terrace of elaborate and intricate parterres as the gardens descend a low hillside from the front of the buildings.

The first of the parterres, which is situated on the same level as the buildings, has double box hedges, with the inner hedges sitting lower than the outer.

Each path or bed edge is marked by box that has been clipped into decorative balls. An avenue of camellias lines the path at the back of the first parterre.

To reach the lower level of the gardens, the route descends through a massive clipped tunnel of cypress, resembling a child's world of gnarled, bare limbs. From outside, the closely clipped tunnel is like a magical monster gliding across the site, and to trim this massive shape, the gardeners have to use a specially constructed, semicircular ladder.

The last parterre of box, which is just a few inches high, is set on a base of light beige gravel. On one side there is a stone *chafariz*, or wall fountain, flanked by two upright, columnar cypresses. This parterre is separated from the others by a highly sculpted, decorative wall of cypress, clipped into a scroll of rounded, sinuous shapes. The land then falls away from the parterre terrace to a streamside walk, giving open views to the vineyards in the valley. BS

Quinta da Aveleda

Porto, Portugal

DESIGNER: Unknown
OWNER: Paolo Amorim
GARDEN STYLE: 16th- to 19th-century rustic and woodland
SIZE: 20 acres (8.1 ha)
CLIMATE: Mediterranean
LOCATION: Penafiel, Porto

The chapel at Quinta da Aveleda was built in 1671, and there has always been a building here since that time. After going through the main gate, ancient cork oak trees (*Quercus suber*) become evident, growing close to a small, nineteenth-century house with a pillared porch. The surrounding woodland is bright with azaleas, rhododendrons, and camellias in spring, and hydrangeas and Japanese maples in summer and fall, with ground cover including vinca and symphytum. To the left stands an unusual stone tower, which is an ornamental goat house, with a spiraling wooden ramp leading to several floors.

The range of trees in the garden was greatly expanded in the late 1800s and now includes cryptomera, liriodendron, taxodium, sequoia, and aesculus, with flowering cherries and pines. Within the woodland is a small lake dotted with islands. Look out for one with a fifteenth-century, richly carved window, which was once part of Prince Henry the Navigator's mansion. The surrounding highlights include more Japanese maples, white arum lilies, and white azaleas. Farther on, providing spatial contrast, is a large, rectangular lawn, the broad steps to the sides leading up to a granite font dedicated to the patron saint of Oporto.

The *quinta* (villa) was developed over many years and blends into the background, thanks to the walls that are covered with climbing roses, clematis, and wisteria. Nearby is the Goose House, a thatched building with a thatched lady on top, in the middle of a landscaped pool in which white geese swim. RChe

Parque de Serralves

Porto, Portugal

DESIGNER: Jacques Gréber
OWNER: The Portuguese State
GARDEN STYLE: 20th-century modernist formal
SIZE: 44.5 acres (18.1 ha)
CLIMATE: Mediterranean
LOCATION: Porto

Surrounding the clean, modern lines of the 1930s, pink-colored facade of Casa de Serralves is a formal parkland with a number of distinct areas that flow naturally from one to the other. The modern house dominates the upper area of the park, with a central axis that moves straight out from the building through a series of different levels featuring sweeping lawns, fountains, and a long, straight water channel.

At the end of this formal garden, a stairway leads down to the small Romantic Lake, which interrupts the central axis before proceeding down to the fields, pastures, and greenhouses. Situated at the far end of the park are some former stables. Back up toward the house, and bearing north, lie the park's fruit orchards and the relatively new gardens of the Museum of Contemporary Art.

The stylish garden was the work of the French architect Jacques Gréber, the main designer of the Paris Exhibition of 1937. The look of the garden is as clear-cut and sharply architectural as the house, and although they are not exactly of the same school, they manage to blend together very well. Close to the building are formal areas with good examples of topiary in box, teucrium, and euonymus.

Long avenues of horse chestnut and *Liquidambar styraciflua*, the latter blazing in fall with its burnished leaves, accentuate the open aspect of the central garden. Other features include a formal rose garden, said to be the largest in Portugal, a sundial garden, and the well-established wisteria pergola, which is truly a breathtaking spectacle. BS

Quinta do Alão

Porto, Portugal

DESIGNERS: Nicolau Nasoni and others

OWNER: Francisco Jacome de Vasconcelos

GARDEN STYLE: 17th-century baroque

SIZE: 2 acres (0.8 ha)

CLIMATE: Mediterranean

LOCATION: Oporto, Porto

This *quinta* (villa) dates back to the fifteenth century; it was once a monastery and, in the seventeenth century, was owned by a relative of King João IV. The entrance drive provides the unbeatable sight of a mass of *Wisteria floribunda*, its long racemes swaying in the slightest breeze. The walls on each side are planted with pink roses and hydrangeas, so that there is color continuing into summer and fall. Once through the gates at the far end, you will see that one wall of the *quinta* is completely covered in superb roses in shades of pink and creamy yellow. In the courtyard, there are orange trees that have been planted alongside camellias and tree ferns.

The main garden, which is situated to one side of the *quinta*, is reached by a path, over which a stone pergola supports a ceiling of pink roses and mauve wisteria; its pillars are covered with evergreen climbers, such as variegated ivies and Japanese honeysuckle. The first of the three gradually ascending, shallow terraces that make up the main garden has an octagonal raised pool with goldfish and a low fountain jet. The broad rectangular areas to each side have weeping willows, red rhododendrons, and azaleas in soft orange and apricot. The central terrace is a parterre of diamonds and circles, and all the beds have box edging with little domed finials, and golden ligustrum and a red Japanese maple as centerpieces, surrounded by anemones, red and yellow tulips, and ranunculus in red, orange, yellow, and white. It looks like a Persian garden.

Dominating the upper terrace of the garden are huge rhododendrons, magnolias, evergreen oaks, and yews. The camellias here are some of the earliest to have been planted in Europe. All these create shade, in contrast to the sunny parterre below. The focal point is a diagonal pool with a boy on a dolphin. Behind this, against a high wall, is a baroque fountain with trimmed ivy accentuating its shape. RChe

Jardim Botânico de Coimbra

Coimbra, Portugal

DESIGNER: William Elsden
OWNER: University of Coimbra
GARDEN STYLE: 18th-century botanical
SIZE: 32 acres (13 ha)
CLIMATE: Mediterranean
LOCATION: Coimbra, Coimbra

Coimbra's botanical garden was originally on a steep slope, but its architect, William Elsden, leveled and terraced it. Because of the high value placed on the plant collection, the entire site was walled and accessed through three large, ornamental iron gates. The garden was created during the eighteenth century as part of the Marquis of Pombal's reforms of Coimbra University. William Elsden was commissioned to design the garden; work began in 1772 and, by 1774, the garden was established. The garden now has several levels, the uppermost consisting of taxonomic beds for botanical study.

You can walk around three sides of the garden on a wide, balustraded upper terrace, with seats set in the wall. Several double stairways descend into the main, rectangular central area with its many small, circular, assymetrical beds, all edged with 20-inch-high (50 cm) box hedges. Topiarized, geometric shapes, with domes and pyramids, are set into the hedging and mark the start of the paths, or the points where paths meet. The lower terrace features a circular pool, fountain, fish, and water lilies.

The best way to gain an overall impression of the garden is to walk along the three sides of the upper terrace, in the shade of the avenues of limes (*Tilia* x *europaea*). There is also a collection of eucalyptus, a large Moreton Bay fig (*Ficus macrophylla*), and many plants from California, South Africa, and South America. The breadth of the collection is the result of the exchange of plants and seed by the garden's nineteenth-century director, Henriques Julio, with Baron Ferdinand von Mueller of Australia's Melbourne Royal Botanic Gardens (see page 894). BS

> "...the collection is the result of the exchange of plants..."

Parco dos Duques de Buçaco

Coimbra, Portugal

DESIGNERS: Benedictine and Carmelite monks
OWNER: The Portuguese State
GARDEN STYLE: 17th-century forest estate
SIZE: 259 acres (105 ha)
CLIMATE: Mediterranean
LOCATION: Buçaco, Coimbra

The Parco dos Duques de Buçaco, or Buçaco Forest, offers the visitor an undulating, ancient landscape. The original oak and pine forest was the site of a Benedictine hermitage in the sixth century, but over the centuries, the monks and government foresters have planted over 400 varieties of Portuguese trees, shrubs, and flowers. Some 300 species from Mexico, Chile, Japan, and elsewhere have also been planted here, brought back to Portugal by a succession of explorers and plant hunters.

The present landscape and plantings date from the middle of the seventeenth century, when Discalced Carmelites built their monastery and the stone walls that surround the forest. Their love of nature resulted in a papal bill threatening anyone who damaged a tree with excommunication, thus ensuring the forest's continued survival. Women were also on the banned list, and were threatened with excommunication if they entered the forest.

The blend of imported, exotic trees, such as ginkgo, cedar, araucaria, palms, sequoias, the Buçaco cedar (*Cupressus lusitanicus*), and Japanese camphor trees (*Cinnamomum camphora*), combines with native trees, all towering above the understory planting of tree ferns, hydrangeas, clivias, camellias, rhododendrons, and lilies, to name but a few.

There are many viewpoints, or *miradoires*, monuments, and hermitages to discover on a walk through the forest. The several routes that you can take are of varying lengths and duration, but make sure that you don't miss the valley of the tree ferns (Vale dos Fetos) and the lake (Lago do Vale dos Fetos). The Cold Fountain (Fonte Fria) is also a marvelous sight, with water flowing down 144 steps to a pool. The most dramatic building in the forest is the Palace Hotel. Once a hunting lodge, it was built between 1888 and 1908 near the site of the seventeenth-century Carmelite monastery. BS

Estufa Fria

Lisboa, Portugal

DESIGNER: Raul Carapinha
OWNER: City of Lisbon
GARDEN STYLE: 20th-century covered, naturalistic
SIZE: 3 acres (1.2 ha)
CLIMATE: Mediterranean
LOCATION: Lisbon, Lisboa

In 1906 a competition was held for the landscape design of an old quarry that was part of Parque Eduardo VII. It was won by the architect Raul Carapinha. The result featured a vast wooden lath roof to the quarry, which creates shade in summer and reduces the wind-chill factor in winter, thereby allowing subtropical plants to survive. Opened in 1930, it is the largest structure of its kind in the world and covers 3 acres (1 ha). In 1975 a heated greenhouse, the Estufa Quente, was added to the park.

Broad paths are overhung with foliage; the lath roof is hardly noticeable, and the slim green supports are completely unobtrusive. Inside the heated area, you will find several kinds of banana, cacti and succulents, towering cereus and euphorbia, as well as star-shaped agaves, furcraeas, and aloes. Paths zigzag up the terraces of natural rock, past hippeastrums in crimson, pink, and white, yellow solandras with their balloonlike buds, and crimson-flowering brachychitons. The view from the top shows clearly what a key role foliage, particularly that of the pineapples and crotons, plays in the design.

A tunnel leads to the upper part of the unheated section, with its fantastic aerial view, looking down on what looks like tropical rainforest. There are the huge leaves of monsteras, philodendrons, and tetrapanax, and many elegant tree ferns, tropical figs, and palms. The shrubs include gardenias, azaleas, and tropical hibiscus in white, pink, scarlet, and yellow, and there are many kinds of climber. As covered gardening goes, it doesn't get much better than this. RChe

Quinta da Capela

Lisboa, Portugal

DESIGNER: Unknown

OWNERS: Arturo de Pereira, Marc Zurcher

GARDEN STYLE: 18th-century formal, rural

SIZE: 3 acres (1.2 ha)

CLIMATE: Mediterranean

LOCATION: Sintra, Lisboa

The Duke of Cadaval's palace at Sintra was destroyed by the great Lisbon earthquake of 1755, then rebuilt in 1773. Today only a supporting wall of the old palace survives, together with the sixteenth-century chapel of Nossa Senhora da Piedade, with its domed ceiling and beautiful tiles depicting the life of Christ.

A simple drive ends near the *quinta* (villa), with lawns leading up to the single-story building. Clipped hedges line the paths that divide the lawns and lead to various focal points. One path leads to a Canary Island palm (*Phoenix canariensis*) and a freestanding bush of wisteria, and on to a large, raised, rectangular water tank. Its walls are partly clothed with ivy, and are topped with posts and chains. Steps lead up one side to a broad, straight walk well furnished by trees, giant white strelitzias, white daturas, white Canary Island marguerites, and carpets of soft, yellow-flowering carpobrotus.

Retracing the walk, you will find a small water tank fed by water gushing from the tall boundary wall, a charming small chapel, and steps leading up to a paved balcony, edged with stone benches. Back on the lawns, a path runs parallel to the tall boundary wall clad with roses, and farther on the arched openings give views out across a citrus grove and the woods to the distant sea. RChe

> "...views out across a citrus grove and the woods to the distant sea"

Palácio dos Marqueses de Fronteira

Lisboa, Portugal

DESIGNER: Marquis of Fronteira
OWNER: Fernando Mascarenhas
GARDEN STYLE: 17th-century formal parterre
SIZE: Parterre garden 0.9 acre (0.3 ha)
CLIMATE: Mediterranean
LOCATION: Benfica, Lisboa

Established in the late seventeenth century, the formal gardens at the Fronteira Palace contain all the characteristics of Portuguese garden architecture.

Visitors to Fronteira should have a look at both the house and the garden. Start with the house, which has breathtaking décor, as well as glimpses of the bold foliage, tiles, and flowers found in the garden. Once outdoors, walk along the Chapel Promenade, with its statuary, arches, niches, and tiled panels, and which leads, unsurprisingly, to a chapel. The walk also overlooks the Jardim de Venus, where mature trees, camellias, and ferns luxuriate, and a bunya-bunya pine (*Araucaria bidwilli*) creates an impressive outline as it towers high above the garden.

The major attraction of Fronteira, though, is the Jardim Grande, a large geometric parterre of squares, diamonds, stars, and wedges. The parterre covers an area of 1 acre (0.3 ha) and has, at its back, a large water tank with a viewing gallery, the Galeria dos Reis. Just as when the garden was first laid out, the sumptuous tilework, the elegant architecture of the Galeria and tank (complete with grottoes and balustrading), and the immaculately kept, box-edged parterres make an unforgettable impact. BS

> "The major attraction…is the Jardim Grande, a large geometric parterre…"

Jardim do Palácio Nacional de Queluz

Lisboa, Portugal

DESIGNER: Jean-Baptiste Robillon
OWNER: The Portuguese State
GARDEN STYLE: 18th-century French baroque
SIZE: 6 acres (2.5 ha)
CLIMATE: Mediterranean
LOCATION: Lisbon, Lisboa

This palace was a favorite residence of the Portuguese royal family, and the gardens as seen today were created in 1757 by the French designer Jean-Baptiste Robillon. They owe much of their inspiration to Versailles (see page 570), but this garden is as homely as the *petit parc* at Versailles is grandiose.

Like Versailles, the garden is made up of a number of different areas. In front of the palace is the Pensile, or Hanging, Garden. With its topiary and intricately patterned twin parterres picked out by low-cut hedges and filled with bedding plants, it is a well-proportioned, highly appropriate setting

for the house. The parterre is complemented by the formal pools with their dynamic fountains (the Fonte de Neptuno is attributed to Gian Bernini), numerous statues (marble ones from Italy, those of lead from England), and the blue and white ceramic urns.

Adjacent to the Pensile Garden is the Malta Garden containing ornately clipped topiary. Originally a formal pool, it dates from 1758 and is slightly sunken. From the elegantly curved and balustraded Lion Staircase, it is a short walk to the garden's most delightful and uniquely Portuguese feature. Built in 1775, the Tiled Canal, with its accompanying bridges, was both an ornamental feature and entertainment. When empty (as it is permanently today), the 55,000 glazed tiles were a beautiful sight, but when the sluices were shut and water from the River Jamor filled the canal, boats would bob about on the water's surface, accompanied by musicians playing in the Lake House, a feature that, sadly, has been lost. TM

Quinta da Regaleira

Lisboa, Portugal

DESIGNER: Luigi Manini
OWNER: Sintra Town Council
GARDEN STYLE: 19th-century manueline Gothic
SIZE: 11 acres (4.5 ha)
CLIMATE: Mediterranean
LOCATION: Sintra, Lisboa

This is a mystical and spiritual place with an old pilgrims' path passing through the forest. In 1715 it was known as Quinta da Torre because of a tower on the site. In 1840 Lady Monteiro da Almeida bought the site and built a fine house, workshops, and a battlemented greenhouse, but in 1893 it was sold to António Augusto Carvalho Monteiro, a Brazilian doctor. He engaged the Italian designer Luigi Manini, who had worked at La Scala in Milan.

A path leads from the gate to a broad, sunny walk called the Threshold of the Gods. It has a line of statues, including Hermes, Ceres, and Mercury, linked by a short box hedge with views back to the *quinta* (villa). Passing a pair of recumbent lions and a small Gothic building with urns and finials, the visitor is led to the Lake of Swans surrounded by tufa cliffs and caves, with a bridge across the trees and ivy draping down. On a terrace above is a curved stone bench, with a thronelike seat and great stone urns decorated with the heads of goats and satyrs. Farther on is the Cascade Lake, a dark pool with sedges and ferns growing from the rocky cliffs. Even higher, there is an outcrop of huge rocks, one of which is imperceptibly hinged and is the entrance point to the Initiation Well. This is followed by the Spiraling Gallery, at the bottom of which is a Knights Templar cross with an eight-pointed star of inlaid marble. The exit is via a dark, twisting stone tunnel that opens to the Guardians' Entrance with two fierce dragons. Other features include the Imperfect Well, Terrace of the Celestial Worlds, and Grotto of Leda. RChe

Quinta de Monserrate

Lisboa, Portugal

DESIGNERS: William Beckford, James Burt, Sir Francis Cook
OWNER: Associação Amigos de Monserrate
GARDEN STYLE: 18th- and 19th-century English romantic
SIZE: 124 acres (50.2 ha)
CLIMATE: Mediterranean
LOCATION: Sintra, Lisboa

Rising majestically from the plain, Sintra enjoys the additional humidity offered by frequent cloud cover and high rainfall. At its Catholic core lies a ruined chapel dedicated to Our Lady of Monserrate, near Barcelona, which gives the park its name.

William Beckford, "England's wealthiest son," rented the park from a British merchant, Gerard de Visme. De Visme built the neo-Gothic palace you see today, framed by an ornate Indian arch and approached along the Perfumed Path. Beckford made the park sublimely picturesque, adding the magnificent falls. Picturesque and ruinous by 1856, Sir Francis Cook bought the park, created the horseshoe pool, or Hippocrene, that represents the myth of Pegasus, and employed landscape architect James Burt. Like his contemporary at Biddulph Grange in Staffordshire, England (see page 254), he created a plantsman's world tour, with Australasian trees, conifers, palms, and camellias. The Fern Valley below Beckford's Falls is massed with mature tree ferns, opening out to views across the tree canopy and the valleys. Monserrate was the first garden in Portugal to boast a lawn and it remains one of the best, here sweeping down the slopes from the palace.

An excellent team of gardeners and the Friends of Monserrate, with local government support, are breathing life back into this sleeping beauty. Monserrate and the two palaces in Sintra make it well worth the easy train ride from Lisbon. CH

Quinta de São Thiago

Lisboa, Portugal

DESIGNER: Unknown
OWNERS: Nicholas Braddell, Maria Teresa Braddell
GARDEN STYLE: Partly 16th-century formal
SIZE: 2 acres (0.8 ha)
CLIMATE: Mediterranean
LOCATION: Sintra, Lisboa

This *quinta* (villa), once a sixteenth-century monks' house, is hidden down a very long, narrow lane that passes through woodlands. Once inside the black studded door in the boundary wall, softened by the curtains of pink passion flowers trailing from above, you are in a courtyard with a raised water tank backed by an ornate wall. The surrounding path has steps leading down to a border planted with strelitzias.

The top of the steps provides views to the ancient *Magnolia grandiflora*, palm, and cycad that create a pleasant frame to the *quinta* and the tall Norfolk Island pine (*Araucaria heterophylla*) behind. The next stop is the tiled, roofed, pillared balcony with honeysuckle and wisteria, followed by the palms, tropical foliage plants, and scarlet anthuriums and bromeliads outside the garden door. Steps and paths then lead down, via a pergola, to the tennis courts and productive garden. Look out for the 8-foot-high (2 m) *Polygala* x *dalmaisiana* that never seems to be without its pealike flowers, and the pink tree fuchsia and red oleander. Steps lead down to a dry bank with succulents, opuntias, agaves, and scarlet aloes. Finally the path leads to lawns with beds of hybrid tea and China roses, and clumps of strelitzias flank the sides of steps down to a rectangular swimming pool.

Visitors are sometimes allowed into the fascinating *quinta* where there is a charming old chapel, and views from the upper balconies to the garden, the woods, and the sea beyond. RChe

Palácio dos Marqueses de Pombal

Lisboa, Portugal

DESIGNER: Carlos Mardel
OWNER: National Institute of Administration
GARDEN STYLE: 18th-century formal parkland
SIZE: Approximately 2 acres (0.8 ha)
CLIMATE: Mediterranean
LOCATION: Oeiras, Lisboa

During the eighteenth century, it was quite common that spaces for both leisure and agriculture would be incorporated into the design of an estate. To this end, the Marquis of Pombal incorporated recreation spaces, gardens, and small holdings for tenant farmers into the design of his palace and garden.

During their eighteenth-century peak, the palace and these luxurious gardens were often used as a backdrop for cultural events such as theater, ballet, and music recitals. The palace, which was also built during the eighteenth century, dominated the site and, today, is used as headquarters of the National Institute of Administration. The surrounding gardens, which are now open to the public on a regular basis, contain numerous pieces of important statuary, Portuguese garden tilework, fountains, and waterfalls. The most impressive tilework can be found on the tiled staircase and fountain leading from the upper to the lower terrace, which is dominated by two mighty specimens of *Araucaria bidwilli*.

Visitors ought to include in their tour around the garden the eighteenth-century grotto, complete with stairway and dripping water, known as the Cascade of the Poets. They should also have a look at the fish tanks, ornamental dairy, and dovecote in the larger parkland, and the many ornamental garden areas within the smooth expanse of lawns. BS

Quinta de Bacalhôa

Setúbal, Portugal

DESIGNER: Afonso de Albuquerque
OWNER: J.P. Vinhos
GARDEN STYLE: 16th-century Italian renaissance
SIZE: Approximately 2 acres (0.8 ha)
CLIMATE: Mediterranean
LOCATION: Azeitão, Setúbal

Quinta de Bacalhôa is a house with a historic past, moving in and out of royal and noble ownership, including Portugal's first Viceroy of the Indies, Afonso de Albuquerque, in 1528. It was De Albuquerque who was largely responsible for laying out the renaissance parts of the house and gardens.

When you enter through a wooden gate into the large courtyard, there is absolutely no hint of the drama and romance that are to come. The first major feature is the precisely clipped box parterre, with not a leaf or stem out of place, followed by a long, raised walkway drawing you onward, past the citrus trees in

a sunken orange grove, and tiled wall benches, to the reflecting pool or water tank. The latter is dominated on one side by an attractively roofed and arcaded pavilion, with interesting tilework, the imagery on one of the panels depicting the biblical story of Susanna and the Elders. From the parapets that surround the tank, there are commanding views over the whole estate, including the vineyard.

In the 1930s the property was bought by an American, Herbert Scoville, who developed the garden. He added flowering shrubs, roses, climbers, and bulbs to the overall design of the garden. BS

> "...a house with a historic past, moving in and out of royal and noble ownership..."

From the hushed, contemplative designs of Japanese and Chinese gardens to the lush, tropical designs of Indonesia, Asian garden styles have had a major impact on Western sensibilities. Yuan Ming Yuan, in Beijing, epitomizes the spare, stylized look in which plants are grown for their shapes rather than their flowers, while geometric, Islamic-inspired Mughal gardens are found across Afghanistan, Pakistan, and India.

ASIA

Jing Shan Gong Yuan

Beijing, China

DESIGNER: Unknown

OWNER: The Chinese State

GARDEN STYLE: 12th- to 20th-century classical imperial

SIZE: 56 acres (23 ha)

CLIMATE: Semiarid

LOCATION: Beijing

TRANSLATION: Mountain of Perspective Park

Jing Shan Park, also known as Feng Shui Park and Coal Hill Park, is the old imperial garden. It dates from the late twelfth century and is almost as old as the city of Beijing. The hill, the most dominant feature of the park, was made in 1420, when the emperor of the Ming dynasty heard that a hill positioned behind the Forbidden City would improve its feng shui. The soil was dug from just outside the Forbidden City, creating a moat as well as a hill to provide protection. The hill was called the Mountain of a Myriad Life, but the last Ming emperor, when he was only thirty-three, hanged himself on a tree here when rebellious peasant troops captured Beijing. The sovereign of the following Qing dynasty (1644–1912) inherited the hill and renamed it Jing Shan, the Mountain of Perspective.

Sitting behind the Forbidden City, the imperial garden is a prominent feature along the central axis of Beijing. It has a formal design that differs from that of naturalistic Chinese gardens. The flattened, triangular hill has five brows along the ridge. To enhance the sense of symmetry, five pavilions were constructed in the mid-eighteenth century, one on each brow, plus a central pavilion lining up with the Forbidden City. Behind the hill, the ancestral temple that had slightly deviated from the axis was rebuilt. The orderliness of this design is tempered by the different tree shapes, bizarre rocks, and zigzag paths to the hill, which add a beautiful sense of quiet relaxation. The view of the Forbidden City from the pavilion 160-feet (49 m) high on the hill is unmissable. LG.

> "...tree shapes, bizarre rocks, and zigzag paths...add a beautiful sense of quiet relaxation"

Beihai Gong Yuan

Beijing, China

DESIGNER: Unknown
OWNER: The Chinese State
GARDEN STYLE: 10th- to 20th-century classical imperial
SIZE: 168 acres (68 ha)
CLIMATE: Semiarid
LOCATION: Beijing
TRANSLATION: Beihai Park

Beihai Park is the former playground of the Chinese emperors and the largest park in the vicinity of the Forbidden City. The first building on site went up during the tenth century, when members of the Liao rulership built a temporary palace. Later the park was landscaped, lakes were created, and mounds were formed using the "spoil." Pavilions, temples, and halls were erected. The Bai Ta, or "White Pagoda", Tibetan-style Buddhist temple, which looks like a giant white onion, was built on one of the islands in 1651.

Daxitian, or "Large Western Heaven," is one of the park's many gardens. This miniature botanical garden contains some plants, such as love-apple (*Solanum aculeatissimum*) and 'Frosty Morn' variegated sedum (*S. alboroseum*), that are now rare even in China.

One garden that should not be missed is Jingxinzhai, otherwise known as the Studio of the Pure Heart. Originally built during the Ming dynasty, it was rebuilt by Emperor Qianlong as a studio or study for the princes. It has a series of rock outcrops covered in parthenocissus, and deep valleys traversed by a maze of narrow paths and covered walkways. The planting is low key, but includes some interesting peach and crab apple trees. The main path winds through deep ravines to cross a central pond by means of a long, very ornate, white marble bridge.

Beihai Park is now open to everyone in Beijing. You can stroll, eat, drink beer, or hire a dragon-shaped boat on one of the lakes that cover more than half the park. SY

Bi Shu Shan Zhuang

Beijing, China

DESIGNER: Unknown
OWNER: The Chinese State
GARDEN STYLE: 18th-century classical imperial
SIZE: 1,360 acres (550 ha)
CLIMATE: Semiarid
LOCATION: Chengde
TRANSLATION: Mountain Resort for Avoiding the Heat

Northeast of Beijing, a 16-mile-long (10 km) wall encloses Bi Shu Shan Zhuang, also known as the Imperial Summer Retreat. It was created by successive generations of Chinese emperor to provide a setting for diplomatic and recreational activities away from the oppressive heat of the Forbidden City.

The garden began development in 1703 under the Emperor Kangx and now fills an entire valley with landscape gardening on the grand scale. The site was probably selected for the interestingly shaped rock formations found in the surrounding hills, including the phallic Anvil Rock, which dominates the skyline. The main palace complexes were constructed in the eighteenth century and are adjacent to the lakes. These vast water features were constructed for boating, so that the emperor and his entourage, including musicians, could be transported in dragon- or phoenix-headed boats to view various temples, mountain pavilions, and lotus flowers in the shallows.

The estate underwent major development in the eighteenth-century reign of the Emperor Qianlong, an avid creator of gardens, who introduced Tibetan-style architectural features, including a representation of the Potala Palace in Lhasa. They were not only impressive garden buildings, but also strong statements of power, clearly indicating to visitors the range and influence of the Chinese empire.

Today there is still much to enjoy at the Imperial Summer Retreat—a microcosm of a past empire that was made a World Heritage Site in 1994. JR

Xie Qu Yuan

Beijing, China

DESIGNER: Unknown
OWNER: The Chinese State
GARDEN STYLE: 18th-century classical imperial
SIZE: 17.3 acres (7 ha)
CLIMATE: Semiarid
LOCATION: Beijing
TRANSLATION: Garden of Harmonious Pleasure

"A garden of gardens within a garden" is how the Garden of Harmonious Pleasure has been described. Located in the northeastern corner of the extensive Summer Palace, this garden is tiny, but not to be missed. When Emperor Qianlong visited the south of China in 1751, he was so impressed with the Ji Chang Garden at Wuxi that he built the Garden of Harmonious Pleasure, which became one of his favorite retreats during the hot Beijing summers.

The garden is composed of various pavilions, halls, and terraces. A 1-mile-long (2 km) walkway, painted with more than 1,400 landscape cameos, links this garden with the rest of the Summer Palace landscape garden. The main building, the Hall of Bestowing Favors, was used as a sitting area for the Dowager Empress Cixi. Another pavilion, close to the complex surrounding the central lotus pool, was used by Cixi for fishing. It is said that when Cixi went fishing, eunuchs would secretly dive into the water to hang fish on her fishing line to entertain her. The garden is a tranquil place; the main pool is packed with lotus and surrounded by willows. The small, water scenery garden echoes the tiny Yang Ren Feng Courtyard in the eastern part of the garden. Both act as foils to the grandeur of the larger garden, making them appear even more exquisite by comparison.

To understand why the garden is so aptly named, try to visit in the evening when it is illuminated. The reflections in the pool and the glow from the buildings are unforgettable. SY

Yi He Yuan

Beijing, China

DESIGNER: Unknown
OWNER: The Chinese State
GARDEN STYLE: 18th-century classical imperial
SIZE: 720 acres (290 ha)
CLIMATE: Semiarid
LOCATION: Beijing
TRANSLATION: Garden of the Preservation of Harmony

Garden design on the grand scale can be seen at Yi He Yuan, also known as the Garden of the Preservation of Harmony, or River Summer Palace, where the Dowager Empress Cixi (1835–1908) liked to stay from the flowering of the magnolias to the withering of the chrysanthemums to escape the hot summers of the Forbidden City.

Although there had been a temporary imperial residence here since 1153, the garden remained undeveloped prior to the reign of the eighteenth-century Emperor Qianlong. He had the lake enlarged in 1749, and the buildings developed both as residences and for holding court. The majority of the landscape is filled to the south with the waters of Kunming Hu, the Vast Bright Lake. To the north, Longevity Hill is covered with flowering trees, ornamental buildings, and smaller, more intimate gardens. The eastern shore is connected to the Island of the Dragon King by a magnificent bridge with seventeen arches. Along the northern shoreline is an intricately painted, covered walk, with each beam and lintel depicting a different scene from literature and legend. Another remarkable feature is a marble boat that appears solidly moored to the shoreline.

The garden was declared a public park in 1924. There are almond, cherry, and plum blossoms on the slopes of Longevity Hill in late winter; wisteria and peonies in the smaller, walled gardens in spring; exotic summer lotus flowers in the lake; and chrysanthemums in fall. JR

Yu Hua Yuan

Beijing, China

DESIGNER: Unknown
OWNER: The Chinese State
GARDEN STYLE: 15th-century classical imperial
SIZE: 2.5 acres (1 ha)
CLIMATE: Semiarid
LOCATION: Beijing
TRANSLATION: Imperial Palace Garden

Kept a secret for 500 years, this tiny garden, built for the sole use of the emperor and his harem, is now open to everyone. The garden was designed during the Ming period as part of the Imperial Palace complex. The pavilion buildings are stunning and are "designed to be in harmony with the universe." This garden was also where the emperor would worship on New Year's Day.

Behind the garden pavilions are a couple of pools, adjacent to a huge rock edifice crowned by the Pavilion of Imperial Prospect. Because this building is so high, it would have been the only place possible for the women of the imperial harem ever to gain a glimpse of the outside world. The garden was originally laid out in a symmetrical style with trees and plants arranged in rows. Amazingly the majority of the plants still present date back to the fifteenth century. There are many old, wizened trees of pine, juniper, and wisteria, as well as an interesting example of the twisted Chinese dragon claw date (*Ziziphus jujuba* 'Tortuosa'). The garden also has a wonderful collection of petrified rocks and wood that is intermingled artistically between the plants, forming "stage sets" that are framed by the windows of the pavilions.

The paths in the garden are some of the best you will see anywhere, containing central sections of pebble designs depicting various plants and animals, including lotus flowers and, of course, one of the Chinese symbols of good luck, the bat. SY

Yuan Ming Yuan

Beijing, China

DESIGNER: Unknown
OWNER: The Chinese State
GARDEN STYLE: 17th- and 18th-century classical imperial
SIZE: 870 acres (352 ha)
CLIMATE: Semiarid
LOCATION: Beijing
TRANSLATION: Gardens of Perfect Brightness

The eighteenth-century Emperor Qianlong (1711–99), whose name keeps appearing in the history of Chinese gardens, was one of the most influential emperors in China. He was the owner and generous patron of various gardens and palaces, including Yuan Ming Yuan, which is also known as the Old Summer Palace and the Garden of Gardens.

At the foot of the Western Mountains, 10 miles (16 km) northeast of the Forbidden City, Yuan Ming Yuan was once the most ostentatious garden in China. First built in the 1700s by the Emperor Yongzheng, it housed the imperial state administration. In 1735 Yongzheng's son, Qianlong, succeeded to the throne and tripled the site of Yuan Ming Yuan. Hundreds of temples were built and scenic features added. Little gardens were created that were modeled on the most famous scenes in the Jiangnan (the lower Yangtze River), a region that had the best gardens of the state. Yuan Ming Yuan kept its fame until 1860, when Anglo-French forces burned it as a punishment to its absent emperor.

Today the site is a wild, quiet place at the corner of a fast developing, intellectual district of Beijing. You can trace the surviving landforms of the hills and lakes, see a handful of added or restored pavilions, the remains of old stones, the wild shrubs and lawns, and what was the most stunning feature, the "Western" palace complex. Although by no means restored, the 17 acres (7 ha) of fragments are well worth visiting. LG

Ge Yuan

Jiangsu, China

DESIGNER: Attributed to Shi Tao
OWNER: The Chinese State
GARDEN STYLE: 18th- and 19th-century classical
SIZE: 5.7 acres (2.3 ha)
CLIMATE: Humid subtropical
LOCATION: Yangzhou, Jiangsu
TRANSLATION: Garden of Self

Ge Yuan's history is uncertain, but it is thought to have been the residence of a wealthy salt merchant. The garden's design has been attributed to the artist and calligrapher Shi Tao in the eighteenth century, though the garden was remodeled in the nineteenth century.

Ge Yuan uses garden rockwork in a highly distinctive way. Different types of rock distinguish various areas and characterize the four seasons. The beds adjacent to the moon gate entrance signify spring. They are planted with bamboos and feature vertical rocks that suggest bamboo shoots, thus playing with the visitor's imagination. Summer is celebrated by a cooling pool of water, surrounded by gray, water eroded limestone in fantastical shapes. A zigzag bridge leads the visitor through a cooling grotto up to a pavilion that surmounts the rockwork, where you can catch any summer breezes. A winding path leading up through a steep hill of yellow rocks evokes the fall, recalling the mountains toward the end of the year. On a smaller scale, white-capped rocks symbolize winter snow on the mountains, and a paved area with irregular white stone represents cracked ice on the surface of a lake. Being able to read the garden in this way certainly adds another dimension.

The reasoning behind the first part of the garden's name is that the leaves of the bamboo are said to resemble the three brushstrokes of the Chinese character ge, which means "self." JR

Canglangting

Jiangsu, China

DESIGNER: Unknown
OWNER: The Chinese State
GARDEN STYLE: 12th- and 19th-century scholar's garden
SIZE: 2.5 acres (1 ha)
CLIMATE: Humid subtropical
LOCATION: Suzhou, Jiangsu
TRANSLATION: Blue Wave Pavilion

Canglangting, or the Blue Wave Pavilion, also known as the Surging Wave Pavilion, is one of the oldest of Suzhou's wonderful collection of private or "scholar's" gardens. The garden's major development began in 1140 as a retirement project for a military official. Subsequent major renovations were carried out in 1874. Its name was inspired by a third-century BCE poem, in which an elderly fisherman suggests that if the blue waves were clean, he would wash his hat ribbons in them, and if the waters were muddy, he would wash his feet. The poem came to represent the need for Chinese officials to adapt to the changing circumstances of political life.

The garden uses one of Suzhou's canals as a boundary feature. It can be viewed from the wonderful Pavilion for Watching the Fish and an adjacent covered corridor. The focal point is a central mound, with arrangements of rocks, and plantings of bamboos and trees. This mountainous representation is a reminder of the natural landscape to which a scholar could retreat to live a hermit's life. The pavilion at the hill's summit has the typical, highly curved roof eaves of the region. White plastered walls with delicately pierced windows provide privacy as well as views to the water. The walls within the garden form a blank canvas against which to view the rockwork and planting.

Many fine rocks are enhanced by the addition of carved calligraphy. They add an additional sense of mystery to this gem of a scholar's retreat. JR

Huanxiu Shanzhuang

Jiangsu, China

DESIGNER: Ge Yuliang
OWNER: The Chinese State
GARDEN STYLE: 18th-century classical private garden
SIZE: 0.2 acre (0.08 ha)
CLIMATE: Humid subtropical
LOCATION: Suzhou, Jiangsu
TRANSLATION: Mountain Villa with Embracing Beauty

This tiny gem of a garden conveys the mountainous scenery of China and apparently was designed by Ge Yuliang, a famous eighteenth-century creator of garden "mountains." It was originally the garden of a private residence belonging to a high official during the reign of the eighteenth-century Emperor Qianlong. It underwent a number of changes in ownership and by 1949 was in a state of dilapidation. Fortunately the rockwork survived. It is considered to be among the finest rock and water garden constructions in Suzhou.

A 23-foot-high (7 m) hill constructed of rockwork and surrounded by an informal pool is the garden's major feature. The rockwork is crossed by a number of winding paths, giving views down into two ravines and the water below. There are also several stone caves, and a stone table and seats. A pretty zigzag bridge seems to float above the water, giving access to more paths through the garden. The quaintly named Asking for Spring Pavilion is situated on an island that can be reached via two low bridges over the water, and one of the garden entrances, set in a white plastered wall, offers a fine example of a vase-shaped doorway, immediately signifying that you have entered a peaceful place.

The planting includes deciduous and coniferous trees and shrubs, which are not planted so densely that they obscure the rockwork, which is the major feature of this amazing garden—a mountain range in a courtyard. JR

Ji Chang Yuan

Jiangsu, China

DESIGNERS: Qin Yao, Zhang Lian, Zhang Qin
OWNER: The Chinese State
GARDEN STYLE: 16th- and 17th-century classical
SIZE: 2.5 acres (1 ha)
CLIMATE: Humid subtropical
LOCATION: Wuxi, Jiangsu
TRANSLATION: Garden of Ecstasy

Ji Chang Yuan, or the Garden of Ecstasy, was originally built by the Qin family on a small piece of flat land in east China. In 1591 Qin Yao was dismissed from his work at court and returned to his home town to channel all his energy into creating a garden, constructing some twenty garden scenes here.

Of developments made by subsequent owners, the creation of a series of hills in the seventeenth century by the artificial mountain designer Zhang Lian and his nephew, Zhang Qin, stands out. They piled up a range of small hills with stone and earth, and added a winding stream. The trees planted on the hills eventually grew very tall and injected a sense of age, and, as hoped, it became difficult to distinguish between the artificial and natural hills.

The best gardens are at Jia Shu Tang, the Hall of Beautiful Trees, and the teahouse, where you can see a rockery bank, an elegant pavilion, and leaning trees framing the view to the distant mountain Xi Shan, topped by a pagoda. All these features, in various layers, are united and reflected by a gourd-shaped lake in the center of the garden.

Ji Chang Yuan has good views of the surrounding landscape, which adds to the garden's effect and helps make it one of the leading gardens in southeast China. The eighteenth-century Emperor Qianlong made seven visits and had an imperial interpretation of Ji Chang Yuan, called Xie Qu Yuan, or the Garden of Harmonious Pleasure, made at his Summer Palace in Beijing. LG

Huqiu Shan

Jiangsu, China

DESIGNER: Unknown
OWNER: The Chinese State
GARDEN STYLE: 19th-century classical private garden
SIZE: 3 acres (1.2 ha)
CLIMATE: Humid subtropical
LOCATION: Suzhou, Jiangsu
TRANSLATION: Tiger Hill

The famous Chinese poet Su Shi said, "It is a lifelong pity if, having visited Suzhou, you did not visit Tiger Hill." He Lu, founder of Suzhou and King of Wu, fell in battle in 496 BCE and is said to have been buried in the hill by his son, Fu Chai, along with 3,000 swords from the vast collection his father had built up. It is said that three days after the burial, a white tiger was seen crouching on He Lu's tomb, and ever since, the garden has been known as Tiger Hill. It is also known as Surging Sea Hill.

The landscaped area around the hill, like many Chinese sites, contains various garden areas, most of which are associated with different buildings. The whole area is dominated by the hill, which is more than 112 feet (34 m) above sea level. The hill is topped by a 154-foot-high (47 m) pagoda that is a major feature in itself. Its foundations have sunk, causing the pagoda to tilt slightly. On the lower slopes of the hill, not far from the entrance, is the recently restored Yongcui Shanzhuang, known as the Verdant Mountain Villa. It was designed to give the most natural and pleasing vistas of the area to the viewer. The garden, which was built in 1884, also contains a huge area of rock and a pool with lotus flowers.

At the Wan Jing Villa, you will find some of the finest and best-kept examples of *peng jing*, the Chinese art of dwarfing single trees and incorporating them into miniature landscapes. There are thousands of specimens on view. These miniature replicas of full-sized gardens are quite amazing and demonstrate this ancient Chinese art at its best. SY

> "...some of the finest...examples of *peng jing*, the Chinese art of dwarfing single trees..."

Liu Yuan

Jiangsu, China

DESIGNERS: Xu Taishi, Liu Rongfeng, Sheng Xuren
OWNER: The Chinese State
GARDEN STYLE: 16th-, 18th- and 19th-century classical
SIZE: 7.4 acres (2.2 ha)
CLIMATE: Humid subtropical
LOCATION: Suzhou, Jiangsu
TRANSLATION: The Garden for Lingering In

Built during the Ming dynasty, the Liu Yuan, or the Garden for Lingering In, is one of the largest and most important classical gardens in Suzhou. It was originally built by a retired official called Xu Taishi, who incorporated many different types of bizarrely shaped rock and stone into the garden, for which it became renowned. One rock alone, from the famous Lake Tai Hu, is more than 20 feet (6 m) tall—it is lean, wrinkled, hollow, and perforated. Sometimes incense is burned at the base so that the smoke wafts up into the rock and out of the perforations.

The planting in the garden is varied and includes bamboos, vines, peonies, and pelargoniums. Look out for the Hall of Five Peaks, which is also known as the Nanmu Hall, after the wood of the same name that was used to construct the furniture and the hall. In front of the hall stands a hill constructed of piled stone with five peaks. The excellent view of the hill from inside the hall is an example of the principle of traveling through hills and valleys without leaving your seat. This is all in contrast to the Stone Forest Courtyard in which eight small-scale scenes have been created, using pillars of stone, banana plants, bamboo, and wisteria.

You can learn an extraordinary amount about Chinese gardens from this one example, which is considered by many to be the most beautiful in the Ming tradition. It is particularly celebrated for its clever use of garden space. No wonder it was declared a World Heritage Site by UNESCO in 1997. SY

Shi Zi Lin

Jiangsu, China

DESIGNER: Monk Tian Ru
OWNER: The Chinese State
GARDEN STYLE: 14th-century classical private garden
SIZE: 2.5 acres (1 ha)
CLIMATE: Humid subtropical
LOCATION: Suzhou, Jiangsu
TRANSLATION: Lion Grove Garden

Shi Zi Lin is one of the four great gardens of Suzhou and is admired for the incredible collection of pitted, eroded rocks that were greatly appreciated by classical Chinese scholars. The garden is part of a temple complex, and its construction dates back to 1342, when it was laid out by disciples of the Buddhist monk Tian Ru, under his guidance. It is thought that the name Lion Grove Garden derives from the lion-like appearance of many of the rocks in its grounds, and from the fact that lions are guardians of the Buddhist faith.

The first point to notice is that there are a number of shaped doorways in the white plaster walls of the courtyards, which provide framed views of the lion-shaped rocks around the garden. Then focus on the pool, which is crossed by a zigzag bridge that widens in the center to form the base of a pavilion that seems to float above the surface of the water, in which the elegant, upswept eaves of its roof are reflected. A recently found stone boat is moored by the edge of the pool and would have been used for entertaining. Such boats were used to symbolize the stability of the owner's position on what could be challenging and changing political seas. There is also a complex arrangement of rocks surrounding the lake. The winding paths within them alter in both elevation and direction to surprise visitors, making the garden seem much larger. The planting softens and contrasts with the water-worn rocks, and elsewhere there are ginkgos (*Ginkgo biloba*), lacebark pines (*Pinus bungeana*), and wisterias in the courtyards.

In the southwest corner of the garden, on top of one of the major rockwork constructions, a lovely fan-shaped pavilion offers fine views over the garden. Thanks to the artist Ni Can, who painted the garden in the fourteenth century, soon after it was completed, it is known what it looked like then—and that a visit today is the "real thing." JR

Wang Shi Yuan

Jiangsu, China

DESIGNER: Song Zongyuan
OWNER: The Chinese State
GARDEN STYLE: 18th-century classical private garden
SIZE: 1.3 acres (0.5 ha)
CLIMATE: Humid subtropical
LOCATION: Suzhou, Jiangsu
TRANSLATION: Garden of the Master of the Fishing Nets

Wang Shi Yuan, or Garden of the Master of the Fishing Nets, with its wonderful litany of imaginatively named pavilions, was begun in 1140. It fell into neglect and was recreated by the bureaucrat Song Zongyuan in 1770. The enclosed complex of house and garden is one of the smallest, most beautiful, and most perfectly proportioned in Suzhou. There are three main areas: a residential section, a central main garden, and an inner garden. The design of the main garden, with its central lake, is a study in using proportion and open and closed spaces to best effect.

The lake shore is flanked by a walkway made from yellow granite arranged to look like mountains from the outside. Inside are grottoes and the delicate, arched, 1-foot-wide (30 cm) Leading to Serenity Bridge. You will also find four pavilions: the Washing My Ribbon Pavilion, which extends over the water; the Moon Comes with Breeze Pavilion; the Japanese Apricot Pavilion; and the Duck-Shooting Veranda.

To the north are various garden buildings, including the Appreciating Paintings Studio Pavilion, the Viewing Pines Pavilion, and the Void Studio. To the south is the Pavilion of Clean Water for Cap-string Washing, the Stick to Peace Mansion, the Lute Chamber around courtyards of quiet seclusion, and the Small Hill Osmanthus Bush Pavilion, near the rockery. The inner western garden is a quiet court featuring the Late Spring Abode as the principal building. It was the model for the Astor Court Ming garden at the Metropolitan Museum of New York. TM

Zhan Yuan

Jiangsu, China

DESIGNER: Unknown
OWNER: The Chinese State
GARDEN STYLE: 14th- and 19th-century classical
SIZE: 1.3 acres (0.5 ha)
CLIMATE: Humid subtropical
LOCATION: Nanjing, Jiangsu
TRANSLATION: Garden of Prospect

Zhan Yuan, built in the early Ming dynasty (1368–1644) as a prince's garden, was used as a local government office during the Qing dynasty (1644–1912). In the mid-nineteenth century, opponents of the Qing Empire, called Taiping Tianguo (the Kingdom of Heavenly Peace), settled in Nanjing and took over Zhan Yuan. In 1864 the last war between the Taiping and the Qing empire destroyed the garden.

Zhan Yuan has since experienced three restorations. The latest began in 1960. Guided by Liu Dunzheng, one of the best garden historians and architects in China at that time, the project improved rather than strictly followed the historical plan. The pond was given a more "natural" form, and evergreens were added to improve the winter view. The restoration upgraded Zhan Yuan in the typical Jiangnan (lower region of the Yangtze River) style, which highlighted the naturalistic look.

To the east is the History Museum of Taiping Tianguo, with its many relics of this bloody episode. The garden to the west retains the artificial miniature mountains, one of only two features inherited from the Ming dynasty (the other being an old wisteria). The mountains are piled high with bizarre Taihu rocks and have leaning, ancient pine trees; they give one of the best views at Zhan Yuan. Keep an eye out for other individual rocks, such as that at the entrance, which are highly rated for their unique forms. Zhan Yuan interweaves the old and the new, the peaceful and the violent, the tangible and intangible. LG

Zhou Zheng Yuan

Jiangsu, China

DESIGNERS: Wang Xianchen, Wang Xinyi, Zhang Luqian
OWNER: The Chinese State
GARDEN STYLE: 16th-, 17th-, and 19th-century classical
SIZE: 16 acres (6.5 ha)
CLIMATE: Humid subtropical
LOCATION: Suzhou, Jiangsu
TRANSLATION: Garden of the Humble Administrator

This huge garden, known as the Garden of the Humble Administrator, is said to have cost a boatload of silver and taken sixteen years to build. The biggest garden in Suzhou, it was built in 1513 by the Imperial Censor, Wang Xianchen, after he had resigned and returned to his hometown. Why did he give the garden this self-effacing name? He felt he could no longer administer anything but the garden, but he certainly did it with style.

Developed by subsequent owners, the garden is now simple, natural, and elegant in typical Ming style, with wild country scenery. Most of its major buildings are constructed beside water or partly submerged in it. The best place to view the garden scenery is the Yihong Pavilion in the middle garden section.

The middle part of the garden is full of arched and stone-slab bridges, weeping willows, and pools, and is stylized like a traditional Chinese painting. Visitors also love the Eighteen Camellia Hall in the western part, which has its own courtyard and eighteen different varieties of camellia, and the Little Blue Waves Pavilion, which has water on both sides. The corridors approaching it give the illusion of a courtyard on water. Close by is Little Flying Rainbow, the only covered bridge in the gardens of Suzhou. Its reflection in the water looks like a rainbow, hence the name. SY

RIGHT Most of the buildings at Zhou Zheng Yuan are built beside—or even partly in—water.

Yu Yuan

Shanghai, China

DESIGNERS: Pan Yunduan, Zhang Nanyang
OWNER: The Chinese State
GARDEN STYLE: 16th-century classical private garden
SIZE: 5 acres (2 ha)
CLIMATE: Humid subtropical
LOCATION: Shanghai
TRANSLATION: Garden of Contentment

In the heart of Shanghai, a bustling commercial district called Cheng Huang Miao (Temple of City God), is a tranquil enclosure—Yu Yuan, the Garden of Contentment. The history of the garden can be traced back more than 400 years to when a Ming official, Pan Yunduan, had it made for his retired father, a minister in the Ming court. As the estate of an educated, powerful, and wealthy family, Yu Yuan was ingenuously designed and well constructed, making it the leading garden in Shanghai. In the later nineteenth and early twentieth centuries, Yu Yuan was occupied and destroyed by warlords. Thankfully the restored site, now half its original size, is in keeping with Yunduan's design.

Entering the garden from the south, you encounter first a grand hall and then the garden's most precious feature, a group of artificial mountains piled up by Zhang Nanyang, the master of garden design in Ming China. The miniature mountains cleverly create mazelike routes to a bridge over water and to a mountain pavilion. Elsewhere the garden is divided and structured by curved walls, water, hills, trees, and buildings. Its seemingly never-ending paths cluster at various garden features, including the Dragon Wall and the giant rock quarried from Lake Taihu, which should not be missed.

Although categorized as a Jiangnan (the lower region of the Yangtze River in southeast China) garden, Yu Yuan is more compact and richly decorated than other such gardens. LG

Xi Hu

Zhejiang, China

DESIGNERS: Bai Juyi, Su Shi
OWNER: The Chinese State
GARDEN STYLE: 9th- and 11th-century classical
SIZE: 14,826 acres (6,004 ha)
CLIMATE: Humid subtropical
LOCATION: Hangzhou, Zhejiang
TRANSLATION: West Lake

Xi Hu, the West Lake, has been a model and inspiration for designers of Chinese landscapes for more then ten centuries, and none of its imitators has ever achieved such mastery.

First a lagoon and then a lake, Xi Hu eventually evolved into its long-term shape through a combination of nature and human power. In the ninth and eleventh centuries, Bai Juyi and Su Shi, two leading poets in the Tang and Song dynasties, were governors of Hangzhou. They noticed that part of the lake was turning into marshland, so they had the sludge removed and piled into two dikes, and built bridges edged with willow and other trees. The two dikes, named Bai Di (Causeway of Bai) and Su Di (Causeway of Su), soon became busy roads and popular sites for touring.

Today, the scenic site of Xi Hu includes the 1,400-acre (567 ha) lake, the surrounding mountains and hills, and nearly 100 gardens and scenic features dotted in the landscape. If you take a circuit along the lake and the causeways, you will get the most marvelous and evocative views of specially created gardens—the famous Ten Scenes of Xi Hu—whose highly descriptive names are a good indication of what you will see. The ten scenes are Fall Moon on the Calm Lake, Melting Snow on Broken Bridge, Listening to the Orioles in the Waving Willows, Evening Bell at Southern Screen Hill, Sunset Glow at Thunder Peak, Three Pools Mirroring the Moon, Observing the Fish at Flower Harbor, Spring Dawn at the Su Di, Peaks in the Cloud, and Lotus in the Breeze at Crooked Garden.

In the mid-eighteenth century, the Emperor Qianlong was so inspired by the Ten Scenes he saw during a visit to Xi Hu that he had the same scenes recreated in his imperial garden, Yuan Ming Yuan, and a similar, but much smaller, lake, Kunming Hu, made in the Summer Palace. LG

Guo Zhuang

Zhejiang, China

DESIGNER: Unknown
OWNER: The Chinese State
GARDEN STYLE: 19th-century classical private garden
SIZE: 2.5 acres (1 ha)
CLIMATE: Humid subtropical
LOCATION: Hangzhou, Zhejiang
TRANSLATION: Guo's Villa

A humble compartment of the Xi Hu (West Lake) Scenic Site, Guo Zhuang is the best existing traditional private garden in Hangzhou. It is one of the garden masterpieces of Jiangnan (the lower region of the Yangtze River in southeast China), thanks to its incomparable surroundings and the smartly managed garden space.

If you stroll along the bamboo lane at the entrance, the first surprise is the sudden view to a square pond that looks bigger than it is because the entrance is quite restrained. Such optical illusion is just the beginning. Keep walking along either the straight bank or the roofed corridor, squeezing through piled rockeries and plantings, and you will see a moon gate, and then there is the great surprise of the sealike lake, Xi Hu. The garden develops with regular switches between tight, closed spaces and sudden, open ones. The key feature, or spirit, is water.

Besides the Xi Hu, there are two superb water "yards." The larger one, a virtually square pond lined by trees, has a strong sense of tranquillity and simplicity. The smaller yard is more homey, with flowering trees and shrubs dotted among its rockery banks. The two yards are connected, as well as divided, by the teahouse Liang Yi Xuan, or Belvedere of Both Good, which has the best view of both yards.

Cleverly juxtaposing shade and light, curved and straight, yin and yang, the garden of Guo Zhuang is a wonderful embodiment of the Chinese wisdom of Tao and the Way of Nature. LG

Xianggang

Hong Kong, China

DESIGNERS: Urban Council, Royal Hong Kong Jockey Club
OWNER: The Chinese State
GARDEN STYLE: 20th-century landscaped public park
SIZE: 20 acres (8.1 ha)
CLIMATE: Humid subtropical
LOCATION: Central, Hong Kong
TRANSLATION: Hong Kong Park

The area comprising Xianggang Gong Yuan, or Hong Kong Park, is some of the most expensive real estate in the world. The high-rise cityscape surrounding it makes its stillness amid the city turmoil seem all the more precious. The park opened in 1991. It was conceived as a microcosm of the universe, with a series of linked views that you discover as you stroll along the winding paths by the lakes, the landscaped gardens, waterfalls, rain-forest aviary, and greenhouses. From an entrance on Cotton Tree Drive, you ascend a white-brick water staircase flanked by lamps and containers of lush, tender perennials. At the top of the steps, the garden unfolds with areas of beautifully groomed landscape composed of lakes, streams, lawns, and plantings. They incorporate trees such as the Chinese banyan (*Ficus microcarpa*), as well as flowering trees such as *Bauhinia tomentosa*, coral trees, callistemon, and holly (*Ilex rotunda*).

Clipped spheres of purple berberis and golden privet (*Ligustrum ovalifolium* 'Aureum') are softened by sprays of vibrantly colored dwarf rhododendron and royal palms (*Roystonea regia*), creating compositions that echo Chinese paintings. Rocks built into the hillside form a mountain waterfall that descends into a pool with dancing fountains, where fish dart and terrapins bask on rocks. There are pools for lotus and tropical water lilies, with purple iris and thalias at the water's edge. A Conservation Corner is a perfect habitat for dragonflies, and there is even a serene Tai Chi Garden. EH

Changdeokgung

Seoul, South Korea

DESIGNER: Unknown
OWNER: The South Korean State
GARDEN STYLE: 15th- and 17th-century landscaped
SIZE: 78 acres (32 ha)
CLIMATE: Continental warm summer
LOCATION: Seoul
TRANSLATION: Palace of Prospering Virtue

Like any modern city, Seoul has its share of bland, high-rise architecture, but there are ancient sites tucked away if you know where to look.

The royal palace of Changdeokgung dates back to 1405, though it was rebuilt in the seventeenth century. It was designed to harmonize with nature as much as possible. Hidden within the palace grounds is the Piwon, or Secret Garden, a woodland retreat that during the Yi dynasty was kept solely for the use of the royal family and the king's concubines. To explore the garden, you must join a tour. Dragonflies

flit in and out of the maple trees, and skim the lily ponds, and somehow, the palace's high stone walls manage to blot out the rumble of Seoul's busy traffic beyond. With the insistent buzz of the cicadas, you may feel as though you are in the middle of the countryside rather than the heart of the metropolis.

The Piwon is one of the best examples of Korean, traditional, natural landscape design. Look out for a 700-year-old Chinese juniper tree that has been designated a national monument, and another said to be 1,000 years old. Also note the pleasure pavilions and elegant stone bridges that span the still pools. The garden's Arch of Longevity is a stunning piece of engineering, carved from a single piece of stone. Spring visitors enjoy the cherry blossoms; in fall there are maples in red, yellow, and brown, and all shades between. Even in the hot and humid Korean summers, the garden provides a peaceful retreat away from the noise of the city streets. SA

Chollipo Arboretum

Ch'ungch'ŏng-Namdo, South Korea

DESIGNER: Min Pyong-gal
OWNER: Min Pyong-gal
GARDEN STYLE: 20th-century arboretum
SIZE: 160 acres (65 ha)
CLIMATE: Continental warm summer
LOCATION: Taean-Gun, Ch'ungch'ŏng-Namdo

A chance purchase of a cliff-top house on the coast about 120 miles (192 km) southwest of Seoul was the starting point for Chollipo Arboretum. Today it boasts one of the finest collections of magnolias in the world, complemented by hollies and other evergreens, and carpets of spring wildflowers.

The arboretum is the life's work of Min Pyong-gal, but behind this seemingly natural Korean name lies an intriguing tale. Min Pyong-gal was formerly known as Carl Ferris Miller, an American who ended up in Korea after World War II as an interpreter for the U.S. Navy. Loving the country, he decided to settle in 1947 and became a Korean citizen. The original site at Chollipo was pressed upon him by an old man desperate to sell. From the first few acres, the site has grown to encompass sand dunes with their unique flora, and ponds converted from rice paddies for water loving species. On Magnolia Hill, more than 1,800 magnolias have been planted with underlying hepaticas, irises, and corydalis in spring.

The tides in this part of the world are dramatic and can vary by 40 feet (10 m), allowing visitors to walk at low tide to an offshore island planted with camellias and groves of hollies. Back inland, the Big Valley rises to a peak of 394 feet (120 m), and is devoted to Korean native wildflowers and shrubs.

The arboretum is funded entirely by Min Pyong-gal: "As a naturalized Korean citizen, it is a contribution to my adopted country. I think of it not in twenty-five or thirty years, but in two hundred years when the plants will carry on after I die." SA

Kenrokuen

Ishikawa, Japan

DESIGNERS: The Maeda family
OWNERS: The Maeda family
GARDEN STYLE: 17th to 19th-century stroll garden
SIZE: 28.2 acres (11.4 ha)
CLIMATE: Humid subtropical
LOCATION: Kanazawa, Ishikawa

The name Kenrokuen means The Garden Displaying Six Qualities, and those qualities are spaciousness, seclusion, artistic intent, maturity, abundant water, and striking vistas. This expansive garden displays all these characteristics, though seclusion can be a challenge because it is a popular destination. The garden opened to the public in the late 1800s, and was declared a National Site of Scenic Beauty in 1922.

Kenrokuen was created as the outer garden of Kanazawa Castle over a 200-year period, from the seventeenth to the nineteenth century. The large garden was designed to offer the strolling visitor a range of views that would bring to mind the natural scenery of Japan. The informal design includes two large ponds and a stream, planted with irises and flanked by cherry trees, that winds through the garden. The water is crossed by a variety of traditional, arching wooden and stone bridges, and a series of stepping-stones arranged in the formation of flying geese. On the bank of the Misty Pond is the famous and much photographed, two-legged Kotoji stone lantern, named after the bridge that supports the strings on a Japanese *koto*, or harp. The oldest fountain in Japan, dating from the latter half of the eighteenth century, can be seen in the garden, producing a spout of water that can reach up to 11.4 feet (3.5 m) high, an extremely unusual feature in a traditional Japanese design. JR

RIGHT An elaborate bracing system at Kenrokuen prevents breakage of branches by the weight of snow.

Kairaku-en

Ibaraki, Japan

DESIGNER: Tokugawa Nariaki
OWNER: The Japanese State
GARDEN STYLE: 19th-century stroll garden
SIZE: 31.4 acres (12.7 ha)
CLIMATE: Humid subtropical
LOCATION: Mito, Ibaraki
TRANSLATION: The Park to Be Enjoyed Together

When Tokugawa Nariaki, the feudal lord of Mito in Ibaraki Province, built himself a magnificent three-story villa in the mid-nineteenth century, he also created a garden to be shared with the people of Mito. It was a pioneering idea that led to the development of public parks in Japan.

He borrowed the surrounding landscape in the traditional *shakkei* style, using nearby Lake Senba as the focal point of the garden, and planted cedar woods, a bamboo grove, and 3,000 plum trees in 100 different varieties around his house, Kobuntei (the name comes from an old word for "plum"). Nariaki planted plum trees so that his people could enjoy their blossom, and also their fruit in times of famine. Today, in late February and March, Kairaku-en hosts Ume Matsuri, a plum festival, when thousands of visitors come to enjoy the blossom and picnic under the trees. Ten Miss Plum Ladies, dressed in pink, red, and white kimonos to match the flowers, greet the visitors, and there is an exhibition of bonsai plum trees covered in blossom. Later in spring, hundreds of cherry trees are covered in flower, and in May bright pink and red azaleas dominate the garden. At the end of the year, the maples turn scarlet and orange.

Whatever the season, do not miss a tour of the traditional Kobuntei villa, with its tatami mats and sliding screens exquisitely painted with plums, cherries, azaleas, and maples. From the top floor, the visitor is rewarded with a view over Lake Senba. The spirit of Nariaki looks on in approval. SG

Canada Garden

Tōkyō, Japan

DESIGNER: Moriyama & Teshima
    Planners Limited
OWNER: Canadian Embassy
GARDEN STYLE: 20th-century modern
SIZE: Approximately 1.6 acres (0.6 ha)
CLIMATE: Humid subtropical
LOCATION: Tokyo, Tōkyō

Imagine the design brief: to create a garden for the Canadian Embassy in Tokyo that will symbolize the wide, open spaces of Canada and still strike a chord with the people of Japan. The result is a triumph.

The eight-story building is split in half, horizontally, at the fourth floor where the garden is located. The lower three floors are leased as office space, and the upper four levels house the embassy. An outside escalator takes thousands of visitors a month up to the fourth-floor entrance lobby. The Canada Garden surrounds the lobby on three sides, entirely visible through its glass walls.

On one side there is a representation of the rugged landscape of the Canadian Shield—a vast area of pre-Cambrian rock that covers most of Canada. This part is horseshoe-shaped, like a warrior's shield. Forests, lakes, rivers, and mountains are suggested, with three stone mounds representing the Rockies. A bronze sculpture symbolizing the connections between Canada and Japan rises from a still, reflective pool. The Shield then dives beneath some water representing the Pacific, and stepping-stones lead across, linking the two geographically distant cultures. The path leads through a stone portal into a traditional Japanese garden. Rocks placed in raked gravel symbolize mountains and water.

Every day hundreds of Tokyo's office workers eat their lunches here, sharing the tranquillity. The garden is not merely a meeting of two cultures, but rejoices in their differences in an entirely Japanese way. SG

Kokyo Higashi Gyoen

Tōkyō, Japan

DESIGNER: Unknown
OWNER: The Imperial Palace, Tokyo
GARDEN STYLE: 20th-century modern
SIZE: 250 acres (101.2 ha)
CLIMATE: Humid subtropical
LOCATION: Tokyo, Tōkyō
TRANSLATION: East Gardens of the Tokyo Imperial Palace

These gardens reflect the ever changing face of Japan and its emperor. Until the nineteenth century, the Tokugawa shōguns ruled Japan. When the shōguns were overthrown, the capital was moved to their former seat at Edo, which was renamed Tokyo. The emperor built a new residence in Edo Castle's grounds, but it was razed by bombs during World War II. In 1968 work was completed on a new palace, and the new East Gardens on the site of the old castle were opened to the people of Tokyo, a reflection of the increasing accessibility of the Imperial family.

The gardens are the epitome of perfect grooming. Every azalea bush is scissor pruned into a dome, and all the trees—the conifers and acers—are cloud pruned every year by a team of diligent gardeners, with needles and twigs being removed by hand from each branch to achieve the perfect pillow of foliage.

But what everyone wants to see is the *sakur*, or spring cherry blossoms. The media give the best time for viewing it in each province, starting in Okinawa in February. When the cherry-blossom front reaches Tokyo in late March, it coincides with a bank holiday. The entire population seems to visit the East Gardens and the palace moat to celebrate the event with a *hanami*, or flower-viewing party. The most popular variety is *Prunus* x *yedoensis* 'Somei Yoshino', which produces pure white, single flowers with a pink eye on bare branches. When the petals start to fall, the tree appears to be white, just for a few fleeting days: the symbol of ephemeral beauty and brief life. SG

Adachi Bijutsukan

Shimane, Japan

DESIGNER: Kinsaku Nakane
OWNER: Zenko Adachi
GARDEN STYLE: 20th-century tree and rock garden
SIZE: 10.5 acres (4.3 ha)
CLIMATE: Humid subtropical
LOCATION: Yasugi, Shimane
TRANSLATION: Adachi Museum of Art

Viewing the gardens of the Adachi Museum of Art is like witnessing the unrolling of a scroll. Areas of the garden are progressively revealed from the windows of the lower story of the building, which form the frames for the living scenes. Though the Adachi Museum houses a magnificent collection of paintings, these are not displayed in areas of the building from which the garden can be seen, and so do not compete with the garden.

A range of garden areas seamlessly surrounds the museum, and includes broad areas of white gravel set with beautifully sculpted pines, an area of moss garden, an informal pool edged with fine rocks, and domed azaleas. The beautifully curved lawn seems to flow down to meet a sea of immaculate gravel. The Waterfall of the Turtle and the Crane, 49.2 feet (15 m) high, surrounded by pine and maple trees, takes the viewer straight to Japan's mountainous landscape.

One specific window frame is well worth studying. It captures the garden with the strong outline of a forked tree trunk in the foreground, the sweeping curve of a lawn with shaped azaleas and rocks in the middle distance, and mountain slopes beyond, the whole being just like a Japanese screen painting. The patron of the garden, Zenko Adachi, said, "Landscaping cannot be done by a single person. An excellent garden can only be realized by having a workforce of skilled gardeners." You only have to visit to see that he was absolutely right. JR

Korakuen

Okayama, Japan

DESIGNER: Ikeda Tsunamasa
OWNERS: The Ikeda family
GARDEN STYLE: 17th-century stroll garden
SIZE: 32.9 acres (13.3 ha)
CLIMATE: Humid subtropical
LOCATION: Okayama, Okayama
TRANSLATION: The Garden for Taking Pleasure Later

The large landscape garden of Korakuen is found on the north bank of the River Asahi, opposite the imposing face of Okayama Castle, which figures in many of the views from the garden. The creation of the garden dates from 1687, and was added to over the next 200 years by a single aristocratic family.

The garden has a large, central lake, the Marshy Pond, which contains three islands said to remind the viewer of the scenery around Lake Biwa, near Kyoto. An artificial hill, Sole Heart Mountain, rises from the lawn just beyond the shore of the lake, and is planted with skillfully pruned azaleas. The hill offers excellent views over the sweeping lawns and other features distributed around the open center. Groves of maples, cherries, and pruned pines appear throughout the garden, along with a small tea plantation and a rice field laid out in the traditional Chinese style.

In addition to the central pond, water is found beyond the central area in the form of winding streams, and occasionally you will find the garden staff wading through them, vigorously using bamboo twig brooms to sweep the pebbles that line the base to remove any algal growth. One of the streams flows through the center of a formal, open-sided pavilion, where parties for poetry composition were held, each participant having to complete a poem before a cup of rice wine floated past. There is also an area planted with irises that can be viewed by crossing a zigzag timber bridge. In all, plenty of enjoyment can be found in this spacious and beautiful site. JR

Nunobiki Hābu-en

Hyōgo, Japan

DESIGNER: Seiko Hirota
OWNER: Nunobiki Herb Park
GARDEN STYLE: 20th-century Japanese, European
SIZE: 40 acres (16 ha)
CLIMATE: Humid subtropical
LOCATION: Kōbe, Hyōgo
TRANSLATION: Nunobiki Herb Garden

The Japanese characters for Kōbe translate as "God's door," and if travel to heaven is upward, the metaphor is extremely apt. A cable car carries you high into the hillside from the skyscraper city, across terraces of planting dominated by herbs in their broadest sense. At its peak is the Tenbou Rest House, where you can walk out onto terraces giving expansive views while, under your feet, a tiny mint (*Mentha requienii*) acts as scented green mortar between the rectangular paving stones. Below, in the Sample Garden, geraniums are planted in quantity and variety, against the distant view of the skyscrapers and port of Kōbe.

In fact color, exuberance, and scent are present almost all the year round, and if you want, you can walk, terrace by terrace, back down to Kōbe or take the aptly named Hiking Course and see the many beautifully maintained herb displays. A large loop in the wide path encompasses the extensive Lavender Garden in Provençal style. There are great kaleidoscopic blocks of salvias, from deep purple with dark leaves through bicolors to pinks, reds, and yellows. A winding set of steps takes you to a demonstration blue garden, the steps being simply, but boldly, flanked by massed feverfew (*Tanacetum parthenium*) and corn poppies (*Papaver rhoeas*). In contrast there is a small, ornamental kitchen garden located at the point where two tracks converge. And do not miss the great swath of sunflowers in August, the forest path to the Wild Flower Garden, and the Nihon (Japanese) Herb Garden. CH

Daisen-in

Kyōto, Japan

DESIGNER: Kogaku Sōkō
OWNER: Daitoku-ji Temple
GARDEN STYLE: 16th-century dry landscape
SIZE: 0.02 acre (0.01 ha)
CLIMATE: Humid subtropical
LOCATION: Kyoto, Kyōto
TRANSLATION: Great Hermit's Temple

Daisen-in reflects a watershed in Japanese history. Until the end of the twelfth century, Japan had been ruled by the aristocrats—courtly, mannered, and romantic. The shōguns who seized power from the nobility had no time for elegant and leisurely promenading. They were frugal, and their gardens were confined, smaller, and urban, imbued with the spirit of the new religion from China: Zen Buddhism.

The garden at Daisen-in is too small for promenading; it is to be explored in the imagination. It is an allegory of life that is represented by a river of white sand. The garden surrounds the abbot's quarters on three sides, starting in the northeast corner, where it erupts from a ravine that signals truth, the source of life. The river swirls wildly in Youth, past the Rocks of Dismay, and over the Barrier of Doubt and Contradiction. Here a little turtle stone, symbolizing sorrow, is vainly trying to swim against the flow, trying to return to the past. Also note the Treasure Ship Stone that has no bow wave. It is not forging ahead, but going with the flow, enjoying the present, laden with the treasures of experience: the joys and disappointments of life. The river finally flows into a sea of raked sand, the Ocean of Nothingness, and the everlasting peace of paradise.

The screens within the abbot's quarters are decorated with monochrome images of hermit scholars and the natural world. To engage with this garden is to step into those sparse, ink-washed paintings that depict life in the sixteenth century. SG

Entsu–ji

Kyōto, Japan

DESIGNER: Unknown, but possibly the monk Gyokuen
OWNER: The Japanese State
GARDEN STYLE: 17th-century Japanese temple garden
SIZE: 0.2 acre (0.1 ha)
CLIMATE: Humid subtropical
LOCATION: Iwakura, Kyōto
TRANSLATION: Large Sad Mountain Prayer Place

This small, contemplative garden, with one of the best surviving examples of *shakkei*, or borrowed scenery, is a beautifully balanced composition of rock and moss. Symbolizing hills by a flowing river, the rocks consist of numerous low stones and two natural rock outcrops, set in a rolling carpet of moss. The low stones appear to be placed in curving rows that imply that the river is flowing from left to right.

A clipped hedge provides the backdrop for the rock and moss composition, and, more important, is the lower part of the "frame" that highlights Mount Hiei, 3.6 miles (6 km) in the distance. Tall cypress and pine trees, between the garden and mountain, form other parts of the framed or borrowed picture, although it is thought that these trees were not in existence when the garden was designed.

It is also thought that the *shoin*, or main building, of Entsu-ji was once part of an imperial palace. Emperor Gomizuno built various country villas in the seventeenth century, including one at this site. When he later moved to the nearby Shugaku-in villas in 1659, which had the advantage of a better water supply, Entsu-ji became a convent, and it is thought that the garden was created around that time.

Entsu-ji shows the restraint of the Zen garden, but, with all the elements softened, is a good example of the blending of styles seen in the Edo period (1603–1867). The severe walls seen at Ryōan-ji (see page 792) have now become clipped hedges, and the groundcover has moss instead of gravel. PCa

Byōdō–in

Kyōto, Japan

DESIGNER: Fujiwara Yorimichi
OWNER: Kyoto City
GARDEN STYLE: 11th-century Japanese Pure Land garden
SIZE: 4.9 acres (2 ha)
CLIMATE: Humid subtropical
LOCATION: Uji-shi, Kyōto
TRANSLATION: The Court Temple

Placed on the UNESCO World Heritage List in 1994, the Byōdō-in (or Byoudou-in) Temple is a monastery garden dedicated to the worship of Buddha Amida (Amitabha). It was designed to recreate paradise on Earth, and is the most beautiful example of Japan's few surviving Pure Land gardens, a style that was popular during the Heian period (792–1192). Only at Byōdō-in is it now possible to see an original Heian building positioned, as intended, in front of its pond.

The building and the pavilions are linked by roofed corridors, and were built in the early eleventh century by Fujiwara Michinaga as part of a country estate. The garden was remodeled in 1053 by his son Yorimichi, who added the Amida Hall, more commonly called the Phoenix Hall, or Hou-do. The architectural style of this Buddhist structure, designed to hold the statue of Amitabha Tathagata, not surprisingly is Chinese. But its position by the pond and the additional pavilions are typically Japanese.

The garden is a masterpiece of natural beauty. Positioned in front of the Amida Hall, the reflective Ajiike Pond gives the impression that the building is floating. The pond contains a *suhama*, or beach of stones, to imitate the shore of the River Uji. The whole—the garden, connecting bridges, reflective pool, and the building—is intended to be an image of the Pure Land, or heaven. TM

RIGHT At Byōdō-in, the hall is connected to the garden by an arched bridge (*soribashi*) and a flat bridge (*hirabashi*).

Tōhan Meiga no Niwa

Kyōto, Japan

DESIGNER: Tadao Ando
OWNER: City of Kyoto
GARDEN STYLE: 20th-century contemporary urban
SIZE: 0.7 acre (0.3 ha)
CLIMATE: Humid subtropical
LOCATION: Kyoto, Kyōto
TRANSLATION: The Garden of Fine Art

The Garden of Fine Art has been created as a multilevel, concrete structure designed by the well-known architect Ando Tadao. The space was developed to enable reproductions of great paintings from around the world to be displayed in an outdoor environment. The paintings, eight in total, have been reproduced by a photographic process onto ceramic plates that are said to be resistant to corrosion and fading. The majority of the reproductions are placed on the concrete walls, though one of Claude Monet's impressionistic water lily paintings is strikingly placed beneath the water's surface in a clear, formal pool.

However, it is the garden's architectural use of space that constitutes the major reason for a visit. The viewer is guided through a series of walkways in this very contemporary setting of concrete and glass, and at all three levels a screen of falling water can be seen and heard at the end of the garden. On the lowest story, the wall of water makes a contrast with a view of the trees above framed by concrete beams. A beautiful concrete support for an upper floor seems to have been inspired by the nodes, or joints, on a bamboo stem.

The Garden of Fine Art is an excellent example of a continuum that began in the gravel gardens of the Zen temples. It cleverly and sensitively fuses the painterly and the spatial, making you rethink your ideas about what constitutes a garden. JR

Konchi–in, Nanzen–ji

Kyōto, Japan

DESIGNER: Kobori Enshu
OWNER: Rinzai Zen
GARDEN STYLE: 17th-century dry landscape
SIZE: 28 acres (11.3 ha)
CLIMATE: Humid subtropical
LOCATION: Kyoto, Kyōto
TRANSLATION: Cottage by a Mountain Stream

The temple complex at Nanzen-ji is a wealth of ancient buildings, teahouses, and gardens. And tucked away in a far corner of the complex lies a hidden jewel, Konchi-in. Ahead of the garden is a sparkling pond, teeming with little turtles and giant koi; a small island, scarlet with maples in fall, is joined to the land by a broken-back bridge to prevent evil spirits from crossing. A formal path, lined with stone lanterns, leads around the pond and through a *tori*, a Shinto-style gate. Down under the clattering bamboos, the path becomes rougher, slowing the footsteps, inviting contemplation, until at last it presents the visitor with a view of an exquisite dry landscape garden; this is Konchi-in.

Step up to the viewing hall, and the sliding screens allow only half of the garden to be seen at a time. An ocean of raked gravel runs from the veranda to a shoreline. Slide the screen to the left, and a flat turtle island appears, solid and still, symbolizing wisdom and longevity. Slide the screen to the right, and a vertical crane island appears in the frame. This bears an ancient plum tree, its trunk silver and contorted, and when it blossoms in spring, it encapsulates both youth and old age. The flowers open, fade, and the petals fall, as transient as a young woman's beauty. And every fall, a maple reddens behind the silver trunk: a poignant reminder of the passing seasons and of life's transience. SG

Ginkaku-ji

Kyōto, Japan

DESIGNER: Soami
OWNER: Sokoji-ji school of the Rinzai sect
GARDEN STYLE: 15th-century dry and stroll garden
SIZE: 7.4 acres (3 ha)
CLIMATE: Humid subtropical
LOCATION: Jisho-ji Temple, Kyoto, Kyōto
TRANSLATION: The Temple of the Silver Pavilion

The dry landscape garden of the Silver Pavilion at Jisho-ji, made a UNESCO World Heritage Site in 1994, is at once enigmatic and startling. A 2-foot-high (0.6 m) platform of sparkling white sand, raked into long parallel lines, lies beside a 6-foot-high (1.8 m) cone of sand with a flat top. It could be Mount Fuji, a mound of rice implying wealth and prosperity, or a pile of sand for replenishing the platform.

When Shōgun Yoshimasa commissioned the Silver Pavilion and its garden, he was planning his retirement and his escape from the civil wars that ravaged fifteenth-century Kyoto. He wanted somewhere to while away peaceful hours burning incense, watching traditional Noh theater, and, above all, writing poetry with friends. The moon is an iconic image in Japanese poetry. It symbolizes unattainable goals and unobtainable beauty, and here, on the veranda overlooking the Moon Viewing Garden, Yoshimasa would sit and seek inspiration for his writing. At certain times of the year, the moon rises over a dip in the surrounding tree line and shines down the long, raked, silvery lines, directly onto the rounded flat top of the mound. It is as if the moon is reflected in a deep lake, its rays lighting the surface of the water. At full moon, it is said that moonlight illuminates the entire Silver Pavilion.

The Silver Pavilion is not actually silver, but austere black and white. Shōgun Yoshimasa had intended to cover the structure with silver leaf, just as his grandfather Yoshimitsu had covered Kinkaku-ji with gold leaf, but the civil unrest that continued throughout most of his rule delayed the completion of the villa, and his final plans were never realized.

Finally note the nearby classic stroll garden, which contrasts with and complements the dry garden. It has meticulously pruned trees, and a pond with Crane and Turtle islands, highly appropriate symbols of longevity and permanence. SG

Tōfuku-ji Temple

Kyōto, Japan

DESIGNER: Mirei Shigemori
OWNER: Sonoisan Said
GARDEN STYLE: 20th-century gravel and moss garden
SIZE: 1.75 acres (0.7 ha)
CLIMATE: Humid subtropical
LOCATION: Tōfuku-ji Temple, Kyoto, Kyōto
TRANSLATION: Garden of Eight Views (Hass no Niwa)

The garden of the Hō-jō (main hall) of the Tōfuku-ji Temple provides a beautiful modernist interpretation of the gravel and moss gardens traditionally found surrounding temple buildings in Kyoto. The garden was created in 1939, and the designer, Mirei Shigemori, said that his main aim was to produce a garden of timeless modernity.

The story begins in 1938 when a temple of the Rinzai school of Zen Buddhism, with minimal financial resources, asked an equally poor and unknown landscape designer to prepare a master plan for the improvement of the surrounding landscape over the next 100 years. The head priest felt that there was an opportunity for the development of some gardens around the Hō-jō, his only stipulation being that, in keeping with the philosophy of the Zen sect, nothing should go to waste, and that the old paving stone should be reused.

Mirei Shigemori created a series of masterpieces. To the south are four stone groupings, representing the islands of the immortals, surrounded by gravel, including some skillfully raked whirlpools. To the western end of the building is a checkerboard planting of pruned azaleas and gravel, inspired by the patterns of rice fields in the landscape. The shaded north side of the building provides the location for the iconic grid pattern of square stones and moss for which this garden is best known; the paving from the original entrance path was used here. The east garden completes the circuit and is composed of cylindrical foundation stones from a former temple building in the celestial arrangement of the Big Dipper, surrounded by rings of raked gravel.

Mirei Shigemori's aim was to develop a contemporary design, and it was an approach he pursued for the rest of his career. For those interested in how design can be informed by, and reinterpret, the past, this is an excellent place to begin. JR

Katsura Rikyu

Kyōto, Japan

DESIGNERS: Prince Toshihito, Kobori Enshu
OWNER: Japanese Royal Family
GARDEN STYLE: 17th-century stroll garden
SIZE: 16 acres (6.5 ha)
CLIMATE: Humid subtropical
LOCATION: Kyoto, Kyōto
TRANSLATION: Detached Palace

Katsura Imperial Villa was built in the early Edo period as a residence for Prince Hachijo no Miya Toshihito. Work commenced in the 1620s; it was continued by Toshihito's son Prince Toshitada. The villa and garden as seen today were completed in 1645. Never intended as a primary residence, the villa was more of a summerhouse. It is notable for its minimalism—a classic example of *sukiya*-style architecture. Even so, life here was refined and luxurious.

As with so many great Japanese gardens, there is a harmonious fusion with the house, and in many ways the two intertwine. Prince Toshihito was the garden's designer, and he was aided by Kobori Enshu, a tea master, government official, and garden designer. The garden contains literary images from the prince's favorite novel, *Tale of the Genji*, which evoked the golden age of the Heian period (795–1192) some 600 years before. However, the garden differs from the Shinden palaces of that period because it has a more compact plan.

The stroll garden to the south of the villa is particularly complex because the paths twist and turn, constantly revealing and screening off breathtaking vistas. There is also a 3.1-acre (1.3 ha) boating lake with beaches, pavilions, sixteen bridges, and islands, with one of the group of three probably representing the mythical Isles of the Blessed. Although the lake has lost one of its islands and a long bridge, it is essentially unaltered. The garden is aligned south to east rather than due south (as it should be according to the principles of feng shui) to best observe the rising of the moon, for which there is a special viewing platform. It also contains a miniature version of the Amanohashidate, one of Japan's most popular scenic wonders.

The villa can be viewed only on tours held by the Imperial Household Agency. It is necessary to obtain permission to visit in advance. TM

Sanbo-in

Kyōto, Japan

DESIGNERS: Toyotomi Hideyoshi, Gien Jugo
OWNER: The Japanese State
GARDEN STYLE: 16th-century stroll garden
SIZE: 1.2 acre (0.5 ha)
CLIMATE: Humid subtropical
LOCATION: Daigo Fushimi-ku, Kyōto
TRANSLATION: The House of Three Treasures

The rather extravagant temple garden of Sanbo-in has an emphasis on pleasure and richness that makes it feel more like a palace than a retreat. The pervading atmosphere was created by its patron, Toyotomi Hideyoshi, a prolific builder who ruled Japan from 1582 to 1598. He was drawn to the area while "cherry viewing," and worked on the design with the abbot of the temple, Gien Jugo. The garden's notable feature is the large number of rocks used, about 800 in all. Prized rocks were used in its creation, one being the Fujita Stone, which was considered so desirable by the garden makers that it was moved from another garden apparently "wrapped in silk, decorated with flowers and brought to the garden with the music of flute, drums, and the chanting of laborers."

The garden—a fine testimony to the Momoyama style—has both real ponds and the *karesansui*, or dry landscape garden, where water is symbolized. Like everything else here, the ponds and dry garden are meant to be seen by strolling along the gravel paths, though in the past visitors would also have surveyed the garden from the water. The high point, though, is clearly the island in the middle of the Broad Pond, which has waterfalls in the background. Other interesting features include the turf bridge over the pond, which looks slightly out of scale, and two visually striking patches of moss surrounded by white gravel, which are said to represent a gourd and sake cup. The patches were apparently created for a flower viewing event in 1598. PCa

Jojakko-ji

Kyōto, Japan

DESIGNER: Unknown
OWNER: Jojakko-ji Temple
GARDEN STYLE: 17th-century stroll garden
SIZE: 2 acres (0.8 ha)
CLIMATE: Humid subtropical
LOCATION: Kyoto, Kyōto
TRANSLATION: Everlasting Pure Land

Kyoto, like Paris, is a city that was constructed to be a capital. Its main streets were laid out in the eighth century in a grid pattern, contained within a natural bowl surrounded by mountains. But, unlike Paris, the city gates were aligned according to the laws of geomancy, and the oldest temples were placed in the wooded hills to commune with natural spirits.

Tucked into the bamboo groves that cover the lower slopes of Mount Ogura in western Kyoto is Jojakko-ji, a temple famous for the brilliance of its fall leaves. It was originally built in 1640 for the priest Nisshin, as a retirement home. It was converted into a temple after his death and given the Buddhist name Jojakko. The temple garden is approached through a formal thatched gate and up a long flight of stone steps, guarded at each side by two seated figures; a small chapel halfway up has benches for resting. To one side of the steps is a hidden waterfall streaming out of the mossy hillside.

The temple buildings are traditional and simple, in keeping with the surroundings, and they provide a good platform from which to view the garden. Look for the small pond surrounded by moss and stones. A further steep, but short, climb leads to an elegant two-story pagoda. The whole temple and its garden pay homage to the passing of the year: a poignant legacy from an elderly priest to his followers. SG

RIGHT At Jojakko-ji, acers in every shade of orange, scarlet, and vermillion light up the garden in fall.

Kinkaku-ji

Kyōto, Japan

DESIGNER: Shōgun Ashikaga Yoshimitsu
OWNER: Shōkoku-ji Temple
GARDEN STYLE: 14th-century paradise garden
SIZE: 11 acres (4.5 ha)
CLIMATE: Humid subtropical
LOCATION: Kyoto, Kyōto
TRANSLATION: The Golden Pavilion

The first sight of Kinkaku-ji, mirrored in the surrounding lake, is—and always was meant to be—breathtaking. Built by Shōgun Yoshimitsu in 1397 to entertain visiting trade delegations from Ming China, its garden was laid out in the Chinese style. After his death, the pavilion became a Zen temple.

Designed to be viewed from the veranda as a three-dimensional painting, the garden surrounds a lake divided by a pine-clad peninsula jutting out from the bank, creating an inner and outer lake. The inner lake is filled with rocks and five islands, and the larger outer lake contains three smaller islands and seems to be boundless, giving an illusion of distance, emphasized by trimming all the pine trees to scale.

The islands are "turtle" islands, being low and flat in profile, with four projecting legs and a head. They allude to the famous Buddhist myth of the five Mystic Isles, each of which floated on the backs of three turtles. All the birds and beasts were white, the flowers were scented, the fruit brought immortality, and the immortals who lived there flew on the backs of cranes. But, one day, an evil giant appeared, netted six of the turtles, and allowed two of the islands to drift away, leaving three islands remaining.

A footpath leads around the lake, passing the Dragon's Gate Cascade. At the base of the waterfall, a stone represents a carp trying to leap up the cascade like a salmon. At the top he will achieve dragonhood and fly away to his heaven. But he has no need. There can be fewer more beautiful places on Earth. SG

Kōdai-ji

Kyōto, Japan

DESIGNER: Kobori Enshu

OWNER: Unknown

GARDEN STYLE: 17th-century stroll garden

SIZE: 2 acres (0.8 ha)

CLIMATE: Humid subtropical

LOCATION: Kyoto, Kyōto

TRANSLATION: Temple of the Kodai-in (a noble title)

When Toyotomi Hideyoshi, one of the most colorful and famous of Japan's military rulers, died in 1598, his widow, Kita-no-Mandokoro, built the grand temple of Kōdai-ji to house his mausoleum. In the late eighteenth century, fires destroyed many of the original temple buildings, but those that remain are well preserved, as is this classic garden.

Kita-no-Mandokoro commissioned the leading designer of the seventeenth century, Kobori Enshu, to create one of the finest gardens of this period. It takes the visitor on a journey of corridors and exquisite buildings. From the stark simplicity of the raked gravel garden in front of the Main Hall, a raised corridor leads across a pond to the Kaisan-do, the Founder's Hall. Whiskered dragons snake across the walls inside the hall, warning of the Reclining Dragon Corridor that arches its back as it rises uphill to Otama-ya, the mausoleum of Hideyoshi and his wife. Its roof is fittingly shaped like the helmet of a samurai warrior. Beyond are two small tearooms by Sen no Rikyo. Kasa-tei, the Umbrella House, with a thatched roof shaped like a parasol, is connected by another corridor to Shigure-tei, the Rainshower House.

The temple and its gardens are delightful to visit by day, but at night they are magical. On specific dates, there are light shows in the garden. Lights line the corridors and paths, buildings and trees are illuminated in different colors, and lasers project images onto the white sand and walls of the Hashin-tei Garden in front of the abbot's chambers. SG

Ryōan-ji

Kyōto, Japan

DESIGNER: Unknown
OWNER: Ryōan-ji Temple
GARDEN STYLE: 16th-century dry landscape
SIZE: 328 square yards (300 sq. m)
CLIMATE: Humid subtropical
LOCATION: Kyoto, Kyōto
TRANSLATION: Temple of the Peaceful Dragon

Of all the enigmatic dry landscape gardens in Japan, Ryōan-ji is perhaps the most baffling to the Western visitor. It is also the most famous, an abstract masterpiece of Japanese garden design.

Created at the end of the sixteenth century as an aid to contemplation for the Rinzai sect of Zen Buddhism, it comprises five groups of three stones, on a sea of raked gravel, running from east to west. All the stones, except one, appear to point upstream. And all the stones, except one, are visible from any one viewpoint. The wall that surrounds the gravel was made of clay boiled in oil, and over time, the oil has seeped out in shadowy shapes that form illusory images, similar to pictures in a fire.

There have been many interpretations of the garden's meaning: islands, mountains piercing low clouds, tiger cubs crossing water, among others. However, the secret of this garden probably is that it has no single meaning. What most commentators do agree on, though, is that the gravel represents the void, the idea of emptiness being a central tenet of Zen Buddhism. The void is also expressed in moments of silence in traditional music, by the distance between players in Noh Theater, and by the spaces left in an ink drawing. The purpose of the barely furnished garden is to encourage the minds of spectators to fill the void with fruits of the imagination. So watch the monks slowly and repetitively rake the white gravel between the stones, and let Ryōan-ji's tranquillity spread its magic. SG

Sanzen-in

Kyōto, Japan

DESIGNER: Saicho

OWNER: Kyoto Prefecture

GARDEN STYLE: 17th-century moss and pond garden

SIZE: 1.2 acres (0.5 ha)

CLIMATE: Humid subtropical

LOCATION: Ohara, Kyoto, Kyōto

TRANSLATION: Temple of Rebirth in Paradise

Sanzen-in is a garden of quiet contemplation, with everything gentle and green, set off by the shallow water of the pond and the Temple of Rebirth in Paradise itself. The garden was built during the Edo period by Saicho, the priest who introduced Buddhism to Japan. It is highly controlled, with the area around the southeast being full of shrubs tightly clipped into small balls set among old lanterns and pagodas. It looks like a series of miniature landscapes because of the undulating contours. When it has snowed, the garden looks magical.

Water is in abundance, both in the shallow pool that has a Crane and a Tortoise Island, and in the superb waterfall. In fact the whole area around the temple has a plentiful supply of water, though it is thought that initially the pond was constructed as a backup reservoir in case of a temple fire. It was only later that it became part of the garden landscape.

The planting ranges from the small-scale to the flashily colorful. Because the humidity here is very high, the garden is fertile, resulting in possibly the best "hair moss" in Kyōto. Here and there in the garden, Japanese maples are planted in such a way that they wave across the moss in the soft, gentle breezes. In fall the leaves look almost artificially positioned as they drop onto the lush moss. As a result, the garden evokes a kind of awakening to all things concerned with earth and heaven. The best views, incidentally, are not from the temple itself, but from outside, in the garden. SY

Omotesenke Fushin'an

Kyōto, Japan

DESIGNER: Unknown
OWNER: Omotesenke Fushin'an Foundation
GARDEN STYLE: Restored 17th-century Japanese tea garden
SIZE: 0.5 acre (0.2 ha)
CLIMATE: Humid subtropical
LOCATION: Kyoto, Kyōto
TRANSLATION: Omotesenke Teahouse

This is one of the schools of tea set up in Kyoto by descendants of the renowned tea master Sen no Rikyu (1521–91), with a series of tranquil garden "rooms" that are a setting for the *roji*, or dewy path to the teahouse. The Omotesenke tea garden is divided into outer, middle, and inner gardens by gateways through which guests pass, releasing their worldly cares before acquiring the quiet, serene state of mind that is required for the tea ceremony. The path consists of natural stepping-stones and is like an unused track through a wild landscape to a hermit's hut that doubles as the teahouse. Two special qualities pervade the garden: *wabi* and *sabi*. *Wabi* is solitude amid nature, and *sabi* is a sense of antiquity.

Guests pass through the outer gate and assemble at a waiting bench before entering through a low gate that necessitates stooping in an act of humility. They then pass through the inner garden before arriving at the Fushin-an teahouse. Everything is made of natural materials, and only trees that are found growing wild on hillsides have been used, with a preference for broadleaved evergreens. Plants with bright or showy flowers are excluded, as are those with strong scents, and the floor covering is of moss or ferns. This is an exquisite garden, seemingly unchanged for hundreds of years, where you feel that every step and view has been designed to create an atmosphere of sensitivity and calm. CH

Shugaku-in Rikyu

Kyōto, Japan

DESIGNER: Gomizuno-ô
OWNER: Imperial household
GARDEN STYLE: 17th-century stroll garden
SIZE: 134 acres (54.3 ha)
CLIMATE: Humid subtropical
LOCATION: Kyoto, Kyōto
TRANSLATION: Shugaku-in Imperial Villa

Shugaku-in was built as a summer retreat for the retired Emperor Gomizuno-ô on the cool, northerly slopes of Mount Hiei. Art, calligraphy, tea ceremonies, and haiku poetry writing were conducted in the small villas, teahouses, and cottages within the garden.

Having removed a convent founded by his daughter to another site, the emperor's builders erected a large dam to create a boating lake and islands. The garden was then divided into three areas, each with its own buildings and character. From the Lower Entrance Villa, a path lined with pine trees leads off to the Middle Villa, the residence of Princess Akenomiya. The rooms have carp painted on the sliding doors; fishing nets were painted over them because it was said that they escaped at night and swam noisily in the lake, disturbing the princess.

The path continues up the slope, bounded by tall hedges that restrict the view and heighten anticipation. At the top, visitors can see the little teahouse, from where the emperor could look out over his lake and beyond, to the borrowed landscape with wooded hills and mountains in the distance,

Finally the path continues down to the boating lake, the Pond of the Bathing Dragon, where once musicians would have performed on dragon boats. An elaborate formal bridge linking two islands is mirrored in the still water. In fall the lake blazes with the reflections of hundreds of colored maples. SG

Shoden-ji

Kyōto, Japan

DESIGNER: Possibly Kobori Enshu
OWNER: The Japanese State
GARDEN STYLE: Late-17th-century Japanese temple garden
SIZE: 0.5 acre (0.2 ha)
CLIMATE: Humid subtropical
LOCATION: Kyoto, Kyōto
TRANSLATION: Divine Teachings Temple

This dramatically simple Zen temple garden, built high into a hillside and reached by a long stair climb, is in the *karesansui*, or dry landscape garden tradition, where water is symbolized, and *shakkei*, or borrowed scenery, is an important element.

The rectangular bed of white gravel is next to the *hojo*, or abbot's quarters, with a series of mounds of clipped azaleas and camellias, known as *karokomi*, arranged rhythmically in groups of three, five, and seven. They are set off in a minimal way by the backdrop of a white wall capped by a clay tile coping.

Karesansui normally involves rocks set in gravel, but here the designer has used clipped plants to represent rocks, adding a further level of symbolism. Shoden-ji is often compared to the nearby Ryōan-ji (see page 792) because they are both Zen gardens incorporating *karesansui*, and are designed to be seen from a fixed vantage point, but the use of clipped plants here is a distinguishing factor.

The Japanese gardening principle of *shakkei*, whereby a view is opened up to a feature outside the garden, making it part of the composition, is facilitated here by the wall, which acts as a division and a link with the landscape beyond, as well as screening the city below. The tile coping of the wall becomes the lower frame of the view that includes both trees and the fine profile of Mount Hiei.

What make this early Edo garden so special, though, are the experimental elements that distinguish it from later dry Japanese gardens. PCa

Shinshinan

Kyōto, Japan

DESIGNER: Ogawa Jihei
OWNER: Matsushita Konosuke
GARDEN STYLE: 19th-century stroll and dry landscape
SIZE: 1 acre (0.4 ha)
CLIMATE: Humid subtropical
LOCATION: Kyoto, Kyōto
TRANSLATION: Doubly Truthful Garden

This garden was constructed in 1890 for Someya, president of the Kanegafuchi Spinning Company, but it was the present owner who renamed the garden Shinshinan. *Shin* means truth, so *shin shin* means doubly true. And that deep respect is evident in the perfection of this garden. No footsteps ever leave a trace, and nothing disturbs even the tiniest detail. Fallen leaves are picked up each day with chopsticks, and the white sand is entirely removed, washed, and replaced each spring. Each task is seen not as a chore, but a pleasure because nothing is allowed to distract the eye from beauty or truth.

Shinshinan is entered through a small-scale copy of a ceremonial gate, whose grass-thatched roof is shaped like the helmet of a samurai warrior. As a sign of welcome, the entrance area is sprinkled with water to settle the dust and refresh the air. A narrow path then leads into the garden and up to a large pond, flashing with orange and gold koi, punctuated by stepping-stones winding across the water. A 1,000-year-old Buddhist stupa stands on a small island, surrounded by contorted, cloud pruned pines angling over the banks, as if they were on a windswept cliff. The path then leads the feet silently over fallen pine needles, through the trees to the northeast corner of the garden, where a small family shrine protects the site from evil spirits. The only sound is of a hidden, burbling stream. The final sight is a grove of cryptomeria trees rising straight from the immaculate expanse of raked white sand. SG

Saiho-ji

Kyōto, Japan

DESIGNERS: Gyoki, Muso Kokushi
OWNER: Koinzan Saiho-ji
GARDEN STYLE: 14th-century pond and dry landscape
SIZE: 4.5 acres (1.8 ha)
CLIMATE: Humid subtropical
LOCATION: Kyoto, Kyōto
TRANSLATION: Koke-dera, or The Moss Temple

Time is the true creator of the ancient, moss-green garden at Saiho-ji. One of the oldest surviving gardens in Japan, a twelfth-century paradise garden, it is believed to have been founded by the priest Gyoki in the eighth century. Then, in the fourteenth century, a monk and Zen gardener called Muso Kokushi redesigned the lower garden around a pond shaped like the Chinese character *kokoro*, which means "heart," and built the first *karesansui*, or dry landscape garden. Two pavilions were erected, neither of which exists now, but they inspired Kinkaku-ji (see page 790), and Ginkaku-ji (see page 785).

Today the lower path leads through carpets of lush moss under evergreen trees that are left to grow naturally, and over bridges to cool, leafy islands. The light filters through, shimmering on the mosses, flashing on the water. In fall the maples ignite with color, their reflections burning in the lake.

The upper dry landscape garden is divided from the natural garden below by a gateway, marking the transition into a man-made world. Rocks are set upright to suggest mountains, and gravel is used to imply a fast flowing stream leading into two ponds. This idea was so realistic that visitors sitting on a certain stone with closed eyes were said to find the image of a burbling stream so intense that water actually seemed to flow before their opened eyes. SG

RIGHT At Saiho-ji, even the bridges are covered by the moss that grows luxuriantly beneath evergreen trees.

Tenryu-ji

Kyōto, Japan

DESIGNER: Muso Soseki
OWNER: Kyōto Prefecture
GARDEN STYLE: 14th-century stroll and pond garden
SIZE: 1 acre (0.4 ha)
CLIMATE: Humid subtropical
LOCATION: Kyoto, Kyōto
TRANSLATION: Heavenly Dragon Temple

Known in Japan as the "garden among gardens," Tenryu-ji was created on a site occupied by the mountain villa of the Imperial Prince Kaneaki, son of the tenth-century Emperor Daigo. In fact it should be known as the Turtle Garden (in Japanese gardens, the turtle symbolizes the human spirit and purity).

The hill behind the temple is known as Turtle Mountain because its silhouette resembles a turtle shell, with the lower slopes representing the turtle's tail. The garden, considered one of the oldest of its kind, was laid out with a lake, also shaped like a turtle, to reflect Turtle Mountain. Other key features of the garden include its rock and waterfall area. One impressive rock group in the area is called the Dragon Gate Waterfall, which includes a stone in the shape of a carp fish. Another group of rocks, known as the Isle of the Blessed, features seven vertical stones that symbolize the Mystic Isles of the Immortals, an essential ingredient in Asian gardens. This group is said to be the most outstanding rock composition of its day. The garden is informed by Chinese paintings and Zen Buddhism, and is probably one of the best examples of the fusion of Chinese and Japanese garden art forms.

Imperial Prince Kaneaki's villa was converted into a temple in 1339 by Muso Soseki, who became the temple's first abbot. A series of fires destroyed that temple, and the present building was erected as late as 1900. Tenryu-ji is now the head temple of the Tenryu-ji branch of Rinzai Zen Buddhism. The garden was designated a World Heritage Site in 1995. SY

"The garden is informed
by Chinese paintings and
Zen Buddhism…"

Daichi-ji

Shiga, Japan

DESIGNER: Attributed to Kobori Enshu or his grandson
OWNER: Daichi-ji Temple
GARDEN STYLE: 17th-century dry landscape
SIZE: 1 acre (0.4 ha)
CLIMATE: Humid subtropical
LOCATION: Mizuguchi-cho, Shiga
TRANSLATION: Daichi-ji Paradise Garden

Zen Buddhist gardens engage with their visitors through symbolism; stones and clipped azaleas are traditionally used to represent mountains, and raked gravel to suggest water. The Horai, or Paradise Garden, at Daichi-ji Temple has other tricks up its sleeve.

The viewing platform is approached by corridors made of scented cypress wood, evoking reveries of the forested glades that grew on this site in the seventeenth century. The sound of dripping water resonates around, and hidden from view is a *suikinkutsu*, a large, buried pot. The main feature, though, next to the *shoin*, or writing hall, is the allegorical dry landscape garden, consisting of undulating mounds of clipped evergreen azaleas set in white gravel against a background of natural hillside. In the center lies a large clipped hedge, evoking the round hull of an early Japanese ship. This represents the vessel of the Seven Gods of Good Fortune, and cubes and spheres within the mound suggest its cargo of treasure being tossed by stormy seas. The gods themselves are symbolized by seven almost invisible stones around the ship.

Beneath the eaves of the platform roof there is a turtle island in the form of a clipped azalea with a projecting stone head, symbolizing longevity. Running alongside, a straight line of cypresses contrasts with the implied chaos of the waves. And just below the platform is a flat-topped rock with a pair of azaleas on either side, inviting you to step down and contemplate the garden. SG

Joju-en, Suizenji Park

Kumamoto, Japan

DESIGNER: Hosokawa Tadatosi
OWNER: Kumamoto Prefectural Government
GARDEN STYLE: 17th-century stroll and pond garden
SIZE: 15 acres (6.1 ha)
CLIMATE: Humid subtropical
LOCATION: Kumamoto, Kumamoto
TRANSLATION: The Garden Within the Park of the Temple

The approach to Suizenji Park is guarded by two of the largest stone lanterns you are ever likely to see in Japan, making you feel like a dwarf in a giant's landscape. Created by the Hosokawa family in 1632, Joju-en is reputed to be one of the six most beautiful landscape gardens in Japan.

Joju-en garden is laid out as a typical Japanese stroll garden, and that means there are miniaturized scenes within the garden depicting various Japanese landscapes. As you stroll from scene to scene, it becomes clear that the garden landscape represents the old highway from Tokyo to Kyoto and even includes, as most important Japanese gardens do, Mount Fuji and Lake Biwa. The garden is best viewed from the teahouse, specially built for the purpose during the Edo period. Here you can enjoy green tea and see the principal view beautifully framed in the doorway of the veranda. Like everything else here, it is immaculately manicured and very impressive.

At certain times of the year, there are special performances of the traditional Noh dance, performed by firelight at the Izumi Shrine, a spring water shrine, in the north of the Suizenji Park. SY

> "Like everything else here, it is immaculately manicured and very impressive"

Cheshmeh-Ali

Semnān, Iran

DESIGNER: Fath Ali Shah
OWNER: Province of Semnān
GARDEN STYLE: 19th-century formal Persian
SIZE: Unknown
CLIMATE: Semiarid
LOCATION: Damghan, Semnān
TRANSLATION: Ali's Spring

With ash trees, poplars, and willows reflected in a deep pool, and the sound of water gushing from a spring, these gardens perfectly fit Vita Sackville-West's description in *Passenger to Teheran* of the meaning of a garden in Persia as a "green cavern full of shadow." In such a parched country, it is not "flowers and their garish colours that your eyes crave for," she wrote, but "pools where gold fish dart, and the sound of little streams."

The gardens of Cheshmeh-Ali are set in a well-watered valley 17 miles (27 km) north of Damghan,

in the foothills of the southern Alborz. Snowmelt from the mountains and a gushing spring provide abundant water for the large pool. The clear spring water emerging from rocks at the western end of the garden is also collected by local Iranians and used to brew *chai*, or tea, at the water's edge.

During the early years of the nineteenth century, Fath Ali Shah (1771–1834) transformed an existing pool at Cheshmeh-Ali into a formal tank by reinforcing the steep sides. He enclosed the garden within walls of brick and baked clay that echo the color of the arid mountains outside the garden. He also built a hunting pavilion on an island in the middle of the water. This, and another building to the east, backed by a stand of white-stemmed poplars (*Populus alba* f. *pyramidalis*), are now open ruins, although the shahs continued to use the garden as a retreat from the summer heat of Tehran until the end of the nineteenth century. EH

Bagh-e Fin

Eşfahān, Iran

DESIGNER: Shah Abbas I

OWNER: Province of Eşfahān

GARDEN STYLE: 16th-century Persian *chahar bagh*, with 19th-century buildings

SIZE: 6.5 acres (2.6 ha)

CLIMATE: Semiarid

LOCATION: Fin, Eşfahān

Water has kept this garden alive for more than four centuries, and is the key to its lingering beauty. This exquisite place is located in Fin, a suburb of the city of Kāshān. Emerging from the shadows of the monumental gateway, the visitor's first and enduring impression is of water glistening in shafts of sunlight and dancing in the shade cast by the massive cypress trees lining the garden's broad central alley. This leads to a two-story pavilion, its arched roof framing blue sky and serving as a reminder of the intense heat beating down on those not fortunate enough to have passed through the gates of paradise.

Massive walls, 23 feet (7 m) high and thick enough to house cool viewing pavilions, protect the garden from the grit-laden winds that sweep across the great salt desert. The first mention of a walled garden at Fin dates to the beginning of the sixteenth century, but the great Shah Abbas I (1571–1629) was responsible for adding buildings to accommodate his court. Most were replaced by later rulers, but the garden's layout of rectangular beds divided by water channels is close to the original *chahar bagh*, or quadripartite design. Grass now grows in place of the pomegranates, jasmine, and shrub roses that would originally have filled the garden with color and scent, but restoration is in progress.

Water is brought by an underground *qanat*, or channel, from the mountains, and also comes from a spring—the Soleimaniyeh—whose discovery legend attributes to King Solomon. Stored in a great cistern, it enters the geometric garden on the highest, northern side, from where it flows into turquoise-tiled channels that run around the perimeter and traverse the terraces. The water lies static and silent in the shade of the central pavilion, shining in square basins like mirrors open to the sky, as though to receive the heavens into a place that excites the imagination as a union of the earthly and the divine. EH

Chehel Sotun

Eşfahān, Iran

DESIGNER: Shah Abbas II
OWNER: Province of Eşfahān
GARDEN STYLE: 17th-century Persian *chahar bagh*
SIZE: 6.7 acres (2.7 ha)
CLIMATE: Semiarid
LOCATION: Eşfahān, Eşfahān

Twenty slender wooden columns, doubled in number by their reflections in the still water of a long pool, account for this royal pleasure garden's name—the Garden of Forty Columns. Each column supporting the painted wooden ceiling of the pavilion's elegant *talar*, or porch, was made from a single plane tree, a rarity in a country so lacking in trees. Their simple, tapering outlines are beautiful, but once they were more ornate, being covered with colored pieces of glass and mirror. This gave an impression of such extreme lightness that the roof appeared to be unsupported and floating on air.

Paintings in the main audience hall show festive scenes that help us to imagine the garden with flowering trees and flower-studded grass spread with carpets. The buildings were hung with sumptuous curtains to keep them cool and, for evening receptions, there would have been flickering light from pyramids of lamps reflected in the mirrored walls and sparkling in the fountains and pools.

The narrow stone watercourses encircling the pavilion are now dry, and if there was a pool to the east, it no longer exists. But the palace is supremely elegant in its garden setting, especially reflected in the long tank to the west that is flanked by tall pines and plane trees, and edged with colorful, modern roses. Native elms (*Ulmus minor*) line the main walks, with massed plantings of sweetly scented Brompton stocks (*Matthiola incana*) in spring, and Banksian roses creating fountains of yellow blossoms. Pots of colorful annuals demonstrate the skill of the gardeners. EH

Bagh-e Shahzadeh

Kermān, Iran

DESIGNER: Naser ad-Douleh
OWNER: Province of Kermān
GARDEN STYLE: 19th-century Persian *chahar bagh*
SIZE: 8.5 acres (3.5 ha)
CLIMATE: Semiarid
LOCATION: Māhān, Kermān

Dominated by brooding mountains to both the north and south, and surrounded by a vast expanse of brown, barren land, Bagh-e Shahzadeh is one of the most awe-inspiring examples of the pleasure gardens created in Iran in the nineteenth century. It was built by the governor of Kermān Province in the 1880s on sloping land near the pilgrimage city of Māhān. The layout is an extended *chahar bagh* quadripartite design with a long central axis, transverse walkways, and buildings at either end.

An entrance gate set in a vast wall at the garden's southern end transports the visitor from the hot, stony desert to a garden that expresses the calm and safety of the oasis. The feeling of having entered into paradise begins in the ruined summer pavilion. This airy, two-story structure affords a view along the wide, terraced, tree-lined waterway, some 800 feet (250 m) long, that bisects the garden and drops at regular intervals to form dashing waterfalls. At the top of the slope, glimpsed at the entrance through a curtain of high water jets, is the governor's residence, now a restaurant, framed by the blue sky and snowcapped mountains beyond.

Water from the mountains, the lifeblood of the garden, is still stored outside the garden in a vast cistern. In a large, rectangular pool in front of the main pavilion, the water acts like a mirror, silent and reflecting, before it begins its cascade from one level of the shaded waterway to the next. It pauses in the pools to bring the heavens down to earth, and create a sense of openness in a space actually enclosed by massive walls and dominated by tall trees. Plane trees and cypresses prevail, overshadowing flower beds planted with modern roses. On either side of the steps flanking the waterway lie shady walks, and orchards of pears and pomegranates, where groups of picnickers spread their rugs on the rough grass and brew tea in the shade. EH

Bagh-e Doulatabad

Yazd, Iran

DESIGNER: Mohammad Taqi Khan
OWNER: Province of Yazd
GARDEN STYLE: 18th-century formal Persian
SIZE: 12 acres (5 ha)
CLIMATE: Semiarid
LOCATION: Yazd, Yazd

As a thriving oasis in the desert, this walled garden offers welcome peace and shade in a town that is reputed to endure hotter summers than any other settlement on the Iranian plateau. Here, to quote the poet, novelist, and gardener Vita Sackville-West, who visited Persia in the 1920s, "everything is dry, crumbling, and decayed; a dusty poverty, exposed for eight months of the year to a cruel sun. For all that there are gardens in Persia," she added, "but they are gardens of trees, not of flowers: green wildernesses."

The cypresses, grapevines, pomegranates, and cherry trees that grow in plots adjacent to the summer pavilion are enough to conjure Bagh-e Doulatabad's former glory. The garden was created in the mid-eighteenth century by Mohammad Taqi Khan, a governor of Yazd. It was used by his family, and also as a setting for public ceremonies and sports. The restored summer palace and ruined winter pavilion, linked by long avenues of pines, terminate vistas along a central area planted with clover.

Essential water, "the symbol of God's mercy," has been brought to the garden for more than two centuries from Mehriz, a town in the foothills of the Shirkush Mountains, 22 miles (35 km) away. It is carried by qanat, the ancient system of underground aqueducts devised to bring melting snow from the mountains to make possible the cultivation of fields and gardens. Since water is so precious and evaporates so quickly in the intense heat, the garden has no ornamental watercourses and only one pool.

Inside the shady, northwest-facing summer pavilion, there are five pools that ripple in the breeze caught by the elegant badgir, or wind tower, that, at 108 feet (33 m), is reputed to be the tallest in the world. From the interior's shadowy coolness, the garden's mantle of green, seemingly miraculous in this searing desert heat, can be glimpsed through pierced screens and stained-glass windows. EH

Bagh-e Eram

Fārs, Iran

DESIGNER: Il-Khan of the Qashqai tribe
OWNER: University of Shirāz
GARDEN STYLE: 19th-century Persian *chahar bagh*
SIZE: 57 acres (23 ha)
CLIMATE: Semiarid
LOCATION: Shirāz, Fārs

The Garden of Heaven, also known more prosaically as Eram Botanical Gardens of the University of Shirāz, features a large reflecting pool. The central waterway and cross-axial brooks were laid out in the mid-nineteenth century, but the extended *chahar bagh* (quadripartite) plan, with lateral sunken beds planted with spring flowering fruit trees, may have been created in the eighteenth century.

Water from a spring on the garden's northwestern side runs between geometric beds in the upper garden before flowing through the pavilion to the large rectangular pool. From this turquoise-tiled reflecting pool, it descends through a series of terraces and spills into the cypress-lined, transverse brooks that irrigate the garden and define its layout.

Displays of terra-cotta flowerpots with scented stocks and marigolds mimic Persian carpets near the entrance. The upper garden is a riot of colorful annuals and irises planted among shrubs. In the lower garden, an avenue of tall cypress trees provides shade for orange groves. There is an area for the display of a great variety of traditional as well as introduced plants, many with labels in Latin. Flowering Judas trees (*Cercis siliquastrum*) predominate in spring and early summer among palms, lilacs, golden rain trees (*Koelreuteria paniculata*), and photinias to create one of the most interestingly planted gardens in Iran. Summer exotics include salvias, zinnias, and four o'clocks (*Mirabilis jalapa*) from the New World. It is worth lingering among the orange trees, white mulberries, and roses to hear a nightingale sing. EH

Naranjestan

Fārs, Iran

DESIGNER: Qavam al-Mulk
OWNER: Province of Fārs
GARDEN STYLE: 19th-century formal Persian
SIZE: 1.6 acres (0.6 ha)
CLIMATE: Semiarid
LOCATION: Shirāz, Fārs

This beautiful garden in the city of Shirāz is known as the Naranjestan for its orange trees. Known also as Bagh-i-Qavam, it demonstrates how the classical Persian garden, enclosed by high walls and shaded by tall trees, could serve the needs of a powerful family in the nineteenth century.

The complex was built by the Qavam al-Mulk, head of the Khamseh tribal federation, in 1870. The single-story entrance building is the *biruni*, or office, from which there is a view along the garden's main axis to the grand *talar*, or reception hall. Between is the elaborately patterned water garden. A narrow, blue-tiled brook, some 250 feet (80 m) long, runs down the center and opens out into deeper, circular and elliptical pools where fountains once played. Transverse pathways allow closer inspection of triangular flower beds set in grass and filled with colorful bedding, including pansies, poppies, and Brompton stocks. Orange trees line the paths, and at the back the beds are filled with roses and perennials shaded by tall date palms (*Phoenix dactylifera*).

Ivy-clad arches at the path ends lead to the area in front of the reception hall, with a reflecting basin that feeds the brook running down the center of the garden. If the awnings that protect the hall from bright sunlight are tied back, the water shimmers, catching the light from the ornate mirrorwork on the hall's ceiling. This conjures a magical scene of the garden in its heyday, when light from chandeliers would be seen dancing off the mirrorwork and the reflecting pool as people walked toward the hall. EH

Bagh-i-Babur

Kābul, Afghanistan

DESIGNER: Zahiruddin Babur

OWNER: Aga Khan Trust for Culture

GARDEN STYLE: 16th to 19th-century formal Mughal

SIZE: 27 acres (11 ha)

CLIMATE: Continental warm summer

LOCATION: Kābul, Kābul

On the Sher-e-Darwaza Mountain on the edge of Kābul, Bagh-i-Babur was one of the first Mughal "paradise gardens." The Emperor Babur laid it out before he founded the Mughal dynasty. The word *paradise* in modern Persian is linked to *pairi*, meaning around, and *diz*, meaning form. For the Mughals, the garden represented the idea of heaven on earth, and Babur demonstrated this in his clever balance of walls, trees, flowers, space, symmetry, and water. In fact he created such a tranquil and harmonious garden that he decided to be buried here, making it the first tomb garden of that period.

Bagh-i-Babur received sporadic attention from subsequent rulers, such as Shah Jahan, the constructor of the Taj Majal, who also built Babur's tomb. Centuries of neglect and war, not to mention years of drought and a large earthquake in 1842, have seen these gardens and their historical buildings deteriorate and decay. In some ways, Bagh-i-Babur, and its need for reconstruction, is a metaphor for Afghanistan. Since 2002, organizations such as AKDN, UNESCO, and local bodies have collaborated in rebuilding the garden to its initial design, and the gardens are nearing completion. With the growth of the seedlings, plants, and saplings, Bagh-i-Babur will soon become a large, open, peaceful public space, with its shallow amphitheater and ornamented stone Mughal terraces, once covered magnificently in plane trees and jasmine flowers, violets, and wild roses, and the carefully engineered waterway that descends from the terraces to the garden's center. MBr

Jahangir's Tomb Garden

Punjab, Pakistan

DESIGNER: Nur Jahan
OWNER: The Government of Pakistan
GARDEN STYLE: 17th-century Islamic-Mughal
SIZE: 67 acres (27.1 ha)
CLIMATE: Semiarid
LOCATION: Lahore, Punjab

The tomb of the fourth Mughal emperor, Jahangir, who reigned from 1605 to 1627, is one of the finest of the great tomb gardens of northern India, and well illustrates the tendency in the Muslim world to make places of rest both beautiful and recreational. With his gifted wife, Nur Jahan, whose less-well-preserved tomb is on the other side of the nearby railroad track, he was responsible for some of the finest gardens in India, notably the Shalimar gardens of Kashmir. Nur Jahan is reputed to have designed this garden, though the building was commissioned by their son Shah Jahan. Construction probably began in 1637.

As with other Mughal tomb gardens, it is the imposing and relentless geometry that so impresses the visitor, although much of the detail awaits restoration, with the outer reaches of the garden fading into wilderness. The tomb itself is shaped like an overturned table, in red and cream sandstone, with a minaret at each corner. Inside, the tombs and their surroundings include marble and semiprecious stone inlay work, incorporating many floral motifs.

Axes, each including what was once a canal, accompanied by regularly spaced, clipped trees, radiate out from the tomb toward four substantial gatehouses. As with other Mughal tomb gardens, each square of the pattern is subdivided and centered on a tank, from which radiate further axes with accompanying canals and trees.

Today the garden functions as a public park where you will see games of cricket, family picnics, and small outdoor religious schools. NK

Shalimar Bagh

Punjab, Pakistan

DESIGNER: Unknown
OWNER: The Government of Pakistan
GARDEN STYLE: 17th-century Islamic-Mughal
SIZE: 40 acres (16.2 ha)
CLIMATE: Semiarid
LOCATION: Lahore, Punjab

Laid out between 1633 and 1642, these pleasure gardens were created for the Emperor Shah Jahan and his court to celebrate the completion of a canal bringing water to Lahore. The scale is vast, making this one of the most rewarding of the surviving Mughal garden complexes. The gardens are arranged in three stepped areas, ascending from the former entrance. The first level is dominated by a wide canal, whose fountains still work, and the second by pavilions and a substantial, highly ornamental tank.

One of the great joys of this garden is the level of surviving ornamentation and the wide array of Mughal garden features. Paths are brick and, although eroding, can be appreciated for their patterning. The central tank and its accompanying pavilions are a particular delight, and it requires little imagination to hear the water and imagine the sights of the opulent Mughal court. Fine marble fretwork is a particularly lovely feature around the main pavilion, along with finely shaped waterways and ranks of carved niches for lights. Originally water would have flowed over a series of slopes, cooling the pavilion and reflecting the light of thousands of oil lamps. The tank has walkways that cross the water to a central platform, and a scalloped border adorns its edge.

The outskirts of Lahore are kept at bay by a great boundary wall of red brick with decorative alcoves and occasional domes. Trees, both natural and shaped, are a notable feature throughout the garden, and the shapes of what were once flower beds are still clearly visible through the grass. NK

Shalamar Bagh

Jammu and Kashmir, India

DESIGNERS: Emperor Jahangir, Emperor Shah Jahan
OWNER: The Indian State
GARDEN STYLE: 17th-century Persian *chahar bagh*
SIZE: 24.2 acres (9.8 ha)
CLIMATE: Humid subtropical
LOCATION: Srinigar, Jammu and Kashmir

A stately atmosphere pervades the Shalamar Bagh, or Abode of Love, the most celebrated of the royal gardens. Set between the hills and the languid waters of Lake Dal, it was built as a summer residence by the Mughal Emperor Jahangir in 1619 for his Empress Nur Jahan. It was completed by his son Shah Jahan.

The ground plan is an extended *chahar bagh*, or quadripartite design, with four terraces and, originally, a pavilion in a rectangular pool at the crossing point of the canals. The transverse channels have long been filled in, but the black marble pavilion built by Shah Jahan has been restored and water,

coming from a spring augmented by snowmelt, still bisects the garden. The water fills a pool at the top of the garden, cascades over shallow terraces, spouts in fountains around the pavilion in the women's garden, the *zenana*, and finally flows through a central canal in the Emperor's Garden and onward to the lake.

It used to be possible to arrive at the garden by boat, via the long canal that still runs through willow groves and rice fields, but the approach has been truncated by a road. From the entrance, the view is of plane trees towering above lawns, clipped hedges, and well-kept flower beds at either side of a central canal edged with stone and fringed by roses. Above the first cascade sits the emperor's throne, a black marble platform reached by stepping-stones; stone bases are all that remain of the Hall of Public Audience. Beyond are the kiosks that flank the entrance to the women's garden. Formerly lamps were lit in the niches behind the cascades. EH

Nishat Bagh

Jammu and Kashmir, India

DESIGNER: Asaf Khan
OWNER: The Indian State
GARDEN STYLE: 17th-century Persian *chahar bagh*
SIZE: 44 acres (17.8 ha)
CLIMATE: Humid subtropical
LOCATION: Srinigar, Jammu and Kashmir

Set on a steeply sloping hill, with the Zabarwan Mountains as its backdrop and views out to the serene Lake Dal, this is the most dramatic of the Mughal gardens in Kashmir. There is a story that soon after Nishat Bagh was built in 1633, Emperor Shah Jahan decided it was too splendid to be owned by a subject, even though the subject in question was Asaf Khan, his prime minister and father-in-law. Envious, perhaps, of the garden's vivacity compared with his peaceful Shalamar nearby, the emperor ordered the water, which also supplied the royal garden, to be diverted. With the fountains silent, Nishat lost its very reason for being until a servant risked his life by restoring the flow. Instead of receiving punishment, his master was allowed to draw water from the stream supplying Shalamar.

Massive plane trees suit the grand scale of the terraces. These ascend the mountain, each rising higher than the one before. Originally the terraces numbered twelve, one for each sign of the zodiac, though the lowest is now cut off from the waterfront by the modern road. Abundant water runs down the terraces in wide channels bisecting the garden, and ripples down carved stone ramps called *chadar*, pausing to dance in rectangular pools with myriad fountains. Stone or marble thrones ornament the head of virtually every waterfall in the garden.

Flower beds at nearly every level add well-orchestrated color to the garden. There are narrow bands of gold marigolds, sheets of mixed poppies, blocks of massed pansies, clarkias, cosmos, and beds of roses and lilies among clipped evergreens. The 18-foot-high (5.5 m) retaining wall of the last terrace runs the full width of the garden to octagonal towers at the perimeter, with inner stairways leading to the secluded women's garden, the *zenana*, high on the hillside. There can be few more exciting views of the lake than those to be had from here. EH

Achabal

Jammu and Kashmir, India

DESIGNER: Nur Jahan
OWNER: The Indian State
GARDEN STYLE: 17th-century Persian
SIZE: 10.9 acres (4.4 ha)
CLIMATE: Humid subtropical
LOCATION: Achabal, Jammu and Kashmir

Children and adults line up for the thrill of crossing the top of the great cascade at Achabal—also known as the Begumabad or Queen's Garden—by way of the stepping-stones that appear to sit precariously near its edge. They leap bravely from stone to stone or crouch to touch the icy water as it ripples by, gathering speed before falling as a roaring torrent.

This huge waterfall is the crowning glory of an especially watery Mughal garden, built into the mountains 31 miles (49.6 km) south of Srinigar. The ancient spring of Achabal, gushing out of the mountainside, is perhaps the largest in Kashmir.

It feeds a waterway that bisects the space, rushing from a reservoir at the top of the garden, down the great cascade, and into a wide, still pool with rows of fountain jets, an airy island pavilion set within it. The water dashes on through a central pavilion at a lower level to fall again, now flanked by beds of standard roses and seasonal bedding as it flows toward the entrance and a river beyond the gates.

Unusually for a Mughal garden, most of which are bisected by a central watercourse, at Achabal there are two stone side channels running parallel to the main one. Here the water ripples over sunlit *chadar*—carved stone ramps that link the terraces—and runs through wide lawns in the shade of vast plane trees. Beside these watercourses, stone platforms are set between the trees as places to sit. Originally these would have been shaded by canopies and spread with carpets, but today they are simply enjoyed as they are by Achabel's hordes of visitors. EH

Pari Mahal

Jammu and Kashmir, India

DESIGNER: Dara Shukoh
OWNER: The Indian State
GARDEN STYLE: 17th-century formal
SIZE: 12.8 acres (5.2 ha)
CLIMATE: Humid subtropical
LOCATION: Srinigar, Jammu and Kashmir

From the shores of Lake Dal, Pari Mahal can be seen by day perched 600 feet (190 m) high on a spur of the Zebanwan Mountain. At night its position—above the other pleasure gardens around the lake—is illuminated to further enhance its romantic name, which means Fairy Palace. It was built in 1640 by Emperor Shah Jahan's favorite son, the ill-starred Mughal prince Dara Shukoh, who was beheaded in 1659 by order of his younger brother, Aurangzeb.

Pari Mahal is thought to have been not only a pleasure garden for the prince and his retinue, but also a school of astrology for his spiritual guide and counselor, Akhund Mullah Shah—astrology was central to the thinking of the Mughals. There were originally seven terraces, representing the known planets. Retained by arched walls, the fifth of these had a pigeon house, and the seventh a square building, possibly an observatory. There are traces of watercourses, fountains, and tanks, including a large rectangular water basin with stone sides, but Pari Mahal differs from other Kashmiri gardens in that there are no water chutes. It seems that most of the water was conducted by underground earthen pipes.

The octagonal bastions at either end of an upper terrace offer panoramic views of the snowcapped Pir Panjal and the tranquil lake, and, midway across, the Char Chenar, the Isle of the Plane Trees, an artificial 0.5-acre (0.2 ha) island that was a favorite Mughal picnic ground. Lying just above water level, the trees, thought to have been planted at each corner by Shah Jahan, seem to float on the water. EH

Vernag

Jammu and Kashmir, India

DESIGNER: Emperor Jahangir
OWNER: The Indian State
GARDEN STYLE: 17th-century formal water garden
SIZE: 9.9 acres (4 ha)
CLIMATE: Humid subtropical
LOCATION: Srinigar, Jammu and Kashmir

Emperor Jahangir so loved Vernag that he prayed with his dying breath to be conveyed there for burial. Sadly the dead emperor was carried instead to Lahore. Today's Vernag is a shadow of its former self, but it is easy to understand why Jahangir and his wife Nur Jahan so loved it. Even now the road from Srinigar along the River Jhelum makes the garden seem remote, but the journey is worthwhile, just to see the octagonal pool of kingfisher-blue water glittering against a backdrop of pine-covered hills.

Vernag's spring is believed to have flowed from the fountain of heaven. The site had long been a place of worship when, in 1609, the emperor ordered the building of stone sides for the pool, "halls with domes and houses about," and a garden with a canal such that "travelers over the world can point out few like it." With a stone walkway surrounded by arcades, the surviving buildings may have formed the fountain court of Jahangir's palace.

The still water in the pool transforms into a rushing torrent as it flows between two huge plane trees. It passes into a stone-edged canal that runs for almost 330 yards (305 m), then down a ruined chute into a pool on what may have been a lower terrace (now a fish farm). At either side of this 12-foot-wide (3.5 m) canal, walkways run between narrow beds of bright flowers, including sweet Williams (*Dianthus barbatus*), pansies, marigolds, and California poppies (*Platystemon californicus*) set in grass panels. Behind low, clipped hedges, emerald lawns spread out, set with plane trees and flowering shrubs. EH

The Rock Garden

Punjab/Haryana, India

DESIGNER: Nek Chand
OWNER: Nek Chand
GARDEN STYLE: 20th-century idiosyncratic, sculptural
SIZE: 25 acres (10.1 ha)
CLIMATE: Humid subtropical
LOCATION: Chandigarh, Punjab/Haryana

The Rock Garden at Chandigarh has been honored with an appearance on an Indian postage stamp, and some call it India's greatest artistic achievement since the Taj Mahal. That is clearly debatable, but the two do share one common characteristic: Both were created by dedicated, passionate individuals.

Located to the northeast of the city, the Rock Garden, with its winding paths and informality (it is actually more of a sculpture garden than a rock garden), provides a contrast with Le Corbusier's regular layout of the city. This very eclectic garden began life some thirty-three years ago when the designer Nek Chand, then a transport official, devoted his evenings after work to clearing a patch of jungle to make a small garden, constructing it from recycled materials. In the intervening years, the garden has grown in size and Nek has gained a well-deserved international reputation.

The Rock Garden, a fantasyland intended to represent a lost kingdom, is now an agglomeration of fourteen courtyards linked by walks, large buildings, a series of waterfalls and streams, and thousands of sculptures, mostly covered in mosaics, and depicting various aspects of Indian society and life, as well as the subcontinent's wildlife.

This is one of the world's most unusual and idiosyncratic gardens, and it is the work of a man with a vision, artistic integrity, and a sense of fun and social responsibility. The beauty is in the detail. It certainly makes an unforgettable contrast with the Taj Mahal, whose gardens need some careful restoration. TM

Bagh-i Hayat Bakhsh

Delhi, India

DESIGNER: Shah Jahan
OWNER: The Indian State
GARDEN STYLE: 17th-century Mughal *chahar bagh*
SIZE: 0.04 acre (0.01 ha)
CLIMATE: Semiarid
LOCATION: The Red Fort, Delhi, Delhi

The fortress palace of Shajahanabad, built by the Mughal Emperor Shah Jahan from 1639 to 1648, and now known as the Red Fort, was conceived as a symbol of good government, a terrestrial image of paradise, described in the Koran as "gardens underneath which rivers flow." Architecturally the complex is superb, but it takes imagination to conjure the cooling effect of the now dry water channel, called the Nahr-i Bihisht (River of Paradise), which links the series of airy pavilions along the terrace. Of the paradisiacal imagery, little remains except exquisite *jail*, or filigree screens, and the *pietra dura*, or semiprecious stone inlay, which turns the walls into ever blooming flower beds.

Of real plants there are few, and it requires a great imaginative leap to see beyond the heat and dust. The largest and most impressive garden, the Bagh-i Hayat Bakhsh, or Life-Giving Garden, is a *chahar bagh*, or quadripartite design, with wide walkways of sandstone bisected by water channels that meet at a central tank, on which stands a summer pavilion. Imagine this screened and cooled by silver fountains—forty-nine on the platform, 119 bordering the sides of the tank, and thirty in each canal—throwing spray high into the air. Replace the grass plots with fruit trees underplanted with yellow, crimson, and purple flowers, and the weeping evergreens with stately rows of shade-giving cypresses. Then the vision of a paradise garden of "perfect freshness and pleasantness," as the emperor's historian described it, will be complete. EH

Gardens of Emperor Humayun's Tomb

Delhi, India

DESIGNERS: Sayyid Muhammad, Mirak Sayyid Ghiyath
OWNER: The Government of India
GARDEN STYLE: 16th-century Persian *chahar bagh*
SIZE: 30 acres (12.2 ha)
CLIMATE: Semiarid
LOCATION: Delhi, Delhi

Sacred ashoka trees (*Saraca indica*) line the enclosure leading to Emperor Humayun's tomb garden. From the entrance, you emerge into bright light to see the mausoleum set in a vast, flat, open space of emerald lawns defined by low, evergreen hedges, and by gravel causeways and narrow water channels.

The sandstone tomb is set on an arcaded, sandstone platform 21 feet (6.4 m) high. It was built by the second Mughal emperor's senior widow, the Persian-born Haji Begum, at his son Akbar's direction, and was completed in 1570. It is set in the center of India's earliest extant Mughal garden, still preserved in its original form, the plot being divided in four by broad gravel walks, with each quarter divided again by narrower walks to make thirty-two square plots.

Water enters the garden by the northern gatehouse, where it trickles down a chevron patterned *chadar*, or carved water chute, to feed narrow, cut-limestone brooks. Some 14 inches (35 cm) wide, these run around the garden's perimeter, down the center of the main walks, and encircle the tomb. Channels bisecting the garden are intersected by square pools, and those running around the tomb meet at octagonal pools at each corner. Cypress trees line the walkways, and tall palms cast shadows near the tomb. There are beautiful trees such as neem (*Azadirachta indica*) and the sacred fig (*Ficus religiosa*), as well as flowering hibiscus and citrus. However, shades of brown and green predominate, with no garish annuals to detract from the garden's purpose as a reflection of paradise beyond the earthly. EH

Rashtrapati Bhavan

Delhi, India

DESIGNER: Edwin Lutyens
OWNER: The Government of India
GARDEN STYLE: 20th-century Islamic-Mughal, English
SIZE: 13 acres (5.3 ha)
CLIMATE: Semiarid
LOCATION: New Delhi, Delhi

A strong case can be made for this being one of the most exceptional gardens of the twentieth century; the designer and writer David Hicks certainly thought so. It is a modern version of a Mughal garden, with definite touches of the 1930s, created by Edwin Lutyens for the viceroy of the British Empire in India. It is now the garden of the official residence of the president of India. Work on the garden began in traditional Mughal style in 1918 as part of the construction of New Delhi, and was partly inspired by the interest of Lady Hardinge, vicereine from 1910 to 1916, and other members of her circle.

Lutyens combined the geometry of the classic Islamic garden with contemporary monumentalism and architectural detailing to create a tour de force that relates to the central axis of the palace, as well as the building's architecture. Its dominant, warm red sandstone with contrasting creamy layers is typical of Mughal monuments in northern India.

Water is a major part of the garden, with a square canal defining a central area of lawn, and several fountains designed to look like lotus leaves. There is a basic framework of trees, including the umbrella-shaped, clipped maulari (*Mimusops elengi*), a classic tree of Mughal gardens, and roses, but the main planting interest comes from the spring display of annuals, all grown in an adjoining nursery and planted out in late winter. Cottage-garden favorites, such as stocks and marigolds, rub shoulders with more vibrant, subtropical species, creating an impression of exuberant abundance. NK

Amber Palace Garden

Rajasthan, India

DESIGNERS: Raja Man Singh, Raja Jai Singh, Sawai Jai Singh
OWNER: Government of Rajasthan
GARDEN STYLE: 16th–18th century mixed Indian
SIZE: 0.5 acre (0.2 ha)
CLIMATE: Semiarid
LOCATION: Amber, Rajasthan

Jaipur was the capital of the powerful Rajput state from 1037 until 1728. The city rose to preeminence with the marriage of the Rajput princess Jodh Bai to Akbar, the third Mughal emperor. The birth in 1569 of her son and his heir, Jahangir, further helped to consolidate Mughal power and Rajput influence. One of the palaces that Akbar built for his favorite wife was at his new capital, Fatehpur Sikri, and the fact that he allowed her to continue to worship as a Hindu demonstrated his religious tolerance.

The Amber Palace stands on a hillside overlooking the Maotha Lake, some 7 miles (11 km) from Jaipur, and the first phase of construction was started in 1592 by Raja Man Singh, a commander in Akbar's army. It was completed about 200 years later by Mirza Raja Jai Singh and Sawai Jai Singh. Like the red sandstone and white marble palace, the gardens—two main ones, a smaller enclosed garden, and the larger lake garden—reflect both Akbar's Islamic beliefs and Jodh Bai's Hinduism. The gardens are based on the Islamic concept of a *chahar bagh* garden, defined by its central water source and quadripartite design, each section being further subdivided into a series of geometric beds.

Set within the lake, the larger garden looks as if it floats upon the surface like a moored ship, its terraces composed of a series of complicated parterres, their pattern picked out in stone. The overriding motif or pattern is the star, which was of particular importance to the Seljuk Turks (who had settled in the area), representing intellectual powers and life itself. TM

Sahelion-ki-Bari

Rajasthan, India

DESIGNER: Maharana Sangram Singh II
OWNER: Government of Rajasthan
GARDEN STYLE: 18th-century Hindu
SIZE: 3 acres (1.2 ha)
CLIMATE: Semiarid
LOCATION: Udaipur, Rajasthan

Water is the source of life and fun in this pleasure garden, which is one of the finest examples of a Hindu "rain" garden. Built by Maharana Sangram Singh II and also known as the Maids of Honor Garden, it is believed to have been designed as a cool summer retreat for the forty-eight maids who accompanied the Maharana's wife as dowry. Later Maharana Bhopal Singhji constructed a pavilion of "rain fountains" to create the illusion of rain dancing to the rhythm of the dancing maids. Maharana Fateh Singh reconstructed the gardens in the late nineteenth century after they were substantially damaged by floods.

Lying at a lower level than Fateh Sagar Lake, the garden's beautiful pools and fountains are gravity-fed. The main pool has a white marble *chhatri*, or umbrella-shaped pavilion, in the center, glimpsed through a curtain of water that splashes down onto a platform. Contrasting black marble *chhatri*s at the four corners of the pond have sculpted birds on the roofs that once spurted water from their beaks.

Marble pathways lined with palm trees lead to extensive lawns, shady walks, fruit trees, and a rose garden with more than 100 varieties, as well as further fountains and exotic pools, including one overlooked by a fine stone throne. Here four marble elephants preside over a circular tank planted with cannas that flower in October. A curtain of "rain" created by fountain jets surrounds the pool, and in its center is a tiered fountain with marble lions. Once the reserve of frolicking royal ladies in the hottest months of the year, the garden is now a popular tourist spot. EH

Udaivilas Gardens

Rajasthan, India

DESIGNER: Bill Bensley
OWNER: Oberoi Hotel Group
GARDEN STYLE: Contemporary
SIZE: 30 acres (12.1 ha)
CLIMATE: Semiarid
LOCATION: Udaipur, Rajasthan

Set on the banks of Lake Pichola, one of the most picturesque lakes in Rajasthan, the recently created Udaivilas Gardens are an exciting and very modern interpretation of traditional styles on a site surrounded by historical references. To the south lie the Aravalli Hills with the Monsoon Palace, built by Maharana Sajjan Singh in 1884, perched on a distant summit. To the east stands the majestic Udaipur City Palace, begun in 1559 by Maharana Udai Singh II, founder of the city. In the lake itself are the island palaces of Jag Niwas, built in 1754, where the James Bond movie *Octopussy* was filmed, and Jag Mandir.

Arriving from the water, the new hotel looks like a yellow sandstone palace set in a landscape of well-watered lawns and flowering shrubs, punctuated by the tall, flowering spikes of agaves. Near the landing stage there are pools packed with pink and mauve lotus, and from here the ground rises through mown grass, where natural and introduced rocky outcrops are planted with ornamental grasses, including purple fountain grass (*Pennisetum setaceum* 'Rubrum').

Arriving by land, a tree-lined avenue leads to an entrance where stone elephants and buildings, and clipped trees set in panels of grass, are mirrored in dark reflecting pools. The first inner courtyard garden has a marble lotus pool as its central feature, with panels of grass and clipped foliage plantings in raised, stone-edged beds. A series of labyrinthine courtyards running through the buildings leads to a Mughal inspired, stepped water garden and an immaculately clipped, star-shaped parterre. EH

Samode Bagh

Rajasthan, India

DESIGNER: Rawal Sheo Singhji
OWNER: Nathawat Singhs of the Samode Hotel Group
GARDEN STYLE: 18th-century formal Mughal *chahar bagh*
SIZE: 20 acres (8 ha)
CLIMATE: Semiarid
LOCATION: Alwar, Rajasthan

After bumping along the dusty road through the dry and rugged Aravalli hills, it is a relief to enter the peaceful Samode Bagh, now restored and open to visitors as a luxurious hotel, where the air is cooled by pools and fountains fed by natural springs and wells. Hidden from prying eyes by 15-foot-high (4.5 m) stone walls, this large, Mughal-style garden paradise was built as a garden for relaxation and privacy by a son of the illustrious Pritviraj Singh Ji of Amber in the mid-eighteenth century.

From the imposing gateway, the view is of a long canal in which fountains dance in dappled sunlight.

Wide raised walkways are at either side, and the water is framed by massed plantings, first of purple hearts (*Tradescantia pallida*) and then by emerald-green groundcover, contained within raised, stone-edged beds. Transverse paths divide the garden into the canonical, Mughal-style *chahar bagh*, or quadripartite garden, with sunken plots in which massive trees cast welcome shade over well-watered lawns.

Through an elegant marble pavilion, there are glimpses of arching fountains in a raised water tank and of the main pavilion, beyond which are other water tanks, one of them packed with lotus. The Samode Bagh served originally as a summer retreat and hunting lodge. The main pavilion is a perfect spot from which to watch the last rays of the sun caught in droplets of fountain water. Be sure to see the bathing pool with its arcaded surrounding walls and steep, marble waterslide—you can almost hear the sound of eighteenth-century laughter. EH

Dhobi Mahal

Rajasthan, India

DESIGNER: Emperor Shah Jahan
OWNER: Unknown
GARDEN STYLE: 17th-century *chahar bagh*
SIZE: 0.4 acre (0.2 ha)
CLIMATE: Semiarid
LOCATION: Bari, Rajasthan

Strung along the shores of Lake Talab Shahi, crumbling *chhatri*, or domed kiosks, their roofs sprouting vegetation, point the way to the small, isolated garden that is now known as Dhobi Mahal, or the Palace of the Washer Man or Woman. Now the garden is overrun with weeds, rubble, and monkeys, and the water channels are dry and barely visible. Nevertheless, the garden and, indeed, the whole crumbling complex offer a fascinating glimpse of the Mughal grandeur associated with the royal hunt.

The ruined garden is one of several walled enclosures that form part of the Lal Mahal, a massive hunting palace built entirely in red sandstone by Emperor Shah Jahan. It was completed in 1637 and later maintained by the rulers of Dholpur. The Dhobi Mahal consists of a waterfront pavilion flanked by pillared wings with a raised terrace that looks out over Lake Talab Shahi, home to a wealth of migratory birds. On the other side, the pavilion terrace has a sunken pool and overlooks a lower, rectangular *chahar bagh*, or quadripartite garden. The once planted areas, now filled with weeds and rubbish, are defined by raised walkways around the perimeter and transverse paths that radiate from a raised central pool, now filled in. The remains of small waterfalls with niches for oil lamps or flowers indicate that the central pool originally supplied water to the shallow channels running along the center of the walkways.

This is a must-see garden, so long as you let history, a vivid imagination, and the abundant wildlife compensate for the lack of horticultural interest. EH

Neemrana

Rajasthan, India

DESIGNER: Aman Nath
OWNER: Neemrana Hotels Group
GARDEN STYLE: Varied
SIZE: 25 acres (10.1 ha)
CLIMATE: Semiarid
LOCATION: Neemrana, Alwar, Rajasthan

Perched on a plateau in the Aravalli Hills, 65 miles (105 km) southwest of Delhi, this raja's fort-palace was built after 1464. It is a vast, eleven-tiered building hanging on to the hillside with countless terraces on different levels, and superb views of the surrounding plain dotted with humpbacked hills. Enormous wooden doors, big enough for an elephant to pass through, form the grand entrance and, wherever there is a pocket of earth or room for a pot, there are flowers and foliage. Annuals in spring are used to make colorful carpets beside the paths, species roses form elegant screens, and the delicate scent of frangipani wafts in the air. Most impressive of all is the bougainvillea, in magenta and white, forming cascades of color down the precipitous walls.

Neemrana fort-palace and gardens have been in the process of restoration and reconstruction as a hotel since 1986. Many-layered hanging gardens have been planted on the terraced hill incorporated within the new fort-palace wings, where queen of the night (*Selenicereus grandiflorus*) sweetens the air after sunset. The Mukut Bagh, or Crown Garden, literally crowns the whole building with top-lit palms and a small sandstone kiosk with a bronze horse. The majesty of the view is awesome. As the former British High Commissioner to India Sir Nicholas Fenn wrote in the visitor's book, "Travel in India is good for the mind; Neemrana is good for the soul." EH

RIGHT The fifteenth-century fort-palace of Neemrana looms majestically over exuberant planting, much of it in pots.

Palace Gardens of Deeg

Rajasthan, India

DESIGNER: Suraj Mal, Rajah of Bharatpur
OWNER: The Indian State
GARDEN STYLE: 18th-century Persian *chahar bagh*
SIZE: 0.02 acre (0.01 ha)
CLIMATE: Semiarid
LOCATION: Bharatpur, Rajasthan

The fountains at the Palace Gardens of Deeg may be silent, but the pavilions, walkways, and the pointed arch of a finely carved, white marble swing are enough to make you envisage these water gardens at their best in the eighteenth century, when the "special effects" included the sound of thunder created by heavy balls rolling around on a roof.

The marble swing, brought to Deeg by Raja Surajmal as a war trophy from the Mughal court of Delhi, is set on a platform under the trees at one end of a watercourse overlooking the garden. Here, on ropes made of scented fiber and covered by wreaths of flowers, the fortunate user could swing through a fountain spray. Bulls harnessed to large leather buckets in a complicated pulley system labored for sixty days to draw water and fill the massive water tank, which fed the swing and the fountains in the middle of the garden. Today for the festival of Holi that marks the end of winter, motorized pumps take twenty-four hours to fill the tank for water displays in all colors of the rainbow.

A broad terrace with a central watercourse leads from the main gate to the palaces and pavilions surrounding a large, square garden that overlooks a bathing tank. The garden plan is in an extended *chahar bagh*, being divided into sixteen sections, first by four raised sandstone walkways with water channels and lotus-bud fountain jets that meet at a central octagonal pool. Sloping water chutes take the water (when it is running) to the lower level, which is further divided by walkways. Lawns and flower beds now fill these plots where originally fruit trees would have blossomed in flower-studded grass.

Inlaid flower patterns that rival the beautiful examples at Agra's Red Fort adorn the marble walls of the *zenana*, or women's quarters, which looks out on to a delightful fourfold garden tucked away in a corner of the complex. EH

I'timad-ud-Daulah's Tomb Garden

Uttar Pradesh, India

DESIGNER: Empress Nur Jahan
OWNER: Archaeological Survey of India
GARDEN STYLE: 17th-century Persian *chahar bagh*
SIZE: 5.7 acres (2.3 ha)
CLIMATE: Semiarid
LOCATION: Agra, Uttar Pradesh

This tomb lies in the center of a *chahar bagh*, or quadripartite garden, as if it were a precious casket set on bands of rubies in a bed of emeralds. The building, known locally today as the "mini-Taj," is exquisite, and the garden is one of the best preserved of those that lined the River Jumna in the Mughal city of Agra. The white marble tomb was built in 1628 by Nur Jahan, Emperor Jahangir's queen, for her father. It stands on a platform of red sandstone and is inlaid with lapis, onyx, topaz, jasper, and cornelian in elaborate geometric and floral designs, including the cypress (symbolizing longevity) entwined with the blossom of rejuvenation. Inside, the tomb is suffused with light coming through *jail*, or filigree screens.

Water entered the garden via a carved chute, and was collected in an octagonal tank that is still visible in the corner on the river, before feeding the channels that delineate the perimeter and the quartered plots of the *chahar bagh* ground plan. Broad, stone walkways, each with a central narrow water channel that widens into a square tank and fountain, divide the garden into quarters and, on the west side, lead to a waterfront pavilion built of red sandstone inlaid with marble shapes depicting vases and bottles. Steps (not in use), with flower beds at either side, descend to the river. There are also bands and rectangles of brightly colored annuals set in the grass plots between the walkways, where fruit trees would have blossomed in the spring. EH

The Garden of Diwan-i Amm

Uttar Pradesh, India

DESIGNER: Emperor Akbar the Great
OWNER: Archaeological Survey of India
GARDEN STYLE: 16th-century Mughal *chahar bagh*
SIZE: 0.4 acre (0.2 ha)
CLIMATE: Semiarid
LOCATION: Fatehpur Sikri, Uttar Pradesh

In the deserted Mughal palace at Fatehpur Sikri, narrow brooks traverse vast paved courtyards, including one marked out as a giant pachisi board where Emperor Akbar the Great played with his courtiers, using sixteen young slaves from his harem as living pieces. But the huge tank that supplied the water now holds little more than a green dribble, and the shallow channels have been dry for centuries— indeed the lack of water is cited as one of the reasons Akbar moved his court to Lahore in 1585, only fifteen years after building the complex of airy, sandstone palaces and courtyards.

Even without water, the sunken garden to the west of the Diwan-i Amm, or public audience chamber, is like a corner of paradise. Here in the shade of the arcaded veranda of the pavilion, Akbar dealt with affairs of state, his throne raised on a dais to emphasize his dominance over the assembly. The garden is of typical Mughal plan, except that it is oblong rather than square and, rather than being quadripartite, is divided into six unequal rectangles by three walkways. Narrow brooks (now dry) were once fed via elegant *chadar*, or carved water chutes, by the channels running around the Pachisi Courtyard. The central pool is rectangular with chamfered corners and aligned with the pavilion where four walkways meet. Annual bedding, such as busy lizzies in spring and celosia in late summer, makes colorful ribbons around the grass plots. EH

Anguri Bagh

Uttar Pradesh, India

DESIGNER: Emperor Shah Jahan

OWNER: The Indian State

GARDEN STYLE: 16th-century Mughal *chahar bagh*

SIZE: 0.4 acre (0.2 ha)

CLIMATE: Semiarid

LOCATION: Red Fort, Agra, Uttar Pradesh

The royal palace within the Red Fort, the great fortress built by Mughal Emperor Akbar and completed in 1565, boasts several garden areas with geometric flower beds, water channels, and tanks. The best-preserved of them is the Anguri Bagh, or Grape Garden, thought to be so named because of wall paintings of vines in the pavilion.

The private garden of the *zenana*, or women's quarters, is enclosed on the waterfront side by the Khas Mahal, or private palace, and is surrounded by two-story buildings on the other three. Red sandstone rings on the arcaded walls of the lower story were used to help support awnings that stretched over the garden, giving shelter and privacy.

In front of the Khas Mahal, which is set on a wide marble platform bordered by a carved marble balustrade, is a beautiful Mughal pool with the corners carved as lotus petals, their exquisite forms more evident for the lack of water. The pool was linked to a marble cascade, set with arched niches for oil lamps by night and vases of flowers by day, which flowed into the garden set at a lower level. It has a typical *chahar bagh,* or quadripartite layout, with four stone walkways intersected by a raised marble tank in the center. The sunken flower beds are laid out as geometrical, stone-edged parterres that would have been massed with flowers at varying heights. The narrow, surrounding border may have been planted with groups of single flowers to complete the impression of a richly colored carpet gained by visitors looking down from the palace. EH

Akbar's Tomb Garden

Uttar Pradesh, India

DESIGNER: Emperor Akbar
OWNER: The Indian State
GARDEN STYLE: 17th-century Persian *chahar bagh*
SIZE: 91.8 acres (37.2 ha)
CLIMATE: Semiarid
LOCATION: Sikandra, Uttar Pradesh

The monumental gateway into Akbar's tomb in Sikandra is covered with floral and calligraphic decorations in white and colored marble, crowned by four white marble minarets. At either side, the walls are pierced with some of the most beautiful sandstone *jail*, or filigree screens, in India. When you emerge into bright sunlight, the mausoleum is spread out before you, a tiered pyramid set on a raised platform with a wide stone causeway.

Akbar, grandson of Babur and son of Humayun, ruled the Mughal Empire from 1556 to 1605. He started building his tomb, and his son Jahangir completed it. Inside, the tomb's walls are adorned with paintings of golden trees of life, vases of flowers, and rich blue and green floral arabesques. In contrast to the rich detail of the buildings, the garden surrounding the tomb could not be simpler: it is a classic, fourfold design, or *chahar bagh*.

The garden verges on the austere, and its perfect proportions set off the building in the center. Four raised causeways from the tomb lead to four "gateways," one of which—on the south wall—is the entrance. When bulls work the wheel that draws water from the well, the narrow brooks running down the center of the walkways feed four tanks in the center platform, interrupted by four further identical square tanks. Water ripples down carved chutes, flanked by stone steps, to irrigate the sunken plots between the causeways. These are now expanses of lawn where deer graze, while langur monkeys play in the palms, pines, plane trees, and cypresses. EH

Mahtab Bagh

Uttar Pradesh, India

DESIGNER: Emperor Shah Jahan
OWNER: Agra Monument Board
GARDEN STYLE: 17th-century Persian *chahar bagh*
SIZE: 360 square yards (300 sq. m)
CLIMATE: Semiarid
LOCATION: Agra, Uttar Pradesh

Mughal Emperor Shah Jahan's Moonlight Garden was designed for pleasure—an earthly paradise as a reward for the faithful. It was part of the original Taj complex built in the early seventeenth century, but whereas the garden of the Taj Mahal on the opposite side of the River Jumna is sacred and a symbol of heavenly paradise, the Mahtab Bagh was mainly intended for viewing the marble mausoleum, reflected in the water by the light of the moon.

The tradition of moonlight gardens in India—places in which to stroll along white plastered walkways to enjoy the cooler night air—predates the Mughal dynasty. As well as fragrant white flowers and blossoming fruit trees, Shah Jahan added pools, fountains, and a cascade. For more than three centuries, visitors who looked across the river from the Taj saw what appeared to be wild dunes and grass, but paintings and historical references show that the single surviving octagonal tower in the southeast corner was once part of a walled enclosure, just like the Taj's quadripartite garden opposite.

The garden is axially as well as dimensionally coordinated with the Taj, with the terrace and octagonal pool matching the tomb. Water from the river was stored in cisterns in the Mahtab Bagh to rise in the fountain and then cascade into a watercourse with a lotus pool in the center. These channels are now ribbons of colorful annuals, but it is a magical experience to gaze at the Taj from here, and imagine the Mughal nobility seeing it by moonlight through water sprays thrown up by twenty-five fountains. EH

Taj Mahal

Uttar Pradesh, India

DESIGNER: Emperor Shah Jahan
OWNER: Archaeological Survey of India
GARDEN STYLE: 17th-century Persian *chahar bagh*
SIZE: 42 acres (17 ha)
CLIMATE: Semiarid
LOCATION: Chandigarh, Uttar Pradesh

The masterpiece of the Mughal dynasty, the tomb of Mumtaz Mahal, built by Shah Jahan between 1632 and 1654, is set in a remarkably beautiful garden that plays a vital role in the impact the building makes on the visitor. When the fountains play, emerging from jets in the shape of lotus buds, the building appears to shimmer in their droplets. From every angle, framed by arches or the foliage of trees, such as the horsetail tree (*Casuarina equisetifolia*) and the massive *Heterophragma adenophyllum* to the left of the entrance, the mausoleum inspires awe. The tomb is set on a great white platform overlooking the River Jumna. The Mahtab Bagh on the opposite shore completes the vast, symmetrical ground plan.

The Taj garden is enclosed to east and west by massive battlemented walls, with ornamental arches and crenellations inlaid with marble. Within is a classical *chahar bagh*, divided into quarters by broad, shallow channels with a red sandstone pavilion at the end of both cross axes, and a raised marble tank at the center. Wide walkways between stately trees and flowering shrubs, nearly all with labels in Latin, are well worth exploring. The tomb's floral designs in marble and inlays of semiprecious stones are well known. A walk down to the river, outside the vast enclosure, affords views of the retaining walls decorated with sandstone panels depicting date palms and crown imperials. EH

RIGHT This classic view of the Taj Mahal is reflected in the long canal, lined by pencil-thin cypresses on either side.

Ram Bagh

Uttar Pradesh, India

DESIGNER: Empress Nur Jahan
OWNER: Agra Monument Board
GARDEN STYLE: 16th-century Persian *chahar bagh*
SIZE: 240 square yards (200 sq. m)
CLIMATE: Semiarid
LOCATION: Agra, Uttar Pradesh

The pavilions of Ram Bagh, also known as Aram Bagh (Garden of Rest) and Bagh-i Nurafshan, are dilapidated and the water channels dry, but the terraces, walkways between sunken flower beds, narrow stone watercourses, and carved water chutes remain to delineate a ground plan that is spectacular in its formal simplicity. Ram Bagh is one of the earliest surviving gardens of the Mughal period and is based on a *chahar bagh* quadripartite grid.

Low-maintenance lawn, punctuated by clipped evergreens, now fills the plots, and bands of bedding line the walkways, but Ram Bagh is fascinating, not only for its quadripartite ground plan. Set on the waterfront at Agra, the views from the riverside terrace over pierced sandstone balustrades are of a broad sweep of the River Jumna. Along the eastern riverbank, ruined walls and red sandstone towers crowned by *chhatri*—domed kiosks resembling umbrellas—indicate the remains of a series of Mughal gardens that may be more than 400 years old. Some sources claim that Ram Bagh dates to Babur's reign and that he was buried here before his body was taken to his garden in Kābul. Others say the garden was renovated a century later, in 1621.

Between the oblong pavilions overlooking the river, there is a stone platform, set in the center of a large, square tank. Sitting here on a warm spring day, it is easy to imagine being a member of the Mughal court enjoying the river breeze, cooled by the water surrounding the platform, with a rich carpet beneath you and the scent of blossoms wafting on the air. EH

Ban Qiao

Taiwan

DESIGNERS: Lin Guo-hua, Lin Guo-fang
OWNER: Taipei City Government
GARDEN STYLE: 19th-century classical Chinese
SIZE: 2.7 acres (1.1 ha)
CLIMATE: Humid subtropical
LOCATION: Panch'iao, Taiwan

At the end of the eighteenth century, a former merchant and government administrator from China, Lin Ping-hou, selected a plot of land on the northern banks of the River Tamshui and commissioned the construction of Bi-Yi Hall. In 1851 two of his five sons, Lin Guo-hua and Lin Guo-fang, laid out the grounds for a garden and added another house. There were further expansions in 1893 with yet another house surrounding five separate courtyards, and then the gardens were also extended. Now known as the Lin Family Mansion and Garden, the estate is considered one of the finest examples of Ching dynasty residential architecture.

The compound is the largest historical garden in Taiwan. With quiet pools and exquisite pavilions, it is immediately understandable why this garden cost twice as much to create as the entire city of Taipei. The garden is revered for its beauty. The koi-filled, banyan shaded ponds and Zenlike features add a contemplative touch that contrasts with the bustling blare of the city. Serenity can be found in the running water and bridges, the bonsai trees, and the brilliance of the symmetrical and technical architecture.

Although Chinese landscaping may sometimes skimp on luscious greenery, these gardens have enough succulent flora, giant water lilies, and richly colored shrubbery to satisfy most tastes. The gardens are an oasis, a treasured reminder of a bygone age. The Lin Family Mansion and Garden were donated in 1987 to the Taiwanese government, and were extensively renovated in 2000. GW

Queen Sirikit Botanic Garden

Chiang Mai, Thailand

DESIGNER: Thai Botanic Garden Organization
OWNER: The Thai State
GARDEN STYLE: 20th-century mainly naturalistic
tropical botanical
SIZE: 2,372.2 acres (960 ha)
CLIMATE: Wet tropical
LOCATION: Mae Rim, Chiang Mai

Lying to the northwest of Chiang Mai, this spectacular botanical garden is located in a protected watershed and conservation area. Established in 1993 as a state enterprise, it was the country's first center for botanical studies at international standards, with a remit to conserve native plants in the wild. The beautiful, mountainous terrain, and plentiful streams and waterfalls make a stunning backdrop for the lush plant collections and dramatic landscape features.

A number of trails weave through the gardens, and one passes through a large arboretum at the heart of the site, featuring figs, bananas, palms, gingers, and pines, as well as ferns, their relatives, and climbers. An area devoted to ornamental beds and borders, where the main stream and waterfalls are also located, is popular for picnicking. The Rock Garden trail displays many more plants on the way to the orchid nursery. This area houses a high proportion of the estimated 600 Thai orchid species thought to exist in the wild. Here plants on the endangered list are micropropagated to increase their numbers.

In 2001 a new greenhouse complex was officially opened, with five exhibition conservatories and eight greenhouses. The largest building is the Tropical Rain Forest House, which holds the garden's collection of native palms, cycads, ferns, and other tropical, Southeast Asian species. The diverse environments in the complex run from arid desert to an aquatic zone. Shade houses contain more orchids, as well as forest cacti and water lilies. The landscape has matured rapidly, and is a must-see for any traveler with a passion for plants and gardens. JHe

Bang Pa-in

Ayutthaya, Thailand

DESIGNER: King Rama V

OWNER: The Thai royal family

GARDEN STYLE: 19th-century mixed Oriental-style and Western-style palace complex

SIZE: Unknown

CLIMATE: Wet tropical

LOCATION: Ayutthaya, Ayutthaya

The history of these spectacular gardens, with their "floating" temples and regal buildings, dates back to the seventeenth century. According to the chronicles, King Prasat Thong founded a monastery on an island in the Chao Phraya River and, in 1632, the year of his son's birth, erected a summer residence there.

The site was revived many years later by King Rama IV (King Mongkut), who built his own palace. This later became the site of a Buddhist monastery, disguised as a Gothic church, complete with steeple and stained-glass windows. Adding to the building's bizarre nature, it is accessible only by cable cars running across the water. The monastery was built by the king's son and heir, Rama V, who is acknowledged as the father of modern Thailand. Most of the buildings seen today were constructed in the latter years of the nineteenth century, the eclectic mixture of influences ranging from sumptuously decorated Thai- and Chinese-style buildings to some with grand, neoclassical facades. The Sages' Lookout, a cross between a lighthouse and a Moorish minaret, gives excellent views of the palace and countryside.

Entering Bang Pa-in, you would be forgiven for thinking that these were the grounds of some English country manor, designed by Capability Brown with lakes and follies, and tree-lined, horse-and-carriage rides. The buildings, linked by elegant bridges and walkways, are serenely reflected in the water. Although it is not as intensely gardened as some places, Bang Pa-in is certainly awe inspiring. *JHe*

The Jim Thompson Garden

Bangkok, Thailand

DESIGNER: Jim Thompson
OWNER: The James H. W. Thompson Foundation
GARDEN STYLE: 20th-century urban jungle oasis
SIZE: 1 acre (0.4 ha)
CLIMATE: Wet tropical
LOCATION: Bangkok, Bangkok

Once the site of lavish, high-society dinner parties, Jim Thompson's former home is now a museum. Built facing a canal, the main house and outbuildings, with their steeply curving roofs, create a series of tranquil spaces among the nearby palms and tropical trees.

Jim Thompson was a U.S. architect whose work in army intelligence took him to Bangkok in 1945. He fell in love with Thailand and its people, and made the capital city his home. He is best remembered for regenerating the country's ailing silk industry, but this entrepreneurial figure was also a passionate collector of Asian art and architecture, and an avid tropical gardener. The house, completed in 1959, was constructed by combining six of the best examples of traditional Thai homes in the country. An existing rain tree (*Samanea saman*) provided shade for the garden, and Thompson added scarlet-flowering flame trees (*Delonix regia*) and the foliage and flowers of many exotic shrubs and climbers.

In 1967 Thompson set off on a walking trip to the Cameron Highlands in Malaysia. He was never heard from again and has since become something of a legend. At the time of his mysterious disappearance the garden was well established, but with Thompson gone it soon succumbed to an invasion of wild figs.

Twenty-five years later, an impenetrable jungle obscured many of the buildings and original features. In 1994–95 a major restoration took place. Local landscaping firms cleared the plot, except for some smaller trees and palms. New paths and terraces were laid, and the beds replanted with diverse foliage plants and ravishing blooms to recapture the garden's former luxuriance. Tracing the winding pathways, visitors discover secret fish pools and, nestling among the greenery, stone sculptures and antique water jars. With the noise and bustle of the city muffled by vegetation, it is hard to believe that this is essentially an urban plot. JHe

Nong Nooch Tropical Garden

Chonburi, Thailand

DESIGNER: Nongnooch Tansacha
OWNERS: Nongnooch Tansacha, Kampon Tansacha
GARDEN STYLE: 20th-century formal, informal tropical
SIZE: 200 acres (81 ha)
CLIMATE: Wet tropical
LOCATION: Pattaya, Chonburi

Imagine a surreal, *Alice in Wonderland*-style pleasure ground that borrows from cultures across the globe, and you will begin to understand what an extraordinary place this "Kew Gardens" of Thailand really is. The gardens were conceived by Nongnooch Tansacha and opened to the public in 1980. Having purchased 600 acres (243 ha) for use as a fruit plantation in 1954, she radically redrew her plans upon returning from her grand tour of Europe.

A little bit of everything is included in this East-meets-West extravaganza. There is even an adaptation of Stonehenge. A formal cascade, also of epic proportions, is reminiscent of those found in Italian renaissance villas. There is a European Garden with classical statues and tall, colonnaded hedges, and the Thai Topiary Garden has a multitude of clipped forms around the shores of a lake. In addition to the traditional shapes that you might find in the grounds of an English country manor, there is cloud pruning and, throughout the gardens, an abundance of abstract topiary and swirling, psychedelic, land art. You will not find European yew and English box here, though, just a myriad of plants and tropical carpet bedding offering every shade of color. Butterfly Hill alone uses 50,000 flowers and ornamental plants.

Everywhere there are magnificent palms and cycads, and, in addition, separate bromeliad, cacti, canna, fern, and bonsai collections. The nurseries that supply the garden extend over almost twice its area. If you are a serious garden buff, give yourself the whole day. You will need it. JHe

Anuradhapura

North Central, Sri Lanka

DESIGNER: King Pandukabhaya
OWNER: The Sri Lankan State
GARDEN STYLE: 3rd-century BCE Buddhist
SIZE: 400 acres (160 ha)
CLIMATE: Dry tropical
LOCATION: Anuradhapura, North Central

In 543 BCE, Buddhist monks successfully rooted a cutting from the sacred bo tree (*Ficus religiosa*), and it still grows at the heart of the ancient city of Anuradhapura. This venerable tree, known as Sri Maha Bodhi, can only be glimpsed, but it imbues its surroundings with a sense of antiquity, and the shape of its upturned leaves has inspired the six forms of the dagoba, or Buddhist domed reliquary. Later, in the third century BCE, some 9,884 acres (4,000 ha) of cityscape, including flower and fruit gardens, were laid out by King Pandukabhaya, though today this is primarily an archaelogical and architectural site.

Water was harnessed on a grand practical and visual scale, the huge water tank stretching as far as the eye can see to ensure a year-round supply. The magnificent *kuttam poluna*, or twin stepped pools, were built for the Buddhist monks to bathe; they are undamaged, and you can see decorations that include rice pots and a five-headed cobra (*naga*). The entrance moonstone is also in excellent condition; the outer flames represent desire; the horses, death; lions, illness; and bulls and elephants, vitality. Life force and prosperity appear as a ring of lianas or creepers encircling geese that surround the lotus flower, or nirvana. Three other extensive water tanks act as mirrors to the sky, with one supplying the Royal Pleasure Gardens, and one shaped as an elephant.

Legend has it that a royal prince fell in love with a low-caste girl who was walking in the grounds, and forsook his throne to marry her. They are known as the Isurumuniya lovers. CH

Brief Gardens

North Western, Sri Lanka

DESIGNER: Bevis Bawa
OWNER: Bevis Bawa Trust
GARDEN STYLE: 20th-century European, Oriental tropical
SIZE: 25 acres (10 ha)
CLIMATE: Wet tropical
LOCATION: Kalawila, North Western

The Burghers—an amalgam of Portuguese, Dutch, British, and Singalese families—lived and traded beside the British and Singalese in Sri Lanka in the early twentieth century. One of them was Bevis Bawa, a landscape artist, sculptor, and bon vivant. His barrister father bought the land here with the proceeds of a legal brief, which explains the name of Brief Gardens. In 1920 Bawa began to clear what had been a rubber plantation to make the gardens.

Today tall flowering shrubs line the drive leading to the gardens, which radiate from an open-plan bungalow surrounded by a creeper-clad veranda. The bungalow and gardens seem fused, with views and vistas framed by iron or stone entrances and exits, in a network of courtyards and terraces.

Bawa, his wife, and a team of gardeners created a world of diverse garden styles and plantings. Much of the paving used in the garden is imprinted with varied leaf patterns. The best features include the exotically planted, Italian-style water staircase that, incidentally, dramatically draws the visitor past Bawa's secluded grave. Also note the small Japanese garden, shaded and mossy, complete with weathered stone lanterns and figurines, providing a moment of quiet; and the "edible" garden, filled with luscious, exotic fruit. The tropical abundance of the planting is brought into focus by close-clipped hedges and mown lawns that also frame the wonderful views to the coast. Bawa died in 1992, leaving the gardens to his gardeners in shares that he set up to correspond to their individual periods of tenure. CH

Peradiniya

Central, Sri Lanka

DESIGNER: Unknown
OWNER: The Sri Lankan State
GARDEN STYLE: 19th-century botanical
SIZE: 147 acres (59.5 ha)
CLIMATE: Wet tropical
LOCATION: Kandy, Central

Kandy was the former capital of the Kandyan kings who ruled the interior—the Hidden Kingdom—until the British arrived in 1802. In 1821, on the site of a former Kandyan palace, the British created the Peradiniya Botanical Gardens to study and propagate the abundant native flora. The gardens maintain strong links with the Royal Botanic Gardens, Kew, in England (see page 386) and play an important part in the global network of botanical gardens. Nestling in a tight bend on the River Mahaweli-Ganga, the gardens remain mercifully free of monkeys.

The magnificent avenue of royal palms (*Roystonea* spp.) was planted in three stages—in 1885, 1905, and 1950—and the entire collection of trees exceeds 10,000. The enormous banyan tree (*Ficus benghalensis*) dominates the site; its branches spread inexorably over the ground around it, putting down epiphytic elbows to support a huge area of groundcover. Also note the spice gardens with mature allspice, cinnamon, clove, and nutmeg trees, and, because of renewed interest in Ayurvedic and alternative medicines, the excellent medicinal borders. There are spectacular orchids and collections of palms, bamboos, and ferns, and even colorful flower displays dotted around a small lake shaped like Sri Lanka, with islands representing cities such as Kandy and Colombo. Many trees have been planted in the gardens to mark auspicious visits, not least Kandy's tenure as South East Asia Command Headquarters during World War II, when Lord Mountbatten was in charge. CH

Kranji War Cemetery

Singapore

DESIGNERS: Sir Reginald Blomfield, Edwin Lutyens
OWNER: Commonwealth War Graves Commission
GARDEN STYLE: 20th-century memorial
SIZE: 1,750 acres (708.8 ha)
CLIMATE: Wet tropical
LOCATION: Kranji, Singapore

In his war sonnet *The Soldier*, the English poet Rupert Brooke wrote, "…there's some corner of a foreign field, that is for ever England." This is the sentiment that underlies the Commonwealth War Graves Commission, established in Britain in 1917. It commemorates the fallen Commonwealth forces of two world wars: 1.7 million men and women in 2,500 war cemeteries in some 150 countries.

These cemeteries were conceived as gardens, and their architects, Sir Reginald Blomfield and Edwin Lutyens, sought to create an immediate, obvious link between the gardens of home and the fields where the soldiers lay. As well as honoring the dead, they also offer mourners a sense of serenity and solace. So, from Normandy to Cyprus, and from Tanzania to Madras, the flowers of English cottage gardens—lavender and lilies, and floribunda roses—are clustered around the long rows of white headstones. In a similar vein, at Vimy Ridge, Canadian pines recall the Canadian troops who fell there, and Australian graves are planted with antipodean species.

During the Japanese invasion of Singapore in 1942, the area around Kranji became the scene of fierce fighting, and after the Allied defeat the Japanese established a prisoner-of-war camp there. Today's Kranji War Cemetery was developed from a small cemetery started by the prisoners held in that camp. It commemorates the names of 24,000 Commonwealth servicemen who gave their lives in Malaysia, many of whom were denied a proper burial by the fortunes of war. In keeping with the vision of Blomfield and Lutyens, Kranji is identical in character to cemeteries of the Commonwealth War Graves Commission the world over. Though the horticultural detail may vary according to the nationality of the soldiers buried there, the impression remains the same: immaculately maintained gardens of dignity, tranquillity, and unexpected cheerfulness. AE

Singapore Botanic Gardens

Singapore

DESIGNER: Singapore Agri-Horticultural Society
OWNER: Singapore National Parks Board
GARDEN STYLE: 19th-century tropical landscape
SIZE: 128.5 acres (52 ha)
CLIMATE: Wet tropical
LOCATION: Singapore, Singapore

Singapore Botanic Gardens are among the greatest botanical gardens in the world. Originally laid out by the Singapore Agri-Horticultural Society, they were handed over in 1874 to the government. Kew-trained directors were then employed to develop the gardens in the London flagship garden's image.

The gardens were first established on the present site in 1859 as a leisure garden and ornamental park. The park remains very popular with the locals, who use it for jogging, practicing tai chi (usually early in the morning), and strolling through the gardens. There are areas of rain forest, formal borders, many heritage specimen trees, ginger and spice collections, including nutmeg, cloves, and cinnamon, and a bold display of the orchid *Vanda* 'Miss Joaquim', Singapore's national flower. The National Orchid Garden, a more recent addition, houses the largest display of tropical orchids in the world with more than 3,000 different species and hybrids. Within this garden is the fabulous Yuen-Peng McNeice bromeliad display with more than 520 cultivars, varieties, and hybrids, as well as the Tan Soon Siang Misthouse, which contains a collection of rare orchids.

When you meander down through the elegant Palm Valley, you will see ancient specimens, the old herbarium buildings, and Burkill Hall, once the garden director's house, used by Henry Ridley, who introduced rubber to Malaysia and developed the technique of tapping trees, and Professor Eric Holttum, well known for his experiments in orchid breeding and hybridization. MB

Singapore Zoo

Singapore

DESIGNER: Lyn de Alwis
OWNER: Tamasek Holdings/Singapore Tourist Board
GARDEN STYLE: 20th-century zoological
SIZE: 69 acres (27.9 ha)
CLIMATE: Wet tropical
LOCATION: Mandai Lake Road, Singapore

Forget the shopping. By far the best thing to do in Singapore is visit the zoo, not only for the animals, but to marvel at the astonishing gardens that have been made around, and even within, the animal enclosures. Two areas (displaying diurnal and nocturnal animals) are arranged on the banks of an artificial lake, surrounded by a belt of rain forest that successfully excludes the modern city. The animals are kept not in cages but in artfully landscaped enclosures, separated from the public by moats and fences. And the range of exotic plants is amazing. Curly-horned antelopes peep through thickets of ginger and bamboo, jackals saunter through a xerophytic rock garden, and monkeys gambol in a lush habitat of tall trees, palms, and spectacular grasses. There are water features everywhere with pools, streams, and even full-sized waterfalls, and the moats, dressed to look like natural riverbanks, are filled with fish.

In the Fragile Forest, you can explore the interrelationship of plant and animal life in the rain forest. There is a huge, walk-through, butterfly area, an Elephant Camp like an Indian riverbank, a delightful Heliconia Garden, and a magical Fragant Walk. Most exciting of all is the baboon enclosure, representing the dramatic landscapes of Ethiopia with impenetrable forest, scorching desert, and the wonders of the Great Rift Valley. At the center is a village hut, and the sequence of gardens that leads to it makes inspired use of Ethiopian artifacts, from stark compositions of rocks and pots to carved figures emerging from a sea of succulents. AE

Batujimbar Pavilions

Bali, Indonesia

DESIGNERS: Geoffrey Bawa, Made Wijawa
OWNER: Donald Friend
GARDEN STYLE: 20th-century indigenous
SIZE: 15 acres (6 ha)
CLIMATE: Dry tropical
LOCATION: Bali, Indonesia

Geoffrey Bawa was Sri Lanka's most influential twentieth-century architect. One of the signatures of his style was the carefully considered relationship between buildings and their surroundings. In many cases, as at Batujimbar, the climate allowed Bawa to blur the boundary between external and internal spaces, fusing the garden and building as one.

Constructed from local materials by local craftsmen, using traditional techniques and styles, Batujimbar was an early example of a sympathetic tourist development. It was the brainchild of the Australian painter Donald Friend, an acquaintance of Bawa's brother. In 1971, after settling in the southeast corner of Bali, next to the sea, at Batujimbar, Friend asked Bawa to be his architect for a development of beach villas on the site, with a museum to house his collection of Balinese sculpture, and an amphitheater to complement his house.

Bawa drew a master plan delineating fifteen plots, each covering an area of 1 acre (0.4 ha), with a beach frontage of about 100 feet (30 m). However, only Friend's museum, with its moat and stone terracing, and two of the houses were built to Bawa's designs, which called for a pool at the center of the plot and a garden. Friend lost control of the project, and most of the development ignored Bawa's master plan. In 1985 Friend's own plot was revamped, and the same decade saw the Australian garden designer Made Wijaya rework many of the gardens. Little of Friend's vision and Bawa's architecture remains, but their masterful museum and garden are still there. TM

Once merely a showcase of European gardening styles, Latin America has long asserted its independence in design. In mid-twentieth-century Brazil Roberto Burle Marx introduced his own contemporary, organic landscapes, highlighting tropical plants in big, bold, sculptural groups. The gardens of Uruguay and Mexico are also outstanding examples of blending Hispano-Moorish and European influences with a purely Latin flair.

CENTRAL AND SOUTH AMERICA

Las Pozas

San Luis Potosí, Mexico

DESIGNERS: Edward James, Plutarco Gastelum, Ivan Hicks
OWNERS: The Gastelum family
GARDEN STYLE: 20th-century surrealist sculpture garden
SIZE: 98 acres (39.7 ha)
CLIMATE: Dry tropical
LOCATION: Xilitla, San Luis Potosí

Edward James, the millionaire patron of surrealist artists Salvador Dalí and René Magritte, created a tropical, leaf–packed, utterly over-the-top garden called Las Pozas in the Mexican jungle. It is full of huge, hidden sculptures, some over 100 feet (30 m) tall, and architectural follies painted red, blue, and gold among butterflies as big as crabs. It is named after its string of pools connected by waterfalls along a winding jungle river.

James began working on this tropical garden in 1949, aided by his friend, Plutarco Gastelum. Ivan Hicks, a British designer of surreal gardens who worked for James, continued developing it throughout his life until his death in 1984. However, Las Pozas has only recently become widely known. Gardening magazines compete over the pictures, all of which get blown up to fill pages in an attempt to convey the multi-tangled density of the jungle that is now slowly creeping back over the sculptures and the brick. At times, hacking and thwacking is the only way back, in or out.

The bizarre entrance to Las Pozas was planned as a giant aviary and monkey cage. The second floor was to be a cinema. Inside are huge concrete leaves and gourds, dolphins, and stairways. Other fantasy structures have names like the House With a Roof Like a Whale, the Archway of the Bats, House With Three Stories That Might Be Five, and the Temple of Ducks. The musician John Lennon visited, as did the magician Alexander Guido, and the artist Pablo Picasso. RR

> "The bizarre entrance to Las Pozas was planned as a giant aviary and monkey cage"

Jardín Botánico de la UNAM

México D.F., Mexico

DESIGNERS: Dr. Faustino Miranda, Dr. Efren del Pozo
OWNER: National Autonomous University of Mexico
GARDEN STYLE: 20th-century botanical, native collection
SIZE: 247 acres (100 ha)
CLIMATE: Dry tropical
LOCATION: Mexico City

Behind Mexico City's Olympic Stadium, the UNAM (National Autonomous University of Mexico) Botanical Garden, also known as the Botanical Garden at Pedregal, enjoys a sheltered location and has much mysterious appeal.

About three-quarters of the Mexican landscape has ecological habitats that combine very variable, harsh weather with scarce rainfall, resulting in an abundance of arid and semiarid vegetation. The garden has marvelous collections of such plants, grouped according to habitat type and temperature zone, including many yuccas and agaves, and a particularly exceptional collection of cactus species in a desert area. All this is laid out on a site that has many volcanic outcrops, creating a highly unusual "other" world, with plenty of mystery emanating from the solidified lava.

The undulating network of paths reveals the garden's areas edged with dark, knobbly rocks, with redder shades of crushed stone making a good mulch that sets off plant foliage. Flowering spikes of agaves tower over your head. In a zone devoted to plants from temperate regions, an arboretum displays a collection of indigenous trees. Fine-needled pines and oak species are prevalent, with firs, loquats, Mexican hawthorn trees, and sweet gums that grow in the more humid, cloud-forest regions.

One section is devoted to plants used for medicinal and culinary purposes, because many traditional Mexican dishes and drinks use native plants and extractions in their recipes. RChi

Casa Luis Barragán

México D.F., Mexico

DESIGNER: Luis Barragán
OWNER: Casa Museo Luis Barragán
GARDEN STYLE: 20th-century Mexican modernist
SIZE: 0.11 acre (0.04 ha)
CLIMATE: Dry tropical
LOCATION: Mexico City

The former home of Pritzker prize-winning Mexican architect Luis Barragán blends into the surrounding streets in a quiet, unassuming way. Looking upward, you have glimpses of colored walls that form the roof terrace, hinting at what lies behind the rather stark facade. Once inside, you become enveloped in a showplace for Barragán's design philosophy. Importantly, he called himself a landscape architect, believing that the garden was just as important as the building. His architecture was based on the use of walls—flat planes, colored, textured—and the way sunlight plays off them, and the necessity for all views from a house to include views of a garden. His own house encapsulates this thinking. A continuous project throughout his life, Barragán's house and garden show visitors how he lived by his ideals. Designed in 1947, its simplicity and minimalism retain a surprisingly contemporary appeal.

The ground floor opens on to the garden, turning the outdoors into an extension of the house. One wall of the living room is a large, four-square window looking on to the west garden, providing a framed view of lush green space with a foreground of square paving. Plants cascade down from above, liana style, casting amazing shadow patterns. Tall walls enclose taller trees while, upstairs, a pure, spatial composition of vertical and horizontal walls completely cuts off the streets below. Walls are colored with a typically Mexican palette of luminous bright pink, rust red, and white. Small square tiles pave the ground.

Being here, you feel as though you are immersed in an abstract painting. Enjoy the house and its views of the garden below as a place of meditation, away from city life. As Barragán said, "You have to make homes become gardens and gardens, home. Intimacy and home should be there, in the enclosed gardens. You can't trust a garden that is open-wide and reveals everything at first sight." RChi

Las Chinampas de Xochimilco

México D.F., Mexico

DESIGNERS: Xochimilco Indians, Aztecs
OWNER: Mexican Federal District
GARDEN STYLE: Market gardens on islands with canals
SIZE: 2,000 acres (810 ha)
CLIMATE: Dry tropical
LOCATION: Mexico City

Known as the Mexican Venice for its network of canals and gondolas, these floating gardens are similar to the French *hortillonages* in Amiens (see page 550). The color, music, and carnival atmosphere make this Mexican version a delight. As you drift past little houses and market gardens in one of the brightly decorated punts, called *trajineras*, floating mariachi and marimba bands serenade you, floating kitchens feed you, and flower vendors in flat-bottomed canoes sell bouquets. In fact everything is on the move except for the floating gardens. They did float once, though, just over 1,000 years ago, when they were devised by the Indians who lived in Xochimilco, which means "place of flowers" in Aztec, and made the lakeside marshes productive.

Large areas were marked out with stakes, fenced with branches, and interwoven with reeds. They were filled in with rocks and aquatic vegetation. In the top layer of fertile mud, corn, beans, and squashes were sown. Willows, planted along the edges, took root and anchored the marshes to the lake bed, after which they gradually grew into tiny islands. With abundant water and cooling breezes, these raised fields, known as *chinampas*, meaning "over the reed fence," were a huge success, first with the Aztecs who arrived in the thirteenth century, and then with the Spanish conquistadors two centuries later. Even today you will find large, cheap markets that supply fruit, vegetables, and flowers for most of Mexico City's markets. The area was declared a World Heritage Site by UNESCO in 1987. VR

Casa Folke Egerstrom

México D.F., Mexico

DESIGNER: Luis Barragán
OWNERS: The Egerstrom family
GARDEN STYLE: 20th-century Mexican modernist
SIZE: Approximately 1.1 acre (0.5 ha)
CLIMATE: Dry tropical
LOCATION: Mexico City

One of the most influential architects of the twentieth century, Luis Barragán made no distinction between indoor and outdoor space. A garden was simply "architecture without a roof." The aim of his architecture was to provide a buffer against the world: to make a still, quiet place that would inspire deep feelings of serenity and repose.

Barragán was born in 1902 to a wealthy land-owning family in Guadalajara, a provincial capital of Mexico. To create his "glorified barnyard," Casa Folke Egerstrom and stables, on the edge of Mexico City, he reached imaginatively back to his childhood. The hitching posts and refreshing pools of the family ranch, the simple shapes and bright, flat colors of the village houses under the blazing Mexican sun, the leaky guttering and rough wooden downspouts, all were reimagined at Casa Folke Egerstrom, broken down into their purest, simplest elements of color and form. Here is a hardworking, practical space honed down into a piece of abstract art, a sculptural composition of water, wall, and tree.

There is nothing complicated in his effects, no more than a splash of paint, and a pattern of light and shade, and his materials are simply adobe, timber, and limewash. He even uses simple masses and simple shapes. Yet, in his hands, this simplicity becomes transcendent. As an old man, in 1980, Barragán wrote of his lifelong yearning to create a perfect garden, describing that elusive perfection as a "serene and silent joy." What better description of the enduring power of Casa Folke Egerstrom? AE

> "...no distinction between indoor and outdoor space. A garden was 'architecture without a roof'"

Jardín Ortega

México D.F., Mexico

DESIGNER: Luis Barragán
OWNER: Casa Museo Luis Barragán
GARDEN STYLE: 20th-century Mexican modernist
SIZE: 0.14 acre (0.06 ha)
CLIMATE: Dry tropical
LOCATION: Mexico City

Casa Ortega was architect Luis Barragán's home from 1943 to 1948, and remains part of the museum complex dedicated to his life and works. The garden shows all the concepts that influenced his architecture and approach to landscape design; for Barragán, the two were inextricably linked.

His influences included French landscape architect Ferdinand Bac, who believed gardens should be enchanted places for meditation and spaces that "bewitch" the visitor. He also drew on the design of Moroccan houses, where the public facade is unassuming and private. Entry does not reveal everything at once; instead buildings unfold as you explore them, large windows giving views on to the garden. Signature Barragán elements include house walls that make abstract planes, cantilevered staircases making zigzag patterns against walls, and low garden walls that draw the eye down and around. He also designed roof terraces and balconies from which shapes and patterns in the garden, and shadows cast by trees can be appreciated.

This garden displays a core of existing structures that Barragán worked into his design. Fragments of an earlier existence include tall perimeter walls with thick buttresses, gnarled rocks, and pockmarked boulders now honored as features, a few standing on stone plinths. It is a totally enclosed space that is almost monastic in spirit. As Barragán said, "Any work of architecture which does not express serenity is a mistake." This garden can be visited by appointment with the Casa Museo Luis Barragán. RChi

Jardín Etnobotánico

Oaxaca, Mexico

DESIGNERS: Francisco Toledo, Luis Zarate
OWNER: State of Oaxaca
GARDEN STYLE: 20th-century native botanical
SIZE: 5.7 acres (2.3 ha)
CLIMATE: Dry tropical
LOCATION: Oaxaca, Oaxaca

The broad plaza in front of the Santo Domingo de Guzmán Cultural Center in the city of Oaxaca stops you in your tracks, exhibiting a dramatic contrast between crisp, modern rows of cacti and succulents with magnificent, towering, old buildings behind. Inside are the wonderful Ethnobotanical Gardens of Oaxaca.

A World Heritage Site, the building complex has a breathtaking scale. The monastery beside the Santo Domingo Church houses a museum whose collections include anthropological articles, jewelry, and artifacts from the Mixtec period. The Mexican army used the walled former monastery orchards for shooting practice until 1994, when artist Francisco Toledo led a petition for the area to be conserved.

Garden director Alejandro de Avila joined Toledo in the bold vision of creating a garden to showcase the state of Oaxaca's huge floral diversity. Today the modern garden featuring Mexican design has a backdrop of imposing, baroque period architecture.

Ornamental brooks zigzag through crisply defined, blue gravel, garden paths, and lead through the garden. Their design derives from the geometric, hieroglyph-based motifs used in indigenous Zapotec art. A stunning "hedge" of tall cacti makes an unusual allée, reflected in a shallow rectangle of water like a collection of huge, green organ pipes. This garden is more than a series of plant collections; it demonstrates the relationship between vegetation and the traditions of Oaxaca. It displays the art of the garden in every sense, and is a source of aesthetic inspiration and intellectual stimulation. RChi

Jardín Botánico Lankester

Cartago, Costa Rica

DESIGNER: Charles H. Lankester
OWNER: University of Costa Rica
GARDEN STYLE: Semiformal tropical forest
SIZE: 27 acres (11 ha)
CLIMATE: Dry tropical/wet tropical
LOCATION: Paraiso, Cartago

Situated in the Central Valley, Lankester Botanical Gardens enjoy a perpetual spring with mild temperatures and regular afternoon showers. The gardens are home to about 1,000 species of native and exotic orchid, as well as palms, bamboos, heliconias, bromeliads, and conifers. The location is dense and leafy, and resonates to the clack of tree bamboos and the rustle of palm fronds.

Cacti and other succulents thrive in the high trees, where drying winds and a scorching sun create an arid environment. On the ground, however, there is high humidity, and a rich scent of gingers and orchids.

Cobblestone paths meander through groves of native bamboo and forested glades where bromeliads, philodendrons, diefenbacchia, and anthuriums grow wild on the trees. Trails wind through groves of heliconias, with their banana-shaped leaves and flowers resembling lobster claws. Blue morpho butterflies float through the forest on their 6-inch-wide (15 cm) wings, hunting for fruit juice.

The garden was founded in the 1940s by the British naturalist and orchidologist Charles H. Lankester. After his death, the importance of preserving the garden became evident. It was finally donated to the University of Costa Rica on the proviso that it remained a botanical garden. It is now one of the region's most important botanical institutions.

According to native Costa Rican tradition, the rose-purple *Cattleya skinneri*, Costa Rica's national orchid, brings happiness and good luck. Masses can be seen flowering here in March and April. CW

Jardín Botánico Wilson

Puntarenas, Costa Rica

DESIGNERS: Robert Wilson, Catherine Wilson
OWNER: Organization for Tropical Studies
GARDEN STYLE: 20th-century botanical and rain forest
SIZE: 30 acres (12.2 ha)
CLIMATE: Dry tropical
LOCATION: San Vito, Puntarenas

Close to the Panamanian border, in the rain forest of the Talamanca mountains, is one of Central America's most important botanical gardens. Established in 1963 by Robert and Catherine Wilson, the garden features magnificently diverse plantings of tropical and subtropical species, such as aroids, bromeliads, ferns, gingers, heliconias, marantas, and palms. The palm collection is one of the finest in the world.

Well-groomed trails wind around the palm-covered hillsides, through banana and heliconia groves, agave and lily beds, and beneath the rain forest canopy. Signs lead you through plantings of related species on the orchid garden loop, the bromeliad walk, the tree fern hill trail, and the bamboo forest. Blue-crowned motmots (*Momotus momota*)—a large bird with a long blue tail and a marvelous black crown—are common to the forested areas, while noisy flocks of chestnut-mandibled toucans (*Ramphastos swainsonii*) roost in the tall cecropia trees.

The garden is part of a network of sites used for research into conservation, horticulture, sustainable development, agro-ecology, and reforestation. The garden and its surrounding preserve are part of La Amistad Biosphere Reserve, consisting of thousands of acres of parkland and buffer zones. Though La Amistad is only 24 miles (39 km) from the garden, it is the largest and least explored park in Central America. The garden and La Amistad are a biological wonderland that should not be missed. CW

Palácio do Itamaraty

Brasília, Brazil

DESIGNERS: Roberto Burle Marx, Oscar Niemeyer
OWNER: Ministry of Foreign Affairs
GARDEN STYLE: 20th-century modernist landscaped
SIZE: 3.9 acres (1.6 ha)
CLIMATE: Dry tropical
LOCATION: Brasília

As a garden designer, Roberto Burle Marx was a cultural phenomenon. He challenged the deep-rooted assumptions of European design, creating an entirely individual, distinctly Brazilian style. He created the first landscape style appropriate to modern architecture and large-scale public buildings.

Nowhere is this seen more clearly than in Brasília, the new capital of Brazil created in the 1950s by urban planner Lúcio Costa, architect Oscar Niemeyer, and landscape architect Burle Marx. The monumental new architecture was all about size, boldness, and flamboyance. Burle Marx responded with equal bravura, and the most dramatic example of his art is the Ministry of Foreign Affairs building, Itamaraty. Marooned in an artificial lake, Itamaraty is approached by narrow concrete bridges and surrounded by "floating" green islands—planters filled with aquatic and moisture-loving plants. Burle Marx collected and grew many of the plants he used himself.

At Itamaraty, the water appears to flow right into the building, under its lofty arches and into an internal garden, where bromeliads swarm up posts set in a pool, and jungle planting threatens to escape down corridors. A second garden uses ferns, organic sculpture, and his signature plant, *Vriesea imperialis,* positioned beneath a colossal concrete pergola, with islands of colored stones. In this symbolic city carved out of the jungle, Itamaraty offers a fascinating study into the mingling of the artificial and the natural. AE

Promenade de Copacabana

Rio de Janeiro, Brazil

DESIGNER: Roberto Burle Marx
OWNER: District of Rio de Janeiro
GARDEN STYLE: 20th-century modernist urban landscape
LENGTH: 2.4 miles (4 km)
CLIMATE: Dry tropical
LOCATION: Rio de Janeiro

Occasionally a landscape architect creates a space that becomes iconic because it sums up the spirit of a city. This is Roberto Burle Marx's great achievement in the linear park he created along the shoreline of Rio de Janeiro. It contains two outstanding set pieces: the Op-Art lawn of the Museum of Modern Art and the swirling sidewalks of Copacabana.

The Copacabana promenade essentially consists of three parallel sidewalks, 2 miles (4 km) in length, which are separated by busy lanes of traffic, and broken up by side streets and underground parking garage entrances. From these very dubious and uninspiring ingredients, Burle Marx created one of Rio's most exciting and exuberant vistas.

Burle Marx believed that gardens were first and foremost works of art—his project plans look like modern abstract paintings, with swirling lines and bold blocks of color. A painter himself, he was heavily influenced by Pablo Picasso. At Copacabana he made swooping, irregular patterns of black, white, and red Portuguese stone mosaic, placing clumps of coconut palms and other salt-resistant trees in the gaps between the garage entrances. He added a rhythmic pattern of black-and-white parabolas along the beach, echoing the wave patterns on the shore. The design is best appreciated from above; the thirty-seventh-floor restaurant of the Le Meridien Hotel offers an excellent vantage point. AE

Jardim de Luiz Cézar Fernándes

Rio de Janeiro, Brazil

DESIGNER: Roberto Burle Marx
OWNER: Luiz Cézar Fernándes
GARDEN STYLE: 20th-century modernist landscape
SIZE: Approximately 10 acres (4 ha)
CLIMATE: Dry tropical
LOCATION: Petrópolis, Rio de Janeiro State

The Serra dos Órgãos (Organ Pipe Mountains) of southern Brazil as a backdrop for drifts of tropical planting make this garden one of the most iconic of the last fifty years. It is an early work by Roberto Burle Marx and one of his most informal, with none of the architectural detailing of his urban projects. The impact is created by water surrounded by masses of vegetation to balance the dramatic mountain view, while the addition of trees helps the garden to blend with its landscape.

Created in 1948 for Odette Monteiro, it was bought by Luiz Cézar Fernándes after her death in 1984. He employed Burle Marx to restore it. Curving paths lead the eye into the landscape, disappearing behind vegetation or grassy banks, leaving the observer unsure where the garden ends and the surroundings begin. Look out for purple-flowered tibouchinas and the lake, with nearby slopes planted with what has become a classic feature of Burle Marx's work: vast, organically-shaped beds of brightly colored plants with an emphasis on structure and foliage, provided in part by large clumps of philodendron. The site of this garden is superb; Burle Marx's gift was to make the most of it and to produce a design that was not in any sense overpowered by it. In so doing, he inspired many other designers. NK

RIGHT Roberto Burle Marx's design bursts with lush tropical flora and merges seamlessly into the surrounding landscape.

Jardim Botânico do Rio de Janeiro

Rio de Janeiro, Brazil

DESIGNER: King João VI of Portugal
OWNER: District of Rio de Janeiro
GARDEN STYLE: 19th-century botanical
SIZE: 330 acres (140 ha)
CLIMATE: Dry tropical
LOCATION: Rio de Janeiro

Rio de Janeiro has a great tropical botanical garden sited close to a large urban forest and only a short distance from the legendary beaches of Ipanema and Copacabana. Founded in 1808 by the then Prince Regent Dom João of Brazil and Portugal, the garden's primary purpose was to acclimatize West Indian plants, such as nutmeg, pepper, and cinnamon, to the Brazilian climate. Portuguese colonial rulers deemed the produce economically beneficial and essential for their way of life.

One of the garden's most striking features is a 2,400-foot-long (731 m) avenue of towering royal palm trees (*Roystonea oleracea*), which stand out from the large palm collection. The original tree, planted by King João VI, became known as the Palma Mater, and the plan was that only the royal family would have access to its seeds. The tree first flowered in 1829, and the seed was supposed to be burned to prevent its use by ordinary subjects. Apparently slaves who worked in the garden smuggled seed out and sold it, and many were able to purchase their freedom on the proceeds. Though lightning destroyed the Palma Mater, its remains are on display in the garden. All the other trees in the avenue, now about 100-foot (30 m) tall, were grown from the original.

Rio de Janeiro Botanical Garden is a beguiling mixture of the formal and informal, with a European layout and a rich biodiversity of Brazilian plants, dotted with a variety of sculptures and fountains. Other sights that will stop you in your tracks are the Frei Leandro pond, with its magnificent, green floating islands of the giant-leaved Amazon water lily *(Victoria amazonica)* and plants bearing fruit large enough to be used for ball games on the nearby beaches. There are also plantings of cocoa, rubber, and the pungent abricó-de-macaco tree. Against the incomparable backdrop of the Corcovado Mountain, Rio de Janeiro Botanical Garden is a heady mix. RChi

Sítio Roberto Burle Marx

Rio de Janeiro, Brazil

DESIGNER: Roberto Burle Marx
OWNER: National Institute for Cultural Heritage
GARDEN STYLE: Modern, abstract
SIZE: 100 acres (40.5 ha)
CLIMATE: Dry tropical
LOCATION: Rio de Janeiro

Roberto Burle Marx was one of the most celebrated landscape designers of the twentieth century. He bought this site in 1949 to store his considerable plant collection. He lived here from 1973 until he died in 1994, during which time he restored the beautiful house and sixteenth-century chapel.

Burle Marx was a renowned plantsman. In his garden, over 3,500 species were combined into multilayered, lush plantings around a series of spaces. The home sits in a forest clearing, and the balance between voids and vegetation is barely kept in a state of equilibrium in the tropical climate. A generous, deep veranda keeps at bay richly textured and colored foliage.

Stone steps are used to link areas, and old stone columns are allowed to push up through vegetation. In openings, swaths of colored groundcover plants swirl around, making bold, dramatic patterns in Burle Marx's signature style. Bromeliads encrust the tree trunks, bright heliconias stand against lush backdrops of foliage, and huge, whale-sized boulders ooze interesting collections of moss.

Burle Marx studied and explored the Brazilian forests, and made significant contributions to plant knowledge—more than thirty plants bear his name. His work has a sense of timelessness achieved through a combination of planting huge groups of the same specimen, keeping colors separate, and using native plants. Burle Marx understood the character of plants and put them together in rich layers to make beautiful, relaxing gardens. RChi

El Cementerio de Tulcán

Carchi, Ecuador

DESIGNER: José María Azael Franco Guerrero
OWNER: Municipality of Tulcán
GARDEN STYLE: 20th-century topiary
SIZE: 12 acres (5 ha)
CLIMATE: Wet tropical
LOCATION: Tulcán, Carchi

"In Tulcán, a cemetery so beautiful that it invites one to die…;" so runs one lyrical description of this extraordinary garden, capturing concisely its powerful allure and unique style. The Andean frontier town of Tulcán, situated on Ecuador's northern border with Colombia, would seem to have little to commend it to the tourist or garden lover. Yet its cemetery is such a source of wonder that it has been declared a national monument.

In 1936 José María Azael Franco Guerrero began landscaping Tulcán's municipal cemetery. His visionary approach was simple enough. He planted hundreds of cypress trees (*Cupressus arizonica*), lining the paths and walkways with these evergreens. As they grew, Guerrero and his team of gardeners began the process of clipping, pruning, trimming, and training that has made the cemetery at Tulcán one of the finest topiary gardens in the world.

The style of the topiary is quintessentially Latin American, and is inspired by the architecture and sculpture of the continent's pre-Columbian cultures. The actual forms that this style takes, however, are eclectic, occasionally bizarre, and always visually stunning. Arches, stonework, animals, human figures, and faces are all marvelously depicted. The quality of the topiary is remarkable, particularly because a huge amount of intricate detail is cut in relief. The local name for the garden is Escultura en Verde del Campo Santo, or Sculpture in Green of the Holy Field. This is a garden of precision, craftsmanship, vision, imagination, and brilliance. AM

El Jardín Botánico de Buenos Aires

Buenos Aires, Argentina

DESIGNER: Carlos Thays
OWNER: The Argentinean State
GARDEN STYLE: 19th-century botanical
SIZE: 20 acres (8.1 ha)
CLIMATE: Humid subtropical
LOCATION: Buenos Aires

The French landscape architect Carlos Thays created this botanic garden, also known as Jardín Botánico Carlos Thays, in 1892. The original range of plants was very wide, with 721 Argentinean species alone, but those from the tropical north and cold south did not survive; until the 1990s, pollution added to the number of losses. Efforts were then made to improve conditions, and Nigel Taylor, curator of the Royal Botanic Gardens at Kew, went there to advise in 1997.

The design integrates the botanical aspect into a parklike, open space. Many hundreds of trees were planted, and today they have an enormous impact because of their botanical interest, beauty, and the way they create shade in summer, and screen out the surrounding apartments and office blocks twenty stories high. The best of the trees include a group of blue jacaranda (*Jacaranda mimosifolia*), with huge, hazy clouds of blue flowers, and *Tabebuia impetiginosa*, with leafless branches dripping with thousands of mauve-pink trumpets. A favorite medium-size native is the common coral tree (*Erythrina crista-galli*) with crimson racemes of big florets, and the yellow jacaranda (*Tipuana tipu*), which looks like a labernum with light yellow flowers. The best of the shrubs include brunfelsia, whose flowers change from purple to mauve and then white; calliandra, with delicate, fine leaves and fluffy red bobbles for flowers, and bird of paradise (*Caesalpinia gilliesii*), whose open clusters of yellow flowers have bright red stamens.

The gardens are English in style, having many areas of lawn and curving paths. There is also a French influence seen in the number of formal pools and statues, particularly of nymphs. One marble nymph stands in a scallop-shaped, marble pool surrounded by white-flowered water lilies, while another stands in a bed of pansies edged with *Festuca glauca* with a lavender-blue jacaranda in the distance. RChe

Paso Correntino

Soriano, Uruguay

DESIGNERS: Rosemarie Symonds Chilibroste, Roy Cheek
OWNER: Rosemarie Symonds Chilibroste
GARDEN STYLE: 20th-century cottage and Robinsonian
SIZE: 7 acres (2.8 ha)
CLIMATE: Humid subtropical
LOCATION: Mercedes, Soriano

Visiting this garden involves traveling through remote countryside, with few vehicles, gauchos on horseback driving cattle, black-necked swans on the lakes, mauve lantana, and *Acacia cavens* in the hedges. An old, single-story house that was once a shop, marks what is a private estate open by appointment.

The central garden is enclosed and kept cool by shady verandas with displays of antique agricultural equipment, including branding irons. A tall Canary Island date palm (*Phoenix canariensis*) towers above everything, owls nesting in the top. The house door is framed in yellow banksian roses with sweet-scented bushes of *Pittosporum tobira* 'Variegatum' at the sides. A Gothic arch has been cut through a hedge of cotoneasters by careful pruning, leading to a statue of St. Fiacre, patron saint of gardeners.

At this point the arboretum merges seamlessly into a cottage garden. A crimson-flowered *Melianthus major* blends in with big, scarlet bottlebrushes loved by hummingbirds that feed on the nectar. All manner of climbers snake over the trunks of old fruit trees with apples, pears, plums, apricots, and figs. Island beds are packed with everything from dahlias to larkspur. Then it's time to wander past an old, gnarled pepper tree (*Schinus molle*), scented pittosporums, and strange shaped boughs on the way to the river. It's hidden by thick trees on the bank, where pruning has created a series of windows through the foliage, giving marvelous views of the water. The hedges are filled with *Lantana montevidensis* and potato vine (*Solanum jasminoides*), and blue butterflies. RChe

Mantua

Montevideo, Uruguay

DESIGNERS: Carol Brown, Roy Cheek
OWNER: Carol Brown
GARDEN STYLE: 20th-century cottage and formal
SIZE: Approximately 1.5 acres (0.6 ha)
CLIMATE: Humid subtropical
LOCATION: Montevideo

Carrasco is the garden suburb of Uruguay's capital, Montevideo. Sandy beaches lie to the south, countryside to the north. The house at Mantua is broad, spacious, and mostly single-story, set in a large, rectangular garden.

The central lawn has a weeping mulberry tree and large pool. An open gazebo is festooned with roses and blue nepeta at each base, and everywhere you look there is a plethora of stunning plants that have been cleverly linked. There is a rare, purple-leaved casuarina, a white-edged ivy around a statue of a cherub with *Saxifraga stolonifera* at its base and, in the little bosquet at the end of the garden, shrubs and shade-tolerant plants that create a subtropical, lush glade. *Pseudopanax lessonii* 'Gold Splash' has handlike leaves and blue flowers, while *Farfugium japonicum* 'Aureomaculatum' has large, round leaves with yellow spots.

A separate, smaller lawn with a central pool and fountain fills the raised terrace by the house. At the far end is a path leading to a colorful mixed border and an informal, cottage-style area spanned by three rose-covered arches. This feature is unexpected and is all the more stunning for it. RChe

> "...everywhere you look there is a plethora of stunning plants that have been cleverly linked"

Esquina Ventosa

Maldonado, Uruguay

DESIGNERS: Mercedes Drever Villar, Roy Cheek
OWNER: Mercedes Drever Villar
GARDEN STYLE: 20th-century cottage and Gertrude Jekyll
SIZE: 4 acres (1.6 ha)
CLIMATE: Humid subtropical
LOCATION: Solis, Maldonado

Also known as Windy Corner, this private garden belongs to the vice president of the International Rose Society. The drive festooned with old roses is a taste of some of the treats ahead. This is followed by a bungalow chimney covered by the violet-blue flowers of oceanblue morning glory (*Ipomoea indica*). The color theme is picked up by a tibouchina shrub at the chimney's base and a nearby pool. An arch of foliage cut in a weeping 'Pendula' mulberry (*Morus alba*) frames the view across the lawn to a gazebo. This feature forms the centerpiece of a small, square garden containing four beds of herbs that have been edged with neatly clipped cotton lavender (*Santolina chamaecyparissus*). Surrounding the arch are short hedges in which bay cones have been cleverly set in the corners.

At the entrance, hedges rise to buttress the arches, garlanded in pink and white rambling roses that smartly stand out against the tall, dark background hedge of Italian cypress (*Cupressus sempervirens*). Across the lawn, a fine group of cedars and a light green swamp cypress form the background to an arched pergola of cascading yellow banksian roses.

The mixed boundary hedge and the tall trees beyond it lead the eye toward a kidney-shaped pool and a fountain with a simple jet. Despite all these features, the extraordinary show of roses is always present. A semicircular, domed rose pergola provides color, scent, rest, and shade, and imaginatively conceals the telephone poles behind. RChe

> "An arch of foliage cut in a weeping mulberry...frames the view across the lawn..."

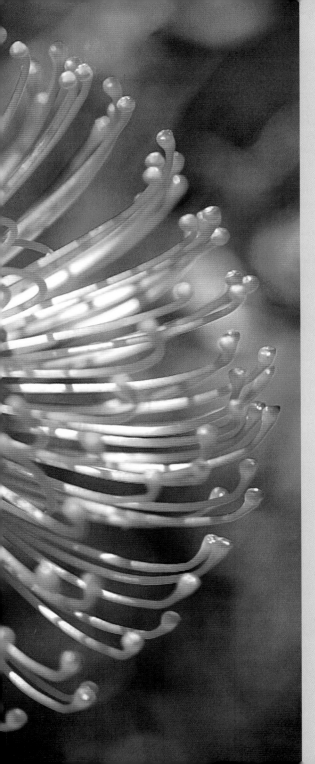

Nature looms large in most African gardens. For raw South African beauty nothing surpasses Namaqualand, a huge semi-desert, where masses of bulbs and wildflowers emerge after the heavy winter rains. In Morocco, Yves Saint-Laurent's renovation of the old walled paradise garden at Majorelle displays the most exotic taste. By contrast, restrained Islamic garden designs with enclosed oases and water features prevail in Egypt.

AFRICA

Al Bahia Palace Gardens

Marrakech-Tensift-El Haouz, Morocco

DESIGNER: Muhammad al Mekki
OWNER: City of Marrakech
GARDEN STYLE: 19th-century formal Islamic-Spanish
SIZE: 20 acres (8.1 ha)
CLIMATE: Mediterranean
LOCATION: Marrakech, Marrakech-Tensift-El Haouz

The Palace of Al Bahia, meaning "The Bright" (or "The Brilliant"), consists of a series of buildings, including a mosque, around paved courtyards, and extensive, flower- and foliage-filled gardens that are reminiscent of Andalucía. Built in the nineteenth century, the palace was designed by the architect Muhammad al Mekki for Ahmed Ibn Moussa, known as Ba Ahmed, the son of the grand vizier or minister, Abd al Rahman. It took nearly fifteen years to complete and contained more than 140 rooms for Ba Ahmed, his family, servants, and guards.

The palace includes a concubines' courtyard, an area reserved for four wives and eighty concubines, decorated with a central basin and surrounded by rooms intended for the concubines. U.S. writer Edith Wharton visited Morocco in 1917 and stayed as a guest in the harem when the palace was still used as a residence. She wrote about her experience in her book *In Morocco* (1920).

The surfaces inside and out are decorated with rich designs, many of them floral, ranging from painted and gilded wooden doorways, and cedar wood ceilings to *zillig*, or mosaic tiles, in geometrical patterns on walls and floors.

The secluded inner courtyards are fourfold *chahar bagh* gardens with marble and glazed-tile paths meeting at a central, circular basin. The quadrants between are set at a lower level and are filled with lush plantings, including tall date palms, orange and banana trees, and fragrant jasmine in the large garden adjacent to the concubines' courtyard. EH

> "The quadrants... are filled with lush plantings, including tall date palms, orange and banana trees..."

Les Jardins de La Mamounia

Marrakech-Tensift-El Haouz, Morocco

DESIGNER: Pasha Mamoun
OWNER: The Mamounia Hotel
GARDEN STYLE: 18th-century formal Arab-Islamic
SIZE: 20 acres (8.1 ha)
CLIMATE: Mediterranean
LOCATION: Marrakech, Marrakech-Tensift-El Haouz

Gnarled olive trees planted two centuries ago still line the Mamounia's main avenue leading to Prince Moulay Mamoun's small, but perfectly proportioned, pavilion. The magnificent gardens, known originally as Arset el Mamoun, were a wedding gift to the prince from his father, Sultan Sidi Mohamed Ben Abdellah, ruler of Marrakech in the eighteenth century. The hotel dates to the French colonial period.

The gardens adjacent to the hotel are formal and floriferous, with roses and massed annuals in beds edged with evergreens beneath swaying palm trees. Fountains bubble over the edges of elegant marble basins to fill tiled pools backed by stands of bamboo and banana. Beyond these intimate and immaculately maintained flower beds, there is a vast oasis, an extended *chahar bagh* fourfold garden enclosed by walls 985-feet-long (300 m) and dripping with bougainvillea. The planted areas, between wide walkways lined with olive trees, consist of well-watered lawns set with flowering shrubs and fruit trees.

The hotel has received a number of well-known guests over the years who have enjoyed the gardens. One of the most renowned is former British Prime Minister Sir Winston Churchill, who chose to stay there because he enjoyed painting the views from the roof, which he described as "paintaceous." The Mamounia has also attracted the attention of filmmakers as a location setting, including director Sir Alfred Hitchcock, who used it in his classic work *The Man Who Knew Too Much* (1956). EH

Al Badia
Palace Gardens

Marrakech-Tensift-El Haouz, Morocco

DESIGNER: Ahmed al Mansur
OWNER: City of Marrakech
GARDEN STYLE: 16th-century formal Islamic-Spanish
SIZE: 7 acres (1.5 ha)
CLIMATE: Mediterranean
LOCATION: Marrakech, Marrakech-Tensift-El Haouz

Massive crumbling walls, now home to storks' nests, enclose the Al Badia (meaning "Incomparable") Palace. which was built between 1578 and 1603 by the most powerful ruler of the Saadian dynasty, Ahmed al Mansur, to commemorate the Moroccan victory over the Portuguese in 1578 at Ksar El Kebir. The wealth from the ransom of Portuguese captives helped build what was a sumptuous and impressive palace in its heyday. Its surfaces were once decorated with marble and onyx, which were removed in 1696 to decorate royal palaces in Meknes; by the eighteenth century, Al Badia was a mere shell.

The huge, enclosed *chahar bagh*, or fourfold garden, consists of a pool 295 feet (90 m) long with a planted island in the center, surrounded by raised, white marble walkways. The quadrants between are 8 feet (3 m) lower than the central pool, and the pipes used for periodic flooding of these planted areas are visible. Fruit trees—citrus, myrtle, and jasmine—in ordered arrangement hint at the garden's former glory, when these sunken beds would have been so lushly planted as to form richly colored carpets when viewed from above. Pavilions at each end of the garden are flanked by rectangular pools and fountains.

From a viewing platform in the palace walls, the prospect of the palace garden's formal layout is magnificent. EH

Le Jardin
Majorelle

Marrakech-Tensift-El Haouz, Morocco

DESIGNER: Jacques Majorelle
OWNER: Association Jardin Majorelle
GARDEN STYLE: 20th-century Islamic art deco
SIZE: 1 acre (0.4 ha)
CLIMATE: Mediterranean
LOCATION: Marrakech, Marrakech-Tensift-El Haouz

Also known as the Majorelle Garden, this garden of lush greens, acid yellows, and dashes of hot red and orange is suffused with the vivid blue that became known as Bleu Majorelle. It was created in the 1920s and 1930s by French painter Jacques Majorelle.

Enclosed by high walls, long, narrow water channels are linked to a square pool, with raised walkways that allow for periodic flooding of planted areas. From the hot, sunlit street, you enter a world of bubbling fountains and luxuriant growth. Dark areas open on to sunlit glades in a constant play of light and shadow. Dramatic plantings of palms and dragon trees cast shadows over bamboos and banana fronds; sharp agaves are interplanted with prickly cactus; and giant euphorbias rub shoulders with spiky aloes. Bougainvilleas make magenta cascades as they climb trees and structures. Above all, there is the excitement of cobalt blue on walls, gates, pergolas, terra-cotta pots, and pond edges.

Majorelle was an avid collector and imported rare varieties, including palms from the South Pacific, water lilies and lotus from Asia, and succulents from South Africa. In 1980 French fashion designers Yves Saint-Laurent and Pierre Bergé bought the property and restored the garden and studio. EH

RIGHT Jacques Majorelle financed plant expeditions and imported cacti from the American Southwest.

Jardins de l'Agdal

Marrakech-Tensift-El Haouz, Morocco

DESIGNER: Sultan Moulay Abderrahmane
OWNERS: The Moroccan Royal family
GARDEN STYLE: 12th- and 19th-century Islamic-Spanish
SIZE: 40 acres (16.1 ha)
CLIMATE: Mediterranean
LOCATION: Marrakech, Marrakech-Tensift-El Haouz

These vast royal gardens, also known as The Aguedal Gardens or The Agdal, were once a profitable, private agricultural estate. The shade of the orchard's fruit trees amid the hot desert landscape provided a welcome haven where sultans could enjoy parties and picnics.

There are orange groves, fig, citrus, pomegranate, and apricot orchards, olive plantations, and vineyards, all irrigated by pools fed by an ancient system of underground channels from the Ourika Valley in the High Atlas. The largest body of water is a mammoth 10-acre (4 ha) tank next to a single-story pavilion, the Dar al Hana, or House of Health. In 1873 Sultan Mohammed IV drowned in this enormous lagoon while boating with his son.

The gardens were established in the twelfth century by Sultan Abd al Mumin, and enlarged over the centuries. By the eighteenth century, the high walls built of mud and clay had been breached by tribesmen whose cattle grazed in the orchards. Sultan Moulay Abderrahmane redesigned the gardens in the mid-nineteenth century, and they have remained in the ownership of the royal family ever since. EH

"These vast royal gardens... were once a profitable, private agricultural estate"

Jardins de Ménara

Marrakech-Tensift-El Haouz, Morocco

DESIGNER: Sultan Moulay Abderrahmane
OWNER: City of Marrakech
GARDEN STYLE: 12th- and 19th-century formal Arab-Islamic
SIZE: 237 acres (96 ha)
CLIMATE: Mediterranean
LOCATION: Marrakech, Marrakech-Tensift-El Haouz

The layout of these peaceful gardens, located to the west of Marrakech, could not be simpler. There is a large, raised, 8-acre (3 ha) tank and olive groves, date-palm plantations, and orchards are enclosed by high mud and brick walls. Horticulturally there is not a great deal to write about, but there is something magical about the light, especially at sunrise and sunset, which makes a visit to the Ménara Gardens an unforgettable experience. It is also a social space where young Moroccans can meet with friends, and chat and listen to music away from the bustle of the city.

In the early morning light, the pleasure pavilion, with its pyramid-shaped, green-tiled roof, is reflected in the still water. Instead of being dwarfed by the vast lake, the elegant building with its arched openings seems to dominate the scene, as if floating at the water's edge above dark cypresses and palms planted at a lower level, with snowcapped mountains away in the distance.

The gardens were laid out in the twelfth century, during the Almohad period, as a resort where the sultans could escape the hardship of the summer heat, relax, and enjoy some shade, but they were redesigned in the middle of the nineteenth century by Sultan Moulay Abderrahmane. He also rebuilt the pavilion, and it is said that he would throw the female companion he had spent the evening with in the pavilion into the lake at dawn. A canal system is also used to irrigate the gardens and orchards. EH

Al Montazah Palace Gardens

Al Iskandariyah, Egypt

DESIGNER: Unknown
OWNER: The Egyptian State
GARDEN STYLE: 19th- and 20th-century formal
　Italianate landscaped
SIZE: 115 acres (46.5 ha)
CLIMATE: Semiarid
LOCATION: Alexandria, Al Iskandariyah

The port of Alexandria has traditionally been a place where wealthy Egyptians escape the oppressive summer heat of Cairo to enjoy the sea breezes of the Mediterranean coast. Al Montazah was such a summer retreat for the Egyptian royal family.

The construction of the Al Montazah complex was started in 1892 by King Abbas II, the last *khedive*, or viceroy, of Egypt, who built a large palace called the Salamlek. Turkish-Florentine in style, the palace's crenellated central tower is a replica of that of the Palazzo Vecchio in Florence, and dominates what is a confection of a building. In 1932, King Fuad I built a larger palace and called it the Haramlik. His son, King Farouk I, built a bridge to the sea to act as a waterfront. The palaces and gardens are bordered by walls to the south, east, and west, and by a beach on the north side. The larger palace was restored by President Anwar Sadat, and today is the summer residence of President Hosni Mubarak. The gardens are open to the public for a small fee, and with sea views, lush lawns, palms, pines, grazing deer, and access to the beach, they attract locals as a place to relax, play music, and picnic. CK

> "...sea views, lush lawns, palms, pines, grazing deer, and access to the beach..."

Al Azhar Park

Al Qāhirah, Egypt

DESIGNER: Sites International, Cairo
OWNERS: Aga Khan Trust for Culture, Governorate of Cairo
GARDEN STYLE: 20th-century Islamic public park
SIZE: 74 acres (30 ha)
CLIMATE: Arid
LOCATION: Cairo, Al Qāhirah

Until the creation of this public park, which opened in 2005, Cairo boasted an average of one footprint, or 3 square inches (19 sq. cm) of green space for each of its seventeen million inhabitants. Al Azhar Park, which rises above the Ayyubid City Wall on one side and the City of the Dead on the other, is therefore a green oasis in a desert of concrete and brick.

This new garden has been created on the site of an earlier one, made during the Fatamid reconstruction of Cairo in the late tenth century. However, for the past half millennium, the site was a rubbish dump, and thousands of tons of soil had to be removed, with environmental cleaning to strip the ground of high levels of salts and pollutants.

The park has expansive views in all directions, and was planned as an Islamic version of the "Mixed Style." It has a rectilinear core and curvilinear surroundings. The difference is that the core draws from a range of Islamic paradise gardens rather than from the baroque, and its prime feature is the main axis. The walkway runs the length of the site, from the high point of the restaurant, past the *chahar bagh* (quadripartite) garden and lake frontage. The axis is enlivened by water features, including fountains, brooks, canals, and *chadar* (water chutes), inspired by regional Islamic gardens. Surrounding this central zone are lawns and informal planting. There are more than 325 different plant species, many native to Egpyt. There is also a *bustan*, or orchard, and covering the circular pool at the top of the cascade are trees in raised containers, creating a shady awning. TM

Karnak

Qinā, Egypt

DESIGNER: Unknown
OWNER: The Egyptian State
GARDEN STYLE: Ancient Egyptian
SIZE: 247 acres (100 ha)
CLIMATE: Arid
LOCATION: Luxor, Qinā

Located by the eastern bank of the River Nile, near to Luxor (ancient Thebes), Karnak, also known as the Festival Temple, was a religious complex. Within the precincts stood temple buildings and residences for the priesthood, and open spaces that were developed as gardens. Ancient Egyptian gardens are the forerunners of today's formal gardens, which use plants as architectural elements, given that gardens in the Nile Valley were on the edge of the desert where natural vegetation is sparse. The gardens created by the Egyptians were based on straight lines and symmetry. Fruit trees, date and doum palms, and vines in symmetrical arrangements, providing food and shade, were common. Gardens were used to grow herbs for culinary, cosmetic, and medicinal purposes, and plants for food. Archaeologists are uncertain what plants were cultivated here, but it is likely that cucumber, onion, lettuce, garlic, radish, melon, and legumes were grown in vegetable beds.

At the center of the Karnak complex was a sacred lake in which the priests of Amun purified themselves for religious rituals. Such water features would have contained water lilies, aquatic lotus (*Nymphaea lotus* and *N. caerulea*), edged by papyrus (*Cyperus papyrus*) and small shrubs grown in large earthenware pots.

Beyond the sixth pylon lies the major work of Thutmose III (ca.1516–1450 BCE), who ruled during the Eighteenth Dynasty of Tutankhamun. His military triumphs are commemorated on the inside walls surrounding the granite sanctuary at Karnak, called Most Splendid of Monuments. He built the Akh-Mnw, or Festival Hall; a part of the vestibule of the latter is called the Botanical Room. Here you can see wall decorations showing plants, animals, and birds brought to Egypt from Syria by the pharaoh in his bid to create what may have been the first ever botanical garden. Plants depicted include iris, caranchoe, palm, pomegranate, and alum. TM

Brenthurst Gardens

Gauteng, South Africa

DESIGNERS: Sir Herbert Baker, Sid Rogers, Joane Pim
OWNER: City of Johannesburg
GARDEN STYLE: 20th-century naturalistic park
SIZE: 42 acres (17 ha)
CLIMATE: Humid subtropical
LOCATION: Johannesburg, Gauteng

The Brenthurst estate, with a house built in 1906 by Sir Herbert Baker, was bought by the Oppenheimer family in 1922. Sir Ernest Oppenheimer had joined a London diamond firm when he was sixteen, before emigrating to South Africa, where he made his fortune in the diamond industry. Baker had described the house as favoring the design of a "beautiful garden with terraces, pergolas, water pools, and a natural rock garden in the lichened rocks."

The garden's character began to emerge after World War II when the head gardener, Sid Rogers, softened Baker's original steep, stone terraces and built the first waterfalls near the house. In the late 1950s, Harry Oppenheimer inherited Brenthurst with his wife, Bridget. In their enthusiasm to reshape the garden, they engaged landscape designer Joane Pim.

Pim suggested building a new terrace in front of the house to link with the lawns below, and reduced the steepness of the steps by introducing two arched bridges. The view from the terrace takes in the round pool, graced by two Chinese storks, and, on the far side, a 1914 cast of Renoir's *Venus Victorieuse*. Pim developed the hillside above as a wild garden for indigenous plants, featuring banks of proteas, Cape flowers, Transvaal bushes, and Namaqualand daisies. Successive gardeners since Pim's death in 1972 have developed the wild garden even further, making it one of the outstanding features of Brenthurst. JHa

LEFT Water features such as waterfalls and ponds contribute to the harmonious mood of Brenthurst.

Namaqualand

Northern Cape, South Africa

DESIGNER: None
OWNER: State owned land and private farmland
GARDEN STYLE: Natural area
SIZE: 23,166 square miles (60,000 sq. km)
CLIMATE: Semiarid
LOCATION: Namaqualand, Northern Cape

Although not a garden in the traditional sense of the word, Namaqualand bursts into a dazzling floral display every spring. The wild flowers that carpet the ground in an array of mauve, yellow, and white transform what is essentially a barren semidesert. Most of the flowers belong to the different species of Asteraceae, or daisies, including *Osteospermum*, *Arctotis*, and *Dimorphotheca*. There are also aloes, gladioli, and lilies; in total, there are about 4,000 different species in the area, flowering from August to October.

Conservation International has recognized this region as the only arid hot spot of biodiversity, placing it among the twenty-five most ecologically valuable places in the world. The colorful areas at Skilpad Nature Reserve, now part of Namaqua National Park, are maintained by a regimen that involves lack of disturbance from grazing animals and plowing after the spring.

There are about 1,000 species of succulent in the area, making up at least one-third of the desert's flora, and one-tenth of the world's succulents. The region is also home to numerous edible and medicinal plants prized by the indigenous Khoi and Nama tribes.

The best place to visit in the area is the Namaqua National Park, open from 8 AM to 5 PM during the spring flower season. The flowers are at their best only in sunshine, and between 10:30 AM and 4 PM Flower tours are booked up well in advance, but independent visitors can call the regional and national "flower hotlines" for information. BS

Durban Botanic Gardens

KwaZulu-Natal, South Africa

DESIGNER: Dr. John Medley Wood
OWNER: Ethekwini Municipality
GARDEN STYLE: 19th-century botanical
SIZE: 37 acres (14.9 ha)
CLIMATE: Dry tropical
LOCATION: Durban, KwaZulu-Natal

Durban Botanic Gardens were established in 1849, making them the oldest surviving botanical garden in Africa. Situated in the center of South Africa's bustling Indian Ocean port of Durban, it is easy to forget that, in the gardens' infancy, elephants, hippos, and even the occasional lion were to be found on its paths.

The gardens began life as an experimental plot on which to trial plants of economic potential. The botanical nature of the gardens was primarily concerned with commerce and with providing crops for Natal's colonists to grow for profit. In fact the source of much of the wealth that was to feed the local economy—sugar and forestry—initially

came from here. Plants from all over the world were cultivated, including specimens of eucalyptus, agathis, and jackfruit tree. More than 130 species of palm now flourish here, in addition to smaller, colorful plants in the Bromeliad Garden and the Orchid House.

It would be wrong, however, to consider the gardens as purely exotic. The emblem of the gardens is the South African cycad (*Encephalartos woodii*), one of the rarest plants in the world. It was named after its discoverer, Dr. John Medley Wood, who was the gardens' curator from 1882 to 1913. The magnificent specimen of this living fossil alone is worth a visit, and is the crowning glory of one of the world's finest collections of cycads. The influence of Dr. Wood on the gardens cannot be overstated. He remains one of South Africa's greatest botanists, but he also oversaw the development of the gardens into what they are today; a mix of exotic and native trees, and cycads that thrill both the amateur and the expert. AM

Natal National Botanical Garden

KwaZulu-Natal, South Africa

DESIGNERS: Pietermaritzburg Botanical Society,
G. W. Mitchell, W. E. Marriot
OWNER: South African National Biodiversity Institute
GARDEN STYLE: 19th-, 20th-, and 21st-century botanical
SIZE: 30 acres (12 ha), within 128 acres (52 ha)
CLIMATE: Dry tropical
LOCATION: Pietermaritzburg, KwaZulu-Natal

This wonderful garden is a beautiful example of both old- and new-style botanical gardens in an area with hot summers, misty winters, and high rainfall. Begun in the 1870s as an experimental station for trialing exotic trees for forestry, the garden now contains indigenous flora of the region, much of which has been eradicated elsewhere. From the outset, the relationship between the old and the new is characterized by lofty, exotic trees from Asia, Europe, and New Zealand, all underplanted with local natives, including kniphofias and dieramas.

An avenue of plane trees greets the visitor near the entrance, and characterizes this nineteenth-century approach to the botanical garden while, at ground level, swaths of local delights, such as crinum and clivias, hold sway. Beyond the older plantings of the garden is an area of woodland full of indigenous trees, with combretum, calodendron, and turraea, bordering a small river and lake. Beyond the woodland is the Midlands Meadow, an area of indigenous grassland plants and a key part of the conservation program. As for plants used by man, the Muthi Garden, a Zulu herbal garden, has a range of local medicinal plants from aloes to agapanthus.

The Natal National Botanical Garden reflects the colonial period during which it was created, but it is now driven by a spirit of conservation, focusing on the extraordinary floral wealth of the region. AM

Sheilam Cactus Garden

Western Cape, South Africa

DESIGNER: Maarten Malherbe
OWNERS: Garth Schwegmann, Minette Schwegmann
GARDEN STYLE: 20th-century nursery and desert
cactus collection
SIZE: 6 acres (2.4 ha)
CLIMATE: Mediterranean
LOCATION: Robertson, Western Cape

Where else in the world would you find beds of cactus shaded by trees laden with apricots? At Sheilam you find this, and more. The garden, situated in the Breede River Valley, looks like a set for a Western movie, with the purple mountains rising as a backdrop.

Sheilam was established in 1954 when nurseryman Maarten Malherbe bought the property. He and his wife, Molly, used the first letter of each of their seven children's names to create the name "Sheilam." Although the property was originally an ostrich and apricot farm, Maarten and Molly brought a collection of cacti with them. People kept asking for seeds or cuttings, and it was from these small beginnings that the nursery and garden evolved. Since 1967 it has been owned by the Schwegmann family (Garth and Minette).

More than 2,000 species of plant can be seen, including the impressive Old Man of Mexico (*Cephalocereus*) and the Golden Barrel (*Echinocactus grusonii*); other plants have bizarre names, including horses' teeth and elephants' feet. The garden is laid out in a fairly austere way in blocks of different species, but it is the style of planting that makes it so impressive, as well as the sheer size, shape, and color. Closer viewing of the plants gives a unique insight into how they use camouflage, self-defense mechanisms, and survival strategies, while displaying an amazing combination of texture and design. SY

Rustenberg Farm Gardens

Western Cape, South Africa

DESIGNER: Rozanne Barlow
OWNERS: Simon Barlow, Rozanne Barlow
GARDEN STYLE: 21st-century formal garden
SIZE: 2.5 acres (1 ha)
CLIMATE: Mediterranean
LOCATION: Stellenbosch, Western Cape

The Rustenberg Wine Estate is most famous for its Stellenbosch wines, and there has been a vineyard at the site since 1682. The current owners, the Barlow family, have run the estate for more than sixty years. The old garden—a farm garden with lawn, fruit trees, a clay tennis court, and swimming pool that is now the koi pond—was cleared and landscaped by Rozanne Barlow in 2001. The new garden is framed by formal paths and enclosed within walls.

To reach the garden, you walk under a century-old pergola, covered with vines and climbers. What immediately stand out are the formality and soft plantings of roses, foxgloves, irises, agapanthus, and nicotiana with a surrounding of old English oaks (*Quercus robur*); beyond are Mount Simonsberg and pastures with Jersey cows. One particularly gentle touch is the small, formal rose garden planted with *Rosa* 'Little Pink Hedge' with lavender in the center. Also look out for the labyrinth made with brick paving and an edging of river stones, which takes ten minutes to walk. After that, it's just a quick step to the winery and tasting rooms. BS

> "...soft plantings of roses, foxgloves, irises, agapanthus and nicotiana..."

Kirstenbosch National Botanical Garden

Western Cape, South Africa

DESIGNER: Professor Harold Pearson
OWNER: South African National Biodiversity Institute
STYLE: 20th-century botanical garden in parkland
SIZE: Garden 89 acres (36 ha), park 1,305 acres (528 ha)
CLIMATE: Mediterranean
LOCATION: Cape Town, Western Cape

The Kirstenbosch National Botanical Garden has become as much a symbol of South Africa as Table Mountain, in whose shadow the garden lies. Established in 1913 on land left to the nation by the colonialist Cecil Rhodes, Kirstenbosch was the first botanical garden in the world whose principal motivation was to preserve its nation's flora. Most of the plants grown in the gardens are indigenous to South Africa. One of the few foreign species is an avenue of camphor trees (*Cinnamonum camphora*) planted to honor Queen Victoria; under the trees' canopy are plantings of shade loving bulbs and herbaceous perennials. On the outer edges of the site, you'll also see the remains of the hedge of wild almonds that was planted in the 1660s to mark the perimeter of the newly established Cape Colony.

Kirstenbosch holds many "living collections" and, within a natural amphitheater, you'll see an imposing group of palmlike *Encephalartos* cycads—living fossils that have changed little since prehistoric times. In the middle of the group, a plant extinct in the wild, *Encephalartos woodii*, is caged to protect it from theft.

Even in midwinter, the gardens are full of color and interest. The crane flower (*Strelitzia reginae*) is the emblem of the garden, and during the winter, there is the imposing yellow form, 'Mandela's Gold'. JHo

RIGHT Set against the eastern slopes of Table Mountain, the world renowned Kirstenbosch National Botanical Garden.

Vergelegen Garden

Western Cape, South Africa

DESIGNER: Ian Ford & Associates

OWNER: Anglo American Farms

GARDEN STYLE: 20th-century formal

SIZE: Garden 150 acres (60.7 ha), estate 7,413 acres (3,000 ha)

CLIMATE: Mediterranean

LOCATION: Somerset West, Western Cape

Vergelegen, meaning "situated far away," earned its reputation as a gardener's paradise soon after the property was granted to the governor of the Cape, Willem Adriaan van der Stel, in 1700. He was a farmer, botanist, forester, and successful horticulturist, and the five camphor trees (*Cinnamomum camphora*) that he planted 300 years ago stand in a row by the homestead.

After six years, Van der Stel had half a million vines, fruit orchards and orange groves, 1,000 cattle, and 1,800 sheep, but his enterprise proved too much for the local Free Burghers, who arranged for the Dutch East India Company to order him back to the Netherlands.

Vergelegen then passed through a succession of owners. Charles and Cynthia Barlow bought it in 1941, and it was during their time that the royal equerry, Peter Townsend, told King George VI and Queen Elizabeth about this "magically beautiful place." During their tour of South Africa in 1947, they were said to be "overcome by Vergelegen's loveliness."

In 1987 the gardens were restored; they now have a White Garden, a Rose Garden, and an Octagonal Garden with a view to the house along 1,312 feet (400 m) of herbaceous borders. The twin, 10-foot-wide (3 m) borders have two seasonal planting times. In spring 8,000 daffodil and tulip bulbs are planted among summer-flowering perennials (with delphiniums, gauras, anemones, and hollyhocks), but annuals, including cleome and nicotiana, are added in September. There is also a project to nurture the return of natural *fynbos* vegetation to the area. JHa

Stellenberg Gardens

Western Cape, South Africa

DESIGNERS: Sandy Ovenstone, David Hicks
OWNERS: Andrew Ovenstone,
  Sandy Ovenstone
GARDEN STYLE: 20th-century formal
SIZE: 6.5 acres (2.6 ha)
CLIMATE: Mediterranean
LOCATION: Kenilworth, Western Cape

Andrew and Sandy Ovenstone inherited the eighteenth-century manor house of Stellenberg in 1974, and much of Sandy's thinking was inspired by three English gardens—Hidcote and Sissinghurst (see pages 305 and 370), and Lady Salisbury's garden at Hatfield House (see page 332)—as well as other gardens in Provence. The house contains the family's collection of modern European and South African art, including work by Maud Sumner and Cecil Higgs.

Seen from the breakfast room window, across a stone terrace and lawn, the White Garden is a delight, stretching opposite the east side of the house with a pair of decorated white columns at one end. On the far side is a collection of white roses backed up by a profusion of white perennials, and on the other side of the house, a gray painted swimming pool nestles in the lawn, within walls and flower beds rich in color and texture. Scented mandevilla and pink and double-white daturas flourish here among 'Albertine' roses, bougainvillea, and hibiscus.

The gates of this garden open on to steps descending either side of a raised stone pool to a formal, walled garden, designed by David Hicks as a silver wedding present from Andrew. Here, backed by the lower slopes of Table Mountain, are low myrtle hedges that, either side of a long tunnel of seven arches of *Rosa* 'New Dawn', are used to create parterres. They contain David Austin roses and massed perennials on one side, and one-color plantings in beds on the other, with bowers of 'Iceberg' roses geometrically placed in the gravel between them. JHa

Old Nectar

Western Cape, South Africa

DESIGNER: Una van der Spuy
OWNER: Una van der Spuy
GARDEN STYLE: 20th-century formal country garden
SIZE: 3.7 acres (1.5 ha)
CLIMATE: Mediterranean
LOCATION: Stellenbosch, Western Cape

The beautiful town of Stellenbosch lies near the head of the Eerste River valley, famed for its vineyards and some of South Africa's finest gardens. One of them, Old Nectar, has become a National Monument, and is the only private garden in South Africa to have such an honor. It is still owned by its creator, Una van der Spuy, who was born in 1912.

She and her husband, General K. R. van der Spuy, bought the Cape Dutch house in 1941 as a rather dilapidated property with a few acres of ground. They saw what a wonderful site it was, set in the Jonkershoek Valley, with mountains rising high in the background. With the general away at war, Una began restoring the house and, in 1942, tackled the garden. Some impressive oaks lining the drive were thought to be worth keeping, and they now provide the backdrop. She began by terracing the steeply sloping site, and you will now find seven small gardens, providing a perfect setting for the house, which is reached by a flight of stone steps covered with erigeron daisies.

The Rose Garden in front is formal with triangular beds, containing one variety of rose each, converging on a central, wrought-iron ornament. The view from here is of wide lawn terraces descending from a round lily pond; lower down, a classically designed, long, stone-edged swimming pool catches the eye. At the bottom, a long, curving, broad walk is covered by pergolas bearing 150 old roses, intertwined with clematis. This tranquil spot is a place for contemplation and relaxation. JHa

> "...a National Monument, and is the only private garden...to have such an honor"

Karoo Desert National Botanical Garden

Western Cape, South Africa

DESIGNER: Jacques Thudichum
OWNER: South African National Biodiversity Institute
GARDEN STYLE: 20th-century botanical garden
SIZE: Garden 27 acres (11 ha), park 355 acres (144 ha)
CLIMATE: Mediterranean
LOCATION: Worcester, Western Cape

The word *karoo* means dry area, and the Karoo Botanical Garden is probably the world's most arid garden. The parched landscape has a lunar appearance that is the perfect setting for the strange and magnificent plants that thrive in this inhospitable environment. Many of the plants here are unique to the area, and more than 300 species are rare or endangered.

In spring the garden is covered with technicolor carpets as thousands of orange, yellow, and cream Namaqualand daisies (gazanias) open in the strengthening sun. Joining them are swaths of ursinias, deep blue heliophilas, and paler blue felicias, and, as the season progresses, iridescent red and purple mesembryanthemums. The extent of the spectacle depends on the previous year's rainfall, but it is always dazzling. In winter, against a backdrop of snow-covered mountains, the aloes burst into flower in orange and red.

Succulents flourish year round, making the site the Southern Hemisphere's largest succulent garden. In the searing heat of summer, when most plants would be baked to dust, the specially adapted stems and roots of succulents help them to prosper and bloom. These unfamiliar and bizarre plants with their swollen stems, sparse, spiky foliage, and fantastic flowers seem otherworldly. Note the specially marked walking trails, with explanatory information panels, throughout the garden. JHo

The Garden Route

Western/Eastern Cape, South Africa

DESIGNER: None
OWNERS: Various
GARDEN STYLE: Natural landscapes
LENGTH: 130 miles (208 km)
CLIMATE: Mediterranean
LOCATION: Western/Eastern Cape

This conservation route is a long strip of coastal plain that stretches between Mossel Bay and Storms River Mouth, with forested areas intersected by rivers that run out to the rocky shore. You'll see areas of indigenous forest, freshwater lakes, wetlands, hidden coves, and long beaches.

The narrow coastal plain is well forested, and is mostly bordered by extensive lagoons that run behind a barrier of sand dunes and white beaches. The region has some of the largest patches of indigenous forest in the country—giant yellow wood trees and wildflowers—as well as commercial plantations of eucalyptus and pine. The existing forested area is, however, a small remnant of the original hardwood forest, now largely replaced by commercial plantations.

One of the main centers on the Garden Route is Knysna, at the heart of the forested area. Trees surround a lagoon, with the only forest dwelling elephants in the country. Knysna and its surrounds are also remarkably rich in what is known in Afrikaans as *fynbos*, the fine bush that abounds in Cape Province. (The best time of year to enjoy the Cape flowers, especially the proteas, is from July to October, depending on the level of winter rainfall.) Within Knysna forest, there is also a network of trails taking in trees of importance, with the Arboretum Trail leading to the "Big Tree," an allegedly 600-year-old yellow wood. BS

The first European settlers brought
a wide range of garden styles to
Australia, yet no one fashion has ever
dominated design. The varied climate
of the continent allows for an amazing
assortment of distinctive, inventive
styles. New Zealand is climatically
just as diverse, and conditions for
cultivation are often superb. In both
countries, traditional designs based
on Asian and European gardens are
given an amusing twist.

AUSTRALIA AND NEW ZEALAND

Kings Park and Botanic Garden

Western Australia, Australia

DESIGNERS: Members of Perth Park Board
OWNER: City of Perth
GARDEN STYLE: 19th-, 20th-, and 21st-century city park
SIZE: 988 acres (400 ha)
CLIMATE: Mediterranean
LOCATION: Perth, Western Australia

Perth's Kings Park is almost certainly the city's best-known tourist attraction. This large public park lies within walking distance of the city center, and from the top of Mount Eliza, there are splendid views over the River Swan and the city's glass-walled offices.

The park is significant for its aboriginal cultural heritage (Mount Eliza, known as *Kaarta gar-up*, is a traditional gathering point for the local Nyoongar people), its large tracts of natural bushland covering more than two-thirds of the area, and landscapes that date from the late nineteenth and early twentieth centuries, beginning with the symbolic planting of a Norfolk Island pine (*Araucaria heterophylla*) by Premier John Forrest in 1895. Early works in the park included the creation of scenic drives, parklands along the ridge overlooking the city, and the terraced gardens and walks along Mounts Bay Road. The park also serves as a national shrine where many of the city's most important monuments are located, including the State War Memorial, unveiled in 1929 and a prominent feature on the park's skyline. The avenues and driveways are particularly eye-catching, especially the one with sugar gums (*Eucalyptus cladocalyx*) forming an entrance archway to the park.

Much of the captivating and unique flora of Western Australia is featured in the 42-acre (17 ha) botanical garden, established over the past three decades. Extensive bushland areas with nature trails, new wildflower display gardens, and generous picnic facilities with children's playgrounds now make the park a top attraction. CR

Flecker Botanic Gardens

Queensland, Australia

DESIGNER: Eugene Fitzalan
OWNER: Cairns City Council
GARDEN STYLE: 19th-century botanical
SIZE: 91 acres (36.8 ha), including native bush
CLIMATE: Wet tropical
LOCATION: Cairns, North Queensland

This compact gem, not far from Cairns, started life in 1886 as a recreational reserve. An idyllic mix of lawns, shady borders, colorful ornamentals, and fruit trees, it is crammed with a staggering variety of the world's tropical plants, most planted in a relaxed, rain forest style. It is the perfect place for a leisurely stroll that will leave you smiling.

It is divided into several themes, including the Gondwanan Heritage Trail, aboriginal plant use, and a tropical rain forest section, featuring foliage plants such as *Johannesteijsmannia magnifica* from Malaysia, with massive leaves like pleated cardboard. Also look out for self-sown seedlings and unusual fungi, and for the quirky such as the bat plant (*Tacca chantrieri*) with its sinister, whiskery flowers. Pride of place goes to the jade vine (*Strongylodon macrobotrys*) with hanging clusters of jade-green, clawlike flowers, and to one of the only two specimens to be found in Australian gardens of the titan arum (*Amorphophallus titanum*) with flowers up to 6 feet (2 m) tall.

There are many beautiful trees packed with tropical ferns, lianas, and dazzling bromeliads, including *Saraca cauliflora* from Thailand, which produces masses of orange-yellow flowers. Most impressive is a giant teak tree (*Tectona grandis*) that towers over the garden and is simply beautiful when the large leaves are punctuated by huge clusters of white flowers. The surrounding lowland swamp forest, also part of the gardens, is accessible by a boardwalk, but when visiting either, do take your insect repellent. MB

Townsville Palmetum

Queensland, Australia

DESIGNERS: Jim Darley, Robert Tucker
OWNER: Townsville City Council Parks Services
GARDEN STYLE: 20th-century botanical and palm collection
SIZE: 43 acres (17.4 ha)
CLIMATE: Wet tropical
LOCATION: Townsville, Queensland

Highlighting palms by planting them in a palmetum was the idea of local plantsman Jim Darley. On a site that was once a dairy farm and mango orchard, more than 320 palm species, from habitats ranging from dry tropics to wet lowlands and rain forest, are gathered together in one location. The aim is to display the palms so that individuals or groups can be appreciated in all their glory.

There are palms of all shapes and sizes, from dwarf and multistemmed species to giants like a *Roystonea oleracea*, which is 98 feet (30 m) high and still growing. Highlights include an avenue of *Carpoxylon macrospermum*, a rare palm from the Vanuatu Islands, that is probably the largest planting of the species in the world, and the legendary coco-de-mer (*Lodoicea maldivica*), whose buttock-shaped seed is about 20 x 14 inches (50 x 35 cm) and can weigh more than 44 pounds (20 kg). Townsville's Japanese sister city, Tokuyama, funded the initial development of the Licuala Walk, which has some of the most handsome palms in the world, usually seen only as single specimens. Also look out for the Tokuyama Garden, completed in 1996 and a symbol of international friendship. It is more ornamental than botanical, with a beautiful central water feature and plantings of cycads, gingers, crotons, frangipani, and palms. There is a central arbor that is regularly used for weddings.

There is a fifteen-year master plan for developing the gardens, and the experience of visiting may become even more thrilling. MB

Carrick Hill

South Australia, Australia

DESIGNER: Ursula Hayward
OWNER: The Australian State
GARDEN STYLE: 20th-century English Edwardian
SIZE: 98 acres (39.6 ha)
CLIMATE: Mediterranean
LOCATION: Adelaide, South Australia

Carrick Hill is one of the few period homes in Australia to survive with its original contents almost completely intact, and its grounds undiminished. The estate centers on an idiosyncratic house in the English Jacobean style, built in the late 1930s by the department store owner Sir Edward Hayward and his wife, Ursula, the daughter of a South Australian pastoralist.

Set on the lower slopes of the Adelaide Hills, the property has sweeping views over Adelaide and the Gulf of St. Vincent. The garden's design reflects Ursula's knowledge of English formal gardens, showing her great love of rare trees, flowering shrubs, and roses. Tuberoses (*Polianthes tuberosa*), lilies, orchids, and hawthorns were particular favorites. It is made up of a hedged inner garden bisected by a superb, pleached pear arbor, a cutting garden, and terraces linked by slate paths. A brook and pools, an orchard, and a nuttery are features of the garden's outer parkland surrounds, with everything ringed by largely untouched bushland, a rare survival in the outskirts of Adelaide.

The garden evolved during the Hayward ownership, and was altered when the property passed to the South Australian government in 1983. The Haywards were passionate collectors of British art, and their magnificent collection of paintings and antiques is an equal delight in concert with the house as a center of stylish living. The garden is also undergoing a major restoration to reflect the Hayward era at its zenith. CR

Adelaide Botanic Gardens

South Australia, Australia

DESIGNERS: George Francis, Dr. Richard Schomburgk
OWNER: The Australian State
GARDEN STYLE: 19th-century botanical
SIZE: 101 acres (40.9 ha)
CLIMATE: Mediterranean
LOCATION: Adelaide, South Australia

Opened to the public in 1857, Adelaide's Botanic Gardens rate among the world's finest. English and French visitors feel particularly at home here because the gardens' original designer, George Francis, is said to have been influenced by the Royal Botanic Gardens at Kew (see page 386), and André Le Nôtre's baroque masterpiece at Versailles (see page 570).

Visitors to the Botanic Gardens can easily spend a day touring the grounds with their vast collection of trees, including the avenue of plane trees, planted in 1874, and huge, gnarled Moreton Bay fig trees (*Ficus macrophylla*), more than a century old. (The Salvation Army held its first Australasian meeting here in 1880, a date marked by a commemorative tree.) Also make sure you visit the Palm House, a superb Victorian greenhouse featuring a display of Madagascan arid flora. The palm house was imported from Germany in 1875, and exquisitely restored in the 1990s. The ultramodern Bicentennial Conservatory is in complete contrast, and was built to celebrate Australia's bicentenary in 1988. This 328-foot-long (100 m), 88-foot-high (27 m), distinctive steel structure is thought to be the largest, single-span conservatory in the Southern Hemisphere, and houses the gardens' collection of lowland tropical rain forest plants. Adding to the mix of building styles is the Museum of Economic Botany, a quaint, Greek-style structure dating from 1881. Also of note is the National Rose Trial Garden, established in 1996. Roses are tested for their suitability to Australian conditions, with the best performers receiving an award. LA

Everglades Gardens

New South Wales, Australia

DESIGNER: Paul Sorensen
OWNER: National Trust of Australia
  (New South Wales)
GARDEN STYLE: 20th-century 1930s classical, informal
SIZE: 13 acres (5.2 ha)
CLIMATE: Temperate
LOCATION: Leura, New South Wales

Thanks to the collaboration of two Euro-Australians, this historic place, hidden away in the Blue Mountains, marked a turning point in Australian garden design. The Belgian industrialist Henry van de Velde acquired the land in 1932, and commissioned the Danish garden designer Paul Sorensen to create an extraordinary landscape. The result was an enchanting terraced garden on a steep slope combining European skills, romantic ideas, and the powerful magic of the Australian bush.

Miles of dry, stone walls and blue stone paths create the structure, and link the various terraces, the most spectacular being the Studio Terrace with its pool, Italianate colonnade, Italian urns, and outdoor stage backed by a grand arch rescued from a Sydney bank. After going past the house, also designed by Sorensen, the visitor encounters the Cherry Terrace, a broad lawn bordered by cherry trees, followed by the Rhododendron Walk and an inviting bench to catch a glimpse of the view. Then follows The Lookout, fenced with art deco wrought iron, where the contrast with the vast, untouched landscape below is breathtaking. Steps down guide you to the enchanting waterfall of the Grotto Pool.

The remarkable appeal of this garden is how vividly it illustrates the meeting of the ancient world with the new, and how it has been done with intelligence, generosity, and an eye for beauty. MO

The Chinese Garden of Friendship

New South Wales, Australia

DESIGNER: Sydney's Chinese sister city, Guangzhou,
  Guangdong Province, China
OWNER: City of Sydney
GARDEN STYLE: 20th-century traditional Chinese
SIZE: 2.5 acres (1 ha)
CLIMATE: Humid subtropical
LOCATION: Sydney, New South Wales

Poised between glitzy Darling Harbor and the busy streets of Sydney's Chinatown is a remarkable garden celebrating the friendship between Sydney and the Chinese city of Guangzhou, or Canton. The Chinese first migrated to Sydney in the mid-1850s, and this garden, created to mark Australia's 1988 bicentenary, was a way of sharing their cultural heritage.

No special knowledge is needed to appreciate this exquisite composition of pools and pavilions, trees and stones. Water is used creatively in brooks, cascades, and glassy pools where strangely shaped rocks rear their "heads" like monsters among the lotus flowers. Walkways meander among thickets of bamboo, opening unexpectedly into sunny courtyards decorated with calligraphy and carvings. Giant willows trail their branches into the lake, dragons writhe on a painted screen, and a tall pagoda, perched on a rock, looks out over a lake.

There is real mastery in the control of space, revealing the garden a little at a time, and presenting views perfectly framed by the circle of a moon gate, the arch of a bough, and the fretwork of a delicately carved screen. The garden is a favorite place for weddings and weekend sorties with children, but go when it is quiet for the authentic experience. AE

RIGHT Sydney's Chinese Garden of Friendship is intended as a contemplative space and is rich in symbolism.

Mount Wilson

New South Wales, Australia

DESIGNERS: Various
OWNERS: Rodger Davidson, Wai Davidson, and others
GARDEN STYLE: 19th- and 20th-century mixed
SIZES: Various
CLIMATE: Temperate
LOCATION: Mount Wilson, New South Wales

Most towns and villages are lucky if they can boast one or, at best, two fabulous gardens. However, in the village of Mount Wilson, just two hours' west of Sydney, there are inspirational gardens around every corner. The abundance of spectacular gardens is largely because of the location: Situated 3,000 feet (914 m) above sea level and surrounded by rain forest, Mount Wilson has an unusually (for Australia) cool climate and rich, volcanic soil. The best time to visit is in spring or fall, when many of the gardens are at their best and are open to the public.

One of the village's most picturesque gardens is Nooroo, established in 1880. It features a wisteria collection, at its best from the end of October to the beginning of November. There is also a bluebell dell, flowering in the first two weeks of October. Windyridge is one of the village's newer gardens. The owners, Rodger and Wai Davidson, have created the perfect setting for their collection of Kurume azaleas, clipped in a Japanese style to produce eye-catching waves of color. The garden also features sculpture, water gardens, a lily pond, and a lawn terrace.

The Yengo Sculpture Gardens were established in 1889, the 20-acre (8 ha) gardens being restored in the 1960s and 1970s. Sculptures by Judith Holmes Drewry and Lloyd Le Blanc are placed among the giant beeches, ancient oaks, shrubs, and bulbs.

If time is short, then just wander down the village's avenues with their rows of plane, lime, elm, beech, liquidambar, and cherry trees. It is a plant-lover's paradise. LA

Eryldene

New South Wales, Australia

DESIGNERS: Professor Ebden Waterhouse, Hardy Wilson
OWNER: The Eryldene Trust
GARDEN STYLE: 20th-century "rooms"
SIZE: 1 acre (0.4 ha)
CLIMATE: Humid subtropical
LOCATION: Sydney, New South Wales

Eryldene is a memorial to Professor Ebden Waterhouse's passion for camellias, and the garden's extensive collection is considered Australia's most significant. Waterhouse, a linguist, became one of the world's foremost authorities on the camellia, planting his first six at Eryldene in 1914. He raised and named many popular varieties, founded Sydney's famous Camellia Grove nursery, and was president of the International Camellia Society. He was an authority on the history and nomenclature of early camellia cultivars, and raised hundreds of seedlings. The hybrids 'E. G. Waterhouse,' 'Margaret Waterhouse,' and 'Lady Gowrie' are among many of Waterhouse's successes, which have remained popular with Australian gardeners since their introduction in 1954.

The house at Eryldene is also worth a visit. Situated on Sydney's North Shore, in the early colonial style with a strong Georgian influence, it's now recognized as the finest, unaltered architectural example of Hardy Wilson's domestic work. The garden, planned by Waterhouse, was designed as an extension of the house in a series of "rooms," each leading to the next, filled with trees, shrubs, and flowers. Superbly proportioned buildings designed by Wilson—a secluded study, temple, Chinese-inspired pavilion with lacquered red columns, and a delightful shingled pigeon house—are used in the "rooms," and contribute to Eryldene's tranquil atmosphere.

Eryldene has remained largely unchanged since it was built in 1913, giving it an important place in Australian architectural and horticultural history. CR

Mount Tomah Botanic Garden

New South Wales, Australia

DESIGNERS: Alfred Brunet, Effie Brunet
OWNER: Sydney Botanic Gardens Trust
GARDEN STYLE: 20th-century botanical
SIZE: 536 acres (217 ha)
CLIMATE: Temperate
LOCATION: Blue Mountains, New South Wales

This spectacular garden is situated in the Blue Mountains, 60 miles (100 km) west of Sydney. The magical blue haze hovering above the eucalyptus forests covering this region, as well as the extraordinary basalt formations (creating natural rainwater reservoirs), and the cooler climate at this higher altitude—3,300 feet (1,000 m) above sea level—all contribute to the success of the garden. Its aim is to increase awareness and understanding of plants, and the need for conservation of endangered species, and it does so with the lightest touch through an outstanding design.

The area was used for cattle grazing and timber milling until it was acquired, in 1934, by a French couple, Alfred and Effie Brunet, who ran a cut-flower garden supplying Sydney's florists, and who also planted unusual conifers. In the 1960s they offered their land as an annex to the Sydney Royal Botanic Gardens, and in 1987 Mount Tomah opened its doors. The visitor has a range of short walks to take in the major features, but you could easily allow a whole day to explore the hilly site. Don't miss the arresting rock garden with plants arranged geographically among basalt columns, pools, and cascades; the dazzling display of the rhododendron collection in full bloom; the plants of the ancient Southern Hemisphere from South Africa to Papua New Guinea; the formal garden with its robust pergola backed by giant eucalyptus; and the preserved Brunet garden, which has a collection of mature trees and shrubs that were planted by the Brunets as their private garden. MO

> "Don't miss the arresting rock garden with plants arranged ...among basalt columns..."

Vaucluse House

New South Wales, Australia

DESIGNER: William Charles Wentworth
OWNER: Historic Houses Trust
GARDEN STYLE: 19th-century picturesque
SIZE: 25 acres (10 ha)
CLIMATE: Humid subtropical
LOCATION: Sydney, New South Wales

Built in 1803 in a prestigious harbor suburb of Sydney, Vaucluse House is one of the few nineteenth-century houses in the area that retains a significant part of its original setting. The fashion for the picturesque had an early impact in Sydney, and Vaucluse is one of the few surviving examples of the "baronial," or imitation castle, look.

The house was once the home of William Charles Wentworth, father of the Australian Constitution, his wife, Sarah, and their family of ten children from 1827 to 1853, and again in 1861 to 1862. They set about making many improvements, including the Gothic iron veranda and the fountain that is the central feature of the lawn at the front of the house. At this time, the estate also supported a large area of orchards, vegetable plots, and vineyards.

After the Wentworths died, the estate slowly became a municipal park, and in 1981, the property was transferred to the Historic Houses Trust of New South Wales, with work commencing on long-term conservation. Originally the estate was set within an untamed "bushland" setting of several hundred acres. A bush-revival scheme has been established to encourage the recovery of the surviving specimens of native plants surrounding the house.

Research and planning have reestablished the original boundaries of the pleasure garden, and details such as gravel paths with brick-edged drains have been restored. A partial reconstruction of the kitchen garden is ongoing, using the written records of growing vegetables and fruit at Vaucluse. CR

Kennerton Green

New South Wales, Australia

DESIGNER: Marylyn Abbott
OWNER: Marylyn Abbott
GARDEN STYLE: 20th-century shrub, woodland, and potager
SIZE: 8 acres (3.2 ha)
CLIMATE: Humid subtropical
LOCATION: Mittagong, New South Wales

Kennerton Green is one of the grand gardens of the Southern Highlands, just over one hour's drive south of Sydney. During the 1950s, the garden was slowly developed as an adornment to a pretty nineteenth-century cottage with its camellia and rhododendron beds, a flowering cherry walk, deciduous trees, and an enclosed formal garden featuring standard hybrid tea roses. A magnificent *Wisteria floribunda* 'Kuchibeni'—a gift from the renowned Australian botanist Dr. Peter Valder—is a showstopping sight in spring.

Since 1988 the garden, under the guidance of Marylyn Abbott, internationally known for her designs, has been further extended in a series of themed "rooms." They include Una's Wood (a thick grove of birches with pure white trunks underplanted with bluebells as a memorial to Abbott's mother), an ornamental vegetable garden, an iris-rimmed lake, a laburnum walk, and a bay-tree parterre. The mature trees and sweeping lawns, with hedges of cypress and box, make a superb background to the massed plantings of bulbs. Roses and perennials, together with annuals, are at their peak in spring and early summer, and recent additions include a paradise courtyard.

Also look out for the small rose garden featuring the 'Yvonne Kenny' rose, named after one of Australia's most famous opera singers. CR

RIGHT Kennerton Green mixes formality and informality through its series of themed garden "rooms."

Government House

New South Wales, Australia

DESIGNER: Mortimer Lewis
OWNER: The Australian State
GARDEN STYLE: 18th-century picturesque and 19th-century formal Italianate
SIZE: 11 acres (4.5 ha)
CLIMATE: Humid subtropical
LOCATION: Sydney, New South Wales

Few gardens can boast a view quite as spectacular as the one from Government House. First laid out in the late eighteenth century, when the fashion was for gardens to have picturesque settings, the grounds are set high on a headland overlooking Sydney Harbor. There is a superb collection of exotic trees and shrubs, largely thanks to the neighboring Botanic Garden that runs most of the estate.

The grounds, which at one time covered 35 acres (14 ha), succumbed to Italianate formality in the late nineteenth century, and are divided into two main terraces: Western and Eastern. The former dates from 1845, built at the same time as the house, and was densely planted as an arboretum with rain forest trees from Queensland and northern New South Wales. The original sandstone walls remain, as do a beautiful *Magnolia grandiflora* and fine olive trees. Follow the carriageway around to the southeast corner of the house, and you will find a magnificent Moreton Bay fig tree (*Ficus macrophylla*).

But by far the most impressive part of the garden is the Eastern Terrace, developed after Sir John Young took up residence as governor in 1860. This area was the public face of the garden, with breathtaking views across Sydney Harbor to Bradley's Head. Low stone walls are laid out symmetrically around an axial path, and a circular pond, fountain, gravel paths, and ornamental garden add to the feeling of English formality, with all its grandeur and nostalgic nods to the homeland. LA

Royal Botanic Gardens Sydney

New South Wales, Australia

DESIGNER: Charles Moore
OWNER: Sydney Botanic Gardens Trust
GARDEN STYLE: 19th- and 20th-century parkland with themed garden areas
SIZE: 74 acres (29.9 ha)
CLIMATE: Humid subtropical
LOCATION: Sydney, New South Wales

The Botanic Gardens act as a green barrier between the tower blocks of Sydney and the opera house, and is bounded on two sides by the sea. Founded in 1816, they are the oldest scientific institution in Australia. Charles Moore, a Scotsman, who was the director from 1848 to 1896, developed the gardens in their modern form, and established the Palm Grove and reclaimed land to increase the size of the site.

A maze of paths weave among a host of well-maintained display gardens and greenhouses, including the Palm House, and the Succulent and Oriental Gardens, and there are many rare and unusual plants. The star in the collection is the Wollemi pine (*Wollemia nobilis*), a recently discovered conifer, found in an isolated canyon in 1994, only 150 miles (240 km) from Sydney. The first seed raised specimen was planted in 1998 in the Rare and Threatened Plant Garden; it is ironic that a plant that was free for millennia is now protected by a cage.

There are sculptures dotted throughout the garden, including one by Henry Moore, as well as indigenous aboriginal art and Mrs. Macquarie's Chair, which was carved in an outcrop of stone in 1816, so that the wife of the governor could sit and watch the ships come in.

It is a tranquil setting worth visiting for its plants, history, and stunning location. Any garden that says in its visitor code, "We also invite you to smell the roses, hug the trees, talk to the birds, and picnic on the lawns" has to be worth a visit. MB

Sculpture Garden, National Gallery of Australia

Australian Capital Territory, Australia

DESIGNERS: Harry Howard and Associates
OWNER: The Australian State
GARDEN STYLE: 20th-century sculpture garden planted with Australian natives
SIZE: 7 acres (2.8 ha)
CLIMATE: Temperate
LOCATION: Canberra, Australian Capital Territory

The National Gallery of Australia in Canberra is home to an impressive art collection, and one of the country's finest gardens. The heritage listed Sculpture Garden is densely planted with native Australian plants, among which are placed twenty-six of the world's best sculptures, sympathetically interacting with eucalyptuses, acacias, and banksias.

Designed in the 1980s by Harry Howard, the garden is divided into different areas based on the seasons of the year, with the plantings chosen for their foliage, flowers, fragrance, height, and habit. Entering through the Winter Garden, there is a serene courtyard planted with winter-flowering *Acacia iteaphylla,* banksias, and correas, and featuring sculptures from the late nineteenth and early twentieth centuries, including Auguste Rodin's *The Burghers of Calais.* From here, an avenue of eucalyptus, acacia, and casuarina planted in informal groupings leads down to Lake Burley Griffin. Running adjacent to the lake is the Spring Garden, itself divided into four distinct "rooms" and planted with eucalyptus, banksia, and grevillea. In the Summer Garden, a bronze Henry Moore sculpture is reflected in a pond planted with lilies and rushes, and a grove of *Casuarina cunninghamiana* forms the backdrop to a group of bronzes by Robert Klippel. LA

Australian National Botanic Gardens

Australian Capital Territory, Australia

DESIGNER: Unknown
OWNER: The Australian State
GARDEN STYLE: 20th-century botanical
SIZE: 98 acres (39.6 ha) in a 200-acre (81 ha) site
CLIMATE: Temperate
LOCATION: Black Mountain, Canberra, Australian Capital Territory

These gardens, magnificently sited on the slopes of the Black Mountain, are devoted exclusively to Australian flora and were opened to the public in 1964. Several decades of planning have gone into establishing the gardens as the premier collection and display of Australian native plants.

During 1970 a misting system was installed in a dry gully near the parking lot. During this decade, the careful selection of plants, along with the artificially increased humidity, saw the development of the Rain Forest Gully as one of the gardens' major attractions. This was a significant horticultural achievement, in addition to helping raise public awareness about rain forests.

About 90,000 plants, representing more than 5,000 species, are grown, and they are arranged in taxonomic and ecological groupings. Note the brilliantly executed rock gardens based on the granite and Hawkesbury sandstone, and the swamp and mallee environments.

Although the gardens have had a relatively short history, there are a number of memorials, commemorative building names, and plaques on the site. In addition there is a range of art and sculpture, including the Friends Cascade flow-form water sculpture, which reminds people that recycling and reinvigorating water can be functional as well as appealing to the senses. CR

The Fulling Garden

Victoria, Australia

DESIGNER: Gordon Ford
OWNER: Gwen Ford
GARDEN STYLE: 20th-century Australian bush with orchard
SIZE: 1.5 acres (0.6 ha)
CLIMATE: Temperate
LOCATION: Eltham, Victoria

Gordon Ford was one of the pioneers of what has become known as the "natural" or bush garden in Australia. On land that was a former orchard at Eltham, which he bought at the end of World War II, he created a natural garden using Australian native plants. A mud-brick house in the center of the garden and pools and waterfalls are the major features. The large upper pool is placed so that the entrance to the living area is approached by steps across the water.

Ford's design philosophy was based on two central ideas. The first was articulated by Brenda Colvin who wrote *Land and Landscape* in 1947, in which she refers to the "asymmetrical juxtaposition of mass and voids," the "mass" being the use of trees, shrubs, and boulders; the "voids" being the grassed areas, paths, and pools. The second key concept, for Ford, was disguising the garden boundary. He did so by planting many Australian trees chosen for their leaf texture and shape rather than flower color. Trees in the garden with these qualities include the prickly paperbark (*Melaleuca styphelioides*), spotted gum (*Eucalyptus maculata*), and apple myrtle (*Angophora cordifolia*), with its salmon-pink bark. The understory of small shrubs, such as correas and grevilleas, merge with the leaf litter to form a bush "floor."

But it is the sensitively placed rocks that make a significant contribution to the quality of the garden landscape at Fulling. CR

Royal Botanic Gardens Melbourne

Victoria, Australia

DESIGNERS: Ferdinand von Mueller, William Guilfoyle
OWNER: City of Victoria
GARDEN STYLE: 19th-century picturesque and parkland
SIZE: 87 acres (35.2 ha)
CLIMATE: Temperate
LOCATION: Melbourne, Victoria

In 1846 Charles La Trobe selected the site for the Royal Botanic Gardens from marshland and swamp. In 1857 Ferdinand von Mueller became its first director. He created the National Herbarium of Victoria and brought in many plants. In 1873 William Guilfoyle became director, and added tropical and temperate plants, creating the design the gardens have today.

Once described as "an oasis of peace in a desert of worldly troubles," the gardens still exude that same charm and serenity many generations later. There are around 13 acres (5 ha) of lawn, punctuated by flower beds, winding paths, lakes, superb specimen trees, and borders. There is a magnificent Fern Gully, Australian Rain Forest Walk, and Alexandra Gardens with an intricate floral clock.

Melbourne's mild climate allows an eclectic mix of tropical and temperate plants to be grown, and there is a collection of around 12,000 species of plant. Beside the familiar plants from cool temperate climates, such as daffodils, tulips, and azaleas, there are also native banksias and wattles. The elegant Fitzroy Conservatory is packed with displays of cineraria and cyclamen. Among the scientific collections are plants from the Canary Islands, New Zealand, and New Caledonia, as well as cycads and viburnums. Bird-watchers should go straight to the main ornamental lake.

The Ian Potter Foundation Children's Garden, opened in 2006, is a great place to play and learn about plants and conservation. It features a bamboo forest and children's kitchen garden. MB

Heronswood

Victoria, Australia

DESIGNERS: Edward Latrobe Bateman, Clive Blazey
OWNER: The Digger's Club
GARDEN STYLE: 19th-century cottage
SIZE: 4.5 acres (1.8 ha)
CLIMATE: Temperate
LOCATION: Latrobe Parade, Dromana, Victoria

The garden at Heronswood, the site of the Australian mail-order seed company The Digger's Club, has a spectacular site on Victoria's Mornington Peninsula, facing north to Port Phillip Bay, but protected from the prevailing southerly winds. The company's founders, Clive and Penny Blazey, have been instrumental in reviving interest in cottage gardening and heirloom vegetables, reintroducing many old cultivars to gardeners and commercial production.

Until recently, Heronswood was primarily a perennial garden with a series of garden "rooms" featuring cottage flowers, vegetables, and perennials for a dry climate. Now the focus is on food-producing plants, particularly vegetables and subtropical fruiting trees that thrive in Australia's hot summers (Clive wrote a book *The Australian Fruit and Vegetable Garden*).

An added attraction at Heronswood is the Gothic revival stone house, designed in 1871 by Edward Latrobe Bateman. The exterior walls of the house were built from granite blocks hewn from a quarry on Arthur's Seat, and local limestone trims the corners. It has a picturesque, bell-shaped roof, built with slate imported from Wales.

Bateman is also credited with the early landscape plans for the garden. Many of the fine specimen trees date from the nineteenth century, including Moreton Bay figs (*Ficus macrophylla*), cypresses, oaks, and an *Araucaria cookii*; these now mature trees frame the views of the bay in a manner strongly reminiscent of French Riviera landscapes. CR

> "...mature trees frame...views of the bay in a manner...reminiscent of French Riviera landscapes"

Mawallok

Victoria, Australia

DESIGNER: William Guilfoyle
OWNERS: Peter Mitchell, Jocelyn Mitchell
GARDEN STYLE: 18th-century English landscaped
SIZE: 8 acres (3.2 ha)
CLIMATE: Temperate
LOCATION: Beaufort, Victoria

Mawallok was laid out in 1909 for the Russell family—Australian pastoral pioneers—by Australian landscape designer William Guilfoyle in the year of his retirement as director from Melbourne's Royal Botanic Gardens.

As with many nineteenth-century properties on the windy plains of western Victoria, the homestead and garden at Mawallok are surrounded by thickly planted belts of trees, especially conifers such as Monterey pines (*Pinus radiata*) and cypresses. Within this sheltering framework of trees, Guilfoyle's plan was designed to complement the newly built home. His style is recognizable by the open lawns flowing through the garden to the dense woodland plantings on the fringes. He added the drama of sentinel-like palms on the sweeping lawns to frame the northern vista in a formal landscape design, with the house as a centerpiece. However, the palms were removed in the 1930s, and the garden was modified, further extending the view across the lawn, a nine-hole golf course, and lake to the distant Mount Cole.

In recent years, renovation has returned paths and garden beds to their position on Guilfoyle's original plan. Sinuous walks weave through the perimeter shrubberies and beneath mature, deciduous trees, including horse chestnut, copper beech (*Fagus sylvatica* Atropurpurea Group), planes, limes, and oaks. With the restoration, Mawallok is an elegant reflection of the style of the eighteenth-century English landscape movement in an Australian context. A visit in any season is rewarding. CR

Rippon Lea

Victoria, Australia

DESIGNER: Sir Frederick Sargood
OWNER: National Trust of Australia
SIZE: 27 acres (11 ha)
GARDEN STYLE: 19th-century landscaped
CLIMATE: Temperate
LOCATION: Elsternwick, Victoria

Rippon Lea is a remarkable example of a late-nineteenth-century landscape around a suburban mansion that has survived almost without alteration. The estate, built and developed between 1868 and 1903, was the creation of the leading Victorian politician and businessman Sir Frederick Sargood. The house was designed in the Romanesque style by Joseph Reed, one of Melbourne's most prominent architects.

Although reduced from its original size, the garden still retains many elements of the Victorian era, including a lake, mound and grotto, fernery, conservatory, serpentine carriageway, and sweeping lawns. The entrance drive, overhung with huge Moreton Bay figs (*Ficus macrophylla*), winds through a shrubbery offering glimpses of lawns, house, and tower and, finally, the entrance front. From the west front of the house, a wide expanse of lawn stretches to the thick perimeter planting of flowering shrubs, towering conifers, and spreading, deciduous trees.

On the far side of the garden is a large, ornamental lake. The curving edges are fringed with willows and poplars, and cast-iron bridges disguised as rustic woodwork link the garden walk. Rippon Lea's vast, iron-framed fernery has been restored, and includes more than 230 species of fern, including tree ferns (*Dicksonia antarctica*), some of which are 132 feet (10 m) high. CR

RIGHT Rippon Lea's fernery is an example of Victorian style. Today it houses more than 230 species of fern.

Garden of St. Erth

Victoria, Australia

DESIGNERS: Tommy Garnett, Penny Garnett,
  The Digger's Club
OWNER: The Digger's Club
GARDEN STYLE: 20th-century cottage
SIZE: 6.5 acres (2.6 ha)
CLIMATE: Temperate
LOCATION: Blackwood, Victoria

A simple sandstone cottage is the focal point of the garden at St. Erth. It was built by a Cornish stonemason, Matthew Rogers, who named his Australian home on the goldfields after his birthplace. It sits beside the garden's central axis, which exactly follows the road of the once-bustling, gold mining town of Simmonds Reef, which was a settlement of 10,000 people in the 1850s. The garden was initially the creation of plantsman Tommy Garnett and his wife, Penny, but today is an integral part of The Digger's Club seeds company in Victoria.

In spring visitors are greeted by thousands of bulbs and, as summer approaches, the blooms of exquisite, cool-climate plants. The Himalayan blue poppy (*Meconopsis betonicifolia*) can grow only in certain places in Australia, and St. Erth is one of them, where it makes a spectacular sight. In the fall, an extensive range of perennials, including richly colored dahlias and salvias, contrasts with bold clumps of ornamental miscanthus and panicum grasses. The old orchard is being revitalized with espaliered varieties of apples, pears, quinces, cherries, and plums. A "food forest" of fruit yielding groundcover and shrubs has also been planted to showcase the idea of "Eden in your backyard."

Renowned for its twice-yearly festivals—with daffodil displays and blossoming fruit trees in spring, and a bold show of perennials in the fall—in a quiet corner of the Australian bush, the Garden of St. Erth has become one of Victoria's best-loved gardens. CR

Wigandia

Victoria, Australia

DESIGNER: William Martin
OWNER: William Martin
GARDEN STYLE: 20th- and 21st-century modern, dry
  country garden
SIZE: 1 acre (0.4 ha)
CLIMATE: Mediterranean
LOCATION: Noorat, Victoria

Central to the creation of this Australian garden is William Martin's idea that foliage and form are more important than flowers, and he divides his plantings into three groups: structural plants that are almost permanent, infill plants that are sometimes changed, and self-seeders. Equally important, the garden is meant to harmonize with the surrounding landscape on the slopes of the extinct volcano Mount Noorat, one of many to be found on the vast, flat plains of western Victoria.

To achieve this, he has filtered out the Northern Hemisphere woodland plants traditionally used, and has concentrated instead on what he calls the "second-rank shrubs of nineteenth-century shrubberies," using broom, cistus, cestrum, teucrium, and rhaphiolepis. Color interest comes from the juxtaposition of foliage and form, with silvery artemisias next to dark green acanthus, pink-stemmed bergenias in a stone sink with echeverias, and clumps of spear lilies next to jelly palm (*Butia capitata*).

Martin knows which plants survive the drought, winds, and high temperatures of an Australian summer. He has assembled an outstanding and eclectic collection of plants, creating a garden that reflects its location. The property takes its name from the unusual shrub *Wigandia carascana*, with its huge, heart-shaped leaves and striking, violet-blue flowers. It epitomizes the type and style of plant to be found in this dramatic country garden. CR

Panshanger

Tasmania, Australia

DESIGNER: Joseph Archer
OWNER: The Mills family
GARDEN STYLE: 19th-century English garden and
    woodland in a natural setting
SIZE: 8 acres (3.3 ha)
CLIMATE: Temperate
LOCATION: Longford, Tasmania

Panshanger is an elegant house in the Greek revival style, built by Englishman Joseph Archer in the 1830s. Both the house and estate were conceived to reflect the increasing wealth and status of its owner. Early lithographs of Panshanger show the house on a commanding point above the Lake River, framed by clumps of trees with the aptly named mountain range—the Great Western Tiers—in the background. These images, ca.1835, relate directly to romanticized Wordsworthian landscapes. The house is known today as one of the finest colonial examples of Greek revival architecture in Australia.

Today, however, the general effect at Panshanger is more one of enclosure than openness. The long entrance avenue and surrounding parkland are heavily wooded. Mature trees—conifers, silver birches, laurels, oaks, and elms—and thick, expansive shrubberies protect the house, screening the view to the river, although the grassy void at the front of the house has been retained. And finely worked, nineteenth-century iron gates open to a flower garden full of roses, created within the projecting wings of the house. But what really stands out is the unique pigeon tower—a crenellated, cylindrical folly—positioned to be seen from the house terrace as an eye-catcher in the classic eighteenth-century manner. A water tower, also castellated, stands nearer the house, a tribute to Joseph Archer's engineering skills in the pumping and distribution of water from the river to house and garden. CR

Woolmers

Tasmania, Australia

DESIGNER: Thomas Archer (walled garden)
OWNER: Woolmers Foundation Inc.
GARDEN STYLE: 19th-century estate and rose garden
SIZE: Rose garden 5 acres (2 ha), original garden
    1 acre (0.4 ha)
CLIMATE: Temperate
LOCATION: Longford, Tasmania

Woolmers is one of the few nineteenth-century Tasmanian gardens in which the layout and detail survive largely intact. The land was granted to Thomas Archer in 1817, and his first house, completed two years later, was almost certainly surrounded by a simple cottage garden, with areas for fruit and produce. Archer's second son, William, an architect, returned to Tasmania from London in 1842, and designed an extension of the house in the fashionable Italianate style. A new garden was created, enclosed by a curved wall and with impressive gateways.

Today this garden, situated on high ground above the Macquarie River, and with views to Longford and the mountains beyond, is a delightful period piece. The central focus is the lawn with its pond and cast-iron fountain, encircled by a gravel carriageway. Two cross axes give the garden its strong structure: One is formed by the drive, and the second by the paths, porches, and archways linking the house, stables, and orchard. Brick-edged paths wind between the shrubberies and flower beds, leading to a Gothic smoking house and an octagonal summerhouse.

The National Rose Garden of Australia has been established at Woolmers, and thousands of roses are displayed in beds according to their origins, from the earliest European roses through to those of today. This area is formal and symmetrical, acknowledging the historical context of the surrounding estate, which is regarded as an outstanding example of a nineteenth-century Australian rural settlement. CR

Butler Point

Northland, New Zealand

DESIGNERS: Lindo Ferguson, Laetitia Ferguson
OWNERS: The Ferguson family
GARDEN STYLE: 19th-century cottage
SIZE: 10 acres (4 ha)
CLIMATE: Temperate
LOCATION: Mangonui, Northland

In 1828 a fourteen-year-old Dorset lad ran away to sea. By the age of twenty-four, William Butler was the captain of a whaling ship that put into the northerly port of Mangonui. Seeing his opportunity, he set up a business here helping whalers. The captain's home is now a museum, standing in a beautiful garden. The setting is superb, separated by just 490 feet (150 m) from Mangonui's seafront. A Maori hill fort rises behind the garden, and ancient pohutukawa trees (*Metrosideros excelsa*) cover the peninsula, including one reputed to be the largest in New Zealand, with a girth of more than 36 feet (11 m).

The Ferguson family rescued the estate from a long decline in 1970, and have restored the old home and garden, surrounding them with orchards of mango, fig, avocado, and macadamia nuts. There is a pretty cottage garden, protected from the sea winds by a fence of ponga, the native New Zealand tree fern (*Cyathea dealbata*), and a shelter belt of native trees. Behind it rises a stupendous *Magnolia grandiflora*, one of Butler's original plantings.

An arch leads to an area of lawns and borders with a riotous jumble of spider lilies (*Hymenocallis*), red hot pokers, and towering echiums jostling among hibiscus and cordylines, with antler ferns (*Platycerium bifurcatum*) and bromeliads sprouting from the trees. In late summer, the garden turns pink as swaths of belladonna lilies bloom among the pohutukawa trees. Between them lie the gravestones of Captain Butler and his family, shaded by the mighty branches. AE

Ayrlies

Auckland, New Zealand

DESIGNER: Beverley McConnell
OWNER: Beverley McConnell
GARDEN STYLE: 20th-century plantswoman's garden
SIZE: 12 acres (4.8 ha)
CLIMATE: Temperate
LOCATION: Whitford, Auckland

In 1967 Beverley McConnell and her husband, Malcolm, began to rebuild their house with a view across farmland to the Hauraki Gulf and the Rangitoto volcano. Once Malcolm had fenced off 3 acres (1ha) of land, they set about planting trees: "500 in one weekend alone." Being aware of the dictates of the local terrain and its contours, they proceeded gently for ten years, and then, in 1977, bulldozed out four good-sized ponds. Driving into Ayrlies now, it is possible to see and hear the water splashing down a series of rock faces, under bridges, and into ponds.

Here, as in most of the garden, New Zealand plants such as huge tree ferns (*Cyathea dealbata*), phormiums, and gunnera are featured, but from the house downward, they merge with the exotics. Red bougainvillea, purple petrea, white jasmine, and the cream tubes of *Pandorea pandorana* give way to magnolias, azaleas, and camellias lower down.

Paths wind around thickly planted pools at the lowest part of the garden, and colors blend happily, particularly in Beverley's Lurid Border with the reds, oranges, and golds of dahlias, crocosmias, and daylilies. The most unexpected part of the garden, though, is near the house, where a reflecting pool has been fashioned into a volcanic crater lake, the inspiration being a lake at the Huntington Botanic Garden in California. Local basalt rocks push out over the water to form high banks. JHa

RIGHT Ayrlies is characterized by informal, but detailed, planting, and water features.

Hamilton Gardens

Waikato, New Zealand

DESIGNER: Unknown
OWNER: City of Hamilton
GARDEN STYLE: 20th-century themed gardens
SIZE: 23.5 acres (58 ha)
CLIMATE: Temperate
LOCATION: Hamilton, Waikato

This is a hugely ambitious project for turning a large public park into a living history of gardens, and has been carried off with considerable aplomb. The star turn is a series of Paradise Gardens that represent "the six principal historic small garden traditions." There is a Chinese Scholar's Garden of the Sung Dynasty, a Japanese Garden of Contemplation, and an English Garden in the Arts and Crafts style. The best are the American Modernist Garden based on Thomas Church's Dewey Donnell garden in California, and the Italian Renaissance Garden of cool and muscular symmetry. Making up the set is a Mughal *chahar bagh*, or quadripartite paradise garden, inspired by a small hunting palace near Agra, India.

In contrast are the gardens based on plant groups, with rhododendron banks and camellia groves, a Victorian Flower Garden, and a rose garden with more than 230 cultivars. Foreign visitors, however, find their greatest inspiration in a New Zealand garden featuring only native plants, along with beautiful areas of both untouched and restored native landscape that provide counterpoints to the flowery display gardens.

Although some garden developments took place in the 1960s, most of this has been achieved since 1982, and development is ongoing. Recent features include a chinoiserie pavilion based on William Kent's Chinese House at Stowe in England (see page 319). And there are plans for a Maori garden on the riverbank, celebrating the plants, techniques, and technology of pre-European, Maori horticulture. AE

Pukeiti Gardens

Taranaki, New Zealand

DESIGNER: John Goodwin
OWNER: Pukeiti Rhododendron Trust
GARDEN STYLE: 20th-century rhododendron collection
SIZE: 890 acres (360 ha)
CLIMATE: Temperate
LOCATION: New Plymouth, Taranaki

Also known as the Pukeiti Rhododendron Trust, this is one of the greatest rhododendron gardens in the world, carved out of lush, temperate rain forest in the shadow of Mount Egmont in North Island, New Zealand. Developed since 1951, there is a large formal lawn with borders packed with rhododendrons, but best of all are those planted in the native temperate rain forest. The collection of around 2,000 different species boasts plants in flower year round, and other woodland gems such as camellias, magnolias, primulas, pleiones, and cobra lilies that luxuriate in the shelter, the mild climate, and heavy rainfall reaching 118–157 inches (3,000–4,000 mm) per year.

The best plants include *Rhododendron protistum*, grown from original Frank Kingdon-Ward seed, with creamy white, rose-flushed flowers, which is the largest example in cultivation in the world, reaching 26 x 39 feet (8 x 12 m). Also there is a breathtakingly beautiful *R. nuttallii* from the warmer areas of northeast Asia, with handsome, leathery leaves, peeling mahogany bark, and glorious, large, white, sweetly-scented flowers.

There is a collection of 400 species and hybrids of 'Vireya' rhododendron growing in a shade house. These species are frost-tender, mostly from the cloud forest mountains of Southeast Asia, and have exquisitely beautiful, dainty flowers. Although sunshine spotlights the plants in the borders and rain forest glades, creating diamond-spangled leaves and flowers, the rain is also a bonus, providing visitors with the ultimate "rhododendron experience." MB

Otari Native Botanic Garden

Wellington, New Zealand

DESIGNERS: Dr. Leonard Cockayne, J. G. McKenzie,
OWNER: City of Wellington
GARDEN STYLE: 20th-century botanical in native forest
SIZE: Collection 12.4 acres (5 ha), forest 247 acres (100 ha)
CLIMATE: Temperate
LOCATION: Wilton, Wellington

In the 1860s, a Wellington farmer, Job Wilton, set aside 17 acres (7 ha) of the virgin forest that his neighbors were busy cutting down. It formed the basis, in 1926, of the Otari Open-Air Plant Museum, a concept promoted by plant ecologist Dr. Leonard Cockayne and J. G. McKenzie, Director of Parks and Reserves for Wellington City. They aimed to protect disappearing native plants and encourage gardeners to use them.

The garden has a comprehensive, 1,200-species-strong collection of New Zealand's flora, with plants from the remote sub-Antarctic islands of the south right through to the subtropical far north. There are impressive collections of phormium, pittosporum, coprosma, and olearia; countless different hebes; spectacular plantings of grasses; and more than sixty types of fern. A glade of grass trees (*Dracophyllum*) is underplanted with a sea of Chatham Island forget-me-nots (*Myosotidium hortensia*), and spiky, juvenile lancewoods (*Pseudopanax crassifolius*) jostle around their parent, and a rock garden displays many rare and endangered alpines.

A walkway through the tree tops gives a bird's-eye view of the forest, including colossal matai *(Prumnopitys taxifolia)* and rimu *(Dacrydium cupressinum)*—one huge specimen is believed to be 800 years old. Other stately remnants of pristine podocarp forest are wreathed in vines and covered by flamboyant epiphytes. Around the garden, new areas of forest are steadily regenerating in parts previously logged. AE

Gardens of the World

Tasman, New Zealand

DESIGNER: Geoff Etherington
OWNERS: Geoff Etherington, Gillian Etherington
GARDEN STYLE: 20th-century themed gardens
SIZE: 6.7 acres (2.7 ha)
CLIMATE: Temperate
LOCATION: Hope, Nelson, Tasman

Never mind going around the world in eighty days; in this corner of New Zealand you can do it in eighty minutes, thanks to Geoff Etherington, who, in 1990, attacked his orchard with a digger. He grubbed up the trees, formed a series of gentle mounds around a central lake, and planted a series of gardens, each with flora from a different continent, making a stroll around the site a botanical world tour. It's handled with delicacy and wit, the implanting making satisfying compositions of texture and form. Asia, New Zealand, and the Americas have shapely evergreens and flowering shrubs; Europe is more floriferous; a miniature Australian gum forest has signs warning about marauding koalas; and Africa is impressive with gigantic proteas and rare trees.

The formal gardens include a rose garden, herb garden, herbaceous borders, and fountain leading to a simple quincunx of golden ash (*Fraxinus excelsior* 'Aurea'), creating an area of austere and shady loveliness. In contrast, a boat crammed with colorful bedding bobs on the central lake, and an exhilarating dry garden offers a combination of tribal sculpture, ferocious cacti, succulents, and fiery African blooms.

Visit on the weekend and there's likely to be a wedding party, since couples can marry in the sheltered amphitheater with its backdrop of lake and surrounding mountains. Geoff and his wife, Gillian, call their garden a "dream come true," and their stated aim is to "conserve unusual plants in a world where there is so much destruction." AE

Ohinetahi

Canterbury, New Zealand

DESIGNER: Sir Miles Warren
OWNER: Sir Miles Warren
GARDEN STYLE: 20th-century formal
SIZE: 3 acres (1.2 ha)
CLIMATE: Temperate
LOCATION: Governor's Bay, Lyttelton, Canterbury

Sir Miles Warren, one of New Zealand's foremost architects, has turned his remarkable skills to garden design with remarkable success. His perfectly proportioned, formal garden demonstrates outstanding attention to detail, a sensitive use of plants, and a taste for contemporary sculpture.

A series of small, but perfectly proportioned, garden "rooms," divided by hedges that protect the garden from strong sea breezes, gives a strong sense of structure. There is simplicity in some of the most effective design, especially where two *Robinia pseudoacacia* 'Frisia' cast shade over a table and chairs, backed by an immaculately clipped, evergreen hedge and framed by two Italian cypresses (*Cupressus sempervirens*). Beyond is a traditional, double herbaceous border with roses and delphiniums, leading to an ogee gazebo straight out of *Alice in Wonderland*. A formal red garden has a belvedere adding height and fine views over the lawn, house, and rose garden with its framework of formal hedging and topiary to the bay beyond. There's also a Gothic-style gate and suspension bridge over a gully, where hostas and other shade-loving plants enjoy life beneath the trees. Even the vegetable border is geometrically shaped and planted for color. What is most memorable is the detail—the razor-sharp formal hedging—the imagination, and the inspirational use of plants. MB

RIGHT Ohinetahi is one of New Zealand's best formal gardens and uses "rooms" to great effect.

This diverse collection of islands have one thing in common: they all feature a wonderful mix of garden design styles. Many of the islands have been colonized several times, with each settler bringing with them a new gardening style. The amalgam of new intertwined with the old creates an unpredictable, evocative mix. From the indigenous to the exotic, island gardens represent the truly awesome power of nature.

ISLANDS

Sausmarez Manor

Guernsey, Channel Islands

DESIGNER: Peter de Sausmarez, Seigneur of Sausmarez
OWNER: Peter de Sausmarez, Seigneur of Sausmarez
GARDEN STYLE: 20th-century subtropical woodland
SIZE: 5 acres (2 ha)
CLIMATE: Temperate
LOCATION: St. Martin, Guernsey

Sausmarez Manor has been the ancestral home of the seigneurs of Sausmarez for almost one thousand years. The current seigneur, Peter de Sausmarez, has devoted himself to maintaining his ancestral home, which incorporates fragments of building dating as far back as the twelfth century. The house standing today dates from the early eighteenth century and has strong hints of a New England influence, thanks to the family's connections with the New World. The building's elegantly proportioned facade is built of gray granite and looks out over a wide lawn that is fringed with tall grasses.

Over the past twenty years, Peter has developed and extended the exotic woodland garden, which features over fifty varieties of camellia, the green foliage providing a marvelous year-round backdrop.

The garden is worth visiting at any time of year from December onward, when the first camellias flower. Beyond an archway smothered with dainty, white *Solanum jasminoides* 'Album', you plunge into groves of exotics, including solid-stemmed South American bamboos. Great stands of *Gunnera manicata* line the stream, while the leaf-strewn paths dip beneath tunnels of more bamboo, or pass tree ferns, palms, bananas from China and Abyssinia, and huge bushes of fuchsia. Echiums also thrive here, as do escallonia and agapanthus. Many different types of hydrangea provide late-season interest. The trees are special, too, with walnuts and a white mulberry tree among the canopy of planes, acers, beech, and horse chestnuts (*Aesculus hippocastanum*). VB

La Seigneurie Gardens

Sark, Channel Islands

DESIGNER: Dame Sibyl Hathaway
OWNER: Michael Beaumont, Seigneur of Sark
GARDEN STYLE: 20th-century formal
SIZE: 5 acres (2 ha)
CLIMATE: Temperate
LOCATION: Sark

La Seigneurie is the home of the seigneur, the lord of the Isle of Sark, the last outpost of British feudalism. Sark has a total area of only 1,347 acres (545 ha), and is 3 miles (5 km) long and 1.5 miles (2.4 km) wide at its widest point. The tiny island has about 600 inhabitants and is remarkable for having no cars.

The house (closed to the public) was built in 1675, but has been added to over the centuries. High walls shelter the gardens from the winds that whip across the island, creating a microclimate in which many delicate, subtropical plants flourish. Doorways leading into the walled garden are frothy with clematis, and a Victorian glasshouse leans along the south-facing wall, planted with peaches. The garden is divided into several areas, with long beds of mixed planting, as well as a rose garden and a Mediterranean corner planted with santolina, helichrysum, and lavender. The garden continues to flower well into fall, the late show being provided by cleomes, asters, salvias, cannas, and mallows, and the ubiquitous Channel Island bulb, the pink nerine (known variously as the Guernsey and Jersey lily). Threaded through these beds are graceful spires of *Verbena bonariensis*. There are also low walls covered with erigeron (known locally as St. Peter Port daisies) and, beyond the well-stocked vegetable garden, a maze of olearia or New Zealand holly. At the bottom of the hill are ancient carp ponds belonging to the sixth-century monastery of St. Magloire, which once stood on the site of the house. They are surrounded by willows, holm oaks (*Quercus robur*), and fuchsias. VB

Creux Baillot Cottage

Jersey, Channel Islands

DESIGNER: Judith Queree
OWNERS: Nigel Queree, Judith Queree
GARDEN STYLE: 20th-century cottage garden
SIZE: 0.25 acre (0.1 ha)
CLIMATE: Temperate
LOCATION: Leoville, Jersey

On an island that made its name for potatoes and bedding plants, it is refreshing to discover a gardener with a botanical slant, and who takes full advantage of the mild climate. Judith Queree, an avid collector and inspired artist, has packed her small garden with unusual plants and elegant features created by her husband, Nigel, an instinctive craftsman.

The garden, wrapped around a 300-year-old granite cottage and set in the side of a shallow valley, is approached by a single track leading straight into a collection of 1,500 different plants, with 250 clematis for year-round flowers and forty primulas, all grown on organic principles. The upper part gently slopes in front of the cottage, and this south-facing microclimate is a haven for plants like Spanish shawl (*Heterocentron elegans*) from Central America and *Pelargonium endlicherianum* that remain outdoors year-round; a nearby raised bed includes most of Judith's salvia collection, and plants usually reserved for British conservatories. Beyond the house, a woodland garden, packed with rarities, is shaded from the sun by a slatted pergola that leads into a bog garden viewed from an elegant boardwalk. The proximity to the sea inspired a maritime theme, with an old rowing boat beached in the shade of palmlike tree ferns, and fishing nets draped around the garden to provide the perfect climbing frame for roses.

Judith's attention to detail and passion for plants gives the garden a sense of structure and guarantees surprises around every corner, skills that made her runner-up in the BBC's *Gardener of the Year 2000*. MB

> "…fishing nets draped around the garden to provide the perfect climbing frame for roses"

El Jardí Botànic de Sóller

Mallorca, Mediterranean Islands

DESIGNER: Fundació Jardí Botànic de Sóller
OWNER: University of Mallorca
GARDEN STYLE: 20th-century ecological, botanical
SIZE: 4 acres (1.6 ha)
CLIMATE: Mediterranean
LOCATION: Sóller, Mallorca

This modest botanical garden for the conservation and study of Mediterranean flora, especially that of the Balearic Islands, opened to the public in 1992. The garden is divided into ecological sections. The main areas include stream beds and cool mountainsides, the seaside, oak forests, shade, mountains, damp and shady places, and sand dunes.

The most colorful native plant area is the mountain garden, where rocks are attractively arranged to give cliff, crevice, paving, and gravel conditions. The endemic pine *Pinus halepensis* var. *ceciliae* grows here with *Hypericum balearicum*, all yellow flowers and tiny, wavy, silver-edged leaves. Balearic Island sage (*Phlomis italica*), with whorls of light mauve flowers, grows with French lavender (*Lavandula dentata)* and Spanish lavender (*Lavandula stoechas*). Also note the yellow-flowering rock roses with gray leaves, and a native, blue-flowered, creeping rosemary that layers but produces no seed.

The oak forest area includes the beautiful Majorcan peony (*Paeonia cambessedesii*) with large pale pink to deep rose flowers and contrasting, creamy white stamens and gray-green foliage. The ornamental plant area has a good collection of cacti, but also sky-blue plumbago, scarlet-flowered bottlebrushes, chestnut-crimson melianthus, and oleanders in several shades. Another notable plant is the ever flowering, pink and magenta myrtle-leaf milkwork (*Polygala myrtifolia*). RChe

The Heidi Gildemeister Garden

Mallorca, Mediterranean Islands

DESIGNER: Heidi Gildemeister
OWNER: Heidi Gildemeister
GARDEN STYLE: 20th-century waterwise, ecological
SIZE 7 acres (2.8 ha)
CLIMATE: Mediterranean
LOCATION: Mallorca

Some determination is needed to visit this very private garden. From the public road, its entrance is just one of a hundred field gates. The track is 2.5 miles (4 km) long and goes up and down over the mountains, with branch tracks and no signs.

From the green valley, you head through woodland that thins as you go, past stunted bushes, blue rosemary, and yellow hawkweed, until the rock is almost bare and you have only an occasional glimpse of the sea through the mountain ridges. Then you come to fine, mature trees of evergreen oak, ancient olives, and carobs. Blending into this scene is an ancient farmhouse set among scattered pines and palms. Four rock steps up and the short meadow grass becomes lawn with carefully clipped shrubs. The house is partly draped with mauve wisteria that also cascades out of nearby trees. Note the palms, the bronze and yellow gazanias swirling around the rocks, and the leaves of *Pittosporum tobira* blending with the olives. There are irises, yuccas, santolina, and white-flowering cistus, a pool framed by pines and shrubs, and steps leading down to a small dell beneath an oak. Here, in this cool and still spot, you will find tree ferns, aquilegias, and hedychiums.

Almost everywhere you look there are framed views of the mountains, with unmistakable similarities to the Table Mountain in South Africa, farther South African echoes being provided by aloes, pelargoniums, osteospermums, and more. RChe

Jardines de Alfabia

Mallorca, Mediterranean Islands

DESIGNER: Benhabet
OWNER: Don José Zaforteza Calvet
GARDEN STYLE: 15th-, 17th-century formal
SIZE: 10 acres (4 ha)
CLIMATE: Mediterranean
LOCATION: Bunola, Mallorca

Set in the Tramuntana Mountains toward Mallorca's northwestern coast, the lush, terraced gardens of Alfabia offer a cool oasis in Mallorca's intense summer heat. A visit to the gardens will enable you to peel back centuries of the island's history.

Alfabia's origins date back to the Moorish rule of the fourteenth and fifteenth centuries. Shortly after the Christian Reconquest, King Jaume I rewarded his ally, Benhabet, with a large estate. Benhabet channeled water from the surrounding mountains to irrigate his gardens, which he designed as a series of shaded "rooms" in the Arabic fashion. Most important of all, he created the garden in such a way that it seems to merge with the surrounding landscape.

There are contrasts throughout, with clipped avenues of low hedging in places and elsewhere a veritable jungle of palms, bamboos, and bulrushes. Watercourses gurgle, a welcome sound on a scorching day, while trellises of jasmine and wisteria shade the paths. Young chusan palms (*Trachycarpus fortunei*) contrast with more substantial, elderly date palms. There are bougainvillea-covered pergolas, stairways among sinewy branches, and fallen trunks. At the very bottom is an exotic, tropical garden with a water lily pond. Beyond are vistas of olive trees, while color is provided by flowers cascading over stone terraces and in large pots. Today's visitors will quickly appreciate that, despite extensive later developments in the garden, Benhabet's spirit lives on. VB

La Real Cartuja de Valldemossa

Mallorca, Mediterranean Islands

DESIGNER: Unknown
OWNER: Muncipal Council of Valldemossa
GARDEN STYLE: 17th-century formal
SIZE: 5 acres (2 ha)
CLIMATE: Mediterranean
LOCATION: Northwest coast, Mallorca

The composer Frédéric Chopin spent the winter of 1838–39 with his mistress, George Sand, at the Carthusian monastery at Valldemossa on the Balearic island of Mallorca. The weather, unusually, was cold and stormy. Chopin was ill, the couple fell out with the locals, and Sand wrote an ill-natured account of their visit, *A Winter in Majorca*. They were clearly not comforted by the matchless position of the monastery, set high up in the Tramuntana Mountains with views to the northwest coast of the island. Most distinctive of all is the ornate, green bell tower, visible from miles around, its shape reminiscent of a minaret. The gardens still have a monastic atmosphere, with quiet cloisters around tall cypresses, and long pathways through bushes of clipped yew and laurel.

Note the bougainvillea-covered balcony offering a breathtaking panorama of the valley far below, and groves of olive and almond trees. There is a rose garden, enclosed by neat hedging and surrounded by tall drum yews, many of them shot through with the bright red, climbing nasturtium (*Tropaeolum speciosum*). There is the odd splash of color, but the gardens are predominantly dark green and gray with tall eucalyptus forming an arch over stone walkways radiating out from the monastery buildings.

Often busy in summer because of the Chopin connections, the monastery nevertheless manages to maintain an air of tranquillity and of timelessness into the twenty-first century. VB

S'Avall

Mallorca, Mediterranean Islands

DESIGNER: Don Juan Panella
OWNER: Doña Carmen Delgado de March
GARDEN STYLE: Formal cacti and succulent garden
SIZE: 20 acres (8.1 ha)
CLIMATE: Mediterranean
LOCATION: Colònia de Sant Jordi, Mallorca

In the dry, flat, southeast of Mallorca is the private estate of Doña Carmen Delgado de March. The first thing you notice upon entering is the vivid cerise bougainvillea covering part of the mansion's high walls, then the avenue of pencil-thin cypresses that leads to the main parterre, filled with scarlet cannas and symmetrical box at the corners.

Beyond the parterre, a glasshouse contains substantial benches with landscaped beds of the best collection of cristate cacti in Europe. A shade house holds a magnificent collection of ferns and other plants needing shade and humidity. Paths then wind on through open shrubbery, where the intense blue flower spikes of echiums contrast with white angels' trumpets, with white and pink rhaphiolepis forming groups beneath. The small, gray-leaved bush germander (*Teucrium fruticans*) is a foil for the large, green leaves and mauve powder-puff flowers of *Eupatorium sordidum*. The center bed is a clear sweep of begonias. The path continues past a fine palm collection, an island, and a bridge to the superbly landscaped cactus and succulent garden.

The gently contoured land includes a pool, viewing platform, and amphitheater. Stone paths wind around, binding the scene together. The cacti and succulents are well grouped, and their contrasting shapes are amazing. There are great fluted columns and tall, ribbed spheres of many sizes and textures. In spring the succulent aloes produce their many poker flowers in yellow, orange, and red. This is one of the best succulent and cacti gardens in the world. RChe

Palazzo Parisio

Malta, Mediterranean Islands

DESIGNER: Unknown
OWNERS: The Scicluna family
GARDEN STYLE: 19th-century Maltese/Italianate baroque
SIZE: 6 acres (2.4 ha)
CLIMATE: Mediterranean
LOCATION: Naxxar, Malta

Marquis Giuseppe Scicluna acquired this property in 1898 and converted it into a palatial stately home, and the Scicluna family still live here.

The baroque walled gardens integrate perfectly with the palace. The second-floor balcony gives a good view of two huge Norfolk Island pines (*Araucaria heterophylla*) that frame the view down to a parterre of four octagonal, grassy panels, each with a central pool and fountain, and a surround of clipped, dwarf hedges. To one side is a long, elegant stone orangery.

At ground level, the main vista leads through a triumphal stone arch to a much larger garden with a central pool, a high water jet, and paths that give it a geometrical structure. The planting is quite diverse. Tall trees of many kinds, including palms, conifers, and tropical figs are well spaced so that adequate light reaches the formal beds below. In spring it is alive with scented stocks and freesias, irises, ranunculus, anemones, and winter pansies.

The main walk is lined with highly scented citrus trees, while to one side a major path leads to a pool backed by a high baroque arch. The planting is subtle with the clean white spaths of arum lilies contrasting with their shiny green leaves. Nearby a section has been replanted, mainly with subtropical fruit trees, palms, loquats, guavas, and several citruses, one of which bears both oranges *and* lemons.

The main vista continues through a gateway with a fine stone arch. Look out for the long avenue of ancient olive trees and, in summer, a number of large-flowering, multicolored hibiscus. RChe

Ras Rihana

Malta, Mediterranean Islands

DESIGNER: Chevalier Maurice Mizzi
OWNER: Chevalier Maurice Mizzi
GARDEN STYLE: 20th-century experimental eclectic
SIZE: 2 acres (0.8 ha)
CLIMATE: Mediterranean
LOCATION: Bidnija, Malta

On the fringe of a remote hilltop village, the house is approached along a narrow lane. It was built in 1969 by John and Diana Charlmers, and in 1978 it was acquired by Maurice Mizzi. The stunning views are a big plus, but the searing winds can be a problem, so protection is important.

Steps by a loggia lead down to the swimming pool. The protecting wall is covered by a range of climbers, including the black coral pea (*Kennedia nigricans*) and cat's claw (*Macfadyena unguis-cati*) with its hooklike tendrils and bright yellow flowers, and the highly scented, white-flowering stephanotis.

The bank of the terrace has drifts of the long-flowering trailing lantana (*Lantana montevidensis*) and, in summer, hibiscus in several colors. Across the formal lawn, a well-branched Mediterranean pine (*Pinus halepensis*) frames the view and, with several carob trees, gives wind protection. The spring flowering includes white almonds, apricots, rose-pink peaches, and white cherries. In summer and fall the fruit gives a succession of colors, while the vegetables below also catch the eye, thickening up with broad beans, green chard, celeriac, and the great, gray, feathery rosettes of globe artichokes.

The final features are a pool set below a bank with cascades of purple osteospermum, and a circular walk with fascinating, unusual trees and shrubs. You return along a straight path to find a cactus and succulent garden, and more shrubs, including a beautiful, yellow-flowering cassia and the brilliant blue spikes of the pride of Madeira (*Echium candicans*). RChe

Villa Barbaro

Malta, Mediterranean Islands

DESIGNERS: The Cremona-St. George family
OWNER: Marquis Anthony Cremona-Barbaro-St. George
GARDEN STYLE: Maltese formal
SIZE: 2 acres (0.8 ha)
CLIMATE: Mediterranean
LOCATION: Tarxien, Malta

The high garden walls of Villa Barbaro, surrounded by houses in the town of Tarxien, give no hint of the private, peaceful, green open space within, one that has developed over hundreds of years. The first things you notice on entering are the bantams: the rooster with its red, yellow, orange, and black feathers, and the white hens, all foraging for garden pests.

Plants suited to this climate are the backbone of the garden. Nothing is forced. So the parterre, which is not clipped too often and so avoids rigid shapes, is made of pink and blue rosemary, with the dark leaves contrasting with silvery artemisias. Elsewhere lavenders, the blue-flowering, gray-leaved bush germander (*Teucrium fruticans*), and pelargoniums take center stage. For contrast there are scented roses, particularly in pink, crimson, and white, mostly grown in terra-cotta pots. The walls are softened by shrubs and climbers. One wall is the backdrop for a white seat with solandra clambering all around it, its balloonlike buds bursting open to reveal yellow flowers, its large, dark leaves contrasting with the light colored, smaller leaves of pittosporum and teucrium. On the other side of the garden is a large, fine-leaved argyranthemum bush that never seems to stop producing its white, daisylike flowers. There is even a pink variety called 'Vancouver'.

One of the highlights is the citrus garden with its magnificent collection of cultivars, some of which are quite ancient. Once you start trying to compare their shapes, color, foliage, and shades of glistening orange, red, and yellow, you will never stop. RChe

> "One of the highlights is the citrus garden with its magnificent collection of cultivars…"

Villa Bologna

Malta, Mediterranean Islands

DESIGNERS: Margaret Strickland, Count Casteletti
OWNER: Chevalier Gerald de Trafford
GARDEN STYLE: 18th-century baroque
SIZE: 8 acres (3.2 ha)
CLIMATE: Mediterranean
LOCATION: Attard, Malta

This grand villa, originally built in 1745, was inherited and restored by Count Gerald Strickland, prime minister of Malta from 1927 to 1932.

Entering the huge gates, one is immediately impressed by the colorful bougainvilleas that clad the 25-foot-high (7.6 m) walls enclosing the courtyard. Well-spaced trees, most planted in 1930, including an araucaria, the sulfur-yellow-flowering silk oak (*Grevillea robusta*), and the yellow-fruiting bead tree (*Melia azedarach*), balance the scale of the building. Next come the borders and a pergola covered with an 'Albéric Barbier' rambling rose, a fine wall fountain, and a triumphal gateway with statues of Bacchus and Pan, which leads to the impressive walled garden. The focal point is the imposing stone fountain and pool, its four pillars topped by fine statues. The whole effect is set off by the urns and troughs on each side, spilling over with fiery-colored geraniums.

A fine, wrought-iron gate opens to the expansive rear gardens with a pool where four columns curve over the water and join, supporting four dolphins. The pool is edged in blue-flowering vinca, its color echoing the flowers of the jacaranda trees, the shutters of the villa, and the clipped rosemary edging the lawn beyond. The final touches are gently restful, a pair of weeping, silvery-leaved schinus trees providing a shady site with views to the sunken pool, and, nearby, a blue and white dovecote. There are also old vines, an ancient wellhead in a pine copse, a new olive grove, a historic carob tree, new peach trees, and much, much more. RChe

> "…a fine wall fountain, and a triumphal gateway with statues of Bacchus and Pan…"

Palácio Sant'Ana

São Miguel, Azores, Atlantic Ocean Islands

DESIGNERS: George Brown, subsequent head gardeners

OWNER: Regional Government of Azores

GARDEN STYLE: 19th-century picturesque eclectic

SIZE: 20 acres (8.1 ha)

CLIMATE: Mediterranean

LOCATION: Ponta Delgada, São Miguel

In 1845 British garden designer George Brown came here from a nursery in Fulham, London, to lay out the Sant'Ana garden for Jacome Correia. Over the next few years, he shipped over plants and brought his family. The palace is now the seat of the president of regional government.

The show begins with an arboretum of mature trees, including, oaks, elms, grevilleas, liriodendrons, crimson-flowering metrosideros, palms, mangoes, and avocados. Views through the trees across sweeping lawns frame the large, pink and white, neoclassical palace, designed in 1846. Farther on is a large, productive garden with a central pool and fountain at the cross paths.

The box-edged beds contain a wide range of cut flowers for official occasions, with dahlias, watsonias, zinnias, and strelitzias topping the list. Against the upper wall are historic lean-to glasshouses and a tall, octagonal, central conservatory. A raised walk with a pergola planted with mauve wisteria, honeysuckle, orange campsis, and bougainvilleas frames a view over the glasshouses to the flowery garden. Beyond this are many trees, including huge metrosideros from New Zealand. In the shade beneath are blue and white agapanthus, giant pink and white crinums, azaleas, and fuchsias in many colors.

In front of the palace are formal flower beds, the Rose Garden, and, in the lowest section, a broad, serpentine pond backed by Norfolk Island pines (*Araucaria heterophylla*), cordylines, cannas, and blue and white agapanthus. RChe

Terra Nostra

Azores,
Atlantic Ocean Islands

DESIGNERS: Visconde da Praia and descendants
OWNER: Bensaude Turismo
GARDEN STYLE: 19th-century picturesque and woodland
SIZE: 30 acres (12.1 ha)
CLIMATE: Mediterranean
LOCATION: São Miguel, Azores

In 1770 American Thomas Hickling built a simple wooden summerhouse here and planted 2 acres (0.8 ha) with trees from his homeland. In 1848 the Visconde da Praia and his wife bought the property, replaced the summerhouse with the present mansion, and laid out a garden with water features, parterres, and woodland. In 1872 the second Visconde added a serpentine canal, grottoes, and avenues. The next major change came in 1990, with the arrival of 3,000 new trees.

The house is set on a mount framed by fine, old araucarias. The curving path leads past fine Japanese maples and mature Chinese camellias toward a bust of Thomas Hickling near the house. Behind the house are views down to the curving lake, its dark waters reflecting the crimson cannas on an island, the blue hydrangeas, and white swans. A path then leads on to several gardens enclosed by pittosporum hedges, one planted in 2000 with raised beds of cycads, and another with native plants such as the Azores blueberry, *Vaccinium cylindraceum*. A maze of paths leads to an avenue of palms, azaleas, and tree ferns, along with ivy-covered concrete prehistoric animals.

By the pool are ducks, geese, and swans. In spring there are red, orange, and yellow rhododendrons, and, in fall, yellow-scented ginger lilies. A fern garden has aspidistras, ophiopogons, and tree ferns. RChe

LEFT A walkway at Terra Nostra reveals a stately fern garden where magnificent tree ferns flourish above the pool.

Quinta da Boa Vista

Madeira,
Atlantic Ocean Islands

DESIGNERS: The Garton family
OWNER: Betty Garton
GARDEN STYLE: 20th-, 21st-century Anglo-Portuguese
SIZE: 12 acres (4.8 ha)
CLIMATE: Mediterranean
LOCATION: Funchal, Madeira

At Quinta da Boa Vista, the entrance leads under a pergola with vines, including clock vine (*Thunbergia mysorensis*) with its long, yellow and red racemes. Beyond are the shade houses where, under a big jacaranda tree, you take the cobbled drive. The land on each side is full of strelitzias (others are grown here commercially). Here the rugged, knobbly trunk of a huge, ancient, false pepper tree (*Schinus molle*) contrasts superbly with its weeping, gray-green foliage. Visitors will also love the bougainvilleas in various colors and the aloes at the top of a slope. Opposite is a large, feathery, pink shower tree (*Cassia javanica*) with its big clusters of pink flowers.

Near the summerhouse is a trio of fantastically scented frangipanis over 6 feet (1.8 m) tall, one entwined with the bright orange blossoms of streptosolen. Farther on is a long drift of agapanthus, their rounded heads of blue flowers backed by the taller stems of leonotis, with soft, orange flowers in whorls. At the end of the lawn, a tall *Eucalyptus ficifolia* tree is covered with crimson-red flowers in early fall. The best part comes last: a series of shade houses with tens of thousands of orchids in every color, including unique, new, award-winning hybrids and their descendants. RChe

> "…tens of thousands of orchids in every color…"

Quinta da Torrinha

Madeira, Atlantic Ocean Islands

DESIGNER: Russell Bode
OWNER: Russell Bode
GARDEN STYLE: 18th-century tropical, formal and informal
SIZE: 1 acre (0.4 ha)
CLIMATE: Mediterranean
LOCATION: Funchal, Madeira

This three-story quinta, which is named after its eighteenth-century viewing turret, has an original terrace with pebble paths, all of which are gently shaded by an old, weeping, false pepper tree (*Schinus molle*), and contrasting ancient palms and cycads. A brick-edged pool forms the focal point of the garden, and is surrounded by an extensive range of bromeliads, ferns, and foliage plants, including the red-edged acalypha and variegated Indian fig (*Ficus indica*). Other beds contain green and white arum lilies, busy lizzies in a wide range of colors, and strelitzias. Paths then lead down through groups of mature trees to an exuberant planting of tropicals, including pink pineapples, brilliant scarlet heliconias, and fine-leaved *Dracaena marginata* 'Variegata', with its narrow pink- and white-striped leaves.

This colorful, informal jungle, with papyrus (*Cyperus papyrus*) sprouting above the rounded discs of white water lilies, and a small stream and pool, leads to a formal garden with a central, rectangular pool, the formality of which is accentuated by vertical conifers. The surrounding area is bright with scarlet fuchsias, white shell ginger (*Alpinia zerumbet*), and large, pink hebes. One exit leads to the Rose Garden, with its elegant pergola and grass paths among beds edged by red iresine. From the formal garden, a pair of curving steps lead up to a pergola with pink roses, before you finally reach views of the cathedral tower and the sea from the upper terrace. RChe

Quinta do Palheiro Ferreiro

Madeira, Atlantic Ocean Islands

DESIGNERS: The Blandy family
OWNERS: The Blandy family
GARDEN STYLE: 19th-, 20th-century formal
SIZE: 30 acres (12.1 ha)
CLIMATE: Mediterranean
LOCATION: Palheiro Ferreiro, Madeira

Set in the hills above Funchal, Quinta do Palheiro Ferreiro, also known as Blandy Gardens, boasts an eclectic mix of plants from warm, temperate climates. The original owner, Conde de Carvalhal, planted many of the trees and established a camellia collection numbering over 10,000 plants, and flowering from November to April. The Blandy family, who bought the quinta in 1885, have continued to develop it, placing emphasis on South African plants.

Around the house are king proteas (*Protea cynaroides*) and, on the terrace below, a fabulous specimen of sweet michelia (*Michelia doltsopa*) with exquisitely scented, magnolialike flowers. There are many notable trees, especially Paraña pine (*Araucaria angustifolia*) from Brazil, the South African silver tree (*Leucadendron argenteum*), and Australian waratah (*Telopea speciosissima*), all confirming Madeira's reputation for having the perfect gardening climate. One of the most spectacular specimens in full flower is a New Zealand Christmas tree (*Metrosideros robusta*), which forms giant red pom-poms.

Other treats include the formal Jardim da Senhora, or Garden of the Ladies, with box-edged beds and fun topiary, and the Inferno—a jungle of climbers and giant, self-seeded rice paper plants (*Tetrapanax papyrifer*). MB

RIGHT A fine collection of rarely seen trees benefits from the superb growing conditions at Quinta do Palheiro Ferreiro.

Jardim Tropical da Quinta do Monte Palácio

Madeira, Atlantic Ocean Islands

DESIGNERS: José Berardo, Eleuterio Soares

OWNER: José Berardo Foundation

GARDEN STYLE: Portuguese-Oriental

SIZE: 21 acres (8.5 ha)

CLIMATE: Mediterranean

LOCATION: Funchal, Madeira

As you step through the main entrance of the garden, which lies toward the highest part, its cool greenness becomes immediately evident as the pebbled paths and steps lead through mature trees, which have been underplanted predominately with the lacy foliage of tree ferns and woodwardias. The greenness of the garden is enhanced by hanging, tasseled, scarlet flowers of fuchsia and, occasionally, by the blue or white of hydrangeas.

As the path curves and descends, you will see a rock pool and cascade before you reach the red Chinese gateway with its guardian lions. Beyond this is a gallery of ceramic pictures depicting the history of the Portuguese discoverers, which is softened by the overlapping tree ferns above and the grasslike ophiopogon beneath. Steps lead down, past Japanese lanterns and a red Oriental bridge that spans the valley, to another Chinese gateway. In summer the blue hydrangeas on the other side of the path cleverly complement the color of the tiles. Note the curving wall with protruding cannon that can actually eject water, and the cascade that discharges a great sheet of water into the lake.

The route continues to the palace with a fine display of historic porcelain and on to the water channels, stepping-stones, and bridge, and the pool, which is packed with carp. Beyond is the most flowery part of the garden, with a plethora of orchids and proteas. After you reach the lowest spot in the garden, the path zigzags up past the best collection of cycads in the world. RChe

"…these gardens are visited and enjoyed by thousands of people from every continent…"

El Jardín del Cactus

Lanzarote, Canary Islands, Atlantic Ocean Islands

DESIGNER: César Manrique
OWNER: Island Council of Lanzarote
GARDEN STYLE: 20th-century contemporary
SIZE: 10 acres (24 ha)
CLIMATE: Mediterranean
LOCATION: Guatiza, Lanzarote

Lanzarote's arid landscape of lava flows and ash is the perfect setting for the contemporary art of César Manrique (1919–92). A painter, sculptor, and protégé of Nelson Rockefeller, Manrique was born in the island's capital, Arrecife. He studied art in Madrid and New York before returning to Lanzarote to become a major influence in the sensitive development of the island as a tourist destination.

At Guatiza, on the edge of an area of volcanic hills known as Las Calderas, several years of pumice removal by local farmers had created a deep, oval hollow. Here Manrique created a living sculpture called El Jardín del Cactus, also known as Lanzarote Cactus Garden. The large amphitheater, set 16.4 feet (5 m) below ground and surrounded by high walls, is inhabited by drought-tolerant plants and is towered over by a restored windmill, guarded by a giant cactus sculpture. Opened in 1990, it contains nearly 10,000 cacti and succulents from 1,400 species, including rare Canary Island natives. The cacti are grouped by genus and are planted on steep terraces that encircle a central display of black, mulched beds dotted with larval "monoliths," fountains, and pools, and crossed by meandering paths of basalt. This magical, surreal display becomes even more extraordinary during showers of rain, when succulents running with drops of water are lit by the sun.

The landscapes at Jameos del Agua and Mirador del Rio are worth visiting, too, while Manrique's organic-shaped "wind mobiles" are on view throughout the island. MB

El Jardín de Sitio Litre

Tenerife, Canary Islands, Atlantic Ocean Islands

DESIGNER: Unknown
OWNER: John Lucas
GARDEN STYLE: 18th-century Anglo-Spanish formal
SIZE: 5 acres (2 ha)
CLIMATE: Mediterranean
LOCATION: Puerto de la Cruz, Tenerife

The first designers of this garden are unknown, but we do know that it was bought in 1774 by Archibald Little, a British merchant. The name "Sitio Litre" is a part phonetic translation from the English, meaning "situation of the Littles."

The older, formal structure of the garden, with pools, pergolas, terraces, and the croquet lawn, gives it a unique Anglo-Spanish style, all attributed to the Littles. Next, Charles Smith and his family owned the garden from 1856 to 1996, when it was bought by John Lucas. In six months the ancient trees and palms were stripped of dead branches, the tangles of tropical shrubs and climbers were pruned and thinned, and soil was brought in for the new plantings. Paths were lifted, pipes and cables laid beneath for irrigation and lighting, and the pergolas, pools, and seats were repaired. The blueprint for the upgrade consisted of twenty-seven paintings (now in the North Gallery at Kew, England) by Marianne North, who stayed here for two months in 1875.

It is a delight to wander in this peaceful, mature garden in the center of Puerto de la Cruz, not least to see the curving pergola with a superb display of orchids. Look out for the large dragon tree (*Dracaena draco*), in excellent condition and approximately 400 years old, predating the garden, and a Norfolk Island pine (*Araucaria heterophylla*), the biggest in the Canary isles, probably planted in 1730. RChe

Jardín d'Aclimatación de la Orotava

Tenerife, Canary Islands, Atlantic Ocean Islands

DESIGNER: Nicolas Eduardo
OWNER: National Institute for Agricultural Research
GARDEN STYLE: 19th-century Spanish-French formal
SIZE: 7 acres (2.8 ha)
CLIMATE: Mediterranean
LOCATION: Puerto de la Cruz, Tenerife

This garden was founded in 1878 by the Marquis of Villanueva del Prado. The geometrical plan, still evident today, was designed by Nicolas Eduardo. Just inside the main entrance of this gently sloping site is a wide, paved area where seats are shaded by trees on which orchids and bromeliads grow. To one side are shaded orchids and, farther on, delicate calliandras with fluffy red and white stamens overhang a path attractively edged with variegated spider plants (*Chlorophytum comosum* 'Variegatum').

Farther on, climbing, endemic canarinas have dangling yellow and orange bells, towered over by the soaring, thorny trunks of chorisia with its orchid-like flowers and pods bursting with silky threads. Look out for African spathodia with clusters of orange and scarlet, tuliplike flowers, and popcorn cassia (*Senna didymobotrya*) with flowers in yellow columns and brown buds that smell of peanuts. There are many palms, including the blue-gray-leaved European fan palm (*Chamaerops humilis*).

In the center of the garden is a circular pool and fountain with interesting bamboo arches. There are several cycad trees, about 200 years old, some with cones over 2 feet (60 cm) high. Huge breadfruit sometimes hang from the trunk of the tree opposite and, farther on, a large bed is dedicated to various different banana trees, including some with huge, red-ribbed leaves, and others with blue flowers. RChe

Hijuela del Botánico

Tenerife, Canary Islands, Atlantic Ocean Islands

DESIGNER: Unknown

OWNER: La Orotava Municipality

GARDEN STYLE: 18th-century botanical

SIZE: 1 acre (0.4 ha)

CLIMATE: Mediterranean

LOCATION: La Orotava, Tenerife

This garden, whose name means "daughter of the botanic garden," is much smaller and more informal than the Jardín d'Aclimatación (see opposite). It is situated in the center of La Orotava behind the neoclassical town hall, and may once have been the kitchen garden of a convent.

Its walls are topped with very fine iron railings, while inside the grand entrance gates is an open space with some antique benches and a large dragon tree (*Dracaena draco*) as the focal point. Clipped box and myrtle shrubs edge the curving paths that lead away, and there is a wide mix of planting, from bright, informal beds with cannas, rinums, and fuchsias, to white angels' trumpets and self-sown busy lizzies. Shady beds contain the the kaffir lily (*Clivia miniata*), its dark, straplike leaves making an excellent background for its scarlet flowers, and the tubular-flowered greentip kaffir lily (*Clivia nobilis*). Elsewhere orange-colored asclepias attract huge, orange-marked monarch butterflies.

Look out for the fascinating old building that appears to be made of rustic timber, but is, in fact, carefully contrived concrete. Its retaining wall is hung with the endemic *Lotus maculatus* with fine, silvery leaves, and yellow and orange pealike flowers. There are also many palms, tree ferns, cedars, junipers, tropical figs, and huge, spiky, white-flowering yuccas, jacarandas, and the orange/scarlet-flowering African tulip tree (*Liriodendron tulipifera*). There are even several kinds of banana tree, including the splendid Abyssinian banana *(Ensete ventricosum)*. RChe

Jardín Botánico Canario Viera y Clavijo

Gran Canaria, Canary Islands, Atlantic Ocean Islands

DESIGNERS: Various garden directors

OWNER: Government of the Eastern Canary Islands

GARDEN STYLE: 20th-century ecological, botanical

SIZE: 67 acres (27.1 ha)

CLIMATE: Mediterranean

LOCATION: Tafira Alta, Gran Canaria

Named after the eighteenth-century naturalist José de Viera y Clavijo, this botanical garden, the biggest in Spain, was established in 1952 by the Swedish botanist Eric Sventenius. Its current director, Dr. David Bramwell, has made many new developments. Since 1983 a seed bank has been developed that focuses on 400 endemic species. The native plants are grouped according to their original geographical locations.

Even in the parking lot, a range of palms is underplanted with native plants, including white and mauve echiums, and limoniums. The big surprise is to find yourself on a high cliff with the whole botanical garden laid out below. The path zigzags down past banks covered with native plants, lotuses tumbling over the edge, evergreen bushes of limonium, and rosettes of aeoniums. The path progresses through a group of dragon trees (*Dracaena draco*), past a fountain dedicated to famous botanists, and on through a wild olive grove to the unique Canary pine forest. On the cliff above are the 8-foot-high (2 m), white flower spikes of tower of jewels (*Echium simplex*) and the gray, organ-pipe clusters of the native Canary Island spurge (*Euphorbia canariensis*).

The cactus and succulent garden is superb, with the white-striped form of century plant (*Agave americana*) and cerise carpets of carpobrotus, along with numerous cacti in soaring columns, sinuous carpets, prickly spheres, and oval pads. There are also aloes of all sizes, with yellow, orange, and red vertical flower spikes contrasting with the marvelous swan neck agave (*A. attenuata*). RChe

> "The cactus and succulent garden is superb, with…numerous cacti in soaring columns…"

El Jardín de la Marquesa de Arucas

Gran Canaria, Canary Islands, Atlantic Ocean Islands

DESIGNERS: Ramón Madam y Uriondo, Vicente Ramos
OWNER: Marchioness of Arucas
GARDEN STYLE: 19th-century picturesque
SIZE: 12 acres (4.9 ha)
CLIMATE: Mediterranean
LOCATION: Arucas, Gran Canaria

The palatial house was constructed in 1880 for Ramón Madam y Uriondo, the first marquis of Arucas, and his wife, Maria. The house is impressive, with grand, colonnaded balconies, the entrance path flanked by stone urns on fern filled pillars. The lush gardens, said to have been designed by a Frenchman, give a very good balance of shade and sunny glades.

Look out for the palms, araucarias, giant strelitzias, pandanus trees with their prop roots, a 500-year-old dragon tree (*Dracaena draco*), the thorny-trunked chorisia with pink, orchidlike flowers, and the brilliant scarlet flowers of the African erythrina. There are also several architectural features, including a stone grotto of volcanic rocks with a pink- and white-tipped, leafy breynia at its base, and a Chinese-style summerhouse linked to a simple, arched bridge over an irregular pool with rocky islands, water lilies, and fish. Peacocks strut around and perch in the trees, while blue plumbago, red cannas, and yellow farfugium give splashes of color. Large shrubs of brunfelsia, with its flowers of dark mauve turning white, and double red hibiscus make a very effective background.

Many paths lead off in all directions, again taking in some excellent planting—brilliant tangerine pyrostegia mixes with climbing blue skyflower (*Thunbergia grandiflora*). Best of all, the smooth-stemmed palms create beautiful avenues, one with a groundcover of pink begonias. RChe

Miriam C. Schmidt Botanical Garden

St. Eustatius, Caribbean Islands

DESIGNER: Miriam C. Schmidt
OWNER: St. Eustatian Government
GARDEN STYLE: 21st-century Caribbean botanical
SIZE: 13 acres (5.3 ha)
CLIMATE: Dry tropical
LOCATION: Southeast coast, St. Eustatius

The importance of the island of St. Eustatius is frequently overlooked. Historically a wealthy trading outpost of the Caribbean, Statia, as it is affectionately called, was the first foreign nation to recognize the newly formed United States of America in 1776. When Dutch traders purchased the island of Manhattan from the indigenous Americans, they used thirty blue beads from Statia as currency.

The island of Statia is as colorful as its beads, and the St. Eustatius National Parks authority aims to maintain the biodiversity of the island. As an islander, Miriam C. Schmidt felt strongly about the loss of endemic trees and plants, such as the morning glory *Ipomoea sphenophylla*. The project commenced in the 1980s with the gift of 13 acres (5 ha) of land from the Statian government. With five anticipated phases, this development is strongly backed by the hard work of many volunteers.

The first phase focused on planting the garden, and was completed in 2005 after four years. Visitors may now enjoy a Sensory Garden, Palm Garden, Kitchen Garden, Lookout Garden, and Bird Trail. Despite an ongoing battle with the Mexican creeper (*Antigonon leptopus*), the second phase commenced in 2006 with more planting. Most important is the attention being paid to the richly exotic native flora and fauna. This is truly a garden in the making, and a timely project for the twenty-first century. AW

Wingfield Plantation

St. Kitts and Nevis, Caribbean Islands

DESIGNER: Unknown
OWNER: Morris Widdowson
GARDEN STYLE: 17th-century Caribbean
SIZE: 10 acres (4 ha)
CLIMATE: Wet tropical
LOCATION: St. Kitts, St. Kitts and Nevis

Lying close to the Black River, this former sugar estate, also known as Romney Manor Estate, is the oldest on the island and, dating from the early seventeenth century, also one of the oldest in the whole Caribbean. Early in the twentieth century, after centralization of the island's cane industry, the estate's water-powered mill was closed. In 2001 cane ceased to be grown here altogether, and 350 years of sugar production came to an end.

Apparently Sam Jefferson II, the great, great, great-grandfather of Thomas Jefferson, once owned this plantation. Although Romney Manor was the first Caribbean estate to free its slaves, it is quite clear whose hands worked the land and laid the groundwork for the current gardens, where the volcanic soil and proximity to the rain forest fuel the rich growth of tropical fruit trees and flowers. In the center of the garden is the 350-year-old rain tree (*Samanea saman*), 24 feet (7.3 m) in diameter, beyond which is an immaculate lawn bordered by a shrubbery and a richness of delicate orchids. There is a fountain and the ruins of the sugar estate factory, now under restoration, and much, much more, all in this wonderful, heavily scented location. GW

"…an immaculate lawn bordered by a shrubbery and a richness of delicate orchids"

Morne L'Etoile

Martinique, Caribbean Islands

DESIGNERS: Littée brothers
OWNER: Unknown
GARDEN STYLE: 19th-century French-Creole
SIZE: 2.5 acres (1 ha)
CLIMATE: Wet tropical
LOCATION: Saint-Pierre, Martinique

Martinique was named Madinina, or "Island of Flowers," by the Arawak and Carib Indians. Two-thirds of the island is classified as a regional national park and is protected land. This house was built at the heart of a banana plantation in 1870 by the Littée brothers. Under the shadow of the volcano Mount Pelée, famous for its eruption in 1902, the fertile land is crammed with cane and avocado, and the sweet scents of banana and pineapple waft on the breeze.

The plantation is of such exceptional beauty that you cannot but be submerged in the Creole atmosphere of yore. A respectful restoration of the house and gardens over more than three years by the new owners has maintained and enhanced the architecture and style of the era.

In the near vicinity of the Morne L'Etoile gardens, the Macintosh Plantation has an abundance of tropical flowers and plants. It is named after the renowned cultivator of the anthurium, Martinique's best-known flower. After an extraordinary wander through the ferns and foliage of the rain forest, you arrive in nearby La Trace. Other enticing natural beauties of the area that should be seen are the Saut Gendarme Waterfall and Le Jardin de la Pelée.

Morne L'Etoile is designated as a World Heritage Site by UNESCO. For the visitor, it promises all the delights of a tropical garden and does not fail to deliver. With its dramatic backdrop of the still-active Mount Pelée, the Morne L'Etoile estate, at an altitude of almost 1,160 feet (350 m), looks out across the city of Saint-Pierre and its sparkling blue bay. AW

Fond Doux Estate

St. Lucia, Caribbean Islands

DESIGNER: Unknown
OWNERS: Lyton Lamontagne, Eroline Lamontagne
GARDEN STYLE: 18th-century Caribbean
SIZE: 135 acres (54.6 ha)
CLIMATE: Wet tropical
LOCATION: Soufrière, St. Lucia

The drive-in volcano on St. Lucia may be high on the list of every visitor to the island, but you should not miss the Fond Doux Estate. Located close to the Piton Mountains on the western side of the island, close to the city of Soufrière, you will find this 250-year-old working estate squirreled away amid the tranquillity of the tropical forests. This huge plantation was one of the first French estates to be built in the region around the middle of the eighteenth century. It is awe inspiring to see the continuity of its production of cocoa, citrus, bananas, coconuts, and vegetables, with many original techniques still on show.

From the porch of the old plantation house, the estate rolls out like a magic carpet packed with tropical greenery. Walking the estate trails, you are immediately struck by the incredible beauty, exotic birds, flourishing trees, and rich range of crops. With three distinctive trails—the Fond Doux Estate Trail, the Chateaubelair Hill Trail, and The East Ruins Trail—incredible diversity and marvelous surprises at every turn keep hikers on their toes. Old military ruins and dramatic views of Pitons and religious shrines abound; the sound effects are provided by the red-neck pigeon and the St. Lucia oriole. AW

> "…the estate rolls out like a magic carpet packed with tropical greenery"

Flower Forest

Barbados, Caribbean Islands

DESIGNERS: Richard Coghlan, Fritz Lundi
OWNER: Flower Forest Ltd.
GARDEN STYLE: 20th-century tropical semiformal
SIZE: 50 acres (20.2 ha)
CLIMATE: Wet tropical
LOCATION: St. Joseph, Barbados

This former sugar plantation is now a cross between a botanical garden and a nature trail, and its flowers and plants will amaze you. The wild and dramatic lushness, the framed formality, and the sheer beauty and diversity of the plant life make this Barbados at its finest. Located in St. Joseph, with spectacular scenery and sweeping views of the rugged east coast, the garden is a mixture of tropical ornamental and economic plants, most well labeled, with banana and breadfruit trees, and indigenous Caribbean flora.

Bearded fig trees (Ficus citrifolia) tower over the garden, and the Barbados cherry (Malpighia punicifolia), with its wide spreading branches and bright-red, juicy fruit, provides the understory. Begonias are massed along the path edges with cinnamon-colored zeanaida doves pecking beneath. One of the most interesting trees is the sandbox (Hura crepitans), which has dark, pointed spines and smooth, brown bark. The sharp spines along the trunk have resulted in the name "monkey-no-climb," although "monkey pistol" might be more apt because it describes the sharp, cracking sound when the seeds burst apart. Despite this particular tree, green monkeys are often seen in the garden.

With the garden at your back, and a comfortable place to sit, one of the great pleasures of a visit to the Flower Forest is sipping a cool drink and looking out over the hilly country, taking note of the coconut palms on the crest of a ridge, the banana plantations crowding the slopes, and the packed breadfruit trees in the valley. CW

Andromeda Botanical Gardens

Barbados, Caribbean Islands

DESIGNER: Iris Bannochie
OWNER: The Barbados National Trust
GARDEN STYLE: 20th-century tropical botanical
SIZE: 6 acres (2.4 ha)
CLIMATE: Wet tropical
LOCATION: St. Joseph, Barbados

The late Iris Bannochie, creator of the Andromeda Gardens, is a legend of Caribbean horticulture, and this intimate, tasteful garden is a testament to her taste, style, and skill. She began developing it on an outcrop of fossil-encrusted limestone in 1954. It now has the widest range of tropical plants in the Caribbean, encapsulating the exotic exuberance of the tropics.

The garden is designed along the axis of a stream that fills several ponds. Narrow paths weave among the vibrant gingers, heleconias, and hibiscus loved by hummingbirds. There are collections of cacti and orchids growing in a shade house, and also in a compost of coconut shells by a swimming pool, in surely one of the finest locations in the world. There is a wonderful collection of trees, including a shady grove of palms. At the center of the upper garden is a majestic, native bearded fig tree (*Ficus citrifolia*) with a thick curtain of roots hanging from the branches. The Portuguese are said to have called the island Los Barbados ("the Bearded Ones") after these figs.

Iris Bannochie regarded her treasure as a botanical garden and noted all new plant arrivals in a diary. She once said, "True gardeners like anything that is different," so it is no surprise to find oddities such as the Barbados gooseberry (*Pereskia aculeata*), an unusual succulent with "leaves" on the fruit. Exiting from the garden, you walk under a pergola supporting a magnificent jade vine (*Strongylodon macrobotrys*) with hanging clusters of turquoise flowers. Effects such as that convince you that you are in one of the world's most desirable gardens. MB

The Priory

Grenada, Caribbean Islands

DESIGNERS: Patrizia Banus, Pietro Banus
OWNER: Patrizia Banus, Pietro Banus
GARDEN STYLE: 20th-century tropical Gertrude Jekyll
SIZE: 0.25 acre (0.1 ha)
CLIMATE: Wet tropical
LOCATION: St. George's, Grenada

In the center of St. George's, the small and attractive capital of Grenada, on a hill between the Anglican and Catholic churches, is a house called The Priory. It is over 200 years old and was once a chapel.

Even before you enter the garden, bushy bougainvilleas and lantanas can be seen peeping through the front railings with jasmine climbing all over them. Color planning is evident, as purple bougainvilleas link with mauve false heather (*Cuphea hyssopifolia*), both contrasting with the pink and white young foliage of a big snow bush (*Breynia nivosa*). The colors turn to red with coleus and copperleaf (*Acalypha wilkesiana*), tangerine with Cape honeysuckle (*Tecoma capensis*), and yellow with coral fountain (*Russelia equisetiformis*).

Near the house, a frangipani gives exquisite scent to a hot color scheme of orange- and red-leaved croton, the red-flowering gout plant (*Jatropha podagrica*), and a yellow-flowering kalanchoe. There is also the climbing flame lily, *Gloriosa superba*, with its exotic, yellow-edged, scarlet flowers. Other climbers include the bright blue tropical pea; quisqualis, whose flowers change from red to white; and the light mauve-pink trumpets of porana.

The center of the garden has a small pool and fountain, and four triangular flower beds. Two are mulched with pebbles, and two are underplanted with creeping, variegated stenotaphrum. The terraces are balanced by an elegant, open pavilion, and the rear garden is like a green balcony with an amazing view of the prettiest capital in the Caribbean. RChe

Bay Gardens

Grenada, Caribbean Islands

DESIGNER: Keith Hugh St. Bernard
OWNER: Albert St. Bernard
GARDEN STYLE: Tropical jungle
SIZE: 7 acres (2.8 ha)
CLIMATE: Wet tropical
LOCATION: Morne Delice, Grenada

These gardens are part of the rain forest and were created by the late Keith Hugh St. Bernard on the site of an old sugar mill over a period of about thirty years. They are now managed by his brother, Albert.

Access to this jungly woodland is by a trail of narrow paths covered by nutmeg husks. Occasionally a fallen tree trunk or a low branch has been deliberately retained. The tour takes in a long sequence of surprises, the twisting paths revealing scene after scene as you turn a corner or move from shade to sunlit openings. The plants may be highlighted, or there may be a pool of tropical fish and turtles. In one particular small, open space, there is a dark green background of trees and palms, with dappled light falling on the bright red, translucent leaves of a copperleaf, *Acalypha wilkesiana* 'Macafeeana', while peppermint dragon, *Dracaena marginata* 'Tricolor', is in full sun, its white- and pink-edged leaves like an exploding firework. In another, bigger, sunnier space, there are the spiky, arching, cream-edged leaves of *Pandanus baptistii* in the background, the striking orange and crimson *Codiaeum* 'Sookhdeo' in front, and a green-edged, yellow-leaved variegated tapioca, *Manihot esculenta* 'Variegata', and an orange-red bougainvillea close by. In other small, sunny glades, you will find black-leaved elephant ear (*Calocasia antiquorum* 'Illustris') shooting up and emerging from the big, green, paddlelike leaves of lobster claw (*Heliconia rostrata*).

Other plants here include bananas with rose and blue fruit and scarlet flowers, the cochlospermum tree with huge, golden flowers, purple tibouchinas, heliconias, and masses of orchids. RChe

> "…twisting paths revealing scene after scene as you turn…"

Sunnyside

Grenada, Caribbean Islands

DESIGNERS: Jean Renwick, Robin Renwick
OWNER: Jean Renwick, Robin Renwick
GARDEN STYLE: 20th-century formal and informal
SIZE: 5 acres (2 ha)
CLIMATE: Wet tropical
LOCATION: St. Paul's, Grenada

Jean and Robin Renwick's garden is set on a hill that offers views over both the Atlantic and the Caribbean. The garden's giant trees are superb and include palms, mahoganies, a large, weeping fig with aerial roots (*Ficus benjamina*), and the only African baobab (*Adansonia digitata*) in Grenada, with its hugely wide, gray trunk. There are also bottle palms with bulbous trunk bases that are endemic to Round Island, an extinct and now partly submerged volcanic island about 15 miles (24 km) north of Mauritius.

The garden features several pools, and one of these has a statue of a voluptuous maiden among sky-blue and mauve water hyacinths, red and yellow carp, and the soft green rosettes of water lettuce. Another pool has a standing statue of a man backed by the big leaves of banana plants, with water hyacinths and the bright blue spikes of pontaderia at the water's edge. You will also see a statue of a little, joyful Buddha surrounded by bromeliads with leaves in a multitude of different colors, including yellow and red, with centers in purple, red, or pink.

Mainly, though, you are likely to be looking upward. One palm has dark leaves arranged like a gigantic fan, while a rounded cashew tree (*Anacardium occidentale*) has nuts emerging from a large, swollen, crimson, pearlike base. Elsewhere there are more palms and a fine groundcover of tradescantias, hemigraphis, and bromeliads.

Jean Renwick will guide you around this impressive garden herself, but visits are possible only if you book a tour in advance. RChe

The Tower

Grenada, Caribbean Islands

DESIGNERS: Unknown
OWNERS: The Slinger family
GARDEN STYLE: 19th-century Caribbean colonial
SIZE: 2 acres (0.8 ha)
CLIMATE: Wet tropical
LOCATION: St. Paul's, Grenada

The home of the Slinger family, where they have lived for over fifty-five years, The Tower is one of the few Victorian colonial houses that is still in private ownership. It is very eclectic in style and building materials, and has a square, crenellated turret.

The terraced garden is 820 feet (250 m) above sea level. Its double, mixed borders are traditional Gertrude Jekyll in style, with a tropical twist. The main color theme is green, yellow, orange, and red, featuring plants such as ti tree (*Cordyline terminalis*), philodendrons, and gout plant, with its red flowers and swollen stem bases. Behind the house is a large games lawn, and to one side is a gazebo covered by the jade vine (*Strongylodon macrobotrys*), whose hanging racemes, up to 3 feet (1 m) long, are covered with beaked flowers of turquoise-green. The adjacent beds have begonias, ferns, anthuriums, and eucharis—a tropical bulbous plant with many white, richly scented flowers on each stem.

Elsewhere the planting is very striking, with tropical foliage in bright and fiery colors, centered around bright crimson ti tree, dark red and yellow acalyphas, and variegated erythrina with green leaves, bright yellow veins, and orange-red flowers. Extending the color theme is red ginger (*Alpinia purpurata*) and a dwarf form of parrot's beak (*Heliconia psittacorum*) with orange-yellow flowers.

There is also a good range of trees grown for fruit. The pickings include cashews, avocados, mangoes, wax apples, and star fruit, a strong reminder that the property is still partly a working plantation. RChe

Laura Herb and Spice Garden

Grenada, Caribbean Islands

DESIGNER: Unknown
OWNER: Cooperatively owned
GARDEN STYLE: Caribbean
SIZE: 8 acres (3.2 ha)
CLIMATE: Wet tropical
LOCATION: St. David's, Grenada

Grenada is known as the "Spice Island of the Caribbean." Nutmeg was first introduced to the island from Indonesia by the Honorable Frank Gurney in 1843, and now the island is the world's third largest nutmeg producer. However, a visit to Laura Herb and Spice Garden reveals that many other spices and herbs are also grown, and the garden's educational tour is an introduction to many fragrant surprises.

Wandering through this specialized garden, the visitor discovers trails that offer breathtaking displays. Beneath nutmeg and bay trees, lemongrass and ginger scent the air. Wafts of pimento and cinnamon vie with the sweet perfumes of mango and banana. In the garden's rich and arable volcanic soil, cinnamon, thyme, basil, and many more aromatic plants are grown for export to restaurants, which include many famous names. Other varieties are grown in the controlled ecosystem for medicinal use and exported worldwide for use in patented medicines.

Laura Herb and Spice Garden is a commercial grower of organic products, and so the garden is always changing. With each season, plants pass through their life phases, to be harvested and replaced by other species. However, for the visitor there are always clear and accurate signs identifying what is currently growing. The garden is a little off the beaten track, near Perdmontemps in St. David, but there is no better introduction to the astonishing horticultural richness of Grenada. GW

St. Rose Nursery and Garden

Grenada, Caribbean Islands

DESIGNER: John Criswick
OWNER: John Criswick
GARDEN STYLE: 20th-century eclectic, naturalistic, tropical
SIZE: 5 acres (2 ha)
CLIMATE: Wet tropical
LOCATION: St. George's, Grenada

This is one of the most interesting ornamental plant nurseries in the Caribbean. It lies a short distance from St. George's, in a deep valley on the fringe of the rain forest, 650 feet (200 m) above sea level. A stream runs through the garden, which has moist, flat, well-drained, and both gentle and steeply sloping areas.

The first thing that strikes you is the boundary fence swathed in *Odontadenia macrantha*, with its apricot flowers and clovelike scent. There is a rare *Saraca thaipingensis* tree with pink young leaves and large, yellow flowers; bananas with fruit in red and blue; angels' trumpets with red, yellow, white, pink, and orange flowers; and a huge range of heliconias, hibiscus, and bougainvilleas, with roses and rhododendrons from China and southeast Asia. The most fascinating area is the Valley Garden, which has a series of pools, tropical water lilies with blue and yellow flowers, and a sacred lotus with circular, silver-gray leaves and pure white or delicate pink flowers.

Bromeliads of every color act as groundcover. Their flowers are of every shape and shade—the most outstanding plant has many rosettes of translucent pink leaves. There are numerous palms, some with smooth, gray-white trunks, and others with mauve flowers. The sealing wax palm (*Cyrtostachys renda*), with its bright red stems, is the most striking. RChe

RIGHT St. Rose Nursery and Garden is a fabulous showcase of tropical plants, including the aquatics of the Valley Garden.

Westerhall Point

Grenada, Caribbean Islands

DESIGNER: Dodo Helgerson
OWNER: Dodo Helgerson
GARDEN STYLE: 20th-century contemporary private garden
SIZE: 2 acres (0.8 ha)
CLIMATE: Wet tropical
LOCATION: St. George's, Grenada

Westerhall Point is a private estate of residential houses with spacious gardens on a narrow promontory midway along the south coast, in one of the driest and windiest parts of Grenada. Dodo Helgerson's house and garden is on a windy ridge dotted with palms and flame trees (*Delonix regia*), with their tiny leaflets and orange-scarlet flowers.

Although the site is very open, the path to the house is sheltered. There are raised beds by the house, and one wall is a cascade of bougainvilleas in lilac, mauve, white, and purple. The purple is echoed by the narrow, arching grass *Pennisetum* 'Burgundy Giant'. There are yet more bougainvilleas in white and magenta, while spiky aloes make a strong contrast with the butterfly-covered, bushy ixoras. The grass walk around the house has magenta and white on the left, and on the right, orange and yellow, and, as the path widens, a Norfolk Island pine (*Araucaria heterophylla*). The pine's symmetry of stiff, horizontal branches complements the long, upright trunks and waving fans of coconut palms.

There are superb views across to the pool, where the lawn sweeps down to the water's edge, to the jetty, and across the bay to the hills beyond. RChe

> "...views across to the pool, where the lawn sweeps down to the water's edge, to the jetty..."

Hawaii Tropical Botanical Garden

Hawaii, Pacific Ocean Islands

DESIGNER: Dan Lutkenhouse
OWNER: Hawaii Tropical Botanical Garden
GARDEN STYLE: 20th-century tropical rain forest
SIZE: 17 acres (7 ha)
CLIMATE: Humid subtropical
LOCATION: Onomea Bay, Hawaii

In 1977 Dan and Pauline Lutkenhouse purchased 17 acres (7 ha) of the beautiful Onomea valley to create a botanical garden. For eight years, Dan worked to clear the thick jungle, preserving the best of the environment, plants, and trees. It was some years before he discovered the magnificent, three-tier waterfall that makes the garden's focal point.

Trails cut by hand wind intriguingly through this superb rain forest garden, which enjoys an annual rainfall of over 160 inches (400 cm). It is a dramatic and natural setting for the vast and fabulous collections of exotic plants and trees. The Heliconia Trail has over 82 species and varieties of heliconia. Vibrant hibiscus and codiaeum introduce a kaleidoscope of color to different areas, while cat's whiskers (*Orthosiphon stamineus*), with its delicate, white, wispy flowers with long stamens, contrasts with the awesome spines of the nibung palm (*Oncosperma tigillarium*). Of outstanding beauty is the Orchid Garden, with a ravishing selection of colorful plants, both great and small, including the tiny *Pleuranthodium* species orchid.

Banyan Canyon has a Jurassic feel with its Indian banyan trees (*Ficus benghalensis*) and bamboo forest, incorporating a selection of bromeliads and tall tree ferns. Trails lead down to viewpoints toward the ocean, where the waves thunder against the volcanic rocks. Topping it all off is the majestic 160-foot-tall (49 m) Cook pine (*Araucaria columnaris*). RL

The Garden of the Sleeping Giant

Viti Levu, Fiji, Pacific Ocean Islands

DESIGNER: Raymond Burr
OWNER: Unknown
GARDEN STYLE: 20th-century tropical landscape
SIZE: 49 acres (19.8 ha)
CLIMATE: Wet tropical
LOCATION: Nausori, Viti Levu

Back in the days of black-and-white television, the U.S. actor Raymond Burr, who died in 1993, played lawyer Perry Mason and investigator Robert Ironside. His passion was orchids and, in 1977, he created his own tropical orchid garden. The site he chose was a lush valley on the Fijian island of Viti Levu, with the backdrop of the Mountain of the Sleeping Giant raising its gaunt profile from the forest. This private collection has grown into the largest orchid display in Fiji, with some 2,000 different varieties, remarkable not only for their beauty, but also for their extraordinary diversity of form.

While the ranks of frilled and freckled potted specimens in the shade tunnels will delight dedicated orchid enthusiasts, the real thrill is seeing indigenous orchids thriving amid Fiji's exuberant native flora. Nearly every Fijian plant is reputed to have some domestic or medicinal use, from the lofty, native tree ferns, or balabala, once used to build thatched huts, to the legendary noni tree (*Morinda citrifolia*), said to relieve all kinds of ailments.

Boardwalks lead through a series of dense, scented groves, beneath cascades of bougainvillea and palms draped with tangles of Spanish moss, to a hidden lake, bright with water lilies and darting fish. A jungle walk continues through native forest, where orchids and bromeliads spangle the tree trunks, and countless exotic ferns unfurl in the shade. It is a long journey to get here, but it is well worth the effort. AE

Seychelles National Botanical Gardens

Mahé, Seychelles, Indian Ocean Islands

DESIGNER: Paul Rivalz Dupont
OWNER: The Seychelles State
GARDEN STYLE: 20th-century botanical
SIZE: 14.8 acres (6 ha)
CLIMATE: Wet tropical
LOCATION: Victoria, Mahé

These gardens are near the center of Victoria, perhaps the greenest capital in the world, and were laid out in 1901 by Mauritian agronomist Paul Rivalz Dupont.

The sloping lawns, stream, ponds, background of tree-clad mountains, and mature trees make a terrific setting. You can see the Seychelles sunbird perched on the pride of Venezuela trees; the Seychelles bulbul; the Seychelles kestrel; and the flying fox, a large, reddish, fruit eating bat. Endemic palms here are latanier hauban (*Roscheria melanochaetes*), with leaves up to 8 feet (3 m) long; latanier mille-pattes (*Nephrosperma vanhoutteanum*) with slightly longer leaves; walking palm (*Verschaffeltia splendida*), a giant nearly 100 feet (30 m) tall with strong aerial roots; cabbage palm (*Deckenia nobilis*), the heart of which is used to make "millionaire's salad"; and the astonishing coco-de-mer (*Lodoicea maldivica*), which grows to 98 feet (30 m) high. The coco-de-mer seed takes seven years to mature, and can weigh 44 pounds (20 kg), making it the largest in the world.

Exotic palms here include the sealing wax palm (*Cyrtostachys renda*) from Borneo, which grows to 15 feet (5m). It has bright green leaves, and amazing, brilliant red stems. The many trees of economic importance include the breadfruit (*Artocarpus altilis*), the elephant apple (*Dillenia indica*), and the durian (*Durio dulcis*), which tastes delicious but smells foul. Spices include cinnamon, and nutmeg with its apricotlike fruit. For color, look no farther than the scarlet poinsettias; yellow, red, and crimson gingers and canna lilies; and flashy bougainvilleas. RChe

Seychelles Ecological Botanical Garden

Mahé, Seychelles, Indian Ocean Islands

DESIGNER: Unknown

OWNER: The Seychelles State

GARDEN STYLE: 20th-century naturalistic

SIZE: 6 acres (2.4 ha)

CLIMATE: Wet tropical

LOCATION: Barbarons, Mahé

The new Ecological Botanical Garden opened in the late 1990s on the southern side of Mahé in an undeveloped area. After some initial clearance, a modern nursery was built. The accent in this garden is on propagating large numbers of endemic and threatened plant species, many of which are intended for replanting on nature reserves throughout the Seychelles. Many beautiful palms are planted not as single specimens but in natural drifts. Other endemics have been planted into this structure to take advantage of the diversity of the terrain and recreate the flora as it was before human settlers. The only area where non-native plants have been used for aesthetic effect is near the entrance.

Tens of thousands of new plants can be seen growing in the wild, including screwpines such as vakwa de rivyer (*Pandanus multispicatus*), a spreading bush with very spiny 5-foot-long (2 m) leaves; the 32-foot-high (10 m) vakwa montany (*P. balfourii*), with its crown of white-edged, straplike leaves; and vakwa parasol (*P. hornei*), with its huge umbrella head of reddish-edged leaves.

There are a number of other superb endemic plants produced. The bois rouge (*Dillenia ferruginea*), has large, copper-colored leaves with red parallel veins. The leaf bases clasp the stem to create a funnel, which directs rainwater toward the roots. Its spike of white flowers, which look like magnolias, is attractive too. The sea poison tree (*Barringtonia asiatica*) flowers at night and its fruit can float on the sea. Wright's gardenia (*Rothmannia annae*) is a rare shrub with spotted white and magenta flowers. RChe

"Tens of thousands of new plants can be seen growing in the wild…"

The Anthelme Garden

Mauritius, Indian Ocean Islands

DESIGNERS: The Anthelme family, Jean-Marie Sauzier
OWNER: The Anthelme family
GARDEN STYLE: 20th-century tropical Gertrude Jekyll
SIZE: 1 acre (0.4 ha)
CLIMATE: Wet tropical
LOCATION: Perebere, Mauritius

Open to visitors by appointment, this pretty private garden is in the north of the island on level land not far from the sea, and as in many of the gardens of this residential area, coconut palms are a feature. The first thing you notice is the long, straight border, backed by a stone wall, which is planted with tropical shrubs in a design that refers to the principles of Gertrude Jekyll. At its boldest, it has orange-flowering ixora, a golden-yellow lantana, and a scarlet russelia.

Opposite the border is the white, painted, two-story house framed by palm trees. A border of soft, orange ixoras to one side; ferns and heliconias on the shady side; and two fine, mature cycads like feathered umbrellas on each side of the main steps.

Passing around the house, the rear garden is quite different. In one corner is a huge, evergreen tropical fig. It is only twenty years old, but its long, beardlike, aerial roots reach the ground and have grown into more than forty smooth, gray trunks. Nearby is a wonderful collection of frangipanis, or plumeria, in white, pale pink, crimson, rose, and yellow—it must be the best collection in the Indian Ocean. Also note an interesting form of chorisia—often called the kapok tree because its seed pods are full of woolly fiber. It has delicate, mauve-pink, orchidlike flowers, and a sturdy trunk covered in gray thorns. From the arbor, a curving path leads back to the house through a garden of evergreen, tropical shrubs planted in groups. RChe

Madame Veerasamy's Garden

Mauritius, Indian Ocean Islands

DESIGNER: Devi Veerasamy
OWNER: Devi Veerasamy
GARDEN STYLE: 20th-century eclectic botanical
SIZE: 1 acre (0.4 ha)
CLIMATE: Wet tropical
LOCATION: North Decotter, Beau Bassin, Mauritius

Devi Veerasamy grows rare and threatened endemic plants from Mauritius, and rare plants from around the world. Her award-winning garden—open to the public by appointment—is set in leafy Beau Bassin on the edge of a ravine. Her single-story white house looks out between the straight trunks of a Chinese fan palm (*Livistonai chinensis*), which has dark turquoise-blue fruit, and a bottle palm (*Hyophorbe lagenicaulis*), with its swollen, flasklike base. Their vertical form is balanced perfectly by the horizontal branches of a magnificent flame tree (*Delonix regia*).

The lawn has a central flower bed of horizontally trained bougainvilleas, which form a carpet of crimson, white, pink, and cerise. Set back from this is a great curve of containers with more bougainvilleas in almost every color imaginable. A second lawn features crotons with leaves varying from the broad and spotted to the narrow and twisting. The range of leaf colors is amazing, and includes green, copper-purple, yellow, red, and orange. The nearby jatrophas are equally spectacular. The many endemic plants are near the drive, including the national flower, boucle d'oreille (*Trochetia boutoniana*), with white-centered, bell-shaped flowers. There is also an elegant fleur de Saint Louis (*Hibiscus genevii*), once thought to be extinct. To the side of the house is a border with more unusual exotic plants, including *Holmskioldia sanguineam* 'Aurea', the uncommon yellow form of the Chinese hat plant. RChe

Sir Seewoosagur Ramgoolam Botanical Garden

Mauritius, Indian Ocean Islands

DESIGNERS: Pierre Poivre, James Duncan
OWNER: The Mauritian State
GARDEN STYLE: 19th-century botanical with palm avenue
SIZE: 92.6 acres (37.5 ha)
CLIMATE: Wet tropical
LOCATION: Pamplemousses, Mauritius

This garden's origins go back to 1735 when Governor Mahé de La Bourdonnais bought a house that he called Mon Plaisir. What began as a humble vegetable garden developed into a major fresh food source for ships calling at Port Louis. In 1768 Mon Plaisir became the home of the French horticulturist Pierre Poivre, who introduced plants from all over the world and raised indigenous species. In 1849 a British horticulturist, James Duncan, took over.

Walking through the main entrance there is a curving avenue of bottle palms with their large, swollen bases, leading to a baobab (*Adansonia digitata*) from central Africa. There is a huge range of palms and trees to see, including roystoneas; lucky nut (*Thevetia peruviana*) with its yellow flowers and seeds that are used as lucky charms; and sandpaper vine (*Petrea volubilis*) with racemes of purple flowers and mauve leaves. The path to the right crosses the stone Bridge of Sighs over the little valley of the Citron River. Look out for the trumpet flowers of climbing blue skyflower (*Thunbergia grandiflora*); cinnamon and Indian almond trees; and a group of prehistoric-seeming cycads.

Of the hundreds of kinds of palm found here, the Indian talipot (*Corypha umbraculifera*) is perhaps the most amazing. It does not flower for thirty to eighty years and then produces a huge fountain of white flowers, 25 feet (8 m) tall. Farther on is an avenue of sweetenia, the true mahogany. The most photographed plants in the garden are the giant Amazonian water lilies (*Victoria amazonica*) in the great canal, with their beautiful, red-backed, corrugated young leaves. The big flowers open white and attract pollinating beetles that become trapped overnight. The next day, the flowers turn pink and open once more to release the pollinators. RChe

Paradise Valley

Mauritius, Indian Ocean Islands

DESIGNERS: James Wilson, the Rountree family
OWNERS: The Rountree family
GARDEN STYLE: 19th-century naturalistic and forest
SIZE: 37 acres (15 ha)
CLIMATE: Wet tropical
LOCATION: Rivière des Anguilles, Mauritius

Once a vanilla plantation, this is now part of the huge, private, sugar estate of the Rountree family. Bel Air Sugar Estate consists of about 2,100 acres (850 ha) of cane land, 99 acres (40 ha) of clifftop pasture land with superb views, and 37 acres (15 ha) of subtropical forest, known as Paradise Valley.

After you enter, the first part of the valley is shady and cool because of the many trees, palms, and giant bamboos. It is a magical place. The Chenille plant, or red-hot cat's tail, (*Acalypha hispida*) grows to over 10 feet (3 m) high here. Its hanging, rose-pink flowers sometimes extend to 2 feet (0.6 m) long, and are quite startling when they dangle over the track with purple-leaved crotons below them. Natural backlighting shines through the rose-colored leaves of ti trees (*Cordyline terminalis*). Other attractions including the white-spotted green leaves of dumbcane (*Dieffenbachia seguine*) 'Maculata'; the beautifully marked leaves of marantas; and colorful walking iris (*Neomarica northiana*), with its three large, radiating white petals, and three curved blue petals with white veins. Gradually the valley opens into full sun. There is a small lake with big travelers' trees, whose green flowers are pollinated by lemurs. The fanlike formation of their leaves catches water in their channellike bases—if you are thirsty, just wedge a knife between them and water gushes out. A series of interconnected ponds, edged by pandanus bushes, leads to a thatched, stone summerhouse. Beyond lies the sea, and a dramatic view of the foam of great waves as they crash against the black rocks. RChe

> "Its hanging, rose-pink flowers... are quite startling when they dangle over the track..."

Le Parc Exotica

Réunion, Indian Ocean Islands

DESIGNERS: Mr. Prugniere, Georges Ango
OWNER: Le Domaine Des Pierres
GARDEN STYLE: 20th-century native and exotic collection
SIZE: 10 acres (4 ha)
CLIMATE: Wet tropical
LOCATION: Saint-Pierre, Réunion

Parc Exotica is an amazing place. You enter through potted palm trees under an enormous elephant's head. The path leads on through a tunnel with owls and lizards into an area with more palms, ponds, and the sight of deer in the distance.

There are many astonishing trees, including the ylang ylang (*Conanga odorata*), with richly scented, hanging green flowers. The flame, or flamboyant, tree (*Delonix regia*) has tiny, feathery leaves and masses of scarlet flowers, while a bank to the west has a row of yellow- and lime-green-centered forms of furcraea. The shade tunnels are equally surprising. The first has hundreds of anthuriums with flamingolike flowers and gigantic spathes. If you look between the tunnels, you will see many mature adeniums in containers. They have strange, swollen, knobbly gray branches, and beautiful white, pink, or rose, flowers.

The orchid shade house is worth a visit, as are the bonsai and topiary borders. The large, rectangular pool has a model of Réunion in the middle. The cactus garden is beautifully landscaped into curved rocky terraces topped by the bleached, twisted trunks and boughs of ancient pines from the Arizona desert. The plants are many and varied, and include echinopsis with its great spherical cushions; melocactus with its dense, hooked spines; elkhorn (*Euphorbia cristata*) with a mass of ribbed, wavy stems and red-tipped crests; and spiny-edged succulents in a huge range of sizes and colors. RChe

Le Conservatoire de Mascarin

Réunion, Indian Ocean Islands

DESIGNER: Unknown
OWNER: The French State
GARDEN STYLE: 20th-century botanical
SIZE: 9.9 acres (4 ha)
CLIMATE: Wet tropical
LOCATION: Saint-Leu, Réunion

The Conservatoire Botanique National de Mascarin is situated on the west coast of Réunion. It was once the center of an agricultural estate that dates back to 1857. In 1986 it became a botanical garden, and it is now spectacular.

At the entrance, broad steps lead up a hill through a green corridor of mature palms, cycads, and other trees underplanted with ferns, red and yellow abutilons, begonias, and chlorophytums. Halfway up is a circular pond full of mauve- and blue-flowering water hyacinths. The terrace at the top has four rectangular beds edged with dwarf bamboo. The side borders include a superb clump of lobster claw (*Heliconia rostrata*) with large, paddlelike leaves. Its stems bend with the weight of large, brilliant red flowers. You reach a villa, behind which are more hedges, lawns, and a huge water tank filled with water lilies and cyperus. Around the corner is a small formal garden set among trees. Its six beds are filled with scarlet salvias, impatiens, and yellow-streaked chlorophytums. Then comes a eucalyptus woodland, and an area devoted to native plants, including *Psiadia retusa*, an evergreen shrub in the daisy family with white clusters of pompom flowers.

In the large Succulent Garden, paths wind through a broad valley filled with threatening agaves, their huge rosettes of thick, succulent leaves edged with hooked teeth. There are stunning euphorbias with pink, crimson, and primrose flowers. RChe

Climate Classification Systems

Two systems have been used to classify the climate of the gardens featured in this book. The first is based on the Köppen climate classification system, which divides the earth into six climatic regions. An adaptation of the Köppen system has been applied to the gardens in every continent apart from those in North America, where the North American climate zone system, based on plant hardiness, has been used.

Köppen Climate Classification System

During the twentieth century, German climatologist and botanist Vladimir Köppen (1846–1940) created the following system to classify the earth's regions by a combination of average annual precipitation, average monthly precipitation, and average monthly temperature.

A	Tropical Humid	Moist and hot tropical climates with no or little dry seasons; tropical rain forests; tropical monsoon climates; dry tropical Savannah climates
B	Dry	Arid desert; low-latitude desert; semiarid steppe; low-latitude steppe
C	Mild Mid-Latitude (Warm Temperate)	Moist and warm mid-latitude climates with dry, hot summers; humid subtropical, Mediterranean climates; Marine West Coast (mild, no dry season, warm summers)
D	Severe Mid-Latitude (Cool Temperate)	Moist, cool, humid continental climate with severe winters and hot or warm summers; subarctic climates with severe dry, cold winters, cool summers
E	Polar	Tundra, no true summer; or Frozen ice cap
H	Highland	High mountain weather conditions (added later)

North American Climate Zones

North America uses a climate system known as the Plant Hardiness Zone. Each zone is distinguished by the lowest temperature that can be expected in that area during the winter months. Plants are categorized by their ability to subsist in the natural landscape, taking into consideration elevation and access to water.

1	Below -50° F	Below -45.6° C	**6b**	-5° to 0° F	-20.5° to -17.8° C
2a	-50° to -45° F	-45.5° to -42.8° C	**7a**	0° to 5° F	-17.7° to -15.0° C
2b	-45° to -40° F	-42.7° to -40.0° C	**7b**	5° to 10° F	-14.9° to -12.3° C
3a	-40° to -35° F	-39.9° to -37.3° C	**8a**	10° to 15° F	-12.2° to -9.5° C
3b	-35° to -30° F	-37.2° to -34.5° C	**8b**	15° to 20° F	-9.4° to -6.7° C
4a	-30° to -25° F	-34.4° to -31.7° C	**9a**	20° to 25° F	-6.6° to -3.9° C
4b	-25° to -20° F	-31.6° to -28.9° C	**9b**	25° to 30° F	-3.8° to -1.2° C
5a	-20° to -15° F	-28.8° to -26.2° C	**10a**	30° to 35° F	-1.1° to 1.6° C
5b	-15° to -10° F	-26.1° to -23.4° C	**10b**	35° to 40° F	1.7° to 4.4° C
6a	-10° to -5° F	-23.3° to -20.6° C	**11**	above 40° F	above 4.5° C

For more information, see the interactive map at www.usna.usda.gov/Hardzone/ushzmap.html

Useful Addresses

North America

American Horticultural Society
7931 East Boulevard Drive
Alexandria, VA 22308-1300
Tel: +1 (703) 768 5700
www.ahs.org

American Public Gardens Association
100 West 10th Street
Suite 614
Wilmington, DE 19801
Tel: +1 (302) 655 7100
www.publicgardens.org

Canadian Society for Horticultural Science
Suite 1112
141 Laurier Avenue West
Ottawa, Ontario K1P 5J3
Tel: +1 (613) 232-9459
www.cshs.ca

National Trust for Historic Preservation
1785 Massachusetts Ave, NW
Washington, DC 20036-2117
Tel: +1 (202) 588 6000
www.nthp.org

UK

Cadw Historic Parks and Gardens
Plas Carew
Unit 5/7 Cefn Coed
Parc Nantgarw
Cardiff CF15 7QQ
Tel: +44 (0)1443 33 6000
www. cadw.wales.gov.uk

English Heritage
Customer Services Dept.
P.O. Box 569
Swindon SN2 2YP
Tel: +44 (0) 870 333 1181
www.english-heritage.org.uk

Garden History Society
70 Cowcross Street
London EC1M 6EJ
Tel: + 44 (0) 20 7608 2409
www.gardenhistory
society.org

Garden History Society in Scotland
The Glasite Meeting House
33 Barony Street
Edinburgh EH3 6NX
Tel/fax: +44 (0) 131 557 5717
www.gardenhistory
society.org

National Trust
P.O. Box 39
Warrington WA5 7WD
Tel: +44 (0) 870 458 4000
www.nationaltrust.org.uk

Royal Horticultural Society
80 Vincent Square
London SW1P 2PE
Tel: +44 (0) 845 260 5000
www.rhs.org.uk

Europe

Deutsche Botanische Gesellschaft (German Botanical Society)
www.deutsche-botanische-
gesellschaft.de

Grandi Giardini Italiani (Great Italian Gardens)
Piazza Cavour, 6
22060 Cabiate
Como
Tel: +39 (0) 31 756211
www.grandigiardini.it

Kungliga Skogs-och Lantbruksakademiens (Royal Swedish Academy of Agriculture and Forestry)
Drottninggaten 95 B
Box 6806
113 86 Stockholm
Tel: +46 (0) 8 54 54 77 00
www.ksla.se

Mediterranean Garden Society
P.O. Box 14
Peania GR-190 02
Greece
Tel/fax: +30 (210) 6643 089
www.mediterraneangarden
society.org

Royal Horticultural Society of Ireland
Cabinteely House, The Park
Cabinteely, Dublin 18
Tel/fax: +353 (1) 2353912
www.rhsi.ie

Sociedad Española de Ciencias Hortícolas (Spanish Society of Horticultural Sciences)
Campus Universitario de Rabanales Edif.
Celestino Mutis
Ctra. Madrid-Cádiz Km 396
14014 Córdoba
Tel/fax: +34 957 218 501
www.sech.info

Società Orticola Italiana (Italian Horticultural Society)
Polo Scientifico Università di Firenze
Viale delle Idee, 30
50019 Sesto Fiorentino (FI)
Tel: +39 (055) 4574070-4067
www.soihs.it

Société Nationale d'Horticulture de France (National Horticultural Society of France)
84, rue de Grenelle
75007 Paris
Tel: +33 (0) 1 44 39 78 78
www.snhf.org

Australia and New Zealand

Australian Garden History Society
Gate Lodge
100 Birdwood Avenue
Melbourne
Victoria 3004
Tel: +61 (03) 9650 5043
www.gardenhistorysociety.
org.au

Australian Institute of Horticulture
P.O. Box 314, Ryde
New South Wales 1680
Tel: +61 (02) 8001 6198
www.aih.org.au

Australian National Botanic Gardens
P.O. Box 1777
Canberra, ACT 2601
Tel: +61 (02) 6250 9450
www.anbg.gov.au

Royal New Zealand Institute of Horticulture
P.O. Box 12
Lincoln University
Canterbury
Tel: +64 (3) 325 2811 Ext.8670
www.rnzih.org.nz

Japan

International Association of Japanese Gardens
P.O. Box 40083
Central Station
Portland, OR 97240
www.japanese-gardens-
assoc.org

Japanese Garden Database
JGarden Network
1911 Brandywine Street
Philadelphia, PA 19130
www.jgarden.org

Africa

Botanical Society of South Africa
Private Bag X 10
Claremont 7735
Tel: +27 (21) 797 2090
www.botanicalsociety.
org.za

South America

Sociedad Argentina de Horticultura (Botanical Society of Argentina)
www.horticulturargentina.org

Sociedad Botánica de México (Botanical Society of Mexico)
Universidad Nacional
Autónoma de México
Campus Morelia
Antigua Carretera a Pátzcuaro 8701
Col. San José de La Huerta
58190, Morelia, Michoacán
www.socbot.org.mx

Sociedade Botânica do Brasil (Botanical Society of Brazil)
UFRGS - BOTANICA
Bloco 4 Prédio 43433
Av. Bento Gonçalves, 9500
CEP: 91501-970
Porto Alegre – RS
www.botanica.org.br

Garden Directory

Afghanistan
Bagh-i-Babur Western slope of Sher-e Darwaza Mountain, southwest of Kabul

Argentina
El Jardín Botánico de Buenos Aires
Avenida Santa Fe 3951
1425 Buenos Aires

Australia
Adelaide Botanic Gardens North Terrace, Adelaide, South Australia 5000
Australian National Botanic Gardens Clunies Ross Street, Black Mountain, Canberra 2601
Carrick Hill 46 Carrick Hill Drive Springfield, South Australia 5062
Chinese Garden of Friendship, The Harbour St, Darling Harbour, Sydney, New South Wales
Eryldene 17 McIntosh Street, East Gordon, New South Wales 2072
Everglades Gardens 37 Everglades Avenue, Leura, New South Wales 2780
Flecker Botanic Gardens Collins Avenue, Cairns, Queensland 4870
Fulling Garden, The 141 Pitt Street, Eltham, Victoria 3095
Garden of St Erth Simmons Reef Rd., Blackwood, Victoria 3458
Government House Macquarie St., Sydney, New South Wales 2000
Heronswood 105 La Trobe Parade, Dromana, Victoria 3936
Kennerton Green Bong Bong Rd, Mittagong, New South Wales 2575
Kings Park and Botanic Garden Fraser Avenue, West Perth, Western Australia 6005
Mawallok near Beaufort, Victoria
Mount Tomah Botanic Garden Bells Line of Rd. via Bilpin, Blue Mountains, New South Wales 2758
Mount Wilson Off Bells Line of Rd., Mount Wilson, New South Wales 2786
Panshanger 366 Panshanger Rd., Longford, Tasmania 7301
Rippon Lea 192 Hotham St., Elsternwick, Victoria 3185
Royal Botanic Gardens Melbourne Birdwood Avenue, South Yarra, Victoria 3141

Royal Botanic Gardens Sydney Mrs. Macquaries Rd., Sydney New South Wales 2000
Sculpture Garden, National Gallery of Australia Parkes Place, Parkes, Canberra, ACT 2601
Townsville Palmetum Nathan St., Douglas, Queensland
Vaucluse House Wentworth Rd., Vaucluse, New South Wales 2030
Wigandia P.O. Box 46, Noorat, Victoria 3265
Woolmers Woolmers Lane, Longford, Tasmania

Austria
Hellbrunn Fürstenweg 37, Salzburg A5020
Mirabellgarten Schloss Mirabell, Mirabellplatz, Salzburg A5020
Salzburger Freilichtmuseum Hasenweg, Grossgmain, Salzburg A5084
Schlossgarten Belvedere Schloss Belvedere, Prinz Eugen Strasse 27, Vienna A1030
Schlossgarten Laxenburg Schlossplatz 1, Laxenburg A2361
Schlossgarten Schönbrunn Schloss Schönbrunn, Vienna A1130

The Azores
Palácio Sant'Ana Rua José Correia, Punta Delgada, São Miguel 9500-077
Terra Nostra Rua Padre José Jacinto Botelho 5, Furnas, São Miguel 9675-061

Barbados
Andromeda Botanical Gardens Bathsheba, St. Joseph
Flower Forest, The Highway 2, Richmond, St. Joseph

Belgium
Château de Beloeil Rue du Château, B7970 Beloeil, Hainaut
Enghien Château d'Enghien, Enghien, Hainaut
Jardins d'Annevoie, Les 37a Rue des Jardins, B5537 Annevoie, Namur
Kalmthout Arboretum Heuvel 2, B2920 Kalmthout, Antwerp

Serres Royale de Laeken Palais Royal, Rue Bréderode 16, B1000 Brussels
Tuinen Van Hex Kasteel Hex, B3870 Heers, Limburg

Brazil
Jardim Botânico de Rio de Janeiro Rua Jardim Botânico 1008, Rio de Janeiro
Jardim de Luiz Cézar Fernándes Petropolis, Rio de Janeiro State
Palácio do Itamaraty Esplanada dos Ministerios, 70170 Brasilia
Promenade de Copacabana Rio de Janeiro
Sítio Roberto Burle Marx Estrada Burle Marx 2019, Barra de Guaratiba, Rio de Janeiro-RJ, CEP: 23020-240

Bulgaria
Ayazmo Park Stara Zagora

Canada
Abkhazi Garden 1964 Fairfield Rd., Victoria, British Columbia V8S 1H4
Annapolis Royal Historic Gardens 441 St. George St., Annapolis Royal Nova Scotia B0S 1A0
Butchart Gardens 800 Benvenuto Avenue, Brentwood Bay Vancouver Island, British Columbia, V8M 1J8
Darts Hill 170 St. & 16 Avenue, Surrey, British Columbia V4A 7M8
Dr. Sun Yat-Sen Classical Chinese Garden 578 Carrall St., Vancouver, British Columbia V6B 5K2
Edwards Gardens 777 Lawrence Avenue East, Toronto, Ontario M3C IP2
Jardin Botanique de Montréal 4101 Sherbrooke East, Montreal, Quebec H1X 2B2
Jardins de Métis Reford Gardens, 200 Route 132, Grand-Métis, Quebec G0J 1Z0
Maison et Jardins Chénier-Sauvé 83 Chénier St., Saint-Eustache, Laurentides J7R 1W9
Minter Gardens 52892 Bunker Rd., Rosedale, British Columbia V2P 6H7
Niagara Parks Botanical Gardens 2565 Niagara Parkway, Niagara Falls, Ontario L2E 6T2

Nitobe Memorial Garden c/o UBC
Botanical Garden, 6804 SW Marine Drive,
Vancouver, British Columbia V6T 1Z4
Parc du Bois-de-Coulonge
1215 Chemin Saint-Louis Sillery
Quebec G1S 1E7
Parc Régional Bois de Belle-Rivière
9009 Arthur-Sauvé, C.P. 3418,
Mirabel, Quebec J7N 2T8
Park and Tilford Gardens 440–333
Brooksbank Ave., Vancouver, British
Columbia V7J 3S8
Parkwood Estate Gardens
270 Simcoe St North, Oshawa
Ontario L1G 4T5
Quatres Vents, Les (CEPS),
3330 Boulevard Malcolm-Fraser
(Rte. 138), La Malbaie, Quebec G5A 2J5
Queen Victoria Park Niagara Parkway
Niagara Falls, Ontario L2E 6S8
Royal Botanical Gardens
680 Plains Rd. West,
Hamilton/Burlington, Ontario L7T 4H4
Thomas Hobbs' Garden
6550 Balaclava St, Kerrisdale
Vancouver, British Columbia V6N 1L9
Toronto Music Garden, The
475 Queen's Quay West
Toronto, Ontario L9Y 4T9
UBC Botanical Garden
6804 SW Marine Drive, Vancouver
British Columbia V6T 1Z4
Van Dusen Botanical Garden
5251 Oak St, Vancouver
British Columbia V6M 4H1

Canary Islands
El Jardín de la Marquesa Arucas
Carretera de Banderas, Arucas, Gran
Canaria 35400
El Jardín del Cactus
35444 Guatiza Village, Lanzarote
El Jardín de Sitio Litre Camino Sitio
Litre, 38400 Puerto de la Cruz, Tenerife
Hijuela del Botánico Calle Tomás
Pérez, La Orotava, Tenerife 38300
**Jardín Botánico Canario Viera y
Clavijo** Carretera del Centro, Las Palmas,
Gran Canaria 35017
**Jardín de Aclimatación de la
Orotava** La Paz, Puerto de la Cruz,
Tenerife 38400

China
Beihai Gong Yuan
(Beihai Park) Jing Shan Qianjie, Beijing
Bi Shu Shan Zhuang (Mountain Resort
for Avoiding the Heat) Chengde, Hebei
Canglangting (Blue Wave Pavilion)
South Suzhou, Jiangsu
Ge Yuan (Garden of Self)
Dong Guan St., Yangzhou, Jiangsu
Guo Zhuang (Guo's Villa)
Hangzhou, Zhejiang
Huanxiu Shanzhuang
(Mountain Villa with Embracing Beauty)
262 Jingde Rd, Suzhou, Jiangsu
Huqiu Shan (Tiger Hill)
8 Huqiu Shan, Suzhou, Jiangsu
Ji Chang Yuan (Garden of Ecstasy)
Wuxi, Jiangsu
Jing Shan Gong Yuan
(Mountain of Perspective Park) Beijing
Liu Yuan (The Garden for Lingering In)
Changmen Gate, Suzhou, Jiangsu
Shi Zi Lin (Lion Grove Garden)
23 Yuanlin Rd, Suzhou, Jiangsu
Wang Shi Yuan (Garden of the Master
of the Fishing Nets) Suzhou, Jiangsu
Xianggang Gong Yuan
(Hong Kong Park) 19 Cotton Tree Drive,
Central, Hong Kong
Xi Hu (West Lake) Hangzhou, Zhejiang
Xie Qu Yuan (Garden of Harmonious
Pleasure) Yi He Yuan, Haidian, Beijing
Yi He Yuan (River Summer Palace)
Haidian, Beijing
Yu Hua Yuan (Imperial Palace
Garden) Beijing
Yu Yuan (Garden of Contentment)
32 Anren Rd, Shanghai
Yuan Ming Yuan
(Gardens of Perfect Brightness)
28 Qinghua West Rd, Beijing 100084
Zhan Yuan (Garden of Prospect)
128 Zhan Yuan Rd, Nanjing, Jiangsu
Zhou Zheng Yuan
(Garden of the Humble Administrator)
178 Dongbei St, Suzhou

Costa Rica
Jardín Botánico Lankester
University of Costa Rica, Cartago
Jardín Botánico Wilson
San Vito, Puntarenas

Croatia
Villa Gučetic Trsteno, Dubrovnik,
Dubrovacko-Neretvanska
Villa Skocibuha Sudurad, Sipan,
Dubrovnik, Dubrovacko-Neretvanska

Czech Republic
Botanická Zahrada a Arboretum
(Botanic Gardens and Arboretum)
Mendel University Agriculture and
Forestry, Zeměděskál, 61300 Brno,
South Moravia
Lednicko-Valticky Areal
(Lednice-Valtice Cultural Landscape)
Breclav District, Jihomoravský Kraj,
South Moravia
Správa Prazského Hradu
(Prague Palace Gardens) Valdstejnske
Square 3, Prague 1
Valdtsějnský Palác
(Wallenstein Palace) Valdstejnske
namestí 3, 11801 Prague
Villa Müller Nad Hradním
vodojemem 14, 16200 Prague
Zahrady Prazský Hradu
(Prague Castle Gardens)
Hradcany, Prague 1, 11908 Prague
Zámek Buchlovice (Buchlovice Castle)
Státní Zámek Buchlovice, 68708
Buchlovice, Zlinsky Kraj
Zámek Jaroměřice (Jaroměřice Castle)
Náměstí Míru 1, 67551 Jaroměřice nad
Rokytnou
Zámek Kroměříž (Kroměříž Castle)
Snĕmovní náměstí 1, 76701 Kroměříž,
South Moravia
Zámek Lysice (Castle Lysice) Zámecká
1, 67971 Lysice, South Moravia
Zámek Milotice (Milotice Castle)
69605 Milotice u Kyjova, Jihomoravský
Kraj, South Moravia
Zámek Průhonice (Castle Průhonice)
25243 Stredočeský Kraj, Central Bohemia
Zámek Troja (Troja Castle) U Trojského
Zámku 1, Prague 7, 17100 Troja
Zámek Veltrusy
(Veltrusy Castle) Státní Zámek Veltrusy,
Stredočeský Kraj, 277 46 Veltrusy

Denmark
Botanisk Have Århus (Århus Botanical
Garden), Møllevejen 10, DK-8000 Århus

Botanisk Have København
(Copenhagen Botanical Garden)
Gothersgade 128 (or Øster
Farimagsgade 2C, entrances),
Øster Farimagsgade 2B (office)
1353 Copenhagen K
Egeskov Slot
(Egeskov Castle), Egeskovgade 18,
Fyn, DK-5772 Kværndrup
Fredensborg Slotshave (Fredensborg
Palace Gardens) (Fredensborg-
Humlebæk Tourist Office), Østrupvej 3,
Frederiksborg, DK-3480 Fredensborg
Frederiksborg Slot (Frederiksborg
Castle), Frederiksborg, DK-3400 Hillerød
Gisselfeld Kloster
(Gisselfeld Manor), Gisselfeldvej 12A,
DK-4690 Haslev
Glorup Slot (Glorup Castle)
Glorupvej 34, Fyn, 5853 Ørbæk
Liselund (Liselund Park)
Langebjergvej 6, Storstrøm (Isle of Møn)
DK-4791 Borre-Møn
Tivoli Tivoli A/S, Vesterbrogade 3,
Postboks 233, DK-1630 Copenhagen V

Ecuador
El Cementerio de Tulcán
Tulcán, Carchi

Egypt
Al Azhar Park Salah Salem St, Cairo
Al Montazah Palace Gardens
Al Montazah, Alexandria
Karnak Karnak Temple Complex, Luxor

England
Abbey House Gardens Market Cross,
Malmesbury, Wiltshire SN16 9AS
Abbotsbury Sub Tropical Gardens
Bullers Way, Abbotsbury,
nr. Weymouth, Dorset DT3 4LA
Alnwick Garden, The Denwick Lane,
Alnwick, Northumberland NE66 1YU
Anglesey Abbey Gardens
Lode, Cambridgeshire CB5 9EJ
Antony House
Torpoint, Plymouth, Cornwall PL11 2QA
Arley Hall Northwich,
Cheshire CW9 6NA
Ascott House Wing, Leighton Buzzard,
Bedfordshire LU7 0PS
**Athelhampton House
and Gardens** Athelhampton,
Dorchester, Dorset DT2 7LG
Audley End House
Saffron Walden, Essex CB11 4JF

**Barbara Hepworth Museum
and Sculpture Garden** 2 Barnoon Hill,
St. Ives, Cornwall TR26 1AD
Barnsley House Barnsley,
Cirencester, Gloucestershire GL7 5EE
Batsford Arboretum Moreton-in-
Marsh, Gloucestershire GL56 9QB
**Bayleaf Farmstead at the Weald
and Downland Museum** Singleton,
Chichester, West Sussex PO18 0EU
Bekonscot Model Village Warwick Rd.,
Beaconsfield, Buckinghamshire HP9 2PL
Belsay Hall Belsay, Newcastle-upon-
Tyne, Northumberland NE20 0DX
Benington Lordship Gardens
Benington, Stevenage,
Hertfordshire SG2 7BS
Beth Chatto Gardens Elmstead
Market, Colchester, Essex CO7 7DB
Bicton Park Botanical Gardens
East Budleigh, Budleigh Salterton,
Devon EX9 7BJ
Biddulph Grange Gardens Biddulph,
Stoke-on-Trent, Staffordshire ST8 7SD
Bide-a-Wee Cottage
Stanton, nr. Netherwitton, Morpeth,
Northumberland NE65 8PR
**Birmingham Botanical Gardens
and Glasshouses** Westbourne Rd.,
Edgbaston, Birmingham B15 3TR
Blenheim Palace Woodstock,
Oxfordshire OX20 1PX
Blickling Hall
Blickling, Norwich, Norfolk NR11 6NF
Borde Hill Garden Balcombe Rd.,
Haywards Heath, West Sussex RH16 1XP
Boughton House
Kettering, Northamptonshire NN14 1BJ
Bourton House
Bourton on the Hill, Moreton-in-Marsh,
Gloucestershire GL56 9AE
Boveridge House
Cranborne, Wimborne, Dorset BH21 5RU
Bowood House and Gardens
Calne, Wiltshire SN11 0LZ
Bramdean House Bramdean,
Alresford, Hampshire SO24 0JU
Bramham Park
Wetherby, West Yorkshire LS23 6ND
Brandy Mount House Gardens
East St, Alresford, Hampshire SO24 9EG
Brantwood
Coniston, Cumbria LA21 8AD
Broadleas Gardens
Broadleas, Devizes, Wiltshire SN10 5JQ
Brodsworth Hall
Doncaster, South Yorkshire DN5 7XJ

Brogdale
Brogdale Rd., Faversham, Kent ME13 8XZ
Brook Cottage Garden
Well Lane, Alkerton, Banbury,
Oxfordshire OX15 6NL
Bryan's Ground
Letchmoor Lane, Stapleton, Presteigne,
Herefordshire LD8 2LP
Burford House Tenbury Wells,
Worcestershire WR15 8HQ
Bury Court
Bentley, nr. Farnham, Surrey GU10 5LZ
Buscot Park
Faringdon, Oxfordshire SN7 8BU
Caerhays Castle Gardens
Gorran, St. Austell, Cornwall PL26 6LY
**Cambridge University Botanic
Garden** Bateman St, Cambridge,
Cambridgeshire CB2 1JF
Castle Bromwich Hall Gardens
Chester Rd., Castle Bromwich,
Birmingham B36 9BT
Castle Drogo
Drewsteignton, Devon EX6 6PB
Castle Howard
York, North Yorkshire YO60 7DA
Charleston Charleston, Firle,
nr. Lewes, East Sussex BN8 6LL
Chatsworth Chatsworth, Bakewell,
Derbyshire DE45 1PP
Chelsea Physic Garden 66 Royal
Hospital Rd, Chelsea, London SW3 4HS
Chenies Manor
Chenies, Rickmansworth,
Buckinghamshire WD3 6ER
Chiswick House Grounds Burlington
Lane, Chiswick, London W4 2RP
Cholmondeley Castle Gardens
Malpas, Cheshire SY14 8AH
Clare College Fellows' Garden
Clare College, Trinity Lane, Cambridge,
Cambridgeshire CB2 1TL
Claremont Landscape Garden
Portsmouth Rd., Esher, Surrey KT10 9JG
Clipsham Yew Tree Avenue
Tree Avenue, Clipsham, Lincolnshire
Cliveden Taplow, Maidenhead,
Berkshire SL6 0JA
Clumber Park
Worksop, Nottinghamshire S80 3AZ
Coach House, The
Bettiscombe, Bridport, Dorset DT6 5NT
Coleton Fishacre House and Garden
Coleton, Kingswear,
Dartmouth, Devon TQ6 0EQ
Concrete Menagerie, The
The Fountain House, Branxton,

Northumberland TD12
Cothay Manor Greenham,
Wellington, Somerset TA21 0JR
Coton Manor Garden Coton,
Northamptonshire NN6 8RQ
Cottesbrooke Hall Northampton,
Northamptonshire NN6 8PF
Cragside Gardens and Estate
Rothbury, Morpeth,
Northumberland NE65 7PX
Cranborne Manor
Cranborne, Dorset BH21 5PS
Croome Park
Severn Stoke, Worcestershire WR8 9JS
Crossing House Garden
78 Meldreth Rd, Shepreth, Royston,
Cambridgeshire SG8 6PS
Dalemain
Dalemain, Penrith, Cumbria
CA11 0HB
Dartington Hall
Dartington, Totnes, Devon TQ9 6EL
David Austin Rose Gardens, The
Bowling Green Lane, Albrighton,
Wolverhampton, Shropshire WV7 3HB
Denmans Gardens Denmans Lane,
Fontwell, West Sussex BN18 0SU
Dorothy Clive Garden, The
Willoughbridge, Market Drayton,
Shropshire TF9 4EU
Duncombe Park Helmsley, York,
North Yorkshire YO62 5EB
East Bergholt Place
East Bergholt, Suffolk CO7 6UP
Eastgrove Cottage Garden
Sankyns Green, nr. Shrawley,
Little Witley, Worcester WR6 6LQ
East Lambrook Manor Gardens
South Petherton, Somerset TA13 5HH
East Ruston Old Vicarage Garden
Old Vicarage, East Ruston,
Norwich, Norfolk NR12 9HN
Easton Walled Gardens Easton
Grantham, Lincolnshire NG33 5AP
Eden Project, The
Bodelva, St. Austell, Cornwall PL24 2SG
Exbury Gardens Exbury,
Southampton Hampshire SO45 1AZ
Exotic Garden, The
6 Cotman Rd., Norwich, Norfolk NR1 4AF
Felbrigg Hall Norwich, Norfolk NR11 8PR
Felley Priory Garden
Underwood, Nottinghamshire NG16 5FL
Fishbourne Palace
Salthill Rd, Fishbourne, Chichester,
West Sussex PO19 3QR
Folly Farm Sulhamstead Abbots,

nr. Reading, Berkshire RG7 4DF
Forde Abbey and Gardens
Chard, Somerset TA20 4LU
Garden House, The Buckland
Monachorum, Yelverton, Devon PL20 7LQ
Garden Organic Ryton
Coventry, Warwickshire CV8 3LG
Garden Organic Yalding Benover Rd,
Yalding, nr. Maidstone, Kent ME18 6EX
Gibberd Garden, The Marsh Lane,
Gilden Way, Harlow, Essex CM17 0NA
Gipsy House Whitefield Lane, Great
Missenden, Buckinghamshire HP16 0BP
Glen Chantry Ishams Chase, Wickham
Bishops, Witham, Essex CM8 3LG
Glendurgan Garden Mawnan Smith,
Falmouth, Cornwall TR11 5JZ
Gnome Reserve, The West Putford,
nr. Bradworthy, North Devon EX22 7XE
Goodnestone Park Gardens
Wingham, Canterbury, Kent CT3 1PL
Gravetye Manor Hotel Vowels Lane,
East Grinstead, West Sussex RH19 4LJ
Great Comp Garden Great Comp Lane,
Platt, Kent TN15 8QS
Great Dixter
Northiam, Rye, East Sussex TN31 6PH
Greencombe Gardens
Porlock, Somerset TA24 5RS
Gresgarth Hall
Caton, Lancashire LA2 9NB
Haddon Hall
Bakewell, Derbyshire DE45 1LA
Hadspen Garden
Castle Cary, Somerset BA7 7NG
Hall's Croft Old Town, Stratford-
upon-Avon, Warwickshire CV37 6BG
Hampton Court Palace
East Molesey, Surrey KT8 9AU
Hannah Peschar Sculpture Garden
Black and White Cottage,
Standon Lane, Ockley, Surrey RH5 5QR
Harewood, Harewood, Leeds LS17 9LQ
Hatfield House
Hatfield, Hertfordshire AL9 5NQ
Hawkstone Historic Park and Follies
Weston under Redcastle,
Shrewsbury Shropshire SY4 5UY
Heale Garden Middle Woodford,
Salisbury, Wiltshire SP4 6NT
Helmingham Hall Gardens
Helmingham, nr. Stowmarket,
Suffolk IP14 6EF
Hergest Croft
Kington, Herefordshire HR5 3EG
Herterton House Hartington Cambo,
Morpeth, Northumberland NE61 4BN

Hestercombe Gardens Cheddon
Fitzpaine, Taunton, Somerset TA2 8LG
Heveningham Hall Heveningham,
Halesworth, Suffolk IP19 0PN
Hever Castle and Gardens
Hever, Edenbridge, Kent TN8 7NG
Hidcote Manor Garden
Hidcote Bartrim, nr. Chipping,
Campden, Gloucestershire GL55 6LR
High Beeches Gardens
Handcross, Sussex RH17 6HQ
Highdown Gardens Littlehampton Rd.,
Worthing, West Sussex BN12 6PG
Highgrove
Tetbury, Gloucestershire GL8 8TN
Hill Top nr. Sawrey, Hawkshead,
Ambleside, Cumbria LA22 0LF
Himalayan Garden at the Hutts, The
Grewelthorpe, Ripon, North
Yorkshire HG4 3DA
Hodnet Hall Gardens
Market Drayton, Shropshire TF9 3NN
Holdenby House Gardens
Holdenby, Northampton,
Northamptonshire NN6 8DJ
Holker Hall Cark-in-Cartmel,
Grange-over-Sands, Cumbria LA11 7PL
Home Covert Garden and Arboretum
Roundway, Devizes, Wiltshire SN10 2JA
Hotel Endsleigh Milton Abbot,
Tavistock, Devon PL19 0PQ
Ickworth House Horringer,
Bury St. Edmunds, Suffolk IP29 5QE
Iford Manor
Bradford-on-Avon, Wiltshire BA15 2BA
Isabella Plantation, The Richmond
Park, Richmond, Surrey TW10 5HS
Jellicoe Roof Garden House of Fraser,
105-111 High St, Guildford GU1 3DU
John Madejski Garden
Victoria and Albert Museum,
Cromwell Rd., London SW7 2RL
Kelmarsh Hall Northampton,
Northamptonshire NN6 9LY
Kelmscott Manor Kelmscott,
Lechlade, Gloucestershire GL7 3HJ
Kiftsgate Court Gardens Chipping
Campden, Gloucestershire GL55 6LN
Killerton
Broadclyst, Exeter, Devon EX5 3LE
Knightshayes Court Bolham,
Tiverton, Devon EX16 7RQ
Kyoto Garden Holland Park,
Kensington High St., London W8
Lady Farm Chelwood, Somerset BS39 4NN
Laskett, The
Much Birch, Hereford, Herefordshire HR2

Leonardslee Lakes and Gardens
Lower Beeding, Horsham,
West Sussex RH13 6PP
Levens Hall Kendal, Cumbria LA8 0PD
Longleat House Warminster,
Wiltshire BA12 7NW
Longstock Park Water Garden
Stockbridge, Hampshire SO20 6JF
Loseley Park
Compton, Guildford, Surrey GU3 1HS
Lost Gardens of Heligan, The
Pentewan, St. Austell, Cornwall PL26 6EN
Lyme Park Disley, Cheshire SK12 2NX
Manoir aux Quat' Saisons, Le Church
Rd., Great Milton, Oxfordshire OX44 7PD
Manor, The Hemingford Grey,
Huntingdon, Cambridgeshire PE28 9BN
Mapperton Gardens
Beaminster, Dorset DT8 3NR
Marchants Hardy Plants
2 Marchants Cottages, Ripe Rd.,
Laughton, East Sussex BN8 6AJ
Melbourne Hall
Melbourne, Derbyshire DE73 1EN
Menagerie, The Newport Pagnell Rd.,
Horton, Northamptonshire NN7 2BX
Merriments Gardens Hawkhurst Rd.,
Hurst Green, East Sussex TN19 7RA
Minterne Gardens Minterne Magna,
Dorchester, Dorset DT2 7AU
Montacute House Montacute,
Yeovil, Somerset TA15 6XP
Mottisfont Abbey Garden
Mottisfont, Romsey,
Hampshire SO51 0LP
Muncaster Castle
Ravenglass, Cumbria CA18 1RQ
Munstead Wood Heath Lane,
Busbridge, Godalming, Surrey GU7 1UN
Museum of Garden History
Lambeth Palace Rd, London SE1 7LB
Myddelton House Gardens
Bulls Cross, Enfield, London EN2 9HG
National Memorial Arboretum, The
Alrewas, Staffordshire DE13 7AR
Ness Botanic Gardens
Neston, Cheshire CH64 4AY
Newby Hall Gardens
Ripon, North Yorkshire HG4 5AE
Nymans Garden Handcross,
Haywards Heath, West Sussex RH17 6EB
Old Zoo, The Cherry Drive, Brockhall
Village, Blackburn, Lancashire BB6 8DX
Osborne House
East Cowes, Isle of Wight PO32 6JY
Packwood House Lapworth,
Solihull, Warwickshire B94 6AT

Painshill Park Portsmouth Rd.,
Cobham, Surrey KT11 1JE
Painswick Rococo Garden
The Stables, Painswick House,
Gloucestershire GL6 6TH
Parham House
Pulborough, West Sussex RH20 4HS
Pashley Manor Gardens Ticehurst,
nr. Wadhurst, East Sussex TN5 7HE
Peckover House and Garden North
Brink, Wisbech, Cambridgeshire PE13 1JR
Penjerrick Garden Budock Water,
Falmouth, Cornwall TR11 5ED
Penshurst Place and Gardens
Penshurst, Tonbridge, Kent TN11 8DG
Pensthorpe Millennium Garden
Pensthorpe Fakenham,
Norfolk NR21 0LN
Plantation Garden, The
4 Earlham Rd., Norwich, Norfolk NR2 3DB
Port Lympne Mansion
Lympne, Hythe, Kent CT21 4PD
**Reading International Solidarity
Centre Roof Garden** 35-39 London St.,
Reading, Berkshire RG1 4PS
Renishaw Hall Gardens Renishaw,
nr. Sheffield, Derbyshire S21 3WB
RHS Garden Harlow Carr
Crag Lane, Beckwithshaw,
Harrogate, Yorkshire HG3 1QB
RHS Garden Hyde Hall
Buckhatch Lane, Rettendon,
Chelmsford, Essex CM3 8ET
RHS Garden Rosemoor Rosemoor,
Great Torrington, Devon EX38 8PH
RHS Garden Wisley
Woking, Surrey GU23 6QB
Rodmarton Manor Rodmarton,
Cirencester, Gloucestershire GL7 6PF
Roof Gardens, The
99 Kensington High St., London W8 5SA
Rousham House Steeple Aston,
Bicester, Oxfordshire OX25 3QX
Royal Botanic Gardens, Kew
Kew, Richmond, Surrey TW9 3AB
St. Michael's Mount
Marazion, Cornwall TR17 0EF
St. Paul's Walden Bury Whitwell,
Hitchin, Hertfordshire SG4 8BP
Saling Hall
Great Saling, Braintree, Essex CM7 5DT
Sandringham House Gardens
King's Lynn, Norfolk PE35 6EN
Savill Garden, The
The Great Park, Windsor, Surrey SL4 2HT
Scampston Hall
Malton, North Yorkshire YO17 8NG

Scotney Castle Garden Lamberhurst,
nr. Tunbridge Wells, Kent TN3 8JN
Sezincote Moreton-in-Marsh,
Gloucestershire GL56 9AW
Sheffield Park Garden
Uckfield, East Sussex TN22 3QX
Sheringham Park
Sheringham, Norfolk NR26 8TL
Shrubland Park Gardens
Coddenham, Ipswich, Suffolk IP6 9QQ
Sir Harold Hillier Gardens
Jermyns Lane, Ampfield, Romsey,
Hampshire SO51 0QA
Sissinghurst Castle Sissinghurst,
Cranbrook, Kent TN17 2AB
Sizergh Castle
Sizergh, nr. Kendal, Cumbria LA8 8AE
Snowshill Manor Snowshill,
Broadway, Gloucestershire WR12 7JU
Somerleyton Hall Somerleyton,
Lowestoft, Suffolk NR32 5QQ
Spetchley Park Spetchley,
Worcester, Worcestershire WR5 1RS
Spinners Garden School Lane, Boldre,
nr. Lymington, Hampshire SO41 5QE
Springhead Mill Mill St., Fontmell
Magna, Shaftesbury, Dorset SP7 0NU
Stancombe Park
Dursley, Gloucestershire GL11 6AU
Sticky Wicket Buckland Newton,
Dorchester, Dorset DT2 7BY
Stoneacre Otham, Maidstone, Kent
ME15 8RS
Stone House Cottage Gardens Stone,
Kidderminster, Worcestershire DY10 4BG
Stourhead Stourton,
Warminster, Wiltshire BA12 6QD
Stowe Landscape Gardens Stowe,
Buckingham, Buckinghamshire MK18 5EH
Studley Royal Water Garden
Ripon, Yorkshire HG4 3DZ
Swiss Garden, The Old Warden,
Biggleswade, Bedfordshire SG18 9ER
Tatton Park
Knutsford, Cheshire WA16 6QN
Tintinhull House Garden
Yeovil, Somerset BA22 8PZ
Trebah Garden Mawnan Smith,
Falmouth, Cornwall TR11 5JZ
Trelissick Gardens
Feock, Truro, Cornwall TR3 6QL
Tresco Abbey
Tresco, Isles of Scilly, Cornwall TR24 0QQ
Trewithen Gardens Grampound Rd.,
Truro, Cornwall TR2 4DD
Turn End Townside, Haddenham,
Aylesbury, Buckinghamshire HP17 8BG

University of Oxford Botanic Garden
Rose Lane, Oxford, Oxfordshire OX1 4AZ
Upton House
Banbury, Warwickshire OX15 6HT
Vale End Albury, Surrey GU5 9BE
Vann
Hambledon, Godalming, Surrey GU8 4EF
Ventnor Botanic Garden Undercliff
Drive, Ventnor, Isle of Wight PO38 1UL
Waddesdon Manor
Aylesbury, Buckinghamshire HP18 0JH
Wakehurst Place Ardingly, nr.
Haywards Heath, West Sussex RH17 6TN
Walmer Castle and Gardens
Kingsdown Rd, Walmer, Deal,
Kent CT14 7LJ
Waterperry Gardens
nr. Wheatley, Oxfordshire OX33 1JZ
Westbury Court Garden Westbury-on-
Severn, Gloucestershire GL14 1PD
West Dean Gardens West Dean,
Chichester, West Sussex PO18 0QZ
West Green House Gardens Hartley
Wintney, Hook, Hampshire RG27 8JB
Westonbirt Arboretum Westonbirt,
Tetbury, Gloucestershire GL8 8QS
Westwell Manor
Burford, Oxfordshire OX18 4JT
West Wycombe Park West Wycombe,
Buckinghamshire HP14 3AJ
Wimpole Hall Arrington,
Royston, Cambridgeshire SG8 0BW
Winkworth Arboretum Hascombe Rd.,
Godalming, Surrey GU8 4AD
Woburn Abbey
Woburn, Bedfordshire MK17 9WA
Wollerton Old Hall Wollerton,
Market Drayton, Shropshire TF9 3NA
Wrest Park Gardens
Silsoe, Bedfordshire MK45 4HS
Wyken Hall Stanton,
Bury St. Edmunds, Suffolk IP31 2DW
York Gate Garden Back Church Lane,
Adel, Leeds, Yorkshire LS16 8DW

Estonia
Kadriorg (Kadriorg Park)
Weizenbergi 37, 10127 Tallinn, Harjumaa

Fiji
Garden of the Sleeping Giant, The
Nausori, Viti Levu

Finland
Villa Mairea Noormarkku,
Pori, Satakunta, Länsi-Suomi

France
Abbaye Saint-Michel de Cuxà
66500 Codalet, Languedoc-Roussillon
Arboretum National des Barres
45290 Nogent-sur-Vernisson, Centre
Bambouseraie de Prafrance, La
Domaine de Prafrance 30140
Générargues, Anduze,
Languedoc-Roussillon
Bois des Moutiers, Le
Route de l'Eglise, 76119
Varengeville-sur-Mer, Haute-Normandie
Cèdres, Les
Rue du Semeria, Provence-Alpes-Côte
D'Azur, 06230 Saint-Jean-Cap-Ferrat
Château d'Ainay le Vieil
Ainay-le-Vieil, 18200 Cher, Centre
Château d'Ambleville 1, Rue de la
Mairie, 95710 Ambleville, Ile-de-France
Château de Beauregard
41120 Cellettes, Centre
Château de Brécy 14480 Saint-Gabriel-
Brécy, Basse-Normandie
Château de Breteuil
78460 Chevreuse, Choisel, Ile-de-France
Château de Chamerolles
45170 Chilleurs-aux-Bois, Centre
Château de Chenonceau
37150 Chenonceaux, Centre
Château de Cormatin
71640 Cormatin, Borgogne
Château de Courances
91490 Courances, Ile-de-France
Château de Fontainebleau
77300 Fontainebleau, Ile-de-France
Château de Hautefort
24390 Hautefort, Aquitaine
Château de la Bourdaisière
37270 Montlouis-sur-Loire, Centre
Château de Miromesnil
76550 Tourville-sur-Arques,
Haute-Normandie
Château de Rambouillet
78120 Yvelines, Ile-de-France
Château de Versailles
78000 Place d'Armes, Ile-de-France
Château du Pin, Le
600 Chemin de la Ronze, Pays de la Loire,
69480 Champtocé sur Loire
Château du Rivau
37120 Lémeré, Centre
Château et Parc de Chantilly
Chantilly, 60500 Picardie
Château Marqueyssac
24220 Vézac, Aquitaine
Chatonnière, La
37190 Azay-le-Rideau, Centre

Cimetière du Père-Lachaise, Le
16 Rue du Repos, 75020 Paris
Clos du Coudray, Le
76850 Etaimpuis, Haute-Normandie
Clos du Peyronnet, Le
Avenue Aristide Briand, Provence-
Alpes-Côte D'Azur, 06500 Menton
Colombières, Les
312 Route de Supergaravan,
Boulevard de Garavan, Provence-
Alpes-Côte D'Azur, 6500 Menton
Domaine du Rayol Avenue des Belges,
83820 Le Rayol-Canadel, Côte d'Azur
**Festival des Jardins de Chaumont-
sur-Loire**, Rive Sud de la Loire,
41150 Chaumont-sur-Loire, Centre
Fontana Rosa
Le Jardin Des Romanciers,
Avenue Blasco Ibanez, Provence-
Alpes-Côte D'Azur, 6500 Menton
Giverny
Fondation Claude Monet, Musée Monet,
27620 Giverny, Haute-Normandie
Hortillonages, Les 54 Boulevard
de Beauvillé, Picardie, 80000 Amiens
Jardins Agapanthe, Les
Grigneuseville, Haute-Normandie
Jardin d'André Eve, Le
Moralles Pithiviers-le-Vieil,
45308 Pithiviers, Centre
Jardins de Kerdalo, Les
22220 Trédarzec, Bretagne
Jardins de Villarceaux, Les
95710 Chaussy, Ile-de-France
Jardins de l'Imaginaire, Les
Les Place du Foirail,
24120 Terrasson-La-Villedieu, Aquitaine
Jardin des Plantes, Le
57 Rue Cuvier, 75005 Paris
Jardin du Bâtiment, Le
Le Bâtiment, 85210 Thiré
Jardin du Luxembourg, Le
6e Arrondissement, 75006 Paris
Jardins du Manoir d'Eyrignac, Les
24590 Salignac, Aquitaine
Jardin du Palais Royal, Le
Place du Palais Royal, (Rue de
Montpensier, Rue de Beaujolais,
Rue de Valois) 1e Arrondissement,
75001 Paris
Jardin Exotique d'Eze, Le
06360 Eze, Provence-Alpes-Côte D'Azur
Jardin d'Erik Borja, Le Domaine des
Clermonts, 26600 Beaumont-Monteux
Jardins des Paradis, Les
Place du Théron, 81170 Cordes-sur-Ciel,
Midi-Pyrenees

Jardin des Rosiers, Le
86260 La Puye, Poitou-Charentes
Jardins des Tuileries, Les
Rue de Rivoli, 75001 Paris
Jardins du Musée Albert Kahn, Les
14 Rue du Port, 92100 Boulogne-
Billancourt, Paris
Jardins du Prieuré de Saint-Cosme,
Les 37520 La Riche, Centre
Jardins du Prieuré d'Orsan
18170 Maisonnais, Centre
Labyrinthe, Le
Rue du Lac, Rhône-Alpes, 74140 Yvoire
Manoir d'Ango 76119 Varengeville-
sur-Mer, Haute-Normandie
Parc André Citroën
Quai André Citroën, 75015 Paris
Parc Botanique du Prieuré
d'Orchaise Place de l'Eglise,
41190 Orchaise, Centre
Parc de Bagatelle Bois de Boulogne
Route de Sèvres-à-Neuilly
et Allée de Longchamp, 75016 Paris
Parc de Bercy
Rue de Bercy, 75012 Paris
Parc de Courson
Courson-Monteloup, 91680 Essonne,
Ile-de-France
Parc de la Pagode de Chanteloup
Route de Bléré,
F-37403 Amboise, Centre
Parc de la Villette
211 Avenue Jean Jaurès, 75019 Paris
Parc de Malmaison
Musée National du Château de
Malmaison, Rue du Château, 92500
Malmaison, Ile-de-France
Parc de Montsouris
Boulevard Jourdan, 75014 Paris
Parc de Saint-Cloud
92210 Saint-Cloud, Ile-de-France
Parc de Sceaux Domaine de Sceaux,
92330 Sceaux, Ile-de-France
Parc des Buttes Chaumont
Rue Botzaris, 75019 Paris
Parc Floral d'Apremont
Parc Floral, Cher, 18150 Apremont-sur-
Allier, Centre
Parc Floral de la Source Avenue du
Parc Floral, 45072 Orléans, Centre
Parc Jean-Jacques Rousseau, Le
1 Rue René de Girardin, Picardie,
60950 Ermenonville
Parc Monceau
Boulevard de Courcelles, 75017 Paris
Parc Oriental de Maulévrier
49360 Maulévrier, Pays de la Loire

Parc Saint Bernard
Montée de Noailles, Provence-Alpes-
Côte D'Azur, 83400 Hyeres
Potager Extraordinaire, Le
La Grange des Mares,
85150 La Mothe-Achard,
Pays de la Loire
Roseraie du Val-de-Marne, La
94240 L'Haÿ-les-Roses,
Ile-de-France
Saint-Jean de Beauregard
91940 Saint-Jean de Beauregard,
Ile-de-France
Serre de la Madone
74 Route de Gorbio, Provence-Alpes-
Côte D'Azur, 06500 Menton
Terre Vivante Domaine de Raud,
Rhône-Alpes, 38710 Mens
Vastérival, Le 76119 Sainte-
Marguerite-sur-Mer, Haute-Normandie
Vauville Botanical Gardens
50440 Beaumont-Hague, Basse-
Normandie
Vaux-le-Vicomte
77950 Maincy, Ile-de-France
Villa Ephrussi de Rothschild
06230 Saint-Jean-Cap-Ferrat,
Provence-Alpes-Côte D'Azur
Villa Noailles 55 Boulevard Guy
de Maupassant, Provence-Alpes-
Côte D'Azur, 06130 Grasse
Villandry 37510 Villandry, Centre

Germany
Barockgarten Grossedlitz Park Strasse
85, 01809 Heidenau, Sachsen
Berggarten und Regenwaldhaus
House Herrenhäuser Strasse 4 a,
30419 Hanover, Niedersachsen
Botanischen Gartens in Göttingen
Grisebach Strasse 1a, 37077 Göttingen,
Niedersachsen
Botanischer Garten München-
Nymphenburg Menzinger Strasse
61- 65, 80638 Munich, Bayern
Branitzer Park Robinienweg 5,
03042 Cottbus, Brandenburg
Englischer Garten Munich, Bayern
Fürst-Pückler Park
02953 Bad Muskau, Sachsen
Gartenanlage-Gedenkstätte
Karl Foerster Am Raubfang 6,
14469 Potsdam-Bornim, Brandenburg
Grosser Garten 30419 Hanover,
Niedersachsen
Hofgarten Eremitage Ludwig Strasse
21, 95444 Bayreuth, Bayern

Insel Mainau 78465 Mainau Island,
Baden-Württemberg
Karlsruhe Schlossgarten
Hans Thorma Strasse 6, 76131 Karlsruhe,
Baden-Württemberg
Klein-Glienicke Königstrasse,
14109 Berlin, Berlin-Zehlendorf
Palmengarten
Palmengarten Strasse, Hessen, 60325
Frankfurt am Main
Park an der Ilm
99423 Weimar, Thüringen
Park Schönbusch
Kleine Schönbuschallee 1,
63741 Aschaffenburg, Bayern
Pfaueninsel Pfaueninselchaussee,
14109 Berlin, Berlin-Zehlendorf
Rockgarden Sanspareil
Haus 29, 96197 Wonsees, Bayern
Rosengarten Gönneranlage
Ludwig Wilhelm Strasse 26, 76530
Baden-Baden, Baden-Württemberg
Sanssouci Maulbeerallee,
14469 Potsdam, Brandenburg
Schloss Belvedere Weimar-Belvedere,
99425 Weimar, Thüringen
Schloss Fantasie Bamberger Strasse 3,
95488 Eckersdorf/Donndorf, Bayern
Schlossgarten Schleissheim
Max Emanuel Platz 1, 85764
Oberschleissheim, Bayern
Schlossgarten Schwetzingen
68723 Schwetzingen,
Baden-Württemberg
Schlossgarten Weikersheim
Schloss Weikersheim, 97990
Weikersheim, Baden-Württemberg
Schlosspark Herrenchiemsee
83209 Herrenchiemsee,
Isle of Chiemsee, Bayern
Schlosspark Linderhof
Linderhof 12, 82488 Ettal, Bayern
Schlosspark Nymphenburg
Eingang 19, 80638 Munich, Bayern
Schlosspark Oranienbaum
06785 Oranienbaum, Sachsen-Anhalt
Schlosspark Rheinsberg
16831 Rheinsberg, Brandenburg
Schlosspark Wilhelmshöhe
34131 Kassel, Hessen
Schloss Pillnitz
01326 Dresden, Sachsen
Sichtungsgarten Hermannshof
Babostrasse 5, 69469 Weinheim, Hessen
Sichtungsgarten Weihenstephan
Am Staudengarten 8,
85354 Freising, Bayern

Stadtgarten Karlsruhe
Ettlinger Strasse 6,
76137 Karlsruhe, Baden-Württemberg
Veitshöchheim Hofgarten
Echterstrasse 10, 97209 Veitshöchheim,
Bayern
WALA Garten WALA Heilmittel GmbH,
Bosslerweg 2, 73087 Bad Boll/
Eckwälden, Baden-Württemberg
Westpark Munich
Eduard Schmid Strasse 36, 81541
Munich, Bayern
Wilhelmsbad Hanau
63454 Hanau-Wilhelmsbad, Hessen
Wörlitzer Anlagen
06786 Wörlitz, Sachsen-Anhalt
Zwinger
Theaterplatz 1, 01067 Dresden, Sachsen

Grenada
Bay Gardens (Albert St. Bernard)
Morne Delice, St. George's
Laura Herb and Spice Garden
Perdmontemps, St. David
Priory, The (Patrizia Banas)
The Priory, Church St, St. George's
St. Rose Nursery and Garden
(John Creswick) PO Box 21,
St. George's Estate, St. George's
Sunnyside
(Jean Renwick) St. Paul's, Grenada
Tower, The (Paul Slinger) Tower
Plantation House, St. Paul's
Westerhall Point (Dod Helgarson)
PO Box 26, St. George's

Guernsey
Sausmarez Manor St. Martins, GY4 6SG

Hawaii
Hawaii Tropical Botanical Garden
27-717 Old Mamalahoa Highway,
PO Box 80, Papaikou, HI 96781

Hungary
Alcsút Alcsút, Fejér
Csákvár Csákvár, Fejér
Eszterháza Fertod, Gyor-Moson-Sopron
Margitsziget
Margaret Island, River Danube, Budapest
Martonvásár Martonvásár, Fejér
Tata Komáron-Esztergom
Városliget Budapest

India
Achabal Jammu and Kashmir
Akbar's Tomb Agra, Uttar Pradesh

Amber Palace Garden
Jaipur, Rajasthan
Anguri Bagh
Agra Red Fort, Agra, Uttar Pradesh
Bagh-i Hayat Bakhsh
Red Fort, Delhi G. PO, Delhi 110006
Dhobi Mahal Rupbas, Rajasthan
Garden of Diwan-i Amm, The
Fatehpur Sikri, Uttar Pradesh
**Gardens of Emperor Humayun's
Tomb** Mathura Rd, Dehli
I'timad-ud-Daulah's Tomb Garden
Agra, Uttar Pradesh
Mahtab Bagh
Agra, Uttar Pradesh Neemrana,
Alwar, Rajasthan 301 705
Neemrana Neemrana, Alwar, Rajasthan
Nishat Bagh
Srinagar, Jammu and Kashmir
Palace Gardens of Deeg
North of Bharatpur, Rajasthan
Pari Mahal
Lake Dal, Jammu and Kashmir
Ram Bagh Agra, Uttar Pradesh
Rashtrapati Bhavan Rajpath, Delhi
Rock Garden, The
Chandigarh, Punjab and Haryana
Sahelion-ki-Bari Nr. Bharatiya Lok Kala
Mandal, Udaipur, Rajasthan
Samode Bagh Alwar, Rajasthan
Shalamar Bagh Srinagar, Jammu and
Kashmir
Taj Mahal Agra, Uttar Pradesh
Udaivilas Gardens Udaipur, Rajasthan
Vernag Anantnag, Jammu and Kashmir

Indonesia
Batujimbar Pavilions Jl. Danau
Tamblingan 76 Sanur, Bali 80228

Iran
Bagh-e Doulatabad Yazd, Yazd
Bagh-e Eram Shirāz, Fārs
Bagh-e Fin Fin, Kashān, Eşfahān
Bagh-e Shahzadeh Mahān, Kermān
Chehel Sotun
Chehel Sotun Palace, Eşfahān
Cheshmeh-Ali
Shahr-e Rey, south of Tehran, Semnan
Naranjestan
Narenjestan-e Qavam, Shirāz, Fārs

Italy
Castello Ruspoli Piazza della
Repubblica 9, Vignanello, Lazio
Foce, La
Chianciano Terme, Siena, Tuscany

Giardini Botanici Hanbury
Corso Montecarlo 43, 18030 La Mortola,
Ventimiglia, Liguria
Giardini della Landriana
Via Campo di Carne,
51-Tor San Lorenzo, Lazio
Giardini La Mortella Via F. Calise 39,
80075 Forio, Ischia, Campania
Giardino di Boboli
Pitti Palace, Florence, Tuscany
Giardino di Ninfa
04010 Doganella di Ninfa, Lazio
Giardino Giusti Verona Via Giardino
Giusti 2, Verona 37129, Veneto
Isola Bella Lake Maggiore, Piedmont
Isola del Garda Lake Garda, Lombardy
Isola Madre 28838 Stresa (Verbania),
Lake Maggiore, Piedmont
Orto Botanico di Padova
University of Padova,
Via Orto Botanico 15, Padua, Veneto
Orto Botanico di Pisa
Via Luca Ghini 5, Pisa, Tuscany
Palazzo Reale di Caserta Piazza
Plebiscito 1, 80132 Naples, Campania
Scarzuola, La Montegabbione, Umbria
Scavi Pompei Pompei, Campania
Villa Adriana Via IV Novembre 23,
19016 Monterosso al Mare, Liguria
Villa Aldobrandini Via Mazzarino 1,
Rome 00184, Lazio
Villa Barbarigo
Noventa Vicentina, Valsanzibio, Veneto
Villa Barbaro
Maser, Treviso district, Veneto
Villa Borghese
Piazzale Flaminio, Rome 00186, Lazio
Villa Carlotta Via Regina 2,
22019 Tremezzo, Lombardy
Villa Chigi Cetinale Villa Chigi Cetinale,
53098 Sovicille, Siena, Tuscany
Villa Cicogna Mozzoni
Piazza Cicogna 8, Bisuschio, Lombardy
Villa Cimbrone Via Santa Chiara 26,
Ravello 84010, Campania
Villa del Balbianello
Lenno, Lake Como, Lombardy
Villa d'Este Piazza Trento 1, Tivoli, Lazio
Villa di Castello
Via di Castello 47, Florence, Tuscany
Villa Farnese
Piazza Farnese, Caprarola, Lazio
Villa Gamberaia Via del Rossellino 72,
Settignano-Florence, Tuscany
Villa Garzoni Collodi, nr. Lucca, Tuscany
Villa I Tatti Via di Vincigliata 26, 50135
Florence, Tuscany

Villa Lante Via Giacopo Barrozzi 71,
Bagnaia, Lazio
Villa La Pietra Via Bolognese 120,
Florence 50100, Tuscany
Villa Le Balze Fiesole, Tuscany
Villa Medici Via Il Prato 42, Florence
50123, Tuscany
Villa Monastero
Varenna, Lake Como, Lombardy
Villa Orsini
Parco dei Mostri, Bomarzo, Lazio
Villa Pisani Via Roma 19, 35040
Vescovana, Veneto
Villa Reale di Marlia
Marlia, 55014 Lucca, Tuscany
Villa San Remigio
Verbania Pallanza, Piedmont
Villa Taranto Via Vittorio Veneto 111,
28922 Verbania Pallanza, Piedmont
Villa Vico Bello Siena, Tuscany

Japan
Adachi Bijutsukan 320 Furukawa-cho,
Yasugi-shi, Shimane-ken 692-0064
Byōdō-in Rengecho, Uji, Kyoto
Canada Garden
Canadian Embassy, 3–38,
Akasaka 7-chome, Minato-ku, Tokyo
Daichi-ji Meisaka, Minakuchi-cho,
Koga-gun, Shiga-ken 528, Minakuchi
Daisen-in Daitokujicho Temple,
Murasakino, Kita-ku, Kyoto
Entsu-ji Entsuji, Iwakura,
Hataeda-cho, Sakyo-ku, Kyoto
Ginkaku-ji 2 Ginkakuji-cho,
Sakyou-ku, Kyoto 606-8402
Jojakko-ji Kyoto
Joju-en, Suizenji Park
8-1 Suizenji Koen, 862 Kumamoto-Shi,
Kumamoto
Kairaku-en Mito, Ibaraki
Katsura Rikyu
Ukyo-ku, Katsura, Shimizu-cho, Kyoto
Kenrokuen 1–4 Kenroku-machi,
Kanazawa-shi, Ishikawa-ken
Kinkaku-ji
1 Kinkaku-ji-cho, Kita-ku, Kyoto 603-8361
Kōdai-ji
Simogawara-cho, Higasiyama-ku, Kyoto
Kokyo Higashi Gyoen
1–1 Chiyoda, Chiyoda-ku, Tokyo
Konchi-in, Nanzen-ji
86-12 Nanzenjifukuchi-cho,
Sakyo-ku, Kyoto
Korakuen
1–5 Korakuen, Okayama-shi, Okayama
Nunobiki Hābu-en Kobe City, Hyogo

Omotesenke Fushin'an Teranouchi-
agaru, Ogawa, Kamigyo-ku, Kyoto
Ryōan-ji 13 Goryonoshita-cho, Ryoanji,
Ukyo-ku, Kyoto
Saiho-ji Nishigyo-ku, Matsuo,
Kamigatani-cho, Kyoto
Sanbo-in Daigo Sanbo-in Palace Garden,
Garan-cho, Daigo, Fushimi-ku, Kyoto
Sanzen-in
540 Ohara Raigoin-cho, Sakyo-ku, Kyoto
Shinshinan Kyoto
Shoden-ji
Chinjuan-cho, Nishigamo, Kita-ku, Kyoto
Shugaku-in Rikyu
Sakyo-ku, Shugakuin, Kyoto
Tenryu-ji Tenryu-ji Temple,
68 Susukinobanba-cho, Saga Tenryuji,
Ukyo-ku, Kyoto
Tōfuku-ji Temple
15 Hon-machi, Higashiyama-ku, Kyoto
Tōhan Meiga no Niwa Hangi-cho,
Shimogamo, Sakyo-ku, Kyoto 606-0823

Jersey
Creux Baillot Cottage Le Chemin des
Garennes, Leoville, St. Ouen, Jersey, JE3 2FE

Lithuania
Palanga Vytauto g. 15, LT-5720 Palanga

Madeira
**Jardim Tropical da Quinta
do Monte Palácio** Caminho do Monte
192, Funchal
Quinta da Boa Vista Rua Lombo
da Boa Vista, 9050 Funchal
Quinta da Torrinha Funchal
Quinta do Palheiro Ferreiro
Caminho da Quinta do Palheiro 32,
São Gonçalo, 9060-255 Funchal

Mallorca
Heidi Gildemeister Garden Pollensa
Jardí Botànic de Sóller, El
Ctra. Palma-Port de Sóller, Km. 30, 5,
Apartat de Correus 44, 07100 Sóller
Jardines de Alfabia
Ctra. de Sóller, km 17, 07110 Bunyola
Real Cartuja de Valldemossa, La
Valldemossa
S'Avall Dona Carmen Delgado March,
Colònia Sant Jordi

Malta
Palazzo Parisio Victory Square, Naxxar
Ras Rihana Bidnija
Villa Barbaro Zejtun Tarxien

Villa Bologna St. Anton St., Attard

Martinique
Morne L'Etoile Habitation Morne
L'Etoile, Saint-Pierre 97250

Mauritius
Anthelme Garden, The
Exotice, Chemin St. Francis, Petit Raffray
Madame Veerasamy's Garden
North Decooter, Beau Bassin
Paradise Valley Bel Air,
Rountree estate, Riviere des Anguilles
**Sir Seewoosagur Ramgoolam
Botanical Garden** Pamplemousses

Mexico
Casa Folke Egerstrom
Los Clubes, Atizapán de Zaragoza
Casa Luis Barragán General Francisco
Ramírez 14, Tacubaya, México D. F.
Chinampas de Xochimilco, Las
Xochimilco, México D. F.
Jardín Botánico de la UNAM
Parques del Pedregal, México D. F.
Jardín Etnobotánico Centro Cultural
Santo Domingo, Reforma s/n esquina
con, Constitución, Oaxaca, Oaxaca
Jardín Ortega General Francisco
Ramírez 20-22, Tacubaya
Pozas, Las Xilitla, San Luis Potosí

Monaco
Jardin Exotique, Le
62 Boulevard du Jardin-Exotique,
MC 98000

Morocco
Badia Palace Gardens, Al
Rue Berrima, Marrakesh-Tensift-el Haouz
Bahia Palace Gardens, Al
Rue Riad Zitoun Djedid,
Marrakesh-Tensift-el Haouz
Jardin Majorelle, La
Marrakesh-Tensift-el Haouz
Jardins de l'Agdal
Marrakesh-Tensift-el Haouz
Jardins de la Mamounia, Les
Avenue Bab Jdid,
40 000 Marrakech-Tensift-el Haouz
Jardins de Ménara Marrakesh-Tensift-
el Haouz

Netherlands
Arboretum Trompenburg Coolsingel
67, 3012 AC Rotterdam, Zuid-Holland
Bulb Fields Zuid-Holland

De Eco-Kathedraal Mildam, Freisland
Hortus Botanicus Amsterdam
Plantage Middenlaan 2a, 1018 DD
Amsterdam, Noord Holland
Hortus Botanicus Leiden
Leiden Botanical Garden,
Rapenburg 73, Leiden, Zuid-Holland
Hortus Bulborum Zuidkerkenlaan 23A,
NL- 1906 AC Limmen, Noord Holland
Huis Bingerden Bingerdenseweg 21,
6986 CE, Angerlo Holland, Gelderland
In de Tuinen van Ruinen
Achterma 20, 7963 PM, Ruinen, Drenthe
ING Bank Bijlmermeer Amsterdam
Jac P. Thijsse Park Prins Bernhardlaan
9, Amstelveen, Noord Holland
Keukenhof Stationsweg 166a,
Postbus 66, 2160 AB Lisse, Zuid-Holland
Kröller-Müller Museum
Houtkampweg 6, Otterlo, Gelderland
Kwekerij Piet Oudolf
Broekstraat 17, Hummelo, Gelderland
Mien Ruys Tuinen Mien Ruys Tuinen,
Moerheimstraat 78, Overijssel, 7701 CG
Dedemsvaart
Museum Beeckestijn Westelijke
Parallelweg, 134 Rijksweg, Noord Holland
Museumpark 25 Rotterdam,
Zuid-Holland
Paleis Het Loo Koninklijk Park 1,
7315-JA, Apeldoorn, Gelderland
Park Rosendael, Rosendael 1,
6891DA Rozendaal, Gelderland
Park Sonsbeek Zypendaalseweg 24a,
6814 CL Arnhem, Gelderland
Park Zorgvliet The Hague, Zuid-Holland
Twickel Twickelerlaan 6, Ambt Delden,
Overijssel
Weldam Diepenheimseweg 114, 7475
MN Markelo, Overijssel
Wiersse, De Wiersse, Wiersserallee 9,
7251 LH Vorden, Gelderland
Zypendaal Zypendaalseweg 44,
6814 CL Arnhem, Gelderland

New Zealand
Ayrlies Potts Road, Whitford,
R.D.1, Howick, Auckland
Butler Point Hihi Rd, R.D.1, Mangonui,
Bay of Islands 0494 Northland
Gardens of the World Clover Rd.,
East Hope, Richmond, Tasman
Hamilton Gardens Cobham Drive
(State Highway 1), Hamilton, Waikato
Ohinetahi Governors Bay, Christchurch
Otari Native Botanic Garden
Wilton Rd., Wellington

Pukeiti Gardens 2290 Carrington Road,
R.D.4, New Plymouth, Taranaki,

Northern Ireland
Mount Stewart
Portaferry Road, Newtownards,
County Down, BT22 2AD
Rowallane Garden
Ballynahinch, County Down, BT24 7LH

Norway
Vigelandsparken (Vigeland Sculpture
Park) Nobelsgt. 32, N-0268 Oslo

Pakistan
Jahangir's Tomb Garden
Lahore, Punjab
Shalimar Bagh Lahore, Punjab

Poland
Ogród Botaniczny Krakowa
(Kracow Botanic Gardens)
27 Kopernika St, Krakow, Malopolskie
Ogród Botaniczny Warszawa
(Warsaw Botanic Gardens) 02-973
Warsawa 76 - ul. Prawdziwka 2,
Mazowieckie
Ogród w Arkadii
(Arkadia Garden) Muzeum w
Nieborowie I Arkadii, oddzia Muzeum
Narodowego w Warszawie, Nieborów-
Palac, Lódzkie, 99-416 Nieborów
Ogród w Nieborowie
(Nieborow Palace Gardens) 00-495
Warsaw, Lódzkie, Al. Jerozolimskie 3
Palac Czartoryskich
(Czartoryski Palace) Lubelskie, Warsaw
Palac Wilanòw (Wilanòw Palace)
Wilanòw, Warsaw, Mazowieckie
Park Lazienkowski
(Lazienki Park) Warsaw, Mazowieckie
Zamek w Lancucie
(Lancut Castle) ul Kkamkowa 1,
37-100 Lancut, Podkarpackie

Portugal
Casa de Mateus Largo Morgados
de Mateus, Mateus, 5000 Vila Real
Casa de Campo Estrada Nacional 8,
Braga, Obidos 2510
Estufa Fria Parque Eduardo VII, Lisbon
Jardim Botânico de Coimbra
Universidade de Coimbra,
Arcos do Jardim, Coimbra
**Jardim do Palácio Nacional
de Queluz** Largo do Palácio,
2745-191 Queluz, Lisbon

**Palácio dos Marqueses
de Fronteira** Largo de Sao
Domingo de Benfica 1, Lisbon
Palácio dos Marqueses de Pombal
2784-540 Oeiras, Lisbon
Parco dos Duques de Buçaco
Buçaco, Coimbra
Parque de Serralves
Rua D. João de Castro 210, Porto
Quinta da Aveleda
Apartado 77P, Penafiel, Porto
Quinta da Capela Estrada Velha
de Colares, Lisbon, Sintra 2710-502
Quinta da Regaleira Rua Barbosa
du Bocage, Lisbon, 2710-567 Sintra
Quinta de Bacalhôa
Vila Fresca de Azeitão, Setubal
Quinta de Monserrate Rua Augusto
dos Santos 2-4, Sintra, Lisbon
Quinta de São Thiago Sintra, Lisbon
Quinta do Alão
Leça do Balio, Matosinhos, Porto

Republic of Ireland
Altamont Garden
nr. Tullow, County Carlow
Annes Grove Castletownroche,
nr. Mallow, County Cork
Ballymaloe Cookery School Gardens
Shanagarry, Midleton, County Cork
Dillon Garden, The
45 Sandford Road, Ranelagh, Dublin 6
Glenveagh Castle Garden
Glenveagh National Park, Churchill,
Letterkenny, County Donegal
Ilnacullin Gardens
Glengarriff, County Cork
Irish National Stud, The
Tully, County Kildare
Kilfane Glen and Waterfall
Thomastown, County Kilkenny
Killruddery House and Gardens
Killruddery Gardens, Bray, County
Wicklow
Larchill Arcadian Garden
Kilcock, County Kildare
Mount Usher Gardens
Ashford, County Wicklow
National Botanic Gardens
Glasnevin, Dublin 9
Powerscourt House and Gardens
Enniskerry, County Wicklow

Réunion
Conservatoire de Mascarin, Le
2 rue du Père Georges, Domaine des
Collimaçons, 97436 Saint-Leu

Parc Exotica, Le Route de l'Entre-
Deux, No.60 CD 26, Pierrefonds,
97410 Saint Pierre

Romania
Cluj Grădina Botănică Strada
Republicii 42, Cluj-Napoca, RO-400015
Regal Grădina in Săvârsin Arad
Târgu Jiu Sculpture Park Gorj

Russian Federation
Aptekarsky Ogorod
Prospect Mira 26, Moscow 129090
Elaginskii Dvorets
(Yelagin Palace) Yelagin Ostrov 1,
St. Petersburg, Leningradskaya Oblast'
Gatchina 1 Krasnoarmeiskaya ulitsa,
Leningradskaya Oblast',
188300 Gatchina
Gorkyi Park (Gorky Park) ul Krymsky Val,
119 049, Moscow
Imperskijj Botanicheskiy Sad
(Imperial Botanic Garden) 2 ul.
Professora Popova, St. Petersburg,
Leningradskaya Oblast'
Khutor Ghorka Solovki State Historical,
Architectural and Natural Museum-
Reserve, 164070, Arkhangel'skaya Oblast'
Kuskovo Kuskovo Estate and Park, ul
Yunosti 2, Moscow 115487
Letniy Sad (The Summer Garden)
191041, Saint-Petersburg 2, Kutuzova
Emb., Letny Sad, Leningradskaya
Oblast'
Marfino Moscovskaya Oblast', Moscow
Mon Repos
188800 Vyborg, Leningradskaya
Oblast'
Moskva Botanicheskiy Sad
(Moscow Botanical Garden)
Russian Academy of Sciences,
Botanicheskaya ul, 4,127276 Moscow
Oranienbaum
48 Dvortsovy prospect, 189510
Lomonosov, Leningradskaya Oblast'
Pavlovsk Revolutsii Str. 20,
St. Petersburg, Leningradskaya Oblast'
Peterhof The Peterhof State-Museum
Reserve, 198516, St. Petersburg, ul.
Razvodnaya 2, Leningradskaya Oblast'
Tzarskoje Selo
(Tsar's Village) 7 Sadovaya St.,
Tzarskoje Selo, Leningradskaya Oblast'

St. Eustatius
Miriam C. Schmidt Botanical Garden
St. Eustatius

St. Kitts and Nevis
Wingfield Plantation
Off Old Road, Basseterre, St. Kitts

St. Lucia
Fond Doux Estate
Chateaubelair, Soufriere

Sark
Seigneurie Garden Sark GY9 0SF

Scotland
Achamore Gardens
Isle of Gigha, Argylll and Bute PA41 7AD
Arduaine Garden
Arduaine, by Oban, Argyll PA34 4XQ
**Ascog Hall Victorian Fernery
and Gardens**
Ascog, Isle of Bute, Scotland PA20 9EU
Attadale Strathcarron,
Highland, Wester Ross IV54 8YX
Benmore Botanic Garden
Dunoon, Argyll and Bute, PA23 8QU
Blair Castle Blair Atholl,
Pitlochry, Perthshire PH18 5TL
Brodick Castle Isle of Arran KA27 8HY
Cally Gardens Gatehouse of Fleet,
Castle Douglas DG7 2DJ
Cambo Estate Cambo House,
Kingsbarns, St. Andrews, Fife KY16 8QD
Castle Kennedy Gardens
Stair Estates, Rephad, Stranraer DG9 8BX
Castle of Mey
Thurso, Caithness, Highland, KW14 8XH
Cawdor Castle Gardens
Highland, Nairn IV12 5RD
**Colonsay House and Woodland
Gardens** Isle of Colonsay, Argyll,
Scotland PA61 7YU
Crarae Garden Minard, Inveraray,
Argyll and Bute PA32 8YA
Crathes Castle
Banchory, Aberdeenshire AB31 5QJ
Culzean Castle and Country Park
Maybole, South Ayrshire KA19 8LE
Dawyck Botanic Gardens Stobo,
nr. Peebles, Scottish Borders EH45 9JU
Dirleton Castle and Gardens
North Berwick, East Lothian, EH39 5ER
Drummond Castle Gardens
Muthill, Crieff, PH5 2AA
Dun Ard
Main Street, Fintry, Stirlingshire G63 0XE
Dunbeath Castle Gardens Dunbeath,
Caithness, Highland KW6 6ED
Earlshall Castle
Leuchars, St. Andrews, KY16 0DP

Edzell Castle Gardens
Edzell, Angus DD9 7UE
Garden of Cosmic Speculation, The
Holywood, Dumfries DG2 0RW
Glenarn Rhu, Dunbartonshire G84 8LL
Glenbervie Drumlithie,
Kincardine, Aberdeenshire
Glendoick Gardens Glencarse,
Perth PH2 7NS
Glenwhan Gardens Dunragit, nr.
Stranraer, Wigtownshire DG9 8PH
House of Pitmuies Gardens
Guthrie, By Forfar, Angus DD8 2SN
Inverewe Garden Garden,
Poolewe, Ross-shire, Highland IV22 2LQ
Kellie Castle and Garden
Pittenweem, Fife, KY10 2RF
Kerrachar Gardens
Kylesku, Sutherland, Highland IV27 4HW
Kildrummy Castle
Alford, Aberdeenshire AB33 8RA
Langwell
Berriedale, Highland KW7 6HD
Little Sparta Dunsyre, nr. Lanark,
Lanarkshire, Scotland ML11 8NG
Logan Botanic Garden
Port Logan, Stranraer DG9 9ND
Mellerstain Gordon, TD3 6LG
Berwickshire, Scottish Borders
Mount Stuart Gardens
Isle of Bute, PA20 9LR
Pitmedden Garden
Ellon, Aberdeenshire, AB41 7PD.
Royal Botanic Garden Edinburgh
Inverleith Row, Edinburgh EH3 5LR
Shepherd House Garden
Inveresk Village, Musselburgh,
East Lothian EH21 7TH
Stirling Castle
Stirling, Stirlingshire FK8 1EJ
Stobo Castle Stobo, Peebles,
Scottish Borders EH45 8NY

Seychelles
**Seychelles Ecological Botanical
Garden** Barbarons, Mahé
**Seychelles National Botanical
Garden**
Jardin Botanique Boîte Postale 445 Mahé

Singapore
Kranji War Cemetery
9 Woodlands Road, Singapore 738656
Singapore Botanic Gardens
1 Cluny Road, Singapore 259569
Singapore Zoo
80 Mandai Lake Road, Singapore 729826

South Africa
Brenthurst Gardens PO Box 1050,
Parktown, Gauteng, Johannesburg
Durban Botanic Gardens
70 St. Thomas Rd., Durban,
KwaZulu-Natal
Garden Route, The Moriarty Env.
Centre, 49 Caledon St., George 6529
**Karoo Desert National Botanical
Garden** Van Riebeeck Park, (off National
Road), PO Box 152, Worcester 6850,
Western Cape
**Kirstenbosch National Botanical
Garden** South African National
Biodiversity Institute, Private Bag X7,
Claremont 7735, Cape Town,
Western Cape
Namaqualand Northern Cape
Natal National Botanic Garden
South African National Biodiversity
Institute, PO Box 21667, Mayors Walk,
Pietermaritzburg, KwaZulu-Natal
Old Nectar PO Box 127,
Stellenbosch 7599, Western Cape
Rustenberg Farm Gardens PO Box 33,
Stellenbosch 7599, Western Cape
Sheilam Cactus Garden
Klaas Voogds West Road (PO Box 157),
Robertson 6705, Western Cape
Stellenberg Gardens Oak Avenue,
Kenilworth, Cape Province, Western Cape
Vergelegen Garden Lourensford Road,
Somerset West 7129, Western Cape

South Korea
Chollipo Arboretum
Ch'ungch'ŏng-Namdo 357 930
Changdeokgung
2–71 Waryong-dong Jongno-gu, Seoul

Spain
Alhambra, La Granada, Andalucía
Carmen de la Victoria Cuesta del
Chapiz 9, Granada, Andalucía
Carmen de los Mártires
Paseo de los Mártires, Granada,
Andalucía
Casa de Don Juan de Bosco Andalucía
Casa de los Bates Motril-Salobreña
Granada, Andalucía
Casa de Pilatos
Plaza de Pilatos, Seville, Andalucía
Casa del Rey Moro Ronda, Andalucía
Casas del Chapiz Cuesta del Chapiz,
Albaicin, Granada, Andalucía
Festival de los Patios Cordobeses, El
Córdoba, Andalucía

Generalife, El
Alhambra, Granada, Andalucía
Granja de San Ildefonso, La
Segovia, Castilla Y León, Central Spain
**Hospital de los Venerables
Sacerdotes** Piazza de los Venerables 8,
Seville, Andalucía
Jardí Botànic Cap Roig
Paratge Cap Roig,
E-17210 Calella de Palafrugell, Cataluña
Jardí Botànic de Barcelona
c/ Dr. Font i Quer 2, Parc de Montjuïc,
Barcelona 08038, Cataluña
Jardí Botànic Marimurtra Fundacion
Carlos Faust No.9 Box 11217300 Blanes,
Provincia Girona, Cataluña
Jardí de Santa Clotilde Avinguda Sta
Clotilde, Lloret de Mar, Girona, Cataluña
Jardín Botánico La Concepción
29014 Málaga, Andalucía
**Jardín de la Finca Puente San
Miguel, El** Barrio del Molino, s/n 39530,
Puente San Miguel, Cantabria
Jardín del Monasterio de El Escorial
El Escorial, Madrid, Central Spain
Jardín del Palacio de Aranjuez
Aranjuez, Madrid, Central Spain
Jardins de Ca L'Artigas, Els Afores,
s/n Camí de la Pobla a Clot del Moro,
La Pobla de Lillet (Berguedà), Cataluña
Jardines de las Reales Alcázares
Alcazar, Plaza del Truinfo, Seville, Andalucía
Jardines de Montforte Plaza de la
Legión Española, 46010 Valencia
Medina Azahara Andalucía
Mirada, La, La Mancha
Monasterio de Piedra Calle Afueras
Nuevalos, Zaragoza 50210, Cataluña
Monestir de Pedralbes Pedralbes
Monastery Museum, Baixada del
Monestir, 9, 08034 Barcelona
Palacio de Galiana Paseo de la Rosa,
s/n, Toledo 45003, Castilla-La Mancha
Palacio de las Dueñas Duque de Alba,
Palacio de las Duenas, C/Duenas no. 15,
Seville, Andalucía
Palacio de los Marqueses de Viana
Plaza de Don Gome 2, Córdoba,
Andalucía
Palacio de Mondragón
Ronda, Andalucía
Parc de Joan Miró
Carrer Tarragona, Barcelona, Cataluña
Parc de la Ciutadella Av. del Marquès
de l'Argentera, Barcelona, Cataluña
Parc de L'Estació del Nord, El
Eixample, Barcelona, Cataluña

Parc del Laberint d'Horta
Horta, Barcelona, Cataluña
Parc Güell
Carrer d'Olot, Barcelona, Cataluña
Parc Samà Cambrils, Cataluña
Parque del Buen Retiro
Between C. Alfonso XII and Avenida
de Menendez Pelayo, Madrid
Parque de María Luisa
Av. de María Luísa, Seville, Andalucía
Pazo de Oca
San Esteban de Oca, Galicia
Pinya de Rosa
Jardin Bótanico Tropical Pinya de Rosa,
Blanes, Costa Brava, Cataluña
Real Jardín Botánico
Plaza de Murillo 2, Madrid 28014

Sri Lanka
Anuradhapura North Central province
Brief Gardens
Kalawila, North Western province
Peradiniya Kandy, Central province

Sweden
Botaniska Trädgården Uppsala
Svartbäcksgatan 27, 753 32 Uppsala
Drottningholms Slott
178 02 Drottningholm, Stockholm
Enköpings Parker
Enköping
Grönsöö Slottspark
Lake Mälaren, Stockholm
Gunnebo Slott
Christina Halls Väg,
431 36 Mölndal, Gothenburg
Hagaparken Brunnsviken, Stockholm
Japanska Trädgården
Brunnsparken, Ronneby, Blekinge
Linnéträdgården
Villavägen 8, 752 36 Uppsala
Millesgården Herserudsvägen 32,
181 34 Lidingö, Stockholm
Skogskyrkogården Stockholm
122 33 Enskede, Stockhom
Slottsträdgården
Malmöhusvägen 8,
211 18 Malmö, Skåne
Sofiero Slott och Slottspark
251 89 Helsingborg, Skåne
Uraniborgs Renässansträdgård
Island of Ven, Skåne

Switzerland
Parco Botanico del Canton Ticino
Brissago Islands, Lake Maggiore, Ticino
Vico Morcote Vico Morcote, Ticino

Taiwan
Ban Qiao 9 XiMen St.,
Banqiao City, Taipei County 220, Taiwan

Thailand
Bang Pa-in Tambon Bang Len,
Ayutthaya Province
Jim Thompson Garden, The
6 Soi Kasemsan 2, Rama 1 Road, Bangkok
Nong Nooch Tropical Garden
Sukhumvit Rd. Pattaya,
Chonburi Province
Queen Sirikit Botanic Garden
PO Box 7, Mae Rim, Chiang Mai 50180

Turkey
Topkapi Sarayi
Sultanahmet, Eminonu, Istanbul

Ukraine
Alupka Respublika Krym, Crimea
Nikitskyi Botanichnyi Sad
(Nikitsky Botanical Gardens) Nikita, Yalta,
Respublika Krym, Crimea
Sophievka
St. Kievskaya 12a, 258900 Uman

United States
**Abby Aldrich Rockefeller Sculpture
Garden, Museum of Modern Art**
11 West 53rd Street, New York, NY 10019
Arnold Arboretum
125 Arborway,
Jamaica Plain, Massachusetts 02130
Atlanta Botanical Garden
1345 Piedmont Avenue Northeast,
Atlanta, Georgia 30309
Bartram's Garden
54th Street and Lindbergh Boulevard,
Philadelphia, PA 19143
Biltmore Estate
1 Approach Road,
Asheville, North Carolina 28803
Blithewold Gardens
101 Ferry Road,
Bristol, Rhode Island 02809
Bloedel Reserve, The
7571 Northeast Dolphin Drive,
Bainbridge Island, WA 98110
Boscobel
1601 Route 9D,
Garrison, New York 10524
British Memorial Garden
Hanover Square, New York, NY 10004
Brooklyn Botanic Gardens
900 Washington Avenue,
Brooklyn, New York 11225

Cà d'Zan Mansion and Gardens
The John and Mable Ringling Museum
of Art, 5401 Bay Shore Road,
Sarasota, Florida 34243
Callaway Gardens 17800 US Highway
27, Pine Mountain, Georgia 31822
Celia Thaxter's Garden
Appledore Island, Isles of Shoals, Maine
Central Park
14 East 60th St., New York, NY 10022
Chanticleer 786 Church Road,
Wayne, Pennsylvania 19087
Chase Garden, The
16015 264th St. East, Orting, WA 98360
Chicago Botanic Garden 1000 Lake
Cook Road, Glencoe, Illinois 60022
Chicago Millennium Park
55 North Michigan Avenue,
Chicago, Illinois 60611
Cloisters, The
Fort Tryon Park, New York, NY 10040
Colonial Williamsburg
PO Box 1776, Williamsburg, VA 23187
Cornerstone Festival of Gardens
23570 Highway 121, Sonoma, CA 95476
**Crystal Springs Rhododendron
Garden**
Southeast 28th Avenue and Woodstock
Blvd., Portland, Oregon 97214
Denver Botanic Gardens 1005 York
Street, Denver, Colorado 80206
Desert Botanical Garden
1201 North Galvin Parkway,
Phoenix, Arizona 85008
**Donald M. Kendall Sculpture
Gardens**
700 Anderson Hill Road,
Purchase, NY 10577
Dow Gardens, The 1809 Eastman
Avenue, Midland, Michigan 48640
Dumbarton Oaks 1703 32nd Street
Northwest, Washington, DC 20007
Edison and Ford Winter Estates
2350 McGregor Boulevard,
Fort Myers, Florida 33901
**Elisabeth Carey Miller Botanical
Garden** The Highlands
Seattle, Washington 98177
Enid A. Haupt Garden
1050 Independence Avenue SW,
Washington, DC 20024
Fairchild Tropical Botanic Garden
10901 Old Cutler Road,
Coral Gables, Florida 33156
Fallingwater
Route 381 (PO Box R),
Mill Run, Pennsylvania 15464

Federal Reserve Garden
20th and C Street Northwest,
Washington, DC 20551
Fells, The
456 Route 103A,
Newbury, New Hampshire 03255
Filoli
86 Cañada Road, Woodside, CA 94062
Forestiere Underground Gardens
5021 West Shaw Avenue,
Fresno, California 93722
Forest Lawn
1712 South Glendale Avenue,
Glendale, California 91205-3320
Garden in the Woods
New England Wild Flower Society,
180 Hemenway Road,
North Framingham, MA 01701
Garland Farm Beatrix Farrand Society,
PO Box 111, Mount Desert, Maine 04660
George Eastman House Gardens
900 East Ave., Rochester, NY 14607
Getty Villa, The 17985 Pacific Coast
Highway, Pacific Palisades, CA 90272
Gibraltar Gibraltar Preservation
Delaware, Inc., 1405 Greenhill Avenue,
Wilmington, Delaware 19806
Greenwood Gardens 274 Old Short
Hills Rd., Short Hills, New Jersey 07078
Gunston Hall 10709 Gunston Road,
Mason Neck, Virginia 22079
Harkness Memorial State Park
275 Great Neck Road,
Waterford, Connecticut 06385
Hearst Castle 750 Hearst Castle Road,
San Simeon, California 93452-9740
Hershey Gardens 170 Hotel Road,
Hershey, Pennsylvania 17033
High Line, The Gansevoort Street
to West 30th Street, New York City
Hollister House 300 Nettleton Hollow
Road, Washington, Connecticut 06793
Huntington Botanical Gardens
1151 Oxford Road,
San Marino, CA 91108
Innisfree Garden
Tyrrel Road, Millbrook, New York 12545
Ira Keller Fountain Park SW 3rd Ave.
and Clay St., Portland, Oregon 97201
Isabella Stewart Gardner Museum
280 The Fenway,
Boston, Massachusetts 02115
Jacob Javits Plaza 26 Federal Plaza,
New York, New York 10278
James Rose Center
506 East Ridgewood Ave.,
Ridgewood, New Jersey 07450

Japanese Garden
611 SW Kingston Ave., Portland, OR 97208
**John P. Humes Japanese
Stroll Garden** 347 Oyster Bay Rd.,
Locust Valley, New York 11560
J. Paul Getty Museum, The
1200 Getty Center Drive,
Los Angeles, California 90049
Ladew Topiary Gardens
3535 Jarrettsville Pike,
Monkton, Maryland 21111
**Lady Bird Johnson Wildflower
Center** 4801 La Crosse Avenue,
Austin, Texas 78739
Leichtag Family Healing Garden, The
3020 Children's Way,
San Diego, California 92123
Lincoln Memorial Garden
2301 East Lake Shore Drive,
Springfield, Illinois 62712
Longhouse Reserve 133 Hands Creek
Road, East Hampton, New York 11937
Longwood Gardens
1001 Longwood Road,
Kennett Square, Pennsylvania 19348
Lotusland 695 Ashley Road,
Santa Barbara, California 93108
Madoo Conservancy 618 Sagg Main
Street, Sagaponack, New York 11962
Manitoga 584 Route 9D,
Garrison, New York 10524
Marie Selby Botanical Gardens
811 South Palm Avenue,
Sarasota, Florida 34236
Middleton Place 4300 Ashley River
Road, Charleston, South Carolina 29414
Missouri Botanical Garden
4344 Shaw Boulevard,
St. Louis, Missouri 63110
Monticello 931 Thomas Jefferson
Parkway, Charlottesville, VA 22902
Mount, The 2 Plunkett Street,
Lennox, Massachusetts 01240–0974
Mount Auburn Cemetery
580 Mount Auburn Street,
Cambridge, Massachusetts 02138
Mount Cuba Barley Mill Road,
Greenville, Delaware 19807-0570
Mount Vernon
3200 Mount Vernon Memorial Highway,
Mount Vernon, Virginia 22121
Naumkeag Garden
Prospect Hill Road,
Stockbridge, Massachusetts 01262
Nemours Gardens Rockland Road,
Wilmington, Delaware 19803
New York Botanical Garden

Bronx River Parkway at Fordham Road,
Bronx, New York 10458
Noguchi Museum
9-01 33rd Road at Vernon Boulevard,
Long Island City, New York 11106
Northwest Garden Nursery
86813 Central Road,
Eugene, Oregon 97402-9284
Oakland Museum and Garden
1000 Oak Street at 10th Street,
Oakland, CA 94607
Ohme Gardens 3327 Ohme Road,
Wenatchee, WA 98801
Old Westbury Gardens
71 Old Westbury Road, PO Box 430,
Old Westbury, New York 11568
Peckerwood Garden
20571 F.M. 359, Hempstead, TX 77445
The Pool Garden at El Novillero
27235 Arnold Drive, Sonoma County,
Sonoma, California
Portland Classical Chinese Garden
127 Northwest 3rd Avenue
Portland, Oregon 97209
Quarryhill Botanical Garden
Sonoma Highway 12,
Glen Ellen, CA 95442
**Rhododendron Species Botanical
Garden** 2525 South 336th Street,
Federal Way, Washington 98003
Ruth Bancroft Garden
1500 Bancroft Rd.,
Walnut Creek, CA 94598
Santa Barbara Botanic Garden
1212 Mission Canyon Road, Santa
Barbara, CA 93105
Stan Hywet Hall and Gardens
714 North Portage Path,
Akron, OH 44303
Steepletop 454 East Hill Road,
Austerlitz, New York 12017
Sunset Garden 80 Willow Road,
Menlo Park, California 94025
Taliesin 5607 County Highway C,
Spring Green, Wisconsin 53588
Taliesin West 12621 Frank Lloyd Wright
Blvd., Scottsdale, Arizona 85259
Tohono Chul Park 7366 N. Paseo del
Norte, Tucson, Arizona 85704-4415
Topiary Garden, The
480 East Town St., Columbus, OH 43215
Tucson Botanical Gardens
2150 North Alvernon Way,
Tucson, Arizona 85712
Vanderbilt Mansion Italian Garden
4097 Albany Post Road,
Hyde Park, New York 12538

Van Vleck House and Gardens
21 Van Vleck Street,
Montclair, New Jersey 07042
Vizcaya Museum and Gardens
3251 South Miami Ave.,
Miami, FL 33129
Wallace Gardens Medina, Minnesota
Walt Disney World Resort
12384 South Apopka, Vineland Road,
Orlando, Florida 32836
**Washington Park Arboretum
and Japanese Garden**
1075 Lake Washington Blvd. East,
Seattle, Washington 98112
Wave Hill Gardens
West 249th St. and Independence
Avenue, Bronx, New York 10471
William Paca Gardens 186 Prince
George Street, Annapolis, MD 21401
Winterthur Garden Route 52, 5105
Kennett Pike, Winterthur, DE 19735
Yew Dell Gardens 6220 Old LaGrange
Road, Crestwood, Kentucky 40014

Uruguay
Esquina Ventosa
Solis, Maldonado
Mantua 7140 Carrasco, Montevideo
Paso Correntino Mercedes Soriano
Uruguay, PO Box CC50, Soriano,
Mercedes T5000

Wales
Aberglasney House and Gardens
Llangathen, Carmarthenshire, SA32 8QH
Bodnant Garden Tal-y-Cafn,
nr. Colwyn Bay, Conwy, LL28 5RE
Chirk Castle Chirk, Wrexham, LL14 5AF
Clyne Gardens Mill Lane, Blackpill,
Swansea, SA3 5BD
Crûg Farm Plants Griffith's Crossing,
Caernarfon, Gwynedd, LL55 1TU
National Botanic Garden of Wales
Llanarthne, Carmarthenshire, SA32 8HG
Plas Brondanw Croesor,
Llanfrothen, Gwynedd, LL48 6SW
Plas Newydd Llanfairpwll,
Anglesey, Gwynedd, LL61 6DQ
Portmeirion
Portmeirion, Gwynedd, LL48 6ET
Powis Castle and Garden
Nr. Welshpool, Powys SY21 8RF
Ridler's Garden
7 St. Peter's Terrace, Cockett,
Swansea, SA2 0FW
Tredegar House
Coedkernew, Newport, NP10 8YW

Picture Credits

Every effort has been made to credit the copyright holders of the images used in this book. We apologize in advance for any unintentional omissions or errors and will be pleased to insert appropriate acknowledgment to any companies or individuals in any subsequent edition of the work.

Aarhus Universitet/Poul Ib Henriksen 210
AA World Travel Library 44, 64, 126, 133, 135, 468, 816, 885, 890, 891, 894
AA World Travel Library/Alamy 790
Aalto Foundation 152
AKG 590
Alamy Jennifer Hart 255
Alamy/nagelestock.com/OJ Photos 216
Andrea Jones/Garden Exposures Photo Library 33, 46, 77, 83, 93, 98, 100, 173, 175, 206, 226, 229, 314, 319, 387, 437, 445, 447, 470, 506, 541, 570, 571, 605, 689, 851, 853, 930
Art Archive/Nicolas Sapieha 468
Art Directors and TRIP Photo Library 21, 22, 34, 57, 76, 78, 91, 95, 104, 112, 121, 147, 148, 151, 196, 204, 212, 214, 215, 460, 472, 479, 480, 487, 498, 501, 537, 550, 551, 572, 576, 577, 582, 591, 632, 640, 644, 687, 696, 707, 711, 718, 735, 736, 756, 757, 759, 760, 762, 766, 767, 785, 786, 787, 791, 793, 798, 803, 809, 810, 833, 834, 846, 883, 887, 938, 939
AYArktos 490
©2006 Barragan Foundation, Birsfelden, Switzerland ProLitteris, Zürich, Switzerland, for the work of Luis Barragán. Photo Armando Salas Portugal 844
Bayerische Verwaltung der staatlichen Schlösser, Gärten und Seen 483
Nicola Browne 309, 534, 708
Château du Rivau 598, 599
Roy Cheek 697, 706, 726, 737, 740, 745, 749, 751, 752, 857, 908, 914, 915, 916, 917, 922, 923, 925, 931, 932, 935, 936, 942
Corbis 777, 806; Paul Almasy 643; Bernard Annebicque/SYGMA 109; Yann Arthus-Bertrand 211, 575; Craig Aurness Hearst Castle CA Park Service 94; B.S.P.I. 754-755; Mark Bolton 18-19; Clive Boursnell 366; Pablo Corral 855; Eric Crichton 375, 377; Richard Cummins 84, 122; Eye Ubiquitous 863; Fridmar Dammzefa 140; Ric Ergenbright 125, 721; Macduff Everton 829; Kevin Fleming 66, 113; Franz-Marc Frei 373; Michael Freeman 832; Chich Gryniewicz/Ecoscene 518; Jason Hawkes 135; Robert Holmes 37, 67, 99; Dave G Houser 75, 120, 132, 502, 831; Adam Jones 73; Wolfgang Kaehler 783; Catherine Karnow 800; Layne Kennedy 42; Richard Klune 473, 507; Bob Krist 129; Robert Landau 97; Lester Lefkowitz 136-137; Chris Lisle 153, 218, 775; Massimo Listri 681; Lawrence Manning 45; Kelly Moonaj Photography, Gail Mooney 619; Michael Nicholson 489; Richard T Nowitz 25; Christine Osborne 835; Clay Perry 221, 251, 252, 265, 323, 403; Sergio Pitamitzzefa 654; Jose Fuste Ragg 866; Steve Raymer 139; Anders Ryman 154; Christiam Sarramon 522; Skyscan 509; Nicolas Sapieha 533; Peter Smithers 652, 653; Paul A Souders 903; Roman Soumar 627; Hubert Stadler 918; Arthur Therenart 805; Andrew Cowin/Travel Ink 494; Penny Tweedie 892; Craig Tuttle 71; Adam Woolfitt 650; Michael S Yamashita 29, 658, 797; Inge Yspeert 539; Fridmar Dammzefa 141; Svenja-Fotozefa 156; Guenter Rossenbachzefa 462, 476; Manfred Mehligzefa 464; Jim Zuckerman 484
Ray Cox 165, 167, 170, 177, 179, 181, 182, 184, 185, 187, 192, 194, 195, 198, 200, 209, 413
Pat Crocker 27, 41, 114, 127
Deborah Dunham 808
George Eastman 47
fotoLibra 568
Christopher Gallagher 743
Lei Gao 770, 771
Garden Collection 748; Gary Rogers, 748, 921
Garden Picture Library Philippe Bonduel 621; Nic Bothmaepa 858-859; Gary Braasch 878-879; Jennifer Broadus 583; Digital Vision 150; Brian Carter 423; Christi Carter 26; Tommy Clander 368; Joe Cornish 455; David Dixon 285; John Ferro 673, 675; Nigel Francis 355; Suzie Gibbons 860; Will Giles 870; John Glover 412, 909; Georgia Glynn-Smith 453, 455; David Hastilow 440; Jean-Claude Hurni 593; Henryk T Kaiser 503; Japack Photo Library 867; Joe Malone 142, 536; David Messent 880; Martine Mouchy 450, 454, 580; Richard Nebesky 628; Michael Paul 385; Douglas Peebles 906-907; Brigitte & Philippe Perdereau 174; Stephen Robson 446, 448; Ellen Rooney 655, 656; Kevin Schafer 840-841; JS Sira 298, 324, 388; Brigitte Thomas 271, 369; Bibikow Walter 505
Garden World Images 566
Getty 557
John Glover 258, 259, 346, 422, 424, 727

Greenwood Gardens 87
Robert Harding Picture Library Upperhall Ltd 638
Harpur Garden Library 36, 50, 51, 53, 55, 59, 65, 68, 79, 85, 89, 101, 102, 103, 115, 116, 117, 124, 134, 168, 230, 232, 233, 244, 249, 262, 276, 278, 286, 291, 301, 305, 307, 316, 318, 329, 331, 333, 334, 335, 336, 338, 340, 349, 353, 357, 358, 364, 365, 371, 378, 379, 395, 400, 401, 405, 408, 421, 442, 443, 458, 471, 482, 547, 561, 562, 569, 579, 682, 690, 693, 792, 802, 807, 817, 861, 868, 874, 875, 876, 895, 901, 905
Charles Hawes 516
M. Heuff 521, 526, 527, 528, 532, 535, 542, 592, 699
Hortus/Alamy 679
Heidi Howcraft 492
John P. Humes 49
Erica Hunningher 801, 804, 811, 812, 813, 818, 819, 820, 821, 823, 824, 826, 827
Isola del Garda 659
Lankester Garden 848
Ickworth House/Jason Hawkes/Corbis 287
Jardinoscope 595
Karolek/Alamy 498
Amanda Knapp 360
Lankester Garden 848
Andrew Lawson Photography 118, 172, 178, 180, 203, 223, 224, 227, 234, 239, 242, 248, 249, 266, 267, 268, 272, 274, 277, 279, 297, 299, 302, 303, 306, 310, 311, 313, 315, 317, 320, 326, 327, 332, 343, 345, 347, 350, 356, 382, 391, 392, 394, 398, 399, 427, 431, 438, 439, 441, 456, 669, 678, 789, 889, 897
Marianne Majerus 284, 549
Nancie Matthews 884
Joëlle & Gilles Mayer Le Scanff 524, 545, 581, 603, 606, 612, 613, 614, 617, 725, 733, 734
The M. S. Hershey Foundation 81
The Mount Kevin Sprague 63
Toby Musgrove 865
Clive Nichols 105, 145, 155, 407, 926
Parkwood Garden Estate 28
Brigitte & Philippe Perdereau 559, 596, 608, 616, 910
Photolibrary 601, 602; Brigitte Merle 611
Photoshot 54, 72, 157, 159, 160, 465, 466, 474, 475, 481, 485, 486, 491, 525, 544, 558, 626, 629, 630, 632, 633, 637, 641, 647, 648, 799
Preservation Delaware Inc. Gibraltar 409
Alex Ramsay 269, 449, 657, 660, 663, 665, 666, 670, 671, 677, 676, 683, 686, 688, 691, 692, 694, 795
Rhododendron Species Foundation Gardens 39
Howard Rice 260
Hervé Rimbault 589
Gary Rogers 107, 128, 143, 463, 588, 738, 741, 746, 764, 769, 772, 773, 838
Royal Botanic Gardens, Ontario, Canada 30, 69
Vivien Russell 111, 166, 169, 176, 183, 188, 189, 190, 193, 197, 199, 201, 205, 207, 222, 231, 261, 281, 294, 321, 344, 363, 372, 374, 396, 414, 418, 434, 540, 546, 555, 556, 585, 586, 587, 609, 615, 618, 623, 625, 661, 667, 685, 713
Barbara Segall 700, 705, 709, 714, 717, 729, 730, 731, 739, 742, 744, 753
Christian Sarramon 554, 578
Singapore Tourist Board 837
Gordon Sinclair/Alamy 728
South American Pictures 842, 843, 845, 852, 854
Spanish Tourist Board 703, 712
Patrick Taylor 191, 225, 236, 240, 241, 246, 250, 254, 256, 273, 280, 283, 288, 312, 325, 330, 339, 351, 352, 361, 374, 389, 390, 393, 397, 411, 416, 428, 429, 430, 451, 452, 457, 553, 584, 747
Travel Ink/Barry Hughes 881
Yew Dell Gardens 106
Christine Walkden 765
Andrew Watson 941
World Pictures 219, 736
Konrad Zelazowski/Alamy 501